The Mentally
Disabled
and the Law

An American Bar
Foundation Study

The Mentally
Disabled
and the Law

Edited by
SAMUEL J. BRAKEL
and RONALD S. ROCK

REVISED EDITION

721829

The University of Chicago Press
Chicago and London

The original edition, edited by Frank T. Lindman
and Donald M. McIntyre, Jr., was published in 1961

International Standard Book Number: 0–226–07090–5
Library of Congress Catalog Card Number: 74–158682

THE UNIVERSITY OF CHICAGO PRESS, CHICAGO 60637
THE UNIVERSITY OF CHICAGO PRESS, LTD., LONDON

AMERICAN BAR FOUNDATION

The American Bar Foundation is the legal research affiliate of the American Bar Association. Its institutional mission is to conduct research that will enlarge the understanding and improve the functioning of law and legal institutions. The Foundation's work is supported by the American Bar Association, the American Bar Endowment, The Fellows of the American Bar Foundation, and by outside funds granted for particular research projects.

Contents

CONTENTS

Tables

Preface to
Revised Edition

This revised edition of *The Mentally Disabled and the Law* has been in part a result of the pervasive attention focused during the sixties upon the plight of the mentally ill. A much needed critical evaluation of our nation's response to the needs of its mentally ill was provided by the final report of the Joint Commission on Mental Illness and Health, *Action for Mental Health* (Basic Books, 1961); by and large the states have responded to the challenges in that report by instituting new programs and enacting laws and procedures for their implementation. Yet much remains to be done.

This revision retains essentially the same format and organization as in the 1961 edition. Its primary focus is still on the laws and processes as they appear in the statutes of the various states. However, our evaluation of those laws has been tempered and enriched by studies, conducted by the Foundation and others, of the day-to-day administration of the laws. What the studies demonstrate is that the promise of a well conceived code is easily vitiated by inept administration or a lack of resources. The extent to which a comprehensive code is buttressed by a corresponding comprehensive range of services and resources finally determines its value for the mentally ill.

Much of what was presented in the original report has been retained as still cogent and relevant, and it is therefore appropriate that we again acknowledge the contribution of Frank T. Lindman and Donald M. McIntyre, Jr., editors of the original report, and the many others who made that report possible.

The task of updating the various charts for this revision was ably completed by a staff of research associates, which included David M. Higbee, Daniel J. Siefer, Stanley H. Meadows, and J. Eric Engstrom. The project secretaries, Blossom Abrams, Maureen McVey, and Joanne Porter worked with accuracy and dispatch in typing the manuscript and charts. Finally, Wendy Bradburn, Jean Luther, and Dorothy Lachmann carefully edited the manuscript and prepared it for publication. As always, the findings and conclusions are ours alone and not necessarily those of the Foundation, its officers and directors, or others associated with its work.

RONALD S. ROCK
SAMUEL J. BRAKEL

Introduction

I. BACKGROUND AND DEVELOPMENT OF THE PROJECT

One of the most troublesome problems in the field of law concerns the legal status of mentally disabled persons.[1] Essentially, the problem is one of determining when and to what extent the law should restrict the rights of these persons. Actions by the state in this area tend to fall into these important categories: (1) restrictions on the rights and privileges of mentally disabled persons in the conduct of their personal and business affairs; (2) positive measures that must be taken by the state to insure proper care and treatment for them; and (3) limiting accountability under the criminal law.

Laws relating to mental disability assume major significance when viewed in terms of the large number of people directly affected and the aggregate economic interests involved. At the beginning of fiscal year 1966 there were 579,859 resident patients in public and private mental hospitals and some 557,000 persons receiving care through outpatient clinics. The total number of admissions to inpatient facilities in that fiscal year reached almost 922,000; outpatient clinics took on almost 630,000 new cases.[2]

Since 1956 there has been a steady decrease in the average daily patient population of state and local public mental hospitals, due in large measure to the introduction of tranquilizers; by controlling the more apparent symptoms of some forms of mental illness, tranquilizers have facilitated not only treatment but also community acceptance of former patients. In 1956, state and local public mental hospitals had almost 559,000 resident patients,[3] whereas provisional data for June 30, 1969, indicate a resident patient population of only about 367,000 patients.[4] During the same period, admissions to these institutions increased from 198,000[5] to almost 380,000[6] yearly. Statistical projections indicate that at the present rate of hospitalization one out of every ten citizens will probably spend a portion of his life in a mental institution. Moreover, tens of thousands of mentally disabled persons are adjudged incompetent and placed under guardianship each year.

Equally impressive is the heavy financial burden imposed on the community by providing for mentally disabled persons and by the economic losses resulting from such disabilities. It has been estimated that in 1957 direct costs, such as actual expenditures for care and research, amounted to $1.7 billion a year, and indirect costs, calculated on the basis of actual loss of production and annual earnings, were about $800 million.[7] If to these figures are added private medical costs other than private psychiatric care, costs for construction of facilities, and depreciation and other cost assessments, the total yearly drain on the economy probably reached the $3 billion mark.[8] More recent estimates place the total yearly economic impact at about $21 billion.[9]

Since mental disability characteristically results in some degree of impairment of the individual's capacity to care for himself and to adapt his conduct to society, it often has legal as well as social consequences. The law deals with a wide variety of problems arising from mental disabilities, including the determination in the first instance of whether certain persons are mentally disabled; their hospitalization and discharge; their care and treatment, rights and status while hospitalized; the personal and property rights

1. The term "mental disability" is used throughout this volume in a generic sense to denote any kind of mental health problem (whether due to a deficiency or a malfunction) which subjects the person so afflicted to laws regulating his social, civil, and personal rights. Mental illness, mental deficiency, alcoholism, drug addiction, and epilepsy are included in this generic term.

2. United States Public Health Service, National Institute of Mental Health, *Patients in State and County Mental Hospitals 1967,* at 10, 11 (1969).

3. United States Department of Commerce, Bureau of the Census, *Statistical Abstract of the United States 1959,* at 80 (1959).

4. United States Department of Health, Education and Welfare, *Mental Health Statistics, Current Facility Reports: Provisional Patient Movement and Administrative Data, State and County Mental Hospitals, United States, July 1, 1968–June 30, 1969,* at 1 (1970).

5. United States Department of Commerce, *supra* note 3.

6. United States Department of Health, Education, and Welfare, *supra* note 4, at 8.

7. Fein, *Economics of Mental Illness* x–xii (Joint Commission on Mental Illness and Health Monograph Series no. 2, 1958).

8. *Id.* at xii.

9. National Clearinghouse for Mental Health Information, "The Cost of Mental Illness, 1968." Statistical Note 30 (Oct. 1970).

of all mentally disabled persons; and the relation of the mentally disabled to the criminal law. The law should be vitally concerned with safeguarding the rights of the mentally disabled and with restoring mental patients to society, following their recovery, in such a way as to obviate any possible stigma. At the same time, the law should recognize that reasonable restrictions must be placed on mentally disabled persons to protect their interests and to insure public safety.

Prior to the appointment in 1944 of the American Bar Association Special Committee on the Rights of the Mentally Ill, various sections and standing committees of the Association had dealt with laws relating to the mentally disabled. For example, the Section of Real Property, Probate and Trust Law, because of its interest in incompetency and guardianship, has consistently dealt with problems of mental disability.[10] Similarly, the Section of Criminal Law has been active in this field because of its concern with criminal irresponsibility or "insanity."[11] The Section of Judicial Administration has also manifested an interest in this subject through its Committee on Procedure in Civil Mental Health Matters.

In 1943 the Board of Governors of the American Bar Association authorized the appointment of an exploratory committee to survey the administrative and judicial procedures relating to mental disability with a view toward determining whether the Bar Association as a whole had sufficient present concern with this field to become active in it.[12] This committee in 1944 recommended to the Board of Governors that a special committee be created to advise the Bar Association whether the then-existing laws adequately safeguarded the rights of the mentally disabled and, if they did not, to submit drafts of appropriate legislation.[13]

Appointed on the exploratory committee's recommendation, the Special Committee on the Rights of the Mentally Ill reported at the 1945 annual meeting of the House of Delegates that before it could discharge its duty it would have to examine existing laws to ascertain their actual effect on the rights of the mentally disabled. The report pointed out, however, that such a study would be possible only if a financial grant were made (either by the Bar Association or some foundation) for the purpose of obtaining a research staff.[14] No action on this recommendation was taken by the House of Delegates. In succeeding years the Special Committee reiterated to the House of Delegates the need for a thoroughgoing study by a permanent research staff.[15]

At the 1954 annual meeting of the House of Delegates a resolution was adopted referring the proposed study to the American Bar Foundation,[16] which had been established two years earlier at the instance of the American Bar Association.

Realizing the complexity of the problem presented to it, the American Bar Foundation decided to undertake first a preliminary study of the existing statutes in a limited number of states and of the Draft Act Governing Hospitalization of the Mentally Ill.[17] The initial study included the Draft Act and the statutes of California, Illinois, Michigan, New York and Pennsylvania.[18] From an examination of the data collected, it was evident that in order to present an accurate and comprehensive report of the law in its application to the mentally disabled a more elaborate study would be necessary. Accordingly, an expanded plan for the project was approved early in 1956 by the Board of Directors of the American Bar Foundation.

As outlined in the expanded plan, the purpose of the project was to analyze, classify, and describe pertinent statutes and important court decisions affecting the rights of the mentally disabled. Treatises and other written literature in the field were to be reviewed to obtain the benefit of all prior research on this subject.

The first step in the study was the preparation of

10. Illustrative of the interest and work of this section is an address by Judge McAvinchey, "The Not-Quite-Incompetent Incompetent," to the ABA Section of Real Property, Probate and Trust Law, Aug. 28, 1956, in the ABA Section of Real Property, Probate and Trust Law, *Proceedings* pt. I, at 18 (1956). See also American Bar Association Section of Real Property, Probate and Trust Law: *Index to Publications of the Section, 1934–1955* (1956).

11. See, for example, ABA Section of Criminal Law, Committee on Medico-Legal Problems, *Annual Report* (1935); Committee on Criminal Procedure, *Annual Report* (1938).

12. 68 *ABA Rep.* 183 (1943).

13. 69 *ABA Rep.* 143, 221 (1944).

14. 70 *ABA Rep.* 338 (1945).

15. 72 *ABA Rep.* 289 (1947); 73 *ABA Rep.* 297 (1948); 77 *ABA Rep.* 318 (1952); 79 *ABA Rep.* 399 (1954).

16. 79 *ABA Rep.* 151 (1954).

17. National Institute of Mental Health, Federal Security Agency, *A Draft Act Governing Hospitalization of the Mentally Ill* (Public Health Service Pub. No. 51, 1952) [hereinafter cited as *Draft Act*]. This Act was prepared not to serve as a uniform code but rather as a guide to the states for the revision of their own statutes. The *Draft Act* appears as Appendix A to this Report.

18. American Bar Foundation, "Hospitalization and Treatment of Mental Cases," mimeographed (February 1955).

charts (hereinafter referred to as tables) showing the provisions of the Draft Act and the statutes of all the (then) forty-eight states and the District of Columbia. Next, all available literature in this area of the law was reviewed. Major court decisions, treatises, law review and bar journal articles, and similar materials were carefully studied to ascertain the status of the law as written. From this study and the information derived from the tables, the text of the 1961 Report was prepared. The preparation of the present revised edition of the Report has followed a similar pattern.

The 1961 Report, a study of written law and other literature, was the first phase of a broad inquiry into the law as it relates to the rights of the mentally disabled. Mindful that the application of the law in day-to-day practice is fully as important as the provisions of the written law, the American Bar Association and the American Bar Foundation next felt that a worthy analysis and presentation of many of the problems in this area could be made only after considerable empirical research, including field studies and conferences with physicians and psychiatrists active in the present system. Only through observation of the processes and procedures actually used by the persons responsible for the administration of the laws, supplemented by interviews and other inquiries, could a truly accurate determination be made of the extent to which the rights of mentally disabled persons are protected. With such an understanding of the problems and inadequacies of the law in action, improvements can be made where needed.

Thus it was contemplated that as a sequel to the 1961 Report a field study was necessary. In 1958 an American Bar Foundation Special Committee on Procedure in Hospitalization and Discharge of the Mentally Ill was appointed to plan and finance the field study project.

The field study was carried out in two separate but related projects: *Hospitalization and Discharge of the Mentally Ill*,[19] a study of civil hospitalization practices in seven states, and *Mental Disability and the Criminal Law*,[20] a corresponding study of the relationship between mental illness and the administration of criminal justice in five states and the District of Columbia. Both studies underscored many of the difficulties originally cited in the 1961 Report. More importantly, they established the need for a "process" view of the hospitalization and release of

the mentally ill and the course of the mentally ill person accused of a crime. That is, in order to gauge the impact of law on the mentally ill, the interaction of the various procedures, practices, resources, and attitudes at all points of the law's contact with the mentally ill must be understood, and quantitative as well as qualitative dimensions of the problem must be taken into account. The present edition of this Report reflects this reconceptualization while maintaining its original character as a survey of the mental health laws of the states. The value of the original Report is attested to by the fact that scarcely an article or monograph related to the laws governing the mentally ill over the last ten years has failed to rely on this Report for some proposition or description. The present revision has sought to maintain the independent value of the Report as originally conceived and executed.

Each chapter of the Report deals with a specific topic within the purview of mental disability and the law. These topics are: historical trends, voluntary admission to hospitals, involuntary hospitalization, release and separation from mental institutions, the rights of hospitalized patients, eugenic sterilization, domestic relations, incompetency, personal and property rights, sexual psychopathy, and criminal "insanity" or irresponsibility.

For practical reasons, some aspects of mental disability law can not be covered here. For instance, the Report does not discuss the problems legislators, judges, and practicing attorneys face in keeping abreast of the rapid advances made in the field of psychiatry and, more important, in appropriately incorporating these advances into the mental disability laws. The answers to many of the most pressing problems in this field must ultimately come from close, intensive cooperation between medical experts and the men and women who make, interpret, and administer the law.

II. TERMINOLOGY, TABLES, AND APPENDIXES

A. TERMINOLOGY

The subject matter of this Report is plagued with terminological difficulties. Standard definitions are not to be found and, consequently, generalizations have been difficult to formulate.

Perhaps the greatest difficulty in drafting legislation lies in defining precisely the class or classes of persons contemplated by the proposed statute. This problem becomes particularly acute when dealing with the mentally disabled. Historically, legislatures

19. Rock, Jacobson, & Janopaul, *Hospitalization and Discharge of the Mentally Ill* (1968).

20. Matthews, *Mental Disability and the Criminal Law* (1970).

and courts have not had much assistance from medical science in accomplishing the twin objectives of the law: preservation of the maximum rights and liberties of the mentally disabled and maintenance of the physical welfare of the patient and the community.

> The lawyer came first; it was he, and not the physician, who had to manage the consequences of mental disease insofar as they affected the interests of the community. The lawyer was then the first who had to see to it that the psychotic disturber of the peace be taken out of circulation, that the homicidal maniac (or criminal insane) be removed from the community and isolated somewhere, that property mismanaged or abandoned by a person mentally deranged be taken care of in some normal, legitimate way. In other words, all the problems which have preoccupied psychiatry ever since it was born existed to the full extent of their urgency before it was born. Attempts at their practical solution were made, precedents established, traditions developed, without benefit of any scientific clinical psychopathology; the very possibility of a development of such psychopathology could not even be fathomed many centuries ago.[21]

Current advances in psychiatric knowledge, including the more accurate use of medical terms, have not appreciably eased the difficulty of relating that knowledge to the law. Perhaps an explanation may be found in the diverse purposes of legal and medical terms. A legal term has a precise meaning which may or may not coincide with popular, religious, or scientific concepts. It is a term of art, used by the persons who make, enforce, and interpret the law, and it aims at achieving certain social goals. For instance, the legal meaning of a term such as "mental illness" may be quite different from that intended where used by a physician, so that the medical meaning of "mental illness" would not necessarily provide the legal criteria for involuntary hospitalization or incompetency.

One of the major sources of confusion in the law has been the use of vague and nebulous descriptive terms. Classic illustrations may be found by comparing the great variety of statutory definitions of "mentally ill," "mentally deficient," "epileptics," "alcoholics," "drug addicts," "incompetents," and "psychopaths."[22]

The same term may be used in different parts of codes or statutes, even though each of these parts may be designed to accomplish a different result and may be intended to apply to a different class of persons. For example, identical terms are often used to describe persons subject to involuntary hospitalization, those incapable of preparing a valid will, and those who should be adjudged incompetent for guardianship purposes. In fact, the law in each of these areas applies to a different mental condition; hence, it is possible to be "mentally ill" for the purpose of involuntary hospitalization but to have at the same time sufficient mental capacity to execute a valid will or to marry.

B. TABLES

Aside from providing important source material for the text, the tables appearing throughout this Report are also a valuable adjunct to the text. First, being limited to statutory provisions, the tables offer a visual comparison of the ways in which the rights of mentally disabled persons have been dealt with by the legislatures of the fifty states and the District of Columbia, as well as by the authors of the Draft Act. (A summary of the hospitalization provisions of the Commonwealth of Puerto Rico, the Virgin Islands, and the Territory of Guam is set forth in Appendix B.) A second function of the tables is to provide an easily accessible reference for locating specific statutory provisions which relate to the many detailed aspects of the law concerning the mentally disabled. Many of these provisions are difficult to find through statutory indexes.

These two objectives were accomplished by preparing separate tables for the several areas of the law affecting mentally disabled persons. In some instances it was necessary to divide what might be considered a single subject into a number of subcategories. For example, Involuntary Hospitalization was divided into thirteen principal subcategories, with thirteen corresponding tables to portray the appropriate statutory provisions. The titles to the tables identify the categories selected. The tables are cited by arabic numerals, the first number designating the chapter to which the table is appended and the second, the sequence in which is appears—e.g., Table 2.3.

Except for the tables which simply list statutory

---

21. Zilboorg, "Legal Aspects of Psychiatry," in *One Hundred Years of American Psychiatry* 511 (Zilboorg & Hall eds. 1944).

22. See, respectively, Table 3.1, Statutory Definitions of the Mentally Ill; Table 3.7, Statutory Definitions of the Mentally Deficient and Epileptics; Table 3.8, Statutory Definitions of

Alcoholics and Drug Addicts; Table 8.1, Statutory Definitions of Incompetents and Persons Subject to Guardianship; Table 10.1, Statutory Considerations of Sexual Psychopaths and Related Offenders.

definitions, each table is subdivided into vertical columns whose headings designate (by the use of key words or phrases) the particular statutory provisions charted. The states and the District of Columbia are listed in the initial vertical left-hand column as part of the citation of the particular statute or code used in the research. The statute or code so cited governs the various titles and sections charted horizontally unless another statute or code is cited for the particular section involved. If a supplement to a statute or code is used as authority for a provision, the date of the supplement will be found in parentheses beneath the section cited.

A list of footnotes follows each table. Statutory provisions which do not precisely fit into the table or column heading under which they are charted have been footnoted; additional comments and explanations may also be found in the footnotes. The reader should be cautioned that in some instances it may be misleading to peruse the tables without taking note of the footnotes. In this regard, it is especially important to refer to the footnotes in the extreme left-hand column for qualifications which may govern the entire charting of the state or jurisdiction involved.

The fact that statutory provisions on certain subjects are absent from the tables should not be interpreted as an indication that no law exists on the subject; case law may exist and in many instances be adequate. Furthermore, it must be pointed out that statutory ambiguities have been resolved solely by reference to the statutory language and (with some obvious exceptions) without any attempt to research cases on the point. However, Table Intro. 1, Summary of Civil Hospitalization Proceedings, shows civil hospitalization procedures by state for the convenience of those who wish to determine quickly the types of procedures available in a particular jurisdiction. For a more detailed view the specific tables for that procedure may be examined.

Since legislation is a continuing process, the statutes of the various states are constantly subject to change. There is sometimes a lag between the legislative sessions and the general distribution of the statutory materials needed to ascertain what changes, if any, have been made. To meet this situation, a cutoff date of October 1969 was set. All pertinent statutory materials available to the researchers at that date were used in preparing the tables.

C. APPENDIXES

The Draft Act, to which the Report makes numerous references, is presently out of print; it is set forth as Appendix A at the end of this volume as an aid to the reader. As mentioned previously, the Commonwealth of Puerto Rico, the territory of Guam and the Virgin Islands are not included in the tables following the various chapters in this Report. However, a summary of the major admission, hospitalization, and discharge provisions found in these jurisdictions is contained in Appendix B.

BIBLIOGRAPHY

American Bar Association. Section of Criminal Law. Committee on Criminal Procedure. *Annual Report.* Chicago: American Bar Association, 1938.

————. Section of Criminal Law. Committee on Medico-Legal Problems. *Annual Report.* Chicago: American Bar Association, 1935.

————. *Section of Real Property, Probate and Trust Law: Index to Publications of the Section. 1934–1955.* Chicago: American Bar Foundation, 1956.

American Bar Association Reports. Chicago: American Bar Association.
68 (1943) 183
69 (1944) 143, 221
70 (1945) 338
72 (1947) 289
73 (1948) 297
77 (1952) 318
79 (1954) 151, 399.

American Bar Foundation. "Hospitalization and Treatment of Mental Cases." Unpublished memorandum. February 1955.

Fein, Rashi. *Economics of Mental Illness.* Joint Commission on Mental Illness and Health. Monograph Series no. 2. New York: Basic Books, Inc., 1958.

McAvinchey, Frank L. "The Not-Quite-Incompetent Incompetent." American Bar Association Section of Real Property, Probate and Trust Law. *Proceedings.* Chicago: American Bar Association, 1956.

Matthews, Arthur R., Jr. *Mental Disability and the Criminal Law: A Field Study.* Chicago: American Bar Foundation, 1970.

National Clearinghouse for Mental Health Information. "The Cost of Mental Illness, 1968." Statistical Note 30. Washington, D.C.: National Institute of Mental Health (Oct. 1970).

National Institute of Mental Health. Federal Security Agency. *A Draft Act Governing Hospitalization of the Mentally Ill.* Public Health Service Pub. no. 51. Washington, D.C.: Government Printing Office, 1952.

Rock, Ronald S.; Jacobson, Marcus A.; and Janopaul, Richard M. *Hospitalization and Discharge of the Mentally Ill.* An American Bar Foundation Study. Chicago: University of Chicago Press, 1968.

United States Department of Commerce. Bureau of the Census. *Statistical Abstract of the United States 1959.* 80th ed. Washington, D.C.: Government Printing Office, 1959.

United States Department of Health, Education, and Welfare. *Mental Health Statistics, Current Facility Reports: Provisional Patient Movement and Administrative Data, State and County Mental Hospitals, United States, July 1, 1968–June 30, 1969.* Washington, D.C.: Government Printing Office, 1970.

United States Public Health Service. National Institute of Mental Health. *Patients in State and County Mental Hospitals 1967.* Public Health Service Pub. no. 1921. Washington, D.C.: Government Printing Office, 1969.

Zilboorg, Gregory. "Legal Aspects of Psychiatry." *One Hundred Years of American Psychiatry.* Edited by Gregory Zilboorg and J. K. Hall for the American Psychiatric Association. New York: Columbia University Press, 1944.

Chapter One Historical Trends

In ancient times the laws that governed mentally disabled persons took the form of taboos and tribal customs.[1] Until the Golden Age of Greece, the prevailing explanation for mental disabilities was that the person so afflicted was possessed by demons. Predicated on the theory that such maladies were a result of supernatural powers imposing punishment, the prophylaxis and cure depended entirely on magic. Exorcising the demon from the mentally disabled person was the chief method of treatment. There were a variety of bizarre, and in some instances inhuman, ways to accomplish this. Brutal physical tortures were used, such as crushing the victim's body or removing sections of a disabled person's skull to drive out, or let out, the evil spirit.

In the highly developed civilization of ancient Egypt, mentally disabled persons were taken to the temples, where the priest-physicians used incantations, threats, and such physical remedies as herbs and oils to restore their patients. In Greece during the fourth century B.C., great strides were made to dispel the previous theory that mental disabilities were supernaturally induced. Hippocrates (460–370 B.C.), the father of medicine, and the Greek physicians and philosophers who followed him recognized mental disabilities as natural phenomena and attempted to classify them. They suggested that the mentally disabled be confined in the salubrious atmosphere of a comfortable, sanitary, well-lighted place. Similar advances in medicine were made during the Roman era, and gradually mental disability came to be regarded as primarily a medical problem rather than a religious one.

One of the earliest legal references to the mentally disabled is contained in the Twelve Tables of Rome, which were promulgated in 449 B.C.

There it was provided:

Si furiosus escit, agnatum gentiliumque in eo pecuniaque ejus potestas esto . . . est ei custos non escit.[2]

[If a person is a fool, let this person and his goods be under the protection of his family or his paternal relatives, if he is not under the care of anyone.]

The term *furiosus* undoubtedly meant any mentally disabled person. Later texts, dating from the time of Cicero, limited the term to those who had moments of lucidity. However, it is unlikely that the early law recognized such comparatively subtle distinctions. The Twelve Tables referred to a person who did not act in the normal manner. Control of the person and goods of the *furiosus* did not depend on a judicial decree or formal pronouncement of a magistrate but rather arose directly by reason of the condition of the *furiosus*. The fact that he did not act like other people was sufficient for his relatives to assume control of his person and goods.

It is interesting to note that this law affected only the head of a family, for it applied only if the mentally disabled person was not under anyone's care. In ancient Roman law, sons and daughters of any age were under the power (*potestas*) of the head of the family and could not hold property. It was therefore unnecessary to appoint an administrator for their affairs, and their personal care was a matter for the head of the family to decide.

Later, when Roman law was fully developed, the magistrate designated a guardian (*curator*).[3] The person who exercised *potestas* over a mentally disabled person usually nominated by testament a guardian to serve in his place in case he should die before the disabled person, and this wish was followed by the magistrate. If the testament contained no nomination, the magistrate was free to choose whomever he pleased. Ordinarily he named as guardian a close relative of the person who needed care.

Roman law was troubled with problems that seem contemporary. What was the legal status of a mentally disabled person during his lucid moments? Was he still under the protection of a guardian? If not, was it necessary to name a new guardian each time the illness returned? And what was the status of a testament made by him during his lucid moments? These questions were answered during the time of Justinian, when it was decided that the guardianship

---

1. For an enlightening account and analysis of the care of the mentally ill in primitive societies, see Biggs, *The Guilty Mind* 3–34 (1955); Deutsch, *The Mentally Ill in America* 1–12 (2d ed. 1949).

2. Bruns, *Fontes Juris Romani Antiqui* 23–24 (Editio alterata aucta amendata, 1871).

3. *Code* 5.70.6; *Institutes* 1.23.3. Under Justinian a proceeding was held before the *curator* was named; the cited passage in the Institutes states that the *curator* will be named "ex inquisitione."

was merely suspended during the person's lucid moments and that it again became operative as soon as the illness returned.[4] In addition, it was held that testaments made during lucid moments were valid.[5]

Problems arose as well in the field of contract and tort law. The Romans held that mentally disabled persons were unable to form the consent necessary to make a valid contract and that, therefore, they were incapable of entering into a contract.[6] Similarly, they were not legally capable of agreeing to the marriage contract. Roman law also held that mentally disabled persons were legally incapable of obligating themselves by delictual acts such as theft, for the offender could not form the intent to take the property of another.

Under fully developed Roman law, the ward lost all legal capacity. He could not, of course, make a testament nor could his guardian do it for him. The guardian, in earlier Roman law, had full and complete power over the goods of the ward. He could buy, sell, and exchange the ward's property. Later this complete power was limited so that the guardian acted solely as the administrator of the ward's patrimony. He could not sell or transfer the real property of the ward, nor make a gift in his name nor liberate his slaves.[7]

When guardianship terminated, through either the ward's recovery or his death, the guardian had to account either to the former ward or to his heirs. This was one method of encouraging honest stewardship.[8]

After the decay of the Western Empire during the fifth century, the *lex barbarorum,* or the law of the Germanic tribes, was applied in Western Europe while Roman law continued to be followed in the Eastern Empire. The Visigothic Code,[9] which was followed in Spain and France, declared that "[a]ll persons who are insane from infancy, or indeed from any age whatever, and remain so without intermis-

sion, cannot testify, or enter into a contract, and if they should do so, it would have no validity. But such as have lucid intervals, shall not be prohibited from transacting business during those periods."[10]

During the Middle Ages, mental disabilities were again considered the product of possession by demons, and exorcism was revived as the accepted method of treatment. This time it was accompanied by ceremonies more elaborate and antidotes more torturous than those used by the ancients.[11] The laws that were promulgated continued to reflect concern for the property of the disabled, with little legal attention given to his person.

In England, sometime between 1255 and 1290, the statute *De Praerogativa Regis* was enacted.[12] This law divided mentally disabled persons into two classes, the idiot and the lunatic, the former being a person who "hath no understanding from his nativity" and the latter "a person who hath had understanding, but . . . hath lost the use of his reason." The king was granted the custody of the lands of "natural fools" (idiots); after providing the "fool" with necessaries, the king could retain the profits from the land. After the "fool's" death the land was to be returned to the "right heirs." The land of those who happened to "fail of their wit" (lunatics) was held by the king, and all of the profits therefrom applied to the maintenance of the mentally ill persons and their households. Any excess was returned to such persons "when they come to right mind."[13] Guardianship over the property of the "idiot" was profitable for the guardian; on the other hand, managing the property of a "lunatic" was a duty, and no profit could be made from it.

In *Beverley*'s case,[14] decided in the early seventeenth century, Lord Coke expounded the law of insanity as it had developed in England. Because of its importance, the opinion is worthy of close examination.

Lord Coke first explained that every act performed by a *non compos mentis* concerned his life, his lands, or his goods. The law of England provided that every act done by him in a court of record should

---

4. *Code* 5.70.6.

5. *Code* 6.22.9; *Institutes* 2.12.1. However, since a *furiosus* is *non compos mentis,* he may not be used as witness to a will; if he should have temporary remission, he might serve during that period. *Institutes* 2.10.6; *Digest* 28.1.20.4.

6. *Institutes* 3.20.8: "The *furiosus* is unable to transact business, for he does not understand what he does."

7. *Digest* 40.1.13.

8. The former ward or his heirs could commence an action *negotiorum gestorum utilis* against the guardian.

9. This code, drafted between A.D. 466 and 485, was edited in Latin and was greatly influenced by Roman law. It served as the basic legislation of the Visigoths for nearly 200 years when it was replaced by a code edited by order of King Receswind.

10. *Visigothic Code* 2.5.10. in Scott, *The Visigothic Code* 67 (1910).

11. Shryock, "The Beginnings," in *One Hundred Years of American Psychiatry* 4 (Zilboorg & Hall eds. 1944).

12. 17 Edw. 1, c. 9; 1 Holdsworth, *A History of English Law* 473 (7th ed. 1956); 2 Pollock & Maitland, *The History of English Law* 464 (2d ed. 1911).

13. 17 Edw. 1, c. 9.

14. 4 Co. 123b, 76 Eng. Rep. 1118 (K.B. 1603).

bind him and his heirs forever while acts done *in pais* (without legal proceedings) should bind him for life and in some cases forever. However, the law of England was that the *non compos mentis* should not lose his life for having committed murder or felony.

The reason for this distinction is clear: the penalties inflicted on the felon were extremely severe, "so that by punishing a few, fear might come to many." However, as Lord Coke pointed out, "the punishment of a man who is deprived of reason and understanding cannot be an example to others." Lord Coke added that the *non compos mentis* was not able to form the felonious intent that was the very heart of the crime and therefore not guilty of murder or felony, although he was subject to conviction for high treason if the circumstances warranted.

Lord Coke listed four types of persons included in the generic term *non compos mentis*. They were:

1. the idiot or natural fool;
2. he who was of good and sound memory, and by the visitation of God has lost it;
3. lunatics, those who are sometimes lucid and sometimes *non compos mentis;*
4. those who by their own acts deprive themselves of reason, as the drunkard.

This distinction had certain important legal consequences. For example, an idiot was required to appear in court in person, while one who had become *non compos mentis* was represented by a guardian if he were under age and by an attorney if he had reached his majority. The lunatic was responsible for acts done by him during his lucid moments, while those acts performed during his nonlucid moments were of the same effect as those performed by an idiot. Lord Coke concluded this phase of his analysis with the observation that those who voluntarily deprived themselves of their reason, such as the drunkard, should not be heard to claim insanity as a defense in a civil or criminal action. Indeed, he argued that it would constitute an aggravation of the offense.

He then made an interesting comparison between the civil and the common law as these laws sought to protect the idiot and his inheritance. He noted that all acts performed by a *non compos mentis* without the accord of his tutor were void in the civil law. The lack of a similar requirement in common law was cited as a defect in the common-law system. He pointed out that the law of England did in fact provide a tutor in the form of the king. As we have seen, under the statute *De Praerogativa Regis,* the person and goods of the idiot were in the custody of the king. Any transfer of property made by the idiot could be

voided by action of the king, and the king could terminate any action against an idiot "brought on any bond or writing that he has made" by sending a *supersedeas* to the court where the suit had been commenced. The king could even void gifts or transfers made by the idiot before he was adjudged incompetent. However, if the idiot died before being adjudged incompetent, no formal inquiry as to his competency could be held, and transfers made by the idiot during his lifetime could not be attacked.

One who became *non compos mentis,* as distinguished from the person who was born an idiot, was also protected by the king. The king was accountable to the lunatic when the latter had lucid moments. Transfers attempted by the lunatic during his nonlucid moments were subject to attack in the same manner as were those made by idiots.

It is clear from *Beverley*'s case that English law by the seventeenth century had established many methods to protect the property of the insane. Similarly, in criminal matters, the law had recognized that the mentally disabled could not form a criminal intent and, therefore, were not guilty of felonies and murders. Lord Coke also related that the king was given custody of the person of the afflicted individual as well as his lands. It would appear, however, that this protection of the person consisted of caring for his needs out of the proceeds from the lands. There is no indication that this care even constituted a drain on the king's treasury. Nonetheless, it is interesting to note this relatively early concern for the person of one who was mentally disabled.

The method of determining an individual's mental status is worthy of attention. When a person was thought to be an idiot, the chancellor, upon petition, issued a writ *de idiota inquirendo,* which was tried by a jury of twelve men. The writ and the procedure employed in the case of lunacy were similar in nature to the writ *de idiota inquirendo,* and juries, simply to avoid heavy exactions by the king, often found for lunacy where idiocy would have been a more accurate finding.[15]

If an incompetent were determined by the jury to be a lunatic, the chancellor committed him to the care of some friend, who received an allowance with which to care for him. The incompetent's heir was generally made the manager of the estate, although, according to Blackstone, "to prevent sinister practices" he was not given the custody of the incompetent. For the custody of the estate the heir was responsible to the court of chancery, to the recovered

15. 1 Blackstone, *Commentaries* 303–7 (9th ed. 1783).

3

lunatic, or to his administrator.[16] The practices of persons charged with the custody of an incompetent and his property gradually developed into a set of customs, rules, and standards for the proper management of a lunatic's property.

During the period between the attack of lunacy and the determination by the jury, the incompetent was cared for by his nearest relatives. It may be that the impecunious *non compos mentis* could not enjoy the privilege of having his sanity determined by a jury, for Blackstone states that one applied to the royal authority for lasting confinement "when the disorder is grown permanent, and the circumstances of the party will bear such additional expense."[17]

The distinction is significant and may serve to explain much of the later development of detention procedures. If one held property, he was able to pay the expenses incurred in the inquiry as to his sanity. Likewise, such an inquiry was necessary to assure the proper administration of the applicant's affairs, while the proceeds from his holdings would pay the cost of administration and provide for his maintenance. On the other hand, those who were not persons of wealth did not require an administrator for their affairs, and there was no method of compensating the nearest relative for their support.

It is apparent that in colonial America the prospect of supporting an indigent incompetent was not a pleasant one, especially during the early years. The colonies were sparsely populated, and communal facilities—not only those for the care of the mentally disabled but others such as fire departments, public schools, and even prisons—were lacking. The family, as the primary social unit, was expected to care for its own. Communal facilities slowly developed to care for those who had neither family nor friends to turn to for support. The position of the mentally disabled with neither means nor family was critical. Since they were unable to secure employment, they formed transient bands, drifting from town to town.

This itinerant group was treated as a monolithic mass; there was no attempt to analyze its components. A "drifter" was a "drifter" and nothing more. Whether he was mentally or physically disabled or simply lazy made no difference to the townspeople, who feared they would have to support him. For these reasons the mentally disabled, during the colonial period, were often subjected to the same treatment as the itinerant poor. In the strongly Puritanical atmosphere of the time, which equated work

and industry with the moral life, it was inevitable that the laws should be aimed at compelling a man to labor, rather than at providing for his needs. In the case of the mentally disabled, these measures led to such grotesque incidents as whipping the hapless. The victims of society wandered aimlessly about the countryside, undergoing ridicule from village children and idlers and eking out an existence by begging.[18]

Early instances of community action seem to have been motivated by a desire to aid the impoverished family in caring for its charge rather than by any desire to aid directly the victim of a mental disability. For example, in Pennsylvania, the Upland court records of 1676 show that a certain Jan Vorelissen of Amesland complained to the court that his son Erik was "bereft of his naturall Senses and is turned quyt madd," and that he, the father, was a poor man and unable to maintain his son. It was therefore ordered that three or four persons be hired "to build a little block-house at Amesland for to put in the said madman."[19] A similar instance occurred in Braintree, Massachusetts, in 1689, where the inhabitants voted that a certain Samuel Speere should construct a small building to contain his sister and also that he should provide for her. The town further voted to pay the expenses incurred by Speere in maintaining his sister.[20] Likewise, instances may be found where the community made maintenance payments to persons not related to but in charge of indigent mentally disabled. This development does not appear to have involved any judicial procedure. Rather, it is quite likely that the members of the community, having a mentally deranged person in the neighborhood who perhaps plagued them by constant begging, decided it would be better for one person, reimbursed by the community, to provide for the needs of that individual. This seems more a practical solution of a problem than a "commitment" to the custody of another.

Of course, if the mentally disabled person was violent, forcible restraint was necessary and recourse was had to the sheriff or constable to detain him. In

18. Deutsch, *supra* note 1, at 25. The situation was not much better in England. Shakespeare, writing of a somewhat earlier period, described one of his characters in this fashion: "Poor Tom, that eats the swimming frogs, the toads, the tadpole, the wall newt and the water newt, that in the fury of his heart, when the foul fiend rages, eats cow dung, fox sallets, swallows the old rat and the ditch dog, drinks the green mantle of the slimy pool; who is shipt from tything to tything, and stocked, punished and imprisoned." (*King Lear,* act 3, scene 4.)

19. Deutsch, *supra* note 1, at 42.

20. Ibid.

16. Ibid.

17. Id. at 305.

some instances the town itself requested the police authority to take such measures. In 1676, Massachusetts enacted a statute ordering the selectmen of towns having dangerously distracted persons to take care of them, "that they doe not damify others."[21] The negative wording of this statute indicates that the sole purpose of the community's action was to restrain the violent. Here again, as in the earlier instances, the laws reflected the state of medical knowledge and the level of community development. Medical knowledge provided no method of treatment, and quite naturally, the community could do no more than protect itself. This Massachusetts statute provided the legal basis for the forcible restraint of the violent.

Though research on this period has uncovered no cases of anyone's requesting his release from forcible detention, it is quite probable that such detention could have been justified on the theory that the community had the right to defend itself collectively against one who would cause it harm. As has been seen, Lord Coke declared it law that a *non compos mentis* could not be guilty of murder or a felony because he could not form the requisite felonious intent. Lord Coke added, however, that a *non compos mentis* could be guilty of high treason, which was a crime against the community.[22] Furthermore, the community had the right to defend itself against acts of violence committed by the *non compos mentis*.

In these early cases, if the derangement and violence were apparent and, more pertinently, the mentally disabled person was without family, there probably was no objection raised about commitment. When a member of a small community acted strangely and constituted a threat to the peace, he was placed in custody. The subtleties of psychiatric diagnosis were for a later day.

The problem of proper commitment procedures did not arise until institutions for the detention and treatment of the mentally disabled had developed and their doors had been opened to less obvious cases of mental disability. Formerly, throwing a potential murderer into prison under the guise of restraining his violent tendencies probably raised no debate; today, restraining a meek and harmless mentally disabled person does raise the problem.

The establishment of hospitals to which the mentally disabled could be sent for treatment developed in the eighteenth century. In response to a petition

drawn by Benjamin Franklin, the Pennsylvania Assembly, in May 1751, authorized the establishment of the first general hospital, to receive and cure the mentally ill as well as the sick poor. In 1773, Virginia erected at Williamsburg the first hospital devoted exclusively to the mentally disabled. It remained the only one of its kind in the country until 1824, when the Eastern Lunatic Asylum was established in Lexington, Kentucky.[23]

As noted earlier, detention by relatives was mentioned by Blackstone as being a common measure at the onset of lunacy. In 1774, Parliament enacted a statute to regulate "private madhouses."[24] Though limited specifically to England, Wales, and the town of Berwick upon Tweed, it is a significant statute, for it demonstrates the concern reflected in more populous regions for the condition of the mentally disabled. It provided that the Royal College of Physicians elect five of its Fellows to grant licenses to operate houses for the reception of lunatics in the larger cities. These commissioners were to visit and inspect at least once every year the licensed houses and those detained therein. Any person could apply to the commissioners for information about the place of detention of a particular person. The secretary of the commissioners was to be informed of each new inmate within three days of his admission "except such pauper lunatics as shall happen to be sent there by parish officers." Such notice of arrival had to contain the name and place of abode of the person by whose direction the lunatic was sent to the house and also the name and place of abode of the physician, surgeon, "or apothecary by whose advice such direction was given." Any keeper of such a house who admitted a purported lunatic

> without having an order, in writing, under the hand and seal of some physician, surgeon, or apothecary, that such a person is proper to be received into such house or place as a lunatic . . . shall . . . pay the sum of one hundred pounds.

In other areas of England, justices of the peace, accompanied by a physician, were authorized to license the houses and conduct visitations. After specifically exempting public hospitals from its provisions, this act concluded with this highly significant paragraph:

> And whereas it is not intended by this act to give the keepers of any house or houses, so to be licensed as aforesaid, or any other person concerned in confining

21. *5 Records of the Governor and Company of the Massachusetts Bay in New England* 80 (1854).

22. Beverley's Case, 4 Co. 123b, 124b, 76 Eng. Rep. 1118, 1121 (K.B. 1603).

23. Deutsch, *supra* note 1, at 59, 71.

24. An Act for Regulating Madhouses, 1774, 14 Geo. 3, c. 49.

any of his Majesty's subjects therein, any new justification from their being able to prove that the person so confined having been sent there by such direction and advice as are required by this act; be it therefore declared and enacted, That in all proceedings that shall be had under his Majesty's writ of *Habeas Corpus,* and in all indictments, informations, and actions, that shall be preferred and brought against any person or persons, for confining or ill-treating any of his Majesty's subjects, in any of the said houses, the parties complained of shall be obliged to justify their proceedings according to the course of the common law, in the same manner as if this act had not been made.[25]

It is clear from these words that habeas corpus was viewed in the common law as an appropriate method for attacking the legality of detention in an asylum. The writ of habeas corpus was highly valued in the colonies, and it was considered an integral part of the rights of Englishmen.[26] From the foregoing, it would appear that the writ of habeas corpus was available to those detained in asylums. However, the nonviolent poor could be imprisoned under the poor laws; the nonviolent and perhaps even the violent rich were cared for privately. Probably only the violent poor were detained in the early asylums, for they constituted a threat to the community. The thorny problems arose with the commitment of the nonviolent. The statute of George III referred to a commitment procedure that depended upon certification by one "physician, surgeon or apothecary." Similarly, certification by one physician was all that was required for commitment to the Pennsylvania hospital.[27]

The gradually emerging responsibility of the community, supplementary to the immediate obligation of the family, for restraining violent persons is well illustrated by a New York statute enacted February 9, 1788,[28] which notes that "there are sometimes persons, who by lunacy or otherwise are furiously madd, or are so far disordered in their senses that they may be dangerous to be permitted to go abroad." The statute then authorizes two or more justices to direct, by warrant, constables to apprehend and keep safely locked up the furiously mad and the dangerous. (If the justices found it necessary, these persons could be chained.) This section of the statute concludes with the injunction that it should not be interpreted to restrain or abridge the power of the chancellor as it pertains to lunatics "or to restrain or prevent any friend or relation or [*sic*] such lunatic from taking them under their own care and protection." Here there can be no doubt that the legislators considered the asylums to be primarily for the care of those violent persons who could not be cared for privately. This attitude is all the more understandable when one recalls that the purpose of commitment was detention and not therapy.

While commitment of the *non compos mentis* was sometimes accomplished on certification of only one physician, or on a warrant issued by only two justices of the peace, there are records of the procedural safeguards employed to preserve the property rights of the *non compos mentis.* In New York, the procedure followed in getting someone declared *non compos mentis* for the purpose of having his affairs administered followed in general the procedure outlined by Blackstone: An individual requested a writ *de lunatico inquirendo* from the chancellor.[29] The chancellor, on the issuance of the writ, empowered a jury to inquire into the mental condition of the respondent. If the jury were persuaded that the respondent was incompetent, the chancellor appointed a guardian; the chancellor could also request the respondent to appear before him for examination. Adequate notice to the respondent was necessary. Similarly, an early Louisiana case, under the civil law system, declared that one could not be deprived of his right to administer his own affairs on *ex parte* evidence and that he should be cited and have the opportunity to cross-examine as in any other suit.[30] The different rules applying to legal representation for idiots and lunatics that were discussed by Lord Coke in *Beverley's* case appeared in this country in 1830, when it was held that a person adjudged a lunatic might have leave to attack the finding of incompetency through an attorney, although an idiot must appear in person.[31]

The common-law right of habeas corpus was available to test the detention of a "mentally disabled" person. It was the device used in the *Oakes* case. In

25. Id. at § 31.

26. The colonists' struggle to secure the right of habeas corpus in the colonies is well described in Perry & Cooper, *Sources of Our Liberties* 194–95 (1959). In some instances, the writ continued to be issued as a common law remedy in the colonies despite the Privy Council's veto of colonial legislation that would have statutorily guaranteed this right to the colonists.

27. Deutsch, *supra* note 1, at 62.

28. *N.Y. Laws of 1788,* ch. 31.

29. *In re* Barker, 2 Johns. Ch. 232 (N.Y. 1816); Blackstone, *supra* note 15, at 305.

30. Stafford v. Stafford, 1 Mart. 551 (La. Sup. Ct. 1823).

31. *In re* Covenhoven, 1 N.J. Eq. 19 (Ch. 1830).

1845 a habeas corpus action was instituted on behalf of one Josiah Oakes,[32] who sought his release from the McLean Asylum in Massachusetts on the ground that he had been illegally committed by his family. The court acknowledged that the United States Constitution prohibited the detention of anyone against his will, unless he be deprived of his liberty by judgment of his peers or the law of the land. The court also acknowledged that private institutions for the insane had been in use and sanctioned by the courts. The court went on to state:

> The right to restrain an insane person of his liberty is found in that great law of humanity, which makes it necessary to confine those whose going at large would be dangerous to themselves or others. . . . And the necessity which creates the law, creates the limitation of the law. The question must then arise in each particular case, whether a patient's own safety, or that of others, requires that he should be restrained for a certain time, and whether restraint is necessary for his restoration, or will be conducive thereto. The restraint can continue as long as the necessity continues. This is the limitation, and the proper limitation.[33]

The significance of this decision is readily apparent: it establishes guideposts to be used in determining the propriety of detention. The old standard of "detention of the violent" has gradually become outmoded. Oakes was not a violent person; he was detained on the allegation that he suffered from hallucinations and displayed unsoundness of mind in conducting his business affairs. The charge grew out of the fact that Oakes, an elderly and ordinarily prudent man, became engaged to a young woman of unsavory character a few days after the death of his wife. The commitment of marginal cases required the courts to render more precise the common-law rules as to detention. Reflecting advances in medical science as well as the change in society's view of mental disability, the court contemplated detention for therapeutic purposes as well as for the more obvious reason of defending society against its deranged members.

In 1849 a case was tried in Philadelphia which demonstrated that concern need also be shown for the protection of hospital officials acting in good faith. A man named Hinchman instituted a civil suit for wrongful detention against his mother, sister, cousins, the physicians of the asylum, and the physician who signed the certificate. He recovered a large sum of money. Dr. Isaac Ray, in reporting the case,[34] stated that the evidence showed beyond a doubt that Hinchman was violently and dangerously insane.

Aid for the mentally disabled rapidly ceased to be the concern of an isolated few; partisans of improvement in psychiatric care organized to work more effectively. In 1844 the American Psychiatric Association was founded in Philadelphia by thirteen hospital superintendents.[35] By pooling their experience and knowledge in the relatively new field of psychiatry, they were able to make prodigious strides in understanding and treating the mentally disabled. Two of the original members of this group deserve special mention. Dr. Benjamin Rush, the father of American psychiatry, was the leader of his period in putting the observation and treatment of mental disability on a scientific basis. Dr. Isaac Ray, who possessed a keen insight into the purely medical aspects of "insanity," published an authoritative exposition of the intricate relationship between law and psychiatry.[36]

While law was progressing by means of judicial decision, and medical science by means of the work of such men as Dr. Rush and Dr. Ray, other voices were heard calling for changes. Two women were especially responsible for improvement: Mrs. E. P. W. Packard, who was interested in reforming commitment procedures and Miss Dorothea Lynde Dix, who stressed the inadequacy of treatment facilities.

Mrs. Packard had been committed to the Illinois State Hospital in 1860 on her husband's petition. Under the commitment statute in force at that time in Illinois, married women and infants could be involuntarily committed on the request of the husband or a guardian without the evidentiary standard applicable in cases involving others having been satisfied.[37]

32. Matter of Josiah Oakes, 8 Law Reporter 123 (Mass. Sup. Ct. 1845).

33. Id. at 125.

34. Ray, *A Treatise on the Medical Jurisprudence of Insanity* 411 (5th ed. 1871).

35. In 1844 the founders adopted the title, Association of Medical Superintendents of American Institutions for the Insane. For twenty-eight years beginning in 1893 the organization was named the American Medico-Psychological Association. In 1921 it assumed its present title, the American Psychiatric Association.

36. Ray's most important work, *A Treatise on the Medical Jurisprudence of Insanity, supra* note 34, was the first systematic treatise on this topic to appear in the English language. Six editions were published in this country, as well as one in England; at the time of his death, a seventh was under way. The book was often cited by appellate courts both in this country and abroad.

37. "Married women and infants, who, in the judgment of the medical superintendents of the state asylum at Jacksonville are

After her release three years later, Mrs. Packard began a campaign for new commitment legislation. Specifically, she urged that a person not be committed as insane solely on the basis of the opinions he might express and that commitment should be based only on irregular conduct which indicates that the individual is so lost to reason as to render him an unaccountable moral agent. In her frequent lectures, as well as in the popular books that she wrote,[38] Mrs. Packard vividly portrayed the horror of being wrongfully placed in a mental institution. Largely through her efforts, Illinois enacted the so-called personal liberty bill, which required a jury trial to determine whether the respondent in the action should be committed to a mental institution.

The influence of Miss Dorothea Lynde Dix was felt by lawmakers and social reformers even more keenly than that of Mrs. Packard. This Massachusetts schoolteacher, who later became Superintendent of Nurses for the Union forces during the Civil War, was so appalled at the lack of adequate facilities for the mentally disabled that she spent the last fifty years of her life crusading for improved hospital conditions. Thirty-two mental hospitals in this country and abroad were founded as a result of her efforts and at least twenty states responded to her appeals by establishing and enlarging mental hospitals. No other individual did more in the nineteenth century to advance the idea of communal responsibility for the welfare of the mentally disabled.[39]

Widespread, popularly supported movements such as these often culminated in the enactment of new commitment laws or the revision of old statutes. The new legislation enacted during the latter part of the nineteenth century constitutes the basic legislative patterns currently in force.

The development of the law as it affects the rights of the mentally disabled has been dependent upon three factors: (1) the extent of medical knowledge of the cause, care, and proper treatment of the mentally disabled, (2) the degree to which the politically organized community has acknowledged its respon-

sibility for the care and treatment of its afflicted citizens, and (3) the legal profession's awareness of the social realities of mental disability, as well as the acuteness of its concern for those who have neither relatives nor close friends to safeguard their rights.

The early law provided fairly adequate protection for the property of the mentally disabled individual, but his body was subjected to torture or he was forced to rely upon the charity of friends, depending on the temper of the times. Later the community distinguished between the violent and nonviolent, confining the former and lumping the latter with the itinerant poor. Still later, the nonviolent who had become burdens on their families were considered the responsibility of the community, and financial aid or public facilities were made available to them.

The factors conducive to a thorough examination and reevaluation of the laws as they relate to the rights of the mentally disabled exist today to a greater extent than ever before. Medical science now knows a great deal about mental disability and can, therefore, furnish fresh insights into the medico-legal problems involved. Furthermore, communities have attained a far greater sense of responsibility for the fate of the mentally disabled, and the legal profession is now more vitally concerned with their status.

The growing community assumption of responsibility for the fate of the mentally ill has taken the form of a conscious policy on the part of the federal government and the states, the latter to a large extent in response to the initiatives of the former. The so-called community mental health services concept is still a novel and developing one, yet its maturation over the past decade—in terms of conceptualization and enabling (funding) legislation, as well as of practical implementation—warrants recognition as a trend of conceivably high historical importance.

Primarily responsible for the development of the community mental health concept has been the widely perceived fact that the large state mental hospitals provided a very inadequate answer to the problems of the mentally disabled in this country.[40] Although they are not meant to replace the state mental hospitals, community mental health centers—the op-

evidently insane or distracted, may be entered or detained at the request of the husband or the guardian of the infant without the evidence required in other cases." *Ill. Laws 1851*, § 10, at 96, 98.

38. Packard, *Mrs. Packard's Prison Life* (1867); Packard, *Modern Persecution* (1887).

39. The greatest single project by Dorothea Lynde Dix was lobbying for the passage of a federal act granting 12,225,000 acres of government land to various states for use in providing for the mentally disabled. The act was passed by both houses of Congress in 1854 but vetoed by President Franklin Pierce. Deutsch, *supra* note 1, at 179.

40. For a discussion of some of the history and rationale behind the community mental health concept, see *U.S. Code Cong. & Ad. News* 1064–65, 88th Cong., 1st Sess. (1963); *U.S. Code Cong. & Ad. News* 1253–54, 90th Cong., 1st Sess. (1967). Stressed therein is the fact that the upward population trend in state mental hospitals had already been reversed; part of the credit is given to existing community mental health efforts, with the implication that a further strengthening of community services would further reduce populations and population pressures in the large hospitals.

erational components of the concept—would work to make the alternatives to long-term institutionalization more realistic and increase their utilization. The community centers themselves would provide a whole range of mental health services from consultation to emergency psychiatric care, from outpatient diagnosis to inpatient treatment. In addition, the centers would function as essential links between the community and the large state hospitals: referrals to the latter institutions could be made by the centers, though presumably only as a last resort. "Community involvement" is the guiding theme. Though rarely articulated, this somewhat nebulous concept derives its meaning and attractiveness from the presumption that localizing the decision-making process would benefit the mentally disabled in a given community in a variety of ways. Individualized or personalized assessment of a person's mental condition would be "better" assessment, more humane and sympathetic; localized dispositional decisions would be similarly advantageous by virtue of their consideration of local circumstances, family situation, employment condition, and so forth; local treatment centers could be more readily geared to the particularized needs of persons whose history and prospects as well as present disability are generally known. Effective counseling could persuade family or friends of the patient to retain or assume a share of the responsibility for his welfare, thus postponing or precluding the need for institutionalization and permitting quicker and more hopeful discharge. Some of these presumptions concerning the advantages of community service may be overly optimistic, particularly in view of the fact that the community programs would be laboring under the burdens and stress of novel development, burdens such as insufficient funding, staffing, and physical facilities. But the proponents of community mental health operate from the inalterable conviction that the inadequacies of the present system—the inherent and latent problems of the huge and often isolated state hospitals—are insurmountable, and any attempts to overcome them economically unfeasible. For that reason they place their trust, philosophically and economically, in the new model of mental health service, the community mental health concept.

In October 1963 the United States Congress enacted the Community Mental Health Centers Act[41] which initiated a program of federal financial support to aid and induce the states to provide localized mental health services. As an inducement to state legislative action, the Act was incontrovertibly a success. Whereas a number of states had engaged in community mental health action for years, and in fact had enacted detailed legislation of this sort prior to 1963 (New York was the first state to enact a Community Mental Health Services Act in 1954; some thirteen other states did so within the next decade), the four years following the 1963 Congressional Act produced similar legislation in twenty additional states, so that by the end of 1968 thirty-four states had Community Mental Health Services Acts.[42]

The 1963 federal Act and later amendments[43] devised a funding program which included the following authorizations for appropriation:

For Fiscal Year Ending:	Construction	Staffing	Alcoholics and Narcotic Addicts
6–30–65	$35,000,000		
6–30–66	50,000,000	$19,500,000	
6–30–67	65,000,000	24,000,000	
6–30–68	50,000,000	30,000,000	
6–30–69	60,000,000	26,000,000	$15,000,000
6–30–70	32,000,000	70,000,000	25,000,000

These funds were (are) to be allocated among the states on the basis of population, financial need, and the extent of the need for community mental health centers. To participate in the federal program, each state has to adopt an approved state plan. Individual Community Centers requesting financial aid have to conform to the state plan as well as to certain federal standards. The federal standards include ten "elements of comprehensive care"; the first five of these —inpatient services, outpatient services, partial hospitalization services, emergency services, and consultation and education services—are mandatory or "essential" elements which must be provided by a center seeking federal assistance. Federal contributions to local efforts are subject to certain limitations:

42. See Scully, "Current Status of State Community Mental Health Services Legislation" (1969), prepared for the Legislative Services Branch of the National Institute of Mental Health. The states recognized as having Community Mental Health Acts are: Arizona, Arkansas, California, Colorado, Connecticut, Idaho, Illinois, Indiana, Kentucky, Louisiana, Maine, Maryland, Massachusetts, Michigan, Minnesota, Montana, Nevada, New Hampshire, New Jersey, New York, North Carolina, North Dakota, Ohio, Oregon, Pennsylvania, Rhode Island, South Carolina, Texas, Utah, Vermont, Virginia, Washington, Wisconsin, and Wyoming.

43. Particularly the Alcoholic and Narcotic Addict Rehabilitation Amendments of 1968, Pub. L. No. 90–574, tit. 3, §§ 300–302, 261–63, Oct. 15, 1968.

41. Pub. L. No. 88–164, tit. 2, §§ 200–207, Oct. 31, 1963. See also U.S.C.A. tit. 42, §§ 2681–87 (1964, Supp. 1969).

The federal share in construction costs is not to exceed two-thirds of actual costs; staffing grants are to run for a maximum of fifty-one months, a 75 percent contribution is permitted for the first fifteen months, 60 percent for the next twelve months, 45 percent for the year thereafter, and 30 percent for the final twelve-month period.

The 1963 Community Mental Health Centers Act represents the first instance of significant federal aid and intervention in the mental health area, and constitutes the first program specifically directed at local community services. To be sure, federal assistance to state and local mental health efforts had been contemplated earlier under two 1946 amendments to the Public Health Service Act—the National Mental Health Act and the Hill-Burton amendment—which provided appropriations for personnel training and for the construction of physical facilities, respectively.[44] The promise of these programs was never realized, however; because of the great demand for *general* health facilities and the priority placed on these demands, only 3 percent of the grant funds appropriated under the Hill-Burton Act were used for *mental health* purposes.[45] What portion of this 3 percent was used for *community* mental health services is not recorded.

The response of the states to the 1963 Act has been encouraging in one sense, but less than hoped for on another level. As indicated before, the response in terms of legislation was extremely favorable: numerous states enacted detailed community mental health acts within a short span after passage of the federal Act. Other states legislated on a more modest level, but with sufficient specificity so that by 1968 a total of forty-three states had become eligible for and were participating in the federal program.[46] However, though widespread, participation was quantitatively limited: by early 1969 only some 350 community mental health centers were listed as participants, only half of these were in fact in operation, and only some 60 centers had been operating for two years or more.[47] The original impetus had lagged; the prospect of 2,000 centers on federal assistance by 1973 was revised to a hope that this number could perhaps be achieved by 1980. Qualitatively, the community centers program suffered as well: many of the centers in operation could not provide the contemplated range of services or cope with patient intake.[48]

Among various discernible factors that may have contributed in differential degrees to the incomplete realization of envisioned goals, it is difficult to ascertain whether and to what extent particular factors have in fact been causative.

The amount of federal appropriations and the actual funds which have become available may have been one of the inhibiting factors. First, the amount of federal support *authorized* is in itself not large as compared to the total costs involved in caring for the mentally ill.[49] Second, Congressional *appropriation* and executive *apportionment* have actually made available for use by the National Institute of Mental Health only about two-thirds of the authorized funds. As a result, between 1964 and 1968 total funds allocated to NIMH under the Community Mental Health Centers Act equalled no more than the amount of money required to run the New York State Department of Mental Hygiene for five months.[50] NIMH officials believe that similar cutbacks on the already modest authorizations are inevitable in the coming years as well: prospects "look far from favorable so long as the Vietnam war goes on" and the administration continues to pursue present fiscal policies, they assert.[51]

There is disagreement over whether state and local mental health agencies have in fact been inhibited by lack of authorizations and available funds. NIMH has not been overwhelmed with applications or required to turn down applications for lack of funds. In the past two years there has even been a falling off in requests for federal assistance. Arguably, however, the relatively modest demand for federal aid may it-

44. See 42 *U.S.C.A.* § 201 et seq., 42 *U.S.C.A.* § 291 et seq. (1969). The National Mental Health Act was enacted July 3, 1946 (ch. 538, Pub. L. No. 487); Hill-Burton was enacted Aug. 13, 1946 (ch. 958, Pub. L. No. 725).

45. *U.S. Code Cong. & Ad. News* 1058, 88th Cong., 1st Sess. (1963).

46. Scully, *supra* note 42.

47. Interview with Dr. Buker, Special Services Division, NIMH, Chevy Chase, Md. (May 13, 1969).

48. See, e.g., Brakel & South, "Diversion from the Criminal Process in the Rural Community," 7 *Am. Crim. L.Q.* 122 (1969), reprinted as American Bar Foundation Research Contribution No. 6 (1969). See also community mental health literature generally: e.g., Glasscote, Sussex, Cumming & Smith, *The Community Mental Health Center: An Interim Appraisal* (1969); Shore & Mannino, *Mental Health and the Community: Problems, Programs and Strategies* (1969); Golann, *Coordinate Index Reference Guide to Community Mental Health*, a bibliography (1969); Rosen, Weiner, Hench, Willner, & Bahn, "A National Survey of Outpatient Psychiatric Clinic Functions, Intake Policies and Practices," 122 *Am. J. Psychiat.* 908 (1966).

49. Glasscote et al., *supra* note 48, at 5.

50. Id. at 6.

51. Interview, *supra* note 47. For much the same prediction see Glasscote et al., *supra* note 48, at 7.

self be a function of the knowledge that the funds are short.

It may be suggested that the difficulty of complying with the federal standards for community mental health service has also been instrumental in delaying rapid development of community centers. Few new centers have the capacity to provide the five "essential" elements of service—inpatient, outpatient, partial hospitalization, emergency, and consultation-education services. Even fewer are capable of complying with the "desirable" (nonmandatory) standards—diagnostic, rehabilitative, and pre- and after-care services, training programs, and research and evaluation programs. NIMH officials claim that they follow a policy of strict adherence to the "essential" service requirements.[52] However, this appears to be more a stated goal than a practice. No center has ever had federal funds cut off on grounds of noncompliance, since "this is too drastic a step and hardly a solution to solving the problems of mental illness."[53] A few applications have been denied because local officials made unreasonable assessments of the local resource situation; more realistic assessment rendered the prospect of successful establishment of a comprehensive community mental health program too remote. In sum, adherence to the federal standards of service under NIMH interpretation is not as ominous a task as appearances would indicate: that is, a community center is judged to comply if it acts as a liaison or referral agency which makes accessible the "essential" services. The center does not have to provide those services on location, but fulfills its role when it refers patients efficiently and properly to institutions and facilities which do provide such services. This may not fully conform to the original conception of community mental health centers, but it does dispel the notion that the establishment of the centers is significantly impeded by too rigid federal standards.

It is possible that one significant factor in the slower-than-anticipated growth of the community mental health service concept is the state legislation in this area. Patterned on the Hill-Burton model, the federal Community Mental Health Act requires the establishment of an acceptable state plan, including an agency, which shall describe the state's community mental health needs, set standards, and channel local requests for federal assistance. Allotments out of the total federal funds available are made annually to the states on the basis of general criteria of population, financial need, and the extent of the need for community facilities, but payments or installments out of the allotments are made only on the showing of specific project estimates, local applications, or costs incurred. To implement and facilitate this showing a majority of states have enacted comprehensive statutes authorizing, financially assisting, and regulating local initiatives, but as an examination of some typical provisions reveals, the statutes have some potentially serious shortcomings.[54]

Under most acts, local jurisdictions are required to secure state legislative authorization for mental health activities they wish to engage in. Express designs for the use of local tax funds, the raising of special taxes or the issuance of bonds are often required. Most states require a minimum population of 50,000 in the jurisdiction or area where the center is to be established with state financial aid. The federal program calls for "catchment areas" of from 75,000 to 200,000 population but this requirement is flexible and exceptions are made. State and local planners should make certain that NIMH will accept their estimates as to the number of persons served. Furthermore, state legislation should authorize the establishment of community services across existing jurisdictional (county or city) lines, as some states already do, in view of the fact that few local jurisdictions have a population of 50,000, let alone from 75,000 to 200,000. Equally important, though administratively more complex, would be for the statutes of neighboring states to permit catchment areas across state lines if population concentrations made this desirable. One prerequisite for community mental health service is accessibility: perhaps this should be the first criterion in the location of a center and the designation of a catchment area.

State aid is commonly granted to local jurisdictions, including counties, cities, towns and villages. In some states, public agencies such as local health departments, hospitals, and school districts are also eligible. Under many of the Community Mental Health Service Acts, not-for-profit agencies generally may participate in the state programs or at the least the provisions permit reimbursement for contractual services rendered by such agencies.

The state laws are less than satisfactory on the question of what types of services are reimbursable.

52. Interview, *supra* note 47.

53. Ibid.

54. See Scully, *supra* note 42; Council of State Governments, Committee of State Officials on Suggested State Legislation, *Suggested State Legislation*, B-2 to B-15 (vol. xxvi of Community Mental Health Services Acts, 1967). The discussion regarding the state acts is based in part on these two studies.

Most statutes are specific in designating certain services as eligible for state support, but in many cases such important services as emergency and partial hospitalization care are conspicuously absent. It would appear that the cause of community mental health would be better served by statutes having more general provisions designating as reimbursable "all services for the prevention and treatment of mental illness."[55] If specificity is deemed desirable, then the provisions should at least include those services indicated in the federal standards for comprehensive care, so as to assure a measure of conformity with federal objectives and make more realistic the expectation of federal assistance.

Similar considerations apply to the state provisions regarding types of patients served under the state programs. Comprehensiveness is absent here as well. Very few states at present provide support for services for alcoholics or narcotics addicts despite the recent federal program supporting such services.[56] Other groups of disabled persons are similarly excluded by implication where the statutes enumerate some disabilities but fail to mention others.

Expenditures reimbursable under the state acts uniformly include "regular operational" expenditures such as staff salaries, maintenance and service costs, and so forth. In several states capital expenditures at one time were excluded from the list of reimbursable costs, but in most instances this anomaly has been corrected. Current state laws, however, still fail to provide for training of personnel and research expenditures, a serious omission in view of the fact that community mental health is still in a very early stage of development. Another shortcoming of some of the state acts is the specific exclusion from reimbursement of expenditures by community centers established prior to the time when the state program was to take effect. Thus communities which have pioneered in providing local services are in a sense penalized by that fact on the questionable assumption that their need for present aid is obviated by a measure of prior success.

The amount of reimbursement is often specifically stated in the statutes. State matching grants for locally incurred costs range from a low of 40 percent to a high of 90 percent. The average state share in 1968 was close to 60 percent. Lack of flexibility is the pri-

mary defect of these provisions. Poverty areas may be unable to raise any local funds or be capable of assuming only a very small share of the costs, thus precluding participation in the state aid programs. The federal government is not authorized to assume the total burden either. It is thus mandatory that the state statutes be revised to permit a flexible approach authorizing matching grants of up to 100 percent if local needs so indicate. Fixed *minimum* state shares rather than fixed maximums might be desirable. States needing to economize might advisedly adopt a system of differential rates for types of services deemed more or less essential than others.

A majority of the states which have Community Mental Health Service Acts consider eligible under the reimbursement program only those patients unable to pay for private services. Some states, however, do permit services to patients who could pay for private care but do not have it available to them. Other statutes limit the services for patients of economic means to diagnosis and/or consultation only, or permit service to them only upon referral by a court, school, or other public and private agency. Since ready availability is at the very core of the community mental health concept, such restrictions should be eliminated. Instead, community centers should provide at least a minimum of service (e.g., further referral) to all patients, and be allowed to collect fees—as they may in some states—if the patient's financial situation so warrants.

This examination of the state acts has revealed some of the actual and potential problems regarding the development of effective community mental health programs. States which do not have detailed acts have not, of course, escaped these problems by refraining from legislating on the matter. The discussion here has been based on the premise that the development of community mental health has so far been somewhat less than smooth and satisfactory. Though no independent evaluative study of community services has been done for this Report, this posture is justified by the evaluative literature available. A 1968 study[57] said much by implication: The study was intended to be a detailed description of eight community mental health centers in representative parts of the country, but as the field work progressed, this format had to be revised and ultimately the programs of only two centers were described because the other six were experiencing such organizational and developmental problems that detailed description would have proved nearly meaningless.

55. Cf. *Ark. Stat. Ann.* § 59-261(c) (Supp. 1969), where "programs of prevention and treatment of mental illness [and] other psychiatric, psychological and social disabilities" are included in the definition of reimbursable community services.

56. The Alcoholic and Narcotic Addict Rehabilitation Amendments of 1968, *supra* note 43.

57. Glasscote et al., *supra* note 48.

NIMH has refrained so far from engaging in any overall evaluation of the programs on grounds that such an attempt would be premature. Upon application the Institute does investigate periodically the performance of individual centers. On this basis, officials point out that in some areas drastic inroads on the work of state hospitals have been made by community centers, including the area of care for severely ill patients. Nonetheless a tacit admission emerges to the effect that the community mental health concept still has a long way to go and that its growth has not been without major disappointments and obstacles.

Aside from the specific problems mentioned in connection with the federal Act and the state acts in response thereto, a major and more general task confronting community mental health administrators is to recognize the need for and to work toward the ideal of *integrating* mental health services. That is to say, the community center's function is one of continuous contact with an individual as prospective patient, patient, and ex-patient. Precare, treatment, and aftercare are the operational components of this function, which require that a community center establish and maintain easy communication—a liaison—between itself and those social and medical agencies which touch the patient at the various stages of his disability. This implies a workable program of interchange with state and private hospitals, rehabilitation centers, welfare agencies, employment centers, and so forth. It also implies meaningful contact with law enforcement and judicial officials. Especially in this latter regard there has been much reluctance, neglect, and even deliberate disassociation: community mental health centers do not wish to overextend themselves by concerning themselves with the problems of policemen and judges which are often regarded a priori as not germane to mental health care; at the same time law and law enforcement officials feel that the services offered by community centers have little relevance to the realm of law enforcement.[58] Such thinking is difficult to adjudicate or legislate out of existence. Yet attempts have been made: several states provide in their commitment statutes that the courts and other agencies of commitment may, in proper situations, utilize available alternatives to hospitalization in the state institutions,[59] and a recent District of Columbia case indi-

cated the same approach.[60] Full and appropriate utilization of the existing community mental health services through integration of all organizations and agencies dealing with disabled persons is one major step in the direction of successful development of the community mental health concept.[61]

BIBLIOGRAPHY

An Act for Regulating Madhouses, 14 Geo. 3, 1774.

Biggs, John, Jr. *The Guilty Mind*. New York: Harcourt, Brace & Co., 1955.

Blackstone, Sir William. *Commentaries on the Laws of England*. 9th ed. by RI. Burn, LL.D., vol. 1. London: W. Strahan, T. Cadell & D. Prince, 1783.

Brakel, Samuel J., and South, Galen R. "Diversion from the Criminal Process in the Rural Community." 7

---

ment, the court may order, for a period not to exceed ninety days:

    (A) Such an individual to a public hospital. . . .

    (B) Such an individual to a community mental hygiene or health clinic."

Compare also the California approach which represents the most pervasive utilization of community mental health services in the country. Integration of local and state resources, with an emphasis on local decision-making, is now statutorily the essence of mental health administration in California under the revised Short-Doyle Act, *Cal. Welf. & Inst'ns Code* §§ 5600–5767 (West Supp. 1970); note also, for example, *Cal. Welf. & Inst'ns Code* § 1053.5 (West Supp. 1970), emphasizing the predisposition for treatment in the community.

60. Lake v. Cameron, 124 U.S. App. D.C. 264, 364 F.2d 657, 661 (D.C.) Cir. (1966). A habeas corpus petition for release from Saint Elizabeths Hospital was remanded for inquiry into alternative courses of treatment such as community mental health and day care services, public health nursing care, foster care, or private care.

61. That Congress continues to support the community approach to mental health problems is evidenced by the passage of the 1970 Amendments to the Community Mental Health Centers Act. The amendments extend the basic aspects of the federal program generally. Support for staffing of community facilities is broadened and the percentage of assistance increased. Furthermore, the commitment for support in this area is extended from the present 51 months to 8 years. Programs of construction and staffing of alcoholism and narcotic addiction centers are maintained. Most importantly, increased federal assistance for community mental health efforts in *poverty areas* is provided for. The federal share to a center serving in a poverty area has been raised to 90 percent in construction; for staffing costs, to 90 percent for the first two years and 75 percent for the remaining six years; and 5 percent of the annual staffing funds are set aside for "initiation and development" of services in poverty areas. Pub. L. No. 9-211; 84 Stat. 54 (March 13, 1970). See *U.S. Code Cong. & Ad. News* 267–77, 91st Cong., 2d Sess. (1970). For a summary of the Amendments, see 1 NIMH Reporter, at 1, cols. 2, 3 and at 8, cols. 1, 2 (Spring 1970).

---

58. See Brakel & South, *supra* note 48.

59. E.g., *Ohio Rev. Code Ann.* § 5122.15 (Baldwin 1964):
"If . . . the court finds that there is probable cause to believe that the individual . . . is mentally ill and in need of treat-

American Criminal Law Quarterly 122 (Spring 1969). Reprinted as *Research Contribution No. 6.* Chicago: American Bar Foundation, 1969.

Bruns, Carolus Georgius. *Fontes Juris Romani Antiqui.* Editio alterata aucta amendata. Tubingae: Libraria Lauppiana, 1871.

Council of State Governments. Committee of State Officials on Suggested State Legislation. *Suggested State Legislation.* Chicago: Council of State Governments, 1967.

Deutsch, Albert. *The Mentally Ill in America.* 2d ed. rev. New York: Columbia University Press, 1949.

Glasscote, Raymond M.; Sussex, James N.; Cummings, Elaine; and Smith, Lauren H. *The Community Mental Health Center: An Interim Appraisal.* Washington, D.C.: Joint Information Service of the American Psychiatric Association and the National Association for Mental Health, 1969.

Golann, Stuart E. *Coordinate Index Reference Guide to Community Mental Health.* New York: Behavioral Publications, 1969.

Holdsworth, Sir William. *A History of English Law.* 7th ed. vol. 1. London: Methuen & Company Ltd., 1956.

Perry, Richard L., and Cooper, John C. *Sources of Our Liberties.* Chicago: American Bar Foundation, 1959.

Pollock, Sir Frederick, and Maitland, Frederick William. *The History of English Law.* 2d ed. vol. 2. London: Cambridge University Press, 1911.

Ray, Isaac. *A Treatise on the Medical Jurisprudence of Insanity.* 5th ed. with additions. Boston: Little, Brown & Co., 1871.

Records of the Governor and Company of the Massachusetts Bay in New England. Vol. 5, 1854.

Rosen, B.; Weiner, J.; Hench, C.; Willner, S.; and Bahn, A. "A National Survey of Outpatient Psychiatric Clinic Functions, Intake Policies and Practices." 122 *American Journal of Psychiatry* 908 (1966).

Scott, S. P. *The Visigothic Code.* Boston: Boston Book Co., 1910.

Scully, Richard A. *Current Status of State Community Mental Health Services Legislation.* National Institute of Mental Health. Legislative Services Branch. Washington, D.C.: Government Printing Office, 1969.

Shore, Milton F., and Mannino, F. V., eds. *Mental Health and the Community: Problems, Programs and Strategies.* New York: Behavioral Publications, 1969.

Shryock, Richard H. "The Beginnings." *One Hundred Years of American Psychiatry.* Edited by Gregory Zilboorg and J. K. Hall for the American Psychiatric Association. New York: Columbia University Press, 1944.

United States Code Congressional and Administrative News. Washington, D.C.: Government Printing Office.
88th Congress, 1st Session, 1963
90th Congress, 1st Session, 1967
91st Congress, 2d Session, 1970.

CASES

Beverley's Case, 4 Coke *123b, *124b, 76 Eng. Rep. 1118 (K.B., 1603).

In re Barker, 2 Johns. Ch. 232 (N.Y. 1816).

In re Covenhoven, 1 N.J. Eq. 19 (Ch. 1830).

Lake v. Cameron, 124 U.S. App. D.C. 264, 364 F.2d 657 (D.C. Cir. 1966).

Matter of Josiah Oakes, 8 Law Reporter 123 (Mass. Sup. Ct. 1845).

Stafford v. Stafford, 1 Martin's Reports 551 (La. Sup. Ct. 1823).

Table 1.1   SUMMARY OF CIVIL HOSPITALIZATION PROCEEDINGS

STATE	ADMISSION: Voluntary (and Informal)	ADMISSION: Involuntary — Emergency Hospitalization or Detention	Short-term or Observational Hospitalization — Direct	Short-term or Observational Hospitalization — Part of Regular Commitment Proceedings	Extended Hospitalization — Medical Certification — Protesting Patient	Extended Hospitalization — Medical Certification — Nonprotesting Patient	Extended Hospitalization — Judicial	Extended Hospitalization — Administrative	DISCHARGE — Administrative	DISCHARGE — Judicial	Habeas Corpus to Determine Present Mental State
Draft Act	X	X		X	X	X	X		X	X	
Alabama							X		X		
Alaska	X	X				X	X		X	X	
Arizona	X	X		X	X	X	X		X	X	
Arkansas	X				X	X	X		X		
California	X	X		X	X	X	X		X	X	X
Colorado	X	X	X					X	X	X	
Connecticut	(X)	X					X		X	X	X
Delaware	X	X			X	X	X	X	X	X	
District of Columbia	X	X			X	X	X		X	X	
Florida	X	X			X	X	X	X	X		
Georgia	(X)	X	X		X	X	X	X	X	X	
Hawaii	X	X			X				X		
Idaho	X			X			X		X	X	
Illinois	(X)	X	X		X	X	X		X	X	
Indiana	X				X	X	X		X	X	X
Iowa	X	X	X	X	X	X	X	X	X	X	X
Kansas	(X)	X	X	X			X		X	X	
Kentucky	(X)	X	X		X	X	X		X	X	
Louisiana	X	X					X		X	X	
Maine	(X)	X			X	X	X		X	X	
Maryland	X				X	X			X	X	
Massachusetts	X	X	X						X	X	
Michigan	X	X		X			X		X	X	X
Minnesota	(X)	X		X		X	X	X	X	X	
Mississippi	X					X			X	X	X
Missouri	X	X		X		X	X		X	X	X

15

Table 1.1   SUMMARY OF CIVIL HOSPITALIZATION PROCEEDINGS   continued

STATE	ADMISSION: Voluntary (and Informal)	ADMISSION: Involuntary — Short-term or Observational Hospitalization — Emergency Hospitalization or Detention	Direct	Part of Regular Commitment Proceedings	Extended Hospitalization — Medical Certification — Protesting Patient	Medical Certification — Nonprotesting Patient	Judicial	Administrative	DISCHARGE — Administrative	Judicial	Habeas Corpus to Determine Present Mental State
Montana	X	X	X				X		X		
Nebraska	X				X	X		X	X	X	X
Nevada	X	X				X	X		X	X	
New Hampshire	(X)	X			X	X	X		X	X	
New Jersey	X	X	X	X			X		X		
New Mexico	X	X		X			X		X	X	
New York	(X)	X	X		X	X	X		X	X	X
North Carolina	X	X		X		X	X		X	X	
North Dakota	X	X						X	X	X	X
Ohio	X	X	X			X	X		X	X	X
Oklahoma	X	X					X		X	X	
Oregon	X	X					X		X		X
Pennsylvania	(X)	X			X	X	X		X		
Rhode Island	X	X			X	X	X	X	X	X	
South Carolina	X	X			X	X	X		X	X	
South Dakota	X			X				X	X		
Tennessee	(X)	X	X	X		X	X		X	X	X
Texas	X	X	X				X		X	X	
Utah	X	X		X	X	X	X		X	X	
Vermont	X	X			X	X	X		X	X	
Virginia	X		X	X		X	X		X		X
Washington	X	X		X					X		
West Virginia	X	X		X	X	X	X	X	X		X
Wisconsin	X	X		X			X		X	X	X
Wyoming	X	X			X	X	X		X		X

Chapter Two
Voluntary Admission

I. INTRODUCTION

The admission of a mentally ill person to a hospital for treatment is closely regulated by statute. In most states it takes the form of a code which purports to govern any hospitalization of a person who is or is thought to be mentally ill. In this respect the hospitalization of a person for mental illness differs from the usual practice and procedure relating to general medical problems—in order for any admission for mental disability to be legally valid it must conform to a statutorily prescribed form of admission. The Illinois code provision is illustrative: "No person may be admitted to a hospital as in need of mental treatment or as mentally retarded except as provided in this act."[1] Thus even the mentally ill person who on his own initiative seeks inpatient mental treatment must follow a prescribed course as must the admitting facility.

In this chapter the voluntary form of admission will be discussed. Involuntary hospitalization, the other major category of hospitalization, and its variants will be discussed in chapter 3. For present purposes it is enough to say that involuntary hospitalization is a procedure which does not rely on the acquiescence or action of the subject of the process in order to achieve hospitalization. Voluntary hospitalization typically posits an affirmative action, personal application, on the part of the person who seeks his own admission.

Since the patient who recognizes his mental illness and seeks or accepts hospitalization is very likely to participate actively in his treatment, the availability of voluntary admission or voluntary hospitalization procedures has been favored by practically every group concerned with drafting effective legislation in this field.[2] An excellent summary of the merits of an approach which places due emphasis on voluntary admission is presented in the Commentary accompanying the Draft Act:

A fully operating program of voluntary admissions will reduce materially the harmful experiences often associated with compulsory hospitalization and at the same time encourage the mentally ill and their families to obtain care at an early stage, when the promise of recovery is greatest. Another important consideration is the need . . . for the patient's cooperation with his physician. This is most likely to be obtained if the patient is in a hospital environment because he recognizes his need for it and affirmatively seeks it. Making hospitalization . . . readily available to the mentally ill . . . should reduce the financial and human cost of mental illness which is greatest when the patient's condition has been aggravated by delay in treatment or by the experience of forcible hospitalization, and when, recovery having become impossible, lifelong custody is the only prospect.[3]

In general, voluntary hospitalizations are reported as increasing in number yearly in almost all states. In 1949, the World Health Organization reported that only 13,848 of 138,253 admissions to state mental hospitals in the United States, slightly more than 10 percent, were voluntary. At approximately the same time European nations were reporting between 30 and 70 percent voluntary admissions.[4] By 1961, voluntary admissions in the United States had risen to 23.7 percent.[5] Although more recent compilations of the proportion of voluntary admissions have not been published, a survey of the reports of forty-five states indicates that in thirty-seven the proportion of voluntary admissions has been steadily increasing. In 1968, forty-five states, which account for about 88 percent of the total state hospital admissions, reported 40 percent of all admissions were voluntary.[6]

---

1. *Ill. Ann. Stat.* ch. 91-1/2, § 3-1 (Smith-Hurd Supp. 1970).

2. Curran, "Hospitalization of the Mentally Ill," 31 *N.C.L. Rev.* 274, 277 (1952–53).

3. National Institute of Mental Health, Federal Security Agency, *A Draft Act Governing Hospitalization of the Mentally Ill,* Commentary, at 19 (Public Health Service Pub. No. 51, 1952) [hereinafter cited as *Draft Act*]. The *Draft Act* appears as Appendix A to this Report.

4. In 1952, for example, nearly 70 percent of the admissions in England and Wales, 67 percent of those in Scotland, and 31 percent of those in France were voluntary. World Health Organization, *Hospitalization of Mental Patients* 15 (1955).

5. American Psychiatric Association and the National Association for Mental Health, *Voluntary and Other Admissions to State Mental Hospitals—1956 and 1961* (Joint Information Service Fact Sheet No. 17, April 1962).

6. Compiled from correspondence with the states, on file. Massachusetts, Mississippi, Montana, Ohio, and Virginia did not respond.

While this increase is laudable, most experts in the field believe that a substantial majority of all patients could be cared for under such a procedure.[7]

Although it may be conceded that voluntary admission is extremely desirable from the viewpoint of effective medical treatment, such an admission raises some problems.[8] In most of the states which authorize voluntary admissions one such problem is the patient who has requested admission and is detained in the hospital for a certain fixed period after he requests release. Moreover, even after this fixed period has elapsed, the hospital authorities may further postpone release in order to initiate compulsory indeterminate hospitalization proceedings.[9]

Many states provide voluntary admission procedures also for one or more of the following groups of the mentally disabled, namely, mental deficients, epileptics, alcoholics, and drug addicts. The admission procedures for these groups in most instances are either identical with or similar to those applicable to the mentally ill. The same statutory provision may be used to admit one or more of the classes of the mentally disabled. This is accomplished either by defining "mental illness" to include one or more of these groups or by expressly enumerating one or more of these groups along with the mentally ill. Moreover, it should be borne in mind that any individual who is addicted to alcohol or drugs, afflicted with epilepsy, or even mentally deficient may also suffer from mental illness in the strict sense of the term.

Because of the consistent approach used by the states in considering and providing for the voluntary admission of these special groups, this chapter is restricted to those statutory provisions employing the term "mentally ill" or a synonymous term; no attempt has been made to set out or discuss any other groups of the mentally disabled. The reader who is interested in voluntary admission for these other groups should check the statutes in his jurisdiction to ascertain which provisions, if any, apply to them. Where such provisions are found, variations may exist, such as designating different types of institutions for these groups.

7. See Katz, Goldstein, & Dershowitz, *Psychoanalysis, Psychiatry and Law* 459–86 (1967).

8. Flaschner, "Analysis of the Legal and Medical Considerations in Commitment of the Mentally Ill," 56 *Yale L.J.* 1178, 1201 (1947).

9. See chap. 3, "Involuntary Hospitalization," § III C, Classification of Involuntary Hospitalization Procedures for the Mentally Ill.

II. HISTORICAL DEVELOPMENT

The first legislative provisions for voluntary admission in the United States were enacted in Massachusetts in 1881.[10] By 1924, twenty-eight states had enacted voluntary admission legislation, hardly uniform in substance or scope.[11] Some such provisions existed by 1969 in all states except Alabama,[12] and in numerous foreign countries.[13] The fundamental principles underlying such legislation appear to have secured general acceptance, but how adequately these principles are implemented in practice remains open to question. The brunt of current criticism of this legislation centers on the lack of statutory assurance in most states that the voluntary admittee is adequately informed of his status and rights.

III. THE MEANING OF VOLUNTARY ADMISSION

As used in this Report, the term "voluntary admission" refers to procedures for admission to a mental hospital which are initiated by the affirmative action of the patient himself or of someone empowered by law to act in the patient's behalf. Generally, the original affirmative action required to commence a voluntary admission procedure is the filing of an application. If a statute provides that such an application may be filed by a friend, spouse, or relative of the patient, with his consent, the procedure has been classified not as voluntary admission but rather as a nonprotested involuntary admission, a type of procedure to be discussed in chapter 3.[14] Also characterized as a nonprotested procedure is one which provides that a friend, spouse, or relative of a patient may present the application to the hospital authorities without the patient's consent to admission, but which also provides that the patient may protest admission. While not determinative for this Report's classification scheme, the right of the admittee to demand and obtain release is an almost universal element of statutorily designated "voluntary" procedures. The implications of this aspect of voluntary admission will be discussed in section VII, Release, below.

10. Deutsch, *The Mentally Ill in America* 432 (2d ed. 1949).

11. Overholser, "The Voluntary Admission Law: Certain Legal and Psychiatric Aspects," 3 *Am. J. Psychiat.* 475, 476 (1924).

12. Ross, "Hospitalization of the Voluntary Mental Patient," 53 *Mich. L. Rev.* 353, 357 (1955).

13. World Health Organization, *supra* note 4, at 15.

14. See chap. 3, "Involuntary Hospitalization," § III C for discussion of nonprotested admission.

A recent development in the area of voluntary admission is the statutory designation of an informal voluntary admission procedure. Eight states currently have procedures of this variety in addition to a regular voluntary procedure.[15] Typical is the Illinois provision:

> Any person desiring admission to a hospital for care and treatment of mental illness or mental retardation may be admitted upon his request without making formal application therefor if, after examination, the superintendent of the hospital considers that person suitable for admission upon an informal basis.
>
> Each patient admitted under this Section must be informed in writing and orally, in a language he understands, at the time of admission, of his right to leave the hospital at any time during the normal daily day-shift hours of operation, which shall include but need not be limited to 9:00 *a.m.* to 5:00 *p.m.* Such right to leave shall commence with the first day-shift hours of operation after his admission."[16]

Characteristically the informal application need not be in writing and the patient must be released upon demand. However, only the Illinois, Maine, New York, Pennsylvania, and Tennessee provisions explicitly require the informally admitted patient to be apprised of his status and right to release.

In view of the fact that "formal" voluntary admission is available in each of these states, the utilization of the "informal" procedure is probably greatest in admissions to general or private psychiatric hospitals where a prospective patient may balk at the execution of formal documents which designate him as mentally ill. The procedure may also be appropriate for patients who are unwilling to accept the delayed release provision of the "formal" voluntary procedure but are willing to accept treatment if release is on demand.

It must be emphasized that the classification undertaken here is "objective" in the sense that it is based solely upon express statutory procedure and does not consider the will or desire of the patient in any particular case. Thus, while it is conceivable that a patient may *request* a friend to present him for admission to a hospital, for the purposes of this Report the admission of this patient would occur not by voluntary but by nonprotested admission. An admission commenced by the parent or guardian of a minor or incompetent, however, is considered voluntary;

despite the state of mind of the minor or ward, the legislature has determined that, for purposes of admission to a hospital, the parent or guardian is *legally* empowered to act in behalf of the minor or ward. A friend, although he may be acting at the patient's request in presenting him for admission, is not legally empowered to act in his behalf.

Some procedures have a dual aspect. Thus, a statutory provision, labeled as a voluntary admission procedure, but providing that a person may be admitted to a hospital upon the filing of an application by the patient or his friend, relative, or spouse, has in this Report been considered as two separate procedures: voluntary admission, since the application may be filed by the patient himself, and nonprotested admission, since the patient may also be presented for admission to a hospital by a friend, relative, or spouse.

The foregoing distinction serves to draw attention to the fact that procedures initiated by friends, relatives, or spouses, to which a patient merely acquiesces or consents, may require more safeguards than procedures initiated by the patient himself. Perhaps the most important of these safeguards is that the patient should be clearly informed of his right to protest admission when he himself has not initiated the procedure. If the proposed patient is not informed of this right it may be that procedures designed for patients who actually desire hospitalization could be employed as a means of hospitalizing unwilling patients.

IV. THE VOLUNTARY PATIENT'S RIGHT TO ADMISSION

A. APPLICATION

With the exception of Alabama, all states make statutory provision for the voluntary admission of the mentally ill, specifying that the patient may apply for his own admission.[17] Thirty-eight states and the Draft Act provide that the application may be made by the parent or guardian of a minor and/or the guardian of an incompetent.[18]

To insure that the consent is truly voluntary, that is, that the patient understands the full implications of his decision, five states specifically require that the patient be mentally competent to make the application.[19] No statute deals with the problem of a pa-

---

15. Connecticut, Illinois, Kansas, Maine, Minnesota, New York, Pennsylvania, and Tennessee. See Table 2.1, Voluntary Admission of the Mentally Ill: Informal Admission column.

16. *Ill. Ann. Stat.* ch. 91-1/2, § 4-1 (Smith-Hurd Supp. 1970).

17. See Table 2.1, Application by Patient column.

18. Ibid.

19. For California, Louisiana, Michigan, and Washington, see Table 2.1 n.8; for Alaska, id. at n.4.

tient who becomes incompetent after voluntary admission. New York, on the other hand, explicitly states: "No requirement shall be made, by rule, regulation or otherwise as a condition to admission and retention pursuant to this section that any person applying for admission shall have the legal capacity to contract."[20] It seems reasonable that the voluntary form of admission should be available to any person who understands that the facility is a mental hospital, that he will receive mental treatment, and that he may leave the hospital upon complying with the statutory conditions.

B. DISCRETION OF ADMITTING HOSPITAL

Hospitals in all states are granted wide discretion in admitting voluntary patients. Although the Draft Act states that a public hospital "shall admit" voluntary patients, the provision is qualified by the explicit condition that suitable accommodations must be available.[21] A number of the existing state statutes specify either that admission is discretionary or that an applicant will be admitted if, in the opinion of the superintendent, he will benefit from treatment.[22]

The large question, of course, is whether the voluntary patient should have an absolute right to be admitted to a public hospital. Much of the evidence now available indicates that in the absence of treatment many of these applicants will be patients in mental hospitals at some time in the future. It would seem advantageous, then, both to the patient's mental health and the finances of the state to admit him when he first seeks treatment.

The Draft Act fails to settle this question of policy. As the Commentary accompanying it points out, if there is to be an absolute right to hospitalization the reference within the Act to the availability of "suitable accommodations" should be eliminated.[23] The phrase "suitable accommodations" is, of course, somewhat ambiguous. It is subject to a variety of interpretations, e.g., that patients are to be admitted only if the hospitals are not crowded, or perhaps only if separate wards are available for voluntary patients. Such a criterion, moreover, makes it difficult to sort out the reasons underlying the limited recourse to voluntary admission: is the relatively low proportion of voluntary patients in mental hospitals determined by lack of space or lack of applicants?

It may also be that the relatively low present percentage of voluntary patients is because some hospital officials do not approve of the existence of certain special statutory procedures governing the admission of voluntary patients. Where hospital officials have the authority to reject a voluntary applicant, for example, their decision may be affected by their attitude toward the release procedures involved. The hospital may feel that the patient's release should depend on its evaluation of his condition rather than on his own momentary wishes. Moreover, hospitals may be reluctant to accept such patients in view of the fact that the patient's consent is required before the hospital may administer certain types of treatment. Again, such a condition may appear to the hospital to forestall treating the patient in what it considers to be the most beneficial manner.

C. MAINTENANCE OF THE VOLUNTARY PATIENT

The Draft Act does not deal with the question of payment for care and treatment. Its remarks on the Scope of the Act, however, state that access to a public mental hospital, whether on a voluntary or involuntary basis, should not be conditional on the patient's ability to pay. The Draft Act recommends that the determination of the patient's ability to finance his hospitalization should be treated as a question separate from that of hospitalization itself.[24] This represents a movement away from the policy underlying the earliest voluntary admission laws, which permitted the admission of patients only when they could pay the costs.[25] Most states now authorize the voluntary admission of indigents to public hospitals at public expense.[26]

The more liberal policy would appear justified on the basis of simple economics as well as loftier humanitarian motives. It is far less expensive to offer the indigent patient voluntary care in the early stages of his illness than to risk its advancing to the point where the only alternative is involuntary hospitalization for the remaining years of his life.

V. RIGHTS OF THE VOLUNTARY PATIENT IN THE HOSPITAL

An examination of the relevant statutes fails to reveal any significant difference between the rights of vol-

---

20. *N.Y. Mental Hygiene Law* § 71-5 (McKinney Supp. 1969).

21. *Draft Act* § 2, at 4.

22. See Table 2.1.

23. *Draft Act,* Commentary, at 19.

24. *Draft Act,* Scope of the Draft Act, at 1.

25. Ross, *supra* note 12, at 368.

26. See Table 3.13, Financial Responsibility for Patient's Support in Hospital.

untary and involuntary patients in regard to correspondence, visitation, mechanical restraint, and the exercise of civil rights.[27] Typically, the statutory provisions which deal with these matters refer only to "patients" without differentiating the form of admission. While it is likely that a more permissive attitude about these matters is displayed towards voluntary patients, no study confirms this fact and the failure to state such a policy explicitly by statute may mean that once hospitalized, voluntary patients receive day-to-day treatment no different in these respects from that given involuntary patients.

Whether voluntary and involuntary patients should possess similar rights would appear to depend on whether there is a difference between the mental condition of the two classes. If the only difference between these patients is willingness or unwillingness to accept treatment coupled with an opportunity to elect such admission, there does not seem to be a rational basis for granting special privileges to one and not to the other simply because of status on admission. The granting of special privileges to voluntary patients might furnish the needed incentive to advance the use of this method of treatment and care. However, such a policy necessarily implies some deprivation to involuntary patients which may be not justifiable on independent grounds.

It may be conceded that some restrictions on a patient's rights are necessary for his medical welfare. To administer treatment properly and to insure the patient's welfare it is sometimes desirable to limit correspondence and visitation rights. Hospital authorities, however, should exercise this power within well-defined limits and subject to any patient's right to demand a review of these decisions.[28]

Aside from the therapeutic value of realistically preparing the patient for his hospital stay, the failure of the hospital to inform the patient of rights that will or may be curtailed is not too important as long as the patient is free to leave the hospital after giving notice. The fact that the voluntary patient whose correspondence and visitation rights are restricted may at any time, or at best after a few days' notice, demand his discharge probably provides an adequate check on such restrictions. The knowledge of potential limitations on the exercise of his rights becomes much more important to the patient, however, if a discharge is difficult to obtain or if he must agree to stay in the hospital for an extended period.

VI. COMPETENCY OF THE VOLUNTARY PATIENT IN THE HOSPITAL

The test ordinarily set forth in the statutes to determine an individual's legal capacity to do such things as enter into a contract, execute a conveyance, or exercise the right to vote is whether or not he is "insane" or of "unsound mind."[29] The question that logically follows is whether or not all patients in mental hospitals must be categorized as "insane" or of "unsound mind."

The legislation of eight states specifically provides that patients do not become incompetent simply as a result of hospitalization.[30] Although it is not explicitly stated, voluntary patients no doubt are included. North Dakota states that both voluntary and involuntary patients retain their competency[31] while Oklahoma does not list voluntary patients among the exceptions to those considered mentally competent.[32] Texas specifically provides that voluntary patients retain their competency and shall be informed of this fact on admission.[33] New York is by far the most explicit in enumerating the rights retained by voluntary patients:

> Notwithstanding any other provision of law to the contrary no person admitted to a hospital by voluntary or informal admission shall be deprived of any civil right solely by reason of such admission nor shall such admission modify or vary any civil right of any such person, including but not limited to civil service ranking and appointment or rights relating to the granting, forfeiture or denial of a license, permit, privilege or benefit pursuant to any law.[34]

Wisconsin is statutorily unique in providing that both voluntary and involuntary hospitalization create a rebuttable presumption of incompetency while the patient is under the jurisdiction of hospital authorities.[35] The Draft Act provides that:

27. See chap. 5, "Rights of Hospitalized Patients."

28. Ibid.

29. See chap. 5, "Rights of Hospitalized Patients" and chap. 9, "Personal and Property Rights."

30. *Cal. Welf. & Inst'ns Code* 5331 (West Supp. 1968); *Del. Code Ann.* tit. 16, § 5126(d) (1953); *D.C. Code Ann.* § 21-564 (1967); *Hawaii Rev. Stat. Ann.* § 334-57 (1968); *Kan. Stat. Ann.* § 59-2933 (Supp. 1968); *Minn. Stat. Ann.* § 253A.18 (Supp. 1969); *Ore. Rev. Stat.* § 426.295(1) (1967); *S.D. Compiled Laws Ann.* § 27-8-5 (1967).

31. *N.D. Cent. Code* § 25-03-20(1)(c) (1960).

32. *Okla. Stat. Ann.* tit. 43A, § 64 (1951).

33. *Tex. Rev. Civ. Stat.* art. 5547-24 (1958).

34. *N.Y. Mental Hygiene Law* § 70-5 (McKinney Supp. 1969).

35. *Wis. Stat. Ann.* § 51.005(2) (1957).

Subject to the general rules and regulations of the hospital and except to the extent that the head of the hospital determines that it is necessary for the medical welfare of the patient to impose restrictions, every patient shall be entitled . . . to exercise all civil rights, including the right to dispose of property, execute instruments, make purchases, enter contractual relationships, and vote, unless he has been adjudicated incompetent and has not been restored to legal capacity.[36]

It should be noted that this Draft Act provision makes the patient's exercise of the enumerated rights subject to the restrictions imposed by the head of the hospital or by the hospital's general rules. The Draft Act and the states which have adopted similar civil rights provisions[37] appear to leave open the extent to which the hospital may restrict the patient's exercise of these rights. The question of the validity of the patient's act, in the event that he has chosen to exercise a right contrary to hospital regulations, also remains unanswered.

It would appear, then, that the status of voluntary patients in most states is unclear. It is conceivable, though difficult to substantiate, that the absence of legislation relating to the competency of voluntary patients may well discourage persons from seeking voluntary hospitalization.

VII. RELEASE

Most commonly a voluntary patient secures release by written application. In the provisions of nine states and the Draft Act, the release is to take place "forthwith," but in the remaining states the hospital may force the patient to remain in the institution for a certain period—ranging from forty-eight hours in Alaska, the District of Columbia, Nevada, and New Mexico to fifteen days in New Hampshire and Oklahoma—after he has submitted his request for release.[38] The legality of this requirement has been attacked as a violation of due process. In *Ex parte Romero*[39] a voluntary patient in New Mexico applied for a writ of habeas corpus to secure his immediate release despite the existence of a statute that authorized his detention for ten days after he had notified the hospital, in writing, of his intention and desire to leave. The respondent urged that by voluntarily seeking admission the patient had in effect contracted to remain in the institution and receive treatment for ten days after the submission of written notice. The Supreme Court of New Mexico rejected this argument.

Obviously, it does not require citation of authority that one may not enforce such a contract made with a person he knows to be so disordered in mind as to require treatment in an institution for the treatment of mental diseases.[40]

The court cited several cases in which it had been held that hospitalizing a person in a mental institution without notice and an opportunity to be heard violated due process. It concluded that the provisions of the statutes in question clearly fell short of the due process of law guaranteed by the Constitution of the United States as well as by that of the state of New Mexico.[41]

It has been suggested that the result of the case is sounder than the rationale upon which it rests.[42] It may be argued, for example, that it is unconstitutional to enforce any agreement which deprives the individual of his liberty regardless of his competency. On the other hand, the contention that any patient who needs treatment is per se incompetent to consent to admission unquestionably runs counter not only to the policy underlying the voluntary admission statutes of forty-nine states but to the weight of contemporary medical and legal opinion. In a recent New York case the Court of Appeals went even further in summarily dismissing for an adjudicated incompetent the contention of a committee that the incompetent did not have the legal capacity to request, consent, or agree to the conversion of his status from involuntary to voluntary after five years of hospitalization. The court said an adjudication of incompetency is in no way a decision or judgment that the person so adjudicated may not act in matters involving his personal status. "He may, for instance, enter into a valid marriage . . . and make a valid will. . . . Moreover, the statute expressly recites that the 'legal capacity to contract' should not be required of any person applying for voluntary admission."[43]

---

36. *Draft Act* § 21(a)(3), at 15.

37. See Table 8.2, Effect of Involuntary Hospitalization on Issue of Legal Competency: Competency Affected by Involuntary Hospitalization column.

38. See Table 2.1, Release upon Notice (Time) column.

39. 51 N.M. 201, 181 P.2d 811 (1947).

40. Id. at 203, 181 P.2d at 813.

41. New Mexico subsequently enacted the voluntary admission provisions of the *Draft Act*.

42. Ross, "Hospitalizing the Mentally Ill—Emergency and Temporary Commitments," *Current Trends in State Legislation 1955–56*, at 540 (1957).

43. *In re* Buttonow, 244 N.E.2d 677, 682 (N.Y. Ct. App. 1968).

It would appear that the notice of detention preceding requested release required by nearly all of the states is predicated on the need for providing the hospital with sufficient time to conduct an adequate prerelease medical examination and to determine if involuntary hospitalization proceedings are advisable. Furthermore, some delay may be advisable to permit the patient to reconsider his request. If the advisability of such an interlude, simply as a matter of public policy, is conceded, then the question of a contractual relationship between the patient and the hospital need not be brought into issue. It is worth noting that the court in the *Romero* case was guided by very similar considerations when it made the decree in that case effective two days after it was issued.

Hospital authorities should be required to advise the voluntary patient of his right to release and to assist him in the exercise of this right. In the absence of such information and assistance, it is entirely possible that the availability of the right may have little or no real meaning as far as the patient himself is concerned. Only nine states specifically require that a voluntary patient be advised of his right to request release.[44] Even the Draft Act ignores this aspect of the problem, although it does include a similar provision applicable to patients who have been hospitalized through a nonjudicial procedure.[45] A case in which this issue arose in regard to voluntary patients is *Roberts v. Paine.*[46] Under an action for the recovery of damages, a patient alleged conspiracy and false imprisonment, claiming that he was tricked into signing an application for voluntary admission and then detained for a substantial period after he had made an oral request for release. The statute required written notice ten days in advance of release. The trial court instructed the jury that the law did not impose any obligation upon the hospital to inform the patient that he could secure his discharge by complying with these requirements. Moreover, the court pointed out, no cause of action would arise even if the jury found that the hospital had intentionally concealed this information. The charge to the jury was upheld on appeal. The appellate court's decision emphasized that patients "are often not in a condition to appreciate what is for their own best interests or what their real desires are."[47]

A continued adherence to this premise might easily

have a deterrent effect on the use of voluntary admission procedures. It would seem reasonable that if a patient is not sufficiently ill to be involuntarily hospitalized, he has a right to his freedom. But his right is an empty formality if he is not entitled to know the steps necessary to secure his discharge or if the hospital, either passively or deliberately, withholds this information. The New York Court of Appeals has gone even further in *Buttonow,* holding that equal protection of the law requires that a person converting from involuntary to voluntary status in addition to being advised of his rights may not be deprived of any of the protections afforded him as an involuntary patient. Such rights included court review at the end of the first six month period, again at the end of one year, and thereafter at two-year intervals; the right to a jury trial; and counsel, study, and review of the admission by the agency charged with such duties with repect to involuntary patients. While not deciding these issues for a person originally admitted as a voluntary patient, the court cites with approval a critical analysis of voluntary admissions which urges the need for external review of all such admissions.[48]

Under the present legislation of twenty-six states as well as the provisions of the Draft Act, the detention period may be extended if the superintendent thinks it necessary to initiate involuntary hospitalization proceedings.[49] Although such a provision may be necessary to prevent the release of dangerous patients, it is questionable whether such persons should, in the first instance, be accepted as voluntary patients. In Idaho, for example, the head of the hospital may refuse voluntary admission if he finds that the welfare of the applicant or of society is better protected by judicial hospitalization.[50] Such a refusal provision, of course, could unduly prevent voluntary treatment of persons who may be potentially dangerous yet seek treatment. In any case, any extension should be only long enough to permit initiation of involuntary procedures; the question of continued interim detention should be determined as in other cases of involuntary proceedings. The existing legislation in some states provides that if the hospital officials decide that a person should continue to be hospitalized, they may notify his family or the proper public authorities to initiate involuntary hospitalization proceedings. Such an arrangement protects both the interests of the patient and those of the com-

44. See Table 2.1, Told of Right to Release or Review column.

45. *Draft Act* § 17(b), at 14.

46. 124 Conn. 170, 199 A. 112 (1938).

47. Id. at 173, 199 A. at 115 (1938).

48. *In re* Buttonow, 244 N.E.2d 677, 680 (N.Y. Ct. App. 1968).

49. See Table 2.1, Extension Provision column.

50. *Idaho Code Ann.* § 66-318 (Supp. 1969).

munity at large. It alleviates some of the objections to placing the power to initiate such proceedings in the hands of the superintendent. A patient may hesitate to apply for treatment during the incipient stages of his illness if he knows that his later requests for release may be denied and he himself hospitalized as an involuntary patient, with the resulting loss of civil rights, for an indefinite period.[51] Moreover, the patient may react unfavorably to the superintendent's initiating the application for hospitalization, become hostile toward the hospital authorities, and thus impede his own recovery.

Nine states and the Draft Act specify that hospitalization proceedings cannot be initiated against a voluntary patient unless he has requested release.[52] The implicit intent of this provision is probably to prevent patients from concerning themselves with the threat of involuntary hospitalization. One wonders, however, if the same provision may not have the effect of making some patients afraid to request release. The states which do not have such a provision presumably can at any time initiate involuntary hospitalization procedures against voluntary patients who exhibit characteristics bringing them within the purview of involuntary hospitalization laws.

Eleven states provide that voluntary admission shall be for a specified period of time.[53] In Virginia and Pennsylvania the period is determinate, with a fifteen-day maximum for Virginia and thirty days for Pennsylvania.[54] At the end of that period the patient must be either released or readmitted for another period of treatment. As an additional protection to the patient, Pennsylvania also provides for release upon ten days' notice.[55] The object of determinate voluntary admission is to assure that a continuing consensual treatment relationship will be maintained, a desirable goal. Such a procedure avoids much of the criticism that arises when affirmative action (release request) of the patient is necessary to terminate hospitalization. Where voluntary hospitalization is determinate, affirmative action by the patient is nec-

essary to *continue* hospitalization. It must be noted, however, that Pennsylvania has one of the nation's lowest rates of voluntary admissions to state hospitals: only 14 percent.[56] The administrative problems presented by a determinate voluntary procedure may be one important factor in the low rate of utilization of voluntary procedures.

In the remaining states a minimum period of hospitalization is stipulated after which the provision for release upon notice becomes effective. In these jurisdictions the period of hospitalization is indefinite and determined only by an administrative discharge decision or patient initiated release. The minimum periods vary from fifteen days in New York to sixty days in New Hampshire.[57] There is some variation in procedure. In Tennessee the minimum period is that period required to complete the diagnosis and evaluation but is in no case more than twenty days.[58] In Washington if a demand for release is submitted within the first eighteen days of hospitalization the patient may be detained for a total of thirty days.[59] The Arkansas legislation provides that a voluntary patient may request release by filing notice thirty days in advance. The hospital is not automatically obligated to release him at the end of this period, but the relevant statutes provide that the hospital is liable for detaining anyone beyond it when the continued detention is arbitrary and unreasonable.[60] The hospital's authority has further limits. *Barbee v. Kolb*[61] held that the superintendent of the state hospital would not have authority to hold a person indefinitely who had not been hospitalized by the proper order of a court of competent jurisdiction.

Only Mississippi and South Dakota make no provision for release upon demand. Judicial discharge by statute and habeas corpus appear to be the only means of securing release if the hospital authorities do not discharge the voluntary patient.[62] South Dakota provides for a release procedure upon application to a special commission, but the procedure reportedly has never been invoked.[63] The only release

51. Ross, *supra* note 12, at 382. Although Ross makes this comment about jurisdictions in which release can be obtained only by judicial action, the argument is also applicable to release procedures where only written request is required.

52. See Table 2.1, n.3.

53. Arkansas, Idaho, Montana, North Carolina, New Hampshire, New York, Pennsylvania, South Carolina, Tennessee, Virginia, and Washington. See Table 2.1, Period columns and footnotes thereto.

54. *Va. Code Ann.* 37.1-79 (Supp. 1968); *Pa. Stat. Ann.* tit. 50, § 4403(b) (1969).

55. *Pa. Stat. Ann.* tit. 50, § 4403(c) (1969).

56. Correspondence, *supra* note 6.

57. See Table 2.1, Period columns and footnotes thereto.

58. *Tenn. Code Ann.* § 33-1204(1) (Supp. 1968).

59. *Wash. Rev. Code Ann.* § 72.23.090 (1962).

60. *Ark. Stat. Ann.* § 59-236 (1947).

61. 207 Ark. 227, 179 S.W.2d 701 (1944).

62. *Miss. Code Ann.* § 6909-12 (1952); *S.D. Compiled Laws Ann.* §§ 27-10-10 to 27-10-15 (1967).

63. *S.D. Compiled Laws Ann.* § 27-10-10 (1967). See Note, "Analysis of Admission and Release Procedures at the Yankton State Hospital," 4 *S.D.L. Rev.* 266, 280 (1969).

provisions available to the private (as opposed to the public) patient in Wisconsin are habeas corpus or investigation by the department of public welfare.[64]

It need not be emphasized that the assistance of counsel is almost essential for the patient who wishes to prepare and present a petition for a writ of habeas corpus or release and then to present his case adequately at a hearing. But even in those jurisdictions where the possibility of habeas corpus is present in practice as well as in theory, the absence of prompt release upon notice may discourage some from seeking voluntary admission.

VIII. CONCLUSIONS AND RECOMMENDATIONS

1. *The use of voluntary admission procedures should be encouraged.*

Both the individual patient and the community in which he lives benefit from voluntary hospitalization. The existence of the procedure encourages early diagnosis and treatment and tends to bring about a more cooperative attitude on the part of the patient. The significance of the latter accomplishment is reflected in the higher percentage of recoveries and the shorter period of hospitalization among such patients. The attendant reduction in the financial and human costs of mental illness is not negligible.

2. *The confusion surrounding the legal status of voluntary patients may unnecessarily deprive them of important rights and privileges and thus reduce the beneficial aspects of the procedure.*

All states should make arrangements for simple and prompt voluntary access to mental institutions, not conditional upon the ability to pay for treatment. Such statutes should make it possible for a patient to enter a mental institution in much the same manner as he enters a general hospital and with as little formality. At the same time, however, the question of the voluntary patient's competency should be clearly settled within the statute. The fact of admission should have no effect on general competency. The civil rights of voluntary patients—e.g., the right to correspond and have visitors—should remain unrestricted, unless in the opinion of the hospital authorities the exercise of such rights would preclude proper treatment of the patient. The right to correspond and consult with an attorney by sealed mail, however, should not be infringed upon under any circumstances. Providing for and advising the patient of the fact that he retains his legal and civil rights, except in

unusual circumstances inconsistent with the requirements of treatment, will serve to enhance the utilization of voluntary forms of admission.

3. *Voluntary patients should be entitled to and informed about prompt release upon request.*

If the hospital authorities are of the opinion that the voluntarily admitted patient should be detained in the face of his request for release, they should be required to initiate involuntary hospitalization proceedings of the judicial type, as discussed in chapter 3 of this Report. Unless these proceedings are commenced promptly the patient should be released upon his request. The right of the voluntarily admitted patient to secure his release upon his request should be fully explained to him upon admission and at reasonable intervals thereafter. This right is an illusory one if the voluntary patient is not aware of its existence.

4. *Involuntary patients, under suitable circumstances and with appropriate safeguards, should be permitted to elect to become voluntary patients.* Where the ability of the patient to understand the significance of the act is questionable, i.e., a senile patient, a hearing may be necessary.

BIBLIOGRAPHY

American Psychiatric Association and the National Association for Mental Health. *Voluntary and Other Admissions to State Mental Hospitals—1956 and 1961.* Fact Sheet no. 17. Washington, D.C.: Joint Information Service of the American Psychiatric Association and the National Association for Mental Health, April 1962.

Curran, William J. "Hospitalization of the Mentally Ill." 31 *North Carolina Law Review* 274 (1952–53).

Deutsch, Albert. *The Mentally Ill in America.* 2d ed. rev. New York: Columbia University Press, 1949.

Flaschner, Franklin N. "Analysis of Legal and Medical Considerations in Commitment of the Mentally Ill." 56 *Yale Law Journal* 1178 (1947).

Katz, Jay; Goldstein, Joseph; and Dershowitz, Alan M. *Psychoanalysis, Psychiatry and Law.* New York: Free Press, 1967.

National Institute of Mental Health. Federal Security Agency. *A Draft Act Governing Hospitalization of the Mentally Ill, Commentary.* Public Health Service Pub. no. 51. Washington, D.C.: Government Printing Office, 1952.

Note, "Analysis of Admission and Release Procedures at the Yankton State Hospital." 4 *South Dakota Review* 266 (1969).

64. *Wis. Stat. Ann.* § 58.05(3) (1957).

Overholser, Winfred. "The Voluntary Admission Law: Certain Legal and Psychiatric Aspects." 3 *American Journal of Psychiatry* 475 (1924).

Ross, Hugh A. "Hospitalization of the Voluntary Mental Patient." 53 *Michigan Law Review* 353 (1955).

————. "Hospitalizing the Mentally Ill—Emergency and Temporary Commitments." *Current Trends in State Legislation 1955–56.* Ann Arbor: Legislative Research Center, University of Michigan Law School, 1957.

United Nations. World Health Organization. *Hospitalization of Mental Patients.* Geneva, 1955.

CASES

Barbee v. Kolb, 207 Ark. 227, 179 S.W.2d 701 (1944).

In re Buttonow, 244 N.E.2d 677 (N.Y. Ct. App. 1968).

Roberts v. Paine, 124 Conn. 170, 199 A. 112 (1938).

Table 2.1 VOLUNTARY ADMISSION OF THE MENTALLY ILL

STATE	APPLICATION BY: Patient	APPLICATION BY: Parent or Guardian or Minor, Ward or Incompetent Adult	MEDICAL CERTIFICATION	FURTHER APPROVAL BY	PUBLIC INSTITUTIONS: All	PUBLIC INSTITUTIONS: State Only	Admission Discretionary on Part of Institution as to: Availability of Suitable Hospital Accommodations	Admission Discretionary on Part of Institution as to: Mental Condition	PRIVATE INSTITUTIONS	PERIOD Definite: Maximum	PERIOD Definite: Minimum	PERIOD Indefinite	RELEASE UPON NOTICE (TIME)	EXTENSION PROVISION	TOLD OF RIGHT TO RELEASE OR REVIEW	INFORMAL ADMISSION
DRAFT ACT	2	2			2		2	2	2			4	fn. 1 forthwith 4(a)(1)	fn. 2, 3 5 days. 4(a)(3)		
ALA. Code (1958)																
ALAS. Stat. (1962)	47.30.020(1) 47.30.040(c)	consent required. 47.30.020(1)					fn. 4 47.30.040(c)					47.30.040(b)	immediately, unless petition is filed within 48 hours. 47.30.040(c) 47.30.050	15 days. 47.30.050(a) (3)		
ARIZ. Rev. Stat. Ann. (1956) (Supp. 1970)	36-502	36-502				36-502		36-502				36-504	5 days. 36-504B	fn. 2 5 days. 36-504B		
ARK. Stat. Ann. (1947)	59-231	59-231		signed in the presence of 2 witnesses. 59-231		59-229; and in Supp. 1967, 59-231	fn. 5 59-229 (Supp. 1967)	fn. 5 59-231			fn. 6 30 days. 59-236	59-231	fn. 6 59-236			
fn. 7 CAL. Welf. & Inst'ns Code (West 1966) (Supp. 1968)	fn. 8 6050 / fn. 8 6000	or conservator. 6000		fn. 9 6001	6000, 6004, 7103	6050		6000, 6004, 7103	6002			6050	fn. 10 at any time. 6000, 6002, 6005	6050		
COLO. Rev. Stat. Ann. (1964)	71-1-2(1)	71-1-2(1)			71-1-2(1)		fn. 11 71-3-4	71-1-2	71-1-2			71-1-2(2)	5 days. 71-1-2(3)(a)			
CONN. Gen. Stat. Ann. (1960)	17-187(a) (Supp. 1969)			hospital superintendent. 17-187(b)	17-187(a) (Supp. 1969)			17-187(a) (Supp. 1969)	17-187(a) (Supp. 1969)				10 days. 17-187(a) (Supp. 1969)			17-187(a) (Supp. 1969) 17-187(b)
fn. 12 DEL. Code Ann. (1953) (Supp. 1970)	16, §5123(a)	16, §5123(c)	fn. 13 16, §5123(b)			16, §5123(a)		fn. 13 16, §5123(a)				16, §5123(d)	5 days. 16, §5123(e)			
D.C. Code Ann. (1967)	21-511	21-511			21-511			21-511	may 21-511			21-511 21-512(b)	48 hours. 21-512(a)			

27

Table 2.1 VOLUNTARY ADMISSION OF THE MENTALLY ILL *continued*

STATE	APPLICATION BY — Patient	APPLICATION BY — Parent or Guardian or Minor, Ward or Incompetent Adult	MEDICAL CERTIFICATION	FURTHER APPROVAL BY	PUBLIC INSTITUTIONS — All	PUBLIC INSTITUTIONS — State Only	PUBLIC INSTITUTIONS — Availability of Suitable Hospital Accommodations	PUBLIC INSTITUTIONS — Admission Discretionary on Part of Institution as to Mental Condition	PRIVATE INSTITUTIONS	PERIOD — Definite Maximum	PERIOD — Definite Minimum	PERIOD — Indefinite	RELEASE UPON NOTICE (TIME)	EXTENSION PROVISION	TOLD OF RIGHT TO RELEASE OR REVIEW	INFORMAL ADMISSION
FLA. Stat. Ann. (1960)	394.20(1)	394.20(1)			394.20(1); & in Supp. 1969 394.20(6)			394.20(1)	394.20(1)			394.20(1)	fn. 1 forthwith. 394.20(3)(a)	fn. 2 5 days. 394.20(3)(a)3		
GA. Code Ann. (1963) (Supp. 1969)	88-503.1	88-503.1			88-503.1			88-503.1				88-503.1	fn. 1 5 days. 88-503.3(a)		88-503.4	
HAWAII Rev. Stat. Ann. (1968)	334.52(a)	334-52(e)			334-1 334-52(a)			334-52(a)	334-52(a)			334-52	334-52(d)			
IDAHO Code Ann. (1949) (Supp. 1969)	66-318	66-318	fn. 14 66-322		66-317(f) 66-318			fn. 15 66-318	66-318		fn. 14 66-322	66-318	fnn. 1, 14 7 days. 66-320(a)(3)	fn. 2 5 days. 66-320(a)(3)		
ILL. Ann. Stat. (Smith-Hurd 1966) (Supp. 1969)	91 1/2, §5-2	91 1/2, §5-2		court, if proceedings instituted. 91 1/2, §3-5	91 1/2, §1-5 91 1/2, §5-1			91 1/2, §5-1	91 1/2, §5-1			91 1/2, §5-1	5 days. 91 1/2, §5-3	pending a final order of court. 91 1/2, §5-3	91 1/2, §5-2	fn. 16 91 1/2, §4-1
IND. Ann. Stat. (1964)	22-1205	22-1205	22-1207			22-1201(5) 22-1204	22-1207	22-1207				22-1205	10 days. 22-1205			
fn. 17 IOWA Code Ann. (1969)	fn. 18 229.4T			district court, if applicant unable to pay. 229.42		229.41	229.41					229.41	3 days. 229.41		229.41	
KAN. Stat. Ann. (1964) (Supp. 1968)	59-2905	59-2905	may require medical certification. 59-2905		59-2902(7), 59-2905		59-2905	fn. 19 59-2905	59-2905			59-2906	5 days. 59-2907			59-2904
KY. Rev. Stat. Ann. (1969)	202.015(1)	202.015(1)		signed in presence of 2 witnesses. 202.015(1)		202.015(1)		202.015(1)				202.015(1)	fn. 1 immediately. 202.015(3)	fn. 2 202.015(4)		fn. 20 202.1T7
LA. Rev. Stat. Ann. (1950) (Supp. 1969)	fn. 8 28:5T				28:51		28:50	28:50	28:50			28:51	fn. 1 forthwith. 28:98.1	fnn. 1, 2, 21 28:98.1	28:51	
ME. Rev. Stat. Ann. (1964)	34, §2291				34, §2291		34, §2291	34, §2291	34, §2291			34, §2291	fn. 1 forthwith. 34, §2293	fnn. 3, 22 10 days. 34, §2293		34, §2290 (Supp. 1969)

Table 2.1 VOLUNTARY ADMISSION OF THE MENTALLY ILL continued

STATE	APPLICATION BY — Patient	APPLICATION BY — Parent or Guardian or Minor, Ward or Incompetent Adult	MEDICAL CERTIFICATION	FURTHER APPROVAL BY	PUBLIC INSTITUTIONS — All	PUBLIC INSTITUTIONS — State Only	Admission Discretionary on Part of Institution as to Availability of Suitable Hospital Accommodations	Admission Discretionary on Part of Institution as to Mental Condition	PRIVATE INSTITUTIONS	PERIOD Definite Maximum	PERIOD Definite Minimum	PERIOD Indefinite	RELEASE UPON NOTICE (TIME)	EXTENSION PROVISION	TOLD OF RIGHT TO RELEASE OR REVIEW	INFORMAL ADMISSION
MD. Ann. Code (1968)	59, §37				59, §37			59, §37	59, §37			59, §37	3 days. 59, §37	59, §31 59, §37		
MASS. Ann. Laws (1965)	123, §86				123, §86		123, §86	123, §86	123, §86			123, §86	3 days. 123, §86	fn. 2 123, §86		
MICH. Comp. Laws Ann. (1967)	fn. 8 330.19a	330.19a			330.19a			330.19a	330.19a			330.19a	5 days. 330.19a			
MINN. Stat. Ann. (1959) (Supp. 1969)	253A.03(2)	253A.03(2)				public: 253A.03(2)		253A.03(2)				253A.03(2)	3 days. 253A.03(2)		253A.05(2)	253A.03(1)
MISS. Code Ann. (1952)	6909-12	6909-12	6909-12		6909-12	6909-12		6909-12				6909-12				
MO. Rev. Stat. (1959)	202.783	202.783			202.783		202.783	202.783	202.783			202.783	fn. 1 forthwith. 202.790	fnn. 2, 3 202.790		
MONT. Rev. Codes Ann. (1961) (Supp. 1969)	38-406.2	38-406.2	fn. 23 38-406.2(2c)			38-406.2	38-406.2(1)	38-406.2(1)			60 days. 34-406.2(2d)		5 days. 38-406.2(4)	fn. 24 38-406.2(4)		
NEB. Rev. Stat. (1966)	83-324					83-324	83-338	83-324				83-324	10 days. 83-324	fn. 25 83-324		
NEV. Rev. Stat. (1967)	433.665	433.665			433.665			433.665	433.665			433.665	48 hours. 433.667		433.729	
N.H. Rev. Stat. Ann. (1964)	134:22	135:22			135:22 135:25			135:22	135:25		60 days. 135:22	135:22	fnn. 1, 26 15 days. 135:22			
N.J. Stat. Ann. (1964) (Supp. 1970)	30:4-46	30:4-46.1		fn. 27 30:4-46	30:4-46			30:4-46	30:4-46			30:4-46	fn. 28 72 hours. 30:4-48			
N.M. Stat. Ann. (1953)	34-2-2	34-2-2			34-2-2		fn. 29 34-2-2	34-2-2	34-2-2			34-2-2	fn. 1 48 hours. 34-2-4(1) 34-2-4(3)	fnn. 2, 3 5 days. 34-2-4(3)		
N.Y. Mental Hygiene Law (McKinney 1951) (Supp. 1970)	71(1)	71(1)			71(1)			71(1)	71		fn. 30 15 days. 71(1)	fn. 30 71(1)	fn. 31 10 days. 71(1)		71(4)	71(2)

Table 2.1   VOLUNTARY ADMISSION OF THE MENTALLY ILL   *continued*

STATE	APPLICATION BY		MEDICAL CERTIFICATION	FURTHER APPROVAL BY	PUBLIC INSTITUTIONS					PERIOD			RELEASE UPON NOTICE (TIME)	EXTENSION PROVISION	TOLD OF RIGHT TO RELEASE OR REVIEW	INFORMAL ADMISSION
	Patient	Parent or Guardian or Minor, Ward or Incompetent Adult			All	State Only	Admission Discretionary on Part of Institution as to Availability of Suitable Hospital Accommodations	Mental Condition	PRIVATE INSTITUTIONS	Definite Maximum	Definite Minimum	Indefinite				
N.C. Gen. Stat. (1964)	122-56		fn. 32 / 122-56			122-56	122-56	122-56	122-79 / 122-81.1		fn. 33 / 122-56	122-56	fn. 34 / 10 days. / 122-56			
N.D. Cent. Code (1960)	25-03-01	25-03-01				25-03-01	25-03-01					25-03-01	fn. 35 / 7 days. / 25-03-06	25-03-06(3)		
OHIO Rev. Code Ann. (Baldwin 1964)	5122.02	5122.02				5122.02	5122.02		5122.02			5122.02	fn. 1 / forthwith. / 5122.03(3)	fnn. 2, 3 / 10 days. / 5122.03(3)		
OKLA. Stat. Ann. (1954)	fn. 36 / 43A, §53, / 43A, §57 / (Supp. 1969)	fn. 36 / 43A, §53 / (Supp. 1969) / 43A, §58				43A, §51		43A, §53 / (Supp. 1969) / 43A, §58	43A, §51			43A, §53 / (Supp. 1969) / 43A, §58	fn. 37 / 15 days. / 43A, §53 / (Supp. 1969)			
ORE. Rev. Stat. (1967)	426.220(1)	426.220(1)				426.220(1)	426.220(1)	426.220(1)				426.220	fn. 38 / 72 hours. / 426.220(1)			
PA. Stat. Ann. (1969)	50, §4403(a)	50, §4403(a)		facility. / 50, §4403(b)	50, §4401			50, §4403(b)	50, §4401	30 days. / 50, §4403(b)			10 days. / 50, §4403(c)		informed of voluntary status each 60 days if under 18 years of age. / 50, §4403(d)	fn. 39 / 50, §4402
R.I. Gen. Laws Ann. (1968)	26-2-18				26-2-18		26-2-18	26-2-18	26-2-18			26-2-18	3 days. / 26-2-18			
S.C. Code Ann. (1962)	32-951 / (Supp. 1968)	32-951 / (Supp. 1968)				32-951 / (Supp. 1968)	32-951 / (Supp. 1968)	32-951 / (Supp. 1968)	32-951 / (Supp. 1968)		fn. 40 / 30 days. / 32-953	32-952	fnn. 1, 40 / 32-953	fn. 2 / 15 days. / 32-953		
S.D. Compiled Laws Ann. (1967)	27-4-12					27-4-12	27-4-12	27-4-12				27-4-12 / 27-4-13				
TENN. Code Ann. (1955) (Supp. 1968)	33-1202	33-1202			33-1201(d) / 33-1202		33-1202	33-1202	33-1201(d) / 33-1202		fn. 41 / 20 days. / 33-1204(1)	33-1202	fn. 41 / 33-1204	fnn. 1, 2, 3 / 33-1204(3) / 33-1204(4)		33-1205
TEX. Rev. Civ. Stat. Ann. (1958)	fn. 42 / 5547-23(a)	fn. 42 / 5547-23(a)		fn. 43	5547-22		5547-22	5547-22	5547-22			5547-22	96 hours. / 5547-25	fnn. 2, 3 / 5547-25	fn. 43 / 5547-24	

Table 2.1   VOLUNTARY ADMISSION OF THE MENTALLY ILL   continued

| STATE | APPLICATION BY | | MEDICAL CERTIFICATION | FURTHER APPROVAL BY | PUBLIC INSTITUTIONS | | Admission Discretionary on Part of Institution as to | | PRIVATE INSTITUTIONS | PERIOD | | | RELEASE UPON NOTICE (TIME) | EXTENSION PROVISION | TOLD OF RIGHT TO RELEASE OR REVIEW | INFORMAL ADMISSION |
| | Patient | Parent or Guardian or Minor, Ward or Incompetent Adult | | | All | State Only | Availability of Suitable Hospital Accommodations | Mental Condition | | Definite | | Indefinite | | | | |
										Maximum	Minimum					
UTAH Code Ann. (1968)	64-7-29	64-7-29				fn. 44 64-7-29		64-7-29				64-7-29	fn. 1 forthwith. 64-7-31	fnn. 2, 3 64-7-31		
VT. Stat. Ann. (1968)	18, §7503				18, §7101(7) 18, §7501			18, §7501	18, §7501			18, §7503	4 days. 18, §8001(3)	10 days. 18, §8001(3)		
VA. Code Ann. (1953) (Supp. 1968)	37.1-65	37.1-65				37.1-1(8) 37.1-65		37.1-65	37.1-65	15 days. 37.1-79						
WASH. Rev. Code Ann. (1962)	fn. 8 72.23.070	72.23.070				72.23.030	72.23.110	72.23.070	71.12.560	fn. 45 72.23.100	fn. 47 72.23.090		fn. 46 71.12.560 72.23.090	fn. 47 30 days. 72.23.090		
W. VA. Code Ann. (1966)	27-4-1	27-4-1				27-4-1	27-4-1	27-4-1				27-4-1	fn. 1 96 hours. 27-4-3	fnn. 2, 3, 48 27-4-3		
WIS. Stat. Ann. (1957)	51.10(1)	51.10(1)	fn. 49 51.10(1)			state or county. 51.10(1)		51.10	58.05(2)				5 days. 51.10(2) (Supp. 1969)	35 days. 51.10 (Supp. 1969)		
WYO. Stat. Ann. (1967)	25-54(a)	25-54(a)				25-54(a)		25-54(a)	25-51			25-54(a)	fn. 1 10 days. 25-56	fnn. 2, 3 25-56		

31

1. Release conditioned on consent of person making application for admission. If under 16 years of age, Draft Act 4(a)(2); Ga. 88-504 (a); Idaho 66-320(2) (Supp. 1969); N.D. 25-03-06 (Supp. 1968). Consent of parent or guardian, N.M. 34-2-4. If minor, Cal. W. & I. 6620; Fla. 394.20(3)(a)2; Ky. 202.015(3); La. 28:98.1 (Supp. 1969); Me. 34, §2293; Mo. 202.790; N.H. 135:22; Ohio 5122.03(3); Ore. 426.220(1); S.C. 32-953; Tenn. 33-1202, 33-1204(3) (Supp. 1968); Utah 64-7-31; W. Va. 27-4-3; Wyo. 25-56.

2. Release may be postponed to allow judicial commitment proceedings to be commenced. Draft Act 4(a)(3); Ariz. 36-504B (Supp. 1970); Fla. 394.20(3); Ga. 88-504(a)(3) (Supp. 1968); Idaho 66-320(a)(3) (Supp. 1969); Ill. 91 1/2, §4-2 (Supp. 1968); Ky. 202.015(4); La. 28:98.1 (Supp. 1968); Mass. 123, §86; Mo. 202.790;N.M. 43-2-4; Ohio 5122.03(3); S.C. 32-911 (Supp. 1968); Tenn. 33-1204(4) (Supp. 1968); Tex. 5547-25; Utah 64-7-31; W. Va. 27-4-3; Wyo. 25-56.

3. Proceedings for judicial hospitalization may not be commenced unless patient has requested release. Draft Act 4(b); Me. 34, §2293; Mo. 202.790; N.M. 34-2-4; Ohio 5122.03(3); Tenn. 33-1204 (Supp. 1968); Tex. 5547-25; Utah 64-7-31; W. Va. 27-4-3; Wyo. 25-56.

4. Admission conditioned on patient's having "at the time sufficient insight or capacity to make responsible application for his own hospitalization." Alas. 47.30.040(c).

5. "If the Superintendent shall be satisfied, that . . . in need of hospital treatment . . . , he may . . ." Ark. 59-231. "The Superintendent shall exercise his discretion in accepting patients . . . beyond the maximum capacity of the State Hospital." Ark. 59-229 (Supp. 1967).

6. No official of the hospital will be liable for the detention of the patient until at least 30 days after the patient has made a written demand for his release and then only if it is shown that the detention was unreasonable and arbitrary. Ark. 59-236.

7. By virtue of Stats. 1967, ch. 1667, §50, the older provisions (charted above) prevail over the newly enacted provisions (charted below).

8. Person must be in condition of mind as to render him competent to make a voluntary application. Cal. W. & I. 6000(Supp. 1968); La. 28:51 (Supp. 1969); Mich. 330.19a; Wash. 72.23.070.

9. Admission to Langley Porter Neuropsychiatric Institute or the Neuropsychiatric Institute, UCLA, requires approval of medical superintendent of institution. Cal. W. & I. 6001 (Supp. 1968).

10. ". . . by giving notice . . . and completing normal hospitalization departure procedures." Cal. W. & I. 6000, 6002, 6005 (Supp. 1968).

11. The number of admissions to the state hospital is unlimited, and no insane person may be denied care. Colo. 71-3-4.

12. Del. 16, §5121, provides: "The Board of Trustees of the Department of Mental Health may establish, under the direction and supervision of the State Hospital, a voluntary admission procedure. . . ." This section has not been repealed, and its relationship to the statutorily described procedure in Del. 16, §5123 (Supp. 1970), is unclear.

13. "If the applicant is under the care and treatment of a medical doctor . . . the application shall be accompanied by a letter from the doctor recommending voluntary hospitalization, and setting forth a description of the behavior and symptoms of the patient. . . . If the applicant is not under the care and treatment of such a medical doctor, he shall not be admitted unless the Superintendent first determines that the applicant has sufficient insight and capacity to make responsible application." Del. 16, §5123(b) (Supp. 1970).

14. Before any person may be voluntarily admitted as a patient, it may be required by the head of the hospital:
1. That he be examined by a competent designated examiner.
2. That an agreement be signed by the patient, witnessed by two persons, obligating him to conform to the regulations of such hospital and that he will stay therein and submit himself to observation, examination and treatment for at least nine weeks, unless sooner discharged subject to his right to be released upon notice. Idaho 66-322 (Supp. 1969).

15. Head of hospital may refuse admission to any applicant if he finds welfare of applicant and/or society are better protected by judicial hospitalization procedure. Idaho 66-318 (Supp. 1969).

16. Patient has a "right to leave the hospital at any time during the normal dayshift hours of operation, which shall include but need not be limited to 9 A.M. to 5 P.M." Ill. 91 1/2, 4-1 (Supp. 1969).

17. An attending physician together with a specialist in mental diseases may apply for a temporary commitment of 30 days for observation with the consent of his patient. On the advice of the institution and with the consent of the attending physician, the observation period may be extended for such time as is recommended. See Table 3.11 below. Iowa 229.1

18. Voluntary patients may be admitted to the psychopathic hospital under regulations to be established by the board of regents. They will not be maintained by the state. Iowa 225.8, 225.9.

19. If in the judgment of the "head of hospital" such person is in need of "care or treatment" therein. Kan. 59-2905 (Supp. 1968).

20. This same provision also appears in Table 3.11 below.

21. To postpone release superintendent must within 48 hours of receipt of receipt file a certificate with the district court stating that release of the patient would be unsafe for the patient and others. La. 28:98.1 (Supp. 1969).

22. If head of hospital files certification with court within 10 days of receipt of request that release is unsafe, it may be postponed for no more than 10 days or for beginning of hearings. Me. 34, §2293.

23. Patient must be certified by a physician who has personally examined the patient and believes he is in need of psychiatric evaluation and treatment. Mont. 38-406.2(2c) (Supp. 1969).

24. The exact length of the extension allowed is not set out in the statute. Mont. 38-406.2(4) (Supp. 1969).

25. Unless county board of mental health or district court authorizes the superintendent to detain the patient. Neb. 83-324.

26. Such notice shall not effect release until 60 days from admission to state hospital. N.H. 135:22.

27. Judicial finding as to legal settlement and financial ability on basis of investigation by county adjuster is required. Such finding is not required if security is deposited. N.J. 30:4-46 (Supp. 1970).

28. Discharge may also be effected by chief executive officer of hospital on certificate of medical director that patient is cured, or further treatment is unnecessary or not desirable. N.J. 30:4-48 (Supp. 1970).

29. Head of hospital may discharge any recovered voluntary patient whose hospitalization he determines to be no longer advisable or when discharge would contribute to the most effective use of the hospital in care and treatment of the mentally ill. N.M. 34-2-3.

30. At least 15 days. N.Y. Mental Hygiene Law, 71 (Supp. 1970).

31. Only after expiration of original 15 day-period. N.Y. Mental Hygiene Law, 71 (Supp. 1970).

32. Application must be accompanied by physician's certificate. N.C. 122-56.

33. There is a 30-day minimum period if deemed advisable for adequate examination by hospital superintendent or examining physician and consented to in application form by applicant. N.C. 122-56.

34. Unless proceedings for involuntary commitment of patient have been initiated. N.C. 122-56.

35. If superintendent thinks release is unsafe for patient or others, he may file application for the person's commitment during this period. N.D. 25-03-06.

36. Any person 18 and older or at least 16 but not over 18 with consent of parent or guardian and guardian of mentally incompetent may petition for admission. Okla. 43A, §53 (Supp. 1969), §58.

37. Voluntary patient may secure release on 15-day notice. (Mental incompetent may seek release by habeas corpus on petition of patient, relative, or friend.) Okla. 43A, §53, §99 (Supp. 1969).

38. Any voluntary patient may, on application and notice to superintendent of hospital, be granted a temporary leave of absence if superintendent believes that such leave will not interfere with successful treatment or examination of the applicant for leave, Ore. 426.220(2), except when a period of longer hospitalization has been imposed as condition of admission, Ore. 426.220(1).

39. It is not clear whether a formal written application is required for admission under this procedure; thus it has been charted in the informal admission column. Pa. 50, §4402.

40. Request for discharge may be denied if made sooner than 30 days after admission; forthwith if patient has been in the hospital at least 30 days. S.C. 32-953.

41. Patient not eligible for release "until the admission diagnostic work-up on such patient has been completed and all laboratory data can be compiled and diagnosis established, provided that said diagnosis shall not require more than twenty . days from the date of admission of such patient." Tenn. 33-1204(1) (Supp. 1968).

42. Application may be made by county judge if patient is not legally of age and has consented. Tex. 5547-23(a)

43. Head of hospital must inform patient at time of admission of his right to release and to habeas corpus and that his civil rights and legal capacity are not affected. Patient must be informed of rights of patients as set forth in the code. Tex. 5547-24.

44. No provisions concerning nonstate hospitals. Utah 64-7-29.

45. One-year maximum. Wash. 72-23.100.

46. Twelve days for a public hospital; 10 days for a private hospital. Wash. 71.02.050, 71.12.560.

47. If notice of voluntary patient's desire to leave is given within less than 18 days from date of admission, superintendent shall have right to detain such patient for a period not to exceed 30 days from time of admission. Wash. 72.23.090.

48. If, within 96 hours of receipt of the request, superintendent of state hospital in which patient is confined files with clerk of county court an application for involuntary hospitalization, release may be postponed pending a decision on the application by mental hygiene commission. W. Va. 27-4-3.

49. Certificate of patient's physician based on personal examination. Wis. 51.10.

Chapter Three Involuntary Hospitalization

I. INTRODUCTION

The procedures governing the involuntary hospitalization of persons with mental disabilities are almost entirely statutory.[1] In the past such procedures were known and designated generally as "commitment" laws.[2] Since this term connotes an order employed in criminal proceedings[3] as well as in the confinement of noncriminal mentally disabled persons it has been replaced in nineteen states and the District of Columbia by the less offensive term "hospitalization."[4]

This chapter touches only briefly on the involuntary hospitalization of the mentally deficient, epileptics, alcoholics, and drug addicts. Although persons suffering from these specific types of mental disability are described separately in most involuntary hospitalization statutes, the procedures for their hospitalization are either identical to or substantially the same as those governing the mentally ill generally.[5] In view of the purpose of this Report, the following discussion will be devoted primarily to an analysis of the various involuntary hospitalization and emergency detention procedures as they apply to the mentally ill. It is to be noted that procedures designed for the speedy processing of emergency situations (including simple detention) technically are not hospitalization procedures. However, in practice, the emergency detention procedures play a significant role in the hospitalization process and they are treated in this chapter so that they can be placed in proper procedural perspective as a functional part of involuntary hospitalization procedures.

II. HISTORICAL BACKGROUND

It is difficult to speak of the history of commitment legislation without at the same time describing the development of legislation relating to the problem of mental disability as a whole. This development has been sketched in some detail in chapter 1. The background offered here will thus be limited and designed only to facilitate an understanding of the present hospitalization laws by placing them in a somewhat larger historical context.

During the colonial period there were no statutes concerned with the hospitalization of the mentally ill. The violent and dangerously insane were handled under the authority of the sovereign's police powers.[6] At the time the first asylums[7] for the mentally ill were established, in the middle of the eighteenth century, and for about one hundred years thereafter, the "commitment" of patients to these hospitals was effected with surprising ease and informality.[8] The request of a friend or relative—or perhaps even an enemy—to a member of the hospital staff for an order of admission would often suffice. The staff member might then hastily scribble a few words on a scrap of paper, sign his name, and the procedure would be completed.[9]

The relative success of the humanitarian movement to secure decent care and treatment for the mentally ill in the third quarter of the nineteenth century served to emphasize the inadequacy of the existing commitment laws.[10] Crusades by Mrs. E. P. W. Packard, Dorothea Dix, and others spurred the enactment of commitment laws which specified the use of judicial procedures designed to guard against

1. Voluntary admission to hospitals is discussed in chap. 2, "Voluntary Admission."

2. Curran, "Hospitalization of the Mentally Ill," 31 *N.C.L. Rev.* 274 (1952–53).

3. *Commitment,* "the warrant . . . by which a court directs an officer to take a person to prison" and "a proceeding for the restraining and confining of insane persons for their own and the public's protection." *Black's Law Dictionary* 341 (4th ed. 1951).

4. Alaska, Florida, Georgia, Hawaii, Illinois, Maine, Minnesota, Nevada, New Mexico, North Carolina, North Dakota, Ohio, South Carolina, Tennessee, Utah, Vermont, Washington, West Virginia, and Wyoming. Both "commitment" and "hospitalization" are used in the statutes of Arizona, Colorado, Minnesota, Missouri, and Texas.

5. Table 3.7, Statutory Definitions of the Mentally Deficient and Epileptics and Table 3.8, Statutory Definitions of Alcoholics and Drug Addicts; see Table 3.9, Hospitalization of the Mentally Deficient, Epileptics, Alcoholics, and Drug Addicts, for statutory citations.

6. Deutsch, *The Mentally Ill in America* 419–20 (2d ed. 1949).

7. The term "hospital" was not in general usage until after 1900. Until that time the terms "asylum," "lunatic asylum," or "insane asylum" were used. Council of State Governments, *The Mental Health Programs of the Forty-eight States* 23 (1950).

8. Deutsch, *supra* note 6, at 62, 420.

9. Id. at 62.

10. Curran, *supra* note 2.

wrongful commitments.[11] The success of these earlier crusades is reflected in the almost single-minded concern with the possibility of wrongful commitment which characterized the legislative approach to the problems of the mentally ill until very recently.

There is some evidence that the contemporary legislative approach is more comprehensive. During the last twenty years many state legislatures have evidenced more concern about the treatment and rehabilitation of the mentally ill than about the problem of wrongful commitment. Moreover, the advances in psychiatric knowledge together with the greater understanding of the attributes of mental health have supplied legislators with the factual basis necessary for the enactment of that legislation most conducive to the effective treatment of persons who are, in fact, mentally disabled.[12] Many of the new laws have incorporated measures advocated by the medical profession, such as hospitalization by medical certification, emergency procedures, and short term or observational procedures. A number of these laws include provisions designed to modernize the terminology used in determining to whom and under what circumstances involuntary hospitalization statutes should be applied. These legislative changes have not been viewed with equal favor by all observers. The propriety, and indeed the constitutionality, of some of the newer hospitalization procedures have been challenged. What constitutes the proper criteria for hospitalization, for example, remains open to question. Some of these problems will be explored in this chapter.

III. INVOLUNTARY HOSPITALIZATION OF THE MENTALLY ILL

A. THE MEANING OF INVOLUNTARY HOSPITALIZATION

Involuntary hospitalization describes the removal of a person judged to be mentally ill from his normal surroundings to a hospital authorized to detain him. The determination of whether a person's mental condition brings him within the statutory criteria for involuntary hospitalization is usually made by a court, an administrative tribunal, or a specified number of physicians. While in most cases a court order will be required to effect the patient's removal, this is dispensed with in some instances. Many states provide more than one involuntary hospitalization proce-

dure.[13] The discussion of these procedures is taken up in section III C of this chapter.

An example of a hospitalization order reads as follows:

In the Matter of the Examination of _____ _____ alleged to be a mentally ill person.

By virtue of a notice filed in the above-entitled matter, I caused the said _____ to be brought before me at _____ in said County of _____, State of _____, at _____ o'clock _____ M.; also caused to appear at the same time and place _____, a competent physician, and proceed to examine the said _____; and find as follows:

That the true name of the person examined is _____; age _____ years; nativity _____; present residence _____; and the cause of such mental illness _____ that _____, a competent physician, and _____, a competent physician, after careful examination have certified on oath that the said _____ is mentally ill and by reason of such mental illness is in need of treatment, care or custody.

IT IS THEREFORE CONSIDERED, ORDERED AND ADJUDGED, That the said _____ _____ is a mentally ill person, and that _____ he be and hereby is committed to the _____ State Hospital at _____ and that _____ he be promptly and safely delivered to the superintendent of the _____ State Hospital.

_____

_____ Judge

The period of hospitalization may be either determinate or indeterminate, although the latter represents the more general practice in this country. This period may be terminated by the death of the patient, his discharge, his release upon improvement or recovery, or upon other statutory conditions.[14]

For the purposes of this Report, all hospitalization procedures are treated as involuntary except those wherein hospitalization is commenced originally by the affirmative action of the patient himself or by someone who is empowered by law to act in the patient's behalf, such as the parent of a minor or the guardian of an incompetent. While the term "involuntary hospitalization" suggests *actual* compulsion it

---

11. Id. at 276.

12. Flaschner, "Analysis of Legal and Medical Considerations in Commitment of the Mentally Ill," 56 *Yale L.J.* 1178 (1947).

13. See Table Intro. 1, "Summary of Civil Hospitalization Proceedings."

14. See chap. 4, "Separation from Mental Hospitals."

should be stressed that this element is not always present. For example, in an involuntary proceeding the patient may stand mute or fail to manifest opposition to the hospitalization. Actual compulsion is involved most often in contested cases, which occur infrequently.[15] All these factors should be kept in mind in evaluating the extent to which the statutes providing for such hospitalization adequately safeguard the interests of the mentally ill.

B. WHO IS SUBJECT TO HOSPITALIZATION

1. PRESENT STATUS OF THE LAW

a) *Mentally Ill Persons*

At common law the restraint of an insane person without legal process was justified as an exercise of the sovereign's police power, but the use of such restraint was limited to situations involving imminent danger to persons or property in the community.[16] Such arrangements left much to be desired. Individuals who exercised this right to restrain assumed the burden of proving the imminent necessity of restraint in the event that civil damage suits were filed against them.[17] The common-law rule was codified shortly after the colonial period.[18] The effective protection of the personal rights of the mentally ill, however, was to require additional legislation recognizing that confinement of the mentally ill was incidental to and necessary for proper medical treatment.[19]

Of the forty-three jurisdictions which now provide some form of judicial hospitalization, only nine phrase the sole criterion for hospitalization in terms of whether the individual is dangerous to himself or others.[20] Eighteen other jurisdictions augment this

provision by stating that the need of the patient for care or treatment may serve as an alternative basis for hospitalization.[21] Six states, on the other hand, provide no other basis for hospitalization than the patient's need for care or treatment.[22]

The Pennsylvania statute, for example, permits the involuntary hospitalization of anyone who suffers from a mental illness which "so lessens the capacity of a person to use his customary self-control, judgment and discretion in the conduct of his affairs and social relations as to make it necessary or advisable for him to be under care."[23] Likewise, the Draft Act provides for the compulsory hospitalization of those who are "in need of . . . care or treatment" and lack sufficient capacity to make responsible decisions regarding admission to a hospital.[24]

Six states specify that a person may be judicially hospitalized when his disability is such that for his own welfare or the welfare of others he requires the care or treatment available in a hospital.[25] The phrase "welfare of others" in such cases need not carry the same meaning as that attached to the term "dangerous." It is conceivable that cases may arise in which the potential threat to the "welfare of others" dictates hospitalization even though the person involved is not judged to be dangerous.

The criteria for judicial hospitalization are not spelled out in the statutes of Colorado and Delaware; presumably anyone meeting the statutory definitions of mental illness or insanity may be hospitalized.[26]

While most statutes simply delineate the protective and curative purposes underlying hospitalization, Massachusetts has added another dimension. Social nonconformity, as well as the exhibition of "dangerous" tendencies, appears to suffice as a basis for hospitalization in that state. According to the statutes, a person "likely to conduct himself in a man-

15. Curran, *supra* note 2, at 279. See also Rock, Jacobson, & Janopaul, *Hospitalization and Discharge of the Mentally Ill* 155–57 (1968).

16. Christiansen v. Weston, 36 Ariz. 200, 284 P. 149 (1930); Bisgaard v. Duvall, 169 Iowa 711, 151 N.W. 1051 (1915); Look v. Dean, 108 Mass. 116 (1871); Keleher v. Putnam, 60 N.H. 30 (1880). See Flaschner, *supra* note 12, at 1178, 1185.

17. Crawford v. Brown, 321 Ill. 305, 151 N.E. 911 (1926); Maxwell v. Maxwell, 189 Iowa 7, 177 N.W. 541 (1920); Boesch v. Kick, 97 N.J.L. 92, 116 A. 796 (Sup. Ct. 1922); Annot., 45 A.L.R. 1464 (1926); Annot., 10 A.L.R. 488 (1921); Flaschner, *supra* note 12, at 1185.

18. For example, in 1788 the state of New York enacted a law permitting "any two or more justices of the peace to cause [persons furiously mad who would be dangerous to go abroad] to be apprehended and kept safely locked up in some secure place. . . ." N.Y. Sess. Laws 1788, ch. 31.

19. N.Y. Sess. Laws 1842, ch. 135, §§ 18–23.

20. See Table 3.1, Statutory Definitions of the Mentally Ill, and

Table 3.2, Judicial Hospitalization of the Mentally Ill—Prehearing Procedures. It should be noted that the statutory definitions of mental illness do not necessarily coincide with the statutory criteria set forth for hospitalization. In 1959 only five states restricted involuntary hospitalization to the "dangerous."

21. Ibid. The number was twelve in 1959.

22. Ibid. In 1959 the number of states was seven.

23. *Pa. Stat. Ann.* tit. 50, § 4102 (1969).

24. National Institute of Mental Health, Federal Security Agency, *A Draft Act Governing Hospitalization of the Mentally Ill* § 9, at 9 (Public Health Service Pub. No. 51, 1952) [hereinafter cited as *Draft Act*]. The Draft Act appears as Appendix A to this Report.

25. See Table 3.2.

26. Ibid.

ner which clearly violates the established laws, ordinances, conventions or morals of the community" is considered mentally ill.[27]

Although in some states the statutory criteria for nonjudicial hospitalization differ from those providing for judicial hospitalization, in most cases they are similar. In the few instances where they do differ, they will almost always fall within one of the categories described above.[28]

b) Mentally Deficient Persons

In all but six states the statutes dealing with the mentally ill also provide for the involuntary hospitalization of the mentally deficient.[29] Most of these states provide that such hospitalization is to be effected in accordance with special statutory provisions similar or identical to those used for the mentally ill.

A mentally deficient person subject to involuntary hospitalization is usually described as a "person with a defect in mental development at birth, or at an early age, and which is of such a degree that he is incapable of caring for himself or managing his affairs and requires supervision, care, training, control or custody for his own welfare or for the welfare of others."[30]

Several state statutes explicitly leave the definition of mental deficiency to experts. For example Wyoming provides that "[m]ental deficiency shall mean mental deficiency as defined by appropriate clinical authorities to such extent that a person so afflicted is incapable of managing himself and his affairs. . . ."[31]

c) Epileptics, Alcoholics, and Drug Addicts

Provisions for the hospitalization of epileptics are found in eight states.[32] Alcoholics may be hospitalized in thirty-seven states[33] and drug addicts in thirty-four states.[34] These provisions often constitute one part of the general provisions applicable to all the mentally ill. It is estimated that there are between 800,000 and 1,500,000 epileptics in the United

States,[35] although there were only about 12,000 epileptic patients in public institutions in 1967.[36] To a considerable extent these figures reflect the progress of medical science in controlling seizures. These advances have made it possible for a large number of epileptics, who are otherwise mentally sound, to avoid being hospitalized. Moreover, with each advance in the treatment of epilepsy the problem of hospitalizing those suffering from it decreases in importance.[37]

There is no universal legislative standard prescribing the degree of alcoholism which must exist before a person may be involuntarily hospitalized. A common definition of an alcoholic is "any person who chronically and habitually uses alcoholic beverages to the extent that said person has lost the power of self-control with respect to the use of such beverages, or who, by reason of alcoholism endangers the health, safety or welfare of himself or others."[38] North Carolina requires that the condition exist for at least one year prior to the proceedings.[39]

Kansas adds, as an additional basis for hospitalization, that one has been "five times convicted of intoxication in any court,"[40] while New Hampshire defines a habitual drunkard as one who "has been three times convicted."[41]

Although it appears that these hospitalization provisions are designed to apply primarily to chronic cases, this distinction is not always spelled out in the statutes.[42]

It is estimated that there are between 1,000,000 and 4,500,000 chronic alcoholics in the country.[43] A recent study states:

> Large numbers of problem drinkers are admitted annually to the 285 state mental hospitals in the United States. As many as 40 percent of all men admitted to the mental hospitals in some states are given a diagnosis of alcoholism. . . .[44]

27. *Mass. Ann. Laws* ch. 123, § 1 (1965).

28. See Tables 3.4 Administrative Hospitalization—Prehearing Procedures, and 3.6, Involuntary Hospitalization by Medical Certification.

29. Table 3.9.

30. *Ky. Rev. Stat. Ann.* § 202.010 (1969).

31. *Wyo. Stat. Ann.* § 25-90 Art. II(g) (Supp. 1969). See also Table 3.7 *infra*.

32. Table 3.9. In 1959, eighteen states had such laws.

33. Ibid. In 1959, thirty-six states had such laws.

34. Ibid. In 1959, thirty-four states had such laws.

35. Barrow & Fabing, *Epilepsy and the Law* 3 (1956).

36. United States Public Health Service, National Institute of Mental Health, *Patients in State and County Mental Hospitals 1967,* at 56 (1969).

37. Barrow & Fabing, *supra* note 35, at 94.

38. *N.Y. Mental Hygiene Law* § 30(a) (McKinney 1951).

39. *N.C. Gen. Stat.* § 35-1.1 (Supp. 1967).

40. *Kan. Stat. Ann.* § 74-4401 (1964).

41. *N.H. Rev. Stat. Ann.* § 172:1(vi) (1964).

42. See Table 3.8.

43. Hewitt, *Alcoholism* 19 (1957).

44. State of Maryland, Department of Mental Hygiene, Statistics Newsletter, vii No. 8, 1966, quoted in Plaut, *Alcohol Problems: Report to the Nation* 65 (1967).

Nationally in 1967, "alcoholic disorders" accounted for 17.8 percent of first admissions to public hospitals, 7.7 percent of those to private mental hospitals, and 11.8 percent of those to general hospitals with psychiatric facilities. The total number of first admissions for alcoholics was 83,497; resident patients in public and private mental hospitals who were diagnosed as alcoholics numbered 22,511.[45] The disparity between admissions and resident patients may be traced to the short period of hospitalization of alcoholics and the consequent high rate of turnover in patients.

Several states, including Indiana, Nebraska, Ohio, and Virginia, define mental illness to include addiction to drugs and thus bring addicts within the purview of statutes providing for hospitalization. The emphasis in such legislation, however, is not on the element of danger to others but rather on the chronic nature of the addiction and its deleterious effect on the addict's power to control his own use of the drugs. Thus, an addict is defined in Massachusetts as a person who is so addicted "to the intemperate use of narcotics . . . as to have lost the power of self control."[46] The therapeutic needs of the patient constitute the fundamental motive for hospitalization in such cases.

On the other hand, several states direct attention to the danger to others which drug addiction may entail. The Michigan statute defines a "drug user" as "any person who habitually uses any habit-forming narcotic drugs so as to endanger the public morals, health, safety, or welfare, or who is so far addicted to use of such habit-forming narcotic drugs as to have lost the power of self-control with reference to his addiction."[47]

In 1952 drug addicts constituted less than 1 percent of all first admissions to state mental institutions[48] and one-tenth of one percent of the resident hospital population.[49] By 1967 these figures had more than doubled, to 2.1 percent[50] and 0.4 percent[51]

respectively. Yet, for all the increase in admissions, the total number of resident patients in 1967 stood at 1,484. In contrast the United States Bureau of Narcotics reported over 57,000 known active addicts in 1965.[52]

While it is clear that the imposition of criminal sanctions to suppress drug traffic, rather than civil hospitalization, continues to be society's primary response to drug addiction, some movement towards treatment is discernible.[53] In 1966 Congress passed the Narcotic Addict Rehabilitation Act of 1966 which provides for civil hospitalization of narcotic addicts.[54] An eligible addict or his relative may apply for up to six months' inpatient treatment followed by a three-year period of follow-up outpatient care. Support for the latter program has recently been placed under the Community Mental Health Centers Act. Authorized appropriations for the rehabilitation of narcotic addicts and alcoholics were $15 million for 1969 and $25 million for 1970.[55]

2. COMMENTARY ON THE SCOPE OF PRESENT INVOLUNTARY HOSPITALIZATION LEGISLATION

a) *Mentally Ill Persons*

Even a limited analysis of the statutes and statistics relevant to the handling of the mentally ill indicates that hospitalization has functioned as a multipurpose remedy. It has served not only to prevent breaches of the peace and harm to persons or property but also to provide for the treatment and rehabilitation of the mentally ill, to relieve the family of responsibility for the care of a disabled member, and to provide a refuge for those people within the society—the destitute aged, the mentally deficient, and the maladjusted —who are unwelcome in any social group or institution.[56] The relative weight to be attached to each of these purposes in the larger pattern of involuntary hospitalization has not always remained the same. It fluctuates with social and technological changes. As long as the medical arts were helpless in the treatment of mental illness, for example, little consideration was given to the curative aspects of compulsory hospitalization.

The role of mental hospitals in caring for the aged, the senile, and others for whom some states provide

45. U.S. Public Health Service, *supra* note 36, at 11.

46. *Mass. Ann. Laws* ch. 123, § 62 (1965). See also Table 3.8.

47. *Mich. Comp. Laws Ann.* § 335.202 (1967).

48. U.S. Public Health Service, *Patients in Mental Institutions* pt. II, Table 8, at 26 (Public Health Service Pub. No. 483, 1952).

49. Id., Table 17, at 50. Partial information from 183 of 204 state hospitals showed 826 first admissions for drug addiction in 1952. However, only 249 drug addicts were listed among the resident patients in these hospitals at the end of that year.

50. U.S. Public Health Service, *supra* note 36, at 21.

51. Id. at 54.

52. Bureau of Narcotics, *Traffic in Opium and Other Dangerous Drugs* 17 (1966).

53. See Eldridge, *Narcotics and the Law* 140 (2d ed. 1967).

54. 42 *U.S.C.* §§ 3401–41 (1970).

55. S. Rep. No. 1454, 90th Cong., 2d Sess. 9 (1968).

56. Belknap, *Human Problems of a State Mental Hospital* 32 (1956).

no special facilities continues to be a source of great concern. The overcrowded conditions which characterize many present day institutions may be traced in large measure to the attempt to fulfill this custodial responsibility. Recently these conditions have been eased somewhat in part because of the benefits available under Title XVII (Medicare) and Title XIX (Medicaid) of the Social Security Amendments of 1965. Most recent figures show that the number of patients aged 65 and over in state and county mental hospitals is decreasing at an annual rate of 1.1 percent. However, this is still the largest single age group, constituting 30 percent of all resident patients.[57] If the hospital is to perform satisfactorily its primary mission, the treatment of mental illness, alternatives must be provided to alleviate the overcrowding engendered by simple custodial utilization of the hospital.

There can be little question that the purposes—whether custodial, curative, or protective—envisaged by the statutes are worthwhile social goals. Moreover, to the extent that involuntary hospitalization statutes accord the mentally ill due process of law, that is, the right to notice and a fair hearing, their constitutionality is well established.[58] Unfortunately the statutes are so broadly worded that they fail to identify with clarity or precision the type and degree of mental illness for which involuntary hospitalization, with the accompanying deprivation of many personal and civil rights, is justified. The statutory language in this area is almost universally obscure or tautological. Thus New York law permits hospitalization of a person who is "afflicted with mental disease to such an extent that for his own welfare or the welfare of others, or of the community, he requires care and treatment."[59] Even those statutes which rely on the concept of dangerousness as a justification for hospitalization are in significant aspects vague.[60] In application, such a standard can become as broad as the ingenuity of the person who must apply it allows.[61]

A recent California statute is unique in dividing the mentally ill into two categories: the "gravely disabled" and the "imminently dangerous." The "gravely disabled" person, defined as one who "as a result of mental disorder or impairment by chronic alcoholism, is unable to provide for his basic personal needs for food, clothing, or shelter,"[62] cannot be directly committed to a mental hospital for an extended period.[63] An "imminently dangerous person" is one who during fourteen days of intensive treatment (a) has threatened, attempted or actually inflicted physical harm upon the person of another after having been taken into custody for evaluation and treatment, and who, as a result of mental disorder or impairment by chronic alcoholism, presents an imminent threat of substantial physical harm to others, or (b) "has attempted or inflicted physical harm upon the person of another, that act having resulted in his being taken into custody and who presents, as a result of mental disorder, an imminent threat of substantial physical harm to others."[64]

Part (b) was added to the statute when it became apparent that part (a) covered only persons who acted in the described manner during the fourteen-day period of intensive treatment, an unduly restrictive condition. Part (b) expands the procedure to include those persons whose dangerous conduct led to the detention whether or not they continued to act in that manner during the fourteen-day period. Such persons may be involuntarily judicially hospitalized for ninety-day periods until they are no longer imminently dangerous.[65]

Illinois too has incorporated the notion of imminently dangerous behavior in its definition of who may be hospitalized without reference to any specific act of his. A person may be hospitalized "if that person, as a result of such mental illness, is reasonably expected at the time the determination is being made or within a reasonable time thereafter to intentionally physically injure himself or other persons."[66]

The Draft Act, as well as the several state statutes which are modeled on it, suffers from another source of interpretative difficulty. It provides that a court may order hospitalization upon a finding that a person is mentally ill, needs treatment in a mental hospital, and, because of his illness, lacks sufficient insight or capacity to make responsible decisions with

---

57. *Supra* note 36, at 13.

58. Hall v. Verdel, 40 F. Supp. 94 (W.D. Va. 1941); Shapley v. Cohoon, 258 F. 752 (D. Mass. 1918). Consult this chapter, note 165 *infra*.

59. *N.Y. Mental Hygiene Law* § 2.8 (McKinney 1964).

60. Dershowitz, "A Knife that Cuts Both Ways," 2 *Psychology Today* 43 (Feb. 1969).

61. Rock et al., *supra* note 15, at 132–39.

62. *Cal. Welf. & Inst'ns Code* § 5008(h) (West Supp. 1970).

63. A conservator is appointed who may arrange for hospitalization with court approval. *Cal. Welf. & Inst'ns Code* § 5358 (West Supp. 1970).

64. *Cal. Welf. & Inst'ns Code* § 5300 (West Supp. 1970).

65. Ibid.

66. *Ill. Ann. Stat.* ch. 91-1/2, § 1-11 (Smith-Hurd Supp. 1969).

respect to his need for hospitalization.[67] The Commentary, explaining the act states:

> . . . without being "dangerous," a mentally ill individual may because of the nature of the stage of his illness lose his power to make choices or become so confused as no longer to have the capacity to make a decision having any relation to the factors bearing on his hospitalization. . . .
>
> It should be emphasized that it is not a question of the individual agreeing or disagreeing with medical judgment as to the nature of his illness or the need for hospital care, but rather of whether he is *capable* of making a responsible, not necessarily a wise decision. . . .[68]

The precise meaning of the term "responsible decision" in the Draft Act and the Commentary is elusive. There is no clear statement of the factors which should be weighed in evaluating the individual's "capacity" to make a "responsible decision." The subtle difference pointed out in the Commentary between the capacity to make a "responsible" decision and the capacity to make a "wise" one proves illusory when one attempts to set up manageable criteria for involuntary hospitalization. It would seem, to cite only one objection, that an unwise decision in itself constitutes some evidence of a lack of capacity to make a responsible decision.[69]

One medical author has interpreted the Draft Act as allowing the involuntary hospitalization of severe psychoneurotics and has contended that such deprivation of liberty could rest neither on the doctrine of *parens patriae* nor on the police powers of the state.[70] That author, however, views the Act as requiring only a finding of mental illness (as defined in Part 1, § 1) and a finding that the patient needs medical care but *does not know it*. He fails to distinguish between lack of sufficient knowledge to make a responsible decision and lack of a sufficient capacity to make a responsible decision. Although criteria for hospitalization based upon the extent of the "knowledge" a person may have of his

mental illness and his need for hospitalization may not properly rest upon the police powers of the state, the question of "capacity" to make responsible decisions regarding his hospitalization is another matter.

One view favoring the liberalized requirements is that which rests on the premise that the hospitalization of nondangerous persons is necessary to prevent their condition from deteriorating.[71] Those who adhere to this understanding contend that the second ground for involuntary hospitalization in the Draft Act, which provides for the hospitalization of those who lack sufficient insight or capacity to make responsible decisions, was in fact aimed largely at patients with early manic depressive and schizophrenic psychoses. Denied proper treatment at an early stage, these individuals could in time become dangerous.[72]

Although it may be desirable from a medical point of view to hospitalize those who are not presently dangerous but who might easily become so in the absence of proper treatment, the question of the propriety of such hospitalization remains a real one in view of the conditions existing in many hospitals. A prime requisite for the success of such a policy is that the hospitals be equipped to offer the care and treatment required by such patients. Many communities have not yet provided the financial resources essential to the establishment and maintenance of such facilities. In the absence of these facilities, of course, there is no justification for broadening the involuntary hospitalization requirements to include nondangerous persons.[73]

Parenthetically, it has also been suggested that commitment of a dangerous person may also be constitutionally suspect under such circumstances.

The Robinson [*Robinson v. California*, 370 U.S. 660 (1962)] dicta suggesting that civil commitment

---

67. *Draft Act* § 9, at 9.

68. Id., Commentary, at 28–29.

69. Guttmacher & Weihofen, *Psychiatry and the Law* 290 (1952); Kadish, "A Case Study in the Significance of Procedural Due Process—Institutionalizing the Mentally Ill," 9 *Western Political Q.* 93, 94 (1956).

70. Whitmore, "Comments on a Draft Act for the Hospitalization of the Mentally Ill," 19 *Geo. Wash. L. Rev.* 512, 522–23 and cases cited in n.48 (1951). But see Curran, *supra* note 2, at 291.

71. Ross, "Hospitalizing the Mentally Ill—Emergency and Temporary Commitments," *Current Trends in State Legislation 1955–56*, at 468 n.38 (1957).

72. Ibid.

73. See Birnbaum, "The Right to Treatment," 46 *A.B.A.J.* 499 (1960) for an excellent brief advocating the proposition that incarceration by the state in a mental hospital without proper treatment is a deprivation of liberty without due process. A bill establishing the right to treatment and a Mental Treatment Standards Committee to promulgate minimum standards for treatment was introduced in the General Assembly of Pennsylvania in 1968 and 1969 but failed to pass both times. The bill is the first of its kind. "Right to Treatment Law of 1969," House Bill No. 1142, General Assembly of Pennsylvania (1969 Session).

is constitutional are in paragraphs expressing a favorable attitude to state action—even compulsory state action—assuring treatment for ill citizens. But commitment of dangerous persons is a harder case, because the chief purpose of such a measure is to afford protection for society, not to ensure treatment for the patient. If a case arose in which medical testimony indicated that a patient could not be helped by treatment (either because no treatment was known for his illness or because the available hospital had inadequate facilities), but he was nonetheless committed as dangerous, the Court might well hold that the state was punishing the patient for an illness and thus inflicting cruel and unusual punishment.[74]

b) The Mentally Deficient, Epileptics, Alcoholics, and Drug Addicts

No attempt has been made in this Report to offer a separate evaluation of the problems and procedures unique to the handling of the mentally deficient, epileptics, alcoholics, and drug addicts. The questions presented in these cases are somewhat different from, although they remain related to, the policy issues raised by the hospitalization of the mentally ill. Tables at the end of this chapter present statutory definitions of these conditions and show where these provisions may be found.[75]

The mental deficient subject to "hospitalization" is usually placed in a special institution designated a "school" rather than in a mental hospital. The program in such a school is designed less to cure the disability than to teach the patient to live satisfactorily with it.[76]

A recent study reports that through the application of modern medical and surgical techniques, epilepsy now remains a disabling disorder in less than 20 percent of the cases.[77] This development has been reflected in recent legislation; a number of states which formerly hospitalized epileptics have ceased, for reasons of economy, to regard this single criterion as sufficient for hospitalization.[78] In those cases where epilepsy is coupled with mental illness

or mental deficiency, or perhaps both, however, hospitalization may still be necessary.

Although the Draft Act does not specifically refer to either alcoholism or mental deficiency, it has been suggested that the coverage of the Act is intended to include persons falling within these categories.[79] As pointed out earlier, alcoholics now constitute 17.8 percent of the first admissions to public mental hospitals. The current arguments in favor of a wider use of the hospitalization provisions for alcoholics will thus have to be reviewed in light of the additional burden that such an influx of patients would place on existing facilities. Moreover, experience with the compulsory hospitalization of such patients places in question the efficacy of such an approach to the treatment of alcoholism.[80]

Drug addicts are usually treated separately, partly because of the relation between addiction and the criminal law and partly because treatment in the average mental hospital has been unsuccessful. Special facilities for the treatment of the narcotic addict are provided by the United States Public Health Hospitals at Lexington, Kentucky, and Fort Worth, Texas. Several experimental programs both public and private have been initiated in the last few years with varying success.[81]

C. CLASSIFICATION OF INVOLUNTARY HOSPITALIZATION PROCEDURES FOR THE MENTALLY ILL

Since there have been almost as many approaches to drafting the various hospitalization-procedure statutes as there are jurisdictions, the problem of classifying the procedures presents considerable difficulty. No claim is made that the classification set forth in this Report is ideal or all-embracing. It was adopted because it seemed to provide the most meaningful vehicle for the communication of the particular analysis undertaken.

The general classification of hospitalization procedures has been mentioned previously in this chapter. The reader will recall that all hospitalization procedures are classified as involuntary except those which are commenced originally by the affirmative action of the patient himself or of someone who is empowered by law to act in the patient's behalf.

It cannot be too strongly emphasized, however, that the classification undertaken here is based en-

74. Note, "Civil Commitment of the Mentally Ill: Theories and Procedures," 79 *Harv. L. Rev.* 1291 (1966).

75. See Tables 3.7 through 3.9. For an excellent discussion of the legal policies which should govern the care of the mentally retarded, see The President's Panel on Mental Retardation, *Report of the Task Force on Law* (1963).

76. Ross, *supra* note 71, at 468 n.39.

77. Barrow & Fabing, *supra* note 35, at 2.

78. Id. at 93, 94, and nn.254, 255. I.e., Illinois, Kansas, Maine, Maryland, Mississippi, New Jersey, New York, North Dakota, Ohio, Oregon, South Carolina, and Wisconsin.

79. Whitmore, *supra* note 70, at 512, 514. But see *Draft Act*, Scope of the Draft Act, at 1.

80. Ross, *supra* note 71, at 468 n.39.

81. Eldridge, *supra* note 53, at 144–60.

tirely on the language of the statutes concerned. No notice has been taken of the actual manner in which the differing statutory schemes have been implemented or interpreted by courts and administrators.

The approach used in classifying the various involuntary procedures was to view these procedures from the standpoints of three important but distinct characteristics: (1) the purpose and length of the hospitalization, (2) the primary authority designated under the statute to decide whether the person shall be hospitalized, and (3) the degree of compulsion.

Viewed in light of the purpose and length of hospitalization (or detention), involuntary procedures have been divided into three categories: (1) Those procedures designed as temporary measures to authorize the immediate taking into custody of a person in a situation which does not permit fulfilling the necessary conditions of the normal hospitalization procedure are grouped under the heading emergency hospitalization or detention. (2) Those procedures in which the purpose appears to be either the observation or treatment, or both, of an alleged mentally ill person for a *specified* and *relatively short* period of time have been grouped under the heading short-term or observational hospitalization. (3) All other involuntary procedures have been considered involuntary extended hospitalization. The earlier edition of this Report used the term indeterminate involuntary hospitalization for this last category. Since then, however, several states have eliminated indeterminate hospitalization as a procedure. Since long-term determinate hospitalization is a functional substitute for the earlier indeterminate hospitalization procedure, we have noted the permissible length of hospitalization on all tables.

The classification based upon the purpose and length of hospitalization can be further subdivided into categories based upon the primary authority which decides on the hospitalization issue: judicial or nonjudicial. In addition, some procedures—particularly the nonjudicial variety—depend upon the lack of opposition to hospitalization on the part of the patient or other relevant person: nonprotested admission. Similarly a judicial procedure which does not require the presence of the alleged mentally ill person at the hearing may be considered a nonprotested admission if that person is the one to determine whether or not he will be present.

Graphically portrayed, the classification schema is as follows:

Purpose	Authority	Degree of Compulsion
Emergency	Judicial or Nonjudicial	Compulsory
Short-Term or Observational	Judicial or Nonjudicial	Compulsory or Nonprotested
Extended-Term	Judicial or Nonjudicial	Compulsory or Nonprotested

The nonjudicial category can be further subdivided into two types: administrative and medical certification. The former refers typically to a designated commission variously constituted but normally including a physician. Medical certification refers to a procedure wherein the opinion of qualified physicians is deemed sufficient to authorize admission to a mental facility.

It should be noted that every jurisdiction has a combination of procedures and may have two or more procedures which are designed to accomplish the same ends. Recent legislation, as will be discussed shortly, has tended to recognize the process implications of hospitalization procedures. A number of steps and preliminary decisions precede any final determination. For example, observational hospitalization prior to a final determination of the issue is specifically provided for in nineteen of the forty-three states which have a judicial procedure. Additionally, emergency hospitalization procedures are provided for by the statutes of thirty-nine states and the District of Columbia. As a result the final determination of the person's status is usually made after he has been hospitalized for a period of time.[82] Thus, although the following exposition of the various procedures is compartmentalized for analytical purposes, it must be kept in mind that weaknesses or strengths of a particular procedure may be altered by prior or subsequent procedures. In other words, it is the interaction of all the procedures and their administration which finally determines the efficiency of the hospitalization and release process. The pages which follow will analyze those procedures in some detail.

D. Emergency Hospitalization or Detention of the Mentally Ill

1. the meaning of emergency hospitalization or detention

Emergency hospitalization or detention is a temporary measure for the speedy processing of emergency

82. Rock et al., *supra* note 15, at 123.

situations. Unlike the other forms of hospitalization which undertake to provide relatively complete measures for the personal treatment, care, and safety of the mentally ill, emergency procedures have only limited short-range goals.[83] They deal with the suppression and prevention of conduct likely to create a "clear and present danger" to persons or property. Under common law, any official or private person has the right to detain a dangerous mentally ill person.[84] The majority of jurisdictions have special statutory provisions for the emergency detention of the mentally ill. Ten states, however, lack such provisions.[85]

The absence of special provisions may create a number of difficult problems: (1) it puts the unduly heavy burden of proving urgency on the detaining officer if the detention is later challenged as illegal; (2) some law enforcement officers may hesitate to take an action which, because it is not specifically authorized, they regard as unlawful;[86] (3) in some instances such detentions may be limited to dangerous persons who are found at large, thus no mentally ill person could be taken into custody from a private home without a warrant;[87] (4) detention is usually limited to those who are violent and it is uncertain whether it is available in cases where an ill person may be dangerous without exhibiting signs of violence; and (5) mentally ill persons detained under the general police powers are often kept in jail. Hospital authorities are strongly opposed to the practice of jail detention as well as to the transportation of patients in police conveyances. The Council of State Governments suggests that since mental illness is a medical problem, detention procedures in no way similar to criminal procedures should be adopted.[88]

2. PROCEDURES FOR DETENTION

In all the forty jurisdictions with statutes for emergency detention, some formal application is required in order to initiate the action. The statutes list the persons authorized to file such an application. Authorization is sometimes granted to any reputable citizen, but in other cases it is limited to attending physicians, selectmen of towns, law enforcement and health officers.[89]

Although detention is usually a function delegated to the police and other administrative officers, judicial approval of the action remains a prerequisite in fourteen states.[90] This power of approval is occasionally vested in the magistrate, county clerk, or prosecuting attorney. In some instances, however, it may be exercised by the local board of health or board of county commissioners. In all but four of the remaining twenty-six jurisdictions such judicial certification is dispensed with but a medical certificate must be secured prior to admission.[91] The power to certify is usually not limited to psychiatrists but is granted to all general practitioners. To prevent abuses, at least one state provides that no person is to be detained in a private institution upon a certificate signed by a physician connected with that institution.[92]

Occasionally, it is also required that the medical certification be based on an examination of the patient made not more than three days prior to the date of the certificate.[93] Certification, in a few instances, may require the action of two physicians. At times it may be restricted to the county physician or some other local health officer, such as the official physician of a city.[94] Another important provision contained in the statutes of some states is that the patient be examined by the physician of the admitting institution upon admission and "released forthwith" if the physician does not concur in the original diagnosis.[95]

The jail is apparently a permissible place of detention for the mentally ill in most states. A few states either specifically prohibit the detention of the mentally ill in jails or permit it only if the jail has special facilities or in cases of extreme emergency.[96] Because of the lack of authority and funds for the establishment of facilities to replace the jail, these statutory prohibitions are frequently ineffec-

83. Ross, *supra* note 71, at 461, 471–72.

84. Id. at 486.

85. Table 3.11, Emergency Detention.

86. Guttmacher & Weihofen, *supra* note 69, at 308.

87. Jillson v. Caprio, 181 F.2d 523 (D.C. Cir. 1950).

88. Council of State Governments, *supra* note 7, at 57–58.

89. Table 3.11, Certification columns and footnotes thereto.

90. Ibid.

91. Ibid.

92. *Ill. Rev. Stat.* ch. 91-1/2, § 6-2 (Supp. 1969).

93. For example, see *Conn. Gen. Stat. Ann.* § 17-183 (Supp. 1969); *Ky. Rev. Stat. Ann* § 202.245(1) (Supp. 1968); *S.C. Code Ann.* § 32-956 (1962).

94. See Table 3.11, Certification columns.

95. See *Ill. Rev. Stat.* ch. 91-1/2, § 7-5 (Supp. 1969); *Ky. Rev. Stat. Ann.* § 202.117(1), (3) (Supp. 1968); *N.M. Stat. Ann.* § 32-2-180 (Supp. 1967).

96. Table 3.11, Jail column.

tive. In Indiana, for example, ten years after the passage of a statute prohibiting the detention of the mentally ill in jails, a special committee was established to study methods for enforcing this law.[97] In twenty-seven states detention may be in a private institution if the institution is willing to accept the patient.[98] Additional protection is afforded by the establishment of central administrative supervision over detentions through the requirement that superintendents of hospitals give notice of all detentions to the state commissioner of mental health.[99] The District of Columbia requires that notice of the admission be served by registered mail within twenty-four hours to the spouse, parent, or legal guardian.[100]

Since detention is an emergency measure, it is justified only until proper legal steps for hospitalization can be taken.[101] Accordingly, special provisions in the statutes set specific limits on the length of emergency detention, ranging from twenty-four hours in a few states to thirty days in others and in the case of Ohio up to sixty days.[102] The more common practice is to permit a detention period of between five and ten days. In some instances, however, no specific number of days is listed; detention is permitted until an examination has been completed.[103] Release may be further delayed in most states if, during the detention, proceedings are commenced for the extended hospitalization of the patient.

Considering that the detention period is intended primarily as a measure of control over an immediate threat, the longer time limits provided by statute appear to be excessive. Where the time limit is thirty or sixty days the emergency procedure becomes more akin to a temporary or observational hospitalization and should be treated as such. It is unlikely that in any jurisdiction it could take thirty days to commence a regular commitment proceeding. Section 13 of the Draft Act provides that the head of the detaining hospital shall arrange an examination for all detained persons; if the examination is not held within five days after the date of admission, or if within that time the examiner

fails to certify the patient as mentally ill and dangerous, the patient is to be discharged immediately.[104] This provision was inserted in the Draft Act in order to "complete" the admission of emergency patients under Sections 7 and 8, so that they would acquire the same status as a patient admitted under the standard nonjudicial procedure provided by Section 6.[105] Under the Draft Act when an emergency patient is examined and certified as mentally ill and dangerous he will be indeterminately hospitalized unless he or someone on his behalf requests release under Section 17 of the Act. The patient must be released within forty-eight hours after his request for release, unless within that time the head of the hospital certifies that it would be unsafe to release the patient and files an application for a judicial proceeding. Release may then be postponed for a maximum of five days or until the commencement of the judicial proceedings.[106]

Certain sections of the *Missouri Revised Statutes,* identical to Sections 7 and 8 of the Draft Act, were held unconstitutional as violations of the due process clause of the Fourteenth Amendment to the Constitution in *State ex rel. Fuller v. Mullinax.*[107] The court in this case recognized that the state, in the exercise of its police power, might provide for the summary apprehension of an alleged insane person, dangerous to himself or others, and provide for his temporary detention (without notice or hearing) until the truth of the charges had been investigated. Nevertheless, the court held that the defects of lack of notice and an opportunity to be heard before being hospitalized were not cured by a statutory provision which was identical to Section 17 of the Draft Act requiring that a patient hospitalized under the emergency procedures either be released on request or be given a judicial hearing. The court pointed out that under Sections 7 and 8 of the Draft Act (as incorporated in the Missouri statutes) hospitalization might conceivably continue for the remainder of the patient's life unless he or someone on his behalf subsequently took the requisite action. The impact of the decision in *Mullinax* is that the state is required to provide promptly a judicial hearing for detained individuals or to release them, as opposed to placing on the individual the burden of requesting his release or a judicial hearing. After the *Mullinax* case, the Missouri statutes were amended

97. Indiana Association for Mental Health, *Progress Report* (September 1956).

98. Table 3.11, Private Institution column.

99. *Conn. Gen. Stat. Ann.* § 17-183 (1958).

100. *D.C. Code Ann.* § 21-522 (1967).

101. Ross, *supra* note 71, at 486–87; Christiansen v. Weston, 36 Ariz. 200, 284 P. 149 (1930).

102. Table 3.11, Maximum Period column.

103. Ibid.

104. *Draft Act* § 13, at 12.

105. *Draft Act,* Commentary, at 32.

106. *Draft Act* § 17, at 14.

107. 364 Mo. 858, 269 S.W.2d 72 (1954).

to provide that notice of all emergency detentions be given to the Probate Court and that if no judicial proceedings are initiated within five days of such notice, the judge is to order the release of the patient.[108] Similarly Illinois's recently enacted emergency admission statute calls for notification of the court and a hearing within five days after admission. In addition the patient, his attorney and his nearest relative other than the one who initiated the hospitalization must be notified of the pending proceedings.[109]

The American Bar Association Special Committee on the Rights of the Mentally Ill stressed in its 1947 report that:

> emergency commitment should be for a period of not longer than seven days in any instance, at the termination whereof the patient should be discharged unless . . . appropriate steps have been taken looking toward a commitment for prolonged hospitalization. . . .
>
> Emergency commitments are both advisable and necessary. The procedure should be simple and ready of accomplishment. For instance, there should be the certificate of at least one duly licensed physician, and the affidavit of one or more relatives, or in the absence of any such relatives, of some one or more responsible persons, authorizing the police or other designated agency to enter premises and remove a mentally disturbed patient to the city, county or state hospital.[110]

Sensible legislation in line with the above suggestions should be encouraged.

E. Temporary or Observational Hospitalization

Temporary or observational hospitalization has been described as "commitment for a specified period of time to permit adequate observation of the case, with the diagnosis being accompanied by at least limited treatment."[111] The use of this type of hospitalization in the United States dates back only twenty-five years, but similar practices have received widespread recognition and have been used extensively in other countries for many years.[112] In England, for example, all initial hospitalization in mental institutions is for a specified period. The patients must either be discharged or the hospitalization renewed at the termination of this period.[113]

The Council of State Governments has strongly recommended the use of this procedure.

> This method of hospitalization offers an opportunity for prompt and effective observation—when it may do the most good—without the delay that accompanies formal admission for an indefinite period. Temporary observational admission should be authorized by all states, with specific legal recourse being provided in case there is any doubt of the need for hospitalization, and with a specific limit being placed on the length of hospitalization under such admission.[114]

Although some states have procedures clearly labeled as temporary and observational, functionally a number of separate procedures may operate to provide a period of inpatient observation prior to the formal decision on mental illness and need for hospitalization. Emergency admission, already discussed, is one such functionally interchangeable procedure. Its use is limited in theory, however, to situations where the requirements of alternative modes of hospitalization cannot be met without undue risk to the person or the community. Yet this preliminary short-term intervention is often utilized to establish a diagnosis and determine what further steps, if any, should be taken.[115]

Similarly, most of the judicial involuntary extended hospitalization procedures to be discussed below authorize, under certain circumstances, interim detention of the alleged mentally ill person between the filing of the petition and the final hearing on the matter. When this authority is coupled with the power of the court to order examination of the person by appointed medical examiners, the normal outcome is a preliminary observational hospitalization prior to the formal determination.

A determinate medical-certification procedure also has elements which permit it to function as an observational hospitalization, particularly in those jurisdictions which explicitly authorize the extention of such hospitalization by judicial procedures if the person's condition requires it at the end of the limited period of hospitalization.

108. *Mo. Rev. Stat.* § 202.805 (Supp. 1970).

109. *Ill. Ann. Stat.* ch. 91-1/2, §§ 7-4, 7-6 (Smith-Hurd Supp. 1969).

110. 72 *ABA Rep.* 295 (1947).

111. Illinois Legislative Council, *Mental Hospital Admissions and Discharges* 17 (January, 1956).

112. Ross, *supra* note 71, at 469–70.

113. Royal Commission on the Law Relating to Mental Illness and Mental Deficiency 1954–57, *Report,* CMND. No. 169, at 81 (1957).

114. Council of State Governments, *supra* note 7, at 5–6.

115. Rock et al., *supra* note 15, at 137.

In addition to these "observational" procedures some twenty-seven states have enacted separate temporary or observational hospitalization procedures, as shown in Table 3.10. However, there are two entirely different versions of this procedure. The one referred to by the Council of State Governments may be termed "independent temporary observational hospitalization," because the procedure may be independent of any regular extended hospitalization procedure. That is, no formal petition or supporting evidence for extended hospitalization is required. This method is available in only twelve states. In three of them the application and certification procedures used are substantially similar to those used for involuntary extended hospitalization by medical certification, and in Montana the court must issue an order for hospitalization upon receipt of an application and supporting medical certificates. In the remaining eight states a judicial (or administrative, in the case of Iowa) determination of the need for observational hospitalization must be made after a hearing on the matter. In no case is the maximum period longer than three months and it is as short as five days in Georgia.

The Draft Act does not have a provision for independent temporary or observational hospitalization, nor does the Commentary offer an explanation for this omission.

At the end of the observational period either the patient must be released or an application for extended hospitalization must be filed by the proper authority.[116]

The other type of temporary or observational hospitalization is used in connection with judicial hospitalization proceedings, typically as an alternative to an indeterminate hospitalization order. Eighteen jurisdictions and the Draft Act make this procedure available.[117] In some of these states the court may adjourn the hearing and order the alleged mentally ill person into a hospital for a specified period of time before making a decision on indeterminate hospitalization in order to provide the court with sufficient knowledge to make an informed decision at the hospitalization hearing.

In other states hospitalization for temporary observation may occur after a full hearing. The Draft Act includes such a provision. Under it the court may order indeterminate hospitalization or temporary observation for a period not to exceed six months.[118]

It has been suggested that temporary or observational hospitalization is less desirable when conducted in connection with a judicial indeterminate hospitalization procedure than when it is made an independent proceeding.[119] Underlying this assertion is the belief that "if temporary commitment is conditioned on the filing of a petition for formal commitment, with the attendant publicity and loss of legal capacity, the relatives or family physician will be reluctant to use this procedure, at an early stage of mental illness, when treatment is most likely to be successful."[120] At the time this criticism was written, alternative nonjudicial procedures were less prevalent than now and most temporary or observational procedures were essentially determinate medical-certification procedures. As mentioned earlier, most of the independent or direct observational procedures now include judicial determination or review. Yet in all but three of the relevant jurisdictions[121] a medical-certification procedure is also available. Of the total of twenty-seven states with a separate observational procedure only eleven do not have the alternative of a medical-certification procedure. Thus where short-term treatment rather than diagnosis is the object of the procedure most states have alternatives which avoid the problems cited.

One of the more important legislative developments over the last ten years is the mandatory observation period prior to any formal resolution of the need for extended hospitalization.

Nine states—California, Georgia, Iowa, Minnesota, New York, North Carolina, Ohio, Texas and Virginia—require temporary observation in all cases prior to extended hospitalization.[122] In part this trend is coextensive with the trend away from indeterminate commitment in any form. In indeterminate commitments the initial formal determination of the need for hospitalization results in an order or au-

---

116. See Table 3.10, Temporary or Observational Hospitalization, Action after Observation columns.

117. See Table 3.10, Procedure Part of Regular Commitment Proceedings columns.

118. *Draft Act* § 9, at 9.

119. Ross, *supra* note 71, at 511. See also Curran, *supra* note 2, at 285.

120. Ross, *supra* note 71, at 511.

121. Indiana, Massachusetts, and Texas.

122. *Cal. Welf. & Inst'ns Code* § 5206 (West Supp. 1970); *Ga. Code Ann.* § 88-505.5 (Supp. 1969); *Iowa Code Ann.* § 229.9 (1969); *Minn. Stat. Ann.* § 253A.07(17) (Supp. 1969); *N.Y. Mental Hygiene Law* § 72 (McKinney Supp. 1970); *N.C. Gen. Stat.* § 122-63 (Supp. 1969); *Ohio Rev. Code Ann.* § 5122.15 (Baldwin 1964); *Tex. Rev. Civ. Stat.* art. 5547-40 (1957); *Va. Code Ann.* § 37.1-79 (Supp. 1968).

thority to retain the patient *until* administrative release takes place or the patient successfully challenges his need for hospitalization at some later date whereas in several states extended hospitalization requires that a series of determinations be made within specified periods of time in order to *retain* the patient.

As with discretionary observational hospitalization, the fundamental purpose is to enhance the reliability and validity of the final decision. In part the procedures are a response to the medical criticism that judicial decisions regarding hospitalization are an inappropriate means of determining who can benefit from hospital treatment. By dividing the decision-making process into a number of stages with clearly delineated responsibilities it is hoped that a better balance between the personal rights, the custodial-safekeeping needs, and the active treatment needs of the mentally ill can be achieved. It is possible that such an elongation of the decision-making process provides a better due process model than existing procedural mandates for an immediate and final determination of the issues involved. Equally important in the enactment of such procedures is the implicit recognition that many if not most patients can be effectively treated and even released in a relatively short period of time. Thus temporary involuntary hospitalization may be all that is necessary to treat the patient successfully or at least prepare him to elect to continue treatment as a voluntary patient. Such a change in status is usually approved by statute. When compared to the effects of indeterminate involuntary hospitalization such a resolution of the issue is highly desirable.

In seven of the nine states having mandatory observational hospitalization, the procedure is basically judicial in that the initial hospitalization must be the result of a judicial hearing. Medical review follows that initial decision and only those cases which require it go on to a final judicial determination. Iowa utilizes a commission procedure while in New York the initial hospitalization is based upon medical certificates with judicial review afforded after hospitalization.

Texas, one of the first states to require an initial period of hospitalization prior to any final judicial determination of the person's mental status, has a unique provision:

Prerequisite to commitment

No Petition for the indefinite commitment of a person to a mental hospital may be filed unless he has been under observation and/or treatment in a mental hospital for at least sixty (60) days pursuant to an Order of Temporary Hospitalization entered within twelve (12) months immediately preceding the filing of the Petition.[123]

No other state has quite the same approach since in all other instances the preliminary hospitalization must immediately precede the extended hospitalization.

California's recently enacted procedure requires several stages, beginning with an initial hospitalization of seventy-two hours which may be extended to fourteen days[124] followed by an additional ninety-day period of hospitalization after a judicial hearing.[125]

Georgia's initial hospitalization period is limited to five days in an evaluation facility.[126] Thereafter a period of up to six months of hospitalization is authorized upon the certification of the evaluation facility.[127] The patient may request a full judicial hearing on the need for such continued hospitalization. Additional periods of hospitalization of not more than one year's duration may be subsequently authorized.[128]

North Carolina provides for the longest initial period of hospitalization, 180 days, while Ohio authorizes 90 days; Minnesota, 60 days; and Virginia, 15 days.[129] Iowa, utilizing an administrative commission to determine hospitalization, provides that all initial commitments shall be to a "screening center" of the hospital. No order of commitment can be issued until the superintendent of the facility ap-

123. *Tex. Rev. Civ. Stat.* art. 5547-40 (1957). The statute was adapted from a New York procedure now repealed in which a judicial commitment did not become final until sixty days after the initial order. N.Y. Laws 1944, c. 665 § 5: amended by N.Y. laws 1945, c. 871, § 2; 1946, c. 731.

124. *Cal. Welf. & Inst'ns Code* §§ 5206, 5250 (West Supp. 1970).

125. *Cal. Welf. & Inst'ns Code* § 5300 (West Supp. 1970). The ninety-day extensions are limited to "imminently dangerous persons." "Gravely disabled persons" may not be directly committed but may be hospitalized by a court-appointed conservator with judicial approval.

126. *Ga. Code Ann.* § 88-505.5 (Supp. 1969). This procedure is limited to counties which have not elected the exclusive use of an alternative judicial procedure. *Ga. Code Ann.* § 88-508.9 (Supp. 1969).

127. *Ga. Code Ann.* § 88-506.3 (Supp. 1969).

128. *Ga. Code Ann.* § 88-506.6 (Supp. 1969).

129. *N.C. Gen. Stat.* § 122-63 (Supp. 1969); *Ohio Rev. Code Ann.* § 5122.15 (Baldwin 1964); *Minn. Stat. Ann.* § 253A 07(17)(a) (Supp. 1969); *Va. Code Ann.* § 37.1-79 (Supp. 1968).

proves the commitment. No time limit is stipulated for such approval or disapproval.[130]

A common element of each of these procedures is the authority of the director of the admitting facility to release the patient immediately upon a determination that hospital care is not required. Furthermore in each case, before the court may order extended custody, the admitting facility must recommend or petition for continued hospitalization. Potentially this authority allows for the screening out of persons who will not benefit from the treatment provided by the institution. Properly utilized it permits the institution to select those persons, from among all who are presented for hospitalization, who will benefit most from inpatient treatment. In this way, the final determination of the need for hospitalization is a more informed and realistic determination of that issue than the more traditional procedure.

In general the protections afforded the alleged mentally ill person subject to these procedures appear to be adequate though they are by no means uniform. For example, the New York procedure permits initial hospitalization, upon presentation of two physicians' certificates, without notice or an opportunity to be heard. However, within five days after admission, notice must be given to the patient, the Mental Health Information Service,[131] the nearest relative other than the petitioner, and up to three other persons designated by the patient.[132] A hearing on the need for hospitalization may be requested by any of the above within sixty days of admission. A full hearing must be held within five days of the request to determine the need to retain the patient. If no request for a hearing is made within sixty days and continued involuntary hospitalization appears necessary, the director of the hospital must apply for court authorization. The patient and the others listed above are again notified of the right to a hearing upon request. If no hearing is requested within five days the court may issue an *ex parte* order to continue hospitalization for six months.[133] That

order in turn may be reviewed *de novo* upon petition by any of the above filed within thirty days of the order. Such review must be by jury trial if not waived.[134] As an additional protection the procedures outlined above must be reinstituted at the end of six months, one year, and every two years thereafter.

Notice and a hearing must be afforded prior to the initial hospitalization in California, Georgia, Minnesota, North Carolina, and Ohio, although the presence at the hearing of the alleged mentally ill person is not required in California and may be dispensed with in Ohio and Minnesota if it would be injurious to him.[135] In Texas and Virginia only notice of the proceedings for continued hospitalization must be given.[136] Only Iowa makes no provision for notice of either the initial or subsequent administrative hearing. However, mandatory representation by counsel at the initial hearing is provided,[137] and habeas corpus is available to test present mental status,[138] as well as a *de novo* appeal from the final order of hospitalization.[139]

While such procedures present some administrative difficulties, in general they are more in keeping with the "new philosophy" of psychiatric hospitalization which stresses early and intensive treatment. Such an approach is seen as a means of avoiding chronicity as well as a more beneficial means of allocating scarce psychiatric resources. The approach also has advantages when viewed from the perspective of procedural safeguards for the patient. The traditional legal notion that a final determination of the need for involuntary indeterminate hospitalization must be speedily made has tended to focus all attention on the initial hospitalization decision. Once that decision was made, the patient was left without effective means of challenging the continuation of his status as a mentally ill person. As a result, the laws of most states provided, if anything, an overabundance of prehospitalization protections and little or no posthospitalization monitoring of the process. It is likely that the development of the law in this area will continue to achieve a better bal-

130. *Iowa Code Ann.* § 229.9 (1969).

131. The Mental Health Information Service is a statutory judicial agency charged with the "duty to review the admission and retention of involuntary patients, inform them of their rights, assemble information for judicial scrutiny whenever a hearing is requested, and advise the patients upon request." Note, "The New York Mental Health Information Service: A New Approach to Hospitalization of the Mentally Ill," 67 *Colum. L. Rev.* 672, 675 (1967). See also *N.Y. Mental Hygiene Law* § 88 (McKinney Supp. 1970).

132. *N.Y. Mental Hygiene Law* § 72 (McKinney Supp. 1970).

133. *N.Y. Mental Hygiene Law* § 73 (McKinney Supp. 1970).

134. *N.Y. Mental Hygiene Law* § 74 (McKinney Supp. 1970).

135. *Cal. Welf. & Inst'ns Code* § 5206 (West Supp. 1970); *Ga. Code Ann.* § 88-502.15 (1969); *Minn. Stat. Ann.* § 253A.07(6) (Supp. 1969); *N.C. Gen. Stat.* § 122-63 (Supp. 1969); *Ohio Rev. Code Ann.* § 5122.15 (Baldwin 1964).

136. *Tex. Rev. Civ. Stat.* art. 5547.33 (1957); *Va. Code Ann.* § 37.1-80 (Supp. 1968).

137. *Iowa Code Ann.* § 229.5 (1969).

138. *Iowa Code Ann.* § 229.37 (1969).

139. *Iowa Code Ann.* § 229.17 (1969).

ance of these two important issues by incorporating the "process" or step-by-step approach to involuntary mental treatment reflected in observational hospitalization and determinate rather than indeterminate authority to retain patients.

In sum, the ancillary protections afforded the alleged mentally ill person under these procedures are similar to (and as diverse as) those generally available under involuntary hospitalization procedures. The essential and perhaps crucial difference is that limited hospitalization itself is used to provide an additional protection against precipitous or unwarranted action.

F. Indeterminate or Extended Involuntary Hospitalization Procedures

1. judicial hospitalization procedures

One form of indeterminate or extended involuntary hospitalization procedure requires that a judge or a jury determine whether a person is mentally ill to such an extent as to require hospitalization and, if so, the court orders the patient hospitalized for an extended or indeterminate period of time.[140] This decision may or may not be based upon the advice of medical experts or administrative boards, and it may or may not follow a prior period of temporary or observational hospitalization.

A procedure has not been classified as judicial unless a judge or jury has discretion to determine, on the merits, whether hospitalization is required by the applicable statutory provision. The mere fact that a judge must sign a hospitalization order or make a perfunctory examination of the hospitalization papers has not been considered sufficient to classify the procedure as judicial. Similarly, a requirement that a judge or magistrate must be a member of the administrative tribunal that determines the need for hospitalization has not been deemed sufficient to warrant classifying the procedure as judicial.

Hospitalization procedures were extremely informal until a century ago. The growing evidence of abuses led at that time to the adoption of more formal procedures. The emphasis then and in subsequent legislation has tended to fall on the formalities and technicalities of due process, including notice, hearing, right to counsel, and a trial by jury. Although these safeguards were primarily for the protection of the patient, they have also served to protect the institutional officers and others concerned with the custody of the mentally ill against

140. See Table 3.2 for the names of courts having jurisdiction.

potential charges of improper hospitalization.[141]

Since hospitalization procedures are largely a matter for state legislation, no uniform procedure is followed nationally. Some states have occasionally copied the procedures existing in other states, and in recent years the provisions of the Draft Act have served as the basis for the law in a number of states. But the unifying influences have been relatively few, and hospitalization procedures continue to vary widely from state to state. They range from those requiring a full-dress judicial hearing and determination to those that eliminate the judicial element entirely, permitting it only on review.[142] Most states have several procedures at their disposal. At present, the Draft Act and forty-two jurisdictions have some form of judicial hospitalization procedures.[143] The procedures usually followed are described below.

a) Initiation of Proceedings

(1) Application.—An application for the hospitalization of an alleged mentally ill person must be made and sworn to by the persons authorized by the statute to initiate such actions. Eighteen jurisdictions permit any person to sign such applications, while Illinois authorizes application to be made by any citizen.[144] In the remaining states, the right to file an application is limited to one or more of the following groups: spouses, relatives, friends, guardians, public officials, physicians, and superintendents of hospitals.[145] An example of the form of such an application is reproduced below:

_____, being first duly sworn upon oath, says: I am acquainted with the condition of _____, I verily believe that the said _____ is insane and a fit subject for care and treatment in the _____ State Hospital, and affiant, therefore asks that the said person be brought before the Judge of this county, for examination and commitment or for such order as may be proper, and that warrant be issued to that effect.

(signed) _____

Sworn to and subscribed before me this _____ day of _____, 19___.

_____
Clerk of District Court

141. Deutsch, _supra_ note 6, at 423.

142. See Table Intro. 1.

143. Table 3.2.

144. Table 3.2, Application By columns.

145. Ibid.

(2) Supporting Medical Evidence at Time of Application.—Eighteen states require that the application be accompanied by one medical certificate affirming the allegations in the application; in Illinois such a certificate may but need not be required by the judge.[146] Nine of these eighteen states emulate the Draft Act and provide that a statement from the applicant, to the effect that the proposed patient refuses to submit to an examination, may be accepted in lieu of the medical certificate.[147] The statutes of three states require that two medical certificates support an application.[148] One example of a physician's certificate is presented below:

THIS IS TO CERTIFY:

That I am duly licensed to practice medicine in the State of _____ and that I am not an employee of or financially interested, either directly or indirectly, in any licensed private institution to which admission of the person named below is sought.

That I personally made examination of _____ _____ residing at _____, on this day of _____, 19__, and found _____ _____. That it is my opinion and conclusion that the aforesaid person is a mentally ill person and that I recommend that said person be committed for care and treatment to a suitable public or private hospital.

Signed at _____
this _____ day of _____, A.D. 19__.
_____ M.D.

_____

One state provides that the prosecuting attorney, before accepting an application for filing, must endorse on the application that he has examined the applicant, has investigated the merit of the application, and believes reasonable grounds exist for filing.[149]

Under one procedure in California before a petition may be filed with the court a prepetition investigation must be conducted by a designated person or agency to determine whether there is probable cause to believe the allegations contained in the petition. If probable cause is not found to exist, the petition is not filed.[150] However, this prepetition investigation applies only to court-ordered evaluations. A person who is admitted as an emergency patient without a court order is not subject to a prepetition inquiry.[151]

In general, the requirement of a formal petition and supporting medical evidence coupled with the imminent judicial determination appears sufficient to prevent groundless applications. In fact, field studies suggest that there is a general reluctance on the part of nonrelatives to initiate proceedings even when they are authorized to do so and the need for intervention is clear.[152]

b) Prehearing Medical Examinations

The various provisions relating to prehearing medical examinations may be found in Table 3.2, Judicial Hospitalization of the Mentally Ill—Prehearing Procedures, Medical Examination columns. This table reveals that of the states having judicial hospitalization procedures all but Arkansas, New Jersey, and Rhode Island make some sort of provision for a prehearing medical examination in all cases. Arkansas and Rhode Island each have one judicial procedure which requires a medical certificate while the alternative procedure does not. New Jersey requires two medical certificates as a condition of petitioning, but is silent as to subsequent examinations for one of three classes of patients. Tennessee, Missouri, and Alabama require that one witness at the hearing be a physician, thus implying that medical testimony based upon an examination is a condition of commitment.

It should be noted that except in New Jersey the prehearing medical examination is supplementary to the medical certificate which may be required to support the application.

The function of the prehearing medical examination is to supply evidence to aid the judge or jury in arriving at a proper decision. Thirteen jurisdictions also have explicit statutory provisions which permit the court to dismiss the proceeding if the prehearing medical examination results in a finding that the patient is not mentally ill.

Usually the examination is conducted by two physicians or by two examiners, the latter often having to meet other statutory requirements besides that of being a physician. In Florida, Oklahoma, and the District of Columbia the examination is conducted by an examining committee consisting of two physicians and a nonmedical member.

Prehearing medical examination provisions seem desirable as a means both of assuring intelligent and

146. Table 3.2, Supporting Evidence columns.

147. Id. and n.2 thereto.

148. Table 3.2, Supporting Evidence columns.

149. *Wash. Rev. Code Ann.* § 71.02.090 (1962).

150. *Cal. Welf. & Inst'ns Code* § 5202 (West Supp. 1970).

151. *Cal. Welf. & Inst'ns Code* § 5150 (West Supp. 1970).

152. Rock et al., *supra* note 15, at 86.

impartial determinations grounded, at least in part, on medical evidence and of minimizing the "battle of the experts" during the hearing. Provisions permitting the court to dismiss a case if the prehearing medical examination results in a negative finding may be justified as a method of avoiding an unnecessary hearing costly in time, money, and strain on the alleged mentally ill person. However, field study findings suggest that in actual application the procedure may become a pro forma exercise, requiring monitoring by the court or the patient's counsel to assure that really independent medical judgment is provided.[153]

c) Notice of Proceedings and an Opportunity to be Heard

Because involuntary hospitalization proceedings are civil in nature,[154] the statutes provide for the arrest and detention of the mentally ill only if the individual is judged dangerous to himself, to others, or to property. When this situation exists, provisions are ordinarily made for the patient's detention without notice or a hearing until a judicial determination can be made on the application.[155]

Whether the person who is alleged to be mentally ill should receive notice and appear at the proceedings instituted for his hospitalization has been the subject of heated controversy. Over the years, numerous psychiatrists have decried the traumatic effect of personal notice on a person who is mentally ill.[156] Legal papers are said to produce only anxiety and confusion in a sick mind. This stand has received the support of some leading legal writers who suggest that "where the person is mentally incapable of understanding the nature of the proceedings or preparing therefor, or is so deranged that notice would do him harm, the purpose of protecting his interest can be more effectively accomplished in some other way than by serving him with legal papers."[157] The humanitarian desire to eliminate or curtail the use of notice in such cases raises certain

questions, however. It may be, for example, that the experience of receiving notice would prove no more traumatic for the patient than the experience of suddenly finding himself detained in a mental institution. One method suggested to lessen the potential traumatic effect of formal legal notice would involve having a doctor or some other competent member of a hospital staff visit the patient for the purpose of explaining the nature of the papers.[158]

The contention that notice is relatively ineffective in such circumstances has also been challenged as prejudging the individual's mental condition before the hearing. In the words of the Kansas Court of Appeals:

> Notice and opportunity to be heard lie at the foundation of all judicial procedures. They are fundamental principles of justice which cannot be ignored . . . it will not do to say that it is useless to serve notice upon an insane person; that it would avail nothing because of his inability to take advantage of it. His sanity is the very thing to be tried.[159]

In addition, the American Bar Association Special Committee on the Rights of the Mentally Ill insists that notice is a constitutional requirement.

> Any person before he is committed to a mental hospital or otherwise deprived of his liberty should be served with notice and given a full opportunity to be heard. On this we, the Committee, insist as a constitutional requirement.

In order to extend additional protection in those cases where the person concerned is incapable of understanding the content or significance of notice, the Committee took the position that notice "should be given to his nearest available relative or, in the absence of such, his nearest available friend."[160] This would be in addition to the notice given to the alleged ill person. As to the form of notice, two recent Illinois decisions found simple written notice insufficient where the respondents in a sexually dangerous person proceeding were of subnormal intelligence. Absent an oral explanation of their rights in addition to written notice the court found that they had been effectively denied their right to counsel.[161]

The courts appear to be divided on whether notice

153. See Scheff, "The Societal Reaction to Deviance: Ascriptive Elements in the Psychiatric Screening of Mental Patients in a Midwestern State," 11 *Social Problems* 401, at 407 (1964); Kutner, "The Illusion of Due Process in Commitment Proceedings," 57 *Nw. U.L. Rev.* 383 (1962); Rock et al., *supra* note 15, at 181.

154. Sorter v. Austin, 221 Ala. 481, 129 So. 51 (1930).

155. See this chapter § III D, Emergency Hospitalization or Detention of the Mentally Ill.

156. Group for the Advancement of Psychiatry, "Commitment Procedures" 2 (Rep. No. 4, April 1948).

157. Guttmacher & Weihofen, *supra* note 69, at 295.

158. Id. at 296.

159. *In re* Wellman, 3 Kan. App. 100, 103, 45 P. 726, 727 (1896).

160. 72 *ABA Rep.* 295 (1947).

161. People v. Breese, 34 Ill. 2d 61, 213 N.E.2d 500 (1966); People v. Couvion, 33 Ill. 2d 408, 211 N.E.2d 746 (1965).

and a hearing prior to hospitalization are required by due process. Some follow *In re* Wellman[162] and hold that notice and a hearing are necessary.[163] In *State ex rel. Fuller v. Mullinax*[164] it was held that Section 6 of the Draft Act, which had been incorporated in a Missouri statute, was unconstitutional. The procedure outlined in that statute provided for hospitalization on the basis of certificates filed by two medical examiners. To the court's mind, the deprivation of liberty without a hearing, even where a posthospitalization hearing could be demanded and habeas corpus was available to test the validity of the hospitalization, constituted a denial of due process. Other courts, however, have held that involuntary hospitalization without a hearing is valid as long as the patient has the unqualified right, either through statutory provisions for a posthospitalization hearing or through habeas corpus, to contest his hospitalization in a judicial hearing.[165] In weighing whether the patient's right to demand such a hearing overcomes the objection that he did not have prior notice of hospitalization, it should be noted that in only seventeen states does the patient have an unrestricted right to communicate with an attorney.[166] The services of counsel are extremely important, perhaps indispensable, at such times. Thus in all the other states the patient's ability to secure a posthospitalization hearing or prepare for it adequately is severely hampered at the very first stage of the process.

At the present time, it is mandatory in twenty-six of the forty-two jurisdictions which have judicial hospitalization procedures that notice be given to the person who is alleged to be mentally ill. In nine other states notice is not necessary if it would be harmful to the patient's condition. A number of the remaining states specify that notice may be served upon the person or someone else on his behalf; the rest have no statutory provisions on the subject.[167] Twelve jurisdictions specify the minimal notice permissible.[168] The ultimate value of notice, of course, is affected by the amount of time it leaves the individual concerned to prepare himself for the hearing. It is dubious whether notice is of much assistance in the two states which specify that twenty-four hours' advance notice is sufficient.[169] In one of the states where no statutory provision for minimal notice existed, it was held that notice on the day of the hearing violated due process and that the order hospitalizing the person alleged to be mentally ill was therefore void.[170]

In recent years the notice problem has received more attention from lawmakers. The creation in 1964 of the Mental Health Information Services for New York[171] and the provision for mandatory judicial consultation in Illinois[172] are both in part concerned with providing effective notice of subsequent proceedings particularly where the judicial hearing is subsequent to hospitalization.

In all jurisdictions except Massachusetts and Virginia, a mandatory hearing is provided for by the judicial hospitalization statutes.[173] Since in these two

162. 3 Kan. App. 100, 45 P. 726 (1896).

163. Statutes which dispense with all requirements of notice and the opportunity to be present at the hearing and do not provide for substitute notice have been held invalid. See *In re* Lambert, 134 Cal. 626, 66 P. 851 (1901); State v. Billings, 55 Minn. 467, 57 N.W. 794 (1893); People *ex rel.* Sullivan v. Wendel, 33 Misc. 496, 68 N.Y.S. 948 (Sup. Ct. 1900).

164. 364 Mo. 858, 269 S.W.2d 72 (1954).

165. *In re* Coates, 9 N.Y.2d 242, 173 N.E.2d 797, 213 N.Y.S.2d 74, *appeal dismissed sub nom.* Coates v. Walters, 368 U.S. 34 (1961), initial hospitalization and later indefinite extension without notice conformed to due process where the patient retained the right to seek judicial review. Hammon v. Hill, 228 F. 999 (W.D. Pa. 1915), justice's commitment order based on medical certificate without notice and hearing constitutional in view of availability of habeas corpus to test necessity of confinement; Payne v. Arkebauer, 190 Ark. 614, 80 S.W.2d 76 (1935), same in light of right to statutory appeal from order of probate court. Hiatt v. Soucek, 240 Iowa 300, 36 N.W.2d 432 (1949), summary confinement of a prisoner to mental hospital at expiration of sentence validated by right to have mental condition determined at any time. *In re* Dowdell, 169 Mass. 387, 47 N.E. 1033 (1897), commitment by police court justice without notice in view of statutory right to have propriety of confinement determined subsequently in judicial proceedings. *In re* Crosswell, 28 R.I. 137, 66 A. 55 (1907), commitment on application and medical certificate without court order upheld. Where the statutes which required notice and presence were not fully complied with, the right to review on the merits of the patient's illness by appeal or habeas corpus proceedings has been held a sufficient safeguard to correct all due process defects occurring in the original commitment procedure. See Paul v. Longino, 197 Ga. 110, 28 S.E.2d 286 (1943); County of Black Hawk v. Springer, 58 Iowa 417, 10 N.W. 791 (1882); *In re* Dowdell, *supra*; *Ex parte* Dagley, 35 Okla. 180, 128 P. 99 (1912); *In re* Crosswell, *supra*.

166. See chap. 5, "Rights of Hospitalized Patients."

167. Table 3.2, Notice of Hearing columns.

168. Id. at Minimum Amount column.

169. Ibid.

170. Snavely v. Snavely, 349 Ill. App. 369, 110 N.E.2d 685 (1953).

171. See generally *supra* note 131.

172. *Ill. Ann. Stat.* ch. 91-1/2, § 6-4 (Smith-Hurd Supp. 1969).

173. Table 3.3, Judicial Hospitalization of the Mentally Ill—Hearing and Posthearing Procedures, Hearing columns.

states an individual may waive a hearing by not requesting a hearing, both states have been classified not only as having judicial hospitalization procedures, but also as having nonprotested admission procedures.

In both states it is mandatory that the patient be informed of his right to have a hearing. Such notice has constitutional significance in those jurisdictions which, following the *Wellman* case,[174] hold notice and hearing to be essential elements of due process of law in involuntary hospitalization cases.

In several jurisdictions the hearing is held or may be held before a referee, special commissioner, or fact-finding commission.[175] A sharp distinction has been drawn between hearings held before commissioners or commissions who merely make findings of fact and/or recommendations upon which the court bases its decision while using its own discretion, and those held before commissions whose findings of fact and/or recommendations are mandatory upon the court. In the latter instance, the court is deprived of discretion. The need for hospitalization is essentially determined nonjudicially and the procedure has been classified accordingly.

There are also variations in the legislation governing the patient's presence at the hearing: eleven jurisdictions make the presence of the patient at the hearing mandatory, six provide either that his presence is at the discretion of the court or that he is to be present unless his presence would prove detrimental to his condition, and fifteen provide for his presence if he demands it.[176] In many of these latter jurisdictions, however, the statutes do not clearly state whether the judge must comply with the patient's request. It has been suggested by one writer that compulsory presence might well be eliminated in the interest of more humane treatment.[177] This writer would apparently limit compelled presence to those cases in which the patient contests hospitalization. The rationale underlying the Draft Act, which provides that patients "shall be afforded an opportunity to appear at the hearing,"[178] is similar. Requiring the patient to decide whether or not to appear seems to rest on the premise that he has either the capacity to make a "responsible decision" or access to and willingness to follow the advice of competent counsel. This may not always be the fact.

It would seem more reasonable for the judge in each case where the patient has not demanded to be present to balance the possible traumatic effects of the hearing upon the patient against the desirability and need for his presence. Where the Draft Act's type of provision is adopted, it should be required that the patient be advised by a responsible agency of his right to attend the hearing. It is perhaps unrealistic to expect him to comprehend the full meaning of the written notice without assistance or to be present at the hearing on his own initiative.

It might be possible, should the recommendation outlined above be adopted, for the judge or court-appointed psychiatrist to see the patient privately before the commencement of the hearing and ask him if he wishes to attend. Even if the patient decides not to attend the hearing, the judge or psychiatrist will at least have had an opportunity to observe his demeanor.[179] Thirty-one states authorize the court to hold the hearing at a place other than a courtroom. In these states, when the hearing is held in a hospital or the patient's home, it would be simple for the judge to make the inquiry. The selection of a medical facility or private place for the hearing is desirable even where the patient's presence is mandatory. The Draft Act and several state statutes require that courts be obligated to conduct the hearing in a physical setting not likely to be injurious to the individual's condition and in as informal a manner as may be consistent with orderly procedure.[180]

d) Trial by Jury

Sixteen jurisdictions authorize the use of a jury to decide the question of hospitalization.[181] Thirteen of these provide that a jury trial is to be conducted only if demanded by the patient or someone on his behalf. Of these thirteen, three states place it within the discretion of the court to grant or refuse the request for such a trial. In Michigan and Oklahoma a jury trial is mandatory if requested by the patient or someone on his behalf and also may be held if the court deems it necessary. Special juries consisting of six persons have been utilized by some of the states. For some years Texas and Kentucky were thought to be the only states in which jury trials were mandatory in all hospitalization cases. The

174. 3 Kan. App. 100, 45 P. 726 (1896).

175. Table 3.3.

176. Table 3.2, Presence of Patient columns.

177. Curran, *supra* note 2, at 282–83.

178. *Draft Act* § 9, at 9.

179. In Wisconsin, for example, the presence of the patient is not mandatory but the judge must observe him. *Wis. Stat. Ann.* § 51.02 (1957).

180. *Draft Act* § 9, at 9. Table 3.3, Hearing Place columns.

181. Table 3.3, Jury Trial columns.

Texas provision was eliminated when the constitution was amended in 1953, and Kentucky repealed its provision in 1968. No state now requires a jury trial in every hospitalization case, but only one state, Ohio, specifically prohibits the use of a jury.[182]

The United States Supreme Court has held that the right of a jury trial in civil and criminal cases at common law is a fundamental feature of our system of federal jurisprudence.[183] But this constitutional right extends only to trials in federal courts created under Article III of the Constitution.[184] The Constitution does not specifically extend the right of trial by jury to cases in the state courts.[185]

Although the guarantee of trial by jury in criminal cases under the Sixth Amendment has recently been interpreted as being included in the due process clause of the Fourteenth Amendment,[186] the Seventh Amendment's guarantee of this right in civil cases has not.[187]

The constitutions of the majority of states, however, generally provide for a right to trial by jury in civil and criminal cases. Thus a jury trial may be guaranteed to every individual, including the mentally ill, even if it is not specifically provided for by the statutes or the Federal Constitution.

The general test used to determine in what cases and under what circumstances jury trials are a matter of constitutional right is the extent to which provision was made for trial by jury at the time the state's constitution was adopted.[188] It is the view of many state courts that there was a right to trial by jury in insanity proceedings at common law and consequently that state constitutional guarantees of trial by jury extend to the preservation of this right.[189] Other courts have held that the absence of the right at common law does not in itself settle the question: if the right existed by virtue of a statute before the adoption of the constitution, it was preserved by the constitutional provisions guaranteeing trial by jury.[190] Consequently it is very likely that an attempt to abolish the right to a jury trial in hospitalization proceedings would be resisted in many states on the ground that the right is protected by the state constitution.

The use of the jury has been criticized by both medical and legal commentators[191] because of the emphasis on lay judgment that the jury represents. However, it is clear that involuntary mental hospitalization is not simply a question of the presence or absence of some complex disease process but also of whether or not the illness, if any, is sufficient to warrant state intervention.[192] Thus stated, the question becomes less dependent upon expert diagnosis and more dependent upon social consensus which the jury can represent.[193]

e) Legal Counsel

Forty-two jurisdictions provide that the patient has the right to be represented by counsel but only twenty-four provide for the appointment of counsel in all hospitalization cases in which the person alleged to be mentally ill has none. Seven jurisdictions provide that such appointments may be made at the discretion of the court, and in five states appointment is mandatory in the event that the patient requests counsel.[194] The importance of counsel in these matters is reflected in the Draft Act's recommendation that counsel be appointed in cases where the individual is without such assistance,[195] as well as in the National Legal Aid and Defender Association Standards which include providing counsel in ". . . proceedings involving possible detention or commitment of minors or alleged mentally ill persons."[196]

182. *Ohio Rev. Code Ann.* § 5122.15 (Baldwin 1964).

183. Jacob v. New York City, 315 U.S. 752 (1941).

184. Campbell v. St. Louis Union Trust Co., 346 Mo. 200, 139 S.W.2d 935 (1940).

185. White v. White, 108 Tex. 570, 196 S.W. 508 (1917).

186. See Duncan v. Louisiana, 391 U.S. 145.

187. See Sharpe v. State *ex rel.* Okla. Bar Ass'n, 448 P.2d 301, *cert. denied,* 394 U.S. 904 (1968).

188. State *ex rel.* Kennedy v. District Court, 121 Mont. 320, 194 P.2d 256 (1948); United States Fidel. & Guar. Co. v. Spring Brook Farm Dairy, Inc., 135 Conn. 294, 64 A.2d 39 (1949); Swanson v. Boschen, 143 Conn. 159, 120 A.2d 546 (1956).

189. Shumway v. Shumway, 2 Vt. 339 (1829); *In re* McLaughlin, 87 N.J. Eq. 138, 102 A. 439 (1916); White v. White, 108 Tex. 570, 196 S.W. 508 (1917); Warker v. Warker, 106 N.J. Eq. 499, 151 A. 274 (1930).

190. State *ex rel.* Pepper v. Holtcamp, 235 Mo. 242, 138 S.W. 521 (1911); Warrick v. Moore County, 291 S.W. 950 (Tex. Civ. App. 1927); *In re* Moynihan, 332 Mo. 1022, 62 S.W.2d 410 (1933).

191. See Curran, *supra* note 2, at 283.

192. This is the view taken in England by the National Council for Civil Liberties in its submissions to the Minister of Health on recommendations of the Royal Commission on the Law Relating to Mental Illness and Mental Deficiency (1957).

193. See Rock et al., *supra* note 15, at 171.

194. Table 3.12, Legal Counsel in Hospitalization Proceedings.

195. *Draft Act* § 9, at 9.

196. National Legal Aid and Defender Association, "Standards For a Defender System" (Standard No. 3. p. 15), in *Handbook of Standards For Legal Aid and Defender Offices,* 1970.

In a recent Tenth Circuit Court of Appeals case, Chief Judge Murrah placed the right to counsel under the due process clause of the Fourteenth Amendment, where the statute provides only that the proposed patient "may be represented."[197]

Every patient should be represented at the hospitalization hearing by counsel, either personally retained or court-appointed. This would be no greater protection than that accorded every indicted felon under the prevailing statutory guarantees. Both groups are subject to a deprivation of liberty through custody or confinement. If a distinction is to be drawn between these two groups, then it is the mentally ill who should be given the benefit of more extensive procedural guarantees. With rare exception, the mentally ill person will be less likely than the felon to comprehend the nature of the proceedings and its consequences. Of particular importance is the need of legal representation for a person who is in fact mentally ill and who, because of the possibility of hospitalization, may suffer economic losses from his business or property. Accurate, detailed information of this type could theoretically escape review by the court under many of the present systems, particularly if there were well-concealed ulterior motives behind the initiation of the procedure. Conceivably, the advisability of declaring the patient incompetent and appointing a guardian might never be called to the court's attention.

Counsel must guard not only against scheming relatives but also against incompetent and lax medical judgment and the improper extension of the hospitalization requirement to borderline cases.[198] In many jurisdictions, where the question of payment for hospitalization must be determined at the hospitalization hearing,[199] counsel's function would

include opposing any attempt to assign a greater weight to financial considerations than to the individual's need for treatment. In some jurisdictions the issue of incompetency as well as that of hospitalization is determined at the hospitalization hearing.[200] In these cases counsel should be especially alert to prevent unwarranted deprivation of civil rights.

The appointment of counsel, however, could turn into a mere formality and his services and participation become perfunctory unless he is given an opportunity to consult with his client as well as adequate time to prepare his case. Colorado, for example, seeks to guarantee the effectiveness of this protection by providing that counsel be given at least two days' notice and requiring that he attend all hearings.[201]

Only twenty-six states provide that the court-appointed counsel is to be compensated by the county or state. Arrangements for adequate compensation are, of course, essential in securing conscientious and effective legal service.

2. NONJUDICIAL INVOLUNTARY HOSPITALIZATION PROCEDURES

Although judicial involuntary hospitalization is the more common method of hospitalizing the mentally ill, nonjudicial procedures—which were initially the rule—have again become important. Thirty-three jurisdictions have provisions for some form of nonjudicial hospitalization; in nine of these states *only* nonjudicial procedures are available.[202]

In general, nonjudicial proceedings can be placed under two broad headings: (1) administrative hospitalization, and (2) involuntary hospitalization by medical certification. These will be considered in turn.

a) Administrative Hospitalization

Administrative hospitalization describes the procedure in which an administrative board, on the basis

197. Heryford v. Parker, 396 F.2d 393 (10th Cir. 1968).

198. Two recent studies indicate that the presence of legal counsel at the hearings and the psychiatrists' findings that the patient did not require hospitalization are closely connected. L. Wenger and R. Fletcher, "The Effect of Legal Counsel on Admissions to a State Mental Hospital: A Confrontation of Professions," *J. of Health and Social Behavior* 66 (1969); Y. Kumasaka, A. Zitrin, M. Herman, R. Gupta, "Civil Commitment and Psychiatric Responsibility" (paper No. 155 presented at the 123rd Annual Meeting of the American Psychiatric Association, May 14, 1970). But see Rock et al., *supra* note 15, at 157–60 for the problems counsel faces.

199. It has been suggested that the common cause underlying the defects in state mental hospitals is the lack of sufficient funds; see Note, "Three Controversial Aspects of New Illinois Mental Health Legislation," 47 *Nw. U.L. Rev.* 100, 109 (1952–53). Generally, the states have enacted legislative

schemes whereby the patient or his family is primarily liable for his support in a mental hospital. If the patient or his family is unable to pay the cost, or any part of it, the deficit is paid by the county or state. The various state provisions for both voluntary and involuntary hospitalization may be found in Table 3.13, Financial Responsibility for Patient's Support in Hospital. This table highlights the order of responsibility for the cost of the patient's support.

200. See Table 8.2, Effect of Involuntary Hospitalization on the Issue of Legal Competency.

201. *Colo. Rev. Stat. Ann.* 71-1-8(1) (1963).

202. See Table Intro. 1.

of a hearing and/or investigation, determines whether an individual is mentally ill to the point of requiring hospitalization and, if so, causes the person to be hospitalized for an indeterminate or extended period of time. The reader should recall that, unlike nonprotested admission procedures, administrative hospitalization procedures are compulsory in that they may be employed over the objections of the patient and without his consent. Administrative hospitalization procedures are found in ten states.

In general, the procedures followed in administrative hospitalization are similar to the judicial hospitalization procedures previously discussed.[203] The statutes are usually vague about the nature of the administrative hearing. No doubt less formality is required than for a judicial hearing. Decisions about the extent to which the technical rules of evidence must be followed, or about the patient's right to be represented by counsel and to cross-examine witnesses or present his own witnesses are by and large left to judicial interpretation.

Section 9(f) of the Draft Act, dealing with judicial procedure, expressly provides that the hearing "shall be conducted in as informal a manner as may be consistent with orderly procedure" and that the court "shall receive all relevant and material evidence which may be offered and shall not be bound by the rules of evidence." This illustrates that it is not necessary to adopt administrative hospitalization in order to provide a more informal hearing.

The advocates of administrative hospitalization believe that examination and hospitalization by a medical board, without any participation by the court, is more effective in convincing the patient that he is being treated rather than punished.[204] In addition, it is said that an administrative board composed entirely or largely of physicians creates a system "more akin to the scientific approach."[205]

The advocates of administrative hospitalization fail to take into consideration the fact that the ultimate decision on hospitalization is a social rather than a medical one. Physicians are no more qualified to balance individual liberty against the social policy of the state or its police powers than are other groups. In fact, physicians may be less qualified than such a group as the judiciary.

There are some jurisdictions that require that a judge or an attorney be a member of the administrative board of the hospital.[206] With the majority of the board consisting of physicians, emphasis is still on medical expertise, but this arrangement does give some recognition to the nonmedical aspects of hospitalization. The judge or the attorney is in a position to aid materially in the social judgments involved. These may range from the need for hospitalization to the advisability of concurrent guardianship proceedings.[207]

At one extreme is the procedure in which the board is empowered to conduct the hearing at a place of its choice and to issue a hospitalization order. At the other extreme is the procedure in which the hearing is held in the courtroom and presided over by a judge who must, in accordance with the findings of the board and its decision, either dismiss the case or issue a hospitalization order.

A hearing appears to be mandatory in all the states, though it may be *ex parte* in Delaware and Nebraska.[208] Although a mandatory hearing before a board composed of a majority of physicians tends to minimize the adversary element, it has been suggested that even further steps in this direction should be taken. For instance, in place of a mandatory hearing, notice that hospitalization is under consideration would be served upon the parties, but no formal hearing of contending parties would be held, unless demanded, and the patient's presence would not be compulsory.[209] The commission or board, at its discretion, could dispense with formal notice to the person. At the formal hearing, the patient, of course, would be entitled to representation by counsel. The decision of the commission would be subject to habeas corpus proceedings and appellate court review. It is believed that the provisions outlined "would minimize the harmful effects of adversary process but preserve fairness and guard against abuse."[210]

Delaware has a procedure similar to the proposal outlined above except that it may be used only in connection with patients already hospitalized.[211]

203. See this chapter, § III F 1, Judicial Hospitalization Procedures, and Tables 3.2 and 3.3.

204. Note, "Constitutionality of Non-judicial Confinement," 3 *Stan. L. Rev.* 109, 110 (1950–51).

205. See Note, *supra* note 199, at 107.

206. Table 3.4, Administrative Hospitalization—Prehearing Procedures, Membership column.

207. See chap. 8, "Incompetency, Guardianship, and Restoration."

208. Table 3.5, Administrative Hospitalization—Hearing and Posthearing Procedures, Mandatory Hearing column.

209. See Note, *supra* note 199, at 107. See also Table 3.5, Presence of Patient columns.

210. See Note, *supra* note 199, at 107.

211. Table 3.4, n.3.

There are, however, no provisions for notice, and the presence of the patient is mandatory during the board's investigation.[212] Any person related to the patient by blood or marriage may request the board to summon a six-man jury. If a jury is not requested, it would appear that the board need not hold a formal hearing but may make its investigation in the presence of the patient and later decide *ex parte* the need for hospitalization.[213] Emphasis would thus be upon impartial fact-finding, expert judgment, and a reduction in unnecessary or harmful formalism.[214] The decision of the board may be reviewed in a hearing before a judge.[215]

The Nebraska statutes permit a patient to be hospitalized without his ever having had an opportunity to request or have a formal hearing. The board is not required to hold a hearing and may make its decision *ex parte*.[216] The patient's only opportunity to be heard is through a request for a review of his hospitalization in a hearing before a judge.[217]

Although the involuntary hospitalization of the mentally ill has been traditionally a judicial function, the federal doctrine of separation of powers does not compel this result.[218] A state may distribute its powers as it sees fit,[219] provided that it does not trespass upon the requirements of due process. The Federal Constitution requires only that the administrative procedures be circumscribed by sufficient safeguards to insure that the due process guaranteed by the Fourteenth Amendment is not violated.[220] Thus the power of the state cannot be used in an arbitrary manner; administrative boards must be provided with definite standards of guidance.[221]

Furthermore, due process may require certain minimal procedural safeguards such as notice and a fair hearing. The questions of whether due process requires notice and a fair hearing and whether a posthospitalization hearing will suffice have been discussed previously with respect to judicial hospitalization procedures. They will be considered again in the section on involuntary hospitalization by medical certification which follows next.

It should be noted that all the states having administrative procedures provide for a review of the hospitalization order through one or more of the following methods: a hearing before a judge, a jury trial, or an enlarged habeas corpus proceeding which permits the patient to test the legality of his hospitalization at the time of the writ.[222]

Problems involving the scope of judicial review arise in the field of administrative hospitalization just as they do in other fields of administrative action. Such problems, not unique to this subject, are dealt with quite adequately in other sources;[223] for this reason, further treatment in this Report is not deemed appropriate.

b) Involuntary Hospitalization by Medical Certification

Involuntary hospitalization by medical certification describes the procedure in which an individual may be hospitalized for an indeterminate or extended period, without his consent or over his objection, on the basis of the certificate(s) of one or more physicians or authorized examiners. The fact that such a procedure may require the approval or endorsement of a judge has not been considered sufficient to classify it as a judicial procedure. Basically, the need for hospitalization is determined by the physicians or examiners and is expressed through their medical certificates. The function of the judge in this procedure is not to review the merits of the certificates or to determine whether, in view of them, hospitalization is desirable or required, but to verify the genuineness of the signatures and the qualifications of the persons who signed the certificates. If the certification meets the statutory requirements and no bad faith or abuse is patent, the judge's duty

212. *Del. Code Ann.* tit. 16, § 5124.d (1953).

213. Ibid.

214. See Note, *supra* note 199, at 107.

215. *Del. Code Ann.* tit. 16, § 5124.e (1953).

216. *Neb. Rev. Stat.* § 83-325 (Supp. 1967).

217. *Neb. Rev. Stat.* § 83-328.03 (1966).

218. See Note, *supra* note 204, at 110. Such a result may be compelled, however, by a state constitution incorporating the doctrine of separation of powers. *In re* Opinion of the Justices, 86 N.H. 597, 166 A. 640 (1941).

219. Teamsters Local 309 v. Hanke, 339 U.S. 470 (1950); Southard v. Jackson, 298 Mich. 75, 298 N.W. 457, *cert. denied*, 314 U.S. 659 (1941).

220. Cf. Nebbia v. New York, 291 U.S. 502 (1943); Yick Wo v. Hopkins, 118 U.S. 356 (1886).

221. Schneider v. Town of Irvington, 308 U.S. 147 (1939); Hague v. CIO, 307 U.S. 496 (1930); Graves v. Minnesota, 272 U.S. 425 (1926).

222. Table 3.5, Right to Judicial Review of Hospitalization Order columns.

223. E.g., 4 Davis, Administrative Law Treatise §§ 29.01 to .11 (1958); Dickinson, "Crowell v. Benson: Judicial Review of Administrative Determinations of Questions of "Constitutional Fact,'" 80 *U. Pa. L. Rev.* 1055 (1932); Hart, "Judicial Review of Administrative Action—A Thesis," 9 *Geo. Wash. L. Rev.* 49 (1941).

is to issue a hospitalization order or to endorse the certificates. Usually, such endorsement or approval authorizes a health or police officer to take the patient into custody and transport him to the hospital.

For the purposes of this discussion, thirty-one jurisdictions are considered as providing hospitalization by medical certification, the nonjudicial procedure advocated by those who object most strenuously to the continued reliance on mandatory judicial procedures.[224] However, the procedure is differentially applicable in at least twelve states, depending upon the patient's condition and his willingness to be hospitalized. In eight states the procedure may not be used to hospitalize a patient who protests. In most states it is difficult to determine exactly which class of patients is to be included. Section 6 of the Draft Act serves as a typical example:

Sec. 6. *Hospitalization on medical certification; standard nonjudicial procedure.*—(a) Any individual may be admitted to a hospital upon

(1) Written application to the hospital by a friend, relative, spouse, or guardian of the individual, a health or public welfare officer, or the head of any institution which (sic) such individual may be, and

(2) certification by two designated examiners that they have examined the individual and that they are of the opinion that
(A) he is mentally ill, and
(B) because of his illness is likely to injure himself or others if allowed to remain at liberty, or
(C) is in need of care or treatment in a mental hospital, and because of his illness, lacks sufficient insight or capacity to make responsible application therefor.

The certification by the designated examiners may be made jointly or separately, and may be based on examination conducted jointly or separately, as the regulations of the (central administration) may prescribe. An individual with respect to whom such certification has been issued may not be admitted on the basis thereof at any time after the expiration of 15 days after the date of examination, exclusive of any period of temporary detention authorized under section 11. The head of the hospital admitting the individual shall forthwith make a report thereof to the (central administration).

(b) Such certification, if it states a belief that the individual is likely to injure himself or others if allowed to remain at liberty, shall upon endorsement for such purpose by the head of the (local health authority) or by a judge of any court of record of the county in which the individual is resident or present, authorize any health or police officer to take the individual into custody and transport him to a hospital designated in the application.[225]

Section 6(a) of the Draft Act has been considered by many as a form of compulsory hospitalization by medical certification.[226] Professor Ross contends that this is a misconception, stemming from the ambiguous wording of the section. He explains:

This section provides that a mentally ill individual may be admitted to a hospital on the certificate of two doctors. This section authorizes admission, not commitment. This section provides for what is usually called "non-protested admission," but fails to provide expressly that admission depends on acquiescence, rather than compulsion. Part B of Section 6 and the commentary to the act make it clear that compulsion can not be used unless the procedure is also an emergency situation.[227]

Consequently, the Draft Act has been included in the Involuntary Hospitalization by Medical Certification table with the limiting criteria noted under the Nonprotesting and Protesting Patient columns.[228] Florida, South Carolina, and Utah have provisions substantially similar to, or just as ambiguous as, Section 6(a) and (b) of the Draft Act. Like the Draft Act, they are shown in both the Protesting and the Nonprotesting Patient columns. There are other medical certification procedures that are either silent on this aspect or equally as ambiguous as those just mentioned. These procedures have been characterized as both nonprotesting and protesting admission procedures and are treated accordingly in both the text and the tables.[229]

As the reader knows, a Missouri law, identical to Section 6 of the Draft Act, was held unconstitutional in *State ex rel. Fuller v. Mullinax.*[230] Since that time Missouri has adopted a new nonjudicial hospitalization law. It provides that the county department of welfare must serve the person who is

224. Table 3.6.

225. *Draft Act* § 6, at 6-7.

226. Ross, "Commitment of the Mentally Ill: Problems of Law and Policy," 57 *Mich. L. Rev.* 945, 975 (1959).

227. Ibid. See also *Draft Act,* Commentary, at 24.

228. Table 3.6.

229. Table 3.6, Nonprotesting Patient column.

230. 364 Mo. 858, 269 S.W.2d 72 (1954).

alleged to be mentally ill with notice that an application has been made for his involuntary hospitalization and that he will be hospitalized unless he notifies the department within five days of his desire to have the matter judicially determined. This request may be oral or written. A printed request, addressed to the department, is delivered with the notice.[231] The Missouri procedure is thus a nonprotested admission (waiver-of-hearing) procedure and is shown in that column.[232] Similarly, seven other jurisdictions require either a signed statement that the patient does not object (District of Columbia, Arizona, Nevada, Tennessee) or a hearing if requested (Virginia, North Carolina); while Ohio permits admission if the patient does not object in writing prior to hospitalization.[233]

All thirty-one states having medical certification proceedings provide either (1) the right to a judicial review of the certification order by a trial *de novo* or an enlarged habeas corpus proceeding, such as the one set forth in the North Carolina statutes,[234] or (2) the patient's right to be released within a designated time after he, or someone else on his behalf, gives notice of the intention to exercise this right.[235] The designation of time ranges from "forthwith" or "on request" to a maximum of "thirty days." Where a definite number of days is specified, it allows the hospital authorities time to initiate a judicial proceeding, if such action is deemed appropriate. In Nebraska, where release is "on request," and in Florida, where release is "forthwith," provisions exist for postponing release under certain circumstances; such provision exists also in Arkansas, where release must be within thirty days.[236] Fourteen of the twenty-three states require that the patient be notified of his right to release upon notice or of his right to judicial review.[237] Missouri, of course, informs the patient of his right to have his hospitalization determined by judicial hearing, instead of by medical certification.[238]

At least one commentator has classified as forms of nonprotested admission the procedures wherein

a patient may protest at the time of admission to the hospital as well as those wherein a patient may protest after admission and thereby secure his discharge within a short time unless compulsory proceedings are instituted.[239] It appears more useful to distinguish carefully between procedures which authorize initial hospitalization and those which provide only for the termination of hospitalization. Therefore, for the purposes of this Report, procedures requiring release after request by the patient have not been classified as nonprotested admission unless protest is possible also prior to admission.

Section 6(b) of the Draft Act provides that if the certification by two medical examiners required by section 6(a) is to the effect that the patient is dangerous, the papers may be endorsed by the judge; the patient can then be taken into custody and transported to a hospital.[240] This is a clear example of involuntary hospitalization by medical certification of a protesting patient.

In at least eight states hospitalization by medical certification cannot be used except to hospitalize persons in state institutions.[241] In some instances, the hospital may veto the hospitalization. Where this veto exists, understaffed and overcrowded state hospitals are not likely to accept borderline cases.[242] Eleven states require further approval of the certification before an individual may be hospitalized.[243]

IV. CONCLUDING OBSERVATIONS ON INVOLUNTARY HOSPITALIZATION

Over the years the medical profession has been quite vocal in its criticism of the continued reliance on traditional court procedures in connection with involuntary hospitalization. Typical of such criticism is the following statement issued on behalf of the American Psychiatric Association and the National Association for Mental Health before the Senate Subcommittee on Constitutional Rights in March 1961:

> From a medical point of view, the worst features of the commitment laws and procedures of the past (and some of these features are still with us in some states) include these: Insistence that the patient

231. *Mo. Rev. Stat.* § 202.797 (1959).

232. Table 3.6, Nonprotesting Patient column.

233. Ibid.

234. Table 3.6, Review columns.

235. Table 3.6, Release upon Notice columns.

236. Ibid.

237. Table 3.6, Patient Told of Right To Object, Release or Review column.

238. Ibid.

239. Ross, *supra* note 226, at 953, 974.

240. *Draft Act* § 6(b), at 7.

241. Table 3.6, Limits on Place of Hospitalization column. In Florida the procedure may only be used for admission to a non-state institution.

242. Ross, *supra* note 226, at 977.

243. Table 3.6, Further Approval By column.

appear personally in court with consequent exposure of his problems to the public; the frequent identification of mental illness with criminality as a result of court procedures; the acceptance of a lay judgment as to the degree of illness as occurs, for example, in a jury trial; frequent acceptance of commitment as tantamount to legal incompetence, thus depriving a mental patient of his civil rights; the use of archaic legal terminology such as "insane," "of unsound mind," "idiot," "feebleminded," etc., all of them conveying a legal, rather than a medical, meaning; and embarrassing inquiries into the patient's financial status at the time of his commitment. . . . In general, psychiatrists favor a simple commitment procedure entailing an application to the hospital by a close relative or friend, and a certification by two qualified physicians that they have examined the subject and found him to be mentally ill.[244]

Without a doubt the effort to dejudicialize hospitalization of the mentally ill has met with considerable success. Presently, some thirty-one jurisdictions provide for admission by medical certification. Voluntary and informal hospitalization is supplanting involuntary hospitalization in many states. The terminology of earlier statutes—"commitment," "summons," "warrant," "complaint," "insane," "of unsound mind"—has been replaced by "hospitalization," "application," "mentally ill person," and "patient" with the hearty endorsement of all groups concerned. Not all the issues, however, have been resolved. Medical certification is typically an alternative procedure to the more traditional judicial commitment procedure which forty-three states currently retain. Furthermore, in a number of states the statutes explicitly limit medical certification to patients who consent or do not object to hospitalization. In an even larger number of states it is unclear whether or not compulsion may be exercised to accomplish hospitalization under the medical certification procedure. Thus judicial hospitalization remains as a significant procedure.

The traditional judicial hospitalization procedures, however, have not escaped criticism even from those who favor them. The minimal requirements of notice and an opportunity to be heard, while adhered to in judicial proceedings, often appear to have little substance in fact. One commentator has stated, "Indeed, elaborate statutory pro-

visions for the protection of the individual are often mere illusions of due process, as many pressures, particularly the demands of medical propriety, require that 'legalistic' corners be cut."[245] Because "mental illness" is a global medical concept with as imprecise a definition as "physical illness," judicial procedures inevitably tend to place dispositive weight on expert medical opinion. For example the American Bar Foundation study of hospitalization and discharge concludes:

> The judicial commitment procedure thus amounts to administrative monitoring, often cursory, of a medically oriented process upon which jural apparatus has been grafted. Under these conditions the court becomes essentially ministerial. The judge has neither the objective legal criteria nor the technical training to decide the treatment questions that are really at stake. As a result, he is often reduced to deciding such ancillary administrative questions as what hospital the patient should be sent to, or passing on such procedural trivialities as the form of medical certificates. The medical treatment questions are determined by medical testimony from examiners whose opinions are rarely at variance and are rarely disputed. The court decides the central issues indirectly through the choice of medical examiners, a matter in which it has no special competence and for which it is not responsible to anyone.[246]

The solution to this problem would appear to be a sound and discriminating qualitative definition not only of mental illness but also of the circumstances under which compulsory hospitalization is appropriate. However, no existing definition of mental illness and of the legal criteria for involuntary hospitalization meets this standard, nor is one likely to be forthcoming. This fact has been recognized in much of the recent legislation governing hospitalization.

Attempts at definitional refinements have been supplanted in recent years by procedural and informational prescriptions designed to improve the clinical quality of the final decision. First of all, several procedures incorporating varying degrees of compulsion are authorized. These procedures range from informal admission through compulsory hospitalization, with explicit or implicit emphasis on those voluntary and informal procedures which incorporate the least compulsion or compulsion over the shortest period of time—as in the case of emer-

244. American Psychiatric Association and the National Association for Mental Health, *Psychiatric Points of View regarding Laws and Procedures Governing Medical Treatment of the Mentally Ill* (Joint Information Service, September 1962).

245. Kutner, *supra* note 153.

246. Rock et al., *supra* note 15, at 259.

gency procedures. In some states indeterminate involuntary hospitalization has been completely eliminated and in others it is delayed until a significant period of observational hospitalization has occurred, permitting a more informed judgment as to the real need for extended compulsory hospital care and preserving the right to elect to receive treatment.

Second, greater emphasis has been placed on understanding the social conditions surrounding the petition or application for hospitalization. Although social investigations prior to hospitalization have been required in the past, their major thrust was to determine the financial status of the proposed patient and his relatives. In some jurisdictions this inquiry has been broadened to determine the circumstances which led to petitioning as well as the possibility of utilizing nonhospital dispositions. The California Code, for example, not only provides for a prepetition screening but also deemphasizes hospitalization by severely limiting direct commitments and providing for the appointment (to be renewed yearly) of a conservator to care for the physical needs of "gravely disabled persons." Hospitalization is permitted only upon court approval.[247] Similarly, North Carolina permits an initial commitment of 180 days of compulsory outpatient care of at least one session per week in lieu of hospitalization prior to a final determination of the issue.[248] In other jurisdictions as well, compulsory outpatient care appears to be permitted.[249]

Given the various alternatives to compulsory extended hospitalization it would appear that the need to invoke such a procedure would be relatively infrequent. According to the Group for the Advancement of Psychiatry, "when a patient is adequately prepared for admission and good medical care is available . . . it is estimated that 90 percent of all patients could be admitted on the basis of medical decisions alone. The remaining 10 percent might

still require hospitalization on a non-voluntary basis."[250]

It would appear that one important function of involuntary judicial hospitalization inquiry should be to assure that the alternatives have been fully explored. Because a person meets the criteria posed for involuntary hospitalization does not mean that he can only be involuntarily hospitalized. The substantive criteria are simply too broad to justify such a conclusion. If the purpose of the inquiry is to assure that persons will not undergo unwarranted deprivations of liberty, attention must be paid not only to whether or not any deprivation of liberty is justified but also to what is the minimum deprivation required.[251]

V. CONCLUSIONS AND RECOMMENDATIONS

1. *Efforts to develop a clear and workable statutory definition of the degree of mental illness which*

247. *Cal. Welf. & Inst'ns Code* §§ 5350, 5358, 5361 (West Supp. 1970).

248. *N.C. Gen. Stat.* § 122-63 (Supp. 1969).

249. Statutes which permit commitment to the care and custody of relatives in lieu of hospitalization, as well as those which have included clinics in their definition of hospitals or broadly permit commitment to "any other suitable place," would qualify. Similarly, conditional discharge procedures could be utilized by requiring outpatient care as a condition of release subsequent to a period of inpatient care. See Table 3.3, Place of Hospitalization columns and Table 4.1, Administrative Discharge, Conditional Discharge columns. See also Bleicher, "Compulsory Community Care for the Mentally Ill," 16 *Clev.-Mar. L. Rev.* 93, 104, 105 (1967).

250. Group for the Advancement of Psychiatry, "Laws Governing Hospitalization of the Mentally Ill" 147 (Rep. No. 61, 1966). In this context "medical decision" means that the physician determines that inpatient mental treatment is necessary and the patient accepts his physician's recommendation. It does not refer specifically to the medical certification procedure described earlier. The critical aspect is the confidence placed by the patient in his physician as determined by the doctor-patient relationship. In the public hospitalization process this element is often lacking.

251. This issue was specifically raised in Lake v. Cameron, 124 U.S. App. D.C. 264, 364 F.2d 657 (D.C. Cir. 1966) when Mrs. Lake sought release through habeas corpus. Judge Bazelon, writing for the majority in a 5–4 decision en banc, remanded the case for findings as to alternative modes of treatment in inpatient care. Mrs. Lake was adjudged somewhat senile, of poor memory, given to wandering about, and totally unable to care for herself. The court found that the statutory provision permitting it to order "any other alternative course of treatment which the court believes will be in the best interests of the person or of the public" [*D.C. Code Ann.* § 21–545(b) (1967)] created a duty to explore alternatives "fashioned as the interests of the person and of the public require in a particular case. Deprivations of liberty solely because of dangers to the ill persons themselves should not go beyond what is necessary for their protection" (364 F.2d 660 (D.C. Cir. 1966)). However, the Supreme Court of New Mexico recently rejected the contention of a judicially hospitalized person that hospitalization imposed a restraint which was much broader than was necessary to protect him from injury to himself. The Court found that absent a statutory duty imposed on the court to seek alternatives to complete institutionalization no duty existed. The Court cited with approval the dissent in Lake which contended, "Neither this Court nor the District Court is equipped to carry out the broad geriatric inquiry proposed or to resolve the social and economic issues involved. . . ." State v. Sanchez, 80 N.M. 438, 457 P.2d 370, at 373 (1969).

justifies involuntary hospitalization should continue.

Statutory language is generally so ambiguous that it is difficult to determine the threshold degree of mental illness that justifies involuntary hospitalization. Courts, hospitals, physicians, and alleged mentally ill persons are entitled to a statutory statement of hospitalization prerequisite that is both clear and workable. Absent such a precise formulation, the present provisions for involuntary hospitalization, especially those which are for an indefinite period, should be conservatively interpreted.

2. *Those statutes which still retain terminology employed in criminal proceedings should be amended.*

The use of such terms as "arrested," "warrant," "accused of insanity," "committed," and "inmate" tends to hinder the recognition, acceptance, and treatment of mental illness in the community. It has been claimed by medical experts that these terms, to some extent, place patients in a state of apprehension and thus delay effective treatment and hinder recovery and community acceptance.

3. *Special provisions providing for the emergency detention of the mentally ill should be adopted.*

Such provisions should explicitly state that they are replacing the common law on this subject. They should specify that mentally ill persons shall not be detained in jails or transported in police vehicles unless the extremity of the situation dictates such action. Sufficient funds and facilities for emergency detention of the mentally ill should be provided. The time limits set for emergency detention should bear a reasonable relation to its purpose. Moreover, if hospitalization procedures are not initiated before the expiration of this limited period, the immediate release of the patient should be mandatory.

4. *Independent proceedings for the temporary or observational hospitalization of the mentally ill should be adopted.*

The adoption of such provisions would allow observation and diagnosis, perhaps even treatment. Treatment is especially appropriate in cases where there are indications that the patient is mentally ill but if given immediate treatment will not require indeterminate hospitalization. The recommendations of the hospital medical staff at the end of this period of observation will possess a much higher degree of medical reliability than would otherwise be the case. Temporary hospitalization need not require judicial sanction. Medical certification by two physicians, with provisions for judicial review, would provide sufficient safeguards for this short-term hospitalization.

5. *In addition to independent temporary or observational hospitalization, provisions should be adopted to assure in every case sufficient time to observe and diagnose alleged mentally ill persons prior to the final hearing on the issue of long term hospitalization.*

6. *Alleged mentally ill persons are entitled to notice and an opportunity to be heard.*

The problem in this area is to devise procedures that will protect the interests of those who do not require hospitalization and at the same time avoid subjecting those in need of hospitalization to injurious conditions. The difficulties posed by the attempt to satisfy both criteria may be resolved in part by the following devices. First, notice should be served by a person who is trained and has experience in dealing with the mentally ill. Such a person would not simply deliver the formal papers but, if necessary, read them to the patient or explain their meaning and consequences to him. Second, notice to the patient should be dispensed with in those cases where the court is convinced that substantial or serious harm would result. In such cases, substitute services of notice to relatives and friends should be required.

Any person being deprived of his liberty is entitled to a hearing and a judicial determination of his status. It is not necessary, however, that the hearing be held in a courtroom and with all the traditional amenities of judicial procedure. It might be held in the hospital, the patient's home, or any other convenient place. The problem of the patient's compulsory presence at the hearing can best be solved by balancing in each case the likelihood and degree of harm against the protections and benefits which may be derived.

7. *Alleged mentally ill persons should be entitled to representation by counsel.*

Personal liberty is of such paramount importance that its possible deprivation should be accompanied by every reasonable protection. Every alleged mentally ill person should have the right to be represented by counsel of his own choice. In the case of an indigent patient, the court should appoint competent counsel, who should be compensated by the state or county. Counsel, whether personally selected or court-appointed, should be given adequate time and opportunity to consult with his client in preparation for the hearing. Counsel should test not only the basis for hospitalization but also the suitability of other modes of care and treatment as well as voluntary admission.

8. *Before any order of involuntary hospitaliza-*

tion is entered, the alternative of voluntary admission should be fully explored and the person should be permitted to elect the voluntary form of admission if that alternative is suitable.

The weight of opinion and observation is that involuntary forms of admission are overutilized. To curb this tendency involuntary admission should be permissible only after a positive showing that the person is unsuitable for voluntary admission or unwilling to undertake it.

9. *Property rights should not be neglected when patients are involuntarily hospitalized.*

Under many of the present involuntary hospitalization statutes no provision is made for a proper inquiry at the time of hospitalization to ascertain whether the patient has any business or property interests. The timely discovery of these interests may be very important to the preservation of the patient's property rights. To guard against the possibility that these interests may be overlooked, particularly in nonjudicial proceedings, statutes should require that at the time of hospitalization a prompt and thorough investigation be made to determine if there are any such business or property interests.

BIBLIOGRAPHY

American Bar Association. Special Committee on the Rights of the Mentally Ill. *Report.* 72 American Bar Association Reports 295. Chicago: American Bar Association, 1947.

American Law Reports Annotated. San Francisco. Bancroft-Whitney Co.; Rochester, N.Y.: Lawyers Co-operative Publishing Co. "Right without Judicial Proceeding to Arrest and Detain One Who Is, or Is Suspected of Being, Mentally Deranged." 10 (1921) 488; 45 (1926) 1464.

American Psychiatric Association and the National Association for Mental Health. *Psychiatric Points of View regarding Laws and Procedures Governing Medical Treatment of the Mentally Ill.* Washington, D.C.: Joint Information Service of the American Psychiatric Association and the National Association for Mental Health, September 1962.

Barrow, Roscoe L., and Fabing, Howard D. *Epilepsy and the Law.* New York: Hoeber Medical Div., Harper & Row, 1956.

Belknap, Ivan. *Human Problems of a State Mental Hospital.* New York: McGraw-Hill Book Co., Inc., 1956.

Birnbaum, Morton, M.D. "The Right to Treatment." 46 *American Bar Association Journal* 499 (1960).

Black, Henry Campbell. *Black's Law Dictionary.* 4th ed. St. Paul: West Publishing Co., 1951.

Bleicher, Beatrice K. "Compulsory Community Care for the Mentally Ill." 16 *Cleveland-Marshall Law Review* 93 (1967).

Bureau of Narcotics. *Traffic in Opium and Other Dangerous Drugs.* Washington, D.C.: Government Printing Office, 1966.

Cooperative Commission on the Study of Alcoholism. *Alcohol Problems: A Report to the Nation.* Edited by Thomas F. Plaut. New York: Oxford University Press, 1967.

Council of State Governments. *The Mental Health Programs of the Forty-Eight States.* Chicago: Council of State Governments, 1950.

Curran, William J. "Hospitalization of the Mentally Ill." 31 *North Carolina Law Review* 274 (1952–53).

Davis, Kenneth Culp. *Administrative Law Treatise.* Vol. 4. St. Paul, Minn.: West Publishing Co., 1958.

Dershowitz, Alan M. "A Knife that Cuts Both Ways." 2 *Psychology Today* 43 (February 1969).

Deutsch, Albert. *The Mentally Ill in America.* 2d ed. rev. New York: Columbia University Press, 1949.

Dickinson, John. "Crowell v. Benson: Judicial Review of Administrative Determinations of Questions of 'Constitutional Fact.'" 80 *University of Pennsylvania Law Review* 1055 (1932).

Eldridge, William B. *Narcotics and the Law.* 2d ed. Chicago: University of Chicago Press, 1967.

Flaschner, Franklin N. "Analysis of Legal and Medical Considerations in Commitment of the Mentally Ill." 56 *Yale Law Journal* 1178 (1947).

Great Britain. National Council for Civil Liberties. Submissions to Minister of Health on Recommendations of the Royal Commission on the Law Relating to Mental Illness and Mental Deficiency (1957).

Great Britain. Royal Commission on the Law Relating to Mental Illness and Mental Deficiency 1954–57. *Report.* Cmnd. No. 169. London: Her Majesty's Stationery Office, 1957.

Group for the Advancement of Psychiatry. *Commitment Procedures.* Report no. 4. New York: Group for the Advancement of Psychiatry, April 1948.

Guttmacher, Manfred S., and Weihofen, Henry. *Psychiatry and the Law.* New York: W. W. Norton & Co., 1952.

Handbook of Standards for Legal Aid and Defender Offices. Chicago: National Legal Aid and Defender Association, 1970.

Hart. "Judicial Review of Administrative Action—A Thesis." 9 *George Washington Law Review* 49 (1941).

Hewitt, Donald W. *Alcoholism.* Philadelphia: Lea & Febiger, 1957.

Illinois Legislative Council. *Mental Hospital Admissions*

and Discharges. Bull. 2–550. Springfield: January 1956.

Indiana Association for Mental Health. *Progress Report.* (September 1956).

Kadish, Sanford H. "A Case Study in the Significance of Procedural Due Process—Institutionalizing the Mentally Ill." 9 *Western Political Quarterly* 93 (1956).

Kumasaka, Y.; Zitrin, A.; Herman, M.; and Gupta, R. "Civil Commitment and Psychiatric Responsibility." Paper no. 155, presented at the 123d Annual Meeting of the American Psychiatric Association, May 14, 1970.

Kutner, Luis. "The Illusion of Due Process in Commitment Proceedings." 57 *Northwestern University Law Review* 383 (1962).

National Institute of Mental Health. Federal Security Agency. *A Draft Act Governing Hospitalization of the Mentally Ill.* Public Health Service Pub. no. 51. Washington, D.C.: Government Printing Office, 1952.

Note, "Civil Commitment of the Mentally Ill: Theories and Procedures." 79 *Harvard Law Review* 1291 (1966).

Note, "Constitutionality of Non-judicial Confinement." 3 *Stanford Law Review* 109 (1950–51).

Note, "The New York Mental Health Information Service: A New Approach to Hospitalization of the Mentally Ill." 67 *Columbia Law Review* 672 (1967).

Note, "Three Controversial Aspects of New Illinois Mental Health Legislation." 47 *Northwestern University Law Review* 100 (1952–53).

Rock, Ronald S.; Jacobson, Marcus A.; and Janopaul, Richard M. *Hospitalization and Discharge of the Mentally Ill.* An American Bar Foundation Study. Chicago: University of Chicago Press, 1968.

Ross, Hugh A. "Commitment of the Mentally Ill: Problems of Law and Policy." 57 *Michigan Law Review* 975 (1959).

————. "Hospitalizing the Mentally Ill—Emergency and Temporary Commitments." *Current Trends in State Legislation 1955–56.* Ann Arbor: Legislative Research Center, University of Michigan Law School, 1957.

Scheff, Thomas J. "The Societal Reaction to Deviance: Ascriptive Elements in the Psychiatric Screening of Mental Patients in a Midwestern State." 11 *Social Problems* 401 (1964).

United States Public Health Service. National Institute of Mental Health. *Patients in State and County Mental Hospitals 1967.* Public Health Service Pub. no. 1921. Washington, D.C.: Government Printing Office, 1969.

United States Public Health Service. *Patients in Mental Institutions.* Public Health Service Pub. no. 483. Washington, D.C.: Government Printing Office, 1952.

Wenger, L., and Fletcher, R. "The Effect of Legal Counsel on Admissions to a State Mental Hospital: A Confrontation of Professions." 10 *Journal of Health and Social Behavior* 66 (1969).

Whitmore, Charles W. "Comments on a Draft Act for the Hospitalization of the Mentally Ill." 19 *George Washington Law Review* 512 (1950–51).

CASES

Bisgaard v. Duvall, 169 Iowa 711, 151 N.W. 1051 (1915).

Boesch v. Kick, 97 N.J.L. 92, 116 A. 796 (Sup. Ct. 1922).

Campbell v. St. Louis Union Trust Co., 346 Mo. 200, 139 S.W.2d 935 (1940).

Christiansen v. Weston, 36 Ariz. 200, 284 P. 149 (1930).

County of Black Hawk v. Springer, 58 Iowa 417, 10 N.W. 791 (1882).

Crawford v. Brown, 321 Ill. 305, 151 N.E. 911 (1926).

Duncan v. Louisiana, 391 U.S. 145.

Ex parte Dagley, 35 Okla. 180, 128 P. 99 (1912).

Graves v. Minnesota, 272 U.S. 425 (1926).

Hague v. C.I.O., 307 U.S. 496 (1930).

Hall v. Verdel, 40 F. Supp. 94 (W.D. Va. 1941).

Hammon v. Hill, 228 F. 999 (W.D. Pa. 1915).

Heryford v. Parker, 396 F.2d 393 (10th Cir. 1968).

Hiatt v. Soucek, 240 Iowa 300, 36 N.W.2d 432 (1949).

In re Coates, 9 N.Y.2d 242, 173 N.E.2d 797, 213 N.Y.S.2d 74, *appeal dismissed sub nom.* Coates v. Walters, 368 U.S. 34 (1961).

In re Crosswell, 28 R.I. 137, 66 A. 55 (1907).

In re Dowdell, 169 Mass. 387, 47 N.E. 1033 (1897).

In re Lambert, 134 Cal. 626, 66 P. 851 (1901).

In re McLaughlin, 87 N.J. Eq. 138, 102 A. 439 (1916).

In re Moynihan, 332 Mo. 1022, 62 S.W.2d 410 (1933).

In re Opinion of the Justices, 86 N.H. 597, 166 A. 640 (1941).

In re Wellman, 3 Kan. App. 100, 45 P. 726 (1896).

International Brotherhood of Teamsters, Chauffeurs, Warehousemen and Helpers Union, Local 309 v. Hanke, 339 U.S. 470 (1950).

Jacob v. New York City, 315 U.S. 752 (1941).

Jillson v. Caprio, 181 F.2d 523 (D.C. Cir. 1950).

Keleher v. Putnam, 60 N.H. 30 (1880).

Lake v. Cameron, 124 U.S. App. D.C. 264, 364 F.2d 657 (D.C. Cir. 1966).

Look v. Dean, 108 Mass. 116 (1871).

Maxwell v. Maxwell, 189 Iowa 7, 177 N.W. 541 (1920).

Nebbia v. New York, 291 U.S. 502 (1943).

Paul v. Longino, 197 Ga. 110, 28 S.E.2d 286 (1943).

Payne v. Arkebauer, 190 Ark. 614, 80 S.W.2d 76 (1935).

People *ex rel.* Sullivan v. Wendel, 33 Misc. 496, 68 N.Y.S. 948 (Sup. Ct. 1900).

People v. Breese, 34 Ill. 2d 61, 213 N.E.2d 500 (1966).

People v. Couvion, 33 Ill. 2d 408, 211 N.E.2d 746 (1965).

Robinson v. California, 370 U.S. 660 (1962).

Schneider v. Town of Irvington, 308 U.S. 147 (1939).

Shapley v. Cohoon, 258 F. 752 (D. Mass. 1918).

Sharpe v. State *ex rel.* Okla. Bar Ass'n, 488 P.2d 301, *cert. denied,* 394 U.S. 904 (1968).

Shumway v. Shumway, 2 Vt. 339 (1829).

Snavely v. Snavely, 349 Ill. App. 369, 110 N.E.2d 685 (1953).

Sorter v. Austin, 221 Ala. 481, 129 So. 51 (1930).

Southard v. Jackson, 298 Mich. 75, 298 N.W. 457, *cert. denied,* 314 U.S. 659 (1941).

State *ex rel.* Fuller v. Mullinax, 364 Mo. 858, 269 S.W.2d 72 (1954).

State *ex rel.* Kennedy v. District Court, 121 Mont. 320, 194 P.2d 256 (1948).

State *ex rel.* Pepper v. Holtcamp, 235 Mo. 242, 138 S.W. 521 (1911).

State v. Billings, 55 Minn. 467, 57 N.W. 794 (1893).

Swanson v. Boschen, 143 Conn. 159, 120 A.2d 546 (1956).

United States Fidelity and Guaranty Co. v. Spring Brook Farm Dairy, Inc., 135 Conn. 294, 64 A.2d 39 (1949).

Warker v. Warker, 106 N.J. Eq. 499, 151 A.274 (1930).

Warrick v. Moore County, 291 S.W. 950 (Tex. Civ. App. 1927).

White v. White, 108 Tex. 570, 196 S.W. 508 (1917).

Yick Wo v. Hopkins, 118 U.S. 356 (1886).

Table 3.1   STATUTORY DEFINITIONS OF THE MENTALLY ILL

STATE AND CITATION	STATUTORY PROVISIONS
DRAFT ACT 1	"Mentally ill individual. An individual having a psychiatric or other disease which substantially impairs his mental health."
ALA. Code (1958) 45, 205	"Insanity defined which renders person eligible as patient. A person shall be adjudged insane who has been found by a proper court sufficiently deficient or defective mentally to require that, for his own or others' welfare, he be removed to the insane hospital for restraint, care and treatment."
ALAS. Stat. (1962) 47.30.340(10)	"'[M]entally ill individual' means an individual having a psychosis or senile changes which substantially impair his mental health to the degree that he is a danger to himself or others; or a mentally deficient and severely mentally retarded person whom the commissioner of health and welfare or his designee admits for treatment subject, however, to all the other admission and discharge procedures provided for in §10-340 of this chapter; the definition does not include an individual suffering from acute alcoholism or drug addiction."
ARIZ. Rev. Stat. Ann. (1956) 36-501.5 (Supp. 1970)	"'Mental illness or mentally ill' means a psychiatric disorder which substantially impairs mental health; or a psychiatric disorder to such a degree that a person having such is likely to be dangerous to himself or the person or property of others; and, in either case, is in need of supervision, care, treatment or hospitalization."
ARK. Stat. Ann. (1947)	
CAL. Welf. & Inst'ns Code (West 1966) 5008(h) (Supp. 1968)	"'Gravely disabled' means a condition in which a person, as a result of mental disorder or impairment by chronic alcoholism, is unable to provide for his basic personal needs for food, clothing, or shelter."
5550 (Supp. 1968)	"For the purpose of this chapter, 'mentally ill persons' means only those persons who are of such mental condition that they are dangerous to themselves or the person or property of others, and are in need of supervision, treatment, care, or restraint. 'Mentally ill persons,' as used elsewhere in this code, means persons who come within either or both of the following descriptions: (a) Who are of such mental condition that they are in need of supervision, treatment, care, or restraint. (b) Who are of such mental condition that they are dangerous to themselves or to the person or property of others, and are in need of supervision, treatment, care, or restraint. "Wherever in this code the term 'insane' or its variants are used, such terms shall be construed to refer to and mean 'mentally ill' or its variants, as defined in this section."
COLO. Rev. Stat. Ann. (1964) 71-1-1(b)	"'Mentally ill person' shall mean a person afflicted with disease, infirmity, old age, or disorder, which impairs his mental or emotional functions to a degree sufficient to require protection, a supervision, treatment, or confinement, for his own welfare or for the welfare or safety of others, or who, by reason thereof, lacks sufficient control, judgment, and discretion to manage his own property or affairs."
CONN. Gen Stat. Ann. (1958) 17-176	"'[M]entally ill person' includes each person afflicted by mental disease to such extent that he requires care and treatment for his own welfare or the welfare of others or of the community, and specifically excludes a person whose sole psychiatric disorder is drug dependence."
DEL. Code Ann. (1953) 1, §302	"'Mentally ill person' includes every idiot, lunatic person or person non compos mentis."

Table 3.1   STATUTORY DEFINITIONS OF THE MENTALLY ILL   continued

STATE AND CITATION	STATUTORY PROVISIONS
D.C. Code Ann. (1967) 21-501	"'[M]ental illness' means a psychosis or other disease which substantially impairs the mental health of a person; 'mentally ill person' means a person who has a mental illness."
FLA. Stat. Ann. (1960) 394.191(4) (Supp. 1969)	"The term 'mentally ill' shall mean the condition of being afflicted with a psychiatric disorder which substantially impairs a person's mental health, and which psychiatric disorder requires care, treatment, observation, diagnosis or detention in the interest of the welfare of such person or the welfare of others in the community."
GA. Code Ann. (1963) 88-501(a) (Supp. 1969)	"'Mentally ill' shall mean having a psychiatric disorder which substantially impairs the person's mental health."
HAWAII Rev. Stat. Ann. (1968) 334-1	"'[M]entally ill person' means a person having psychiatric disorder or other disease which substantially impairs his mental health."
IDAHO Code Ann. (1949) 66-317(b) (Supp. 1969)	"'[M]entally ill person or individual' shall mean a person or individual who comes under either or both of the following descriptions: (1) Who is in such mental condition that he is in need of supervision, care or restraint; (2) Who is of such mental condition that he is dangerous to himself or to the person or property of others and is in need of supervision, care or restraint."
ILL. Ann. Stat. (Smith-Hurd 1966) 91½, §1-11 (Supp. 1969)	"'Person in Need of Mental Treatment' . . . means any person afflicted with mental illness, not including a person who is mentally retarded . . . , if that person, as a result of such mental illness, is reasonably expected at the time the determination is being made or within a reasonable time thereafter to intentionally or unintentionally physically injure himself or other persons, or is unable to care for himself so as to guard himself from physical injury or to provide for his own physical needs."
IND. Ann. Stat. (1964) 22-1201(1), 22-1201(2) (Supp. 1969)	"(1) The term 'mentally ill person' shall mean a person who is afflicted with a psychiatric disorder which substantially impairs his mental health; and, because of such psychiatric disorder, requires care, treatment, training or detention in the interest of the welfare of such person or the welfare of others of the community in which such person resides. "(2) The term 'psychiatric disorder' means any mental illness or disease and shall include, but not be limited to, any mental deficiency, epilepsy, alcoholism or addiction to narcotic drugs."
IOWA Code Ann. (1969) 4.1(6)	Chapter 4, Construction of Statutes: "The words 'mentally ill person' include mental retardates, lunatics, distracted persons, and persons of unsound mind."
229.40	Chapter 229, Commitment and Discharge of Mentally Ill Persons: "The term 'mental illness' . . . includes every type of mental disease or mental disorder."
KAN. Stat. Ann. (1964) 59-2902(1) (Supp. 1970)	"The term 'mentally ill person' shall mean any person who is mentally impaired, except by reason of mental deficiency only, to the extent that he is in need of 'care and treatment' and who is or probably will become dangerous to himself or the person or property of others if not given 'care and treatment' and "(A) who lacks sufficient understanding or capacity to make responsible decisions with respect to his need for 'care or treatment,' or "(B) who refuses to seek 'care and treatment': <u>Provided</u>, That no person who is being treated by prayer in the practice of the religion of any church which teaches reliance on spiritual means alone through prayer for healing shall be determined to be a 'mentally ill person' unless substantial evidence is produced

Table 3.1   STATUTORY DEFINITIONS OF THE MENTALLY ILL   continued

STATE AND CITATION	STATUTORY PROVISIONS
KAN. Stat. Ann. (1964)--continued 59-2902(1) (Supp. 1968)	upon which the probate court finds that the 'proposed patient' is or who probbably will become dangerous to himself or the person or property of others, or unless his guardian, if any, consents to such determination."
KY. Rev. Stat. Ann. (1969) 202.010(1)	"'Mentally ill person' means a person having a psychiatric or other disease which substantially impairs his mental health."
LA. Rev. Stat. Ann. (1950) 28:2(3)	"'Mentally ill' means a person who is suffering from an illness which so lessens his capacity to use his customary self-control, judgment, and discretion in the conduct of his affairs and social relations as to make it necessary or advisable for him to be under care, supervision, guidance, or control. The term includes persons suffering from mental disease, mental disorder, lunacy, unsoundness of mind, and insanity."
ME. Rev. Stat. Ann. (1964) 34, §2251(5)	"'Mentally ill individual' means an individual having a psychiatric or other disease which substantially impairs his mental health. For the purposes of this chapter the term 'mentally ill individual' does not include mentally retarded or sociopathic individuals."
MD. Code Ann. (1968)	
MASS. Ann. Laws (1965) 123, §1	"'Mentally ill' person, for the purpose of involuntary commitment to a mental hospital or school under the provisions of this chapter, shall mean a person subject to a disease, psychosis, psychoneurosis or character disorder which renders him so deficient in judgment or emotional control that he is in danger of causing physical harm to himself or to others, or the wanton destruction of valuable property, or is likely to conduct himself in a manner which clearly violates the established laws, ordinances, conventions or morals of the community."
MICH. Comp. Laws Ann. (1967) 330.54	"The term 'mentally ill' or 'mentally ill person' as used in this act includes every species of insanity and extends to every mentally deranged person and to all of unsound mind, other than mentally handicapped, epileptics, and persons who manifest the general deterioration of mental processes, including disorientation, confusion or impairment of memory, associated with senility, but without psychotic implications, and may include persons whose sexual behavior is characterized by repetitive or compulsive acts which indicate a disregard of consequences or the recognized rights of others, or by the use of force upon another person in attempting sex relations or either a heterosexual or homosexual nature or by the commission of sexual aggressions against children under the age of sixteen."
MINN. Stat. Ann. (1959) 253A.02(3) (Supp. 1969)	"'Mentally ill person' means any person having a psychiatric or other disorder which substantially impairs his mental health and who is in need of treatment or supervision."
MISS. Code Ann. (1952) 698	"The term 'unsound mind,' when used in any statute in reference to persons, shall include idiots, lunatics, and persons non compos mentis."
MO. Rev. Stat. (1959) 202.780(5)	"'Mentally ill individual,' an individual having a psychiatric or other disease which substantially impairs his mental health who may or may not be legally insane."
MONT. Rev. Codes Ann. (1961)	

Table 3.1 STATUTORY DEFINITIONS OF THE MENTALLY ILL continued

STATE AND CITATION	STATUTORY PROVISIONS
NEB. Rev. Stat. (1966) 83-306(3)	"The term 'mentally ill' as used in this act, shall include persons suffering from any type of mental illness whatsoever, whether hereditary or acquired by internal or external conditions, diseases, narcotics, alcoholic beverages, accident, or any other condition or happening."
NEV. Rev. Stat. (1967) 433.653	"'Mentally ill person' means any person who has a mental illness but does not include a person committed to a private or public hospital in the State of Nevada by order of the court in a criminal proceeding."
433.655	"'Mental illness' means any psychosis or other disease which substantially impairs the mental health of an individual."
N.H. Rev. Stat. Ann. (1964) 135:21	"'Mental illness' shall mean mental disease to such extent that a person so afflicted requires care and treatment for his own welfare, or the welfare of others, or of the community."
N.J. Stat. Ann. (1964) 30:4-23 (Supp. 1970)	"'Mental illness' shall mean mental disease to such an extent that a person so afflicted requires care and treatment for his own welfare, or the welfare of others, or of the community."
N.M. Stat. Ann. (1953) 34-2-1a	"Mentally ill individual. An individual having a psychiatric or other disease which substantially impairs his mental health."
N.Y. Mental Hygiene Law (McKinney 1951) 2.8	"A 'mentally ill person' means any person afflicted with mental disease to such an extent that for his own welfare or the welfare of others, or of the community, he requires care and treatment."
N.C. Gen. Stat. (1964) 122-36(d)	"The words 'mental illness' shall mean an illness which so lessens the capacity of the person to use his customary self-control, judgment and discretion in the conduct of his affairs, and social relations as to make it necessary or advisable for him to be under treatment, care, supervision, guidance, or control. The words 'mentally ill' shall mean a person with a mental illness."
N.D. Cent. Code (1960) 25-01-01(1)	"'Mentally ill individual' means an individual having a psychiatric or other disease which substantially impairs his mental health."
OHIO Rev. Code Ann. (Baldwin 1964) 5122.01(A)	"'Mentally ill individual' means an individual having an illness which substantially impairs the capacity of the person to use self-control, judgment, and discretion in the conduct of his affairs and social relations and includes 'lunacy,' 'unsoundness of mind,' and also cases in which such lessening of capacity for control is caused by such addiction to narcotics, sedatives, alcohol, or stimulants as to make it necessary for such person to be under treatment, care, supervision, guidance, or control."
5122.01(B)	"'Mentally ill individual subject to hospitalization by court order' means a mentally ill individual who, because of his illness, is likely to injure himself or others if allowed to remain at liberty, or is in need of care or treatment in a mental hospital, and because of his illness lacks sufficient insight or capacity to make responsible decisions with respect to his hospitalization."
OKLA. Stat. Ann. (1954) 43A, §3(c) (Supp. 1969)	"'Mentally ill person' means any person afflicted with a mental illness to such an extent that he is incapable of managing himself and his affairs, and for his own welfare and the welfare of others it is necessary or advisable for him to be under care."

Table 3.1   STATUTORY DEFINITIONS OF THE MENTALLY ILL   continued

STATE AND CITATION	STATUTORY PROVISIONS
ORE. Rev. Stat. (1967)	
PA. Stat. Ann. (1969) 50, §4102	"'Mental disability' means any mental illness, mental impairment, mental retardation, or mental deficiency, which so lessens the capacity of a person to use his customary self-control, judgment and discretion in the conduct of his affairs and social relations as to make it necessary or advisable for him to be under care as provided in this act. It shall include conditions and terms heretofore defined as 'insanity,' 'unsoundness of mind,' 'lunacy,' 'mental disease,' 'mental disorder,' 'feebleminded,' 'moron,' 'idiot' and 'imbecile.' The term shall not include senility, unless mental illness or mental retardation is superimposed."
R.I. Gen. Laws Ann. (1968) 43-3-7	"Insane person defined. The words 'insane person' shall be construed to include every idiot, person of unsound mind, lunatic and distracted person."
S.C. Code Ann. (1962) 32-911(1)	"'Mentally ill person' means a person afflicted with a mental disease, alcoholism and drug addiction as such being excluded, to such an extent that, for his own welfare or the welfare of others or of the community, he requires care, treatment, hospitalization or training."
S.D. Compiled Laws Ann. (1967) 27-1-1	"The phrase 'mentally ill' as used in this title includes any species of mental illness or mental derangement but no mentally retarded person as defined in §27-1-2 shall be admitted into a hospital for the mentally ill."
TENN. Code Ann. (1955) 33-1201(a) (Supp. 1968)	"(a) Mentally ill individual--An individual having a psychiatric or other disease which substantially impairs his mental health who is a bona fide resident of the State of Tennessee" (refers to voluntary patients).
33-302(f) (Supp. 1968)	"Mentally ill individual--An individual who, in the opinion of a licensed physician, has a psychiatric disorder."
TEX. Rev. Civ. Stat. Ann. (1958) 5547-4(K) (Supp. 1969)	"'Mentally ill person' means a person whose mental health is substantially impaired. For purposes of this Code the term 'mentally ill person' includes a person who is suffering from the mental conditions referred to in Art. 1, Sec. 15a of the Constitution of the State of Texas."
UTAH Code Ann. (1967) 64-7-28(a)	"Mentally ill individual. An individual having a psychiatric or other disease which substantially impairs his mental health."
VT. Stat. Ann. (1968) 18, §7101(11)	"'Mentally ill individual' means an individual who is afflicted with mental disease or incapacity to the extent that he requires hospitalization, care or treatment; or an individual who is afflicted with mental disease or incapacity to the extent that he presents a substantial risk of injury to himself, or others if allowed to remain at liberty; or an individual who is afflicted with mental disease or incapacity to the extent that he lacks sufficient insight or capacity to make a responsible decision concerning his mental condition and is in need of hospitalization, care or treatment."
VA. Code Ann. (1953) 37.1-1(15) (Supp. 1968)	"'Mentally ill' means any person afflicted with mental disease to such an extent that for his own welfare or the welfare of others, or of the community, he requires care and treatment; provided, that, for purposes of chapter 2 (§37.1-63 et seq.) of this title, the term 'mentally ill' shall be deemed to include any person who is afflicted with mental deficiency or mental retardation or is a drug addict or inebriate."

Table 3.1   STATUTORY DEFINITIONS OF THE MENTALLY ILL   *continued*

STATE AND CITATION	STATUTORY PROVISIONS
WASH. Rev. Code Ann. (1962) 71.02.010	"'Mentally ill person' shall mean any person found to be suffering from psychosis or other disease impairing his mental health, and the symptoms of such disease are of a suicidal, homicidal, or incendiary nature, or of such nature which would render such person dangerous to his own life or to the lives or property of others."
W. VA. Code Ann. (1966) 27-1-2	"A 'mentally ill' person is one having a psychiatric or other disease which substantially impairs his mental health."
WIS. Stat. Ann. (1957) 51.001 (Supp. 1969)	"Mental illness means as defined in §51.75."
51.75 (Art. II(f)) (Supp. 1969)	"Mental illness means mental disease to such an entext that a person so afflicted requires care and treatment for his own welfare, or the welfare of others or of the community."
WYO. Stat. Ann. (1967) 25-49(a)	"Mentally ill individual. An individual having a psychiatric or other disease which substantially impairs his mental health."

Table 3.2 JUDICIAL HOSPITALIZATION OF THE MENTALLY ILL--PREHEARING PROCEDURES

STATE	APPLICATION BY — Any Person	Limited Group	COURT	CRITERIA FOR HOSPITALIZATION ORDER TO ISSUE — Dangerous or Likely to Cause Injury	In Need of Treatment	Other	SUPPORTING EVIDENCE FOR APPLICATION — No. of Medical Certificates	Other Evidence	PREHEARING MEDICAL EXAMINATION ORDERED BY COURT	DISMISSAL AFTER MEDICAL EXAMINATION	INTERIM DETENTION PENDING HEARING OR REMOVAL TO HOSPITAL	NOTICE OF HEARING — Guardian	Relative	Patient Mandatory	Patient Unless Harmful	Minimum Amount
DRAFT ACT		fn. 1 9	probate 9	9(g)	9(g)		fn. 2 one. 9(a)		2 designated examiners 9(c)	9(e)	24	9(b)	9(b)		9(b)	5 days 9(e)
ALA. Code (1958)	45, §208		probate judge. 45, §208			for his own or others' welfare. 45, 205			1 witness at hearing must be physician. 45, §210							
ALAS. Stat. (1962)	fn. 3 47.30.070(a)		superior court. 47.30.070(a)	47.30.070(i)(1)	fn. 4 47.30.070(i)(2)				fn. 5 1 or more medical examiners. 47.30.070(c) 47.30.070(d)	47.30.070(e)	47.30.090	47.30.070(f)		47.30.070(f)		
ARIZ. Rev. Stat. Ann. (1957)		fn. 6 36-509A (Supp. 1970)	superior court. 36-509A (Supp. 1970)	36-514C (Supp. 1970)					2 physicians 36-501.2 36-514B (Supp. 1970)		36-510 (Supp. 1970)	fn. 7 36-513D (Supp. 1970)	fn. 7 36-513D (Supp. 1970)		fn. 7 36-513A, 36-513D (Supp. 1970)	2 days. 36-513A (Supp. 1970)
ARK. Stat. Ann. (1947)	59-101	fn. 8 / fn. 9 59-234 (Supp. 1967)	probate 59-234 (Supp. 1967); probate 59-101	59-234 (Supp. 1967)	not stated	best interests of patient. 59-234 (Supp. 1967)	1 59-234 (Supp. 1967)				59-103	certification to be delivered to the person affected thereby, or to his guardian, or to his nearest relative. 59-234 (Supp. 1967)				
CAL. Welf. & Inst'ns Code (West 1966)		fn. 10 professional person in charge of the facility, or his designee. 5301 (Supp. 1968)	superior 5301 (Supp. 1968)	fn. 11 5304 (Supp. 1968)				affidavits describing behavior in detail. 5300, 5301 (Supp. 1968)						on same day as filing. 5301 (Supp. 1968)		
COLO. Rev. Stat. Ann. (1964)																
CONN. Gen. Stat. Ann. (1958)	17-177		probate 17-177	17-178 (Supp. 1969)	fn. 12 17-178 (Supp. 1969)				2 physicians, including 1 psychiatrist. 17-178 (Supp. 1969)		17-178 (Supp. 1969)	17-178 (Supp. 1969)	17-178 (Supp. 1969)	17-178 (Supp. 1969)		
DEL. Code Ann. (1953)																
D.C. Code Ann. (1967)	fn. 14 21-54T(a)		U.S. District Court for D.C. 21-544	21-544 21-545(b)			1 21-541(a)(1)	fn. 15 21-54T(a)(2)	commission on mental health. 21-542(a)	21-544 by commission.	21-528	attorney 21-545(a)		21-545(a)		5 days 21-545(a)
FLA. Stat. Ann. (1960)	fn. 16 394.22(2)(a) to 394.22(2)(e)		county or circuit. 394.22(1)	394.22(11)(a)					examining committee: 1 citizen, 2 physicians. 394.22(6)(a) (Supp. 1969)	394.22(6)(b)	394.22(5)	394.22(4)	394.22(4)	394.22(4)		

72

Table 3.2 JUDICIAL HOSPITALIZATION OF THE MENTALLY ILL--PREHEARING PROCEDURES   continued

STATE	APPLICATION BY: Any Person	APPLICATION BY: Limited Group	COURT	CRITERIA FOR HOSPITALIZATION ORDER TO ISSUE: Dangerous or Likely to Cause Injury	In Need of Treatment	Other	SUPPORTING EVIDENCE FOR APPLICATION: No. of Medical Certificates	Other Evidence	PREHEARING MEDICAL EXAMINATION ORDERED BY COURT	DISMISSAL AFTER MEDICAL EXAMINATION	INTERIM DETENTION PENDING HEARING OR REMOVAL TO HOSPITAL	NOTICE OF HEARING: Guardian	Relative	Patient Mandatory	Patient Unless Harmful	Minimum Amount
fn. 10 GA. Code Ann. (1963)	88-505.2 (Supp. 1969)		court of ordinary. 88-505.2 (Supp. 1969)	88-505.2(a)(1) 88-505.2(b)(1) (Supp. 1969)		incapable of caring for physical health and safety. 88-505.2(a)(1) and (b)(1) (Supp. 1969)	1 88-505.2(b) (Supp. 1969)	investigation by county health department. 88-505.2(b) (Supp. 1969)				representatives 88-505.3 (Supp. 1969)	representatives 88-505.3 (Supp. 1969)	88-505.3 (Supp. 1969)		
HAWAII Rev. Stat. Ann. (1968)																
IDAHO Code Ann. (1949)	fn. 1 66-329(a) (Supp. 1969)		probate 66-328 (Supp. 1969)	66-329(h) (Supp. 1969)	66-329(h) (Supp. 1969)		fn. 2 1 66-329(a) (Supp. 1969)		fn. 17 1 designated examiner. 66-317(e) 66-329(b) (Supp. 1969)	66-329(b) (Supp. 1969)	66-329(d) (Supp. 1969)	66-329(d) (Supp. 1969)	66-329(d) (Supp. 1969)		66-329(d) (Supp. 1969)	
ILL. Ann. Stat. (Smith-Hurd 1966)	any citizen 91½, §8-1 (Supp. 1969)		county circuit courts. 91½, §2-1 (Supp. 1969)	91½, §1-11 (Supp. 1969)	91½, §1-11 (Supp. 1969)		fn. 18 1 optional 91½, §8-3 (Supp. 1969)	fn. 19 91½, §8-1	91½, §9-3 (Supp. 1969)				fn. 20 91½, §8-7 (Supp. 1969)	91½, §8-7 (Supp. 1969)		2 days 91½, §8-7 (Supp. 1969)
IND. Ann. Stat. (1964)	a reputable resident. 22-1212 (Supp. 1969); 22-1215		circuit 22-1215				fn. 21 1 22-1212 (Supp. 1969); 22-1215		fn. 22 2 physicians 22-1215		22-1222			22-1216		
fn. 23 IOWA Code Ann. (1969)	225.10		district or superior. 225.10		225.10				1 physician 225.12			fn. 24 225.14		fn. 24 225.14		
KAN. Stat. Ann. (1964)	59-2913 (Supp. 1968)		probate 59-2913 (Supp. 1968)			"mentally ill person" 59-2917 (Supp. 1968)	1 59-2913 (Supp. 1968)	fn. 25 59-2913 (Supp. 1968)	optional, 1 physician 59-2914(f) (Supp. 1968)		59-2915(A) (Supp. 1968)			fn. 26 59-2916 (Supp. 1968)		5 days 59-2916 (Supp. 1968)
KY. Rev. Stat. Ann. (1969)		fn. 27 202.135(1)	circuit. 202.135(1)	202.135(6)(b)	202.135(6)(a)			202.135(1)(a) to 202.135(1)(e)	2 physicians 202.135(4)	202.135(4)	202.277	202.135(5)	202.135(5)		202.135(5)	5 days 202.135(4)
LA. Rev. Stat. Ann. (1950)	28:52 (Supp. 1969)		district 28:52 (Supp. 1969)			fn. 28 Best interest of patient and community. 28:53(A) (Supp. 1969)	1 28:52 (Supp. 1969)		optional, coroner and 1 or 2 physicians. 28:54		28:52.1 (Supp. 1969)					
ME. Rev. Stat. Ann. (1964)	34, §2334	34, §2334	probate 34, §2334	34, §2334	34, §2334		1 34, §2334	fn. 29 34, §2334	2 physicians 34, §2334	34, §2334		fn. 30 34, §2334	fn. 30 34, §2334		34, §2334	72 hours 34, §2334
MD. Ann. Code (1968)																
MASS. Ann. Laws (1965)	not stated		superior or district. 123, §50			proper subject for treatment and custody. 123, §50			2 physicians and 1 psychiatrist, if available. 123, §51 123, §53			123, §51	123, §51	123, §51		fn. 31 48 hours 123, §51 72 hours 123, §51

Table 3.2   JUDICIAL HOSPITALIZATION OF THE MENTALLY ILL--PREHEARING PROCEDURES   continued

STATE	APPLICATION BY: Any Person	Limited Group	COURT	CRITERIA FOR HOSPITALIZATION ORDER TO ISSUE: Dangerous or Likely to Cause Injury	In Need of Treatment	Other	SUPPORTING EVIDENCE FOR APPLICATION: No. of Medical Certificates	Other Evidence	PREHEARING MEDICAL EXAMINATION ORDERED BY COURT	DISMISSAL AFTER MEDICAL EXAMINATION	INTERIM DETENTION PENDING HEARING OR REMOVAL TO HOSPITAL	NOTICE OF HEARING: Guardian	Relative	Patient Mandatory	Patient Unless Harmful	Minimum Amount
MICH. Comp. Laws Ann. (1967)	fn. 32 330.21		probate 330.21			"mentally ill" 330.21			2 physicians 330.21			fn. 33 330.21	330.21		fn. 34 330.21	24 hours 330.21
fn. 10 MINN. Stat. Ann. (1959)	253A.07(1) (Supp. 1969)		probate 253A.07(1) (Supp. 1969)			welfare of patient and protection of society 253A.07(17)(a) (Supp. 1969)	1 253A.07(1) (Supp. 1969)	fn. 35 253A.07(1) (Supp. 1969)	fn. 36 2 physicians 253A.07(2) (Supp. 1969)		253A.07(3) (Supp. 1969)		fn. 37 253A.07(9) (Supp. 1969)	253A.07(9) (Supp. 1969)		5 days 253A.07(9) (Supp. 1969)
MISS. Code Ann. (1952)																
MO. Rev. Stat. (1959)		fn. 1 202.807(1)	probate 202.807(1)		202.807(5)		fn. 2 202.807(1)		1 physician who has examined must be a witness 202.807(3)		202.805(3) 202.833	202.807(2)	202.807(2)	202.807(2)		
MONT. Rev. Codes Ann. (1961)	not stated		district 38-201	38-201					2 physicians 38-203				38-201	38-201		
NEB. Rev. Stat. (1966)																
NEV. Rev. Stat. (1967)		433.685	district 433.685	433.685			one 433.685	fn. 29 433.685	fn. 38 433.69		433.683		433.687	433.687		
fn. 39 N.H. Rev. Stat. Ann. (1964)	135:19		probate 135:19, 135:20	135:19					2 physicians 135:20 135:21		135:19					
N.J. Stat. Ann. (1964)		fn. 40 30:4-27 (Supp. 1970)	county, domestic relations or juvenile. 30:4-23 (Supp. 1970)			"mentally ill" 30:4-27 (Supp. 1970)	2 30:4-29 (Supp. 1970)			fn. 41 30:4-39 (Supp. 1970)	30:4-37		fn. 41 30:4-41 (Supp. 1970)	fn. 41 30:4-41 (Supp. 1970)		
N.M. Stat. Ann. (1953)	fn. 1 34-2-5(a)	fn. 1 34-2-5(a)	district 34-2-5(a)	34-2-5(g)(2)	34-2-5(g)(3)		fn. 2 34-2-5(a)		1 or more licensed physicians. 34-2-5(c)	34-2-5(e)	34-2-7(b) 34-2-18(g)	34-2-5(f)	34-2-5(f)	34-2-5(f)		5 days 34-2-5(e)
N.Y. Mental Hygiene Law (McKinney) 1951																
fn. 10 N.C. Gen. Stat. (1964)	some reliable person having knowledge of the facts shall make and file in writing an affidavit. 122-60		superior court of county. 122-60	122-61					2 physicians 122-62		122-61			122-63		
N.D. Cent. Code (1960)																

Table 3.2   JUDICIAL HOSPITALIZATION OF THE MENTALLY ILL--PREHEARING PROCEDURES   *continued*

STATE	Application By: Any Person	Application By: Limited Group	COURT	Criteria: Dangerous or Likely to Cause Injury	Criteria: In Need of Treatment	Criteria: Other	Supporting Evidence: No. of Medical Certificates	Supporting Evidence: Other Evidence	Prehearing Medical Examination Ordered by Court	Dismissal After Medical Examination	Interim Detention Pending Hearing or Removal to Hospital	Notice: Guardian	Notice: Relative	Notice: Patient Mandatory	Notice: Patient Unless Harmful	Minimum Amount
fn. 10 OHIO Rev. Code Ann. (Baldwin 1964)	5122.11		probate 5122.11	5122.11	5122.11		fn. 42 1 5122.11	fn. 42 5122.11	at least 1 physician. 5122.14		5122.11 5122.17	5122.12(E)	fn. 43 spouse 5122.12(E)		5122.12	
OKLA. Stat. Ann. (1954)		fn. 44 43A, §55 (Supp. 1969)	county 43A, §55 (Supp. 1969)		43A, §55 (Supp. 1969)			fn. 45 43A, §55 (Supp. 1969)	fn. 46 2 physicians 43A, §54, §55 (Supp. 1969)		43A, §55 (Supp. 1969)		fn. 47 43A, §55 (Supp. 1969)	43A, §55 (Supp. 1969)		1 day 43A, §55 (Supp. 1969)
ORE. Rev. Stat. (1967)		fn. 48 426.070	fn. 49 any court having probate jurisdiction. 426.060 426.070		426.070 426.120				fn. 50 2 physicians 426.110		426.140(2)					
PA. Stat. Ann. (1969)	fn. 51 50, §4406(a)(1)		fn. 52 common pleas 50, §4406(a)		50, §4406(a)		at least 1. 50, §4406(a)		2 physicians or hospital report. 50, §4406(a)(4)		optional 50, §4406(a)(4)(ii)			fn. 53 50, §4406(a)(3)(iii)		
R.I. Gen. Laws Ann. (1968)	not stated		district 26-2-1	26-2-1		necessary for his own welfare. 26-2-1	2 26-2-2									
	not stated		fn. 54 supreme court 26-2-9		26-2-8	necessary for his own welfare or others. 26-2-9			fn. 55 3 commissioners 26-2-12	26-2-12				26-2-11		
S.C. Code Ann. (1962)		fn. 56 32-958	probate 32-958		32-960		fn. 2 1 32-958		2 physicians 32-960	32-961	32-1015	32-959 32-962	32-959 32-962		32-959 32-962	
S.D. Compiled Laws (1967)																
TENN. Code Ann. (1955)		fn. 57 33-604(a) (Supp. 1968)	county judge 33-604(2) (Supp. 1968)			mentally ill 33-604(d) (Supp. 1968)	fn. 2 2 33-604(a) (Supp. 1968)		1 witness must be a physician. 33-604(c) (Supp. 1969)		33-604(h) 33-607(b)	parent, guardian, spouse or adult next of kin. 33-604(b) (Supp. 1968)		33-604(b) (Supp. 1968)		
fn. 10 TEX. Rev. Civ. Stat. Ann. (1958)	5547-41		county 5547-41			fn. 58 5547-41(7)	1 5547-42	5547-41	2 physicians 5547-49(d) (Supp. 1969)			5547-44	5547-44	5547-44		7 days 5547-44
UTAH Code Ann. (1967)		fn. 59 64-7-36A	district 64-7-36A	64-7-36H(2)	64-7-36H(3)		fn. 2 1 64-7-36A		2 designated examiners. 64-7-36C	64-7-36F	64-7-38	64-7-36B 64-7-36G	64-7-36B 64-7-36G	64-7-36G		
VT. Stat. Ann. (1968)		fn. 60 18, §7601	probate 18, §7601	18, §7607(2)(A)	18, §7607(2)(B)		fn. 2 1 18, §7601		physician 18, §7603	18, §7605	18, §7506	18, §7606		18, §7606		
fn. 10 VA. Code Ann. (1953)	37.1-67 (Supp. 1968)		county and municipal. 37.1-1(11), 37.1-67 (Supp. 1968)			mentally ill 37.1-67 (Supp. 1968)					37.1-72 (Supp. 1968)			37.1-67 (Supp. 1968)		

Table 3.2   JUDICIAL HOSPITALIZATION OF THE MENTALLY ILL--PREHEARING PROCEDURES   continued

STATE	APPLICATION BY			CRITERIA FOR HOSPITALIZATION ORDER TO ISSUE			SUPPORTING EVIDENCE FOR APPLICATION		PREHEARING MEDICAL EXAMINATION ORDERED BY COURT	DISMISSAL AFTER MEDICAL EXAMINATION	INTERIM DETENTION PENDING HEARING OR REMOVAL TO HOSPITAL	NOTICE OF HEARING				Minimum Amount
	Any Person	Limited Group	COURT	Dangerous or Likely to Cause Injury	In Need of Treatment	Other	No. of Medical Certificates	Other Evidence				Guardian	Relative	Patient		
														Mandatory	Unless Harmful	
WASH. Rev. Code Ann. (1962)	71.02.090		superior 71.02.090	71.02.090				fn. 61 71.02.090	2 physicians 71.02.170		71.02.120	71.02.140	71.02.140		71.02.140	
W. VA. Code Ann. (1966¹)																
WIS. Stat. Ann. (1957)		fn. 62 51.01(1a) (Supp. 1969)	fn. 63 county 51.01(1a) (Supp. 1969)		51.02(5c)				1 physician and 1 psychiatrist if available. 51.01(2a)						51.02(1a) (Supp. 1969)	
WYO. Stat. Ann. (1967)		fn. 59 25-60(b)	fn. 64 district 25-60(a)	25-60(j)(ii)	25-60(j)(iii)		fn. 65 1 25-60(b)(f)	fn. 65 25-60(b)(ii)	1 or more examiners or physicians. 25-60(e)	25-60(f)	25-62	25-60(d) 25-60(h)	spouse also 25-60(d) 25-60(h)	25-60(h)		

1. Application may be made by a friend, relative, spouse, guardian, licensed physician, a health or public welfare officer, a head of a private or public hospital in which such individual may be. Draft Act 9; Idaho 66-329(a) (Supp. 1969); Mo. 202.807; N.M. 34-2-5(a).

2. Or statement from applicant that person refuses to submit to an examination. Draft Act 9(a); Idaho 66-329(a) (Supp. 1969); Minn. 253A.07 (Supp. 1969); Mo. 202.807; Nev. 433.685; N.M. 34-2-5(a); S.C. 32-958; Tenn. 33-604(a) (Supp. 1968); Utah 64-7-36; Vt. 18, §7601.

3. Interested party, licensed physician, peace officer, head of an institution, or department of health and welfare. Alas. 47.30.070.

4. "and because of his illness, lacks sufficient insight or capacity to make responsible decisions concerning hospitalization." Alas. 47.30.070(i)(2).

5. The court may consider the patient's choice in appointing an examiner. The court may direct that he be taken into custody and detained pending a hearing. Alas. 47.30.070(c), (d).

6. "A friend, relative, spouse or guardian, a health, public welfare or peace officer, attending physician or the head of any institution in which the proposed patient may be, may file in the Superior court. . . ." Ariz. 36-509A (Supp. 1970).

7. Notice may be dispensed with "on order of the court if two physicians state in writing under oath that personal service would in their opinion be detrimental to the proposed patient." If notice to patient is dispensed with, notice may be served on guardian, spouse, or adult next of kin, or person on whose premises the proposed patient is living. Ariz. 36-513A, D (Supp. 1970).

8. Arkansas has two methods of judicial hospitalization. The method charted above pertains to state residents outside the hospital who are dangerous to themselves or society. This method may be initiated by any health officer or licensed physician who certifies the above facts to the Probate Court for a hearing. 59-234 (Supp. 1967). The second method, charted in the lower row, may be initiated by any person. Ark. 59-101.

9. Any health officer or any regularly licensed or practicing physician shall make application. Ark. 59-234 (Supp. 1967).

10. Seven states give no authority for indeterminate commitment on initial disposition of the judicial proceeding. California, 90 days, W. & I. 5304 (Supp. 1968); Georgia, 5 days, 88-505.5 (Supp. 1969); Minnesota, 60 days, 253A.07(17)(c) and (25) (Supp. 1969); North Carolina, 180 days, 122-63; Ohio, 90 days, 5122.15; Texas, 60 days, 5547-40; and Virginia, 15 days, 37.1-79 (Supp. 1968).

11. "has threatened, attempted, or actually inflicted physical harm upon the person of another after having been taken into custody for evaluation and treatment, and, as a result of mental disorder or impairment by chronic alcoholism, presents an imminent threat of substantial physical harm to others." Cal. W. & I. 53-04 (Supp. 1968).

12. "is mentally ill, and a fit subject for treatment in a hospital for mental illness or that he ought to be confined. . . ." Conn. 17-178 (Supp. 1969).

13. D.C. has a prehearing examination, then a hearing before a commission, followed by a hearing in court. The latter hearing takes place only if the commission finds the person not sane. We have charted the final or court hearing. D.C. 21-541 to 21-545.

14. "by his spouse, parent, or legal guardian, by a physician, by a duly accredited officer or agent of the Department of Public Health, or by an officer authorized to make arrests." D.C. 21-541(a).

15. A medical certificate or a sworn written statement by petitioner that: "(A) the petitioner has good reason to believe that the person is mentally ill, and, because of the illness, is likely to injure himself or other person if allowed to remain at liberty; and (B) the person has refused to submit to examination by a physician." D.C. 21-541(a)(2).

16. Parent, sibling, spouse, child, next of kin, any 3 citizens, or, if none of the above, the sheriff; the patient, with a medical certificate; or the superintendent of the state prison farm. Fla. 394.22(2)(a) to 394.22(2)(e).

17. Two examiners are required if the individual has refused to submit to an examination prior to the filing of the application. Idaho 66-329(h) (Supp. 1969).

18. If no certificate accompanies the petition, the court may order an examination of the person. Ill. 91½, §8-1 (Supp. 1969).

19. Petition shall state names of witnesses by which alleged facts may be proven, and of the spouse, or nearest relative, or guardian, if known. Ill. 91½, §8-1 (Supp. 1969).

20. Two nearest relatives known to reside in the county. Ill. 91½, §8-7 (Supp. 1969).

21. If patient refuses to submit to an examination, the procedure charted in table 3.10 may be used. See Ind. 22-2903 to 22-2909.

22. If practicable, at least one of the examining physicians shall be

23. a qualified psychiatrist. Ind. 22-1215. Examinations are to be made separately. Ind. 22-1215.

24. There are two methods of involuntary hospitalization in Iowa: judicial and administrative. The "judicial" proceedings are used only to hospitalize persons in the state psychopathic hospital. Iowa 225.10, 225.14.

25. Judge of district or superior court shall cause person, or those legally responsible for him, to be served with notice of the hearing. Iowa 225.14.

26. Petition must state names of 2 witnesses by whom the truth of petition may be proved. If no certificate, court may allow such application to be accompanied by a verified statement by applicant that the "proposed patient" has refused to submit to an examination by a "physician." Kan. 59-2913 (Supp. 1968).

27. Notice to appointed attorney and to such other persons as the court shall direct. Kan. 59-2916 (Supp. 1968).

28. Application may be made by a friend, relative, or spouse or the individual's guardian, or by an authorized staff physician of a hospital or institution in which such individual is residing, or by any other physician or health officer. Ky. 202.135(1).

29. If hospitalization is in the best interest of the patient and of the community. La. 28:53(A) (Supp. 1969).

30. If no certificate, a written statement by applicant that the individual has refused to submit to examination by licensed physician. Me. 34, §2334; Nev. 433.685.

31. Spouse or parent or one of his adult children, or if such are unavailable, then to patient's next of kin or to a friend. Me. 34, §2334.

32. Notice is to inform patient that he has 48 hours to demand a hearing and may have an additional 72 hours to prepare his case. Mass. 123, §51.

33. Such petition to contain statement giving the facts and not the conclusions on which the application of such mental illness is based and because of which the application for the order is made. Mich. 330.12.

34. Notice of hearing may be served on relatives, and on person with whom mentally ill person may reside or at whose house such person may be, or on some person designated by the court. Mich. 330.21.

35. Court may use substitute service but must certify reasons for so doing. Guardian ad litem must be appointed if substitute service is used. Mich. 330.21.

35. Written statement that petitioner has been unable to obtain examination or it could not be performed. Minn. 253A.07(1) (Supp. 1969).

36. Two examiners shall be appointed, at least 1 of whom shall be a licensed physician, if the proposed patient is alleged to be mentally ill; otherwise the court shall appoint 2 licensed physicians and in addition thereto may appoint a person skilled in ascertaining mental deficiency to examine the proposed patient. Minn. 253A.07(2) (Supp. 1969).

37. Notice to be given to proposed patient, his counsel, 1 interested person other than his counsel, the petitioner and such other persons as the court directs. Minn. 253A.07(9) (Supp. 1969).

38. Examined by a psychiatrist or other qualified physician. Nev. 433.691.

39. This procedure may be ex parte. It is limited to insane persons in such condition as to be dangerous if left at large. The examination by 2 physicians is not mandatory, nor is a hearing. Ex parte hospitalization, however, is permitted only upon such examination and certification of 2 physicians that the patient is insane, and such other evidence as can be produced. The patient need not be given notice of the pending examination. In addition, the genuineness and respectability of the signatures to the medical certificate must be certified by a judge or other listed public official. N.H. 135:19, 135:20, 135:21.

40. Application may be made by a relative, spouse, guardian or public officer. N.J. 30:4-27 (Supp. 1970).

41. The provisions are only in reference to the hospitalization of persons already temporarily confined in institutions. N.J. 30:4-41 (Supp. 1970).

42. An application may be accompanied, or the probate court may require that it be accompanied, by a certificate of a licensed physician stating that he has examined the individual and is of the opinion that he is mentally ill and should be hospitalized, or a written statement by the applicant under oath, that the individual has refused to submit to an examination by a licensed physician. Ohio 5122.11.

43. Any one person designated by the individual named in the affidavit, or, if no selection, his attorney or adult next of kin. Ohio 5122.-12(E).

44. Father, mother, husband, wife, brother, sister or child over 18; or sheriff, superintendent or physician in charge of mental hospital or institution, or peace officer in county of patient's residence. Okla. 43A, §55 (Supp. 1969).

45. Statement of facts upon which allegation of mental illness is based. Okla. 43A, §55 (Supp. 1969).

46. Prehearing examination by commission to be composed of 2 physicians and 1 attorney. Okla. 43A, §54.

47. Father, mother, husband, wife or in their absence adult next of kin of full age; and also person with whom mentally ill person resides. Okla. 43A, §55 (Supp. 1969).

48. Notification may be made in writing under oath by 2 persons or by the county health officer or any magistrate. Ore. 426.070.

49. Or the circuit court if its jurisdiction has been extended to include commitment of the mentally ill pursuant to Ore. 3.275, 426.060, 426.070 (1967).

50. Two physicians, unless the county population is under 10,000, in which case one is sufficient. Alleged mentally ill person or his guardian, relative, or friend may nominate 1 additional physician. Ore. 426.110.

51. "The petition may be made by a relative, guardian, friend . . . or any responsible person." Pa. 50, §4406(a)(1).

52. "[A] petition may be presented to the court of common pleas of the county in which a person resides, or is . . ." Pa. 50, §4406(a).

53. When the hearing is to be held, the court shall notify the parties in interest. Pa. 50, §4406(a)(3)(iii).

54. On petition to a supreme court justice for hospitalization, the justice may appoint 3 commissioners to examine the subject and report their findings and recommendations. R.I. 26-2-9.

55. Supreme court justice may confirm or disallow commissioners' findings with or without further hearing. R.I. 26-2-12.

56. Application may be made "by a friend, relative, spouse or guardian of the individual or the superintendent of any public or private institution in which such individual may be." S.C. 32-958.

57. Application may be made by the parent, guardian, spouse or a responsible adult relative of the individual, or by any licensed physician, health or public welfare officer, or by the head of any institution in which the individual may be, or by any officer authorized to make arrests in Tennessee. Tenn. 33-604 (Supp. 1968).

58. "requires hospitalization in a mental hospital for his own welfare and protection or the protection of others. . . ." Tex. 5547-41(7).

59. Application may be made "by a friend, relative, spouse or guardian of the individual, or by a licensed physician, a health or public welfare or peace officer, or the head of any public or private institution in which such individual may be." Utah 64-7-36A; Wyo. 25-60.

60. "An interested party, a licensed physician, a head of a hospital, a selectman, a town service officer, or the commissioner . . ." Vt. 18, §7601.

61. Prosecuting attorney of the county, where the court has not designated some other person, must endorse on the application that he has examined the applicant, investigated the merits of the application, and believes reasonable grounds exist for filing same. Wash. 71-02-090.

62. Written application may be made "by at least three adult residents of the state, one of whom must be a person with whom the patient resides or at whose home he may be or a parent, child, spouse, brother, sister or friend of the patient, or the sheriff or a police officer or public welfare or health officer." Wis. 51.01(1a).

63. If judge of county court is unavailable, application may be made to any court of record. Wis. 51.01 (1b) (Supp. 1968).

Table 3.3   JUDICIAL HOSPITALIZATION OF THE MENTALLY ILL--HEARING AND POSTHEARING PROCEDURES

STATE	HEARING Mandatory	HEARING If Requested by Patient	HEARING HELD BEFORE REFEREE OR FACT-FINDING COMMISSION	HEARING PLACE Courtroom	HEARING PLACE Discretionary	PRESENCE OF PATIENT Mandatory	PRESENCE OF PATIENT Unless Harmful	PRESENCE OF PATIENT If Requested by Patient	JURY TRIAL Mandatory If Demanded by Patient	JURY TRIAL Left to Discretion of Judge	DISMISSAL OF JURY VERDICT OR FINDINGS	INSTITUTION'S DISCRETION — Suitable Hospital Accommodations Available	INSTITUTION'S DISCRETION — Mental Condition	REVIEW De Novo	REVIEW De Novo Jury Trial	PLACE OF HOSP. Public	PLACE OF HOSP. Private	PLACE OF HOSP. Home of Relatives	PERIOD OF HOSPITALIZATION
DRAFT ACT	9(e)		special commissioner optional. 9(i)		9(f)			9(f)				5				1(e)	1(e)		indeterminate or observational period not exceeding 6 months. 9(g)
ALA. Code (1958)	45, §210									45, §210		fn. 1 / 45, § 206	fn. 1 / 45, § 206			45, § 206			indeterminate. 45, § 210
ALAS. Stat. (1962)	47.30.070 (e)				47.30.070 (g)			47.30.070 (f)	47.30.070 (h)							47.30.070 (j)			indeterminate. 47.30.070 (f)
ARIZ. Rev. Stat. Ann. (1956) (Supp. 1970)	36-513			fnn. 2, 3 / 36-513B	36-513B											36-514C	36-514C		indeterminate. 36-514C
ARK. Stat. Ann. (1947)		59-234 (Supp. 1967)		fn. 4 / 59-234 (Supp. 1967)			fn. 5 / 59-234 (Supp. 1967)									59-234 (Supp. 1967)	59-234 (Supp. 1967)		indeterminate. 59-234 (Supp. 1967)
				59-101		59-101				59-101	fn. 6 / 59-105					fn. 7 / 59-103	59-234		indeterminate. 59-103
CAL. Welf. & Inst'ns Code (West 1966) (Supp. 1968)	5303			5303		patient is kept in custody, but must be represented by counsel. 5302, 5303			5303							5304	5304		90 days. 5304
COLO. Rev. Stat. Ann. (1964)																			
CONN. Gen. Stat. Ann. (1958)		17-178 (Supp. 1969)			17-178 (Supp. 1969)		fn. 8 / 17-178 (Supp. 1969)									17-182; & in Supp. 1969, 17-178 and 17-187a	17-182; & in Supp. 1969, 17-178 and 17-187a	fn. 9 / 17-176, 17-178 (Supp. 1969)	indeterminate. 17-178 (Supp. 1969)
DEL. Code Ann. (1953)																			

Table 3.3   JUDICIAL HOSPITALIZATION OF THE MENTALLY ILL--HEARING AND POSTHEARING PROCEDURES   *continued*

STATE	HEARING Mandatory	HEARING If Requested by Patient	HEARING HELD BEFORE REFEREE OR FACT-FINDING COMMISSION	HEARING PLACE Courtroom	HEARING PLACE Discretionary	PRESENCE OF PATIENT Mandatory	PRESENCE OF PATIENT Unless Harmful	PRESENCE OF PATIENT If Requested by Patient	JURY TRIAL Mandatory If Demanded by Patient	JURY TRIAL Left to Discretion of Judge	DISMISSAL OF JURY VERDICT OR FINDINGS	INSTITUTION'S DISCRETION — Suitable Hospital Accommodations Available	INSTITUTION'S DISCRETION — Mental Condition	REVIEW De Novo	REVIEW De Novo Jury Trial	PLACE Public	PLACE Private	PLACE Home of Relatives	PERIOD OF HOSPITALIZATION
(see fn. 13, Table 3.2) D.C. Code Ann. (1967)	21-545(a)		(See fn. 13 Table 3.2) 21-542(a)						21-545(a)							21-545(b) 21-548	21-545(b) 21-548	21-545(b)	indeterminate. 21-545(b)
FLA. Stat. Ann. (1960)	394.22(4)				394.22(4)	394.22(4)										394.22(13)	394.22(13)		indeterminate. 394.22(11) (a)
GA. Code Ann. (1963) (Supp. 1969)	88-505.3				88-505.3											evaluating facility. 88-505.5			5 days. 88-505.5
HAWAII Rev. Stat. Ann. (1968)																			
IDAHO Code Ann. (1949) (Supp. 1969)	66-329(d)		special commissioner optional at discretion of court. 66-329(f)		66-329(e)			66-329(g)								66-329(h)			indeterminate or observational period not exceeding 6 months. 66-329(h)
ILL. Ann. Stat. (Smith-Hurd 1966) (Supp. 1969)	91 1/2, §8-7		fn. 10 / 1 or more physicians optional. 91 1/2, § 9-3		91 1/2, §9-1		fn. 11 / 91 1/2, § 9-4		fn. 12 / 91 1/2, §9-2		91 1/2, §9-5	private only. 91 1/2, §9-6				91 1/2, §9-6	91 1/2, §9-6	91 1/2, §9-6	indeterminate or 1 year if placed in care and custody of private person. 91 1/2, §9-7
IND. Ann. Stat. (1964)	22-1217				22-1216						fn. 13 / 22-1208	22-1220 22-1225 22-1226				22-1201(5) (Supp. 1969) 22-1218			indeterminate. 22-1218
IOWA Code Ann. (1969)	225.14								225.14				225.15			225.14			indeterminate. 225.16 225.17
KAN. Stat. Ann. (1964) (Supp. 1968)	59-2917		2 physicians unless jury is demanded. 59-2917		in a physical setting not likely to have a harmful effect on the "proposed patient." 59-2917				fn. 14 / 59-2917			conditioned upon consent of such facility. 59-2917				59-2917	59-2917		indeterminate. 59-2917

Table 3.3 JUDICIAL HOSPITALIZATION OF THE MENTALLY ILL--HEARING AND POSTHEARING PROCEDURES *continued*

STATE	HEARING Mandatory	HEARING If Requested by Patient	HEARING HELD BEFORE REFEREE OR FACT-FINDING COMMISSION	HEARING PLACE Courtroom	HEARING PLACE Discretionary	PRESENCE OF PATIENT Mandatory	PRESENCE OF PATIENT Unless Harmful	PRESENCE OF PATIENT If Requested by Patient	JURY TRIAL Mandatory If Demanded by Patient	JURY TRIAL Left to Discretion of Judge	DISMISSAL OF JURY VERDICT OR FINDINGS	INSTITUTION'S DISCRETION Suitable Hospital Accommodations Available	INSTITUTION'S DISCRETION Mental Condition	REVIEW De Novo	REVIEW De Novo Jury Trial	PLACE Public	PLACE Private	PLACE Home of Relatives	PERIOD OF HOSPITALIZATION
KY. Rev. Stat. Ann. (1969)	202.135(4)				202.135(5)		fn. 15 202.135(5)					202.230(1)				202.010(6) 202.135(6)	202.010(6) 202.135(6)		indeterminate. 202.135(6)
LA. Rev. Stat. Ann. (1950)	28:55 (Supp. 1969)		coroner and 2 physicians optional. 28:54		28:55 (Supp. 1969)	28:55 (Supp. 1969)										28:2(8)	28:2(8)		indeterminate. 28:55 (Supp. 1969)
ME. Rev. Stat. Ann. (1964)	34, §2334		special commissioner optional. 34, §2334		34, §2334			34, §2334								34, §2334	34, §2334		indeterminate. 34, §2334
MD. Ann. Code (1968)																			
MASS. Ann. Laws (1965)		fn. 16 123, § 51			123, § 51			123, § 51								123, § 51	123, § 51		indeterminate. 123, § 51
MICH. Comp. Laws Ann. (1967)	330.21				330.21		fn. 17 330.21		fnn. 18, 19 330.21	fn. 18 330.21		330.21				330.21	330.21		indeterminate or limited period of intensive treatment (60 days). 330.21
MINN. Stat. Ann. (1959) (Supp. 1969)	253A.07(8)				253A.07(13)			253A.07(12)	253A.07(17)			upon consent. 253A.07(17)				253A.07(17)	253A.07(17)		60 days; indeterminate if further care required. 253A.07(17)(c) 253A.07(25)
MISS. Code Ann. (1952)																			
MO. Rev. Stat. (1959)	202.807(2)				202.807.4			202.807.3				202.793				202.793	202.793		indeterminate or observational period not exceeding 6 months. 202.807(5)
MONT. Rev. Codes Ann. (1961)	38-201(1)				38-201(3)	38-201(3)									38-213	38-208			indeterminate. 38-208

82

Table 3.3 JUDICIAL HOSPITALIZATION OF THE MENTALLY ILL--HEARING AND POSTHEARING PROCEDURES *continued*

STATE	HEARING — Mandatory	HEARING — If Requested by Patient	HEARING HELD BEFORE REFEREE OR FACT-FINDING COMMISSION	HEARING PLACE — Courtroom	HEARING PLACE — Discretionary	PRESENCE OF PATIENT — Mandatory	PRESENCE OF PATIENT — Unless Harmful	PRESENCE OF PATIENT — If Requested by Patient	JURY TRIAL — Mandatory If Demanded by Patient	JURY TRIAL — Left to Discretion of Judge	JURY TRIAL — Dismissal of Jury Verdict or Findings	INSTITUTION'S DISCRETION AS TO ADMISSION — Suitable Hospital Accommodations Available	INSTITUTION'S DISCRETION AS TO ADMISSION — Mental Condition	REVIEW OF HOSPITALIZATION ORDER — De Novo	REVIEW OF HOSPITALIZATION ORDER — De Novo Jury Trial	PLACE OF HOSPITALIZATION — Public	PLACE OF HOSPITALIZATION — Private	PLACE OF HOSPITALIZATION — Home of Relatives	PERIOD OF HOSPITALIZATION
NEB. Rev. Stat. (1966)																			
NEV. Rev. Stat. (1967)	433.691(1)				433.691(1)	433.691(2)										433.697			indeterminate. 433.695(2)
N.H. Rev. Stat. Ann. (1964)	fn. 20 135:19	fn. 20											fn. 21 135:23			135:1 135:19	135:25		indeterminate. 135:19
N.J. Stat. Ann. (1964) (Supp. 1970)	30:4-41		fn. 22 county adjuster optional. 30:4-42	not stated.			30:4-41			30:4-42						30:4-56 to 30:4-59	30:4-27		indeterminate. 30:4-107
N.M. Stat. Ann. (1953)	34-2-5(f)		fn. 23 special commissioner optional. 34-2-5(i)		34-2-5(f)			34-2-5(f)								fn. 24 34-2-5(i)	34-2-5(j)		indeterminate or observational period not exceeding 6 months. 34-2-5(g)(3)
fn. 25 N.Y. Mental Hygiene Law (McKinney 1951) (Supp. 1970)		72.3	referee optional. 72.3		72.3									fn. 26 74	fn. 26 74	72.3	72.3	at some place other than a hospital. 72.3	period not to exceed 6 months. 73.1
N.C. Gen. Stat. (1964)	122-63 122-64				122-64	122-64						122-63				122-63			period not exceeding 180 days. 122-63
N.D. Cent. Code (1960)																			
OHIO Rev. Code Ann. (Baldwin 1964)	5122.15		referee optional. 5122.15		5122.15			5122.15	fn. 27 specifically prohibited. 5122.15							5122.15	5122.15	5122.15	90 days. 5122.15
OKLA. Stat. Ann. (1954) (Supp. 1969)	43A, §55 (Supp. 1969)			not stated.			fn. 28 43A, §55 (Supp. 1969)		fn. 29 43A, §55 (Supp. 1969)	fn. 29 43A, §55 (Supp. 1969)						43A, §51	43A, §55; 43A, §183 (Supp. 1969)		indeterminate. 43A, §55 (Supp. 1969)
ORE. Rev. Stat. (1967)	426.120			not stated.		426.070										426.060	fn. 30 426.130	fn. 30 426.130	indeterminate. 426.120

Table 3.3   JUDICIAL HOSPITALIZATION OF THE MENTALLY ILL--HEARING AND POSTHEARING PROCEDURES   *continued*

STATE	HEARING Mandatory	HEARING If Requested by Patient	HEARING HELD BEFORE REFEREE OR FACT-FINDING COMMISSION	HEARING PLACE Courtroom	HEARING PLACE Discretionary	PRESENCE OF PATIENT Mandatory	PRESENCE OF PATIENT Unless Harmful	PRESENCE OF PATIENT If Requested by Patient	JURY TRIAL Mandatory If Demanded by Patient	JURY TRIAL Left to Discretion of Judge	DISMISSAL OF JURY VERDICT OR FINDINGS	INSTITUTION'S DISCRETION AS TO ADMISSION Suitable Hospital Accommodations Available	INSTITUTION'S DISCRETION AS TO ADMISSION Mental Condition	REVIEW De Novo	REVIEW De Novo Jury Trial	PLACE Public	PLACE Private	PLACE Home of Relatives	PERIOD OF HOSPITALIZATION
PA. Stat. Ann. (1969)	50, §4406(a)(3)			not stated.		50, §4406(a)(3)(i)										50, §4102 50, §4406(b)			indetermi-nate. 50, §4406(b)
R.I. Gen. Laws Ann. (1968)	26-2-1				fn. 31 26-2-2	26-2-1										26-2-3	26-2-3		indetermi-nate. 26-2-3
26-2-11	26-2-11		3 commis-sioners. 26-2-9			26-2-11					26-2-12					26-2-9	26-2-9		indetermi-nate. 26-2-12
S.C. Code Ann. (1962)	32-961				32-962			32-962							32-967	32-963	32-965		indetermi-nate. 32-963
S.D. Compiled Laws Ann. (1967)																			
Tenn. Code Ann. (1955) (Supp. 1968)	33-604(c)		county judge or chairman of the county court. 33-604(c)		33-604(c)			33-604(c)							33-604(e)				indetermi-nate or ob-servational period not exceeding 6 months. 33-604(d)
TEX. Rev. Civ. Stat. Ann. (1958)	5547-43				5547-49(a) (Supp. 1969)			5547-49(b) (Supp. 1969)	5547-48					5547-57	5547-57	5547-58	5547-58		60 days. 5547-40
UTAH Code Ann. (1967)	54-7-36F		special commis-sioner. 64-7-36(J)		64-7-36(G)			64-7-36(G)								64-7-38	64-7-38		indetermi-nate or ob-servational period not exceeding 6 months. 64-7-36 (H)(3)
VT. Stat. Ann. (1968)	18, §7605				18, §7606			18, §7606					18, §7702			18, §7101 (7)	18, §7101 (7)		indetermi-nate. 18, §7607 (2)(B)
VA. Code Ann. (1953) (Supp. 1968)		37.1-67, 37.1-81				37.1-67, 37.1-81							37.1-70			37.1-1(8)	37.1-1(8)		indetermi-nate after hearing or judicial approval within 6 months. 37.1-83

84

Table 3.3 JUDICIAL HOSPITALIZATION OF THE MENTALLY ILL--HEARING AND POSTHEARING PROCEDURES *continued*

STATE	HEARING		HEARING PLACE			PRESENCE OF PATIENT			JURY TRIAL			INSTITUTION'S DISCRETION AS TO ADMISSION		REVIEW OF HOSPITALIZATION ORDER		PLACE OF HOSPITALIZATION			PERIOD OF HOSPITALIZATION
	Mandatory	If Requested by Patient	Hearing Held Before Referee or Fact-Finding Commission	Courtroom	Discretionary	Mandatory	Unless Harmful	If Requested by Patient	Mandatory If Demanded by Patient	Left to Discretion of Judge	Dismissal of Jury Verdict or Findings	Suitable Hospital Accommodations Available	Mental Condition	De Novo	De Novo Jury Trial	Public	Private	Home of Relatives	
WASH. Rev. Code Ann. (1962)	71.02.140				71.02.160				71.02.210			71.02.450 (Supp. 1968)	fn. 32 72.23.270			71.02.240 (1)	71.02.240 (3)	71.02.240 (4)	indeterminate. 71.02.240
W. VA. Code Ann. (1966)																			
WIS. Stat. Ann. (1957)	51.02(2)				51.02(2)	Judge must personally observe patient before decision. 51.02(2)			51.03							51.05(1)			indeterminate. 51.05(1) (Supp. 1969)
WYO. Stat. Ann. (1967)	25-60(f)		fn. 33 25-60(k)		25-60(h)			25-60(h)	25-60(i)					25-72(b)					indeterminate. 25-60(j)

Notes to Table 3.3   JUDICIAL HOSPITALIZATION OF THE MENTALLY ILL--HEARING AND POSTHEARING PROCEDURES

1. When the hospitals are crowded, the superintendent may limit his acceptances to patients who are offensively troublesome, vicious, etc., and may decline those who are harmless or helpless. He may arrange with the probate judge to exchange harmless patients in the hospital for those who are dangerous. Ala. 45, §206.

2. Hearing must be held in open court if demanded by patient, his guardian, spouse, or adult next of kin, or by his attorney. Ariz. 36-413E (Supp. 1970).

3. Hearing shall be held in the courtroom or other place within the county which the court may designate to insure humane treatment. Ariz. 36-513B (Supp. 1970).

4. "Whereupon said court shall hold a hearing either in regular term or in vacation in chambers. . . ." Ark. 57-234 (Supp. 1967).

5. "The presence of such person before the Court need not be required." Ark. 59-234 (Supp. 1967).

6. The judge may set aside the jury's verdict if just cause appears; when 2 juries concur in any case, the verdict shall not be set aside. Ark. 50-105 (Supp. 1967).

7. ". . . the lunatic asylum, if there be one in the State." Ark. 59-103.

8. "[C]ourt may also issue a warrant for the apprehension and bringing before it of the person complained of, and shall see and examine such person, if in its judgment his condition or conduct renders it necessary or advisable to do so, or state in its final order why it was not necessary or advisable to do so." Conn. 17-178 (Supp. 1969).

9. ". . . for his commitment to a hospital for mental illness. . . ." Conn. 17-178 (Supp. 1969).

10. If no such demand is made, the court may appoint a commission of 1 or more physicians to conduct an examination and make findings. Ill. 91½, §9-2 (Supp. 1969).

11. If it is harmful for the patient to appear, then the judge, and jury if there is one, shall personally observe and confer with the patient. Ill. 91½, §9-4 (Supp. 1969).

12. A person alleged to be mentally ill, his spouse, any relative or friend, or an attorney may demand a jury trial by 6 persons. Ill. 91½, §9-2 (Supp. 1969).

13. If at any time during judicial proceedings the patient applies for voluntary admission to the psychiatric hospital in the district where he has legal settlement or to a federal or private institution, the court may dismiss the proceedings provided the head of the hospital concerned consents to the patient's admission. Ind. 22-1208.

14. The jury is to consist of 6 persons. Kan. 59-2917 (Supp. 1968).

15. Oath or affidavit of 2 physicians is required to dispense with patient's presence. Ky. 202.130.

16. If the person does not request a hearing, the court may order hospitalization on the application, medical certification (from prehearing medical examination), and any other evidence it may require. Mass. 123, §51.

17. Patient has right to be present at hearing unless 2 physicians or the medical superintendent in charge of the hospital where patient is under observation certify that his appearance would be improper and unsafe. Mich. 330.21.

18. If the court shall deem it necessary, or if patient or any relative of person with whom patient resides shall so demand, the issue shall be tried by a jury of 6 freeholders. Mich. 330.21.

19. Selection of such jury shall be done in the same manner as is provided for the selection of a jury for the condemnation of land for railroad purposes. Mich. 330.21.

20. Statute provides: "[T]he judge of probate . . . may commit such insane person . . . and such petition may be filed, notice issued, and hearing had in vacation or otherwise." N.H. 135:19.

21. Pursuant to rules and regulations established by the superintendent of the state hospital, the hospital may receive and detain therein as a patient any person who is emotionally or mentally ill. N.H. 135:23.

22. Examination of witnesses may be referred to county adjuster. N.J. 30:4-42 (Supp. 1970).

23. Commissioner recommends disposition of case to court after an examination and before a hearing. N.M. 34-2-5(i).

24. Includes provision for hospitalization in U.S. government hospital if eligible and space available. N.M. 34-2-6.

25. These procedures refer to a judicial hearing conducted after the expiration of 60-day medical certification.

26. If the retention order has been authorized, the patient or his relative or friend have 30 days thereafter to demand a jury trial in a proceedings to review the order. N.Y. Mental Hygiene Law 74.7, 76 (Supp. 1970).

27. The hearing shall be conducted without a jury. Ohio 5122.15.

28. Sanity commission or hospital where patient is temporarily hospitalized must certify that his presence will be improper and unsafe. Okla. 34A, §55 (Supp. 1969).

29. If the court or judge deem it necessary, or at the request of the patient, a relative, a friend, or person with whom he resides, a jury of 6 persons shall be summoned. Okla. 43A, §55 (Supp. 1969).

30. If the patient is nondangerous, he may be paroled to a relative or friend for placement in a facility satisfactory to the judge. This parole can be revoked upon finding that it is in the best interest of the patient. Ore. 426.130.

31. If 2 physicians certify that to testify in open court would prejudice welfare of patient. R.I. 26-2-2.

32. "No case of idiocy, imbecility, harmless chronic mental unsoundness, or acute mania a potu shall be hospitalized in a state hospital; and whenever, in the opinion of the superintendent after careful examination of the case of any person hospitalized, it shall be ascertained that such person comes within the rule of exemptions provided for by this section, the superintendent shall have the authority to discharge such person and return him to the county which ordered him hospitalized." Wash. 72.23.270.

33. The court is authorized to appoint a special commissioner to assist in the conduct of hospitalization proceedings. Regularly appointed court commissioners may also function herein in the absence of the district judge from the county. Wyo. 25-60(k).

Table 3.4 ADMINISTRATIVE HOSPITALIZATION--PREHEARING PROCEDURES *

STATE	APPLICATION By	APPLICATION To	SUPPLEMENTARY MEDICAL CERTIFICATE	CRITERIA: Dangerous or Likely to Cause Injury	CRITERIA: In Need of Treatment	CRITERIA: Other	TRIBUNE: Membership	TRIBUNE: Standing Tribunal	TRIBUNE: Court Appointment for Each Case	TRIBUNE: Quasi-judicial Powers	PREHEARING MEDICAL EXAMINATION	INTERIM DETENTION PENDING HEARING OR REMOVAL TO HOSPITAL	NOTICE: Relatives	NOTICE: Guardian	NOTICE Patient: Mandatory	NOTICE Patient: Unless Harmful	MINIMUM NOTICE
COLO. Rev. Stat. Ann. (1964)	any reputable person. 71-1-5(1) (Supp. 1966)	district or probate court. 71-1-5(1) (Supp. 1966)	licensed physician. 71-1-5(1) (Supp. 1966)		71-1-7(2)(c)	welfare of self and others. 71-1-7(2)(b)	2 licensed doctors. 71-1-6(1) (Supp. 1966)		71-1-6(1) (Supp. 1966)	71-1-7(1)		71-1-5 (Supp. 1966)		fn. 1 71-1-5(1) (Supp. 1966)	71-1-6(2) (Supp. 1966)		2 days to guardian ad litem. 71-1-5(1) (Supp. 1966) 5 days to patient. 71-1-6(2)
DEL. Code Ann. (1953)	fn. 2	board of trustees of the dept. of mental health. 16, §5124(a)			suffering from mental or nervous disease. 16, §5124(c)		2 physicians or jury of 6 persons. 16-5124(b)		fn. 3 16, §5124(a) 16, §5124(b)	16, §5124(d)							
GA. Code Ann. (1963) (Supp. 1969)	any person. 88-507.2	court of ordinary. 88-507.2	88-507.2	88-507.1(a)		incapable of caring for physical health and safety. 88-507.1(b)	fn. 4 2 physicians, 1 attorney. 88-507.3(b)		88-507.3(b)	88-507.3(f)		88-507.3(d)	representatives. 88-507.3(c)	representatives. 88-507.3(c)	88-507.3(c)		
IOWA Code Ann. (1969) fn. 5	any person. 229.1	superintendent of the state hospital. 229.1			229.9		clerk of district court, physician, attorney. 228.2	fn. 6 228.3		229.3	1 physician 229.6	229.2, 229.24 (Supp. 1969)					
MISS. Code Ann. (1952)	any citizen. 6909-03	chancery. 6909-03		6909-03	6903-03		2 physicians. 6909-04		6909-04			6909-03					
NEB. Rev. Stat. (1966)	any person. 83-323	county board of mental health. 83-322 83-325 (Supp. 1967)			fn. 7 83-328 (Supp. 1967)		fn. 8 clerk of district court, 1 physician, and 1 lawyer appointed by judge of district court. 83-317	fn. 8 83-317	for 2 or 3 days. 83-317	83-320	1 physician. 83-326						
N.D. Cent. Code (1960)	guardian, friend, relative, spouse, physician, public official. 25-03-11(1)	mental health board. 25-03-11(1)	fn. 9 25-03-11(1)	25-03-11(7a)	25-03-11(7b)		county judge, 1 physician, 1 attorney. 25-02-11	fn. 10 25-02-11		25-02-16	1 physician. 25-03-11(3)	25-03-13(b) 25-03-23	25-03-11(5) (2)	25-03-11(5) (2)		25-03-11(5) (2)	
R.I. Gen Laws Ann. (1968)		supreme court. 26-2-9				welfare of such person or others. 26-2-9	3 commissioners. 26-2-9		26-2-9	26-2-11		26-2-10			26-2-11		
S.D. Compiled Laws Ann. (1967)	any person. 27-7-2	chairman of county board of mental illness. 27-7-2			fn. 11 27-7-2		county judge, state's attorney, 1 physician. 27-6-1	21-6-2, 27-6-1		27-6-5			27-7-6			27-7-5	5 days 27-7-8
W. VA. Code Ann. (1966)	fn. 12 27-5-4	clerk of county court. 27-5-4	1 certificate 27-5-4	27-5-4		27-5-4	judge, county clerk, prosecuting attorney. 27-3-1	27-3-1		27-5-4	2 physicians, 27-5-4		27-5-4	27-5-4	27-5-4		5 days 27-5-4

*The Notes for Table 3.4 follow Table 3.5.

Table 3.5 ADMINISTRATIVE HOSPITALIZATION--HEARING AND POSTHEARING PROCEDURES

STATE	MANDATORY HEARING	HEARING PLACE		PRESENCE OF PATIENT			RIGHT TO JUDICIAL REVIEW OF HOSPITAL ORDER		ENLARGED STATUTORY PROVISION FOR HABEAS CORPUS	PLACE OF HOSPITALIZATION			PERIOD OF HOSPITALIZATION
		Court Room	Discretionary	Mandatory	Mandatory Unless Harmful	If Patient Requests	Hearing Before Judge	Jury on Review		Public	Private	Home of Relative	
COLO. Rev. Stat. Ann. (1964)	71-1-6(2) (Supp. 1966)		71-1-6(3) (Supp. 1966)		not stated		71-1-13(1) (Supp. 1966)	6 persons. 71-1-13(2)		71-1-11(2) (Supp. 1966)	71-1-11(2) (Supp. 1966)	71-1-11(2) (Supp. 1966)	Indeterminate, 71-1-11(2) (Supp. 1966)
fn. 2 DEL. Code Ann. (1953)	fn. 13 ex parte. 16, §5124(d)	not stated	not stated	fn. 13 16, §124(d)			16, §5124(e)	16, §5126(b)		16, §5124(a)			Indeterminate, 16, §5124(a)
GA. Code Ann. (1963)	88-507.3(b) (Supp. 1969)		88-507.3(f) (Supp. 1969)		not stated				88-502.11(2) (Supp. 1969)	treatment facility, 88-507.3(h) (Supp. 1969)			6 months. 88-507.3(j) (Supp. 1969)
IOWA Code Ann. (1969)	229.2	not stated	not stated		229.4		229.17	229.17	229.37	229.9	229.9		Indeterminate. 229.9 (Supp. 1969)
MISS. Code Ann. (1952)	6909-05	fn. 14 6909-05		fn. 14 6909-05			6909-08			2909-07			Indeterminate. 6909-07
NEB. Rev. Stat. (1966)	can be ex parte. 83-325 (Supp. 1967)		office of clerk of court. 83-318		unless deemed unnecessary or injurious, 83-325 (Supp. 1967)		83-328.03		83-343	83-328 (Supp. 1967)			Indeterminate, 88-328
N.D. Cent. Code (1960)	25-03-11(5)		25-03-11(6)			25-03-11(6)			fn. 15 25-03-21	02-03-11(7)	or other suitable place, 25-03-11(7)	25-03-11(7)	Indeterminate. 25-03-11(7)
R.I. Gen. Laws Ann. (1968)	26-2-11					26-2-11			26-3-10	26-2-15	26-2-15		Indeterminate. 26-2-12
S.D. Compiled Laws Ann. (1967)	27-7-5	not stated	not stated			27-7-13	not stated			27-7-18			Indeterminate. 27-7-18
W. VA. Code Ann. (1966)	27-5-4		27-3-2			fn. 16 27-5-4	27-5-5			27-5-4	fn. 17 27-5-4	fn. 17 27-5-4	Indeterminate or observational period not exceeding 6 months. 27-5-4

Notes to Table 3.4 & 3.5   ADMINISTRATIVE HOSPITALIZATION--PREHEARING, HEARING, AND POSTHEARING PROCEDURES

1. Appointment of guardian ad litem is mandatory. Colo. 71-1-8 (1964). This method of hospitalization is used for any mental hospital except psychopathic hospital at the state medical school.

2. Del. 16, §5124, provides for administrative hospitalization for an indeterminate period of patients of the state mental hospital. However, the operative application-- a report by the superintendent--is no longer provided for in the Delaware statutes. It thus appears that the procedure set out here cannot be commenced.

3. Commission is appointed by board of trustees. Any person related to patient by blood or marriage can request board to summon a 6-man jury. Del. 16, §5124(a).

4. Three reputable persons, two of whom are practicing medical physicians in good standing, said physicians to be residents of the county, if that number reside therein, and the county attorney, or some attorney of the county. Ga. 88-507.3(b) (Supp. 1969).

5. Commission first orders temporary hospitalization at the screening center. No final hospitalization order can be issued until superintendent of hospital where screening center is located shall find and recommend that such order shall be issued. Iowa 229.9.

6. Commission is appointed by district court for 2-year terms arranged so that the tenure of one member will expire each year. Iowa 228.3.

7. If the board finds that the person alleged to be mentally ill is mentally ill and should be admitted to a state hospital, and whether or not his legal settlement is in its county, and if not in its county, where it is, if ascertained (Neb. 83-328 (Supp. 1967)), it shall issue a warrant authorizing the superintendent of the hospital to receive him. Neb. 83-328 (Supp. 1967).

8. Appointed by judge or judges for 2-year terms. Neb. 83-317.

9. Or statement from applicant that person refuses to submit to an examination. N.D. 25-03.11(1).

10. Physician and attorney appointed by board of county commissioners for 2-year terms. N.D. 25-02-11.

11. Fit subject for treatment and custody in hospital. S.D. 27-7-2.

12. Parent, guardian, adult next of kin, spouse, friend, physician, health officer, public welfare caseworker familiar with the case, or the head of any institution in which such individual may be. W.Va. 27-5-4.

13. No investigation by the jury or commission shall be had except in the presence of the patient. The jury or commission may take testimony and administer oaths. Del. 16, §5124(d).

14. Inquiry and examination must be held in presence of the clerk and in the courtroom, or clerk's office unless the patient is physically unable to appear there. Miss. 6909-05.

15. All patients confined or hospitalized as mentally ill or as requiring treatment or observation in any hospital shall be entitled to the benefit of the writ of habeas corpus, and the question of mental illness or of the necessity of treatment or observation in a hospital shall be decided at such a hearing. N.D. 25-03-21.

16. The proposed patient shall be afforded an opportunity to appear at the hearing, but his presence shall not be required; a guardian ad litem who is a competent attorney shall be appointed and shall be present at the hearing to protect the individual's interests. W.Va. 27-5-4.

17. "In lieu of ordering the patient to a State hospital, the mental hygiene commission may order him delivered to some responsible person who will agree to take care of him, and take from such responsible person a bond in the penalty of at least five hundred dollars, . . . with condition to restrain and take proper care of such person until the further order of the court or judge. But if the person found to be a mentally ill or mentally retarded person is not dangerous to himself or others, or is found harmless, he may be delivered to any responsible person who will agree to take proper care of him without such bond . . . ." W. Va. 27-5-4.

Table 3.6 INVOLUNTARY HOSPITALIZATION BY MEDICAL CERTIFICATION

STATE	LIMIT ON PLACE OF HOSPITALIZATION	APPLICATION BY — Any Person	APPLICATION BY — Health, Welfare, or Peace Officer or Hospital Physician	APPLICATION BY — Attorney, Guardian, Relative, Friend, Spouse, or Person at Whose House Residing	NUMBER OF CERTIFICATES REQUIRED	FURTHER APPROVAL BY	CRITERIA FOR ADMISSION — Pro-testing Patient	CRITERIA FOR ADMISSION — Nonpro-testing Patient	HOSPITAL ADMISSION REPORTED TO	ADMISSION DISCRETIONARY — Availability of Suitable Accommodations in Hospital	ADMISSION DISCRETIONARY — Mental Condition	ADMISSION DISCRETIONARY — Unspecified	PATIENT TOLD OF RIGHT TO OBJECT, RELEASE, OR REVIEW	REVIEW — By Superior Court or Habeas Corpus	REVIEW — Jury on Review	ADMINISTRATIVE RELEASE	RELEASE UPON NOTICE — Release on Patient's Request	RELEASE UPON NOTICE — Release on Other's Request	RELEASE UPON NOTICE — Time After Notice	RELEASE UPON NOTICE — Extension Provision	MAXIMUM PERIOD OF HOSPITALIZATION
DRAFT ACT			5(a), 6(a)(1), Commentary 5	5(a), 6(a)(1), Commentary 5	2 designated examiners. 6(a)(2)	Judge or court of record or local health board. 6(b)	likely to injure himself or others. 6(a)(2)	in need of treatment. 6(a)(2)(c)	central administration 6(a)	5			17(b)			15	17(a)	fn. 1 17(a)	48 hours 17(a)	5 days 17(a)	indeterminate 6
ALAS. Stat. (1962)	state-operated or state-designated. 47.30.020	47.30.020 (2)	47.30.020 (2)	by interested party. 47.30.020 (2)	47.30.020 (2)		likely to injure himself or others. 47.30.040 (b)	in need of treatment. 47.30.040 (b)	legal guardian, parent, spouse, or next of kin, if known. 47.30.120			47.30.020	47.30.050 (b)	47.30.100		47.30.040 (b)	47.30.050 (a)	47.30.050 (a)	fn. 2 48 hours 47.30.050 (a)(3)	15 days 47.30.050 (a)(3)	indeterminate 47.30.040 (b)
fn. 3 ARIZ. Rev. Stat. Ann. (1956) (Supp. 1970)	state or other designated. 36-505A.2	36-505A.1	36-505A.1	36-505A.1	2 designated examiners. 36-505A.2	fn. 3 superior court. 36-505A.1	judicial procedure only. 36-509	mentally ill 36-505A.2	fn. 4 guardian, spouse, adult next of kin. 36-519			36-505(A)	fn. 5 36-505B			36-506A	36-506B	36-506B	72 hours 36-506B	fn. 6 5 days 36-506B	indeterminate 36-505C 36-506A
fn. 7 ARK. Stat. Ann. (1947)	state 59-232 (Supp. 1967)		59-232 (Supp. 1967)		1 59-232 (Supp. 1967)		harmful to self or society. 59-234 (Supp. 1967)	acute psychosis 59-232 (Supp. 1967)				59-232 (Supp. 1967)		habeas corpus 59-236		59-236	59-236		fn. 8 30 days 59-236	fn. 8 59-236	indeterminate 59-232 (Supp. 1967)
fn. 9 CAL. Welf. & Inst'ns Code (West 1966) (Supp. 1968)	county designated. 5250(c)		5250(a)		2 5251	facility providing intensive treatment. 5250(c)	danger to self or others, or gravely disabled. 5250(a)		patient's attorney, district attorney, public defender, facility providing intensive treatment, state dept. of mental hygiene, and a person designated by patient. 5253	5250(c)			5252 5275 5276	5275 5276		mandatory after 14 days 5254	5275	5275	fn. 10 5276		14 days 5254
DEL. Code Ann. (1953)	state hospital 16, §5125 (Supp. 1970)				fn. 11 2 physicians 16, §5125 (Supp. 1970)		16-5124 (4)(i) likely to injure himself. 16, §6125 (4) (Supp. 1970)	in need of treatment. 16, §5125 (d) (Supp. 1970)				16, §5121 to 16, §5124 (Supp. 1970)		chancery 16, §5126	mandatory 16, §5126	16, §5132 (a) (Supp. 1970)					indeterminate 16, §5125 (Supp. 1968)

Table 3.6 INVOLUNTARY HOSPITALIZATION BY MEDICAL CERTIFICATION *continued*

STATE	LIMIT ON PLACE OF HOSPITALIZATION	APPLICATION BY — Any Person	APPLICATION BY — Health, Welfare, or Peace Officer or Hospital Physician	APPLICATION BY — Attorney, Guardian, Relative, Spouse, Friend, or Person at Whose House Residing	NUMBER OF CERTIFICATES REQUIRED	FURTHER APPROVAL BY	CRITERIA FOR ADMISSION — Protesting Patient	CRITERIA FOR ADMISSION — Nonprotesting Patient	HOSPITAL ADMISSION REPORTED TO	ADMISSION DISCRETIONARY — Availability of Suitable Accommodations in Hospital	ADMISSION DISCRETIONARY — Mental Condition	ADMISSION DISCRETIONARY — Unspecified	PATIENT TOLD OF RIGHT TO OBJECT, RELEASE, OR REVIEW	REVIEW — By Superior Court or Habeas Corpus	REVIEW — Jury on Review	ADMINISTRATIVE RELEASE	RELEASE UPON NOTICE — Release on Patient's Request	RELEASE UPON NOTICE — Release on Other's Request	RELEASE UPON NOTICE — Time After Notice	RELEASE UPON NOTICE — Extension Provision	MAXIMUM PERIOD OF HOSPITALIZATION
D.C. Code Ann. (1967)	public or private. 21-513			friend or relative. 21-513	fn. 12 21-513		judicial determination only. 21-513	in need of treatment. 21-513		private only 21-513	21-513		21-513	21-514		21-514	written 21-514		none 21-514	fn. 13 21-514	indeterminate 21-513
FLA. Stat. Ann. (1960) (Supp. 1969)	no state 394.191(1)		394.201(1)(a)1	394.201(1)(a)1	2 physicians 394.201(1)(a)2	fn. 14 394.201(1)(b)	likely to injure himself or others 394.201(1)(a) 2a	in need of treatment. 394.201(1)(a) 2b	county judge, guardian or next of kin. 394.201(1)(a)2			394.201(1)(a)	394.201(3)(a)	394.201(5)(c)		394.201(5)(4)	394.201(4)	394.201(4)	forthwith 394.201(4)	5 days 394.201(4)(b)	indeterminate 394.201(1)(a)
fnn. 9, 15 GA. Code Ann. (1963) (Supp. 1969)	public 88-506.3		superintendent 88-506.3		2 88-506.3		if in need of continued hospitalization. 88-505.3 88-505.5					88-506.3	88-506.3	88-506.3		88-506.3					6 months 88-506.3
HAWAII Rev. Stat. Ann. (1968)	public or private. 334-1 334-53(2)	any responsible person. 334-53(a)		334-53(a)	2 334-53(a)	administrator or his deputy. 334-53(b)	mentally ill 334-53(a)		spouse, relative, or friend. 334-53(c)			334-53	334-53(c) 334-81				fn. 16 334-81	fn. 16 334-81			indeterminate 334-53(a)
fn. 9 ILL. Ann. Stat. (Smith-Hurd) 1966	state or licensed private. 91½, §6-1 (Supp. 1969)	91½, §6-1 (Supp. 1969)			1 91½, §6-1 (Supp. 1969)	1 psychiatrist, upon examination instigated by hospital superintendent. 91½, §6-2 (Supp. 1969)	physically unable to injure himself or others. 91½, §1-11, 91½, §6-1 (Supp. 1969)	unable to care for himself. 91½, §1-11, 91½, §6-1 (Supp. 1969)	court of the county of the hospital; patient's attorney; patient's nearest relative reasonably ascertainable; and at least 2 of any persons designated by the patient. 91½, §6-3 (Supp. 1969)			91½, §6-1 (Supp. 1969)	91½, §6-3 (Supp. 1969)	fn. 17 91½, §6-4, 91½, §6-6; & in Supp. 1969 91, §9-1, 91, §9-13	91½, §6-5, 91½, §9-2 (Supp. 1969)	91½, §10-4 (Supp. 1969)	91½, §6-5 (Supp. 1969)	91½, §6-5 (Supp. 1969)			60 days unless continued hospitalization is ordered by court. 91½, §6-6
IOWA Code Ann. (1969)	227.15				2 227.15		mentally ill 227.15					227.15		229.37		229.30					indeterminate 227.15
fn. 18 KY. Rev. Stat. Ann. (1969)	state 202.117(4)		staff physician or a hospital. 202.117(4)	relative, spouse, friend or guardian. 202.117(4)	2 202.117(4)		mentally ill 202.117(4)					202.117(4)	202.265(1)	202.275							indeterminate 202.117(4)

Table 3.6 INVOLUNTARY HOSPITALIZATION BY MEDICAL CERTIFICATION *continued*

STATE	LIMIT ON PLACE OF HOSPITALIZATION	APPLICATION BY: Any Person	APPLICATION BY: Health, Welfare, or Peace Officer or Hospital Physician	APPLICATION BY: Attorney, Guardian, Relative, Friend, Spouse, or Person at Whose House Residing	NUMBER OF CERTIFICATES REQUIRED	FURTHER APPROVAL BY	CRITERIA: Protesting Patient	CRITERIA: Nonprotesting Patient	HOSPITAL ADMISSION REPORTED TO	DISC: Availability of Suitable Accommodations in Hospital	DISC: Mental Condition	DISC: Unspecified	PATIENT TOLD OF RIGHT TO OBJECT TO RELEASE, OR REVIEW	REVIEW: By Superior Court or Habeas Corpus	REVIEW: Jury on Review	ADMINISTRATIVE RELEASE	RELEASE: on Patient's Request	RELEASE: on Other's Request	RELEASE: Time After Notice	RELEASE: Extension Provision	MAXIMUM PERIOD OF HOSPITALIZATION
ME. Rev. Stat. Ann. (1964)	state and private. 34, §2331 (Supp. 1969)		fn. 19 34, §2332 (Supp. 1969)	fn. 19 34, §2332 (Supp. 1969)	2 physicians 34, §2332 (Supp. 1969)	endorsement 34, §2332 (Supp. 1969)	likely to injure himself or others. 34, §2332 (Supp. 1969)	in need of treatment. 34, §2332 (Supp. 1969)	fn. 20 34, §2371			34, §2332	34, §2376			34, §2374	34, §2376	34, §2376	within 10 days. 34, §2376	34, §2376	indeterminate 34, 2332 (Supp. 1969)
fn. 21 MD. Ann. Code (1968)	state or licensed private. 59, §32 hospital or some other place better suited. 59, §1		59, §32 county commissioners or department of welfare if in Baltimore. 59, §1	59, §32	2 59, §32 / 2 59, §1		lunatic or insane. 59, §32 / judicial determination only. 59, §1	lunatic or insane. 59, §32 / lunatic or insane. 59, §1				59, §32 / 59, §1		59, §20 / 59, §20	59, §21 / 59, §1	59, §32 / 59, §42	59, §32	59, §32	fn. 22 59, §32	fn. 22 59, §32	indeterminate 59, §32 / indeterminate 59, §1
MISS. Code Ann. (1952)	state 6909-12	6909-12			2 6909-12	director and staff of hospital. 6909-12	likely to become dangerous. 6909-12	in need of treatment. 6909-12			6909-12			chancery 6909-12			fn. 23 6909-12	fn. 23 6909-12			indeterminate 6909-12
MO. Rev. Stat. (1959)	public or private. 202.793		202.797.1 (1)	202.797.1 (1)	202.797.1 (2)		judicial determination only. 202.797(3)	in need of treatment. 202.797.1 (2)	guardian, spouse or next of kin. 202.817	202.793		fn. 24 202.793	fn. 25 202.797	probate court. 202.797		202.833	202.833.1	202.833.1	48 hours 202.833.1	5 days 202.833.1	indeterminate 202.797
NEB. Rev. Stat. (1966)	state or licensed private. 83-322.01		officer of any charitable institution or agency. 83-322.01	83-322.01	2 physicians 83-322.01		mentally ill 83-322.01	mentally ill 83-322.01		83-338		83-322.01					83-322.01	83-322.01	on request 83-322.01	83-322.01	indeterminate 83-322.01
fn. 26 NEV. Rev. Stat. (1967)	public or private. 433.669			433.669	referral from a practicing physician. 433.669	admitting psychiatrist or physician. 433.669	judicial determination only. 433.669	in need of treatment. 433.669			433.669		433.669 (2)				written 433.669	433.729	433.669		indeterminate 433.669
N.H. Rev. Stat. Ann. (1964)			fn. 27 135:15	fn. 27 135:15	2 physicians 135:21	fn. 28 135:21	own welfare or welfare of others. 135:21					135:15		superior court 135:30 (Supp. 1967)		fn. 29 135:28					indeterminate 135:21
fn. 9 N.Y. Mental Hygiene Law (McKinney 1951) (Supp. 1970) certification by two physicians			72.1	72.1	2 72.1	confirmed by hospital. 72.1	mentally ill 72.1	mentally ill 72.1	fn. 31 72.2		72.1		72.2	74	74		fn. 32 72.3	fn. 32 72.3			60 days unless continued hospitalization is ordered by court. 72.3
fn. 30 certification by one physician only			72.1, 75	72.1, 75	1 75	confirmed by hospital. 75		in need of treatment. 75			75		75	74, 75	74, 75		fn. 32 72.3, 75	fn. 32 72.3, 75			

Table 3.6   INVOLUNTARY HOSPITALIZATION BY MEDICAL CERTIFICATION   *continued*

STATE	LIMIT ON PLACE OF HOSPITALIZATION	APPLICATION BY: Any Person	APPLICATION BY: Health, Welfare, or Peace Officer or Hospital Physician	APPLICATION BY: Attorney, Guardian, Relative, Friend, Spouse, or Person at Whose House Residing	NUMBER OF CERTIFICATES REQUIRED	FURTHER APPROVAL BY	CRITERIA FOR ADMISSION: Protesting Patient	CRITERIA FOR ADMISSION: Nonprotesting Patient	HOSPITAL ADMISSION REPORTED TO	ADMISSION DISCRETIONARY: Availability of Suitable Accommodations in Hospital	ADMISSION DISCRETIONARY: Mental Condition	ADMISSION DISCRETIONARY: Unspecified	PATIENT TOLD OF RIGHT TO OBJECT, RELEASE, OR REVIEW	REVIEW: By Superior Court or Habeas Corpus	REVIEW: Jury on Review	ADMINISTRATIVE RELEASE	RELEASE UPON NOTICE: Release on Patient's Request	RELEASE UPON NOTICE: Release on Other's Request	RELEASE UPON NOTICE: Time After Notice	RELEASE UPON NOTICE: Extension Provision	MAXIMUM PERIOD OF HOSPITALIZATION
fn. 9 N.C. Gen. Stat. (1964)	state and private 122-58(a)				2 122-58(a)		judicial determination only. 122-58(b) 122-63	in need of treatment. 122-58(a)			no discretion 122-58(a)					122-66 through 122-68.1	fn. 33 122-58(b)	fn. 33 122-58(b)			180 days 122.63
fn. 9 OHIO Rev. Code Ann. (Baldwin 1964)	public or private 5122.01(f) 5122.06		5122.06(A)		2 physicians 5122.06(B)		judicial determination only. 5122.06	mentally ill 5122.06(B)	guardian, spouse, or next of kin. 5122.18			5122.06					5122.24	5122.24	10 days 5122.24	10 days 5122.24	90 days 5122.06
PA. Stat. Ann. (1969)		50, §4404 (a)			2 physicians 50, §4404 (b)		mentally ill 50, §4404(a)	mentally ill 50, §4404(a)				50, §4404 (c)		habeas corpus 50, §4426		50, §4420					indeterminate 50, §4404 (c)
R.I. Gen. Laws Ann. (1968)				26-2-8	2 physicians 26-2-8		insane 26-2-8					26-2-8		habeas corpus 26-3-10	26-3-10	26-3-3		26-3-3	forthwith 26-3-3		indeterminate 26-2-8
S.C. Code Ann. (1962)	state 32-954	medical hospital superintendent 32-954(1)		32-954(1)	2 registered examiners. 32-954(2)	fn. 34 probate judge 32-955	likely to injure himself or others. 32-954(2)(b)	in need of treatment. 32-954(2)(b)	guardian, spouse, or next of kin. 32-971	32-954			32-973				32-972 (Supp. 1968)	fn. 35 32-972 (Supp. 1968)	fn. 36 7 days 32-972 (Supp. 1968)	fn. 37 15 days 32-972 (Supp. 1968)	indeterminate 32-954
TENN. Code Ann. (1955) (Supp. 1968)				33-602(a)	2 33-602(a)		judicial determination only. 33-602(a)	in need of treatment. 33-602(a)		33-602(a)	33-602(a)		33-602(a)				33-602(b)	parent, guardian, spouse, or next of kin 33-602(b)	72 hours 33-602(b)	5 days 33-602(b)	indeterminate 33-602
UTAH Code Ann. (1968)	state 64-7-33A		67-7-33A(1)	64-7-33A(1)	2 64-7-33A(2)	fn. 38 64-7-33B	likely to injure himself or others. 64-7-33B (2)(b)	in need of treatment. 64-7-33B(2)(b)	guardian, spouse, or next of kin. 64-7-39			64-7-33	64-7-44(a)	64-3-44(b)		64-7-42 64-7-43	64-7-44(a)	64-7-44(a)	48 hours 64-7-44(a)	5 days 64-7-44(a)	indeterminate 64-7-33A
VT. Stat. Ann. (1968)		fn. 39 an interested party. 18, §7504 (Supp. 1969)			1 18, §7504 (1) (Supp. 1969)		substantial risk of injury to himself or others. 18, §7504 (1) (Supp. 1969)	mentally ill 18, §7504 (1) (Supp. 1969)				18, §7504 (Supp. 1969)	18, §7701	18, §7801							indeterminate 18, §7504 (Supp. 1969)
fn. 9 VA. Code Ann. (1953) (Supp. 1968)	public or private. 37.1-1(8), 37.1-66	any responsible person. 37.1-66			2 physicians or 1 physician and 1 clinical psychologist. 37.1-66	endorsement only after a hearing by a justice. 37.1-66	need for hospitalization. 37.1-66	need for hospitalization. 37.1-66				37.1-66	37.1-80	37.1-103		37.1-98					6 months unless continued hospitalization is ordered by court. 37.1-83

Table 3.6 INVOLUNTARY HOSPITALIZATION BY MEDICAL CERTIFICATION continued

STATE	LIMIT ON PLACE OF HOSPITALIZATION	APPLICATION BY			NUMBER OF CERTIFICATES REQUIRED	FURTHER APPROVAL BY	CRITERIA FOR ADMISSION		HOSPITAL ADMISSION REPORTED TO	ADMISSION DISCRETIONARY ON PART OF INSTITUTION AS TO			PATIENT TOLD OF RIGHT TO OBJECT, RELEASE, OR REVIEW	REVIEW		ADMINISTRATIVE RELEASE	RELEASE UPON NOTICE				MAXIMUM PERIOD OF HOSPITALIZATION
		Any Person	Health, Welfare, or Peace Officer or Hospital Physician	Attorney, Guardian, Relative, Friend, Spouse, or Person at Whose House Residing			Pro-testing Patient	Nonpro-testing Patient		Availability of Suitable Accommodations in Hospital	Mental Condition	Unspeci-fied		By Superior Court or Habeas Corpus	Jury on Review		Release on Patient's Request	Release on Other's Request	Time After Notice	Extension Provision	
W. VA. Code Ann. (1966)	state 27-5-1		27-5-1(a)	27-5-1(a)	2 27-5-1(b)		likely to injure himself or others. 27-5-1(b)(1)	in need of treatment. 27-5-1(b)(2)				27-5-1	27-5-6			27-7-1	27-5-6	27-5-6	not specified 27-5-6	none 27-5-6	indeterminate 27-5-1
WYO. Stat. Ann. (1967)	public or private. 25-49(e) 25-54		25-54(b)	25-54(b)	1 or more designate examiners or physicians. 25-54(b)		likely to injure himself or others. 25-54(b)	in need of treatment. 25-54(b)	fn. 40 25-66			25-54				25-69	25-56	25-56	10 days 25-56	postpone-ment 25-56(d)	indeterminate 25-54

Notes to Table 3.6 INVOLUNTARY HOSPITALIZATION BY MEDICAL CERTIFICATION

1. "... or in writing, by his legal guardian, spouse, or adult next of kin...." Draft Act, 17(a).

2. "... except if the head of a designated hospital, within 48 hours after receiving the request, files with the superior court a certification that in his opinion the discharge of the patient would be unsafe to the patient or others, the discharge may be postponed for not more than 5 days to begin commitment proceedings...." Alas. 47.30.050 (a)(3).

3. Arizona might also be considered as having a judicial procedure since, in the procedure charted, the court is to approve the petition only if it believes it to be in the best interests of the patient. Ariz. 36-505(C)(Supp. 1970). However, since it is an ex parte procedure not initiated by the patient, is based upon medical certification, and cannot be used over the objection or protest of the patient, it has been included in this classification.

   The procedure is as follows: a person may be hospitalized upon the petition of those persons designated by the statute and the certification of two medical examiners. The proposed patient is served with a copy of the petition and certifications together with a form of notice and consent. Within 15 days from the date of filing the petition, certifications, and the executed notice and consent, the court shall approve the petition if it believes that to do so would be in the patient's best interest; otherwise it is to deny the petition. Ariz. 36-505(A), (B), and (C) (Supp. 1970).

4. Unless the petition was filed by the guardian, spouse, or adult next of kin. Ariz. 36-519 (Supp. 1970).

5. "The proposed patient... shall be served... with a form of notice and consent... setting forth his right to release." Ariz. 36-505B (Supp. 1969).

6. The superintendent shall file a certificate seeking postponement of discharge until proceedings for judicial commitment can be arranged. Ariz. 36-506(B) (Supp. 1970).

7. See also Ark. 59-234 (Supp. 1967).

8. "Neither the Superintendent nor any other official or employee of the State Hospital shall be liable for the detention of any person who may be a patient of the hospital, until thirty [30] days after the patient has made demand in writing for his release from detention, and then only if it be shown that such detention was unreasonable and arbitrary." Ark. 59-236.

9. Seven states give no authorization for indeterminate commitment in conjunction with medical certification proceedings. California, 14 days, 5254 (Supp. 1968); Georgia, 6 months, 88-506.3 (Supp. 1969); Illinois, 60 days, 91½, §6-6 (Supp. 1969); New York, 60 days, 72.3 (Supp. 1970); North Carolina, 180 days, 122.63; Ohio, 90 days, 5122.06; Virginia, 15 days, 37.1-79 (Supp. 1968).

10. The court shall grant a writ of habeas corpus or order an evidentiary within 1 judicial day after the petition is filed. Cal. W. & I. 5276 (Supp. 1968).

11. If reasonably possible, 1 of the medical doctors shall be a psychiatrist. Del. 16, §5125(1) (Supp. 1970).

12. No referral from a physician is necessary if the need for immediate admission is apparent to the admitting psychiatrist. D.C. 21-513.

13. Immediate release is required unless proceedings for hospitalization by court order have been initiated. D.C. 21-514.

14. By county judge if patient is to be taken into custody over his protests. Fla. 394.201(1)(b) (Supp. 1968).

15. This is not an ordinary medical certification procedure because only those patients who have previously been committed to an evaluating facility are subject to this type of commitment. Also, only if a patient does not request a hearing is he actually committed for hospitalization on the basis of a medical certificate. Ga. 88-506.3 (Supp. 1969).

16. "... may obtain a judicial determination of the regularity of his admission or of the need for his continued hospitalization...." Hawaii 334-81.

17. Consultation, at the hospital, with the judge of the county is required within 5 business days of admission. Ill. 91½, §6-4 (Supp. 1969).

18. Where a person is hospitalized by this provision the hospital must initiate without delay an application for an involuntary hospitalization order unless the patient agrees to reman voluntarily. Ky. 202.117(4) (Supp. 1968).

19. Friend, relative, spouse or guardian of the individual, a health or public welfare officer, or head of any institution in which individual may be. Me. 34, §2332 (Supp. 1969).

20. On application of any person other than the patient's legal guardian spouse or next of kin, the head of hospital shall notify those persons if known. Me. 34, §2371.

21. The procedure charted on the lower line is limited to the hospitalization of lunatics or insane who are also indigent. Md. 59, §1.

22. Patient or anyone on his behalf may request release, and superintendent shall comply with the request unless he forthwith files a petition for judicial hospitalization proceedings in which a jury may be demanded. Md. 59, §21, 69, §32.

23. "[S]hall have the right to appeal and hearing before the chancery court and to apply for a writ of habeas corpus. . . ." Miss. 6909-12.

24. "The head of a private or public hospital subject to the availability of suitable accommodations may receive therein for observation, diagnosis, care and treatment, any individual whose admission is applied for under the following procedures. . . ." Mo. 202.793.

25. If the patient does not request a judicial hearing after having been sent a request form for such a hearing, he may be transported to and admitted to the hospital. If he requests a judicial hearing, notice is to be given the person who made the application for his hospitalization, and judicial proceedings must be begun within five days. Mo. 202.797.

26. May be accepted by any private hospital and shall be accepted for examination and treatment by any public hospital if, in the judgment of the admitting psychiatrist or physician, the need is indicated on the basis of the person's mental condition and such person signs a statement at the time of such admission stating that he does not object to hospitalization. Nev. 433.669.

27. Limited to parent, guardian or friends. In addition, the board of selectmen in towns, chief of police in cities, or board of county commissioners in counties may make application. N.H. 135:15.

28. Judge of superior or probate court, county commissioner, mayor, city clerk, justice of municipal court of city, or selectman of town. Town clerk must certify genuineness of signatures and respectability of signers. N.H. 135:21.

29. Superintendent or justice of superior court may order discharge when hospitalization is no longer necessary. N.H. 135:28.

30. Only a nonprotesting patient may be hospitalized under the latter procedure.

31. Notice is given to the mental health information service and personally or by mail to the nearest relative and to as many as 3 additional persons if designated in writing by the person alleged to be mentally ill to receive such notice. N.Y. Mental Hygiene, 72.2 (Supp. 1970).

32. "[R]equest for hearing on the question of need for hospitalization. . . ." N.Y. Mental Hygiene Law, 72.3 (Supp. 1970)

33. "If after admission, the patient or any member of his family shall object to the admission of the alleged mentally ill person . . . the clerk receiving such affidavit shall then proceed to hold the hearing required by G.S. 122-64." N.C. 122-58(b).

34. "If [the medical certificate] states a belief that the individual is likely to injure himself or others, [it] shall upon endorsement by a judge of any probate court of the county . . . require any police officer. . . to take the individual into custody and transport him to the hospital designated in the application." S.C. 32-955.

35. Request for release may be made by spouse, adult next of kin, legal guardian, friend, or person who made application for admission. S.C. 32-972 (Supp. 1968).

36. Superintendent may deny request if it is made within 30 days of admission. S.C. 32-972 (Supp. 1968).

37. Judicial commitment proceedings may be commenced within this period. S.C. 32-972 (Supp. 1968).

38. If the certificate states that the individual is likely to injure himself or others, the head of the local board of health, judge of district court or a member of the board of county commissioners shall authorize any officer to take the individual into custody and transport him to the Utah State Hospital. Utah 64-7-33B.

39. ". . . an interested party, by a selectman or town service officer, by the commissioner, or by the head of a hospital in which the individual may be. . . ." Vt. 18, §7504 (Supp. 1969).

40. Whenever a patient has been admitted to a hospital for examination on application of any legal guardian, spouse, parent, child, or sibling, the head of the hospital shall immediately notify 1 of such persons if known. Wyo. 25-66.

Table 3.7   *STATUTORY DEFINITIONS OF THE MENTALLY DEFICIENT AND EPILEPTICS*

STATE AND CITATION	STATUTORY PROVISIONS
DRAFT ACT	
ALA. Code (1958) 45, §236	"The terms 'feeble-minded' and 'mentally inferior or deficient'. . . shall include every person with such a degree of mental defectiveness from birth, or from an early age, that he is unable to care for himself and to manage his affairs with ordinary prudence, or that he is a menace to the happiness or safety of himself or of others in the community, and requires care, supervision, and control either for his own protection or for the protection of others. It is specifically recognized that the greatest danger which the feeble-minded constitute to the community lies in the frequency of the passing on of mental defect from one generation to another."
ALAS. Stat. (1962)	
ARIZ. Rev. Stat. Ann. (1956)	
ARK. Stat. Ann. (1947) 59-301 (Supp. 1969)	"Child or children means mentally deficient persons without regard to chronological age."
CAL. Welf. & Inst'ns Code (West 1966) 6500 (Supp. 1968)	"'[M]entally retarded persons means those persons, not psychotic, who are so mentally retarded from infancy or before reaching maturity that they are incapable of managing themselves and their affairs independently, with ordinary prudence, or of being taught to do so, and who require supervision, control, and care, for their own welfare, or for the welfare of others, or for the welfare of the community."
COLO. Rev. Stat. Ann. (1964) 71-1-1(c)	"'Mentally deficient person' shall mean a person whose intellectual functions have been deficient since birth or whose intellectual development has been arrested or impaired by disease, or physical injury to such an extent that he lacks sufficient control, judgment, and discretion to manage his property or affairs, or who by reason of this deficiency, for his own welfare, or the welfare or safety of others, requires protection, supervision, guidance, training, control or care."
CONN. Gen. Stat. Ann. (1958)	
DEL. Code Ann. (1953)	
D.C. Code Ann. (1967) 21-1101	"'Feeble-minded person' means a person afflicted with mental defectiveness from birth or from an early age, so pronounced that he is incapable of managing himself and his affairs, or being taught to do so, and who requires supervision, control, and care for his own welfare, or the welfare of others, or for the welfare of the community, and is not mentally ill to such an extent as to require his commitment to Saint Elizabeth's Hospital."
FLA. Stat. Ann (1960)	
GA. Code Ann. (1963) 88-2502 (a) (Supp. 1968)	"'Mental retardation' means a state of subaverage general intellectual functioning which originates during the developmental period and is associated with impairment in adaptive behavior."
HAWAII Rev. Stat. Ann. (1968) 333-25	"Mentally retarded persons, as referred to in section 333-24 are persons: (1) Who are afflicted with (A) a deficiency of general mental development associated with chronic brain syndrome, or (B) a deficiency of intelligence arising after birth, due to infection, trauma, or other disease process, or (2) who are afflicted with general intellectual subnormality not due to known organic factors."

STATE AND CITATION	STATUTORY PROVISIONS
IDAHO Code Ann. (1949) 66-317 (3) (Supp. 1969)	"'Mentally deficient or mentally retarded person,' . . . shall mean a person or individual not psychotic, who is so mentally retarded from infancy or before reaching maturity, that he is incapable of managing himself or his affairs independently, with ordinary prudence, or of being taught to do so, and who requires supervision or control, and care for his own welfare, the welfare of others or the welfare of the community. . . ."
ILL. Ann. Stat. (Smith-Hurd 1966) 91½, § 1-12 (Supp. 1969)	"'Mentally retarded and mental retardation' refer to subaverage general intellectual functioning which originates during the developmental period and is associated with impairment in adaptive behavior. Impaired adaptive behavior may be reflected in delayed maturation or reduced learning ability or inadequate social adjustment."
IND. Ann. Stat. (1964) 22-1703	The term "feeble-minded" includes idiotic, epileptic and paralytic children.
22-1201(2)	"The term 'psychiatric disorder' means any mental illness or disease and shall include, but not be limited to, any mental deficiency, epilepsy, alcoholism or addiction to narcotic drugs."
IOWA Code Ann. (1969) 222.2.4	"'Mental retardation' or 'mentally retarded' means a term or terms to describe children and adults who as a result of inadequately developed intelligence are significantly impaired in ability to learn or to adapt to the demands of society."
KAN. Stat. Ann. (1964)	
KY. Rev. Stat. Ann. (1969) 202.010(2)	"'Mentally defective person' means a person with a defect in mental development at birth, or at an early age, and which is of such a degree that he is incapable of caring for himself or managing his affairs and requires supervision, care, training, control or custody for his own welfare or for the welfare of others."
LA. Rev. Stat. Ann. (1950) 28:2(4)	"'Mental defective' means a person who is not mentally ill but whose mental development is so retarded that he has not acquired enough self-control, judgment, and discretion to manage himself and his affairs, and for whose own welfare or that of others, care, supervision, guidance, or control are necessary or advisable. The term includes feeble-minded, idiot and imbecile."
28:2(5)	"'Epileptic' means a person suffering from any condition which brings about lapses of consciousness which may or may not be accompanied by convulsive seizures, and which may become chronic."
ME. Rev. Stat. Ann. (1964) 34, § 2562(3)	"'Mental deficiency' shall mean mental deficiency as defined by appropriate clinical authorities to such extent that a person so afflicted is incapable of managing himself and his affairs, but shall not include mental illness."
MD. Ann. Code (1965) 41, § 322(7)	"'Mental deficiency' shall mean mental deficiency, as defined by appropriate clinical authorities, to such extent that a person so afflicted is incapable of managing himself and his affairs, but shall not include mental illness as defined herein."
MASS. Ann. Laws (1965) 123, § 1	"'Mentally deficient' person, a person whose intellectual functioning has been abnormally retarded, or has demonstrably failed, the deficiency being manifested by psychological signs."

STATE AND CITATION	STATUTORY PROVISIONS
MICH. Comp. Laws Ann. (1967) 330.54	"The term 'mentally handicapped' shall include morons, idiots, imbeciles and those as to whom congenital defects have produced the same deficiency . . . and whenever reference to 'feeble-minded' is made in the laws of this state, reference shall be deemed to be made to 'mentally handicapped.'"
MINN. Stat. Ann (1959) 253A.02(5) (Supp. 1969)	"'Mentally deficient person' means any person, other than a mentally ill person, so mentally defective as to require treatment or supervision, for his own or the public welfare."
MISS. Code Ann. (1952) 698	"The term 'unsound mind,' when used in any statute in reference to persons, shall include idiots, lunatics, and persons non compos mentis."
MO. Rev. Stat. (1962)	
MONT. Rev. Codes Ann. (1961) 64-104	Persons of unsound mind, within the meaning of this code, are idiots, lunatics, imbeciles, and habitual drunkards.
NEB. Rev. Stat. (1966) 83-218 (Supp. 1967)	". . . mentally handicapped as to require residential care. . . "
NEV. Rev. Stat. (1967)	
N.H. Rev. Stat. Ann. (1964)	
N.J. Stat. Ann. (1964) 30:4-23 (Supp. 1970)	"'Mental deficiency' shall mean that state of mental retardation in which the reduction of social competence is so marked that persistent social dependency requiring guardianship of the person shall have been demonstrated or be anticipated. "'Mental retardation' shall mean a state of significant subnormal intellectual development with reduction of social competence in a minor or adult person; this state of subnormal intellectual development shall have existed prior to adolescence and is expected to be of life duration."
N.M. Stat. Ann. (1953) 34-3-1 (Supp. 1969)	"'[M]ental defective' means any person not classified as insane but mentally underdeveloped or faultily developed, or mentally backward or retarded, to the degree that he is incapable of managing himself and his affairs, and requires supervision, care and control for his own welfare, or for the welfare of others, or for the welfare of the community, irrespective of whether any such person is capable of being trained to acquire skills useful to himself and others . . . . "
N.Y. Mental Hygiene Law (McKinney 1951) 2.9	"'Mental defective' means any person afflicted with mental defectiveness from birth or from an early age to such an extent that he is incapable of managing himself and his affairs, who for his own welfare or the welfare of others or the community requires supervision, control or care and who is not mentally ill or of unsound mind to such an extent as to require his certification to an institution for the mentally ill. . . . "
2.10 (Supp. 1970)	"An 'epileptic' . . . is a person suffering from epilepsy as defined in medical practice, to such an extent that for his own welfare and the welfare of others, or of the community, he requires care and treatment in an institution."

STATE AND CITATION	STATUTORY PROVISIONS
N.C. Gen. Stat. (1964) 122-36	"The words 'mentally retarded' shall mean a person who is not mentally ill but whose mental development is so retarded that he has not acquired enough self-control, judgment, and discretion to manage himself and his affairs, and for whose own welfare or that of others, supervision, guidance, care, or control is necessary or advisable."
N.D. Cent. Code (1960) 25-01-01 (2) (Supp. 1969)	"'[M]entally deficient person' means any person, . . . other than a mentally ill person, who is so defective mentally as to be incapable of managing himself and his affairs and to require supervision, control and care for his own or the public welfare. . . ."
OHIO Rev. Code Ann. (Baldwin 1964) 5125.011	"Mentally retarded . . . means having subnormal intellectual functioning originating in the development period prior to age eighteen and is characterized by reduced learning capacity including accompanying inadequate social adjustment as determined by comprehensive evaluation or as determined by a court of record upon such evidence as is deemed satisfactory by such court to established the existence of mental retardation."
OKLA. Stat. Ann. (1954) 43A, § 3(g) (Supp. 1969)	"'Mentally retarded person' means a person afflicted with mental defectiveness from birth or from an early age to such an extent that he is incapable of managing himself and his affairs, who for his own welfare . . . or the welfare of the community requires supervision, control or care and who is not mentally ill or of unsound mind to such an extent as to require his certification to an institution for the mentally ill. . . ."
43A, § 3(g) (Supp. 1969)	"'[M]entally incompetent person' means any person afflicted with mental disease to such an extent that he is incapable of managing himself and his affairs but who does not need to be hospitalized."
ORE. Rev. Stat. (1967)	
PA. Stat. Ann. (1969) 50, § 4102	"'Mental retardation' means subaverage general intellectual functioning which originates during the developmental period and is associated with impairment of one or more of the following: (1) maturation, (2) learning and (3) social adjustment."
R.I. Gen. Laws Ann. (1968) 26-6-1 (Art. II(g)	"'Mental deficiency' shall mean mental deficiency as defined by appropriate clinical authorities to such extent that a person so afflicted is incapable of managing himself and his affairs, but shall not include mental illness as defined herein."
S.C. Code Ann. (1962) 32-911(2) (Supp. 1968)	"'Mentally defective person' or 'mentally deficient person' or 'mentally retarded person' means a person who, because of inadequately developed intelligence, is significantly impaired in his ability to learn and to adapt to the demands of society."
S.D. Compiled Laws Ann. (1967) 27-1-2	"The term 'mental retardation' is a state of subnormal development of the human organism in consequence of which the individual affected is mentally incapable of fully assuming those responsibilities expected of the socially adequate person such as self-direction, self-support and social participation. The terms 'mental retardation' and 'mental deficiency' shall be deemed synonymous."

STATE AND CITATION	STATUTORY PROVISIONS
TENN. Code Ann. (1955) 33-302(g) (Supp. 1968)	"Mentally retarded individual or mentally deficient individual--An individual who is not mentally ill but whose intellectual functions have been deficient since birth, or whose intellectual development has been arrested or impaired by disease or physical injury occurring before maturity and who, being unable to care for himself and manage his affairs, requires care, treatment and training in a hospital and school for his own welfare or the welfare of others or of the community."
TEX. Rev. Civ. Stat. Ann. (1966) 3871b-3(1)	"'Mentally retarded person' means any person, other than a mentally ill person, so mentally deficient from any cause as to require special training, education, supervision, treatment, care or control for his own or the community's welfare."
UTAH Code Ann. (1968) 64-8-13 (Supp. 1969)	"A mentally retarded person shall mean a person in whom there has been found, by comprehensive evaluation, a condition of mental retardation of such a nature and degree as to constitute a substantial, continuing, prospective, educational, vocational, and social hardship."
VT. Stat. Ann. (1968) 18, § 7101(12)	"'Mental defective' means an individual included in one of the following clinical classifications of mental deficiency: mild, moderate, severe, or profound; to the extent that he is incapable of managing himself and his affairs independently, with ordinary prudence, and who requires supervision for his own welfare or that of the community."
VA. Code Ann. (1953) 37.1-1 (Supp. 1968)	"(13) 'Mental retardation' means subaverage general intellectual functioning which originates during the developmental period and is associated with impairment in adaptive behavior. . . . "(14) 'Mentally deficient' means any person afflicted with mental defectiveness from birth or early childhood to such an extent that he is incapable of caring for himself or managing his affairs, who for his own welfare or the welfare of others or of the community requires supervision, control or care. . . ."
WASH. Rev. Code Ann. (1962) 72.33.020	"'Mental deficiency' is a state of subnormal development of the human organism in consequence of which the individual affected is mentally incapable of assuming those responsibilities expected of the socially adequate person such as self-direction, self-support and social participation."
W.VA. Code Ann. (1966) 27-1-3	"A 'mentally retarded' person is one having an inadequately developed or impaired intellect, and who because thereof is significantly disabled in his ability to learn and to adapt to the demands of society."
WIS. Stat. Ann. (1957) 51.75 (Art. II(g)) (Supp. 1969)	"Mental deficiency means mental deficiency as defined by appropriate clinical authorities to such an extent that a person so afflicted is incapable of managing himself and his affairs, but shall not include mental illness . . . ."
WYO. Stat. Ann. (1967) 25-90 (Art. II (g)) (Supp. 1969)	"'Mental deficiency' shall mean mental deficiency as defined by appropriate clinical authorities to such extent that a person so afflicted is incapable of managing himself and his affairs . . . ."

Table 3.8   STATUTORY DEFINITIONS OF ALCOHOLICS AND DRUG ADDICTS

STATE AND CITATION	STATUTORY PROVISIONS
DRAFT ACT	
ALA. Code (1958) 22, §249	"[H]abitually uses any narcotic drugs. . . . so as to endanger the public morals, health, safety or welfare or who is or has been so far addicted to the use of such drugs as to have lost the power of self-control with reference to his or her addiction. . . ."
ALAS. Stat. (1962) 47.30.500(3) (Supp. 1969)	"'[A]lcoholic' means a person who chronically and habitually uses alcoholic beverages to the extent that he loses the power of self-control with respect to the use of alcoholic beverages; or a person who chronically and habitually uses alcoholic beverages to the extent that he becomes a menace to the public morals, health, safety or welfare."
ARIZ. Rev. Stat. Ann. (1956)	
ARK. Stat. Ann. (1947) 83-703(c)	"'Alcoholic' means any person who chronically and habitually uses alcoholic beverages to the extent that said person has lost the power of self-control with respect to the use of such beverages, or while chronically and habitually under the influence of alcoholic beverages endangers public morals, health, safety or welfare."
CAL. Welf. & Inst'ns Code (West 1966, Supp. 1968) 5008(h)	"'Gravely disabled' means a condition in which a person, as a result of . . . impairment by chronic alcoholism, is unable to provide for his basic personal needs for food, clothing, or shelter."
5225	". . . who appears, as a result of chronic alcoholism, to be a danger to others, to himself, or to be gravely disabled."
6350	"A 'narcotic drug addict' . . . is any person who habitually takes or otherwise uses to the extent of having lost the power of self-control any opium, morphine, cocaine, or other narcotic drug."
6400	"A 'habit-forming drug addict' . . . is any person who is so far addicted to the intemperate use of habit-forming drugs, other than narcotic drugs . . . as to have lost the power of self-control." "Habit-forming drugs" are designated in Article 8 (§4210 et seq.) of Chapter 9, Division 2, of the Business and Professions Code.
COLO. Rev. Stat. Ann. (1964)	
CONN. Gen. Stat. Ann. (1958) 17-155(g) (Supp. 1969)	"When any person has become so addicted to the intemperate use of alcohol as to have lost the power of self-control. . . [such person can be committed as an alcoholic]."
19-443(10)	"'Drug-dependent person' means any person who has developed a state of psychic or physical dependence, or both, upon a controlled drug following administration of that drug upon a repeated periodic or continuous basis."
DEL. Code Ann. (1953)	
D.C. Code Ann. (1967) 21-1301	"[H]abitual user of intoxicating liquors, opium, cocaine, or similar substance, or compound or derivative thereof . . . ."
FLA. Stat. Ann. (1960)	

STATE AND CITATION	STATUTORY PROVISIONS
GA. Code Ann. (1963) 88-402(a) (Supp. 1968)	"An 'alcoholic' means any person who chronically and habitually uses alcoholic beverages to the extent that he has lost the power of self-control with respect to the use of such beverages, or while chronically and habitually under the influence of alcoholic beverages endangers public morals, health, safety or welfare."
79A-818(a) (Supp. 1968)	Proceedings against addicts--"Whenever an affidavit . . . setting forth that any person named or described therein habitually uses any narcotic drug as defined in this Chapter, so as to endanger the public morals, health, safety, or welfare, or who is or has been so far addicted to the use of such drugs as to have lost the power of self-control with reference to his addiction. . . ."
HAWAII Rev. Stat. Ann. (1968) 281-1	"'Addicted to the excessive use of intoxicating liquor' refers to one who has acquired the habit of using intoxicating liquor excessively to deprive himself of reasonable self-control, a common drunkard, or a habitual drunkard."
334-1	"'Person habituated to the excessive use of drugs or alcohol' means a person who repeatedly and compulsively uses narcotic, stimulant, depressant, or hallucinogenic drugs or alcohol to an extent which interferes with his personal, social, family, or economic life."
IDAHO Code Ann. (1949) 67-3109 (Supp. 1969)	"'Alcoholic,' as used in this act, means any person who habitually uses alcoholic beverages to such an extent that he endangers the health, morals, safety or welfare of himself, or any other persons or groups of persons."
37-2722 (Supp. 1969)	"'Narcotic addict,' as used in this act, means any person who habitually and unlawfully consumes narcotic drugs to satisfy a physical and/or psychological need for narcotic drugs induced by prior usage."
ILL. Ann. Stat. (Smith-Hurd 1966) 91½, §120.3-3 (Supp. 1969)	"'Addict' means any person who has developed a compulsion to continue taking a narcotic drug or any person who has developed a psychic or physical dependence on the effects of narcotics or dangerous drugs or who abuses the use of narcotic or dangerous drugs so that the person or society is harmed."
IND. Ann. Stat. (1964) 22-1502(b) (Supp. 1969)	"The term 'alcoholic' means any person who chronically and habitually uses alcoholic beverages to the extent that he loses the power of self-control with respect to the use of alcoholic beverages; or any person who chronically and habitually uses alcoholic beverages to the extent that he becomes a menace to the public morals, health, safety or welfare of the members of society in general."
10-3538a(b) (Supp. 1969)	"Any person habitually or frequently using narcotic drugs . . . , or any person who habitually, or with regularity, obtains such narcotic drugs from sources of supply prohibited by the laws of this state, shall, if found in any public place, or in a place of ill repute, be deemed to be a common drug addict . . . ."
IOWA Code Ann. (1969) 224.1	"Persons addicted to the excessive use of intoxicating liquors, morphine, cocaine, or other narcotic drugs. . . . "
KAN. Stat. Ann. (1964) 74-4401	"An 'alcoholic,' 'dipsomaniac' and 'habitual drunkard' hereinafter referred to as an alcoholic, shall mean any person who chronically and habitually uses alcoholic beverages to the extent that he has lost the power of self-control with respect to the use of such beverages, or while chronically and habitually under the influence of alcoholic beverages endangers public morals, health, safety and welfare, or who has been five times convicted of intoxication in any court, or who has been legally determined to have lost the power of self-control from the intemperate use of spirituous or intoxicating liquors."

104

STATE AND CITATION	STATUTORY PROVISIONS
KY. Rev. Stat. Ann. (1969) 222.110(2)	"'Alcoholic' means any person who chronically and habitually uses alcoholic beverages to the extent that he loses the power of self-control . . . or any person who chronically and habitually uses alcoholic beverages to the extent that he becomes a menace to the public morals, health, safety or welfare of the members of society in general."
LA. Rev. Stat. Ann. (1950) 28:2(6)	"'Inebriate' means a person who is habitually so addicted to the use of alcohol or other intoxicating or narcotic substances as to be unwilling or unable without help to stop the excessive use of such substances. The term includes dipsomaniac, habitual drunkard, person addicted to the use of alcoholic drink, absinthe, opium, morphine, chloral, or other intoxicating liquors or drugs as to be a proper subject for restraint, care, and treatment in a hospital or asylum, and persons habitually so addicted to the use of alcohol or narcotic drugs as to be a proper subject for restraint, care and treatment."
40:961(1) (1965)	"Addict means a person who habitually uses one or more of the narcotic drugs defined in this section to such an extent as to create a tolerance for such drug, or drugs, and who does not have a medical need for the use of such drug or drugs."
ME. Rev. Stat. Ann. (1964) 22, §1355	"A person alleged to be suffering from the effects of the use of an opiate, cocaine, chloral hydrate, other narcotic, barbiturate or the excessive use of alcohol may be committed to the care of any hospital, including any state hospital for the mentally ill. . . ."
MD. Code Ann. (1968) 2C, §103(b)	"The term 'chronic alcoholic' means any person who chronically and habitually uses alcoholic beverages (1) to the extent that it injures his health or substantially interferes with his social or economic functioning, or (2) to the extent that he has lost the power of self-control with respect to the use of such beverages."
16, §48	"A drunkard . . . shall be deemed to include any person who has acquired the habit of using spirituous, malt or fermented liquors, cocaine or other narcotics to such degree as to deprive him of reasonable self-control."
MASS. Ann. Laws (1965) 123, §62	". . . any male or female person who is an alcoholic, or who is so addicted to the intemperate use of narcotics, habit-forming stimulants or sedatives as to have lost the power of self-control."
MICH. Comp. Laws Ann. (1967) 330.18	"[S]uch persons as may have been or may hereafter be adjudged to be so addicted to the excessive use of intoxicating liquors, or narcotics or noxious drugs, as to be in need of medical and sanitary treatment or care may . . . be taken to or restrained in any suitable institution or hospital for treatment and care of the insane. . . ."
335.202	"The term 'drug user' means any person who habitually uses any habit-forming narcotic drugs so as to endanger the public morals, health, safety, or welfare, or who is so far addicted to the use of such habit-forming narcotic drugs as to have lost the power of self-control with reference to his addiction."
MINN. Stat. Ann. (1959) 253A.02(d) (Supp. 1969)	"'Inebriate person' means any person incapable of managing himself or his affairs by reason of the habitual and excessive use of intoxicating liquor, narcotics, or other drugs."
MISS. Code Ann. (1952) 436-01(a)	"An 'alcoholic' shall mean any person who chronically and habitually uses alcoholic beverages to the extent that he has lost the power of self-control with respect to use of such beverages, or while chronically under the influence of alcoholic beverages endangers public morals, health, safety or welfare."

STATE AND CITATION	STATUTORY PROVISIONS
N.M. Stat. Ann. (1966) 46-12-7 (Supp. 1969)	"The district courts, . . . shall commit . . . any habitual drunkard, chronic alcoholic, any dipsomaniac . . . five (5) times convicted of intoxication in any court, or . . . legally determined to have lost the power of self-control from the intemperate use of spirituous or intoxicating liquors."
(1962) 54-7-3	"State board of public health is authorized to make rules and regulations . . . for the treatment of drug addicts. . . ."
N.Y. Mental Hygiene Law (McKinney 1951) 201.2 (Supp. 1970)	"The term 'narcotic addict' means a person who is at the time of examination dependent upon opium, heroin, morphine or any derivative or synthetic drug of that group or who by reason of the repeated use of any such drug is in imminent danger of becoming dependent upon opium, heroin, morphine, or any derivative or synthetic drug of that group; provided, however, that no person shall be deemed a narcotic addict solely by virtue of his taking of any such drugs pursuant to a lawful prescription issued by a physician in the course of professional treatment for legitimate medical purposes."
301(a)	"'Alcoholic' and 'chronic alcoholic' means any person who chronically and habitually uses alcoholic beverages to the extent that said person has lost the power of self-control with respect to the use of such beverages, or who, by reason of alcoholism endangers the health, safety or welfare of himself or others."
423.1	"[S]uch person is over the age of eighteen years, and is incapable or unfit to properly conduct himself or herself, or his or her affairs, or is dangerous to himself or herself or others by reason of periodical, frequent or constant drunkenness, induced either by the use of alcoholic or other liquors, or of opium, morphine, or other narcotic or intoxicating or stupefying substance. . . ."
N.C. Gen. Stat. (1964) 122-65.6 (Supp. 1967)	(1) "'Chronic alcoholic' shall mean any person who has been found by any court to have the illness or condition known as chronic alcoholism. . . ." (2) "'Chronic alcoholism' shall mean the chronic and habitual use of alcoholic beverages by a person to the extent that he has lost the power of self-control with respect to the use of such beverages."
35-1.1 (Supp. 1967)	"Any person who habitually, whether continuously or periodically, indulges in the use of intoxicating liquors, narcotics or drugs to such an extent as to stupefy his mind and to render him incompetent to transact ordinary business with safety to his estate, or who renders himself, by reason of the use of intoxicating liquors, narcotics or drugs, dangerous to person or property, or who, by the frequent use of liquor, narcotics or drugs, renders himself cruel and intolerable to his family, or fails from such cause to provide his family with reasonable necessities of life, shall be deemed an inebriate: Provided, the habit of so indulging in such use is at the time of inquisition of at least one year's standing."
122-36(c)	"The word 'inebriate' shall mean a person habitually so addicted to alcoholic drinks or narcotic drugs or other habit forming drugs as to have lost the power of self-control and that for his own welfare or the welfare of others is a proper subject for restraint, care, and treatment."
N.D. Cent. Code (1960)	
OHIO Rev. Code Ann. (Baldwin 1964) 5122.01	See Table 3.1, "Statutory Definitions of the Mentally Ill."
OKLA. Stat. Ann. (1954)	
ORE. Rev. Stat. (1967)	

STATE AND CITATION   STATUTORY PROVISIONS

MISS. Code Ann. (1952)--continued
  436-01(d)   "A 'drug addict' shall mean any person who chronically and habitually uses any
                           form of habit forming drugs. . . ."

MO. Rev. Stat. (1962)
  195.010(1)   "'Addict' means a person who habitually uses one or more narcotic drugs to such
                           an extent as to create a tolerance for such drugs, and who does not have a medical
                           need for such drugs."

MONT. Rev. Codes Ann. (1961)
  66-1516   "'An habitual user of such drugs' or 'drug addict' is defined as follows:
                           'Any person who has needed or demanded the prescribing for, dispensing or adminis-
                           tering, or in any manner the giving of opium or coca leaves or any of their
                           derivatives, salts, preparations, or compounds, at more or less regular intervals
                           for thirty consecutive days prior to the day such person applies to a physician
                           or to a physician of any institution for the prescribing for, dispensing, adminis-
                           tering, or the giving in any way of any such drugs or their derivatives.'"

NEB. Rev. Stat. (1966)
  83-159(1)   "Alcoholic shall mean any person who habitually uses alcoholic beverages to the
  (Supp. 1967)   extent that he has lost the power of self-control with respect to the use of such
                           beverages, or who is chronically or habitually under the influence of alcoholic
                           beverages and endangers the health, morals, safety, or welfare of himself or any
                           other persons or group of persons."

  83-701   "Drug user shall mean any person . . . who uses any habit-forming narcotic drugs
  (Supp. 1967)   so as to endanger the public morals, health, safety, or welfare, or who is so far
                           addicted to the use of such habit-forming narcotic drugs as to have lost the power
                           of self-control with reference to his addiction."

NEV. Rev. Stat. (1967)
  433.248.1   "'Alcoholic' means a person who is so far addicted to the intemperate use of alcoholic
                           beverages as to have lost the power of self-control."

  433.248.2   "'Drug addict' means a person who: (a) Habitually takes or otherwise uses any
                           narcotic or habit-forming drug; or (b) is so far addicted to the use of any stimulant
                           or depressant drug as to have lost the power of self-control."

N.H. Rev. Stat. Ann. (1964)
  172:1 (IV)   "'Chronic alcoholic' means a person who, in consequence of prolonged excessive
                           drinking has developed a diagnosable bodily disease or mental disorder.

  172:1 (V)   "'Compulsive drinker' or 'alcoholic addict' means a person affected by an uncontrolla-
                           ble craving for alcoholic beverages, or a person who chronically and habitually uses
                           alcoholic beverages to the extent that he has lost the power of self-control with
                           respect to the use of such beverages, or while chronically or habitually under the
                           influence of alcoholic beverages endangers public morals, health, safety or welfare.

  172:1 (VI)   "'Habitual drunkard' means a person who is frequently or regularly intoxicated from
                           the use of alcoholic beverages or has been three times convicted for a violation of
                           section 14 of chapter 570, RSA.

  172:1 (VII)   "'Excessive drinker' means a person who drinks to an extent which exposes him to
                           the risk of becoming a compulsive drinker or a chronic alcoholic.

  172:1 (VIII)   "'Inebriate' means any person included in any of the following classifications: an
                           excessive drinker, a compulsive drinker, an alcoholic addict, an habitual drunkard
                           or a chronic alcoholic."

N.J. Stat. Ann. (1953)
  3A:1-1(h)   "'Mental incompetent' means a person who as a result of . . . habitual drunkenness
                           is incapable of governing himself and managing his affairs."

STATE AND CITATION   STATUTORY PROVISIONS

PA. Stat. Ann. (1969)
  50, §2061(1)
                                      "'Addict' or 'drug addict,' a person who is or is thought to be so habitually
                                      addicted to the use of opiates as to be unable or unwilling to stop the use of
                                      such substances without help . . . ."

R.I. Gen. Laws Ann. (1968)
  27-8-1
                                      "Alcoholic--chronically addicted to the excessive use of alcohol . . . ."

  21-28-56   ". . . any person within the county . . . addicted to the use of drugs so as to
                                      be dangerous to the peace or safety of the people of the state, or so as to render
                                      his restraint and treatment necessary for his own welfare . . . ."

S.C. Code Ann. (1962)
  32-995
  (Supp. 1968)   "(1) 'Addict' means any person who has the illness known as alcoholism or drug
                                      addiction.

                                      "(2) 'Alcoholism' means the compulsive use of alcoholic beverages excessively to
                                      the extent that he has lost the power of self-control with respect to the use of
                                      such beverages.

                                      "(3) 'Drug addiction' means the compulsive use of drugs and a dependence on the
                                      effects of drugs."

S.D. Compiled Laws Ann.
  (1967)

TENN. Code Ann. (1955)
  33-803
  (Supp. 1968)   "An alcoholic means any person who chronically and habitually uses alcoholic
                                      beverages, stimulants or sedatives to the extent that he has lost the power of
                                      self-control with respect to use of such beverages, stimulants or sedatives, or
                                      while chronically or habitually under the influence of the same endangers public
                                      morals, safety and welfare."

TEX. Rev. Civ. Stat. Ann.
  5561c-3(c)
                                      "An 'alcoholic' means any person who chronically and habitually uses alcoholic
                                      beverages to the extent that he has lost the power of self-control with respect
                                      to the use of such beverages, or while chronically and habitually under the in-
                                      fluence of alcoholic beverages endangers public morals, health, safety or welfare."

UTAH Code Ann. (1968)
  55-13-3
                                      "The term 'alcoholic' . . . means any person who habitually uses alcoholic beverages
                                      to such an extent that he endangers the health, morals, safety or welfare of himself,
                                      or any other person or group of persons."

VT. Stat. Ann. (1968)
  18, §8401
                                      "(1) 'Alcoholic' means a person who because of his use of alcohol in any form shows
                                      signs of mental illness or who has an uncontrollable desire for alcoholic beverages. . . ."

                                      "(3) 'Drug addict' means a person who shows signs of mental illness because of his
                                      use of drugs, hallucinogens, stimulants or sedatives or who has an uncontrollable
                                      desire for their use or consumption. . . ."

VA. Code Ann. (1953)
  37.1-1
  (Supp. 1968)   "(5) 'Drug addict' means a person who, through use of habit-forming drugs has become
                                      dangerous to the public or himself or unable to care for himself or his property or
                                      family. . . ."

                                      "(9) 'Inebriate' means a person who through use of alcoholic liquors has become
                                      dangerous to the public or himself or unable to care for himself or his property
                                      or his family. . . ."

WASH. Rev. Code Ann. (1962)
  70.96.020(4)
                                      "'Alcoholics' are those persons addicted to the excessive use of alcohol, and those
                                      problem drinkers whose dependence upon or addiction to alcohol has attained such a
                                      degree that it causes a noticeable mental disturbance or an interference with their

Table 3.8   STATUTORY DEFINITIONS OF ALCOHOLICS AND DRUG ADDICTS   continued

STATE AND CITATION	STATUTORY PROVISIONS
WASH. Rev. Code Ann. (1962)--*continued*	
70.96.020(4)	bodily and mental health, their inter-personal relations, and their social and economic functioning."
69.32.010	"The term 'narcotic addict' means a person who habitually uses a narcotic drug or drugs."
72.48.020	"Any person shall be held to be a 'drug addict' . . . who unlawfully administers to himself or unlawfully has administered to himself by others, any habit forming narcotic drug."
W.VA. Code Ann. (1966) 27-1-4	"An inebriate person is anyone over the age of eighteen years who is incapable or unfit to properly conduct himself or herself, or his or her affairs, or is dangerous to himself or herself or others by reason of periodical, frequent or constant drunkenness, induced either by the use of alcoholic or other liquors or of opium, morphine, or other narcotic or intoxicating or stupefying substance."
WIS. Stat. Ann. (1957)	
WYO. Stat. Ann. (1967)	

Table 3.9 HOSPITALIZATION OF THE MENTALLY DEFICIENT, EPILEPTICS, ALCOHOLICS, AND DRUG ADDICTS

State	Mentally Deficient	Epileptics	Alcoholics	Drug Addicts
Draft Act				
ALA. Code (1958)	45, §239			22, §249 / 22, §250
ALAS. Stat. (1962)	47.30.340(10)			
ARIZ. Rev. Stat. Ann. (1956)				
ARK. Stat. Ann. (1947)	59-304-306 (Supp. 1967)		59-232, 59-234, 83-709 (Supp. 1967)	59-232, 59-234 (Supp. 1967)
CAL. Welf. & Inst'ns Code (West 1966)	6250-6254 / 6500-6512 / 6715-6719 / 6740-6741 (Supp. 1968)		5000-5153 / 5225-5368 (Supp. 1968)	3000-3305 / 6250-6254 / 6350-6408 / 6700-6713 / 6725-6732 (Supp. 1968)
COLO. Rev. Stat. Ann. (1964)	71-1-5 (Supp. 1966)			
CONN. Gen. Stat. Ann. (1958)	17-172d (Supp. 1969)	17-172d (Supp. 1969)	17-155g (Supp. 1969)	17-185
DEL. Code Ann. (1953)	16-5521 to 16-5523 (Supp. 1970)		16-5321(5)	16-4714 / 16-5321(5)
D.C. Code Ann. (1967)	21-1103 to 21-1108			
FLA. Stat. Ann. (1960)	393.021, 393.03, 393.031, 393.11 (Supp. 1969)		396.061	398.18
GA. Code Ann. (1963)	88-2507 (Supp. 1968)		88-405 (Supp. 1968)	79A-818 (Supp. 1968)
HAWAII Rev. Stat. Ann. (1968)	333-26		334-53-55	334-53-55
IDAHO Code Ann. (1949)	66-329 (Supp. 1969)			
ILL. Ann. Stat. (Smith-Hurd 1966)	91½, §§7-1 to 7-6; & in Supp. 1969, 91½, §§8-1 to 9-13			
IND. Ann. Stat. (1964)	22-1234, 22-1719, 22-2903 to 22-2911; & in Supp. 1969, 22-1209	22-1719; & in Supp. 1969, 22-1209	22-1234, 22-2903 to 22-2911; & in Supp. 1969, 22-1209	22-1234, 22-2903 to 22-2911; & in Supp. 1969, 22-1209
IOWA Code Ann. (1969)	222.16 to 222.40		224.1 to 224.5	224.1 to 224.5
KAN. Stat. Ann. (1964)			fn. 1 / 74-4408	
KY. Rev. Stat. Ann. (1969)	202.010 to 202.130		222.020 to 222.195	
LA. Rev. Stat. Ann. (1950)	28:53, 28:54, 28:56, 28:57, 28:60, 28:61; & in Supp. 1969, 28:52, 28:52.1, 28:55	28:54, 28:56, 28:57, 28:60, 28:61; & in Supp. 1969, 28:52, 28:52.1, 28:55	28:53, 28:54, 28:56, 28:57, 28:60, 28:61; & in Supp. 1969, 28:52, 28:52.1, 28:55	28:53, 28:54, 28:56, 28:57, 28:60, 28:61; & in Supp. 1969, 28:52, 28:52.1, 28:55

State	Mentally Deficient	Epileptics	Alcoholics	Drug Addicts
ME. Rev. Stat. Ann. (1964)	34, §2563		22, §1353	22, §1353
MD. Ann. Code (1968)	41, §323		2C, §306 / 16, §43	
MASS. Ann. Laws (1965)	123, §66A	123, §69	123, §62	123, §62
MICH. Comp. Laws Ann. (1967)	330.21	330.21	330.18	330.18
MINN. Stat. Ann. (1959)	253A.07 (Supp. 1969)	253A.03 to 253A.07 (Supp. 1969)	253A.03 to 253A.07 (Supp. 1969)	253A.03 to 253A.07 (Supp. 1969)
MISS. Code Ann. (1952)	6909-03		436-02 to 436-05	436-02 to 436-05
MO. Rev. Stat. (1959)	202.595 / 202.601			202.360
MONT. Rev. Codes Ann. (1961)				66-1517
NEB. Rev. Stat. (1966)	83-222 (Supp. 1967)	fn. 2 / 83-306(4)	83-306(4)	83-306(4)
NEV. Rev. Stat. (1967)			433.280	433.280
N.H. Rev. Stat. Ann. (1964)	169:18, 171:5 to 171:18		172:13 (II) (Supp. 1967)	
N.J. Stat. Ann. (1964)	30:4-24 (Supp. 1970)			
N.M. Stat. Ann. (1953)	34-3-6 (Supp. 1969)		46-12-7 (Supp. 1969)	54-7-35 / 54-7-36 / 54-7-38 / 54-7-41 / 54-7-51
N.Y. Mental Hygiene Law (McKinney 1951)	121, 123, 124 (Supp. 1970)	151, 153 to 155 (Supp. 1970)	307, 423 (Supp. 1970)	206, 423 (Supp. 1970)
N.C. Gen. Stat. (1964)	122-70 (Supp. 1967)		122-63; & in Supp. 1967, 122-7, 122-65.8	122-63
N.D. Cent. Code (1960)	25-04-04 to 25-04-07 (Supp. 1969)		25-03-08 / 25-03-10 / 25-03-11 (Supp. 1969)	25-03-08 / 25-03-10 / 25-03-11 (Supp. 1969)
OHIO Rev. Code Ann. (Baldwin 1964)	5125.25 / 5125.28 / 5125.30			
OKLA. Stat. Ann. (1954)	43A, §57 / 43A, §58 (Supp. 1969)			minors only. 43A, §431 (Supp. 1969)
ORE. Rev. Stat. (1967)	427.015 to 427.065			475.645
PA. Stat. Ann. (1969)	50, §4406			
R.I. Gen. Laws Ann. (1968)	26-5-9 to 26-5-12		33-15-30 / 40-12-15 to 40-12-17 (1956)	21-28-57 to 21-28-60
S.C. Code Ann. (1962)	32-982 to 32-989		32-995.4 to 32-995.11 (Supp. 1968)	32-995.4 to 32-995.11 (Supp. 1968)
S.D. Compiled Laws Ann. (1967)			27-8-1 to 27-8-4	

Table 3.9   HOSPITALIZATION OF THE MENTALLY DEFICIENT, EPILEPTICS, ALCOHOLICS, AND DRUG ADDICTS   continued

State	Mentally Deficient	Epileptics	Alcoholics	Drug Addicts	State	Mentally Deficient	Epileptics	Alcoholics	Drug Addicts
TENN. Code Ann. (1955)	33-501 to 33-510 (Supp. 1968)		fn. 3 33-810 (Supp. 1968)		VA. Code Ann. (1953)	37.1-63 37.1-66 37.1-67 (Supp. 1968)		37.1-63 37.1-66 37.1-67 (Supp. 1968)	37.1-63 37.1-66 37.1-67 (Supp. 1968)
TEX. Rev. Civ. Stat. Ann. (1958)	3871b.4 to 3871b.8 (1966)	fn. 4 3232b.6 (1968)	5561c-12	3196c-1 (1968)	WASH. Rev. Code Ann. (1962)	72.33.130		70.96.110	69.32.070 72.48.030
UTAH Code Ann. (1968)	64-8-15 to 64-8-20				WIS. Stat. Ann. (1957)	51.065 (Supp. 1969)		51.09 (Supp. 1969)	51.09 (Supp. 1969)
VT. Stat. Ann. (1968)			18, §8402	18, §8402	WYO. Stat. Ann. (1967)			25-32	

1. Article on Commission on Alcoholism has been nonoperative for several years. Kan. 74-4408.

2. "Persons suffering from any type of mental illness whatsoever, whether hereditary or acquired by internal or external conditions, diseases, . . . or any other condition of happening." Neb. 83-306(4).

3. Alcoholics include a person who uses alcoholic beverages, stimulants, or sedatives to such an extent that he has lost the power of self-control in respect to use of same. Tenn. 33-803 (Supp. 1968).

4. Epilepsy shall not bar admission of any person to a state institution or school. Tex. 3232b.6 (1968).

Table 3.10   TEMPORARY OR OBSERVATIONAL HOSPITALIZATION

STATE	INDEPENDENT TEMPORARY OBSERVATIONAL PROCEDURE — Application by: Relative or Guardian	Health or Welfare Officer	Hospital or Physical	Any Citizen	Medical Certificate	No. of Physicians	Further Approval by	PROCEDURE PART OF REGULAR COMMITMENT PROCEEDINGS — During Hearing	After Hearing	Decision by Court	MAXIMUM PERIOD	ACTION AFTER OBSERVATION PERIOD — By Court: Dismissal	By Court: Proceed with a Hearing	By Court: Commitment for Indeterminate Period	By Hospital: Dismissal	By Hospital: Apply for Commitment
DRAFT ACT									9(g)	9(g)	6 months 9(g)	9(g)	9(g), 18	9(g)		9(g)
ALA. Code (1958)																
ALAS. Stat. (1962)																
ARIZ. Rev. Stat. Ann. (1956) (Supp. 1970)									36-515	36-515	fn. 1 / 30 days / 36-515		36-514, 36-515	36-514, 36-515	36-515	
fn. 2 ARK. Stat. Ann. (1947)																
CAL. Welf. & Inst'ns Code (West 1966) (Supp. 1968)										fn. 3 / 5201	72 hours 5206, 5213	5206			5206	5206
COLO. Rev. Stat. Ann. (1964) (Supp. 1966)				71-1-4(1)	fn. 4 / 71-1-4(1), 71-1-4(7)	1 / 71-1-4(1)	district attorney 71-1-4(1) court 71-1-4(4)				3 months 71-1-4(4)	71-1-4(7), 71-1-4(10)	71-1-4(6), 71-1-4(7)	fn. 5 / 71-1-4(8) / 71-1-4(11)		71-1-4(6)
DEL. Code Ann. (1953)																
D.C. Code Ann. (1967)																
FLA. Stat. Ann. (1960)								394.22(12)(a)		fn. 6 / 394.22(12)(a)	6 months 394.22(12)(a)				394.22(12)(b)	394.22(12)(c)
GA. Code Ann. (1963) (Supp. 1969)				88-404.2	88-505.2(b)	1 / 88-505.2(b)	88-505.2(a)				5 days 88-505.5					88-506.3
HAWAII Rev. Stat. Ann. (1968)																
IDAHO Code Ann. (1949) (Supp. 1969)									66-329(h)	66-329(h)	6 months 66-329(h)(3)	66-329(h)(3)	66-329(h)(3)	66-329(h)(3)		66-329(h)(3)
ILL. Ann. Stat. (Smith-Hurd 1966)																
fn. 7 IND. Ann. Stat. (1964)	any peace officer 22-2911			a reputable resident. 22-1212 (Supp. 1969) a reputable citizen. 22-2904	22-1212 (Supp. 1969) fn. 9 22-2904	1 22-1212 (Supp. 1969) 1 22-1213 (Supp. 1969)	court 22-1213 (Supp. 1969) Judge of municipal court. 22-2905				fn. 8 / 90 days / 22-1213 (Supp. 1969) fn. 10 / 10 days / 22-2906	22-1213 (Supp. 1969) 22-2910	22-1213 (Supp. 1969)		22-1213 (Supp. 1969) 22-2910	22-1213 (Supp. 1969) to circuit court. 22-2909

113

Table 3.10   TEMPORARY OR OBSERVATIONAL HOSPITALIZATION   *continued*

STATE	INDEPENDENT TEMPORARY OBSERVATIONAL PROCEDURE							PROCEDURE PART OF REGULAR COMMITMENT PROCEEDINGS				ACTION AFTER OBSERVATION PERIOD				
	Application by				Medical Certificate	No. of Physicians	Further Approval by	During Hearing	After Hearing	Decision by Court	MAXIMUM PERIOD	By Court			By Hospital	
	Relative or Guardian	Health or Welfare Officer	Hospital or Physician	Any Citizen								Dismissal	Proceed with a Hearing	Commitment for Indeterminate Period	Dismissal	Apply for Commitment
fn. 11 IOWA Code Ann. (1969)			fn. 12 229.1		fn. 12 229.1	fn. 12 2 229.1			229.9	commission 229.9	fn. 13 30 days 229.1			commission 229.9	fn. 14 229.1	fn. 14 229.1
KAN. Stat. Ann. (1964) (Supp. 1968)								fn. 15 prior to hearing. 59-2918			90 days 59-2918	59-2918	59-2918		59-2918	
KY. Rev. Stat. Ann. (1969)				202.100		2 202.100					60 days 202.100	202.115(2)	202.115(1)			
LA. Rev. Stat. Ann. (1950)																
ME. Rev. Stat. Ann. (1964)																
MD. Ann. Code (1968)																
MASS. Ann. Laws (1965)					123, §77	2 123, §77	judge 123, §77				40 days 123, §77				123, §77	123, §77
MICH. Comp. Laws Ann. (1967)								330.21		330.21	fn. 16 60 days 330.21		330.21	330.21		330.21
MINN. Stat. Ann. (1959) (Supp. 1969)									253A.07(17)	253A.07(17)	60 days 253A.07(17)	253A.07(24)		253A.07(25)		253A.07(25)
MISS. Code Ann. (1952)																
MO. Rev. Stat. (1959)									202.807(5)	202.807(5)	6 months 202.807(5)	202.807(5)	202.807(5)	202.807(5)		202.807(5)
MONT. Rev. Codes Ann. (1961)					38-402	2 38-203	judge 38-402				fn. 17 2 to 4 weeks 38-402			38-405	38-404	38-405
NEB. Rev. Stat. (1966)																
NEV. Rev. Stat. (1967)																
N.H. Rev. Stat. Ann. (1964)																
N.J. Stat. Ann. (1964)	30:4-46.1		30:4-46.1		30:4-46.1	1 30:4-46.1		before hearings by certifying physicians. 30:4-46.1			7 days 30:4-46.1 20 days 30:4-37			30:4-46.1	30:4-46.1	

Table 3.10   TEMPORARY OR OBSERVATIONAL HOSPITALIZATION   continued

STATE	INDEPENDENT TEMPORARY OBSERVATIONAL PROCEDURE — Application by — Relative or Guardian	Health or Welfare Officer	Hospital or Physician	Any Citizen	Medical Certificate	No. of Physicians	Further Approval by	PROCEDURE PART OF REGULAR COMMITMENT PROCEEDINGS — During Hearing	After Hearing	Decision by Court	MAXIMUM PERIOD	ACTION AFTER OBSERVATION PERIOD — By Court — Dismissal	Proceed with a Hearing	Commitment for Indeterminate Period	By Hospital — Dismissal	Apply for Commitment
N.M. Stat. Ann. (1953)									34-2-5(g)(3)	34-2-5(g)(3)	6 months 34-2-5(g)(3)	34-2-5(g)(3)	34-2-5(g)(3)	34-2-5(g)(3)		34-2-5(g)(3)
N.Y. Mental Hygiene Law (McKinney 1951)(Supp. 1970)				fn. 18 73(1) 78(1)	72						30 days 78(1)				78(2)	78(2)
N.C. Gen. Stat. (1964)								122-61	122-63	clerk 122-63	180 days 122-63	122-63 122-65	122-65	122-65	122-66.1	122-65
N.D. Cent. Code (1960)																
OHIO Rev. Code Ann. (Baldwin 1964)	5122.06(A)	5122.06(A)	5122.06(A)		5122.06(B)	2 5122.06(B)					90 days 5122.06					
OKLA. Stat. Ann. (1954)																
ORE. Rev. Stat. (1967)																
PA. Stat. Ann. (1969)																
R.I. Gen. Laws Ann. (1968)																
S.C. Code Ann. (1962)																
S.D. Compiled Laws Ann. (1967)								27-7-19			reasonable time. 27-7-19		27-7-19	27-7-19		27-7-19
TENN. Code Ann. (1955)			fn. 19 33-603(c)(Supp. 1968)				judge 33-603 (Supp. 1968)		33-604(d)(Supp. 1968)	33-604(d)(Supp. 1968)	6 months 33-604(d)(Supp. 1968) / 14 days 33-603(c)	33-604(d)(Supp. 1968)	33-604(d)(Supp. 1968)	33-604(d)(Supp. 1968)		33-604(d)(Supp. 1968)
TEX. Rev. Civ. Stat. Ann. (1958)				5547-31	5547-32	2 5547-32	judge 5547-38				90 days 5547-38					
UTAH Code Ann. (1968)									64-7-36H	64-7-36H	6 months 64-7-36H	64-7-36H	64-7-36H	64-7-36H		64-7-36H
VT. Stat. Ann. (1968)																
VA. Code Ann. (1953)(Supp. 1968)				37.1-66	37.1-66	2 37.1-66	justice 37.1-66	37.1-67		37.1-67	15 days 37.1-79				37.1-79	37.1-79

Table 3.10 TEMPORARY OR OBSERVATIONAL HOSPITALIZATION   continued

| STATE | INDEPENDENT TEMPORARY OBSERVATIONAL PROCEDURE | | | | | | | PROCEDURE PART OF REGULAR COMMITMENT PROCEEDINGS | | | | ACTION AFTER OBSERVATION PERIOD | | | | |
| | Application by | | | | Medical Certificate | No. of Physicians | Further Approval by | During Hearing | After Hearing | Decision By Court | MAXIMUM PERIOD | By Court | | | By Hospital | |
	Relative or Guardian	Health or Welfare Officer	Hospital or Physician	Any Citizen								Dismissal	Proceed with a Hearing	Commitment for Indeterminate Period	Dismissal	Apply for Commitment
WASH. Rev. Code Ann. (1962)								71.02.130		71.02.130	fn. 20 60 days 71.02.130		71.02.130			
W. VA. Code Ann. (1966)									27-5-4	27-5-4	6 months 27-5-4	27-5-4	27-5-4	27-5-4		27-5-4
WIS. Stat. Ann. (1957)								51.04(3)		51.04(3)	fn. 21 30 days 51.04(3)		51.04(3)			51.04(3)
WYO. Stat. Ann. (1967)																

1. The observation period may be extended only if the superintendent certifies to the judge that such extension is necessary. Ariz. 36-515 (Supp. 1970).

2. Circuit courts may commit for observation. Ark. 59-242 (Supp. 1967).

3. Any individual may apply to the person or agency designated by the county, who shall file the petition "if satisfied that there is probable cause to believe that the person is, as a result of mental disorder, a danger to others, or to himself, or gravely disabled, and that the person will not voluntarily receive evaluation or professional counseling." Cal. W. & I. 5201 (Supp. 1966).

4. "Upon motion of the guardian ad litem, or upon the court's own motion, the court shall issue an order requiring the doctor attending the respondent to file a written report with the court within 10 days thereafter." Colo. 71-1-4(7) (Supp. 1965).

5. The court may extend the initial period of 3 months for an additional period, not to exceed a total of 6 months.   §11 provides for the court, in case of need of continued hospitalization, to proceed on its own motion as if a petition under involuntary commitment had been filed. Colo. 71-1-4(8), (11) (Supp. 1965).

6. If the examining committee finds that the patient is temporarily ill and may speedily be restored. Fla. 394.22(12)(a).

7. The procedure charted above is for a determinate commitment by the court, to be contrasted with the regular indeterminate commitment charted on tables 3.3 and 3.4. The procecure charted below is to be utilized for observation of a person who has refused to submit to an examination so that regular proceedings could not be initiated.

8. Period may be extended for another 90 days at hospital's request. Ind. 22-1213 (Supp. 1969).

9. The superintendent of the psychopathic ward of the city hospital shall hear the facts and may then file the application affidavit

10. May be extended by court upon request of hospital. Ind. 22-2906.

11. The procedure charted above is an independent procedure which can be used only with the written consent of the patient. Iowa 229.1 (Supp. 1968). The procedure charted below is used in conjunction with administrative hospitalization proceedings by the mental health commission. If commission finds person insane, it shall first order his observation and treatment at a screening center located in a hospital. The final hospitalization order cannot be issued until the hospital superintendent so recommends. Iowa 229.9.

12. Attending physician and another physician experienced in the treatment of mental diseases. Iowa 229.1.

13. If the superintendent recommends a further period of observation, the attending physician may authorize same. Iowa 229.1.

14. At expiration of the first observation period: if the hospital finds the person mentally ill, it is merely to report its findings to the mental health commission. After the expiration of the extended period: if commission does not act on hospital's recommendation for hospitalization within 5 days, the superintendent may dismiss the patient. Iowa 229.1.

15. If patient requests in writing that hearing be continued for 90 days, the court may make an order of referral for short-term "care or treatment." Kan. 29-2918 (Supp. 1968).

16. Unless extended by the court for a period not exceeding 60 days. Mich. 330.21.

17. May be extended to 8 weeks. Mont. 38-403.

18. "The director of any hospital (other than a licensed private institution) maintaining adequate staff and facilities . . . may receive or retain . . . as a patient . . . any person alleged to be in need of immediate observation, care or treatment for mental illness." N.Y. Mental Hygeine Law 78(1) (Supp. 1970).

19. After emergency detention of no more than 3 days, the patient may be detained for observation and treatment for a period not exceeding 14 days upon the superintendent's filing of a written petition with the county court and the issuance of an order for such detention. Tenn. 33-603(c) (Supp. 1968).

20. Such observation and treatment period shall not exceed 60 days unless a jury trial has been demanded. Wash. 71.02.130.

21. May be extended for an additional 60 days. Wis. 51.04(3).

with the municipal court. Ind. 22-2904. The superintendent shall file the application with the court if the applicant is a peace officer. Ind. 22-2911.

Table 3.11   EMERGENCY DETENTION

STATE	APPLICATION BY				CERTIFICATION			CONDITION REQUIREMENT		DETENTION PLACE				MAXIMUM PERIOD
	Any Person	Relative, Friend, Spouse, or Guardian	Public Official	Doctor	Medical	Judicial	Other	Dangerous	Need of Aid	Jail	Public Hospital	Private Institution		
fn. 1 DRAFT ACT	7(a)(1)		fn. 2 / 8(a)		fn. 3 / 7(a)(2)	fn. 3 / 7(b)	fn. 3 / 7(b)	7(a)(1), 8(a), 8(b)			7(b), 8(b)	1(e), 7(b), 8(b)		fn. 4
ALA. Code (1958)														
ALAS. Stat. (1962)		47.30.030(a) 47.30.030(b)	peace officer. 47.30.030(a) 47.30.030(b)		47.30.030(a)		47.30.030(b)	47.30.030(a) 47.30.030(b)		fn. 5 47.30.090(a)	47.30.030(a) 47.30.030(b)	47.30.090(a)		48 hours unless certified. 47.30.040(b) release on request unless petition for commitment is filed. 47.30.050(a)
ARIZ. Rev. Stat. Ann. (1956) (Supp. 1970)		36-507A.1	36-507A.1		36-507A.2	fn. 6 / 36-507C, 36-512		36-507A			36-507C	fn. 6 / 36-507C / 36-512		fn. 6 / 10 days / 36-508 / 36-512
ARK. Stat. Ann. (1947)														
CAL. Welf. & Inst'ns Code (West 1966) (Supp. 1968)			fn. 7 / 5150				fn. 8 / 5150	5150			5150	5150		72 hours / 5150
COLO. Rev. Stat. Ann. (1964)			peace officer. 71-1-3(1)					71-1-3(1)		fn. 9 / 71-1-3(1)	fn. 9 / 71-1-3(1)	fn. 9 / 71-1-3(1)		fn. 10 / 24 hours / 71-1-3(3)(a)
CONN. Gen. Stat. Ann. (1958) (Supp. 1969)					17-183		fn. 11 / 17-183	17-183			17-183	17-183		fn. 12 / 30 days / 17-183
fn. 13 DEL. Code Ann. (1953) (Supp. 1970)	16-5122(b)				16-5122(c)			16-5122(a)			16-5122(c)			72 hours / 16-5122(d)
fn. 14 D.C. Code Ann. (1967)			health official or peace officer. 21-521	family physician, 21-521	psychiatrist on duty at hospital, 21-522			21-522			acceptance mandatory. 21-522	acceptance mandatory. 21-522		48 hours 21-523
FLA. Stat. Ann. (1960) (Supp. 1969)			peace officer. 394.201(2)(a)	394.201(2)(a)	394.201(2)(a)		394.201(2)(a)	394.201(2)(a)			except state. 394.191(1) 394.201(2)(a)	394.201(2)(a) 394.201(2)(b)		fn. 15 / 394.201(4)
GA. Code Ann. (1963)				88-504.2 (Supp. 1969)	88-504.2 (Supp. 1969)			88-504.2 (Supp. 1969)			emergency receiving facility. 88.504.2			24 hours 88-504.4 (Supp. 1969)
HAWAII Rev. Stat. Ann. (1968)			334-54(c)	334-54(a)	334-54(a)			334-54(a)			334-1, 334-54(a)	334-1, 334-54(a)		48 hours 334-54(b)
IDAHO Code Ann. (1949)														

Table 3.11 EMERGENCY DETENTION continued

STATE	APPLICATION BY				CERTIFICATION			CONDITION REQUIREMENT		DETENTION PLACE			MAXIMUM PERIOD
	Any Person	Relative, Friend, Spouse, or Guardian	Public Official	Doctor	Medical	Judicial	Other	Dangerous	Need of Aid	Jail	Public Hospital	Private Institution	
ILL. Ann. Stat. (Smith-Hurd 1966) (Supp. 1969)	fn. 16 / 91½, §7-1				fn. 17 / 91½, §7-1			91½, §1-11 / 91½, §7-1	91½, §1-11 / 91½, §7-1		91½, §7-1	91½, §7-1	fn. 18 / 91½, §7-6
IND. Ann. Stat. fn. 19 (1964)			health or police officer. 22-1234					22-1234			22-1234		15 days 22-1234
IOWA Code Ann. (1969)													
KAN. Stat. Ann. (1964) (Supp. 1968)	59-2909(C)		any peace officer. 59-2908 59-2909(B)		59-2909	59-2908		59-2908 59-2909(B)(3) 59-2909(C)(3)			fn. 20 59-2908 59-2909	59-2908 59-2909	fn. 21 59-2908
KY. Rev. Stat. fn. 22 Ann. (1969)	202.027(2) 202.117(1)		any peace officer. 202.027(1) 202.245(1)		202.027(1) fn. 23 202.117(1) 202.245(1)	202.027(2) 202.117(1) 202.245(1)		202.027(1) 202.245(1)	202.117(1) 202.245(1)	fn. 24 202.245(1)	202.027(3) 202.117(1) 202.245(1)	202.027(3)	7 days 202.027(5) 48 hours 202.117(1) 7 days 202.245(1)
LA. Rev. Stat. Ann. (1950)		28:57	28:57		28:57				28:57		28:2(8), 28:57	28:2(8), 28:57	30 days 28:57
ME. Rev. Stat. Ann. (1964) (Supp. 1969)	34, §2333		34, §2333		34, §2333	endorsement 34, §2332		34, §2332			34, §2333	34, §2333	fn. 25
MD. Ann. Code (1968)													
MASS. Ann. Laws (1965)			fn. 26 / 123, §78	fn. 26 / 123, §78	fn. 27 / 123, §78			123, §78	fn. 26 / 123, §78	fn. 28 / 123, §82	123, §78	123, §78	5 days 123, §78
MICH. Comp. Laws Ann. (1967) (Supp. 1969)			judge, justice of peace, police justice, or peace officer. 330.19		2 physicians. 330.19	prosecuting attorney. 330.19		public safety. 330.19		330.19	330.19	330.19	fn. 29 5 days. 330.19
MINN. Stat. Ann. (1959) (Supp. 1969)			peace or health officer. 253A.04(2)	253A.04(1)	253A.04			fn. 30 253A.04			consent of head of hospital. 253A.04	consent of head of hospital. 253A.04	72 hours 253A.04
MISS. Code Ann. (1952)													
MO. Rev. Stat. (1959)	202.800		fn. 2 / 202.803		fn. 31 / 202.800	fn. 31 / 202.800		202.800 202.803			202.800 202.803	202.800 202.803	fn. 4
MONT. Rev. Codes Ann. (1961)			38-208.1		fn. 32 / 38-208.1			fn. 33 / 38-208.1			38-208.1		5 days 38-208.2

Table 3.11   EMERGENCY DETENTION   *continued*

STATE	APPLICATION BY				CERTIFICATION			CONDITION REQUIREMENT		DETENTION PLACE			MAXIMUM PERIOD
	Any Person	Relative, Friend, Spouse, or Guardian	Public Official	Doctor	Medical	Judicial	Other	Dangerous	Need of Aid	Jail	Public Hospital	Private Institution	
fn. 34 NEB. Rev. Stat. (1966)													
NEV. Rev. Stat. (1967)	433.672				psychiatrist or physician 433.673	fn. 35 433.672		fn. 35 433.672			fn. 35 433.672		48 hours or court order not to exceed 7 days. 433.677
N.H. Rev. Stat. Ann. (1964)					fn. 36 1 or 2 physicians 135:21-a			fn. 37 135:21-a			135:21-a		fn. 36 24 hours 135:21-a
N.J. Stat. Ann. (1964)	34:4-38	30:4-27	constables and police officers 30:4-26.3 (Supp. 1970)		2 physicians 30:4-38	fn. 38 30:4-38		30:4-26.3 (Supp. 1970) 30:4-38			fn. 39 30:4-26.3 (Supp. 1970) 30:4-38		20 days 30:4-38 15 days 30:4-26.3 (Supp. 1970)
N.M. Stat. Ann. (1953) (Supp. 1969)		34-2-18A(1)	34-2-18A(1)		1 physician 34-2-18A(2)			fn. 40 34-2-18D			34-2-18B	fn. 41 34-2-18B	fn. 42 5 days 34-2-18F 34-2-18G
N.Y. Mental Hygiene Law (McKinney 1951) (Supp. 1970)			peace officer 78.3					fn. 43 78.3			78.3		30 days 78
N.C. Gen. Stat. (1964) (Supp. 1967)	122-59				fn. 44 122-59	fn. 44 122-59		122-59			122-59	122-59	20 days 122-59
N.D. Cent. Code (1960) (Supp. 1969)			25-03-08	25-03-08		25-03-08		25-03-08			25-03-08	25-03-08	fn. 45 25-03-08
OHIO Rev. Code Ann. (Baldwin 1960)	5122.08		5122.10		5122.08	5122.09		5122.08 5122.10			5122.08 5122.10	5122.08 5122.10	60 days with medical certificate. 5122.08 5 days without medical certificate. 5122.10
OKLA. Stat. Ann. (1954) (Supp. 1969)			43A, §55			43A, §55		43A, §55		fn. 46 43A, §55			30 days 43A, §55
ORE. Rev. Stat. (1967)	fn. 47 426.180						fn. 48 426.180		426.180		426.180		15 days 426.210
PA. Stat. Ann. (1969)		50, §4405(a)	50, §4405(a)		50, §4405(a)(1)			50, §4405(a)(2)			50, §4401	50, §4401	10 days 50, §4405(f)
R.I. Gen. Laws Ann. (1968)			26-2-1		fn. 49 26-2-2			26-2-1			fn. 50 26-2-1		

Table 3.11 EMERGENCY DETENTION *continued*

STATE	APPLICATION BY				CERTIFICATION			CONDITION REQUIREMENT		DETENTION PLACE			MAXIMUM PERIOD
	Any Person	Relative, Friend, Spouse, or Guardian	Public Official	Doctor	Medical	Judicial	Other	Dangerous	Need of Aid	Jail	Public Hospital	Private Institution	
S.C. Code Ann. (1962)	32-956(1)				32-956(2)	fn. 51 / 32-957		32-356(1)			32-356		fn. 52 / 32-972
S.D. Compiled Laws Ann. (1967)													
TENN. Code Ann. (1955) (Supp. 1968)			fn. 53 / 33-603(a)	33-603(a)	fn. 27 / 33-603(b)			33-603(b)			33-603(b)	33-603(b)	3 days / 33-603(c)
TEX. Rev. Civ. Stat. Ann. (1958) (Supp. 1969)			health or peace officer. 5547-27		5547-28(C)	fn. 51 / 5547-27		5547-27			5547-27	5547-27	24 hours / 5547-27
UTAH Code Ann. (1968)		64-7-34	fn. 2 / 64-7-34 / 64-7-35		fn. 54 / 64-7-34	fn. 54 / 64-7-34	fn. 54 / 64-7-34	64-7-34, 64-7-35			64-7-34, 64-7-35		fn. 4
VT. Stat. Ann. (1968)			police officer 18, §7505(2)			18, §7505(a)		18, §7507(a)			18, §7101(7) / 18, §7505(a)	18, §7101(7) / 18, §7505(a)	fn. 55 / 5 days / 18, §7803
VA. Code Ann. (1953)													
WASH. Rev. Code Ann. (1962)													
W. VA. Code Ann. (1966)	27-5-3 (Supp. 1969)		27-5-2, 27-5-3 (Supp. 1969)		27-5-2 (Supp. 1969)	27-5-3 (Supp. 1969)	27-5-3 (Supp. 1969)	27-5-2, 27-5-3 (Supp. 1969)			27-5-2, 27-5-3 (Supp. 1969)		fnn. 4, 56 / 27-5-6
WIS. Stat. Ann. (1957)	fn. 57 / 51.04(1) (Supp. 1969)			fn. 57 / 51.04(1) (Supp. 1969)	51.04(1) (Supp. 1969)			51.04(1) (Supp. 1969)			51.04(4)	51.04(4)	fn. 58 / 51.04(1) (Supp. 1969)
WYO. Stat. Ann. (1967)			fn. 59 / 25-58(a)	25-58(a)	25-58(b)	25-58(b)		25-58(a) / 25-58(b)		fn. 60 / 25-58(a) / 25-62	25-58(a) / 25-62	25-58(a) / 25-62	fn. 61 / 48 hours / 25-58(d)

Notes to Table 3.11   EMERGENCY DETENTION

1. Draft Act provides for 2 emergency procedures: hospitalization on medical certification, §7, and hospitalization without endorsement on medical certification, §8. Both are charted.

2. If a peace or health officer has reason to believe that a person cannot be allowed to go unrestrained pending an examination, he may transport him to a hospital without process, even if there has been no medical certification. Draft Act 8(b); Mo. 202.803; Utah 64-7-35.

3. When the medical certificate has been endorsed by a judge or the central agency, it authorizes any health or peace officer to take the person into custody and transport him to a hospital. Draft Act 7(b).

4. Although there is no specified maximum period of detention, if an examination is not arranged by the head of the hospital within 5 days after admission, the patient must be released. Draft Act 13; Utah 64-7-40; W. Va. 27-5-6.

   Also, release must be granted within 48 hours of request by patient except that the court may, upon certification by the head of the hospital that release would be unsafe, postpone such release for 5 days pending commencement of proceedings for judicial commitment. Draft Act 17; Mo. 202.833; Utah 64-7-44.

5. Only "because of and during an extreme emergency." Alas. 47.30-.090(a).

6. Application must be approved by the judge before the alleged mentally ill person may be taken into custody. However, if a person becomes ill at night, on a legal holiday or at some other time when a judge is not available, he may be taken to any hospital except the state hospital upon the presentation of the petition. Application must be presented to the judge within 48 hours unless a legal holiday falls on Saturday or Monday, and then it must be presented within 72 hours. Ariz. 36-507C, 36-512 (A&B) (Supp. 1970).

7. Peace officer or other professional person designated by the county. Cal. Welf. & Inst'ns 5150 (Supp. 1968).

8. "Application in writing stating the circumstances under which the person's condition was called to the officer's or professional person's attention, and stating that the officer or professional person believes as a result of his personal observations that the person is, as a result of a mental disorder, a danger to others, or to himself, or gravely disabled." Cal. Welf. & Inst'ns 5150 (Supp. 1968).

9. ". . . place him in a suitable place of custody. . . ." Colo. 71-1-3(1).

10. Saturday, Sunday, and legal holidays excluded. Colo. 71-1-3(3)-(a).

11. No detention if the doctor of the patient's own choosing finds he is not mentally ill. Conn. 17-183 (Supp. 1969).

12. If a complaint for commitment is filed within the 30 days, confinement may be continued, without court order, for an additional 30 days. Conn. 17-183 (Supp. 1969).

13. Upon the petition of any person, alleging dangerous mental illness, a peace officer may immediately take the subject into custody and transport him to a licensed medical doctor for examination. The doctor shall, if possible, give telephonic notice to the nearest known relative. The doctor may either discharge the subject or have him transferred to the state hospital, certifying his actions and reasons in either case. The superintendent of the state hospital shall examine the subject within 72 hours, excluding Saturdays, Sundays, and holidays, and shall either discharge him or seek admission or commitment under another provision. Del. 16-5122 (Supp. 1970).

14. Within 24 hours after admission, notice shall be served, by registered mail, to the spouse, parent or legal guardian. D.C. 21-522.

15. Release is to be forthwith when written request is made by patient, spouse, guardian, or next of kin. However, if within 1 (business) day of request the superintendent certifies to the county judge that release would be dangerous, it may be postponed for not more than 5 days for the commencement of judicial proceedings. Fla. 394.201-(4) (Supp. 1969).

16. Application must be verified and must include names of witnesses by whom facts alleged may be proven. Ill. 91½, §7-1 (Supp. 1969).

17. No medical certificate is required if the petition alleges that it was impossible to have the patient examined, but in such case the patient may not be detained for more than 24 hours unless a certificate is provided to or by the hospital. Ill. 91½, §7-2, §7-3 (Supp. 1969).

18. The hospital must file a petition for a court hearing within 24 hours of admission. The court hearing must be held within 5 business days, according to the procedure for a judicial hospitalization order. The patient may be detained pending such proceedings. Ill. 91½, §7-6 (Supp. 1969).

19. The procedure charted is limited to the Beatty Memorial Hospital. Ind. 22-1234.

20. To any "general hospital" or "psychiatric hospital" but if not available, peace officer may detain in any other suitable place within his jurisdiction. Kan. 59-2908, 59-2909 (Supp. 1968).

21. Until the close of the first day on which the probate court is "available." Kan. 59-2908 (Supp. 1968).

22. The procedure charted above is the emergency detention provision for dangerous mental patients. §§202.117 and 202.245 charted below apply to a temporary admission of a person presented to the state hospital and an admission based upon a personal examination by a health officer, respectively.

23. The admission is conditioned upon certification by a hospital staff physician that the person is in need of immediate treatment and is incapable of making responsible application. Ky. 202.117(1) and (3).

24. If the patient is certified to be dangerous, he may be confined, if hospital facilities are not available, in the county jail for a period not to exceed 48 hours. Ky. 202.245(1).

25. No specified time, but admission must be within 3 days after the date of examination. Me. 34, §2333 (Supp. 1969).

26. A second procedure provides that proceedings can be initiated on request of any doctor or public official; persons in need of care may be detained for 10 days. Mass. 123, §79.

27. Two required. Mass. 123, §78; Tenn. 33-603(b) Supp. 1968).

28. Maximum period of detention in jail, if required in case of emergency, is 12 hours. Mass. 123, §82.

29. Any peace officer, with the approval of the prosecuting attorney, is authorized to confine dangerous persons for not more than 48 hours, Sundays and legal holidays excluded. Mich. 330.19 (Supp. 1969).

30. If person is mentally ill or inebriate and is in imminent danger of causing injury to himself or others if not immediately restrained, and if an order of the court cannot be obtained in time to prevent such anticipated injury. Minn. 253A.04 (Supp. 1969).

31. Medical certificate endorsed by a judge authorizes health and peace officers to take patient to hospital. Mo. 202.800.

32. County physician of county in which patient resides. Mont. 38-208.1.

33. Person must be suffering from acute mania or circular insanity and require immediate hospitalization. Mont. 38-208.1.

34. Any state or licensed private institution may receive a patient upon written application of relatives or friends and accompanied by a certification by 2 licensed physicians that the person is mentally ill. The request must be granted unless involuntary commitment proceedings are instituted. The patient may be held until he or anyone in his behalf requests release. Neb. 83-322.01. Also see 83-357.

35. District attorney may, if satisfied a person is likely to injure

---

himself or others, issue an order to any peace officer for the immediate apprehension of such person and his transportation to a public hospital for emergency observation and diagnosis. Nev. 433.672.

36. "In an emergency a person may be admitted . . . on the certificate of one examining physician; provided, however, that the person so admitted shall not be detained at said hospital for a period longer than twenty-four hours unless a second examining physician shall certify in writing that in his opinion such person is in need of institutionalization by reason of mental illness, based upon a personal examination made within twenty-four hours after admission to the hospital." N.H. 135:21-a.

37. Person's mental state is disturbed so as to constitute a threat to his own life and/or a danger to his family or the community. N.H. 135:21-a.

38. The court must issue an order of temporary commitment before detention, unless impossible. If impossible, the order must be made after commitment. N.J. 30:4-38.

39. Counties are also to provide mental hospital facilities for temporary detention of patients for purposes of observation, examination, and treatment. Detention in such facilities is limited to 15 days unless extended by a court order. N.J. 30:4-26.3 (Supp. 1970).

40. Unless certified in need of care and custody by hospital physician, the patient shall be released immediately. N.M. 34-2-18D (Supp. 1969).

41. Only private institutions which have been approved by state department of public health as suitable for custody and care of such patients. N.M. 34-2-18B (Supp. 1969).

42. Unless hospital superintendent or admitting physician commences judicial hospitalization proceedings. N.M. 34-2-18F (Supp. 1969).

43. "[I]s conducting himself in a manner which in a sane person would be disorderly. . . ." N.Y. Mental Hygiene Law 78.3 (Supp. 1970).

44. Affidavit, sworn to before notary or deputy sheriff, or any qualified physician, or certified by the clerk of superior court. N.C. 122-59 (Supp. 1967).

45. Patient must be released within 5 days after valid request for release unless superintendent of institution or county judge who consented to emergency admission or the county mental health board apply for postponement of release for a period up to 20 days so as to commence proceedings for a judicial determination. N.D. 25-03-10 (Supp. 1969).

46. "[S]ome suitable place. . . ." Okla. 43A, §55 (Supp. 1969).

47. Any 2 persons. Ore. 426.180.

48. County health officer or, if that officer is unable to act or is related to such person by blood or marriage, then by 2 physicians not related to such person. Ore. 426.180.

49. "Whenever such complaint shall be accompanied by a certificate. . . ." R.I. 26-2-2.

50. "[A]t such time and place within the district as shall be named in the warrant." R.I. 26-2-1.

51. Judicial order must be obtained within 48 hours in South Carolina and within 24 hours in Texas after patient has been taken into protective custody by public officer. S.C. 32-957; Tex. 5547-27 (Supp. 1969).

52. Release within 7 days after request unless superintendent starts commitment proceedings. S.C. 32-953(4). Request for release from hospital may be denied if made sooner than 30 days after admission. S.C. 32-972.

53. Any state, county, or municipal officer authorized to make arrests in Tennessee. Tenn. 33-603(a) (Supp. 1968).

54. Medical certificate endorsed by judge, local board of health, or a member of the board of county commissioners. Utah 67-7-34.

55. Patient shall be discharged within 5 days from date of admission unless within that period proceedings for his hospitalization are commenced. Vt. 18, §7803.

56. Until commitment proceedings which must be petitioned for within 30 days after hospitalization. W. Va. 27-5-6.

57. Application by 3 persons, 1 of whom must be a physician, enables the sheriff or other peace officer to take into custody an alleged mentally ill person; however, the sheriff or peace officer may take into custody any person who is violent, threatens violence or appears irresponsible or dangerous. Wis. 51.04(1) (Supp. 1969).

58. Upon medical certification, a police officer may confine the patient for 5 days. Upon endorsement by a court, however, the period may be 10 days. Wis. 51.04(1) (Supp. 1969), 51.04(2).

59. "Any head of a hospital or general hospital, physician, public health, welfare, or peace officer who has evidence that an individual is mentally ill. . . ." Wyo. 25-58(a).

60. A patient taken into custody may be detained in his home, in a local general hospital, or other suitable facility. Only during extreme emergency shall individuals be detained in a nonmedical facility used for the detention of individuals charged with or convicted of penal offenses. Wyo. 25-62.

61. If after examination it is certified that the individual should be hospitalized, according to requirements, he may be detained for 48 hours after such examination, exclusive of Sundays and holidays, at the end of which the patient shall be released unless the district judge or commissioner shall have authorized immediate transportation to a hospital or protective custody. Wyo. 25-58.

Table 3.12   LEGAL COUNSEL IN HOSPITALIZATION PROCEEDINGS

| STATE | RIGHT TO BE REPRESENTED | COURT-APPOINTED COUNSEL IF PATIENT NOT REPRESENTED | | | COUNSEL COMPENSATED BY COUNTY OR STATE |
		Mandatory	Discretionary	Mandatory on Patient's Request	
Draft Act	9(f)	9(f)			
ALA. Code (1958)					
ALAS. Stat. (1962)	47.30.070(h)	47.30.070(h)			
ARIZ. Rev. Stat. Ann. (1956)	36-514A (Supp. 1970)	36-514A (Supp. 1970)			
ARK. Stat. Ann. (1947)					
CAL. Welf. & Inst'ns Code (West 1966)	5206, 5276, 5302 (Supp. 1968)	5302 (Supp. 1968)		5276 (Supp. 1968)	public defender. 5276, 5302 (Supp. 1968)
COLO. Rev. Stat. Ann. (1964)	71-1-8	fn. 1 71-1-8			county 71-1-18(1)
CONN. Gen. Stat. Ann. (1960)	17-178 (Supp. 1969)				17-196
DEL. Code Ann. (1953)					
D.C. Code Ann. (1967)	21-543	21-543			21-543
FLA. Stat. Ann. (1960)	394.22(4)		394.22(4)	"may" if indigent. 394.22(7)(b)	county of indigent 394.22(7)(b)
GA. Code Ann. (1963)	88-505.3(a) (Supp. 1969)			88-505.3(a) (Supp. 1969)	88-508.2(d) (Supp. 1969)
HAWAII Rev. Stat. Ann. (1968)	on appeal 334-82		334-82		334-6
IDAHO Code Ann. (1949)	66-329(g) (Supp. 1969)	66-329(g) (Supp. 1969)			county. 66-329(g) (Supp. 1969)
ILL. Ann. Stat. (Smith-Hurd 1966)	91 1/2, §6-4, 91 1/2, §9-4 (Supp. 1969)	91 1/2, §6-4, 91 1/2, §9-4 (Supp. 1969)			91 1/2, §9-4 (Supp. 1969)
IND. Ann. Stat. (1964)	22-1209 (Supp. 1969)				
IOWA Code Ann. (1969)	229.5	229.5			county. 229.5
KAN. Stat. Ann. (1964)	59-2914(c) (Supp. 1968)	59-2914(c) (Supp. 1968)			59-2934 (Supp. 1968)
KY. Rev. Stat. Ann. (1969)	202.136	202.136			
LA. Rev. Stat. Ann. (1950)	fn. 2 28:141				if patient unable, parish of domicile 28:141
ME. Rev. Stat. Ann. (1964)	34, §2334	34, §2334			34, §2421(1)

Table 3.12   LEGAL COUNSEL IN HOSPITALIZATION PROCEEDINGS   continued

| STATE | RIGHT TO BE REPRESENTED | COURT-APPOINTED COUNSEL IF PATIENT NOT REPRESENTED | | | COUNSEL COMPENSATED BY COUNTY OR STATE |
		Mandatory	Discretionary	Mandatory on Patient's Request	
MD. Ann. Code (1968)					
MASS. Ann. Laws (1965)	123, §51				
MICH. Comp. Laws Ann. (1967)	330.21				
MINN. Stat. Ann. (1959)	253A.07.15 (Supp. 1969)	fn. 3 253A.07.15 (Supp. 1969)			county. 253A.20.1 (Supp. 1969)
MISS. Code Ann. (1952)					
MO. Rev. Stat. (1959)	202.807.4	202.807.4			
MONT. Rev. Codes Ann. (1961)					
NEB. Rev. Stat. (1966)	83-325 (Supp. 1967)			83-325.01 (Supp. 1967)	fn. 4 county. 83-325.04 (Supp. 1967)
NEV. Rev. Stat. (1967)	433.693(1)		fn. 5 433.693(1)		county or state. 433.693(2)
N.H. Rev. Stat. Ann. (1964)					
N.J. Stat. Ann. (1964)	30:4-41 (Supp. 1970)				
N.M. Stat. Ann. (1953)	34-2-5(f)	34-2-5(f)			fn. 6 county. 34-2-20
N.Y. Mental Hygiene Law (McKinney 1951)	77 (Supp. 1970)				county or city. 77 (Supp. 1970)
N.C. Gen. Stat. (1964)					
N.D. Cent. Code (1960)	25-03-11(6) (Supp. 1969)			25-03-11(6) (Supp. 1969)	county where patient cannot pay. 25-03-11(6) (Supp. 1969)
OHIO Rev. Code Ann. (Baldwin 1964)	fn. 7 5122.12(E) 5122.15		fn.8 5122.12 5122.15		
OKLA. Stat. Ann. (1954)	fn. 9 43A, §4 (Supp. 1969)				
ORE. Rev. Stat. (1967)	426.100(1)		fn. 10 426.100(1)	426.100(1)	county. 426.100(2)
PA. Stat. Ann. (1969)					
R.I. Gen. Laws Ann. (1968)	26-2-11	26-2-13			state 26-2-13

Table 3.12   LEGAL COUNSEL IN HOSPITALIZATION PROCEEDINGS   continued

| STATE | RIGHT TO BE REPRESENTED | COURT-APPOINTED COUNSEL IF PATIENT NOT REPRESENTED | | | COUNSEL COMPENSATED BY COUNTY OR STATE |
		Mandatory	Discretionary	Mandatory on Patient's Request	
S.C. Code Ann. (1962)	32-962	32-962			
S.D. Compiled Laws Ann. (1967)	27-7-7 27-7-13				
TENN. Code Ann. (1955)	33-604(c) (Supp. 1968)	33-604(c) (Supp. 1968)			
TEX. Rev. Civ. Stat. Ann. (1958)	5547-43 5547-44	5547-43 5547-44			
UTAH Code Ann. (1968)	64-7-36G	64-7-36G			county. 64-7-44
VT. Stat. Ann. (1968)	18, §7602 18, §7802	18, §7802			
VA. Code Ann. (1953)	37.1-67 (Supp. 1968)	37.1-67 (Supp. 1968)			county or city. 37.1-89
WASH. Rev. Code Ann. (1962)	71.02.140 71.02.190				county. 71.02.230
W. VA. Code Ann. (1966)	fn. 11 27-5-4	fn. 11 27-5-4			county court. 27-5-4
WIS. Stat. Ann. (1957)	fn. 12 51.02		fn. 8 51.02		
WYO.					
WYO. Stat. Ann. (1967)	25-60(d)(g)	25-60(d)(g)			district court funds for county. 25-60(g)

1. He must be given at least 2 days notice of the proceedings and must attend all meetings of the medical commission. Colo. 71-1-8(1).

2. If the patient is unable to pay, parish of domicile in the case of a resident or the state mental health department in the case of a nonresident shall compensate counsel. La. 28:141.

3. In all such proceedings the county attorney shall appear and represent the petitioner. The proposed patient shall be afforded an opportunity to be represented by counsel, and if neither the proposed patient nor others provide counsel, the court at the time the examiners or licensed physicians are appointed shall appoint counsel to represent the proposed patient. Minn. 253A.07.15 (Supp. 1969),

4. In counties having a public defender he shall defend as patient's counsel. Neb. 83-325.03 (Supp. 1967).

5. If person fails or refuses to obtain counsel, the court shall advise him and his guardian or next of kin, if known, of such right to counsel and may appoint counsel. Nev. 433.693(1).

6. General cost of commitment to be paid by county. N.M. 34-2-20.

7. Notice of hearing sent to patient's nominee or attorney if no nomination is made. Ohio 5122.12(E).

8. Court may appoint guardian ad litem. Ohio 5122.12; Wis. 51.02(4).

9. "Right to be represented by counsel may be at discretion of judge--The County Attorneys . . . shall represent the state in all proceedings under the mental health law wherein the alleged mentally ill person is represented by counsel." Okla. 43A-4 (Supp. 1969).

10. If no request for legal counsel is made, the court may, at its discretion, appoint legal counsel. Ore. 426.100(1).

11. "The mental hygiene commission shall appoint a guardian ad litem who shall be a competent attorney, for the individual, and said guardian shall be present at the hearing to protect the interests of the individual." W. Va. 27-5-4.

12. "At the hearing any party in interest . . . may examine . . . witnesses . . . and . . . offer evidence. The hearing . . . shall be open . . . to persons in interest and their attorneys and witnesses." Wis. 51.02(2).

Table 3.13   FINANCIAL RESPONSIBILITY FOR PATIENT'S SUPPORT IN HOSPITAL

STATE Draft Act	PATIENT		FAMILY		COUNTY		STATE	
	Voluntary Admission	Involuntary Admission	Voluntary Admission	Involuntary Admission	Voluntary Admission	Involuntary Admission	Voluntary Admission	Involuntary Admission
ALA. Code (1958)		45, §212 to 45, §214		45, §213				45, §212
ALAS. Stat. (1962)	47.30.270(a) 47.30.270(d)	47.30.270(a) 47.30.270(d)	47.30.270	47.30.270			47.30.270	47.30.270
ARIZ. Rev. Stat. Ann. (1956)	36-503 (Supp. 1970)	36-520B if other than state hospital 36-520H (Supp. 1970)		if other than state hospital 36-520H (Supp. 1970)			36-503 (Supp. 1970)	state hospital only. 36-520H (Supp. 1970)
ARK. Stat. Ann. (1947)	59-230 59-230.1, 59-230.2 (Supp. 1967)	59-230 59-230.1, 59-230.2 (Supp. 1967)	59-230 59-230.2 (Supp. 1967)	59-230 59-230.2 (Supp. 1967)			59-230	59-230
CAL. Welf. & Inst'ns Code (West 1966)	6050 (Supp. 1968)	7279 (Supp. 1968)	6050 (Supp. 1968)	7275 (Supp. 1968)				7275 (Supp. 1968)
COLO. Rev. Stat. Ann. (1964)	71-7-1(1) (Supp. 1965)	71-7-1(1) (Supp. 1965)	71-7-1(1) (Supp. 1965)	71-7-1(1) (Supp. 1965)			71-7-1(1) (Supp. 1965)	71-7-1(1) (Supp. 1965)
CONN. Gen. Stat. Ann. (1958)	17-182	17-182	17-185	17-182			17-182	17-182
DEL. Code Ann. (1953)	16-5127(a)	16-5127(a)	fn. 1 16-5127(a)	fn. 1 16-5127(a)			16-5127	16-5127
D.C. Code Ann. (1967)	21-586(a)	21-586(a)	21-586(a)	21-586(a)			21-586	21-586
FLA. Stat. Ann. (1960)	394.12; & in Supp. 1969, 394.20(5)	394.12, 394.22(13); & in Supp. 1969, 394.201(6)	394.12	394.12			394.12	394.22(13)
GA. Code Ann. (1963)	88-508.8(a) (Supp. 1969)	88-508.8(a) (Supp. 1969)	88.508.8(b) (Supp. 1969)	88-508.8(b) (Supp. 1969)	88-508.8(c) (Supp. 1969)	88-508.8(c) (Supp. 1969)		
HAWAII Rev. Stat. Ann. (1968)	334-6	334-6	fn. 2 334-37	fn. 2 334-37			334-6	334-6
IDAHO Code Ann. (1949)	66-354(a) (Supp. 1969)	66-354(a) (Supp. 1969)	66-354(a) 66-354(b) (Supp. 1969)	66-354(a) 66-354(b) (Supp. 1969)			66-354 (Supp. 1969)	66-354 (Supp. 1969)
ILL. Ann. Stat. (Smith-Hurd 1966)	91 1/2, §12-12 (Supp. 1969)	91 1/2, §12-12 (Supp. 1969)	91 1/2, §1-19, 91 1/2, §12-12 (Supp. 1969)	91 1/2, §1-19, 91 1/2, §12-12 (Supp. 1969)			91 1/2, §12-12 (Supp. 1969)	91 1/2, §12-12 (Supp. 1969)
IND. Ann. Stat. (1964)	22-410(a)	22-410(a)	22-410(a)	22-410(a)			22-411	22-411
IOWA Code Ann. (1969)	230.15	230.15	230.15	230.15	230.1 230.20	230.1 230.20	fn. 3 230.1	fn. 3 230.1
KAN. Stat. Ann. (1964)	59-2006 (Supp. 1968)	59-2006 (Supp. 1968)	59-2006 (Supp. 1968)	59-2006 (Supp. 1968)			59-2006 (Supp. 1968)	59-2006 (Supp. 1968
KY. Rev. Stat. Ann. (1969)	203.080(1) 210.275	203.080(1) 210.275	203.080(2)	203.080(2)			210.320	210.320
LA. Rev. Stat. Ann. (1950)	28:143	28:143	28:143	28:143			28:143	28:143

STATE	PATIENT Voluntary Admission	PATIENT Involuntary Admission	FAMILY Voluntary Admission	FAMILY Involuntary Admission	COUNTY Voluntary Admission	COUNTY Involuntary Admission	STATE Voluntary Admission	STATE Involuntary Admission
ME. Rev. Stat. Ann. (1964)	34, §2512	34, §2512	34, §2512	34, §2512			34, §2512	34, §2512
MD. Ann. Code (1968)	59, §5	59, §5	59, §5	59, §5	59, §1	59, §1		
MASS. Ann. Laws (1965)	123, §96	123, §96	123, §96	123, §96			123, §96	123, §96
MICH. Comp. Laws Ann. (1967)	330.19a, 330.21	330.21	330.21	330.21	330.21	330.21	330.21	330.21
MINN. Stat. Ann. (1959)	246.51 (Supp. 1969)	246.51 (Supp. 1969)	246.51 (Supp. 1969)	246.54 (Supp. 1969)	246.54 (Supp. 1969)	246.51 (Supp. 1969)		
MISS. Code Ann. (1952)	6909-13	6909-13	6909-13	6909-13	6913	6913		
MO. Rev. Stat. (1959)	202.863.3	202.863.3			202.220 202.863.3	202.863.3		
MONT. Rev. Codes Ann. (1961)	38-119 (Supp. 1969); 38-410	38-119 (Supp. 1969)	38-119 (Supp. 1969); 38-410	38-119 (Supp. 1969)			38-119 (Supp. 1969)	38-119 (Supp. 1969)
NEB. Rev. Stat. (1966)	83-352 (Supp. 1967)	83-352 (Supp. 1967)	83-352 (Supp. 1967)	83-352 (Supp. 1967)	83-345	83-345	fn. 4 83-348	fn. 4 83-348
NEV. Rev. Stat. (1967)	433.698	433.699		433.699			433.698	433.699
N.H. Rev. Stat. Ann. (1964)	8:43	8:43	8:41 8:43	8:41 8:43			8:46	8:46
N.J. Stat. Ann. (1964)	30:4-46 (Supp. 1970); 30:4-66	30:4-66	30:4-46 (Supp. 1970); 30:4-66	30:4-66	30:4-68, 30:4-73 (Supp. 1970)	30:4-68, 30:4-73 (Supp. 1970)	30:4-46, 30:4-69 (Supp. 1970)	30:4-69 (Supp. 1970)
N.M. Stat. Ann. (1953)	34-2-21	34-2-21					34-2-21	34-2-21
N.Y. Mental Hygiene Law (McKinney 1951)	24.4(a) (Supp. 1970)	24.4(a) (Supp. 1970)	24.4(a) (Supp. 1970)	24.4(a) (Supp. 1970)			24 (Supp. 1970)	24 (Supp. 1970)
N.C. Gen. Stat. (1964)	122-44	122-44	122-44	122-44			122-44	122-44
N.D. Cent. Code (1960)	fn. 5 25-09-02 25-09-03	fn. 5 25-09-02 25-09-03	fn. 6 25-09-04	fn. 6 25-09-04			fn. 7 25-09-01 25-09-02	fn. 7 25-09-01 25-09-02
OHIO Rev. Code Ann. (Baldwin 1964)	5121.04 (Supp. 1968); 5121.06	5121.04 (Supp. 1968); 5121.06	5121.06	5121.06			5121.01	5121.01
OKLA. Stat. Ann. (1954)	43A, § 53, 43A, § 111 (Supp. 1969)	43A, § 111 (Supp. 1969)					43A, §53 (Supp. 1969)	43A, §51 (Supp. 1969)
ORE. Rev. Stat. (1967)	179.620	179.620	179.630	179.630			179.750	179.750
PA. Stat. Ann. (1969)	50, §4501	50, §4501	50, §4502	50, §4502			50, §4503	50, §4503
R.I. Gen. Laws Ann. (1968)		26-2-14 state: 26-3-17		state: 26-3-17				if private hospital: 26-2-14, 26-3-11 if state: 26-3-17

STATE	PATIENT		FAMILY		COUNTY		STATE	
	Voluntary Admission	Involuntary Admission	Voluntary Admission	Involuntary Admission	Voluntary Admission	Involuntary Admission	Voluntary Admission	Involuntary Admission
S.C. Code Ann. (1962)	32-1026	32-1026	32-1028	32-1028			32-1027	32-1027
S.D. Compiled Laws Ann. (1967)	27-9-3	27-9-3	27-9-3	27-9-3	27-9-9	27-9-9		
TENN. Code Ann. (1955)	33-402, 33-1213 (Supp. 1968)	33-402 (Supp. 1968)	fn. 8 33-402 "sponsor": 33-1213 (Supp. 1968)	fn. 8 33-402 (Supp. 1968)			33-402, 33-1213 (Supp. 1968)	33-402 (Supp. 1968)
TEX. Rev. Civ. Stat. Ann. (1958)								
UTAH Code Ann. (1968)	64-7-6, 64-7-15, 64-7-18	64-7-6 64-7-18	64-7-6 64-7-15	64-7-6			64-7-6, 64-7-15, 64-7-20	64-7-6 64-7-20
VT. Stat. Ann. (1968)	18, §8101	18, §8101	18, §8101	18, §8101			18, §8101	18, §8101
VA. Code Ann. (1953)	37.1-105 (Supp. 1968)	37.1-105 (Supp. 1968)	37.1-105 (Supp. 1968)	37.1-105 (Supp. 1968)			37.1-105 (Supp. 1968)	37.1-105 (Supp. 1968)
WASH. Rev. Code Ann. (1962)	72.23.120	71.02.230 (Supp. 1968)	72.23.120	71.02.230 (Supp. 1968)		71.02.230 (Supp. 1968)	72.23.120	
W. VA. Code Ann. (1966)	27-8-1 (Supp. 1969)	27-8-1 (Supp. 1969)	27-8-1 (Supp. 1969)	27-8-1 (Supp. 1969)	27-8-2	27-8-2	27-8-1 (Supp. 1969)	27-8-1 (Supp. 1969)
WIS. Stat. Ann. (1957)					51.08 (Supp. 1969)	51.08 (Supp. 1969)	51.08 (Supp. 1969)	51.08 (Supp. 1969)
WYO. Stat. Ann. (1967)	25-81	25-81	25-81	25-81			25-85	25-85

1. "Nothing . . . shall relieve from liability . . . any person liable under any other law of this State." Del. 16-5127.

2. The administrator of a psychiatric facility operated by the state or a county may accept voluntary contributions on behalf of any patient. Hawaii 334-37.

3. By the state when such person has no legal settlement in a county, or when such settlement is unknown. Iowa 230.1.

4. State will bear expenses of patients whose legal settlement is outside of the state or unknown. Neb. 83-348.

5. Expenses chargeable against estate except for provisions for family hardship. N.D. 25-09-02, 25-09-03 (Supp. 1969).

6. "In the event of patient's inability to pay for costs of care and treatment, responsible relatives or such patient (spouse, mother, father, or children) of patients . . . shall pay the actual cost incurred by state or such lesser amount as shall be determined." N.D. 25-09-04 (Supp. 1969).

7. All operational and administrative expense of state hospital, state school, and tuberculosis sanatorium shall be appropriated from state treasury. N.D. 25-09-01 (Supp. 1969).

8. Responsible relatives have liability for costs. Tenn. 33-402 (Supp. 1968).

Chapter Four

Separations from Mental Hospitals

I. INTRODUCTION

At present there are four principal ways in which a hospitalized person may be separated from a mental hospital. The patient may be transferred to another institution, die, be released subject to certain conditions, or be granted an unconditional discharge.

The function of the mental hospital when first established as an institution separate and apart from jails was basically custodial. Few patients were discharged as "cured" or "improved"; death accounted for most of the separations. This fact, together with the possibility of "railroading," stimulated the use of the writ of habeas corpus as an additional method of separation. Since the progress of medical science now makes it possible for many patients to improve significantly and perhaps recover completely, discharge procedures have become an important part of hospital administration.

The necessity for the development of effective separation procedures is given an additional dimension by the overcrowded conditions of hospital facilities. Most state hospitals for the mentally ill have consistently operated above their rated bed capacity. Often the responsible hospital authorities have little, if any, control, over the hospitalizing agencies, and there continues to be a constant, largely unregulated flow of patients into these already overtaxed institutions. If the hospitals are to continue their operations in the face of this mounting influx, they must arrange for separations.

II. TRANSFERS OF PATIENTS

Of the 525,584 separations from public hospitals for the mentally ill in fiscal 1969, approximately 24,274 (roughly 5 percent) were accounted for by transfers.[1] Such transfers may entail movement from a state institution to federal facilities, to an institution in another state, or to a different institution within the same state.[2] Under the provisions of the Draft Act, for example, one state may transfer patients to specially equipped federal treatment centers in another state without having to initiate hospitalization proceedings in the second state. Transfers to the institutions of another state, to consider the second of these three categories, generally come about through statutory residence qualifications which bar the treatment of nonresidents and specify that these patients must be sent to institutions in their state of origin.[3] Transfers within the same state may involve moving the patient to another hospital of the same type or perhaps to an institution designed to deal with a different type of patient. For example, a patient might be transferred from one hospital for the mentally ill to another hospital specially equipped and staffed to deal with drug addicts.

Transfers are often occasioned by the crowded conditions within the sending institution or the availability of special treatment in the receiving institution. Such a transfer, whether within the state or outside it, generally does not change a patient's legal status. Usually no new hospitalization order is necessary for his detention in the receiving institution.[4] The power to effect such transfers, however, is not without limitations. The Supreme Court, in *Baxstrom v. Herold,*[5] found a denial of equal protection of the law where an administrative transfer procedure for a mentally ill prisoner at the expiration of his sentence failed to provide the same protections afforded any alleged mentally ill person under the New York Code. The court also held that Baxstrom had the right to a judicial hearing to determine whether or not he was so dangerously mentally ill that his commitment to a mental facility operated by the Department of Corrections was

---

1. United States Department of Health, Education, and Welfare, *Mental Health Statistics, Current Facility Reports: Provisional Patient Movement and Administrative Data, State and County Mental Hospitals, United States, July 1, 1968–June 30, 1969,* at 5.

2. National Institute of Mental Health, Federal Security Agency, *A Draft Act Governing Hospitalization of the Mentally Ill* § 14(b), at 12–13 (Public Health Service Pub. No. 51, 1952) [hereinafter cited as *Draft Act*]. The *Draft Act* appears as Appendix A to this *Report*.

3. See chap. 5, "Rights of Hospitalized Patients," § IX, Transfer of Patients, and Table 5.7, Special Residence Provisions Applicable to Hospitalization and Deportation of Mental Patients.

4. Table 5.3, Provisions Relating to Major Medical Treatment. See also Table 5.8, Transfer of Patients within the State, New Adjudication column.

5. 383 U.S. 107 (1966).

warranted. While the court found the fact that the facility was operated by the Department of Corrections sufficient to distinguish it from the facilities of the Department of Mental Hygiene, it also indicated that if significant differences existed between the sending and receiving hospitals within the same department an unreviewable administrative transfer may be improper.[6] Unreviewable administrative transfers from the institutions of one state to those of another state are even more questionable. Such transfers may easily lead to injustices since hospitalization standards and procedures vary considerably from state to state. It would seem inadvisable in view of this consideration to permit hospitalization in one state upon an order issued in another state.

The Draft Act specifies that a central state agency be assigned the power to transfer patients within a state.[7] Centralizing this authority in the hands of such an agency should lead to a more rational and equitable distribution of patients among the general and specialized facilities available in the state. Such transfers, according to this Act, must be consistent with the medical needs of the patient and "due consideration" is to be given whether the transfer will "maintain relationships and encourage visits beneficial to the patient."[8] In addition, this section of the Act provides that written notice of such transfer must be given to the patient's legal guardian, parents, and spouse; or, if none, then to his nearest known relative or friend.

III. DEATH OF PATIENTS

Death accounted for about 7 percent of the separations from institutions for the mentally ill in 1969.[9] The death rate within the general population for this same period was slightly less than 1 percent.[10] According to one of the recognized studies of mortality rates in mental hospitals reported in 1953, 36 percent of the male first admissions and 32.8 percent of the female first admissions died within three years after admission; in both cases almost half of these deaths occurred within the first three months after admission.[11] To a considerable extent

this high death rate may be traced to the fact that people of advanced age constitute a large proportion of the total population of mental institutions.[12] The death rate for some kinds of mental disorders has been reduced materially because of new therapies.[13]

IV. CONDITIONAL RELEASE

The procedure for conditional release makes it possible for an improved patient to leave the hospital, although his continued absence hinges on his compliance with certain conditions. One quite common condition is that he receive outpatient treatment from a local clinic or psychiatrist or perhaps periodically return to the institution for follow-up care. The patient's failure to adjust to his external circumstances or to comply with any of the special conditions attached to his release may result in his being returned to the hospital. A new hospitalization proceeding is unnecessary in such cases since the patient, although actually living with friends or relatives, remains in the legal custody of the hospital. Statutory arrangements providing for conditional release exist in forty-six states.[14] The period of release is generally one year, although it may be for an indefinite time.[15] The case is reviewed at the end of the stipulated period. On the basis of this review the patient may be rehospitalized, the period of release may be extended, or the patient may receive an absolute discharge. One authority has described the procedure of conditional release as

a means of finishing off the rehabilitative processes begun under medical supervision in the hospital. From the point of view of . . . reestablishment of the individual in society, it is the only logical means of safely bridging over the gap between hospital care and self-directed life in the community. From the point of view of the hospital management, it does serve to reduce population and thus it diminishes the public expense for the maintenance of the insane. . . . [M]any patients can be discharged under supervision and become self-supporting under these conditions

6. Id. at 113.

7. *Draft Act* § 14(a), at 12.

8. Ibid.

9. *Supra* note 1, at 5.

10. Bureau of the Census, *Statistical Abstract of the United States 1969* 56 (90th ed. 1969).

11. Malzberg, "Rates of Discharge and Rates of Mortality

among First Admissions to the New York Civil State Hospitals," 37 *Mental Hygiene* 619, 625 (1953). The first two parts appeared in 36 *Mental Hygiene* 104–20 and 618–38 (1952).

12. Id. at 653–54.

13. Id. at 654.

14. Table 4.1, Administrative Discharge, Type of Discharge, Conditional column.

15. Id. at Period of Conditional Discharge column.

when it would be unsafe to discharge them absolutely from hospital supervision.[16]

In addition to providing a period of transition for the improved patient, the conditional release may also serve as a device for providing nonhospital care for patients who do not require hospital facilities.

The Draft Act uses the term "convalescent status" for conditional release and provides that such release "shall include provisions for continuing responsibility to and by the hospital, including a plan for treatment on an outpatient or nonhospital patient basis."[17] Under the provisions of this act the releasing hospital is required to examine the mental status of the released patient prior to the end of the first year of his release and at least once a year thereafter in order to determine whether his condition warrants a complete discharge.[18] There can be no question that these provisions for outpatient care and periodic reexamination constitute an extremely significant statutory advance in the treatment of the mentally ill. But these requirements will be of little practical value unless adequate outpatient facilities are established in each jurisdiction to work in close cooperation with mental institutions. Under ideal circumstances these outpatient facilities would be available in the home community. Returning to the state hospital at regular intervals for medical advice and treatment is often difficult for former patients.

The practice of conditional release is not without its imperfections. As Deutsch has observed:

Unfortunately, there are some states in which the practice of parole is grossly abused and perverted. In several backward states the parole system is nothing more than a mockery and a sham. Patients are "paroled" without any adequate supervision or follow-up care and protection. Little or no effort is made to follow the progress of the patient after removal from the hospital. Lacking continued psychiatric treatment and advice or the helpful guidance of competent social workers in the critical early period of attempted rehabilitation many a patient who, under proper supervision, might have found adjustment in society, fails to do so and has to be returned to the hospital.[19]

An increasing number of conditionally released patients live in foster homes under what are known as family care plans. Under such a plan a socially adjusted patient is maintained by a family at public expense.[20] Although he lives outside the institution, as a conditionally released patient he is considered to be in the constructive custody of the hospital; further legal process is not needed to return the patient to the hospital proper.[21] The foster family is expected to provide shelter and apprise the hospital of significant changes in the patient's behavior. This system is more widely practiced than an examination of the statute books would lead one to believe. Between 1965 and 1968, twenty-two states expended more than $28,500,000 for mentally ill or retarded patients actually boarded with families under such plans.[22] In at least one state, Maryland, foster home care is occasionally used in lieu of any hospitalization.[23]

In some states conditional release is the only means of justifying continued expenditures for drugs or other necessary therapy once the patient leaves the hospital. Since the patient remains "on the books" of the institution treatment expenditures are permitted. Such technical requirements should be eliminated, for conditional release carries with it effects which are disadvantageous to the patient. For example, automatic restoration to competency is usually dependent upon an absolute discharge. Thus the patient may be held incompetent to transact his business, or exercise other rights and privileges simply because he needs some additional posthospitalization treatment.

The provisions for indeterminate conditional release should also be done away with for similar reasons. Since a conditionally released patient may be returned to the hospital at any time without the need for a fresh determination of his need for inpatient hospitalization, the person is under constant threat of loss of liberty. It would appear that conditional release of no more than one year is sufficient to test the patient's recovery. Upon the expiration of that period a patient who has not been returned to

16. Haines, "Lessons from the Principles Governing the Parole Procedure in Hospitals for the Insane," *Proceedings of the National Conference of Social Work* 159, 160 (1920).

17. *Draft Act* § 16(a), at 13.

18. Ibid.

19. Deutsch, *The Mentally Ill in America* 438 (2d ed. 1949).

20. Id. at 447–48.

21. Guttmacher & Weihofen, *Psychiatry and the Law* 316 (1952).

22. Council of State Governments, *Action in the States in the Fields of Mental Health, Mental Retardation and Related Areas* at Table 10 (1969).

23. Hitchman & Salomon, "Foster Care: An Alternative to Hospitalization," *Current Psychiatric Therapies: 1966,* at 306 (1966).

the hospital should be granted an absolute discharge automatically.

V. ABSOLUTE DISCHARGE

The last of the four separation procedures consists of a complete termination of the legal relationship between the institution and the patient. Once such a discharge is effected, the former patient may not be returned to the institution without the initiation of a new hospitalization proceeding.

There is, unfortunately, a widespread belief that hospitalized patients are rarely discharged. Statistics for recent years show, however, that slightly more patients are discharged each year than are admitted to public state and county mental hospitals. In fiscal 1969, for example, there were 495,077 admissions and a total of 525,584 discharges.[24]

Discharge is considered an administrative function in all states and is normally made the responsibility of the superintendents of mental institutons or the central state agency. The responsible official is seldom directed to consult with the hospitalizing authority before initiating the discharge action, although he may be required to give formal notice of the action.[25] Thirty-five states authorize an additional discharge procedure by permitting the courts to discharge patients upon the application of the patient or some other interested party.[26] A request for discharge, moreover, may be initiated under a habeas corpus proceeding. But only twelve states explicitly provide for release based upon the present mental status of the patient.[27]

A. ADMINISTRATIVE DISCHARGE

Hospital authorities would appear to be best qualified to exercise the major responsibility for discharging involuntary patients.

> That discharge should be by institutional authorities is entirely logical. It should require no argument to demonstrate that the authorities of the hospital where the patient is under daily supervision and to whom the facts of his previous history and of his mental state are best known are the persons who should determine his fitness to be returned to the community.[28]

But the situation which institutional discharge creates is potentially a difficult one. The division of authority between those responsible for hospitalization and those responsible for discharge has at times resulted in a diversity of policies and thus in confusion. The requirements for hospitalization, for example, are established by the courts; the requirements for retention in an institution are established quite independently by the institution. The two sets of standards may easily be inconsistent. Under such an arrangement it is entirely possible for a person to be considered in need of hospitalization by a court and yet at the same time ready for immediate discharge under the standards guiding the decisions of the hospital authorities. Conversely, a patient may be ineligible for release under the discharge policies established by the institution even though he no longer falls within the criteria under which he was originally hospitalized.[29]

The processing of administrative discharges of involuntary patients is usually the function of the hospital. Only one state, South Carolina, vests this power solely in the central state agency responsible for the supervision of mental institutions. Nine other states give the power of discharge to both the institution and the central agency.[30] Placing this authority in the hands of the central agency means, of course, that the ultimate decision is to be made by an agent somewhat divorced from the source of the facts. It is unlikely that the opportunity to establish more uniform discharge policies counterbalances undesirable aspects. Administrative monitoring by the central agency of the local decision-making process is a better solution.

Since discharge is thought to depend upon the medical status of the involuntary indeterminately hospitalized patient, there are no statutory procedures leading to administrative discharge that can be initiated by the patient. In those states that have adopted the provisions of the Draft Act the patient does have some assurance that the question of his discharge will be reconsidered every six months.[31] This reconsideration does not entail a formal hearing but rather consists of a mental examination designed to ascertain the patient's condition at that time. A formal hearing can be obtained only by application to the courts.

In practice the periodic review provision may not

24. *Supra,* note 1.

25. See Table 4.1, Notice of Discharge To columns.

26. See Table 4.2, Judicial Discharge.

27. In thirty-seven states and the District of Columbia habeas corpus is a statutory right. Id. at Habeas Corpus columns.

28. Weihofen & Overholser, "Commitment of the Mentally Ill," 24 *Texas L. Rev.* 307, 333 (1946).

29. Rock, Jacobson, & Janopaul, *Hospitalization and Discharge of the Mentally Ill* 222 (1968).

30. Table 4.1, Discharging Agency columns.

31. *Draft Act* § 15, at 13.

have any significant effect on hospital practices.[32] The nature and quality of the examinations are not regulated and there does not appear to be any means of enforcing the provisions short of judicial action. Because of the difficulties inherent in providing adequate posthospitalization safeguards, at least two states—California and New York—have eliminated indeterminate hospitalization, and several others require a significant period of observational hospitalization before indeterminate hospitalization will be ordered. Such an approach constitutes the most direct means of assuring that the patient's status will be periodically reviewed.[33]

The criteria governing discharge vary considerably from state to state. Although most states do not require full recovery as a condition for discharge, four states provide for the discharge of recovered patients only.[34] Forty-three states and the District of Columbia authorize discharge in the event of improvement.[35] Patients who have not demonstrated any improvement are eligible for discharge in fifteen states, three of which limit such discharges to cases considered either incurable or unlikely to benefit from further institutional treatment. Five others condition such discharges on the willingness and ability of the patient's family or friends to offer a certain minimum degree of care. Several states permit the discharge of senile patients who require only custodial care. West Virginia provides that institutions may require the family to post a bond of at least $500 guaranteeing good behavior before an unimproved patient is discharged.

Of some significance is the fact that at least three states permit even dangerous persons to be administratively discharged in the event that they do not improve under institutional treatment.[36] Such a practice is obviously inconsistent with one of the two basic purposes of hospitalization—the protection of society—and there appears to be little justification for continuing it as an integral part of a state's policy. While hospitalization is conceded to be a last resort, it is clear that there should be statutory safeguards for the protection of the public. Minnesota is perhaps overly stringent, providing that a person

certified by the committing court as dangerous can be discharged only by a three-judge court appointed by the chief justice of the supreme court.[37]

Thirty states require that notice of the discharge be given to the hospitalizing court, and in sixteen states notice to the central state agency responsible for mental institutions is necessary.[38] In thirteen states the guardian or relative of the former patient is to be notified of the discharge.[39] In Mississippi the sheriff of the discharged patient's county must receive notification of the action.[40] This requirement appears to be little more than a formality. There is no evidence to indicate that notice is given for the purpose of facilitating or assisting the discharged patient's rehabilitation.

Although some observers have expressed concern about the possibility of abuse ever present in the handling of the discharge function, most writers believe that improper detention is extremely unlikely. The following statement is typical of this view.

> Practically all of the public institutions in the country are crowded so that the pressure on the authorities is constantly in the direction of granting discharges. Furthermore, the heads of these institutions are public officials and presumably, like judges and other public officials, carry out their duties properly. As a matter of fact the public is probably inclined to agree that very little improper detention is practiced in the public institutions. Doubts, if any, may be entertained with respect to those institutions not operated by the public which are voluntary and often proprietary.[41]

In order to forestall the development of abuses in the discharge practices of privately operated hospitals, it has been recommended that the state exercise a much closer supervision over these institutions than has been the practice in the past. The 1950 report on the mental health programs of the states prepared by the Council of State Governments emphasized the absence of any significant degree of state authority over private hospitals; only seven states reported that they exercised actual supervision over such institutions.[42] That report echoed the concern evidenced in 1947 by the American Bar Association's Special Committee on the Rights

32. See Rock et al., *supra* note 29, at 218.

33. See chap. 3, "Involuntary Hospitalization."

34. Table 4.1, Type of Discharge columns.

35. Ibid.

36. For authority setting forth this and the preceding statements concerning discharge though unimproved see Table 4.1, Type of Discharge, Absolute, Unimproved column and footnotes thereto.

37. *Minn. Stat. Ann.* § 253A.15 (Supp. 1969).

38. Table 4.1, Notice of Discharge To columns.

39. Ibid.

40. *Miss. Code Ann.* § 6919 (1952).

41. Weihofen & Overholser, *supra* note 28, at 333.

42. Council of State Governments, *The Mental Health Programs of the Forty-eight States* 65 (1950).

of the Mentally Ill, which urged that serious consideration be given to a requirement that all establishments caring for the mentally ill report to a duly established governmental agency concerning each case. It was believed that such a requirement would do much to insure proper treatment under competent auspices.[43]

In spite of the generally shared and perhaps somewhat sanguine opinion that the abuse of discharge procedures is more likely to be found in private than in public institutions, there is some evidence that the latter are not beyond criticism on this score. The very overcrowding which makes early releases necessary can also lead to unexamined continuation of hospitalization:

> While it cannot be said that the institution acts with improper motives, conditions are often such that patients can, and do, become "lost." For example, in one institution visited a single doctor was responsible for more than 950 patients, and doctor-patient ratios of 1 to 600 were typical in other large institutions.[44]

The problem of discharge is rendered even more complex by the number of patients who remain in mental hospitals simply because they have nowhere to go. A study of Texas mental institutions, for example, reported that "seventy percent of all the patients don't need to be in a mental hospital."[45] This particular group generally includes a large percentage of elderly people as well as a number of others who could be effectively treated either at home, in clinics, or in other institutions. Many hospitals refuse to release a patient if he has no assurance of assistance in his struggle for rehabilitation.[46] The failure of the local community to equip itself to handle these patients, combined with an unwillingness or inability on the part of the immediate family to assume the financial and emotional burden of caring for the patient, means that the hospital, in many instances, is obliged to retain custody.

An additional source of delay in arranging for discharges may spring from the shortage of qualified hospital personnel. In the course of compiling the data for the Texas study mentioned above, the commentator discovered that of 134 patients in one ward, 45 had never been diagnosed. No one knew

what, if anything, was the matter with them. This situation was not unique. "Similar conditions were found in other Texas hospitals. About 30 percent of all the patients had received no diagnosis."[47] The hospital's inability to screen incoming patients has a number of important consequences. It obviously emasculates one of the most important checks on improper hospitalization—the immediate or early detection of those borderline cases which might be treated more effectively elsewhere. In addition, understaffing seems to have a definite effect on the volume of discharges. "According to the American Psychiatric Association, discharges from mental hospitals are directly proportionate to the size of their staffs."[48] The truth of this observation is supported by a study of the state hospital at Topeka, Kansas, a hospital in which there is one psychiatrist for every twenty-five patients. The study reported that

> The average population for a single year [was] reduced from a high of 1,800 to 1,440. And in the last six months of 1954 the hospital was able to admit as many patients as it did in 1950, 1951, and 1952 combined.[49]

The evidence presented in the report suggests that understaffed institutions not only fail to detect and prevent improper hospitalizations but also prove of little positive value to the patient once he has been admitted. Patients who, if given the proper treatment, would ordinarily recover tend instead to become permanent state wards whose mental condition is, if anything, less satisfactory than it was when they originally entered the institution. Moreover, poorly staffed hospitals are often unable to take the necessary steps to discover those who have improved under institutional care and are perhaps ready for discharge.

The potential evils outlined here may be relieved by adherence to the Draft Act's provisions pertaining to discharge. Under these provisions the head of the hospital is to have each patient examined at least every six months in order to determine whether the patient might be discharged at that time.[50] The practical success of such an arrangement for periodic screening depends, of course, upon the size and training of the staff, but the cost of providing sufficient personnel would seem relatively small if it could prevent a patient's permanent disappearance

43. American Bar Association, Special Committee on the Rights of the Mentally Ill, "Report," 72 *ABA Rep.* 289, 296 (1947).

44. Rock et al., *supra* note 29, at 225.

45. Gainfort, "How Texas Is Reforming Its Mental Hospitals," 19 *The Reporter,* November 19, 1956, at 18, 19.

46. Ibid. See also Rock et al., *supra* note 29, at 215–18.

47. Gainfort, *supra* note 45, at 20–21.

48. Id. at 20.

49. Ibid.

50. *Draft Act* § 15, at 13.

into ward life. Practical difficulties, however, too often prevent periodic and meaningful examinations. In one state with just such a requirement a hospital superintendent commented:

> Whether or not we follow the statute depends on what is meant by "examination." I suppose every patient is seen by a doctor at least once every six months but not necessarily to determine whether he should be released. In theory the requirement is good, and we tried it in one building. Some 720 patients were examined by a team of doctors during a two-month period. A number of discharges and revisions of treatment programs resulted. However, we haven't done it since because it simply took too long. Under present conditions of staffing the requirement is a pious expression of hope, impossible to conform to on a hospital-wide basis.[51]

Periodic redetermination of the involuntary patient's need for hospitalization as a condition to continued retention appears to be a better solution of the problem. New York and California presently have such requirements. It has been argued that the result of such a procedure would be substantially to lessen treatment because of the professional time involved in making such determinations. However, the number of patients who will require involuntary extended care is likely to be relatively small and manageable.

The prevailing emphasis upon release statistics as an indication of the relative quality of an institution is not an unmixed blessing. Some hospitals have become release conscious and strive to match the release record of better-staffed and -equipped institutions. The evil of unnecessary retention may thus be more than matched by an equally futile attempt to establish an impressive rate of patient turnover. It is possible that some patients may be released from such a hospital without ever having been properly diagnosed. Such practices obviously would run counter to the spirit of existing legislation. In the absence of exhaustive field research to determine whether such practices exist and, if so, the extent of their effect on the patient and on the community, it is impossible to make any general statement concerning the practice in the United States.

B. JUDICIAL DISCHARGE

Thirty-five states have enacted legislation to insure the availability of judicial discharge as an additional protection of the patient's interests. The necessary judicial proceedings may be initiated upon the application of the patient, his family, his legal guardian, or any citizen.[52] Eight of these states and the District of Columbia require that the application be accompanied by a medical certificate attesting to the competency of the patient;[53] nineteen provide that the court shall order a medical examination of the patient.[54] Nineteen states require that notice of the application be given to the family or guardian of the patient; twelve specify that it must be sent to the superintendent of the supervising institution.[55] Existing legislation, however, generally does not require that interested parties be given a full opportunity to appear and present their views.

The provisions of the statutes authorizing judicial discharge are not limited in their applicability to the release of recovered patients. In some sixteen states the discharge of improved patients is permitted.[56] Three states specifically allow the discharge of unimproved patients.[57] In three states, before releasing a patient the court is entitled to require security, perhaps in the form of a bond, as a guarantee of the patient's future conduct.[58] Twenty states have attempted to forestall repetitious and nonmeritorious requests by restricting the frequency with which applications for judicial discharge may be filed.[59] These restrictions generally specify that an application may not be made more often than once every six months, or once a year.

All states recognize the patient's right to seek a writ of habeas corpus as a means of securing his discharge if he believes he is being improperly detained. This writ has traditionally been available in Anglo-American jurisprudence to any person, including a mental patient, who asserts that he is being illegally detained and deprived of his liberty.[60] In some jurisdictions, as at common law, the writ is available only to test the legality of the original detention. Thus the protection afforded does not extend to a patient who was originally legally detained but who later recovered and is entitled to release under existing institutional standards.[61] Some

---

51. See Rock et al., *supra* note 29, at 218–19.

52. Table 4.2, Application By columns.

53. Id. at Medical Certification in Support of Petition column.

54. Id. at Court-Appointed Medical Examiners (Number) column.

55. Id. at Notice of Hearing To column.

56. Id. at Condition column.

57. Ibid.

58. Id. at Security for Release column.

59. Id. at Restriction on Petition Frequency column.

60. Guttmacher & Weihofen, *supra* note 21, at 316.

61. Ross, "Commitment of the Mentally Ill: Problems of Law and Policy," 57 *Mich. L. Rev.* 945, 977 (1959).

courts, however, as illustrated by *Hiatt v. Soucek,*[62] have broadened the scope of the writ to permit inquiry into the petitioner's mental condition at the time he requests the writ. Sixteen states have sought to resolve this question by specifically providing that a full determination of the patient's mental status should be made at the time of the habeas corpus proceeding.[63] Under these provisions the mental condition of the patient at the time of the proceeding and not the validity of his initial hospitalization serves as the basic criterion for retention or discharge.

Even more recently the writ of habeas corpus has been utilized to test the legality of detention where it is alleged that an involuntary patient is not being provided adequate treatment.[64]

It is extremely difficult to assess how well these two procedures, judicial discharge and habeas corpus, equip the patient to protect himself against the possibility of improper hospitalization. There are very few statistics detailing the extent to which these procedures have been employed, and thus it is impossible to generalize with any assurance of accuracy. Guttmacher and Weihofen report considerable variation in the use of the writ of habeas corpus from one jurisdiction to another. "In some jurisdictions the writ is resorted to almost not at all by mental patients, whereas in others the number of petitions has at times attained such proportions as to call for judicial attention and correction."[65] In the District of Columbia, to cite an example at one end of the spectrum, one person had submitted fifty petitions, another twenty-seven, and a third twenty-four in a period of less than five years.[66]

Despite evidence of isolated instances of what might be termed an excessive use of habeas corpus procedures, there is reason to believe that many patients in mental institutions have not availed themselves of this procedure. Of course, it should be recognized that in many cases patients have desired to attack the legality of their hospitalization. In many instances, as a practical matter, they cannot secure the benefit of counsel. It is asserted by a former patient that some members of the legal profession openly admit that they would, without further ques-

tion, consign all habeas corpus applications from mental hospital patients to the wastebasket.[67]

Although both attorneys and courts are understandably hesitant about processing requests for release in the face of the detaining hospital's judgment that the patient is not ready for discharge, such requests are not always without merit. The Detroit Legal Aid Office, for example, has handled cases in which it was established that the petitioners should have been released even though such an action had been consistently opposed by the administrators of the hospital.[68] Similarly, a survey conducted by the Veterans Administration of patients who had been judicially discharged in the face of institutional opposition illustrated that such patients showed a better rate of adjustment to the outside community than those patients whose discharge had not been contested by the hospital authorities.[69] A recent international study of contested releases indicates that about 12 percent are successful in the United Kingdom, 23 percent in Ontario, Canada, and 17 percent in New York.[70] While this evidence is sketchy and hardly conclusive, it serves to indicate the desirability of permitting such cases to be reexamined under the aegis of a habeas corpus action.

VI. CONCLUSIONS AND RECOMMENDATIONS

1. *Certain types of patients presently in institutions for the mentally ill could be as well or better cared for in other ways.*

The statutes providing for administrative discharge are so worded as to permit discharge whenever the particular case appears to merit such an action. The force of such statutes is blunted, however, when the outside community is unable or unwilling to provide the limited care essential to the rehabilitation of released patients. A considerable number of improved patients are forced to remain in already crowded institutions for no other reason

62. 240 Iowa 300, 36 N.W.2d 432 (1949).

63. Table 4.2, Habeas Corpus columns.

64. See chap. 5, § V, Periodic Examination, Judicial Review, and the Right to Treatment.

65. Guttmacher & Weihofen, *supra* note 21, at 316–17.

66. Id. at 317.

67. Moore, "The Patient and Legal Aid," *Search* 6 (October 1957). See also Rock et al., *supra* note 29, at 234–41.

68. Klein, "Improper Commitments in Detroit," 15 *Brief Case* 118–20 (1957).

69. Shawver and Boquet, "A Survey of Patients Discharged by Court Order" 29, 33 (United States Veterans Administration, Department of Medicine and Surgery, Psychiatry and Neurology Service, *Information Bulletin*, Sept. 21, 1956).

70. Greenland, "Appealing against Commitment to Mental Hospitals in the United Kingdom, Canada, and United States of America, an International Review" (paper No. 235 presented at the 122d Annual Meeting of the American Psychiatric Association, May 9, 1969).

than this failure on the part of the community. The facilities of these same institutions are further taxed by the continued presence of unimproved patients for whom the institution cannot perform, and most likely never could perform, worthwhile treatment service. Administrative difficulties as well as overcrowded conditions prevent the transfer of these patients to more suitable facilities. These two weaknesses combine to impose a tremendous drain on the limited institutional resources now available and tend to prevent the full provision of services which these institutions should offer.

2. *Statutory provisions should be enacted and adequate funds made available to assure that the need for continued hospitalization will be redetermined periodically.*

Indeterminate hospitalization should be replaced by a procedure which assures that the patient's status will be carefully reexamined at appropriate intervals as a condition for continued involuntary retention. Existing periodic-review statutes are uneven in effect and fail to provide effective means of securing such rights for the patients.

3. *Every patient should be entitled to legal representation and independent medical examination and testimony at hearings concerning judicial discharge or continuation of hospitalization.*

It is essential to provide applicants for judicial discharge or patients subject to continued hospitalization qualified legal counsel and independent medical experts to aid in the preparation of the prehearing material, to represent the patient in the proceedings, and to help in any subsequent appeal therefrom. Because of a patient's lack of financial resources, he may often have difficulty in securing counsel and other assistance. Statutes should provide for the retention and compensation of counsel and expert witnesses where necessary if each patient is to have an opportunity to present his case properly.

BIBLIOGRAPHY

American Bar Association. Special Committee on the Rights of the Mentally Ill. *Report.* 72 American Bar Association Reports 289. Chicago: American Bar Association, 1947.

Bureau of the Census. *Statistical Abstract of the United States 1969.* 90th ed. Washington, D.C.: Government Printing Office, 1969.

Council of State Governments. *Action in the States in the Fields of Mental Health, Mental Retardation and Related Areas.* Chicago: Council of State Governments, 1969.

————. *The Mental Health Programs of the Forty-Eight States.* Chicago: Council of State Governments, 1950.

Deutsch, Albert. *The Mentally Ill in America.* 2d ed. rev. New York: Columbia University Press, 1949.

Gainfort, John. "How Texas Is Reforming Its Mental Hospitals." 19 *The Reporter* 18 (November 19, 1956).

Greenland, Cyril. "Appealing against Commitment to Mental Hospitals in the United Kingdom, Canada, and United States of America, an International Review." Paper no. 235, presented at the 122d Annual Meeting of the American Psychiatric Association, May 9, 1969.

Guttmacher, Manfred S., and Weihofen, Henry. *Psychiatry and the Law.* New York: W. W. Norton & Co., 1952.

Haines, Thomas H. "Lessons from the Principles Governing the Parole Procedure in Hospitals for the Insane." *Proceedings of the National Conference of Social Work* (Forty-seventh Annual Session, April 1920), p. 159. Chicago: University of Chicago Press, 1920.

Hitchman, I., and Salomon, E. "Foster Care: An Alternative to Hospitalization." *Current Psychiatric Therapies: 1966.* Edited by Jules H. Masserman. New York: Grune & Stratton, Inc., 1966.

Klein, Harry. "Improper Commitments in Detroit." 15 *Brief Case* 118 (1957).

Malzberg, Benjamin. "Rates of Discharge and Rates of Mortality among First Admissions to the New York Civil State Hospitals." 37 *Mental Hygiene* 619 (1953).

Moore, Bill. "The Patient and Legal Aid." *Search* (October 1957).

National Institute of Mental Health. Federal Security Agency. *A Draft Act Governing Hospitalization of the Mentally Ill.* Public Health Service, Pub. no. 51. Washington, D.C.: Government Printing Office, 1952.

Rock, Ronald S., Jacobson, Marcus A., and Janopaul, Richard M. *Hospitalization and Discharge of the Mentally Ill.* An American Bar Foundation Study. Chicago: University of Chicago Press, 1968.

Ross, Hugh A. "Commitment of the Mentally Ill: Problems of Law and Policy." 57 *Michigan Law Review* 945 (1959).

Shawver, J., and Boquet, R. "A Survey of Patients Discharged by Court Order." United States Veterans Administration. Department of Medicine and Surgery, Psychiatry and Neurology Service. *Information Bulletin.* Washington, D.C.: Government Printing Office, September 21, 1956.

United States Department of Health, Education, and Welfare. *Mental Health Statistics, Current Facility Reports: Provisional Patient Movement and Administrative Data, State and County Mental Hospitals, United States, July 1, 1968–June 30, 1969.* Washington, D.C.: Government Printing Office, 1970.

Weihofen, Henry, and Overholser, Winfred. "Commitment of the Mentally Ill." 24 *Texas Law Review* 307 (1946).

CASES

Baxstrom v. Herold, 383 U.S. 107 (1966).

Hiatt v. Soucek, 240 Iowa 300, 36 N.W.2d 432 (1949).

Table 4.1 ADMINISTRATIVE DISCHARGE

STATE	DISCHARGING AGENCY — Institution	DISCHARGING AGENCY — Central Agency	TYPE OF DISCHARGE — Absolute — Recovered	Absolute — Improved	Unimproved	Conditional	CONDITIONAL DISCHARGE — Institution — Public	Institution — Private	Period of Conditional Discharge	Administrative Return	NOTICE OF DISCHARGE TO — Central Agency	Court	Relative, Friends, or Guardian
DRAFT ACT	15		15	15		16	16	16	fn. 1 / 1 year / 16	16	15, 16		
ALA. Code (1958)	45, §218 / 45, §219		45, §218 / 45, §219	45, §218		45, §218 / 45, §219	45, §218 / 45, §219	45, §218 / 45, §219	6 months. / 45, §219	up to 6 months. / 45, §219			45, §218
ALAS. Stat. (1962)	47.30.220		47.30.220	47.30.220		47.30.200	47.30.200		indefinite. / 47.30.200	47.30.210	47.30.220	47.30.220	47.30.220
ARIZ. Rev. Stat. Ann. (1956)	36-524 (Supp. 1970)		36-524D (Supp. 1970)	36-524D (Supp. 1970)		36-524A (Supp. 1970)	fn. 2 / 36-501.9 / 36-524A (Supp. 1970)		fn. 3 / 1 year. / 36-524B (Supp. 1970)	36-524B (Supp. 1970)		36-524B (Supp. 1970)	36-524F (Supp. 1970)
ARK. Stat. Ann. (1947)	59-235		59-235	59-235								59-235	
CAL. Welf. & Inst'ns Code (West 1966)	5152, 5254, 5305, 5329, 7105 (Supp. 1968)		no longer in need of care or treatment, 5152, 5254, 5305, 5359, 7105 (Supp. 1968)	improved sufficiently to leave 5254 (Supp. 1968)	no longer constitutes an imminent threat of substantial physical harm to others. 5305 (Supp. 1968)	temporary 5258 (Supp. 1968)	5258 (Supp. 1968)					5305 (Supp. 1968)	conservator 5359 (Supp. 1968)
COLO. Rev. Stat. Ann. (1964)	71-1-28(1) (Supp. 1965)					71-1-28(1) (Supp. 1965)	71-1-28(1) (Supp. 1965)		1 year, 71-1-28(1) (Supp. 1965)	71-1-28(2)		71-1-28(1) (Supp. 1965)	
CONN. Gen. Stat. Ann. (1958)	17-198 (Supp. 1969) / 17-192		17-192	17-192		17-198 (Supp. 1969)	17-198 (Supp. 1969)	17-198 (Supp. 1969)	temporary. 17-198 (Supp. 1969)	17-198 (Supp. 1969)			
DEL. Code Ann. (1953)	16-5132(a) (Supp. 1970)		16-5132(a) (Supp. 1970)	16-5132(a) (Supp. 1970)		16-5132(b)	16-5132(b)		fn. 1 16-5132(d) (Supp. 1970)	16-5133 (Supp. 1970)			
D.C. Code Ann. (1967)	21-546 / 21-548		21-546 / 21-548	21-546 / 21-548									
FLA. Stat. Ann. (1960)	394.22(16) (Supp. 1969)		394.22(16)(a) (Supp. 1969)			394.272 (Supp. 1969)	state, 394.272 (Supp. 1969)					394.22(16)(b)	
GA. Code Ann. (1963)	88-506.7 (Supp. 1969)		88-506.7 (Supp. 1969)	88-506.7 (Supp. 1969)		88-506.8 (Supp. 1969)	88-506.8 (Supp. 1969)		fn. 1 6 months. 88-506.8 (Supp. 1969)	88-506.8 (Supp. 1969)		88-506.7 (Supp. 1969)	representatives 88-506.7 (Supp. 1969)
HAWAII Rev. Stat. Ann. (1968)	334-76		334-76(1)	334-76(2)(A)	334-76(2)(B)	334-75	334-1 / 334-75	334-1 / 334-75		334-75			
IDAHO Code Ann. (1949)	66-317(g) / 66-337 (Supp. 1969)	66-337 (Supp. 1969)	66-337 (Supp. 1969)	66-337 (Supp. 1969)		66-338(a) (Supp. 1969)	66-317(f) / 66-338(a) (Supp. 1969)	66-317(f) / 66-338(a) (Supp. 1969)	fn. 1 1 year. 66-338(a) (Supp. 1969)	fn. 4 / 66-338(b) / 66-339 (Supp. 1969)		66-337 / 66-338(a) (Supp. 1969)	
ILL. Ann. Stat. (Smith-Hurd 1966)	91½, §10-4 (Supp. 1969)	fn. 5 / 91½, §10-2 (Supp. 1969)	91½, §10-4 (Supp. 1969)	91½, §10-4 (Supp. 1969)		91½, §10-4 (Supp. 1969)	91½, §10-4 (Supp. 1969)	91½, §10-4 (Supp. 1969)	fn. 6 1 year. 91½, §10-4 (Supp. 1969)	91½, §10-4 (Supp. 1969)		91½, §10-4 (Supp. 1969)	

143

Table 4.1 ADMINISTRATIVE DISCHARGE continued

STATE	DISCHARGING AGENCY		TYPE OF DISCHARGE				CONDITIONAL DISCHARGE				NOTICE OF DISCHARGE TO		
			Absolute				Institution						
	Institution	Central Agency	Recovered	Improved	Unimproved	Conditional	Public	Private	Period of Conditional Discharge	Administrative Return	Central Agency	Court	Relative, Friends, or Guardian
IND. Ann. Stat. (1964)	22-1307		22-1307	22-1307		22-1306(9) 22-1307	22-1306(3) 22-1307					22-1308 22-1309	
IOWA Code Ann. (1969)	226.19	fn. 7	226.19	fn. 7 226.18 (Supp. 1969)	fn. 7 226.18 (Supp. 1969)	226.23 (Supp. 1969)			1 year. 226.23			226.19	
KAN. Stat. Ann. (1964)	59-2924 (Supp. 1968)		59-2924 (Supp. 1968)	59-2924 (Supp. 1968)		59-2924 (Supp. 1968)	59-2902(7) 59-2924 (Supp. 1968)	59-2902(7) 59-2924 (Supp. 1968)	1 year. 59-2924 (Supp. 1968)	59-2924 (Supp. 1968)		59-2925 (Supp. 1968)	
KY. Rev. Stat. Ann. (1969)	202.239		fn. 8 202.239	202.239		202.242(1)			6 months. 202.242(1)	202.242(2)		202.242(1)	
LA. Rev. Stat. Ann. (1950)	28:96, 28:96.1 (Supp. 1969)		28:96A, 28:96.1 (Supp. 1969)	fn. 9 28:96A (Supp. 1969)	fnn. 10, 11 28:96E (Supp. 1969)	28:100.1 (Supp. 1969)	28:100.1 (Supp. 1969)	28:100.1 (Supp. 1969)	1 year. 28:100.1 (Supp. 1969)	28:100.1 (Supp. 1969)	fn. 12 28:97		28:96.1 (Supp. 1969)
ME. Rev. Stat. Ann. (1965)	34, §2374		fn. 13 34, §2374	fn. 13 34, §2374		34, §2375	34, §2375	34, §2375	34, §2375	34, §2375	34, §2374		
MD. Ann. Code (1968)	59, §42		59, §42	59, §42	fnn. 9, 14, 15 59, §42	59, §41	59, §41	59, §41	1 year. 59, §41	59, §41			
MASS. Ann. Laws (1965)	123, §89	fn. 16 123, §90	123, §89	123, §89		123, §88	123, §88	123, §88	1 year. 123, §88	123, §88	fn. 16 123, §90		123, §90
MICH. Comp. Laws Ann. (1967)	330.35		330.35	330.35	discharge shall not be detrimental to the public nor the patient. 330.35a	330.36	330.36		330.37	330.37		330.39(a)	330.36
MINN. Stat. Ann. (1959)	253A.15.1 (Supp. 1969)		fn. 17 253A.15(1) (Supp. 1969)	fn. 17 253A.15(1) (Supp. 1969)		253A.15(4) (Supp. 1969)	253A.15(4) (Supp. 1969)	253A.15(4) (Supp. 1969)	1 year. 253A.15(4) (Supp. 1969)	253A.15(7) (Supp. 1969)	notice to welfare board of county of patient's residence. 253A.15(11) (Supp. 1969)	253A.15(9) (Supp. 1969)	
MISS. Code Ann. (1952)	6919		6919	6919	fn. 9 6919							sheriff of patient's county of residence. 6919	6919
MO. Rev. Stat. (1959)	202.827		202.827	202.827		202.830.1	202.830.1		fn. 1 1 year. 202.830.1	202.830.2			
MONT. Rev. Codes Ann. (1961)	38-502 (Supp. 1969)		38-506			38-503	38-502 (Supp. 1969)		2 years. 38-506	38-504 (Supp. 1969)		38-506	
NEB. Rev. Stat. (1966)	83-340		83-340	83-340	fn. 18 83-340	83-340.01 (Supp. 1967)	83-340.01 (Supp. 1967)					83-342	
NEV. Rev. Stat. (1967)	433.550 433.717(1)		433.717(1)	433.717(1)		433.570	433.550					fn. 19 433.550	
N.H. Rev. Stat. Ann. (1964)	135:28		135:28	135:28		135:31	135:31	fn. 20 135:31	1 year. 135:31	135:31	fn. 21	fn. 19 433.550 ... fn. 21 135:18	
N.J. Stat. Ann. (1964)	30:4-107 (Supp. 1970)		fn. 22 30:4-107 (Supp. 1970)	fn. 22 30:4-107 (Supp. 1970)	fn. 22 30:4-107 (Supp. 1970)	fn. 22 30:4-107 (Supp. 1970)	30:4-107 (Supp. 1970)	30:4-107 (Supp. 1970)	30:4-107 (Supp. 1970)	fn. 22 30:4-107 (Supp. 1970)			

Table 4.1   ADMINISTRATIVE DISCHARGE   continued

STATE	DISCHARGING AGENCY — Institution	DISCHARGING AGENCY — Central Agency	TYPE OF DISCHARGE — Absolute Recovered	TYPE OF DISCHARGE — Absolute Improved	TYPE OF DISCHARGE — Unimproved	TYPE OF DISCHARGE — Conditional	CONDITIONAL DISCHARGE — Institution Public	CONDITIONAL DISCHARGE — Institution Private	CONDITIONAL DISCHARGE — Period of Conditional Discharge	CONDITIONAL DISCHARGE — Administrative Return	NOTICE OF DISCHARGE — Central Agency	NOTICE OF DISCHARGE — Court	NOTICE OF DISCHARGE — Relative, Friends, or Guardian
N.M. Stat. Ann. (1953)	34-2-10		fn. 13 34-2-10	fn. 13 34-2-10		34-2-11	34-2-11	fn. 23 34-2-11	fn. 1 1 year, 34-2-11	34-2-11			
N.Y. Mental Hygiene Law (McKinney 1951)	87 (Supp. 1970)		87 (Supp. 1970)	fn. 9 87 (Supp. 1970)	fn. 9 87 (Supp. 1970)	87 (Supp. 1970)	87 (Supp. 1970)	87 (Supp. 1970)	fn. 24 87 (Supp. 1970)	fn. 24 87 (Supp. 1970)	87 (Supp. 1970)		
N.C. Gen. Stat. (1964)	122-66.1		122-66.1	122-66.1		122-67 122-67.1 122-68	122-67	122-82.1	fn. 25 1 year, 122-67 122-68	122-67	fn. 26 122-68.1	fn. 27 122-66.1 122-67 122-82.1	
N.D. Cent. Code (1960)	25-03-15 (Supp. 1969)	25-03-15 (Supp. 1969)	fn. 13 25-03-15 (Supp. 1969)	fn. 13 25-03-15 (Supp. 1969)		25-03-16 (Supp. 1969)	25-03-16 (Supp. 1969)		fn. 1 1 year 25-03-16 (Supp. 1969)	25-03-16(2) (Supp. 1969)	25-03-15 (Supp. 1969)		
OHIO Rev. Code Ann. (Baldwin 1964)	5122.21 (Supp. 1968)		5122.21 (Supp. 1968)	5122.21 (Supp. 1968)			5122.22	5122.22	5122.23	5122.23		5122.21 (Supp. 1968)	
OKLA. Stat. Ann. (1954)	43A, §73 (Supp. 1969)		43A, §73(1) (Supp. 1969)	fn. 9, 14 43A, §73(2) (Supp. 1969)		fn. 28 43A, §75(b) (Supp. 1969)	43A, §73	43A, §186	public: 12 months 43A, §73(6) (Supp. 1969) private: 6 months 43A, §186 (Supp. 1969)	43A, §73(b) (Supp. 1969)			
ORE. Rev. Stat. (1967)	426.300(1)		426.300(1)(a)		fn. 9 426.300(1)	426.280	Ch. 426 concerns state hospital only. 426.280		426.280	426.290		426.300(1)	
PA. Stat. Ann. (1969)	50, §4419	50, §4420	50, §4420			50, §4419(a)	50, §4419		fn. 30 1 year, 50, §4419(a)	fn. 31 50, §4419(b)			
R.I. Gen. Laws Ann. (1968)	26-3-4	26-3-4	fn. 32 26-3-4	fn. 32 26-3-4	fn. 32 26-3-4	26-3-25	26-3-25		6 months, 26-3-25	26-3-25			
S.C. Code Ann. (1962)		fn. 33 32-974 32-1020	32-1020	32-974		fn. 34 32-974	32-974		fn. 35 1 year 32-974	32-975			
S.D. Compiled Laws Ann. (1967)	27-10-2		27-10-2	27-10-3									
TENN. Code Ann. (1955)	33-609(d) (Supp. 1968)		fn. 13 33-609(d) (Supp. 1968)	fn. 13 33-609(d) (Supp. 1968)		33-612(a) (Supp. 1968)	33-302(a), 33-612(a) (Supp. 1968)	33-302(a), 33-612(a) (Supp. 1968)	1 year, 33-612(a) (Supp. 1968)	fn. 36 33-612(b) (Supp. 1968)		33-609(d) (Supp. 1968)	fn. 37 33-609(d) (Supp. 1968)
TEX. Rev. Civ. Stat. Ann. (1958)	5547-80(a)		5547-80(a)	5547-80(a)		5547-79	5547-79	5547-79	18 months. 5547-80(b)	5547-79		5547-80(d)	
UTAH Code Ann. (1968)	64-7-42		64-7-42	64-7-42		fn. 34 64-7-43	64-7-43		fn. 1 1 year, 64-7-43	64-7-43	64-7-42	64-7-42	
VT. Stat. Ann. (1968)	18, §7802		18, §7802	18, §7802		18, §8002	18, §7101(7) 18, §8002	18, §7101(7) 18, §8002	fn. 1 1 year, 18, §6002	18, §8004		18, §7802	18, §7802

Table 4.1   ADMINISTRATIVE DISCHARGE   *continued*

STATE	DISCHARGING AGENCY		TYPE OF DISCHARGE				CONDITIONAL DISCHARGE				NOTICE OF DISCHARGE TO		
			Absolute				Institution						
	Institution	Central Agency	Recovered	Improved	Unimproved	Conditional	Public	Private	Period of Conditional Discharge	Administrative Return	Central Agency	Court	Relative, Friends, or Guardian
VA. Code Ann. (1953)	37.1-98 (Supp. 1968)		37.1-19(a) (Supp. 1968)		fn. 9 37.1-98(c) (Supp. 1968)	37.1-98(d) (Supp. 1968)	37.1-98(d) (Supp. 1968)	37.1-99 (Supp. 1968)	37.1-98(d) (Supp. 1968)				
WASH. Rev. Code Ann. (1962)	72.23.140		72.23.140			72.23.140	72.23.140		fn. 1 1 year, 72.23.140	fn. 38 72.23.140		72.23.180	72.23.180
W. VA. Code Ann. (1966)	27-7-1		27-7-1	27-7-1	$500 bond required, 27-7-3	fn. 29 27-7-2	27-7-2	27-7-2	fn. 1 1 year; 27-7-2	27-7-4 (Supp. 1969)	27-7-1	27-7-1	
WIS. Stat. Ann. (1957)	51.12(4) (Supp. 1969)	51.12(1)	51.12(4) (Supp. 1969)	51.12(4) (Supp. 1969)	fn. 9 51.12(4) (Supp. 1969)	fn. 29 51.13(1) (Supp. 1969)	51.13(1) (Supp. 1969)		1 year; 51.13(3)	51.13(1) (Supp. 1969)	51.12(4) (Supp. 1969)	51.14 (Supp. 1969)	
WYO. Stat. Ann. (1967)	25-68		25-68	25-68		25-69	25-69	25-69	1 year 25-69	25-69	25-68 25-69		

Notes to Table 4.1   ADMINISTRATIVE DISCHARGE

1. Reexamination once a year. Draft Act, 16; Del. 16-5132(d) (Supp. 1970); Idaho 66-338(a) (Supp. 1969); Mo. 202.830; N.M. 34-2-11; N.D. 25-03-16 (Supp. 1969); Utah 64-7-43; Vt. 18, §8002; Wash. 72.23.140; W. Va. 27-7-2.

2. On the condition that he will receive outpatient or nonhospital treatment or on such other reasonable conditions as the superintendent may specify. Ariz. 36-524 (Supp. 1970).

3. Within 1 year from the date of a conditional discharge, the patient shall be reexamined and then either rehospitalized, continued on conditional discharge or given a complete discharge. Ariz. 36-524B (Supp. 1970).

4. Mandatory upon request of 2 physicians, health or peace officers, judge or prosecuting attorney. Patient may appeal to court within 30 days. Idaho 66-339, 66-340 (Supp. 1969).

5. Once during the first year, and once during each 2-year period thereafter, the superintendent must file a report with the department setting forth the reasons which justify continued hospitalization. Ill. 91½, §10-2 (Supp. 1969).

6. May be extended. Ill. 91½, §10-4 (Supp. 1969).

7. The state director may discharge persons who are not insane, or who can be cared for after discharge without danger to others. They may also discharge dangerous patients when fully satisfied that relatives or friends will provide necessary supervision, care and restraint. Iowa 226.18, 226.26.

8. Condition justifying hospitalization no longer exists. Ky. 202.239.

9. If not detrimental to patient or public welfare (or not dangerous to self or others; quiet and harmless). La. 28:96A (Supp. 1969); Md. 59, §42; Miss. 6919; N.Y. Mental Hygiene Law, 87 (Supp. 1970); Okla. 43A, §73(2) (Supp. 1969); Ore. 425.300; Va. 37.1-98(c) (Supp. 1968); Wis. 51.12(4) (Supp. 1968).

10. If patient is dangerous, he cannot be released without consent of the central agency and some guarantee from a person responsible for him that the public welfare will be safeguarded. La. 28:96E (Supp. 1969).

11. If he can be safely cared for and supervised by relatives or friends. La. 28:96E (Supp. 1969).

12. The superintendent, if the discharge is granted by the central agency. La. 28:97.

13. Discharge is authorized whenever the the superintendent finds that conditions justifying hospitalization no longer exist. Ohio 5122.21;

14. If incurable and not likely to benefit from further treatment. Md. 59, §42; Okla. 43A, §73(2) (Supp. 1969).

15. If friends or relatives are paying, they may remove a dangerous patient but superintendent must notify them of danger. Md. 59, §42.

16. Those unrecovered who have attempted violence or who are likely to become dangerous to others shall not be discharged without central agency approval. Mass. 123, §90.

17. Head of hospital shall discharge any patient admitted as mentally ill or inebriate when certified by him to be no longer in need of institutional care and treatment. Minn. 253 A.15(1) (Supp. 1969).

18. Relatives, with consent of director of public institutions, can remove a patient not susceptible of cure and not dangerous to be at large. Neb. 83-340.

19. Notice is required to the county clerks in the case of discharge of committed persons, and to the committing judge in instances where the committed person exhibited violence prior to hospitalization. Nev. 433.550.2, 433.550.5.

20. All laws relative to the hospitalization of insane persons to the New Hampshire State Hospital shall govern the hospitalization of insane persons to any other places in the state where insane persons are confined. N.H. 135:25.

21. Notice must be given immediately to the county attorney of the county from which such person was sent to the hospital and the county attorney must cause the person to be immediately removed from the hospital. N.H. 135:18.

22. Absolute and conditional discharge is by administrative regulation. N.J. 30:4-107 (Supp. 1970).

23. Hospital: a public or private hospital or institution, or part thereof, equipped to provide inpatient care and treatment for the mentally ill. N.M. 34-2-1 (d).

24. In accordance with rules prescribed by a commissioner. N.Y. Mental Hygiene Law, 87 (Supp. 1970),

25. Patient may be released without supervision, for 30-day period if it would not be injurious to the patient or dangerous to the community. N.C. 122-68.

26. Notice to and approval by the commissioner of mental health and state department of mental health is required for parole of unusually dangerous mentally disordered patient. N.C. 122-68.1.

27. Notice to the clerk of the superior court of county of patient's residence if there is a conditional discharge. N.C. 122-67.

28. Convalescent leave is granted rather than a discharge when the patient's complete recovery can be determined only by permitting him to leave the institution. At the end of 12 months' convalescent leave, a patient on convalescent leave shall become a discharge patient. Okla. 43A, §75(6) (Supp. 1969).

29. In addition to conditional discharge, hospital may board out harmless patients, who are still considered inmates on leave. W. Va. 27-8-3; Wis. 51.13(1) (Supp. 1969).

30. If extended, not to exceed 1 year. Pa. 50, §4419(a).

31. A leave of absence may be terminated by the director of the facility. Pa. 50, §4419(b).

32. "[A]lthough not restored to sanity. . . ." R.I. 26-3-4.

33. Mental Health Commission approval required for conditional discharges. Absolute discharges following conditional discharge must be made by the commission. S.C. 32-974.

34. May require outpatient treatment as condition. S.C. 32-974; Utah 64-7-43.

35. Whenever conditional discharge exceeds 1 year, the patient or his committee may request the superintendent make it absolute. S.C. 32-974.

36. If, in the case of a patient hospitalized under a court order, there is reason to believe that it is to the best interest of the patient to be rehospitalized, the department or the superintendent may issue an order for the immediate rehospitalization of the patient. Such an order, if not voluntarily complied with, shall, upon the endorsement of the court which ordered the patient's hospitalization or the county court where the patient resides or is found, authorize any police officer to take the patient into custody and transport him to the hospital. Tenn. 33-612(b) (Supp. 1968).

37. Superintendent shall make a report of the release to the person or persons upon whose application the patient was admitted. Tenn. 33-609(d) (Supp. 1968).

38. When the superintendent of the hospital revokes the parole of any patient he may request the superior court to order the detention of the patient. The court shall thereupon order the apprehension of such patient. Wash. 72.23.140. The court should take similar steps when it is made to appear to it that any paroled patient has become unsafe. Wash. 71.02.620.

Table 4.2 JUDICIAL DISCHARGE

STATE	APPLICATION BY			COURT WITH JURISDICTION	RESTRICTION ON PETITION FREQUENCY	MEDICAL CERTIFICATION IN SUPPORT OF PETITION	NOTICE OF HEARING TO		HEARING	NO. OF COURT-APPOINTED MEDICAL EXAMINERS	CONDITION			SECURITY FOR RELEASE	HABEAS CORPUS	
	Patient	Family or Guardian	Anyone				Family or Guardian	Superintendent of Institution			Recovered	Improved	Unimproved		Provision for	Determination of Illness at Time of Writ
DRAFT ACT	18	18		probate court of residence or hospital county. 18	fn. 1 / 1 year / 18		9(f) 18		9(f), 18	2 9(c), 18	fn. 2 / 18				22	
ALA. Code (1958)																
ALAS. Stat. (1962)	47.30.060	or a peace officer. 47.30.060		superior 47.30.060	fn. 1 47.30.060		47.30.060 47.30.070(f)		47.30.060 47.30.070	1 or more. 47.30.060 47.30.070(c)	47.30.070(i)	47.30.070(i)			47.30.100	
ARIZ. Rev. Stat. Ann. (1956) (Supp. 1970)	36-516	36-516		superior court 36-516	1 year 36-516		36-513(D) 36-516		36-514 36-516	2 or more. 36-514(B) 36-516	fn. 2 / 36-516					
ARK. Stat. Ann. (1947)															59-236	
CAL. Welf. & Inst'ns Code (West 1966) (Supp. 1968)	5275	attorney 5275		superior court 5276					5276		5276	5276			5275	5276
COLO. Rev. Stat. Ann. (1964)			any reputable person. 71-1-26	county court 71-1-26 71-1-27		71-1-26 71-1-27				2 71-1-26	71-1-26					
fn. 3 CONN. Gen. Stat. Ann. (1958)			17-192	probate court 17-192							17-192				17-201	17-201
			17-200	superior court 17-200	6 months 17-200				fn. 4 17-200		17-200	fn. 4 17-200			17-201	17-201
DEL. Code Ann. (1953)	16, §5126(a)	16, §5126(a)	fn. 5 16, §5126(a)	chancery court 16, §5126(a)	none 16, §5126(a)				16, §5126(b)		fn. 7 16, §5126(b)					
D.C. Code Ann. (1967)	21-546	attorney, guardian, spouse, parent, nearest relative. 21-546		U.S. District Court (D.C.). 21-546	6 months, or 90 days after commitment. 21-546	fn. 8 21-546					21-546	21-546		21-550	21-549	
FLA. Stat. Ann. (1960)		394.22(15)(2)		county court of commitment, residence or hospital. 394.22(15)(a)		fn. 9 394.22(16)(a) (Supp. 1969)	394.22(15)(c)	fn. 10 394.22(15)(c)	394.22(15)(c)		394.22(15)(d)	394.22(15)(d)			394.45 (Supp. 1969)	
GA. Code Ann. (1963)																
HAWAII Rev. Stat. Ann. (1968)	334-81	334-81		family court 334-81					334-82		334-84	334-84				
IDAHO Code Ann. (1949) (Supp. 1969)	66-343 (Supp. 1969)	66-343 (Supp. 1969)		probate court of hospital county. 66-343 (Supp. 1969)	fn. 1 / 1 year / 66-343 (Supp. 1969)		66-329(d) 66-343 (Supp. 1969)		66-329(j) 66-343	2 66-329(b) 66-343 (Supp. 1969)	fn. 2 / 66-343 (Supp. 1969)				66-347 (Supp. 1969)	

Table 4.2 JUDICIAL DISCHARGE *continued*

STATE	APPLICATION BY — Patient	APPLICATION BY — Family or Guardian	APPLICATION BY — Anyone	COURT WITH JURISDICTION	RESTRICTION ON PETITION FREQUENCY	MEDICAL CERTIFICATION IN SUPPORT OF PETITION	NOTICE OF HEARING TO — Family or Guardian	NOTICE OF HEARING TO — Superintendent of Institution	HEARING	NO. OF COURT-APPOINTED MEDICAL EXAMINERS	CONDITION — Recovered	CONDITION — Improved	CONDITION — Unimproved	SECURITY FOR RELEASE	HABEAS CORPUS — Provision for	HABEAS CORPUS — Determination of Illness at Time of Writ
ILL. Ann. Stat. (Smith-Hurd 1966) (Supp. 1969)	91½, §10-1		on patient's behalf 91½, §10-1	county court which hospitalized. 91½, §10-1	at discretion of court. 91½, §10-3	91½, §10-1	attorney, nearest relative, and at least 2 of any other persons designated by patient. 91½, §10-3	or person having custody. 91½, §10-3	91½, §9-1 to 9-5, 10-3	if no medical certificate 91½, §10-3	91½, §10-3	91½, §10-3			91½, §10-6	
IND. Ann. Stat. (1964)															22-1307 22-2914	fn. 11 22-1307
IOWA Code Ann. (1969)			229.31	district court in county of settlement or hospital location. 229.31	fn. 1 6 months 229.36				229.33	not more than 3 persons. 229.31	229.33				229.37	229.37
KAN. Stat. Ann. (1964) (Supp. 1968)	59-2923		59-2923	probate court which issued order for care and treatment. 59-2923	6 months 59-2923		59-2916, 59-2923	fn. 12 59-2923	59-2917 59-2923		59-2923				59-2938	
KY. Rev. Stat. Ann. (1969)	202.360			county court 202.360					202.360		202.360	202.360		202.360	202.275	
LA. Rev. Stat. Ann. (1950)				committing court. 28:98					28:98		28:98	28:98			28:171(6)	
ME. Rev. Stat. Ann. (1965)	34, §2377	34, §2377		probate court 34, §2377	fn. 1 1 year 34, §2377	34, §2334 34, §2377	34, §2334 34, §2377		34, §2377	2 34, §2334 34, §2377	34, §2377	34, §2377			34, §2255	
MD. Ann. Code (1968)			59, §21	county or Baltimore city court. 59, §21	fn. 13 1 year 59, §21						59, §21				59, §20	59, §20
MASS. Ann. Laws (1965)			123, §91 123, §94A	supreme court justice 123, §91	fn. 14 1 year 123, §94A			123, §92 123, §94A	123, §92	fn. 15 123, §94A	123, §93	123, §93	fn. 16 123, §90 123, §93		123, §92	123, §91
MICH. Comp. Laws Ann. (1967)	330.39			probate court 330.39				fn. 17 330.39	330.39	fn. 18 2 330.39	330.39	330.39	330.35(5)	330.35		
MINN. Stat. Ann. (1959)			253A.19(1) (Supp. 1969)	committing court. 253A.19(1)			253A.19(2) (Supp. 1969)	fn. 19 253A.19(2) (Supp. 1969)	253A.19(2) (Supp. 1969)	2 253A.19(3) (Supp. 1969)	253A.19(5) (Supp. 1969)	253A.19(5) (Supp. 1969)				
MISS. Code Ann. (1952)		6909-08	6909-08	committing court 6909-08				6909-08	6909-08		fn. 7 6909-08				6909-08	
MO. Rev. Stat. (1959)	202.837	202.837		committing court. 202.837			202.807(2) 202.837		before special commissioner. 202.807 202.837	1 202.807(3) 202.837	fn. 2 202.837				202.850	

150

Table 4.2 JUDICIAL DISCHARGE   continued

STATE	APPLICATION BY — Patient	APPLICATION BY — Family or Guardian	APPLICATION BY — Anyone	COURT WITH JURISDICTION	RESTRICTION ON PETITION FREQUENCY	MEDICAL CERTIFICATION IN SUPPORT OF PETITION	NOTICE OF HEARING TO — Family or Guardian	NOTICE OF HEARING TO — Superintendent of Institution	HEARING	NO. OF COURT-APPOINTED MEDICAL EXAMINERS	CONDITION — Recovered	CONDITION — Improved	CONDITION — Unimproved	SECURITY FOR RELEASE	HABEAS CORPUS — Provision for	HABEAS CORPUS — Determination of Illness at Time of Writ
MONT. Rev. Codes Ann. (1961)																
NEB. Rev. Stat. (1966)															83-343	83-343
NEV. Rev. Stat. (1967)	433.713	433.713		433.715	90 days after order, then 6 months. 433.713	433.713			433.715		433.713	433.713			433.040	
N.H. Rev. Stat. Ann. (1964) (Supp. 1967)			135:30	superior court 135:30			optional 135:30	optional 135:30			135:30	135:30				
N.J. Stat. Ann. (1964)															2A:67-13(e) 30:4-24.2 (Supp. 1970)	
N.M. Stat. Ann. (1953)	34-2-12	34-2-12		committing or district court. 34-2-12	fn. 1 1 year 34-2-12		34-2-5(b) 34-2-12		34-2-5 34-2-12	1 34-2-5 34-2-12	fn. 2 34-2-12				34-2-16	
N.Y. Mental Hygiene Law (McKinney 1951)															426	426
N.C. Gen. Stat. (1964)			fn. 20 122-65				patient 122-65				122-65	122-65				
N.D. Cent. Code (1960)	25-03-17	25-03-17		county court and mental health board. 25-03-11	fn. 1 1 year 25-03-17		25-03-11 25-03-17	25-03-11 25-03-17	fn. 21 25-03-11 25-03-17	1 25-03-11 25-03-17	fn. 2 25-03-17				25-03-21	25-03-21
OHIO Rev. Code Ann. (Baldwin 1964)		fn. 22 5122.25		probate court 5122.25					5122.25		fn. 2 5122.25				5122.30	
OKLA. Rev. Stat. (1954)	43A, §75 (Supp. 1969)	43A, §75 (Supp. 1969)	fn. 23 43A, §75 (Supp. 1969)	court where patient resides. 43A, §75 (Supp. 1969)			fn. 24 43A, §75 (Supp. 1969)		43A, §75 (Supp. 1969)	2 43A, §75 (Supp. 1969)	43A, §75 (Supp. 1969)				43A, §99	43A, §99
ORE. Rev. Stat. (1967)															426.380	
fn. 25 PA. Stat. Ann. (1969)															50, §4426	50, §4426
R.I. Gen. Laws Ann. (1968)	26-3-5		26-3-5	supreme court justice. 26-3-5		fn. 26 26-3-6	fn. 27 26-3-6		fn. 26 26-3-6		26-3-5		fn. 28 26-3-4		26-3-10	26-3-10
S.C. Code Ann. (1962)	32-968	32-968		probate court 32-968	fn. 1 1 year 32-968		32-962 32-968		32-962 32-968	2 32-960 32-968	fn. 2 32-968				fn. 29 32-915	
S.D. Compiled Laws Ann. (1967)																

Table 4.2 JUDICIAL DISCHARGE continued

STATE	APPLICATION BY Patient	APPLICATION BY Family or Guardian	APPLICATION BY Anyone	COURT WITH JURISDICTION	RESTRICTION ON PETITION FREQUENCY	MEDICAL CERTIFICATION IN SUPPORT OF PETITION	NOTICE OF HEARING TO Family or Guardian	NOTICE OF HEARING TO Superintendent of Institution	HEARING	NO. OF COURT-APPOINTED MEDICAL EXAMINERS	CONDITION Recovered	CONDITION Improved	CONDITION Unimproved	SECURITY FOR RELEASE	HABEAS CORPUS Provision for	HABEAS CORPUS Determination of Illness at Time of Writ
TENN. Code Ann. (1955)															33-1209 (Supp. 1968)	33-316 (Supp. 1968)
TEX. Rev. Civ. Stat. Ann. (1958)	5547-82(a)	5547-82(a)		court of hospital county. 5547-82(a)	fn. 30 2 years 5547-82(g)	5547-82(c)		5547-82(b)	5547-82(d)	5547-82(d)	fn. 2 5547-82(a)				5547-85	
UTAH Code Ann. (1968)	64-7-45	64-7-45		court of hospital or residence. 64-7-45	fn. 1 1 year 64-7-45		64-7-36 64-7-45		64-7-36 64-7-45	2 64-7-36 64-7-45	fn. 2 64-7-45				64-7-49	
VT. Stat. Ann. (1968)	18, §7801(a)	18, §7801(a)		probate court 18, §7801(a)	fn. 1 18, §7801(a)		18, §7606 18, §7801(b)		18, §7606 18, §7801(b)	1 18, §7603 18, §7801(b)	fn. 2 18, §7801				18, §8005	
VA. Code Ann. (1953)															37.1-103 (Supp. 1968)	37.1-103 (Supp. 1968)
WASH. Rev. Code Ann. (1961)															7.36.020	
W. VA. Code Ann. (1966)																
WIS. Stat. Ann. (1957)	51.11(1)		51.11(1)	court of hospital committing court. 51.11	1 year 51.11(8)		51.11(4)	51.11(3a)	51.11(4)	2 51.11(3)	fn. 2 51.11				292.01	292.01
WYO. Stat. Ann. (1967)															25-72(b)	25-72(b)

Notes to Table 4.2   JUDICIAL DISCHARGE

1. Or 6 months from the order of hospitalization. Draft Act 18; Alas. 47.30.060; Idaho 66-343 (Supp. 1969); Iowa 229.36; Me. 34, §2377; N.M. 34-2-12; N.D. 25-03-17; S.C. 32-968; Utah 64-7-45; Vt. 18, §7801(a).

2. Patient is entitled to a reexamination of the hospitalization order. Draft Act 18; Ariz. 36-516 (Supp. 1970); Idaho 66-343 (Supp. 1969); Mo. 202.837; N.M. 34-2-12; N.D. 25-03-17; Ohio 5122.25; S.C. 32-968; Tex. 5547-82(a); Utah 64-7-45; Vt. 18, §7801; Wis. 51.11.

3. "[Probate] court may . . . when it finds it to be for the best interest of the person so committed, revoke such order of commitment." Conn. 17-178 (Supp. 1969).

4. Judge may appoint commission of not less than 2 persons, who shall have 1 or more private interviews with patient; if the committee finds that patient is cured, or confinement is no longer beneficial or advisable, the judge shall order his discharge. Conn. 17-200.

5. Any 3 persons may also make application for judicial discharge. Del. 16, §5126.

6. Court shall order writ de lunatico inquirendo to be issued to sheriff of county, commanding him to summon a jury within 5 days of service of writ; jury shall determine sanity of committed person and make return of same to court within 2 days after finding.

7. The condition has reference to whether the patient is sane or insane, not whether there has been any recovery. Del. 16, §5126(b); Miss. 6909-08.

8. Hospital examination. Patient may have physician participate at patient's expense (if indigent, provided by department of public health). Hearing only if 1 or more physicians find patient not mentally ill, but chief of service refuses discharge. D.C. 21-546.

9. Superintendent may issue certificate of sanity which is prima facie proof of sanity at judicial hearing. Fla. 394.22(16) (Supp. 1969).

10. County or state's attorney. Fla. 394.22; Minn. 525.78.2.

11. Edenharter v. Conner (1916), 185 Ind. 643, 114 N.E. 212.

12. Notice of time and place to be given to the "psychiatric hospital" or "other facilities for care or treatment" to which the "involuntary patient" was ordered for "care and treatment." Kan. 59-2923. (Supp. 1968).

13. If less than a year, need affidavit showing substantial improvement. Md. 59, §21.

14. The restriction applies only to adjudications of insanity and not to discharge proceedings. Mass. 123, §94A.

15. Two physicians certified by American Board of Psychiatry and Neurology. Mass. 123, §94A.

16. If not detrimental to patient or public welfare (or not dangerous to self or others; quiet and harmless). Mass. 123, §93; Pa. 50-1304.

17. "[A]nd to such other persons as the court shall direct." Mich. 330.39.

18. Judge may not require a medical examination when superintendent and 1 other physician certify in writing that patient is of sound mind. Mich. 330.39.

19. ". . . ten days notice of which shall be given to the county attorney and to the commissioner. . . . Notice shall be given to the patient, his legal counsel, the head of the hospital . . . and such other persons and in such manner as the court directs." Minn. 253A.19(2) (Supp. 1969).

20. Written report filed with clerk by hospital superintendent, after initial 180-day period, as to whether or not further treatment is needed. If not, clerk will discharge or order a second hearing. The hearing may be waived in writing by the patient. N.C. 122-65.

21. Only if the board finds the patient to be mentally ill shall a hearing be held. N.D. 25-03-11, 25-03-17.

22. Upon the request of the private hospital, county home, relative, friend, or facility other than a public hospital who has custody of the patient. Ohio 5122.25.

23. Superintendent. Okla. 43A, §75 (Supp. 1969).

24. If petition is made by person adjudged mentally incompetent, notice to person upon whose application he was committed, if found within county. Okla. 43A, §75 (Supp. 1969).

25. Discharge is made by the Department of Public Welfare. Pa. 50, §§4102, 4420.

26. An examination by the commissioners appointed by the court is required, at which time the patient and petitioner may present evidence. R.I. 26-3-6.

27. The patient shall be served with notice and be allowed to have counsel and be present at the commissioner's examination. R.I. 26-3-6.

Notes to Table 4.2 JUDICIAL DISCHARGE *continued*

28. Any person hospitalized by a supreme court justice may be discharged, although not recovered, by a supreme court justice upon recommendation of the trustees and superintendent of the hospital. R.I. 26-3-4.

29. Under habeas corpus provision, no test of factual issue of petitioner's sanity but the legality of the proceedings or judgment under which he was committed and is being confined. Douglas v. Hall, 297 S.C. 550, 93 S.E.2d 891 (1956).

30. Or within 1 year of commitment order. Tex. 5547-82 (g).

Chapter Five
Rights of Hospitalized Patients

I. INTRODUCTION

The phrase "rights of the mentally ill" popularly carries a strong connotation of procedural protection in the area of involuntary hospitalization. This chapter will focus on the kinds of restrictions that are placed on the rights of persons once they are hospitalized. These restrictions confronting mental patients concern rights which the average citizen takes for granted, such as written communication, visitation, and compensation for work. This chapter will also discuss the rights and restrictions surrounding the question of *treatment* of hospitalized patients.

In discussing principles which should govern the hospitalization of the mentally ill, the Council of State Governments said in 1950:

> Patients while in a hospital should be protected in the enjoyment of personal rights to the extent consistent with required treatment and detention. This principle is based on the very simple . . . idea that an individual hospitalized for mental illness is only sick. The principle goes beyond such obvious matters as the right to receive visitors and to communicate with relatives, public officials, and others.[1]

Recognition of these principles has been slow in evolving. Today, some twenty years later, an examination of the state statutes and administrative regulations indicates that the right to receive visitors or to correspond with persons outside the institution is still less than fully recognized. Moreover, only about half of the states have statutes regulating the use of mechanical restraints, the use of certain kinds of medical treatment, or the use of patients as hospital employees. The persistence of this neglect is attributable at least in part to the traditional and unremitting notion that all mentally disabled persons are incapable of comprehending or exercising their personal rights. Modern medico-legal opinion rejects this overgeneralization. This is not to say that in modern times mental patients should retain all their personal rights. Effective treatment in many instances necessitates a withdrawal of certain patient rights. Considerations of orderly hospital adminis-

tration may also necessitate the imposition of some restrictions. The crux of the problem may be primarily the extent to which discretion to control the patient's freedom should be vested in the hands of hospital authorities.

II. COMMUNICATION

The right of communication is exercised by hospitalized patients primarily in two ways: through visitation (to be discussed in detail later in this section) and through correspondence. The Group for the Advancement of Psychiatry more than twenty years ago endorsed, as a fundamental proposition, the right of patients to communicate, when at all possible, with persons outside the institution.[2]

The right of communication was the first to receive recognition and in most states was the only right to be guaranteed by statute.[3] Today, all but ten of the states have statutory provisions on the subject of patient correspondence, and more than half of all the states have provisions concerning visitation.[4] Without actual observation of hospital practices, it is impossible to discern what rights patients have in those states which do not have statutory provisions in these areas. Unfortunately, comparable uncertainties exist regarding the actual protection of patients' rights in many of the states which do guarantee these rights by statute.

A. CORRESPONDENCE

The basis of many laws granting communication rights to patients is that such communication exposes cases of wrongful hospitalization. Improperly detained individuals are permitted an opportunity to protest their confinement by the free posting of letters. These laws place little or no emphasis on the intrinsic right of a bona fide mental patient to com-

1. Council of State Governments, *The Mental Health Programs of the Forty-eight States* 69 (1950).

2. Group for the Advancement of Psychiatry, "Commitment Procedures" 3 (Rep. No. 4, April 1948).

3. Ross, "Hospitalizing the Mentally Ill—Emergency and Temporary Commitments," *Current Trends in State Legislation 1955–1956,* at 459, 526 (1957).

4. See Table 5.1, Correspondence and Visitation, for the particular provisions made by the states which attempt to safeguard these rights.

municate with the outside world.[5] As a result, the guarantee of correspondence is often limited to correspondence with named public officials or the central hospital agency for the state.[6] A typical provision is contained in the Draft Act, which states:

> Notwithstanding any limitations authorized under this section on the right of communication, every patient shall be entitled to communicate by sealed mail with the [*central administration*] and with the court, if any, which ordered his hospitalization.[7]

Since the power of the hospital to deny the patient visitation or correspondence rights may be misused to the point of depriving him of his right to a writ of habeas corpus, this type of provision is extremely important to the patient. In two New York cases, the state hospital's failure to forward letters to attorneys was held to constitute an unreasonable restraint on the patient's right to a writ of habeas corpus.[8]

In both cases the hospital superintendent—who had the authority to, and in fact did, restrict correspondence—knew that the letters were to an attorney and knew also that they related to habeas corpus proceedings. Although New York patients at that time did not have a right to unrestricted correspondence with an attorney, they did have a right to correspond with the governor, attorney general, judges, district attorneys, and officers of the Department of Mental Hygiene. In the earlier of these two cases, the court, explaining that the exceptions were too restrictive, said:

> Depriving a person confined in a large institution . . . of the right to send a letter to a lawyer . . . imposes an unreasonable restraint upon him never contemplated by the law.[9]

New York, as a result of these cases, enacted legislation which accorded to mental patients the right to unrestricted correspondence with attorneys.[10] Some seventeen other jurisdictions presently have similar statutory provisions.[11] The establishment in New York of the Mental Health Information Service,[12] generally intended as an ever-present safeguard of all patient rights, serves on the specific level to make more realistic the right of the patient to communicate with an attorney. The Service's functions consist of informing all patients of their rights, assisting in the assertion of these rights, reviewing admission and retention procedures and rationales, and aiding the courts in assembling information in the event of judicial hearings. Headquarters of the Service are located in or near the Appellate Division courthouses of each of the four judicial departments, while branch offices are maintained in state and local hospitals throughout each department. Personnel qualifications range from attorneys trained and experienced in law and psychiatry to social workers and former probation officers. In any case, legal assistance—whether through direct or indirect contact—is always readily available to the hospitalized patient in New York.[13]

The question may arise of correspondence which impedes the patient's recovery or even constitutes a

5. "Although a few modern statutes appear to recognize that a patient's rights of communication are worth protecting as such, most statutes clearly indicate that these rights are ancillary to the right to release." Ross, *supra* note 3, at 526.

6. See Table 5.1.

7. National Institute of Mental Health, Federal Security Agency, *A Draft Act Governing Hospitalization of the Mentally Ill* 15 (Public Health Service Pub. No. 51, 1952) [hereinafter cited as *Draft Act*]. The *Draft Act* is reproduced as Appendix A to this Report.

8. Hoff v. State, 279 N.Y. 490, 18 N.E.2d 671 (1939); People *ex rel.* Jacobs v. Worthing, 167 Misc. 702, 4 N.Y.S.2d 630 (1938).

9. People *ex rel.* Jacobs v. Worthing, 167 Misc. 702, 705, 4 N.Y.S.2d 630, 634 (1938). In this case the patient had been institutionalized for four years. From a time early in his confinement, he sought his release from the hospital, endeavoring at all times to communicate his plight to lawyers by "smuggled

mail." When he finally was able to contact an attorney, this case was instituted. In granting the writ of habeas corpus the court said in 4 N.Y.S.2d at 633–34: "The query suggests itself. Why is that one person, who is wholly free to act; who is fully equipped by training and experience to investigate; who is ready and willing to serve (even at times, as in this case, without compensation); who is bound by his oath to give his all to the cause that he espouses; who has the right to appear in court and possesses the power to produce the results required—the attorney at law—omitted from that group to whom inmates may send unexamined mail?"

10. New York Department of Mental Hygiene, Mental Hygiene Law and General Orders, General Order No. 11(e), Correspondence of Patients (All Institutions), at 191 (Supp. I). See also Table 5.1, Restrictions column, *infra* and footnotes thereto for the specific regulations imposed by states which allow correspondence and visitation rights. Presently, see *N.Y. Mental Hygiene Law* § 15 (McKinney Supp. 1970): "[P]atients shall be allowed to correspond without restriction with any public official and with the mental health information service."

11. See Table 5.1, Restrictions column and footnotes thereto.

12. *N.Y. Mental Hygiene Law* § 88 (McKinney Supp. 1970).

13. For a description and performance evaluation of the mental health information service, see Note, "The New York Mental Health Information Service: A New Approach to Hospitalization of the Mentally Ill," 67 *Colum. L. Rev.* 672 (1967). See also Meyer, "Lawyer in a Mental Hospital: The New York Experiment," 53 *Mental Hygiene* 14 (1969).

danger to his immediate welfare. Some of the more recent statutes attempt to meet this dilemma by granting a *qualified* privilege of correspondence and visitation. The Draft Act, for example, provides that every patient is

> entitled to communicate by sealed mail or otherwise with persons, . . . subject to the general rules and regulations of the hospital and except to the extent that the head of the hospital determines that it is necessary for the medical welfare of the patient to impose restrictions.[14]

Under the same rules and regulations, patients are also entitled to receive visitors. Whenever the head of the hospital limits either of these rights, the limitation must be entered on the patient's clinical record.[15]

At first glance the Draft Act seems to offer adequate protection of correspondence and visitation rights, but the dilemma remains. It is often stated that mental hospitals are understaffed and medical personnel so overworked that they have little time to devote to the individual patient;[16] if such is the case it is probable that decisions on a patient's correspondence would be delegated to subordinates— possibly to nonmedical attendants. Certainly a ward attendant should not be the one to decide what civil restrictions are necessary for the patient's medical welfare.

Some measure of safety against abuse is covered in the Draft Act by the requirement that correspondence limitations be made a part of the clinical record. The provision, however, is devoid of adequate enforcement procedures. There is no requirement that the head of a hospital or a central administration check these records. Moreover, the right of an interested or affected party to examine the records would also have to include authority and opportunity to investigate the circumstances and, if appropriate, to cause the restrictions to be lifted.

Another problem with correspondence is the failure of statutes to differentiate between incoming and outgoing mail. Assuming that the purpose behind correspondence limitations is the patient's medical welfare, it would seem that restrictions should lay more emphasis on incoming mail. The British Royal Commission on laws relating to mental illness covers the incoming mail situation by recommending

that hospitals be given the authority to withhold from the patient any harmful incoming letters, but that this power be used very sparingly and all letters withheld from the patient be returned to the writer.[17]

Patients with certain types and at various stages of mental illness are apt to express hostility toward individuals or the outside world, and their letters may contain threatening and perhaps "offensive" material. The language may be libelous or may violate postal regulations. It has also been said that disturbed patients often write to their relatives of the "horrors" of their confinement; the natural reaction of relatives is sometimes to initiate discharge proceedings without a factual basis. The thrust of these propositions is that hospital restrictions on outgoing mail are eminently appropriate and the patient upon recovery will be grateful that the hospital authorities interceded, saving him from acute embarrassment or even legal liability. Accordingly, some hospitals have specific administrative provisions forbidding the posting of letters which contain the names of other patients, obscene material, threats, statements which might embarrass the patient or his family, or unreliable comments concerning discharge.[18]

Such pervasive restrictions may be seen as less than desirable, however. Alternative solutions exist which appear to strike a better balance. One procedure which safeguards the patient's right of communication while according some measure of protection to the public has been effectuated in some institutions, where a small printed notice is inserted in all outgoing mail to the effect that the writer is in a mental hospital and the communication should be treated accordingly. Another approach is offered by the British Royal Commission, which has recommended that

> there should be no censorship of out-going letters from patients . . . except at the request of individual addressees who ask for letters addressed to themselves to be scrutinised or withheld because they find them distressing.[19]

Some fifteen states require that writing materials be furnished to the patients. In addition, some states require that stamps be furnished and that a mailbox

---

14. *Draft Act* § 21(a)(1), at 15.

15. Id. at § 21(a)(2), (c).

16. See, for example, Council of State Governments, *supra* note, 1, at 4.

17. Royal Commission on the Law Relating to Mental Illness and Mental Deficiency 1954–1957, Cmnd. No. 169 § 299, at 103 (1957).

18. Wisconsin, Mendota State Hospital, Administrative Regulations 5 (1949).

19. Royal Commission, *supra* note 17, § 299, at 103.

be made available for patients.[20] Field work is necessary to determine the extent to which this practice is followed in states without the requisite statute. If the patient is unable to obtain writing materials for himself, then his right to correspond depends solely upon the extent to which the hospital sees fit to provide them. Serious thought should therefore be given to regulations which would prevent possible abuses under this system.

B. VISITATION

The situation with regard to visitation raises similar problems. Some thirty states have statutes on the subject.[21] Fourteen of these follow the Draft Act, which contains procedures and restrictions on visitation substantially similar to those on correspondence. Unfortunately, the Draft Act itself, as well as those states adopting it or like statutes, delegates to the hospital broad powers to control visitation.[22] As a result, the rules and regulations of some institutions allow visiting for only one hour once during the work week. Since most institutions are in remote areas, this sort of regulation tends to discourage visitors. Hospital authorities, moreover, have broad discretion in curtailing these rights, and in most states no effective provisions for recourse exist for patients who suffer abuses of this discretion.

Thus, the matter of discretion in the hands of hospital authorities is the primary area of concern here. This is not to say that in the interest of the patient's welfare and his successful treatment the hospital should not have a strong voice in visitation rules. Such, indeed, is the reason given for the broad language of the Draft Act.[23] Nonetheless, serious thought should be given to the advisability of having a reviewing agency oversee the exercise of this discretion.

Among the sixteen other states having statutory

provisions in this area, eight specifically allow unrestricted visits from clergymen; ten are concerned with the right to see an attorney and six allow visits of the patient's private physician. Some statutes simply provide for visits during reasonable hours or at the discretion of the institution's physician.[24]

An important point to consider in assessing the relative merits of visitation freedoms is the success some hospitals have had in exerting little or no restrictions. Practical considerations of hospital administration may require certain regulations; but the success, both here and abroad, of the "open ward" or even the "open hospital" indicates that such independence for patients is feasible.[25]

Many hospitals have recognized that the patient's contact with persons outside the hospital is both beneficial to the patient and educational to the public. Consequently, they have encouraged visits by the public and, more importantly, have solicited volunteer workers. The aim of this movement is to impress upon the community the importance of adequate facilities[26] and to give patients the benefit of normal relationships.

III. MECHANICAL RESTRAINTS

Mechanical restraints which serve to inhibit movement are still used in a few mental hospitals despite the fact that their abolition has been strongly advocated for more than a century.

In 1815 a British parliamentary investigation revealed horribly cruel treatment of patients in private and public asylums. This investigation led progressive leaders to seek means of reducing the use of mechanical restraints to a minimum. In 1856 Dr. John Connelly, medical superintendent of the Middlesex Asylum located at Hanwell, England, published a book entitled *The Treatment of the Insane without Mechanical Restraints*. The book was more than an argument for the removal of mechanical restraints. Connelly advocated kindness, patience, and understanding on the part of the staff, the removal of the prisonlike aspects (which caused patients to feel as if they were being punished for misdeeds), and the planning of healthful recreations and con-

---

20. See Table 5.1, Writing Material Furnished column and footnotes thereto.

21. Id. at Visitation columns. See also *Draft Act* § 21, at 15.

22. The *Draft Act* reads:

Sec. 21. Right to communication and visitation ...

   (a) Subject to the general rules and regulations of the hospital and except to the extent that the head of the hospital determines that it is necessary for the medical welfare of the patient to impose restrictions, every patient shall be entitled

     (1) to communicate by sealed mail or otherwise with persons, including official agencies, inside or outside the hospital;

     (2) to receive visitors; ...

23. *Draft Act*, Commentary, at 34–35.

24. Table 5.1, Visitation columns.

25. See Garber, "Legal Implications of the Open Hospital," 9 *Mental Hospitals* 24–26 (1958); Keane, "An Open Psychiatric Ward in a General Hospital," 8 *Mental Hospitals* 27–32 (1957).

26. See Stevenson, *Mental Health Planning for Social Action* 67 (1956).

genial occupations.[27] The nonrestraint system was widely adopted in England after its successful introduction at the Middlesex Asylum. In nineteenth century America, however, there was no comparable legislative or medical interest in the policy of nonrestraint. In 1844, at its founding meeting, the Association of Medical Superintendents (the forerunner of the American Psychiatric Association) adopted as its very first rule the following:

> Resolved that it is the unanimous sense of this convention that the attempt to abandon entirely the use of all means of personal restraint is not sanctioned by the true interests of the insane.[28]

The arguments for the use of restraint brought forward by Dr. Isaac Ray in 1844 and later expanded by others have been summarized as follows:

1. [T]he ideal of nonrestraint could never be completely realized. . . . Some forms of forcible restraint would always be necessary to the proper discipline of a mental hospital. . . . [L]imitation on the bodily movements of the patient by means of external devices . . . would continue to be required in very special instances. . . . This being the case, it was more honest to champion restraint in principle, rather than nonrestraint.
2. The abolition of mechanical restraint meant merely the substitution of another form of coercion— "manual restraint." . . .
3. To supplant mechanical restraint by attendants would necessitate larger staffs and consequently greater expense.
4. Suicidal, destructive and unmanageable patients required . . . some . . . restraints. . . . Mechanical appliances were least onerous and most effective.
5. Mechanical restraints were also required for patients who were prone to exhaust their energy and to lower their vitality by excessive physical excitement.
6. The patients in European institutions, accustomed as they were to unquestioned acceptance of authority, might willingly submit to "moral" restraint, but not your liberty-loving American who, sane or insane, would never agree placidly to the imposition of authority by an individual. . . .
7. [W]here the abolition of mechanical restraint had been tried, it had resulted in dismal failure. . . .[29]

However, even at that time there were some hospitals in the United States which believed in nonrestraint. In 1838 the first superintendent of Columbus Hospital in Columbus, Ohio, wrote proudly that restraint was seldom required if patients were treated with "kindness and forbearance."[30] A very interesting observation has been made by the former chief of the Mental Health Section of the World Health Organization:

> One can find records of hospitals which abolished restraint, unlocked doors, and developed within the hospital an effective and to some extent democratic society . . . and then the Superintendent retired or died; in ten years' time the doors were locked again, the padded rooms were in use, new strait jackets bought, and the hospital was back where it was before that Superintendent had created this therapeutic community.[31]

The attitude toward restraints in this country has changed considerably since the 1800s. The use of restraints is no longer openly advocated, and usually such practices are seized upon in mental hospital exposes. The Council of State Governments, after an intensive study of their use, concluded: "Mechanical restraint is rarely if ever justified."[32] Though improvements in treatment have curtailed their use, mechanical restraints continue to play a role in some treatment programs. Only about half of the states and the Draft Act have attempted to regulate the use of mechanical restraints by statute.[33] These provisions specify that restraint be used only when it is necessary to meet the patient's medical needs, and most provisions require that the restraint order be signed by a physician and be made part of the patient's clinical record.

In view of the alleged condition of mental hospitals, statutory regulations alone may not be adequate to protect the patient's freedom of movement. For example, the requirement that a physician sign the order is an attempt to make certain that restraints are used only for medical necessity; yet one physician may be responsible for hundreds of patients and therefore obliged to rely on an attendant's

27. Deutsch, *The Mentally Ill in America* 214, 228 (2d ed. 1949).

28. Id. at 215.

29. Id. at 216.

30. Martin, "Inside the Asylum," *Saturday Evening Post,* Nov. 10, 1956, at 130.

31. Lebensohn, "Impressions of Hospital Psychiatry in Holland," 7 *Mental Hospitals* 22, 26 (1956).

32. Council of State Governments, *supra* note 1, at 12.

33. See Table 5.2, Mechanical Restraints, and footnotes thereto citing the conditions and reasons for imposing restraints.

recommendation rather than on a personal investigation.

Although some of the hospital regulations specifically state that "restraints will not be used as punishment, nor will patients be threatened with restraints,"[34] there is considerable opinion that their use may be and is too easily abused. Accounts by ex-patients and mental hospital exposés by outsiders have related that restraints are used as a tool for imposing discipline. Accusations are often made that some attendants use restraints for purposes of personal revenge and satisfaction. An account of allegedly extreme and unjustified cruelty tells of a child who was placed in a straitjacket "in the middle of the ward for a whole day."[35]

The recent appearance of literature in the field of psychotherapy advocating punishment in the form of physical restraints or painful stimuli for purposes of treatment[36] indicates that more is involved here than merely a problem of responsible but overburdened hospital physicians guarding against abuses by vindictive attendants. When punishment is justified as a form of therapy and the methods (restraints) employed are cloaked in language such as "aversive conditioning," the detection of abuse becomes a much more difficult matter.[37]

A minimum requirement designed to prevent unwarranted restraints would be for any restraint order to be entered on the patient's clinical record. The success of this procedure depends, however, on who may see the record and on his authority. A look at protective measures in other countries would be enlightening at this point. In England and Wales, full particulars concerning restraints must be reported in a medical certificate, and reports of restraint are sent quarterly from the hospital to the Board of Control, a central agency supervising the practices of all institutions. Norway also requires that quarterly reports on restraint be sent to a control commission.[38] The periodic report to an outside

agency would seem to afford the patient better protection against unauthorized use of physical restraints than a mere entry in his clinical record, which may go unnoticed.

Even when restraint is absolutely necessary, there still remain questions of patients' rights with respect to the means and duration of restraint. Among the physical restraints used in mental institutions are muffs, straps, belts and wristlets, camisoles, dry packs, lock chairs, and sheet restraints. Some of these are more confining and dehumanizing than others. A strap on one arm, for example, might provide sufficient restraint and at the same time leave the patient free to perform functions, while another type of restraint might totally immobilize him. Obviously there is no justification for the use of a greater amount of restraint than is necessary to prevent the patient from committing destructive physical acts.[39]

The length of time a restraint may be applied varies from state to state and even from hospital to hospital. In some hospitals, an order for the use of a physical restraint must be renewed within two hours, while in others the use of restraints may be continued without a renewal order for a period as long as thirty days. Most hospitals set a three-day limit.[40] Here again, it is necessary that the period be confined to the patient's needs.

Recent developments in the use of tranquilizing (psychotropic) drugs have been instrumental in reducing the incidence of and need for physical restraints.

The utilization of drugs appears to have become a major feature of the programs in today's mental institutions. The marketing and advertising of large varieties of tranquilizing agents have become a very noticeable preoccupation of many psychiatric journals.[41] Whereas a decade ago the cost of drugs may have been prohibitive for many hospitals, preventing

34. Missouri Department of Public Health and Welfare, Official Rules and Regulations, Rule 11.2, at 11 (1954).

35. 6 *League for Emotionally Disturbed Children News*, February 1967, at 3, col. 3.

36. E.g., Ludwig, Marx, Hill, & Browning, "The Control of Violent Behavior Through Faradic Shock," 148 *J. Nerv. & Ment. Disease* 624 (1969); Simmons & Lovaas, "Use of Pain and Punishment as Treatment Techniques with Childhood Schizophrenics," 23 *Am. J. Psychother.* 23 (1969).

37. For a further elaboration see this chapter, § IV, Major Medical Treatment.

38. World Health Organization, *Hospitalization of Mental Patients* 78 (1955).

39. Grimes, *When Minds Go Wrong* 79–80 (1954). Grimes gives a pungent account of the twenty-four-hour-a-day straitjacketing of patients whom the hospital attendants term "soilers."

40. Council of State Governments, *supra* note 1, at 193, 354–57.

41. E.g., current issues of *Hospital & Community Psychiatry* (a journal of the American Psychiatric Association). See also National Clearinghouse for Mental Health Information, *Community Mental Health Center Data Systems* 37 (1969), reproducing a "Summary of Medications" of one mental health center. The summary implies the extensive use of drugs and indicates some of the kinds used. Thorazine, a trade name for chlorpromazine, is still one of the most widely used drugs. Cf. Martin, *supra* note 30, at 144–45.

large-scale procurement and utilization, today even in the less affluent hospitals located in economically disadvantaged areas high percentages of the patient populations are admittedly under the continuous influence of tranquilizers.[42]

The elimination of mechanical or physical restraints is of course laudable. It does not follow, however, that indiscriminate overuse of drugs represents a desirable means of achieving this goal. The present vogue in hospital administration—the "open door" policy where patients may move about "freely" in the wards—means little if accomplished by means of wide utilization of a different form of restraint. The line between physical restraint by mechanical device and by drugs may be a very thin one in many cases. The latter method may be as open to abuse as the former.[43]

IV. MAJOR MEDICAL TREATMENT

A. PSYCHOSURGERY

Little or no legislative attention has been given to how far mental hospitals may go in administering treatments involving danger to the patient. The rules relating to such treatment in a nonmental hospital are quite clear.[44] Except in emergency cases, before a physician performs an operation he must obtain the consent of the patient or that of the parent or guardian if the patient is a minor. The hospital also has the legal duty to see that the operative permit is secured and made part of the record. Violation of this rule renders the physician liable for damages. Usually the patient or the guardian is willing to con-

sent, so the administration of the rule presents few difficulties.[45]

Mental hospitals, however, have special problems. Many mental patients are also incompetent, and their consent might therefore be considered ineffective by a court. Many patients do not have estates and consequently may not have guardians. Others may have become estranged from their families or may be hospitalized in places away from their own communities. Even if the patient is competent, there would be a question of whether he would feel really free to withhold his consent when his release from the hospital and his other personal rights are determined primarily by the hospital officials seeking his consent.

Only a small minority of the states have dealt with this problem by statute.[46] The general gist of these statutes is that the consent of the patient, or of a relative or guardian in case the patient is incompetent, shall be required before surgery may be performed. Most statutes also provide that in case of a serious emergency consent shall not be necessary and/or may be given by the superintendent of the hospital.[47] The existence of an emergency must generally be substantiated and documented.[48] California simply provides that patients have the right to refuse shock treatment or lobotomy.[49] Ohio and Oklahoma require only notice to the patient or guardian, as opposed to consent, in the case of a major operation.[50] Illinois at one time was the only state to provide that neither notice nor consent was required for major surgery since the fact of involuntary commitment vested the superintendent with authority to utilize standard methods of treatment including surgery.[51] This provision has been repealed.

Some states have administrative regulations which require consent for brain surgery or lobotomy.[52]

42. See Brakel & South, "Diversion from the Criminal Process in the Rural Community," 7 *Am. Crim. L.Q.* 122, 145 (1969). Field reports for this study include this typical response from a hospital official: "Most of the patients are on tranquilizing drugs, to reduce the level of their anxiety."

43. This recognition should serve to offset somewhat the optimism implied in findings such as provided by the Wisconsin Department of Public Welfare, 1957 *Report*, at 6: "[T]he use of these drugs had reduced the use of the shock therapies. Between 1955 and 1956 the number of patients started in insulin treatment dropped from 244 to 179. During the same period the number of patients on electro-convulsive treatment declined from 412 to 293. Lobotomy operations were entirely eliminated. The average number of disturbed patients who had to be restrained dropped from 73 per month in 1954 to 65 per month in 1955, to 33 per month in 1956." Furthermore, it should be pointed out that in addition to doubts regarding the primary effects of drug utilization, there may be undesirable side effects which are not yet known because the use of various drugs is still in the experimental stage.

44. See Hayt & Hayt, *Law of Hospital, Physician and Patient* 168 (1947).

45. Ross, *supra* note 3, at 533. See also Waltz & Scheuneman, "Informed Consent to Therapy," 64 *Nw. U.L. Rev.* 628 (1969).

46. See Table 5.3, Provisions Relating to Major Medical Treatment.

47. E.g., *Ariz. Rev. Stat. Ann.* § 36-528 (Supp. 1969); *Ill. Ann. Stat.* ch. 91-1/2, § 1-8 (Smith-Hurd Supp. 1969).

48. Ibid.

49. *Cal. Welf. & Inst'ns Code* § 5325 (West Supp. 1968).

50. *Ohio Rev. Code Ann.* § 5123.03 (Baldwin 1964); *Okla. Stat. Ann.,* tit. 43A, § 96 (1951).

51. *Ill. Ann. Stat.* ch. 91-1/2, § 5-18 (Smith-Hurd 1956), For the present Illinois law regarding surgery, see ch. 91-1/2, § 1-8 (Supp. 1969).

52. See, for example, Kentucky Department of Mental Health, Policies and Procedures, Reg. 2-2 (1958).

Furthermore, almost every state has some general statutory provision allowing the hospital to treat the patient; but it is difficult to determine whether these statutes cover surgery, and there are no cases on this point. One school of thought maintains that public mental hospitals need not obtain consent for surgery on the grounds that the rights of patients hospitalized for mental disabilities should be distinguished from the rights of patients in a general hospital:

> The argument is that mentally ill persons are considered wards of the state. The state as *parens patriae* must provide necessary care and treatment. The care and treatment of mental patients is a governmental function, and the basic consideration in the exercise of this function is the patient's welfare, not what the patient or his relatives believe to be in his interests.[53]

Yet in contemplation of such major treatment as psychosurgery,[54] the above argument raises serious doubts. Although considered a magic remedy at one time, psychosurgery is now being used less and less —partly because many doctors question the wisdom and even the morality of psychosurgery. One form of the operation, prefrontal lobotomy, has caused some patients to become apathetic and unconcerned with life and activity. Observers have described them as "vegetables"[55] or as having "lost [their] soul[s]."[56] The technical characterization of the state as *parens patriae* of the mentally disabled is a poor justification for dispensing with the minimal protections of notice, consent, and documentation of the need for surgery.

B. ELECTROSHOCK TREATMENT

A discussion of the rights of mental patients relating to the use of electroshock treatment may be classified under the following main topics: (1) consent to treatment, (2) the use of treatment for its tran-

quilizing or restrictive effects, and (3) the recovery of damages resulting from such treatment.

There is almost no law on the subject of electroshock treatment. Of the few states which have provisions concerning major medical treatment only California specifically refers to shock treatment, giving the patient an unqualified right to refuse it.[57] Alaska requires consent under ordinary circumstances to the "psychiatric therapies which the department determines,"[58] which conceivably include electroshock treatment. The remaining statutes are concerned only with surgery.

One of the few detailed discussions of the legal and medical problems involved in shock treatment is an advisory opinion of the Pennsylvania Department of Justice, which states that

> The superintendents of State mental hospitals, in their sound discretion may administer to patients of State mental hospitals, electric shock and such other treatments, which in the exercise of reasonable skill and judgment, are indicated, after observation and diagnosis, as being necessary and proper for the patients' best welfare, without first obtaining written permission for such treatments from such patients, their friends, relatives, guardians or other persons who may be legally entitled to give such consent on behalf of such patients; while such consent may be desirable in some cases, it is not essential under the laws of this Commonwealth.[59]

This viewpoint is as open to criticism with regard to electroshock treatment as it is with reference to psychosurgery. Consent to shock treatment is of great importance because electroshock is an extensively used therapy, the merits of which have provoked, and still provoke, a great deal of controversy. A study undertaken by the Council of State Governments in 1950 reported that of 190 hospitals concerned, only 10 indicated they did not use electroshock treatment, and 6 of those 10 stated that they would do so if the requisite facilities and staff were available.[60] Recent developments in the use of psychotropic drugs have led to a reduction in the need for and use of shock treatment,[61] but the issue is as yet far from resolved.

---

53. Ross, *supra* note 3, at 534.

54. Psychosurgery is the treatment of serious psychiatric disorders by brain surgery. Certain brain nerve fibers are cut to reduce the tension and distress associated with chronic emotional suffering. American Psychiatric Association, *Psychiatric Glossary* 39 (1957). Among the forms of psychosurgery are lobotomy (amputation of the prefrontal areas of the brain) and thalamectomy (destroying the lower brain stem nuclei that are connected to the cortical areas). Group for the Advancement of Psychiatry, "Research on Prefrontal Lobotomy" 2 (Rep. No. 6, June 1948).

55. Martin, *supra* note 30, at 144.

56. Group for the Advancement of Psychiatry, *supra* note 54, at 1.

57. *Cal. Welf. & Inst'ns Code* § 5325 (West Supp. 1968). See generally Table 5.3.

58. *Alaska Stat.* § 47.30.130 (Supp. 1969).

59. 64 Pa. D. & C. 35 (1948), as quoted in Ross, *supra* note 3, at 526.

60. Council of State Governments, *supra* note 1, at 184.

61. See Wisconsin, Department of Public Welfare, *supra* note 43, at 6, regarding the impact of drug utilization on the number of shock therapies and lobotomy operations.

Opponents of shock therapy contend that despite its widespread use it has no beneficial results. One journalist has written:

Patients at Columbus State get EST once, twice, or three times a week, and in a few cases oftener. . . . Some patients break bones during EST convulsions. About once in every 2,000 treatments, one dies. . . . Nobody knows why EST works. Some doctors deny that it does work, and some regard it as torture.[62]

The Council of State Governments reported that "although its mode of action is unknown there is much evidence to suggest its usefulness in a great number of the present mental illnesses."[63] However, the study also emphasized that no reputable psychiatrist would recommend its use without careful preparation and follow-up.[64] It is questionable whether understaffed state hospitals could carry out such preparation and follow-up.[65]

The controversy regarding electroshock treatment is reflected also in administrative regulations. For example, Kentucky's regulations state that obtaining consent is not necessary because the treatment is an accepted therapy beyond the stage of experimentation.[66] Michigan[67] and New York,[68] on the other hand, require permission from a legally responsible person before administering such treatment, and New York emphasizes that shock treatment entails risk of serious injury or death.[69]

The question of restricting the use of shock treatment is raised, too, by those who charge that the treatments are used as a disciplinary measure.[70] Some attendants reportedly make threats of electro-shock treatment in order to keep peace and quiet in the ward or to control those patients who do not satisfy the attendant's standards of behavior. One attendant, for example, admitted having put a patient on the "shock list" in order to give himself and the ward some rest from a particularly boring story.[71]

The administration of shock treatment is sometimes carried out within the view of patients. Since the "convulsions often resemble those of an accident victim in death agony and are accompanied by choking gasps and at times by a foaming overflow of saliva from the mouth,"[72] the patient may serve as a frightful spectacle to the onlookers. The patient himself usually does not remember the treatment. Regardless of any benefits which may result from the use of electroshock as a treatment, it can hardly be justified in these surroundings.

Electroshock administered for punitive or disciplinary reasons is particularly offensive because of the serious dangers involved. The legal task of preventing this type of abuse is complicated, however, by a larger, more subtle problem which is prevalent in some of our hospitals. The apparent notion that the mentally disabled are entitled to something less than full human and civil rights in many instances results in the too-ready application of experimental treatment methods to institutionalized patients without regard to their rights, desires, or individuality and the potential psychic or bodily harm which may result. The equation made in some psychotherapeutic circles between treatment and punishment (aversive conditioning) is another dimension which adds to the intricate task of protecting patients from abuse. Two recent articles[73] describing punitive

62. Martin, *supra* note 30, at 81.

63. Council of State Governments, *supra* note 1, at 184.

64. Ibid.

65. See also Group for the Advancement of Psychiatry, "Shock Therapy" (Rep. No. 1, Sept. 15, 1947), warning against such abuses of electroshock therapy as (a) its use in office practice; (b) its indiscriminate administration to patients in any and all diagnostic categories; (c) its immediate use to the exclusion of adequate psychotherapeutic attempts; (d) its use as the sole therapeutic agent, to the neglect of a complete psychiatric program.

66. Kentucky, Department of Mental Health, *supra* note 52.

67. Michigan, Department of Mental Health, Rules and Regulations, Reg. 4-4 at 13 (1954).

68. New York, Department of Mental Hygiene, Mental Hygiene Law and General Orders, Gen. Order No. 57, at 271 (Supp. I).

69. Ibid.

70. Martin, *supra* note 30, at 81; Belknap, *Human Problems of a State Mental Hospital* 191–95 (1956).

71. Belknap, *supra* note 70, at 193.

72. Id. at 194.

73. Ludwig et al., *supra* note 36; Simmons & Lovaas, *supra* note 36. To the uninitiated these studies resemble parodies on the discipline, confirming many of the popular misgivings concerning certain aspects of psychotherapy. Reading them is recommended. The humor is on the grim side, however. At one point it is stated (Simmons & Lovaas at 30) that during the initial period of aversive conditioning by use of the "shock stick," the "result was a diminution in the index behaviors, but the child [4 years of age] showed marked aversion to the experimenter for several days." In Ludwig et al. (at 625) the point is made that faradic shock treatment is a very diverse remedy: "The conditions treated by this means include cases of compulsive gambling, homosexuality, compulsive eating, fetishism, transvestism, car stealing, obsessional ruminations, smoking, writer's cramp, alcoholism, and even habitual blushing, compulsive copulation with sheep and marital infidelity." This is not to say that aversive therapy is per se repugnant to ordinary sensibilities: There may be instances or emergencies where its application is warranted. The objection to the studies in ques-

therapy experiments using electric floor grids and cattle prods on patients are illustrative. Unfortunately, these are not isolated occurrences, but widespread,[74] and in a sense symptomatic of a more general problem of attitude towards the mentally disabled.

The relevance of the above to the question of electroshock treatment lies in recognition that the electroshock for sound medical purposes and clearly abusive shock treatment are only extremes in a more continuous spectrum of therapeutic practices and theories. Electroshock, like drugs, faradic shock, or other new or little-known forms of treatment, can be used—sometimes interchangeably—[75] for a variety of reasons and purposes which are very difficult to circumscribe by law. Nevertheless, any legislation in the area should deal with all these various methods, and with great strictness. Protections should be provided similar to those which have been advocated for psychosurgery. Electroshock (electroconvulsive) treatment in particular should require the consent of the patient or his representative whenever possible. Unchecked discretion on the part of the hospital should be eliminated; documentation of medical need should be obtained; and the fact of treatment recorded.

Case law touching on shock treatment concerns compensation for injuries resulting from the treatment. Three reported cases have turned on negligence resulting in physical injury during shock treatment.[76] The plaintiff in each case suffered a severe fracture or fractures. In each instance the doctrine of *res ipsa loquitur* was invoked; the courts not only refused to apply the doctrine but also refused to submit the cases to the jury on the issue of negligence. However, in the California case there was a strong dissent, urging that the fact that a plaintiff who was to be treated for a mental condition had emerged with deformed hips and broken legs brought the case within the *res ipsa loquitur* doctrine.[77] This dissent pointed out that such a decision would not allow the plaintiff automatically to prevail but would merely require the defendant to rebut the presumption of negligence by furnishing a reasonable explanation for the cause of the injury.

These cases make it difficult for the patient either to protect himself from injury or to recover damages for negligence or gross negligence, inasmuch as he is often forced to submit to the treatment and is unable to testify about what happened to him while he was unconscious. In addition, the patient is not extended the privilege of selecting a physician or technician who he believes will observe the necessary precautions.

The law's predisposition to hold the attending physician exempt from liability for physical injuries due to electroshock treatment points up the drastic aspect of the therapy and underscores the desirability of a consensual relationship between the patient and the doctor.

In view of the present lack of statutory protections from the dangers of electroshock treatment, the judicial unwillingness to enforce some minimum standards of care in this area seems particularly unfortunate.

V. PERIODIC EXAMINATION, JUDICIAL REVIEW, AND THE RIGHT TO TREATMENT

The main reason for requiring periodic examinations is to guarantee that patients involuntarily hospitalized will not be forced to remain in the hospital after the medical and statutory conditions justfying hospitalization no longer exist.[78] Examinations help to determine not only whether the patient should be discharged or conditionally released but also whether he should be transferred to another institution or ward or given new and different treatment. Recent developments in medical research and treatment of mental illness make it more likely that patients will recover and be able to resume a normal life in the community. This achievement gives added weight to the importance of the right to periodic examinations.

An ideal system of examinations would require careful initial diagnosis of all patients at the time of

---

tion centers on the inordinate faith exhibited with regard to essentially experimental and potentially harmful therapy, its seemingly excessive application to the end of producing what the experimenters consider acceptable behavior, and its disregard of the question of the patient's consent (in the Simmons & Lovaas study the shock therapy was given "against the expressed will of the patient").

74. See citations and references in Ludwig et al. and Simmons & Lovaas, *supra* note 36.

75. See Wisconsin, Department of Public Welfare, *supra* note 43, at 6, concerning the impact of drug utilization on the use of shock therapy.

76. Quinley v. Cocke, 183 Tenn. 428, 192 S.W.2d 992 (1946); Farber v. Olkon, 246 P.2d 710 (Cal. Ct. App. 1952), *aff'd*, 40 Cal. 2d 503, 254 P.2d 520 (1953); Johnston v. Rodis, 151 F. Supp. 345 (D.D.C. 1957).

77. Farber v. Olkon, 40 Cal. 2d 503, 510, 511, 254 P.2d 520, 527, 528 (1953).

78. *Draft Act* § 15, at 13, Commentary, at 32.

their admission. If there were no other reason, such an examination would add one more safeguard against the possibility of a wrongful hospitalization. In addition, the diagnosis would provide the hospital with sufficient basic data about the condition of the patient; often the hospitalization order and accompanying documents do not contain adequate information.

Twenty states provide by statute for such post-admission examinations.[79] The Draft Act requires that an examination be held "as soon as practicable" after admission of every involuntary patient[80] and comments that for a large proportion of hospitalized patients this "examination would be the first by physicians specially trained in psychiatry."[81]

Periodic reviews are intended to provide an opportunity for discovering changes in the patient's condition. Many patients improve rapidly enough to warrant their release in a relatively short time. Although in some cases the family or the patient himself may be aware of the improvement and may attempt to change his status, the major responsibility for recognizing a change in the patient's mental health should rest with the hospital. The hospital staff has easy access to the medical facts and should take the initiative in this matter.

The Draft Act requires the head of the hospital either to examine each patient or to have him examined as frequently as practicable but at least once every six months.[82] Twenty-two states require periodic examinations. Eight of these do not specify the frequency, eleven follow the Draft Act, and three require examinations once a year.[83]

Although some statutes specify the frequency of the examinations, they do not prescribe their scope. It is impossible to tell from these statutes whether the patient is to be examined in person or whether only his written record is to be reviewed. Nor is it clear whether the patient should be examined by the whole hospital staff or one doctor. Where the statutory requirement does not specify the frequency of the examination, there is no way of determining if any systematic examination practice exists; needless to say, even less protection is afforded by states that are totally lacking in examination provisions.

To assure full protection for hospitalized patients, periodic medical examinations must be complemented by periodic judicial review. Significant strides in this direction have been made in recent years; the statutory trend, observable in many jurisdictions, toward observational and determinate commitments—as opposed to indeterminate commitments—represents an important implementation of the concept of periodic judicial review. Initial hospitalization orders are limited to observational or otherwise-labeled short-term periods, after which the hospital must obtain renewed authorization by way of a full court hearing if continued hospitalization of the patient appears necessary. Specifically,[84] some nine states presently call for mandatory observational hospitalization prior to long-term indeterminate hospitalization. More than half the states provide for observational commitment which may be utilized at the option of the court. And in several jurisdictions, notably California and New York,[85] the notion of indeterminate hospitalization is statutorily defunct: commitment can be only for relatively short-term periods. Periodic court review is thus assured.

A novel and potentially significant development in the law relating to hospitalization is the emergence of the "right to treatment." This new right assumes much of its importance against the background of required periodic medical examination and judicial review. A showing that hospital officials failed to conduct periodic examinations of the patient may constitute a denial of the right to treatment[86] and entitle the patient to release. At the same time, the right to judicial review permits litigation of the issue of the right to treatment.[87]

The concept of the patient's right to treatment while he is hospitalized received its major judicial impetus in the case of *Rouse v. Cameron*,[88] decided

79. See Table 5.4, Examinations after Hospitalization, Post-admission column.

80. *Draft Act* § 13(a), (b), at 12, Commentary, at 31.

81. Id. at 31.

82. Id. § 15, at 13.

83. See Table 5.4 for the states requiring examinations and for provisions on frequency.

84. For an enumeration of the states and statutes to which these specific provisions pertain, see chap. 3, "Involuntary Hospitalization," and the tables thereto, especially Table 3.10.

85. *Cal. Welf. & Inst'ns Code* § 5304 (West Supp. 1968); *N.Y. Mental Hygiene Law* § 73 (McKinney Supp. 1969). In New York the initial hospitalization is for six months; continued hospitalization must be authorized by court order which in turn must be judicially reviewed within one year and thereafter every two years.

86. E.g., Whitree v. State, 56 Misc. 2d 693, 290 N.Y.S.2d 486 (Ct. Cl. 1968).

87. The issue may also be raised by habeas corpus petition as indicated by the landmark case on right to treatment, Rouse v. Cameron, 373 F.2d 451 (D.C. Cir. 1966).

88. Ibid.

by the United States Court of Appeals for the District of Columbia Circuit. Judge Bazelon's opinion placed considerable emphasis on the existence of a provision in the District of Columbia Code granting in effect a "*statutory* right to treatment."[89] However, court decisions and literature prior and subsequent to the *Rouse* case indicate that there is a more general premise for the patient's right to treatment, not necessarily based on the interpretation of a specific statutory provision: the principle, simply stated, is that the involuntary hospitalization of a person carries with it the obligation to provide the treatment which is its justification and that if such treatment is not forthcoming the patient shall be entitled to an improvement in his situation, including transfer, release, or even damages.[90]

Opposition to an enforceable right to treatment has focused mainly on the difficulty of setting intelligible standards of treatment. The argument goes that treatment methods do and must vary from institution to institution and from patient to patient (some patients may not be treatable at all) and that furthermore the courts are not designed or equipped to inquire into and fix standards of treatment and are ill advised to do so.[91] On the whole, the courts themselves have not disputed this argument: judicial inquiries into treatment methods have been quite limited in most cases.[92] But as Judge Bazelon has stated, this does not mean that the right to treatment should be abolished or that the courts should relinquish the function of enforcing it. It does mean that the courts should be aided in their inquiry by the enactment of legislative and administrative standards of treatment as implemented by internal hospital review.[93]

89. Id. at 453. The reference is to *D.C. Code Ann.* § 21-526 (1967), which states that a patient shall "be entitled to medical and psychiatric care and treatment."

90. See chaps. 10, "The Sexual Psychopath and the Law," and 11, "Mental Disability and the Criminal Law," for discussions of cases and articles on the right to treatment as applied to sexual psychopaths, persons acquitted by reason of insanity, and those incompetent to stand trial.

91. E.g., Council of the American Psychiatric Association, "Position Statement on the Question of Adequacy of Treatment," 123 *Am. J. Psychiat.* 1458 (1967).

92. E.g., Tribby v. Cameron, 379 F.2d 104 (D.C. Cir. 1967); Commonwealth v. Hogan, 341 Mass. 372, 170 N.E.2d 327 (Mass. 1960). Often the appeals court decisions merely remand for further inquiry into the adequacy of treatment: Rouse v. Cameron, 373 F.2d 451 (D.C. Cir. 1966).

93. Bazelon, "Implementing the Right to Treatment," 36 *U. Chi. L. Rev.* 742 (1969); to be effective, hospital review must of course include a separation of functions. See also the detailed

In the context of this particular chapter, a very interesting possibility concerning right to treatment is suggested in the recent case of *Dobson v. Cameron.*[94] In *Dobson,* though the court did not reach the issue, there was a hint that the denial of rights and privileges of visitation and communication with the outside world, as well as other arbitrary restrictions on the patient's liberty, if not dispositive of the right-to-treatment issue may at the least constitute persuasive evidence of the denial of this right.[95]

VI. EMPLOYMENT OF PATIENTS

Most states do not have statutory provisions governing the employment and compensation of patients. Even where the subject is covered by statute, it is not always clear what the purpose of the law is and under what circumstances the work may be performed. Pennsylvania, for example, provides that every patient shall have the right

> [t]o be employed at a useful occupation in so far as the condition of the patient may benefit therefrom and the facility is able to furnish useful employment to such person.[96]

In Iowa, patients may be "required to render" services and the board of control may pay the "inmates" wages if it deems it practicable to do so.[97]

In general it is unclear whether the purpose of statutes authorizing patient labor is to provide occupational and vocational therapy for the patients, as appears to be the case in Pennsylvania, or to provide free labor for the institution, which might be the case in Iowa. In addition, most statutes fail to provide a clear answer to the question of payment for the patient's work.

Therapeutically, no doubt many benefits are derived from occupational activities in the hospital community. These activities, if properly selected and supervised, can become an integral part of the therapy program and an aid in training the patient for his postrelease vocation. Patient services also go a long way in helping the hospital to maintain the buildings and grounds.

Yet patient labor can be easily abused. This danger was recognized by the Council of State Gov-

and comprehensive Pennsylvania H.B. No. 1142 (Session of 1969) on the right to treatment of patients in state institutions.

94. 383 F.2d 519 (D.C. Cir. 1967).

95. Id. at 520 n.1.

96. *Pa. Stat. Ann.* tit. 50, § 4423 (1969).

97. *Iowa Code Ann.* §§ 218.40, 218.42 (1969).

ernments in its survey of mental health programs:

> Obviously, no hospital worthy of the name would use this situation exploitatively in relation to the patient. No hospital worthy of the name would regard a patient as a source of cheap or free labor, nor would it assign a patient to work except in his interest and in an occupation that was suitable for him in view of his condition and his requirements.[98]

Whether this admonition is generally observed by mental hospitals is difficult to determine. It is sometimes said that so long as compulsory, nontherapeutic work is not injurious to the patient's medical interests, the state supporting him should be able to require the work. One-third of the hospitals surveyed in the Council's study paid the patients for their labor; but no information was available on the rate of pay, work hours, and variations in practices from state to state.[99] By contrast, a magazine article charged that it found patients working from ten to fourteen hours a day for little or no pay.[100]

It has been contended that some hospitals are negligent in that they do not discharge recovered patients who are performing tasks for the hospital.[101] A magazine article on patients who do not belong in mental hospitals gave the following as one of the reasons for delays in discharge:

> Money-desperate hospitals use unpaid patient labor to man farms, kitchens, laundries. Experts *Parade* talked to characterized this bluntly as "slave labor which prolongs hospital stays."[102]

The article further quoted hospital personnel who admitted that "we try to keep a good patient worker because there aren't very many."[103]

VII. PROPERTY CONTROL WITHOUT GUARDIANSHIP

Although hospitalization is not intended to deal with the property of mentally ill persons and the hospital is not designated as the patient's guardian or conservator, many states grant the institutions varying degrees of authority over his property.[104]

This authority, which is usually limited to the control of money or property not to exceed a specified amount or value, may be exercised by the mental institution whether the patient has a guardian or not. For patients without guardians these provisions may provide considerable safeguards against the dissipation of property, though the hospitals are not always subject to the same accounting requirements applicable to guardians generally. Management and control of the patient's property often provides an extra guarantee of the hospital's recovery of the payments due for the patient's hospitalization.

Well over half the states have no statutory provision covering property control in the absence of an adjudication of incompetency and the appointment of a guardian.[105] The Draft Act fails to deal with the subject, on the assumption that hospitalization and guardianship (which would include property control) should be dealt with separately. As a matter of practice, however, it turns out that many hospitals exercise some degree of control over the patient's property regardless of whether the patient's legal status is one of formal incompetence or not.[106] The relevant question to be considered is therefore whether the patient's property is adequately protected by the hospital which is not obligated to observe the procedures followed by regularly appointed guardians.

The provisions which exist on this subject are of great variety.[107] The amounts over which institutions are able to exercise control vary from no specified minimum to a maximum of $1,000. The authority may be limited to property found on the person of the patient or may extend to any of his property. The custody of the property may be granted to the hospital, the superintendent, the central agency responsible for institutions, or an appointed hospital representative. In some cases the money is to be held in trust for the patient; in others it is to be applied to costs of hospitalization; and in still others the money is to be used for the "benefit" of the patient. The last situation is interpreted differently in the various states. Some provide that the patient may handle small sums of money; some require that

---

98. Council of State Governments, *supra* note 1, at 187.

99. Ibid.

100. Goldman & Ross, "The Patients Who Shouldn't Be In," *Parade,* Part I, Nov. 11, 1956, at 17.

101. See, e.g., Grimes, *supra* note 39, at 80–83.

102. Goldman & Ross, *supra* note 100, at 11.

103. Id. at 17.

104. See Table 5.5, Property Control without Guardianship,

Control of Property by Institution column. See also Allen, Ferster, & Weihofen, *Mental Impairment and Legal Incompetency* (1968), especially chap. 4, "Guardianship and Incompetency."

105. See Table 5.5 for the thirty-two states lacking provisions on this subject.

106. See chap. 8, "Incompetency, Guardianship, and Restoration," for greater detail.

107. See Table 5.5 and footnotes thereto.

money be put in the hospital's canteen to be used for the patient's tobacco and personal items; and others demand that any money belonging to the patient be put in a trust fund.

It is not clear from the statutes of most states whether personal property found on the patient is to be inventoried by the hospital and a receipt given. Many states do not specify who is to have custody of the personal property and how it is to be disposed. Without close supervision it is possible that some personal effects might be misappropriated.

VIII. UNWARRANTED HOSPITALIZATION

The most effective safeguard against unwarranted hospitalization is a judicious application of adequate hospitalization procedures, covered in chapter 3, and periodic reviews by responsible authorities of the hospitalized person's progress toward recovery. Nevertheless penalties for unwarranted hospitalization exist as an additional protection for the patient.

The statutes in thirty-four jurisdictions[108] and the Draft Act[109] designate that willful or unlawful conduct which causes unwarranted hospitalization is a criminal offense. Typical of these statutes is the Draft Act, which provides:

> Any person who willfully causes, or conspires with or assists another to cause (1) the unwarranted hospitalization of any individual under the provisions of this Act, or (2) the denial to any individual of any of the rights accorded to him under the provisions of this Act, shall be punished by a fine not exceeding $_____ or imprisonment not exceeding _____, or both.

Twenty-four states classify the offense as a misdemeanor and ten as a felony. New York provides a civil remedy in a statute which in terms of emphasis gives considerable protection to the prospective defendant.[110] The provision begins by stating that "[n]o civil action shall be brought against a state official in his personal capacity . . . without leave of a judge of the Supreme Court, first had and obtained." Furthermore, no liability shall attach if the defendant "acted in good faith, with reasonable care upon probable cause." The statute goes on to imply that a claim for damages against the

state—as opposed to an official in his personal capacity—may be a more promising route.

A common-law action for the recovery of damages resulting from false imprisonment or confinement effected through judicial or quasi-judicial hospitalization proceedings is another remedy available to any person so abused.[111] The essential element of such an action is that the defendant must be shown in some way to be responsible for the unlawful confinement of the plaintiff; however, confinement authorized by process regular on its face and issued by a court of competent jurisdiction is lawful and cannot result in an action for false imprisonment even though process was erroneously or improvidently issued. Such process protects those who participated in the proceedings, and also those acting under the order or warrant.[112] Nevertheless, in such instances, an action for malicious prosecution may lie.[113]

While protection of the patient should be a primary concern of the law, the existence of criminal and civil penalties for unwarranted hospitalization has been shown to have indirect adverse effects. It has been observed that in some areas the fear of liability has inhibited officials (notably the police) in the discharge of their responsibility: appropriate involvement has been avoided and proper procedures have been circumvented.[114] This is not to say that there should be no remedy for wrongful hospitalization. It does suggest, however, that a proper legal balance will be exceptionally difficult to attain since even the remotest prospect of liability may be inhibiting, especially for those professionals who may tend to view involvement in mental health problems as distasteful or not part of their function in the first place.

IX. TRANSFER OF PATIENTS

There are extensive statutory provisions and administrative regulations concerning the transfer of patients.[115] The Draft Act requires that a transfer be

---

108. See Table 5.6, Unwarranted Hospitalization, Penalties column, for the specific statutory provisions in the various states.

109. *Draft Act* § 26, at 17.

110. *N.Y. Mental Hygiene Law* § 44 (McKinney Supp. 1970).

111. See cases noted in 145 A.L.R. 728 (1943).

112. Id. at 729–30.

113. Fisher v. Payne, 93 Fla. 1085, 113 So. 378 (1927). See generally 145 A.L.R. 705 (1943).

114. From field work conducted by the American Bar Foundation in connection with studies done under the Foundation's general program on Mental Illness and the Law. See Rock, Jacobson, & Janopaul, *Hospitalization and Discharge of the Mentally Ill* 91 (1968).

115. See Table 5.8, Transfer of Patients within the State. See also chap. 4, § II, Transfers of Patients.

approved by the central hospital administration and that it be consistent with the medical needs of the patient.[116] It also requires that written notice be given the guardian or a friend of the patient and that transfers be arranged so that beneficial visits and relationships with the family may be encouraged. In contrast to the power of discharge, which is vested in the head of the hospital, the act grants the power of transfer to the central agency responsible for mental institutions, on the theory that the latter is more likely to assure the proper distribution of patients among the state's facilities.

Most of the state statutes are similar to the Draft Act. Typically, these statutes are concerned exclusively with transfers between state institutions and not with transfers between private hospitals. Some statutes fail to require notice to the guardian or relative before this kind of transfer.[117] Some, on the other hand, require a new hospitalization adjudication if the transfer is to an institution of a different type, e.g., a transfer from an institution for the mentally deficient to one for the mentally ill. The new adjudication is a necessary safeguard because this sort of transfer indicates a change in the original diagnosis of the patient.

The Draft Act provides for transfers to a facility run by the United States.[118] This provision is based on the Uniform Veterans' Guardianship Act,[119] which has been adopted verbatim or in essence in twenty-three states. According to the Guardianship Act, a patient eligible for treatment by the Veterans Administration or other agency of the United States may be transferred to a facility of the United States either inside or outside the patient's state provided that notice be given to the court issuing the original hospitalization order.[120] Both the Draft Act and the Uniform Veterans' Guardianship Act seek to

> facilitate the placing of patients in appropriate Federal institutions especially equipped to treat a particular type of mental trouble and save the patient distress and sometimes definite harm incident to a second adjudication experience in the State to which transferred.[121]

116. *Draft Act* § 14(a), at 12.

117. See Table 5.8, Notice of Any Transfer columns.

118. *Draft Act* § 14(b), at 12.

119. Reference is here made to both the original and the revised Uniform Veterans' Guardianship Act. For the revised act see 9C *Uniform Laws Annotated* 196 (Supp. 1968).

120. 9C *U.L.A.* at § 18(1), (3) (1957).

121. *Draft Act* 30.

A possible defect in this procedure is that although the patient is spared the traumatic effects of a second adjudication, he may be deprived summarily of visits from his friends and relatives, who now find it inconvenient to make such visits.

X. RESIDENCE CONSIDERATIONS IN HOSPITALIZATION AND DEPORTATION

Residency requirements for hospitalization are imposed primarily because the states resist expending public funds for the hospitalization and treatment of nonresidents. Moreover, since state mental institutions are already crowded, the possibility exists that nonresident mental patients may crowd out resident patients. Considerations of public safety, as well as the difficulties in ascertaining residence prior to hospitalization proceedings, have resulted in the avoidance by most states of the issue of residency until after hospitalization. The requisites for establishing residence, domicile, or settlement are usually recited in local statutes. Many of these requisites have developed from the common law or by court decision or from practices of administrative agencies responsible for determining the residence status of hospitalized patients. Whatever their source, these requirements vary, and they illustrate problems common to the field of conflict of laws.[122] For example, the requirements for establishing residency range from a determination of "intention" to the more precise requirements of one year of continuous "physical presence" or two years of "actual residence."[123] The problems raised by these local variations[124] hinder admissions,[125] as a hypothetical case might serve to demonstrate: a person may lose his residence in State A before acquiring a new residence in State B; if he becomes mentally ill, he is not legally entitled to treatment in either State A or State B.[126]

State statutes and administrative rulings also at-

122. See Table 5.7, Special Residence Provisions Applicable to Hospitalization and Deportation of Mental Patients, for specific provisions relating to the establishment of residence.

123. For a historical discussion of the relation between the indigent mentally disabled and settlement laws, see Deutsch, *supra* note 27, at 44–46.

124. See Table 5.7, Loss of Residence column.

125. Council of State Governments, *supra* note 1, Summary and Recommendations No. 16.

126. The harsh solution to the problem reached in colonial America was to spirit the mentally ill person away to another jurisdiction in the hope of thus ridding the community of the burden of supporting him. Deutsch, *supra* note 27, at 45.

tempt to cover the questions of derivative residency. One interesting and frequent provision specifies that the residence of the wife and minor child follows that of the husband and father. Acute transfer problems arise under such a provision when parents are divorced or separated, when minor children reach majority, and when children are illegitimate. For example, if a wife or minor child is hospitalized in one state and the husband or father acquires residency in another, there is a question whether the residency of the hospitalized person has changed and whether the change necessitates transfer. Statutes and administrative rulings resolve this question in a number of different ways.[127] Some states provide that the residency of a wife or minor child remains fixed from the time of hospitalization. Others direct that a man may not acquire residency when he has a wife or dependent child hospitalized in a public or private institution in another state whose support is not providing for. Furthermore, some states deny residency to a person who is himself a public charge or who has dependents who are likely to become public charges.

The inconsistent treatment of the same special situation by the transferring state and the receiving state may create difficult legal problems. When the hospitalizing state has determined that the patient is not a resident, it will notify the state of which he is a resident of its intention to transfer him. The receiving state, like the sending state or hospitalizing state, will resist spending public funds for care and treatment of a patient unless he meets the local qualifications for establishing resident status. Further, since the patient normally has been hospitalized already, the receiving state is not faced with the immediate problems of public safety which may have caused the state that hospitalized the patient to relax its residency requirement at the time of the hospitalization. The result is that the receiving state may tend to apply its residency laws rigidly in order to avoid the expense which would result from a transfer.

To effect a smoother functioning of interstate transfers of mental patients, compacts or reciprocal agreements have been adopted by many of the states.[128] Such arrangements are most often made between states having the same or similar laws on residency. Those states having a requirement of one year's continuous presence have been most successful in entering into interstate compacts with one another. A few states are prohibited by their constitutions from entering into reciprocal agreements.

In 1955, at the request of the Council of State Governments, representatives of the states of Connecticut, New Jersey, New York, and Pennsylvania met in New York to discuss the possibility of entering into reciprocal agreements under which they would accept transferees. At this meeting the following points were noted:

1. By and large the experience of the states has been that the number of persons repatriated to other states equalled the number received from other states within a given period of time.
2. In the field of public assistance the goal has been to provide aid for the needy wherever and whenever they are found.
3. The decision as to where a person should be hospitalized requires a judgment based on the medical welfare of a patient and is not primarily related to a determination of his residence.
4. Simple reciprocal arrangements among individual states could not accomplish the objectives.[129]

As a result of that meeting an Interstate Compact on Mental Health was drafted:

(1) To assure that any party state will give care and treatment to any person found in that state who is in need of institutionalization by reason of mental illness or mental deficiency;
(2) To permit the transfer of such a patient to an institution in another state when clinical determinations indicate that such a transfer would be in the best interests of the patient;
(3) To provide interstate cooperative machinery for after care or supervision of patients on convalescent status or conditional release;
(4) To authorize additional supplementary agreements between party states "for the provision of any service or facility or for the maintenance of any institution on a joint or cooperative basis" when any two or more states wish to do so.[130]

Since the compact was established, thirty-four states have adopted it.[131] If this trend continues,

127. See Table 5.7, Special Provisions column.

128. Council of State Governments, *supra* note 1, at 66, 221, 224.

129. State of New York, Joint Legislative Committee on Interstate Cooperation 1956, at 304–22 (Legislative Document No. 66, 1956).

130. Council of State Governments, *Suggested State Legislation,* Program for 1958, at 72 (October 1957).

131. See Table 5.7. Also, Council of State Governments, *The Interstate Compact on Mental Health: What It Is and Does* (rev. ed. Dec. 1968).

most of the residency problems of mental patients will be solved.

As a footnote to the question of residence requirements for hospitalization, consideration might be given to the recent case of *Shapiro v. Thompson*[132] in which the United States Supreme Court struck down the residency requirements affecting eligibility to receive welfare. Since the majority opinion in *Shapiro* explicitly limited the scope of its decision, stating that residence requirements in other areas were not affected,[133] the relevance of *Shapiro* to hospitalization may be limited to the proposition that its holding represents further evidence of the general erosion of residency requirements which are not justified by an obvious or compelling state interest. As stated in *Shapiro,* the invalidity of a residence requirement depends first of all on its interference with the fundamental right to travel. To interfere with the right to travel the requirement must cause the denial of another fundamental right or need—such as, by implication in *Shapiro,* the right to welfare. Finally, no compelling state interest exists to justify the infringements. That the residency requirements pertaining to hospitalization conform to the negative conditions which prompted their invalidation in the welfare area is decidely not an inevitable conclusion.[134] Speculation about the proper perspective and reach of *Shapiro* should include, however, consideration of the impact of current developments in the laws of hospitalization such as the increased acceptance of the Interstate Compact on Mental Health. That is, the Compact may come to demonstrate that the individual state purposes served by residence requirements can be overcome and that the "compelling" state interest in maintaining these requirements is not so compelling. Furthermore, spreading use of the Compact may be illustrative of the fact that many of the states do in fact regard hospitalization as a fundamental right, restrictions on which do inhibit the right to travel. The Compact could thus be instrumental in stretching the applicability of *Shapiro* to hospitalization.[135]

132. 394 U.S. 618 (1969).

133. Id. at 638.

134. See Note, "*Shapiro v. Thompson:* Travel, Welfare and the Constitution," 44 *N.Y.U.L. Rev.* 989 (1969), analyzing the *Shapiro* decision and its implications for other residency requirements.

135. As this volume goes to print, the decision of a district court in Arizona confirms the prediction regarding the applicability of *Shapiro* to the mental health field: in Vaughan, et al. v. Bower (Civ. No. 70–10, [May 15, 1970, Dist. Ct. Ariz.]), a three-judge court invalidated an Arizona provision which sub-

XI. CONCLUSIONS AND RECOMMENDATIONS

1. *Statutes by and large do not adequately protect the rights of patients who have been hospitalized.*

Though it is true that hospital doctors and administrators are often in the best position to determine which freedoms or restrictions are most likely to benefit the patient's medical needs, it remains the function of the law to circumscribe the decision-making powers of hospital officials. In many states, owing to the absence of legal guidelines and reviewing machinery, hospital officials in effect have unlimited discretion in areas ranging from correspondence, visitation, and employment to mechanical restraints and major medical treatment. The fact that decisions in most or all of these areas involve considerations other than purely medical ones reinforces the point that patient rights are not sufficiently protected.

2. *Patients should have the right of unrestricted correspondence with attorneys, the court through which they were hospitalized, and the central hospital agency for the state. It should be the duty of the hospital to facilitate the exercise of this right by furnishing the necessary materials.*

There are no persuasive arguments for limiting the patient's right to communicate with legal and mental health officials or agencies. It is further arguable that there should be no restrictions on outgoing patient mail, regardless of destination. To protect the sensitivities of those outside the hospital or to save the patient from potential embarrassment, it appears more desirable to indicate on the outgoing mail that the sender is hospitalized than to give the hospital officials authority to check all correspondence. On the question of incoming mail from sources other than legal or mental health agencies, a different balance might be struck, and hospital officials should be allowed to withhold material which could aggravate the patient's condition. To make the right to correspondence a realistic one, the hospital should make the appropriate materials available to the patient.

3. *Provisions should be made for maximum visitation.*

Liberal visitation rights are an essential component of a therapeutic environment. While hospital officials must have adequate discretion to restrict vis-

jected state mental patients with less than a year's residence in the state to the discretionary removal power of the superintendent, who was allowed to return them to the proper authorities in the state of their residency. The decision was squarely based on the *Shapiro* case.

itation consistent with considerations of administrative capacity and the patient's welfare, the exercise of this discretion should be recorded and reviewable.

4. *The use of mechanical restraints and psychotropic drugs should be regulated by requiring the hospital to record their use. The record should include a substantiation and documentation of the need therefor and should be subject to review.*

Protective measures in this area must reach beyond obviously abusive practices such as the sadistically punitive imposition of mechanical restraints on a patient in full view of other patients. Other practices exist which pose a more subtle threat. The indiscriminate use of drugs on patients for the convenience of hospital officials should be guarded against. The utilization of drugs may in specific instances be as inappropriate and dehumanizing as any mechanical restraint. A convincing and reviewable showing of the need for the imposition of mechanical or nonmechanical restraints is therefore an essential requirement.

5. *The consent of the patient or his guardian should be required as a minimum protection before a hospital may use psychosurgery or any other major medical treatment.*

In view of the controversy surrounding the benefits of treatment methods such as electroshock or psychosurgery and the serious consequences which might result therefrom, these forms of therapy should be applied only as a last resort and only after maximum consideration has been given to the patient's wishes. The requirement of consent may be less meaningful in some instances than in others, however. The consent or refusal of the patient to undergo major medical treatment loses significance if he is so incapacitated or influenced as to be unable to assess the nature of the treatment. On the other hand, the validity of the guardian's consent—irrespective of the guardian's understanding—is always open to doubt because it is only substituted consent to a matter of ultimate personal concern. The competing considerations emphasize that the consent problem has no easy resolution. Serious consideration should be given to a rule granting the patient an absolute right to refuse major medical treatment. Another suggestion of merit is to provide for an independent reviewing agency which shall assess, in all but immediate emergencies, the need for major medical treatment *prior* to its performance.

6. *The circumstances and conditions surrounding services performed by patients need clarification.*

There are too few statutes dealing with the services of patients. Even in the states where statutes exist, it is difficult to determine the intent of the legislation as to the distinction or correlation between therapeutic and remunerative patient services. The statutes are silent about whether patients are to be paid, and if so, the rate of compensation. Whatever the state's policy on the subject of patient services, it should be clarified to prevent possible abuses.

BIBLIOGRAPHY

Allen, Richard C.; Ferster, Elyce Z.; and Weihofen, Henry. *Mental Impairment and Legal Incompetency.* Englewood Cliffs, N.J.: Prentice-Hall, Inc., 1968.

American Law Reports Annotated. San Francisco: Bancroft-Whitney Co.; Rochester, N.Y.: Lawyers Cooperative Publishing Co. "Action for False Imprisonment or Malicious Prosecution Predicated upon Imprisonment of, or Conduct in Connection with, Lunacy Proceedings." 145 (1943) 728.

American Psychiatric Association. *Hospital & Community Psychiatry.* A journal of the association. *See* current issues.

————. *Psychiatric Glossary.* Washington, D.C.: American Psychiatric Association, 1957.

Bazelon, David L. "Implementing the Right to Treatment." 36 *University of Chicago Law Review* 742 (1969).

Belknap, Ivan. *Human Problems of a State Mental Hospital.* New York: McGraw-Hill Book Co., Inc., 1956.

Brakel, Samuel J., and South, Galen R. "Diversion from the Criminal Process in the Rural Community. 7 *American Criminal Law Quarterly* 122 (Spring 1969). Reprinted as *Research Contribution No. 6.* Chicago: American Bar Foundation, 1969.

Council of the American Psychiatric Association. "Position Statement on the Question of Adequacy of Treatment." 123 *American Journal of Psychiatry* 1458 (1967).

Council of State Governments. *The Interstate Compact on Mental Health: What It Is and Does.* Rev. ed. Chicago: Council of State Governments, 1968.

————. *The Mental Health Program of the Forty-Eight States, A Report to the Governors' Conference.* Chicago: Council of State Governments, 1950.

————. *Suggested State Legislation, Program for 1958.* Chicago: Council of State Governments, October 1957.

Deutsch, Albert. *The Mentally Ill in America.* 2d ed. rev. New York: Columbia University Press, 1949.

Garber, Robert S. "Legal Implications of the Open Hospital." 9 *Mental Hospitals* 24 (1958).

Goldman, Robert, and Ross, Sid. "The Patients Who Shouldn't Be In." Part I, *Parade* (November 11, 1956).

Great Britain. Royal Commission on the Law Relating to Mental Illness and Mental Deficiency 1954–57. *Report.* Cmnd. No. 169. London: Her Majesty's Stationery Office, 1957.

Grimes, John Maurice. *When Minds Go Wrong.* New York: Devin-Adair Co., 1954.

Group for the Advancement of Psychiatry. *Commitment Procedures.* Report no. 4. New York: Group for the Advancement of Psychiatry, April 1948.

———. *Research on Prefrontal Lobotomy.* Report no. 6. New York: Group for the Advancement of Psychiatry, June 1948.

———. *Shock Therapy.* Report no. 1. New York: Group for the Advancement of Psychiatry, September 1947.

Hayt, Emanuel, and Hayt, Lillian R. *Law of Hospital, Physician and Patient.* New York: Hospital Textbook Co., 1947.

Keane, Keith M. "An Open Psychiatric Ward in a General Hospital." 8 *Mental Hospitals* 27 (1957).

Kentucky Department of Mental Health. *Policies and Procedures.* Louisville, January 1, 1958.

League for Emotionally Disturbed Children News. Official publication of the League for Emotionally Disturbed Children, Inc. (February 1957).

Lebensohn, Zigmond. "Impressions of Hospital Psychiatry in Holland." 7 *Mental Hospitals* 22 (October 1956).

Ludwig, A., Marx, A., Hill, P., and Browning, R. "The Control of Violent Behavior through Faradic Shock." 148 *Journal of Nervous and Mental Disease* 624 (1969).

Martin, John Bartlow. "Inside the Asylum." *Saturday Evening Post.* (November 10, 1956).

Meyer, E. "Lawyer in a Mental Hospital: The New York Experiment." 53 *Mental Hygiene* 14 (1969).

Michigan Department of Mental Health. *Rules and Regulations.* Lansing, October 1954.

Missouri. Department of Public Health and Welfare. Division of Mental Diseases. *Official Rules and Regulations Governing the Duties of State Hospitals.* Kansas City: Inter-City Press, Inc., 1954.

National Clearinghouse for Mental Health Information. "Summary of Medications." *Community Mental Health Center Data Systems* 37 (1969).

National Institute of Mental Health. Federal Security Agency. *A Draft Act Governing Hospitalization of the Mentally Ill.* Public Health Service Pub. no. 51. Washington, D.C.: Government Printing Office, 1952.

New York. Department of Mental Hygiene. *Mental Hygiene Law and General Orders.* Albany, 1955.

———. Joint Legislative Committee on Interstate Cooperation 1956. Legislative Document no. 66. Albany, 1956.

Note, "The New York Mental Health Information Service: A New Approach to Hospitalization of the Mentally Ill." 67 *Columbia Law Review* 672 (1967).

Ross, Hugh A. "Hospitalizing the Mentally Ill—Emergency and Temporary Commitments." *Current Trends in State Legislation 1955–56.* Ann Arbor: Legislative Research Center, University of Michigan (1957), 459.

Simmons, J., and Lovaas, O. "Use of Pain and Punishment as Treatment Techiques with Childhood Schizophrenics." 23 *American Journal of Psychotherapy* 23 (1969).

Stevenson, George S. *Mental Health Planning for Social Action.* New York: McGraw-Hill Book Co., Inc., 1956.

United Nations. World Health Organization. *Hospitalization of Mental Patients.* Geneva, 1955.

Waltz, Jan. R., and Scheuneman, Thomas W. "Informed Consent to Therapy." 64 *Northwestern University Law Review* 628 (1969).

Wisconsin. Department of Public Welfare. *Report for Quarter Year Ending March 31, 1957.* Madison, 1957.

———. Mendota State Hospital. *Administrative Regulations.* Madison, 1949.

———. "*Shapiro v. Thompson:* Travel, Welfare and the Constitution." 44 *New York University Law Review* 989 (1969).

CASES

Commonwealth v. Hogan, 341 Mass. 372, 170 N.E.2d 327 (Mass. 1960).

Dobson v. Cameron, 383 F.2d 519 (D.C. Cir. 1967).

Farber v. Olkon, 246 P.2d 710 (Cal. Ct. App. 1952), *aff'd,* 40 Cal. 2d 503, 254 P.2d 520 (1953).

Fisher v. Payne, 93 Fla. 1085, 113 So. 378 (1927).

Hoff v. State, 279 N.Y. 490, 18 N.E.2d 671 (1939).

Johnston v. Rodis, 151 F. Supp. 345 (D.D.C. 1957).

People *ex rel.* Jacobs v. Worthing, 167 Misc. 702, 4 N.Y.S.2d 630 (1938).

Quinley v. Cocke, 183 Tenn. 428, 192 S.W.2d 992 (1946).

Rouse v. Cameron, 373 F.2d 451 (D.C. Cir. 1966).

Shapiro v. Thompson, 394 U.S. 618 (1969).

Tribby v. Cameron, 379 F.2d 104 (D.C. Cir. 1967).

Whitree v. State, 56 Misc. 2d 693, 290 N.Y.S.2d 486 (Ct. Cl. 1968).

Table 5.1 CORRESPONDENCE AND VISITATION

STATE	CORRESPONDENCE — Special Provision as to: Central Agency	Specified Official	Counsel	Single Personal Correspondent	Restrictions	Restrictions Recorded	Censorship	Writing Material Furnished	General Freedom of Correspondence	VISITATION — Special Provision as to: Restrictions	Restrictions Recorded	Family & Friends	Counsel	Minister	Physician	Time — Specified	Time — Any Reasonable	General Freedom of Visitation
Draft Act	21(b)	committing court. 21(b)			fn.1 21(a)(1)	21(c)				fn.2 21(a)(2)	21(c)							
ALA. Code (1958)																		
ALAS. Stat. (1962)	47.30.150 (b)	governor, superior court. 47.30.150 (b)			fn.1 47.30.150 (a)(1)	47.30.150 (c)				fn.2 47.30.150 (a)(2)	47.30.150 (c)							
ARIZ. Rev. Stat. Ann. (1956)																		
ARK. Stat. Ann. (1947)																		
CAL. Welf. & Inst'ns Code (West 1966)(Supp. 1968) fn.3					for good cause. 5326	5326		5325		for good cause. 5326	5326							
COLO. Rev. Stat. Ann. (1964)(Supp. 1965)		judge. 71-1-23(2)	71-1-23(2)	fn.4 71-1-23(2)														
CONN. Gen. Stat. Ann. (1958)					fn.5 17-190 (Supp. 1969)			17-190 (Supp. 1969)		fn.6 17-189		fn.6 17-189	fn.6 17-189		fn.6 17-189		17-189	
DEL. Code Ann. (1953)																		
D.C. Code Ann. (1967)			fn.7 21-561(a)(2)				incoming. 21-561(b)		21-561(a)(1)								21-561(c)	
FLA. Stat. Ann. (1960)(Supp. 1969)				fn.8 394.13			394.13	394.14										
GA. Code Ann. (1963)(Supp. 1969)	88-502.5(e)	public officials. 88-502.5(e)			fn.1 88-502.5(a)	88-502.5(f)				88-502.5(g)								
HAWAII Rev. Stat. Ann. (1968)																		

Table 5.1 CORRESPONDENCE AND VISITATION *continued*

STATE	CORRESPONDENCE — Special Provision as to: Central Agency	Specified Official	Counsel	Single Personal Correspondent	Restrictions	Restrictions Recorded	Censorship	Writing Material Furnished	General Freedom of Correspondence	VISITATION — Restrictions	Restrictions Recorded	Special Provision as to: Family & Friends	Counsel	Minister	Physician	Time — Specified	Time — Any Reasonable	General Freedom of Visitation
IDAHO Code Ann. (1949) (Supp. 1969)		committing court. 66-346(b)			fn. 1 / 66-346(a) (1)	66-346(c)				fn. 2 / 66-346(a) (2)	66-346(c)							
ILL. Ann. Stat. (Smith-Hurd 1966) (Supp. 1969)	fn. 9 / 91½, §12-2	fn. 9 / 91½, §12-2	fn. 9 / 91½, §12-2		fn. 1 / 91½, §12-2	91½, §12-2				fn. 2 / 91½, §12-2	91½, §12-2							
IND. Ann. Stat. (1964)										fn. 10 / 22-1034						22-1034		
IOWA Code Ann. (1969)	226.13 226.15						fn. 11 / 226.13 226.15	226.14	fn. 11 / 226.13					fn. 12 / 218.26		fn. 12 / 218.26	218.26	
KAN. Stat. Ann. (1964) (Supp. 1968)	59-2929	fn. 13 / 59-2929	59-2929		fn. 14 / 59-2929								fn. 15 / 59-2929		fn. 15 / 59-2929		fn. 15 / 59-2929	
KY. Rev. Stat. Ann. (1969)	210.220		210.220											210.130				
LA. Rev. Stat. Ann. (1950)	28:171(1)		28:171(1)		fn. 16 / 28:171(5)		fn. 16 / 28:171(5)	fn. 16 / 28:171(5)		fn. 16 / 28:171(9)		28:171(9)	28:171(1)	28:171(2)	28:171(8)		28:171(9)	
ME. Rev. Stat. Ann. (1965)	34, §2254(1)	committing court. 34, §2254(1)	clergyman also included. 34, §2254(1)		34, §2254		fn. 17 / 34, §2254			34, §2254 (2)			34, §2254 (2)	34, §2254 (2)			34, §2254 (2)	
MD. Ann. Code (1968)	59, §35			59, §35				59, §35										
MASS. Ann. Laws (1965)	123, §98				fn. 18 / 123, §98								fn. 19 / 123, §97				123, §97	
MICH. Comp. Laws Ann. (1967)																		
MINN. Stat. Ann. (1959) (Supp. 1969)	253A.17.2	fn. 20 / 253A.17.2	253A.17.2	253A.17.3	253A.17.5	253A.17.5		253A.17.4		253A.17.6			253A.17.6	253A.17.6	253A.17.6		253A.17.6	
MISS. Code Ann. 1952																		
MO. Rev. Stat. (1959)	202.847.2	committing court. 202.847.2			fn. 1 / 202.847.1 (1)	202.847.3				fn. 2 / 202.847.1 (2)	202.847.3							

Table 5.1 CORRESPONDENCE AND VISITATION continued

STATE	C O R R E S P O N D E N C E — Special Provisions as to									V I S I T A T I O N — Special Provisions as to						Time		
	Central Agency	Specified Official	Counsel	Single Personal Correspondent	Restrictions	Restrictions Recorded	Censorship	Writing Material Furnished	General Freedom of Correspondence	Restrictions	Restrictions Recorded	Family & Friends	Counsel	Minister	Physician	Specified	Any Reasonable	General Freedom of Visitation
MONT. Rev. Codes Ann. (1961)				38-112				38-113	fn. 21 fn. 22 38-114 38-116									
NEB. Rev. Stat. (1966)				fn. 23 / 83-314	fn. 23 / 83-314		fn. 23 / 83-314	83-314										
NEV. Rev. Stat. (1967)	433.719				fn. 24 / 433.719		fn. 24 / 433.719		433.719								fn. 25 / 433.719	433.719
N.H. Rev. Stat. Ann. (1964)	135:33							135:33										
N.J. Stat. Ann. (1964) (Supp. 1970)	official agencies, court. 30:4-24.2	commissioner, court. 30:4-24.2	30:4-24.2	fn. 1 / 30:4-24.2		30:4-24.2		on request. 30:4-24.2		fn. 2 / 30:4-24.2	30:4-24.2							
N.M. Stat. Ann. (1953)	34-2-15	committing court. 34-2-15b		fn. 1 / 34-2-15						fn. 2 / 34-2-15(a)								
N.Y. Mental Hygiene Law (McKinney 1951) (Supp. 1970)		fn. 26 / 15		fn. 1 / 15														
N.C. Gen. Stat. (1964)	122-46(b)	committing court. 126-46(b)		122-46(a)(1)	122-46(a)(1)	122-46(c)				122-46(a)(2)	122-46(c)		fn. 27 / 122-46(b)					
N.D. Cent. Code (1960)	25-03-20(2) (Supp. 1969)	mental health board. 25-03-20(2) (Supp. 1969)		fn. 1 / 25-03-20(2) (Supp.1969)	fn. 1 / 25-03-20(a) (1)	25-03-20(3)				fn. 2 / 25-03-20 (b)(1)	25-03-20 (3)	25-03-20 (3)		25-03-20 (4)				
OHIO Rev. Code Ann. (Baldwin 1964)	5122.29		5122.29	fn. 28 / 5122.29	fn. 1 / 5122.29	5122.29				fn. 2 / 5122.29	5122.29				fn. 29 / 5122.29			
OKLA. Stat. Ann. (1954)	43A, §93	committing court. 43A, §93			fn. 1 / 43A, §93	43A, §93				fn. 2 / 43A, §93	43A, §93							
ORE. Rev. Stat. (1967)	426.375(2)	committing court. 426.375(2)	426.375(2)	fn. 1 / 426.375(1)		426.374(3)				fn. 2 / 426.375(a)(2)	426.375(3)							
PA. Stat. Ann. (1969)	50, §4423 (1)	committing court. 50, §4423 (1)	50, §4423	50, §4423 (5)	50, §4423 (5)			50, §4423 (5)				50, §4423 (1)	50, §4423 (1)					50, §4423 (1)

Table 5.1 CORRESPONDENCE AND VISITATION *continued*

STATE	CORRESPONDENCE — Special Provision as to									VISITATION — Special Provision as to						Time		
	Central Agency	Specified Official	Counsel	Single Personal Correspondence	Restrictions	Restrictions Recorded	Censorship	Writing Material Furnished	General Freedom of Correspondence	Restrictions	Restrictions Recorded	Family & Friends	Counsel	Minister	Physician	Specified	Any Reasonable	General Freedom of Visitation
R.I. Gen. Laws Ann. (1968)	26-3-20		26-3-20		26-3-20	fn. 22 26-3-20		fn. 30 26-3-20					26-3-6			fn. 31 26-3-6		
S.C. Code Ann. (1962)	32-1021	committing court. 32-1021		fn. 1 32-1021	fn. 1 32-1021	32-1021				fn. 2 32-1021	32-1021							
S.D. Compiled Laws Ann. (1967)			27-7-42	27-7-42	27-7042	fn. 22		27-7-45										
TENN. Code Ann. (1955) (Supp. 1968)		33-1207							33-1207							at regular visiting hours. 33-1207		33-1207
TEX. Rev. Civ. Stat. Ann. (1958)	5547-86 (a) (4)	courts & attorney general. 5547-86(a) (4)	5547-86 (a) (4)	fn. 32 5547-86	fn. 32 5547-86	5547-86(b)				fn. 2 5547-86 (1)	5547-86(b)							
UTAH Code Ann. (1968)	64-7-48(2)	committing court. 64-7-48(2)		fn. 1 64-7-48(1)	fn. 1 64-7-48(1)	64-7-48(2)				fn. 2 64-7-48(1)	64-7-48(3)		fn. 33 64-7-48(2)	fn. 33 64-7-48(2)				
VT. Stat. Ann. (1968)	18, §7705(b)	18, §7705(b)	18, §7705(b)	18, §7705(a)(1)	18, §7705(a)(1)					18, §7705 (a)(2)			18, §7710	18, §7710				
VA. Code Ann. (1953)																		
fn. 34 WASH. Rev. Code Ann. (1962)					fn. 35 71.12.570		72.23.220	fn. 36 72.23.220										
W. VA. Code Ann. (1966)																		
fn. 37 WIS. Stat. Ann. (1957)	51.35(1)	fn. 38 51.35(1)	51.35(1)				fn. 39 51.35											
WYO. Stat. Ann. (1967)		governor. 25-72(a)	25-72(a)		fn. 1 25-72(a)					fn. 2 25-72(a)								

Notes to Table 5.1   CORRESPONDENCE AND VISITATION

1. Every patient is entitled to communicate by sealed mail or otherwise with persons including official agencies inside or outside the hospital, subject to the general rules and regulations of the hospital and except to the extent that the head of the hospital determines that it is necessary for the medical welfare of the patient to impose restrictions. Draft Act 21(a)(1); Alas. 47.30.-150; Ga. 88-502.5(a) (Supp. 1969); Idaho 66-346(a)(1) (Supp. 1969); Ill. 91½, §12-2 (Supp. 1969); Mo. 202.847.1; N.M. 34-2-15a; N.Y. Mental Hygiene Law 15 (Supp. 1970); N.D. 25-03-20(a)(1); Ohio 5122.29; Okla. 43A, §93; Ore. 426.325(2)(1); S.C. 32-1021; Utah 64-7-48; Wyo. 25-72.

2. Every patient is entitled to receive visitors subject to the general rules and regulations of the hospital and except to the extent that the head of the hospital determines that it is necessary for the medical welfare of the patient to impose restrictions. Draft Act 21(a)(2); Alas. 47.30.150; Idaho 66-346(a)(2) (Supp. 1969); Ill. 91½, §12-2 (Supp. 1969); Mo. 202.847.1; N.J. 30:4-24.2 (Supp. 1970); N.M. 34-2-15a; N.D. 25-03-20(b)(1); Ohio 5122.29; Okla. 43A, §93; Ore. 426.375(a)(2); S.C. 32-1021; Utah 64-7-48; Wyo. 25-72.

3. "to have reasonable access to telephones, both to make and receive confidential calls." Cal. W. & I. 5325(d) (Supp. 1968).

4. With spouse and relatives. Colo. 71-1-23(2) (Supp. 1965).

5. Patient may correspond with any suitable person. Conn. 17-190 (Supp. 1969).

6. Visits by any member of the family, relative, or friend are allowed: if the superintendent does not think they will be injurious, if approved by the welfare commissioner, or if ordered by the court. Conn. 17-189.

7. May receive uncensored mail from "his attorney or personal physician." D.C. 21-561(a)(2).

8. The chosen correspondent's return mail is also to be delivered unopened. Fla. 394.15 (Supp. 1969).

9. The patient may send mail to or receive mail from the governor, members of the General Assembly, the attorney general, judges, state's attorneys, officers of the department, or licensed attorneys-at-law without examination. Ill. 91½, §12-2 (Supp. 1969).

10. Visitors shall be allowed, subject to such rules, regulations, and restrictions as the superintendent may prescribe, on week days between 2:00 P.M. and 5:00 P.M. Ind. 22-1034.

11. If letters written to patients are not delivered, they must be returned to the sender with the reason patient could not receive them. Iowa 226.15. Letters sent by the patient may be inspected by the state director, the patient is assured the delivery to any addressee of 1 letter per week. Iowa 226.13.

12. Patients are to be allowed at least 1 hour each Sunday to receive spiritual advice from any recognized clergyman who represents their religious belief. Iowa 218.26.

13. "absolute right to communicate by letter with the state department of social welfare, the 'head of the hospital,' any court, 'physician' or attorney. Kan. 59-2929 (Supp. 1968).

14. "The 'head of the hospital' may impose reasonable rules and regulations on any 'patient' concerning his communication by letter or otherwise with any other person or agencies and concerning his right to receive visitors." Kan. 59-2929 (Supp. 1968).

15. "any 'patient' shall have the right to be visited by any 'physician' or attorney at any reasonable hour. Kan. 59-2929 (Supp. 1968).

16. Rights of general correspondence and visitation are to be exercised at the physician's discretion. La. 28:171(5), 28:171(9).

17. To communicate by mail in accordance with the regulations of the hospital. Me. 34, §2254.

18. Letters to or from the patient may be sent as addressed, or else to his parent, legal guardian, or most interested friend. Mass. 123, §98.

19. If in the opinion of the superintendent the visit would not be injurious or if a judge first orders in writing that such visit be allowed. Mass. 123, §98.

20. "Any patient may correspond by sealed mail or otherwise, freely without censorship, with the governor, the commissioner, the court, and any official agency, and may communicate without censorship by sealed mail or any other means with his physician and one or more attorneys." Minn. 253A.17.2 (Supp. 1969).

21. All letters are to be mailed in a United States postoffice box by the patient. Mont. 38-114.

22. Notice of the law must be posted in the institution. Mont. 38-116; R.I. 26-3-22; S.D. 27-7-48.

23. Letters may be censored for obscenity, indecency, and threats; also those which are otherwise clearly improper to be mailed. Neb. 83-314.

24. Patient may receive uncensored mail from his attorney or personal physician. All other incoming mail or communications may be read before being delivered to the patient if necessary for patient's medical welfare. Nev. 433.719.

25. Reasonable rules regarding visitation hours and the use of telephone and telegraph facilities may be made. Nev. 433.719.

26. All such patients shall be allowed to correspond without restriction with any public official and with the mental health information service. N.Y. 15 (Supp. 1970).

27. "Notwithstanding any limitations, every patient shall be entitled . . . to receive his or her attorney if accompanied by a medical member of the hospital staff." N.C. 122-46.

28. Unrestricted communication with personal physician. Ohio 5122.29.

29. The patient's personal physician shall be admitted at all times. Ohio 5122.29.

30. The patients shall be afforded "every facility for making such communications." R.I. 26-3-20.

31. After a petition for release has been submitted, the patient may be visited by counsel with the approval of the court or with the superintendent's permission. R.I. 26-3-6.

32. Subject to the general rules of the hospital and except to the extent that the head of the hospital determines that it is necessary for the welfare of the patient to impose restrictions, every patient is entitled to communicate with persons outside the hospital and to communicate by uncensored and sealed mail with legal counsel, the board, the courts, and the attorney general of the state. Tex. 5547-86(a).

33. In no case shall the superintendent deny a patient a visit with a friend, relative, spouse, guardian of the individual, mental health or peace officer, or his legal counsel or clergy of the patient's choice. Utah 64-7-48(2).

34. "All letters directed to the patients shall be delivered to them if, in the judgment of the superintendent, their contents are not prejudicial to the mental condition of the patient." Wash. 72.23.-220.

35. No person in a private institution shall be restrained from sending written communications of the fact of his detention to a friend, relative or other person. If the physician in charge finds it impossible or inadvisable to send any such communication within 24 hours, notice of the patient's detention is to be given to the prosecuting attorney of the county in which the institution is located, and to the Department of Institutions, giving the name and address of the patient and the names and addresses of the person or persons who arranged for his admission. Wash. 71-12-570.

36. Materials shall be furnished for writing at least 1 letter a week. Wash. 72.23.220.

37. Communications from the governor, attorney-general, judges, district attorneys, the department, or licensed attorneys shall be delivered to the patient. Wis. 51.35(1).

38. Attorney general, judges of courts of record, district attorneys. Wis. 51.35(1).

39. Communications and packages for or addressed to a patient may be examined and withheld if there is any good reason therefor. Wis. 51.35(2).

Table 5.2   MECHANICAL RESTRAINTS

State	Medical Needs	Part of Record	State	Medical Needs	Part of Record
DRAFT ACT	fn.1 20	fn. 2 20	MISS. Code Ann. (1952)		
ALA. Code (1958)			MO. Rev. Stat. (1959)	fn. 1 202.843	fn. 2 202.843
ALAS. Stat. (1962)	fn. 1 47.30.140	fn. 2 47.30.140	MONT. Rev. Codes Ann. (1961)		
ARIZ. Rev. Stat. Ann. (1956)			NEB. Rev. Stat. (1966)	fn. 6	
ARK. Stat. Ann. (1947)			NEV. Rev. Stat. (1967)	fn. 7 433.723	fn. 2 433.723
CAL. Welf. & Inst'ns Code (West 1966)			N.H. Rev. Stat. Ann. (1964)		
COLO. Rev. Stat. Ann. (1964)			N.J. Stat. Ann. (1964)	30:4-24.1 (Supp. 1970)	fn. 2 30:4-24.1 (Supp. 1970)
CONN. Gen. Stat. Ann. (1958)			N.M. Stat. Ann. (1953)	fn. 1 34-2-14	fn. 2 34-2-14
DEL. Code Ann. (1953)			N.Y. Mental Hygiene Law (McKinney 1951)		
D.C. Code Ann. (1967)	prescribed by physician 21-563	fn. 2 21-563	N.C. Gen. Stat. (1964)	fn. 1 122-47	fn. 2 122-47
FLA. Stat. Ann. (1960)			N.D. Cent. Code (1960)	fn. 1 25-03-19	fn. 2 25-03-19
GA. Code Ann. (1963)	fn. 1 88-502.4 (Supp. 1969)	fn. 2 88-502.4 (Supp. 1969)	OHIO Rev. Code Ann. (Baldwin 1964)	fn. 1 5122.28	fn. 2 5122.28
HAWAII Rev. Stat. Ann. (1968)			OKLA. Stat. Ann. (1954)	fn. 1 43A, § 92	fn. 2 43A, § 92
IDAHO Code Ann. (1949)	fn. 1 66-345 (Supp. 1969)	fn. 2 66-345 (Supp. 1969)	ORE. Rev. Stat. (1967)	fn. 1 426.385	fn. 2 426.385
ILL. Ann. Stat. (Smith-Hurd 1966)			PA. Stat. Ann. (1969)	50, § 4422	
IND. Ann. Stat. (1964)			R.I. Gen. Laws Ann. (1968)		
IOWA Code Ann. (1969)			S.C. Code Ann. (1962)		
KAN. Stat. Ann. (1964)	fn. 3 59-2928 (Supp. 1968)	fn. 2 59-2928 (Supp. 1968)	S.D. Compiled Laws Ann. (1967)		
KY. Rev. Stat. Ann. (1969)	202.269	202.269	TENN. Code Ann. (1955)	fn. 8 33-307 (Supp. 1968)	
LA. Rev. Stat. Ann. (1950)			TEX. Rev. Civ. Stat. Ann. (1958)	fn. 9 5547-71	fn. 2 5547-71
ME. Rev. Stat. Ann. (1965)	fn. 1 34, § 2253	fn. 2 34, § 2253	UTAH Code Ann. (1968)	fn. 1 64-7-47	fn. 2 64-7-47
MD. Code Ann. (1968)			VT. Stat. Ann. (1968)	fn. 1 18, §7704	fn. 2 18, §7704
MASS. Ann. Laws (1965)	fn. 4 123, § 35	fnn. 2, 5 123, § 37	VA. Code Ann. (1953)		
MICH. Comp. Laws Ann. (1967)			WASH. Rev. Code Ann. (1962)		
			W. VA. Code Ann. (1966)		
			WIS. Stat. Ann. (1957)		
MINN. Stat. Ann. (1959)	fn. 1 253A.17(1) (Supp. 1969)	fn. 2 253A.17(1) (Supp. 1969)	WYO. Stat. Ann. (1967)	fn. 1 25-71	fn. 2 25-71

1. Determination of need is to be made by the head of the hospital or his designee. Draft Act, 20; Alaska, 47.30.140; Ga. 88-515 (Supp. 1968); Idaho 66-345 (Supp. 1969); Me. 34, § 2253; Minn. 253A.17(1) (Supp. 1969); Mo. 202.843; N.M. 34-2-14; N.C. 122-47; N.D. 25-03-19; Ohio 5122.28; Okla. 43A, § 92; Ore. 426.385; Utah 64-7-47; Vt. 18, § 7704; Wyo. 25-71.

2. The reason for the use of restraint is to appear on the patient's record. Draft Act, 20; Alaska 47.30.140; D.C. 21-563; Ga. 88-515 (Supp. 1968); Idaho 66-345 (Supp. 1969); Kan. 59-2928 (Supp. 1968); Maine 34, § 225; Mass. 123, § 37; Minn. 253A.17(1); Mo. 202.843; Nev. 493.723; N.J. 30:4-24.1 (Supp. 1970); N.M. 34-2-14; N.C. 122-47; N.D. 25-03-19; Ohio 5122.28; Okla. 43A, § 92; Ore. 426.385; Tex. 5547-71; Utah 64-7-47; Vt. 18, § 7704; Wyo. 25-71.

3. "The head of the hospital" or a member of the medical staff shall sign a statement explaining the medical necessity for the use of any restraints. Kan. 59-2928 (Supp. 1968).

4. Restraint is to be applied only in the presence of the superintendent, the physician or an assistant physician on his written order. In the case of an emergency it may be applied in the physician's absence or without a written order but immediately after the imposition of the restraint, its use is to be reported to the physician who is to investigate the case and approve or disapprove the restraint imposed. Restraints are to be applied only in cases of extreme violence, infliction of self-injury, active homicidal or suicidal condition, or physical exhaustion. Mass. 123, § 35 to 123, § 38.

5. The reason for restraint, the person ordering its use, and the length of time the restraint was used is to appear on the record. Mass. 123, § 37.

6. The liberty of any person supposed to be mentally ill shall not be restrained by any person not acting under the authority of the county board of mental health except to the extent for the period that may be necessary for the safety of persons and property, and until authority can be obtained. Neb. 83-357.

7. No mechanical restraint shall be applied to any patient hospitalized in any public or private hospital for a mental illness unless the use of restraint is prescribed by a physician. Nev. 433.723.

8. Patient may be held under such restraint as may be necessary for the welfare of the patient. Tenn. 33-307 (Supp. 1968).

9. Restraints are to be applied only if prescribed by a physician and are to be removed as soon as possible. Tex. 5547-71.

Table 5.3   PROVISIONS RELATING TO MAJOR MEDICAL TREATMENT

STATE AND CITATION	STATUTORY PROVISIONS
ALAS. Stat. (1962) 47.30.130 (Supp. 1969)	"Consent to surgery, the psychiatric therapies which the department determines, and autopsies must be obtained for a patient before the undertaking of the surgery, psychiatric therapies or autopsies from one of the following persons: spouse, guardian, either parent or oldest adult child. If none of these persons is found in this state within a reasonable time, or in the case of an emergency, the commissioner of health and welfare or his designee, upon being notified of the pertinent medical facts, may give the consent. However, when the head of the hospital is of the opinion that the patient has insight or capacity to make a responsible decision, the patient's consent shall be obtained before the surgery or psychiatric therapies; his consent shall be determinative, and no other consent is necessary. However, in the case of a minor, consent shall also be obtained from the parent or guardian. The person giving the consent, or a person who acts after the consent is given and is authorized to perform the act undertaken by him is not liable civilly or criminally if the act is done by him in his official capacity. . . ."
ARIZ. Rev. Stat. Ann. (1956) 36-528 (Supp. 1970)	"When, in the written opinion of a patient's attending physician, a true medical emergency exists and a surgical operation is necessary to save the life, physical health, eyesight, hearing or member of the patient, the superintendent may give consent to such surgical operation, provided that the consent of the proper relatives or guardian cannot be had in time to effect such saving and time will not permit the obtaining of appropriate judicial authority."
CAL. Welf. & Inst'ns Code (West 1966) 5325 (Supp. 1968)	"Each person involuntarily detained for evaluation or treatment under provisions of this part shall have the [right] . . . (f) to refuse shock treatment, (g) to refuse lobotomy."
ILL. Ann. Stat. (Smith-Hurd 1966) 91½, §1-8 (Supp. 1969)	"Surgery may be performed on patients only if the consent of the patient, of the parent of a patient under 18 years of age, or the guardian of any patient is first obtained, but if an emergency exists and the life of the patient is threatened, consent need not be obtained, provided substantiation of the emergency is documented."
MINN. Stat. Ann (1959) 253A.17.8 (Supp. 1969)	"The head of a state hospital shall obtain consent for a surgical operation necessary to save the life, health, eyesight, hearing, or a limb of any patient, from the proper relatives or guardian. If such persons cannot be found after diligent search, or in the case of an emergency, the head of the hospital, upon being notified of the pertinent medical facts, may give such consent."
OHIO Rev. Code (Baldwin 1964) 5123.03	"Before proceeding with any major operation which in the judgment of the superintendent of an institution is advisable or necessary, the superintendent shall notify the patient's personal or family physician and the spouse, parent, guardian, or one of the next of kin residing in Ohio, if such information is shown by the records on file with the superintendent. In cases of grave emergency where the medical staff feels that surgical or other intervention is necessary to prevent serious consequences or death, authority is hereby given to proceed with such measure."
OKLA. Stat. Ann. (1954) 43A, §96	"Before proceeding with any major operation which in the judgment of the superintendent of the institution is advisable or necessary, the superintendent shall notify or cause to be notified the spouse, parent or guardian or one of the next of kin residing in Oklahoma, if such information is shown by the records on file with the superintendent and a copy of said notice shall be filed in the patient's records; except that in cases of grave emergency where the medical staff feels that surgical or other intervention is necessary to prevent serious consequences or death, authority is hereby given to proceed with such measure."

Table 5.3   PROVISIONS RELATING TO MAJOR MEDICAL TREATMENT   continued

<u>STATE AND CITATION</u>   <u>STATUTORY PROVISIONS</u>

TENN. Code Ann. (1955)
   33-307
   (Supp. 1968)

Patient may be given such standard treatment including surgery as may be necessary for patient's welfare. However, surgery may be performed on such patient only if the consent of the patient or the parent, guardian, spouse, or adult next of kin is first obtained.

VT. Stat. Ann. (1968)
   18, §7708

"If the superintendent finds that a patient supported by the state requires a surgical operation or that a surgical operation would promote the possibility of his discharge from the hospital, the superintendent, with the consent of the patient, his attorney or his legally appointed guardian, if any, or next of kin, if any be known, may make the necessary arrangements with some surgeon and hospital for the operation. The expense of the operation shall be borne by the state in the same proportion as the patient is supported by the state."

Table 5.4 EXAMINATION AFTER HOSPITALIZATION

STATE	POSTADMISSION	PERIODIC EXAMINATIONS		STATE	POSTADMISSION	PERIODIC EXAMINATION	
		Frequency Specified	As Practicable			Frequency Specified	As Practicable
Draft Act	13(a)	not less often than every 6 months. 15		ME. Rev. Stat. Ann. (1965)	34, §2372	not less often than every 12 months. 34, §2374	
ALA. Code (1958)				MD. Ann. Code (1968)			
ALAS. Stat. (1962)			47.30.220	MASS. Ann. Laws (1965)			
ARIZ. Rev. Stat. Ann. (1956)			as frequently as necessary. 36-524D (Supp. 1970)	MICH. Comp. Laws Ann. (1967)			
ARK. Stat. Ann. (1947)	59-229 (Supp. 1967)			MINN. Stat. Ann. (1959)	253A.06.1 253A.07.23 (Supp. 1969)	not less often than annually. 253A.17.7 (Supp. 1969)	
CAL. Welf. & Inst'ns Code (West 1966)	7251 (Supp. 1968)		from time to time. 7251 (Supp.1968)	MISS. Code Ann. (1952)			
COLO. Rev. Stat. Ann. (1964)				MO. Rev. Stat. (1959)	202.820		202.827
CONN. Gen. Stat. Ann. (1958)				MONT. Rev. Codes Ann. (1961)			
DEL. Code Ann. (1953)				NEB. Rev. Stat. (1966)			
D.C. Code Ann. (1967)		not less often than every 6 months. 21-548		NEV. Rev. Stat. (1967)	433.681	not less often than every 6 months. 433.717	
FLA. Stat. Ann. (1960)				N.H. Rev. Stat. Ann. (1964)			
GA. Code Ann. (1963)				N.J. Stat. Ann. (1964)			
HAWAII Rev. Stat. Ann. (1968)				N.M. Stat. Ann. (1953)	34-2-8	not less often than every 6 months. 34-2-10	
IDAHO Code Ann. (1949)	66-324, 66-333 (Supp. 1969)		66-337 (Supp. 1969)	N.Y. Mental Hygiene Law (McKinney 1951)			
ILL. Ann. Stat. (Smith-Hurd 1966)	$91\frac{1}{2}$, §§6-2, 7-5 (Supp. 1969)	not less often than every 6 months. $91\frac{1}{2}$, §10-1 (Supp. 1969)		N.C. Gen. Stat. (1964)			
IND. Ann. Stat. (1964)				N.D. Cent. Code (1960)	25-0311(10)	at least every 6 months. 25-03-15	
IOWA Code Ann. (1969)	225.15			OHIO Rev. Code Ann. (Baldwin 1964)	5122.19		5122.21
KAN. Stat. Ann. (1964)				OKLA. Stat. Ann. (1954)			
KY. Rev. Stat. Ann. (1969)	202.237	not less often than every 6 months. 202.239		ORE. Rev. Stat. (1967)			
LA. Rev. Stat. Ann. (1950)		not less often than every 6 months. 28:96B (Supp. 1969)		PA. Stat. Ann. (1969)			

Table 5.4   EXAMINATION AFTER HOSPITALIZATION   continued

STATE	POSTADMISSION	PERIODIC EXAMINATIONS	
		Frequency Specified	As Practicable
R.I. Gen. Laws Ann. (1968)			
S.C. Code Ann. (1962)	32-1017	not less often than annually. 32-1020	
S.D. Compiled Laws Ann. (1967)			
TENN. Code Ann. (1955)	33-609(2) (Supp. 1968)	not less often than every 6 months. 33-609(d) (Supp. 1968)	
TEX. Rev. Civ. Stat. Ann. (1968)		not less often than every 6 months. 5547-77	
UTAH Code Ann. (1968)	64-7-40		64-7-42

STATE	POSTADMISSION	PERIODIC EXAMINATIONS	
		Frequency Specified	As Practicable
VT. Stat. Ann. (1968)	18, §7702		
VA. Code Ann. (1953)	37.1-70		
WASH. Rev. Code Ann. (1962)			
W. VA. Code Ann. (1966)	27-5-6		27-7-1
WIS. Stat. Ann. (1957)			
WYO. Stat. Ann. (1967)	25-65	not less often than every 6 months. 25-68	

Table 5.5   PROPERTY CONTROL WITHOUT GUARDIANSHIP

STATE	ASSETS RECORDED BY COURT CERTIFICATION TO HOSPITAL	CONTROL OF PROPERTY		USE OF PROPERTY		EXAMINATION OF PROPERTY		MAXIMUM SUM THAT THE HOSPITAL CAN CONTROL
		By Institution	By Others	For Patient	For Institution Expense	With Court Order	Without Court Order	
DRAFT ACT	See page 2 of "The Scope of the Draft Act," in Appendix A of this volume							
ALA. Code (1958)								
ALAS. Stat. (1962)								
ARIZ. Rev. Stat. Ann. (1956)		36-520.01 (Supp. 1970)			36-520.01 (Supp. 1970)			
ARK. Stat. Ann. (1947)								
CAL. Welf. & Instn's Code (West 1966)	5210, 5229 (Supp. 1968)		central agency. (Supp. 1968)	7281 (Supp. 1968)			7278 (Supp. 1968)	
COLO. Rev. Stat. Ann. (1964)								
CONN. Gen. Stat. Ann. (1958)								
DEL. Code Ann. (1953)								
D. C. Code Ann. (1967)								
FLA. Stat. Ann. (1960)								
GA. Code Ann. (1963)								
HAWAII Rev. Stat. Ann. (1968)		334-23		334-23				"small amounts of cash". 334-23
IDAHO Code Ann. (1949)	66-352 (Supp. 1969)	66-352, 66-503 (Supp. 1969)		66-352, 66-502 (Supp. 1969)	for maintenance of patient. 66-503 (Supp. 1969)			fn. 1 66-352 (Supp. 1969)
ILL. Ann. Stat. (Smith-Hurd 1966)			fn. 2 central agency 3, §118b (Supp. 1969)					$1,000 3, §118b (Supp. 1969)
IND. Ann. Stat. (1964)		22-518		22-518				
IOWA Code Ann. (1969)								
KAN. Stat. Ann. (1964)								
KY. Rev. Stat. Ann. (1969)								
LA. Rev. Stat. Ann. (1950)	22:172, 28:173 (Supp. 1969)				interest on funds used for recreational purposes. 28:173 (Supp. 1969)			
ME. Rev. Stat. Ann. (1964)								
MD. Ann. Code (1968)								
MASS. Ann. Laws (1965)		123, §39 (Supp. 1968)		123, §39 (Supp. 1968)				
MICH. Comp. Laws Ann. (1967)			medical superintendent. 330.52a	330.52a				established for each hospital by the department of mental health. 330.52a
MINN. Stat. Ann. (1959)			fn. 3 state treasurer. 246-15 (Supp. 1969)	246.15 (Supp. 1969)				
MISS. Code Ann. (1952)								

Table 5.5   PROPERTY CONTROL WITHOUT GUARDIANSHIP   continued

STATE	ASSETS RECORDED BY COURT CERTIFICATION TO HOSPITAL	CONTROL OF PROPERTY		USE OF PROPERTY		EXAMINATION OF PROPERTY		MAXIMUM SUM THAT THE HOSPITAL CAN CONTROL
		By Institution	By Others	For Patient	For Institution Expense	With Court Order	Without Court Order	
MO. Rev. Stat. (1959)								
MONT. Rev. Codes Ann. (1961)	38-210 (Supp. 1969)	38-210 (Supp. 1969)			38-210 (Supp. 1969)			$100, 38-210 (Supp. 1969)
NEB. Rev. Stat. (1966)								
NEV. Rev. Stat. (1967)		433.440, 433.470		433.440.4	433.440.3			$150 433.440.3
N.H. Rev. Stat. Ann. (1964)								
N.J. Stat. Ann. (1964)		30:4-67.1			30:4-67.1	30:4-67.1		
N.M. Stat. Ann. (1953)								
N.Y. Mental Hygiene Law (McKinney 1951)		personal property, 50, 51 (Supp. 1970)			fn. 4 51 (Supp. 1970)	fn. 5 51a (Supp. 1970)		
N.C. Gen. Stat. (1964)								
N.D. Cent. Code (1960)		25-01.1-20 (Supp. 1969)		25-01.1-20 (Supp. 1969)				
OHIO Rev. Code Ann. (Baldwin 1964)	fn. 6 5123.42	fn. 6 5123.42		5123.42				$50 5123.42
OKLA. Stat. Ann. (1954)								
ORE. Rev. Stat. (1967)								
PA. Stat. Ann. (1969)								
R.I. Gen. Laws Ann. (1968)								
S.C. Code Ann. (1962)								
S.D. Compiled Laws Ann. (1967)								
TENN. Code Ann. (1955)								
TEX. Rev. Civ. Stat. Ann. (1958)								
UTAH Code Ann. (1968)								
VT. Stat. Ann. (1968)								
VA. Code Ann. (1953)								
WASH. Rev. Code Ann. (1962)		72.23.230		72.23.230(1)	over $300, 72.23.230(2)			$1,000 collection of moneys owed to inmate only, 72.23.240
W.VA. Code Ann. (1966)			fn. 7 27-11-4	27-11-4				
WIS. Stat. Ann. (1957)								
WYO. Stat. Ann. (1967)								

1. Any moneys, or other things of value, found on the person of a mentally ill person at the time of proceedings for involuntary hospitalization. Idaho 66-352 (Supp. 1969).

2. An employee of the agency may serve, without fee, as a conservator of personal estate of a patient in a state mental hospital if the value of the estate is less than $1,000. Ill. 3, §118b (Supp. 1969).

3. "The chief executive officer of each institution shall have the care and custody of all moneys belonging to the inmates thereof which may come into his hands . . . ." Minn. 246.15 (Supp. 1969).

4. The institution is entitled to the interest which was accrued or shall accrue on monies belonging to the patient upon approval of the director of the budget. N.Y. Mental Hygiene Law. 51 (Supp. 1970).

5. If examination and control of patient's property, other than his personal property, is desired, a court order is necessary. N.Y. Mental Hygiene Law, 51-a (Supp. 1970).

6. Superintendent is to file with the court a list of all money and valuables on the person of the patient within 10 days of patient's admission. If the patient has more than $50, the court may appoint a special guardian. Ohio 5123.42.

7. County court appoints a committee for a person found to be mentally ill or retarded. W. Va. 27-11-1. This committee takes possession of the estate and manages it, using such funds as necessary for the maintenance of the patient and his family. W. Va. 27-11-4.

Table 5.6   UNWARRANTED HOSPITALIZATION

STATE AND CITATION	PENALTIES
DRAFT ACT 26	"Any person who willfully causes, or conspires with or assists another to cause, (1) the unwarranted hospitalization of any individual . . . , shall be punished by a fine not exceeding $_____ or imprisonment not exceeding _____, or both."
ALA. Code (1958)	
ALAS. Stat. (1962) 47.30.330 (Supp. 1969)	"A person who intentionally causes, or attempts to cause, or conspires with another person to cause an individual to be committed to a hospital, . . . knowing or having reasonable grounds for believing that the individual is not mentally ill, and in need of hospitalization, is punishable by a fine of not more than $10,000, or by imprisonment for not less than one year nor more than 10 years, or by both. The court may order all or part of the fine paid to the injured individual."
ARIZ. Rev. Stat. Ann. (1956)	
ARK. Stat. Ann. (1947) 59-234 (Supp. 1967)	"No action shall be brought . . . to recover damages . . . ; provided that the immunity herein granted shall not be held to extend to any person who shall wilfully make and sign a false certificate to a hospital that a person is suffering from psychosis, nor to any one who confines, or detains a person in a hospital with knowledge that any such certificate is wilfully false."
CAL. Welf. & Inst'ns Code (West 1966) 5203 (Supp. 1968)	"Any individual who seeks a petition for court-ordered evaluation knowing that the person for whom the petition is sought is not, as a result of a mental disorder, a danger to himself, or to others, or gravely disabled is guilty of a misdemeanor . . . and may be held liable in civil damages by the person against whom the petition is sought."
5255	"Any individual who is knowingly and willfully responsible for detaining a person for more than 14 days in violation of the provisions of Section 5254 is liable to that person in civil damages."
COLO. Rev. Stat. Ann. (1964) 71-1-24	"Any person who wilfully causes, or who conspires with or assists another to cause, unwarranted hospitalization or confinement under the provisions of this article shall be liable in damages to the person so hospitalized or confined."
CONN. Gen. Stat. Ann. (1958) 17-184	"Any person who wilfully causes, or attempts to cause, or who conspires with any other person to cause, any person who is not mentally ill to be committed . . . , and any person who wilfully certifies falsely to the mental illness of any person in any certificate . . . , and any person who . . . willfully reports falsely to any court or judge that any person is mentally ill, shall be fined not more than one thousand dollars or imprisoned in the State Prison not more than five years, or both."
DEL. Code Ann. (1953) 16-5134 (Supp. 1970)	"Any person who wilfully causes, or conspires with or assists another to cause (1) the unwarranted hospitalization of any individual in the Delaware State Hospital under the provisions of this chapter, or (2) the denial to any individual of any of the rights accorded to him under the provisions of this chapter, shall be punished by a fine not exceeding $500, or imprisonment not exceeding one year, or both."

D.C. Code Ann. (1967)
21-591
	"Whoever:
	(1) without probable cause for believing a person to be mentally ill:
	    (A) causes or conspires with or assists another person to cause the hospitalization, under this chapter, of the person first referred to; or
	    (B) executes a petition, application, or certificate pursuant to this chapter, by which he secures or attempts to secure the apprehension, hospitalization, detention, or restraint of the person first referred to; or

Table 5.6   UNWARRANTED HOSPITALIZATION   continued

STATE AND CITATION	PENALTIES

D.C. Code Ann. (1967)--*continued*
21-591

(2) causes or conspires with or assists another person to cause the denial to a person of a right accorded to him by this chapter; or
(3) being a physician or psychiatrist, knowingly makes a false certificate or application pursuant to this chapter as to the mental condition of a person--shall be fined not more than $5000 or imprisoned not more than three years, or both."

FLA. Stat. Ann. (1960)
394.192
(Supp. 1969)

(1) <u>Conspiracy to hospitalize;   penalty.</u>
"(a) Any person who knowingly furnishes false information for the purpose of securing the involuntary hospitalization of any individual to any facility for the mentally ill shall, upon conviction, be punished by a fine not exceeding $5,000.00 or imprisonment in the county jail not exceeding one year, or by both such fine and imprisonment.
"(b) Any individual who without probable cause for believing a person to be mentally ill.
  "1. Causes or conspires with or assists another to cause the involuntary hospitalization of any such person under this act, or
  "2. Causes or conspires with or assists another to cause the denial to any person of any right accorded to him under this act. Shall, upon conviction, be punished by a fine not exceeding $5,000.00 or imprisonment in the county jail not exceeding one year, or by both such fine and imprisonment.
"(c) Any individual who without probable cause for believing a person to be mentally ill executes a petition, application, or certificate pursuant to this act, by which such individual secures or attempts to secure the involuntary apprehension, involuntary detention, involuntary hospitalization, or involuntary restraint of any such person, and any physician who knowingly makes any false certificate or application pursuant to this act as to the mental condition of any person shall, upon conviction, be punished by a fine not exceeding $5,000.00 or imprisonment in the county jail not exceeding one year, or by both such fine and imprisonment.
"(2) <u>Freedom from liability; good faith.</u>
The Director of the Division of Mental Health or the administrator of any hospital acting pursuant to the provisions of this act shall be entitled to rely in good faith upon the representations made for admission by any individual or any certification with respect to any individual made by a licensed physician or any court. All persons acting in good faith, reasonably and without negligence, in connection with the preparation or execution of petitions, applications, certificates or other documents or the apprehension, detention, discharge, examination, transportation or treatment of an individual under the provisions of this act shall be free from all liability, civil or criminal, by reason of such acts."

GA. Code Ann. (1963)
88-502.18
(Supp. 1969)

"Any person who by wilful action or gross negligence, violates or abuses any provision of this Chapter shall be liable to the patient for any damages which the patient suffers by reason of such wrongful conduct."

HAWAII Rev. Stat. Ann.
(1968)

IDAHO Code Ann. (1949)

ILL. Ann. Stat.
(Smith-Hurd 1966)
91½, §15-1
(Supp. 1969)

"Any person who conspires unlawfully to cause, or unlawfully causes any person to be adjudicated as mentally retarded or in need of mental treatment . . . , or to be detained at, or admitted to or hospitalized in any hospital . . . shall, upon conviction, be fined not less than $500 nor more than $1,000, or imprisoned not exceeding one year . . . , or both."

IND. Ann. Stat. (1964)

IOWA Code Ann. (1969)

Table 5.6   UNWARRANTED HOSPITALIZATION   continued

STATE AND CITATION

PENALTIES

KAN. Stat. Ann. (1964)
59-2932
(Supp. 1968)

"Any person acting in good faith and without negligence shall be free from all liability, civil or criminal, which might arise out of acting pursuant to this act. Any person who for a corrupt consideration or advantage, or through malice, shall make or join in making or advise the making of any false application, report or order provided for in this act shall be guilty of a misdemeanor and punished by a fine of not more than one thousand dollars or by imprisonment in the county jail for not more than one thousand dollars or by imprisonment in the county jail for not more than one year."

KY. Rev. Stat. Ann. (1969)
210.991

"Any person who willfully causes or conspires with or assists another in causing (1) the unwarranted hospitalization of any individual under the provisions of KRS Chs. 202, 203, and 210 . . . shall be punished by a fine not exceeding five thousand dollars or imprisonment for a term not to exceed five years or both."

LA. Rev. Stat. Ann. (1950)
28-181
(Supp. 1969)

"Any person who, alone or in conspiracy with others, unlawfully, wilfully, maliciously, and without reasonable cause, commits or attempts to commit to any mental institution any person not sufficiently ill to require care shall be fined not more than one-thousand dollars, or imprisoned for not more than one year, or both."

ME. Rev. Stat. Ann. (1965)
34, §2259

"Any person who wilfully causes, or conspires with or assists another to cause, the unwarranted hospitalization of any individual under this chapter, or the denial to any individual of any of the rights accorded to him under this chapter, shall be punished by a fine of not less than $100 nor more than $1000, or by imprisonment for not less than one year nor more than 5 years, or by both."

MD. Ann. Code (1968)
59, §26, 59, §31,
59, §33

"Any officer or other person in charge of the insane or feeble-minded who may refuse to comply with any of the provisions . . . [these provisions concern the qualifications of the physicians signing the medical certificate and the procedures to be followed in using physician's certificates for hospitalization] shall be deemed guilty of a misdemeanor and, on conviction of same, shall be fined or imprisoned, in the judgment of the court. . . ."

MASS. Ann. Laws (1965)
123, §110

"Whoever wilfully conspires with a person unlawfully or improperly to commit . . . a person who is not insane or wilfully assists in or connives at such a commitment shall be punished by fine or imprisonment, at the discretion of the court."

MICH. Comp. Laws Ann.
(1967)
330.62

"Any violation of the provisions of this and the preceding sections is a misdemeanor and on conviction thereof the person guilty shall be confined a sum not to exceed $300, or by imprisonment not to exceed 90 days, or both. In the event of a corporation violating such provisions, such corporation shall be fined as herein provided and the officers of such corporation shall be considered the same as though individuals not connected with corporations and fined and imprisoned as herein set forth."

MINN. Stat. Ann. (1959)
253A.21.1
(Supp. 1969)

"Any person who wilfully makes, joins in, or advises the making of any false petition or report or knowingly or wilfully makes any false representation for the purpose of causing such petition or report to be made or for the purpose of causing an individual to be improperly hospitalized . . . is guilty of a gross misdemeanor and may be punished by imprisonment in the state prison for not more than one year or by a fine of not more than $500."

MISS. Code Ann. (1952)

Table 5.6   UNWARRANTED HOSPITALIZATION   continued

STATE AND CITATION	PENALTIES
MO. Rev. Stat. (1959) 202.870	"Any person who wilfully causes or conspires with or assists another to cause, the unwarranted hospitalization of any individual . . . shall be punished by a fine not exceeding five thousand dollars or imprisonment not exceeding five years, or by both such fine and imprisonment."
MONT. Rev. Codes Ann. (1961)	
NEB. Rev. Stat. (1966) 83-315	"Any person who willfully and knowingly violates any of the provisions of section 83-314 [includes commitment procedures for the mentally ill] shall upon conviction thereof be punished by imprisonment . . . not exceeding three years nor less than six months, or by a fine not exceeding five hundred dollars, or both, and shall not be eligible to any office in a state hospital thereafter."
NEV. Rev. Stat. (1967) 433.620	"Any public officer or employee who transports or delivers or assists in transporting or delivering or detains or assists in detaining any person pursuant to this chapter shall not be rendered civilly or criminally liable thereby unless it shall be shown that such officer or employee acted maliciously or in bad faith or that his negligence resulted in bodily injury to such person."
433.739	"1.) Any person who, without probable cause for believing a person to be mentally ill, causes or conspires with or assists another to cause the hospitalization of any such person . . . shall be punished by a fine not exceeding $3,000 or by imprisonment in the state prison for not less than 1 year nor more than 3 years, or by both fine and imprisonment. "2.) Any person who, without probable cause for believing another person to be mentally ill, executes a petition, application or certificate, . . . by which such person secures or attempts to secure the apprehension, hospitalization, detention or restraint of any such person . . . or any physician or psychiatrist who knowingly makes any false certificate or application . . . shall be punished by a fine not exceeding $5,000 or by imprisonment in the state prison for not less than 1 year nor more than 3 years or by both fine and imprisonment."
N.H. Rev. Stat. Ann. (1964)	
N.J. Stat. Ann. (1964) 30:4-33 (Supp. 1970)	"A person who shall sign an application or certificate or written statement of a practicing physician for the commitment of a person to an institution for the mentally ill, mentally retarded or tubercular in this state for any purpose or motive other than the care and treatment of the patient or who shall in any manner aid or abet in any such application shall be guilty of a misdemeanor."
N.M. Stat. Ann. (1953) 34-2-25 (Supp. 1969)	"Any person who wilfully causes or conspires with or assists another to cause (1) the unwarranted hospitalization . . . of any individual . . . (2) shall be punished by a fine not exceeding one thousand dollars ($1,000) or imprisonment not exceeding one (1) year, or both."
N.Y. Mental Hygiene Law (McKinney 1951) 44 (Supp. 1970)	"No civil action shall be brought . . . for alleged damages because of any act done or failure to perform any act, while discharging his official duties, without leave of a judge of the supreme court . . . . Any such officer or employee in any such action shall not be liable for damages if he shall have acted in good faith, with reasonable care and upon probable cause."
N.C. Gen. Stat. Ann. (1964) 122-51	"Nothing contained in this chapter shall be held or construed to relieve from liability in any suit or action instituted in the courts of this State, any husband, wife, guardian, or physician, who unlawfully, maliciously and corruptly attempts to hospitalize any person or patient to any hospital for the mentally ill or center for the mentally retarded under the provisions of this chapter."

Table 5.6   UNWARRANTED HOSPITALIZATION   continued

STATE AND CITATION	PENALTIES
N.D. Cent. Code (1960) 25-03-28	"Any person who wilfully and maliciously causes or conspires with or assists another to cause the unwarranted hospitalization of any individual . . . shall be punished by a fine of not exceeding $1,000 or by imprisonment of not more than one year, or by both such fine and imprisonment."
OHIO Rev. Code Ann. (Baldwin 1964)	
OKLA. Stat. Ann. (1954) 43A, §131	"Any person who shall knowingly contrive or conspire to have ordered or admitted any person to an institution for the mentally ill, or mentally retarded, unlawfully or maliciously shall be guilty of a misdemeanor, and upon conviction, shall be fined not to exceed . . . ($1,000) or confined in jail not to exceed one (1) year, or both."
43A, §139	"Any physician who falsely certifies to the mental illness or mental retardation of any person, or whose false certificates as to mental illness or retardation of any person is proved to be the result of negligence or deficient professional skill, or who signs such a certificate for pecuniary reward, or promise thereof, or other consideration of value or operating to his advantage, other than the professional fee usually paid for such service, shall be guilty of a misdemeanor, and upon conviction . . . shall be sentenced to pay a fine not to exceed . . . ($500) or to imprisonment not to exceed one (1) year, or both."
ORE. Rev. Stat. (1967)	
PA. Stat. Ann. (1969) 50, §4605	"(4) It shall be unlawful for any person, corporation, partnership or association to wilfully cause or conspire with or assist another to cause the unwarranted detention or commitment of any person under the provisions of this act, or the denial to any person of any of the rights accorded to him under the provisions of this act. . . . "(6) It shall be unlawful for any physician to knowingly make any false statement, certificate or report which aids in or causes a person to be admitted, committed or detained pursuant to the provisions of this act."
R.I. Gen. Laws Ann. (1968) 26-2-19	"Any physician who wilfully conspires with any person unlawfully or improperly to commit to any lunatic hospital or asylum . . . any person who is not insane, shall be punished by a fine not exceeding . . . ($5,000) or imprisonment not exceeding . . . (5) years, at the discretion of the court."
S.C. Code Ann. (1962) 32-916	"Any person who wilfully causes or conspires with or assists another to cause, (a) the unwarranted confinement of any individual under the provisions of this chapter or (b) the denial to any individual of any of the rights accorded to him under the provisions of this chapter, shall be fined not exceeding $1000 or imprisoned for not exceeding one year, or both."
S.D. Compiled Laws Ann. (1967) 27-1-4	"Any officer required to perform an act, and any person accepting an appointment under the provisions of this title, who shall willfully refuse or neglect to perform his duty as herein prescribed, shall be guilty of a misdemeanor, besides being liable to an action for damages."
27-1-6	"Every overseer of the poor, constable, keeper of a jail, or other person who confines any mentally retarded or mentally ill person in any other manner or in any other place than is authorized by law, is guilty of a misdemeanor."

Table 5.6   UNWARRANTED HOSPITALIZATION   continued

STATE AND CITATION	PENALTIES
Tenn. Code Ann. (1955) 33-1212 (Supp. 1968)	"Any person who willfully causes, or conspires with or assists with another to cause, (1) the unwarranted hospitalization, without probable cause, of any individual . . . or (2) the unwarranted detention, without probable cause, of any patient . . . shall be punished by fine not exceeding five hundred dollars ($500) or by imprisonment not exceeding twelve (12) months or both, in the discretion of the court, provided, however, that the head of any hospital acting pursuant to the terms and provisions of this chapter shall be entitled to rely in good faith upon the representations made for admission by any individual, or any certification with respect to said patient by any reputable physician . . . or by any court of record in the county of such individual's residence or presence."
Tex. Rev. Civ. Stat. Ann. (1958) 5547-19	"Any person who willfully causes or conspires with or assists another to cause the unwarranted commitment or hospitalization of any individual to a mental hospital is guilty of a misdemeanor and upon conviction shall be punished by a fine not exceeding five thousand ($5,000) or by imprisonment in the county jail not exceeding two (2) years or by both."
UTAH Code Ann. (1968) 64-7-21	"If any person in anywise attempts to introduce another into the hospital contrary to the provisions of this chapter, he is guilty of a misdemeanor, and shall be fined in any sum not less than $50 nor more than $300."
VT. Stat. Ann. (1968) 18, §7104	"Any person who wilfully causes, or conspires with or assists another to cause: (1) the hospitalization of an individual knowing that the individual is not mentally ill or in need of hospitalization or treatment as a mentally ill or mentally defective individual; or (2) the denial to any individual of any rights granted to him under this Part of this title; or (3) the voluntary admission to a hospital of an individual knowing that he is not mentally ill or eligible for treatment thereby attempting to defraud the state; or (4) the elopement of any patient or student from a hospital or training school or who knowingly harbors any sick person or who aids in abducting a patient or student who has been conditionally discharged from the person or persons in whose care and service that patient or student has been legally placed; shall be fined not more than $500.00 or imprisoned not more than one year, or both."
VA. Code Ann. (1953) 37.1-154 (Supp. 1968)	"It shall be unlawful for any person to knowingly and maliciously contrive or conspire to procure the admission of any person to any hospital."
37.1-155 (Supp. 1968)	"Any person found guilty of violating any provision of this chapter shall be fined not exceeding one thousand dollars or confined in jail not exceeding one year, either or both in the discretion of the jury or the court trying the same."
WASH. Rev. Code Ann. (1962)	
W. VA. Code Ann. (1966) 27-12-1	"Any physician who shall sign a certificate respecting the mental condition of any person without having made the examination as provided for by this chapter, or shall make any statement in such certificate maliciously for the purpose of having such person declared mentally ill, mentally retarded or inebriate, and any person who shall maliciously make application to any circuit court or mental hygiene commission for the purpose of having another person declared mentally ill, mentally retarded, or inebriate, shall be guilty of a misdemeanor, and, upon conviction thereof, shall be fined not exceeding five hundred dollars, or imprisoned not exceeding one year, or both fined and imprisoned at the discretion of the court."
WIS. Stat. Ann. (1957)	

Table 5.6   UNWARRANTED HOSPITALIZATION   continued

STATE AND CITATION

WYO. Stat. Ann. (1967)
   25-89

PENALTIES

"Any person who wilfully causes or conspires with or assists another to cause:
(a) the unwarranted hospitalization of any individual-or (b) the denial to any
individual of any of the rights accorded to him under the provisions of this act,
shall be guilty of a felony, and upon conviction shall be punished by a fine not
exceeding $5000.00 or imprisonment not exceeding five years, or both."

Table 5.7   SPECIAL RESIDENCE PROVISIONS APPLICABLE TO HOSPITALIZATION AND DEPORTATION OF MENTAL PATIENTS

State	Establishment of Residence	Loss of Residence	Special Provisions	Statutory Provisions for Service to Nonresidents	Adoption of Interstate Compact of Mental Health
Draft Act					
ALA. Code (1958)					
ALAS. Stat. (1962)	superior court makes finding as to residence. 47.30.170(a), 47.30.070(j)			"if the patient is certified by the head of a hospital to be mentally ill and (1) dangerous to himself or to others if allowed at liberty, or (2) in need of immediate custody and care or treatment, and lacking sufficient insight and capacity to make responsible decisions concerning hospitalization." 47.30.170(a)	47.30.180
ARIZ. Rev. Stat. Ann. (1956)	1 year 36-522(B) (Supp. 1970)			superintendent may return a nonresident to proper authorities in the state of his residence. 36-522A (Supp. 1970)	
ARK. Stat. Ann. (1948)	59-229 (Supp. 1967)			mentally ill and in urgent need of immediate hospitalization. 59-229 (Supp. 1967)	59-401 (Supp. 1967)
CAL. Welf. & Inst'ns Code (West 1966)	one year continuously; time in public institution for the care of the mentally ill or mental defectives or on parole not counted. 4120 (Supp. 1968)	"who has not acquired residence in another state by living continuously therein for at least one year subsequent . . . ." 4120 (Supp. 1968)		prompt and humane return. 4119, 4121 (Supp. 1968)	
COLO. Rev. Stat. Ann. (1964)	1 year; time in public institution or on parole not counted. 71-1-22(2) (Supp. 1965)	insane person does not lose residency until he gains residence elsewhere by living therein for at least 1 year subsequent to his residence in Colorado. 71-1-22(2) (Supp. 1965)	71-1-22 (Supp. 1965)	until arrangements can be made to return them to their home state. 71-1-22(1) (Supp. 1965)	74-11-1 (Supp. 1965)
CONN. Gen. Stat. Ann. (1958)					17-258
DEL. Code Ann. (1953)				may receive nonresident "who is able to pay for his maintenance and support." 16-5129(a)	16-6101 (Supp. 1966)
D.C. Code Ann. (1967)	1 year prior to filing commitment petition. 21-551			patient is to be returned if an institution in that state is willing to accept him. 21-551	
FLA. Stat. Ann. (1960)	1 year continuously, immediately preceding. 394.27		residence may not be established while a person is, by any state, adjudicated incompetent. 394.271	nonresident may not be admitted pending transfer, 394.27(1); nonresident who is dangerous may be hospitalized, at discretion of the director of the division of mental health, if the patient cannot be transferred. 394.27(2)	

Table 5.7   SPECIAL RESIDENCE PROVISIONS APPLICABLE TO HOSPITALIZATION AND DEPORTATION OF MENTAL PATIENTS   *continued*

State	Establishment of Residence	Loss of Residence	Special Provisions	Statutory Provisions for Service to Nonresidents	Adoption of Interstate Compact of Mental Health
GA. Code Ann.	88-501(f) (Supp. 1969)			88-504 (Supp. 1969)	
HAWAII Rev. Stat. Ann. (1968)					335-1
IDAHO Code Ann. (1949)	1 year's actual residence immediately prior to hospitalization. 66-356 (Supp. 1969)		if patient is a minor, residence requirement must be met by guardian. 66-357 time spent by nonresident in institution does not contribute toward residency requirements. 66-359 (Supp. 1969)	hospitalization to be based on medical merits of the case and not on residence. Once hospitalized, indigent patients, when their welfare is not being jeopardized, are to be deported to the state of their residence provided that they will be received in an appropriate hospital. If hospitalization of paying nonresident in no wise interferes with hospitalization of local indigent resident patients, they may remain in the state of Idaho hospitals, but may be deported after 1 year. 66-336 (Supp. 1969)	66-1201 (Supp. 1969)
ILL. Ann. Stat. (Smith-Hurd 1966)	1 year continuously, excluding time in public or private hospitals. 91 1/2, §1-13 (Supp. 1969)	not a resident of another state. 91 1/2, §1-13 (Supp. 1969)		if arrangements cannot be made for patient to be received in the state of his residence. 91 1/2, §12-7 (Supp. 1969)	91 1/2, §50-1 (Supp. 1969)
IND. Ann. Stat. (1964)	1 year continuously, immediately prior to application. 22-213			nonresidents may be admitted where settlement cannot be ascertained or where the circumstances of the case constitute, in the judgment of the commission, a sufficient reason for the suspension of the residence rules. 22-213	22-225
IOWA Code Ann. (1969)				If a hospitalized patient is discovered to be a nonresident, he may be deported if his condition permits such transfer. 230.7 If court finds legal settlement is unknown or not in U.S., patient may be hospitalized at state expense. 230.14	218A.1
KAN. Stat. Ann. (1964)	1 year continuously prior to application. 39-111		minor derives residency from parents. 39-111	state department of social welfare may waive residency requirements in cases where: (1) residence cannot be determined; or (2) a medical emergency exists. 39-111	department may enter into agreements with authorities of other states for arbitration. 39-110 (Supp. 1967) compact adopted. 65-3101 to 65-3106 (Supp. 1968)
KY. Rev. Stat. Ann. (1969)					210.520

Table 5.7   SPECIAL RESIDENCE PROVISIONS APPLICABLE TO HOSPITALIZATION AND DEPORTATION OF MENTAL PATIENTS   *continued*

State	Establishment of Residence	Loss of Residence	Special Provisions	Statutory Provisions for Service to Nonresidents	Adoption of Interstate Compact of Mental Health
LA. Rev. Stat. Ann. (1950)				state will apprehend and detain any person who has fled from another state to (1) escape detention (2) avoid proceedings initiated to declare him insane, and (3) avoid the results of legal proceedings in which he was found insane. 28:503	28:721 (Supp. 1969)
ME. Rev. Stat. Ann. (1965)					34, §2561
MD. Ann. Code (1968)				59, §46	41, §319
MASS. Ann. Laws (1965)					123, §1
MICH. Comp. Laws Ann. (1967)	a mentally diseased person having a legal settlement in this state is entitled to care in the state hospitals when legally admitted thereto. 330.33			may receive temporary care, pending his return to his home. 330.33	330.81
Miss. Code Ann. (1952)	6909-13			temporary care pending return to residence. 6909-21	
MO. Rev. Stat. (1959)	1 year 202.100 (Supp. 1969) 202.415	202.415		may be returned to state of residency. 202.875	202.880
MONT. Rev. Codes Ann. (1961)				"An insane person, nonresident of this state, may be received . . . for a period not to exceed thirty days pending return to the state of his residence." 38-120 (Supp. 1969)	
NEB. Rev. Stat. (1966)	83-323			nonresidents may be accepted on same terms as private pay patients. Nonresidents must make quarterly payment in advance. 83-355	
NEV. Rev. Stat. (1967)	1 year; time spent in or on parole from a public institution is not counted in determining residency. 433.030			nonresident shall be transferred to the state of his residence if an appropriate institution of that state is willing to accept him. 433.697	

Table 5.7   SPECIAL RESIDENCE PROVISIONS APPLICABLE TO HOSPITALIZATION AND DEPORTATION OF MENTAL PATIENTS   *continued*

State	Establishment of Residence	Loss of Residence	Special Provisions	Statutory Provisions for Service to Nonresidents	Adoption of Interstate Compact of Mental Health
N.H. Rev. Stat. Ann. (1964)				the director, division of mental health, in consultation with the advisory commission, may enter into an agreement with the similar board or officer of any other state for the transfer of indigent insane persons from one state to the other where they may be deemed equitably to belong, after an investigation of the facts connected with the case. 135:37	135A:1
N.J. Stat. Ann. (1964)	continuous residence in county for 5 years immediately preceding the date of application for commitment excluding the time, if any, spent by the patient in any charitable or correctional institution or public hospital. 30:4-49 (Supp. 1970)	30:4-49.6 (Supp. 1970)	alien in county for 3 years has legal settlement. 30:4-49 30:4-59 (Supp. 1970)		30-7B-1
N.M. Stat. Ann. (1953)					141
N.Y. Mental Hygiene Law (McKinney 1951)	1 year; time in institution or on military reservation or on parole from out-of-state institutions cannot be included, but time prior and subsequent to commitment or residence on military reservation may be accumulated for purpose of the 1-year requirement. 2.14, 60 (Supp. 1970)	1-year absence unless absence is due to military service. 2.14 (Supp. 1970)	where there is no reciprocal agreement, requirements to obtain residence in N.Y. shall "not be less than those required for the acquisition of residence in the state from which the nonresident comes." 2.14(b) (Supp. 1970)	where there is no reciprocal agreement, nonresidents are to be deported except that the commissioner may defer such action where removal would cause the patient undue hardship and the interest of the state or other patients would not be materially harmed by such deferment. 23.4	
N.C. Gen. Stat. (1964)	The "county of residence" of an alleged mentally ill, mentally retarded, or inebriate person shall be the county of his actual residence at the time of his hospitalization notwithstanding that such person may have been temporarily out of the county of his residence, in a hospital, or under court order a patient of some other state institution at the time of his hospitalization. A county of residence shall not have been changed by virtue of a person being temporarily out of his county in a hospital, or confined under court order. N.C. 122-26(a)		122-37 122-39 122-40 (Supp. 1967)	patient is committed to state hospital until arrangement can be made to send him back to the state of residence. 122-38	122-99
N.D. Cent. Code (1960)				nonresidents may be admitted if they defray the actual cost of hospitalization, but not to exclusion of residents. 25-02-06	25-11-01 (Supp. 1969)
OHIO Rev. Code Ann. (Baldwin 1964)	12 consecutive months next preceding date of application; shall not have received relief or custodial care during such 12 months. 5123.31		no care need be provided if condition existed before patient acquired residence. 5123.31	in making transfers, commissioner of mental health insofar as practicable is to employ nurses or attendants instead of law officers and is to employ female nurses or attendants to accompany female patients. 5123.32	5123.63

Table 5.7   SPECIAL RESIDENCE PROVISIONS APPLICABLE TO HOSPITALIZATION AND DEPORTATION OF MENTAL PATIENTS   continued

State	Establishment of Residence	Loss of Residence	Special Provisions	Statutory Provisions for Service to Nonresidents	Adoption of Interstate Compact of Mental Health
OKLA. Stat. Ann. (1954)	live continuously within the state 1 year immediately preceding certification exclusive of time spent in institutions. 43A, §3(k) (Supp. 1969)			the director of mental health is to keep a list of all hospitalized nonresidents and to make every effort possible for the deportation of mentally ill and mentally retarded persons cared for at public expense. 43A, §§14(12), 71 (Supp. 1969)	43A, §501 (Supp. 1969)
ORE. Rev. Stat. (1967)	1 year exclusive of time spent in institutions. 428.210(6)	continues until new one acquired. 428.210(6)		nonresident patients returned to state of residence; costs paid by the state. 428.230	428.310
PA. Stat. Ann. (1969)					62, §1121 (1968)
R.I. Gen. Laws Ann. (1968)				director of social welfare is authorized to remove nonresident paupers who have been committed to state institutions to the state of their residence. 26-2-4	26-6-1
S.C. Code Ann. (1962)				notice is to be given to state of residence of committed nonresidents, and arrangements are to be made for their delivery. 32-1024	32-1051
S.D. Compiled Laws Ann. (1967)					27-19-1
TENN. Code Ann. (1955)				temporary care until transfer to state of residency is arranged. 33-319, 33-1106 (Supp. 1968)	
TEX. Rev. Civ. Stat. Ann. (1958)	1 year; time spent in public institution or on leave of absence therefrom shall not be counted on determining residency. 5547-4(n) (Supp. 1969)	"and who has not acquired residence in another state by living continuously therein for at least one (1) year subsequent . . . ." 5547-4(n) (Supp. 1969)		"board" may return nonresidents to state of residency. 5547-16	
UTAH Code Ann. (1968)	1 year immediately preceding application for admittance. 64-7-14	see "Establishment of Residence" column.		Temporary care of persons stricken with mental illness while traveling through or temporarily sojourning in state. The director of division of mental health upon the recommendation of the superintendent of hospital may admit patients from other states upon the request of the patient's physician; provided that a sum not less than is now charged for voluntary patients is to be paid in advance monthly for their care. 64-7-14	
VT. Stat. Ann. (1968)	18, §7101(15)				

Table 5.7   SPECIAL RESIDENCE PROVISIONS APPLICABLE TO HOSPITALIZATION AND DEPORTATION OF MENTAL PATIENTS   *continued*

State	Establishment of Residence	Loss of Residence	Special Provisions	Statutory Provisions for Service to Nonresidents	Adoption of Interstate Compact of Mental Health
VA. Code Ann. (1953) (Supp. 1968)	1 year 37.1-1 (12)			same proceedings shall be held with regard to him as if he were a resident. 37.1-91	
WASH. Rev. Code Ann. (1962)	maintenance of domiciliary residence in state for a period of 1 year preceding commitment to a state institution without receiving assistance from any tax-supported organization and who has not subsequently acquired a domicile in another state. 72.25.020 (Supp. 1969)			arrangement with the U.S. Department of Interior or the Bureau of Immigration for the deportation of insane aliens to such points as may be designated by the Department of Interior or Bureau of Immigration. 72.25.010 (Supp. 1969) return of all nonresident insane to the state of legal residence. Expenses of return shall be paid by state of Washington. 72.25.020 (Supp. 1969)	72.27.010 (Supp. 1969)
W. VA. Code Ann. (1966)	1 year 27-1-8				27-14-1
WIS. Stat. Ann. (1957)					51.75 (Supp. 1969)
WYO. Stat. Ann. (1967)				expense of returning nonresident patients shall be paid by Wyoming. 25-76	25-90

Table 5.8   TRANSFER OF PATIENTS WITHIN THE STATE

STATE	TRANSFER FROM STATE HOSPITAL				TRANSFER FROM PRIVATE HOSPITAL		NOTICE OF ANY TRANSFER		NEW ADJUDICATION
	One State Institution to Another	Approval or Initiation by	State to Private Hospital	Approval by Initiation by	Initiation by	Approval by	Guardian, Spouse, or Relative	Other	
DRAFT ACT	14(a)	central administration 14(a)	1(e); 14(a)	central administration 1(e); 14(a)	central administration 1(e); 14(a)		14(a); 14(b)	committing court 14(b)	
ALA. Code (1958)									
ALAS. Stat. (1962)	fn. 1 47.30.160(a)	47.30.160(a)	fn. 1 47.30.160(a)	department of health and welfare. 47.30.160(a)			47.30.160(c)	superior court, if judicially hospitalized. 47.30.160(c)	
ARIZ. Rev. Stat. Ann. (1956) (Supp. 1970)	designated facility 36-523A	superintendent initiates; written consent of patient, parents, spouse, or guardian. 36-523A	other designated facility. 36-523A	superintendent initiates; written consent of patient, parents, spouse, or guardian. 36-523A			consent needed 36-523A		
ARK. Stat. Ann. (1947) (Supp. 1967)	fn. 2 59-234	fn. 2 59-234	59-234	fn. 2 59-234		59-234 (Supp. 1967)	fn. 2 59-234 (Supp. 1967)		
CAL. Welf. & Inst'ns Code (West 1966) (Supp. 1968)	4122; 7300	initiated by director of institutions or at request of relatives or friends. 7300; 7302							
COLO. Rev. Stat. Ann. (1964)									
CONN. Gen. Stat. Ann. (1958)	17-192	probate court 17-192 superintendent with approval of commissioner. 17-193	17-192 17-193	probate court 17-192 superintendent with approval of commissioner. 17-193	probate court 17-192 superintendent with approval of commissioner 17-193			court 17-193	fn. 3 17-193
DEL. Code Ann. (1953)	16-5324(a)	committing court 16-5324(a)							
D.C. Code Ann. (1967)									
FLA. Stat. Ann. (1960)	394.18 (Supp. 1969)	board of commissioners of state institutions. 394.18 (Supp. 1969)							
GA. Code Ann. (1963) (Supp. 1969)	88-502.13(b)	administrator 88-502.13(b)	88-502.13(a)	88-502.13(a)	88-502.13(a)	88-502.13(a)	representatives 88-502.13(a)		
HAWAII Rev. Stat. Ann. (1968)	334-1; 334-71(a)	administrator 334-71(a)	334-71; 334-71(a)	administrator 334-71(a)	334-71; 334-71(a)		334-71(c)	family court 334-71(c)	
IDAHO Code Ann. (1949) (Supp. 1969)	66-317(f); 66-334(a)	state board of health or its designee. 66-334(a)	66-317(f); 66-334(a)	state board of health or its designee. 66-334(a)	state board of health or its designee. 66-334(a)		66-334	friend 66-334	
ILL. Ann. Stat. (Smith-Hurd 1966) (Supp. 1969)	91½, §12-4	central agency 91½, §12-4	or relative 91½, §12-4	patient or relative initiates; court must approve. 91½, §12-4	hospital, patient or relative. 91½, §12-4	court 91½, §12-4			

Table 5.8 TRANSFER OF PATIENTS WITHIN THE STATE *continued*

STATE	TRANSFER FROM STATE HOSPITAL				TRANSFER FROM PRIVATE HOSPITAL		NOTICE OF ANY TRANSFER		NEW ADJUDICATION
	One State Institution to Another	Approval or Initiation by	State to Private Hospital	Approval by / Initiation by	Initiation by	Approval by	Guardian Spouse, or Relative	Other	
fn. 4 IND. Ann. Stat. (1964)	22-303	mutual consent of superintendents. 22-303							
IOWA Code Ann. (1969)		state director or commission. 227.11	227.11	state director or commission. 227.11	"on application" 227.10; 229.29	state director 227.10 central agency 227.29			if more than 6 months since adjudication. 229.29
KAN. Stat. Ann. (1964) (Supp. 1968)	59-2924	state director of institutions. 59-2924							
KY. Rev. Stat. Ann. (1969)	202.235(1)	commissioner 202.235(1)					202.235(1)		
fn. 5 LA. Rev. Stat. Ann. (1950)	28:94A	superintendent or central agency may initiate. 28:94A	28:94A	joint application of superintendent and guardian or person liable for support. 28:94A	superintendent and guardian or person liable for support. 28:94A				
ME. Rev. Stat. Ann. (1965)	fn. 6 34, §2373	department 34, §2373	34, §2373		department 34, §2373		34, §2373		
MD. Ann. Code (1968)	59, §40	commissioner of mental hygiene. 59, §40					59, §40		
fn. 7 MASS. Ann. Laws (1965)		department of mental health. 123, §20		department of mental health. 123, §20	department of mental health, hospital, and guardian 123, §20	central agency 123, §20	123, §20		
MICH. Comp. Laws Ann. (1967) (Supp. 1969)	330.19b	fn. 8 330.19b			330.19b		330.19b	court which ordered admission. 330.19b	
MINN. Stat. Ann. (1959) (Supp. 1969)	fn. 9 253A.14	commissioner of public welfare. 253A.14					253A.14	court 253A.14	
MISS. Code Ann. (1952)	6778								
MO. Rev. Stat. (1959)	202.823	division of mental diseases. 202.823					202.823		
MONT. Rev. Codes Ann. (1961)	38-301								
NEB. Rev. Stat. (1966)	from county institution. 83-334	county board members. 83-334							
NEV. Rev. Stat. (1967)									
N.H. Rev. Stat. Ann. (1964)									

Table 5.8   TRANSFER OF PATIENTS WITHIN THE STATE   *continued*

STATE	TRANSFER FROM ONE STATE INSTITUTION TO ANOTHER		TRANSFER FROM STATE HOSPITAL		TRANSFER FROM PRIVATE HOSPITAL		NOTICE OF ANY TRANSFER		NEW ADJUDICATION
	One State Institution to Another	Approval or Initiation by	State to Private Hospital	Approval by Initiation by	Initiation by	Approval by	Guardian Spouse, or Relative	Other	
N.J. Stat. Ann. (1964) (Supp. 1970)	fn. 10 30:4-83; 30:4-84.1	fn. 11 commissioner 30:4-83					30:4-83.1	commissioner 30:4-83.1	
N.M. Stat. Ann. (1953)	fn. 12 34-2-10	head of hospital. 34-2-10							
N.Y. Mental Hygiene Law (McKinney 1951)									
N.C. Gen. Stat. (1964)	122-13; 122-13	fn. 13 122-13	122-80					fn. 14 122-80	
N.D. Cent. Code (1960)	25-03-14	state hospital superintendent. 25-03-14	25-03-14	relative or guardian. 25-03-14			25-03-14		
OHIO Rev. Code Ann. (Baldwin 1964)	5122.20; 5123.46	fn. 15 5122.20; 5123.46					5122.20		
OKLA. Stat. Ann. (1954)	43A, §62	director of mental health and board of control of neuropsychiatric unit. 43A, §62			fn. 16 43A, §188 (Supp. 1969)	state hospital superintendent. 43A, §188 (Supp. 1969)			
ORE. Rev. Stat. (1967)									
PA. Stat. Ann. (1969)	50, §4416(a)	50, §4416(a)					50; §4416(e)		
R.I. Gen. Laws (1968)	Butler Hospital to state hospital. 26-2-4	director of social welfare. 26-2-4							
S.C. Code Ann. (1962)	32-1018	health commission 32-1018					32-1018	friend 34-1018	
S.D. Compiled Laws Ann. (1967)									
TENN. Code Ann. (1955) (Supp. 1968)	fn. 17 33-309; 33-1206	33-309	33-309	33-309	33-309	33-309	fn. 18 33-1206	committing authority 33-309	
TEX. Rev. Civ. Stat. Ann. (1958)	5547-73(a)	board 5547-73(a)	5547-74	patient, head of private hospital. 5547-74	hospital, head of private hospital. 5547-73(b)			court, central agency. 5547-73; 5547-74(c)	
UTAH Code Ann. (1968)	64-7-41(1)	division of mental health. 64-7-41(1)					at least 10 days prior to transfer. 64-7-41(1)		
VT. Stat. Ann. (1968)	18, §7901	commissioner 18, §7901					18, §7901	attorney 18, §7901	
VA. Code Ann. (1953) (Supp. 1968)	37.1-48; 37.1-86	commissioner 37.1-48; 37.1-86	37.1-1(8); 37.1-48; 37.1-86	commissioner 37.1-48; 37.1-86					

Table 5.8 TRANSFER OF PATIENTS WITHIN THE STATE   *continued*

| STATE | TRANSFER FROM STATE HOSPITAL | | | | TRANSFER FROM PRIVATE HOSPITAL | | NOTICE OF ANY TRANSFER | | NEW ADJUDICATION |
	One State Institution to Another	Approval or Initiation by	State to Private Hospital	Approval by Initiation by	Initiation by	Approval by	Guardian Spouse, or Relative	Other	
WASH. Rev. Code Ann. (1962)	72.23.290	superintendent 72.23.290							
W.VA. Code Ann. (1966)									
WIS. Stat. Ann. (1957)	51.12(1); 51.125	department 51.12(1); 51.125						court 51.12; 51.125	
WYO. Stat. Ann. (1967)	25-67	board 25-67	25-49(e); 25-67	board 25-67	board 25-67		or friend 25-67		

205

1. In the determination, consideration shall be given to the maintenance of the relationship of the patient to his family, legal guardian, or friends and the encouragement of visits beneficial to the patient. Alas. 47.30.160(a).

2. With certification of licensed, regularly practicing psychiatrist and at discretion of head or board of hospital. Ark. 59-234 (Supp. 1969).

3. Upon application by a conservator, overseer, member of the family, or friend of the patient, the committing court shall hold a hearing to determine whether the transfer agreement should be revoked, modified, or affirmed. Conn. 17-193.

4. Section 22-302, which may or may not be in force, provides for notification of the transfer to the court, and limits transfers to no more than 1 in 5 years. Ind. 22-302.

5. A voluntary patient shall be transferred only with his written consent. La. 28:94A(3).

6. Department may transfer a patient from one hospital to another either within or out of state if the department determines it would be consistent with the medical needs of the patient to do so. Me. 34, §2373.

7. Voluntary patients and those under observational hospitalization may not be transferred. Mass. 123, §20.

8. Department of mental health may, upon recommendation of the medical superintendent involved, transfer patients. Mich. 330.19b (Supp. 1969).

9. From one state hospital or institution to any other hospital or other institution. Minn. 253A.14 (Supp. 1969).

10. Transfers may be temporary or indefinite. N.J. 30:4-83, 30:4-84.1 (Supp. 1970).

11. By order of the commissioner or upon application of the chief executive officer. N.J. 30-483 (Supp. 1970).

12. Transfer to United States facilities. N.M. 34-2-9, 10.

13. Usually the transfer is to be in accordance with rules and reculations promulgated by the North Carolina State Board of Mental Health. N.C. 122-13. However, transfers from the Psychiatric Training and Research Center at Chapel Hill to a state hospital or institution may be effected upon recommendation of the director of the inpatient service of the Research Center and approval of the superintendent of the appropriate state hospital. N.C. 122-13.1.

14. A certificate of transfer must be filed with the committing court only in the case of transfers from a state hospital to a private facility. N.C. 122-80.

15. Approval by the board of county commissioners must be secured for any transfer to a county home. Ohio 5123.46.

16. Transfer may be initiated by the attending physician, the person in charge of the private facility, or the petitioner, relative, or guardian of the patient. Okla. 43A, §188 (Supp. 1969),

17. An involuntary patient may be transferred from a public institution to a private institution, or vice versa, upon application of the patient or his spouse, guardian, or a responsible relative and approval of the commissioner and the superintendent of the private institution. Tenn. 33-309 (Supp. 1968).

18. For transfer of a voluntary patient, notice shall be given to patient's guardian, parent, spouse, or other person upon whose application such patient was originally admitted. Tenn. 33-1206 (Supp. 1968).

Chapter Six Eugenic Sterilization

I. INTRODUCTION

Sterilization is the surgical means by which both male and female are rendered incapable of reproduction. The operation is much more serious in women than in men. In females the surgeon must do an abdominal operation, removing segments of the fallopian tubes (salpingectomy) and tying the cut ends. In men the operation is relatively simple. Small scrotal skin incisions are made, segments of the vas deferens are removed (vasectomy), and the proximal ends of the vas are tied. Neither operation interferes with the desire for sexual intercourse or with its gratification.[1] Sterilization operations are effective in nearly 100 percent of the cases: failure actually to sterilize occurs in 1 to 2 percent of operations performed on both males and females. Salpingectomy is at present irreversible, although research to effect reversibility is continuing. Vasectomy is reversible on occasion: some estimates place the chance of success at between 35 and 40 percent, others profess a 50-percent chance of restoration.[2]

Four fundamental considerations have been advanced for the use of sterilization: (1) therapeutic purposes,[3] such as the cure or treatment of certain diseases or malfunctions, or the preservation of the health of a woman when it can be reasonably calculated by competent medical authority that pregnancy or childbirth would be fatal; (2) socioeconomic reasons prompting a number of people to undergo the operation purely for birth control purposes in states where there are no statutes prohibiting the operation for this purpose;[4] (3) punitive purposes in some states[5] authorizing the sterilization of hereditary criminals and sex offenders; and (4) eugenic purposes. This last consideration is based on the assumption that certain types of individuals are socially more desirable than others and that the improvement of future generations can be accomplished by increasing the proportion of individuals of the desirable types through decreasing the rate of propagation of the inferior individuals.[6] Proponents of this principle, relying on scientific claims that certain types of mental disabilities are inheritable traits, advocate the sterilization of persons possessing these traits.

This chapter deals with laws permitting the involuntary sterilization of the mentally disabled.

Although statutes authorizing sterilization for eugenic purposes have existed in the United States for approximately sixty years, the controversy over the constitutionality and the practicality of the laws still waxes strong. Before deciding whether the rights of the mentally disabled are protected in this field, there are many factors to consider in addition to contents of the statutory provisions. Why were sterilization statutes originally passed? Do they accomplish their purposes? Is it possible that the conditions which were originally thought to justify the creation of such statutes no longer exist?

II. HISTORICAL BACKGROUND AND SCOPE

Until the end of the nineteenth century sterilization was impractical because castration, the only method known at the time, caused undesirable changes in secondary sex characteristics and was considered too radical an operation to use for eugenic reasons.[7] In the last decade of the century, however, Dr. Harry C. Sharpe of the Indiana State Reformatory developed a method of sterilizing males (vasectomy), and at about the same time the now stand-

---

1. Deutsch, *The Mentally Ill in America* 371 (2d ed. 1949).

2. Comment, "Sterilization: A Continuing Controversy," 1 *U.S.F.L. Rev.* 159, 161 (1966), citing St. John-Stevas, *Law and Morals* 95 (1964); Landman, *Human Sterilization* 233 (1932); Woodside, *Sterilization in North Carolina: A Sociological and Psychological Study* 162 (1950).

3. Clarke, *Social Legislation* 195 (2d ed. 1957).

4. Ibid. See also Christensen v. Thornby, 192 Minn. 123, 255 N.W. 620 (1934), holding that a voluntary operation to sterilize a man in order to protect his wife from conception and the grave dangers of childbirth is not against public policy where the statutes do not prohibit such operations.

5. See O'Hara & Sanks, "Eugenic Sterilization," 45 *Geo. L.J.* 20, 34, 42 (1956). California, Delaware, Georgia, Idaho, Iowa,

Oklahoma, Oregon, Utah, and Wisconsin provide for compulsory sterilization of "hereditary criminals"; and California, Georgia, Idaho, Iowa, Michigan, and Oregon include in their statutes such groups as sex offenders and syphilitics.

6. Jennings, "Eugenics," 5 *Encyclopedia of Social Science* 618, 619 (1931).

7. O'Hara & Sanks, *supra* note 5.

ard method of sterilizing females (salpingectomy) was developed in France.[8]

The United States was the pioneer in the field of sterilization legislation, but this lead came only after much legislative and judicial opposition.[9] Although the first bill on the subject was introduced in a state legislature almost immediately after the perfection of the new surgical techniques, it was thirty years before the constitutionality of compulsory sterilization of the mentally disabled was sustained by the United States Supreme Court.[10]

The first bill was introduced in 1897 in the state of Michigan, but is was defeated.[11] In 1905, the Pennsylvania legislature passed a sterilization bill "for the prevention of idiocy," which has been summarized as follows:

> It provided that upon enactment, "it shall be compulsory for each and every institution in the State, entrusted . . . with the care of idiots . . . to appoint" a neurologist and a surgeon "to examine the mental and physical condition of the inmates." If this examination showed that there was "no probability of improvement of the mental condition of the inmate" and "procreation is inadvisable," the surgeon was authorized "to perform such operation for the prevention of procreation as shall be decided safest and most effective."[12]

The bill was vetoed by the governor, who returned it with this message:

> This Bill has, what may be called with propriety, an attractive title. If idiocy could be prevented by an Act of Assembly, we may be quite sure that such an act would have long been passed and approved in this State, and . . . in all civilized countries. . . . The nature of the operation is not described, but it is such an operation as they shall decide to be safest and most effective. It is plain that the safest and most effective method of preventing procreation would be to cut the heads off the inmates, and such authority is given by the Bill to this staff of scientific experts. . . .[13]

Indiana finally enacted the first compulsory sterilization law in 1907.[14] Even before 1907, superintendents of mental hospitals in several states were secretly having mentally deficient persons sterilized. In fact, it is asserted that Dr. Sharpe, who perfected the vasectomy operation, secretly and illegally sterilized several hundred males at the Indiana State Reformatory before the passage of the Indiana law.[15] The Indiana statute was later declared unconstitutional,[16] as were other similar statutes which came before the courts prior to 1925.[17]

In 1925 the highest courts of Michigan[18] and Virginia[19] held that the sterilization statutes of their respective states were constitutional. Two years later the constitutionality of the Virginia statute was upheld by the United States Supreme Court in *Buck v. Bell*.[20]

In the ten years following this Supreme Court decision, twenty states passed sterilization statutes, most of them closely resembling the Virginia law.[21] In all, thirty-two states and the Commonwealth of Puerto Rico have enacted sterilization statutes, five of which have been declared unconstitutional.[22] Controversy continues over the merits of this legis-

8. Ibid.

9. Landman, "The History of Human Sterilization in the United States—Theory, Statute, Adjudication," 23 *Ill. L. Rev.* 463, 472 (1929).

10. Buck v. Bell, 274 U.S. 200 (1927).

11. O'Hara & Sanks, *supra* note 5, at 22.

12. Challener, "The Law of Sexual Sterilization in Pennsylvania," 57 *Dick. L. Rev.* 298 (1952).

13. Pennsylvania, Vetoes by the Governor of Bills Passed by the Legislature, Session of 1905, p. 26. Cited in Challener, *supra* note 12, at 299 n.1.

14. Ind. Acts 1907, ch. 215. Cited in O'Hara & Sanks, *supra* note 5, at 22 n.17.

15. Deutsch, *supra* note 1, at 370.

16. Williams v. Smith, 190 Ind. 526, 131 N.E. 2 (1921).

17. Smith v. Bd. of Exmrs. of Feeble-minded, 85 N.J.L. 46, 88 A. 963 (1913); Haynes v. Lapeer Circuit Judge, 201 Mich. 138, 166 N.W. 938 (1918); *In re* Thompson, 103 Misc. 23, 169 N.Y.S. 638 (Sup. Ct. 1918), *aff'd mem. sub nom.* Osborn v. Thompson, 185 App. Div. 902, 171 N.Y.S. 1094 (3d Dep't 1918).

18. Smith v. Command, 231 Mich. 409, 204 N.W. 140 (1925). This decision upheld Mich. Pub. Acts 1923, No. 285, which authorized the sterilization of mentally deficient persons but did not include mentally ill persons.

19. Buck v. Bell, 143 Va. 310, 130 S.E. 516 (1925), *aff'd,* 274 U.S. 200 (1927). This decision upheld Va. Pub. Acts 1924, ch. 394, which, like the Michigan statute (*supra* note 18), authorized the sterilization of mentally deficient persons and did not include mentally ill persons.

20. 274 U.S. 200 (1927).

21. Note, "Human Sterilization," 35 *Iowa L. Rev.* 251, 253 n.12 (1950).

22. The sterilization laws of Nevada, New Jersey, New York, and Washington have been declared unconstitutional and have not been reenacted. The Alabama law was held unconstitutional in an advisory opinion by the Alabama Supreme Court—*In re* Opinion of the Justices, 230 Ala. 543, 162 So. 123 (1935). The Alabama law remains on the statute books (*Ala. Code* tit. 45, § 243 (1959)), but it has been inoperative since the 1935 opinion. See Ferster, "Eliminating the Unfit—Is Sterilization the Answer?" 27 *Ohio St. L.J.* 591 (1966).

lation, though the balance appears to have shifted more in the direction of opposition to such legislation. In the past few years, Kansas and Montana have repealed their sterilization laws. Connecticut, Nebraska, and North Dakota recently repealed the compulsory aspects of their statutes, and now permit only voluntary sterilization.

Opposition to the sterilization laws has also come in the form of medical and legal criticism. In 1965 the Board of Directors of the Association for Voluntary Sterilization, formerly known as the Human Betterment Association, "unanimously voted that this Association is opposed to compulsion of any kind [in regard to sterilization], either directly or implicit."[23] In April 1969, the American Civil Liberties Union Board of Directors adopted a similar policy statement.[24] Even more significantly perhaps, opposition is shown in the decline in actual application of the sterilization laws. The number of sterilizations has decreased steadily during the past twenty-five years. Reaching a peak during the 1920s and 1930s, sterilizations under the statutes dropped to a low of 467 in 1963. In fact, the Human Betterment Association stopped tabulating such sterilizations after that year, concluding that the figures had become statistically insignificant.[25] Currently, some five states are not using their sterilization statutes at all and have not done so for over a decade.[26] Only six or seven states have averaged more than fifteen sterilizations per year over the past two decades.[27]

One state, North Carolina, in 1963 accounted for 240 sterilizations—more than 50 percent of all sterilizations under the statutes in the United States —but all were claimed to have been performed with the consent of the patient or a relative.[28]

Decrease in the utilization of the sterilization statutes is "probably due to a rejection of the view that mental illness and mental retardation are hereditary."[29] The decrease was *not* caused by court decisions. Sterilization orders have rarely been attacked in the courts during the period of decline. Few amendments of the sterilization laws have been made by state legislatures. Recently the United States Supreme Court seemed ready to take the opportunity to follow through on the practiced rejection of the sterilization statutes and rule so as to invalidate all sterilization statutes which include the probability of compulsion, but the case which would have provided this opportunity was later dismissed.[30]

III. COMPARATIVE ANALYSIS OF STATUTORY PROVISIONS

The procedure for authorizing an involuntary sterilization varies considerably from state to state. Some states have detailed requirements concerning hearing, counsel, medical evidence, and appeal, while others offer little or no procedural protection of the rights of patients. Table 6.1, Sterilization, ap-

23. Letter to the American Bar Foundation from the Association of Voluntary Sterilization, Inc. (John R. Rague, Executive Director, July 7, 1969). The Association, while strongly opposed to compulsory sterilization, advocates voluntary sterilization—provided it is truly voluntary—as the only effective birth control method. The Association notes that while compulsory sterilization in the United States is declining, voluntary operations are becoming increasingly popular. The estimate is that some 2,000,000 living Americans had chosen voluntary contraceptive sterilization by 1963. The Association recently provided legal assistance on the plaintiff's side in the California case of *Jessin v. County of Shasta*, 79 Cal. Rptr. 359 (1969), wherein a woman was suing the county and the county hospital for refusing to provide her with a requested sterilization operation; the Association has notified the American Bar Foundation that the *Jessin* case has been decided in favor of the plaintiff.

24. Personal letter, *supra* note 23.

25. Ibid.

26. Ferster, *supra* note 22, at 599. The states not using their statutes are Arizona, Mississippi, Montana, Oklahoma, and West Virginia. As noted earlier, Alabama's law has been inoperative for some thirty-five years as the result of an adverse advisory opinion by its Supreme Court.

27. Georgia, Iowa, Michigan, North Carolina, Oregon, Virginia, and possibly Delaware. Ferster, *supra* note 22, at 599.

28. Id. at 601. Doubts have been expressed concerning the voluntariness of "voluntary" or "consensual" sterilizations. This point will be discussed later in this chapter at § IV C 3, Procedural Due Process.

29. Id. at 599.

30. The Association for Voluntary Sterilization, *supra* note 23, stated in July 1969: "A landmark rule on the question of mandatory sterilization of mentally retarded persons may be made this year by the United States Supreme Court. The action stems from a June 1968 Nebraska Supreme Court ruling upholding its earlier decision that the state law permitting sterilization of mentally deficient persons is constitutional. In a case involving Gloria Cavitt, a medical board concluded that she could be released from the state mental institution if she would agree to sterilization. The woman's lawyer challenged the action of the Nebraska Court, and the United States Supreme Court agreed in February 1969 to rule on the authority of a state to sterilize 'mentally defective' persons on the ground that their children might be improperly cared for or might become welfare cases. The Nebraska Legislature has repealed the mandatory sterilization law, but the repealer does not take effect until after November of this year, which gives the U.S. Supreme Court ample time to act on the Cavitt appeal." See *In re* Cavitt, 182 Neb. 712, 157 N.W.2d 171 (1968); *rehearing*, 183 Neb. 243, 159 N.W.2d 566 (1968). On February 1969, the United States Supreme Court noted "probable jurisdiction" (393 U.S. 1078 (1969)), but on January 8, 1970 the *Cavitt* case was "dismissed . . . under rule 60." (396 U.S. 996 (1970)).

pearing at the end of this chapter, gives a ready comparison of the provisions of the sterilization statutes of the states having such legislation.

Although it has been claimed that today most operations are performed with the consent of the patient,[31] only Connecticut, Minnesota, Nebraska, North Dakota, and Vermont require that the operation be performed on that basis alone.[32] Connecticut and North Dakota changed from involuntary sterilization provisions to voluntary ones as recently as 1965. The Nebraska legislature repealed the mandatory part of its statute in 1969.[33] The remaining twenty-one states which have statutes on the subject provide for involuntary or compulsory sterilization of the mentally disabled. The statutes in all of the states providing for involuntary sterilization are applicable to patients in state institutions; eight of these states further provide that persons outside of such institutions also come within the purview of compulsory sterilization laws.[34]

The sterilization statutes of all the states list the mentally deficient as subject to sterilization, and with a few exceptions the mentally ill are similarly identified as being within the scope of the statutes.[35] Thirteen states still include epileptics in their designation of the classes of persons subject to such laws.[36] Other classifications or groups not considered in this chapter, such as "hereditary criminals," sex offenders, and syphilitics, are also included in a significant number of the compulsory sterilization statutes.[37]

The involuntary procedure may be commenced in nineteen states by an application from the superintendent of the institution where the patient is confined for an order authorizing the operation.[38] In the remaining states as well as in some of the states where the hospital superintendent is authorized to do so, the application may be submitted by such other individuals and agencies as physicians, guardians, relatives, state welfare commissions,

sheriffs, superintendents of the poor, supervisors of townships, and boards and commissions supervising public welfare.[39]

Sixteen of the states having involuntary sterilization statutes designate an administrative agency with authority to order sterilization.[40] One of these—Delaware—fails to provide expressly for a hearing before that agency.[41] Three states provide for a judicial hearing in addition to the administrative procedure.[42] In Arkansas and Michigan the judicial hearing is the exclusive procedure. Three states provide for neither a hearing procedure nor a hearing agency.[43] In those states where the statutes designate administrative agencies with authority to order sterilization, the superintendent of the state mental institution is usually a member of such agency, but otherwise these agencies vary considerably in type and composition from state to state.[44]

As far as notice of the application and hearing are concerned, seventeen states provide for notice to the patient; several states must notify the patient's closest kin or relatives; three states provide for notification to the central state hospital agency; and all but a few states provide for notice to the patient's guardian.[45] Most of these states specify a definite period of time in their notice provisions, usually requiring a minimum of thirty days, though three states require only ten days, and one twenty days.[46]

In addition to designating certain classes of the

31. Guttmacher & Weihofen, *Psychiatry and the Law* 188 (1952). See also the North Carolina experience alluded to in text accompanying note 28 *supra*.

32. See Table 6.1, Sterilization, for the statutory citations.

33. See personal letter, *supra* note 23. The repealer became effective in November 1969; it has not yet been codified.

34. See Table 6.1, Applicability columns.

35. Ibid.

36. Ibid.

37. See O'Hara & Sanks, *supra* note 5, at 34, 42; Ferster, *supra* note 22.

38. See Table 6.1, Application By columns.

39. Ibid.

40. Id. at Hearing Agency columns.

41. Ibid.

42. Id. at Hearing and Hearing Agency columns: Idaho, Indiana, and Iowa.

43. Id.: Alabama, Maine, and South Dakota.

44. Id. at Hearing Agency columns. Illustrative of this variation are the following administrative agencies or persons specified by the various statutes: State Board of Medical Examiners, Director of Mental Hygiene, Hospital Superintendent and two outside surgeons appointed by him, Superintendent and one physician and one alienist appointed by the Department of Welfare, State Board of Eugenics (composed of the Directors of the Social Security Board, State Board of Health and the Superintendents of the State Hospitals), State Counsel for Mental Health, Superintendent of State Mental Hospitals with the Chief Medical Officer and the Secretary of the Board of Health, Board of Directors or Board of Trustees of the hospital, five members of the Board of Examiners, Executive Committee of the State Board of Health, three competent physicians and surgeons appointed by the Board of Examiners, Board of Mental Health, Executive Committee of the State Board of Health, State Hospital Board, and Public Health Counsel.

45. See Table 6.1, Notice columns.

46. Id. at Minimum Notice Required column.

mentally disabled, the statutes in most instances require certain conditions to be met or reasons to be given before sterilization may be authorized.[47] In almost all states the statutes specifically provide that the operation may be performed to prevent procreation. About half of these states have an alternative provision which allows the operation for the improvement of the patient's condition. In several states, statutes permit sterilization of patients for such other reasons as the advancement of the best interests of the patient and society or the probability that the patient's offspring would become a social menace or a ward of the state, or simply in "a proper case."

All but four of the states provide for judicial appeal from the hearing. Idaho and Iowa have automatic judicial review where sterilization has been ordered by the administrative agency, but such judicial determination is limited to cases where consent, as defined by the statute, has not been given to the performance of the operation. The right to counsel at the initial hearing is set forth in the statutes of about fifteen states, but only a few of them provide for the appointment of counsel if the patient has none.[48]

IV. REEVALUATION OF STERILIZATION LAWS

A. Scientific Validity of Sterilization

Some eugenicists, claiming that scientific evidence shows many mental disabilities to be inherited, theorize that the chief prophylactic measure is prevention of procreation. They advocate a widespread use of sterilization of the mentally disabled on the grounds that the number of such persons is constantly increasing and that propagation of the mentally unfit is a serious threat to the welfare of the race.[49]

1. THE MENTALLY DEFICIENT

It is generally agreed at the present time that mentally deficient persons cannot be cured. Thus it would appear that any solution to the problem of mental deficiency must lie in preventing its occurrence. This is the basis for the position of those advocating the sterilization of the mentally deficient. But while there is sufficient evidence to show that mentally deficient persons are more likely to produce subnormal children than are persons of normal intelligence,[50] it is also recognized that in addition to the heredity factor there are other causes for mental deficiency, including birth injuries and thyroid deficiency.[51]

This scientific uncertainty was highlighted more than thirty years ago by the American Neurological Association Committee for the Investigation of Eugenical Sterilization, which recommended that an institute for the continuing study of human heredity be established to conduct research for a period of at least one hundred years for the purpose of recording scientifically the lives of people of several generations, and that under the present state of knowledge about heredity, any law concerning sterilization should be voluntary rather than compulsory.[52] The Committee further made the following replies to the traditional arguments of the advocates of eugenic sterilization laws:[53]

> 1) There is nothing to indicate that mental disease and mental defect are increasing, and from this standpoint there is no evidence of a biological deterioration of the race.
>
> 2) The reputedly high fecundity of the mentally defective groups . . . is a myth based on the assumption that those who are low in the cultural scale are also . . . biologically defective.[54]
>
> 3) Nothing in the acceptance of heredity as a factor in the genesis of any condition considered by this report excludes the environmental agencies of life as equally potent, and in many instances as even more effective.

That these views and recommendations have retained their validity is evidenced by the more recent literature on this subject.[55]

---

47. Id. at Condition Requirement columns.

48. Id. at Hearing Agency, Judicial Appeal, and Right to Counsel columns.

49. American Neurological Association, Committee for the Investigation of Eugenical Sterilization, *Report* 24–25 (1936). See also Cook, "Eugenics or Euthenics," 37 *Ill. L. Rev.* 287 (1943); Landman, *supra* note 2, at 4.

50. Myerson, "Certain Medical and Legal Phases of Eugenic Sterilization," *Yale L.J.* 618, 629–30 (1943).

51. Id. at 622.

52. American Neurological Association, *supra* note 49, at 178–79, 181–83.

53. Findings of the Committee as reported in Ferster, *supra* note 22.

54. In fact there is some evidence to demonstrate that the marriage rate and the birth rate among the feebleminded are low. Along these lines there is also some evidence indicating that the death rate among the feebleminded is proportional to the degree of feeblemindedness and is greater than that of the normal population. See Myerson, *supra* note 50, at 627–28.

55. See, for example, the arguments against sterilization as

2. THE MENTALLY ILL

Sterilization of the mentally ill is on even more precarious scientific ground than sterilization of the mentally deficient. Little is known about the organic pathology of the two major mental diseases, schizophrenia and manic-depressive psychosis. It is not known what hereditary mechanisms, if any, are involved in transmitting these diseases, nor what may be the relative causal roles of environmental as opposed to hereditary factors.

An illustration of relatively recent medical opinion about sterilization of the mentally ill is provided by responses to a questionnaire sent to twenty Kansas psychiatrists. They expressed the view that even limited sterilization "offers more pitfalls than benefits to society." Questions were raised about the effect of the operation on the patients, and serious doubts were expressed about whether "the diseases for which the sterilized patients were institutionalized were hereditary."[56] The general increase in admissions of mentally ill people to institutions has been attributed almost solely to "a growing public consciousness that mental disease is treatable,"[57] and the very fact that mental illness responds to treatment in many cases indicates strongly that the hereditary factor plays only a small part, if any, in the development of the mental condition.

3. EPILEPTICS

In thirteen states the sterilization laws still specifically include epileptics.[58] At the time most of the sterilization laws were passed, epilepsy was considered to be hereditary and incurable and to result in progressive mental deterioration. But advances in medical and surgical treatment today allow 80 percent of all epileptics to lead normal and productive lives.[59] It is now recognized that epilepsy is not inherited, although a predisposition to it may exist as a recessive trait, as may be the case with any other physical disorder. For this reason, applicability of the sterilization laws to this group of people appears the least defensible.

4. SUMMARY ON SCIENTIFIC VALIDITY

When considered in the light of recent scientific thinking the validity of sterilization for eugenic purposes is certainly open to serious question. In evaluating the advisability of compulsory sterilization it is important to keep in mind that mental illness and epilepsy have shown increasing responsiveness to medical treatment. It is also important to remember that although there is some relationship between heredity and mental deficiency, it has been estimated that about 89 percent of inheritable mental deficiency is passed on by individuals not themselves deficient.[60] At the present time there is no way of ascertaining who these normal carriers are. Thus, if it were possible to sterilize collectively all the feebleminded, their number in the following generation would be cut down by only about 11 percent. While this in itself is not a conclusive argument against sterilization of the mentally deficient, it affirms the assertion that there is no scientifically acceptable plan to eliminate the problem of mental deficiency. Recognition of this fact in turn serves to reinforce opposition based on religious, moral, or legal (constitutional) grounds.

B. RELIGIOUS AND MORAL OPPOSITION

There has been growing opposition to sterilization based not only on scientific but also social, moral, and theological grounds.[61] Foremost in this opposition has been the Roman Catholic Church with its strong position against sterilization.[62] It has been said that Catholic opposition has contributed to the defeat of such legislation in several states.[63]

C. CONSTITUTIONAL PROBLEMS OF STERILIZATION STATUTES

Statutes permitting involuntary sterilization have been attacked as not meeting the following constitutional requirements: (1) substantive due process, involving broad issues of public policy and the basic scientific validity of eugenic sterilization; (2) equal protection, involving the scope and limitations of

---

summarized in 1960 by Bernard L. Diamond, quoted in Ferster, *supra* note 22, at 603–4. Note also the ACLU and Association for Voluntary Sterilization positions against compulsory sterilization at text accompanying notes 23 and 24 *supra*.

56. Comment, "What Has Happened to Kansas' Sterilization Laws?" 2 *Kan. L. Rev.* 174, 179 (1953).

57. Myerson, *supra* note 50, at 626.

58. See Table 6.1, Applicability columns.

59. Barrow & Fabing, *Epilepsy and the Law* 1–2, 7, 13 (1956).

60. Deutsch, *supra* note 1, at 373–74.

61. Id. at 373.

62. Pope Pius XI, "Casti Connubii: Encyclical Letter on Christian Marriage" (1930) in *The Papal Encyclicals in Their Historical Context* 235, 236 (Mentor ed. 1956). The Roman Catholic Church's official position against sterilization, and particularly against involuntary sterilization, remains firm. (From a telephone conversation with the Rev. Joseph T. Mangan of Loyola University of Chicago, Nov. 17, 1969).

63. O'Hara & Sanks, *supra* note 5, at 37–38.

the statutes in their designation of persons covered by such laws; (3) procedural due process, with the attention of the courts being directed to matters of hearing, notice, counsel, and appeal; and (4) the avoidance of cruel and unusual punishment, under statutes which designate "hereditary criminals" and sex offenders as persons subject to compulsory sterilization.

1. SUBSTANTIVE DUE PROCESS

In the leading sterilization case, *Buck v. Bell*,[64] the United States Supreme Court held that sterilization of a mentally deficient woman who had a mentally deficient mother as well as a mentally deficient daughter did not violate substantive due process.

Proceeding on the assumption that the defects were hereditary, Justice Holmes, speaking for the Court, said that the statute was a valid exercise of the state's police power and compared it to statutes requiring compulsory vaccination. With regard to this comparison, it is interesting to note that when the constitutionality of the vaccination statute was upheld in Massachusetts in 1903—later affirmed by the United States Supreme Court—the Massachusetts Supreme Court said:

> If a person should deem it important that vaccination should not be performed in his case, and the authorities should think otherwise, it is not in their power to vaccinate him by force, and the worst that could happen to him under the statute would be the payment of the penalty of $5.[65]

It has been argued that the Massachusetts vaccination statute and the Virginia sterilization statute are not analogous because "so far as concerns liberty there would appear to be a real difference between assessing a fine and compelling submission."[66] Intuitively most people would probably agree that there is a "real difference" between a fine of five dollars and compulsory sterilization, and the excess of legalism displayed in this argument may be seen with some humor. In any case, a further objection to the analogy is that the scientific findings relating the prevention of smallpox with vaccination are far more conclusive than the highly controverted claim that mental disorders are largely hereditary.

Justice Holmes also made another analogy in

Buck v. Bell, to the effect that if the nation can call upon its best citizens to sacrifice their lives in time of war, it should be able to ask a lesser sacrifice of those who are already a burden to it. This analogy has been criticized on the ground that there is "a necessity and an urgency that causes us to sacrifice men in self-defense which is wholly lacking in the case of eugenic sterilization."[67]

Some recent critics of the decision in *Buck v. Bell* have addressed themselves mainly to the proposition that the right to parenthood is a fundamental liberty. They tend to suggest, against the arguments of Justice Holmes, that the right of procreation far outweighs the contribution to the public welfare of compulsory sterilization.[68]

Even before *Buck v. Bell,* the dangers inherent in the logic of compulsory sterilization were discerned by the Supreme Court of New Jersey:

> There are other things besides physical or mental diseases that may render persons undesirable citizens, or might do so in the opinion of a majority of a prevailing legislature. Racial differences, for instance, might afford a basis for such an opinion in communities where that question is unfortunately a permanent and paramount issue.[69]

In opposing the clear holding of *Buck v. Bell,* its critics have thus contended that compulsory sterilization violates substantive due process and would violate it even if the eugenic effectiveness of sterilization were to be proved by scientific evidence. Interestingly enough, the issue of whether the eugenicists' beliefs are upheld by scientific evidence does not seem to have been raised in *Buck v. Bell,* and has been ignored or assumed away in subsequent sterilization cases. Thus, in *State v. Troutman*[70] the Idaho Supreme Court said there was "no doubt in our minds that heredity plays a controlling part in the blight of feeblemindedness." To assume the scientific validity of eugenic sterilization seemed not unreasonable in the *Troutman* case, which presented startling documentation in favor of the eugenic viewpoint: The defendant was himself a congenital defective; his mother, father, five brothers and six sisters were also feebleminded; his mother's sister

---

64. 274 U.S. 200 (1927).

65. Commonwealth v. Pear, 183 Mass. 242, 66 N.E. 719, 722 (1903), *aff'd*, 197 U.S. 11 (1905).

66. Gest, "Eugenic Sterilization: Justice Holmes vs. Natural Law," 23 *Temp. L.Q.* 306, 308 n.3 (1950).

67. O'Hara & Sanks, *supra* note 5, at 29–30.

68. Gest, *supra* note 66; Berns, *"Buck v. Bell:* The Sterilization Decision and Its Effect on Public Policy" 26, 127–28 (Thesis, University of Chicago, 1951).

69. Smith v. Bd. of Exmrs. of Feeble-minded, 88 A. 963, 966 (1913).

70. 50 Ida. 673, 299 P. 668, 670 (1931).

had seven children, three of whom were feeble-minded; and one of these three had ten children, all ten of whom were feebleminded.[71] The tragedy of the Troutman family, however, does not of itself validate the eugenic argument in regard to mental defectives, must less justify or support the wisdom, workability, effectiveness, or constitutionality of involuntary sterilization applied to the broad class of the mentally disabled.

2. EQUAL PROTECTION OF THE LAWS

In 1918 two sterilization statutes were successfully attacked on the grounds that they applied only to inmates of public institutions and therefore violated the Fourteenth Amendment's guarantee of equal protection of the laws.[72] However, in 1925 the Virginia Supreme Court of Appeals, holding to the contrary that a law applying solely to inmates in state institutions did not violate this clause, said that "there can be no discrimination . . . since the woman on the outside, if in fact feeble-minded, can, by the process of commitment, and afterwards a sterilization hearing, be sterilized under the act."[73] When the United States Supreme Court considered the case,[74] it also decided that there was no denial of equal protection. In ruling on this question, the Court stated:

> [T]he law does all that is needed when it does all that it can, indicates a policy, applies it to all within the lines, and seeks to bring within the lines all similarly situated so far and so fast as its means allow. Of course so far as the operations enable those who otherwise must be kept confined to be returned to the world, and thus open the asylum to others, the equality aimed at will be more nearly reached.[75]

Subsequent to this decision only one sterilization statute has been invalidated by the United States Supreme Court on the grounds that it violated the equal protection clause.[76]

71. Ibid.

72. Haynes v. Lapeer Circuit Judge, 201 Mich. 138, 166 N.W. 938 (1918); *In re* Thompson, 103 Misc. 23, 169 N.Y.S. 638 (Sup. Ct. 1918), *aff'd mem. sub nom.* Osborn v. Thompson, 185 App. Div. 902, 171 N.Y.S. 1094 (3d Dep't 1918).

73. Buck v. Bell, 143 Va. 310, 130 S.E. 516 (1925), *aff'd,* 274 U.S. 200 (1927).

74. Buck v. Bell, 274 U.S. 200 (1927).

75. Id. at 208.

76. Skinner v. Oklahoma *ex rel.* Williamson, 316 U.S. 535 (1942), held unconstitutional an Oklahoma statute which provided for the sterilization of habitual criminals. The statute

From a practical viewpoint, it has been said that sterilizing only institutionalized persons is ineffective. Even if all institutionalized mentally deficient persons were sterilized, it becomes apparent that the problem is far from solved when we consider that only 10 percent of all such persons are in institutions and only 11 percent of all feebleminded children are the offspring of parents so afflicted.[77]

3. PROCEDURAL DUE PROCESS

With regard to procedure, due process means fair process—a procedure by which one's rights are determined in conformity with at least minimum standards of fairness and orderliness. Ordinarily these standards include the requirements of adequate notice and an opportunity to be heard. The question of what constitutes the minimum standards of procedural due process in sterilization cases has never been decided by the United States Supreme Court, and on only a few occasions has the question been brought before state courts.

In connection with the procedural protection afforded by sterilization statutes, it is interesting to note that in *Buck v. Bell* Justice Holmes, prior to stating that the "attack is not upon the procedure but upon the substantive law,"[78] stressed that under the Virginia law involved "there can be no doubt that so far as procedure is concerned the rights of the patient are most carefully considered."[79] Holmes also gave the following detailed description of the procedure set out in the Virginia statute:

> The superintendent first presents a petition to the special board of directors of his hospital or colony, stating the facts and the grounds for his opinion, verified by affidavit. Notice of the petition and of the time and place of the hearing in the institution is to be served upon the inmate, and also upon his guardian, and if there is no guardian the superintendent is to apply to the Circuit Court of the County to appoint one. If the inmate is a minor notice also is to be given to his parents, if any, with a copy of the petition. The board is to see to it that the inmate may attend the hearings if desired by him or his guardian. The evidence is all to be reduced to writing, and after the board has made its order for or against the operation, the superintendent, or the inmate, or his guardian,

excepted from its operation persons convicted of embezzlement, and the court decided that a distinction between embezzlement and larceny violated the equal protection clause.

77. Deutsch, *supra* note 1, at 374.

78. Buck v. Bell, 274 U.S. 200, 207 (1927).

79. Ibid.

may appeal to the Circuit Court of the County. The Circuit Court may consider the record of the board and the evidence before it and such other admissible evidence as may be offered, and may affirm, revise, or reverse the order of the board and enter such order as it deems just. Finally any party may apply to the Supreme Court of Appeals, which, if it grants the appeal, is to hear the case upon the record of the trial in the Circuit Court and may enter such order as it thinks the Circuit Court should have entered.[80]

A comparison of the various statutes analyzed in Table 6.1, Sterilization, with the Virginia statute shows the protection of the patient's rights offered by many of these statutes to be substantially less than that offered by the statute of Virginia.[81] Considering the emphasis placed by the United States Supreme Court on the existence of procedural protection in *Buck v. Bell,* it would seem likely that if the Supreme Court had been called upon to pass on the procedural aspect of these statutes, it would have declared some of them unconstitutional.

There is a certain amount of conflict in the holdings of the few state cases on the subject. A North Carolina case held that procedural due process was denied where there was no provision for notice and an opportunity to be heard,[82] and an Indiana case reached the same decision where a statute did not grant a public hearing and an opportunity to cross-examine and otherwise controvert the issues.[83] But contrary to these cases, a California court in effect approved a sterilization statute lacking requirements of notice and an opportunity to be heard.[84] On another phase of the question, a Kansas case held that it was not essential that there be a provision giving

the right to appeal from a sterilization order made by the examining board where notice and an opportunity to be heard were adequately provided for in the administrative proceedings.[85] However, according to an advisory opinion of the Alabama Supreme Court, a sterilization statute, in addition to requiring notice and a hearing, must provide a subsequent right of appeal to the courts.[86] In Washington the court held that even though the patient had a right to appeal from the board's order, procedural due process had been denied him since no provision existed for notice or a hearing prior to the decision of the board, and the patient had the burden of appealing after being served with the sterilization order of the board.[87]

The sufficiency of the procedural safeguards has not been challenged to any appreciable extent. In fact, the Human Betterment Association up until 1958 counted a total of only twenty-three occasions where cases involving sterilization of institutionalized patients had come before the courts.[88] The last ten years have produced proportionately few challenges to the procedural or substantive fairness of the sterilization laws. The Human Betterment Association concludes that all this "speaks well not only of the care and forethought state legislators have given to the consideration of the provisions of the laws but also of the care exercised in their application by administrators."[89] This optimistic conclusion ignores a number of other factors of at least equal probability; the lack of representation by counsel for persons already disadvantaged by mental condition and institutionalization is at least one other explanation for the infrequency of legal contests in the sterilization area.

The belief that today a large proportion of the relatively limited number of sterilizations performed under the statutes are performed with the consent of the patient or those legally responsible for him may be another reason for the apparent lack of legal contest and concern. It should be pointed out, however, that even if it is true that most sterilizations today are technically "voluntary" or by con-

80. Id. at 206–7.

81. See, for example, Alabama, where the statute merely authorizes the superintendent and the assistant superintendent of the institution for mental deficients to sterilize any inmate, if after consultation these officials deem it advisable. *Ala. Code* tit. 45, § 243 (1940). In 1951 a legislative committee strongly recommended that the statute be repealed and the superintendent instructed not to perform any more operations. The committee believed the statute to be unconstitutional in view of a 1935 advisory opinion of the Alabama Supreme Court to the governor concerning procedural due process in connection with certain proposed sterilization legislation (*In re* Opinion of the Justices, 230 Ala. 543, 162 So. 123 (1935)). *Reports of the Special Joint Legislative Committee Investigating the Alabama Hospitals* 9, 10 (1951).

82. Brewer v. Valk, 204 N.C. 186, 167 S.E. 638 (1933).

83. Williams v. Smith, 190 Ind. 526, 131 N.E. 2 (1921).

84. Garcia v. State Dep't of Inst'ns, 36 Cal. App. 2d 152, 97 P.2d 264 (1939).

85. State *ex rel.* Smith v. Schaffer, 126 Kan. 607, 270 P. 604 (1928).

86. *In re* Opinion of the Justices, 230 Ala. 543, 162 So. 123 (1935).

87. *In re* Hendrickson, 12 Wash. 2d 600, 123 P.2d 322 (1942).

88. Human Betterment Association of America, *Summary of U.S. Sterilization Laws* 2 (1958), as cited in Ferster, *supra* note 22, at 598.

89. Ibid.

sent, this does not assure proper protection of the patient's rights. With reference to the mentally disabled, generally, one question arises concerning the value—legal or otherwise—of the consent of an incompetent patient: Does he have "capacity"? Some mentally disabled persons may be capable of understanding the nature and consequences of the operation, but others are not. In the setting of the mental institution, a different problem also obtains, as was perceived in the American Neurological Association *Report:*[90]

> [T]he word voluntary is frequently a mere subterfuge, in that it is often a condition of discharge from the institution that the patient be sterilized, and consequently the individual involved is in the position of being confined or confinable until he gives his consent for sterilization, which hardly makes the bargain free and equal and nullifies the real meaning of the word voluntary.

The relevance today of this observation made over thirty years ago is illustrated by the 1968 decision *In re Cavitt.*[91] In the *Cavitt* case, the Nebraska Supreme Court upheld the constitutionality of a statute providing for the sterilization of mentally defective persons as a prerequisite for parole or release from a state institution. Two recent California cases—*Andrade* and *Hernandez*[92]—demonstrate that similar doubts about the voluntariness of voluntary sterilizations obtain even in cases involving persons of normal mental condition. In these two cases the choice was between jail and probation on condition of sterilization. Andrade, who had been charged with failure to make child-support payments, chose sterilization and submitted to the operation. He subsequently petitioned the California Supreme Court to the effect that he be authorized to seek surgery to undo the operation without having his probation revoked. The court denied without opinion the relief sought; the United States Supreme Court later denied certiorari.[93] The Hernandez case grew out of a narcotics charge; the same choice—probation on condition of sterilization—was given to the defendant. She chose not to be sterilized, was sentenced to jail, and appealed. The California Superior Court

suspended the jail sentence which had been imposed on the defendant for violation of the probation condition. Three years' routine probation was ordered.[94]

A final problem with voluntary sterilizations is their application to children. North Carolina and Virginia, for example, sterilize very young children under their laws which specify no minimum age. A case concerning a six-year-old boy is reported from Virginia; 30 percent of North Carolina's sterilizations from 1962 through 1964 were performed on children between ten and nineteen years old.[95] The fact is that such operations are often far from voluntary, being performed with the consent of—or even on the petition of—the parent or guardian.[96]

4. CRUEL AND UNUSUAL PUNISHMENT

Proponents of statutes providing for the sterilization of criminals argue for such laws on eugenic grounds, as do those who favor the sterilization of the mentally disabled. These proponents urge that laws for the sterilization of criminals be viewed as a protection for society rather than as a punishment for offenders. It has sometimes been contended, however, that the sterilization of criminals constitutes cruel and unusual punishment. The courts are not in agreement on this question. The Supreme Court of Washington did not regard a vasectomy as cruel in a case where the defendant was adjudged guilty of statutory rape of a girl under the age of ten years.[97] But at least two federal courts, in cases involving the sterilization of criminals, have taken the position that although not cruel in the physical sense, the operation was degrading, humiliating, and productive of mental suffering, and therefore was legally cruel.[98] Since the sterilization of mentally disabled persons is in no way connected with "punishment,"[99] the argument of cruel punishment cannot properly be made with regard to the mentally disabled. However, it should be noticed that the effects of the operation which the federal courts considered in regard to criminals—degradation, humiliation, and

---

90. American Neurological Association, *supra* note 49, at 7–8.

91. 182 Neb. 712, 157 N.W.2d 171 (1968). For a more detailed discussion of *Cavitt,* see this chapter, § IV D, Alternative Rationales for Sterilization.

92. The cases—*Andrade* (1964) and *Hernandez* (1966)—are reported in Comment, *supra* note 2; see source citations therein.

93. *In re* Andrade, 380 U.S. 953 (1965).

94. Comment, *supra* note 2.

95. Ferster, *supra* note 22, at 621.

96. Ibid.

97. State v. Feilen, 70 Wash. 65, 126 P. 75 (1912).

98. Davis v. Berry, 216 F. 413 (S.D. Iowa 1914), *rev'd for mootness,* 242 U.S. 468 (1916); Mickle v. Henrichs, 262 F. 687 (D. Nev. 1918). The Iowa and Nevada statutes involved in these cases were found unconstitutional because they prescribed cruel and unusual punishment.

99. E.g., *In re* Cavitt, 182 Neb. 712, 157 N.W.2d 171 (1968); Smith v. Command, 231 Mich. 409, 204 N.W. 140 (1925), disavowing punishment as an end.

mental anguish—would be just as apt to result when the subject of compulsory sterilization is a mentally disabled person.

D. ALTERNATIVE RATIONALES FOR STERILIZATION

Despite criticisms and suggestions to the contrary, *Buck v. Bell* at present is still the law. Though sterilizations have decreased in number, and many of those performed are labeled "voluntary," the statutes are still operative in varying degrees, while problems of substantive and procedural propriety remain.

The California *Andrade* case and the Nebraska Supreme Court's *Cavitt* decision demonstrate the dubiousness of "voluntary" sterilization. Consent to sterilization is hardly voluntary when it is made a precondition for release, probation, or parole from a prison or mental institution. These cases, however, also indicate a shift away from eugenic grounds in the rationale for sterilization. In *Andrade,* there was no question of mental deficiency. In *Cavitt,* the defendant had an I.Q. of 71, and the doctors agreed that she was mentally deficient. But what really prompted the sterilization order was the fact that she and her eight children "were provided for largely by public aid."[100] Eugenic consequences did not figure in the decision. There was no proof or allegation that her children were mentally deficient. In fact, "none of these doctors had investigated the mental condition of her parents or of her children," as the court readily admitted.[101] One commentator has appropriately concluded, therefore, that sterilization has found new support "among those seeking to reduce the welfare rolls." "This time we will be promised salvation from 'poor parents' rather than 'poor heredity.' "[102]

Many of the current statutes provide for sterilization for other than eugenic reasons and are applied accordingly. It is reported, for example, that North Carolina, where more than half of the sterilizations in the United States were performed in 1963, "bases its sterilization program primarily on fitness for parenthood."[103] In this context it is of interest to mention the 1962 Ohio probate court decision *In re Simpson.*[104] In that case sterilization of an eighteen-year-old mentally defective girl who had had one illegitimate child was ordered, despite the fact that Ohio does not even have a sterilization statute. The court justified the compulsory order on the basis of its general equity powers. Considerable emphasis was placed on the "additional burdens upon the county and state welfare departments" that would result if people like the defendant "continued to bring children into the world."[105] *Simpson,* like *Andrade* and *Cavitt,* illustrates that illegitimacy, poor parenthood, and potential burden on public funds have replaced eugenic considerations in many instances.

The noneugenic grounds for involuntary sterilization are as lacking in sociological and constitutional validity as the eugenic arguments are in scientific justification. Furthermore, irrespective of the rationales advanced, the sterilization laws as they are presently worded fail, through their all-inclusiveness and lack of procedural protections, to guard against misapplication. Their use or misuse must therefore depend largely on the judgment of individual judges, prosecutors, or probation officers, or often, in the case of the mentally disabled, on the views and philosophies of state hospital superintendents.[106]

---

100. *In re* Cavitt, 157 N.W.2d 171, 175 (1968).

101. Id. at 175. On rehearing before the Nebraska Supreme Court it was specifically held that there was no requirement under the statute for a finding that offspring of the party to be sterilized would likely be defective. The court concluded its affirmation of the statute and its prior holding by stating the myth that "[t]he order does not require sterilization. . . . The choice is hers." *In re* Cavitt, 159 N.W.2d 566, 568 (1968).

102. Ferster, *supra* note 22, at 619, 591. The author also notes (at 623) that bills for compulsory sterilization of unwed mothers have been seriously debated in several states and advocated in many others.

103. Id. at 616. There is some evidence that children of mentally disabled parents are adversely affected by the psychosis of their parents: see Anthony, "Clinical Evaluation of Children with Psychotic Parents," 126 *Am. J. Psychiat.* 177 (1969). The evidence, however, is not conclusive. Many questions remain concerning the permanency and seriousness of these effects and the type of disability that is likely to produce them. In any case, none of this evidence can be construed as an argument in favor of compulsory sterilization.

104. 180 N.E.2d 206 (Ohio P. Ct. 1962).

105. Id. at 208.

106. Ferster, *supra* note 22, at 614. "The attitude of the state towards its sterilization law is principally a reflection of the views of the institution superintendent. . . . For example, Delaware sterilizations declined between 1952 and 1962 but in 1963 it had the highest number of reported state sterilizations per 100,000 population. Delaware also appointed a new superintendent of hospitals in July 1961 who believed it would be possible to release more patients if they had been sterilized so 'I began to push the matter and more patients were released. . . .' Georgia's annual sterilization rate dropped from 112 in 1959 to an all-time low of 7 operations in 1963. There were no changes in the sterilization law during that period. 'The changes have been in the philosophy of the superintendent, not making it necessary for the Eugenics Board to make any decision.' "

Some commentators have designated expressions of alarm or concern about this fact as excessive in view of the recent sparing use of the sterilization laws—only 467 sterilizations were reported to have taken place under the statutes in 1963 compared to 1638 in 1943[107]—but simply to acquiesce in the fact that appropriate, noncoercive, and procedurally fair utilization of the sterilization laws depends on the individual judgments of a few is a greater excess.

V. CONCLUSIONS AND RECOMMENDATIONS

1. *Statutes authorizing involuntary sterilization should be repealed.*

Involuntary sterilization of criminals for punitive purposes is cruel and unusual punishment. Involuntary sterilization of groups of criminals and of mentally disabled and physically disabled persons for eugenic reasons is also not justifiable. Eugenic arguments are of very dubious scientific validity; the hereditary nature of criminality is almost universally rejected today, and, while heredity may be a factor in some mental and physical disabilities, many reasons remain for rejecting involuntary sterilization as a solution to the problem of illness. Because it is scientifically uncertain which disabilities are hereditary, any statute authorizing sterilization will have considerable difficulty in rationally identifying those groups of disabled persons who should be subject to its proceedings, and will therefore be legally suspect. Moreover, moral opposition may be expressed towards attempts by the state to purify the human race by designating certain groups of individuals as more or less desirable than others and prohibiting reproduction of the less desirable through one of the most drastic means available. Any such attempts would fail as a practical matter as well, since among those persons not afflicted with congenital disability there are carriers of such illnesses, while among those so afflicted many are not carriers of the disability. Rationales for sterilization which have recently come to supplant the discredited eugenic arguments are no more acceptable. Saving society from "poor parenthood" is an equally dangerous role for the state to assume, particularly if effectuated through involuntary sterilization.

2. *Statutes authorizing voluntary sterilization, especially as applied to the mentally disabled, should afford every reasonable substantive and procedural protection to assure that the sterilization is truly voluntary.*

An individual probably has a right to be sterilized if he so desires. Since sterilization is at present irreversible for females and less than 50 percent reversible for males, and since other methods of contraception are available, though perhaps less certain in effect, the statutes authorizing voluntary sterilization should imply and explicate a sense of hesitancy. For example, such statutes should inquire into the possibility of coercion by way of outside influence, personal circumstances, present mental condition or emotional state, and so forth. In other words, prior to granting the applicant's request, a determination must be made that the operation is "truly desired" and "truly voluntary." As applied to the mentally disabled, and particularly those in institutions, this means that no statute shall authorize sterilization requested as the result of a condition imposed for probation, or discharge from, or entrance into, an institution, and that all statutes shall require an inquiry with respect to such possibilities. "Voluntary" sterilizations, by substituted consent, of individuals who are incapable of giving valid personal consent should be approached with even more care. Every effort should be made to communicate to the incapacitated person the nature of the operation; the disabled person should be adequately represented at any hearings; consent should be given only by a guardian or relative whose interests must be found to coincide with those of the disabled person; and there should be convincing evidence of medical need for the operation.

BIBLIOGRAPHY

American Neurological Association. Committee for the Investigation of Eugenical Sterilization. *Report.* 1936.

Anthony, E. James. "Clinical Evaluation of Children with Psychotic Parents." 126 *American Journal of Psychiatry* 177 (1969).

Barrow, Roscoe L., and Fabing, Howard D. *Epilepsy and the Law.* New York: Hoeber Medical Div., Harper & Row, 1956.

Berns, Walter. "*Buck v. Bell:* The Sterilization Decision and Its Effect on Public Policy." Unpublished thesis, University of Chicago Library. June 1951.

Challener, William A., Jr. "The Law of Sexual Sterilization in Pennsylvania." 57 *Dickinson Law Review* 298 (1952).

Clarke, Helen I. *Social Legislation.* 2d ed. New York: Appleton-Century-Crofts, Inc., 1957.

107. Id. at 599.

Comment, "Sterilization: A Continuing Controversy." 1 *University of San Francisco Law Review* 159 (1966).

——— "What Has Happened to Kansas' Sterilization Laws?" 2 *Kansas Law Review* 174 (1953).

Cook, Walter Wheeler. "Eugenics or Euthenics." 37 *Illinois Law Review* 297 (1943).

Deutsch, Albert. *The Mentally Ill in America*. 2d ed. rev. New York: Columbia University Press, 1949.

Ferster, Elyce Z. "Eliminating the Unfit—Is Sterilization the Answer?" 27 *Ohio State Law Journal* 591 (1966).

Gest, John B. "Eugenic Sterilization: Justice Holmes vs. Natural Law." 23 *Temple Law Quarterly* 306 (1950).

Guttmacher, Manfred S., and Weihofen, Henry. *Psychiatry and the Law*. New York: W. W. Norton & Co., 1952.

Jennings, H. S. "Eugenics." *Encyclopedia of Social Science*, vol. 5. New York: Macmillan Co., 1931.

Landman, J. H. "The History of Human Sterilization in the United States—Theory, Statute, Adjudication." 23 *Illinois Law Review* 463 (1929).

———. *Human Sterilization*. New York: Macmillan Co., 1932.

Letter to the American Bar Foundation from the Association of Voluntary Sterilization, Inc., John R. Rague Executive Director. July 7, 1969.

Myerson, Abraham. "Certain Medical and Legal Phases of Eugenic Sterilization." 52 *Yale Law Journal* 618 (1943).

Note, "Human Sterilization." 35 *Iowa Law Review* 251 (1950).

O'Hara, James B., and Sanks, T. Howland. "Eugenic Sterilization." 45 *Georgetown Law Journal* 20 (1956).

Pope Pius XI. "Casti Connubii: Encyclical Letter on Christian Marriage" (1930). *The Papal Encyclicals in Their Historical Context*. New York: New American Library, 1956.

St. John-Stevas, Norman. *Law and Morals*. Twentieth Century Encyclopedia of Catholicism, vol. 148. Englewood Cliffs, N.J.: Hawthorn Books, Inc., 1964.

Woodside, Moya. *Sterilization in North Carolina: A Sociological and Psychological Study*. Chapel Hill: University of North Carolina Press, 1950.

CASES

Brewer v. Valk, 204 N.C. 186, 167 S.E. 638 (1933).

Buck v. Bell, 143 Va. 310, 130 S.E. 516 (1925), *aff'd*, 274 U.S. 200 (1927).

Christensen v. Thornby, 192 Minn. 123, 255 N.W. 620 (1934).

Commonwealth v. Pear, 183 Mass. 242, 66 N.E. 719 (1903), *aff'd*, 197 U.S. 11 (1905).

Davis v. Berry, 216 F. 413 (S.D. Iowa 1914), *rev'd for mootness*, 242 U.S. 468 (1916).

Garcia v. State Dep't of Institutions, 36 Cal. App. 2d 152, 97 P.2d 264 (1939).

Haynes v. Lapeer Circuit Judge, 201 Mich. 138, 166 N.W. 938 (1918).

In re Andrade, 380 U.S. 953 (1965).

In re Cavitt, 182 Neb. 712, 157 N.W.2d 171 (1968); *rehearing*, 183 Neb. 243, 159 N.W.2d 566 (1968); *prob. juris. noted*, 393 U.S. 1078 (1969); *appeal dismissed*, 396 U.S. 996 (1970).

In re Hendrickson, 12 Wash. 2d 600, 123 P.2d 322 (1942).

In re Opinion of the Justices, 230 Ala. 543, 162 So. 123 (1935).

In re Simpson, 180 N.E.2d 206 (Ohio P. Ct., 1962).

In re Thompson, 103 Misc. 23, 169 N.Y.S. 638 (Sup. Ct. 1918), *aff'd mem. sub nom*. Osborn v. Thompson, 185 App. Div. 902, 171 N.Y.S. 1094 (3d Dep't 1918).

Jessin v. County of Shasta, 79 Cal. Rptr. 359 (1969).

Mickle v. Henrichs, 262 F. 687 (D. Nev. 1918).

Skinner v. Oklahoma *ex rel*. Williamson, 316 U.S. 535 (1942).

Smith v. Board of Examiners of Feeble-minded, 85 N.J.L. 46, 88 A. 963 (1913).

Smith v. Command, 231 Mich. 409, 204 N.W. 140 (1925).

State *ex rel*. Smith v. Schaffer, 126 Kan. 607, 270 P. 604 (1928).

State v. Feilen, 70 Wash. 65, 126 P. 75 (1912).

State v. Troutman, 229 P. 668 (Idaho Sup. Ct.) 1931.

Williams v. Smith, 190 Ind. 526, 131 N.E. 2 (1921).

Table 6.1 STERILIZATION

STATE	APPLICABILITY Patients in State Institutions	Outside State Institutions	Mentally Ill	Mentally Deficient	Epileptics	APPLICATION BY Institution Superintendent	Others	NOTICE Patient	Relatives	Central Agency	Guardian	MINIMUM NOTICE REQUIRED	MEDICAL CERTIFICATE	INDEPENDENT MEDICAL EXAMINATION	HEARING	PRESENCE OF PATIENT	HEARING AGENCY Judicial	Administrative	CONDITION REQUIREMENT Improve Condition	Prevent Procreation	Other	JUDICIAL APPEAL	RIGHT TO COUNSEL
DRAFT ACT																							
ALA. Code (1958)	45, §243		45, §243																				
ALAS. Stat. (1962)																							
ARIZ. Rev. Stat. Ann. (1956)	36-531		36-531	36-531	36-531	36-531			if infant notice to parents if known. 36-534		fn.1 36-533	30 days 36-533A			36-535	36-535A		fn.2 36-535		36-536B		36-537	
ARK. Stat. Ann. (1947)	§4 Act 127-1969	§4 Act 127-1969	§1(c)(i) §4 Act 127-1969	§1(c)(i) §4 Act 127-1969			Guardian §4 Act 127-1969	§5(b)(1) §5(c) Act 127-1969	§5(b)(2) §5(b)(3) §5(b)(5) Act 127-1969		§5(b)(4) Act 127-1969	20 days §5(b) Act 127-1969	§7 Act 127-1969	§7(a) Act 127-1969	§7(b) Act 127-1969	§7(b) Act 127-1969	§7(b) Act 127-1969			§1(c)(ii) Act 127-1969		§11 Act 127-1969	§7(b) Act 127-1969
CAL. Welf. & Inst'ns Code (West 1966) (Supp. 1966)	7254		7254	7254		7254		7254	7254	7254	7254	30 days 7254			if written objection filed within 30 days 7254			fn.3			"a proper case" 7254	7254	
COLO. Rev. Stat. Ann. (1964)																							
CONN. Gen. Stat. Ann. (1958) (Supp. 1969) [fn.4]	17-19		17-19	17-19		17-19												fn.4 17-19	17-19	17-19			
DEL. Code Ann. (1953)	16-5701 16-5702	16-5702	16-5701 16-5702	16-5701 16-5702	16-5701 16-5702	institution board 16-5701	fn.5 16-5702		fn.6 16-5701(c)		16-5701(c)	30 days 16-5701 (c)						fn.7 16-5701(a) 16-5702(b)		16-5701(b)			
D.C. Code Ann. (1967)																							
FLA. Stat. Ann. (1960)																							
GA. Code Ann. (1968)	99-1303		99-1303	99-1303		99-1303		99-1305	99-1305		99-1305		99-1304		99-1306	if requested 99-1306		fn.8 99-1301		99-1303		fnn. 9, 10 99-1310	
HAWAII Rev. Stat. Ann. (1968)																							
IDAHO Code Ann. (1949)	66-802		66-802	66-802	66-802	66-802		66-804 66-807	66-804		66-804 66-807	20 days 66-807			66-808	66-807	fn.11 66-808	fn.11 66-803		66-803		66-810	66-808
ILL. Ann. Stat. (Smith-Hurd 1966)																							
IND. Ann. Stat. (1964)	22-1601		22-1601	22-1601	22-1601	22-1601		22-1602	22-1602	22-1602	fn.1 22-1602	30 days			22-1602	fn.12 22-1602	fn.13 22-1613 22-1614	fn.14 22-1602		22-1602		22-1603	22-1602

220

Table 6.1 STERILIZATION   continued

STATE	Patients in State Institutions	Outside State Institutions	Mentally Ill	Mentally Deficient	Epileptics	Institution Superintendent	Others	Patient	Relatives	Central Agency	Guardian	Minimum Notice Required	Medical Certificate	Independent Medical Examination	Hearing	Presence of Patient	Hearing Agency: Judicial	Hearing Agency: Administrative	Improve Condition	Prevent Procreation	Other	Judicial Appeal	Right to Counsel
IOWA Code Ann. (1969)	145.2	145.2	145.2	145.2	145.9	145.2		145.3				10 days 145.3			145.4	fn. 12 145.4 145.5	fn. 11 145.17	fn. 11 145.5		145.9		fn. 10 145.15	fn. 15 145.4 145.17
KAN. Stat. Ann. (1964)																							
KY. Rev. Stat. Ann. (1969)																							
LA. Rev. Stat. Ann. (1950)																							
ME. Rev. Stat. Ann. (1965)	34, §2462	fn. 16 34, §2461	34, §2461 34, §2462	34, §2461 34, §2462		fn. 17 34, §2462	fn. 18 34, §2461	fn. 19 34, §2464	fn. 19 34, §2464	fn. 20 34, §2463	fn. 19 34, §2464			fn. 21 34, §2461					34, §2461	34, §2461 34, §2462		fn. 9 34, §2464 34, §2465	fn. 15 34, §2464
MD. Ann. Code (1968)																							
MASS. Ann. Laws (1965)																							
MICH. Comp. Laws Ann. (1967)	720.304	720.305	720.301	720.301		fn. 22 720.304	fn. 22, 23 720.304	if above age 10, 720.305	720.305		fn. 1 720.305	10 days 720.305		fn. 24 720.306	720.307	fn. 25 720.307	fn. 26 720.306			720.304, 720.305		720.309	fn. 15 720.307
MINN. Stat. Ann. (1959)	256.08		fn. 27 256.08	fn. 28 256.07																			
MISS. Code Ann. (1952)	6957		fn. 29 6957	fn. 29 6957	fn. 29 6957	5958			6958		6958				6958	6958		fn. 30 6958			fn. 31 6957	6960	6958
MO. Rev. Stat. (1959)																							
MONT. Rev. Codes Ann. (1961)																							
fn. 32 NEB. Rev. Stat. (1966)	83-504			83-501							fn. 1 83-505		fn. 33 83-504		83-505	83-505		fn. 34 83-502		83-501		83-505	83-505
NEV. Rev. Stat. (1967)																							
N.H. Rev. Stat. Ann. (1964)	174:1	174:1	174:1	174:1	174:1	174:1		174:3			fn. 1 174:2	fn. 35 174:3		fn. 36 174:2	174:4	fn. 37 174:4		fn. 38 174:4		174:6	fn. 39 174:1	174:7	
fn. 40 N.J. Stat. Ann. (1964)																							
N.M. Stat. Ann. (1953)																							
N.Y. MENTAL HYGIENE LAW (McKinney 1951)																							

221

Table 6.1 STERILIZATION *continued*

STATE	APPLICABILITY — Patients in State Institutions	Outside State Institutions	Mentally Ill	Mentally Deficient	Epileptics	APPLICATION BY — Institution Superintendent	Others	NOTICE — Patient	Relatives	Central Agency	Guardian	Medical Certificate	Independent Medical Examination	Hearing	Presence of Patient	HEARING AGENCY — Judicial	Administrative	CONDITION REQUIREMENT — Improve Condition	Prevent Procreation	Other	Judicial Appeal	Right to Counsel
N.C. Gen. Stat. (1964)	35-36 (Supp. 1969)	35-37 (Supp. 1969)	35-36 (Supp. 1969)	35-36 (Supp. 1969)	35-36 (Supp. 1969)	35-37 (Supp. 1969)	fn. 41 35-37 (Supp. 1969)	35-44	35-44		fn. 1 35-44	35-43		35-45	35-45		fn. 43 35-45	35-39(1)	35-39(3)	public good. 35-39	35-48 35-50	35-45
N.D. Cent. Code (1960) (Supp. 1969)	25-04.1-01			25-04-01 25-04.1-01	25-04-01 25-04.1-01	25-04.1-01	25.04.1-01 25.04.1-08		fn. 44 25-04.1-01		fn. 44 25-04.1-01	fn. 45 25-04-.1-01						25-04-.1-01		protection of society 25-04-.1-01		
OHIO Rev. Code Ann. (Baldwin 1964)																						
OKLA. Stat. Ann. (1954)	43A, §341		43A, §341	43A, §341	43A, §341	43A, §341		43A, §342	43A, §342		fn. 1 43A, §342			43A, §342	fn. 37 43A, §342		fn. 46 43A, §342	43A, §342	43A, §342	fn. 47 43A, §342	43A, §343	43A, §342
ORE. Rev. Stat. (1965)	436.030		436.070	436.070	436.070		fn. 48 436.025	436.041 436.090	436.090		fn. 49 436.090			436.050			436.020		436.050		436.110	fn. 15 436.120(4)
PA. Stat. Ann. (1969)																						
R.I. Gen. Laws Ann. (1968)																						
S.C. Code Ann. (1962)	32-671		32-671	32-671	32-671	32-671		32-672	32-672		32-672			32-673	32-673		fn. 50 32-672	32-675	32-675		32-676	32-673
S.D. COMPILED LAWS Ann. (1967)	27-11-1		27-11-1	27-11-5	27-11-1	27-11-3	27-11-1	27-11-4	27-11-4		27-11-4	27-11-3							27-11-1		27-11-5	
TENN. Code Ann. (1955)																						
TEX. Rev. Civ. Stat. Ann. (1958)																						
UTAH Code Ann. (1968)	64-10-1	64-10-1	64-10-1	64-10-1	64-10-1	64-10-1		64-10-3	64-10-5		fn. 1 64-10-4	64-10-4		64-10-4	fn. 37 64-10-5		64-10-2	64-10-7 (Supp. 1967)	64-10-7 (Supp. 1967)		64-10-8	64-10-6 (Supp. 1967)
fn. 51 VT. Stat. Ann. (1968)	18, §8701	18, §8701	18, §8701	18, §8701	18, §8701		fn. 27 18, §8702					fn. 52 18, §8702						18, §8702	18, §8702			
VA. Code Ann. (1953) (Supp. 1968)	37.1-156		37.1-156	37.1-156	37.1-156	37.1-156		37.1-159	37.1-160		fn. 1 37.1-160			37.1-159	fn. 37 37.1-161		fn. 53 37.1-158	37.1-156	37.1-156		37.1-168 37.1-169	37.1-165
WASH. Rev. Code Ann. (1962)																						

Table 6.1 STERILIZATION *continued*

STATE	APPLICABILITY					APPLICATION BY		NOTICE					MEDICAL CERTIFI-CATE	INDEPENDENT MEDICAL EXAMINATION	HEARING	PRESENCE OF PATIENT	HEARING AGENCY		CONDITION REQUIREMENT			JUDICIAL APPEAL	RIGHT TO COUNSEL
	Patients in State Institutions	Outside State Institutions	Mentally Ill	Mentally Deficient	Epileptics	Institution Superintendent	Others	Patient	Relatives	Central Agency	Guardian	MINIMUM NOTICE REQUIRED					Judicial	Administrative	Improve Condition	Prevent Procreation	Other		
W. VA. Code Ann. (1966)	16-10-1 (Supp. 1969)		fn. 54 16-10-1 (Supp. 1969)	16-10-1 (Supp. 1969)	16-10-1 (Supp. 1969)	16-10-1 (Supp. 1969)		16-10-1 (Supp. 1969)	16-10-1 (Supp. 1969)		16-10-1 (Supp. 1969)	30 days 16-10-1 (Supp. 1969)			16-10-1 (Supp. 1969)	fn. 37 16-10-1 (Supp. 1969)		fn. 55 16-10-1 (Supp. 1969)	16-10-1 (Supp. 1969)	16-10-1 (Supp. 1969)		16-10-2 16-10-3	16-10-1 (Supp. 1969)
WIS. Stat. Ann. (1957)	46.12		46.12	46.12			fn. 56 46.12	46.12	46.12		46.12	30 days 46.12		fn. 57 46.12						46.12			
WYO. Stat. Ann. (1967)																							

Notes to Table 6.1   STERILIZATION

1. If the patient has no guardian, one must be appointed for him. Ariz. 36-533B; Ind. 22-1602; Mich. 720.306; Neb. 83-505 (Supp. 1967); N.H. 174:3; N.C. 35-44 (Supp. 1969); Okla. 43A, §342; Utah 64-10-4; Va. 37.1-160 (Supp. 1968).

2. State board of medical examiners. Ariz. 36-535.

3. If an objection to sterilization is filed, the director of the department of mental hygiene is to make full inquiry into the matter. Cal. W. & I. 7254 (Supp. 1968).

4. A board at each institution shall be composed of the physician in charge and 2 skilled surgeons appointed by the physician in charge. The board shall examine any patient recommended for sterilization and may authorize such operation. However, if the board determines the patient to be competent, no such operation shall be performed without the consent of the patient; if incompetent, consent of the next of kin or guardian or, if none, the board of trustees is required. Conn. 17-19 (Supp. 1969).

5. Institution board, upon the report and recommendation of the mental hygiene clinic or the superintendent of the state hospital. Del. 16-5702(a).

6. Notice to person with whom patient last resided is sufficient if no relative or guardian can be located. Del. 16-5701(c).

7. The superintendent and 1 physician and 1 alienist appointed by the department of welfare. Unanimous decision of the board plus the written consent of the department is necessary to authorize sterilization. If person is not institutionalized, board is to consist of 2 physicians and 1 alienist. Del. 16-5701, 16-5702.

7. State board of eugenics, which is composed of the directors of the department of family and children services and the state board of health and the superintendent of the state hospital. Any 2 of the above may act as the board. Ga. 99-1301.

9. Sterilization order states that the patient or his legal representative has the right to judicial appeal. Ga. 99-1309; Me. 34, §2464.

10. Jury trial is available on demand. Ga. 99-1313; Iowa 145.17.

11. The state board of eugenics inquires into the condition of the patient and, if proper, orders sterilization. However, unless the patient (or, if patient is insane or feebleminded, his guardian or next of kin) consents to the operation, there must be a full civil proceeding in a district court. Idaho 66-803, 66-804, 66-806 (Supp. 1969), 66-807, 66-808; Iowa 145.4, 145.5, 145.9, 145.15, 145.17.

12. The patient is to be allowed to attend the hearings, if he or his guardian or next of kin so request. Ind. 22-1602; Iowa 145.5, 145.4.

13. Court may enter order for sterilization on the basis of the examining doctor's certificate at the same time as commitment order is made. Ind. 22-1613, 22-1614.

14. The governing board of the institution must report its findings to the commissioner of mental health who may approve or reverse the decision. Ind. 22-1602.

15. Court will appoint attorney if defendant does not have one. Iowa 145.17; Me. 34, §2464; Mich. 720.307; Ore. 436.120.

16. Sterilization for patients outside of institution must be voluntary or with the consent of a relative if the patient is incapable of consenting. Me. 34, §2461.

17. Medical staff or institution physician or any institution in the state. Me. 34, §2462.

18. Physician in case of noncommitted persons. Me. 34, §2461.

19. Notice of the sterilization order and right to appeal must be sent to the patient and his or her father or mother, husband or wife, or legal guardian. In the absence of such relatives or guardian the court shall appoint an attorney to protect the rights of the patient, and he shall receive such notice. Me. 34, §2464.

20. The central agency may approve the recommendation for inmate's sterilization, but the order cannot be carried out without the further approval of 2 of the 3 state hospital superintendents. Me. 34, §2463.

21. Physician in charge of the case must call in a physician and surgeon to examine the patient and to decide if he is capable of consenting to the operation. Me. 34, §2461.

22. In Michigan 2 procedures for sterilization exist: 720.304 is applicable to patients where action is commenced by the superintendent and upon the written consent of a defective patient over the age of 16, not otherwise incapable of giving consent, together with a similar consent in writing by his or her legal guardian, if any, and also by one or more of the following persons, in the order named, husband, wife, father, mother--but without a court order; 720.305 permits the husband, wife, father, or mother to apply for a sterilization order to render a defective person incapable of procreation, but this requires a court order for effect.

23. Guardian, relatives, state welfare commission, sheriff, superintendent of the poor, or supervisor of township. Mich. 720.305.

24. Two physicians are to be appointed by court. Mich. 720.306.

25. Unless 2 reputable physicians certify that it would be improper and unsafe. Mich. 720.307.

26. Court shall appoint 2 reputable physicians who shall make investigation and examination of mental and physical condition and personal and family condition of such defective. Mich. 720.306.

27. Written consent of patient and also consent of spouse or nearest kin or guardian is necessary. Written consent of patient of, if person is incppable of understanding that he or she cannot procreate children after the operation, written consent of guardian. Vt. 18, §8702.

28. Spouse or nearest kin must consent. If none be found, commissioner of public welfare may consent as legal guardian. Minn. 256-07.

29. Afflicted with hereditary forms of insanity that are recurrent: idiocy, imbecility, feeblemindedness, or epilepsy. Miss. 6957.

30. Board of directors or trustees of hospital. Miss. 6958.

31. Best interests of the patient and society. Miss. 6957.

32. No person who has been adjudged an imbecile, or a feebleminded person, or a person who has been adjudged afflicted with hereditary epilepsy or hereditary insanity shall marry in this state until after he or she has been submitted to an operation for sterilization. Neb. 42-102 (Supp. 1967).

33. Unless patient is released by court order, decision regarding sterilization must be made by panel of 5 physicians before patient can be paroled or discharged. Neb. 83-504.

34. The five members of board of examiners. Majority must agree to any decision. Neb. 83-501, 83-502.

35. Not less than 14 days before presentation of such petition to said board. N.H. 174:3.

36. Two or more physicians with 2 years' experience who are registered in state. N.H. 174:2.

37. If patient or guardian so desires. N.H. 174:4; Okla. 43A, §342; Utah 64-10-5; Va. 37.1-161 (Supp. 1969); W. Va. 16-10-1 (Supp. 1969).

38. Board of the institution. N.Y. 174:2, 174:4.

39. In the best interest of inmate and society. N.H. 174:1.

40. "Nothing in this act . . . shall give the licensing authority or agency herein provided for the the power or authority to require any hospital to practice or permit sterilization of human beings . . . contrary to beliefs of any well established religious body." N.J. 30-11-9.

41. Director of public welfare, next of kin, or legal guardian if not committed. N.C. 35-37 (Supp. 1969).

42. Twenty days' notice of time and place of presentation of such petition to such board. N.C. 35-44.

43. Eugenics board. N.C. 35-40, 35-45.

44. Within 14 days after notification of recommendation for sterilization is received, court-appointed guardian, parent, or spouse shall express consent or nonconsent to sterilization operation. No such operation shall be performed without written consent of court-appointed guardian, parent, or spouse. If written notice of nonconsent is not received within 14 days after notification, then consent to proceed with operation shall be deemed to have been denied. No further request for consent to sterilize shall be made for at least 1 year from date of denial. N.D. 25-04.1-02 (Supp. 1969).

45. Superintendent may make recommendation on obtaining unanimous approval of board composed of 3 competent physicians, 1 professional psychologist, and a professional social worker. N.D. 25-04.1-01 (Supp. 1969).

46. Mental health board. Okla. 43A,§342.

47. If patient will continue to be public or partial public charge or supported in any manner or form by charity. Okla. 43A, §341.

48. "Any two persons or any person licensed to practice medicine . . . may file a petition." Ore. 436.041 (2).

49. In all cases copy of the notice must be served on public defender. Ore. 435.041(2).

50. Executive committee of state board of health. S.C. 32-672.

51. Statutes provide for voluntary sterilization only. Vt. 18, §§8701 to 8704.

52. Certificates by 2 physicians and surgeons must show whether person is capable of understanding that he cannot procreate children. Certificates must be sworn to before notary public or justice of the peace. Vt. 18, §8702.

53. State hospital board. Va. 37.1-158 (Supp. 1968).

54. Applicable to inmate afflicted with any hereditary form of insanity. W.Va. 16-10-1 (Supp. 1968).

55. W.Va. board of health. W.Va. 16-10-1 (Supp. 1968).

56. Department of public welfare. Wis. 46.12.

57. Psychiatrist and surgeon. Wis. 46.12.

Chapter Seven

Domestic Relations

I. INTRODUCTION

Severe mental disability prevents the afflicted person from functioning in normal domestic relationships. Laws have been passed which are designed to lessen the resulting domestic disruption by forbidding the mentally disabled to marry. When one of the marriage partners suffers from a mental disability, heavy burdens are often placed upon the other spouse and upon the children. Under these circumstances, many jurisdictions allow the family relationship to be terminated through divorce and adoption.

II. MARRIAGE OF MENTALLY DISABLED PERSONS

A. DEVELOPMENT OF THE LAW

Prohibitions against the marriage of mentally disabled persons appear in the common law. The law's concern with this topic may be attributed to two separate policies: to prevent the creation of a marital contract when one of the partners is incapable of understanding the nature of the relationship and to prevent reproduction by persons whose issue may become a public charge. The first of these policies is the older and has played the more prominent part in legislation. The English laws on this subject appear to be based on this reason.[1] The latter concern over propagation of the mentally disabled stems from the more recent eugenic movement, which is also responsible for the sterilization laws, and is reflected in the statutes of only a few states.[2]

Possession of sufficient mental capacity to consent is a prerequisite for a valid marriage by statute and at common law.[3] Although no general test of capacity is universally recognized, the usual test is the person's mental ability to understand the nature of the marriage relation and the duties and obligations involved.[4]

States opposing the marriage of the mentally disabled for eugenic reasons adhere to the theory that mental illness and deficiency are hereditary and that it is the state's duty to prevent their perpetuation.[5] In nine states eugenic considerations are apparently at the core of the law, since mentally disabled persons are permitted to marry when sterilization has been performed or when the woman is over forty-five years of age, or, as in Michigan, when the ex-patient or adjudicated person can show by means of medical certification that there is no probability that he or she will transmit mental defects to the issue of the marriage.[6] Medical evidence discovered in recent years has challenged and undermined the validity of eugenic theories by raising questions regarding the role of heredity in some or even most types of mental illness and deficiency. However, the basis of the argument against such marriages has merely been transferred from heredity to environment.[7] The major argument now propounded is that mentally disabled persons, whether their condition is inherited or not, are unfit parents and should not be permitted to bear children.

B. PERSONS PROHIBITED FROM MARRYING

There is no uniformity in the language of the statutes which prohibit marriage of the mentally disabled. The list of terms describing the persons affected by these laws is almost endless. Among the most com-

---

1. For an analysis of English laws concerning marriage of the mentally disabled, see Royal Commission on the Law Relating to Mental Illness and Mental Deficiency 1954–57, CMND. No. 169, *Report,* at 294 (1957).

2. See Table 7.1, Marriage and Mental Disability. See also chap. 6, "Eugenic Sterilization."

3. 35 *Am. Jur.* "Marriage" § 17 (1941).

4. Kingsley, "What Are the Proper Grounds for Granting An-

nulments?" 18 *Law & Contemp. Prbl.* 39, 40 (1953). Allen, Ferster, & Weihofen, in *Mental Impairment and Legal Incompetency* 301 (1968), note the exception of eight states where the test for capacity to marry is statutorily the test for capacity to contract generally ("ordinary" contracts). The authors point out, however, that the courts in these states do not interpret such statutory language strictly against the incapacitated party. These courts have recognized that the marriage contract differs in terms of its demands, duties, and presumptions from any other civil contract and that the test for capacity should vary accordingly. Thus, mental ability to understand the nature of the marriage relation and its duties and obligations appears in fact to be the test even in these eight jurisdictions.

5. 1 Vernier, *American Family Laws* § 41 (1931).

6. See Table 7.1, Exception to Prohibition column. See also chap. 6, "Eugenic Sterilization."

7. See chap. 6, "Eugenic Sterilization," for an analogous development in the rationales supporting sterilization of the mentally disabled.

mon of these terms are: idiots, insane, weak-minded, lunatics, feebleminded, imbeciles, persons incapable of contracting, and persons of unsound mind.[8]

A commentary on this statutory variety, written nearly forty years ago, stated:

> The totally unscientific character of the statutes dealing with a scientific subject in this modern age of scientific enlightenment is revealed in connection with the inconsistent . . . statements defining the classes of incompetents. . . . There are all degrees of mental incapacity and many varieties of insanity, some curable, some incurable; some acquired and some hereditary. Perhaps these defy legal description or definition, but it is certain that their different degrees and characteristics have hardly been recognized at all by the legislation of the Nation in dealing with the marriage problem.[9]

Statutory terminology has improved only slightly since this criticism was made. The only significant difference has been the deletion of epileptics from the descriptive list on the part of some twelve states since 1960. Otherwise it is still difficult to determine to whom the statutes apply and whether their scope is related to medical knowledge. For example, many statutes still do not specify whether they include hospitalized persons, incompetents, or other subclasses of the mentally disabled.

C. Methods of Enforcement

The effectiveness of the various statutes prohibiting marriage of persons with mental infirmities is highly questionable. Only twenty states have attempted to establish any machinery to enforce the prohibitions.[10] Eighteen states provide criminal punishment for violations. Penalties vary from minor fines to a maximum of five years' imprisonment. The punitive measures apply usually to the incompetent person himself, often also to the clerk or official granting the marriage license, and in a few states also to anyone "advising," "abetting," or "causing" the marriage. North Carolina, North Dakota, and Oregon require that a medical certificate avowing the absence of the prohibited conditions be produced before any marriage license can be issued. Kansas requires the county clerk to ask the applicants if they have ever been adjudicated "an incapacitated person" and if so, whether they have been discharged

as restored. In the absence of such specific statutory instruction, clerks can hardly be expected to ask such a question. One Texas clerk, queried on the point, reportedly replied, "Are you serious? How can I ask a person if he's crazy?"[11] It has been concluded that the statutes preventing marriages of people with mental disabilities have in fact prevented very few such marriages[12] and have "thus far . . . invariably proved worthless, chiefly because of the lack of adequate provision for the identification or diagnosis of the mental status of applicants for marriage licenses."[13]

Many states do not specifically prohibit marriage of the mentally disabled but instead allow annulment or divorce as a relief.[14] Of course, the threat of a severed marriage is not an effective deterrent to one who is incapable of understanding the marriage relationship, nor is dissolution an effective enforcement measure when it is dependent upon the voluntary initiative of one of the parties to the disapproved relationship. In essence, such divorce or annulment provisions are not designed, and are probably not intended, to function in a deterrent or prohibiting capacity.

If the state actually wishes to control marriages that it considers unadvised, it should take more direct action. The most effective method might be to check all applications for marriage licenses against a central record file for all incompetent and hospitalized persons. In New Hampshire, such procedures were in effect prior to 1961. All public and private schools were required to report annually the names of all epileptic, imbecile, feebleminded, idiotic or insane pupils who had left school or had become fourteen years of age during the preceding year. Also, the state hospital and the state school for the retarded were required to file the names of all patients discharged or paroled.[15] These requirements were repealed, however, in 1961. Requirement of a physician's certificate stating the absence of the prohibited conditions would also be a direct and effective method of control, since it would act as a check on persons who are mentally disabled but have not been so adjudicated. Whatever the merits —social desirability or practical effectiveness—of these methods, any enactment of such enforcement provisions should at the least guarantee at some

8. See Table 7.1, Description of Persons Prohibited from Marrying column.

9. 1 Vernier, *supra* note 5, at 190.

10. See Table 7.1, Enforcement column.

11. Allen et al., *supra* note 4, at 303.

12. Id. at 299.

13. Deutsch, *The Mentally Ill in America* 377 (2d ed. 1949).

14. See Table 7.1, Status column.

15. Allen et al., *supra* note 4, at 304.

point the right to a judicial determination of the issue of competency to marry. That is, where denial of the marriage license is based on the fact of *prior* institutionalization, there must be a right to a judicial hearing on *present* mental condition; likewise, where denial stems from inability to obtain a physician's certificate of approval, a right to judicial review of such medical opinion should obtain.

D. HOSPITALIZED PATIENTS

While persons outside institutions have been shown to be rarely affected by laws regulating or prohibiting marriage of the mentally disabled, the situation appears to be radically different for hospitalized persons. The statutes of several states specifically include persons under commitment to institutions in their description of persons prohibited from marrying.[16] Whereas other designations are subject to interpretation and are rendered escapable by lack of enforcement machinery, "the prohibition against committed persons is rigid and absolute. . . . Even in the *absence* of such prohibitory statutes, patients in the state hospitals on compulsory commitment can be and ordinarily are prevented from marrying."[17]

E. EFFECT OF PROHIBITED MARRIAGES

The legal effect of prohibited marriages varies from state to state. In some states the parties are subject to criminal penalties but the marriage is valid. In three states—Maine, Michigan, and Wyoming—the marriages are specifically stated to be void without any need for a judicial decree.

A number of other states similarly employ the label "void" or "absolutely void," but nonetheless grant relief only through formal proceedings for divorce or annulment.[18] Several jurisdictions call such marriages "voidable," and nearly half the state statutes today merely declare that mental incompetency is a ground for annulment without using the terms "void" or "voidable."[19] Theoretically a void marriage ought to raise serious questions about the spouses' rights to property and the legitimacy of children of the marriage, but in fact the strict logical conclusions are often avoided.

> It is not at all certain . . . that even in those states [which use the language of voidness] the courts would inexorably apply all the orthodox consequences of voidness. The statutes themselves frequently make an exception by declaring that children of such void marriages shall nevertheless be legitimate. Others specifically forbid attack on the marriage after the death of the parties. Although, logically, a void marriage cannot be ratified, only one court seems to have denied the right to ratify, and that court later reversed itself.[20]

Considerable variation exists with regard to who may institute divorce or annulment proceedings. In some jurisdictions only the person with mental disability may seek relief, while in others only the person without it may do so. A few jurisdictions specify that either party may initiate proceedings, and other states provide no statutory guidance.[21] Again theoretically, if a marriage is "void" under the statute, either party to the marriage and even interested third parties should be able to assert the defect. But generally the logic has not been so extended. Designation of the person or persons who may sue for dissolution of the marriage appears to bear little relationship to whether such marriages are deemed void or voidable.[22] Collateral or third-party attack has been allowed in some cases to deprive the surviving spouse of inheritance rights upon the death of the other spouse, but on the whole such actions have been disfavored.[23] Courts have often refused to allow voidness to deprive a spouse of a share of the property acquired during the relationship, and, as indicated before, several state statutes specifically forbid attack on the marriage after the death of the parties.[24]

Most states authorize annulment or divorce on the ground of prenuptial mental disability. Although the possession of sufficient mental capacity to consent to the relationship is prerequisite to a valid marriage, it is presumed that a person who has entered into a marriage was capable of legally contracting it and the burden of proving incapacity is

16. See Table 7.1, Description of Persons Prohibited from Marrying column.

17. Allen et al., *supra* note 4, at 304. (Emphasis added.) On the other hand, marriages do take place among patients on temporary leave—i.e., those technically still under commitment but beyond the immediate control of the institution. Hospital superintendents generally refrain from taking steps to nullify such marriages.

18. See Table 7.1, Status . . . and Spouse . . . columns.

19. Ibid. See also Allen et al., *supra* note 4, at 307.

20. Allen et al., *supra* note 4, at 307.

21. See Table 7.1, Spouse column. See also Harper, *Problems of the Family* 298–300 (1952).

22. See Table 7.1.

23. Allen et al., *supra* note 4, at 307–8.

24. Ibid.

on the party seeking divorce or annulment.[25] It is held that the determining fact should be mental condition at the time of the marriage ceremony rather than the condition prior to, or subsequent to, the marriage, even though the interval may be very short.[26] In England, under the common law, a marriage is void *ab initio* if either party at the time of the marriage is suffering from insanity to such an extent as to be incapable of understanding the nature of the ceremony or as to have insane delusions on the subject.[27] The Matrimonial Causes Act of 1950 makes a marriage voidable if either party to the marriage was at the time of the marriage of unsound mind, a mental defective, or subject to recurrent fits of insanity or epilepsy. The Royal Commission on laws relating to mental illness recommended certain changes in 1957: (1) The provision on unsoundness of mind should be redrafted so as to make it clear that it applies only when a person has gone through a ceremony of marriage with a full understanding of the nature of the ceremony and what it imports, but was nevertheless of unsound mind at the time. This change was thought to provide a clearer distinction between marriages which are voidable on these grounds and those which are void *ab initio*. (2) The wording should be altered to "subject to recurrent attacks of insanity or epilepsy." (3) Only the sane spouse may seek judicial relief.[28] The desirability of the Commission's recom-

mendations is debatable. One aspect is clear, however: the reason for such provisions is to afford *relief* to an "innocent" sane spouse rather than a desire on the part of the state to invalidate the marriage.

III. POSTNUPTIAL MENTAL ILLNESS

A. HISTORICAL BACKGROUND

Divorce is designed to dissolve marriages for postnuptial causes, annulment for causes existing at the time of the marriage.[29] Postnuptial mental illness, or "insanity" as it is often termed by the statutes, is usually the only type of mental disability for which a *divorce* may be granted because other types of mental disability such as mental deficiency and epilepsy are present from the time of birth or early childhood.

Postnuptial mental illness as a ground for divorce in this country has had a slow growth. It is a matter of academic dispute whether Arkansas, in a statute of 1843, or Washington, in 1886, was the first state to permit divorce for postnuptial mental illness.[30] In 1931 only thirteen states were reported to have statutory provisions allowing divorce for postnuptial mental illness.[31] Fifteen years later twenty-six states had such statutes.[32] At the present time the number has increased to thirty-one.[33] England and Puerto Rico also have such provisions.

Mental disability as a ground for divorce has always been the subject of violent controversy. It has been objected to not only by those who are generally opposed to divorce but also by those who recognize the need for divorce in some cases but believe it should be restricted to situations in which there is "fault" on the part of one spouse. One of the general arguments is as follows:

> A concealed hereditary taint which breaks out after marriage is sometimes made cause of divorce by our legislatures . . . and yet devoted kindness and for-

25. 35 *Am. Jur.* "Marriage" § 113 (1941).

26. In Littreal v. Littreal, 253 S.W.2d 247 (Ky. Civ. App. 1952), where a wife brought a separate maintenance action wherein committee for the husband sought an annulment on the ground that the husband had been adjudicated incompetent prior to the marriage, the court denied the annulment on the ground that the prior adjudication merely raised a presumption that the incapacity continued thereafter. It was the court's view that the presumption as to the validity of the marriage is so strong that a presumption of incompetency would not overcome it unless the marriage ceremony and the incompetency decree were reasonably simultaneous. Similarly in Forbis v. Forbis, 274 S.W.2d 800 (Mo. Ct. App. 1955), it was the opinion of the court that a person's being of unsound mind eleven months after a marriage did not necessarily mean that the condition had existed at the time of the marriage.

27. Royal Commission, *supra* note 1, at 294.

28. The sane spouse must meet the following requirements: (1) at the time of the marriage he was ignorant of the facts alleged; (2) he has refrained from marital intercourse since his discovery of the alleged facts; (3) he must bring the action within a year of the marriage. Although this procedure avoids property and legitimacy problems and appears to offer reasonable protection to the rights of both marital partners, it does not effectively prevent such marriages from occurring. Royal Commission, *supra* note 1, at 294–95.

29. McCurdy, "Insanity as a Ground for Annulment or Divorce in English and American Law," 29 *Va. L. Rev.* 771, 774 (1943).

30. Gordon, "Insanity and Divorce," 5 *J. Crim. L. & Crim.* 544–48 (1914–15); Stimson, *American Statute Law* § 6201 (1886); 2 Vernier, *supra* note 5, at § 72 (1932); Comment, 35 *Cal. L. Rev.* 99, 105 (1947). It is interesting to note that while Sweden has allowed divorce for insanity for over a century, by 1915 only Germany, Switzerland, Monaco, Bulgaria, and Portugal had laws allowing such divorce. Gordon, *supra* at 544.

31. 2 Vernier, *supra* note 5, at § 72.

32. Keezer, *On the Law of Marriage and Divorce.* § 451 (3d ed. 1946).

33. See Table 7.2, Divorce and Mental Disability, Grounds for Divorce columns.

bearance not only afford the surest hope of restoring the sufferer, diseased in mind or body, to health once more, but may bring the highest blessings to the patient's spouse. The constancy of husband and wife to one another in sickness or health, in accordance with the marriage vow, is the crown of matrimony. . . .[34]

A more direct attack is delivered by another writer:

One objection to making insanity a ground for divorce is that not only is there absence of fault but renunciation of duty for mere misfortune. . . . Another objection is that if insanity is made a ground for divorce why should not any other disease if it results similarly in irreparable disruption of the cohabitational aspects of the marriage. A distinction may perhaps be found in the fact that insanity unlike other diseases results in substantial change in personality.[35]

Such criticism notwithstanding, divorce on the ground of postnuptial mental disability, which had been the minority policy, became the practice in a majority of states within a span of about fifteen years. Identification of the factors responsible for this change may be helpful in assessing future legislative development. It is important to note that two-thirds of the statutes allowing divorce on the ground of agreed separation for a certain period were passed within approximately the same fifteen-year period. The growth of the concept of divorce without "fault" seems to have brought about the latter development. The movement to substitute the "forward-looking" consideration of "cooperation" for the outdated principle of "guilt" has gained strength in many countries. "Nowhere," say its proponents,

is the justification for such a change of attitude more obvious than in the law of divorce. . . . Countries which refuse to impose a business partnership on an unwilling party do not hesitate to impose on unwilling spouses this most intimate of human relations.[36]

Since divorce on the ground of mental illness can be characterized as divorce without "fault," it would seem that the increasing acceptance of this latter concept is at least partly responsible for the additional statutes allowing divorce on the ground of mental illness.[37] Other reasons are also offered for this change:

The possibility of defective offspring,[38] the apparent unfairness of considering a person legally married whose spouse is incurably insane, and the effect upon other persons not responsible for the unfortunate situation have been factors in bringing about this attitude.[39]

Not all of these arguments are new. Many were propounded forty and fifty years ago.[40] But today, with the steady increase in hospitalization of the mentally disabled and greater public interest in this area, these ideas have become more generally accepted.

B. Present Status of Postnuptial Mental Illness as a Ground for Divorce

There is substantial similarity among the statutes of the thirty-one states that allow postnuptial mental illness as a ground for divorce. All but one (Utah) require the condition to have persisted for a specified period,[41] which in most jurisdictions appears to refer to time spent in a mental institution. In fifteen states the necessary period is five years; in the remainder it is from two to three years except in Alaska where it is eighteen months. A trend toward reducing the length of time during which the illness and/or confinement must have persisted is discernible: a few states have altered their requirement from five to three, or from three to two, years. Almost all the states require the condition to be incurable and most require that this fact be established by medical testimony; in twelve states such testimony must be given by more than one medical expert.[42] However, some eight states fail to require that the condition of in-

---

34. 2 Schouler, *Marriage, Divorce, Separation and Domestic Relations* 1787 (1921).

35. McCurdy, *supra* note 29, at 804–5.

36. Silving, "Divorce without Fault," 29 *Iowa L. Rev.* 527, 557 (1944), cited in Keezer, *supra* note 32, at § 451 n.10.

37. Comment, *supra* note 30, at 105–6.

38. The argument regarding the possibility of defective offspring is not a very compelling one. Divorce is technically appropriate only in cases of postnuptial insanity—i.e., forms of mental disturbance that the affected person was *not* born with. Eugenic theories about hereditary illness are least acceptable when applied to these types of mental disabilities (see chap. 6, "Eugenic Sterilization"). More compelling is the notion that divorce may be appropriate because the home environment with a mentally ill parent is damaging to a child's development. Instances have been recorded—systematically in at least one study—where the child actually participates in the symptomatology of the afflicted parent's psychosis. See Anthony, "Clinical Evaluation of Children with Psychotic Parents," 126 *Am. J. Psychiat.* 177 (1969).

39. Keezer, *supra* note 32, at § 450.

40. E.g., Gordon, *supra* note 30.

41. See Table 7.2, Period column.

42. Id. at Incurable and Medical Testimony columns.

curability be established by experts in the field of mental illness.[43]

The main problem that might arise under these requirements turns upon the term "incurable." Incurability is closely related to length of institutional confinement, since one of the chief factors in establishing incurability is a showing that the patient has not responded to accepted methods of treatment over a period of time. However, if the assertion is valid that a majority of patients in state hospitals do not receive adequate treatment because of overcrowding and understaffing, it is difficult to see how an accurate statement in regard to incurability could be made solely on this basis. Alternatively, it appears equally tenuous to equate a patient's discharge with curability or recovery. Many state hospitals today are gradually reducing the average length of stay for inpatients, but it is far from clear whether an institution's discharge policy bears a significant relationship to recovery.[44] It is even more doubtful whether the discharge criterion has any bearing on whether the marriage relationship should be forced to continue in opposition to the desire of a plaintiff spouse.

Only a few cases touch on these problems,[45] and they do little to clarify the real issues at stake. A California case[46] denied divorce to the plaintiff husband where the wife had entered the hospital as a voluntary patient rather than being confined under order of court. It is difficult to see why the legal status of the afflicted spouse should be determinative of whether divorce is or is not appropriate. Decisions in Kansas[47] and North Carolina[48] came closer to dealing with the relevant problems, indicating that curability is the primary issue while length of institutionalization—either as an independent criterion or as evidence of incurability—is of lesser import. These cases held that the statutory requisite regarding length of confinement does not necessarily mean a continuous period of confinement: intervening periods of outpatient treatment or parole (especially when such intervals are *not* spent with the "sane"

spouse) do not operate to preclude the granting of divorce.

California requires that for purposes of the divorce statute the mentally ill spouse be confined within the state.[49] In *Dribin v. Superior Court,*[50] the plaintiff, in a divorce suit seeking a California decree, offered in evidence a deposition from the Minnesota State Hospital stating that the "defendant was incurably insane." The plaintiff urged that the California requirement of confinement within the state was unconstitutional because there would seem to be no logical reason for such discrimination and the restriction amounted to discrimination on the basis of state citizenship. The California Supreme Court decided that this was not an arbitrary requirement:

> The legal concept of "insanity" may well vary considerably in the different jurisdictions and in different applications of the term (. . . "insanity is a broad, comprehensive, and generic term, of ambiguous import, for all unsound and deranged conditions of the mind"). In this state a definition of such concept in respect of civil proceedings has been expressly set forth . . . and in addition . . . [the] code . . . throws about an alleged insane or incompetent person various safeguards by way of notice, service of process, hearing, evidence, jury trial, etc., before an adjudication of insanity and commitment therefor may be made. . . . The Legislature in requiring proof of confinement in California may have had in mind that the same safeguards might not be afforded before adjudication and confinement in other jurisdictions.[51]

The court's reasoning is not completely persuasive. Confinement in a California institution can occur for an entire spectrum of mental conditions ranging from partial personality disorder to severe psychosis with total impairment of social functioning capacity. At the same time, the range of procedural protections accorded a prospective patient in California undoubtedly also varies significantly with the legal route employed as well as with the prevailing

43. Ibid.

44. See chaps. 2, 3, and 4 on civil hospitalization and separation from mental hospitals regarding population trends, admission and discharge policies, in state institutions.

45. See Annot., 15 A.L.R.2d 1135–37 (1951).

46. Riggins v. Riggins, 139 Cal. App. 2d 712, 294 P.2d 751 (1956).

47. Katz v. Katz, 191 Kan. 500, 382 P.2d 331 (1963).

48. Mabry v. Mabry, 243 N.C. 126, 90 S.E.2d 221 (1955).

49. See Table 7.2, Commitment column. *Cal. Civ. Code* § 108 (West Supp. 1967).

50. 37 Cal. 2d 345, 231 P.2d 809 (1951). The statute under consideration required that the incurably insane spouse be confined in a California institution for a period of at least three consecutive years before divorce was to be allowed. The couple in that case had married in the state of Illinois and had separated two and a half years later. Subsequently, the defendant was adjudged "insane" in Minnesota on the application of her mother. At the time of the divorce suit, she had been a patient in the Minnesota State Hospital for more than five years.

51. Id. at 349, 231 P.2d at 813.

practices (e.g., availability of legal services) in different locales within the state. If three years' confinement in California is viewed as an adequate test, there is really little reason why five years in a Minnesota institution should not suffice. The point is, of course, that confinement in an institution is by itself an insufficient standard for determining the degree of mental disability that would warrant divorce, regardless of where the confinement takes place. If on the other hand lengthy confinement is perceived as an indication of irreparable disruption of the communal aspects of the marriage, and the granting of divorce is predicated on that consideration, then proof of extended institutionalization should be conclusive, variation in substantive and procedural standards of admission among the states being irrelevant.

Following the *Dribin* holding, it was reasonable to expect that similar problems would arise with frequency in different jurisdictions. The increasing mobility of the population made it likely. Many states had divorce statutes which were open to equally restrictive interpretation.[52] It appeared that unless the terminology and involuntary hospitalization procedures of the different states became more uniform, many courts would adopt the California view and permit divorce only when hospitalization had been within the boundaries of their own state. These predictions did not materialize, however.[53] The factors inhibiting the anticipated undesirable developments are a matter of speculation. Perhaps the *Dribin* type of factual situation remains even today a rare occurrence. Or, the general tendency toward facilitating divorce may have made the lower courts less strict on the residence requirement. Residence has already been relegated to a less-than-controlling consideration on a different level: the Interstate Compact on Mental Health—regarding transfers of patients among the states—explicitly places the patient's therapeutic interests over traditionally primary legal and administrative interests based on residence. The Compact's rapidly growing acceptance among the states over the past decade[54]

may be viewed as a trend in the direction of emphasizing personal considerations over governmental ones, a trend which has applicability to the problem of divorce as well.

Most of the states permitting divorce on the ground of mental illness make provision for the future support of the mentally ill person, and about half of them expressly provide by statute that financial responsibilities of the plantiff are not to be changed by divorce.[55] The California code attempted to go further by requiring the plaintiff to prove ownership of property sufficient to support the mentally ill spouse for the remainder of his life. However, this provision was declared unconstitutional because it created an unreasonable class discrimination between persons of different financial resources. Said the court in the same *Dribin* case:[56]

No compelling necessity has been found by the Legislature or suggested to us for generally denying divorce to the poor and making it available to the wealthy. Here the state has guarded against financial dependency of the insane spouse by providing that the divorce of an insane spouse does not relieve the other spouse of any obligation imposed by law as a result of the marriage for the support of the insane spouse . . . [I]n view of such provision, the additional requirement of proof of possession of financial ability appears arbitrary. . . . Since full liability for support perdures, after divorce as during marriage, and since the court can exact security as in any case according to the means of the spouse securing the decree, the only basis left for the classification is wealth as against poverty. In this application it is not a valid classification.

Only about two-thirds of the states provide by statute for a guardian *ad litem* or counsel for the

---

52. See Table 7.2, Commitment column, for citations to the statutes.

53. Research has uncovered only Georgia as having adopted the California *Dribin* view by judicial decision: Shelton v. Shelton, 209 Ga. 454, S.E.2d 5 (1963).

54. The Interstate Compact on Mental Health was developed in 1955 by a group of state officials representing the ten northeastern states. The Compact was first ratified by Connecticut in late 1955. By November 1968, thirty-five other states had adopted it: Alaska, Arkansas, Colorado, Delaware, Hawaii,

Idaho, Illinois, Indiana, Iowa, Kansas, Kentucky, Louisiana, Maine, Maryland, Massachusetts, Michigan, Minnesota, Missouri, New Hampshire, New Jersey, New York, North Carolina, North Dakota, Ohio, Oklahoma, Oregon, Pennsylvania, Rhode Island, South Carolina, South Dakota, Vermont, Virginia, Washington, West Virginia, and Wisconsin. See Council of State Governments, "The Interstate Compact on Mental Health: What It Is and Does" (rev. ed. Dec. 1968).

55. See Table 7.2, Continuing Financial Liability column.

56. Dribin v. Superior Court, 37 Cal. 2d 345, 348, 231 P.2d 809, 812 (1951). The court decided this issue first, adding that the unconstitutional portion of the statute did not invalidate the rest of the statute. The court then proceeded to deny the divorce on the basis of the valid portion (confinement within the state) of the statute. It is not clear why the court felt compelled to rule on the first issue, financial dependency, at all.

defendant.[57] In addition, numerous states do not require personal service of process on the mentally ill person. Instead, provision is made for service on the guardian or proper hospital authority,[58] who may in a few states decide, in the best interest of the patient, that he not be personally served or notified. Thus the defendant may be totally ignorant of the divorce proceeding. Though it may be debatable whether vigorous contest to preserve a marriage unwanted by at least one of the parties is desirable, the laws of most states are predicated on the assumption that it is. Accordingly, provisions for notice to and representation for the defendant would be appropriate elements within this scheme.[59] More persuasive perhaps is the point that notice and representation are essential to assure that the defendant receive adequate protection in terms of the financial and property aspects of an eventual divorce decree.

C. MENTAL ILLNESS AS A DEFENSE IN DIVORCE ACTIONS GENERALLY

The question of mental illness as a defense to divorce commonly arises in jurisdictions which do not recognize postnuptial mental illness as a ground for divorce. In those states, that defense will bar a divorce based upon misconduct which occurred during the illness. It is introduced primarily in cases where divorce is sought on the grounds of cruelty, desertion, or adultery. In those jurisdictions where postnuptial mental illness is a valid ground, the defense will generally have only a temporary effect since a divorce may subsequently be granted after the statutory waiting period.

Many courts have taken the view that if the nature of the mental illness is such that it deprives the defendant of the ability to differentiate right from wrong, he may not be held legally accountable for the consequences of his acts that would otherwise be grounds for divorce, any more than he could be held accountable for them in a criminal action. It appears that a rule akin to a strict *M'Naghten* is applied, for if the defendant knows the difference between right and wrong, mental illness is no defense to the divorce action even though the defendant acted under the compulsion of a diseased mind.[60]

It is generally accepted that if the conduct providing a ground for the divorce action occurred before the defendant became insane, the divorce will be granted even if mental illness intervened before the action was brought.[61] Since the defense of mental illness is introduced primarily in divorce actions where there is, in fact, "fault" by the defendant, it is understandable that the courts have felt that a mentally ill person should not be held to the same responsibility for his actions as one who is not mentally ill.

It has been argued, however, that since divorce is a civil action, it is curious to insist upon the right-and-wrong standard of criminal responsibility, and that the standards of civil hospitalization would be more appropriate.[62] This line of reasoning is not entirely convincing: if "fault" is indeed the basis for divorce, then absence of fault, as a defense, could well be appropriately predicated on a formula involving knowledge of right and wrong. The essential point is that "fault" is a misplaced standard in divorce actions, whether disproved by criminal or by civil criteria. Instead, focus should be on the degree or type of mental disability and its effects on the marriage (including the children) in determining whether dissolution or continuation of the relationship would be in the best interest of the parties to it (and of the state, which sees its function as preserving the institution of marriage generally).

D. THE RIGHT OF A MENTALLY ILL SPOUSE TO SUE FOR DIVORCE

Whereas in the case of prenuptial mental illness most states allow the mentally disabled party to seek annulment (or divorce),[63] in cases where illness developed subsequent to the marriage only two jurisdictions—Alabama and Massachusetts—grant the mentally ill spouse (as well as the "sane" party) the

---

57. See Table 7.2, Guardian *Ad Litem* and Court Appointed Counsel columns.

58. See Table 9.1, Personal and Property Rights of the Mentally Disabled, Procedures Relating to Service of Process column.

59. Arguably, these elements are so central to fairness that their denial would constitute a violation of due process. Regarding substituted notice, for instance, a *minimum* requirement for this manner of proceeding should be a case-by-case finding that such would be in the best interest of the patient.

60. See Harper, *supra* note 21, at 706–8.

61. Annot., 19 A.L.R.2d 144, 181 (1951).

62. Another view on the subject is found in the position of some English judges that the purpose of divorce is not to punish the defendant for offenses but to protect the offended spouse against violation of his marital rights. It is immaterial to the offended party that his marital partner was mentally incapable of understanding the legal consequences of the acts being cited as grounds for divorce. According to this view, mental illness is never a defense to an action for divorce. This view has not been favored by American courts. Annot., *supra* note 61, at 148.

63. See Table 7.1, Spouse Authorized to Petition column.

right to seek divorce.[64] In Massachusetts an express statutory provision[65] gives the guardian or next friend, appointed by the court for that purpose, the power to file an action for divorce on behalf of a mentally ill person. In Alabama, however, the right exists by judicial interpretation[66] of a statute which contains only a general provision such as is found in all states allowing a guardian of a mentally ill person to sue and be sued for his charge.

The vast majority of the courts that have been confronted with the question of the right of a mentally ill person to sue for divorce have held that a guardian or next friend may *not* maintain the action.[67] It has been held that general statutes giving the guardian, committee, or next friend the power to sue do not apply to divorce actions on the theory that a divorce is so personal that it cannot be maintained by a person who is not a party to the marriage. Another line of reasoning is that a petition in a divorce proceeding must be personally verified, and mentally ill persons are incapable of doing this.[68]

It may conceivably be urged that the advisability of permitting mentally ill persons to sue for divorce be considered with caution, since mentally ill persons not infrequently see things in an entirely different light when, if ever, they recover, and they may not wish to have a divorce after their recovery. On the other hand, denial of the right to sue for divorce may result in hardship to the mentally ill spouse. For example, the "sane" spouse may be left in physical control of property owned by the mentally ill spouse, quite possibly to the latter's detriment. Whatever the pros and cons of the argument for allowing the mentally ill to sue for divorce, it is interesting to note that while thirty-one states allow marital partners of the mentally ill to obtain divorces

without any showing of misconduct on the part of the mentally ill, only Alabama and Massachusetts permit mentally ill persons to obtain a divorce and then only when there is "fault" on the part of the sane spouse. Owing to the inactive role of the mentally ill as members of the community, there is apparently less pressure for legislation concerning the marital rights of the mentally ill.

IV. ADOPTION OF CHILDREN OF MENTALLY DISABLED PARENTS

A. HISTORICAL BACKGROUND

Adoption dates back to biblical times.[69] In both England and the United States, however, adoption is not part of the common law but is based entirely upon statutes. Massachusetts enacted the first adoption statute in the United States in 1851; England did not have a provision on the subject until 1926.[70]

The power of the state legislature to provide for adoption is universally recognized, and the welfare of the child is considered the primary objective. Consent of the natural parents or surviving parent to an adoption proceeding is quite uniformly required in the statutes of the various states and lies at their very foundation.[71]

Parental consent is not required, however, in cases where the conduct of the parents has been deleterious to the welfare of the child.[72] Early statutes dispensed with consent only when there was parental misconduct such as abandonment, neglect, or cruelty.[73] In recent years, nonconsensual adoptions have been extended to include cases where the parents of the children to be adopted are mentally disabled. This extension has probably resulted from the view that mentally disabled persons are incapable of consenting to adoption of their children.[74] Pres-

64. See Annot., 6 A.L.R.3d 681 (1966).

65. *Mass. Ann. Laws* ch. 208, § 7 (1955).

66. Campbell v. Campbell, 242 Ala. 141, 5 So. 2d 401 (1941). An intermediate view was expressed in a Tennessee case which held that the question of a person's possession of the requisite volition to seek a divorce or the capacity to take the oath "is a fact to be found by the trial court just as is any other." Turner v. Bell, 198 Tenn. App. 232, 279 S.W.2d 71, 80 (1955). This holding is essentially in agreement with the majority rule. Although it does not recognize a previous adjudication of insanity as a bar to the bringing of a divorce suit, it nevertheless makes the sanity of the plaintiff a criterion for his right of action. It seems reasonable to assume, therefore, that Tennessee would follow the majority in denying a mentally ill person the right to sue if the court finds the plaintiff lacking the requisite personal volition and capacity to take the statutory oath.

67. Annot., *supra* note 61, at 182–83.

68. Annot., 149 A.L.R. 1284, 1285–86 (1944).

69. Exodus 2:10.

70. Note, "Due Process Rights of Mentally Ill Parents in Nonconsensual Adoptions." 30 *Ind. L.J.* 431, 433 n.9 (1954–55).

71. 1 *Am. Jur.* "Adoption of Children" §§ 4, 36 (1936).

72. In such cases the issue is, technically speaking, not *adoption* but *termination* of the parent-child relationship. The termination/adoption distinction is made much of in some circles and will be alluded to below. However, the language of adoption is commonly used in reference to the subject matter—in disregard of terminological niceties and perhaps of substantive considerations. On the whole this section follows the traditional approach, using the language of adoption to speak of both that and termination on grounds of mental disability.

73. See Keal v. Rhydderck, 317 Ill. 231, 148 N.E. 53 (1925).

74. 1 *Am. Jur.* "Adoption of Children" § 36 (Supp. 1959). See

ently, there are forty-one jurisdictions having statutes which include mental illness as a ground for dispensing with the need for parental consent to adoption.[75]

Adoption of children of mentally disabled parents involves two separate issues or sets of circumstances. One situation concerns parents who may be willing to have their children adopted, but who because of mental disability are incapable of giving valid legal consent. Statutory authorization for consent by a friend or relative in such instances is aimed at securing the legality of transfer of parental rights and serves mainly to protect the rights of the adopting parents. The other situation, involving parents who may *not* want to have their parental rights abrogated or whose consent is not considered, is one where the parent's mental disability is cause for a petitioner (the state, a welfare agency, the "sane" parent, etc.) to seek a transfer of parental custody. The question is thus one of unfitness for parenthood, analogous to parental delinquency, and what is sought is legal justification for *termination*[76] of the rights of the natural parents. The distinction is often disregarded in the literature on the subject as it is in the statutory provisions. However, in considering the social or philosophical justification for nonconsensual adoption it is important to keep these separate circumstances in mind.

Adoption, and especially termination, without the consent of the mentally disabled parent involves an intricate problem of balancing interests as between parent and child. The complexity of this balancing process is aggravated by the lack of firm scientific or sociological knowledge in this area.[77] Even at that, it appears that state legislatures have failed to take sufficient notice of the inherent complexities or to utilize the knowledge that is available. For instance, some mental disorders may be curable, others not; but the adoption statutes rarely consider this. At present, mental deficiency and organic mental disorders are *not* considered to be curable, and parents hospitalized for serious conditions of this sort are not likely to be discharged. Therefore, adoption in these cases would seem to be in the best interest of the child. However, some of the psychoses are controllable, and the parent may be released after only a short period of confinement. There is a real danger that if adoption is allowed in these circumstances, the parent-child relationship would be severed unjustifiably.[78] In addition to generally failing to take these substantive considerations into account, the statutes are often procedurally inadequate.

B. STATUTORY REQUIREMENTS FOR ADOPTION

Of the forty-one jurisdictions which allow children of the mentally ill to be adopted without the parents' consent, only five demand that the parental disability be "hopeless" or "incurable," and of those only Nevada provides for a fixed period of disability. Among the thirty-six which do not require an incurable affliction, only Kentucky sets a definite period —one year—through which the disability must have persisted.[79] Only Illinois states that the disability must be established by medical evidence, "evidence by 2 qualified physicians selected by the court that such parent continues to be mentally ill, in need of mental treatment or mentally retarded,

---

generally 45 A.L.R.2d 1379 (1952) for an annotation specifically dealing with mental illness as a ground for adoption of children.

75. See Allen et al., *supra* note 4, at 321. See also Table 7.3, Adoption and Mental Disability, Consent column. The count of forty-one jurisdictions as including mental disability as a ground for dispensing with consent is open to some variation, the inclusion being a matter of interpretation with regard to some statutes. E.g., *D.C. Code Ann.* § 16-304(e) (1967) states that lack of consent shall not be binding if it is "contrary to the best interests of the child." *Mont. Rev. Codes Ann.* § 61-205 (1961) and *Idaho Code Ann.* § 16-1504 (Supp. 1969) dispense with consent if the parents have been deprived of their civil rights generally. It seems likely that parental mental disability would come under the catchall language of these provisions; the issue is simply less clear than in a more typical statute such as *Ariz. Rev. Stat. Ann.* § 8-103A1(a) (Supp. 1970), which explicitly declares that consent shall not be necessary if the parent is "legally declared insane or incompetent."

Allen et al., *supra* note 4, at 314 emphasize the need for specific statutory authority in this area: "As is true of consensual acts generally, valid consent requires mental capacity to understand the nature of the transaction being consented to. A parent who lacks such capacity cannot legally consent to relinquishment of his parental rights. And in the absence of a statute authorizing proceedings by which parental rights may be terminated without consent, neither the courts nor other authorities are empowered to take a child from the custody of a mentally ill or hospitalized parent."

76. See note 72 *supra.*

77. E.g., Allen et al., *supra* note 4, at 319, documenting some prevailing judicial sentimentalism about natural parenthood, while noting that "[s]cientific studies indicate that biological parenthood is of less importance to the maturing child than psychological parenthood." And see Anthony, *supra* note 38, concerning the adverse effects of parental psychosis on the child. However, the "scientific" evidence on these and related questions is often still less than conclusive, and certainly far from universally accepted.

78. Note, *supra* note 70, at 434.

79. See Table 7.3, Consent of Parent column.

and will not recover . . . in the foreseeable future."[80]

The legal rights of the mentally disabled are thus less fully protected by adoption statutes than by divorce statutes. Both involve a permanent severance of the family relationship. All states, save one, that grant divorce on the ground of mental illness allow the suit to be maintained only after a fixed period of disability,[81] and Utah, the exception, requires medical testimony to establish that the disability is incurable.

Adoptions involving mentally ill parents have rarely been litigated on the appellate level. The constitutionality of this type of legislation was, however, challenged in Illinois in 1954 in the *Nabstedt* case.[82] The Illinois adoption statute provided that the parent must have been mentally ill for a period of three years and required that two qualified physicians selected by the court testify that the parent was not expected to recover in the foreseeable future. The law also authorized the court appointment of a guardian *ad litem* to represent the parent and to consent to adoption. The principal attack on the statute was based on the argument that it violated the substantive due process requirement of the Fourteenth Amendment because of the possibility that the parent might be restored to reason, but could not regain the custody and companionship of the child. The court conceded the possibility, but considered it too remote to invalidate the law and concluded:

> The concern of the legislature for the interest of the parent shows in its requirements that the mental illness must have continued for a period of three years and must, in the opinion of two qualified physicians, be such that there will not be recovery in the foreseeable future. . . . We note that a majority of the statutes of other states do not contain a requirement that insanity must have existed for a prescribed period of time before the entry of an adoption decree. Nor are they so strict in their requirements concerning medical evidence as to the permanent character of the mental illness.[83]

Illinois has since dispensed with this three-year requirement.[84]

80. *Ill. Ann. Stat.* ch. 4, § 9.1-8(3) (Smith-Hurd Supp. 1969).

81. See Table 7.2, Period column.

82. People *ex rel.* Nabstedt v. Barger, 3 Ill. 2d 511, 121 N.E.2d 781 (1954).

83. Id. at 514, 121 N.E.2d at 784.

84. *Ill. Ann. Stat.* ch. 4, § 9.1-8(e) (Smith-Hurd 1966).

The *Nabstedt* case also dealt with the question of adequate notice. Though the "insane" parent in *Nabstedt* had been personally served, counsel argued that the statute was void for failing to *require* such notice. The court met the argument by stating that notice was indeed constitutionally required in petitions of the first instance, but that it was *not* required in "supplemental petitions," where the court had continuing jurisdiction over the case on the basis of a prior decree involving guardianship. The soundness of this dictum may be questioned in view of the fact that many years may elapse (four years in the *Nabstedt* case) between the appointment of a guardian and the petition for adoption: the natural parent should be entitled to dispute the presumption of continued unfitness.[85] Nonetheless, Illinois is among the minority of some eight states that provide for at least some measure of notice to the parent whose consent is not necessary because of mental disability. Several states require only notice to the guardian, guardian *ad litem,* or other representative of the natural parents. Most states have no specific notice provisions whatsoever.[86]

Lack of procedural protections is a serious defect in the adoption statutes of most states,[87] one which has received insufficient attention. In the event of a petition for adoption the natural parents should be notified, a hearing held to determine *present* mental condition and fitness for parenthood, and legal representation afforded. The issue of whether consent of the natural parents can be dispensed with should be considered in light of the crucial difference between those parents who are willing but legally unable to consent and those whose parental rights the state is seeking to terminate. Perhaps it would be profitable to maintain the adoption-termination distinction with some rigor, for purposes of clarifying the substantive issues as well as the procedural questions.[88]

85. Cf. Child Saving Institute v. Knobel, 372 Mo. 609, 37 S.W.2d 920 (1931). See also Annot., 76 A.L.R. 1077, 1079 (1932).

86. See Table 7.3, Consent of Parent column.

87. Cf. Uniform Adoption Act, as in *Okla. Stat.* tit. 10, §§ 60.1 to 60.23 (1961) or *Mont. Rev. Codes Ann.* §§ 61-201 to 61-218 (1947). See also the Model Termination Act: U.S. Dep't of HEW, Children's Bureau, An Act for Termination of the Parent-Child Relationship, Legislative Guides for the Termination of Parental Rights and Responsibilities and the Adoption of Children 37 (1961).

88. The rights to notice and counsel and a hearing on the issue of present mental condition assume their greatest significance in the context of termination proceedings. More technical questions such as the proper place for bringing the proceedings

Relative to other grounds such as abandonment, mental disability as a ground for dispensing with consent is a comparatively infrequent occurrence. Still, a New York survey reported that mental illness prevented obtaining parental consent in a significant 12 percent of cases.[89] Considering the disadvantaged status of the mentally disabled and the socially fundamental nature of the right to parenthood, the adoption laws as applied to the mentally disabled merit critical attention.

C. ANNULMENT OF ADOPTIONS

Seven states allow the annulment of adoptions if the child develops feeblemindedness, epilepsy, or insanity as a result of conditions existing prior to the adoption and of which the adopting parents had no notice. Three states permit annulment of adoptions for "good or sound cause shown." Annulment proceedings may be brought within a specified period of time designated by statute.[90] These statutes are apparently attempting to protect the adopting parents from responsibility for a child with inherited mental disabilities. However, some modern medical authorities do not consider mental illness or epilepsy inheritable conditions.[91] On the other hand, since feeblemindedness is a condition which is generally present at birth, the period of time for annulment specified by most statutes appears unnecessarily long. Furthermore, the statutes make no provision as to the nature of the proof required, fail to provide a guardian *ad litem* for the child, and neglect to provide for the disposition of the child whose adoption is annulled. From the statutes it appears that little consideration is given to the rights of the child.

V. CONCLUSIONS AND RECOMMENDATIONS

1. *The law should not attempt to prohibit the mentally disabled from marrying, since the premise that mentally disabled persons as a group are less fit for the marriage relationship than any other groups of persons is scientifically tenuous and therefore legally arbitrary, while the eugenic arguments advanced to support such prohibition are similarly unsound.*

Though capacity to understand the meaning of the marriage contract is of itself not an unreasonable prerequisite to formal (governmental) sanction of a marriage, the legislative enactment of blanket prohibitions against the mentally disabled is an ill-conceived means of implementing this goal. Many of the mentally disabled may be quite "capable" of entering into and maintaining the personal relationship of marriage. In short, the statutes must avoid resolution of the capacity issue by the designation of inapposite medico-legal classes of persons. That this is more easily said than done is abundantly clear. Presently existing statutory prohibitions epitomize the difficulty of rationally identifying those groups of persons thought not to be fit for marriage. The provisions are usually indiscriminately applicable to the broad class of the mentally disabled—including in some cases even persons with disabilities such as epilepsy—thereby accentuating the basic sociological and legal dubiousness of legislative interference in this area. Marital prohibitions to prevent the propagation of "undesirable types" are lacking in scientific validity. (See chapter 6, "Eugenic Sterilization.") The related, though non-eugenic, rationale that children of mentally disabled parents may be circumstantially affected by the parents' disability has some evidentiary basis, but the data is inconclusive and provides no justification for categorical denial of the right to marry.

The virtual absence of enforcement and enforcement machinery characterizing the existing laws may reflect existing doubts regarding the need for and wisdom of this legislation. If a marriage relationship proves to be unworkable because of the mental disability of one or both parties, the laws of divorce or annulment permitting termination of the relationship should suffice to alleviate personal hardship and protect the personal and property rights of the parties and children. The extensive use of the dissolution laws by "normal" persons may be viewed as a further argument against legislation which singles out mentally disabled persons as incapable of or unfit for marriage.

2. *Mental disability shall be a ground for divorce or annulment provided that the statutes adequately protect the mentally disabled by substantive and procedural rules.*

Though *prior* restraints on marriage by reason of

---

may also be dependent on the termination adoption distinction. See Allen et al., *supra* note 4, at 321–22: "Modern social-work thinking distinguishes between termination of the rights of the natural parents and adoption of the child by others." Allen et al. discuss some of the implications of the distinction.

89. Allen et al., *supra* note 4, at 321.

90. See Table 7.3, Annulment of Adoption column.

91. Myerson, "Certain Medical and Legal Phrases of Eugenic Sterilization," 52 *Yale L.J.* 618 (1942–43); Comment, "What Has Happened to Kansas' Sterilization Laws?" 2 *Kan. L. Rev.* 174 (1953–54); Barrow & Fabing, *Epilepsy and the Law* 14, 34 (1956).

mental disability are undesirable, it does not follow that mental illness may not be a ground for termination of the marriage relationship. Mental disability—whether prenuptial or postnuptial in development—may be such as to preclude or greatly diminish the chances of maintaining or achieving an acceptable marriage relationship. In these cases annulment or divorce would be appropriate. Statutes on this point should avoid the defects of existing laws. Notions of fault should be recognized as irrelevant whether proffered as grounds for, or as a defense to, a divorce decree. Incurability should be rejected as a standard of mental condition that warrants divorce: medical opinion today has generally discarded such absolutes, and the laws should be brought into conformity therewith. Length of institutionalization as a criterion for divorce should be approached cautiously: long-term hospitalization may well be, but sometimes is not, an indication of severe disability; long-term separation of the parties to the marriage through hospitalization may or may not signify irreparable disruption of the relationship. The basic inquiry should instead be into the desirability of continuing the marriage relationship *as affected* by the severity of the disability, the prospects of substantial recovery, the length of separation as resulting from past and predicted institutionalization. Procedurally, statutes should protect the mentally disabled by providing for notice of, and counsel at, the divorce proceedings. Mentally disabled persons should be allowed to sue for divorce in appropriate circumstances.

3. *Statutes authorizing nonconsensual adoption or termination of the parent-child relationship should be worded so as to assure a careful weighing of the interests of the child and of the natural parents.*

Many of the considerations relevant to divorce and mental disability are applicable to the issue of nonconsensual adoption or termination. Legal standards of disability bearing scant relation to present medical knowledge and terminology should be avoided. Focus should be on the effects of conditions and circumstances on the parent-child relationship rather than on these factors themselves as if they constituted independent determinants. The procedural protections of notice and counsel are eminently applicable to adoption actions.

BIBLIOGRAPHY

Allen, Richard C.; Ferster, Elyce Z.; and Weihofen, Henry. *Mental Impairment and Legal Incompetency.* Englewood Cliffs, N.J.: Prentice-Hall, Inc., 1968.

American Jurisprudence. San Francisco: Bancroft-Whitney Co.; Rochester, N.Y.: Lawyers Co-operative Publishing Co.
"Adoption of Children." 1 (1936) §§ 4, 36.
"Marriage." 35 (1941) §§ 17, 113.

American Law Reports Annotated. San Francisco: Bancroft-Whitney Co.; Rochester, N.Y.: Lawyers Co-operative Publishing Co.
"Necessity of Notice to Parents or Legal Custodian before Adoption of Child." 2d ser. 76 (1932) 1077.
"Right of Guardian or Committee of Incompetent to Maintain Action for Divorce or Annulment of Marriage." 2d ser. 149 (1944) 1284.
"Requisites of Proof of Insanity as a Ground for Divorce." 2d ser. 15 (1951) 1135.

Anthony, E. James. "Clinical Evaluation of Children with Psychotic Parents." 126 *American Journal of Psychiatry* 177 (1969).

Barrow, Roscoe L., and Fabing, Howard D. *Epilepsy and the Law.* New York: Hoeber Medical Div., Harper & Row, 1956.
"Insanity as Affecting Right to Divorce or Separation on Other Grounds." 2d ser. 19 (1951) 144.
"Mental Illness as a Ground for Adoption of Children." 2d ser. 45 (1952) 1379.
"Power of Incompent Spouse's Guardian, Committee or Next Friend to Sue for Granting or Vacation of Divorce or Annulment of Marriage, or to Make a Compromise or Settlement in Such Suit." 3d ser. 6 (1966) 681.

Comment, "Divorce: Statutory Abolition of Marital Fault." 35 *California Law Review* 99 (1947).

———. "What Has Happened to Kansas' Sterilization Laws?" 2 *Kansas Law Review* 174 (1953).

Council of State Governments. *The Interstate Compact on Mental Health:What It Is and Does.* Rev. ed. Chicago: Council of State Governments, 1968.

Deutsch, Albert. *The Mentally Ill in America.* 2d ed. rev. New York: Columbia University Press, 1949.

Gordon, Alfred. "Insanity and Divorce." 5 *Journal of Criminal Law and Criminology* 544 (1914).

Great Britain. Royal Commission on the Law Relating to Mental Illness and Mental Deficiency 1954–57. *Report.* Cmnd. No. 169. London: Her Majesty's Stationery Office, 1957.

Harper, Fowler V. *Problems of the Family.* Indianapolis: Bobbs-Merrill Co., 1952.

Keezer, Frank H. *On the Law of Marriage and Divorce.* 3d ed. by John W. Morland. Indianapolis: Bobbs-Merrill Co., 1946.

Kingsley, Robert. "What Are the Proper Grounds for Granting Annulments?" 18 *Law and Contemporary Problems* 39 (1953).

McCurdy, William E. "Insanity as a Ground for Annulment or Divorce in English and American Law." 29 *Virginia Law Review* 771 (1943).

Myerson, Abraham. "Certain Medical and Legal Phases of Eugenic Sterilization." 52 *Yale Law Journal* 618 (1943).

Note, "Due Process Rights of Mentally Ill Parents in Nonconsenual Adoptions." 30 *Indiana Law Journal* 431 (1954–55).

Schouler, James. *Marriage, Divorce, Separation and Domestic Relations*. Vol. 2, 6th ed. by Arthur W. Blakemore. Albany, N.Y.: Matthew Bender & Co., 1921.

Silving, Helen. "Divorce without Fault." 29 *Iowa Law Review* 527 (1944).

Stimson, Frederick J. *American Statute Law*. Boston: Charles C. Soule, 1886–92.

United States Department of Health, Education, and Welfare. Children's Bureau. Model Termination Act. *An Act for Termination of Parental Rights and Responsibilities and the Adoption of Children*. Washington, D.C.: Government Printing Office, 1961.

Vernier, Chester G. *American Family Laws*. Palo Alto, Cal.: Stanford University Press, 1931–32.

CASES

Campbell v. Campbell, 242 Ala. 141, 5 So. 2d 401 (1941).

Child Saving Institute v. Knobel, 372 Mo. 609, 37 S.W.2d 920 (1931).

Dribin v. Superior Court, 37 Cal. 2d 345, 231 P.2d 809 (1951).

Forbis v. Forbis, 274 S.W.2d 800 (Mo. Ct. App. 1955).

Katz v. Katz, 191 Kan. 500, 382 P.2d 331 (1963).

Keal v. Rhydderck, 317 Ill. 231, 148 N.E. 53 (1925).

Littreal v. Littreal, 253 S.W.2d 247 (Ky. Civ. App. 1952).

Mabry v. Mabry, 243 N.C. 126, 90 S.E.2d 221 (1955).

People *ex rel.* Nabstedt v. Barger, 3 Ill. 2d 511, 121 N.E.2d 781 (1954).

Riggins v. Riggins, 139 Cal. App. 2d 712, 294 P.2d 751 (1956).

Shelton v. Shelton, 209 Ga. 454, 74 S.E.2d 5 (1953).

Turner v. Bell, 198 Tenn. App. 232, 279 S.W.2d 71 (1955).

Table 7.1   MARRIAGE AND MENTAL DISABILITY

State	Description of Persons Prohibited from Marrying	Exception to Prohibition	Enforcement of Prohibition	Status of Marriage of Mentally Ill	Spouse Authorized to Petition for Judicial Dissolution
Draft Act					
ALA. Code (1958)					
ALAS. Stat. (1962)				if either party is incapable of consenting for want of sufficient understanding, the marriage is voidable. 25.05.031 (1965) voidable if either party is of unsound mind. 09.55.090(2)	party under disability. 25.05.031 (1965)
ARIZ. Rev. Stat. Ann. (1956)					
ARK. Stat. Ann. (1947)	persons who are incapable of consenting to marriage. 55-106			when either party to a marriage is incapable of consenting to any marriage, that marriage shall be void from the time its nullity is declared by a court of competent jurisdiction. 55-106	
CAL. Civ. Code (West 1954)	imbecile or insane. 69 (Supp. 1970)			annulment if 1 party was of unsound mind unless there was free cohabitation after coming to reason. 82(three)	either party. 82(Three)
COLO. Rev. Stat. Ann. (1964)	person who cannot make a civil contract. 90-1-1			annulment if 1 or both parties were mentally incapable of giving consent. 46-3-1	any real party in interest. 46-3-4
CONN. Gen. Stat. Ann. (1958)					
DEL. Code Ann. (1953)	persons of unsound mind, or a person who is or has been a patient in an insane asylum. 13, §101(b): (1) & (2)	patient or expatient may marry if he files with the clerk a certificate stating that he is fit to marry, signed by the institution superintendent. 13, §101(b)(2)	$100 fine or 30 days imprisonment upon default. 13, §102	annulment for insanity. 13, §1551(5)	sane party or committee of lunatic or lunatic on regaining reason. 13, §1551(5)
D.C. Code Ann. (1967)	idiot or person adjudged to be a lunatic. 30-103			annulment on court decree. 16-903, 19-904, 30-103	
FLA. Stat. Ann. (1960)					
GA. Code Ann. (1961)	persons not "of sound mind." 53-102 (Supp. 1968)			marriages of persons unable to contract shall be void. 53-104 may be annuled if no children. 53-601	either party or next friend for party of unsound mind. 53-602
HAWAII Rev. Stat. Ann. (1968)				that 1 of the parties was, at the time of the marriage, an idiot or lunatic is grounds for annulment. 580-21(4), 580-26	sane party, or relative or next friend of insane party, or insane party after restoration to reason. 580-26
IDAHO Code Ann.(1963)	persons of unsound mind. 29-101 (1967) persons who cannot make a civil contract. 32-201			annulment if 1 party was of unsound mind unless there was free cohabitation after coming to reason. 32-501(3)	sane party or relative or guardian of the party of unsound mind. 32-502(3)
ILL. Ann. Stat. (Smith-Hurd 1966)	an imbecile, or insane. 89, §6		penalties for false affidavit or knowingly issuing a license to parties not having legal capacity to marry. 89, §13		
IND. Ann. Stat. (1965)	imbeciles, persons of unsound mind, or under guardianship as such. 44-207		penalties vary for clerk or person authorized to solemnize marriage, and others. 44-210, 44-211, 44-212	void if either party insane or idiotic. 44-104 annulment if incapable of contracting from want of understanding. 44-106	insane party. 44-106

Table 7.1 MARRIAGE AND MENTAL DISABILITY continued

State	Description of Persons Prohibited from Marrying	Exception to Prohibition	Enforcement of Prohibition	Status of Marriage of Mentally Ill	Spouse Authorized to Petition for Judicial Dissolution
IOWA Code Ann. (1950)	mentally ill or retarded, mental retardate or under guardianship as incompetent & those disqualified from making any civil contracts. 595.3			annulment where either party mentally ill or a mental retardate at time of marriage. 598.19(4) (Supp. 1969)	
KAN. Stat. Ann. (1964)	persons adjudicated incapacitated. 23-120 (Supp. 1968)	woman 45 years & over & man marrying woman over 45. 23-120 (Supp. 1968)	officer issuing marriage license is required to ask: "Have either of you ever been adjudicated an incapacitated person? if your answer is yes, have you been discharged as restored?" Persons who knowingly violate the marriage act may be fined not more than $1000 or imprisoned for not more than 3 years or both. 23-121 (Supp. 1968); & 22-123		
KY. Rev. Stat. Ann. (1969)	idiots, lunatics. 402.020		fines for aiding, abetting, solemnizing or issuing license for prohibited marriage. 402.990	void. 402.020	
LA. Rev. Stat. Ann. (1950)					
ME. Rev. Stat. Ann. (1964)	insane, feebleminded persons, idiots. 19, §32		any person $100 fine. 19, §3	void. 19, §§32, 631	(no decree necessary). 19, §631
MD. Ann. Code (1957)					
MASS. Ann. Laws (1955)	insane person, idiot, feebleminded person under commitment to institution for feebleminded, to the custody of the department of mental health or to an institution for mental defectives. 207, §5			annulment. 207, §14	either party. 207 §14
MICH. Comp. Laws Ann. (1967)	insane or idiot; persons who have been confined in any public institution or asylum as feebleminded, imbecilic or insane, or persons who have been adjudged feebleminded, imbecilic or insane. 551.6	if expatient or adjudicated person files in the office of the county clerk certificate of 2 physicians that the person is cured and that there is no probability that they will transmit any such defects to the issue of such marriage. 551.6	fine of not more than $1000 or imprisonment for 1 to 5 years to any person of sound mind who intermarries with prohibited person, or who shall advise & abet, cause or procure or assist in procuring any such marriage. 551.6	void. 552.1	(no decree necessary). 552.1
MINN. Stat. Ann. (1969)	imbeciles, insane or feebleminded persons. 517.03	mentally deficient persons committed to the guardianship of commissioner of public welfare may marry on his written consent. 517.03		prohibited marriages are absolutely void. Annulment is allowed in cases where either party is incapable of assent through want of understanding. 518.01, 518.02	injured party. 518.02
MISS. Code Ann. (1956)	insane or imbecile. 461(f) (Supp. 1968)			relief is by divorce action. 2735	injured party unless he or she knew of the insanity at the time of marriage. 2735
MO. Rev. Stat. (1949)	insane, feebleminded or mentally imbecile. 451.020 (Supp. 1969)		official misdemeanor. 451.020 (Supp. 1969)	void. 451.020 (Supp. 1969)	
MONT. Rev. Codes Ann. (1961)	feebleminded, legally incompetent. 48-105, 48-120			marriage of feebleminded is void, while that of person of unsound mind is voidable. 48-201, 48-202(3)	sane party or relative or guardian of party of unsound mind. 48-203(3)
NEB. Rev. Stat. (1968)	persons adjudged imbecile, or feebleminded or afflicted with hereditary insanity. 42-102	unless sterilized. 42-102		void when either party is insane or an idiot at the time of marriage, & the term idiot shall include all persons who from whatever cause are mentally incompetent to enter into the marriage relation. 42-103	either party. 42-119

241

Table 7.1   MARRIAGE AND MENTAL DISABILITY   continued

State	Description of Persons Prohibited from Marrying	Exception to Prohibition	Enforcement of Prohibition	Status of Marriage of Mentally Ill	Spouse Authorized to Petition for Judicial Dissolution
NEV. Rev. Stat. (1967)	persons incapable of contracting. 122.010			void from the time invalidity declared. 125.330	either party. 125.330
N.H. Rev. Stat. Ann. (1968)	imbeciles, feebleminded, idiots, or insane. 457:10	woman over 45 or permission granted by department of health. 457:10	it is the duty of town clerk to forward all applications of persons suspected of having the prohibited condition to the state board. 457:15		
N.J. Stat. Ann. (1953)	imbecile, or persons of unsound mind; also inmates of mental institutions unless they have been satisfactorily discharged. 2A:124-2 (Supp. 1970) 37:1-9 (1968)		misdemeanor to married person with prohibited conditions. 2A:124-2 (Supp. 1970)	nullity from time so declared by court. 2A:34-1	either party. 2A:34-1
N.M. Stat. Ann. (1962)	persons not capable of consenting to a contract. 57-1-1		practicing deceit to be married contrary to law is punishable by a fine of $50 to $100 and/or imprisonment for 10 to 60 days. 7-1-17		
N.Y. Dom. Rel. (McKinney 1964)	persons not capable of making a contract. 10			annulment if one party was incapable of consenting from want of understanding. 7.2 or has been incurably insane for 5 years or more. 6, 7.5; & in Supp. 1970, 141	either party. 7; & in Supp. 1970, 141
N.C. Gen. Stat. (1966)	persons adjudged idiot, imbecile, mental defective, or of unsound mind. 51-12(Supp. 1967)	unless sterilized. 51-12 (Supp. 1967)	license cannot be granted until presentation of medical certificate showing absence of these conditions. 51-9(Supp. 1967) fine for anyone aiding in violation of prohibitions. 51-13	prohibited marriages declared void upon suit; annulment if party incapable of consent due to want of will or understanding. 50-4, 51-3	either party. 50-4
N.D. Cent. Code. (1960)	mental deficient, insane, or person afflicted with hereditary insanity. 14-03-07 (Supp. 1969)	woman over 45. 14-03-07 (Supp. 1969)	license cannot be granted until presentation of medical certificate showing absence of these conditions. 14-03-17 (Supp. 1969)	annulment where either party was of unsound mind unless cohabitation after restoration of reason. 14-04-01.3	sane party or relative or guardian of party of unsound mind. 14-04-02.3
OHIO Rev. Code (Baldwin 1964)	imbeciles or insane persons. 3101.06				
OKLA. Stat. (1961)	any party or parties legally incompetent to consent to a civil contract. 43-1 (1954)			annulment if either party was incapable because of lack of understanding. 12-1283	incapable party or parent or guardian of such party. 12-1283
ORE. Rev. Stat. (1967)	persons incapable of consenting from want of understanding; to obtain a marriage license, person must be declared free from feeblemindedness or mental illness by a physician. 106.030, 106.071(3)(c), 106.071(6)			void from time so declared by court. 106.030	when either party has not sufficient understanding, marriage may be declared void at suit of either party. 106.030, 107.020 cohabitation after restoration to understanding precludes annulment. 107.020
PA. Stat. Ann. (1965)	insane, weakminded, of unsound mind or person who is under guardianship as person of unsound mind. 48,§1-5(d)(Supp. 1969) if applicant has been within the last 5 years an inmate of an institution for weakminded, insane, or persons of unsound mind, he cannot marry unless orphan's court judge permits license to issue. 48, §1-5(e)	unless a judge of the orphan's court shall decide that it is for the best interest of such applicant & the general public to issue the license. 48, §1-5(d) (Supp. 1969)		void since insane incapable of entering into marriage. 48, §1-5	
R.I. Gen. Laws Ann. (1956)	idiots & lunatics. 15-1-5			absolutely void. 15-1-5 relief by divorce action. 15-5-1	

Table 7.1   MARRIAGE AND MENTAL DISABILITY   continued

State	Description of Persons Prohibited from Marrying	Exception to Prohibition	Enforcement of Prohibition	Status of Marriage of Mentally Ill	Spouse Authorized to Petition for Judicial Dissolution
S.C. Code Ann. (1962)	mentally incompetent person. 20-1			may be declared void for inability to contract. 20-43	
S.D. Compiled Laws Ann. (1967)					
TENN. Code Ann. (1955)	insane or imbecile. 36-411		"Any county court clerk, or deputy clerk, who shall issue a marriage license without compliance with the provisions of [§36-411] and not in good faith shall be guilty of a misdemeanor and shall be punishable by fine of not less than $25 or more than $250." 36-413 (Supp. 1968)	voidable. Hunt v. Hunt, 412 S.W.2d 7 (1965)	
TEX. Rev. Civ. Stat. Ann. (1960)					
UTAH Code Ann. (1953)	idiots, lunatics. 30-1-2(1) (Supp. 1967)		one who solemnizes prohibited marriage $1000 fine or imprisonment for not more than 3 years or both. 30-1-15	void. 30-1-2 (Supp. 1967)	
VT. Stat. Ann. (1968)	persons non compos mentis. 18, §5142(3)		clerk knowingly violating provision fined maximum of $20. 18, §5143	voidable by court. 15, §512, 15, §514	insane only. 15, §514
VA. Code Ann. (1960)	idiot, imbecile, or insane person. 20-45, 20-46, 20-47 (Supp. 1968)	woman over 45. 20-46 (Supp. 1968)	any person. $100 maximum fine and/or 90 days confinement in jail. 20-46	void from time so declared by court. 20-45 (Supp. 1968)	either party. 20-45 (Supp. 1968)
WASH. Rev. Code Ann. (1961)	imbecile, feebleminded, idiot, insane person, or person who has been afflicted with hereditary insanity. 26.04.030	woman over 45. 26.04.030	any person; $1000 fine or imprisonment for not more than 3 years or both. 26.04.230	voidable by court action. 26.04.130	insane only. 26.04.130
W.VA. Code Ann. (1966)	"all marriages solemnized when either of the parties was an insane person, feebleminded person, idiot, imbecile, . . . shall be void from the time they are so declared a decree of nullity." 48-2-1 (Supp. 1969)			void. 48-2-1 (Supp. 1969)	either party. 48-2-2 (Supp. 1969)
WIS. Stat. Ann. (1957)	because of insanity or idiocy lacks capability of assenting to marriage. 245.03 (Supp. 1969)			annulment. 247.02 (Supp. 1969)	sane party if ignorant of spouse's insanity at time of marriage or guardian of lunatic or incompetent. 247.02 (Supp. 1969)
WYO. Stat. Ann. (1957)	insane or idiot. 20-32 (second)			void. 20-32 (second)	either party; no decree necessary. 20-34

Table 7.2 DIVORCE AND MENTAL DISABILITY

| STATE | GROUNDS FOR DIVORCE | | PERIOD | COMMITMENT | MEDICAL TESTIMONY | | INCURABLE | CONTINUING FINANCIAL LIABILITY | GUARDIAN AT LITEM | COURT-APPOINTED COUNSEL |
	Yes	No			No. of Witnesses	Qualifications				
DRAFT ACT										
ALA. Code (1958)	34, §20.7		5 years 34, §20.7	34, §20.7	1 34, §20.7	superintendent or assistant superintendent of institution in which confined. 34, §20.7	34, §20.7			
ALAS. Stat. (1962)	09.55.110(8)		18 months 09.55.110(8)	09.55.110(8)			09.55.110(8)	09.55.110(8)		
ARIZ. Rev. Stat. Ann. (1956)		25-312								
ARK. Stat. Ann. (1962) (Supp. 1967)	32-1202		3 years 34-1202	34-1202	2 34-1202	2 reputable physicians; physician and/or superintendent of institution. 34-1202	34-1202	34-1202	34-1202	
CAL. Civ. Code (West 1954)	92		3 years 108 (Supp. 1968)	must be in state. 108 (Supp. 1968)	1 108 (Supp. 1968)	member of medical staff or institution. 108 (Supp. 1968)	108 (Supp. 1968)	108 (Supp. 1968)	108 (Supp. 1968)	
COLO. Rev. Stat. Ann. (1964)	46-1-1(i)		3 years 46-1-1(i)					46-1-1(i)		
CONN. Gen. Stat. Ann. (1958)	46-13		5 years 46-13	46-13	2 or more (on request of either party. 46-19	psychiatrists who are diplomates of the American Board of Psychiatry and Neurology, who are not on the staff of any state hospital. 46-19		but of a sane wife after her remarriage. 46-20	46-19	
DEL. Code Ann. (1953)	13, §1522(10) 13, §1523 (Supp. 1970)		5 years 13, §1522(10) (Supp. 1970)	13, §1522(10) (Supp. 1970)	5 13, §1522(10) (Supp. 1970)	state psychiatrist, a licensed physician, an attorney, and 2 laymen of good character. 13, §1522(10) (Supp. 1970)	for divorce from bed and board. 13, §1523(7)	such order as superior court deems fitting. 13, §1522(10) (Supp. 1970)		
D.C. Code Ann. (1967)		16-904								
FLA. Stat. Ann. (1969)		61.041								
GA. Code Ann. (1952) (Supp. 1968)	30-102(2) 30-102(11)		2 years 30-102(11)	30-102(11)	2 30-102(11)	superintendent of institution and 1 other physician. 30-102(11)	30-102(11)	30-102(11)	30-102(11)	

Table 7.2 DIVORCE AND MENTAL DISABILITY continued

STATE	GROUNDS FOR DIVORCE		PERIOD	COMMITMENT	MEDICAL TESTIMONY		INCURABLE	CONTINUING FINANCIAL LIABILITY	GUARDIAN AD LITEM	COURT-APPOINTED COUNSEL
	Yes	No			No. of Witnesses	Qualifications				
HAWAII Rev. Stat. Ann. (1968)	580-41(4)		3 years 580-41(4) 580-43					580-49	32-802	county attorney 32-803
IDAHO Code Ann. (1963)	32-603(2) 32-801		3 years 32-801	32-801			32-801	as in other cases. 32-801		
ILL. Ann. Stat. (Smith-Hurd 1966)		40, §1 (Supp. 1969)								
IND. Ann. Stat. (1968)	3-1201 (eighth)		5 years 3-1201 (eighth)	3-1201 (eighth)			3-1201 (eighth)	3-1201 (eighth)		
IOWA Code Ann. (1950)		598.8 (Supp. 1969)								
KAN. Stat. Ann. (1963)(Supp. 1968)	60-1601		3 years 60-1601	person filing must have 1 year residency. 60-1603	2 of 3 60-1601	all court appointed. 60-1601	poor prognosis for recovery. 60-1601	60-1601		
KY. Rev. Stat. Ann. (1969)	403.020		5 years 403.020	403.020	2 403.020	physicians competent in psychiatry. 403.020	403.020	discretionary 403.020		
LA. Rev. Stat. Ann. (1965)	9:301		2 years 9:301							
ME. Rev. Stat. Ann. (1964)		19, §691								
MD. Ann. Code (1966)	16, §26		3 years 16, §26	16, §26	2 16, §26	competent in psychiatry. 16, §26	16, §26	discretionary 16, §26	Maryland Rules of Procedure S72. 16, §26	Maryland Rules of Procedure S72. 16, §26
MASS. Ann. Laws (1955)		208, §1 (Supp. 1968)								
MICH. Comp. Laws Ann. (1967)		552.1								
MINN. Stat. Ann. (1969)	518.06(7)		5 years 518.06(7)	518.06(7)			518.06(7)	518.06(7)		
MISS. Code Ann. (1956)	2735		3 years 2735	2735	2 2735	superintendent or member of medical staff of state hospital or Veterans Administration hospital and one other physician; both must be experts in mental disease. 2735	2735	2735	2735	
MO. Rev. Stat. (1949)		452.010								
MONT. Rev. Codes Ann. (1967)	21-103		5 years 21-104	21-104		competent physicians. 21-104	21-104	21-104		

Table 7.2 DIVORCE AND MENTAL DISABILITY *continued*

STATE	GROUNDS FOR DIVORCE		PERIOD	COMMITMENT	MEDICAL TESTIMONY		INCURABLE	CONTINUING FINANCIAL LIABILITY	GUARDIAN AD LITEM	COURT-APPOINTED COUNSEL
	Yes	No			No. of Witnesses	Qualifications				
NEB. Rev. Stat. (1968)	42-301		5 years 42-301	42-301	3 42-302.01	qualified physicians including superintendent of state hospital if patient is confined there. 42-302.01	42-301	discretionary with court. 42-318.01	42-302.02	
NEV. Rev. Stat. (1967)	125.010		2 years 125.010					125.010		
N.H. Rev. Stat. Ann. (1968)		458:7								
N.J. Stat. Ann. (1952)		2A:34-2								
N.M. Stat. Ann. (1953)	22-7-7		5 years 22-7-7	committed or not committed.	3 22-7-9	court-appointed physicians. 22-7-9	22-7-7		22-7-8	22-7-8
N.Y. Dom. Rel. (McKinney 1964)		170 (Supp. 1970)								
N.C. Gen. Stat. (1966)	50-5(6)		5 years 50-5(6)	50-5(6)	2 50-5(6)	reputable physicians 50-5(6)	50-5(6)	50-5(6)	50-5(6)	
N.D. Cent. Code (1960) (Supp. 1969)	14-05-03.7		5 years 14-05-03.7	14-05-03.7	3 14-05-03.7	superintendent of state hospital or Veterans Administration hospital and 2 court-appointed physicians. 14-05-03.7	14-05-03.7			
OHIO Rev. Code (Baldwin 1964)		3105.01								
OKLA. Stat. (1961)	12, §1271		5 years 12, §1271	12, §1271	3 12, §1271	superintendent of hospital in which defendant is confined; and 2 court-appointed physicians. 12, §1271	poor prognosis for recovery. 12, §1271	12, §1271	12, §1271	
ORE. Rev. Stat. (1967)	107.030(7)		2 years 107.030(7)	adjudication of mental illness. 107.030(7)	2 107.030(7)	physicians licensed by state board of medical examiners. 107.030(7)	107.030(7)			
PA. Stat. Ann. (1955)		23, §10, note 12								
R.I. Gen. Laws Ann. (1956)		15-5-2								
S.C. Code Ann. (1962)		20-101								

Table 7.2 DIVORCE AND MENTAL DISABILITY *continued*

STATE	GROUNDS FOR DIVORCE		PERIOD	COMMITMENT	MEDICAL TESTIMONY		INCURABLE	CONTINUING FINANCIAL LIABILITY	GUARDIAN AD LITEM	COURT-APPOINTED COUNSEL
	Yes	No			No. of Witnesses	Qualifications				
S.D. Compiled Laws Ann. (1967)	25-4-18		5 years 25-4-18	25-4-18			25-4-18			
TENN. Code Ann. (1955)		36-801								
TEX. Rev. Civ. Stat. Ann. (1960) (Supp. 1969)	4629(6)		5 years 4629(6)	4629(6)			4629(6)			
UTAH Code Ann. (1953)	30-3-1(9)			30-3-1(9)	competent witnesses 30-3-1(9)	either party may request that defendant be examined by 2 or more physicians. 30-3-1(9)	30-3-1(9)		30-3-1(9)	
VT. Stat. Ann. (1958)	15, §551		5 years 15, §631	15, §631			15, §631	15, §634	15, §632	15, §633
VA. Code Ann. (1961)		20-91 (Supp. 1968)								
WASH. Rev. Code Ann. (1961)	26.08.020(10)		2 years 26.08.020(10)			competent medical testimony. 26.08.020(10)	chronic 26.08.020(10)			
W. VA. Code Ann. (1966) (Supp. 1969)	48-2-4(8)		3 years 48-2-4(8)				48-2-4(8)	48-2-4(8)		
WIS. Stat. Ann. (1957)		247.07 (Supp. 1969)								
WYO. Stat. Ann. (1957)	20-39		2 years 20-39	20-39			20-39	20-39	20-40	20-40

Table 7.3   ADOPTION AND MENTAL DISABILITY

State	Consent of Parent Not Necessary If	Annulment of Adoption Allowed If	State	Consent of Parent Not Necessary If	Annulment of Adoption Allowed If
DRAFT ACT			ILL. Ann. Stat. ---continued (Smith-Hurd 1966)	will not occur in the for-seeable future, and may appoint a guardian ad litem having the authority to consent 4, §9.1-8 (Supp. 1969)	
ALA. Code (1958)	parent is insane or otherwise incapacitated from giving consent 27, §3		IND. Ann. Stat. (1968)	parent judicially declared incompetent or mentally defective 3-120(g)(5) (Supp. 1969)	
ALAS. Stat. (1962)	parent was more than 1 year prior to the filing of a petition for adoption adjudged to be insane 30.10.040(1) (Supp. 1969)		IOWA Code Ann. (1950)	parent is hopelessly mentally ill 600.3 (Supp. 1969)	within 5 years of adoption child develops mental retardedness, epilepsy, or mental illness as a result of conditions existing prior to the adoption of which the adopting parents had no knowledge 600-7 (Supp. 1969)
ARIZ. Rev. Stat. Ann. (1956)	parents declared insane or incompetent 8-103A.1(a) (Supp. 1970)				
ARK. Stat. Ann. (1947)	parent is insane or otherwise incapacitated from giving consent 56-106(b) (III)	"within 5 years of adoption child has developed feeble-mindedness, insanity . . . as a result of a condition existing prior to adoption unknown to the adopting parents." 56-110(c)	KAN. Stat. Ann. (1964)	parent incapable of giving consent 59-2102 (Supp. 1968)	
CAL. Civil Code (West 1954)		"within five years of adoption child shows evidence of being feeble-minded, or insane, as a result of conditions prior to the adoption, and of which conditions the adopting parents . . . had no notice." 227b	KY. Rev. Stat. Ann. (1969)	parent has been adjudged incompetent at least a year before petition filed 199.500	
			LA. Rev. Stat. Ann. (1965)		good cause is shown within 2 years after entry of "interlocutory decree" other than mere withdrawal of consent by parent 9:431
COLO. Rev. Stat. Ann. (1964)					
CONN. Gen. Stat. Ann. (1958)		"sound cause" is shown during judicially ordered interlocutory period 45-63 (Supp. 1969)	ME. Rev. Stat. Ann. (1964)	parent is hopelessly mentally ill or intemperate or not entitled to custody of child 19, §532 (Supp. 1969)	"good cause" is shown 19, §538
DEL. Code Ann. (1953)	parent legally incompetent by virtue of insanity 13, §908(1)(B)		MD. Ann. Code (1966)	court finds consents are withheld contrary to the child's best interests 16, §74	
D.C. Code Ann. (1967)	court finds after a hearing that consents are withheld contrary to the child's best interests 16-304(e)		MASS. Ann. Laws (1955)	parent is adjudged hopelessly insane by court hearing to the adoption petition 210, §3 (Supp. 1968)	
FLA. Stat. Ann. (1960)			MICH. Comp. Laws Ann. (1967)	a general guardian has been appointed for the parent because of mental incompetency 710.3(4)	
GA. Code Ann. (1964)	parent is insane or otherwise incapacitated 74-403(2) (Supp. 1968)				
HAWAII Rev. Stat. Ann. (1968)	living legal parent legally adjudged to be mentally ill or mentally incompetent to an extent requiring institutional care, or otherwise incapacitated 578-2		MINN. Stat. Ann. (1969)	parent is adjudged insane or incompetent 259.24(d) (Supp. 1969)	"within five years of adoption child develops feeble-mindedness, epilepsy, insanity, . . . as a result of conditions existing prior to the adoption of which the adopting parents had no knowledge or notice . . . ." 259.30
IDAHO Code Ann. (1947)	parent is deprived of civil rights 16-1504 (Supp. 1969)				
			MISS. Code Ann. (1956)	parent is mentally or otherwise unfit to raise child 1269-09 (Supp. 1968)	
ILL. Ann. Stat. (Smith-Hurd 1966)	parent has been adjudicated incompetent by reason of mental impairment, or mentally ill, or in need of mental treatment, or mentally retarded; however, the court must find from evidence of 2 physicians that such mental condition continues and that recovery		MO. Rev. Stat. (1949)	parent is adjudged incompetent 453.040-1 (Supp. 1969)	within 5 years after adoption the child develops feeblemindedness 453.130

Table 7.3 ADOPTION AND MENTAL DISABILITY *continued*

State	Consent of Parent Not Necessary If	Annulment of Adoption Allowed If	State	Consent of Parent Not Necessary If	Annulment of Adoption Allowed If
MONT. Rev. Codes Ann. (1961)	parent is deprived of civil rights, or rights have been terminated by judicial proceedings 61-205(1)(a), 61-205(3), 61-205(4), 61-205(5)		PA. Stat. Ann. (1963)	parent is adjudged a person of unsound mind 1, §2(c)	
NEB. Rev. Stat. (1968)	parent incapable of consenting 43-104(3)(d)		R.I. Gen. Laws Ann. (1956)	parent is insane or under guardianship. The court shall proceed as if parent were dead. It may appoint a next friend to give or withhold consent 15-7-7 (Supp. 1967)	
NEV. Rev. Stat. (1967)	parent has been adjudged insane for 2 years and the court is satisfied by proof that such insanity is incurable 127.040(2)		S.C. Code Ann. (1962)		
N.H. Rev. Stat. Ann. (1968)	insane, but other parent must consent. No specific provision if both parents are insane 461:3		S.D. Compiled Laws Ann. (1967)	parent is adjudged by a court of competent jurisdiction to be mentally incompetent 25-6-4(3)	
N.J. Stat. Ann. (1960)		"public policy of the state is to protect the adopting parents from assuming responsibility for a child without sufficient knowledge of the child's heredity and capacity for physical and mental development . . . ." 9:3-17	TENN. Code Ann. (1955)	parent is incompetent to given consent; a guardian ad litem shall be appointed for the incompetent parent to give or withhold consent 36-108 (Supp. 1968)	
N.M. Stat. Ann. (1953)	child is dependent or neglected or has no responsible parent or guardian 13-9-1, 13-9-2 a parent has been adjudicated mentally ill and commited to a mental institution continuously for 3 years next preceding the filing of the petition to adopt 22-2-6(A)(4) (Supp. 1969)		TEX. Rev. Civ. Stat. Ann. (1959)	consent not required of parents whose parental rights have been terminated by court order 46a.6c (Supp. 1969)	
N.Y. Dom. Rel. (McKinney 1964)	parent is insane or has been judicially declared incompetent or mentally defective as defined by the mental hygiene law 111.4		UTAH Code Ann. (1953)	a father or mother has been deprived of custody on account of cruelty, neglect, or desertion or has voluntarily relinquished custody to an agency licensed to receive children for adoption 70-30-4 (1968)	within 5 years of adoption child develops feeblemindedness, epilepsy, or insanity, as a result of conditions existing prior to the adoption of which the adopting parents had no notice 78-30-13
N.C. Gen. Stat. (1966)	one or both parents have been adjudged mentally incompetent. The court may appoint a next friend who shall investigate whether such parent is incurably insane and report to court. This next friend may give or withhold consent 48-9(d)		VT. Stat. Ann. (1958)	parents are incompetent; consent for adoption is to be given by department of social welfare 15, §435	
N.D. Cent. Code (1960)	parent is insane; consent is to be given by child's guardian or by the director of the division of child welfare 14-11-04 notice of hearing must be given to insane parents 14-11-10 (Supp. 1969)		VA. Code Ann. (1968)	court finds consents are withheld contrary to the child's best interests 63.1-225(4)	
OHIO Rev. Code (Baldwin 1964)	parent has been adjudged incompetent by reason of mental disability. The court shall appoint a guardian ad litem who shall investigate the situation surrounding the parent and the child and if satisfied that the adoption should be completed shall execute the consent 3107.06(3)		WASH. Rev. Code Ann. (1961)	parents are adjudged mentally ill or otherwise incompetent and if the court finds that the child's interests will best be served by permanent deprivation of custody 20.32.040(3) notice must be given to parents unless there had been a court order depriving them of custody 26.32.080(1)	
OKLA. Stat. (1966)	parent deprived of civil rights 10, §60.6		W. VA. Code Ann. (1966)	parent is insane, but must have consent of legal guardian or person having legal custody 48-4-1	
ORE. Rev. Stat. (1967)	where the parent is mentally ill and the court finds that the child will be best promoted through the adoption of the child 109.322		WIS. Stat. Ann. (1957)	parental rights have been terminated 48.84(1) mental deficiency which renders parent incapable of giving the child proper care is cause for termination of parental rights 48.40(1)(e)	
			WYO. Stat. Ann. (1957)	parent is adjudged incompetent, or insane; the consent of the parent's guardian to the adoption is sufficient 1-717	

Chapter Eight

Incompetency, Guardianship, and Restoration

I. INTRODUCTION

This chapter will be concerned with mentally disabled persons who are incapable of managing their business and financial transactions. Some persons may need hospital care and yet be capable of handling their affairs. Others may be incapable of managing their property but otherwise perfectly capable of living in society.

The question of an individual's capacity to conduct his affairs is generally determined in an incompetency proceeding. In order that the assets of a person found to be incompetent might be safeguarded, he is prohibited, for example, from writing checks, selling property, and entering into business. To engage in such transactions in his behalf, a guardian is usually appointed.[1] In the event that the incompetent recovers from his disability a special restoration proceedings is usually held to determine if he is able to resume management of his own affairs. In this chapter attention will be focused on the functions and mechanics of incompetency and restoration proceedings.

II. HISTORICAL BACKGROUND

Incompetency proceedings are of a much earlier origin than hospitalization proceedings. For example, in Rome at the time of Cicero elaborate provisions were made for the protection of the property of the mentally disabled, while none at all existed for their person. This pattern was followed in England and also in colonial America, where several of the colonies passed legislation designed to protect the estates of "insane persons" long before the colonial governments became concerned with the personal welfare of the mentally disabled.[2]

No institution for the care of the mentally disabled existed in England until long after the Norman Conquest. Guardianship of the mentally disabled in medieval England was the function of the lord of the manor, who was to protect their proprietary and personal interests. This guardianship actually applied to both the person and the property of the "insane"; but the chief reason for its existence was apparently proprietary, stemming from the desire to prevent the mentally disabled from becoming a public burden or dissipating their assets to the detriment of their heirs.

It would seem that originally this guardianship, or tutorship as it was called, was applicable only to mentally deficient persons.[3] By the beginning of the fourteenth century, however, guardianship was expanded to include mentally ill persons and was formally recognized as a duty of the Crown.[4]

The king's guardianship was exercised through the Lord Chancellor, by virtue of a special commission issued to him by the Crown rather than by the general authority of the chancery court. In exercising the power, the Chancellor held an inquisition to inquire into the condition of the mentally disabled person and to appoint a committee for his person and property if he was adjudged an "idiot" or a "lunatic." It was the further duty of the chancery court to supervise and control the conduct of such a committee.

In the United States responsibility for incompetents was deemed to be vested in the people. Either by inheritance from the common law or by express constitutional and statutory provisions, jurisdiction over the person and property of incompetents was assumed by the courts of equity.[5] Currently, other courts also exercise jurisdiction over incompetency proceedings.[6]

III. ORDERS OF INCOMPETENCY AND OF HOSPITALIZATION COMPARED

Incompetency and hospitalization are two distinct legal concepts determining separate issues and leading to different results. An order of incompetency and an order for hospitalization in a mental institution fulfill different purposes, but their functions

---

1. For a discussion of the concept and function of guardians see this chapter, § IX, Guardianship.

2. Deutsch, *The Mentally Ill in America* 40 (2d ed. 1949).

3. 2 Shelford, *A Practical Treatise on the Law Concerning Lunatics, Idiots and Persons of Unsound Mind* 7 (1833); 2 Reeves, *History of English Law* 307–8 (1814).

4. De Praerogativa Regis, 17 Edw. 2, cs. 9, 10 (1324).

5. For a general history see 29 *Am. Jur.* "Insane and Other Incompetent Persons" § 32 (1960).

6. See Table 8.3, Independent Determination of Incompetency, Court column.

are often confused. The involuntary hospitalization of a mentally disabled individual is usually ordered for one or more of the following reasons: (1) to protect the public against acts of violence; (2) to protect the individual from self-inflicted injury or peril; (3) to provide therapeutic measures in order to alleviate his condition. The main purpose of an incompetency determination, on the other hand, is to safeguard the assets of an individual incapable of managing his affairs and to protect his person by methods short of hospitalization when he is unable to care for himself. The confusion between the two legal concepts may well have arisen because old cases and statutes used the term "insanity" indiscriminately to describe both concepts.[7]

Statutory terminology today shows some improvement, but the confusion persists.[8] Most of the statutes still fail to make the proper distinctions. Many provisions still employ terms such as insane, lunatic, idiocy, and the like. Some of the incompetency statutes do not use the term "incompetent" at all, but simply state that a guardian may or shall be ap-

pointed for a person who suffers from a designated mental or physical disability. Such statutes thus predicate loss of the right to conduct one's business not on a finding of incapacity to do so, but on the determination of some medical-diagnostic condition. Even those statutes which include the term "incompetent" often similarly lack the proper focus; generally, these provisions merely define an incompetent person as one who suffers from insanity or other adverse condition. Determinations of incompetency under these statutes are hence equally likely to be based on medical classifications, to the exclusion of more precise considerations on the issue of whether the person in question is capable of managing his own affairs. Moreover, or perhaps as a result, the term "incompetent" itself often appears to be perceived (or even intended by the statutes) as a "diagnostic entity"[9] rather than a term of legal status identifying or suggesting a limitation on legal rights. This perception thus produces the rather startling logic that a person is incompetent because he is incompetent. It also supports the proposition that mere improvement in statutory terminology is unlikely to resolve all problems in the competency law.

Although it has been alleged that an adjudication of incompetency is entirely for the benefit of the individual and the protection of his estate, whereas hospitalization is intended for the protection of the public,[10] this distinction does not withstand analysis. Many will dispute even the second part of this pro-

7. Ross, "Hospitalizing the Mentally Ill—Emergency and Temporary Commitments," *Current Trends in State Legislation 1955–56*, at 459, 513 (1957).

8. See Table 8.1, Statutory Definitions of Incompetents and Persons Subject to Guardianship. See also Allen, Ferster & Weihofen, *Mental Impairment and Legal Incompetency* (1968); chap. 2, "The Semantics of Incompetency," at 32–45 gives a ready comparison of the statutory terminology by listing the key phrases of the incompetency provisions of the various states. The term "incompetent" has become more prominent in the statutes (twenty-seven jurisdictions), but the old designations still abound; "insane" (twenty-four states), "lunatic" (eleven states), "unsound mind" (nine states), and so forth.

9. Allen et al., *supra* note 8, at 37.

10. Guttmacher & Weihofen, *Psychiatry and the Law* 325 (1952).

	Incompetency	Hospitalization
Test	Unable to care properly for one's property or person because of one of the following conditions:	Dangerous to self or others, or in need of treatment, because of one of the following conditions:
Applicable to cases of	Mental illness Mental deficiency Drug addiction Alcoholism Senility Physical disability Spendthrifts	Mental illness Mental deficiency Drug addiction Alcoholism Epilepsy
Purposes	Protect estate from dissipation and provide protection for persons unable to care for themselves	Removal from society for protection of the individual or of society and/or for treatment of the illness
Primary right affected	Civil rights	Freedom to be at large
Comparable to	Legal status of a minor	Person removed from society for a contagious disease

position, but—more relevant for purposes of this chapter—the assertion that an adjudication of incompetency is solely for the benefit of the incompetent is also questionable. It seems clear that incompetency and guardianship are intended not only to protect the assets of the ward for his own sake but also to prevent him from becoming a financial burden on the public. This is the admitted primary purpose of guardianship in cases of spendthrifts. In other cases of incompetency, it also appears that the state is acting to protect its treasury as well as to protect the assets of the individual. Furthermore, the public has a direct interest in other phases of incompetency. Incompetency not only deprives the individual of power to dispose of his property but also curtails other rights which may be of direct concern to the public,[11] such as that of driving an automobile.

Although there is considerable variation in legislation, in general the main differences between incompetency and hospitalization may be summarized in the table on page 251.

IV. WHO MAY BE DECLARED INCOMPETENT

Just as the state is not interested in hospitalizing all persons who may need treatment, so is it not interested in declaring incompetent all persons who cannot properly care for their property. Many of the mentally ill may obtain treatment and care through means other than hospitalization. The policy underlying hospitalization is based largely upon social criteria and thus usually takes into account whether other means are available for handling cases. Likewise, an incompetency proceeding is often not considered necessary unless property of considerable value is involved and a danger of dissipation seems to exist. Even then, proper evidence and the petition of interested persons are prerequisites to the establishment of incompetency and guardianship.

Changes in the economy of the United States probably require a reevaluation of this attitude toward incompetency and guardianship. With the growth of veterans' benefits, pension plans, insurance policies, annuities, and social security, the number of persons with property interests requiring at least some management is on the increase. Thus, while in the past guardianship was necessary for only

a limited number of the mentally disabled, the same may not be true today.[12]

To protect adequately the property interests of all hospitalized persons, it may be necessary to provide machinery whereby the need for a declaration of incompetency and guardianship would be examined in all instances of hospitalization rather than merely in those where such a declaration is specifically requested. A further justification for such machinery relates to nonproperty rights, such as the right to vote. It may be desirable to limit these nonproperty rights through an incompetency proceeding even though the hospitalized person has no property whatever.

There is considerable variation among the states in the designation of the classes of persons who may be declared incompetent.[13] Mentally ill and mentally deficient persons appear to be subject to incompetency proceedings in all states: the statutes often specifically designate these classes or otherwise refer to them in the more archaic terms of "insanity." In about half of the states persons incapacitated by old age or physical infirmity may be declared incompetent as well. Drug addicts and alcoholics are specifically included in a somewhat smaller number of jurisdictions, and spendthrifts fall explicitly within the incompetency provisions in several states. Most significant, however, virtually all the state statutes contain some broad catchall language to the effect that a person may be declared incompetent for "any other cause" or disability in addition to the enumerated infirmities.

V. INCOMPETENCY MERGED WITH HOSPITALIZATION

Legal incompetency may be the result of an independent judicial action brought for the specific purpose of determining competency, or it may be one of the issues decided at a hospitalization proceeding. Although the chief function of a hospitalization hearing is to determine whether a person requires confinement in a hospital, in many states the hospitalization order may also affect, in varying degrees, the bundle of rights associated with the question of incompetency. In only a few of these states does a

11. For a discussion of some of these nonproperty rights which are affected by an adjudication of incompetency, see chap. 9, "Personal and Property Rights."

12. See Allen et al., *supra* note 8, at 47–48: "It is probable that there are many patients with substantial assets who do not have a guardian." The authors note that in the Denver area, for example, officials estimated that 35–50 percent of the adjudicated patients had sufficient funds to warrant appointment of a conservator.

13. See Table 8.1 and Table 8.3, Applicable Cases columns.

hospitalization order automatically constitute a finding of complete or general incompetency,[14] but in several it may serve to curtail automatically some of the rights which a finding of incompetency curtails. In other states the hospitalization order may incorporate a finding of incompetency if the judge deems such a finding warranted by the person's condition; in yet another group of states, hospitalization creates a rebuttable presumption of incompetency. Even among the few states which do make the hospitalization order itself the equivalent of an adjudication of incompetency, several do not appoint a guardian for the afflicted person.[15] Thus, in cases where no guardian is appointed, the incompetent is in the unfortunate position of being incapable of managing his own affairs while at the same time having no one legally authorized to act for him. That this is a pervasive problem in these jurisdictions has been confirmed by recent field research: investigations in the early 1960s in Colorado, the District of Columbia, and Ohio—states where complete incompetency was merged with hospitalization—revealed that guardians were appointed in less than a fourth of the hospitalizations. Estimates as to the need for guardianships—based on patients' assets—ranged as high as 50 percent of those committed.[16] The laws in these jurisdictions have since undergone considerable revision. In the District of Columbia, hospitalization and competency have been clearly separated.[17] In Colorado and Ohio, these issues and determinations are still merged, but the guardianship provisions have been strengthened.[18] It is not clear at this point, however, to what extent these statutory changes have affected the practices.

There is considerable controversy over whether persons who are in need of confinement in a mental hospital are also necessarily incapable of managing their own affairs. It has been asserted that "from a medical viewpoint, there is no necessary relationship between commitability and competency."[19] It has been further stated that many patients in mental

hospitals sign and endorse checks, make out their tax returns, and are entirely competent to do so.[20] Still, the opposite view is not entirely devoid of psychiatric support, as the following statement made at the American Psychiatric Association Mental Hospital Institute indicates:

> If they aren't competent to look after themselves outside the hospital, they are not competent to transact business. . . . The idea that a person is allowed to sell real estate while he is deprived of the right to walk the streets, I find difficult to comprehend.[21]

The equation of hospitalization with incompetency—though probably a minority view in medical circles—is bolstered by considerations of a purely practical nature. Doubtlessly the institutionalization of an individual inhibits his ability to conduct his business, regardless of mental capacity. It would appear that the appointment of a guardian in many instances serves the interest of one who has been separated from society. The essential question might be whether the element of compulsion is desirable in this area: does hospitalization call for automatic, nonconsensual relinquishment of the right to conduct business, or is a voluntary delegation of such authority more appropriate? The latter proposition, however, raises the problem of the patient's capacity to make this decision. The sum of these various considerations appears to be that general competency is best determined as a question separate from hospitalization, but the fact of hospitalization should have a bearing on the issue of competency.

The legal profession is also divided on this matter. The Orphans Court of Delaware County, Pennsylvania, had no difficulty in separating ability to live outside of a hospital from competency to do business when it dismissed the Commonwealth's petition for the appointment of a guardian for the estate of an alleged incompetent confined in the state hospital.[22] The court found that the alleged incompetent

14. See Table 8.2, Effect of Involuntary Hospitalization on the Issue of Legal Competency, Competency Affected by Involuntary Hospitalization column. Colorado, Ohio, and West Virginia are the only states where there is still a complete merger of hospitalization and incompetency.

15. See Table 8.2.

16. See Allen et al., *supra* note 8, at 47–48.

17. *D.C. Code Ann.* § 21-564 (1967).

18. See *Colo. Rev. Stat. Ann.* §§ 71-1-11, 153-9-2 (Supp. 1965); *Ohio Rev. Code Ann.* §§ 5121.09, 5122.36 (Baldwin 1964).

19. Davidson, *Forensic Psychiatry* 196 (1952).

20. Guttmacher & Weihofen, *supra* note 10, at 339.

21. American Psychiatric Association, *Better Care in Mental Hospitals* 43 (Blain ed. 1949). See also Allen et al., *supra* note 8, at 36: though the authors themselves advocate rigid separation between the issues of hospitalization and competency, their study does document the prevalence of the opposite view. One California psychiatrist of high official responsibility is quoted as saying: "I simply tell the court whether the man is psychiatrically sane or not . . . [M]any lawyers don't agree with me. They ask me, 'What does that have to do with whether he is competent?' I tell them that insanity and incompetency amount to the same thing. I have had some trouble with lawyers on this."

22. Streda Estate, 137 *Legal Intell.* No. 97, at 1, col. 3 (Del. Cty. Orphans Ct., Nov. 6, 1957).

was suffering from dementia praecox and had delusions of persecution. He was convinced that his neighbors had joined in a conspiracy to fill his home with poison gas. The superintendent of the state hospital had testified that the alleged incompetent was of "unsound mind and might dissipate his estate or become the victim of designing persons." However, he did not testify to any facts in support of his opinion and admitted that he had not questioned the "incompetent" concerning the extent of his property, claims against the estate, and the like. The alleged incompetent testified in his own behalf and according to the court "demonstrated an intelligent grasp of his financial situation, recited detailed facts such as the mortgage arrangements relating to his home, and convinced the court he is well familiar with the nature and extent of any property now or heretofore owned by him." In denying the petition the court stated that

> the criterion is not the mental illness but rather the inability to manage property by reason of mental illness. Unless the mental illness produces or results in such inability to manage property, the court is not warranted in appointing the guardian for the estate of a mentally ill person.[23]

On the other hand, field studies on the administration of incompetency cases[24] indicate that the distinction between mental illness (hospitalization criteria) and incompetency—so meticulously maintained by this Pennsylvania court—is often ignored in many other courts and legal circles.

The various state statutes still reflect the division of opinion, though the legislative trend today is clearly toward a complete separation between hospitalization and incompetency. The Draft Act intentionally omits incompetency; its preface states as a fundamental thesis of the act that an order of hospitalization decides no more than the need of hospitalization, making the status of incompetency neither a prerequisite to nor a consequence of hospitalization.[25] Very few states—Colorado, Ohio and West Virginia—maintain the complete merger of incompetency with involuntary institutionalization as part of their statutory scheme, and the provisions of several states specifically disavow any such in-

exorable connection.[26] The statutes of a number of states assert that commitment shall not raise even a presumption of incompetency.[27]

This legislative trend may well be hailed as significant and salutary reform by those various commentators and committees which have long advocated separation of the issues of competency and hospitalization.[28] An optimistic assessment, however, may be somewhat premature in view of the fact that the practices in most jurisdictions do not as yet conform to the theory of separation outlined in the statutes.

That incompetency and hospitalization are in effect still "merged" despite statutory directives to the contrary is most clearly observable in those jurisdictions which consider the issues separately but in the same proceeding. Tennessee and Texas[29] are the only states where a determination as to competency *must* be made at the commitment hearing, but in several other states[30] the statutes allow the committing court discretion to decide the competency issue in the same proceeding.

The Texas experience has been analyzed in detail by observers in the field,[31] whose findings—quite likely applicable to other states as well—are illustrative of the fact that separation is largely an illusion. Random sampling and direct observation of hospitalization cases in Texas disclosed that *all* persons committed were also "found" incompetent.[32] It is

23. Id. at 8, col. 2.

24. See Allen et al., *supra* note 8, at 50–54.

25. National Institute of Mental Health, Federal Security Agency, *A Draft Act Governing Hospitalization of the Mentally Ill*, Scope of the Draft Act, at 2 (Public Health Service Pub. No. 51, 1952) [hereinafter cited as *Draft Act*]. The *Draft Act* is reproduced as Appendix A to this Report.

26. See Table 8.2.

27. E.g., *Hawaii Rev. Stat. Ann.*, §334-57 (1968); *Del. Code Ann.* tit. 16, § 5126(d) (1953); *Cal. Welf. & Inst'ns Code* § 5331 (West Supp. 1968).

28. For some of the more recent proposals of separation of the issues, see Allen et al., *supra* note 8, at 49–51 and nn.24, 25. As mentioned earlier, the authors themselves argue for such separation; they state that 88 percent of a total of 182 attorneys, psychiatrists, and psychologists interviewed in their field study advocated the same; they also cite in support the Group for the Advancement of Psychiatry, *Laws Governing Hospitalization of the Mentally Ill* 156–57 (Rep. No. 61, 1966), and Canadian Mental Health Association, *The Law and Mental Disorder* 30 (1964). The Canadian study records the following astonishing finding: One psychiatric hospital, which treats only certified acutely ill patients and whose superintendent has discretionary powers to advise on competency, has recommended *no* patient incompetent in the last 1,500 admissions.

29. *Tenn. Code Ann.* § 33-313 (Supp. 1968); *Tex. Rev. Civ. Stat.* art 5547-51 (1958).

30. See Table 8.2, Where Involuntary Hospitalization and Incompetency May Be Determined by the Same Hearing column.

31. Allen et al., *supra* note 8, at 50–54.

32. Contrast this with the experience of the Canadian hospital, *supra* note 28, where not one patient in the last 1,500 admissions has been recommended for incompetency.

virtually inconceivable that truly independent consideration of the competency issue would have produced this result. The description of the hearing procedures is explanatory: hearings were held at the hospital, lasting about one minute and a half per patient; the patient himself was present in some 10 percent of the cases only; the attorneys selected by the judge were young and inexperienced and their preparation was minimal or nil; most had never seen, or had any prior contact with, the patient they represented; judge, attorneys, and hospital personnel were said to exhibit considerable lack of understanding of the competency issue.

Jurisdictions where the statutes do not permit or provide for determination of hospitalization and competency in the same proceeding are somewhat less likely to exhibit the defects just described. Nonetheless, even in these states separation of the issues appears to be a theory not followed in practice. The presumption of incompetency flowing from commitment—operative in perhaps still a majority of the states[33]—tends to dim the separation of the issues as contemplated by the statutes. More significant, however, in many states administrative regulations result in de facto incompetency for institutionalized patients irrespective of legal determination of that issue. On the basis of interviews with hospital officials and observation of hospital practices, a recent study concluded that:

> legal status as a "competent" or "incompetent" person is not determinative of whether he may execute a legal instrument, drive an automobile, marry, etc. While he is in the hospital, the policies and procedures of the hospital determine the extent to which he manages his own affairs and exercises his civil rights. Indeed legal status is not even an important factor in such policies and procedures.[34]

A final factor which tends to perpetuate merger of the issues of competency and hospitalization despite statutory language to the contrary is the logically inconsistent language and/or utilization of the restoration provisions in several states.[35] That is to say, the statutes provide that patients discharged from institutions routinely go through formal judicial proceedings for restoration of competency re-

gardless of whether their competency was ever affected by commitment as such or by independent adjudication of incompetency. It is quite possible to argue that formal restoration serves only to make clear—to the patient as well as to the business community—the patient's legal status, a none-too-superfluous process in view of the widespread ignorance (perhaps excusable, considering the perplexities posed by the changing competency law) concerning the collateral effects of hospitalization.[36] Others assert, however, that the restoration situation is merely another indication that separation of incompetency from commitment is more myth than reality.[37]

The factors alluded to here as militating against meaningful separation of competency and involuntary hospitalization—presumption, administrative regulations, and restoration—will be discussed more elaborately in subsequent sections, following the section on the effect of hospitalization on voluntary and temporary patients.

VI. VOLUNTARY AND TEMPORARY PATIENTS

It is difficult to ascertain from the statutes how or whether voluntary or temporary hospitalization affects legal competency. Jurisdictions such as Illinois, Ohio, Texas, and Washington formerly provided specifically that voluntary patients were not to suffer loss of their civil rights.[38] South Dakota used to specify the competency of temporary patient was not affected.[39] Today, though a few states specifically provide that voluntary or temporary patients shall not lose their civil rights,[40] the more common approach is to "resolve" this question by implication.

Logically it would appear that voluntary or temporary admission to an institution should have no

33. See this chapter, § VIII C, Admissibility and Weight of Evidence of Hospitalization.

34. Allen et al., *supra* note 8, at 59. For a more detailed discussion see this chapter, § VII, Administrative Regulations.

35. See Allen et al., *supra* note 8, at 53–54, on restoration proceedings in California, Massachusetts, New York, North Carolina, and Texas.

36. Id. at 49, 53, 58.

37. Ibid. The authors view the restoration provisions as demonstrating legislative ambivalence on the question of separating competency and commitment, though they themselves argue for greater clarity concerning the effects on legal competency of hospitalization and discharge.

38. *Ill. Rev. Stat.* ch. 91-1/2, § 4-8 (1956); *Ohio Rev. Code Ann.* § 5123.57 (Baldwin 1958); *Tex. Rev. Civ. Stat.* art. 5547-24 (Supp. 1958); *Wash. Rev. Code* § 71.02.650 (1956).

39. *S.D. Code* § 30.01A07 (Supp. 1952).

40. E.g., of the states listed above only Texas retains such a provision: *Tex. Rev. Civ. Stat.* art. 5547-24 (1958). See also *N.D. Cent. Code* § 25-03-20 (1)(c) (1960), which provides generally that voluntary or involuntary hospitalization shall not be an adjudication of incompetency. And see N.Y. Mental Hygiene Law § 70-5 (McKinney Supp. 1969).

formal impact on competency. In states such as Ohio, where—as was mentioned earlier—the questions of commitment and competency were and still are merged, a determination regarding competency presupposes, is part of, a formal adjudication as to hospitalization. But voluntary or temporary hospitalization is no formal adjudication of *any* issue; hence competency is not affected, and a statute stating the same only repeats a logically compelled conclusion. A statutory provision to the effect that voluntary or temporary patients shall not lose their civil rights is of course also redundant in jurisdictions (e.g., Texas) where the issue of competency must be determined separately from the question of hospitalization. Thus the Texas provision, like the former Ohio provision, is technically superfluous, and its only conceivable intent a reemphasis of the concept that persons hospitalized do not become incompetent by the mere fact of hospitalization. Such clarification of the patient's legal status may of itself be useful, considering the changing and complex state of the laws. However, it can be argued that the failure to relate this to the logic of the total statutory scheme on competency leads to confusion: it obscures the overall relationship between hospitalization and incompetency contemplated in the particular jurisdiction—whether separation or merger; it obscures the fact that voluntary or temporary patients may still be subjected to independent hospitalization proceedings; and it obscures the possibility of hospital-administrative restrictions on the personal, civil, and property rights of such patients.

The applicability of administrative competency regulations to voluntary and temporary patients is a more clear-cut matter. The statutes of a number of states expressly provide that limitations on legal competency may be imposed by the hospital despite the fact that formal or complete incompetency shall not be an automatic consequence of hospitalization.[41] Similar administrative restrictions obtain as a practical matter in jurisdictions where there is no explicit statutory authorization on this score.[42] Neither the statutes on administrative regulations nor the relevant practices distinguish between voluntary and involuntary patients or between temporarily and indeterminately hospitalized patients, and in fact these regulations are applied either ad hoc or systematically[43] to any patient. De facto incompetency by

way of administrative regulations can thus obtain for patients regardless of any legal adjudication of incompetency and irrespective of the legal form of admission.

The prospect of formal and complete incompetency for voluntary and temporary patients would appear to be remote under the statutes, and the suggestion that its specter tends to discourage the use of temporary and voluntary procedures is somewhat farfetched. A more real concern for voluntary patients is the imposition of administrative limitations. However, the negative inferences to be drawn from such imposition can be minimized. Hospital rules applied ad hoc to the proper situations may even be an inducement toward voluntary or temporary entrance into an institution. A patient assured that he will be allowed to perform those functions he is capable of, while responsibly represented in those he cannot perform, is far less likely to be hesitant about leaving the community for a period of time. In fact the principle of only partial or ad hoc incompetency may be the answer to the problems of the competency law in general; loss of *all* civil rights is a dehumanizing and unnecessary experience for the great majority of the mentally disabled, whether accomplished by judicial or administrative means, and whether the patient be voluntary or involuntary.

VII. ADMINISTRATIVE REGULATIONS

As a matter of practice, hospitals in all jurisdictions appear to impose administrative restrictions on the civil rights of patients.[44] The statutes of several states expressly permit this.[45] The restrictions are applied to patients who are legally competent as well as to those legally incompetent. On the other side of the coin, patients who are legally incompetent are not always restrained from exercising their civil rights and in some instances are allowed to execute contracts, deeds, and wills with express permission of the hospital.[46] Administrative regulations may be propounded ad hoc by individual institutions or, as for example in Massachusetts and New York, be issued on a more systematic level by the state department of mental health.[47]

41. See Table 8.2, Competency Affected by Involuntary Hospitalization column.

42. Allen et al., *supra* note 8, at 55, 56, 59–68.

43. Ibid. For a fuller discussion see this chapter, § VII, Administrative Regulations.

44. See Allen et al., *supra* note 8, at 59.

45. See Table 8.2, Competency Affected by Involuntary Hospitalization column.

46. Allen et al., *supra* note 8, at 59. Of course patients on temporary leave also perform various business and personal functions without the hospital's knowledge and despite their incompetency. Hospitals, upon learning of such transactions, usually do not attempt to nullify them.

47. Id. at 55–56, esp. nn. 49, 50. The regulations of the depart-

The Draft Act, which does not make incompetency a consequence of hospitalization, is typical of those statutes which expressly permit the imposition of administrative regulations. Section 21 of the Act provides:

(a) Subject to the general rules and regulations of the hospital and except to the extent that the head of the hospital determines that it is necessary for the medical welfare of the patient to impose restrictions, every patient shall be entitled

. . . .

(3) to exercise all civil rights, including the right to dispose of property, execute instruments, make purchases, enter contractual relations, and vote, unless he has been adjudicated incompetent and has not been restored to legal capacity.

. . . .

(c) Any limitations imposed by the head of the hospital on the exercise of these rights by the patient and the reasons for such limitations shall be made a part of the clinical record of the patient.[48]

The commentary of the Draft Act interprets this section as guaranteeing the patient full enjoyment of his personal rights.[49] However, a close reading of the section indicates that this guarantee has limited value and contains inherent hazards. Section 21 permits the hospital to impose restrictions and to curtail the patient's rights both because of the practical needs of hospital administration and the needs of the patient's medical welfare. It is not specified how far the hospital may proceed in curtailing a patient's rights; but, in actuality, it is given authority to accomplish through administrative action what a finding of incompetency achieves through a judicial proceeding. The fact that any limitation must be recorded may provide some safeguard against arbitrary restrictions, but only if effective review procedures are made available to patients.

A problem which could arise under the Draft Act or a similar provision is illustrated by *In re Alexieff's Will*.[50] A general order of the New York Depart-

ment of Mental Hygiene provided that no patient could execute a will without the permission of the Commissioner of Mental Hygiene or a court. The case concerned the validity of a will executed by a patient who did not obtain such permission. The court, assuming without deciding that the procurement of such an order was a condition precedent to the execution of the instrument as a will, held that, nevertheless, the failure to procure the order did not affect the validity of the instrument as a will. There was evidence that the patient was in fact competent, and consequently the will was admitted to probate.[51] What other courts would decide in similar situations is uncertain.

Commentators have expressed reservations about the discretionary aspects of administrative regulations. Abuse may occur in the imposition of restraints not absolutely essential to the proper operation of the hospital nor relevant to the mental condition of the patient. Administratively imposed restraints are further criticized for the fact that they generally deny the patient the right to dispute the issue of capacity. It has been suggested, therefore, that if the hospital doubts a patient's competency and wishes to restrict his activities even though he is legally competent, it should be required to initiate formal competency proceedings. Several countervailing arguments exist, however. To require the hospital to initiate proceedings in every instance may be too burdensome and impractical. Second, the presumption that formal proceedings assure the patient of a meaningful hearing with due procedural protections may be no more than just that—a presumption.[52] Most significant, an adjudication of complete incompetency is likely to be unnecessary and undesirable for the patient in question. In view of all these factors, a more promising approach would be to assure the opportunity for a judicial review of hospital or departmental administrative decisions as applied to the patient.

VIII. INCOMPETENCY INDEPENDENT OF HOSPITALIZATION

As noted earlier, virtually all the states today have abandoned the complete merger of incompetency and hospitalization. Though the practices and even some of the subsidiary statutory provisions often

---

ment of mental health often include allowing a judge or hospital official to make ad hoc determinations of a patient's competency to perform a specific act.

48. *Draft Act* § 21, at 15.

49. *Draft Act,* Commentary, at 20.

50. 94 N.Y.S.2d 32 (Sur. Ct. 1949), *aff'd,* 227 App. Div. 790, 97 N.Y.S.2d 532 (1950), *motion for leave to appeal denied,* 277 App. Div. 901, 98 N.Y.S.2d 582 (1950).

51. See chap. 9, "Personal and Property Rights," for a general discussion of the effect of hospitalization on testamentary capacity.

52. Recall the discussion of the Texas practices at text accompanying note 32 *supra.*

militate against actual separation and truly independent consideration of the competency issue, technically competency today is an independent determination in all but a few states and will be examined as such in this section.

A. INITIATION OF INCOMPETENCY PROCEEDINGS

The procedure governing a determination of incompetency is substantially similar to that used in judicial hospitalization proceedings. Although in a very few states a petition can be presented only by a relative or a friend, in most states it can be brought by any interested person.[53] Notice to the alleged incompetent is a statutory requirement in a vast majority of states.[54] Even where statutes do not make notice a requirement, the courts usually have held it to be essential on the theory that a statute which made notice unnecessary would be a violation of due process.[55] However, in a few jurisdictions the judge may, if it is deemed necessary, dispense with notice altogether.[56] In a few others the court has discretion to reduce, for good cause, the length of time between the service of notice and the holding of the hearing.[57] About half the states require that notice be given to one or more relatives in addition to the notice served upon the alleged incompetent.[58] In only some ten to twelve states do statutes require that a medical certificate of the incompetent's mental condition accompany the petition. However, some other states require medical evidence at the hearing or an investigation of the petition by a commission of doctors.[59]

B. HEARING AND TESTIMONY

The person alleged to be incompetent is entitled to produce evidence and witnesses in order to dispute the allegations set out in the petition and the evidence against him. About half the states make some provision for the appointment of counsel or a guardian *ad litem*.[60] In a number of these states such appointment is discretionary with the court. In some others the prosecuting attorney is to act as counsel for the alleged incompetent unless the latter is able to furnish his own.[61] Because the proceedings may result in the loss of the person's civil rights[62] as well as the loss of control over his property, representation by counsel would appear to be a necessary protection. Ordinarily the incompetent must be present at the hearing unless it is shown to the court's satisfaction that his presence should be dispensed with.[63]

With a view toward facilitating as fair and efficient a hearing as is possible in the absence of the alleged incompetent, it has been proposed that an extensive investigation be conducted by a court-appointed commission composed of a psychiatrist, a clinical psychologist, and an attorney.[64] Under this plan the alleged incompetent would be represented by counsel; his own presence, however, "would in most instances not only be unnecessary but undesirable."[65] It has been contended that the incompetency determination should be conducted in this fashion "both because it is the most effective way of getting a real understanding of the individual and because it does less violence to his peace of mind."[66] The desirability of these proposals is not beyond dispute, however. Firm medical evidence for the contention that the mentally ill are adversely affected by being present at hearings dealing with their condition is lacking. The suggestion of such effect is perhaps even more tenuous with regard to alleged incompetents, as distinguished from persons thought to be mentally ill. The provision for representation by counsel has merit, but substituted presence does not of itself obviate the due process problem posed by denial of the fundamental right of personal presence at a hearing where significant personal and property rights are at stake.

Under the federal Constitution, neither the due process clauses of the Fifth and Fourteenth Amendments nor the right to trial by jury in criminal cases guaranteed by the Seventh Amendment appear to give an alleged incompetent the right to demand a jury.[67] Several state courts have held, however, that

53. See Table 8.3, Application By columns.

54. Id. at Notice columns.

55. 25 *Am. Jur.* "Guardian and Ward" § 40 (1940).

56. E.g., Illinois: *Ill. Rev. Stat.* ch. 3, § 117(a) (1967).

57. E.g., Arkansas: *Ark. Stat. Ann.* § 47-611(c) (Supp. 1967).

58. See Table 8.3, Notice columns.

59. Id. at Medical Certificate column.

60. Id. at Counsel or Guardian *Ad Litem* column.

61. Ibid.

62. In addition, some states allow a guardian to hospitalize his ward. Ross, *supra* note 7. See also *Cal. Welf. & Inst'ns Code* § 5358 (West Supp. 1967).

63. Table 8.3, Presence in Court columns.

64. Guttmacher & Weihofen, *supra* note 10, at 332.

65. Ibid.

66. Id. at 332–33.

67. See Ward v. Booth, 197 F.2d 963 (9th Cir. 1952); Simon v. Craft, 182 U.S. 427 (1901); Barry v. Hall, 98 F.2d 222 (D.C. Cir. 1938).

there was a right to trial by jury in incompetency proceedings at common law and that state constitutional guarantees of trial by jury consequently extend and preserve such a right; and some jurisdictions have held that even though the right did not exist at common law, it existed by statute before the adoption of the state constitution and was, therefore, incorporated in the constitutional provisions guaranteeing jury trials.[68] Nonetheless, the states generally recognize no original or common-law right to trial by jury in incompetency cases.[69] About one-third of the states presently provide by statute for either mandatory or optional juries in such cases;[70] but, as in most civil proceedings, the right to have a jury determine incompetency may be waived.[71]

In some jurisdictions, the alleged incompetent's failure to demand a jury trial is deemed to be a waiver of his right.[72] In this circumstance his right to a jury trial would not be effective unless he were informed of his right to demand such a procedure. This problem is not so acute in those states where the court is required to appoint counsel or a guardian *ad litem* for incompetency proceedings,[73] but where the alleged incompetent is not represented by counsel, it is quite likely that he would not be cognizant of his right to a jury.

C. Admissibility and Weight of Evidence of Hospitalization

It is difficult to state what the evidence must demonstrate concerning the type and degree of mental impairment to warrant a finding of incompetency. The statutes are not specific, and apparently the courts determine each case on the particular facts and circumstances involved. However, some idea of the general standards used can be obtained from the following discussion of the case law:

> [I]t is not essential, to justify the appointment of a guardian or committee, . . . that he be shown to be insane in the technical sense. . . . [I]t seems to be the prevailing view that proof of the entire absence of reason, understanding or memory is not required in order to justify the appointment of a guardian or committee of the estate. . . . It generally is . . . suffi-

cient to show that he is as incapable of managing his affairs as if he were insane, and according to some decisions, the test . . . is whether there is such mental impairment as renders the subject incapable of understanding and acting in the ordinary affairs of life. On the other hand . . . a guardian cannot be appointed merely because a person cannot manage his property judiciously. . . . The unsoundness of mind which will justify an appointment must be more than mere debility or impairment of memory.[74]

A majority of states have held that evidence of the person's hospitalization is admissable.[75] The weight that this evidence carries varies among the states and is dictated by case law in most jurisdictions. In a number of states the statutes deal with this question, but with little uniformity.[76] The statutory provisions of California, Delaware and Hawaii expressly state that the fact of hospitalization shall raise no presumption as to incompetency.[77] At the other extreme, the statutes of Indiana and North Carolina provide that hospitalization accompanied by a certificate from a physician or hospital superintendent regarding the patient's general disability shall be equivalent to an adjudication of incompetency.[78] A Wisconsin statute provides that hospitalization creates a rebuttable presumption of incompetency.[79] The Wisconsin provision reflects the prevailing view as found in the case law of most states.

Judicial decisions in a few states have treated the presumption as conclusive.[80] An Arkansas case concerning the appointment of a guardian for a mental patient is illustrative.[81] It was contended in this case that the appointment was invalid because notice of the incompetency proceedings had not been served on the patient. Apparently the only evidence introduced at the incompetency proceedings was a letter addressed "to whom it may concern,'" stating

---

68. See Annot., 33 A.L.R.2d 1145 (1954).

69. Id. at 1155.

70. See Table 8.3, Jury Trial columns.

71. Annot., 33 A.L.R.2d 1145, 1162; 29 *Am. Jur.* "Insane Persons" § 21 (1960).

72. See Table 8.3, Jury Trial columns.

73. Id. at Counsel or Guardian *Ad Litem* column.

74. 25 *Am. Jur.* "Guardian and Ward" § 18 (1940).

75. Ross, *supra* note 7, at 518.

76. See Table 8.2, Competency Affected by Involuntary Hospitalization column.

77. *Cal. Welf. & Inst'ns Code* § 5331 (West Supp. 1968); *Del. Code Ann.* tit. 16, § 5126(d) (Supp. 1970); *Hawaii Rev. Stat. Ann.* § 334-57 (1968).

78. *Ind. Ann. Stat.* § 8-120 (1964); *N.C. Gen. Stat.* § 35-3 (1966).

79. *Wis. Stat. Ann.* § 51.005(2) (1957).

80. Ross, *supra* note 7, at 516–17.

81. Sanders v. Omohundro, 204 Ark. 1040, 166 S.W.2d 657 (1942).

that the patient was mentally ill, was confined to a private mental hospital in Michigan, and was incapable of taking care of her property. The letter was signed by a physican on the hospital staff. The Arkansas court, stating that incompetency is presumed from the fact of confinement, upheld the appointment of the guardian.

Treating the presumption as conclusive is in effect a type of delayed merger. In view of the fact that the legislative trend in the great majority of states has been expressly to separate the issues of hospitalization and competency, it appears doubtful that the holding in the Arkansas decision would be reiterated today.

A few decisions have adopted the position that evidence of hospitalization is not merely inconclusive on the issue of capacity but is totally inadmissible.[82] However, these cases appear to have dealt not with whether a hospitalization order is admissible in an incompetency hearing, but rather with whether such an order is admissible in suits involving the validity of legal acts already performed by the alleged incompetent.[83]

IX. GUARDIANSHIP

When incompetency is determined independently of hospitalization, a guardian is usually appointed for the incompetent. But in those jurisdictions where incompetency is merged with hospitalization, frequently no guardian is appointed even though the hospitalized person automatically becomes incompetent.[84] Guardianship may be limited to guardianship of the person or guardianship of the estate, or may include both.[85] In most states one guardian may be appointed for the person of the incompetent and another appointed for the estate. Corporations may act as guardians in about one-third of the states.[86] In some jurisdictions the term "conservator," "curator," "committee," or "tutor" is used

instead of "guardian." "Conservator" or "curator" are applied especially to guardians of the estate.

A guardian of the estate engages in the usual activities of property management, buys and sells on behalf of the ward, makes contracts for him, and represents him in legal proceedings.[87] As an agent of the court, the guardian is answerable to it for the judicious use of the ward's funds. He must obtain the court's permission for certain activities, as would be required if he were the guardian of a minor, and must submit the same kind of accounts. In general, the guardian has greater powers over his ward's personal property than over his real property. Usually, a court order must be secured before a sale of the ward's real property can be consummated.[88] A guardian of the person has essentially the same duties and obligations toward his ward as the person having the custody of a minor.

An interesting problem concerning the legal authority of the guardian of a person relates to his power to hospitalize his ward or make application for his admission to a mental hospital. In almost all jurisdictions, a guardian is an "interested party" under the hospitalization statutes and therefore may initiate involuntary proceedings.[89] In California today, hospitalization by a conservator is statutorily the standard procedure for hospitalizing the "gravely disabled."[90] Furthermore, several states authorize a guardian to make application for the "voluntary admission" of his ward.[91] It is usually necessary in such instances for the guardian to obtain the approval of the court which supervises him.[92] Other states specifically provide that no patient may be confined in a mental hospital except as authorized by the hospitalization statutes; in these states it is clear that the guardian cannot act to hospitalize his ward unless the hospitalization statutes so provide.[93]

A few guardianship statutes are so broad in their grant of authority that they might be construed as authorizing the guardian to hospitalize his ward despite the fact that the hospitalization statutes do not so provide.[94] On the other hand, many states

82. Leggate v. Clark, 111 Mass. 308 (1873); Knox v. Haug, 48 Minn. 58, 50 N.W. 934 (1892).

83. Ibid.

84. This problem is no longer as serious as it once was in view of the fact that today very few states (Colorado, Ohio, and West Virginia) retain complete merger by statute. As recently as eight years ago, however, this was still perceived as one of the main failings of the competency laws: see Allen et al., *supra* note 8, at 37, regarding the situation as it prevailed in Colorado, the District of Columbia, and Ohio in 1962.

85. See Table 8.2, Guardian Of columns, and Table 8.3, Guardians columns.

86. Table 8.3, Corporations Permitted column.

87. 25 *Am. Jur.* "Guardian and Ward" § 107 passim (1940).

88. Id. at §§ 108, 124.

89. See Table 3.2, Judicial Hospitalization of the Mentally Ill—Prehearing Procedures, Application By columns.

90. *Cal. Welf. & Inst'ns Code* § 5358 (West Supp. 1968).

91. See chap. 2, "Voluntary Admissions," and tables thereto.

92. Ross, *supra* note 7, at 473.

93. Id. at 472–73.

94. Id. at 473.

have provisions which imply that the hospitalization statutes provide the sole methods of hospitalizing persons.[95]

The question remains whether a guardian should be permitted to hospitalize his ward against his will and without recourse to the normal statutory hospitalization procedure. If the guardian is permitted to do so, the incompetency determination assumes unusual importance in that it makes the incompetent person subject to compulsory hospitalization at his guardian's discretion and without the customary statutory safeguards. Since the criteria underlying the incompetency determination may differ from those upon which hospitalization is based, it would appear undesirable to permit a guardian to hospitalize his ward against his will without using the normal statutory procedures.

Only slightly more than half the states have statutory provisions for supervising the treatment of the ward.[96] Louisiana, one of the states providing for supervision, requires the court to appoint a superintendent for an incompetent person. This superintendent is to report to the court every three months on the state of the incompetent's health and the type of treatment he is receiving. In addition, Louisiana authorizes the judge to visit the ward outside the presence of the guardian whenever the judge deems it expedient.[97]

One of the primary aims of guardianship laws should be to assure that guardians or representatives are in fact appointed for those adjudicated or administratively designated as incompetent and that such appointments coincide temporally with the fact of incompetency. The statutes which formerly merged the issues of hospitalization and competency often failed to accomplish these objectives.[98] The decline of merger in favor of separation of the issues in the great majority of jurisdictions has resolved only part of the problem. An independent judicial determination of incompetency assures virtually by definition the appointment of a guardian, but such a determination may never take place, or if it does it may occur long after the fact of hospitalization, while in the meantime the hospitalized patient remains de facto incompetent by virtue of institution-alization or by express administrative regulation. The hospitals themselves often manage patients' funds and may to some extent perform the functions of guardianship generally; the laws, however, need to make it clear that whichever agency or person acts as the representative of a de facto incompetent patient must comply with the standards of responsibility and disinterest that this fiduciary function implies.

It must be noted that the private court-appointed guardian—usually a friend or relative of the incompetent—is not the only and exclusive type of guardian. Limited guardianships are operative in the administration of veterans' benefits and social security. These types, in numbers alone, far surpass the traditional private guardian.[99] Public guardians have been created in a number of states. The New York hospital system has its "Reimbursement Agent." State guardianship in Minnesota has come under intensive study, and its type has become known as the "Minnesota Plan."[100] The functions and operations of these alternatives to private guardianship will not be discussed here. Their workability and potential for resolving the problems in this area are dealt with in other more detailed studies on competency.[101]

X. RECORDS OF INCOMPETENCY

Contracts entered into by a person after he has been adjudged incompetent are usually void even though the other contracting party had no actual notice of the incompetency determination.[102] To be protected against the possibility of unknowingly dealing with an incompetent person, the businessman must have a method of ascertaining the legal status of persons with whom he may wish to transact business. This is not an easy task because very few states have central statewide registration of incompetents, and the only record of incompetency is found in the court in which the incompetency was adjudicated.[103]

95. Ibid.

96. See Table 8.3, Continuing Court Supervision column.

97. *La. Civ. Code Ann.* arts. 424, 425 (West 1952).

98. See Allen et al., *supra* note 8, at 47–48: "[F]ewer than one out of four of the patients in any of these jurisdictions [had] a guardian." When a guardian was appointed, a considerable period of time, even a number of years, might have elapsed between adjudication and appointment; see 48 n.13.

99. Id. at 97.

100. Id. at chap. 5, "State Guardianship: The Minnesota Plan," 99–112.

101. See generally Allen et al., *supra* note 8, and citations therein to derivative studies.

102. 29 *Am. Jur.* "Insane and other Incompetent Persons" § 67 (1960).

103. Only four states have installed a system of central registration, and one of these pertains only to incompetents who have been hospitalized. Two other states have attempted to mitigate the problem of notice by requiring newspaper publication of the incompetency adjudication. See Table 8.3, Central Registration of Incompetency column.

It is quite possible that a person adjudged incompetent in one county may have his property or business located in other counties. Therefore, the present record-keeping system offers little practical protection to a person dealing with an incompetent.[104] The situation is even more difficult in states where the law is not clear on the relationship between hospitalization and incompetency. In these states, there would seem to be considerable uncertainty surrounding business transactions involving mental patients or former mental patients.

XI. RESTORATION TO COMPETENCY

A. THE MEANING OF RESTORATION

Restoration is a legal determination that an individual previously adjudged incompetent has regained the ability to manage his business and personal affairs adequately. Restoration can be accomplished through a separate judicial proceeding to determine competency, or it may occur in connection with a patient's discharge from a mental hospital.[105]

The complex interrelationships between hospitalization and incompetency are paralleled by those between discharge and restoration. In a significant number of states discharge is equivalent to restoration of civil rights; however, the statutes usually specify or contemplate that only "final" or "regular" discharge shall have this effect.[106] The implication is that conditional discharge does not restore the patient to competency. This would appear to make sense were it not for the fact that discharge terminology often does not correspond to the simple "final"/"conditional" dichotomy. Patients may be discharged as "cured," "improved," "unimproved," and so on; the impact of such dispositions on restoration is far from clear in the statutes. The uncertainty surrounding the patient's legal status is further compounded by the fact that the patient himself is usually not informed of his competency status upon

discharge.[107] In those jurisdictions where discharge and restoration are not merged by statute, independent restoration proceedings must presumably be instituted to effectuate reinstatement of civil rights. However, a few of these states have no specific restoration procedure.[108] A different type of complication exists in those states where, despite the fact that discharge and restoration are not merged, a certificate of discharge signed by the hospital superintendent raises a presumption of legal competency.[109]

The statutory variations on the restoration theme and the resulting or inherent lack of clarity with regard to the legal status of a discharged patient are matched by practices often dissonant or inconsistent with the probable meanings of the statutes. Some of these practices will be outlined below.[110]

B. RESTORATION MERGED WITH DISCHARGE

Although automatic restoration appears to be limited to persons who have been discharged both unconditionally and as recovered, there are numerous variations in the manner in which such restoration is effected. In a few jurisdictions the mere fact of absolute discharge is sufficient to restore the patient to competency.[111] The usual procedure is for the hospital to notify the probate court that the patient has been discharged as "recovered."[112] The court is then required to issue an order of restoration. Under this procedure it is unnecessary for the patient to take any legal action or to appear in court. However, in some states where this procedure is followed it is reported that judges, believing restoration to be a judicial function, refuse to issue such restoration orders automatically.[113]

In Minnesota, where restoration is automatic upon discharge, the State Department of Welfare has said:

> In the literal language of the statutes, outright and final discharge acts to restore the patient to full capacity and restores his rights and responsibilities.

---

104. For an example of the problems in this area see Rohrer v. Darrow, 66 Colo. 463, 182 P. 13 (1919). Mrs. Rohrer had been hospitalized in a private institution in 1901 and conditionally released in 1903. No discharge was ever obtained. Thereafter she engaged in buying and selling real estate in her own name. In 1917 a deed she executed was successfully challenged on the ground that she had been declared incompetent when hospitalized and was still incompetent because of the failure to obtain absolute discharge. See also Ross, *supra* note 7, at 516–17.

105. See Table 8.4, Independent Restoration Proceedings, Restoration Merged with Discharge column.

106. Ibid.

107. Allen et al., *supra* note 8, at 49.

108. E.g., New Hampshire; see Table 8.4.

109. Ibid. E.g., Nevada: *Nev. Rev. Stat.* § 41.300 (1967).

110. For descriptions of restoration practices based on field studies in several jurisdictions, see Allen et al., *supra* note 8, at chap. 3; Rock, Jacobson, & Janopaul, *Hospitalization and Discharge of the Mentally Ill*, chap. 10, 424–52 (1968).

111. See Table 8.4, Restoration Merged with Discharge column.

112. Ibid.

113. Cram, *Mental Health in Kansas: Community Action* 25 (1957).

However, in the eyes of many lawyers, there is question as to whether this status would stand up in any contest; these persons hold that only the committing court has the right to restore. Hence, it would be well to advise patients to seek legal advice in effecting important contracts or undertaking other legal transactions in which the legal status of competency is of primary importance. Such patients may wish to use the legally established procedures for restoration to capacity and through petition and hearing in the appropriate probate court.[114]

In those instances where patients are discharged as improved or unimproved or where conditional discharge has become "final" following the lapse of a statutorily specified time period, the consequences for legal competency are especially dubious. Accordingly, the advice of the Minnesota Welfare Department would be especially pertinent for patients discharged under those conditions.

C. INDEPENDENT RESTORATION

In the states where discharge and restoration are not merged, a variety of procedures and practices operate to effect the return to legal competency. Generally, it can be said that the procedure followed in independent restoration proceedings closely parallels that required in incompetency proceedings. A few states, however, have no specific restoration procedure but merely provide that the court is to discharge the guardian when the cause for which the guardianship was granted has ceased or is removed.[115]

Patients discharged as improved or unimproved as well as those discharged as cured may initiate proceedings in the majority of states. In many states any interested person or relative of the incompetent may do so. To prevent improper or premature applications, a number of states have statutory restrictions on the frequency of filing such applications.[116]

In states where there is a separation of incompetency and hospitalization, patients often may bring restoration proceedings while still in a mental hospital. In several states in which there is a close connection between discharge and restoration, patients were formerly specifically prohibited from bringing restoration proceedings until after discharge.[117] These provisions have since been repealed, but the rule may still be in force by way of judicial decision.[118]

In many of the states which do not make restoration an automatic consequence of discharge, the release of a patient from a mental hospital nevertheless has some effect on his status as an incompetent. In some states the discharge of a patient may be accompanied by a discretionary certificate from the hospital authorities that the person released has recovered sufficiently to manage his own affairs, in which case the patient is automatically restored to competency. In other states discharge provides the occasion for an automatic judicial inquiry into the competency of the former mental patient, although the outcome of that hearing is not predetermined by the fact of discharge. A few states have stipulated that discharge shall constitute prima facie evidence of the patient's return to competency, while in other states it creates a presumption of renewed legal capacity.[119] Because of the great confusion in this area of the law, the discharged patient's safest course of action in any of these states would appear to be the instigation of regular restoration proceedings. In the absence of counsel, however, it is unlikely that the patient will be aware that such action is advisable.

The practice or advisability of instituting formal restoration proceedings even though restoration may theoretically have already been accomplished by the fact of discharge is even reflected in some of the statutes. In Texas, for example, a recent amendment to the competency statute provides that any person who has been committed to a mental hospital and since discharged therefrom may apply in court "for an order adjudicating that he is not now mentally ill or incompetent."[120] But in Texas, discharge of a patient who has been found incompetent already terminates the incompetency,[121] and patients not "found" incompetent are not rendered so by the mere fact of hospitalization.[122] The amendment concerning judicial restoration is thus clearly super-

114. Minnesota Department of Public Welfare, Patient Movement, pt. 3, chap. 2, at 20 (Jan. 30, 1956).

115. See Table 8.4 and especially footnotes thereto. E.g., *N.H. Rev. Stat. Ann.* § 462:30 (1964).

116. See Table 8.4, Frequency of Restoration Applications column. E.g., Illinois, Iowa, Kansas.

117. E.g., Kentucky and North Carolina.

118. North Carolina: *In re* Harris, 241 N.C. 179, 84 S.E.2d 808 (1954).

119. See Table 8.4.

120. *Tex. Rev. Civ. Stat.* art. 5547-83(c) (Supp. 1970).

121. *Tex. Rev. Civ. Stat.* art. 5547-81(b) (1958).

122. In Texas, hospitalization is *not* determinative of incompetency, but the two issues are decided in the same proceeding. *Tex. Rev. Civ. Stat. Ann.* art. 5547-51 (1958).

fluous and has been criticized to the effect that its inconsistency jeopardizes the meaning of the remaining competency-restoration provisions.[123] Such criticism may be ill-conceived, however: the importance of certainty surrounding a discharged patient's legal status cannot be over-emphasized. The clearer the fact of restoration is made to the ex-patient and to the business community, the more confidently the former will be able to engage in "normal" activities such as driving an automobile, signing checks, and so forth, and the easier will be his task of rehabilitation.

XII. CONCLUSIONS AND RECOMMENDATIONS

1. *The statutes should make it clear that incompetency is to be determined as an issue separate from hospitalization, although the fact of hospitalization may be introduced as evidence in the determination of the competency question.*

The statutes of virtually all the states today technically separate hospitalization and incompetency, but on the practical level the issues are still often fused. Especially where hospitalization and competency are determined in the same proceeding, the separation is not effectively maintained. The statutes often contribute to the blurring of proper distinctions: incompetency is defined in diagnostic medical terms; hospitalization raises variously weighted presumptions as to competency; or medical certification of the fact of hospitalization is held as dispositive of the competency question. The elimination of such provisions appears desirable. Medical evaluation of alleged incompetents may be appropriate, but incompetency statutes must avoid using language and criteria applicable to mental conditions that warrant hospital treatment. Evidence of hospitalization may be relevant and may indicate incompetency for some purposes and as such should be admissible in a determination of the competency issue; but such evidence should not be elevated to the stature of presumption, conclusive or otherwise, and indiscriminately applicable to all cases.

2. *It is desirable that competency determinations be more discriminating and that they specify those functions which the incompetent should not and may not perform while stating those rights and functions which he remains entitled to assert or perform.*

For the majority of the mentally disabled loss of all civil rights and social rights is unnecessary and undesirable. There is therapeutic value in permitting

123. See Allen et al., *supra* note 8, at 53–54.

mentally ill persons to perform certain normal functions which they are capable of performing, and in fact hospitals at times allow patients to do so despite the fact that they may be formally incompetent.

3. *Hospitalized patients not formally adjudicated as incompetent may be subjected to certain administrative limitations on competency, provided the restrictions be only those essential to the welfare of the patient or to the orderly administration of the hospital and provided that certain safeguards be observed, such as the recording of such restrictions, including a showing of need therefor, and the opportunity of the patient to challenge them.*

It would be undesirable to take away the power of the hospital to place reasonable restrictions on the conduct of patients who may be legally competent. Requiring the hospital to initiate formal competency proceedings in all such instances would be impractical. Some measure of administrative discretion, checked by the safeguards of recording and the right of the patient to contest, though not without its advantages, would appear to strike the best possible balance. If the administrative regulation affects the patient's right to conduct business, it must be accompanied by a limited guardianship.

4. *Upon discharge from the hospital the patient's legal status as competent or incompetent should be clarified.*

Upon discharge, neither the patient nor the business community is cognizant of the former's legal status. This major problem should be remedied by requiring an official documentation and explanation of the patient's competency, incompetency, or partial incompetency when the patient leaves the hospital. The relationship between discharge and restoration to competency should be guided by, and involve considerations substantially similar to, those affecting the relationship between hospitalization and incompetency (see recommendations 1–3).

BIBLIOGRAPHY

Allen, Richard C.; Ferster, Elyce Z.; and Weihofen, Henry. *Mental Impairment and Legal Incompetency.* Englewood Cliffs, N.J.: Prentice-Hall, Inc., 1968.

American Jurisprudence. San Francisco: Bancroft-Whitney Co.; Rochester, N.Y.: Lawyers Co-operative Publishing Co.

"Guardian and Ward." 25 (1940) §§ 18, 40, 107 *passim*, 108, 124.

"Insane and Other Incompetent Persons." 29 (1960) §§ 21, 32, 67.

American Law Reports Annotated. San Francisco:

Bancroft-Whitney Co.; Rochester, N.Y.: Lawyers Co-operative Publishing Co.

"Constitutional Right to Jury Trial in Proceeding for Adjudication of Incompetency or Insanity or for Restoration." 2d ser. 33 (1954) 1145.

American Psychiatric Association. *Better Care in Mental Hospitals.* Edited by Daniel Blain. Washington, D.C.: American Psychiatric Association, 1949.

Canadian Mental Health Association. *The Law and Mental Disorder.* "One: Hospital and Patient Care." A report of the Committee on Legislation and Psychotic Disorder; a committee of the National Scientific Planning Council. Toronto, Ont.: Canadian Mental Health Association, 1964.

Cram, Margaret. *Mental Health in Kansas: Community Action.* Lawrence: Governmental Research Center, University of Kansas, 1957.

Davidson, Henry A. *Forensic Psychiatry.* New York: Ronald Press Co., 1952.

Deutsch, Albert. *The Mentally Ill in America.* 2d ed. rev. New York: Columbia University Press, 1949.

Group for the Advancement of Psychiatry. *Laws Governing Hospitalization of the Mentally Ill.* Report no. 61. New York: Group for the Advancement of Psychiatry, 1966.

Guttmacher, Manfred S., and Weihofen, Henry. *Psychiatry and the Law.* New York: W. W. Norton & Co., 1952.

Minnesota Department of Public Welfare. *Patient Movement.* Minneapolis, January 30, 1956.

National Institute of Mental Health. Federal Security Agency. *A Draft Act Governing Hospitalization of the Mentally Ill.* Public Health Service Pub. no. 51. Washington, D.C.: Government Printing Office, 1952.

Reeves, John. *History of English Law.* 3d ed. vol. 2. London: Reed & Hunter, 1814.

Rock, Ronald S.; Jacobson, Marcus A.; and Janopaul, Richard M. *Hospitalization and Discharge of the Mentally Ill.* An American Bar Foundation Study. Chicago: University of Chicago Press, 1968.

Ross, Hugh A. "Hospitalizing the Mentally Ill—Emergency and Temporary Commitments." *Current Trends in State Legislation 1955–56.* Ann Arbor: Legislative Research Center, University of Michigan Law School, 1957.

Shelford, Leonard A. *A Practical Treatise on the Law Concerning Lunatics, Idiots, and Persons of Unsound Mind.* Vol. 2. Philadelphia: J. S. Littell, 1833.

CASES

Barry v. Hall, 98 F.2d 222 (D.C. Cir. 1938).

In re Alexieff's Will, 94 N.Y.S.2d 32 (Sur. Ct. 1949), *aff'd,* 227 App. Div. 790, 97 N.Y.S.2d 532 (1950), *motion for leave to appeal denied,* 277 App. Div. 901, 98 N.Y.S.2d 582 (1950).

In re Harris, 241 N.C. 179, 84 S.E.2d 808 (1954).

Knox v. Haug, 48 Minn. 58, 50 N.W. 934 (1892).

Leggate v. Clark, 111 Mass. 308 (1873).

Rohrer v. Darrow, 66 Colo. 463, 182 P. 13 (1919).

Sanders v. Omohundro, 204 Ark. 1040, 166 S.W.2d 657 (1942).

Simon v. Craft, 182 U.S. 427 (1901).

Streda Estate, 137 Legal Intell. No. 97 (Del. Cty. Orphans Ct. November 6, 1957).

Ward v. Booth, 197 F.2d 963 (9th Cir. 1952).

STATE AND CITATION	STATUTORY PROVISIONS
DRAFT ACT	
ALA. Code (1958) 21, §9	"The court of probate has authority, and it is a duty, to appoint guardians for persons of unsound mind . . . having an estate."
ALAS. Stat. (1962) 20.05.080	The court may appoint a guardian to take care, custody, and management of the estate of an insane person or any other person who is incapable of conducting his affairs, maintaining his family and educating his children.
ARIZ. Rev. Stat. Ann. (1956) 14-861	The words "incompetent," "mentally incompetent," and "incapable" mean a person who, though not insane, is, because of old age, disease, weakness of mind, or other cause, unable to manage and take care of himself or his property without assistance, and is likely to be imposed upon by artful or designing persons.
ARK. Stat. Ann. (1947) 57-601a (Supp. 1969)	"A 'guardian' is one appointed by a court to have the care and custody of the person or of the estate, or of both, of an incompetent."
57-601c(2) (Supp. 1969)	"An 'incompetent' is any person who is . . . incapable, by reason of insanity, mental illness, imbecility, idiocy, senility, . . . or other mental incapacity, either of managing his property or caring for himself."
CAL. Prob. Code (1956) 1460 (Supp. 1969)	"Any superior court . . . may appoint a guardian for . . . an insane or an incompetent person. . . . [T]he phrase 'incompetent person' . . . shall be construed to mean or refer to any person, whether insane or not, who by reason of old age, disease, weakness of mind, or other cause, is unable, unassisted, properly to manage and take care of himself or his property, and by reason thereof is likely to be deceived or imposed upon by artful or designing persons."
1751 (Supp. 1969)	"[T]he superior court . . . shall appoint a conservator [for] . . . any adult person who by reason of advanced age, illness, injury, mental weakness, intemperance, addiction to drugs or other disability, or other cause is unable properly to care for himself or for his property, or who for said cause or for any other cause is likely to be deceived or imposed upon by artful or designing persons, or for whom a guardian could be appointed . . . , or who voluntarily requests the same and . . . establishes good cause therefor."
CAL. Welf. & Inst'ns Code (West 1966) 5350 (Supp. 1968)	"A conservator . . . may be appointed for any person who is gravely disabled as a result of mental disorder or impairment by chronic alcoholism."
5008(h) (Supp. 1968)	"'Gravely disabled' means a condition in which a person, as a result of mental disorder [or impairment by chronic alcoholism], is unable to provide for his basic personal needs for food, clothing, or shelter."
COLO. Rev. Stat. Ann. (1964) 71-1-1(1)(b)	"'Mentally ill person' shall mean a person afflicted with disease, infirmity, old age, or disorder, which impairs his mental or emotional functions to a degree sufficient to require protection, supervision, treatment, or confinement, for his own welfare or for the welfare or safety of others, or who by reason thereof, lacks sufficient control, judgment, and discretion to manage his own property or affairs. The terms, 'insane person,' 'mental incompetent' or 'lunatic,' shall hereafter be deemed to mean and be included within the words, 'mentally ill person,' within the present statutes of the state of Colorado, unless context otherwise indicates a mentally deficient person."

STATE AND CITATION	STATUTORY PROVISIONS
COLO. Rev. Stat. Ann.--*continued* (1964) 71-1-1(1)(c)	"'Mentally deficient person' shall mean a person whose intellectual functions have been deficient since birth or whose intellectual development has been arrested or impaired by disease, or physical injury to such an extent that he lacks sufficient control, judgment, and discretion to manage his property or affairs, or who by reason of this deficiency, for his own welfare or the welfare or safety of others, requires protection, supervision, guidance, training, control, or care. The terms, 'idiot,' 'feeble-minded person,' 'mental incompetent,' or 'weak-minded person,' shall hereafter be deemed to mean and be included within the words 'mentally deficient person,' within the present statutes of the state of Colorado, unless the context otherwise indicates a mentally ill person."
CONN. Gen. Stat. Ann. (1958) 45-70 (Supp. 1969)	"When any person having property is found to be incapable of managing his affairs . . . such court shall appoint a conservator of such person, who, upon giving a probate bond, shall have charge of the person or the estate or both of such incapable person."
DEL. Code Ann. (1953) 12, §3914(a) (Supp. 1970)	Guardians may be appointed for persons not mentally ill who, because of advanced age or mental infirmity or physical incapacity, are unable to manage and care for their property and consequently are in danger of dissipating or losing such property or of becoming the victim of designing persons.
12 §3701 (Supp. 1970)	"The Court . . . shall have the care of mentally ill persons . . . so . . . as to appoint trustees . . . to take charge of them and manage their estates."
D. C. Code Ann. (1967) 21-1501	"When an adult . . . is unable, by reason of advanced age, mental weakness not amounting to unsoundness of mind, mental illness . . . or physical incapacity, to properly care for his property the [court] . . . may . . . appoint a fit person to be conservator of his property."
21-501	"Mental illness" means a psychosis or other disease which substantially impairs a person's mental health.
FLA. Stat. Ann. (1964) 744.03(5)	"An 'incompetent' is any person who, because of minority, senility, lunacy, insanity, imbecility, idiocy, drunkenness, excessive use of drugs, or other physical or mental incapacity, is incapable of either managing his property or caring for himself, or both."
GA. Code Ann. (1965) 49-601	"The ordinaries . . . may appoint guardians for persons who are mentally ill, mentally retarded, or mentally incompetent to the extent that they are incapable of managing their estates."
HAWAII Rev. Stat. Ann. (1968) 551-26	"If . . . it appears to the judge that the person in question is insane, the judge shall appoint a guardian."
551-27	"The words 'insane person' are intended to include every idiot, non-compos, lunatic and distracted person."
IDAHO Code Ann. (1947) 15-1815	"When . . . any person is insane, or from any cause mentally incompetent to manage his property . . . ."
15-1816 (Supp. 1969)	"[T]he court must appoint a guardian of his person and estate. . . ."

267

STATE AND CITATION	STATUTORY PROVISIONS
ILL. Ann. Stat. (Smith-Hurd 1961) 3, §112 (Supp. 1969)	"An 'incompetent' . . . includes any person who because of insanity, mental illness, mental retardation, old age, physical incapacity, or imperfection or deterioration of mentality, is incapable of managing his person or estate and any person who because of gambling, idleness, debauchery or the excessive use of intoxicants or drugs, so spends or wastes his estate as to expose himself or his family to want or suffering."
3, §113 (Supp. 1969)	The court may adjudge a person incompetent and appoint a conservator for him.
3, §265(a), (b), and (c)	Courts have the power to appoint conservator.
IND. Ann. Stat. (1953) 8-101(c)(2)	"An 'incompetent' is any person who is incapable by reason of insanity, mental illness, imbecility, idiocy, senility, old age, infirmity, or other incapacity, of either managing his property or caring for himself or both."
8-106	"A guardian of the estate [or] . . . of the person may be appointed for any incompetent."
IOWA Code Ann. (1964) 633.552	"Any person may file . . . for the appointment of a guardian. The petition shall state . . . 2. That the proposed ward is: . . . a mental retardate, mentally ill, senile, . . . or a spendthrift."
633.566	"Any person may file . . . for the appointment of a conservator. The petition shall state . . . 2. That the proposed ward is: . . . a mental retardate, mentally ill, senile, . . . or a spendthrift."
KAN. Stat. Ann. (1964) 59-3002(1) (Supp. 1968)	"The term 'incapacitated person' shall mean any person who is impaired by reason of mental illness, mental deficiency, physical illness or disability, advanced age . . . or other cause to the extent that he lacks sufficient understanding or capacity to make or communicate responsible decisions concerning either his person or his estate.
59-3002(2)	"The term 'guardian' shall mean any person who has been appointed by a court of competent jurisdiction to exercise control over the person of an incapacitated person or of a minor."
KY. Rev. Stat. Ann. (1969) 203.010(2)	"'Incompetency' or 'incompetent person' shall apply to a person of unsound mind who from confirmed bodily infirmity is unable to make known to others by speech, sign or otherwise his thoughts or desires and by reason thereof is unable to manage his estate, or one whose mind because of mental illness or infirmity or old age has become so disabled as to render him unable to manage his estate."
LA. Civ. Code Ann. (West 1952) Art. 389	"No person . . . who is subject to an habitual state of imbecility, insanity or madness, shall be allowed to take care of his own person and administer his estate, although such person shall, at times, appear to have the possession of his reason."
ME. Rev. Stat. Ann. (1964) 18, §3601	A guardian may be appointed for: "(1) All persons, including those mentally ill or of unsound mind and married women who, by reason or infirmity or mental incapacity, are incompetent to manage their own estates or to protect their rights. . . ."
MD. Ann. Code (1966) 16, §135	"The court shall have the power also to appoint a committee or trustee to take charge of and manage the property of any person incompetent by reason of mental disability. . . . "

STATE AND CITATION	STATUTORY PROVISIONS
MASS. Ann. Laws (1955) 201, §§ 6, 8, 16 (Supp. 1968)	"A guardian may be appointed for any mentally ill person . . . who so spends, wastes or lessens his estate as to expose himself or his family to want or suffering, or any town to charge or expense for his or their support; or for any person of mental weakness who is 'unable to properly care for his property. . . .'"
MICH. Comp. Laws Ann. (1967) 703.1	The judge of probate may appoint guardians "(4) of all persons who are insane, imbecile, idiotic, or who by reason of old age or disease are mentally incompetent to have the care, custody and management of their estate. . . ."
MINN. Stat. Ann. (1969) 525.54	A guardian may be appointed for any person who because of "imperfection or deterioration of mentality is incompetent to manage his person or estate, or any person who because of idleness, or debauchery, so spends or wastes his estate or injures his person as to be likely to expose himself or his family to want or suffering. . . ."
MISS. Code Ann. (1957) 432	A guardian may be appointed for a person adjudicated to be a lunatic or of unsound mind and also for those persons "who have not been adjudged to be of unsound mind, or who may have been so adjudged in proceedings which did not fully comply with the law in effect at the time of such adjudications, provided such persons (1) have been continuously confined in a mental hospital . . . for a period of more than one year and are still so confined, (2) are of unsound mind, (3) are mentally incapable of taking care of their estates, and (4) are incapable of responding to process."
MO. Rev. Stat (1956) 475.010(1)	"A 'guardian' is one appointed by a court to have the care and custody of the person or of the estate, or of both, . . . or of an incompetent. . . .
475.010(3)	"An 'incompetent' is any person who is incapable by reason of insanity, mental illness, imbecility, idiocy, senility . . . or other incapacity, of either managing his property or caring from himself or both. . . ."
MONT. Rev. Codes Ann. (1964) 91-4701	A guardian may be appointed for any person who "is insane, or from any cause mentally incompetent to manage his property. . . ."
NEB. Rev. Stat. (1968) 38-201	A guardian may be appointed for "any mentally ill person or any person who, by reason of extreme old age or other cause, is mentally incompetent to have the charge and management of his property. . . ."
NEV. Rev. Stat. (1967) 159.100.1	A guardian may be appointed for any person who is insane or "who by reason of extreme old age, or for any other cause, is mentally incompetent to manage his or her property. . . ."
N.H. Rev. Stat. Ann. (1968) 464:2, 464:5, 464:6	A guardian may be appointed for any person who is decreed to be mentally incompetent or who by inability to manage his affairs with prudence, or from vicious habits of any kind, so wastes, spends or lessens his estate or so neglects to attend his business as to expose himself or any of his family to want or suffering, or the town in which he resides to expense for the support of himself or any of his family.
N.J. Stat. Ann. (1953) 3A:1-1	"'Mental incompetent' means a person who as a result of idiocy, insanity, lunacy, unsoundness of mind . . . is incapable of governing himself and managing his affairs."

STATE AND CITATION	STATUTORY PROVISIONS
N.M. Stat. Ann. (1953) 32-2-1	"For the purpose of this act, a person shall be deemed incompetent who, though not insane, is, by reason of mental disability or habitual drunkenness, incapable of properly caring for himself or managing his property. . . ."
32-2-3 (Supp. 1967)	A guardian may be appointed for a person adjudged insane or incompetent.
N.Y. Mental Hygiene Law (McKinney 1951) 100 (Supp. 1970)	The supreme court and the county courts outside the city of New York have jurisdiction over the custody of a person and his property if he is incompetent to manage himself or his affairs by reason of age, drunkenness, mental illness or other cause, or is a patient and unable adequately to conduct his personal or business affairs.
N.C. Gen. Stat. (1965) 35-2	A guardian may be appointed for any person found to be a mental defective, inebriate, or mentally disordered or incompetent. Where the person is found to be incompetent from want of understanding to manage his affairs, by reason of physical and mental weakness on account of old age and/or disease, and/or like infirmities, a clerk may appoint a trustee instead of guardian.
N.D. Cent. Code (1960) 30-10-02	"The county court may appoint a guardian . . . of a person . . . who is of unsound mind or from any cause mentally or otherwise incompetent to manage his own property."
OHIO Rev. Code (Baldwin 1964) 2111.01(D)	"'Incompetent' means any person who, by reason of advanced age, improvidence, or mental or physical disability or infirmity, chronic alcoholism, mental deficiency, lunacy, or mental illness, is incapable of taking proper care of himself or his property or fails to provide for his family or for other persons for whom he is charged by law to provide, or any person indeterminately hospitalized pursuant to section 5122.15 [hospitalization of the mentally ill] and not subsequently found competent pursuant to section 5122.36 [legal effect of indeterminate hospitalization]."
OKLA. Stat. (1965) 58-852	A guardian may be appointed for the person and/or estate of any insane or incompetent individual.
ORE. Rev. Stat. (1967) 126.006(3)	"Incompetent includes any person who, by reason of mental illness, mental deficiency, advanced age, disease, weakness of mind or any other cause, is unable unassisted to properly manage and take care of himself and property."
PA. Stat. Ann. (1969) 50, §3102	"'Incompetent' means any person who, because of mental infirmities of old age, mental illness, mental deficiency, drug addiction or inebriety, is unable to manage his property, or is liable to dissipate it or become the victim of designing persons."
R.I. Gen. Laws Ann. (1956) 33-15-8	"A guardian may be appointed for an idiot, lunatic, or person of unsound mind, . . . who, from want of discretion in managing his estate, so spends, wastes or lessens his estate, or is likely so to do that he may bring himself or his family to want or suffering, or may render himself or his family chargeable upon the town for support."

STATE AND CITATION	STATUTORY PROVISIONS
S.C. Code Ann. (1962) 32-1039	"If . . . the court finds that the individual, being mentally ill or mentally deficient, is incapable of caring for and managing his own estate, a committee may be appointed. . . ."
S.D. Compiled Laws Ann. (1967) 30-27-6	"A county court . . . may appoint a guardian . . . of a person who is insane or for any cause mentally or physicially incompetent. . . ."
TENN. Code Ann. (1955) 33-313 (Supp. 1968)	In any judicial proceeding for hospitalization of any individual to a mental hospital, the court shall consider evidence bearing on the competency of the individual to manage himself and his estate; this question shall be decided separately and apart from the question of mental illness. If the court finds the individual incompetent and he has no legal guardian, it shall appoint one. Whenever a mentally retarded individual is hospitalized, the court shall enter an order of incompetency and appoint a guardian, if there is none.
34-1008 (Supp. 1968)	If a person by reason of mental weakness is incapable of managing his own estate, the court upon petition may appoint a conservator to have charge and management of the property of such person, and, if the court deems it advisable, also to have charge and custody of the person, subject to the direction of the appointing court.
TEX. Rev. Civ. Stat. Ann. (1958) 5547-4(ℓ) (Supp. 1969)	"'Mentally incompetent person' means a mentally ill person whose mental illness renders him incapable of caring for himself and managing his property and financial affairs."
UTAH Code Ann. (1953) 75-13-20	"The words 'incompetent,' 'mentally incompetent' and 'incapable,' . . . mean any person who, though not insane, is, by reason of old age, disease, weakness of mind, or from any other cause, unable, unassisted, to properly manage and take care of himself or his property, and by reason thereof would be likely to be deceived or imposed upon by artful or designing persons."
75-13-19	"[T]he district court . . . may appoint guardians. . . ."
VT. Stat. Ann. (1958) 14, §2683 (Supp. 1969)	"On the application of a relative or friend of an insane person, or of a person mentally incapable of taking care of himself or his property . . . the probate court many appoint a guardian of such person. . . ."
VA. Code Ann. (1953) 37-140	"A guardian may be appointed for any person 'who by reason of advanced age or impaired health, or physical disability, has become mentally or physically incapable of taking proper care of his person or properly handling and managing his estate. . . ."
WASH. Rev. Code Ann. (1967) 11.88.010	"Guardians may be appointed for the persons and estates of incompetents. An incompetent is a person incapable by reason of insanity, mental illness, imbecility, idiocy, senility . . . or other mental incapacity, of either managing his property or caring for himself or both."
W. VA. Code Ann. (1966) 27-11-1	"When a person is found mentally ill or mentally retarded . . . the county court shall appoint a committee for him."

STATE AND CITATION   STATUTORY PROVISIONS

WIS. Stat. Ann. (1958)
  319.01
                          Guardians may be appointed for a person who is "incapable of managing his pro-
                          perty or caring for himself by reason of mental illness, deficiency or infirmity,
                          chronic inebriety, durg addiction or other like incapacity;" or for a person "who
                          because of the use of intoxicants or drugs or of gambling, idleness or debauchery
                          or other wasteful course of conduct is unable to attend to business or thereby
                          is likely to affect the health, life or property of himself or others so as to
                          endanger the support of himself and his dependents or expose the public to such
                          support."

WYO. Stat. Ann. (1957)
  3-29.1
  (Supp. 1969)
                          "The district court of each county, or the judge thereof, may appoint a guardian
                          for the person and estate, or either of them, of mentally incompetent or incom-
                          petent persons who reside or have estates within the county, and who have no
                          legally appointed guardian within this state, . . . 'mentally incompetent person'
                          shall mean an individual who is unable, unassisted, to properly manage and take
                          care of himself or his property or both as the result of mental illness, mental
                          deficiency, or mental retardation; and 'incompetent person' shall mean an individ-
                          ual who is unable unassisted to properly manage and take care of himself or his
                          property as a result of the infirmities of advanced age, physical disability,
                          disease, alcoholism or addiction to drugs."

Table 8.2   EFFECT OF INVOLUNTARY HOSPITALIZATION ON THE ISSUE OF LEGAL COMPETENCY

STATE	COMPETENCY AFFECTED BY INVOLUNTARY HOSPITALIZATION	INVOLUNTARY HOSPITALIZATION AND INCOMPETENCY MAY BE DETERMINED BY THE SAME HEARING	APPOINTMENT OF GUARDIAN			
			Mandatory	Conditional	Property	Guardian of Person
Draft Act	although generally separated in the Act, Commentary sec. 21, limitations may be imposed by the hospital. 21(a)(3) 21(c)					
ALA. Code (1958)						
ALAS. Stat. (1962)	Limitations may be imposed by the hospital. 47.30.150(c)(a)(3)					
ARIZ. Rev. Stat. Ann. (1956)	the court may, in addition to ordering commitment, also adjudge the patient incompetent; however, unless adjudged incompetent, the patient shall be considered competent and retain his civil rights. 36-514D (Supp. 1970)			upon discretion of court. 36-514D (Supp. 1970)	36-514D (Supp. 1970)	
ARK. Stat. Ann. (1947)						
CAL. Welf. & Inst'ns Code (West 1966)	no person may be presumed to be incompetent because he or she has been evaluated or treated for mental disorder. 5331 (Supp. 1968)	upon the creation of a conservatorship for a gravely disabled person, the conservator may have the authority to hospitalize or otherwise have treated such gravely disabled person. 5358 (Supp. 1968)				
COLO. Rev. Stat. Ann. (1964)	upon a finding of mental illness or mental deficiency, the court may designate some proper person to take custody of the respondent and assume his custody, care and maintenance, as an alternative to commitment. 71-1-11(2); 71-1-11(3) (Supp. 1965). the county court shall appoint a conservator of the estate of a person who has been adjudicated mentally ill or mentally deficient. 153-9-2(1) (Supp. 1965)	71-1-11(2), 71-1-11(3) (Supp. 1965)	if incompetent is a resident of county, or has property therein requiring conservation. 153-9-2(1) (Supp. 1965)	upon discretion of court. 71-1-11(2), 71-1-11(3) (Supp. 1965)	153-9-2(1) (Supp. 1965)	71-1-11(2), 71-1-11(3) (Supp. 1965)
CONN. Genn. Stat. Ann. (1958)	the commissioner of finance and control, or his deputy, or the superintendent of the institution may apply to the court for the appointment of a conservator of the person or an administrator of the estate of a patient having property who is maintained at the expense of the state. 4-68g (Supp. 1969)			upon application to and order of the probate court. 4-68g (Supp. 1969)	administrator 4-68g (Supp. 1969)	conservator 4-68g (Supp. 1969)

Table 8.2   EFFECT OF INVOLUNTARY HOSPITALIZATION ON THE ISSUE OF LEGAL COMPETENCY   *continued*

| STATE | COMPETENCY AFFECTED BY INVOLUNTARY HOSPITALIZATION | INVOLUNTARY HOSPITALIZATION AND INCOMPETENCY MAY BE DETERMINED BY THE SAME HEARING | APPOINTMENT OF GUARDIAN | | | |
			Mandatory	Conditional	Guardian of Property	Guardian of Person
DEL. Code Ann. (1953)	commitment shall not raise any presumption of insanity. 16,§ 5126(d) where the person named in an application for the appointment of a trustee is an inmate of an institution for the mentally ill, the court may appoint a trustee for such person without issuing a writ to inquire by a jury, except that such a writ is required if requested by the inmate, his spouse or a relative. 12, § 3702(b) (Supp. 1970)			upon discretion of court. 12, § 3701(b) (Supp. 1970)	12, § 3701 12, § 3702(b) (Supp. 1970)	12, § 3701 12, § 3702(b) (Supp. 1970)
D.C. Code Ann. (1967)	"A patient . . . may not by reason of the hospitalization, be denied the right to dispose of property, execute instruments, make purchases, enter into contractual relationships, vote, and hold a driver's license, unless the patient has been adjudicated incompetent." 21-564					
FLA. Stat. Ann. (1964)		the procedure calls for a determination of competency (394.22(1)) with provisions for hospitalization if necessary. (394.22(11)(a))		upon discretion of court. 744.31	744.31	744.31
GA. Code Ann. (1965)	at any time during procedures for hospitalization of a patient an evaluation can be made to determine if the person is incapable of managing his estate. 49-604(a)(1) (Supp. 1969)	court may combine in one proceeding the hearings on the issue of hospitalization and on the issue of the appointment of a guardian. 49-604(a)(3) (Supp. 1969)	49-604(b) (Supp. 1969)	49-604(a) (Supp. 1969)	49-604(b) (Supp. 1969)	49-604(b) (Supp. 1969)
HAWAII Rev. Stat. Ann. (1968)	no presumption of insanity or legal incompetency shall exist with respect to any patient by reason of his admission to a psychiatric facility. 334-57					
IDAHO Code Ann. (1949)	limitations may be imposed by the hospital. 66-346(a)(3), 66-346(c) (Supp. 1969)					
ILL. Ann. Stat. (Smith-Hurd 1961)	"An authenticated transcript of the evidence taken in a proceeding [for commitment] . . . is admissable in evidence at the hearing [on incompetency]. 3, § 117(c) (Supp. 1969) The dept. of mental health may, with the approval of the court, designate an employee to serve as conservator of the estate of a patient in the state hospital when the estate does not exceed $1000. 3, § 118(b) (Supp. 1969)					

Table 8.2   EFFECT OF INVOLUNTARY HOSPITALIZATION ON THE ISSUE OF LEGAL COMPETENCY   *continued*

STATE	COMPETENCY AFFECTED BY INVOLUNTARY HOSPITALIZATION	INVOLUNTARY HOSPITALIZATION AND INCOMPETENCY MAY BE DETERMINED BY THE SAME HEARING	APPOINTMENT OF GUARDIAN			
			Mandatory	Conditional	Property	Guardian of Person
IND. Ann. Stat. (1953)	commitment to a hospital for the insane is equivalent to a prior adjudication of incompetency if a medical certificate is filed alleging incapability of caring for self or property, and no contradictory affidavit is filed. 8-120 hospital employee may without hearing be appointed guardian if estate of patient is less than $300. 22-1256 (1964)			a medical certificate is required. 8-120 if estate of less then $300. 22-1256 (1964)	8-120 22-1256 (1964)	8-120
IOWA Code Ann. (1949)						
KAN. Stat. Ann. (1964)	fn. 1 59-2933 (Supp. 1968)			fn. 2 upon discretion of court. 59-3006 (Supp. 1968)	conservator 59-3002(4) (Supp. 1968)	guardian 59-3002(2) (Supp. 1968)
KY. Rev. Stat. Ann. (1969)	limitations may be imposed by the hospital. 202.272(3), 202.273(5)					
LA. Rev. Stat. Ann. (1952)						
ME. Rev. Stat. Ann. (1964)						
MD. Ann. Code (1968)						
MASS. Ann. Laws (1965)						
MICH. Comp. Laws Ann. (1967)		if in the judgment of the court a guardian is needed before one can be regularly appointed, the court may summarily appoint a guardian by a separate order and without further notice. 330.22		330.22	330.22	330.22
MINN. Stat. Ann. (1959)	fn. 3 253A.18 (Supp. 1969)	incompetency proceedings may be before, during, or after commitment proceedings, and jointly. 253A.18(2) (Supp. 1969)		upon request. 525.54, 525.541 (1969) if person to be committed is minor or owns property of value & appears incompetent. 253A.18 (Supp. 1969)	525.551 (1969)	appoint guardian, either general or special. 253A.18(Supp. 1969) 525.551 (1969)
MISS. Code Ann. (1952)						
MO. Rev. Stat. (1959)	although generally separated in the statute, restrictions may be imposed by the hospital. 202.847.1(3) 202.847.3			letters of guardianship of the person or estate, or both, may be granted for any person adjudged incompetent. 475.030.1 (Supp. 1969)	475.030.1 (Supp. 1969)	475.030.1 (Supp. 1969)
MONT. Rev. Codes Ann. (1961)	state hospital shall hold moneys of all persons adjudged insane and committed to such state hospital. 38-210 (Supp. 1969)					
NEB. Rev. Stat. (1960)						

Table 8.2   EFFECT OF INVOLUNTARY HOSPITALIZATION ON THE ISSUE OF LEGAL COMPETENCY   *continued*

STATE	COMPETENCY AFFECTED BY INVOLUNTARY HOSPITALIZATION	INVOLUNTARY HOSPITALIZATION AND INCOMPETENCY MAY BE DETERMINED BY THE SAME HEARING	APPOINTMENT OF GUARDIAN			
			Mandatory	Conditional	Guardian of Property	Guardian of Person
NEV. Rev. Stat. (1967)	a guardian shall be appointed upon the request of any interested person if the committed person adjudged mentally ill has income aggregating $500 annually; hospital superintendent is authorized to receive personal property if its total value does not exceed $300. 433.230.1, 433.450			upon the request of any interested person if the committed person has income aggregating $500 annually. 433.230.1	433.230.1	
N.H. Rev. Stat. Ann. (1964)		a guardian may be appointed for a person alleged to be insane, or who has been legally declared to be insane. 135:40		135:40		
N.J. Stat. Ann. (1964)	fn. 4 30:4-65			30:4-65	30:9-05	
N.M. Stat. Ann. (1953)	although generally separated in the statute, restrictions may be imposed by the hospital. 34-2-15a(3)					
N.Y. Mental Hygiene Law (McKinney 1951)	although generally competency and hospitalization are separate, Mental Hygiene Law, 34.14, allows commissioner to authorize directors of state institutions to perform limited acts for patient who has no committee or upon his discharge from a committee. (Supp. 1970)					
N.C. Gen. Stat. (1966)	while competency and hospitalization are separate, 35-3 provides that a certificate of a superintendent of a hospital for insane stating that confined person is of insane mind and memory shall be sufficient evidence to authorize clerk to appoint a guardian for such insane person.					
N.D. Cent. Code (1960)	voluntary and involuntary hospitalization under the provisions of this chapter shall not be in adjudication of incompetency. 25-03-20(1)(c)					
OHIO Rev. Code (Baldwin 1964)	indeterminate hospitalization is an adjudication of legal competency; legal incompetency is sufficient grounds for the appointment of a guardian. 5122.36	5121.02 5122.36		if estate is sufficient for inmate's support and no guardian has been appointed, department shall petition for appointment. 5121.09	2122.02	2122.02

Table 8.2 EFFECT OF INVOLUNTARY HOSPITALIZATION ON THE ISSUE OF LEGAL COMPETENCY *continued*

| STATE | COMPETENCY AFFECTED BY INVOLUNTARY HOSPITALIZATION | INVOLUNTARY HOSPITALIZATION AND INCOMPETENCY MAY BE DETERMINED BY THE SAME HEARING | APPOINTMENT OF GUARDIAN | | | |
			Mandatory	Conditional	Property	Guardian of Person
OKLA. Stat. (1954)	no person admitted to any institution shall be considered legally mentally incompetent except those admitted in accordance with the provisions of the sections entitled "Court certification--Procedure--Notice--Order for admission," "Admission on petition of guardian of mentally incompetent person," and those under the section entitled "Residents of state in institutions of other states--Admission to Oklahoma institution" who have been declared legally mentally incompetent elsewhere. 43A, § 64		if in the judgment of the court the mentally ill person needs a guardian prior to his admission to the hospital, the court may by separate order and without further notice appoint summarily a guardian of the person only, which guardianship shall continue only until such person is admitted to the hospital. 43A, § 55. a guardian of the estate of such person shall be regularly appointed. 43A, § 55. If it is found that the person is mentally incompetent but that it is not necessary to hospitalize him, the judge of the county court must issue an order adjudging the person mentally incompetent and must appoint a guardian of his personal estate. 43A, § 65.		43A, § 55 43A, § 65	until admission to hospital. 43A, § 55 43A, § 65
ORE. Rev. Stat. (1967)	no person admitted to a state hospital for the treatment of mental illness shall be considered by virtue of the admission incompetent. 426-295(1)					
PA. Stat. Ann. (1969)						
R.I. Gen. Laws Ann. (1968)						
S.C. Code Ann. (1962)	if any patient of a state mental health facility has no legally appointed committee, the superintendent of the facility may receive and accept for the use and benefit of such patient a sum not in excess of $2500 in any one calendar year, which may be due such patient by inheritance, gift, pension, or otherwise. 32-1042 (Supp. 1968)	the court may appoint a committee for the person hospitalized & may make further orders for the custody & control of the estate of the person. 32-966			32.966	
S.D. Compiled Laws Ann. (1967)	the commitment of a person under this chapter shall not affect his property rights nor his legal capacity. 27-8-5.					
TENN. Code Ann. (1955)		in any judicial proceedings for hospitalization, the court shall hear and consider evidence bearing on the competency of the individual to manage himself and his estate. 33-313 (Supp. 1968)	If adjudged incompetent. 33-313 (Supp. 1968)		33-313 (Supp. 1968)	33-313 (Supp. 1968)
TEX. Rev. Civ. Stat. Ann. (1968)		the court, or the jury as the case may be, shall determine whether he is mentally incompetent. 5547-51				

277

STATE	COMPETENCY AFFECTED BY INVOLUNTARY HOSPITALIZATION	INVOLUNTARY HOSPITALIZATION AND INCOMPETENCY MAY BE DETERMINED BY THE SAME HEARING	APPOINTMENT OF GUARDIAN			
			Mandatory	Conditional	Guardian of Property	Guardian of Person
UTAH Code Ann. (1968)	limitations may be imposed by the hospital. 64-7-48					
VT. Stat. Ann. (1968)	limitations may be imposed by the hospital. 18, § 7705(a)(3)					
VA. Code Ann. (1953)						
WASH. Rev. Code Ann. (1962)						
W. Va. Code Ann. (1966)	the entry of an order ordering hospitalization for an indeterminate period shall relieve the patient of legal capacity. 27-5-4		county court shall appoint a committee if person found mentally ill by county mental hygiene commission. 27-11-1		committee 27-11-4	committee 27-11-4
WIS. Stat. Ann. (1957)	hospitalization, whether by voluntary admission or commitment, raises a rebuttable or disputable presumption of incompetency while patient is under jurisdiction of hospital authorities. 51.005(2)					
WYO. Stat. Ann. (1957)		a petition for appointment of a guardian for an alleged mentally incompetent person may be merged and heard simultaneously with a petition for the involuntary hospitalization of such person unless objected to by the alleged incompetent or his attorney; whenever two such petitions are pending the court shall first determine the petition for involuntary hospitalization. 3-29.12 (Supp. 1969)			3-29.7 (Supp. 1969)	3-29.7 (Supp. 1969)

1. "Neither an order of referral nor an order for 'care or treatment' made pursuant to this act shall imply an adjudication of incapacity, nor shall either order create any presumption that the 'proposed patient' or 'involuntary patient' is an 'incapacitated person.'" Kan. 59-2933 (Supp. 1968).

2. "The probate court having jurisdiction and venue. . .may appoint. . .a guardian for an incapacitated person who is unable to make or communicate responsible decisions concerning his person. . .or for a minor; a conservator may be appointed for an adult who has made application. . .for an incapacitated person who is unable to make or communicate responsible decisions concerning his estate. . .or for a minor." Kan. 59-3006 (Supp. 1968).

3. Except as otherwise provided. . .no person by reason of commitment, hospitalization, or treatment. . .shall be deprived of any legal right, including but not limited to the right to dispose of property, sue and be sued, execute instruments, make purchases, enter into contractual relationships, vote, and hold a driver's license. Commitment, hospitalization, or treatment of any patient. . .is not a judicial determination of legal incompetency except to the extent [necessary to save life or health by operation in an emergency]. Minn. 253A.18 (Supp. 1969).

4. Where, on final hearing, it appears patient has real or personal property, and no arrangements have been made for payment of patient's maintenance, and no guardian has been appointed, an action may be brought in the county court in which the proceeding for commitment was brought for appointment of some competent person as guardian of the estate during such commitment.

    Such guardian is to conserve the estate for the purpose of maintaining the patient in the institution in which he may be lawfully confined. The chief executive officer of the institution or the county treasurer in the institution's county may be appointed guardians. N.J. 30:4-65.

Table 8.3 INDEPENDENT DETERMINATION OF INCOMPETENCY

See "Commentary" 21(a)(3) in the Draft Act in Appendix A of this volume

STATE	APPLICATION BY				APPLICABLE CASES					SUPPORTING EVIDENCE		NOTICE				PRESENCE IN COURT			JURY TRIAL			COUNSEL OR GUARDIAN AD LITEM	GUARDIANS		CORPORATIONS PERMITTED	CENTRAL REGISTRATION OF INCOMPETENCY	NOTICE TO COUNTY OF RESIDENCY	CONTINUING COURT SUPERVISOR
	COURT	Relative	Alleged Incompetent	Any Interested Person	Mentally Ill or Unsound Mind	Deficient	Alcoholics	Drug Addicts	Others	Verified Petition	Medical Certificate	HEARING	Incompetent Person	Relatives	Period of Time	Mandatory	Except When Harmful	Discretionary	Number on Jury	Mandatory	Optional		For Both Person and Property	Separation Optional				
fn.1 DRAFT ACT																												
ALA. Code (1958)	probate 21, §9 21, §11	21, §11		friends 21, §11	21, §11 21, §25		fn.2 7, §1064			21, §11		21, §12	fn.3 21, §15		not more than 30 days, 21, §11	21, §12			6 21, §12	21, §12		fn.3 21, §11 21, §15						
ALAS. Stat. (1962)	superior 22.10-.020(a) (Supp. 1969)	20.05-.090		20.05-.090	20.05-.090		20.05-.110		spendthrifts, 20.05-.110 missing persons, 20.05-.130	20.05-.090		20.05-.090	20.05-.090		not less than 10 days, 20.05-.090	Tuppela v. Chichagoff Min. Co., 267 F. 753							20.05-.100					verified account of estate must be filed annually with court. 20.05-.190
ARIZ. Rev. Stat. Ann. (1956)	14-862	14-862		friend 14-862	14-862	14-861			old age or other cause. 14-861	14-862		14-862	14-862		5 days 14-862	if able to attend 14-862							14-863-.A	14-863-.A				annual inventory. 14-807-.A
ARK. Stat. Ann. (1948) (Supp. 1967)	probate 57-604	57-609		57-609	57-601c (2)	57-601c (2)	57-601c (2)	57-601c (2)		57-609	fn.4 57-615b	57-615b	57-611b (1)	57-611b (1), 57-611b (2), 57-611b (5)	57-611b court may reduce but not less than 3 days. 57-611c			57-615b				not necessary to appoint guardian ad litem. 57-611c	57-601a 57-616	57-601a 57-616	estate only 57-607d			57-642a
fn.5 CAL. PROB. Code (West 1956) guardian	superior 1460 (Supp. 1969)	1461 (Supp. 1969)		friend 1461 (Supp. 1969)	1460 (Supp. 1969)	1460 (Supp. 1969)			old age 1460 (Supp. 1969)	1461 (Supp. 1969)		1462 (Supp. 1969)	1461 (Supp. 1969)	1461 (Supp. 1969)	10 days 1461 (Supp. 1969)		inability must be certified 1461						1462 (Supp. 1969)	1462 (Supp. 1969)				
conservator	superior 1751 (Supp. 1969)	1754 (Supp. 1969)	1754 (Supp. 1969)	not a creditor 1754 (Supp. 1969)	1751 (Supp. 1969)	1751 (Supp. 1969)	1751 (Supp. 1969)	1751 (Supp. 1969)	1751 (Supp. 1969)	1754 (Supp. 1969)		1754 (Supp. 1969)	1754 (Supp. 1969)	1754 (Supp. 1969)	15 days 1754 (Supp. 1969)		inability must be certified. 1754 (Supp. 1969)						1751 (Supp. 1969)	1751 (Supp. 1969)				1960, 1904 (Supp. 1969)
CAL. Welf. & Inst'ns Code (West 1966) conservator for gravely disabled	superior 5352 (Supp. 1968)			fn.6 mental health officer 5352	gravely disabled 5350 (Supp. 1968)		5350 (Supp. 1968)				conservatorship investigation 5354 (Supp. 1968)	5350 (Supp. 1968) Prob. 1754 (Supp. 1969)	5350 (Supp. 1968) Prob. 1754 (Supp. 1969)	5350 (Supp. 1968) Prob. 1754 (Supp. 1969)	15 days 5350 (Supp. 1968) Prob. 1754 (Supp. 1969)		inability must be certified, 5350 (Supp. 1968) Prob. 1754 (Supp. 1969)				5350(d) (Supp. 1968)		fn.7 5357, 5358 (Supp. 1968) Prob. 1852 (Supp. 1969)	5350 (Supp. 1968) Prob. 1751 (Supp. 1969)				fn.8 5361 (Supp. 1968)

Table 8.3   INDEPENDENT DETERMINATION OF INCOMPETENCY   *continued*

STATE	Court	Relative	Alleged Incompetent	Any Interested Person	Mentally Ill or Unsound Mind	Deficient	Alcoholics	Drug Addicts	Others	Verified Petition	Medical Certificate	HEARING	Incompetent Person	Relatives	Period of Time	Mandatory	Except When Harmful	Discretionary	Number on Jury	Mandatory	Optional	Counsel or Guardian ad litem	For Both Person and Property	Separation Personal / Property (Optional)	Corporations Permitted	Central Registration of Incompetency	Notice to County of Residency	Continuing Court Supervisor
fn. 9 COLO. Rev. Stat. Ann. (1964)	See Table 8.2, "Effect of Involuntary Hospitalization on the Issue of Legal Competency"																											
CONN. Gen. Stat. Ann. (1958)	probate 45-70 (Supp. 1969)	45-70 (Supp. 1969)		fn. 10 45-70 (Supp. 1969)					person incapable of managing his affairs. 45-70 (Supp. 1969)	written application. 45-70 (Supp. 1969)		45-71 (Supp. 1969)	45-71 (Supp. 1969)	fn. 11 45-71 (Supp. 1969)	5 days 45-71 (Supp. 1969)								45-70 (Supp. 1969)	45-70 (Supp. 1969)			fn. 12 45-74	
fn. 13 DEL. Code Ann. (1953)	chancery 12, §3914(a) (Supp. 1970)	12, §3914(a) (Supp. 1970)	12, §3914(a) (Supp. 1970)	12, §3914(a) (Supp. 1970)	fn. 13	mentally infirm 12, §3914(a) (Supp. 1970)			aged - 12, §3914(a) (Supp. 1970)	petition under oath. 12, §3914(a) (Supp. 1970)	whenever possible Ch. Ct. R. 175 (d) (Supp. 1968)	12, §3914(b) (Supp. 1970)	12, §3914(b) (Supp. 1970)	such persons as court deems desirable. 12, (b) (Supp. 1970)	reasonable 12, §3914(b) (Supp. 1970)			Ch. Ct. R. 177 (Supp. 1968)					property only 12, §3914(a) (Supp. 1970)		service of process upon corporate guardian provided for Sup. Ct. R. 4(f)(1) (II)(c) (Supp. 1968)			Ch. Ct. R. 179 (Supp. 1968)
D.C. Code Ann. (1967)	U.S. District 21-1501	21-1501	21-1501	21-1501	21-1501	mental weakness not amounting to unsoundness of mind. 21-1501			age, physically incapacitated. 21-1501	21-1501		21-1502	to this person and also to such others as court may direct. 21-1502 (a)		14 days 21-1502 (a)							court may appoint guardian ad litem, 21-1052 (b)	conservator of property only 21-1502 (b) but a person may be appointed at any time to be responsible for personal welfare, 21-1506				21-1507	21-1502 (b)

Table 8.3 INDEPENDENT DETERMINATION OF INCOMPETENCY *continued*

STATE	COURT	APPLICATION BY			APPLICABLE CASES					SUPPORTING EVIDENCE		HEARING	NOTICE			PRESENCE IN COURT			JURY TRIAL			COUNSEL OR GUARDIAN AD LITEM	GUARDIANS		CORPORATIONS PERMITTED	CENTRAL REGISTRATION OF INCOMPETENCY	NOTICE TO COUNTY OF RESIDENCY	CONTINUING COURT SUPERVISOR
		Relative	Alleged Incompetent	Any Interested Person	Mentally Ill or Unsound Mind	Deficient	Alcoholics	Drug Addicts	Others	Verified Petition	Medical Certificate		Incompetent Person	Relatives	Period of Time	Mandatory	Except When Harmful	Discretionary	Number on Jury	Mandatory	Optional		For Both Person and Property	Separation Optional				
fn. 14 FLA. Stat. Ann. (1960)	county 394.22 (1) 744.06	394.22 (2)(a)	incompetent must present 1 medical certificate, 394.22-(2)(d)	sheriff or any 3 citizens 394.22-(2)(b)	includes any person unable to manage property, or spendthrift. 394.22 (1)		394.22 (1)	394.22 (1)	744.03 (5)	394.22 (1)	examination by 2 physicians and a responsible citizen. 394.22 (6)	394.22 (4) 744.06	394.22 (4)	394.22 (4)	reasonable 394.22 (4)							right to counsel with appointment discretionary 394.22 (4), 394.22 (7)(b)	744.31	744.31	a trust company or bank 744.27 (3)	notice to director of mental health only if incompetent committed, 394.22 (11)(b)		744.54
fn. 16 GA. Code Ann. (1965)	ordinaries 49-601 49-604		fn. 16 49-604 (Supp. 1969)		49-601	49-601	49-601	49-601		application on oath 49-604 (b) (Supp. 1969)	49-604 (b) (Supp. 1969)	fn. 17 49-604 (b), 88-507-.3 (Supp. 1969)	49-604 (b), 88-507-.3 (Supp. 1969)	representatives 49-604, 88-507-.3 (Supp. 1969)		must be examined by commission which acts as court. 49-604 (b) 88-507.3 (Supp. 1969)						49-604 (b), 88-507.3 (Supp. 1969)	fn. 18 49-604 (b) (Supp. 1969)	49-604 (b) (Supp. 1969)				
HAWAII Rev. Stat. Ann. (1968)	circuit 551-1	551-27	friends 551-27		551-26		551-26		spendthrifts 551-26	551-27		551-27	551-27	551-27	14 days 551-27							if no such person can be found & served with notice, guardian may be appointed. 551-27	551-27 551-28	551-27 551-28				
IDAHO Code Ann. (1947)	probate 15-1815	15-1815	friend 15-1815		15-1815	15-1815				15-1815	15-1815	15-1816 (Supp. 1969)	15-1815	15-1815	5 days 15-1815		"if able to attend" 15-1815						fn. 19 15-1816 (Supp. 1969)		15-1808	15-1808		15-1825 (Supp. 1969)
ILL. Ann. Stat. (Smith-Hurd 1961)	circuit 3, §113 3, §2 (a) (Supp. 1969)	3, §113 (Supp. 1969)	any reputable citizen of state. 3, §113 (Supp. 1969)		3, §112 (Supp. 1969)	3, §112 (Supp. 1969)	3, §112 (Supp. 1969)	3, §112 (Supp. 1969)	spendthrifts 3, §112 (Supp. 1969)	3, §113 (Supp. 1969)		3, §117 (a) (Supp. 1969)	unless good cause shown, supported by affidavit. 3, §117 (a) (Supp. 1969)	3, §117 (a) (Supp. 1969)	3 days 3, §117 (a) (Supp. 1969)				6 or 12 3, §117 (Supp. 1969)		3, §117 (b) (Supp. 1969)	court may appoint guardian ad litem 3, §118	conservator 3, §118 (Supp. 1969)	3, §119 (Supp. 1969)	3, §119 (Supp. 1969), 3, §271	3, §119 (Supp. 1969)		3, §122

Table 8.3   INDEPENDENT DETERMINATION OF INCOMPETENCY *continued*

STATE	COURT	Application By: Relative	Application By: Alleged Incompetent	Application By: Any Interested Person	Applicable Cases: Mentally Ill or Unsound Mind	Deficient	Alcoholics	Drug Addicts	Others	Supporting Evidence: Verified Petition	Medical Certificate	HEARING	Notice: Incompetent Person	Notice: Relatives	Notice: Period of Time	Presence in Court: Mandatory	Except When Harmful	Discretionary	Jury Trial: Number on Jury	Mandatory	Optional	Counsel or Guardian Ad Litem	Guardians: For Both Person and Property	Separation	Optional	Corporations Permitted	Central Registration of Incompetency	Notice to County of Residency	Continuing Court Supervisor
IND. Ann. Stat. (1953)	probate 8-104			8-111	8-101(c) (2) 8-106	8-101 (c)(2) 8-106	8-101 (c)(2) 8-106	8-101(c) (2) 8-106	senility 8-101 (c)(2) 8-106	8-111		8-119	8-114 (c)(1) (Supp. 1969)	persons having custody and any other the court directs 8-114 (c)(2) (Supp. 1969)	court may reduce for good cause; but must be 3 days 8-114 (Supp. 1969)	8-119	8-119				8-119	fn. 20 8-114 (Supp. 1969) 8-119	8-101(a) 8-106 8-121	8-101(a) 8-106 8-121	8-101(a)	8-123(b)			8-132 8-133
IOWA Code Ann. (1964)	probate 633.10 (3)	fn. 21		633.552 & in Supp. 1969, 633.566	633.552 633.566 (2)	633.552 633.566 (2)	633.552 633.566 (2)	633.552 633.566 (2)	senile, spendthrift 633.552 633.566 (2)	633.552; and in Supp. 1969, 633.566		633.555 633.569	633.554 633.568								633.555 633.569	633.555 633.569	fn. 22 633.556 633.570	fn. 22 633.627 633.628		633.64			633.669 633.670 668.24
KAN. Stat. Ann. (1964)	probate 59-301 (6) (Supp. 1968)			59-3007 59-3009 (Supp. 1968)	59-3009 (Supp. 1968)					59-2201	may be required 59-3009 (Supp. 1968)	59-3008 59-3010 (Supp. 1968)	59-3008 59-3012 (Supp. 1968)	spouse 59-3012 (Supp. 1968)	5 days 59-3012 (Supp. 1968)		59-3010 (Supp. 1968)		6 59-3013 (Supp. 1968)		fn. 23 59-3013 (Supp. 1968)	59-2205 (Supp. 1968) 59-3010	59-3013 (Supp. 1968)	59-3013 (Supp. 1968)				59-3009 (Supp. 1968)	59-3014 59-3018 59-3019 (Supp. 1968)
KY. Rev. Stat. Ann. (1969)	circuit 203.012 (1)			any reputable resident 203.012 (1)	203.010 (2) 203.012 (1)				old age 203.010 (2) 203.012 (1)	verified affidavit or on information & belief 203.012 (1)		203.022	203.016	if named in petition 203.016	3 days 203.016	203.016				203.022 (2)	203.022		203.022 (2)	203.022 (2)					
fn. 24 LA. Civ. Code (1952)	Judge of parish	relative and spouse 390		stranger or Judge ex-officio 391	389, 422	389 422			fn. 25 all persons under any infirmity 422		393											administrator, curator pro tempore for estate 394	administrator-curator, under-curator 404						424, 425
LA. Code Civ. Pro. Ann. (1961)	district court of parish 4541	4543		4543							Judge may appoint expert to examine defendant. 4547	4547	4544	as in ordinary proceedings. defendant does not appear, court shall appoint an attorney who will be served notice 4544								4544	4353				4552		appeal from judgment. appointing or removing curator can be taken within 30 days. 4548

Table 8.3 INDEPENDENT DETERMINATION OF INCOMPETENCY continued

STATE	COURT	Relative	Alleged Incompetent	Any Interested Person	Mentally Ill or Unsound Mind	Deficient	Alcoholics	Drug Addicts	Others	Verified Petition	Medical Certificate	HEARING	Incompetent Person	Relatives	Period of Time	Presence Mandatory	Except When Harmful	Discretionary	Number on Jury	Jury Mandatory	Jury Optional	Counsel or Guardian ad litem	Guardians For Both Person and Property	Separation Person / Property Optional	Corporations Permitted	Central Registration of Incompetency	Notice to County of Residency	Continuing Court Supervisor
ME. Rev. Stat. Ann. (1964)	probate 18, §3601	18, §3601		friends, creditors, or municipal officers or overseers of the poor of the town where they reside. 18, §3601	18, §3601(1)	18, §3601 (1)	18, §3601 (2)		18, §3601			18, §3602	18, §3602		14 days 18, §3602							18, §3651	fnn. 26 & 27 18, §§ 3605, 3701					18, §3702
MD. Ann. Code (1966)	circuit Rule 71.a 16, §132			next friend 16, §135	16, §132	fn. 28 16, §149			fn. 28 16, §149	16, §135	2 16, §135	16, §135								16, §134		Rule 119b 205e2	fn. 28 16, §132 16, §135					
MASS. Ann. Laws (1955)	probate 201, §1 (Supp. 1968)	2 or more. 201, §6 (Supp. 1968)		fn. 29 201, §6 (Supp. 1968)	201, §6 (Supp. 1968)		fn. 30 201, §8		fn. 30 201, §8		201, §6 (Supp. 1968)	201, §6 (Supp. 1968)	201, §7 (Supp. 1968)	201, §7 (Supp. 1968)	201, §7 (Supp. 1968)							person under a disability 201, §34 208, §15	201, §6 (Supp. 1968)	fn. 31 201, §16				
MICH. Comp. Laws Ann. (1967)	probate 703.1	703.2	703.2	703.2	703.1 (4)	703.1 (4)	703.1 (6)	703.1 (6)	age 703.1 (7) spendthrift 703.1 (3)	703.2		703.2	703.2	703.2	14 days 703.2							703.12	703.1	703.1				703.29
MINN. Stat. Ann. (1969)	fn. 32 probate 525.01			525.541	525.54	525.54	525.54		525.54	525.54		525.551	525.55	525.55	14 days 525.55								525.551	525.551	525.551			525.56 525.58
MISS. Code Ann. (1952) fn. 32	chancery 432 (1956) drunkards and drug addicts 435 (1956) unsound mind, 6903-02	drunkard or drug addict. 435 (1956) unsound mind, 6909-02	6909-02	drunkard or drug addict. friend. 435 (1956) unsound mind, 6909-02	6909-02	6909-02	435 (1956)	435 (1956)		if not adjudicated, sworn petition, 6909-02		435 (1956) 6909-02	435 (1956) 6909-02		5 days 6909-02	435 (1956) 6902-02						1309 (1956)	435 (1956) 6909-02	435 (1956) 6909-02				411 (1956)
MO. Rev. Stat. (1956)	probate 472.020 (1956)	475.060		475.060	475-.010.3 475.060	475-.010.3 475.060	475-.010.3 475.060	475-.010.3 475.060	475-.010.3 475.060	petition 475.060		475-075	475-.075.2	to spouse if directed by court, 475.075.2	reasonable 475-.075.2			fn. 34 475-.075.2			475.075-.1	475.075-.1 475.075-.2 475.075-.3	475.075-475.090	475.090 475.090	475.055-.3 (Supp. 1969)	fn. 35 475.140		475.270

284

Table 8.3 INDEPENDENT DETERMINATION OF INCOMPETENCY *continued*

STATE	COURT	App. By: Relative	App. By: Alleged Incompetent	App. By: Any Interested Person	Applicable: Mentally Ill or Unsound Mind	Applicable: Deficient	Applicable: Alcoholics	Applicable: Drug Addicts	Applicable: Others	Supporting: Verified Petition	Supporting: Medical Certificate	Notice: HEARING	Notice: Incompetent Person	Notice: Relatives	Notice: Period of Time	Presence: Mandatory	Presence: Except When Harmful	Presence: Discretionary	Jury: Number on Jury	Jury: Mandatory	Jury: Optional	Counsel or Guardian ad Litem	Guardians: For Both Person and Property	Guardians: Separation Optional	Corporations Permitted	Central Registration of Incompetency	Notice to County of Residency	Continuing Court Supervisor
MONT. Rev. Codes Ann. (1963)	district 91-4701	91-4701		friend 91-4701	91-4701				91-4701	91-4701		91-4702	91-4701		5 days 91-5701	if able to attend, 91-4701						R. Civ. P., 4D(2)(a), 17(c) (Supp. 1969) 93-2806	91-4702					91-4703
NEB. Rev. Stat. (1968)	county 38-201	38-201		38-201	fn. 36 includes old age or other cause. 38-201	38-301	38-301					38-202	38-201		14 days 38-201							7-13	38-202					
NEV. Rev. Stat. (1967)	district 159.100-.1	159-.100.1		fn. 37 159.100-.1	includes old age or any other cause, 159.100-.1					159.100-.1		159.130	fn. 38 159.100-.1	fn. 38 159.100-.2	5 days 159.100-.2	if able to attend, 159.100-.2							159.130	159.130				159.540 et seq.
N.H. Rev. Stat. Ann. (1968)	probate 464:1	fn. 39 464:1					464:5 464:7		fn. 40 464:5	inquisition by 3 suitable persons. 464:1		464:1 464:2	fn. 41 464:1									462:1	462:4 464:1 to 464:3			fn. 42 135:40	464:8	
N.J. Stat. Ann. (1964)	county or superior 3A:6-36 (Supp. 1970)	Rule 4: 102-1 (a) (1968)		Rule 4: 102-1(a) (1968)	Rule 4 102-1(a) (1968)	idiocy Rule 4: 102-1 (1968)	3A:6-41 Rule 4: 102-1 (1968)			affidavit Rule 4: 102-2(a) (1968)	2 affidavits, 1 to be from superintendent of institution if confined. Rule 4: 102-2(b) (1968)		also serve any person having custody. Rule 4: 102-4 (1968)	Rule 4: 102-4 (1968)	20 days court may shorten for good cause. Rule 4: 102-4 (1968)		Rule 4: 102-5 (1968)			3A:6-35 Rule 4: 102-6 (a) 102-6 (b) (1968)	3A:6-35 Rule 4: 102-6 (b) (1968)	expressly no guardian ad litem to be appointed, but incompetent may have counsel, Rule 4: 102-4	3A:6-36		32-3-2			
N.M. Stat. Ann. (1953)	district 32-2-2	32-3-1		32-3-1	32-3-1		32-3-1		fn. 43 spendthrift 32-3-1	32-3-1		32-3-1	32-3-1		5 days 32-3-1						if demanded 32-3-1	fn. 44 32-3-1	estate only, 32-2-3 (Supp. 1967); 32-3-2					
N.Y. Mental Hygiene Law (McKinney 1951) (Supp. 1970)	county or supreme 101(2)	101(1)	101(1)	if none applies than a local official, 101(1)	incompetent applies, 101(1)				fn. 45 patient of state institution 102	101(2) 101(3)			unless court orders otherwise. 101(4)	spouse; court may require further notice in any manner it deems proper, 101(4)					12 to 24 101(6)	101(5)	or a commission 101(5)	101(8) (b)						

Table 8.3 INDEPENDENT DETERMINATION OF INCOMPETENCY   *continued*

STATE	COURT	APPLICATION BY Relative	Alleged Incompetent	Any Interested Person	APPLICABLE CASES Mentally Ill or Unsound Mind	Deficient	Alcoholics	Drug Addicts	Others	SUPPORTING EVIDENCE Verified Petition	Medical Certificate	HEARING	NOTICE Incompetent Person	Relatives	Period of Time	PRESENCE IN COURT Mandatory	Except When Harmful	Discretionary	JURY TRIAL Number on Jury	Mandatory	Optional	COUNSEL OR GUARDIAN AD LITEM	GUARDIANS For Both Person and Property	Separation Optional	CORPORATIONS PERMITTED	CENTRAL REGISTRATION OF INCOMPETENCY	NOTICE TO COUNTY OF RESIDENCY	CONTINUING COURT SUPERVISOR
N.C. Gen. Stat. (1966)	superior 35-2			35-2	anyone mentally disordered 35-2	35-2	35-2	35-2		35-2		35-2	35-2						12 35-2	35-2								
N.D. Cent. Code (1960)	county 30-10-02	30-10-02(1)		30-10-02(1)	30-10-02(4)	30-10-02(4)	30-10-02(2)		spend-thrifts 30-10-02(3)	30-10-05(1)		30-10-05(4)	others as court may direct 30-10-05(3)(b)									court may appoint 30-10-24	30-10-02 30-10-09	30-10-02 30-10-09				
OHIO Rev. Code (Baldwin 1964)																							fn. 46 2111.02	2111.02 2111.06	2111.01 2111.01 (A)			
OKLA. Stat. (1965)	county 58, §851	58, §851		friend 58, §851	from any cause incompetent 58, §851					58, §851		58, §851	58, §851		5 days 58, §851	fn. 47 58, §851							58, §852		58, §775 (Supp. 1969)			fn. 48 58, §871
ORE. Rev. Stat. (1967)	probate 126.106 426.295 (2)	426.295 (2)	426.295 (2)	creditor, guardian or interested person 426.295 (2)	person committed to a state hospital 426.295					426.295 (2)		426.295 (2)		guardian who is not the petitioner 426.295 (2)	3 days 426.295 (2)								fn. 49 126.020 126.020	fn. 49 126.020				126.320
PA. Stat. Ann. (1969)	orphans 50, §3102(2) 50, §3301(a)	spouse or relative 50, §3301(a)		creditor, debtor or other person 50, §3301(a)	50, §3102(3)	50, §3102(3)	50, §3102(3)	50, §3102(3)	old age 50, §3102(3)	50, §3301(a)		50, §3301(a)	50, §3301(a)	fn. 50 50, §3301(a)			or absent from the Commonwealth 50, §3301(a)					expressly unnecessary 50, §3301(a)	guardian of estate or person 50, §3301(a)	guardian or guardians of person or estate 50, §3301(3)	50, §3313(a)			50, §3601
R.I. Gen. Laws Ann. (1956)	probate 33-15-8	33-15-8		33-15-8	33-15-8	idiot 33-15-8	33-15-8		fn. 40 33-15-8	33-15-8		33-15-8	fn. 51 33-15-8 33-15-9		14 days 33-15-9 33-15-17							33-15-9	fn. 52 33-15-8 33-15-28 33-15-29	33-15-8	trust company as guardian of estate 14-5-6			33-15-19 33-15-26
fn. 53 S.C. Code Ann. (1962)	probate 32-1035	32-1035		32-1035	32-1035	32-1035	32-1035		32-1035	fn. 54 32-1035 32-1036	fn. 54 32-1035 32-1036	fn. 54 32-1036 32-1038	32-1035	32-1035								fn. 55 32-1035						
S.D. Compiled Laws Ann. (1967)	county 30-27-6 11	30-27-11		30-27-11 30-27-6	fn. 56 30-27-5 30-27-6					30-27-13		30-27-14	fn. 57 30-27-15	fn. 57 30-27-15	fn. 57 reasonable 30-27-15			30-27-16					30-27-18	30-27-18				

Table 8.3 INDEPENDENT DETERMINATION OF INCOMPETENCY *continued*

STATE	APPLICATION BY — COURT	Relative	Alleged Incompetent	Any Interested Person	APPLICABLE CASES — Mentally Ill or Unsound Mind	Deficient	Alcoholics	Drug Addicts	Others	SUPPORTING EVIDENCE — Verified Petition	Medical Certificate	HEARING	NOTICE — Incompetent Person	Relatives	Period of Time	PRESENCE IN COURT — Mandatory	Except When Harmful	Discretionary	JURY TRIAL — Number on Jury	Mandatory	Optional	COUNSEL OR GUARDIAN AD LITEM	GUARDIANS — For Both Person and Property	Separation	Operational	CORPORATIONS PERMITTED	CENTRAL REGISTRATION OF INCOMPETENCY	NOTICE TO COUNTY OF RESIDENCY	CONTINUING COURT SUPERVISOR
TENN. Code Ann. (1955) (Supp. 1968) fn. 58	probate or county 34-1008	34-1008	34-1008	friends 34-1008	mental weakness 34-1008				old age or physical incapacity, 34-1008	34-1008	2 physicians who have at least 3 years. 34-1008	34-1010	34-1009	34-1009	7 days 34-1009							fn. 58 34-1010	34-1012		34-1012				
TEX. Prob. Code Ann. (1956) fn. 59 fn. 60	county and probate 3(e) 4	fn. 61 111 112		fn. 61 111 112	3(p) 109(c) 112	3(p) 109(c) 112	3(p) 109(c) 112					113 114 115	fn. 62 130(d)	fn. 63 33(f)(2) (Supp. 1969) 130(a) 130(b)	10 days 33(f)(1) 33(f)(2) (Supp. 1969)			115			115		7(b) 111(f)	7(b) 111(f)		3(x) 78(e) 109(c)(2)			399, 400 (Supp. 1969)
UTAH Code Ann. (1953)	district 75-1-6	75-13-19		friend 75-13-19	75-13-19	75-13-19 75-13-20			fn. 64 75-13-19 75-13-20			75-13-19 75-14-19 75-14-17 75-14-18	fn. 65 75-13-19		fn. 66 75-13-19						75-14-18		75-13-19				7-4-3 (1)		75-13-36 75-13-37
VT. Stat. Ann. (1958) fn. 67	probate 14, §2601 14, §2602	14, §2683 (Supp. 1969)		friend or commissioner of social welfare, 14, §2683 (Supp. 1969)	also includes person mentally incapable of taking care of himself or his property. 14, §2683 (Supp. 1969)					14, §2683		14, §2684 14, §2685	14, §2664	fn. 68 14, §2664	6 days; 10 days if out of state. 14, §2684								14, §2691					14, §2689	14, §2921
VA. Code Ann. (1953) (Supp. 1968)	courts of record—as to determination of legal incompetency, city or county courts. 37.1-127			judge may also do so on own motion 37.1-128	fn. 69 37.1-128	fn. 69 37.1-128			advanced age 37.1-132	"written complaint and information". 37.1-128		37.1-128	37.1-128			37.1-128					37.1-128		37.1-138 37.1-139						
WASH. Rev. Code Ann. (1967)	superior 11.88-.010	11.88-.030		11.88-.030	11.88-.010	11.88-.010	11.88-.010	11.88-.010		11.88-.030		11.88-.040	also on persons having care, custody or control. 11.88-.040	spouse 11.88-.040	10 days 11.88-.040							fn. 70	11.88-.010		11.88-.010	fn. 71 11.88-.100 30.08-.110 30.08-.150(9)			11.88-.120 11.88-.100 11.92-.010 11.92-.050

Table 8.3 INDEPENDENT DETERMINATION OF INCOMPETENCY *continued*

STATE	APPLICATION BY				APPLICABLE CASES					SUPPORTING EVIDENCE		HEARING	NOTICE			PRESENCE IN COURT			JURY TRIAL			COUNSEL OR GUARDIAN AD LITEM	GUARDIANS		CORPORATIONS PERMITTED	CENTRAL REGISTRATION OF INCOMPETENCY	NOTICE TO COUNTY OF RESIDENCY	CONTINUING COURT SUPERVISOR
	COURT	Relative	Alleged Incompetent	Any Interested Person	Mentally Ill or Unsound Mind	Deficient	Alcoholics	Drug Addicts	Others	Verified Petition	Medical Certificate		Incompetent Person	Relative	Period of Time	Mandatory	Except When Harmful	Discretionary	Number on Jury	Mandatory	Optional		For Both Person and Property	Separation Optional				
W. VA. Code Ann. (1967)																												
WIS. Stat. Ann. (1958)	county 319.05	319.07	fn. 72 319.31	fn. 73 319.07	319.01 (1) 319.01 (3) 319.03 319.07	319.01 (1) 319.01 (3) 319.03 319.07	319.01 (1) 319.01 (3) 319.03 319.07	319.01 (1) 319.01 (3) 319.03 319.07	fn. 74 319.01 (1) 319.01 (4) 319.03 319.07 319.08 (2)			319.08 319.12	also on custodian if in custody or confinement 319.08 (1) (Supp. 1968)	319.06 (1) (Supp. 1969)	10 days 319.08 (1) (Supp. 1969)	if able to attend 319.08 (1)						court may appoint guardian ad litem 319.11	319.03	319.03	223.10		319.215	319.25 (Supp. 1969)
WYO. Stat. Ann. (1957)	district 3-29.1 (Supp. 1969)	3-29.2 (Supp. 1969)		3-29.2 (Supp. 1969)	3-29.1 (Supp. 1969)	3-29.1 (Supp. 1969)	3-29.1 (Supp. 1969)	3-29.1 (Supp. 1969)	old age, physical disability 3-29.1 (Supp. 1969)	3-29.2 (Supp. 1969)	fn. 75 3-29.3 (Supp. 1969)	3-29.4 (Supp. 1969)		3-29.2, 3-29.5 (Supp. 1969)	10 days 3-29.5 (Supp. 1969)		3-29.3 (Supp. 1969)				3-29.6 (Supp. 1969)	3-29.5 (b) (Supp. 1969)	3-29.7 (Supp. 1969)		4-12 7-121 13-98			3-28 3-29

Notes to Table 8.3   INDEPENDENT DETERMINATION OF INCOMPETENCY

1. Under the theory of the Draft Act, a determination that hospitalization is justified is entirely different and separate from an adjudication of incompetency. Commentary Sec. 21.

2. Relatives may file applications in the chancery court for the preservation of the estate of male alcoholics. A jury is not used. Ala. 7, §1064.

3. If person alleged to be of unsound mind has been committed and is in a hospital, notice is not necessary but guardian ad litem must be appointed. Guardian is to employ counsel at alleged incompetent's expense. Ala. 21, §15.

4. Evidence of incompetency must include the oral testimony or sworn written statement of at least 1 qualified medical witness whose qualifications are to be set forth in his testimony. Court may appoint medical examiners to examine alleged incompetent and report their findings to the court. Ark. 57-615b (Supp. 1967).

5. Three separate procedures are relevant. The first, charted in the upper row, is for the appointment of a guardian. The second, charted in the center row, is for the appointment of a conservator. The third, charted in the lower row, applies only to the appointment of a conservator for gravely disabled persons. Cal. Prob. 1460 et seq., 1750 et seq., W. & I. 5350 et seq. (Supp. 1968).

6. Petition may be filed only by the professional person in charge of an agency providing intensive mental treatment when a gravely disabled patient is unwilling or unable to accept voluntary treatment. Cal. W. & I. 5352 (Supp. 1968).

7. A conservator of a gravely disabled person may be given, by the court, the right to place his conservatee in a state or state-licensed institution. Cal. W. & I. 5358 (Supp. 1968).

8. Conservatorship of a gravely disabled person automatically terminates after one year. Cal. W. & I. 5361. (Supp. 1968).

9. The same procedure is followed whether it is alleged that a person is mentally ill or mentally deficient. In either case, if found mentally ill or mentally deficient, he may be committed to the appropriate state institution, or, in the discretion of the court, to the care and custody of a proper person. A conservator of the estate is to be appointed in either situation if the person has real or personal property. Colo. 71-1-11 (Supp. 1965), 153-9-2(1) (Supp. 1965).

10. Selectmen of town of incompetent's residence or domicile, state welfare commission if person is receiving state aid, or board of directors of a charitable organization. Conn. 45-70 (Supp. 1969).

11. If relative made the application, selectmen of the town are to get notice. Conn. 45-71 (Supp. 1969).

12. Conservator must register fact of incompetency on land records of any town in which conservatee has an interest in real property. Conn. 45-74.

13. A trustee is to be appointed for all mentally ill persons. See Del. 12, 3701 et seq. (Supp. 1970), and Ch. Ct. R. 100 et seq. (Supp. 1968). This requires the issuance of a writ de lunatico inquirendo, unless the person alleged to be mentally ill is an inmate at an institution for the mentally ill. A verified petition may be filed by any person, supported by the certificates of 2 physicians; 10 days' notice of the intent to make application and to execute the writ must be given to interested adult parties; a jury is required if the respondent is at large, and is available upon request if respondent is confined; respondent may be produced for inspection by the jury.

14. A judicial finding of incompetency is a necessary prerequisite for involuntary hospitalization. Fla. 394.22(11). After such finding of incompetency, a guardian may be appointed, whether or not the incompetent is hospitalized. Fla. 744.31. Thus the judicial hearing on the appointment of a guardian is fully merged with the hearing on hospitalization.

15. The same procedure is used whether the petition is for the appointment of a guardian of the estate or commitment to a hospital. Ga. 49-604-(b) (Supp. 1969).

16. If one application fails on its merits, another will not be allowed unless verified by 3 disinterested neighbors besides the applicant. Ga. 49-607.

17. The ordinaries court shall issue a commission directed by 3 reputable persons, 2 of whom shall be physicians, requiring them to examine and hear witnesses under oath, and return its findings to the court. Ga. 88-507.3, 49-604(b) (Supp. 1969).

18. Guardians are authorized to arrange for a suitable place for the custody, care, treatment, or hospitalization of the ward, or to place them in the care of the state department of health. Ga. 49-604(b) (Supp. 1969).

19. Guardian of the estate only may be appointed if it appears person is capable of taking care of himself but not his estate. Idaho 15-1816 (Supp. 1969).

20. Prosecuting attorney is to defend the alleged incompetent if there is a jury trial. It is not necessary for the court to appoint a guardian ad litem. Ind. 8-114 (Supp. 1969), 8-119.

21. A mental retardate or mentally ill person may not file a voluntary petition. Iowa 633.557, 633.572.

22. Separate but identical procedures are provided for the appointment of a guardian of the person and a conservator of the property.

23. Court hearing only unless person requests in writing, at least 48 hours prior to hearing, a hearing before a commission or a jury. Kan. 59-3013.

24. Louisiana Code of Civil Procedure consolidates procedural rules applicable generally to civil actions and proceedings covered in the Code of Practice in the Revised Statutes and in the Civil Code.

25. Not only lunatics and idiots are liable to be interdicted, but likewise all persons who, owing to any infirmity, are incapable of taking care of their persons and administering their estates. La. Civ. Code art. 422.

26. "If, upon such hearing, he adjudges that such person is mentally ill . . . or incapable . . ., he shall appoint a guardian." Me. 18, §3602.

"Such guardians shall have the custody of the persons of their wards, if resident in the state, except so far as the court of probate may from time to time otherwise order . . ." Me. 18, §3605.

27. A person who deems himself unfit by reason of infirmities of age or physical disability to manage his estate may make application for the appointment of a conservator of his estate. Me. 18, §3701.

28. There is a specific procedure governing the appointment of a conservator for a person unable "by reason of advanced age, mental weakness (not amounting to unsoundness of mind), or physical incapacity," to care for his property. Md. 16, §149.

29. Two or more friends, or the mayor and alderman of a city, or the selectmen of a town in which he is an inhabitant or resident, or the department of mental health may so petition. Mass. 201, §6 (Supp. 1968).

30. There is a specific procedure covering the spendthrift, which has not been charted. Mass. 201, §8.

31. A conservator, who is to have charge only of the property, may be appointed if a person is unable to take care of his property due to advanced age or mental weakness. Mass. 201, §16.

32. In the guardianship provisions which appear in the Probate Code, the reference is only to the "court," but it is obvious that the court designated is the probate court. Minn. 525.54 to 525.612.

33. The chancery court may also appoint guardians of the estate of residents where there has been no adjudication of incompetency or where

the adjudication proceedings were not in full compliance with the law, provided certain statutory requirements are met. Miss. 432 (1956).

34. Patient must be notified that he has the right to attend. Mo. 475.-075.2.

35. Notice of guardianship to be published in paper once a week for 4 consecutive weeks. Mo. 475.140.

36. "Spendthrift" is intended to include every person who is liable to be put under guardianship on account of excessive drinking, gambling, idleness, debauchery, or lack of discretion in managing any benefits received from public funds. The provisions for hearing, etc., are very similar to those depicted on the chart. Neb. 38-301 et seq.

37. If no person has been duly appointed legal guardian for an incompetent person receiving any form of state aid, the state welfare department may petition for the appointment of a guardian of the estate of the incompetent person. Nev. 159.110.1.

38. A citation shall be served on the alleged incompetent and also on the person with whom or in whose custody the insane or incompetent may be. Incompetent person is required to show cause why guardian should not be appointed. Nev. 159.100.2.

39. Or overseers of the poor of the town where alleged incompetent resides. N.H. 464:1, 464:6

40. In New Hampshire a spendthrift includes a person who, by excessive drinking, gaming, idleness, debauchery, inability to manage his affairs with prudence, or vicious habits of any kind, so wastes his estate as to expose his family to hardship or town to a burden. N.H. 464:5.

41. Rhode Island has a very similar provision, but does not denote such a person a spendthrift. All categories are included within that class for which a guardian may be appointed. R.I. 33-15-8.

41. Statute speaks of notice but does not specify to whom it is to be given. N.H. 464:1.

42. Whenever a guardian is appointed for a person who has been legally declared to be insane, the register of probate shall within 1 week after such appointment, transmit to the director, division of mental health, the name and residence of both guardian and ward. N.H. 135:40.

43. Applies to any person by reason of mental disability (or habitual drunkenness, as the case may be), incapable of caring for himself properly, of of managing his property. N.M. 32-3-1.

44. Court to appoint counsel if person does not have one or has not chosen his own. N.M. 32-3-1.

continued

45. A similar procedure for an order of incompetency is used for persons legally committed or admitted to an institution. N.Y. Mental Hygiene Law 102 (Supp. 1970).

46. A guardian of an incompetent shall also be guardian of the children of the ward. Ohio. 2111.02.

47. If able to attend. Okla. 58, §851.

48. Guardian must file inventory within 3 months and report to court once a year. Guardian's annual inventory "must be recorded by the judge." Okla. 58, §871.

49. Separate proceeding for appointment of guardian; any person may file with clerk of court for the appointment of a guardian. Ore. 126.126.

50. Notice of the petition and hearing shall be given in such manner as the court shall direct to the alleged incompetent, to all persons residing within the Commonwealth who are sui juris and would be entitled to share in the estate of the alleged incompetent if he died intestate at that time, and to such other parties as the court may direct. Pa. 50, §3301(a).

51. When application is made for the appointment of a guardian for any person confined in an asylum for the insane, the court shall order personal notice to be served upon such person. The server shall apply to the physician in charge of the asylum and, if in the opinion of the physician that service on the inmate will be injurious to his mental health, the physician shall so note on the service of notice, and return it to the court. R.I. 33-15-9. In all other cases notice shall be by publication. R.I. 33-15-8.

52. A conservator may be appointed to care for the property of any person who "by reason of advanced age or mental weakness, is unable to care for his property." These proceedings differ only slightly from proceedings depicted on the table. R.I. 33-15-44.

53. If the alleged incompetent is hospitalized, the procedure varies in that (a) a certificate is required from the physician in charge and the superintendent of the institution, to the effect that the patient is mentally ill or mentally deficient and incapable of caring for or managing his estate, (b) a further certificate is required from the commission stating that the person has been admitted to a mental health facility and is subject to the control of the commission, and (c) there is a different hearing procedure. S.C. 32-1036, 32-1037, 32-1038.

54. If alleged incompetent is not a patient or trainee at a state mental health facility the court shall appoint 2 designated examiners to examine the person and report to the court their findings as to his mental condition and in particular his capacity to care for and manage his own affairs. A hearing shall be held if requested by a party in interest, relative, friend, or in the discretion of the probate judge. S.C. 32-1036.

55. Notice to secure a guardian ad litem is to be served on alleged incompetent, his legal guardian, if any, and his nearest known relative or friend. Court may appoint a guardian ad litem if no appearance or answer is made by him or by anyone in his behalf within 20 days. S.C. 32-1035.

56. Pertinent statutory use in 30-27-6 is "person who is mentally ill or for any cause mentally . . . incompetent to manage his own property." S.D. 30-27-6.

57. Unless good cause is shown for dispensing with notice, the court must direct that reasonable notice, the manner and method thereof to be determined by the court, be given any person having the care or custody of the alleged incompetent and such relatives or other persons as the court determines. S.D. 30-27-15.

58. The procedure charted is for appointment of a conservator for a person who by reason of "mental weakness" is incapable of managing his own estate. Tenn. 34-1008 (Supp. 1968). Another procedure exists; if the superintendent of any hospital has reason to believe that any patient not having been adjudged incompetent and having no guardian is in fact unable to manage himself of his estate, he may apply by written petition for a competency hearing for such patient and the appointment of a guardian for him. The patient may, but is not required to, be present at the hearing. Tenn. 33-313 (Supp. 1968). The court shall appoint a guardian ad litem to look after the interest of the person in question, which guardian ad litem shall be present at the hearing. Tenn. 34-1010 (Supp. 1968).

59. The procedure charted for Texas is the procedure related to Part 3 of ch. V of the Probate Code (Tex. Prob. Code Ann., §108 to §127), "Estates of Minors and Incompetents." This Code also has another procedure, in ch. IX, entitled "Specific Provisions Relating to Persons of Unsound Mind and Habitual Drunkards." The provisions of ch. IX (Tex. Prob. Code Ann., §415 to §426) have not been charted.

60. The definition section of the Probate Code provides in part, "When used in this Code, unless otherwise apparent from the context: . . . (e) 'County Court' and 'Probate Court' are synonymous and denote county courts in the exercise of their probate jurisdiction and courts especially created and organized for the sole purpose of exercising probate jurisdiction." Definitions of "County Judge," "Probate Judge," and "Judge," and "Court" are to the same effect. Tex. Prob. Code Ann. §§3(e), 3(f), 3(g).

61. The Probate Code provides that the county judge (which, by definition, includes the probate judge) may also cause an application to be filed. Tex. Prob. Code Ann. §§3(f), 112.

62. While 130(c) of the Probate Code provides for personal service of the citation on persons alleged to be of unsound mind and drunkards, 130(d) provides that no citation need be issued or served if it is presented under oath in the application that, within 6 months before

or mental deficiency. Va. 37.1-128 (Supp. 1968).

In a similar procedure a committee is appointed for a person adjudged to be an epileptic and committed to a hospital or colony and is found by the superintendent to be mentally ill to such a degree that the superintendent believes him to be legally incompetent. Va. 37.139.1 (Supp. 1966).

70. "It shall not be necessary that the person for whom guardianship is sought shall be represented by a guardian ad litem in proceedings." Wash. 11.88.040(3).

71. Only trust companies and national banks, and then only as guardian of the estate. This power is subject to certain preferred rights of certain classes of persons to be so appointed. Wash. 30.08.110, 30.08.150(9).

72. An adult resident who believes that he is unable properly to manage his property or income may voluntarily apply for a conservator, who shall have powers and duties of a guardian of the estate of an incompetent person. Appointment of a conservator is not evidence of the competency or incompetency of a person whose estate is being so administered. Wis. 319.31.

73. There is also a procedure where a patient in any state or county hospital or asylum for the insane or in any state institution for the mentally deficient appears to have property in the state of Wisconsin and does not have a guardian. Certain public officials may apply to the county court for the appointment of a guardian. Wis. 319.295 (Supp. 1968).

74. A guardian may be appointed for a spendthrift. While there are some differences in the provisions as they relate to spendthrifts, these differences have not been charted. Wis. 319.01(1), 319.01(4), 319.03, 319.07, 319.08(2).

75. If the alleged incompetent's presence at the hearing on the petition cannot reasonably be expected because of the condition of his health, or because he is a patient in a hospital or in the custody of a state institution, the petition shall be accompanied by written statements of a licensed physician and a court-designated examiner that attendance at the hearing would be injurious to the patient's health and describing the conditions of the person. Wyo. 3-29.3 (Supp. 1969).

filing, the person concerned has been adjudged by a court of competent jurisdiction in the state of Texas, after due notice, to be a person of unsound mind or an habitual drunkard. Tex. Prob. Code Ann. §§130(c), 130(d).

63. Notice by posting is given to all persons interested in the welfare of the person for whom guardianship is sought. The notice must be posted at the courthouse for not less than 10 days. Tex. Prob. Code Ann. §§33(f)(2) (Supp. 1969), 130(a).

64. 73-13-19 designates "persons who are . . . from any cause mentally incompetent to manage their property" as a group for whom guardians may be appointed. 73-13-20 provides that "mentally incompetent" shall be construed to mean "any person who, though not insane, is by reason of old age, disease, weakness of mind, or from any other cause, unable, unassisted, to properly manage and take care of himself or his property, and by reason thereof would be likely to be deceived or imposed upon by artful or designing persons." Utah 75-13-19, 75-13-20.

65. Notice is also given to such persons as the court may designate. Utah 75-13-19.

66. 75-13-19 provides for appointment "after such notice of the time and place of the hearing as the court may direct." Utah 75-13-19.

67. In Vermont there are procedures by which (1) an infirm person may himself apply to the probate court for the appoint of a guardian (Vt. 14, §2671) and (2) by which the Commissioner of Social Welfare may apply for the appointment of a guardian for a spendthrift. Vt. 14, §2682 (Supp. 1969). These procedures are not charted.

68. If a wife is the alleged incompetent, notice must also be served on the husband. Vt. 14, §2684.

69. There is a procedure for a person in a mental hospital under legal commitment, whereby the court (circuit court of the county or corporation or circuit court of the city of residence of such a person, with other courts designated as to Richmond) shall, after reasonable notice to this person and on sworn certificate of the hospital superintendent as to his legal incompetency due either to mental illness or mental defectiveness, or such other evidence as the court may require, determine if the person is legally incompetent because of mental illness

Table 8.4   INDEPENDENT RESTORATION PROCEEDINGS

Draft Act row note: See page 2 of "Scope of the Draft Act," Guardianship and Incompetency, in Appendix A of this volume

STATE	RESTORATION MERGED WITH DISCHARGE	APPLICATION BY — Ward	APPLICATION BY — Relative	APPLICATION BY — Anyone	COURT — Incompetency Court	COURT — Other	SUPPORTING EVIDENCE — Medical Certificate	SUPPORTING EVIDENCE — Verified Petition	SUPPORTING EVIDENCE — Other	NOTICE TO — Guardian	NOTICE TO — Relatives	NOTICE TO — Others	HEARINGS	PRESENCE IN COURT	JURY TRIAL — Mandatory	JURY TRIAL — Optional	JURY TRIAL — Right of Incompetent	JURY TRIAL — Right of Others	RESTORATION — Full	RESTORATION — Partial	FREQUENCY OF RESTORATION APPLICATIONS	APPEALS	APPLICABLE TO ALL INCOMPETENTS
Draft Act																							
fn. 1 ALA. Code (1958)	probate court decrees restoration to sanity upon certificate from hospital. 45, §218	21, §16		by next friend. 21, §16	probate. 21, §16		2 physicians or 2 competent persons. 21, §16	21, §16		21, §17		the person at whose instistence original inquisition was made. 21, §17	if contested by guardian or other person. 21, §18	optional. 21, §12; 21, §18	fn. 2 21, §18				21, §19				21, §16
ALAS. Stat. (1962)					20.05 .220														20.05.220				
ARIZ. Rev. Stat. Ann. (1956) fn. 3 36-524G (Supp. 1970)		or guardian. 14-864A	14-864A	friend. 14-864A	superior. 14-864A			14-864A		if any. 14-864A	spouse & parents. 14-864A		14-864C			14-864B		petitioner. 14-864B	14-864C				14-864A
ARK. Stat. Ann. (1947) fn. 4 59-235				57-457	probate. 57-457			57-457					fn. 5 57-457						57-457				fn. 6 57-457; & in Supp. 1967, 57-601
fn. 7 CAL. Prob. Code (1956)		or guardian. 1470	1470	any friend. 1470	superior. 1470			1470		1471	1471	incompetent. 1471	1472			1471	1471		1472				
CAL. Welf. & Inst'ns Code (West 1966)	application for reappointment of conservator for gravely disabled persons may be made only by existing conservator; unless such application is made, conservatorship automatically terminates after 1 year, & court will so decree. 5361, 5362 (Supp. 1968)	or conservator. 1755 (Supp. 1968)	1755 (Supp. 1968)	any friend. 1755 (Supp. 1968)	superior. 5361 (Supp. 1968)		2 physicians. 5361 (Supp. 1968)	1755 (Supp. 1968)		conservator. 5362 (Supp. 1968)	1754, 1755 (Supp. 1968)	conservatee. 5362 (Supp. 1968)	5350, 5361 (Supp. 1968) 1754, 1755 (Supp. 1968)			5362 (Supp. 1968)	5362 (Supp. 1968)		5362 (Supp. 1968)		fn. 8 5364 (Supp. 1968)		
COLO. Rev. Stat. Ann. (1964) fn. 9 71-1-26				any reputable person. 71-1-26	county. 71-1-26		1 doctor. 71-1-26	71-1-26	court shall appoint 2 physicians to examine patient. 71-1-26				fn. 10 71-1-26						71-1-26				71-1-26

Table 8.4 INDEPENDENT RESTORATION PROCEEDINGS continued

STATE	RESTORATION MERGED WITH DISCHARGE	APPLICATION BY			COURT		SUPPORTING EVIDENCE			NOTICE TO			HEARINGS	PRESENCE IN COURT	JURY TRIAL				RESTORATION		FREQUENCY OF RESTORATION APPLICATIONS	APPEALS	APPLICABLE TO ALL INCOMPETENTS
		Ward	Relative	Anyone	Incompetency Court	Other	Medical Certificate	Verified Petition	Other	Guardian	Relatives	Others			Mandatory	Optional	Right of Incompetent	Others	Full	Partial			
CONN. Gen. Stat. Ann. (1958)				fn. 11	probate. 45-77 (Supp. 1969)							fn. 12 45-77 (Supp. 1969)	45-77 (Supp. 1969)						45-77 (Supp. 1968)			fn. 13 45-288	45-77 (Supp. 1968)
DEL. Code Ann. (1953) (Supp. 1970)		12, §3914(e)		having sufficient interest. 12, §3914(e)	chancery. 12, §3914(e)								fn. 14						§3914(e)				12, §3914(e)
D.C. Code Ann. (1967)	21-1504	21-1504			district. 21-1504														21-1504				21-1504
FLA. Stat. Ann. (1960)	394.22 (16) (Supp. 1969)		includes spouse. 394.22 (15)(a)	next friend. 394.22 (15)(a)	county. 394.22 (15)(a)	if in hospital, county court of that county. 394.22 (15)(a)	fn. 15 394.22 (16)(a) (Supp. 1969)	394.22 (15)(b)		394.22 (15)(b)		state's attorney. 394.22 (15)(b)	mandatory. 394.22 (15)(c)	394.22 (15)(c)					394.22 (15)(d)			394.22 (15)(f) (Supp. 1969)	394.22 (15) 394.22 (16)
fn. 16 GA. Code Ann (1965) (Supp. 1969)	if guardian appointed. 49-605(a)	personally or by attorney. 49-605(b)			ordinaries. 49-605(b)		49-605(b)			if any, 49-605(b)	representatives. 49-605(b)		fn. 17 49-605(b)	49-605(b)					49-605(b)			49-605(b)	
HAWAII Rev. Stat. Ann. (1968)		551-62		fn. 18 551-62	judge. 551-62														551-62				551-62
IDAHO Code Ann. (1947)	fn. 19 15-1818	or guardian. 15-1818	15-1818	any friend. 15-1818	probate. 15-1818			15-1818		if any, 15-1818	spouse, parent. 15-1818		15-1818			15-1818	15-1818	"petitioner" 15-1818	15-1818				15-1818
fn. 20 ILL. Ann. Stat. (Smith-Hurd 1961)	fn. 20 9T 1/2, §10-7 (1966) (Supp. 1969)	3, §129 (Supp. 1969)			circuit. 3, §129 (Supp. 1969)			3, §129 (Supp. 1969)		conservator. 3, §130 (Supp. 1969)		other interested persons as court directs. 3, §129 (Supp. 1969)	3, §129 (Supp. 1969)			3, §129 (Supp. 1969)	3, §129 (Supp. 1969)	any interested party. 3, §129 (Supp. 1969)	3, §129 (Supp. 1969)		fn. 21 3, §129 (Supp. 1969)		3, §129 (Supp. 1969)
IND. Ann. Stat. (1953)	22-1308 (1964)			8-148	probate. 8-104 8-147(a) (3) (Supp. 1969) 8-148			8-148											8-147(c) (Supp. 1969)				8-148

Table 8.4 INDEPENDENT RESTORATION PROCEEDINGS *continued*

STATE	RESTORATION MERGED WITH DISCHARGE	APPLICATION BY — Ward	APPLICATION BY — Relative	APPLICATION BY — Anyone	COURT — Incompetency Court	COURT — Other	SUPPORTING EVIDENCE — Medical Certificate	SUPPORTING EVIDENCE — Verified Petition	SUPPORTING EVIDENCE — Other	NOTICE TO — Guardian	NOTICE TO — Relatives	NOTICE TO — Others	HEARINGS	PRESENCE IN COURT	JURY TRIAL — Mandatory	JURY TRIAL — Optional	JURY TRIAL — Right of Incompetent	JURY TRIAL — Right of Others	RESTORATION — Full	RESTORATION — Partial	FREQUENCY OF RESTORATION APPLICATIONS	APPEALS	APPLICABLE TO ALL INCOMPETENTS
IOWA Code Ann. (1964)	certificate sent to courts no effect on fiduciary. 226.19 (1969)	633.679			probate. 633.10														633.679		fn. 22 every 6 months. 633.680		633.679
KAN. Stat. Ann. (1964) (Supp. 1968)		59-3027		59-3027	probate. 59-3027	or to which venue transferred. 59-3027				59-3012		fn. 23 59-3012	59-3013				59-3013		59-3027		fn. 24 6 months 59-3027	59-2401 (19)	59-3033
KY. Rev. Stat. Ann. (1969)		or guardian. 203.024 (1)	203.024 (1)	next friend. 203.024 (1)	circuit. 203.024 (1)			203.024 (1)		if not petitioner. 203.024 (1)	if not petitioner. 203.024 (1)	county attorney & committee, if any. 203.024 (1)	203.024 (2)			203.024 (2)		court. 203.024 (2)	203.024 (3)			203.510	203.024 (1)
fn. 25 LA. Code Civ. Pro. Ann. (West 1961)													summary trial. 4546	4547								4548	
ME. Rev. Stat. Ann. (1964)		dismiss conservator. 18, §3702		fn. 26 18, §3607	probate 18, §3601																		18, §3607
MD. Ann. Code. (1966)		16, §145			16, §145								16, §145		16, §145		16, §145		16, §145			fn. 27 5, §6	16, §145
MASS. Ann. Laws (1955) (Supp. 1968)		201, §13		201, §13	probate. 201, §13							department of mental health. 201, §13							201, §13				201, §13
MICH. Comp. Laws Ann. (1967)		703.23		fn. 18 703.23	probate. 703.23														703.23				703.23
MINN. Stat. Ann. (1969)	253A.19 (1959) (Supp. 1969)	525.61		525.61	probate. 525.61		fn. 28 525.61					525.61	525.61						525.61			525.71(14)	525.61
MISS. Code Ann. (1952)				fn. 29 6909-14	chancery. 6909-14				fn. 29 6909-14				6909-14	"all interested persons." 6909-14					6909-14				6909-14

295

Table 8.4 INDEPENDENT RESTORATION PROCEEDINGS *continued*

STATE	RESTORATION MERGED WITH DISCHARGE	APPLICATION BY Ward	Relative	Anyone	COURT Incompetency Court	Other	SUPPORTING EVIDENCE Medical Certificate	Verified Petition	Other	NOTICE TO Guardian	Relatives	Others	HEARINGS	PRESENCE IN COURT	JURY TRIAL Mandatory	Optional	Right of Incompetent	Right of Others	RESTORATION Full	Partial	FREQUENCY OF RESTORATION APPLICATIONS	APPEALS	APPLICABLE TO ALL INCOMPETENTS
MO. Rev. Stat. (1956)				fn. 11	probate. 475.360			475.360					475.360		fn. 30 475.360				475.365.1			475.365.3	475.360
MONT. Rev. Codes Ann. (1963)		91-4704	91-4704	friend. 91-4704	district. 91-4704			91-4704		91-4704	91-4704	91-4704	91-4704		if requested by petitioner. 91-4704		91-4704	91-4704	91-4704				91-4704
fn. 31 NEB. Rev. Stat. (1968)																							
NEV. Rev. Stat. (1967)	certificate of discharge signed by state hospital chief establishes presumption of legal capacity. 41.300			41.320		district. 41.310		"petition" 41.320				as the court may order. 41.320	41.310						41.300 41.310				41.300 41.310 41.320
fn. 32 N.H. Rev. Stat. Ann. (1964)																							
N.J. Stat. Ann. (1953)		Rule 4:102-7 (1968)		some interested person. Rule 4:102-7 (1968)	county. 3A:6-43	superior. 3A:6-43		complaint verified by affidavit. Rule 4:102-7 (1968)	facts evidencing return to competency. Rule 4:102-7 (1968)				Rule 4:102-7 (1968)			Rule 4:102-7 (1968)			3A:6-43; Rule 4:102-7 (1968)				3A:6-43; Rule 4:102-7 (1968)
N.M. Stat. Ann. (1953)		or through his attorney. 32-2-9			district 32-2-9								fn. 33 32-2-9						32-2-9				32-2-9
fn. 34 N.Y. Mental Hygiene Law (McKinney 1951) (Supp. 1970)	112(2)				112(2)														112(2)				112(2)
N.C. Gen. Stat. (1966)	fn. 3 35-5	or guardian. 35-4	35-4	friends. 35-4	fn. 35 superior. 35-4		fn. 36 35-4.1 35-4.2	35-4		35-4 35-4.1 35-4.2			35-4 35-4.1 35-4.2		fn. 36 35-4 35-4.1	35-4.1 35-4.2	fn. 36 35-4 35-4.1 35-4.2		35-4 35-4.1 35-4.2 35-5			35-4 35-4.1	35-4 35-4.1 35-4.2 35-5
N.D. Cent. Code (1960)		or guardian. 30-10-20	within 3d degree. 30-10-20	30-10-20	county. 30-10-20			30-10-20		30-10-20	spouse; father or mother if living in county. 30-10-20		30-10-20						30-10-20				30-10-20

Table 8.4 INDEPENDENT RESTORATION PROCEEDINGS *continued*

STATE	RESTORATION MERGED WITH DISCHARGE	APPLICATION BY Ward	APPLICATION BY Relative	APPLICATION BY Anyone	COURT Incompetency Court	COURT Other	SUPPORTING EVIDENCE Medical Certificate	SUPPORTING EVIDENCE Petition Verified	SUPPORTING EVIDENCE Other	NOTICE TO Guardian	NOTICE TO Relatives	NOTICE TO Others	HEARINGS	PRESENCE IN COURT	JURY TRIAL Mandatory	JURY TRIAL Optional	JURY TRIAL Right of Incompetent	JURY TRIAL Right of Others	RESTORATION Full	RESTORATION Partial	FREQUENCY OF RESTORATION APPLICATIONS	APPEALS	APPLICABLE TO ALL INCOMPETENTS
OHIO Rev Code (Baldwin 1964)	fn. 37 final discharge. 5122.36	fn. 38 or guardian. 5122.38		head of hospital. 5122.38	probate. 5122.38			5122.38		5122.38	spouse. 5122.38	party filing petition for commitment. 5122.38	5122.38						fn. 37 5122.38				
OKLA. Stat. (1965)		or guardian. 58, §854	58, §854	friend. 58, §854	county. 58, §854			58, §854		58, §854	spouse; father or mother. 58, §854		58, §854						fn. 39 58, §854 58, §855				58, §854
ORE. Rev. Stat. (1967)	fn. 40 426.295 (3)	fn. 40 426.295 (3)	426.295 (3)	426.295 (3)	426.295 (3)			426.295 (3)					426.285 (3)						426.295 (3)				
PA. Stat. Ann. (1969)				fn. 11 50, §3323	orphan's 50, §3102, §3323				"good cause." 50, §3323			such notice as court shall direct. 50, §3323	50, §3323						50, §3323				50, §3323
R.I. Gen. Laws Ann. (1968)		26-3-5		anyone in wards behalf. 26-3-5		justice of supreme court. 26-3-5		26-3-5				person confined as insane 26-3-6	fn. 42 commission shall examine patient in hospital. 26-3-6						26-3-6 26-3-8				
S.C. Code Ann. (1962)	regular discharge shall restore legal rights. 32-1032			fn. 43 32-1045	probate. 32-1045		2 32-1045	32-1045					32-1045						32-1046			32-1047	applicable to all not actually confined or on conditional discharge from a state mental health facility. 32-1045
S.D. Compiled Laws Ann.		or guardian. 30-31-3	within 3d degree. 30-31-3	friends. 30-31-3	county. 30-31-3			30-31-3		30-31-4	husband or wife or mother or father. 30-31-4	& incompetent. 30-31-4	30-31-5						30-31-6	30-31-7			30-31-3
TENN. Code Ann. (1955)	if superintendent certifies competency 33-314 (Supp. 1968)	fn. 44 33-315 (Supp. 1968); 34-1016			33-315 (Supp. 1968); 34-1016		2 33-315 (Supp. 1968); 34-1016						33-315 (Supp. 1968); 34-1016						33-315 (Supp. 1968); 34-1016				34-1016 (Supp. 1968)

297

Table 8.4 INDEPENDENT RESTORATION PROCEEDINGS continued

STATE	RESTORATION MERGED WITH DISCHARGE	APPLICATION BY — Ward	Relative	Anyone	COURT — Incompetency Court	Other	SUPPORTING EVIDENCE — Medical Certificate	Verified Petition	Other	NOTICE TO — Guardian	Relatives	Others	HEARINGS	PRESENCE IN COURT	JURY TRIAL — Mandatory	Optional	Right of Incompetent	Right of Others	RESTORATION — Full	Partial	FREQUENCY OF RESTORATION APPLICATIONS	APPEALS	APPLICABLE TO ALL INCOMPETENTS
TEX. Prob. Code (1956)	"presumption until discharged." Tex. Rev. Civ. Stat. Ann. (1958) 5547-83 (a) (Supp. 1969)	426(a)		426(a)	"court" denotes & includes both a county court in exercise of its probate jurisdiction & court especially created. 423(g) 426				guardian to appear. 426(a)	426(a)			if facts be doubtful. 426(b)			fn. 45 426(b)			426(b)				only as to persons adjudged to be of unsound mind or habitual drunkards. 426(b)
UTAH Code Ann. (1953)		or guardian. 75-13-10 75-13-21	75-13-21	any friend. 75-13-21	75-13-10 75-13-21			75-13-21		75-13-21	husband, wife, father, or mother. 75-13-21		75-13-21						75-13-21				75-13-21
VT. Stat. Ann. (1958)		where guardian certifies guardian is not needed & court declines to discharge guardian, ward may make application to probate court. 14, §3008 (Supp. 1969)			14, §3006; & in Supp. 1969, 14, §3008														14, §3006 14, §3010			14, §3041	applicable to insane, spendthrift, absconding person or person mentally incapable of taking care of himself. 14, §3008 (Supp. 1969)
fn. 46 VA. Code Ann. (1953) (Supp. 1968)	37.1-44																		37.1-144				37.1-144
fn. 47 WASH. Rev. Code Ann. (1962)	71.02.650																						
fn. 48 W. Va. Code Ann. (1966)	27-7-1																		27-7-1				only those discharged from a mental hospital. 27-7-1

Table 8.4   INDEPENDENT RESTORATION PROCEEDINGS   *continued*

STATE	RESTORATION MERGED WITH DISCHARGE	APPLICATION BY			COURT		SUPPORTING EVIDENCE			NOTICE TO			HEARINGS	PRESENCE IN COURT	JURY TRIAL				RESTORATION		FREQUENCY OF RESTORATION APPLICATIONS	APPEALS	APPLICABLE TO ALL INCOMPETENTS
		Ward	Relative	Anyone	Incompetency Court	Other	Medical Certificate	Verified Petition	Other	Guardian	Relatives	Others			Manda-tory	Optional	Right of Incompetent	Right of Others	Full	Partial			
fn. 48 WIS. Stat. Ann. (1958	319.26 (1)(c) 319.26 (2)(c)																						319.26(1)(c) 319.26(2)(c)
WYO. Stat. Ann. (1957)	upon discharge guardian shall petition court for judicial determination of restoration of competency. 3-29.11 (Supp. 1969)	3-29.10 (Supp. 1969)	3-29.10 (Supp. 1969)	3-29.10 (Supp. 1969)	district 3-29.10 (Supp. 1969)			3-29.10 (Supp. 1969)	fn. 50 3-29.10 (b) (Supp. 1969)	3-29.11 (d) (Supp. 1969)	spouse; children, & if none, brothers or sisters. 3-29.11 (d) (Supp. 1969)		3-29.11 (Supp. 1969)						3-29.11 (e) (Supp. 1969)				those discharged. 3-29.11 others. 3-29.10 (Supp. 1969)

Notes to Table 8.4   INDEPENDENT RESTORATION PROCEEDINGS

1. There is another brief procedure which is not on the chart. If the guardian becomes satisfied that his ward has been restored to sanity and is capable of managing his estate, and the probate judge views, from the proof and facts stated, such representation as correct, he must make an order discharging the guardian and restoring the estate to the ward. Ala. 21, §20.

2. Not necessary if neither guardian nor person instituting incompetency proceedings contests the application. Ala. 21, §18.

3. Although restoration is not merged with discharge, full restoration is automatic if person secures certificate from superintendent of the hospital stating that he has been restored to competency. The court thereupon shall order that the person has been restored to full competency and full civil rights. Ariz. 36-524G (Supp. 1970); N.C. 35-5.

4. When patient has been adjudicated incompetent by a probate court for the purpose of guardianship and is later discharged by the superintendent after having recovered mentally, the superintendent shall certify this fact to the probate court of the county in which the patient resides, and the court shall issue an order removing his disability and restoring him to his normal legal status. Ark. 59-235.

5. Court shall cause the facts to be inquired into in such manner as it may direct. Ark. 57-457.

6. Drug addicts and deficients are included in the definition of incompetents but not in restoration proceedings, perhaps because the incompetency chapter was for the most part repealed and rewritten and the restoration section was not changed. Ark. 57-457; 57-601 (Supp. 1967).

7. Three procedures are relevant. The first (upper row) is for removal of a guardian and restoration. The second (center row) is for termination of a conservatorship. The third (lower row) is for reappointment of a conservator for gravely disabled persons; such conservatorship automatically terminates 1 year after creation. Cal. Prob. 1470 et seq., 1755 (Supp. 1968), W. & I. 5361 (Supp. 1968).

8. At any time, but not to exceed once every 6 months, the conservatee may petition the superior court for a rehearing as to his status as a conservatee. Cal. W. & I. 5364 (Supp. 1968).

9. Superintendent of a state hospital may discharge any person adjudicated incompetent who, in his opinion, is no longer incompetent. The superintendent shall so certify to the committing court. The court may, on its own motion, enter an order of competency. Colo. 71-1-27. An administrative [conditional] discharge by a hospital superintendent shall not constitute an adjudication of competency. Colo. 71-1-28(3).

10. Court is to appoint 2 physicians to cause the facts to be inquired into. If after the inquiry the court finds the person restored to reason, it will enter a restoration order. It is not a hearing in actuality; no provision for notice, witnesses, jury, etc. Colo. 71-1-26.

11. Statute does not prescribe who may file the application in restoration proceedings. Conn. 45-77 (Supp. 1969); Mo. 475.360; Pa. 50, §3323 (Supp. 1969).

12. After such notice as the court prescribes. Conn. 45-77 (Supp. 1969).

13. Appeal may be taken from any order, denial, or decree of the probate court by any "aggrieved party." Conn. 45-288.

14. If it appears to the court that the guardianship is no longer necessary. Del. 12, §3914(e) (Supp. 1970).

15. If a certificate has been received from the hospital stating that a committed person has recovered his sanity, it will be prima facie proof that the person is sane. Fla. 394.22(16)(a) (Supp. 1969).

16. Identical procedures are provided for termination of guardianship. Ga. 49-605(b) (Supp. 1969).

17. Procedure is same as for commitment or for an adjudication of incompetency. A commission of 2 physicians and an attorney is to conduct a hearing, to hear witnesses, and to file a report with the court. Counsel is to be appointed if the petitioner is unable to employ counsel. Ga. 49-605(b) (Supp. 1969).

18. Guardian of any insane person (or of any other person) may be discharged by judge of probate when it shall appear to him on application of the ward, or otherwise, that such guardianship is no longer necessary. Hawaii 551-62; Mich. 703.23.

19. When adjudged incompetent is discharged from the hospital as "cured," superintendent is to file a certificate to this effect with probate court of the county in which he was adjudged incompetent. The certificate shall be prima facie evidence of sanity. Upon filing such certificate of discharge, court shall make an order restoring such person to sanity and to all his rights as a citizen. Idaho 15-1818.

20. Procedures relating to release and restoration are also found at Ill. 91½, §10-1 to 91½, §10-3 (Supp. 1969) and 91½, §10-7 (1966) (Supp. 1969).

21. Cannot file a petition to have ward adjudged competent within 1 year after adjudication of incompetency except by leave of court. Ill. 3, §129 (Supp. 1969).

22. Application cannot be made until there has been a guardianship

300

for at least 6 months, and subsequent applications must be at least 6 months apart. Iowa 633.680.

23. To attorney, spouse, and to such other persons as the court shall direct; notice shall also be given to any natural guardian, custodians, or conservator. Kan. 59-3012 (Supp. 1968).

24. No application will be heard for 6 months from the date of the original adjudication finding the ward or conservatee to be an incapacitated person or for 6 months from the date of any subsequent hearing on an application for restoration. Kan. 59-3027 (Supp. 1968).

25. The provisions on restoration are: "Interdiction ends with the causes which gave rise to it. Nevertheless the person interdicted cannot resume the exercise of his rights, until after the definitive judgment by which the repeal of the interdiction is pronounced." Also interdiction "can only be revoked by the same solemnities which were observed in pronouncing it." La. Civ. Code Ann. 420, 421 (West 1952).

26. When on application of person under guardianship or otherwise the judge finds a guardian no longer necessary, the property of the ward is restored to the ward. Me. 18, §3607.

27. Appeal rights are not stated in the provisions governing restoration. However in the Appeals article it is stated that any party may appeal from a final decree, or order in the nature of a final decree, entered by a court of equity. Me. 5, §6.

28. Court may appoint 2 physicians to examine patient. Minn. 525.61.

29. The statute does not say who may file the application, but only that "upon the filing of a proper petition therefor supported by such proof as the chancellor may deem sufficient," the proper chancery court may adjudicate. Miss. 6909-14.

30. "If the court, upon the inquiry, finds that the person is not restored to his right mind, and such person, or anyone for him, within ten days after such finding, files with the court an allegation in writing, verified by oath or affirmation that the person is of sound mind and is aggrieved by the action and finding of the court," the court shall then cause the facts to be inquired into by a jury." Mo. 475.360.

31. For the restoration of competency provision under the Uniform Veteran's Guardianship Act see Neb. 38-416.

32. The only provision in any manner dealing with restoration to competency reads: "Revocation of Guardianship. If the cause for which any guardianship was granted has ceased or is removed, such guardianship, upon like petition and notice, shall be revoked." N.H. 462:30.

33. The court shall inquire into the fact of such person's insanity or incompetency and make such finding as it deems proper. N.M. 32-2-9.

34. No specific restoration provision is provided. However, if the incompetent is declared competent, the court shall order the committee to restore to him the property remaining in his hands. N.Y. Mental Hygiene Law 112(2) (Supp. 1970).

35. This procedure may not be used by persons confined to an institution. N.C. 35-4.

36. A person discharged from an institution may have a hearing with a jury before the clerk, if he so wishes. The clerk is to appoint at least 1 physician to examine the person. N.C. 35-4.1, 35-4.2.

37. The person discharged or his guardian may make a motion in the probate court to terminate the guardianship. Ohio 5122.36.

38. Two methods of restoration of competency in Ohio: (1) automatic restoration with final discharge from hospital. 512.36. (2) Each individual hospital entitled to an adjudication of competency or incompetency. 5122.38.

39. Whenever a guardian for an incompetent is discharged by the proper court by final order thereof, and no other guardian has been appointed for such person, such person shall be presumed to be fully restored and shall be presumed to be fully capable and competent to make contracts and transact any and all business as though said person had never been declared to be incompetent. Okla. 58, §855.

40. When a person committed to a state hospital has been declared incompetent and is discharged from the hospital, the superintendent of the hospital shall advise the court which entered the order of incompetency whether or not on the basis of medical evidence the person is competent. If the superintendent advises that the person is not competent, upon petition of the person, his guardian, relative or creditor or other interested person, the court shall hold a hearing to determine whether or not the discharged person is competent. Ore. 426.295(3).

41. Two procedures for commitment and restoration are provided. The chart depicts the system involving a justice of the supreme court. As to the method of restoration through the district court, see R.I. 26-2-3.

42. The justice of the supreme court shall appoint a commission of 3 members which shall examine the alleged insane in the institution where detained. The commission acts much like a court in hearing witnesses and the like (see specific procedures, 26-2-9 et seq.). The commission shall report to the justice of the supreme court, and the latter may either confirm or disallow the same and order the recommitment or discharge of such person, or dismiss the petition

altogether. R.I. 26-3-6, 26-3-7, 26-3-8.

43. Application to be filed by the guardian ad litem or the committee of the incompetent. S.C. 32-1045.

44. Section 34-1016 of the 1967 supplement to the Tennessee code refers to sections 33-310 to 33-313; these sections have been repealed, and their function is served by section 33-315 (Supp. 1968).

45. Jury need not be called if judge feels that there is no doubt as to the facts. Tex. Prob. Code 426(b).

46. No specific restoration provision is provided. However, the fiduciary shall surrender the ward's estate, or so much as he may be accountable for, to the ward if he shall be restored. Va. 37.1-144 (Supp. 1968).

47. A guardianship is terminated by an adjudication of competency. Wash. 11.88.140.

48. No specific restoration provision is provided. However, the regular administrative discharge of a confined individual restores said patient to legal capacity. W. Va. 27-7-1.

49. No specific independent restoration provisions are provided. Only reference thereto is: (1) "A guardianship of the person shall terminate . . . when the court adjudicates a former incompetent to be competent"; (2) "A guardianship of the estate shall terminate when the court adjudicates a former incompetent to be capable of handling his property." Wis. 319.26(1)(c), 319.26(2)(c).

50. Whenever a person previously adjudged mentally incompetent has been hospitalized in or committed to a public or private institution, the petition shall be accompanied by an affidavit issued by the head of the hospital or other qualified person administering treatment setting forth the affiant's evaluation of the person's mental condition. If the affiant declares that in his opinion the person is free from mental illness, mental deficiency, or mental retardation to such a degree that such person is competent to manage himself, his property, or both, such affidavit shall be prima facie evidence of the mental competency of such person. Wyo. 3-29.10(b) (Supp. 1969).

302

Chapter Nine Personal and Property Rights

I. INTRODUCTION

The right of a mentally disabled person to execute a document, initiate litigation, participate in business and professional activities, and exercise such political rights and privileges as voting and holding office is limited by statute. Similarly, eligibility to receive such special assistance as veterans' benefits is subject to statutory regulation. In order to provide adequate protection to the mentally disabled person, his family, and those with whom he or his guardian must necessarily deal, it is imperative that these statutes clearly set forth the restrictions they seek to impose. Unfortunately, the task of extracting precise and meaningful information from existing statutes is well-nigh impossible.

A partial list of terms employed to describe persons prohibited from exercising a particular right includes lunatic, idiot, insane, mentally unfit, and mentally disordered. Difficulty lies in the absence of statutory provisions establishing the identity of these people. Research shows that typically this sort of statute

1. not only neglects to say whether a person's rights are suspended when that person enters a mental hospital and becomes a patient there, but also fails to differentiate between voluntary and compulsory hospitalization;

2. fails to state whether a formal legal adjudication of mental disability is required before personal and property rights are restricted;

3. does not say whether nonhospitalized mentally ill persons are prohibited from exercising particular rights;

4. is silent as to the rights of a person who, although adjudged incompetent, does not need hospitalization;

5. fails to indicate whether prohibition of rights applies to a person who is in fact incompetent but who has not been so adjudicated;

6. neglects to spell out administrative procedures enforcing the suspension of rights;

7. is unclear about whether the denial of rights is based on the premise that any person who is in need of hospitalization is incapable of exercising them or on the premise that a person who does not possess the ability to manage his own affairs is also unqualified to exercise other rights; and

8. fails to specify when or how reinstatement of any suspended rights occurs.

The typical statute is thus deficient in scope, lacking in clarity, and based on outdated information. It is primarily from the concept of incompetency that the various personal and property disabilities discussed hereafter appear to be derived. Many of these limitations are merely a detailed listing of the effects or by-products of incompetency. Since, historically, compulsory hospitalization is an outgrowth of incompetency, the disabilities of incompetency have almost always been assumed to be attached to the hospitalized person. However, many legal and medical experts now believe that a person may be in need of hospital treatment and yet be capable of performing many ordinary personal, civil, and business functions. The competency statutes have begun to reflect this thinking: in all but a few jurisdictions, merger of the issues of hospitalization and competency no longer obtains as a matter of theory. Insofar as the statutes limiting personal and property rights are extensions of the competency provisions, the trend apparent in competency legislation has an impact on the question of personal and property rights. By the same token, many of the issues discussed in the previous chapter on competency—the practical implementation of the separation theory, the desirability of complete separation, problems related to guardianship, restoration, and so forth—are of equal relevance to this chapter. To avoid needless duplication, these general issues will not be reconsidered here.

One general principle, however, will be reiterated: that is, limitations on personal and property rights should obtain only to the extent necessitated by the mental condition of the individual, and in the case of hospitalized patients any additional limitations must extend no further than those essential to the proper administration and operation of the institution. Loss of the total bundle of personal and property rights is unnecessary and undesirable for the great majority of the mentally ill. The competency statutes have failed to take this principle into account; the related provisions affecting specified rights are, by their relation to the competency issue, similarly defective.

II. PARTICIPATION IN LEGAL MATTERS

A. EXECUTION OF LEGAL DOCUMENTS

1. CONTRACTS AND CONVEYANCES

Under the early common law it was permissible to claim mental disability in order to avoid any contractual obligations which occurred during a period of such disability. Subsequently the view developed that no one, mentally disabled or recovered, could assert his inability to avoid his acts during the illness.[1] However, the modern view adopts no arbitrary position with respect to the right of avoiding obligations incurred while mentally disabled. The right is made dependent upon factors calculated to protect the interests of both the mentally disabled and the parties dealing with him.

Most courts distinguish between the contracts[2] and conveyances of an incompetent made prior to an adjudication of his condition and those executed after such an adjudication.[3] A majority hold that contracts made prior to an adjudication of incompetency are voidable; under certain conditions they may be disaffirmed by the incompetent, but they remain in full force until disaffirmed.[4] This reasoning is also the majority rule with regard to conveyances.[5] A minority of courts have held that the contracts of incompetents, even if their incompetency has not been adjudicated, are absolutely void. These holdings are based on the premise that a valid contract presupposes a meeting of minds of the parties, which requirement cannot be fullfilled if one party is incompetent.[6]

Legal transactions made by an incompetent after a guardian has been appointed are usually void, except that in some jurisdictions they may be enforced for the benefit of the incompetent. The basis for this rule is that it would be almost impossible for the guardian to preserve the estate if every time the ward made a transaction the guardian were obliged to go before a jury upon the question of the ward's competency.[7]

In many jurisdictions when a mental incompetent is not under guardianship, his contracts, in the absence of a statute to the contrary, are considered voidable rather than void.[8] The rule that his contracts are voidable probably resulted from an effort to allow the incompetent who had no one to act for him to make transactions which would be to his benefit.

There is a general presumption that incompetency continues from the time of the adjudication until such time as there is a judicial declaration of restoration. However, most courts tend to treat the adjudication as prima facie evidence of incapacity to contract or as a rebuttable presumption rather than as a conclusive one.[9]

Patients committed to mental hospitals are deprived of the right to contract if their commitment constitutes an automatic adjudication of incompetency—as in the few "merger" jurisdictions—or, alternatively, when they have been found incompetent in an independent proceeding. Additionally, patients' rights to contract may be restricted by the administrative regulations of hospitals or state mental health agencies. This occurs both in states where there is specific statutory authorization to this effect and in those where there is not.[10] The extent of the permitted administrative restrictions is not specified in the states having statutes on this matter, and there have been no court decisions concerning the validity of contracts made in violation of administrative restrictions.[11] Some statutes state that a contract executed by a patient is valid if he is a voluntary patient.[12] Such provisions appear to be analogous to the common rule that the contracts of persons not adjudicated incompetent are valid until disaffirmed, as opposed to the invalidity of transactions made by adjudicated incompetents.

---

1. 2 Blackstone, *Commentaries* 291 (1783).

2. Negotiable instruments are treated as ordinary contracts in this section.

3. See Table 9.1, Personal and Property Rights of the Mentally Disabled, Validity of Contracts column.

4. Ibid.

5. Note, 3 *Wayne L. Rev.* 73, 74 (1956).

6. Comment, "The Mentally Ill and the Law of Contracts," 29 *Temp. L. Rev.* 380, 383 (1956).

7. Annot., 7 A.L.R. 568, 594 (1920). For a discussion of the guardian's duties and obligations see chap. 8, "Incompetency, Guardianship, and Restoration," § IX, Guardianship.

8. Rubenstein v. Dr. Pepper Co., 228 F.2d 528 (8th Cir. 1955); 2 Williston, *Contracts* § 251 (3d ed. 1959).

9. Comment, *supra* note 6, at 384.

10. See chap. 8, "Incompetency, Guardianship, and Restoration."

11. But compare *In re* Alexieff's Will, 94 N.Y.S.2d 32 (Sur. Ct. 1949), aff'd, 227 App. Div. 790, 97 N.Y.S.2d 532 (1950), *motion for leave to appeal denied*, 277 App. Div. 901, 98 N.Y.S.2d 582 (1950).

12. E.g., *Tenn. Code Ann.* § 33-1207 (Supp. 1967); *Tex. Rev. Civ. Stat. Ann.* art. 5547-24(c) (Supp. 1967).

All jurisdictions hold mentally disabled and incompetent persons responsible for necessaries. However, these persons are liable for the value of the necessaries rather than for any agreed figure. Many problems arise in determining what constitutes necessaries. The disabled person's liability for necessaries also extend to those furnished a spouse or other members of the family entitled to his support whenever sufficient provision for such support has not been made by him or his guardian.[13]

2. WILLS

In Anglo-American law the right to make a will is one created by statute. A person's ability to make a will is known as his testamentary capacity. The first Wills Act[14] granted this right to everyone without qualification as to sanity, but was soon amended to exclude idiots "or any person de non sane memory."[15] Modern statutes usually describe testamentary capacity as "sound mind and memory."[16] It should be emphasized here that "sound mind" apropos of the ability to make a valid will does not mean the same thing as it does when hospitalization is being considered or when incompetency is being determined.

The use of the term "sound mind" for purposes of testamentary capacity does not cause confusion even though the term is not defined by the statutes, because a fairly uniform definition has been established by case law. To be of sound mind for the purpose of making a will the testator must be able to

1. know, without prompting, the nature and extent of the property of which he is about to dispose;
2. know the nature of the act he is about to perform;
3. know the names and identity of the persons who are to be the objects of his bounty;
4. know his relation toward them;
5. have sufficient mind and memory to understand all of these facts;
6. appreciate the relations of these factors to one another;
7. recollect the decision which he has formed.[17]

The fact that a testator is under guardianship does not mean that he is assumed to be incapable of passing these tests. Maryland and the District of Columbia require that a testator be capable of making a valid deed or contract, which would preclude persons under guardianship from making a will in those jurisdictions. However, they are the only jurisdictions which equate contractual and testamentary capacity.[18]

Even if the testator executes the will in a mental hospital, the mere fact of hospitalization does not necessarily invalidate the will. Moreover, the fact that a testator suffers from delusions does not invalidate his will unless he lacks the ability to form a clear conception of his relation to persons and things.[19] For example, a delusion that he is being pursued and molested by devils or evil spirits would not invalidate a person's will.[20] However, if the testator disinherits his daughter under the delusion that she is trying to poison his food, the will would be invalid because of the testator's inability to evaluate his relations toward those whom the will affects. The rule in a recent case is quite typical of the predominant attitude on delusions as affecting testamentary capacity.

> An insane delusion that will avoid a will must affect or enter into the execution of the will; and even if the testator has an insane delusion on certain subjects, still if he has mental capacity to know his property and the objects of his bounty, and to make a disposition of his property according to a plan formed by him, the will cannot be set aside on the ground of mental incapacity. A mental disturbance, therefore, may or may not reach the state where one loses his capacity to make a valid will.[21]

In some jurisdictions, the statutes provide that a person "of unsound mind" may not make conveyances or contracts until his restoration to capacity has been judicially determined.[22] Although Oklahoma and South Dakota have such statutes, they alone add a clause which states that if such person of unsound mind is "actually restored to capacity,"

13. Williston, *supra* note 8, at § 255.

14. 32 Hen. 8, c. 1 (1540).

15. Green, "Public Policies Underlying the Law of Mental Incompetency," 38 *Mich. L. Rev.* 1189, 1203–4 (1940).

16. See Table 9.2, Statutory Descriptions of Persons Who May Make a Will.

17. 1 Page, *Wills* § 132 (1941).

18. *Md. Ann. Code* art. 93, § 349 (1964); *D.C. Code Ann.* § 18-102 (1967).

19. Page, *supra* note 17, at §§ 135, 140–46.

20. Banks v. Goodfellow, L.R. 5 Q.B. 549 (1870).

21. Roller v. Kurtz, 6 Ill. 2d 618, 627, 129 N.E.2d 693, 697 (1955).

22. See Table 9.2.

he may make a will even though his restoration has not been judicially determined.[23]

In some states a mental patient may be prohibited by administrative regulation from making a will.[24] The validity of a will prepared in disregard of the prohibition is not clear, but the only case in which such a situation arose held that the regulation did not affect the validity of the will.[25] However, even if other jurisdictions follow this decision, it would seem extremely difficult from a practical point of view for a patient to make a will without the hospital's cooperation, especially where such matters as securing legal advice and the presence of witnesses are concerned.

Evaluating charges of testamentary incapacity is difficult because there is no opportunity to question the testator. If there is to be psychiatric testimony at the hearing, it is therefore necessary that it be in the form of a hypothetical question, because in most cases the psychiatrist has never examined the testator.

It has been suggested that many will contests could be avoided and dispositions made in greater accord with the testator's wishes if the testator, were examined by a psychiatrist at the time the will is executed. Such an examination would cover points of law raised by statutes and court decisions bearing on testamentary capacity and would be extensive enough to satisfy the psychiatrist as to the testator's capacity. This examination could be made with special propriety (in the legal sense of the word) if the psychiatrist were a subscribing witness, for as such it would be his duty to satisfy himself as to the testator's competency at the time of the execution of the will.[26]

The proponents of this psychiatric examination believe that it may also afford valuable information concerning the independent issue of whether the testator was subjected to undue influence.[27] The psychiatrist, alone with the testator, can observe the latter's suggestibility, mood, fears, and degree of contact with reality. These observations, the facts upon which they are based, and the conclusions drawn therefrom would be included in the notes of the psychiatric examination.[28] They would then be available as a basis for testimony if the will is later challenged on the grounds of undue influence.

The two main advantages claimed for the examination are that a more accurate picture is acquired of the testator's mental condition at the time of the will's execution and that the number of will contests is reduced. The latter claim is based on the belief that in a substantial number of cases will contests are without merit and that even when there is a bona fide dispute, more cases would be settled out of court if it were known that accurate evidence of the testator's mental condition existed.

B. RIGHT TO SUE AND BE SUED

Early common law prohibited "idiots" and "lunatics" from instituting suits in their own behalf, since they lacked the requisite reason and understanding. However, by the time of Lord Coke, the common-law rule had been changed to allow lunatics to maintain suits.[29] The modern rule is that an incompetent person may sue or be sued in the same way as a sane person, unless he has been divested of the power to act for himself through an adjudication of incompetency and the appointment of a guardian. Where there is a guardian, suit is brought by him on behalf of his ward, and many states have statutes allowing the appointment of a guardian *ad litem* for this purpose when the regular guardian is unwilling or unable to act. Modern authorities generally regard the requirement that a guardian sue or be sued for the incompetent as a protection of the interests of the incompetent rather than as a limitation on his capacity to institute suit.[30]

Problems are most apt to arise when mentally disabled persons have been adjudged incompetent but do not have a guardian, or when they are hospitalized but are not incompetent. If a patient is unaware that he has a cause of action or a valid defense, or if he is restricted by hospital rules and regulations from corresponding or consulting with his counsel, his right to obtain legal redress is extremely limited.[31]

23. Ibid. *Okla. Stat. Ann.* tit. 15, § 24 (1966); *S.D. Compiled Laws Ann.* §§ 27-2-3, 29-2-3 (1967).

24. See chap. 8, "Incompetency, Guardianship, and Restoration," § VII, Administrative Regulations.

25. *In re* Alexieff's Will, 94 N.Y.S.2d 32 (Sur. Ct. 1949), *aff'd*, 227 App. Div. 790, 97 N.Y.S.2d 532 (1950), *motion for leave to appeal denied*, 277 App. Div. 901, 98 N.Y.S.2d 582 (1950).

26. Stephens, "Probate Psychiatry—Examination of Testamentary Capacity by a Psychiatrist as a Subscribing Witness," 25 *Ill. L. Rev.* 276, 277–78 (1930).

27. Id. at 279. The theory underlying the doctrine of undue influence is that the testator is "induced by various means, to execute an instrument which, although his, in outward form, is in reality not his will, but the will of another person which is substituted for that of testator." Page, *supra* note 17, at § 184.

28. Stephens, *supra* note 26, at 280.

29. 29 *Am. Jur.* "Insane and Other Incompetent Persons" § 117 (1960).

30. Ibid.

31. See chap. 5, "Rights of Hospitalized Patients."

To some extent, the disabilities of mentally ill persons to institute suit are alleviated by statutory extensions on the time limitations of actions.[32] The extension of a statute of limitations in favor of a mentally ill person is not of the same importance if a guardian has been appointed, since the guardian has the power to institute legal action.

Most states have statutory procedures for the service of process on mentally ill persons and incompetents. If there is a guardian, service must usually be made on both the ward and the guardian. In some jurisdictions copies of process served on hospitalized persons must be left with the superintendent of the hospital or with a central agency concerned with mentally ill persons. In some states the hospital superintendent is to decide whether it will endanger the ill person to be served with process.[33]

III. ENGAGEMENT IN BUSINESS AND PROFESSIONAL ACTIVITIES

A. PROFESSIONAL LICENSING

The purpose of statutes suspending or revoking the professional licenses of persons suffering from mental disabilities is presumably to protect the public by preventing unqualified persons from practicing their professions. Although nearly all states have such provisions, the statutes in most cases are difficult to interpret.[34] For example, these statutes refer to persons who are insane, of unsound mind, or incompetent, without specifically defining these terms. Moreover, most states place the power of suspension or revocation of licenses in the hands of the appropriate professional licensing board. Because the board is not likely to have any knowledge of the practitioner's mental condition unless he has been hospitalized or adjudged incompetent, the chance of appropriate and timely exercise of these powers is very remote.

It is physically impossible for most patients to practice their professions while in a hospital. Therefore, the statutes are obviously more applicable to patients who have been released or to those persons who are incompetent but not hospitalized. If a released patient is still mentally ill, though not to the extent that he needs hospital treatment, prohibiting him from practicing his profession seems a reasonable protection of the public interest. However, when a patient is discharged as cured the prohibition is not necessary, and proper care should be exercised to see that no such barrier blocks the former patient in his effort to resume his position in the community.

It is not clear in a number of states whether a person is entitled to have his license reinstated once he has been absolutely discharged or restored to competency. In some states a person who is involuntarily hospitalized in a mental institution is permanently deprived of his previous license.[35] In other states the license of even a voluntary patient is permanently revoked.[36] Such a provision is apt to discourage a prospective patient from applying for voluntary admission, and since the hospitalized patient is not likely to practice his profession, the provision, in most instances, is in effect a penalty unnecessarily imposed on a person willing to undergo treatment.

Professional persons usually spend many years in training and are not equipped to practice any other occupation than the one for which they have been licensed. Although this is not sufficient reason to allow them to engage in activities which they cannot perform properly, society must be extremely cautious in making any decisions which will deprive persons of their livelihood.

B. APPOINTMENT OF AGENTS

Incompetent persons are limited in their power to appoint agents just as they are in other contracts.[37] Not only is an incompetent prohibited from appointing an agent, but any simple agency that was created when the principal was competent is terminated when the principal becomes incompetent.[38]

Proposals have been made—one before the Mississippi Bar Association[39] and another by the chairman of an American Bar Association Committee[40] —recommending enabling legislation by which a person could anticipate either temporary or per-

32. See Table 9.1, Restrictions on Capacity To Sue and Be Sued columns.

33. See Table 9.1, Procedures Relating to Service of Process column.

34. See Table 9.3, Engagement in Occupations, for statutory restrictions on the practice of licensed professions by mentally disabled persons.

35. Ibid.

36. Ibid.

37. See Table 9.1, Restrictions on Making Contracts columns.

38. American Law Institute, *Restatement of the Law of Agency* §§ 122, 133 (1958).

39. See Wynn, "Management of Infants' and Incompetents' Property," ABA Section of Real Property, Probate and Trust Law, *Proceedings* Part I, 96 (1956).

40. Wynn, "A Vacuum in Our Law-Management of Property of Quasi Incompetent Persons," ABA Section of Real Property, Probate and Trust Law, *Proceedings* Part I, 27 (1956).

manent incompetency in the same way as he may now anticipate death: by drawing a will and appointing an executor. Under such a plan a person would select a personal representative to act for him if at some future time he should become incapable of acting for himself. The ABA chairman said in part:

> I have always felt that there was one thing paramount in the matter of wills . . . namely, so long as it did not violate the public policy, so long as it was legal, the wish of the testator should prevail. I still think that principle is sound. I suggest there is no reason why a thinking man, realizing that he may at any moment by reason of accident or illness or old age become incompetent, should not anticipate that incompetency; or should not be given machinery by which he can anticipate that incompetency. And in those circumstances, his wishes should prevail, just as his wishes should prevail in the matter of his will.[41]

The aim of such proposals, of course, is to abolish the rule whereby the incompetency of the principal terminates the agency. Whether the agent is labeled an executor or some otherwise designated representative, whatever terms are employed or analogies drawn regarding the document of the appointment, in essence the proponents are saying that, in view of the similarity of their respective situations, there is little reason for a rule which fails to give an incompetent the same privilege as a testator.

C. Driver's Licenses

A person's inability to operate a motor vehicle properly can endanger public safety and is thus a matter of concern to the state. In most states mentally ill and mentally deficient persons cannot be issued driver's licenses,[42] and in many jurisdictions the restriction applies also to alcoholics, drug addicts, epileptics, and incompetents. Most of the statutes make the prohibition dependent upon an adjudication of the mental condition.[43] However, it is often difficult to determine by reading the statutes whether the adjudication required is for hospitalization in a mental institution or for incompetency. Some states suspend the license as soon as a person enters a mental hospital, whether as a voluntary or a compulsory patient; some do not take action unless the patient has been involuntarily hospitalized, and others are not

concerned unless there has also been an adjudication of incompetency.

Where statutes, in addition to prohibiting the original issuance, also provide for suspension or revocation, there are very few enforcement provisions.[44] While a patient is in the hospital there is no problem, but once he is released he may have access to automobiles and may become a threat to public safety.

If the motor vehicle laws are to protect the public and safeguard the rights of the mentally disabled, several questions must be decided: To whom should the restriction apply? Should the right be renewed when the patient is released on a conditional discharge or only when he receives an absolute discharge? Perhaps the ability to drive varies from patient to patient and should be determined by the hospital when the patient is discharged, either absolutely or conditionally.

Although it is important to prevent persons likely to endanger themselves or others from operating motor vehicles, it is equally important to see that persons are not unnecessarily deprived of this privilege. A discharged patient faces many problems in learning to live again in society. Opportunities for employment and recreation are essential to his rehabilitation and the operation of a motor vehicle is an important aid and factor in this convalescence.

IV. POLITICAL ACTIVITIES

A. The Franchise Right

According to most laws the right to vote—like many other rights and privileges of citizenship—cannot be exercised by the "feebleminded" or "insane."[45] What these terms mean with reference to the right to vote is not established by statutes or by case law.

Are all patients in mental institutions automatically excluded from this right? Puerto Rico specifically says that mental patients may not vote.[46] The lack of a definition in most state statutes makes it difficult to determine whether the prohibition is applicable only to persons hospitalized in mental institutions, whether it extends only to those legally adjudged incompetent, whether both classes are encompassed, or whether the law is even broader and applies to any mentally ill person, hospitalized or at large, adjudged incompetent or not.

Although some states and the Draft Act provide that patients may vote unless they have been adjudi-

---

41. Id. at 29.

42. See Table 9.4, Voting, Holding Office, Jury Service and Driver's License, Driving columns.

43. Ibid.

44. Ibid.

45. See Table 9.4, Voting columns.

46. *P.R. Laws Ann.* tit. 16, § 10 (1961).

cated incompetent, the exercise of voting rights by competent patients may be restricted by considerations of hospital administration and each patient's medical welfare.[47] Even where the patient's right to vote is not affirmatively withdrawn, it is still not known whether hospitals do in fact provide an opportunity for the patient to exercise the right. Unless a balloting place is provided on the premises or the patient is permitted to go to a public polling place, the right cannot be actually exercised except by absentee ballot. Even if state laws permit him to vote by absentee ballot, in many states the patient may not do so freely because of correspondence restrictions.[48]

Very few states have any administrative machinery for disenfranchising persons other than those in mental institutions.[49] Minnesota requires judges to report persons who have been placed under guardianship to the Commissioner of Registrations, who is to destroy the incompetent's registration card.[50] Persons who have been restored to capacity or discharged from a mental hospital are also reported to the commissioner, and he is required to inform them that they must reregister if they desire to vote.[51] A few other states provide by statute that the registration of patients is to be cancelled, but give no explanation of how this is to be accomplished.

B. Public Office and Jury Service

The problems connected with the effect of mental illness upon the holding of public office are quite similar to those in the area of voting: most statutes on the subject state that one of the requirements for holding public office is that the person be a qualified voter.[52]

With the rather recent enactment in many states of temporary or observational hospitalization provisions, there has been an increase in the number of persons able to return to their normal activities within a short time. For this reason it might be advisable to allow the temporary or observational period to expire before depriving the patient of his right to hold office. Only if indeterminate hospitalization is necessary should this right be finally abridged.

By and large, the problems of jury service are also substantially the same as those having to do with voting: many jurisdictions require a candidate for jury duty to be a qualified voter.[53] From the practical standpoint of initially selecting prospective jurors, the mentally disabled who are hospitalized present no problem. Problems do arise, however, with persons who are conditionally released or who although not hospitalized are under an adjudication of incompetency. Because of screening procedures both at the initial selection of prospective jurors and at the *voir dire* examination in each jury trial, the incapacity of a person is more apt to be detected there than when the person attempts to vote.

C. Payment of Taxes

Incompetents are not granted general relief from all tax burdens. Yet, many states exempt from certain types of taxation persons who have mental disabilities and/or are under guardianship. The most common exemption is from payment of the poll tax,[54] which is probably based on the fact that the tax is a prerequisite to voting and that such persons cannot vote. A few states allow partial exemption from property taxes. For example, Alabama exempts the property of "insane" persons to the extent of $3,000,[55] and New Hampshire allows selectmen to make just and reasonable deductions whenever the estate is insufficient to support the "insane" person.[56] This type of exemption appears properly to be based on the premise that persons suffering from certain mental disabilities are less capable of assuming burdens of taxation than are average citizens.

In many jurisdictions the period for redeeming property which has been sold for unpaid taxes is extended in cases of persons who were suffering from mental disabilities at the time of the sale.[57] Such a provision is necessary to protect two types of incompetents. The first is incompetents who have no guardians. Despite the fact that these persons

47. National Institute of Mental Health, Federal Security Agency, *A Draft Act Governing Hospitalization of the Mentally Ill* § 21 (a) (3), at 15 (Public Health Service Pub. No. 51, 1952) [hereinafter cited as *Draft Act*]. The *Draft Act* is reproduced as Appendix A to this Report. See also Table 9.4, Voting column.

48. See chap. 5, "Rights of Hospitalized Patients," and Table 5.1, Correspondence and Visitation.

49. See Table 9.4, Voting Enforcement column.

50. Ibid. *Minn. Stat.* § 201.15 (Supp. 1969).

51. Ibid.

52. See Table 9.4, Holding Public Office columns.

53. Id. at Jury column.

54. E.g., *Neb. Rev. Stat.* § 77-1611 (1966); *N.H. Rev. Stat. Ann.* § 72:1 (1955).

55. *Ala. Code* tit. 51, § 2(f) (1958).

56. *N.H. Rev. Stat. Ann.* § 75:6 (1955).

57. *Ark. Stat. Ann.* §§ 84-1201, 84-1211 to 1216 (1960); *Iowa Code Ann.* § 447.7 (1949).

may have assets which are more than adequate to pay their taxes, their disability may prevent them from understanding their financial position and obligations. The extra time would allow them to acquire a guardian or to recover to competency. The second type consists of persons whose illness has affected their income to the extent that they are unable to pay their taxes. The extension period allows them time to acquire the income necessary to redeem their property.

A United States Supreme Court case, *Covey v. Town of Somers*,[58] illustrates the problems in this area. The incompetent had been a long-time resident of a New York community and was known to be incompetent by local residents and tax officials. She did not pay her property taxes over a period of years, but was at all times able to meet her financial obligations. In accordance with a New York statute, she was notified by mail and publication that a foreclosure action would be brought if the taxes were not paid within a specified period. After the expiration of the statutory period for redemption or answer, a judgment of foreclosure was entered. Shortly after this action the incompetent was hospitalized in a mental institution and a guardian was appointed. The guardian failed in an attempt to redeem the land and sought appellate relief, alleging that the New York statute as applied in this case violated the due process clause of the Fourteenth Amendment of the United States Constitution. The Supreme Court of the United States upheld his contention and said:

> Assuming . . . that the taxpayer . . . was wholly unable to understand the nature of the proceedings against her property (from which it must be inferred that she was unable to avail herself of the statutory procedure for redemption or answer), *and* that the town authorities knew her to be an unprotected incompetent, we must hold that compliance with the statute would not afford notice to the incompetent and that a taking under such circumstances would be without due process of law.[59]

While the court held for the incompetent in this case, the decision probably will not aid the average tax-delinquent incompetent. The court placed great emphasis on the fact that the officials concerned in the foreclosure action knew that the taxpayer was incompetent.[60] This may not be true in the average

58. 351 U.S. 141 (1956).

59. Id. at 147.

60. Cf. Merchant v. Davies, 224 F.2d 347, 348 (D.C. Cir. 1957).

community, and it is doubtful, therefore, that the *Somers* decision will be applicable to a different fact situation. Consequently, the best protection for the incompetent appears to be a statute similar to that of West Virginia, which allows the redemption of real estate by the payment of the amount required for redemption at any time within one year after removal of the disability but in no event more than twenty years after the sale was confirmed.[61]

V. SPECIAL BENEFITS

A. Pensions and Veterans' Benefits

In order to evaluate the rights of the mentally disabled in connection with pension rights, two questions must first be answered: (1) Are there pension rights or benefits which would take effect because of a mental disability? (2) When mentally ill persons are entitled to pensions or benefits for any reason, are the payments distributed in a manner different from that used for "normal" persons?

Veterans are entitled to benefits for mental as well as for physical disabilities. It is not known how many other pension or benefit plans come into effect upon the occurrence of mental disability. Whether persons should be entitled to pensions for mental disability would depend to some extent on the theory underlying the granting of such benefits for physical disabilities. If the physical disability must be of a permanent nature before benefits accrue, this requirement should also apply to mental disorders. Mental illness is often sufficiently curable for persons to reestablish normal, productive lives, and the condition would have to exist for a period of time before its incurability could be determined. In most of the states that grant divorce on the grounds of incurable mental illness, the illness must have lasted for at least three years before it is considered incurable;[62] a similar provision might prove workable for pensions.

An intensive investigation of pension policies would have to be undertaken before a decision is reached on whether mental and physical disabilities should be treated similarly. However, it should be remembered that a person whose mental disability is incurable is less capable of supporting himself than most persons suffering from physical disabilities.

Many mentally disabled persons may be covered by pension plans providing benefits because of age, accident, or physical disease. Various agencies and

61. *W. Va. Code Ann.* § 11A-4-34 (1966).

62. See chap. 7, "Domestic Relations."

insurers have different rules for the disposition of these benefits when the recipient is mentally disabled. Some will continue to send installments to the disabled person or will pay them to the family. Others will turn the money over to a guardian or keep it for the person until he is discharged from the mental institution.

The Uniform Veterans' Guardianship Act[63] provides a procedure for the protection of persons who are beneficiaries of money disbursed by the United States Veterans Administration. Most states have adopted, with some variations, either the original Act of 1928 or the 1942 revision which superseded it.[64] This Uniform Act provides that any relative or friend of a veteran, or any person authorized by law, may petition for the appointment of a guardian, and if the designated persons cannot or do not petition then any resident of the state may file therefor.[65] If a petition requesting the appointment of a guardian for a mentally incompetent veteran is filed, then the certificate from the administrator or his duly authorized representative stating that the person has been rated incompetent by the Veterans Administration is prima facie evidence of the necessity for such appointment.[66] The Act is a laudable attempt to simplify the difficult problems of the Veterans Administration in dealing with large numbers of mentally disabled persons who are entitled to veterans' benefits.

The revision in 1952 of the Illinois Mental Health Act appears to have been an attempt to solve this problem of guardianship for veterans. Under the former law there was only one classification: "mentally ill person"; such a person was defined in part as being "incapable of managing and caring for his own estate."[67] This meant that a guardian was necessary in all cases of mentally ill veterans. The 1952 revision created two classes of mental patients: the "mentally ill person," who is incapable of managing his property, and the "person in need of mental treatment," whose ability to manage his property is not at issue.[68] This distinction appears to have been developed primarily to enable dealing with veterans without appointing a guardian.[69] Although the idea that not all persons who need hospitalization are incompetent is a sound one, this law was criticized as lending itself to arbitrary administration. Today the Illinois Mental Health Code defines mental illness in terms of the need for treatment, while the competency of mentally ill persons is a separate question dealt with in a different part of the statutes.[70]

B. INSURANCE

1. MENTALLY DISABLED PERSONS AS PARTIES INSURED

Contracts of insurance made with mentally disabled persons are subject to the same rules concerning validity as apply to ordinary contracts made with such persons.[71]

Interesting and difficult questions arise when the insured becomes mentally ill and is unable to comply with the condition of the policy. If the insured does not pay his premiums, the insurer is discharged from the contract even though the nonperformance is wholly due to the insured's mental disability.[72] Some courts, however, have held that where the "insanity" of the insured is the cause of his failure to pay premiums, and where proof of such disability "would entitle the insured to have the premium payment waived, insanity will excuse his failure to give the required notice."[73] Furthermore, if the mental disability of the insured person interferes with his ability to comply with his contractual obligations of giving notice and proofs of loss, the insurer is not relieved of his liability under the insurance contract.[74]

An insured person who is mentally disabled cannot change his beneficiary or execute a valid assessment of his policy.[75] In these matters the courts

63. 9C *Uniform Laws Annotated* 323 (1957).

64. 9C *U.L.A.* at 67 (Supp. 1959); National Conference of Commissioners on Uniform State Laws, *Handbook* 241–42 (1967).

65. Uniform Veterans' Guardianship Act (as revised) § 5(1) in 9C *U.L.A.* 326 (1957).

66. Id. § 7, 9C *U.L.A.* at 328.

67. Ch. 91-1/2, § 1 [1945] Ill. Laws 63d Gen. Assembly 871 (repealed 1951).

68. Ch. 91-1/2, §§ 1-8, 1-9 [1951] Ill. Laws 67th Gen. Assembly 1585 (repealed 1963).

69. Illinois Legislative Council, "Mental Hospital Admissions and Discharges" 3, 29 (Bull. No. 2-550, January 1956).

70. Ill. Rev. Stat. ch. 91-1/2, § 1-8 (1969); Ill. Rev. Stat. ch. 3, §§ 112, 113 (1969). For a criticism of the two-definitions solution of the 1952 revision, see Illinois Legislative Council (Bull. 1956), *supra* note 69. See also chap. 8, "Incompetency, Guardianship, and Restoration," regarding the general legislative trend toward separation of the issues of hospitalization and competency.

71. Vance, *Insurance* 151 (1959).

72. Id. at 152.

73. Ibid.

74. Ibid.

75. For change of beneficiary see Sluder v. National Americans, 101 Kan. 320, 166 P. 482 (1917); Taylor v. United States, 113

apply essentially the same test as that applied in determining whether a person has the mental capacity to execute other legal instruments.[76] However, when a question of double payment by the insurance company arises from its having paid the proceeds of the policy to the insured's assignee or second-designated beneficiary without knowledge that the insured was mentally disabled at the time he made the assignment or changed the beneficiary, the courts consistently protect the company by denying recovery to the original beneficiary.[77]

2. HEALTH INSURANCE PLANS—COVERAGE FOR MENTAL ILLNESS

Health insurance coverage for mental illness takes on added significance when we consider that the some six hundred thousand persons confined in mental hospitals in the United States are but a very small portion of the people in this country suffering from a mental illness serious enough to need treatment.[78] It was estimated a decade ago that in this country about 116 million people had some health insurance coverage for hospital care; 101 million for surgical service; 65 million for medical service in the hospital; and 9 million for physician service in the office, clinic, or home.[79] But in the midst of the multitude of health insurance plans, coverage for mental illness stood out—and to a large extent still does—as "one of the major unsolved problems of health insurance."[80]

Under growing pressure from subscribers, from public officials at both federal and state level, and

from labor's increasing militancy at the bargaining table, coverage for mental illness is now slowly expanding.[81] The commercial insurance companies—notably the Blue Cross and Blue Shield plans—demonstrate appreciable improvement in coverage of psychiatric illness, yet the benefits are still far more limited than for physical illness. There is particular resistance to covering partial hospitalization and outpatient treatment costs. In a day when emphasis is increasingly placed on community treatment to the exclusion of long-term institutionalization, such resistance is extremely inappropriate. The cost of drugs is also excluded from coverage in the standard policy. Yet the rising significance of drugs in treating hospitalized and discharged patients and in efforts to obviate the need for hospitalization argues strongly against this limitation on coverage. A step in the right direction is the Federal Employees Health Benefits program covering more than two million federal employees and some four million family members. One aspect of the program is an optional plan for outpatient care including a limited number of visits to a private psychiatrist. Medicare similarly provides some measure of comprehensiveness in mental health insurance coverage. The landmark in insurance planning, however, is the United Auto Workers Contract of 1964, which provides not only generous inpatient benefits but also major outpatient benefits and drug costs for some two and one-half million workers and their dependents. Its terms "embody the most enlightened principles of progressive psychiatric coverage." It encourages workers to *seek* treatment by providing the first five visits for therapy at no cost. "This is the obverse of most existing plans which insist upon a high deductible and heavy early co-insurance to deter utilization."

It is beyond the scope of this report to give more than this rough sketch of mental health insurance or to attempt to analyze or evaluate all existing health insurance plans. Instead the subject has been touched upon here to point out some general problem areas, to indicate the great need for adequate and comprehensive mental health insurance, and to give some notion regarding possible solutions in this area.

One commentator has stated that the major problems in extending benefits for mental illness are difficulty in terminology describing the different

---

F. Supp. 143 (W.D. Ark. 1953); assignment, Farmer's State Bank v. Kelley, 115 Ga. 733, 118 S.E. 197 (1923;) change of beneficiary and assignment, New York Life Ins. Co. v. Federal Nat'l Bank, 151 F.2d 537, 162 A.L.R. 536 (10th Cir. 1945), *cert. denied,* 327 U.S. 778 (1946).

76. Lynn v. Magness, 191 Md. 674, 62 A.2d 604 (1948); Rapp v. Rapp, 238 S.W.2d 80 (Mo. Cir. Ct. App. 1951); Taylor v. United States, 113 F. Supp. 143 (W.D. Ark. 1953).

77. See Metropolitan Life Ins. Co. v. Bramlett, 224 Ala. 437, 140 So. 752 (1932); Wodell v. John Hancock Mut. Life Ins. Co., 320 Mass. 4, 67 N.E.2d 469 (1946); change of beneficiary and assignment, New York Life Ins. Co. v. Federal Nat'l Bank, *supra,* note 75.

78. Porterfield, "Mental Health Insurance," 60 *Best's Insurance News* 32 (August 1959).

79. Reed, "Health Insurance Coverage for Mental Illness," 73 *Public Health Reports* 185 (1958).

80. Weil, "Voluntary Health Insurance," 81 *Medical Times* 477 (April 1959). See also Reed, *supra* note 79, at 185; Bennett, Hargrove, & Eagle, "Voluntary Health Insurance and Nervous and Mental Disease," 151 *A.M.A.J.* 202 (1953).

81. See National Committee Against Mental Illness, *What Are the Facts About Mental Illness in the United States?* 51 (1966). The remainder of the paragraph in the text, including quotes, is based on this source at 51–60.

mental illnesses and personality and character disorders, lack of actuarial information, and the high cost of psychiatric treatment.[82] Another commentator ascribes the lack of such coverage, in part, to the long duration of mental illness, to its having been traditionally considered as separate and apart from other illnesses, and to the fact that much of the hospitalization for mental illness is provided in government hospitals at little or no cost to the mentally ill person or his family.[83]

In many cases, adequate coverage for mental illness would be extremely beneficial to the mentally ill person. In view of the present overcrowded and understaffed condition of many state institutions, private care—financed through hospitalization insurance—would afford a mentally ill person a better alternative for treatment of his illness than hospitalization in large public institutions.

Better coverage for mental illness could, among other things, result in an increase in private facilities for therapeutic treatment, thus relieving some of the present burden on public institutions and reducing the cost to taxpayers. One writer comments: "If the voluntary hospitals are going to construct short-term psychiatric units, the prepaid medical care plans have the responsibility of attempting to extend broader coverage for mental illness."[84] The question of what role hospitalization insurance can play in the treatment of mental illness is one that deserves most careful study and research. It involves not only such questions as cost and whether they can be determined but also how mental hospitals should be financed and the parts that the patient, private insurance, and government should play in this financing.[85]

VI. CONCLUSIONS AND RECOMMENDATIONS

1. *Insofar as limitations on personal and property rights are related to the competency issue or are in fact affected by competency determinations, the recommendations and conclusions made in chapter 8 apply here.*

2. *Effective enforcement provisions should be part of every statute granting certain rights or privileges or prohibiting certain acts on the part of the mentally disabled.*

82. Weil, "Health Insurance and Mental Illness," 33 *J. Am. Hospital Ass'n* 103 (Mar. 1, 1959).

83. Reed, *supra* note 79, at 185.

84. Weil, *supra* note 82, at 48.

85. Reed, *supra* note 79, at 189–90.

If society is to be protected in those areas in which protection is deemed necessary, proper enforcement machinery must accompany statutory prohibitions. By the same token, protection should be afforded to the mentally disabled by machinery which facilitates the exercise of those rights they retain.

BIBLIOGRAPHY

American Jurisprudence. San Francisco: Bancroft-Whitney Co.; Rochester, N.Y.: Lawyers Co-operative Publishing Co.
"Insane and Other Incompetent Persons." 29 (1960) § 117.

American Law Institute. *Restatement of the Law of Agency.* St. Paul: American Law Institute Publishers, 1958.

American Law Reports Annotated. San Francisco: Bancroft-Whitney Co.; Rochester, N.Y.: Lawyers Co-operative Publishing Co.
"Admissibility and Probative Force on Issue as to Mental Condition, of Evidence that One Had Been Adjudged Incompetent or Insane, or Had Been Confined in Insane Asylum." 7 (1920) 568.

Bennett, A. E., M.D.; Hargrove, E. A., M.D.; and Engle, Bernice, M.A. "Voluntary Health Insurance and Nervous and Mental Disease." 151 *Journal of the American Medical Association* 202 (January 17, 1953).

Blackstone, Sir William. *Commentaries on the Laws of England.* 9th ed. by RI. Burn, LL.D., vol. 1. London: W. Strahan, T. Cadell, & D. Prince, 1783.

Comment, "The Mentally Ill and the Law of Contracts." 29 *Temple Law Review* 380 (1956).

Green, Milton D. "Public Policies Underlying the Law of Mental Incompetency." 38 *Michigan Law Review* 1189 (1940).

Illinois Legislative Council. *Mental Hospital Admissions and Discharges.* Bull. 2-550. Springfield: January, 1956.

National Committee Against Mental Illness. *What Are the Facts About Mental Illness in the United States?* Washington, D.C.: National Committee Against Mental Illness, Inc., 1966.

National Conference of Commissioners on Uniform State Laws. *Handbook.* Baltimore: Lord Baltimore Press, Inc., 1959.

National Institute of Mental Health. Federal Security Agency. *A Draft Act Governing Hospitalization of the Mentally Ill.* Public Health Service Pub. no. 51. Washington, D.C.: Government Printing Office, 1952.

Note, "Real Property—Validity of Conveyance by Mental Incompetents." 3 *Wayne Law Review* 73 (1956).

Page, William Herbert. *Treatise on the Law of Wills.* Vol. 1. Cincinnati: W. H. Anderson Co., 1941.

Porterfield, John D., M.D. "Mental Health Insurance." 60 *Best's Insurance News* 32 (August 1959).

Reed, Louis S. "Health Insurance Coverage for Mental Illness." United States Department of Health, Education, and Welfare. Public Health Service. 73 *Public Health Reports* 185 (1958).

Stephens, S. "Probate Psychiatry—Examination of Testamentary Capacity by a Psychiatrist as a Subscribing Witness." 25 *Illinois Law Review* 276 (1930).

Uniform Laws Annotated. Brooklyn: Edward Thompson Co.
"Uniform Veterans' Guardianship Act." 9C (1957) 318.

Vance, William R. *Vance on Insurance.* 3d ed. by Buist M. Anderson. (Previous editions under title of *Handbook of the Law of Insurance.*) St. Paul: West Publishing Co., 1951.

Weil, Thomas P. "Health Insurance and Mental Illness." 33 *Journal of the American Hospital Association* 48 (March 1, 1959).

———. "Voluntary Health Insurance." 81 *Medical Times* 477 (April 1959). East Stroudsburg, Pa.: Romaine, Pierson Publishers, Inc.

Williston, Samuel. *A Treatise on the Law of Contracts.* 3d ed. vol. 2. Mount Kisco, N.Y.: Baker, Voorhis & Co., Inc., 1959.

Wynn, James O. "Management of Infants' and Incompetents' Property." American Bar Association Section of Real Property, Probate and Trust Law. *Proceedings,* Part 1. Chicago: American Bar Association, 1956.

———. "A Vacuum in Our Law—Management of Property of Quasi Incompetent Persons." American Bar Association Section of Real Property, Probate and Trust Law. *Proceedings,* Part 1. Chicago: American Bar Association, 1956.

CASES

Banks v. Goodfellow, L.R. 5 Q.B. 549 (1870).

Covey v. Town of Somers, 351 U.S. 141 (1956).

Farmers State Bank v. Kelley, 115 Ga. 733, 118 S.E. 197 (1923).

In re Alexieff's Will, 94 N.Y.S.2d 32 (Sur. Ct. 1949), *aff'd* 227 App. Div. 790, 97 N.Y.S.2d 532 (1950), *motion for leave to appeal denied,* 227 App. Div. 901, 98 N.Y.S.2d 582 (1950).

Lynn v. Magness, 191 Md. 674, 62 A.2d 604 (1948).

Merchant v. Davies, 244 F.2d 347 (D.C. Cir. 1957).

Metropolitan Life Ins. Co. v. Bramlett, 224 Ala. 437, 140 So. 752 (1932).

New York Life Ins. Co. v. Federal Nat'l Bank, 151 F.2d 537, 162 A.L.R. 536 (10th Cir. 1945), *cert. denied,* 327 U.S. 778 (1946).

Rapp v. Rapp, 238 S.W.2d 80 (Mo. Cir. Ct. App. 1951).

Roller v. Kurtz, 6 Ill. 2d 618, 129 N.E.2d 693 (1955).

Rubenstein v. Dr. Pepper Co., 228 F.2d 528 (8th Cir. 1955).

Sluder v. National Americans, 101 Kan. 320, 166 P. 482 (1917).

Taylor v. United States, 113 F. Supp. 143 (W.D. Ark. 1953).

Wodell v. John Hancock Mut. Life Ins. Co., 320 Mass. 4, 67 N.E.2d 469 (1946).

Table 9.1 · PERSONAL AND PROPERTY RIGHTS OF THE MENTALLY DISABLED

| STATE | RESTRICTIONS ON MAKING CONTRACTS | | | LIABILITY FOR NECESSARIES | RESTRICTIONS ON CAPACITY TO SUE AND BE SUED | | PROCEDURES RELATING TO | |
	Incompetent	Mentally Ill	VALIDITY OF CONTRACTS		Incompetent	Mentally Ill	Service of Process	Extension of Time Limitation on Actions
DRAFT ACT	fn. 1 21(a)(3)	fn. 1 21(a)(3)	valid unless adjudicated incompetent. 21(a)(3)					
ALA. Code (1958)	9, §43	9, §43	void generally, 9, 43; however, subject to suit upon a ward's contract. 7, §106 except that conveyances of and mortages upon real property are not void, but insane party may have an action. 9, §41; 9, §42	7, §106; 9, §43; 57, §8	personal injury 7, §103; other than personal injury 7, §104; guardian may sue for use of ward 7, §105	wife or mother may prosecute or defend where husband or father confined but not declared insane. 7, §100	insane resident--guardian or guardian ad litem with or without service on insane person, as court directs. 7, §196 insane nonresident defendant--on defendant, but if guardian or if hospitalized, then on guardian or person in charge of hospital. 7, §200	20 years. 7, §36 no default judgment. 33, §53 contested wills. 61, §66 claims against insolvent estate. 61, §401
ALAS. Stat. (1962)	fnn. 1, 2 47.30.150(a)(3)	fnn. 1, 2 47.30.150(a)(3)	valid unless adjudicated incompetent. 47.30.150(a)(3)					for workmen's compensation: so long as incompetent has no guardian. 23.30.105 action to claimed escheated property: limitation extended until 1 year after disability ceases. 09.50.110 generally: limitation extended until 2 years after disability ceases. 09.10.140(2)
ARIZ. Rev. Stat. Ann. (1956)		insanity of a general partner dissolves the partnership. 65-320(1966)			incompetent must be represented. R. Civ. P. 14-809C 17(g)		adjudicated insane or mentally incompetent--on person & guardian; if no guardian, then on person & such other person as court designates. R. Civ. P. 4(d)(4) nonresident insane or incompetent person--motor vehicle cases--same as if sui juris nonresident. R. Civ. P. 4(d)(5) in decedent estate matters--on guardian of insane or incompetent person. 14-1222	limitation runs from removal of disability. 12-502 recovery of real property. 12-528 actions against state. 12-822
ARK. Stat. Ann. (1947)					where there is guardian of estate, he represents ward. 57-627 (Supp. 1967)		on insane person & guardian; if no guardian, on wife, person having his care, or with whom he lives, or keeper of asylum. 27-337 (1962) on ward and guardian of estate. 57-627 (Supp. 1967)	3 years after removal of disability. 37-226 (1962) redemption of lands forfeited to the state. 84-1211 (1960)
CAL. Civ. Code (West 1954)	after adjudication of incapacity, person of unsound mind cannot contract. 40 (Supp. 1968)	person entirely without understanding has no power to contract. 38 contracts of person of unsound mind but not without understanding--before adjudication, subject to rescission. 39	invalid if one party is without capacity to contract. 1557 subject to rescission if one party is of unsound mind, but not entirely without understanding. 39	person entirely without understanding liable for reasonable value of things necessary for support of himself or his family. 38	guardian or conservator to represent ward, unless another person appointed. Prob. 1501, 1852 (1956) (Supp. 1968) guardian ad litem may be appointed. Civil Pro. 372 (Supp. 1968)	guardian ad litem may be appointed. Civil Pro. 372 (Supp. 1968)	on incompetent person and on conservator or guardian if one has been appointed. Civil Pro. 411.4 (Supp. 1968)	generally, limitation runs from removal of disability. Civil Pro. 352 (1968) but in certain actions, disability may not exceed 20 years. Civil Pro. 328 (1968)

Table 9.1 PERSONAL AND PROPERTY RIGHTS OF THE MENTALLY DISABLED *continued*

STATE	RESTRICTIONS ON MAKING CONTRACTS — Incompetent	RESTRICTIONS ON MAKING CONTRACTS — Mentally Ill	VALIDITY OF CONTRACTS — Incompetent	VALIDITY OF CONTRACTS — Mentally Ill	LIABILITY FOR NECESSARIES	RESTRICTIONS ON CAPACITY TO SUE AND BE SUED — Incompetent	RESTRICTIONS ON CAPACITY TO SUE AND BE SUED — Mentally Ill	PROCEDURES — Service of Process	PROCEDURES — Extension of Time Limitation on Actions
COLO. Rev. Stat. Ann. (1964)	person making a contract with an insane person may be bound. 71-1-27	person making a contract with an insane person may be bound. 71-1-21	contracts void as against insane person; person making contract with insane person may be bound at election of insane person's conservator. 71-1-21			incompetent must be represented. R. Civ. P. 17(c)		upon conservator, R. Civ. P. 4(e)(3); if no conservator, then upon mental incompetent. 153-10-27	limitation runs from removal of disability. 87-1-17 87-2-1 to 87-2-7
CONN. Gen. Stat. Ann. (1958)	during pendency of application. 45-73		when application for conservator pending--if application recorded, no contract between time of recordings and adjudication shall be valid without court approval. 45-73					if person confined in institution for mentally ill, to superintendent of institution and commissioner of finance & control. 4-68(f) (Supp. 1969)	4 years after gaining legal capacity on contract under seal; 52-573; & 3 years on simple or implied contracts. 52-576
DEL. Code Ann. (1953)	with regard to property forming subject matter of guardianship. 12, §3914(e) (Supp. 1970)					shall be represented by guardian or trustee; if neither, by guardian ad litem. Ch. Ct. R. 17(c); Super. Ct. R. 17(c)		upon trustee or guardian. Super. (Civ.)Ct. R. 4(f)(1)(ii)(c) (Supp. 1968) 10, §362	3 years after removal of disability. 10, §8115
D.C. Code Ann. (1967)	21-564(a)		valid unless adjudicated incompetent. 31-564(a) void if made after filing for conservatorship. 21-1507		21-1507	conservator may sue or be sued in representative capacity. 21-1503 appointment of guardian ad litem if non compos mentis. Fed. R. Civ. P. 17(c); Ct. of Gen. Sess. R. 17(b)	appointment of guardian ad litem if non compos mentis. Fed. R. Civ. P. 17(c); Ct. of Gen. Sess. R. 17(b)	on person non compos mentis and committee or guardian ad litem. 13-333	generally, limitation as runs from removal of disability. 12-301(a)
FLA. Stat. Ann. (1964)	394.22(10)(a)		after adjudication, person presumed incapable of making any contract binding on him or his estate; filing of judgment is notice of incapacity. 394.22(10)(a)			guardian to be joined in any action, unless his interest is adverse to that of ward; then, guardian ad litem to be appointed. 744.61		incompetents 48.041 (Supp. 1969)	for 12 months after appointment of guardian. 744.62, 744.63 95.05, 95.20 (Supp. 1969) 95.31
GA. Code Ann. (1963)	if adjudged insane, lunatic or non compos mentis, contracts are void, and even if restored to sanity, void until guardianship dissolved. 20-206 (1965)	contract of an insane person, a lunatic or a person non compos mentis, who has never been adjudicated to be insane, a lunatic or of unsound mind, is not absolutely void, but only voidable, except that a contract made by a person during a lucid interval is valid without ratification. 20-206 (1965)	void if adjudicated insane or incompetent; voidable if not so adjudicated. 20-206 (1965)		one may recover for necessaries furnished an insane person, a lunatic or a person non compos mentis. 20-206 (1965)	by guardian, or if none, by next of friend or guardian ad litem. 81A-117(c) 81A-125(b) (1967)		on incompetent, and on guardian if any. 81-212 (Supp. 1968)	limitation runs from removal of disability. 3-801, 3-802 (1962)
HAWAII Rev. Stat. Ann. (1968)	551-32	fn. 1 334-57	fn. 3 valid unless right to contract is suspended by the hospital. 334-57, 551-32		fn. 3 551-32			fn. 4 334-58	limitation runs from removal of disability. 657-34
IDAHO Code (1947)	no capacity if adjudicated incompetent. 32-108 (1963)	fn. 1 66-346(a)(3) (Supp. 1969)	subject to recission if made before adjudication of incompetency. 32-107(1963)			fn. 5 to be represented by guardian or guardian ad litem. 5-306	fn. 5 to be represented by guardian or guardian ad litem. 5-306	an incompetent and guardian. 5-507.5	time of disability is not a part of time limited. 5-230

316

Table 9.1   PERSONAL AND PROPERTY RIGHTS OF THE MENTALLY DISABLED   *continued*

STATE	RESTRICTIONS ON MAKING CONTRACTS — Incompetent	RESTRICTIONS ON MAKING CONTRACTS — Mentally Ill	VALIDITY OF CONTRACTS	LIABILITY FOR NECESSARIES	RESTRICTIONS ON CAPACITY TO SUE AND BE SUED — Incompetent	RESTRICTIONS ON CAPACITY TO SUE AND BE SUED — Mentally Ill	PROCEDURES RELATING TO — Service of Process	PROCEDURES RELATING TO — Extension of Time Limitation on Actions
ILL. Ann. Stat. (Smith-Hurd 1961)	29, §2	hospitalization for mental treatment does not deprive a patient of his right to enter into contractual relationships. 91½, §9-11 (1966) (Supp. 1969)	fn. 6 29, §2 void against incompetent. 3, §126 valid unless adjudicated incompetent. 91½, §9-11 (1966) (Supp. 1969)		fn. 5 to be represented by conservator. 3, §124			2 years after removal of disability. 83, §22 (1966)
IND. Ann. Stat. (1953)			void. 8-141		guardian to appear and represent the ward in all actions. 2-803 (1967) 8-137(a)		process to be served on guardian. 2-803 (1967), 8-137(a)	2 years after removal of disability. 2-605 (1967)
IOWA Code Ann. (1964)	no power to convey, encumber or dispose of property. 633.637		presumption of fraud in all contracts made after filing of petition for conservator. 633.638		guardian or conservator to represent ward. R. Civ. P. 12 and 13 (1951) (Supp. 1969) 633.646(1)	guardian ad litem appointed to defend. R. Civ. P. 12 and 13 (1951) (Supp. 1969)	upon person and guardian or conservator, or upon head of hospital. R. Civ. P. 56(c) to 56(e) (1951) (Supp. 1969)	1 year after termination of disability. 614.8 (1950) (Supp. 1969)
KAN. Stat. Ann. (1964)	59-1402 (Supp. 1968)	subject to hospital regulations. 59-2930 (Supp. 1968)	59-2930 (Supp. 1968)		a guardian shall appear in defense of all incapacitated persons. 59-2205, 60-217 (Supp. 1968)		service to be made upon an incapacitated person by personal service, & guardian service to be made in the same manner. 60-304 (Supp. 1968)	1 year after removal of disability. 60-515(a) (Supp. 1968)
KY. Rev. Stat. Ann. (1969)		fn. 1 202.272(1)(3) (Supp. 1969)	valid unless adjudicated incompetent. 202.272(1)(3)		guardian to represent the ward. 287.130, 287.230(1)			3 years after removal of disability. 413.020
LA. Civ. Code Ann. (West 1952)	32	insane disqualified. 31	31 void. 1788 if suit is by the incapable--enforceable. 1791		mental incompetent does not have the procedural capacity to sue; curator enforces interdict's rights. Code Civ. Pro. Ann. 684 (1960)			3522
ME. Rev. Stat. Ann. (1964)	18, §3603	fn. 1 34, §2254(3) (Supp. 1969)	void. 18, §3603; valid unless adjudicated incompetent. 34, §2254(3) (Supp. 1969)	18, §3603	guardian to appear. 18, §3505	18, §3507		within the time limited after the disability is removed. 14, §853
MD. Ann. Code (1963)	court has power to delegate person's right or power to manage his property or estate, if such is adjudged a lunatic or non compos mentis. 16, §147 (1966)				guardian or committee is to appear, answer & defend for party. Rules 205d, 205e (Supp. 1968)	Rules 205d, 205e (Supp. 1968)	service on party & parent or guardian of disabled person. Rules 119, 306c4 (Supp. 1968)	within the respective times so limited after the disability is removed. 57, §2 (1968)
MASS. Ann. Laws (1955)	spendthrifts. 201, §10		void. 201, §10	201, §10	guardian is to represent the ward in all suits. 201, §37			personal action may be commenced within the time hereinbefore limited after the disability is removed. 260, §7 (1968) real actions within 10 years after such disability is removed. 260, §25 (1968)
MICH. Comp. Laws Ann. (1967)				330.27, 600.2928(1)	fn. 5 703.18		service upon guardian. 600.1913	1 year after disability is removed. 600.5851(1)

Table 9.1   PERSONAL AND PROPERTY RIGHTS OF THE MENTALLY DISABLED   *continued*

| STATE | RESTRICTIONS ON MAKING CONTRACTS | | | | RESTRICTIONS ON CAPACITY TO SUE AND BE SUED | | PROCEDURES | RELATING TO |
	Incompetent	Mentally Ill	VALIDITY OF CONTRACTS	LIABILITY FOR NECESSARIES	Incompetent	Mentally Ill	Service of Process	Extension of Time Limitation on Actions
MINN. Stat. Ann. (1969)	525.543		fn. 3 525.543	fn. 3 525.543 525.56.3(1) 525.56.3(2)	fn. 5 525.56.3(3)		501.27(1947)	5 years after removal of disability in foreclosure sale. 580.20(1947) suspension until disability is removed. 541.15 (1947) (Supp. 1969)
MISS. Code Ann. (1956)							fn. 7 1864, 6946-08 (1952)	within time limits after removal of disability. 738
MO. Rev. Stat. (1962)	subject to hospital regulations. 202.847.1(3)		fn. 8 valid unless adjudicated incompetent. 202.847.1(3) 475.345 (1956)		fn. 5 475.130.3 (1956) (Supp. 1969)		fn. 9 472.100.2(1), 472.100.5 (1956) (Supp. 1969) 506.150 (1949)	within 3 years after removal of disability for real actions. 516.030 (1949) within respective times after removal of disability for personal actions. 516.170 (1949)
MONT. Rev. Codes Ann. (1961)	13-201, 13-202(1967) 64-108, 64-110, 64-112	fn. 10 64-111	fn. 11 64-112	64-108	fn. 5 R. Civ. P. 17(c) 93-2806.3 (1963)		fn. 12 R. Civ. P. 4D(2)(d)(1963) (Supp. 1969)	fn. 13 R. Civ. P. 4D(2)(d)(1963) (Supp. 1969)
NEB. Rev. Stat. (1968)	real estate 38-701 to 38-705	38-701 to 38-705	38-301, 38-304	38-304	fn. 5 38-502			5 years after removal of disability for recovery of estate sold by guardian 38-628 any action within respective time limits after removal of disability. 25-213
NEV. Rev. Stat. (1967)		435.725	valid unless adjudicated incompetent. 433.725		fn. 5 159.270.2 Justices' Courts R. Civ. P. 17(e) Nev. R. Civ. P. 17c		Justices' Courts R. Civ. P. 4(d)(4) Nev. R. Civ. P. 4(d)(4)	2 years on real property action. 11.180.2 time of disability shall not be part of time limit in all other actions. 11.250.2 1 year on right to sue. 11.280
N.H. Rev. Stat. Ann. (1968)	462:27, 464:9		invalid. 462:27, 464:9		fn. 5 462:28		462:1, 462:4	5 years after removal of disability on real actions. 508:3 2 years after disability is removed in personal actions. 508:8
N.J. Stat. Ann. (1953)	fn. 14 3A:22-1, 3A:22-3		fn. 14 3A:22-1		fn. 15 2A:15-1 (1952)			2A:14-21
N.M. Stat. Ann. (1953)	34-2-15a(3)	fn. 1 34-2-15a(3)	valid unless adjudicated incompetent. 34-2-15a(3)		fn. 5 21-1-1(17)(a), 21-6-13, 21-6-14, 21-6-16, & in Supp. 1967, 32-2-3	21-1-1(17)(c), 21-6-13, 21-6-14, 21-6-16, 21-6-17; & in Supp. 1967, 32-2-3	fn. 16 21-3-12	1 year after termination of disability. 23-1-10, 23-1-22
N.Y. Mental Hygiene Law (McKinney 1951)	100(7) (Supp. 1970)			100.105(2)	Debt & Cred. Law 250 (1945)		committee & incompetent; court has discretion to waive as to incompetent. Civ. Prac. (1963) 309(b)	3 years after the disability ceases. Civ. Prac. (1963) 208
N.C. Gen. Stat. (1953)	35-2 to 35-4 (1966)				1-64, 1-65.1 (Supp. 1967) 1-66, 1-67		fn. 7 committee or guardian & insane person. 1-66, 1-97.3	within times herein limited after removal of disability. 1-17.2, 1-19, 1-20

Table 9.1 PERSONAL AND PROPERTY RIGHTS OF THE MENTALLY DISABLED *continued*

STATE	RESTRICTIONS ON MAKING CONTRACTS			LIABILITY FOR NECESSARIES	RESTRICTIONS ON CAPACITY TO SUE AND BE SUED		PROCEDURES RELATING TO	
	Incompetent	Mentally Ill	VALIDITY OF CONTRACTS		Incompetent	Mentally Ill	Service of Process	Extension of Time Limitation on Actions
N.D. Cent. Code (1960)	fn. 17 9-02-02, 9-02-01, 14-01-01, 14-01-03	fn. 18 rescission 14-01-02	14-01-01	14-01-01	guardian must appear for & represent his ward in all suits. 30-14-06		guardian ad litem or guardian of incompetent or both. N.D. Rules of Civ. Proc. 4(d)(3)	time of such disability is not part of time limited for commencement of action. 28-01-14, 28-01-25, 28-01-30, 28-01-31 within 3 years on tax redemption. 57-26-04
OHIO Rev. Code (Baldwin 1964)	1301.03	1301.03			guardian or trustee. 2307.11, 2307.13		guardian and incompetent. 2101.27(C), 2101.29(B), (C), (E)	2305.04, 2305.16 (Supp. 1968) 2325.11
OKLA. Stat. Ann. (1966)	fn. 19 15, §11; 15, §12; 15; §16; 15, §22; 15, §44	15, §16; 15, §23	15, §22; 15, §23	15, §22	58, §803; 58, §804 (1965)		fn. 20 43A, §321; 58, §810 (1965)	2 years in actions to recover real property. 12, §94 (1960) 1 year in other types of actions. 12, §96 (1960)
ORE. Rev. Stat. (1967)	126.280		voidable if made at time ward incompetent. 126.280	126.280	guardian or guardian ad litem. 13.051		guardian and incompetent. 15.080(4)	disability shall not be part of time limited for commencement of action. 12.160(2), 12.170, 12.180
PA. Stat. Ann. (1969)	incapable to contract after adjudication. 50, §3511; 50, §3512		50, §3511		R. Civ. P. 2051 to 2075		guardian or incompetent. R. Civ. P. 2055	subject to regular limits upon removal of disability in personal actions. 12, §35 (1953) 10 years in real actions. 12, §73; 12, §82 (1953)
R.I. Gen. Laws Ann. (1956)	void after appointment of guardian & recording. 33-15-13		void 33-15-13	33-15-13	33-18-16 to 33-18-20		guardian and incompetent. 35-15-9, 33-15-25	within such time as hereinbefore limited, after such impediment is removed. 9-1-19
S.C. Code Ann. (1962)	fn. 21 32-1046				10-231, 10-236		fn. 22 guardian and incompetent. 10-435, 10-436, 10-437	time of disability is not part of time limit. 10-104(2), 10-105, 10-106 10 years in any action to recover real property. 10-128(2)
S.D. Compiled Laws Ann. (1967)	fn. 17 27-2-3	fn. 18 rescission 27-2-2, 53-2-1, 53-2-2	27-2-1	27-2-1	15-6-17(c)		fn. 7 15-6-4(d)(6)	time of disability is not part of time limited for commencement of action. 15-2-22(2), 15-2-23, 15-2-24 in real property actions. 15-3-14(2)
TENN. Code Ann. (1955)		33-1207 (Supp. 1968)	valid unless adjudicated incompetent--voluntary patients only. 33-1207 (Supp. 1968)					28-107 within regular time limitation after removal of disability. 28-107
TEX. Rev. Civ. Stat. Ann. (1958)		5547-83(b) (Supp. 1969)	voluntary patient--valid. 5547-24(c) mentally ill without adjudication--valid. 5547-83(b) (Supp. 1969)		lunatics or persons non compos mentis by guardian or next friend. 1894			time of disability is not part of time limit. 5518.3 (Supp. 1969) 5535 (Supp. 1969)

Table 9.1   PERSONAL AND PROPERTY RIGHTS OF THE MENTALLY DISABLED   continued

STATE	RESTRICTIONS ON MAKING CONTRACTS				RESTRICTIONS ON CAPACITY TO SUE AND BE SUED		PROCEDURES RELATING TO	
	Incompetent	Mentally Ill	VALIDITY OF CONTRACTS	LIABILITY FOR NECESSARIES	Incompetent	Mentally Ill	Service of Process	Extension of Time Limitation on Actions
UTAH Code Ann. (1968)	fn. 1 64-7-48(1)(c)	fn. 1 64-7-48(1)(c)	valid unless adjudicated incompetent. 64-7-48(1)(c)		insane or incompetent by general guardian or guardian ad litem. R. Civ. P. 17(b) (1953)		upon guardian--personal service. R. Civ. P. 4(e)(3) (1953) guardian unnecessary--in rem, unknown party. R. Civ. P. 17(b) (1953)	time of disability is not part of time limited for commencement of action. 78-12-36 (1953)
VT. Stat. Ann. (1958)	14, §2689	fn. 1 18, §7705(a)(3) (1968)	void 14, §2688; 14, §2689 valid unless adjudicated incompetent. 18, §7705(a)(3) (1968)		adjudged insane. 14, §2693, 12, §974 (Supp. 1969)			within times respectively limited after disability is removed. 12, §551
VA. Code Ann. (1953)					fn. 23		in personam. Rule 2:4 (1957)	10 years on action to recover land. 8-7 (1957) within time allowed after removal of disability in personal actions. 8-30 (1957)
WASH. Rev. Code Ann. (1962)	loss of legal capacity where indeterminate commitment. 27-5-4				insane person by guardian or guardian ad litem. 4.08.060		guardian 4.28.080(12) (Supp. 1968)	time of disability not be part of time limited for commencement of action. 14.16.190
W. VA. Code Ann. (1966)					if there is guardian must sue by guardian; otherwise by next friend. Rule of C.P. 17(c)		56-4-10	within regular limits after becoming sane in personal actions. 55-2-15 5 years in real estate actions. 55-2-3, 55-2-4 3 years in ejectment actions. 55-4-27
WIS. Stat. Ann. (1958)	296.02, 319.215		specific performance of contract made before incompetent. 296.02 void upon filing of petition for guardian. 319.215		general guardian or guardian ad litem. 260.22		guardian & defendant. 262-06(2)(b) (Supp. 1969)	writs of errors & appeals. 274.01(1) (Supp. 1969) time of disability is not part of time limit. 893.33 (1966)
WYO. Stat. Ann. (1957)		fn. 1 25-72 (1967)	valid unless adjudicated incompetent. 25-72(c)				guardian, person having legal custody, or guardian ad litem. R. Civ. P. 4(d)(2)	within 3 years after disability is removed. 1-22

1. Subject to the general rules and regulations of the hospital and except to the extent necessary for patient's medical welfare to impose restrictions, every patient may exercise all civil rights, including the right to enter contracts, unless he has been adjudged incompetent and not restored to legal capacity. Draft Act 21(a)(3); Alas. 47.30.150(a)(3); Hawaii 334.57; Idaho 66-345(a) (Supp. 1969); Ky. 202.272(1)(3); Me. 34, §2254(3) (Supp. 1969); N.M. 34-2-15a(3); Utah 64-7-48(1)(c); Vt. 18, §7705(a)(3); Wyo. 25-72(c).

2. If partner is declared a lunatic or shown to be of unsound mind, court shall decree a dissolution of the partnership. Alas. 32.05.270(1).

3. If guardian is appointed for incompetent after filing of petition lis pendens, all contracts except for necessaries and all transactions of real or personal property made by ward after such filing and before termination of guardianship shall be void. Hawaii 551-32; Minn. 525.543.

4. Neither administrator nor anyone connected with a psychiatric facility shall accept service of process on behalf of a patient. A legal process served on a patient shall be filed with records of the patient, and administrator or his deputy shall immediately inform the court from which the process issued, in writing, of date of service and mental and physical condition of patient. Hawaii 334-58.

5. Guardian is to appear and represent the ward in all actions. Idaho 5-306; Ill. 3-124; Mich. 703.18; Minn. 525.56; Mo. 475.130.3 (Supp. 1969); Mont. Civ. P. 17(c), 93-2806.3; Neb. 38-502; Nev. Justices' Courts R. Civ. P. 17(e), Nev. R. Civ. P. 17(c), 65.010, Nev. Rev. Stat. 159.270.2; N.H. 462:28; N.M. 21-1-1(17)(c), 21-6-13, 21-6-16, 21-6-17, 32-2-2 (Supp. 1969).

6. Void against the incompetent person but a competent party is bound. Ill. 3, §126. Contract is binding on conservator if made before adjudication of incompetency. Ill. 29, §2.

7. If institution's superintendent states that process cannot be served without danger or injury to insane person, it need not be served; the reason is to be endorsed on the summons. Miss. 1864, 6946-08; N.C. 1-97.3; S.D. 15-6-4(d)(6).

8. Contract invalid without consent of guardian and approval of court. Mo. 475.345 (1956).

9. Service is to be on guardian; if no guardian appointed, deliver personally on the incompetent or qualified members of his family or agent. Mo. 472.100.2(1), 472.100.5 (Supp. 1969), 506.150.

10. Conveyance or contract of person of unsound mind but not entirely without understanding made before his incapacity has been judicially determined is subject to recission. Mont. 64-111.

11. After his incapacity has been judicially determined, person of unsound mind may make a contract where such contract confers a beneficial interest in his estate, but he may make no others. A discharge or parole with a certificate showing "improved condition" creates a presumption of competency. Mont. 64-112.

12. Service is to be on guardian of person adjudged of unsound mind or for whom guardian has been appointed. If no guardian, court shall appoint guardian ad litem. If party is alleged, but not adjudged, to be of unsound mind, process may be on him personally. Mont. Civ. Pro. Rule 4D(2)(d) (Supp. 1969), Mont. 93-3007, 93-3007.4.

13. Court may stay any action pending against a person on learning that such person is of unsound mind. Mont. R. Civ. P. 4D(2)(d) (Supp. 1969).

14. Court may compel specific performance of a bargain, contract, or agreement made by mental incompetent when he was mentally competent, and direct his guardian to perform all acts and execute all conveyances for that purpose. N.J. 3A:22-3.

15. Every person must be of sound mind to maintain a suit. N.J. 2A:15-1.

16. If there is a guardian, service is to be on him. If no guardian, service is to be made on ward in same manner as on competent or sane person. N.M. 21-3-12.

17. After his incapacity has been judicially determined, person of unsound mind can make no conveyance or other contract, nor delegate any power nor waive any right until restored to capacity. N.D. 14-01-03; S.D. 27-2-3.

18. Conveyance or other contract of person of unsound mind, but not entirely without understanding, made before his incapacity has been determined judicially on application for appointment of guardian, is subject to recission as provided by the laws of this state. N.D. 14-01-02; S.D. 27-2-2.

19. Persons of unsound mind and persons deprived of their civil rights are incapable of contracting. Okla. 15, §11.

20. Service on committed persons is to be made by superintendent of institution. Okla. 43A, §321. Service for noncommitted persons is to be made on guardian. Okla. 58, §810.

21. Probate court determination of sanity restores incompetent's legal status to property and contractual rights. S.C. 32-1046.

22. Service is on both incompetent and guardian. S.C. 10-435. If person is committed, service is made by institution's superintendent. S.C. 10-436, 10-436.1.

23. Appointment of guardian whether person served or not. Va. 8-88 (1957). Committee may sue or be sued for ward. 37.1-139 (Supp. 1968). No action or suit on any claim or demand shall be instituted by or against ward by committee after ward's commitment and until his discharge. 37.1-140 (Supp. 1968). All actions or suits to which ward is party at time of his commitment shall be prosecuted or defended at the committee. 37.1-141 (Supp. 1968).

Table 9.2   STATUTORY DESCRIPTIONS OF PERSONS WHO MAY MAKE A WILL

STATE AND CITATION

STATUTORY PROVISIONS

DRAFT ACT

ALA. Code (1958)
  61, §§1, 2

"Every person   . . . of sound mind, may, by his last will, devise his lands, tenements, or hereditaments, or any interest, therein. . . . All persons . . . of sound mind, and no others, may also, by their last will dispose of all their personal property."

ALAS. Stat. (1962)
  13.05.010
  (Supp. 1969)

"Every person of sound mind.. . . ."

ARIZ. Rev. Stat. Ann. (1956)
  14-102

"Every person of sound mind . . . ."

ARK. Stat. Ann. (1947)
  60-401
  (Supp. 1967)

"Any person of sound mind . . . ."

CAL. Prob. Code
    (West 1956)
  20
  (Supp. 1969)

"Every person of sound mind . . . ."

COLO. Rev. Stat. Ann. (1964)
  153-5-1

"Every person . . . of sound mind and memory . . . ."

CONN. Gen. Stat. Ann. (1958)
  45-160

"Any person . . . of sound mind . . . ."

DEL. Code Ann. (1953)
  12-101

"Any person . . . of sound and disposing mind and memory . . . ."

D.C. Code Ann. (1967)
  18-102

"A will, testament, or codocil is not valid . . . unless the person making it is . . . at the time of executing or acknowledging . . . of sound and disposing mind and capable of executing a valid deed or contract."

FLA. Stat. Ann. (1959)
  731.04

"Any person . . . of sound mind . . . ."

GA. Code Ann. (1959)
  113-201

"Every person may make a will, unless laboring under some legal disability arising . . . from a want of capacity. . . ."

  113-202

"An incapacity to contract may coexist with a capacity to make a will. The amount of intellect necessary to constitute testamentary capacity is that which is necessary to enable the party to have a decided and rational desire as to the disposition of his property. His desire must be decided, as distinguished from the wavering, vacillating fancies of a distempered intellect. It must be rational, as distinguished from the ravings of a madman, the silly pratings of an idiot, the childish whims of imbecility, or the excited vagaries of a drunkard."

  113-204

"An insane person generally may not make a will. A lunatic may, during a lucid interval. A monomaniac may make a will, if the will is in no way the result of or connected with his monomania. In all such cases it must appear that the will speaks the wishes of the testator, unbiased by the mental disease with which he is affected."

  113-205

"Eccentricity of habit or thought does not deprive a person of the power of making a will; old age and weakness [of] intellect resulting therefrom does not, of itself, constitute incapacity. If the weakness amounts to. imbecility, the testamentary capacity is gone. In cases of doubt as to the extent of this weakness, the reasonable or unreasonable disposition of his estate should have much weight in the decision of the question."

STATE AND CITATION	STATUTORY PROVISIONS
HAWAII Rev. Stat. Ann. (1968) 536-1	"Every person . . . of sound mind . . . ."
IDAHO Code Ann. (1947) 14-301	"Every person . . . of sound mind . . . ."
ILL. Ann. Stat. (Smith-Hurd 1961) 3, §42	"Every person . . . of sound mind and memory . . . ."
IND. Ann. Stat. (1953) 6-501	"Any person of sound mind . . . ."
IOWA Code Ann. (1964) 633.624	"Any person of . . . mind . . . ."
KAN. Stat. Ann. (1964) 59-601	"Any person of sound mind . . . ."
KY. Rev. Stat. Ann. (1969) 394.020	"Any person of sound mind . . . ."
LA. Civ. Code Ann. (West 1952) Art. 1475	"To make a donation either inter vivos or mortis causa, one must be of sound mind."
ME. Rev. Stat. Ann. (1964) 18, §§1, 3607	"A person of sound mind . . . ." [However, the latter statute provides that a person over 21 who is under guardianship cannot dispose of his property "otherwise than by his last will."]
MD. Ann. Code (1964) 93, §349	"[P]erson . . . of sound and disposing mind, and capable of executing a valid deed or contract."
MASS. Ann. Laws (1966) 19, §1	"Every person of . . . sound mind . . . ."
MICH. Comp. Laws Ann. (1967) 702.1	"Every person of . . . sound mind . . . ."
MINN. Stat. Ann. (1969) 525.18	"Every person of sound mind . . . ."
MISS. Code Ann. (1956) 657	"Every person . . . of sound and disposing mind . . . ."
MO. Rev. Stat. (1956) 474.310	"Any person . . . of sound mind . . . ."
MONT. Rev. Codes Ann. (1963) 91-101	"Every person . . . of sound mind . . . ."
NEB. Rev. Stat. (1964) 30-201	"Every person of . . . sound mind . . . ."
NEV. Rev. Stat. (1967) 133.020	"Every person of sound mind . . . ."
N.H. Rev. Stat. Ann. (1955) 551:1	"Every person . . . of sane mind . . . ."

STATE AND CITATION	STATUTORY PROVISIONS
N.J. Stat. Ann. (1953) 3A:3-1 (Supp. 1970)	"A will made . . . by . . .[a] lunatic or person of unsound mind and memory, shall not be valid. . . ."
N.M. Stat. Ann. (1953) 30-1-1	"Any person . . . in sound mind . . . ."
N.Y. Est. Powers & Trusts (McKinney, 1967) 3-1.1	"Every person . . . of sound mind and memory . . . may by will dispose of real or personal property."
N.C. Gen. Stat. (1966) 31-1	"Any person of sound mind . . . ."
N.D. Cent. Code (1960) 56-02-01	"Any person eighteen years of age or older . . . may make a will. . . ."
14-0.1-03	"After his incapacity has been determined judicially upon application for the appointment of a guardian, a person of unsound mind can make no conveyance or other contract, nor delegate any power, nor waive any right until his restoration to capacity is determined judicially. If actually restored to capacity, he may make a will, though his restoration is not determined judicially."
OHIO Rev. Code (Baldwin 1964) 2107.02	"A person . . . of sound mind and memory . . . ."
OKLA. Stat. 84, §41 (1970)	"Every person . . . of sound mind . . . ."
15, §24 (1966)	[The latter statute provides that after incapacity has been judicially determined, a person of unsound mind can make no conveyance or other contract, until his restoration to capacity is judicially determined. But if actually restored to capacity, he may make a will, though his restoration is not thus determined.]
ORE. Rev. Stat. (1965) 114.020	"Every person . . . of sound mind . . . ."
PA. Stat. Ann. (1950) 20, §180.1 (Supp. 1969)	"Any person of sound mind . . . ."
R.I. Gen Laws Ann. (1956) 33-5-2	"Every person of sane mind . . . ."
S.C. Code Ann. (1962) 19-201	A will is not valid unless testator was of sound mind.
S.D. Compiled Laws Ann. (1967) 29-2-3	"Every person of sound mind . . . ."
27-2-3	[The latter statute provides that after incapacity has been judicially determined, a person of unsound mind can make no conveyance or other contract until his restoration to capacity has been judicially determined. If actually restored to capacity, he may make a will, though his restoration is not thus determined.]
TENN. Code Ann. (1955) 32-102	"Any person of sound mind . . . ."
TEX. Prob. Code (1956) 88(b)(1)57	Testator must have been of sound mind.

Table 9.2   STATUTORY DESCRIPTIONS OF PERSONS WHO MAY MAKE A WILL   continued

STATE AND CITATION	STATUTORY PROVISIONS
UTAH Code Ann. (1953) 74-1-1	"Every person . . . of sound mind . . . ."
VT. Stat. Ann. (1959) 14, §1	"A person . . . of sound mind . . . ."
VA. Code Ann. (1968) 64.1-47	"No person of unsound mind . . . shall be capable of making a will. . . ."
WASH. Rev. Code Ann. (1967) 11.12.010	"[P]erson of sound mind . . . ."
W. VA. Code Ann. (1966) 41-1-2	"No person of unsound mind . . . shall be capable of making a will."
WIS. Stat. Ann. (1957) 238.01	"Every person . . . being of sound mind may devise" lands, etc.
238.05	"Every person . . . being of sound mind, may, by last will . . . bequeath . . . personal estate."
WYO. Stat. Ann. (1957) 2-47	"Any person . . . of sound mind . . . ."

Table 9.3   STATUTORY PROVISIONS REGARDING ENGAGEMENT IN OCCUPATIONS

DRAFT ACT
    No provisions

ALA. Code (1958)
    46, §162:   "The Board shall have the power
    to annul and revoke any certificate of
    registration [as a medical technician]
    for incompetency . . . ."

    46, §187(12):   "The board shall have the
    power to revoke any certificate of regis-
    tration [as a registered nurse] for incom-
    petency, . . . [or] for mental incapac-
    ity . . . ."

    46, §257(a20) (Supp. 1967):   "The board
    may revoke, suspend or place on probation
    the license of any pharmacist . . . . (g)
    Whenever in the judgment of the board,
    the person is no longer . . . mentally
    capable of performing his duties . . . ."

    46, §257(21)(23):   The board may also sus-
    pend or revoke the license of a licensee
    [in the healing arts, including physicians,
    osteopaths, chiropodists, chiropractors,
    physical therapists, and podiatrists]
    found to be mentally incompetent to a de-
    gree and of a character which renders the
    licensee unsafe or unreliable as a prac-
    titioner.

ALAS. Stat.
    21.27.020 (1966):   Licenses are not issued
    to incompetents for insurance agents, bro-
    kers, solicitors, or adjustors.

    13.20.010(4) (1966) (Supp. 1969):   Persons
    of unsound mind are not qualified to act
    as executors or administrators.

    08.36.310(6) (1962):   A license and regis-
    tration for dentistry may be revoked, sus-
    pended, or annulled if the licensee is in-
    sane.

    08.68.270(7) (1962):   A license for profes-
    sional or practical nursing may be denied,
    suspended, or revoked if the licensee is
    mentally ill or incompetent.

    08.84.120(7) (1962):   A registration as a
    physical therapist may be refused, revoked,
    or suspended if the applicant or registrant
    has been declared mentally ill by a court
    and has not thereafter been lawfully de-
    clared sane.

ARIZ. Rev. Stat. Ann. (1956)
    14-492A: If an executor or administrator
    becomes insane, he may no longer act.

    Certificates of
    32-2042A.4:   physical therapists and
    32-1452D.3:   practitioners in medicine or
                   surgery
    may be revoked or suspended if the holder
    has been declared insane.

ARIZ. Rev. Stat. Ann. (1956) -- *continued*
    Licenses of
    32-1290.1:   dentists and
    32-1663.5 (Supp. 1970):   nurses
    who are mentally incompetent may be re-
    voked or suspended.

    32-2081(4) (Supp. 1970):   Certificate of a
    psychologist under commitment or under
    medical certificate to an institution for
    the mentally ill may be revoked.

    28-413(5):   Person suffering from a mental
    disability shall not be licensed as a
    chauffeur.

ARK. Stat. Ann. (1957)
    75-309(5) (Supp. 1967):   Persons of mental
    disability or disease cannot be licensed
    as operators or chauffeurs.

    71-874:   Licenses of cosmetologists who
    have been adjudged insane or legally in-
    competent shall be suspended.

    72-613(10) & (11) (Supp. 1967):   Licenses
    of practitioners in medicine and surgery
    who have been adjudged insane or mentally
    ill, or have been voluntarily committed,
    or who become medically incompetent to
    practice to such an extent as to endanger
    the public, may be revoked or suspended.

    71-2217(10) (Supp. 1967):   License as a
    polygraph examiner may be refused, or sus-
    pended or revoked, where the license hold-
    er has been adjudged mentally incompetent.

    72-1040(4) (Supp. 1967):   License as a
    pharmacist may be refused, or suspended
    or revoked, if the licensee has become in-
    sane or has been adjudged to be of unsound
    mind.

    72-1328(g) (Supp. 1967):   Registration as
    a physical therapist may be refused, or
    revoked, if the registrant has been de-
    clared insane and has not thereafter been
    lawfully declared sane.

    71-310.1(j):   Registration as an architect
    may be revoked if the holder has been ad-
    judged mentally incapable.

    72-560(3):   The privilege of practicing un-
    der license as a dentist or dental hygien-
    ist may be revoked or suspended for insan-
    ity, or for adjudication of insanity or
    mental incompetency if deemed detrimental
    to patients.

CAL. Bus. & Prof. Code (West 1964)
    Licenses of
    23102:   alcoholic beverage license holders
              and
    9028:   social workers
    are suspended or revoked upon adjudica-
    tion of insanity or incompetency.

326

COLO. Rev. Stat. Ann. (1964)
13-4-3(2)(E) (Supp. 1965): No person shall be issued a chauffeur's license who is suffering from any mental disability or disease.

97-4-20(1)(a)(g) (Supp. 1967): Board may deny, revoke, or suspend any license to practice as a licensed practical nurse upon proof that the person is mentally incompetent.

CONN. Gen. Stat. Ann.
20-59(h) (1958): Certificates of chiropodists may be revoked, suspended, or annulled upon mental illness or deficiency of practitioner.

DEL. Code Ann. (1953)
12, §1508: Letters testamentary or of administration will not be granted to a person of unsound mind.

No person previously adjudged to be mentally ill or an idiot, lunatic, or feebleminded may be issued
21, §2762(4) (Supp. 1970): a taxicab driver's license, or
24, §2706(b)(4) (Supp. 1970): chauffeur's license.

Licenses to practice
24, §1741(a)(7), (8) (Supp. 1970): medicine or surgery or
24, §1755 (Supp. 1970): osteopathy may be refused, revoked, or suspended for (7) any mental disability which renders the further practice dangerous; or for (8) mental incompetence or mental illness, when determined by a court of competent jurisdiction. Such adjudication shall require an automatic suspension of the license.

24, §1921(a)(5) (Supp. 1970): Licenses to practice nursing may be refused, suspended, or revoked for mental incompetency.

D.C. Code Ann. (1967)
2-605: Licenses of pharmacists who are suffering from mental disease may be revoked.

Licenses of
2-433(6): practical nurses and
2-462(6): physical therapists may be denied, revoked, or suspended if licensee is mentally incompetent.

FLA. Stat. Ann.
734.11(1) (1964): Any personal representative may be removed and his letters revoked for insanity.

458.12(1) (1965): Insane persons are disqualified to practice medicine until their sanity is restored.

FLA. Stat. Ann.--*continued*
465.101(1)(d)3 (1965): The license of a pharmacist may be revoked or suspended by reason of insanity.

464.21(2)(a) (1965): The board may deny or refuse to renew the license of a nurse who has been adjudged incompetent.

459.14(1)(i) (1965) (Supp. 1969): Osteopathic license may be refused, suspended, or revoked upon a judicial determination of incompetency.

466.24(1) (1965) (Supp. 1969): The license of a dentist may be suspended or revoked if the licensee is afflicted with psychiatric disorders deemed dangerous to the public health.

GA. Code Ann.
80-106 (1964): Licenses of mentally deranged pilots may be revoked or suspended.

79A-408(1)(b), (4) (1964): The license of a pharmacist may be suspended or revoked if the licensee become unfit or incompetent by reason of any abnormal mental condition; or if the licensee has been adjudicated incompetent.

84.412.2(8) (1955) (Supp. 1968): A certificate of registration of a barber or manicurist may be refused, suspended, or revoked if such persons sustain any mental disabilities which render them unable to pursue their occupations.

84.916(15) (1955) (Supp. 1968): The license of a medical practitioner may be refused, suspended, or revoked if the licensee sustains any mental disability which renders the further practice of medicine dangerous.

84-1509.2 (1955) (Supp. 1968): The license of a veterinarian may be revoked or suspended upon an adjudication of insanity.

84.3010(g) (1955): The registration of a physical therapist may be refused, suspended, or revoked if the registrant has been declared insane.

HAWAII Rev. Stat. Ann. (1968)
286-104(5): A chauffeur's license shall not be issued to any person suffering from any physical or mental disability or disease.

467-14(16): The license of a real estate broker may be suspended or revoked if the licensee is adjudicated insane or incompetent.

457-19(5): A license to practice nursing may be denied, suspended, or revoked upon proof that the licensee is mentally incompetent.

HAWAII Rev. Stat. Ann. (1968)--*continued*

    471-10(6):   A veterinarian's license may be refused, suspended, or revoked for insanity.

IDAHO Code Ann.

    54-1810(k) (1957):   Licenses held in medicine and surgery are subject to revocation or suspension when holder has been declared insane.

    49-309.5 (1967):   No license shall be issued to any person as a chauffeur or operator who has been previously adjudged to be suffering from mental disability or disease and has not been restored to competency.

   Persons adjudged incompetent may not act as

    15-317.4 (1947):   administrators,
    15-302.3 (1947):   executors, or
    15-1848 (1947):   guardians.

    54-218(d) (1957) (Supp. 1969):   The license of a certified public accountant is subject to revocation or suspension if he has been declared insane.

    54-305.1(d) (1957) (Supp. 1969):   A license to practice architecture may be refused, suspended, or revoked upon an adjudication of mental incompetency or insanity.

    54-1220(b) (1957) (Supp. 1969):   The certificate of an engineer or surveyor may be revoked or suspended if the holder is found guilty of insanity.

    54-1422(6) (1957) (Supp. 1969):   A license to practice nursing may be denied, revoked, or suspended for mental incompetence.

    54-2040(i) (1957) (Supp. 1969):   Licenses of real estate salesmen and brokers may be suspended or revoked upon a declaration of insanity.

ILL. Ann. Stat. (Smith-Hurd)

   The entry of a decree establishing that any licensee is in need of mental treatment operates as a suspension of the licenses or certificates of registration of

    16 3/4, §14.80 (1963) (Supp. 1969): barbers,
    16 3/4, §26.2 (1963)(Supp. 1969): beauty culturists,
    91, §81 (1966) (Supp. 1969): chiropodists,
    91, §62.2 (1966)(Supp. 1969): dentists,
    111$\frac{1}{2}$, §73.20 (1956): funeral directors and embalmers,
    91, §35.46 (1966)(Supp. 1969): nurses,
    91, §55.13 (1966): pharmacists,
    91, §22.15 (1966)(Supp. 1969): physical therapists,
    91, §16a (1966)(Supp. 1969) those licensed in medicine, surgery, human ailments, midwifery.

ILL. Ann. Stat. (Smith-Hurd)--*continued*

   Persons of unsound mind or adjudged incompetent cannot act as

    3, §94 (1961):   administrators or
    3, §77 (1961):   executors.

    95$\frac{1}{2}$, §6-103.5, 6-205(b) (1958) (Supp.1969):   Licenses of chauffeurs and operators shall not be issued or renewed or shall be revoked if person was previously adjudged to be afflicted with any mental disability and has not been restored to competency by law.

    3, §276(a)(2) (1961) (Supp. 1969):   An executor, administrator, guardian, or conservator may be removed if such person is adjudged in need of mental treatment or is adjudged an incompetent.

    48 $\frac{1}{2}$, §49.4 (1966) (Supp. 1969):   Licenses of professional engineers may be refused, suspended, or revoked if the licensee has been declared mentally ill or in need of mental treatment.

    16$\frac{3}{4}$, §14.80(g) (1963):   Certificates of barbers may be refused, suspended, or revoked if the holder is afflicted with any mental ailment, illness, or impairment which renders the holder incompetent or a danger to the public.

IND. Ann. Stat.

    63-518(2) (1961) (Supp. 1969):   Licenses of dentists are suspended or revoked upon adjudication of unsound mind.
    12-509(9) (1956):   No permit to sell beer shall be issued to a person non compos mentis.
    47-2704(d) (1965):   Persons adjudged insane and not restored to competency may not be licensed to operate a motor vehicle.
    63-925(e) (1961):   A license to practice nursing may be revoked, suspended, or denied if the holder is mentally incompetent.

IOWA Code Ann.

    321.177(5) (1966):   No person shall be licensed as an operator or chauffeur who has been adjudged to be afflicted with or suffering from any mental disability or disease or who is believed
    321.177(7) (1966) (Supp. 1969):   to have a mental disability making unsafe the operation of a motor vehicle.
    633.64(1) (1964):   A mental retardate or mentally ill person may not act as a fiduciary.

KAN. Stat. Ann. (1964)

    65-1627 (Supp. 1968):   Board may revoke or suspend any license of any pharmacist when the registrant has been adjudged an incapacitated person.

KY. Rev. Stat. Ann. (1969)
Licenses of
314-250(1):   registered or
314-390(1):   practical nurse
may be denied, revoked, or suspended if
person is "mentally incompetent."
Licenses of
311.595(1)(g):   physicians, osteopaths and
chiropodists may be revoked or suspended
if holder has developed such mental disability that continued practice is dangerous to patient or to the public.
313.130(7):   dentists or dental specialists
may be revoked, suspended, or refused if
the licensee has a mental disability such
that continued practice would be dangerous
to patients or to the public.
317.590(1)(c):   barbers and cosmetologists
shall be refused or revoked upon proper
showing of mental health that would endanger public health or safety.

327.070(7):   The license of any physical
therapist who has been declared insane may
be refused, suspended, or revoked.
329.070(8):   The license of a detection of
deception examiner may be denied, suspended, or revoked where the licensee has been
adjudged mentally ill, mentally deficient,
or in need of mental treatment.

LA. Rev. Stat. Ann. (1950)
37:930(5):   Licenses of nurses may be suspended or revoked if holder is mentally
incompetent.

ME. Rev. Stat. Ann. (1965)
32, §3053:   The license of a physical therapist who has been declared insane by a
court and not thereafter declared sane
may be suspended.
32, §2105:   License of nurse may be revoked
or suspended if mentally incompetent.

MD. Ann. Code (1964)
93, §59 (Supp. 1968):   Persons of unsound
mind cannot act as executors.

MASS. Ann. Laws
Persons who are mentally ill cannot act as
201, §33 (1969):   guardians or conservators
60, §96 (1964):   or tax collectors.

112, §61 (1965):   Any certificate, registration, license, or authority issued by the
boards of medicine, pharmacy, veterinary
medicine, and the board of dental examiners may be revoked or suspended if it appears to the board that the holder of such
certificate, registration, license, etc.,
is insane.

MICH. Comp. Laws Ann. (1967)
257.303(5), (6):   Licenses as chauffeurs
or operators shall not be issued to

MICH. Comp. Laws Ann. (1967)--*continued*
persons adjudged idiots or suffering from
mental disability or disease.
257.303a: Licenses of chauffeurs or operators may be revoked or suspended if holder has become afflicted with mental infirmities or disabilities rendering him
an unsafe driver.
338.362:   Certificates of licenses of
nurses may be revoked, denied, or suspended upon proof that the nurse is unfit
or incompetent by reason of mental disability.
338.1115(d):   Licenses of pharmacists may
be revoked for insanity.

MINN. Stat. Ann.
525.501 (1969):   Representatives who are
insane or otherwise mentally incompetent
may be removed as estate or trust representatives.
171.04(5) (1960) (Supp. 1969):   No license
shall be issued to any person who has
been adjudged legally incompetent by reason of mental illness, mental deficiency,
or inebriation, and has not been restored
to capacity, unless the department is
satisfied that such person is competent
to operate motor vehicle.
148.251(5) (1946):   License of nurse may
be revoked, suspended, or denied for mental incompetency.

MISS. Code Ann. (1956)

MO. Rev. Stat. (1956)
473.140:   Letters of an executor or administrator may be revoked if he becomes of
unsound mind.

MONT. Rev. Codes Ann. (1961)
66-1240(5):   Licenses of nurses may be denied, revoked, or suspended upon proof of
mental incompetence.

NEB. Rev. Stat.
38-507 (1960):   Guardians who are insane
may be removed by the court upon notice
to them.
71-1.104.01 (1966):   License to practice
medicine and surgery shall be suspended
when licensee because of mental illness
or mental deterioration is not qualified
to practice.
71-1.132.29 (1960):   Licenses of nurses
may be denied, revoked, or suspended on
proof of mental incompetency.

NEV. Rev. Stat. (1967)
630.030.15:   The practice of medicine,
surgery, and obstetrics by one who is
adjudicated insane constitutes unprofessional conduct,

NEV. Rev. Stat. (1967)--*continued*
  630.300:   and licenses are refused, sus-
    pended, or revoked if holder is guilty
    of unprofessional conduct.

  Licenses of
    632.220.5:   professional and
    632.320.5:   practical nurses
      may be revoked, suspended, or denied for
      mental incompetence.

  Licenses of
    637.150.1:   ophthalmic dispensers and
    640.160.7:   physical therapists
      may be refused, suspended, or revoked when
      holder is adjudicated insane and not
      thereafter lawfully declared sane.

    636.295.6:   Licenses of optometrists may
      be suspended or revoked if licensee is
      afflicted with any mental disorder or
      disturbance seriously impairing his com-
      petency as an optometrist.

N.H. Rev. Stat. Ann.
  564:9 (1955):   A trustee who becomes insane
    may, after notice to him, be removed.
  329:17 (1966):   Licenses for practice
    of medicine may be revoked or suspended
    if the holder is insane, or
  329:17-a (1966):   suspended if the li-
    censee is involuntarily committed to
    the state hospital in order that his
    sanity may be determined.
  328-A:9 (1966):   Registration of physical
    therapists may be revoked or suspended if
    registrant is insane.
  330-A:14(d) (1966):   Certificates of psy-
    chologists may be suspended or revoked if
    holder is or has been committed to an in-
    stitution for the mentally ill.
  305:21 (1966):   Insanity of business part-
    ner may dissolve partnership.

N.J. Stat. Ann.
  3A:11-4.e (1953):   A fiduciary may be re-
    moved if of unsound mind or mentally in-
    capacitated.
  12:8-19.c (1968):   License of pilot may be
    declared null and void if he is laboring
    under a mental derangement so as to be in-
    capable of attending to business.
  52:17B-41.22(a) (1955):   Licenses of oph-
    thalmic dispensers or technicians who are
    adjudicated insane may be refused, sus-
    pended, or revoked.
  52:14-13 (1955):   Persons committed to in-
    stitutions for the insane cannot serve
    as state officers.

N.M. Stat. Ann. (1961):
  Licenses of
    67-6-39(5):   nurses,
    67-4-10(b),(4):   dentists, and dental hy-
      gientists and
    67-9-10(e) (Supp. 1969):   pharmacists,
    67-11-20(2) (Supp. 1969):   veterinarians,

N.M. Stat. Ann. (1961)--*continued*
  Licenses of--*continued*
    67-30-12(7) (Supp. 1969):   psychologists,
    67-31-10(d) (Supp. 1969):   polygraphers,
      and
    67-10-12:   physical therapists
      may be denied, suspended, or revoked upon
      adjudication of insanity or mental incom-
      petence.

    64-13-40(f) (Supp. 1969):   Mentally dis-
      abled, insane, or diseased persons may not
      be licensed as chauffeurs and operators.

N.Y. Educ. Law (McKinney 1953)
  6514.2(c):   The license or registration of
    a practitioner of medicine, osteopathy,
    or physiotherapy may be revoked, suspend-
    ed, or annulled if he becomes insane.
  6911.1(f):   The license and registration
    of any person licensed to practice nurs-
    ing may be revoked or suspended upon
    proof that such licensee has become men-
    tally incompetent.

N.C. Gen. Stat. (1965)
  Licenses of
    90-14:   persons practicing medicine or
      surgery,
    90-65 (Supp. 1967):   pharmacists, and
    90-171.5(7)(Supp. 1967):   registered
      nurses
      may be revoked or suspended if licensee
      is mentally incompetent.

    20-9(d) (Supp. 1967):   Applicants adjudged
      insane may not be licensed as chauffeurs
      or operators.

N.D. Cent. Code (1960)
  Licenses of
    43-06-15.3:   chiropractors and
    43-14-20.3:   osteopaths
      may be refused or revoked for mental
      aberrations.

    43-28-19.4:   Certificate of registration
      of any dentist may be revoked or suspend-
      ed if holder has been adjudged insane.

OHIO Rev. Code (Baldwin 1964)
  4723.28:   Certificate or license of regis-
    tered or practical nurses may be denied,
    suspended, or revoked upon proof that
    person is mentally incompetent.

OKLA. Stat.
  59, §48(1) (1963):   Chiropodists' licenses
    may be revoked in case of a mental weak-
    ness which incapacitates the licensee.
  59, §167 (1963):   The original or renewal
    license, or both, of any chiropractor who
    becomes   incompetent to practice because
    of insanity may be suspended.

OKLA. Stat.--*continued*
59,§327.30(1) (1963): The board may revoke or suspend a dentist's license if he has been proven mentally unsound.
59, §567.8(a)(5) (1963): The board may deny, revoke, or suspend any registered or practical nurse who is judicially determined to be mentally incompetent.
59, §637(g) (1963): The board may refuse to issue or may suspend or revoke any license for an osteopath who has been adjudicated insane and committed to an institution for the insane.
59, §880(e) (1963): The board shall refuse to grant registration or renewal of registration to a physical therapist if he has been declared mentally incompetent by a court and has not theretofore been lawfully declared sane.
59, §516 (1963): The license or certificate of any physician or surgeon may be suspended when such physician or surgeon becomes incompetent to practice medicine because of insanity.
47, §6.103.5 (1962): The commissioner shall not issue any license to any operator or chauffeur who has been adjudged afflicted with or suffering from any mental disability or disease.
47, §6.207 (1952): The holder of an operator's or chauffeur's license established to have a mental disease may, in the discretion of the commissioner, have his license cancelled.

ORE. Rev. Stat. (1967):
675.070(1)(f): Certification of a psychologist may be revoked or refused if he is mentally or emotionally unfit to practice psychology.
684.100(1)(e): Licenses of chiropractors may be suspended or revoked on the grounds of commitment to a mental institution.
679.165: The entry of a decree by any court establishing the mental disease of any dentist operates as a suspension of his license.
677.225(1)(a), (b): The board shall suspend a person's license to practice medicine and surgery if he is adjudged to be mentally ill or admitted voluntarily to a state hospital.
482.120(2): No operator's or chauffeur's license shall be issued to any applicant who has previously been committed, or been determined to be mentally ill or mentally retarded, until released or restored to competency by judicial decree.

PA. Stat. Ann.
20-320.331(2), (3) (1950): A personal representative shall be removed when he has been adjudged a lunatic, or has become incompetent to discharge the duties of his office because of mental incapacity and his incompetency is likely to continue to the injury of the estate;

PA. Stat. Ann.--*continued*
20-320.921(1) (1950): the same conditions are true for a trustee;
20-320.1031(1) (1950): the same conditions are true for a guardian.
63-42.16(6) (1968): License or registration of a podiatrist (includes chiropodist) may be refused, revoked, or cancelled if he or she shall become mentally incompetent.
63-390.5(4) (1968): License of any pharmacist may be revoked or suspended upon proof that he is unfit or unable to practice pharmacy by reason of a physical or mental disease or disability.
63-410 (1968): License of a physician may be refused, revoked, or suspended for any condition which impairs intellect and judgment to such an extent as to incapacitate for the performance of professional duties.
License of a
63-666 (1968): practical nurse or a
63-224(6) (1968): professional nurse may be suspended or revoked where the the licensee has become mentally incompetent.

R.I. Gen. Laws Ann.
5-34-28(5) (1956): Licenses to practice nursing may be denied, revoked, or suspended upon proof of mental incompetence.
5-34-30 (1956): If the nurse is hospitalized for mental illness, the board may suspend or refuse to renew the license.
31-10-3(5) (1968): Chauffeurs or operators adjudged to be afflicted with or suffering from any mental disability or disease may not be licensed.

S.C. Code Ann. (1962)
56-572(3)(c), (d): The license of any dentist or dental hygienist may be suspended or revoked for insanity or adjudication of insanity.
56-1349.3: Licenses of physical therapists are suspended or revoked upon declaration of insanity.
56-734: Certificate of registration of engineers and land surveyors may be revoked by board where there is a declaration of insanity by a court of competent jurisdiction.

S.D. Compiled Laws Ann. (1967)
36-9-49: Mental incompetence is ground for denial, revocation, or suspension of nurse's license.
36-4-32: Suspension of license for mental incompetence of physician or surgeon.
36-10-14(7): Mental illness is ground for denial, suspension, or revocation of physical therapist's license.

TENN. Code Ann. (1955)
35-117: Trustees who are insane, lunatic, or non compos mentis may be removed.
8-2801(7): Public officers by adjudication of insanity or
19-114: justices of the peace who shall have become permanently insane, or of such mental imbecility as not to be competent to perform the duties of the office, shall be removed.

63-752(e) (Supp. 1968): Licenses of nurses who are mentally incompetent may be denied, revoked, or suspended.

TEX. Rev. Civ. Stat. Ann. (1960)
Licenses of
4563(e): optometrists,
4542a:12(e): pharmacists,
4549(a): dentists,
4528c-10: licensed vocational nurses, and
6687b-30: chauffeurs or operators
are revoked or suspended if holder has become insane or has been adjudged of unsound mind.

TEX. Prob. Code
78(b) (1956): Executor or administrator is not qualified to serve if he is incompetent.

UTAH Code Ann. (1963)
58-8-11(a): Licenses of dental hygienists may be revoked for mental incompetency to practice the profession.
58-31-14(a)(5): License to practice nursing may be revoked or suspended if the person is mentally incompetent.

VT. Stat. Ann. (1968)
26, §1559(a)(5): Board may revoke or suspend any license to practice nursing upon proof the licensee is mentally incompetent.
26, §2156: Physical therapist who is insane will be refused registration.

VA. Code Ann.
54-317.1(2) (1967): Licenses of persons practicing medicine, osteopathy, chiropractic, naturopathy, chiropody, or physical therapy may be denied or suspended if holder has been adjudged insane or incompetent by a court and not declared restored.
24-147 (1969): Whenever any public officer shall be adjudged a lunatic or insane person, the office shall become vacant.

VA. Code Ann.--*continued*
46.1-360 (1967): Persons previously adjudged insane and not restored shall not be licensed as chauffeurs or operators;
46.1-427(a) (1967): and licenses of chauffeurs and operators shall be suspended when holder is adjudged mentally ill.

WASH. Rev. Code Ann. (1961)
18.72.030(14) (Supp. 1968): Members of the medical profession who are declared mentally incompetent are guilty of "unprofessional conduct" for which their licenses may be revoked or suspended.
18.74.080(5): Licenses of physical therapists are refused or revoked if person has been declared insane and not thereafter declared sane.

W. VA. Code Ann. (1966)
Licenses of
30-7-11(e): registered or
30-7A-10(4) (Supp. 1969): practical nurses
are revoked or suspended if person is mentally incompetent.

30-20-9(g): License for physical therapy practice may be refused to one declared mentally incompetent.

WIS. Stat. Ann. (1957)
149.07 (Supp. 1969): Licenses of registered and practical nurses are revoked or suspended for mental incompetence.
152.07(7) (Supp. 1969): Licenses or certificates and registration of dentists who are in a hospital for mental diseases are suspended.
152.08 (Supp. 1969): This provision also applies to dental hygienists.
258.28(6) (Supp. 1969): Attorney's license is suspended when mental illness will endanger clients' interests.

WYO. Stat. Ann. (1957)
3-14: A guardian who becomes insane can be removed by the court.
33-143(j): Unlawful to practice chiropractic while adjudged mentally incompetent or insane.
33-288: Nurse's license may be revoked or suspended for mental incompetence.
33-340: Unlawful to practice medicine while having any mental disability which renders the practice of medicine and surgery dangerous.

Table 9.4   VOTING, HOLDING OFFICE, JURY SERVICE, AND DRIVER'S LICENSE

STATE	VOTING — Prohibitions	VOTING — Enforcement	VOTING — Commitment or Adjudication of Prohibited Condition Required	HOLDING PUBLIC OFFICE — Prohibitions	HOLDING PUBLIC OFFICE — Office Specified	HOLDING PUBLIC OFFICE — Adjudication Required	JURY PROHIBITIONS	DRIVING — Prohibitions	DRIVING — Commitment or Adjudication Required	DRIVING — Enforcement--Suspension or Revocation	CIVIL RIGHTS — Retention of	CIVIL RIGHTS — Loss of
DRAFT ACT	restriction by hospital, or an adjudication of incompetency. 21(a)(3)		incompetency requires adjudication. 21(a)(3)								subject to hospital regulations or adjudication of incompetency. 21(a)(3)	
ALA. Code (1958)	all idiots or insane persons, Const. Art. VIII, §182			not qualified electors, 41, §5(1)	governor. Const. Art. V, §128 state officials Const. Art. V, §136	adjudication of insanity vacates office. 41, §164 Const. Art. V, §128, Const. Art. V, §136	challenge for cause, 30, §55(9)	insane or an idiot, 36, §66	adjudged insane. 36, §66	suspension, 36, §68		
ALAS. Stat. (1962)	unsound mind. Const. V, §2 15.05.040 restriction by hospital, or an adjudication of incompetency. 47.30.150(a)(3)		"judicially determined." Const. V, §2 15.05.040 incompetency requires adjudication. 47.30.150(a)(3)				sound mind required. 05.20.010	mental disability or disease. 28.15.030(5)	adjudged mental disability or disease. 28.15.030(5)		subject to hospital regulations or adjudication of incompetency. 47.30.150(a)(3)	
ARIZ. Rev. Stat. Ann. (1956)	under guardian, non compos mentis or insane. Const. Art. VII, §2 registration: insane person or under guardian, 16-101			"shall be qualified elector" Const. Art. VII, §15 insane or under guardian--not qualified to register, 16-101; also Const. Art. VII, §2 office deemed vacant if adjudicated insane, 38-291(2)		office deemed vacant if adjudicated insane, 38-291(2)	unsound mind, 21-201	mental disability or disease. 28-413(5) (Supp. 1970)	adjudged mental disability or disease. 28-413(5) (Supp. 1970)	suspend if incompetent to drive, 28-446 (Supp. 1970)	unless adjudged incompetent, 35-514D (Supp. 1970)	
ARK. Stat. Ann. (1947)	idiot or insane person, Const. Art. III, §5 insane, 3-101 (1956)			must possess qualifications of elector, Const. Art. XIX, §3 insane person not entitled to privileges of elector, 3-101 (1956)				mental disability or disease. 75-309(5)(1957) (Supp. 1967)	adjudged mental disability or disease, 75-309(5) (1957) (Supp. 1967)	suspend if incompetent to drive, 75-334(a)(5) (1957) (Supp. 1967)		
CAL. Codes	idiot or insane person. Const. Art. II, §1 (1954) Elections (West 1961) 100	registration to be cancelled when insanity of person registered is legally established. Elections 383(b) (Supp. 1969)	registration to be cancelled when insanity legally established. Elections 383(b) (Supp. 1969)	no person eligible who is not an elector, Gov't 275 (1960) insane person shall not ever exercise privileges of an elector, Const. Art. II, §1 Elections (West 1961) 20			not in possession of natural faculties, not of ordinary intelligence, or decrepit. Civil Pro. (West 1954) 198, 199	insane or feebleminded or an idiot or an imbecile; also where it appears by examination or other evidence that person is unable to operate motor vehicle safely because of mental defect. Vehicle (West 1960) 13805 (Supp. 1969)	.	suspend or revoke or restrict or require examination. Vehicle (1960) 13800(e) (Supp. 1969), 13801 (1960)	"Every person involuntarily detained . . . shall return all rights not specifically denied him . . .." W. & I. 5327 (Supp. 1968)	
COLO. Rev. Stat. Ann. (1963)	under guardian, non compos mentis or insane, 49-3-2(2)			must be elector, 49-3-5				mental disability or disease. 13-4-4 (Supp. 1965)	adjudged mental disability or disease, 13-4-3 (Supp. 1965)	mandatory revocation. 13-4-22(1)(i) (Supp. 1965)		

Table 9.4   VOTING, HOLDING OFFICE, JURY SERVICE, AND DRIVER'S LICENSE   *continued*

STATE	VOTING			HOLDING PUBLIC OFFICE			JURY PROHIBITIONS	DRIVING			CIVIL RIGHTS	
	Prohibitions	Enforcement	Commitment or Adjudication of Prohibited Condition Required	Prohibitions	Office Specified	Adjudication Required		Prohibitions	Commitment or Adjudication Required	Enforcement--Suspension or Revocation	Retention of	Loss of
CONN. Gen. Stat. Ann. (1958)	idiot or mentally ill person. 9-12 (1967) Also see Const. Art. VI, §2 (1965)			every elector shall be eligible for any office. Const. Art. VI, §10 (1965) no mentally ill person shall be admitted as an elector 9-12 (1967)			must be electors with no permanent disability. 51-217 (Supp. 1969)	must be free from any disease that might affect operation of a motor vehicle. 14-36 (1969)				
DEL. Code Ann. (1953)	idiot or insane person. Const. Art. V, §2 (4) [Del. Laws, Ch. 57, effective 5/7/53, provided that words "mentally ill" be substituted for "insane" whenever appearing in the Del. Code and that said words "shall have same legal connotation that the word 'insane' possessed heretofore in that Code." (Supp. 1970)] no idiot or insane person. 15, §1701 (Supp. 1970)	refuse registration. Const. Art. V, §4 procedure for striking names of persons disqualified from voting. 15, §1706 (Supp. 1970)					only qualified electors may serve as jurors. 10, §4504(a) (Supp. 1970)	fn. 1 27, §2706(b)(4) (Supp. 1970) 21, §2706(b)(5)	such adjudication is grounds for refusal. 21, §2706(b)(4) (Supp. 1970) but is not required for refusal. 21, §2706(b)(5)	immediate suspension. 21, §2733(a)(3) revocation upon hearing. 21, §2733(b)		
D.C. Code Ann. (1967)	mentally incompetent. 1-1102(2)(d)	denial of registration. 1-1107(b)(2)	1-1102(2)(d) 21-546(b)				incapable by reason of mental infirmity. 11-2301(a)(3)	must be mentally qualified. 40-301(a)(1)		suspension or revocation. 40-302(a)	unless adjudicated incompetent. 21-564(a)	
FLA. Stat. Ann. (1960)	under guardianship. 97.041(5)(b) (Supp. 1969) mentally incompetent. 97.041(5)(c) (Supp. 1969) under guardianship, non compos mentis, or insane. Const. Art. VI, §4		97.041(5)(c) (Supp. 1969)				mentally infirm 40.01(3); persons not of sound mind and discretion. 40.07(3)(1961)	mental disability or disease. 322.05(5)(1968)	adjudged mental disability or disease. 322.05(5)(1968)	suspend if incompetent to drive. 322.27(1)(c) (1968)		
GA. Code Ann. (1948)	idiots and insane persons. Const. 2-701, 2-704, 2-801	insane not permitted to register. Const. 2-801		insane may not hold any office, or appointment of honor, or trust. Const. 2-801/ person of unsound mind is ineligible to hold any civil office. 89-101.5 (1963)			idiots, lunatics and insane are not qualified to serve as grand jurors. 59-201(1965) idiot or lunatic may be challenged and for this cause excluded from jury service. 59-804.3(1965)				fn. 2	

Table 9.4 VOTING, HOLDING OFFICE, JURY SERVICE, AND DRIVER'S LICENSE continued

STATE	VOTING			HOLDING PUBLIC OFFICE			JURY PROHIBITIONS	DRIVING			CIVIL RIGHTS	
	Prohibitions	Enforcement	Commitment or Adjudication of Prohibited Condition Required	Prohibitions	Office Specified	Adjudication Required		Prohibitions	Commitment or Adjudication Required	Enforcement--Suspension or Revocation	Retention of	Loss of
HAWAII Rev. Stat. Ann. (1968)	non compos mentis Const. Art. II, §2 hospital has power of temporary suspension 334-57						not in possession of natural faculties, or decrepit. 690-1(2)	mental disability. 286-104(5)			subject to hospital regulations or adjudication of incompetency. 334-57	
IDAHO Code Ann. (1947)	under guardianship, idiotic, or insane Const. Art. VI, §3 34-402 (1963) restriction by hospital or an adjudication of incompetency 66-346(a)(3) (Supp. 1969)		incompetency requires adjudication, 66-346(a)(3) (Supp. 1969)	under guardianship, idiotic, or insane Const. Art. VI, §3	any civil office Const. Art. III, §6		under guardianship, idiotic, or insane. Const. Art. VI, §3	afflicted with or suffering from any mental disability or disease. 49-309(5)(1967)	49-309(5)(1967)	immediate suspension; revocation after hearing, 49-330(3)(1967)	subject to hospital regulations or adjudication of incompetency. 66-346(a)(3) (Supp. 1969)	
ILL. Ann. Stat. (Smith-Hurd 1958)	fn. 3						Jurors must be in the possession of natural faculties and not infirm. 78, §2 (1966)	mental disability, 95½ §6-103(5)	95½ §6-103(5)	revocation, 95½ §6-205(b) (Supp. 1969)		
IND. Stat. Ann. (1965)							insane challenge for cause. 5-811(1968)	insane, feeble-minded, idiot, imbecile, 47-2704(d) mental disability or disease. 47-2704(e)		suspension or revocation, 47-1081(a)(3)		
IOWA Code Ann. (1966)	idiot or insane person, Const. Art. II, §5						unsound judgment, 607.1 609.2(3)(1950)	fn. 4 adjudged mental disease or disability, 321.177(5) believed to have mental disability, 321.177(7) (Supp. 1969)		suspension without hearing; revocation upon hearing, 321.210.4 (Supp. 1969)		
KAN. Stat. Ann. (1964)	under guardianship, non compos mentis, insane. Const. Art. V, §2			incapacity 59-203	probate judge 59-203, 59-205	incapacitated person 59-205		mental disability or disease. 8-237(6)	8-237(6)	suspension, 8-255(a) (Supp. 1968)		
KY. Rev. Stat. Ann. (1969)	idiots and insane persons. Const. sec. 145.3 117.605 restriction by hospital or an adjudication of incompetency 202.272(1)(3)	purged or not allowed to register. 117.605 117.810(1)	incompetency requires adjudication, 202.272(1)(3)				indiscreet or not of good demeanor. 29.025(1)	insane or an idiot, imbecile or feebleminded. 186.440(5)	186.440(5)	suspension, 186.570(1)(c)	subject to hospital regulations or adjudication of incompetency, 202.272(1)(3)	
LA. Rev. Stat. Ann. (1950)	insane or interdicted. 18:42(5) Const. Art. VIII, §6			Const. Art. VIII, §6			interdicted or insane person cannot hold position of trust Const. Art. VIII, §6	mentally ill, 32:408 32:414(8)		32:414	La. Civ. Code Ann. 33 (West 1952)	

335

Table 9.4 VOTING, HOLDING OFFICE, JURY SERVICE, AND DRIVER'S LICENSE— *continued*

STATE	VOTING			HOLDING PUBLIC OFFICE			JURY PROHIBITIONS	DRIVING			CIVIL RIGHTS	
	Prohibitions	Enforcement	Commitment or Adjudication of Prohibited Condition Required	Prohibitions	Office Specified	Adjudication Required		Prohibitions	Commitment or Adjudication Required	Enforcement--Suspension or Revocation	Retention of	Loss of
ME. Rev. Stat. Ann. (1965)	under guardianship. Const. Art. II, §1 restriction by hospital or an adjudication of incompetency. 34, §2254 (Supp. 1969)		incompetency requires adjudication. 34, §2254 (Supp. 1969)								subject to hospital regulations or adjudication of incompetency. 34, §2254 (Supp. 1969)	
MD. Ann. Code (1957)	under guardianship, non compos mentis. Const. Art. I, §2							mentally ill. 66½, §88(5)	66½, §88(5)	66½, §104(d) 66½, §105(c)		
MASS. Ann. Laws (1957)	under guardianship. 51, §1 Const. Articles of Amendment Art. III, §105							incompetent person. 90, §22 (Supp. 1968)		suspension. 90, §32 (Supp. 1968)		
MICH. Comp. Laws Ann. (1967)							600.1215(3)	fn. 1 257.303(5)	fn. 1 adjudged an idiot. 257.303(5) commitment. 257.303a	fn. 5 257.304		
MINN. Stat. Ann. (1947)	insane, under guardianship, non compos mentis Const. Art. VII, §2	fn. 6 201.15 (1962) (Supp. 1969)		insane, under guardianship, non compos mentis Const. Art. VII, §§2, 7	fn. 7 525.052 (1969)	fn. 7 525.052 (1969)	unsound mind, 628.43 mentally unfit, 628.49 insane, 628.54(4)	fn. 1 171.04(5), 171.04(9)(1960) (Supp. 1969)	fn. 1 171.04(5)(1960) (Supp. 1969)	adjudged incompetent. 171.18(5)(1960)		
MISS. Code Ann. (1956)	insane. 3130, 3235 (Supp. 1968) Const. Art. 12, §241			insane, unsound mind. 4053 Const. Art. 12, §250 (Supp. 1968)	4053	unsound mind. 4053	1762; Const. Art. 12, §264	fn. 1 8093(d) 8093(f)	fn. 1 8093(f)	incompetent: suspension. 8107(a)15		
MO. Rev. Stat. (1959)	restriction by hospital or an adjudication of incompetency. 202.847.1(3) (1962) insane. Const. Art. VIII, §2 idiot or insane, 111.060 (1966)		incompetency requires adjudication. 202.847.1(3) (1962)	incompetent, insane. Const. Art. VII, §1 475.350 (1956)		475.350 (1956)	mentally incapable. 494.020(6) 497.030(1949) (Supp. 1969)	302.010(18) 302.060(5)	302.010(18) 302.060(5)	incompetent: revocation or suspension. 302.291	subject to hospital regulations or adjudication of incompetency. 202.847.1(3) (1962)	
MONT. Rev. Codes Ann. (1967)	insane. Const. Art. IX, §8 23-310	23-518.4	fn. 8 23-518.4	Const. Art. IX, §11 59-602.2(1961)		59-606.2 (1961)	93-1301.2 93-1304 (1964)	adjudged mentally disabled or diseased. 31-127.5(1961)	31-127.5(1961)	suspension. 31-147.5 31-148 (1961)		
NEB. Rev. Stat. (1960)	non compos mentis. Const. Art. VI, §2 32-1048			fn. 9 Const. Art. IV, §12	fn. 9 Const. Art. IV, §12		unsound mind. 25-1601(1)	fn. 10 60-419 (Supp. 1967)	fn. 10 60-419 (Supp. 1967)	incompetent: revocation. 60-425.5		
NEV. Rev. Stat. (1967)	insane. Const. Art. 2, §1	registration cancelled. 293.540.2	293.540.2 433.725	Const. Art. 15, §3 281.040	all 281.040		6.010	fn. 11 483.250.7	433.725 483.250.5	incompetent: suspension. 483.470.1(e)		

Table 9.4 VOTING, HOLDING OFFICE, JURY SERVICE, AND DRIVER'S LICENSE *continued*

STATE	VOTING: Prohibitions	VOTING: Enforcement	VOTING: Commitment or Adjudication of Prohibited Condition Required	HOLDING PUBLIC OFFICE: Prohibitions	HOLDING PUBLIC OFFICE: Office Specified	HOLDING PUBLIC OFFICE: Adjudication Required	JURY PROHIBITIONS	DRIVING: Prohibitions	DRIVING: Commitment or Adjudication Required	DRIVING: Enforcement--Suspension or Revocation	CIVIL RIGHTS: Retention of	CIVIL RIGHTS: Loss of
N.H. Rev. Stat. Ann. (1955)				incapacity or unfitness. 4:1	state treasurer; insane. 6:15	public hearing. good cause. 4:1		incompetent. 262:40 (1966)		262.40(1966)		
N.J. Rev. Stat. Ann. (1964)	insane. 19:4-1 Const. Art. 2, §6	19:33-1		52:14-13(1955)		52:14-13(1955)	2A:69-1 (1952) (Supp. 1970)	39:3-10 (1961) (Supp. 1970)				
N.M. Stat. Ann. (1953)	insane. 3-2-5l; Const. Art. VII.1 restriction by hospital or an adjudication of incompetency. 34-2-15a(3)		3-2-21(2) (Supp. 1969) incompetency requires adjudication. 34-2-15a(3)	Const. Art. VII, §2 5-3-4,5				fn. 12 64-13-40(F) (Supp. 1969)		incompetent. 64-13-60.5	subject to hospital regulations or adjudication of incompetency. 34-2-15a(3)	
N.Y. Mental Hygiene Law (McKinney 1951)										permissive suspension or revocation if mentally disabled or if court commitment to department of mental hygiene. Veh. and Traf. 510.3(b) (1960)		
N.C. Gen. Stat. (1963)	lunatics. Const. VI, §1-4 163-55 (Supp. 1967)				Judges, clerks, Const. IV, §§33 and 32			fn. 1 20-9(d), 20-9(e). (Supp. 1967)	suspension if adjudged insane. 20-9(d) (Supp. 1967) 20-17.1	suspension and revocation of incompetent to drive. 20-16(a)(4) revocation if adjudged insane. 20-17.1		
N.D. Cent. Code (1960)	under guardianship, non compos mentis or insane. 16-01-04 Const. Art. V, §127			must be a qualified elector. 44-01-01	44-11-01	office becomes vacant if adjudged insane. 44-02-01.2	must be an elector of sound mind. 27-09-01	mentally incapable of safe driving; adjudged insane. 39-06-03.4			subject to hospital regulations or adjudication of incompetency. 25-03-20	
OHIO Rev. Code (Baldwin 1964)	Const. Art. V, §6 insane. 3503.18	cancel registration. 3503.18		no office unless qualified elector, Const. Art. XV, §4			must be an elector; insane or idiot not an elector. 2313.06	fn. 1 4507.08(b) 4507.08(c) (Supp. 1968)	suspension of adjudged mentally incompetent. 4507.161	4507.161		
OKLA. Stat. (1962)	no person shall be a qualified elector who is a patient in an institution for mental retardation or who has been committed by judicial order to an institution for mental illness. Const. Art. 3, §1 (1952) (Supp. 1969)						must be qualified elector, of sound mind and discretion. 38-28 (1958) (Supp. 1969)	adjudged suffering from mental disability or disease; those not adjudged, discretionary with commissioner. 47-6-103.5 47-6-207	47-6-103.5	cancellation, if in discretion of commissioner, person may temporarily lose control. 47-6-207		

337

Table 9.4 VOTING, HOLDING OFFICE, JURY SERVICE, AND DRIVER'S LICENSE *continued*

STATE	VOTING Prohibitions	VOTING Enforcement	VOTING Commitment or Adjudication of Prohibited Condition Required	HOLDING PUBLIC OFFICE Prohibitions	Office Specified	Adjudication Required	JURY PROHIBITIONS	DRIVING Prohibitions	DRIVING Commitment or Adjudication Required	DRIVING Enforcement--Suspension or Revocation	CIVIL RIGHTS Retention	CIVIL RIGHTS Loss of
ORE. Rev. Stat. (1967)	mentally diseased. Const. Art. II, §3			fn. 13 236.010(6)		fn. 13 236.010(6)	must possess natural faculties and sound mind. 10.030(1)(d) 17.130	no license if determined mentally ill or retarded; discretionary if competency restored or suffering from mental deficiency 482.120(2) 482.130 482.240	482.120(2)	suspend and revoke if incompetent or afflicted with mental disability. 482.450		
PA. Stat. Ann. (1960)								fn. 1 75, §604(6) 75, §604(7)	75, §604(7)	permissive suspension if incompetent to drive safely, or mentally disabled 75, §618(a)(1) 75, §618(b)(5)		
R.I. Gen. Laws Ann. (1956)	lunatic, non compos mentis, or under guardianship. Const. Art. XXIV, §1			only qualified electors, which excludes lunatics, persons non compos mentis, or under guardianship. Const. Art. IX, §1	governor, lieutenant governor, secretary of state, attorney general, or general treasurer; remove if any becomes insane or otherwise incapacitated. Const. Art. II, §3 17-2-2 (Supp. 1967)		must be a qualified elector. 9-9-1	fn. 1 31-10-3(5), 31-10-3(8) (1968)	31-10-3(5) (1968)			
S.C. Code Ann. (1962)	insane and idiots. Const. Art. 2, §6; 23 §62 (Supp. 1968)			must be qualified elector which excludes insane persons. Const. Arts. 2, §2; 17, §1			each juror must be a qualified elector, which excludes insane persons. Const. Art. 5, §22 (Supp. 1968)	must be mentally fit to drive. 46-162		may revoke or suspend license of any person afflicted with mental disability. 46-174		
S.D. Compiled Law Ann.	under guardianship non compos mentis, insane. Const. Art. VII, §8						person suffering from any mental disability or disease. 32-12-32	person suffering from any mental disability or disease 32-12-32	no license shall be issued to any person adjudged to be mentally incompetent. 44.03B03(4) (Supp. 1960) 32-12-32	suspension. 32-12-49(4)		
TENN. Code Ann. (1955)	incompetent, 33-1207 (Supp. 1968)		33-1207 (Supp. 1968)	insane, 8-2801(7)		8-2801(7)	unsound mind. 22-102	mental disability or disease, 59-705(e) and (g) (1968)	59-705(e)(1968)	incompetent: suspension; 59-713.5(1968)	33-1207 (Supp. 1968)	adjudicated incompetent. 33-1207 (Supp. 1968)
TEX. Rev. Civ. Stat. Ann. (1969)	lunatics and idiots, Election Code Ann. 5.01 (1967) VI, §1 Second (1955)			ineligible to hold office under state constitution, e.g., senators, qualified state elector. Election Code Ann. 1.05 (1967) Const. Arts. III, §6; VI, §1 Second (1955)			Code Crim. Proc. 35.16(a)(1) and (5)(1966)	6687b.4.6 6687b.4.8	6687b.4.6	revocation. 6687b.30		

Table 9.4   VOTING, HOLDING OFFICE, JURY SERVICE, AND DRIVER'S LICENSE   *continued*

STATE	VOTING			HOLDING PUBLIC OFFICE			JURY PROHIBITIONS	DRIVING			CIVIL RIGHTS	
	Prohibitions	Enforcement	Commitment or Adjudication of Prohibited Condition Required	Prohibitions	Office Specified	Adjudication Required		Prohibitions	Commitment or Adjudication Required	Enforcement--Suspension or Revocation	Retention of	Loss of
UTAH Code Ann. (1953)	insane, idiot. Const. Art. IV, §6 restriction by hospital or an adjudication of incompetency, 64-7-48(1)(c)		incompetency requires adjudication, 64-7-48(1)(c)	Const. Art. IV, §6			sound mind and discretion, 78-46-8(5)	mental disability or disease. 41-2-5(4) 41-2-5(5) (Supp. 1967)	41-2-5(4) (Supp. 1967)	41-2-19(3) (Supp. 1967)	subject to hospital regulations or adjudication of incompetency. 67-7-48(1)(c)	
VT. Stat. Ann. (1968)	restriction by hospital, or an adjudication of incompetency, 18, §7705(a)(3)		incompetency requires adjudication, 18, §7705(a)(3)					mentally unfit, 23, §603			subject to hospital regulations or adjudication of incompetency 18, §7705(a)(3)	
VA. Code Ann. (1969)	insane. Const. Art. II, §23 (1968) 24-18					office declared vacant when officer adjudged insane, 24-147	8-175(1), 8-175(3) (1957)	insane or suffering from a mental disease or disability, 46.1-360 46.1-361 (1967)	46.1-360 (1967)			
WASH. Rev. Code Ann. (1962)	Const. Art. VI, §3 (1966)			Const. Art. VI, §3 (1966) 42.04.020(1961)			in full possession of his faculties & of sound mind. 2.36.070(4) (1961)	insane. 46.20.030(4)	46.20.030(4)	suspension. 46.20.290(3)		
W. VA. Code Ann. (1966)	Const. Art. IV, §1			Const. Art. IV, §1, 4			52-1-2	mental disability or disease, 17B-2-3(5)	17B-2-3(5)	incompetent to drive--suspension, 17B-3-6(5)		
WIS. Stat. Ann. (1958)	persons under guardianship, non compos mentis, or insane. 6.01(1)(a)(1967) Const. Art. 3, §2 (1957)	12.59(1967)					must be possessed of their natural faculties. 255.01(2)(3) (Supp. 1969)	mentally ill or deficient, mental disability or disease. 343.06(5), (7)	343.06(5)	cancellation. 343.25(4)		
WYO. Stat. Ann. (1957)	restriction by hospital or an adjudication of incompetency. Const. Art. 6, §6		incompetency requires adjudication, 25-72(a)(c) (1967)	must be a qualified elector. Const. Art. 6, §15			natural faculties. 1-77.2 court must discharge a person where it appears he is not competent. 1-79			suspension 31-273(3)(f) (1967)	subject to hospital regulations or adjudication of incompetency. 25-72 (1967)	

1. Department shall not issue driver's license to any person who has previously been adjudged insane (or an idiot: Mich. 257.303(5); Ohio 4507.08(b) (Supp. 1968)) until restored to capacity, and not then unless the department is satisfied that such person is competent to operate a motor vehicle with safety to persons or property. Mich. 257.303(5); Minn. 171.04 (5) (Supp. 1969); N.C. 20-9(d) (Supp. 1967); Ohio 4507.08(c) (Supp. 1968); Pa. 75-604(6); R.I. 31-10-3 (5). Or to any person when, in the opinion of the commissioner, such person is afflicted with or suffering from such mental disability or disease as will affect such person in a manner to prevent him from exercising reasonable and ordinary control over a motor vehicle. Del. 21-27-06(b)(4) (Supp. 1970); Mich. 257.303(6); Minn. 171.04(9) (Supp. 1969); Miss. 8093(d), (f); N.C. 20-9(e); Ohio 4507.08(c) (Supp. 1968); Pa. 75-604(7); R.I. 3-10-3(8).

2. All persons non compos mentis or who are otherwise incapable of managing their own affairs, may have their persons and estates, or either of them, placed in control of guardians. Such persons retain all rights of citizens which they have the capacity to enjoy, and which are compatible with their situations. Ga. 79-209 (1964). Among the rights of citizens are the enjoyments of personal security, of personal liberty, private property and disposition thereof, the elective franchise, the right to hold office unless disqualified by the constitution and laws, to appeal to the courts, to testify as a witness, to perform any civil function, and to keep and bear arms. Ga.79-205 (1964).

3. There is no statutory disqualification for mental incapacity. In Wilch v. Shumway, 232 Ill. 54, 83 N.E. 549 (1907), it was held that the vote of a person non compos mentis ought not to be received, but where the voter is able to understand the nature of his act, it is sufficient.

4. A license may be issued when said mentally ill person is placed on parole or convalescent leave, when such issuance has been recommended by the institution medical staff. Iowa 321.177(5).

5. Duty of probate court to report to secretary of state the relevant data of every person adjudged to be insane or feebleminded. Mich. 257.304.

6. Persons placed under guardianship must be reported by the probate judge to the commissioner of registration, who may destroy registration cards of such person. Persons restored or discharged must also be reported, and if not registered, the commissioner must notify them to register. Minn. 201.15 (Supp. 1969).

7. Probate judge removed by governor after adjudication of insanity or mental incapacity. Minn. 525.052 (1969).

8. Although state constitution and a statute (Const. Arts. 9, §8; 23, §310) prohibit the right to vote to idiots and insane persons, registration cards must be canceled only for those persons whose insanity has been legally established. Mont. 23-518.4.

9. Governor shall have power to remove any officer, whom he may appoint, in case of incompetency, and may declare his office vacant. Neb. Const. Art. IV, §12.

10. Licenses of all persons committed to state institutions are revoked; mental defective must have certificate of competence to operate motor vehicle, to be issued by superintendent at his discretion, before license is restored. Neb. 60-419 (Supp. 1967).

11. Shall not issue license to any person who has previously been adjudged to be afflicted with or suffering from any mental disability and who has not been restored to capacity. Shall not issue license to any person when the administrator has good cause to believe that such person by reason of mental disability would not safely operate a motor vehicle. Nev. 483.250.5, 483.250.7.

12. Department shall not issue any license to any person, as an operator or chauffeur, who is afflicted with or suffering from any mental disability or disease which would render him unable to operate a motor vehicle with safety, and who has not at the time of application been restored to health. N.M. 64-13-40F (Supp. 1969).

13. An office shall become vacant before the expiration of the term if the incumbent is found to be a mentally diseased person by the decision of a competent tribunal. Ore. 236.010(6).

Chapter Ten

The Sexual Psychopath and the Law

I. INTRODUCTION

Chapters 1 through 9 of this Report have dealt largely with the law relating to the noncriminal mentally disabled individual. Chapters 10 and 11, on the other hand, will take up mentally disabled persons who have offended the criminal law. When such persons are accused and/or convicted of criminal offenses, they are as a rule hospitalized rather than incarcerated in penal institutions.

The concern of this chapter will be with those persons whose antisocial and criminal conduct is motivated by sexual deviation and who as a consequence are subject to involuntary hospitalization. Such treatment results from special legislation existing in twenty-eight of the states.[1] In several states there is legislation broad enough to permit the involuntary hospitalization of mentally disabled persons who have a propensity toward the commission of anti-social and criminal acts. Not all such persons, however, are motivated by sexual deviation. Since these statutes are seldom used except in connection with sexual deviates, and because of the marked similarity between the procedures followed under them and sexual deviate legislation, discussion will be limited to the latter provisions.

1. The legislation of twenty-eight jurisdictions is considered in this chapter and the appended tables. The table headings indicate the main features of the sex psychopathy laws. Michigan, New York, and South Dakota, which are sometimes included in lists of states having sexual psychopath laws, have been excluded here. The South Dakota statutory authorization for distinctive handling of sex offenders is limited to the post-sentencing transfer of child-molester prisoners to the state hospital for examination and possible hospitalization. Definition of a class of offenders, special hearing procedures, and provisions for release or parole are absent from this brief scheme (*S.D. Compiled Laws Ann.* §§ 22-22-9 to 22-22-10 (1967)). The inclusion elsewhere of New York has been predicated on former § 1940 of the *N.Y. Penal Law,* which provided for indeterminate sentencing and discretionary hospitalization of certain types of habitual offenders. No equivalent of § 1940 has been reenacted in the revised Penal Law of 1965. A bill providing for a comprehensive scheme regarding sex offenders failed in New York in 1947 by veto of the governor. Michigan's sexual psychopath statute (the Goodrich Act) was recently repealed in its entirety and the legal category of criminal sexual psychopath abolished (Public Act 143, effective Aug. 1, 1968). Michigan retains provisions on "sexually delinquent" persons who may be sentenced to prison indeterminately (*Mich. Comp. Laws Ann.* §§ 750.10a, 750.335a et seq. (1968)).

Quite often special legislation concerning sexual deviates and sex offenders is the result of great public uproar over the commission of a brutal sex crime or the execution of a notorious sex offender.[2] For example, Michigan's former sexual psychopath statute was commonly called the Goodrich Act,[3] after a defendant, Martin Goodrich, who was convicted of a heinous sex crime. At the time of the trial considerable evidence was brought out that many persons in the community were aware of Goodrich's abnormal sexual activity, and the psychiatrist's report indicated that if Goodrich had been hospitalized earlier and given psychiatric treatment, the brutal crime might never have occurred. These circumstances were largely responsible for the enactment of the Michigan statute.[4]

It had long been recognized that many sex crimes were committed by individuals who evidenced varying degrees of mental disability. Until the passage of special legislation, persons who had committed sex crimes, unless they were encompassed by one of the traditional tests of insanity, were held responsible for their crimes and consequently incarcerated, even in cases where it was medically clear that incarceration would have no deterrent or rehabilitative effect. This special legislation represents an effort to protect the public through the proper disposition of "persons with criminal propensities to the commission of sex offenses."[5] The statutes are premised upon the assumption that the relatively new science of psychiatry is able to identify, isolate, and treat such individuals. More will be said about this assumption later.

A. MENTALLY DEFICIENT PERSONS

Mentally deficient persons, sometimes referred to as mental defectives, are those mentally disabled persons, not mentally ill, who suffer from organic or

2. Hacker & Frym, "The Sexual Psychopath Act in Practice: A Critical Discussion," 43 *Cal. L. Rev.* 766, 767 (1955); Sutherland & Cressey, *Principles of Criminology* 127 (5th ed. 1955).

3. The Goodrich Act was recently repealed; see note 1 *supra.*

4. ABF Pilot Project Report, "Survey of the Administration of Criminal Justice in the United States, 1958" (unpublished report of the American Bar Foundation).

5. Sutherland, "The Sexual Psychopath Laws," 40 *J. Crim. L.C. & P.S.* 547 (1950).

hereditary disorders affecting their intellectual development.[6] These individuals may be criminally responsible but, nevertheless, unable to make a proper social adjustment. When these persons commit crimes, they are subject to hospitalization under the "defective delinquent" statutes.[7]

B. PSYCHOPATHS

The broadest statutes are those that apply to psychopaths in general. Although the term "psychopath" is not susceptible of precise definition,[8] it is usually

> applied to various inadequacies and deviations in the personality structure of individuals who are neither psychotic nor feebleminded, the defect existing particularly in the connative, emotional and characterological aspects of the personality. These aspects are not so organized and adapted to each other as to operate as a harmonious unit to permit co-ordination of the individual with his environment.[9]

Such individuals are apt to run afoul of the criminal law at some point in their lives. Thus far Pennsylvania, Maryland, and Connecticut have enacted special legislation in regard to them.

Pennsylvania's Greenstein Act,[10] now repealed,

gave the trial judge power, if petitioned by district attorney, defendant, or defendant's counsel, to provide for a mental examination of any convicted criminal. If the defendant was found not criminally insane but mentally ill or mentally deficient, the judge could hospitalize him in an institution until further order of the court.

Section 5 of the Maryland Defective Delinquent statute defines a defective delinquent as:

> An individual who, by the demonstration of persistent aggravated anti-social or criminal behavior, evidences a propensity toward criminal activity and who is found to have either such intellectual deficiency or emotional unbalance, or both, as to clearly demonstrate an actual danger to society so as to require confinement and treatment.[11]

The statute may be applied to criminals convicted and sentenced for (1) a felony or a misdemeanor punishable by imprisonment in a penitentiary, (2) a crime of violence, or (3) a sex crime; it may also be applied to (4) a person having two or more convictions for any offense punishable by imprisonment. Recent legislation in Connecticut[12] has established similar procedures applicable to any person convicted of a sex crime or an offense penalized by imprisonment in a state prison.

The Connecticut and Maryland laws represent the farthest step in the direction of applying psychiatric knowledge to the criminal field. Under such statutes any person convicted of a given category of crimes may be hospitalized in a mental institution rather than incarcerated in a penal institution. The procedure for the hospitalization and treatment of the psychopath roughly parallels that for the sexual psychopath. For the purpose of this chapter the Connecticut and Maryland statutes will be considered as sexual psychopath laws.

Likewise, because most defective delinquent laws have been incorporated into the sexual psychopath statutes or, in those states where they are still separate, the procedures involved correspond closely to the sexual psychopath laws, the remainder of this

6. For statutory definitions of mentally deficient persons who may be subject to civil hospitalization, see Table 3.7, Statutory Definitions of the Mentally Deficient and Epileptics.

7. The first such legislation, enacted in Massachusetts in 1911 (*Mass. Acts & Resolves* 1911, ch. 595, §§ 1–12) recognized "defective delinquents" as a distinct class of criminal offenders. Section 1 authorized the court, where the offense was not punishable by death or imprisonment for life, to commit the offender to a "department for defective delinquents" if "it shall appear that the offender has committed the offense for which he is charged, is mentally defective, and is not a proper subject for the schools for the feeble minded, or for commitment as an insane person." The statute, amended many times, presently appears in *Mass. Ann. Laws* ch. 123, §§ 113–24 (1965) under the heading "Defective Delinquents and Drug Addicts." Massachusetts also has a sexual psychopath law ("Sexually Dangerous Persons") at *Mass. Ann. Laws* ch. 123A, §§ 1–11 (1965, Supp. 1968).

8. See Note, "The Psychopathic Personality," 10 *Rutgers L. Rev.* 425 (1955). Although some authorities presently prefer the term "sociopath" or "sociopathic personality," the older term "psychopath" has been retained in this chapter because it is used in most of the relevant statutes.

9. Noyes, *Modern Clinical Psychiatry* 504 (1940). For similar definitions see Hoag & Williams, *Crime, Abnormal Minds and the Law* 105 (1923); Weiss & English, *Psychosomatic Medicine* 549 (1943). See also the definition given by the American Psychiatric Association, at text accompanying note 82 *infra*.

10. This act was passed as Pa. Public Law 224 (1933), amended by Pa. Public Law 352 (1935), *Pa. Stat. Ann.* tit. 19, §§ 1153–56, and repealed by Pa. Public Law 533, art. X, § 1001

(1951). For the text of the law see Michigan, *Report of the Governor's Study Commission on the Deviated Criminal Sex Offender* 131 (1951) [hereinafter referred to as *Michigan Report*].

11. *Md. Ann. Code* art. 31B, § 5 (1967). See Sas v. Maryland, 334 F.2d 506 (4th Cir. 1964) for a reference to the controversy regarding the constitutionality of legislation like the Maryland statute.

12. *Conn. Gen. Stat. Ann.* § 17-244 (1960).

chapter will be concerned only with sexual psychopath statutes.

C. SEXUAL PSYCHOPATHS

There are as many definitions or descriptions of the sexual psychopathic personality as there are statutes on the subject. Generally, though, the common denominator in the various statutes is the reference to the person's inability to control his own sexual acts or perversions.[13] How this inability is demonstrated is the subject of variation.

Many of the sexual psychopath statutes expressly stipulate that the sex offender's mental condition fall somewhere short of legal insanity for the statute to apply; contemplated is a type of mental disability not legally recognized as sufficiently severe to render the individual criminally irresponsible.[14] It may be questioned whether such a description of mental condition is medically or legally defensible: an arbitrary designation of certain forms of deviant behavior as "mental abnormality short of insanity" assumes a theory of human conduct deemed unacceptable in many psychiatric circles today. Moreover, it assumes the legal question of responsibility rather than determining it. The defect is especially obvious in statutes which explicitly state the causal relation of the individual's mental condition to the illegal act which calls the statute into play.[15] For instance, if, as in some jurisdictions, the test of criminal responsibility turns on whether the offense was the product or result of mental disease,[16] in what sense can the sexual psychopath's mental condition be said to fall short of legal insanity or fail to absolve from criminal responsibility? And if a mental condition such as sociopathy is a mental disease or defect for purposes of criminal responsibility, as it is in some jurisdictions,[17] or for purposes of diagnosis or treatment, as it is according to prevailing psychiatric thought,[18] what is the justification of a statute in which psychopathy is not?

Irrespective of their various wordings, the sexual psychopath statutes appear to be predicated on the view that prison sentences are not a deterrent to sexual psychopaths and that medical treatment may make them useful citizens again.[19] The legislation has been viewed by some writers as an extension of the traditional concept of insanity in criminal proceedings.[20] The aim is twofold: (1) to protect society by providing for indeterminate confinement of sexually deviated offenders, and (2) during confinement, to provide medical treatment for the cure of their abnormality.

II. PROCEDURES

The material in this section is presented graphically in Table 10.2, Psychopathy and the Law, *infra*. On the basis of the scope of their jurisdiction the statutes may be divided into two major groups: (1) preconviction statutes, under which jurisdiction extends to persons merely charged with crime, and (2) postconviction statutes, which require that the alleged psychopaths actually be convicted of a criminal offense before the statute may apply.

The postconviction statutes represent the more recent trend in special legislation aimed at sex offenders. Of the twenty-eight jurisdictions presently having such legislation, only a third follow the preconviction model. Since 1950, most states enacting sex offender legislation have adopted the postconviction type. The exceptions to this trend are Florida and Iowa, as well as Alabama, which in 1961 converted its statute to the preconviction form.[21]

13. See Table 10.1, Statutory Considerations of Sexual Psychopaths and Related Offenders, for statutory definitions. For studies of the various sexual psychopath statutes see Bensing, "A Comparative Study of American Sex Statutes," 42 *J. Crim. L.C. & P.S.* 57 (1951); Group for the Advancement of Psychiatry, "The Sexual Psychopath Laws," in *Psychiatrically Deviated Sex Offenders,* App. A (1950); Swanson, "Sexual Psychopath Statutes," 51 *J. Crim. L.C. & P.S.* 215 (1960).

14. Typical provisions are, e.g., *D.C. Code Ann.* § 22-3503(1) (1967); *Fla. Stat. Ann.* § 917.12 (Supp. 1969). *Ala. Code* tit. 15, § 434 (Supp. 1967) begins: "Any person who is suffering from a mental disorder but is not mentally ill or feebleminded to an extent making him criminally irresponsible . . . ."

15. E.g., *Cal. Welf. & Inst'ns Code* § 6300 (West Supp. 1968): "Mentally *disordered* sex offender means any person who *by reason of mental defect*, disease, or disorder, is predisposed to the commission of sexual offenses. . . ." California has a different definition for a separate class of mentally *abnormal* sex offenders: *Cal. Welf. & Inst'ns Code* § 6450 (West Supp. 1968). (Emphasis added.)

16. See Durham v. United States, 214 F.2d 862 (D.C. Cir. 1954). See generally chap. 11, "Mental Disability and the Criminal Law." Cf. also the rule of criminal responsibility in *Model Penal Code* § 4.01.

17. See Blocker v. United States, 274 F.2d 572 (D.C. Cir. 1959), 320 F.2d 800 (D.C. Cir. 1963).

18. Ibid.

19. Hirning, "The Sex Offender in Custody," in *Handbook of Correctional Psychology* 233, 255 (1947).

20. See *In re* Mundy, 97 N.H. 239, 244, 85 A.2d 371, 374 (1952); Maryland, Report of the Legislative Council, *An Indeterminate Sentence Law for Defective Delinquents* (no. 29 at 2, 1950); Mihm, "A Re-examination of Our Sex Psychopath Statutes," 44 *J. Crim. L.C. & P.S.* 716–17 (1954).

21. Comment, "The Validity of the Segregation of the Sexual

The majority of the postconviction statutes apply only to persons who commit certain named sex offenses. However, some psychiatrists are of the opinion that many crimes, not in themselves sex crimes, may nevertheless in some instances be motivated by sexual deviation. Several of the postconviction statutes, therefore, apply also to persons convicted of any criminal offense in which sexual deviation appears to have been an element.[22]

The law's preoccupation with sex offenses and offenders is pointedly reflected in a California statute which provides that convicted sex offenders must register with the sheriff or chief of police of the county or city of their residence or temporary domicile within thirty days of their arrival there.[23] It is far from clear whether this concern is always necessary and/or humanitarian.

A. INITIATION OF PROCEEDINGS

Under the preconviction statutes the petition alleging sexual psychopathy is filed prior to, during, or after the trial for the criminal offense but in any event prior to the time sentence is pronounced.[24]

Under these statutes it is usually the rule that the filing of the petition alleging sexual psychopathy will be sufficient to cause the court to suspend or postpone any criminal proceedings that may be in progress until the issue of sexual psychopathy is determined.[25]

Psychopath under the Law," 26 *Ohio St. L.J.* 640, 646 (1965). See Table 10.2, Psychopathy and the Law, Time of Proceedings columns. Florida's statute may be applied prior to as well as subsequent to conviction. (*Fla. Stat. Ann.* § 917.12(2) [Supp. 1969]).

22. See Table 10.1.

23. *Cal. Penal Code* § 290 (West Supp. 1968); see also *Cal. Penal Code* § 290.5 and *Cal. Welf. & Inst'ns Code* § 6302. See People v. Jones, 42 Cal. 2d 219, 266 P.2d 38 (1954); Lambert v. California, 355 U.S. 225 (1957).

24. The District of Columbia, Florida, and Indiana also permit the filing of the petition after sentencing if the defendant has been placed on probation and the probationary period has not yet expired. For statutory citations to this material see Table 10.2.

25. However, in Washington the petition alleging that the defendant is a sexual psychopath must be filed and served on the defendant ten days prior to trial of the criminal charge. The court may proceed to hear the criminal charge. If the defendant is convicted or has previously pleaded guilty to the charge, sentence is pronounced; the court then proceeds to hear the sexual psychopathy allegations. Acquittal does not suspend the hearing on the issue of psychopathy, but provisions authorizing transfer of a committed sexual psychopath to a correctional institution do *not* apply to the committed sexual psychopath

Generally, the preconviction statutes permit hospitalization proceedings to be initiated only by the district attorney or the attorney general. A number of states also permit the court to initiate proceedings on its own motion or on motion of the defense. The typical provision authorizes the prosecuting attorney, at his discretion, to file a petition alleging sexual psychopathy if he has reasonable ground to believe that the defendant is the type of sex offender defined by the statute.

Procedures under the postconviction statutes, unlike those of the preconviction laws, carry the trial on the criminal offense to the stage of conviction before making a determination on the issue of psychopathy.

Some postconviction statutes do not provide for a separate hearing on the issue of psychopathy.[26] The judge makes his decision on the basis of the report and recommendations of the medical examiners. In states that do provide for a separate hearing, the procedures set forth are similar to those of the preconviction statutes.[27]

B. MEDICAL EXAMINATIONS

Both the preconviction and postconviction statutes provide for a prehearing medical examination of the defendant, to be conducted by two or more medical examiners appointed by the court. It is generally required that the examiners be psychiatrists. However, a limited number of states[28] merely require that the examiners be "physicians" and not specifically psychiatrists or specialists in the diagnosis of mental diseases. Some of the statutes require only that the examination consist of one or more interviews with the examiners, while others provide for temporary hospitalization in a special institution for observation and diagnosis.[29] Such hospitalization is usually limited to thirty or sixty days. Pennsylvania provides for the longest period of observation: ninety days plus the possibility of an additional thirty-day extension upon request of the psychiatric

---

who has been acquitted of the criminal charge. *Wash. Rev. Code Ann.* § 71.06.020 (1962) and § 71.06.030 (Supp. 1968).

26. Under the recent ruling of the United States Supreme Court in Specht v. Patterson, 386 U.S. 605 (1967), statutes failing to provide for a separate hearing on the issue of psychopathy are probably unconstitutional if applied accordingly. Cf. Williams v. New York, 337 U.S. 241 (1949). See this chapter, § V D 4, Standard Procedural Protections of the Criminal Trial.

27. See Table 10.2, Hearing column.

28. See Table 10.2, Medical Examination columns.

29. See Table 10.2, Commitment Period columns.

examiner.[30] In Washington the observation period "shall not exceed 60 days unless a jury trial has been demanded."[31] The statutes are often unclear regarding the need for a "second hearing" on the issue of indeterminate hospitalization following the period of observational hospitalization. In Indiana, for example, the statute ambiguously states that following a diagnostic report from the hospital that the defendant is a sexual psychopath, "the court shall then determine the question of the psychopathy of the accused person."[32] The correct interpretation of this language may be a point of debate, but it is clear that as a matter of practice in Indiana, the accused is sometimes not returned to the court following the observation period.[33]

The laws of the District of Columbia and Indiana expressly require that the defendant answer the questions asked by the medical examiners under penalty of contempt of court.[34] The same rule exists by judicial interpretation in several other states.[35] The constitutionality of this type of rule has been upheld by the courts on the grounds that the proceedings are civil in nature and the customary safeguards of a criminal trial need not be observed; also, the statutes of these states generally provide that any evidence which may be brought out during the psychopathy hearing and which tends to prove criminal activity by the defendant may not be used against him in any other civil or criminal action. The trend in recent years, however, seems to be toward requiring observation of the safeguards of a criminal trial at sexual psychopath proceedings;[36]

30. *Pa. Stat. Ann.* tit. 19, § 1168 (Supp. 1969).

31. *Wash. Rev. Code Ann.* § 71.02.130 (1962).

32. *Ind. Ann. Stat.* § 9-3404(d) (Supp. 1968). The "first hearing" determines "probable psychopathy" and leads to observational hospitalization.

33. Granucci & Granucci, "Indiana's Sexual Psychopath Act in Operation," 44 *Ind. L.J.* 555, 557 (1969). The controversy may well be entirely academic: when "second hearings" *are* held the courts virtually never disagree with the hospital's findings.

34. *D.C. Code Ann.* § 22-3506 (1967); *Ind. Ann. Stat.* § 9-3404(a) (Supp. 1968). The Indiana provision was recently upheld by the Indiana Supreme Court in Haskett v. Marion Criminal Court, 234 N.E.2d 636 (1968). The Haskett decision has been attacked as inconsistent with the principle of Specht v. Patterson, 386 U.S. 605 (1967). See Note, "Indiana's Sexual Psychopath Statute," 44 *Ind. L.J.* 242 (1969).

35. Mihm, *supra* note 20.

36. See Annot., 24 A.L.R.2d 350 (1952, esp. Later Case Service 1965 and Supp. 1969); Specht v. Patterson, 386 U.S. 605 (1967); Gerchman v. Maroney, 355 F.2d 302 (3d Cir. 1966). For an elaboration on this trend, see this chapter, § V D 4, Standard Procedural Protections of the Criminal Trial.

thus, merely barring use of the evidence obtained at the medical examination in proceedings *other* than the psychopathy hearing for which the examination was conducted may be viewed as an insufficient protection.

A number of the states which provide for medical examination by two or three examiners require that, before the court may proceed with the case, the examiners agree, either unanimously or by majority, that the defendant is the type of sex offender defined in the statute.[37]

When a separate hearing on the question of psychopathy is held, the medical examiners are commonly required to be witnesses, and they may be examined by both parties. The defendant is usually allowed to have a psychiatrist of his own choosing examine him at the expense of the state.

C. RIGHT TO COUNSEL AND TRIAL BY JURY

Under both post- and preconviction statutes the defendant has the right to have counsel represent him at the psychopathy hearing. However, only Iowa, Minnesota, and Nebraska provide that when the defendant is unable to obtain counsel by his own efforts the court shall appoint counsel for him. Despite the scarcity of such provisions, an American Bar Foundation study[38] has noted that as a practical matter "counsel is provided to some extent in virtually every state that has such a proceeding." The phrase "to some extent" is not clarified; further, the question remains whether anything less than the fullest extent is constitutionally permissible.[39]

In most states the preconviction statutes set out that the defendant may demand a jury hearing on the issue of psychopathy or that either party is entitled to a jury hearing upon demand.[40] Missouri leaves the use of a jury to the discretion of the judge; New Hampshire explicitly denies the defendant the right to a jury hearing, and the Minnesota statute is silent on this point.[41]

D. SENTENCE

Upon a finding of sexual psychopathy all the preconviction statutes authorize indeterminate hospital-

37. See Table 10.2, Medical Examination columns.

38. Silverstein, *Defense of the Poor* 144 (1965).

39. See subsequent discussion on the applicability of criminal trial procedures to sexual psychopath hearings, this chapter, § V, Critical Evaluation.

40. See Table 10.2, Jury column.

41. *Mo. Rev. Stat.* § 202.720(4) (1962); *N.H. Rev. Stat. Ann.* § 173:5(VI) (1964); *Minn. Stat. Ann.* § 526.10 (1947).

ization in a mental institution. Three allow the defendant to appeal the finding.[42] Sentence under the postconviction statutes is usually for an indeterminate period with no minimum or maximum time prescribed; such sentence is in lieu of the sentence provided by the regular criminal code, and as such is appealable.[43]

In a majority of the statutes, both pre- and postconviction, a finding of sexual psychopathy and subsequent hospitalization do not serve as a defense to a later trial or to sentencing on the original criminal offense.[44] However, in the latter type of statute the time spent under the hospitalization order is to count as time served under the criminal sentence. No sound reasons exist for not crediting time served upon a preconviction hospitalization order. Moreover, recent case law suggests that the defense of double jeopardy may be held to apply in the context of sexual psychopath proceedings.[45]

E. RELEASE

The release procedures for the preconviction and postconviction statutes are similar. Release may be predicated upon a medical finding that the prisoner is cured or "fully recovered" and is no longer a psychopath or, more often, that he has improved sufficiently to be no longer dangerous to others. Thus, his release would not be dangerous to the public. The release procedure most often followed requires that the patient be certified by the superintendent of the institution in which he is hospitalized as cured or improved and then returned to the court for a prerelease hearing. If the court decides that the defendant is to be released, a common procedure is to place him on probation prior to granting a complete discharge.[46] The rule in most jurisdic-

tions is that habeas corpus may be used to effect release under these statutes.[47]

The release procedures of jurisdictions which stipulate that the patient must be cured or fully recovered from his psychopathy have been criticized as too stringent or unrealistic. The identification and treatment of sexual psychopaths remain a very uncertain process; thus, criteria of release based on improvement rather than permanent cure or total recovery seem more appropriate.[48]

III. CONSTITUTIONAL PROBLEMS

Illinois and Michigan were the first states to enact sexual psychopath statutes. The Illinois provisions were passed in 1938.[49] In 1937, Michigan had enacted a statute applicable to sexual psychopaths,[50] but the statute was immediately challenged and declared unconstitutional on the grounds of double jeopardy and lack of a jury trial.[51] The defendant in that case, having been previously convicted of gross indecency, was serving his sentence in the reformatory at Ionia. After the passage of the 1937 Act, the Commissioner of Pardons and Paroles filed a petition to have the defendant committed to a state hospital on the grounds—in the language of the statute—that the defendant, "though not insane, appears to be a sex degenerate, and appears to be suffering from a mental disorder characterized by marked sex deviation, with tendencies dangerous to public safety."

The finding of unconstitutionality was based primarily on the fact that the law was an amendment and an addition to a section of the Michigan Criminal Code. Although the attorney general contended that the proceeding authorized by the statute was a civil one analogous to statutory inquests relating to insane prisoners, the majority of the court held the proceeding to be criminal in nature; as such it violated the right of the accused to a trial by a jury from the locale of the crime, as secured by the Constitution, and also placed him in the position of being sentenced a second time for the same crime.

Shortly after the 1937 Act was declared uncon-

42. *Ind. Ann. Stat.* § 9-3406 (1956); *Iowa Code* § 225A.5 (Supp. 1969); *Mo. Rev. Stat.* § 202.720(4) (1962).

43. See Annot., *supra* note 36.

44. See Table 10.2, Disposition of Original Offense columns. Florida and New Hampshire expressly provide that a person found to be a sexual psychopath may not later be tried on the offense for which he originally stood charged. Connecticut, Massachusetts, New Jersey, Ohio, Oregon, Pennsylvania, Wisconsin, and Wyoming either protect a person from further sentencing when released as cured or provide that the total period of incarceration may not exceed the maximum period for which he could have been sentenced for commission of the criminal offense. See Table 10.2, Commitment Period columns.

45. See Specht v. Patterson, 386 U.S. 605 (1967); Gerchman v. Maroney, 355 F.2d 302 (3d Cir. 1966).

46. See Table 10.2, Release columns.

47. Mihm, *supra* note 20, at 725.

48. See, e.g., Cohen, "Administration of the Criminal Sexual Psychopath Statute in Indiana," 32 *Ind. L.J.* 450 (1957), to the effect that it is impossible for a psychiatrist to know that a sexual psychopathic patient has fully recovered.

49. *Ill. Rev. Stat.* ch. 38, §§ 820.01–825 (1957); presently *Ill. Rev. Stat.* ch. 38, §§ 105-1.01 to 105-12 (1967).

50. Mich. Public Acts 1937, No. 196, at 305.

51. People v. Frontczak, 286 Mich. 51, 281 N.W. 534 (1938).

stitutional, the Michigan legislature enacted a new statute as part of the Civil Code;[52] this new statute was similar in most respects to the old one. In 1942 the new law was held to be constitutional in *People v. Chapman*.[53]

It was contended in the *Chapman* case that the statute was unconstitutional in that (1) it denied the defendant the equal protection of the laws because it limited "the class of criminal sexual psychopathic persons who might be brought within its provision only to those who are charged with a criminal offense," and (2) it arbitrarily created a special group out of this class by giving the attorney general or the prosecuting attorney discretion in initiating proceedings.[54]

The court answered the first contention by stating that it was well recognized that the legislature might make classifications of persons, provided such classifications were based on reasonable and substantial distinctions and were in accord with the aims to be achieved. On the second contention, the court held that such delegation of discretion was reasonably essential to the administration of the statute and did not deny the defendant equal protection of the laws.

The court further found that proceedings under the new statute were civil proceedings and therefore were not circumscribed by the constitutional and statutory requirements surrounding a person accused of or tried for a crime.

After the passage of legislation in Illinois and Michigan, psychopath statutes were enacted in California, Massachusetts, Minnesota, Ohio, and Wisconsin. In 1940 the constitutionality of the Minnesota act was upheld by the United States Supreme Court in the case of Minnesota ex rel. *Pearson v. Probate Court*.[55] It was contended by the petitioner in *Pearson* that the definition of persons to whom the statute was to apply was too vague and indefinite to meet the standards of due process and that since the statute carved a special group out of a class, it failed to extend to the defendant the equal protection of the laws.

The Supreme Court, adopting the construction of the statute set forth by the Minnesota Supreme Court, held that the statute as interpreted by that court was not so vague as to be unconstitutional.[56] The court further stated that the statute did not deprive the defendant of the equal protection of the laws, since the legislature was free to recognize different degrees of harm and could confine its restrictions to those classes of cases where it deemed the need to be greatest.

Traditionally, the question of the constitutionality of the sex psychopath statutes has been stated as follows:

> In determining the constitutionality of the sex psychopath statutes, the crux of our consideration rests upon the judicial determination of whether the proceedings under the act are criminal or civil. No one questions the power of the state to commit to institutions mentally unbalanced persons who become dangerous to the peace and safety of the community. The care, treatment and indeterminate commitment of persons who are insane, mentally deranged, emotionally or mentally ill, has long been considered as a civil rather than a criminal proceeding. The object of the state is to offer a method for protecting society from the acts of such persons by placing them in such confinement as would be favorable to their cure. This commitment is not regarded as a punishment or a sentence. Consequently, the normal guarantees so jealously guarded by the courts in criminal proceedings do not apply to civil commitment procedures.[57]

Today, this view and its rationale are still uttered by some courts, but with considerably less certainty and conviction. The substantive constitutionality of the sex psychopath laws is still accepted; but the procedural inadequacies and their traditional justification by means of designating the laws as "civil" rather than "criminal" have recently been seriously and at times effectively challenged.[58]

52. *Mich. Comp. Laws* §§ 780.501–780.509 (1948). These provisions, originally enacted as Mich. Public Acts 1939, No. 165, at 323, are now repealed; see note 1 *supra*.

53. 301 Mich. 584, 4 N.W.2d 18 (1942).

54. Id. at 596–97, 4 N.W.2d at 23–24.

55. 309 U.S. 270 (1940).

56. The Minnesota Supreme Court held: "It can reasonably be said that the language of Section 1 of the act is intended to include those persons who, by a habitual course of misconduct in sexual matters, have evidenced an utter lack of power to control their sexual impulses and who, as a result, are likely to attack or otherwise inflict injury, loss, pain or other evil on the objects of their uncontrolled and uncontrollable desire. It would not be reasonable to apply the provisions of the statute to every person guilty of sexual misconduct nor even to persons having strong sexual propensities. Such a definition would not only make the act impracticable of enforcement and, perhaps, unconstitutional in its application, but would also be an unwarranted departure from the accepted meaning of the words defined." State *ex rel.* Pearson v. Probate Court, 205 Minn. 545, 555, 287 N.W. 297, 302 (1939), *aff'd*, 309 U.S. 270 (1940).

57. Mihm, *supra* note 20, at 718.

58. One commentator has noted that many of the sexual psy-

IV. NUMBER OF HOSPITALIZATIONS

In view of the constitutional as well as the practical doubts regarding the utilization of the sex psychopath laws, the statutes today are not widely applied. With a few notable exceptions, such as California and Wisconsin, the courts of most jurisdictions "seem uneasy" about the use of sex psychopath provisions.[59] Numerically, therefore, the problems surrounding sex psychopath legislation might not be of the greatest significance; in terms of principle and the potential for individual injustices, however, a critical evaluation of the sex psychopathy concept is of high importance.

V. CRITICAL EVALUATION

Critics challenge the sexual psychopath laws upon four distinct grounds: (1) the basic assumptions underlying the need for such laws, (2) the inability to identify the sexual psychopath, (3) the nonexistence or inadequacy of treatment for such individuals, and (4) the lack of protection of individual rights. A fifth ground for criticism, which runs through the other four, is the unwarrantedly broad scope of these laws.

---

chopath statutes are saved only by the fact that they have not come before the United States Supreme Court. Gorrell, "The Sexual Psychopath Laws: Validity and Construction," 14 *Baylor L. Rev.* 93 (1962). See also Annot., *supra* 36, listing decisions which undercut the traditional view. See especially the recent case of Specht v. Patterson, 386 U.S. 605 (1967).

59. Comment, *supra* note 21, at 656, citing Bowman & Engle, "Sexual Psychopath Laws," *Sexual Behavior and the Law* 757, 761–62 (Slovenko ed. 1965).

On the other hand, the utilization of the sex offender statutes often appears to be underestimated in the popular conception. See Granucci & Granucci, *supra* note 33, at 555 n.3: "One reason for this lack of attention [regarding the Indiana statute] has been the mistaken belief that the statute is not used." The article indicates that the Indiana sex offender law has been used more than 450 times in the past decade.

In California the number of sex offenders admitted to institutions via the statutory provisions totalled 812 in 1964, 804 in 1966, and 707 in 1968. (Letter from the Cal. Dep't of Mental Hygiene, Bureau of Biostatistics, July 25, 1969.)

In Wisconsin, since 1951 over 3,000 convicted sex offenders have been examined under the law and over half of these were recommended for institutional treatment. Over the past decade, the policy of the state's Sex Crimes Facility has been to admit only individuals committed under the "mandatory" aspect of the statute and to exclude "permissive" referrals. It is estimated that a less restrictive policy would result in a caseload of some 400, far beyond the institution's capacity. Under the existing policy, the Wisconsin institution had on Dec. 31, 1968, a residency of 143 offenders: 118 commitments and 25 cases for presentence examination. (Letter from the Wis. Dep't of Health and Social Services, Bureau of Clinical Services, July 31, 1969.)

A. NEED FOR SEXUAL PSYCHOPATH LAWS

There is available a relatively large body of material that challenges the underlying assumptions of the sex deviate laws. The assumptions most often attacked are: (1) the sex deviate is more dangerous than other types of criminals; (2) there is a high degree of recidivism among sex deviates—higher than among other criminals; (3) such sex deviates can be isolated; and (4) there are in existence both methods of treatment and necessary facilities for treatment that will lead to recovery.

Many studies have been made to determine how dangerous the sex deviate actually is. The report of the Illinois Commission on Sex Offenders concludes that "not more than about 5% of convicted sex offenders are dangerous."[60] Another author has stated:

There are very few aggressive and dangerous sex offenders in the criminal population. Most of the deviates are mild and submissive, more an annoyance than a menace to the community.[61]

In addition to the fact that the danger represented by sex offenders is overemphasized,[62] it appears that the sexual psychopath statutes are not designed, or are interpreted as not being designed, to deal with those sex offenders who *are* dangerous. The practice in many jurisdictions has been to apply the sex offender statutes primarily to those whose acts are passive or merely morally offensive, while more violent offenders are subjected to the regular criminal processes.[63] This policy may even be reflected in the

---

60. Illinois, *Report of the Illinois Commission on Sex Offenders to the Sixty-eighth General Assembly of the State of Illinois* 11 (1953) [hereinafter referred to as *Illinois Report*].

61. Tappan, "Sentences for Sex Criminals," 42 *J. Crim. L.C. & P.S.* 332, 336 (1951).

62. Some other studies making this point include: California, Dep't of Mental Hygiene, *California Sexual Deviate Research* 15, 39 (1953) [hereinafter referred to as *California Report 1953*]; California, Dep't of Mental Hygiene, *California Sexual Deviate Research* 98–100 (1954) [hereinafter referred to as *California Report 1954*]; New Jersey, *Report of the Commission on the Habitual Sex Offender* 13–14 (1950) [hereinafter referred to as *New Jersey Report*]; Sutherland, *supra* note 5, at 543–48; Ellis & Brancale, *The Psychology of Sex Offenders* 32–33 (1956).

63. See Burick, "An Analysis of the Illinois Sexually Dangerous Persons Act," 59 *J. Crim. L.C. & P.S.* 254, 255 (1968), citing *Illinois Report, supra* note 60, at 14; Smith, "Their Therapeutic Possibilities and the Legal Difficulties Encountered in a 20-Year Experience in the Psychiatric Division," Illinois Department of Public Safety, Menard, Illinois (1963); Tappan, *Crime, Justice and Correction* 414 (1960).

See also Note, *supra* note 34, at 261: "[The Indiana] statute

statutes themselves: thus, while the sex offender laws were ostensibly enacted in response to violent sex offenders who pose a serious threat to society, a statute such as Indiana's, for instance, expressly excludes from its coverage those charged with murder, manslaughter, or statutory rape.[64]

The belief that sexual psychopaths have higher recidivism rates than other offenders has also come under increasing attack. It would be only natural, of course, to expect sex offenders who fit the definitions of the statutes to be highly recidivist, since that is how the statutes define them. Moreover, as indicated previously, the statutes in many jurisdictions are applied primarily to nonviolent offenders, and there is evidence that minor offenders such as exhibitionists are indeed much more recidivist than more violent offenders.[65] But sexual psychopaths, as a whole, appear to have lower rates of prior conviction and parole violation than any other type of prisoner, and certain types of sex offenders have extremely low rates of recidivism. According to a California statistical study,[66] only 7.2 percent of sex offenders had been in prison two or more times previously, as compared with 16 percent of all prisoners. The "proportion of sex offense prisoners without prior criminal commitment ranged from 37.9 for sodomists to 58.5 percent for those imprisoned for incest." It is concluded that "one-half of all sex offenders committed to California prisons have a prior commitment record for some type of offense, and about one-fifth have a prior prison record." California has similar statistics on parole violators.[67] Less than 10 percent of paroled sex offenders commit new crimes of a serious nature while on parole. With regard to total violation rate on parole, sex offenders have only a 31.8 percent violation rate as compared to a rate of 50.3 percent for other prisoners.

Paul W. Tappan concludes:

Our sex offenders are among the least recidivous of all types of criminals. They do not characteristically repeat as do our burglars, arsonists, and thugs.[68]

The thrust of these critics is not that there are no recidivist sex offenders, but rather that if the reason for establishing such legislation is the elimination of recidivism among criminals, other types of criminals pose a greater need for such legislation.

Closely related to recidivism is the theory that sex deviates progress from minor sex crimes to major sex crimes of force and violence. Studies have shown that such is not the case.[69]

Studies have also been made to determine whether sex crimes are on the increase in this country. Thus far the results may be termed inconclusive: the statistical methodology appears to have been defective, and—possibly for that reason—the studies fail to agree with each other.[70]

The statistical attack on the underlying assumptions of the sex psychopathy laws has been complemented by more generally polemical criticism. Argues one study:

[I]n the face of the patent fallacies used to support indefinite treatment of the sex deviate, is it not apparent that in reality other motives have guided most of the recent legislation? Perhaps the anxiety and guilt feelings that are associated with sex in the American mentality? Individual treatment by open-ended sen-

is made available to a prosecuting attorney where the result will be an enormous increase in the period of incarceration of a misdemeanant but . . . not . . . to a defendant charged with a felony even when that felony is a serious sex offense."

64. *Ind. Ann. Stat.* § 9-3401 (Burns 1956).

65. See Burick, *supra* note 63, at 256, citing Ellis & Brancale, *supra* note 62, at 33–37.

66. *California Report* 1953, *supra* note 62, at 21.

67. See *California Report* 1953, *supra* note 62, at 20–25; *California Report* 1954, *supra* note 62, at 100. See also Schnur, "Prison Conduct and Recidivism," 40 *J. Crim. L.C. & P.S.* 36, 38 (1949).

68. Tappan, *supra* note 61, at 336. See also *Michigan Report, supra* note 10, at 4; *Illinois Report, supra* note 60, at 11; *New Jersey Report, supra* note 62, at 14, 22–24; Ellis & Brancale, *supra* note 62, at 33–37; Ploscowe, *Sex and the Law* 216–17 (1951); Sutherland, *supra* note 5, at 547.

69. *Illinois Report, supra* note 60, at 11–19; *Michigan Report, supra* note 10, at 4; *New Jersey Report, supra* note 62, at 14; Sutherland, *supra* note 5, at 547; Tappan, "Some Myths about the Sex Offender," 19 *Fed. Probation* 7, 9 (June 1955); and Guttmacher & Weihofen, *Psychiatry and the Law* 11 (1952), who state that "a graduation from minor offenses, such as exhibitionism, to major offenses, such as rape, is almost unknown."

70. There is a dearth of recent scientific evidence on all these topics. Much of the literature continues to rely on studies done during the 1950s. What new evidence is available usually comes by way of personal correspondence, interviews, or unpublished reports. If anything can be concluded from these sources it is that information about the increase, dangerousness, and recidivism of sex offenders—while continuing to confirm the doubts about the underlying assumptions of sexual psychopath laws—remains inconclusive and unsubstantiated. See, e.g., including source citations therein, Comment, *supra* note 21; Comment, "The Plight of the Sexual Psychopath," 41 *Notre Dame Law.* 527 (1966); Birnbaum, "Primum Non Nocere: How to Treat the Criminal Psychopath," 52 *A.B.A.J.* 69 (1966); Bowman & Engle, *supra* note 59; Note, *supra* note 34; Granucci & Granucci, *supra* note 33; Burick, *supra* note 63.

tences reflects our underlying need to punish the sex deviate more severely than other criminals.[71]

The misapplication of the sex offender laws lends support to this point. The fact that the "truly dangerous offender is usually subjected to the criminal sanctions, and the minor offender is caught up in the sex-psychopathy procedures"[72] clearly belies one major rationale of the laws.

Yet dubiousness of rationale and potential for misapplication are not in themselves mandates for repeal or voidance on constitutional grounds. Other criticisms remain, however, which have been interpreted as such.

B. IDENTIFICATION OF THE SEXUAL PSYCHOPATH

One of the principal problems encountered in the administration of the sexual psychopath statutes has been the difficulty of identifying the class of persons to whom the statutes are applicable. The problem centers around the use of the term "psychopath."

1. LEGAL STANDARDS OF IDENTIFICATION

A major function of any law is to define clearly that class of persons to which the law applies. In this respect the sex deviate laws have failed. While purporting to deal with the same personality in their sex deviate laws, some twenty-eight jurisdictions give that many different definitions or descriptions of the psychopath. These definitions, set forth in Table 10.1, Statutory Considerations of Sexual Psychopaths and Related Offenders, include such phrases as: "not mentally ill or feeble-minded to an extent making him criminally irresponsible," "affected in a degree constituting a menace," "psychopathic personality," "marked departures from normal personality," "utter lack of power to control his sexual impulses," "threat of bodily harm to members of the public," "any person convicted of an offense involving physical force or violence," "disparity of age between an adult or a minor," "sexual

act of a compulsive or repetitive nature."[73] In an effort to avoid the problems connected with the use of the term "psychopath," some states recently enacting or amending their statutes have not used the word "psychopath" alone but have either substituted other terms or appended descriptive adjectives. For example, various statutes designate the individuals as sexual psychopaths, mentally abnormal sex offenders, sexually dangerous persons, criminal sexual psychopaths, sex offenders, or psychopathic personalities.

Medical observers almost universally decry the failure of the sexual psychopath laws to establish an effective definition or legal criteria for identifying the sexual psychopath. "The sex psychopath laws fail miserably in this vital task. . . . The vagueness of these criteria is immediately apparent. By definition, any ordinary psychosis which can be clinically recognized by a competent psychiatrist is excluded."[74]

Recognition of the legal insufficiency of statutory definitions is not confined to the medical profession. Almost all legislative research committees have pointed out the problem.[75] In addition, the lack of adequate definition has raised the constitutional problem of vagueness.[76]

2. MEDICAL STANDARDS OF IDENTIFICATION

Much of the difficulty in definition stems from the fact that psychiatrists themselves disagree widely about the connotation of the term "psychopath." The state of medical confusion over the term "sexual psychopath" is ascertainable from the 1950 *New Jersey Report,* where twenty-nine medical authorities give twenty-nine different definitions.[77] This listing and a study of over 200 terms applied to the psychopath[78] are sufficient to create a great

71. Tappan, *supra* note 61, at 335–36.

72. Comment, *supra* note 21, at 654, citing Ploscowe, *supra* note 68, at 229. See also Note, *supra* note 34, at 251 and Burick, *supra* note 63, at 256. The suggestion in these articles is that the sex psychopathy provisions often serve as legal ploys whereby prosecutors obtain harsh penalties against offenders of public morality in cases where sufficient evidence is wanting and/or where the criminal penalties would be less severe. There is some evidence that the last decade has seen an attempt to curb some of these practices, but data to substantiate this point are lacking. See Burick, *supra* note 63, at 255 n.15, regarding the practices in Cook County, Illinois.

73. For a comparison of these statutes see Group for the Advancement of Psychiatry, *Psychiatrically Deviated Sex Offenders* 4 (Rep. No. 9, February 1950); also *New Jersey Report, supra* note 62, at 68.

74. Ploscowe, *supra* note 68, at 235–37.

75. *California Report* 1953, *supra* note 62, at 106–8; *Illinois Report, supra* note 60, at 8–9; *New Jersey Report, supra* note 62, at 26–32, 36–42.

76. See Minnesota *ex rel.* Pearson v. Probate Court, 309 U.S. 270 (1940); see this chapter, § III, Constitutional Problems.

77. *New Jersey Report, supra* note 62, at 37, 40–42.

78. Cason, "The Psychopath and the Psychopathic," 4 *J. Crim. Psychopathology* 522 (1943). See also Cason, "The Symptoms of the Psychopath," 61 *Public Health Reports* 1833 (1946) and Apfelberg, Pfeffer, & Sugar, "Psychiatric Study of 250 Sex Offenders," 100 *Am. J. Psychiat.* 762 (1944).

doubt whether a psychiatrist can adequately isolate any individual as a sexual psychopath. Not only does the psychiatrist find it difficult to recognize the sexual psychopath,[79] but he has further difficulty in marshaling other psychiatrists to support his findings, both in the individual case and in the establishment of criteria to apply to all cases.

A related problem is that the psychiatrist is often unable to distinguish among various types of sex offenders:

> Much of the current confused thinking about sex offenders and sex deviates results from researchers' and clinician's frequent inability to distinguish among: (A) normal sex offenders, who are not sex deviates; (B) sexual deviates who are actually performing illegal sex acts, but who are sufficiently stable and well adjusted to maintain their deviational patterns without getting into official difficulties; (C) sexual deviates who are performing illegal sex acts, and who are also so psychiatrically deviated or emotionally disturbed that they frequently, and perhaps usually, come to official attention as sex offenders, and (D) psychiatrically deviated and pathological but sexually non-deviated or normal offenders, who also frequently come to official attention.[80]

A Michigan commission[81] of the 1950s studied and abstracted more than 500 books and articles, concluding with as much relevance for today as then that:

> In general, recent literature does little more than to make glaringly apparent the present confused state

of psychiatric, psychological, and sociological theory in the sex deviation field. Psychiatrists are dissatisfied with the concept of psychopathic personality. Psychologists emphasize the inadequacy of personality that characterizes so many sex offenders. A leading sociologist (the late Dr. Sutherland) regarded sexual psychopath laws as ineffective. Clinically studied cases are almost never checked against control groups. Statistical studies give interesting information but do not touch dynamics. The constant refrain is the need for more and better research.

The term "sexual psychopath" appears in fact to be primarily a legal term, there being no generally accepted medical-diagnostic counterpart for the type of personality the statutes describe. The American Psychiatric Association's psychiatric glossary, though it does define psychopathy and sexual deviation, does so separately only:

> *Psychopathic Personality (Psychopath):* A person whose behavior is predominantly amoral or antisocial and characterized by impulsive, irresponsible actions satisfying only immediate and narcissistic interests without concern for obvious and implicit social consequences accompanied by minimal outward evidence of anxiety or guilt. *The term "psychopath" is considered unsatisfactory by many but is still used....*
>
> *Sexual Deviation:* Sexual behavior at variance with more or less culturally accepted sexual activities.[82]

Collapsing these two descriptions into one definition of sexual psychopathy might lead to a measure of uniformity in expert thought and testimony in sex offender proceedings. It remains highly doubtful, however, whether mere consistency in labeling (or mislabeling) on the part of forensic psychiatrists would do much to improve the socio-legal determinations contemplated by the sexual psychopath laws. Rather than solidify the unsatisfactory, it might be more profitable to acknowledge that the term "sexual psychopath," as it is "employed in legal and psychiatric procedure, is not a sufficiently clear

---

79. This difficulty is augmented by the fact that several states do not require that a psychiatrist examine the sex offender; see Table 10.2, Medical Examination columns. A physician untrained in psychiatry has an even more difficult time.

80. Ellis & Brancale, *supra* note 62, at 28. See also Bowman and Rose, "A Criticism of the Current Usage of the Term 'Sexual Psychopath,'" 109 *Am. J. Psychiat.* 177, 178 (1952). The criminal law, like the sex psychopathy law, also exhibits a wide variation in approach. Thus while an act of sodomy performed between consenting adults in private is not a crime under the new Illinois criminal code, in Nevada it may lead to a sentence of up to life imprisonment. What import this has for the application of the sex psychopath laws is not always clear. Presumably, however, if the criminal law no longer proscribes certain conduct, the applicability of the sexual psychopath statute would be similarly limited. This would be true even under preconviction statutes, since there must still be a criminal charge to trigger the sex psychopath proceedings. One could conclude that a liberalization of the criminal law with regard to sex offenses would spell some (if not proportionate) progress in the operation of the sexual psychopath laws.

81. *Michigan Report, supra* note 10, at 38–39.

82. American Psychiatric Association, Committee on Public Information, *A Psychiatric Glossary* (1964). (Emphasis added.) See also Burick, *supra* note 63, at 255, where psychopathy is referred to as "the now rejected psychiatric term." See also Katz, Goldstein, & Dershowitz, *Psychoanalysis, Psychiatry and Law* 506–14 (1967) and Noyes & Kolb, *Modern Clinical Psychiatry* (1964), where the sexual psychopath is similarly absent as a psychiatric entity. See Gebhard, Gagnon, Pomeroy, & Christenson, *Sex Offenders* (1965); this clinical study contains a chapter (chap. 36) on the sexual psychopath, but concludes that sex psychopathy is a legal rather than a medical phrase.

diagnostic entity to apply to most sex offenders, nor to justify legislation relating to sex criminals."[83]

C. TREATMENT OF THE SEXUAL PSYCHOPATH

Sex psychopathy legislation appears to be an example of an area where the law has assumed a state of medical (and perhaps social) advancement that has not yet been attained, particularly in relation to the question of treatment of the sexual psychopath. At present there is insufficient scientific knowledge to assure meaningful diagnosis and effective treatment—a medical problem greatly aggravated by the sociological one that personnel resources and physical facilities for sexual psychopathic patients are lacking.

The population pressures on mental institutions have been somewhat reduced over the past decade,[84] yet most hospitals still operate at capacity or near-capacity level—if not in terms of bed-space, then certainly in terms of the patient-physician ratio.[85]

But whether alleviating the shortage of physical facilities would solve most of the problems concerning treatment of the sexual psychopath is extremely dubious. The *New Jersey Report* of the 1950s concluded that even where facilities existed, treatment was still "almost purely custodial."[86] In part such failure may be attributed to the lack of an adequate number of *trained* personnel in these facilities. But the problem appears to go deeper than that: even assuming total adequacy of staff and space resources, serious questions remain about the ability of medical science to cure or substantially improve the vast majority of sexual psychopaths. Interviews with state hospital staff members have yielded the following representative statements: "[T]here was not much to do for him as there is not much treatment for the psychopathic sexual pervert"; "The

treatment in cases like this consists solely in a long program of re-education. There are no drugs or specific treatment for this type of psychopath. Actually the hospitalization of such an individual is more a legal matter than a medical one."[87]

A study of the literature on treatment methods fails to reveal any widely accepted techniques. With considerable persuasiveness the *New Jersey Report* summed up the situation accordingly: "An underlying difficulty is the lack of psychiatric knowledge today of methods than can be employed effectively to deal with psychopathic offenders."[88]

The past decade appears to have produced no major breakthrough in the treatment of sex psychopaths. A 1963 study of sex offenders in California[89] noted that various reports released on the subject "claim varying levels of success from treatment programs, but as yet there has been no single method of treatment, with or without custody, which has been demonstrated to be more successful than any other." The study itself goes on to concentrate on determining recidivism rates of various types of hospitalized sex offenders; it makes no comparisons with non-hospitalized deviates. Other articles and studies of recent origin are no more optimistic: one such study[90] records the experiences of various states, the least unfavorable conclusions being that the statistics on treatment results are inconclusive or unreliable. A commentator on the Texas experience ventured the following opinion: "When the first [sex offender] is cured that will be one hundred percent more than is being cured in Texas."[91]

Claims to the contrary have been put forth. One relatively recent article[92] states that "psychotherapy [for sex psychopaths] . . . has shown some encouraging results," but immediately adds a disclaimer to the effect that "it is generally conceded that medical knowledge at present is inadequate to determine the extent to which this mode of treatment will prove successful."[93] Experiences with the treatment of

---

83. Ellis & Brancale, *supra* note 62, at 41; see also Bowman & Rose, *supra* note 80, at 181.

84. See "Introduction" and chap. 3, "Involuntary Hospitalization," for a discussion of population trends in mental hospitals.

85. It has been postulated that in addition to the legal and constitutional doubts surrounding the sexual psychopath laws, one other reason for their sparing use in some jurisdictions has been the fear of overtaxing the existing medical facilities for treatment of the mentally ill: the fear that persons already hospitalized will be released without proper recovery simply to make room for incoming patients, or that certain personality types who would normally be hospitalized will not be hospitalized simply because there is no room. (See, e.g., Birnbaum, *supra* note 70, to the effect that the fear of overburdening physical and personnel resources still looms very large.)

86. *New Jersey Report, supra* note 62, at 32.

87. Comment, "Sexual Psychopathy—A Legal Labyrinth of Medicine, Morals and Mythology," 36 *Neb. L. Rev.* 320, 342 (1957).

88. *New Jersey Report, supra* note 62, at 32.

89. Frisbie, "Recidivism Among Treated Sex Offenders," California Dep't of Mental Hygiene (1963).

90. Bowman & Engle, *supra* note 59, at 757–78.

91. Gorrell, *supra* note 58, at 107, cited in Bowman & Engle, *supra* note 59, and 769.

92. Comment, *supra* note 21, 655.

93. Ibid., citing Bowman & Engle, *supra* note 59, at 768–69 and Comment, *supra* note 87, at 342 on the point that it is highly

sex offenders in Denmark[94] also raises some hopes of curability. The fact remains, however, that certainly in this country, treatment of the sexual psychopath represents an ideal which is not attained in practice. Instances of successful rehabilitation are few and are purchased at the high cost of subjecting certain groups of individuals labeled as sexual psychopaths to prolonged detention without meaningful treatment and hence limited, perhaps questionable, impact on the general public safety.[95]

The lack of treatment constitutes a basic condemnation of the sex psychopathy laws, since the very philosophy behind, and justification for, such legislation is that sex offenders should be treated rather than punished. Lack of treatment destroys any otherwise valid reason for differential consideration of the sexual psychopath.[96] The courts in some jurisdictions have already indicated that the mentally disabled patient has a "right to treatment."[97]

It would be anomalous not to extend this right to the sexually deviant patient. In fact, the logic of several recent judicial decisions concerning the disposition of sex psychopath cases already suggests that a "right of treatment" applies to such offenders.[98]

D. PROTECTION OF INDIVIDUAL RIGHTS: ADDITIONAL IMPLICATIONS OF "DUE PROCESS"

Section III, Constitutional Problems, discussed sex deviate statutes which have in fact presented, in the form of litigation, certain substantive constitutional problems. Some of the questions to be dealt with at this point are also of constitutional dimension, but less directly so in the sense that they are more or less tangential to the constitutional issues traditionally perceived as central. This section will also discuss constitutional rights of the procedural variety. Needless to say, the distinction between substantive and procedural issues is not always clear. Moreover, since appropriate "procedural" protections may do much to obviate so-called substantive inadequacies of the law, the focus of reform in the area of sex psychopathy laws has to a large extent been on the application of procedural safeguards. Hence also the somewhat amorphous grouping of rights in this section.

1. THE CRIME OF SEXUAL PSYCHOPATHY

Anglo-Saxon legal tradition has long recognized that a man could not be punished for activities which were not a completed crime and proven so in a formal manner. The sexual psychopath laws come very close to violating this tradition; they do not "punish" the individual for one isolated sex act but are directed toward those individuals who have manifested a pattern of deviation in sexual matters in the past or indicate they will establish such a pattern in the future. There is no requirement that this pattern be found only on police or court records; it may also be found in answers the accused makes to the court psychiatrist. Quite frequently the accused will "confess" prior acts that never have and never will come before a criminal court. Nevertheless, these acts may be the basis for the

---

questionable whether the psychopathic personality can be cured by psychotherapy. On the point that many sex offenders are not treatable, see also Burick, *supra* note 63, at 256, relying primarily on Ellis & Brancale, *supra* note 62, at 33–37. See also Granucci & Granucci, *supra* note 33, indicating poor diagnostic and treatment practices at state institutions for sex offenders.

94. Stürup, *Treating the "Untreatable"* (1968), describing the treatment program for psychopaths at Herstedvester, Denmark.

95. For a discussion of the conflicting social and philosophical values regarding the commitment of sexual psychopaths and mentally disabled persons for detention and/or treatment purposes, see Comment, "Due Process for All—Constitutional Standards for Involuntary Civil Commitment and Release," 34 *U. Chi. L. Rev.* 633 (1967).

96. Tappan, *supra* note 69, characterizes as "atrocious" the "policy of those jurisdictions that commit noncriminals and minor deviates for indefinite periods to mental hospitals where no therapy is offered." It would be fair to conclude that in such cases imprisonment for a short period would be a more humane alternative. And the *New Jersey Report, supra* note 62, at 47, concludes that "a great majority of the sex deviates, even those who may be considered abnormal psychologically, are not sick in the ordinary sense as applied to psychotic patients: psychiatric institutions are not presently suited in their space or methods to receive and treat 'garden varieties' of psychopathic, neurotic, schizoid, and constitutional sex variant. Cures cannot be expected through mere hospitalization—unless some individuals simply 'grow out of' their illness, as these might do more speedily under the active program of a correctional institution."

97. See chap. 5, "Rights of Hospitalized Patients," regarding the right to treatment as applicable to civil patients, and chap. 11, "Mental Disability and the Criminal Law," for the treatment rights of "criminal" patients. A considerable amount of literature has recently come out on this subject. For some of the latest discussions see articles on "The Mentally Ill and the Right to Treatment," 36 *U. Chi. L. Rev.* (1969): Bazelon, "Implementing the Right to Treatment," at 742; Katz, "The Right to

---

Treatment—An Enchanting Legal Fiction?" at 755; Morris, "Criminality and the Right to Treatment," at 784.

98. E.g., Millard v. Cameron, 373 F.2d 468 (D.C. Cir. 1966); Commonwealth v. Page, 339 Mass. 313, 159 N.E.2d 82 (1959), holding unconstitutional the imprisonment of an offender where the proceedings were under the sex offender statute.

psychiatric finding that the individual is a sexual psychopath. Thus in such instances, hospitalization or confinement might rest not upon the act for which the individual was accused or convicted but rather on prior unrecorded, unconfirmed acts to which the individual confesses or of which he is accused.

A number of recent cases have held explicitly that an individual may not be punished for the status of being a narcotics addict[99] or an alcoholic.[100] Clearly then, it is equally unconstitutional to punish a person for being a sexual psychopath. Whether the disposition is under the preconviction or postconviction type of statute would make little difference, since under the latter type of statute conviction is not the basis of the disposition but serves rather as that necessary element which permits or triggers differential handling.[101]

The traditional reply to the suggestion of unconstitutionality is that the goal of sex offender legislation is not to "punish" but to "treat." The sincerity of such argument is at times less than obvious; a California court stated:

> The law was never intended to be a legal bypass whereby certain privileged perverts might be kept in mental hospitals for a short term and then released. . . . In the proper administration of the sexual psychopathy law there should be no hope of early release for any sexual psychopath[!][102]

Considering that a finding of sex psychopathy and subsequent indeterminate commitment may be based on such nondangerous display of deviancy as voyeurism or indecent exposure,[103] judicial language of

99. Robinson v. California, 370 U.S. 660 (1962).

100. Driver v. Hinnant, 356 F.2d 761 (4th Cir. 1966); Easter v. District of Columbia, 361 F.2d 50 (D.C. Cir. 1966). For the limitations of these holdings see the recent United States Supreme Court decision in Powell v. Texas, 392 U.S. 514 (1968).

101. On this point see Specht v. Patterson, 386 U.S. 605 (1967), which explicitly distinguishes postconviction dispositional decisions under the sexual psychopath statutes from ordinary postconviction sentencing discretion.

102. *Ex parte* Gross, 115 Cal. App. 2d 502, 252 P.2d 416 (1953). See also Specht v. Patterson, 386 U.S. 605, 608 (1967), to the effect that the disposition in sexual psychopath proceedings constitutes "criminal punishment."

103. See note 63 *supra* on the Indiana statute. A recent leading decision by the Indiana Supreme Court on sexual psychopathy involved a window-peeper: Haskett v. Marion Criminal Court, 234 N.E.2d 636 (1968). A few cases have held that application of the sexual psychopath statutes is inappropriate in cases involving nondangerous social offenses. E.g., Millard v. Cameron, 373 F.2d 468 (D.C. Cir. 1966) to the effect that the

this nature is—to put it mildly—highly inappropriate.[104]

2. THE RIGHT TO TREATMENT

It has already been pointed out that commitment of the sex offender to a mental institution does not at all assure treatment, irrespective of the sincerity of legislative or judicial intentions. The judiciary in the District of Columbia has taken explicit note of this, ruling that habeas corpus is available to the sexual psychopath to show that treatment is not being given at the hospital. Thus in *Millard v. Cameron* the right of treatment was extended to a sexual psychopath confined in St. Elizabeth's Hospital; said the court, "[I]ndefinite commitment under the Sexual Psychopath Law is justifiable only upon a theory of therapeutic treatment.[105]

The courts in other jurisdictions have not gone so far as to allow inquiry into the treatment programs of mental institutions. Commitment or transfer of sexual psychopaths to *prison* facilities, however, has been invalidated on grounds of absence of therapy. A 1951 study severely criticized the sending of sex offenders to the Michigan State Prison at Jackson where a separate cell block was set aside as the official clinic for sexual psychopaths:

> The only apparent difference between the regimen of prisoners and that of the sex psychopaths was that the latter were designated as "visitors," though, like the man who came to dinner, they were apparently there for a long stay. The only treatment provided was an occasional visit by a prison psychiatrist.[106]

Perhaps responding to this criticism, the Michigan Supreme Court in *In re Maddox* (1957)[107] held that the transfer of a sexual psychopathic patient from a mental institution to a prison facility without a judicial determination was unconstitutional. The court in the *Maddox* case, though emphasizing the treatment issue, based its holding primarily on the

offense must be more than merely socially repulsive or repugnant.

104. Note the irony of another California case: People v. Hymes, 161 Cal. App. 2d 668, 327 P.2d 219, 222 (1958), the court stating that "having invoked the *beneficent provisions* of the [sexual psychopath] law, . . . appellant cannot be heard to question the constitutionality of the law." (Emphasis added.)

105. Millard v. Cameron, 373 F.2d 468, 473 (D.C. Cir. 1966), citing Miller v. Overholser, 206 F.2d 415, 419 (D.C. Cir. 1953) as anticipating its holding.

106. Ploscowe, *supra* note 68, at 235.

107. *In re* Maddox, 351 Mich. 358, 88 N.W.2d 470 (1957).

constitutional point of denial of trial: as is possible under a preconviction statute such as Michigan's, the petitioner had never been tried or convicted for an offense.

A 1959 Massachusetts case[108] placed the emphasis more clearly on the lack of treatment in invalidating the imprisonment of a person adjudged to be a sex offender under the statute. Expressly refraining from outlining standards for adequate treatment, the court simply held that the state had failed to establish that a treatment center in fact existed at the prison facilities. That this decision represented only a limited step was illustrated a year later in *Commonwealth v. Hogan*[109] which held that there would be no in-depth inquiry into (the prison's) treatment practices: a measure of segregation from convicted criminals and the availability of medical personnel was deemed sufficient to satisfy the non-penal character of commitment.

3. MEDICAL EXAMINATIONS

Examinations to determine the medical status of an alleged sex offender also pose problems which need to be remedied by substantive or procedural rules. A few states as yet do not require the medical examiners to be psychiatrists specifically trained to make such determinations.[110] However, serious problems persist even in jurisdictions where the technical competence of the examiner is statutorily assured. One writer, describing the criminal justice system in this country, has said that the psychiatrist "has become in many instances a *threat* to offenders."[111] In the context of sexual psychopath proceedings, this suggestion is confirmed to some de-gree by a variety of situations and practices. First, since the sexual psychopath statutes do not provide psychiatrically recognizable standards, the examiner must look elsewhere for a basis for his decision as to whether the offender should be subjected to the special dispositions called for in the statutes. "The result is that fundamentally social-legal determinations are made by the psychiatrist as a medical expert."[112] Despite the psychiatrist's lack of expertise in socio-legal matters, virtually conclusive weight is given to his testimony or reports. For example, a study of Indiana's sexual psychopath act in operation found that in *every* case in which the examining physicians concluded that the defendant was a sexual psychopath, the courts committed the defendant for observation. As for indeterminate commitment, out of 397 cases the courts differed only 8 times with the hospital psychiatrist's observational report.[113] This situation is all the more serious in view of the finding that "large numbers" of psychiatric reports address themselves to the wrong questions: instead of sex psychopathy, the issues considered are criminal responsibility, competency, or need of treatment. Very little guidance is provided by the courts.[114] In addition, psychiatric reports are often entirely conclusionary. Some judicial and statutory correctives on this latter practice have recently been effected. The District of Columbia Circuit Court of Appeals in *Millard v. Cameron*[115] based its reversal of a sex psychopathy finding in part on the fact that the committing court had predicated its decision on a totally inadequate "boiler-plate" report, thus depriving the defendant of a meaningful hearing. The statutes of a few states are worded in order similarly to improve medical testimony. In California, for example, each psychiatrist must make "a separate written report of the *result* of his exam-

108. Commonwealth v. Page, 339 Mass. 313, 159 N.E.2d 82 (1959). The promise of the *Page* decision was that the court avoided the procedural grounds for reversal and chose instead the lack of treatment. Though Massachusetts is a postconviction jurisdiction, the *Page* court could have reversed on denial of a full trial (cf. *In re* Maddox, *supra* note 107,) since the defendant had already served his sentence on the conviction and was being "transferred" after an adjudication of sex psychopathy at which hearing he had been denied certain fundamental protections.

109. 341 Mass. 372, 170 N.E.2d 327 (1960).

110. See Table 10.2, Medical Examination columns. A Michigan study in the 1950s stated: "The Committee further recommends that the standards of physicians qualified to make mental examination in commitment proceedings be raised. Ideally, the mental condition should be determined by psychiatrists and the Committee urges their use whenever possible; *but that requirement is impossible as long as there is a shortage of such specialists.*" *Michigan Report, supra* note 10, at 186. (Emphasis added.)

111. Blumberg, *Criminal Justice* 35 (1967).

112. Comment, *supra* note 21, at 645. Of course, much the same holds true for the psychiatrist's contribution where the issue is civil hospitalization, criminal responsibility, or competency to stand trial (see chap. 5, "Rights of Hospitalized Patients" and chap. 11, "Mental Disability and the Criminal Law"). The undue weight given to psychiatric determinations is one aspect of the problem. A second difficulty lies in the fact that a psychiatrist functioning outside of his field of expertise is more likely to be influenced by persons or predispositions prejudicial to the case. See Blumberg, *supra* note 111, or Matthews, *Mental Disability and the Criminal Law* (1970), generally on the point of lack of independence of the courtroom psychiatrist.

113. Granucci & Granucci, *supra* note 33: an analysis of the case files of some 400 persons adjudicated under the Indiana sex offender statute from 1959 to 1969.

114. Id. at 569.

115. Millard v. Cameron, 373 F.2d 468 (D.C. Cir. 1966).

ination, together with [and thus distinguished from] his conclusions and recommendations."[116] Additionally, there must be a finding "as to whether or not the person would benefit by care and treatment in a state hospital."[117]

The California requirement of a special finding of amenability to treatment prior to commitment may represent an important emerging right in sex psychopath proceedings. A recent case decided by the California Supreme Court held that in the absence of full and fair hearing on all the issues, including amenability to treatment, commitment—even observational commitment—is invalid.[118] By the same token, the Wisconsin Supreme Court decided in 1967 that commitment of a sexual psychopath cannot be mandatory or automatic upon conviction (Wisconsin, like California, has a post-conviction type of statute), but that the defendant is entitled to a special hearing on his need for specialized treatment.[119] The holding has been implemented by an administrative directive to "all [Wisconsin] personnel involved in the clinical aspects of the Sex Crimes Law." Henceforth one of "the criteria to be followed in considering a recommendation for specialized treatment under the Sex Crimes Law [is]: . . . Is the individual *potentially* responsive to *available* specialized treatment assuming adequate motivation?"[120] This approach would seem to have many advantages over the commitment procedures of most jurisdictions where consideration of this most basic issue—the offender's amenability to treatment—is neglected or, as in Illinois, even precluded.[121]

4. STANDARD PROCEDURAL PROTECTIONS OF THE CRIMINAL TRIAL

The well-known procedural protections applicable to criminal trials—such as the right against self-incrimination, the right of confrontation, and the right to counsel—have in the past often been denied

to defendants in sexual psychopath proceedings.[122] The rationale for such denial has normally been that such proceedings are civil in nature and as such not subject to these safeguards. It may be safely stated that today this nominal rationale is no longer generally accepted, with the result that in several jurisdictions the procedural safeguards of criminal proceedings are gradually being made applicable to sex psychopathy proceedings where formerly not even the *civil* standards of procedure were met.[123]

Perhaps the most important decision on the above point is *Specht v. Patterson*.[124] The United States Supreme Court in that case broadly stated what had long been argued: that sex psychopathy proceedings "whether denominated civil or criminal are subject both to the Equal Protection Clause of the Fourteenth Amendment as we held in *Baxstrom v. Herold,* 383 U.S. 107, and to the Due Process Clause."[125] The court held that the application of the Colorado Sex Offenders Act, a postconviction statute which fails to provide for a separate determination of the issue of sex psychopathy, violated those basic rights. As to that issue, "there was no hearing in the normal sense, no right of confrontation and so on."[126] Then outlining what would constitute acceptable procedure, the court added that "[d]ue process . . . requires that [the defendant] be present with counsel, have an opportunity to be heard, be confronted with witnesses against him and to offer evidence of his own. And there must be findings adequate to make meaningful any appeal that is allowed."[127] Logically, these guarantees should

116. *Cal. Welf. & Inst'ns Code* § 6308 (West Supp. 1967). (Emphasis added.)

117. Ibid.

118. People v. Succop, 67 Cal. 2d 785, 433 P.2d 473 (1967).

119. Huebner v. State, 33 Wis. 2d 505, 147 N.W.2d 646 (1967).

120. Memo from Asher R. Pacht, Ph.D., Chief of Clinical Services, State of Wisconsin Dep't of Public Welfare, Div. of Corrections, April 5, 1967. (Emphasis in original.)

121. Burick, *supra* note 63, at 256: "At the hearing itself, psychiatric testimony of the person's amenability to treatment at a mental hospital is *not* permitted." (Emphasis added.)

122. For a listing of judicial decisions denying criminal procedural protections to the sex psychopath, see 24 A.L.R.2d 350 (1952). Note also the statutory abrogation of the right against self-incrimination: *D.C. Code Ann.* § 22-3506 (1967) and *Ind. Ann. Stat.* § 9-3404 (Supp. 1968) provide that the defendant must answer the questions put by the psychiatrist under pain of contempt proceedings.

123. For the applicability of the due process clause in civil commitment proceedings see, e.g., Fuller v. Mullinax, 364 Mo. 858, 269 S.W.2d 72 (1954); Heryford v. Parker, 396 F.2d 393 (10th Cir. 1968). Note also the parallel development in juvenile proceedings: e.g., *In re* Gault, 387 U.S. 1 (1967).

124. 386 U.S. 605 (1967).

125. Id. at 608. The court goes on to point out that punishment under the statute "is criminal punishment even though it is designed not so much as retribution as it is to keep individuals from inflicting future harm."

126. Ibid. Note that the court distinguished the dispositional phase of the sexual psychopath hearing from the regular sentencing proceedings in criminal trials. Id. at 606; cf. Williams v. New York, 337 U.S. 241 (1949).

127. 386 U.S. 605, 610 (1967).

apply equally to preconviction sexual psychopath hearings.

The *Specht* decision was preceded by state and federal court cases which anticipated its holding, and has been followed by subsequent decisions elaborating on its principles. A selective look at these will reveal the reach of due process and equal protection principles as applied to the sexual psychopath law, and will describe what, in view of the United States Supreme Court's mandate by way of *Specht,* is a very salutary trend in the field of sex offender laws.

Gerchman v. Maroney,[128] decided by the Court of Appeals for the Third Circuit in 1966, one year prior to *Specht,* provided the primary precedent for the *Specht* decision. The court in *Maroney* held that the right to confrontation and cross-examination could not be denied in proceedings under the Pennsylvania sex offenders statute: the defendant was entitled to "the full panoply of the relevant protections which due process guarantees in state criminal proceedings."[129] Like *Specht,* the *Maroney* case dealt with the application of a postconviction sex offender statute. No convincing reasons have been advanced why these protections should not obtain in preconviction proceedings, and in fact recent case law in Illinois—a preconviction jurisdiction—confirms that the procedural safeguards vouched for in *Specht* and *Maroney* are not confined to postconviction statutes. The Illinois Supreme Court in *People v. Breese*[130] asserted that "in proceedings under the [Illinois Sexually Dangerous Persons] Act the defendant must be accorded the essential protections available in a criminal trial, even though such proceedings are said to be civil in nature." Specifically, the court held that the defendant could not be said to have waived counsel, and that counsel must be provided by the court when the accused is indigent. Lower court cases in Illinois have extended these principles of due process and equal protection to include most of the other safeguards of criminal proceedings: the right against self-incrimination, the right to a speedy trial, and some of the rules of evidence regarding incompetent testimony.[131]

The logic of applying the fundamental proce-

dural protections to sexual psychopath proceedings seems inescapable, not because such proceedings may be more criminal than civil in nature, but because sexual psychopath proceedings involve an equal or even greater risk of deprivation of liberty than criminal proceedings. The rights to counsel[132] and to notice and hearing[133] have in some courts been upheld even in civil commitment cases—proceedings decidedly "civil" in nature. Likewise, protections such as the right against self-incrimination have been held applicable in juvenile cases on grounds that the defendant was "threatened with a deprivation of his liberty."[134]

Though a general acceptance of the theory that the procedural safeguards of a criminal trial should be made available to defendants in sex psychopath proceedings would appear to be a significant step forward, there must additionally be assurance of practical implementation and more than mere ritualistic observance of this principle at the actual trial level. That such implementation is not a matter of course has been demonstrated in a very recent study which noted that

> even in the presence of such protections erroneous decisions are being made. The bar's inability to obtain adequate medical reports and its reluctance to actively utilize such protections as the right of cross-examination have resulted in the neutralization of these protections.[135]

VI. OVERVIEW

Though principles of substantive and procedural due process are emerging in the field of sexual psychopathy law, they are as yet far from universally established. Two relatively recent state supreme court decisions will illustrate the point.

In the Indiana case of *Haskett v. Marion Criminal Court,*[136] the court ignored the language of the *Maroney* and *Specht* decisions[137] and upheld the statutory requirement that the accused answer the

128. 355 F.2d 302 (3d Cir. 1966).

129. *Id.* at 312.

130. 34 Ill. 2d 61, 213 N.E.2d 500 (1966). See also People v. Capoldi, 10 Ill. 2d 261, 139 N.E.2d 776 (1957).

131. See People v. Beshears, 65 Ill. App. 2d 88, 213 N.E.2d 55 (1965); People v. Potter, 85 Ill. App. 2d 151, 228 N.E.2d 238 (1967).

132. Heryford v. Parker, 396 F.2d 393 (10th Cir. 1968); Dooling v. Overholser, 243 F.2d 825 (D.C. Cir. 1957); see also Rogers v. Stanley, 17 N.Y.2d 256, 270 N.Y.S.2d 573, 217 N.E.2d 636 (1966). There are, however, many cases *contra.*

133. Fuller v. Mullinax, 364 Mo. 858, 269 S.W.2d 72 (1954).

134. *In re* Gault, 387 U.S. 1, 50 (1967).

135. Granucci & Granucci, *supra* note 33, at 571.

136. Haskett v. Marion Criminal Court, 234 N.E.2d 636 (Ind. 1968), upholding *Ind. Ann. Stat.* § 9-3404(a) (Supp. 1968).

137. Specht v. Patterson, 386 U.S. 605 (1967); Gerchman v. Maroney, 355 F.2d 302 (3d Cir. 1966).

questions posed by examining physicians. Adhering to the discredited civil-criminal distinction, the court stated that the right against self-incrimination did not obtain in sex offender proceedings and that the statutory grant of immunity—to the effect that the evidence so obtained could not be used in any other proceeding—constituted sufficient protection to the defendant.[138]

The *Haskett* case also illustrates the problems of scope and classification inherent in the sexual psychopath statutes. The defendant in *Haskett* was a window-peeper. As noted earlier, it has been found that the sexual psychopath statutes in many jurisdictions fail, both in language and application, to distinguish between sex offenders who pose a threat to society and those whose behavior is a mere social nuisance, between those who are in need of treatment and indeed treatable and those who are not. The statutes in some areas are applied *to the exclusion* of serious or dangerous sex offenders, while aiming their thrust at behavior which in some instances may even be engaged in by a large percentage of the population. This is not to say that some nuisance-type sex offenders may not be as much in need of psychiatric help as major offenders: the compulsive behavior of many exhibitionists or window-peepers is evidence of their need of treatment. But the point is that a sensible process of selection must take place, and this does not now occur under the statutes or in their application. Moreover, the selection of those to whom the statutes will be applied should take into account certain realities regarding the lack of treatment resources and the limitations of present therapeutic techniques. If confinement is the only available "treatment," as is often the case, then the laws should be restricted in their application to those who should be confined for the safety of society.

Of relevance to the confinement problem is the *Tinsley* case,[139] decided in 1961. The Colorado Supreme Court held that there was no violation of equal protection where the defendant was sentenced to life imprisonment *in the state penitentiary* under the sexual psychopath statute, even though a sentence of such severity could not have been given for the same offense under the regular criminal statutes of Colorado. This is a questionable decision.

Indeterminate incarceration to prevent future misconduct is anomalous in a system which purports to punish only for specific acts that must be proved beyond a reasonable doubt in a court. In regard to such dispositions, questions may be raised not only of equal protection, but also of Eighth Amendment guarantees against cruel and unusual punishment.[140] Commitment to the penitentiary of course destroys all possible justification based on such notions as the benefits of treatment for the accused. Since the probabilities of successful treatment in mental institutions are not high and since amenability to treatment is a factor not usually considered, it may certainly also be argued that indeterminate commitment to hospitals is subject to similar constitutional doubts.

VII. CONCLUSIONS AND RECOMMENDATIONS

1. *The desirability of special legislation with regard to sex offenders is quite questionable in view of the difficulty of identifying those sex offenders who will respond to known methods of treatment.*

While it is probably true that most sex offenders do not benefit from custodial incarceration and that some would benefit from a measure of psychiatric care, the same might be said of any and all offenders. Differential handling of sex offenders is justified only if successful treatment methods exist and if those persons most likely to respond thereto can be selected with a degree of confidence. At present this does not appear to be the case. Any attempts at special legislation in this area will therefore virtually unavoidably reiterate the defects of existing sexual psychopathy legislation—making reference to broad, amorphous groups of offenders; tending to misapplication, willful or otherwise; and resulting in meaningless, inappropriate, or even harmful institutionalization for a large percentage of those to whom the statutes are applied.

2. *Such special legislation respecting sex offenders as now exists or is enacted should observe certain substantive and procedural standards in order to maximize the possibility of benefit to persons to whom the legislation is applied and minimize the potential for adverse effects.*

If, despite reservations expressed in conclusion 1, the need and desirability of special sex offender laws is thought to persist, such laws should con-

---

138. But see *In re* Gault, 387 U.S. 1 (1967), that the characterization of a proceeding as noncriminal is no justification for denying the right against self-incrimination. Also Specht v. Patterson, 386 U.S. 605 (1967); Gerchman v. Maroney, 355 F.2d 302 (3d Cir. 1966).

139. Trueblood v. Tinsley, 148 Col. 503, 366 P.2d 655 (1961).

140. For a discussion of the cruel and unusual punishment point in relation to sex psychopathy statutes, see, e.g., Burick, *supra* note 63, at 263.

form to certain substantive and procedural standards. It may be argued that the criminal laws and the laws of civil hospitalization can be utilized conjunctionally to handle sex offenders needing and likely to benefit from psychiatric treatment, but such utilization would involve the same problems of selection and identification that confront the special sex offender laws. What the criminal and civil-hospitalization laws do suggest, however, are standards and safeguards which the sexual psychopath laws should comply with. The recommendations that follow below will reflect these standards as well as other considerations which would make the sex offender laws more compatible with notions of fairness and rationality.

3. *A person sought to be tried under a sexual psychopath statute shall be given prior notice of that fact and be entitled to a special hearing on the issue of sexual psychopathy. The determination of that issue shall be based on examination and/or observation by impartial experts whose testimony shall include consideration of the person's amenability to treatment.*

Notice and a hearing on the primary issue to be determined at trial are essential elements of due process that are often not complied with, especially under the postconviction type of sex psychopathy statute. Though sexual psychopathy is not a psychiatrically recognized diagnostic entity and an evaluation in this regard hence poses troublesome questions for conscientious psychiatrists, it would be undesirable for a court to determine the issue without expert aid. At the very least, therefore, the defendant should be informed of the availability of expert examination or observation. To assure impartiality, the defendant should be given a voice in the selection of any panel of experts, and he shall retain the right to present his own expert witnesses. Amenability to treatment is a difficult issue to resolve in view of the intractability of the factors that cause or prevent sexually deviant behavior, yet an attempt to predict response to treatment should be made. Institutionalization in disregard of amenability to treatment is not justifiable.

4. *Initial disposition under the sexual psychopath statutes should be limited to observational hospitalization. If it is concluded that the patient is indeed in need of treatment and will likely benefit therefrom, there may ensue a subsequent judicial order for lengthier hospitalization, provided that periodic review of the patient's condition shall be assured.*

Observational hospitalization is desirable in that it facilitates the difficult task of identifying those persons who will respond to available methods of treatment. If continued hospitalization is indicated, a judicial hearing on this issue shall be accorded the patient. Periodic review of the patient's condition will be the safeguard thereafter: at stated intervals the hospital shall be required to obtain from the court a reauthorization for its hold on the patient. A determination of continued institutionalization shall be founded on assessments or predictions concerning continued need of treatment, chances of recidivism, or dangerousness. Length of hospitalization should not necessarily be limited to the length of sentence possible for the offense under the criminal law; as the great disparity among the various states in sentences for the same offense indicates, such sentences reflect only disparate notions of social and moral outrage and have little relevance to the rehabilitation of the offender or the protection of society.

5. *The procedural safeguards of a criminal trial should be applied in sexual psychopathy proceedings.*

Whether labeled criminal or civil in nature, psychopathy proceedings should accord the defendant the same protections as in a criminal trial because both proceedings involve the possibility of significant loss of liberty. The right to counsel and the right against self-incrimination are among the most important in this context.

6. *Any special legislation regarding sex offenders should include provisions for medical and sociological research in this area as well as provisions assuring adequate treatment facilities for those affected by the laws.*

Only continued research in the area of sexual deviancy will increase the likelihood that sex offender laws can succeed either in differentiating dangerous from nondangerous offenders and "disordered" from "normal" offenders or in identifying those for whom special treatment is appropriate. Assuming that the laws will help make possible fair and rational selection, then the establishment of adequate facilities with well-trained personnel is essential to implement the purpose of the law.

BIBLIOGRAPHY

American Bar Foundation. "Survey of the Administration of Criminal Justice in the United States." Vol. 3 of the Pilot Project Report, 1958. Unpublished. Chicago, 1958.

American Law Reports Annotated. San Francisco:

Bancroft-Whitney Co.; Rochester, N.Y.: Lawyers Co-operative Publishing Co.

"Statutes Relating to Sexual Psychopaths." 24 (1952) 350.

American Psychiatric Association. *Psychiatric Glossary*. Washington, D.C.: American Psychiatric Association, 1957.

Apfelberg, Benjamin; Pfeffer, Arnold; and Sugar, Carl. "Psychiatric Study of 250 Sex Offenders." 100 *American Journal of Psychiatry* 762 (1944).

Bazelon, David L. "Implementing the Right to Treatment." 36 *University of Chicago Law Review* 742 (1969).

Bensing, Robert C. "A Comparative Study of American Sex Statutes." 42 *Journal of Criminal Law, Criminology and Police Science* 57 (1951).

Birnbaum, Morton. "*Primum Non Nocere:* How to Treat the Criminal Psychopath." 52 *American Bar Association Journal* 69 (1966).

Blumberg, Abraham S. *Criminal Justice*. Chicago: Quadrangle Books, 1967.

Bowman, K., and Engle, B., in *Sexual Behavior and the Law*. Edited by Ralph Slovenko. Springfield, Ill.: Charles C Thomas, 1965.

Bowman, Karl M., and Rose, Milton. "Criticism of the Current Usage of the Term 'Sexual Psychopath.' " 109 *American Journal of Psychiatry* 177 (1952).

Burick, Lawrence T. "An Analysis of the Illinois Sexually Dangerous Persons Act." 59 *Journal of Criminal Law, Criminology and Police Science* 254 (1968).

California. Department of Mental Hygiene. *California Sexual Deviate Research*. Sacramento, 1953.

———. *California Sexual Deviate Research*. Sacramento, 1954.

Cason, Hulsey. "The Psychopath and the Psychopathic. 4 *Journal of Criminal Psychopathology* 522 (1943).

———. "The Symptoms of the Psychopath." 61 *Public Health Reports* 1833 (1946).

Cohen, Elias S. "Administration of the Criminal Sexual Psychopath Statute in Indiana." 32 *Indiana Law Journal* 450 (1957).

Comment, "Due Process for All—Constitutional Standards for Involuntary Civil Commitment and Release." 34 *University of Chicago Law Review* 633 (1967).

———. "The Plight of the Sexual Psychopath." 41 *Notre Dame Lawyer* 527 (1966).

———. "Sexual Psychopathy—A Legal Labyrinth of Medicine, Morals and Mythology." 36 *Nebraska Law Review* 320 (1957).

———. "The Validity of the Segregation of the Sexual Psychopath under the Law." 26 *Ohio State Law Journal* 640 (1965).

Ellis, Albert, and Brancale, Ralph. *The Psychology of Sex Offenders*. Springfield, Ill.: Charles C Thomas, 1956.

Frisbie, L. *Recidivism among Treated Sex Offenders*. California Department of Mental Hygiene. Sacramento, 1963.

Gebhard, P.; Gagnon, J.; Pomeroy, W.; and Christenson, C. *Sex Offenders*. New York: Harper & Row, 1965.

Gorrell, Jack. "The Sexual Psychopath Laws: Validity and Construction." 14 *Baylor Law Review* 93 (1962).

Granucci, Anthony, and Granucci, Susan Jamart. "Indiana's Sexual Psychopathic Act in Operation." 44 *Indiana Law Journal* 555 (1969).

Group for the Advancement of Psychiatry. "The Sexual Psychopath Laws," *Psychiatrically Deviated Sex Offenders*. Appendix A of Report no. 9. New York: Group for the Advancement of Psychiatry, February 1950.

Guttmacher, Manfred S., and Weihofen, Henry. *Psychiatry and the Law*. New York: W. W. Norton & Co., 1952.

Hacker, Fredrick J., and Frym, Marcel. "The Sexual Psychopath Act in Practice: A Critical Discussion." 43 *California Law Review* 766 (1955).

Hirning, L. Clovis. "The Sex Offender in Custody." *Handbook of Correctional Psychology*. Edited by Robert M. Lindner, Ph.D., and Robert V. Seliger, M.D. New York: Philosophical Library, 1947.

Hoag, Ernest Bryant, and Williams, Edward Huntington. *Crime, Abnormal Minds and the Law*. Indianapolis: Bobbs-Merrill Co., 1923.

Illinois. Commission on Sex Offenders. *Report to the Sixty-eighth General Assembly of the State of Illinois* Springfield, 1953.

Katz, Jay. "The Right to Treatment—An Enchanting Legal Fiction?" 36 *University of Chicago Law Review* 755 (1969).

Katz, Jay; Goldstein, Joseph; and Dershowitz, Alan M. *Psychoanalysis, Psychiatry and Law*. New York: Free Press, 1967.

Maryland. *An Indeterminate Sentence Law for Defective Delinquents*. Report no. 29 of the Legislative Council. Annapolis, 1950.

Matthews, Arthur R., Jr. *Mental Disability and the Criminal Law*. Chicago: American Bar Foundation, 1970.

Michigan. Governor's Study Commission on the Deviated Criminal Sex Offender. *Report*. Lansing, 1951.

Mihm, Ferd Paul. "A Re-examination of Our Sex Psychopath Statutes." 44 *Journal of Criminal Law, Criminology and Police Science* 716 (1954).

Morris, Grant H. "Criminality and the Right to Treatment." 36 *University of Chicago Law Review* 784 (1969).

New Jersey. Commission on the Habitual Sex Offender. *Report.* Trenton, 1950.

Note, "Indiana's Sexual Psychopath Statute." 44 *Indiana Law Journal* 242 (1969).

———. "The Psychopathetic Personality." 10 *Rutgers Law Review* 425 (1955).

Noyes, Arthur Percy. *Modern Clinical Psychiatry.* Philadelphia: W. B. Saunders, 1940.

Noyes, Arthur Percy, and Kolb, Laurence C. *Modern Clinical Psychiatry.* 6th ed. Philadelphia: W. B. Saunders, 1963.

Ploscowe, Morris. *Sex and the Law.* New York: Prentice-Hall, 1951.

Schnur, Alfred C. "Prison Conduct and Recidivism." 40 *Journal of Criminal Law, Criminology and Police Science* 36 (1949).

Silverstein, Lee, ed. *Defense of the Poor.* Vol. 1. Chicago: American Bar Foundation, 1965.

Smith. *Their Therapeutic Possibilities and the Legal Difficulties Encountered in a 20-Year Experience in the Psychiatric Division.* Illinois Department of Public Safety. Menard, 1963.

Stürup, Georg K. *Treating the "Untreatable."* Baltimore: Johns Hopkins Press, 1968.

Sutherland, Edwin H. "The Sexual Psychopath Laws." 40 *Journal of Criminal Law, Criminology and Police Science* 543 (1950).

Sutherland, Edwin H., and Cressey, Donald R. *Principles of Criminology.* 5th ed. Philadelphia: J. B. Lippincott, 1955.

Swanson, Alan H. "Sexual Psychopath Statutes." 51 *Journal of Criminal Law, Criminology and Police Science* 215 (1960).

Tappan, Paul W. *Crime, Justice and Correction.* New York: McGraw-Hill Book Co., Inc., 1960.

———. "Sentences for Sex Criminals." 42 *Journal of Criminal Law, Criminology and Police Science* (1951).

———. "Some Myths about the Sex Offender." 19 *Federal Probation* 7 (1955).

Weiss, Edward, and English, O. Spurgeon. *Psychosomatic Medicine.* Philadelphia: W. B. Saunders, 1943.

CASES

Blocker v. United States, 274 F.2d 572 (D.C. Cir. 1959), 320 F.2d 800 (D.C. Cir. 1963).

Commonwealth v. Hogan, 341 Mass. 372, 170 N.E.2d 327 (1960).

Commonwealth v. Page, 339 Mass. 313, 159 N.E.2d 82 (1959).

Dooling v. Overholser, 243 F.2d 825 (D.C. Cir. 1957).

Driver v. Hinnant, 356 F.2d 761 (4th Cir. 1966).

Durham v. United States, 214 F.2d 862 (D.C. Cir. 1954).

Easter v. District of Columbia, 361 F.2d 50 (D.C. Cir. 1966).

Ex parte Gross, 252 P.2d 416 (Cal. Dist. Ct. App. 1953).

Fuller v. Mullinax, 364 Mo. 858, 269 S.W.2d 72 (1954).

Gerchman v. Maroney, 355 F.2d 302 (3d Cir. 1966).

Haskett v. Marion Criminal Court, 234 N.E.2d 636 (Ind. 1968).

Heryford v. Parker, 396 F.2d 393 (10th Cir. 1968).

Huebner v. State, 33 Wis. 2d 505, 147 N.W.2d 646 (1967).

In re Gault, 387 U.S. 1 (1967).

In re Maddox, 351 Mich. 358, 88 N.W.2d 470 (1957).

In re Mundy, 97 N.H. 239, 85 A.2d 371 (1952).

Lambert v. California, 355 U.S. 225 (1957).

Millard v. Cameron, 373 F.2d 468 (D.C. Cir 1966).

Miller v. Overholser, 206 F.2d 415 (D.C. Cir. 1953).

People v. Beshears, 65 Ill. App. 2d 88, 213 N.E.2d 55 (1965).

People v. Breese, 34 Ill. 2d 61, 213 N.E.2d 500 (1966).

People v. Capoldi, 10 Ill. 2d 261, 139 N.E.2d 776 (1957).

People v. Chapman, 301 Mich. 584, 4 N.W.2d 18 (1942).

People v. Frontczak, 286 Mich. 51, 281 N.W. 534 (1938).

People v. Hymes, 327 P.2d 219 (Cal. Dist. Ct. App. 1958).

People v. Jones, 42 Cal. 2d 219, 266 P.2d 38 (1954).

People v. Potter, 85 Ill. App. 2d 151, 228 N.E.2d 238 (1967).

People v. Succop, 67 Cal. 2d 785, 433 P.2d 473 (1967).

Powell v. Texas, 392 U.S. 514 (1968).

Robinson v. California, 370 U.S. 660 (1962).

Rogers v. Stanley, 17 N.Y.2d 256, 270 N.Y.S.2d 573, 217 N.E.2d 636, (1966).

Sas v. Maryland, 334 F.2d 506 (4th Cir. 1964).

Specht v. Patterson, 386 U.S. 605 (1967).

State *ex rel.* Pearson v. Probate Court of Ramsey County, 205 Minn. 545, 287 N.W. 297 (1939), *aff'd,* Minnesota *ex rel.* Pearson v. Probate Court of Ramsey County, 309 U.S. 270 (1940).

Trueblood v. Tinsley, 366 P.2d 655 (Colo. 1961).

Williams v. New York, 337 U.S. 241 (1949).

Table 10.1   STATUTORY CONSIDERATIONS OF SEXUAL PSYCHOPATHS AND RELATED OFFENDERS

STATE AND CITATION	STATUTORY PROVISIONS
DRAFT ACT	
ALA. CODE (1958) 15, §434 (Supp. 1967)	"Any person who is suffering from a mental disorder but is not mentally ill or feebleminded to an extent making him criminally irresponsible for his acts, such mental disorder being coupled with criminal propensities to the commission of sex offenses, is hereby declared to be a <u>criminal sexual psychopathic person</u>."
ALAS. Stat. (1962)	
ARIZ. Rev. Stat. Ann. (1956)	
ARK. Stat. Ann. (1964)	
CAL. Welf. & Inst'ns Code (West 1966) 6300 (Supp. 1968)	"<u>Mentally disordered sex offender</u> means any person who by reason of mental defect, disease, or disorder, is predisposed to the commission of sexual offenses to such a degree that he is dangerous to the health and safety of others."
6450 (Supp. 1968)	"<u>Mentally abnormal sex offender</u> . . . means any person who is not mentally disordered or mentally retarded, and who by any habitual course of misconduct in sexual matters has evidenced an utter lack of power to control his sexual impulses and who, as a result is likely to attack or otherwise inflict injury, loss, pain or other evil upon the objects of his uncontrolled and uncontrollable desires."
COLO. Rev. Stat. Ann. (1964) 39-19-1	<u>Sex offenders</u> are "persons convicted of the crimes of indecent liberties, incest, assault with intent to commit unnatural carnal copulation, unnatural carnal copulation, assault with intent to commit rape, or rape, if the district court is of the opinion that any such person, if at large, constitutes a threat of bodily harm to members of the public, or is an habitual offender and mentally ill. . . ."
CONN. Gen. Stat. Ann. (1960) 17-239	"There shall be a security treatment center for the care of . . . persons convicted of any offense enumerated in section 17-244 whose mental state has been determined in examination by the staff of the diagnostic unit of the center . . . [and have been found] to demonstrate clearly such actual danger to society or to himself as to require custody, care and treatment. . . ."
17-244(a)	"When any person . . . is convicted . . . of a sex crime involving (1) physical force or violence, (2) disparity of age between an adult and a minor or (3) a sexual act of a compulsive or repetitive nature . . . ."
DEL. Code Ann. (1953)	
D.C. Code Ann. (1967) 22-3503(1)	"'Sexual psychopath' means a person, not insane, who by a course of repeated misconduct in sexual matters has evidenced such lack of power to control his sexual impulses as to be dangerous to other persons because he is likely to attack or otherwise inflict injury, loss, pain, or other evil on the objects of his desire."
FLA. Stat. Ann. (1944) 917.12 (Supp. 1969)	"All persons suffering from a mental disorder and not insane, which mental disorder has existed for a period of not less than four months immediately prior to the appointment of the psychiatrists provided for . . . coupled with criminal propensities to the commission of sex offenses and who may be considered dangerous to others are hereby declared to be <u>mentally disordered sex offenders</u>."
GA. Code Ann. (1960)	
HAWAII Rev. Stat. Ann. (1968)	

STATE AND CITATION	STATUTORY PROVISIONS
IDAHO Code Ann. (1947)	
ILL. Ann. Stat. (Smith-Hurd 1964) 38, §105-1.01	"All persons suffering from a mental disorder, which mental disorder has existed for a period of not less than one year, immediately prior to the filing of the petition hereinafter provided for, coupled with criminal propensities to the commission of sex offenses, and who have demonstrated propensities toward acts of sexual assault or acts of sexual molestation of children, are hereby declared <u>sexually dangerous persons</u>."
IND. Ann. Stat. (1956) 9-3401	"Any person over the age of sixteen years who is suffering from a mental disorder and is not insane or feebleminded which mental disorder is coupled with criminal propensities to the commission of sex offenses, is hereby declared to be a <u>criminal sexual psychopathic person</u>."
IOWA Code Ann. (1969) 225A.1	"All persons charged with a public offense, who are suffering from a mental disorder and are not a proper subject for the schools for the mentally retarded or for commitment as a mentally ill person, having criminal propensities toward the commission of sex offenses, and who may be considered dangerous to others, are hereby declared to be '<u>criminal sexual psychopaths</u>.'"
KAN. Stat. Ann. (1964) 62-1534 (Supp. 1969)	<u>Sex offenders</u> are persons who are convicted of "any offense against public morals and decency, as relating to crimes pertaining to sex, in which perversion or mental aberration appears to be or is involved or where the defendant appears to be mentally ill . . . ."
KY. Rev. Stat. Ann. (1969)	
LA. Rev. Stat. Ann. (1967)	
ME. Rev. Stat. Ann. (1964)	
MD. Ann. Code (1967) 31B, §5	"A <u>defective delinquent</u> shall be defined as an individual who, by the demonstration of persistent aggravated anti-social or criminal behavior, evidences a propensity toward criminal activity, and who is found to have either such intellectual deficiency or emotional unbalance, or both, as to clearly demonstrate an actual danger to society so as to require such confinement and treatment, when appropriate, as may make it reasonably safe for society to terminate the confinement and treatment."
MASS. Ann. Laws (1965) 123A, §1	A <u>sexually dangerous person</u> is "[A]ny person whose misconduct in sexual matters indicates a general lack of power to control his sexual impulses, as evidenced by repetitive or compulsive behavior and either violence, or aggression by an adult against a victim under the age of sixteen years, and who as a result is likely to attach [sic] or otherwise inflict injury on the objects of his uncontrolled or uncontrollable desires."
MICH. Comp. Laws Ann. (1967)	
MINN. Stat. Ann. (1969) 526.09	<u>Psychopathic personality</u> means "the existence in any person of such conditions of emotional instability, or impulsiveness of behavior, or lack of customary standards of good judgment, or failure to appreciate the consequences of his acts, or a combination of any such conditions, as to render such person irresponsible for his conduct with respect to sexual matters and thereby dangerous to other persons."
MISS. Code Ann. (1952)	

STATE AND CITATION	STATUTORY PROVISIONS
MO. Rev. Stat. (1959) 202.700	Criminal sexual psychopath means "all persons suffering from a mental disorder and not insane or feeble-minded, which mental disorder has existed for a period of not less than one year immediately prior to the filing of the petition . . . coupled with criminal propensities to the commission of sex offenses, and who may be considered dangerous to others . . . ."
MONT. Rev. Codes Ann. (1961)	
NEB. Rev. Stat. (1964) 29-2901	"Sexual psychopath shall mean any person who, by a course of misconduct in sexual matters, has evidenced an utter lack of power to control his sexual impulses and who, as a result, is likely to attack or otherwise inflict injury, loss, pain, or other evil on the objects of his uncontrolled and uncontrollable desires."
NEV. Rev. Stat. (1967)	
N.H. Rev. Stat. Ann. (1964) 173-A: 2 (Supp. 1969)	"The term 'dangerous sexual offender' as used in this chapter means any person suffering from such conditions of emotional instability or impulsiveness of behavior, or lack of customary standards of good judgment, or failure to appreciate the consequences of his acts, or a combination of any such conditions, as to render such person irresponsible with respect to sexual matters and thereby dangerous to himself, or to other persons."
N.J. Stat. Ann. (1953) 2A:164-3, 2A:164-5 (Supp. 1970)	Sex offender means "a person who is convicted of the offense of rape, carnal abuse, sodomy, open lewdness, indecent exposure or impairing the morals of a minor, or of an attempt to commit any of the aforementioned offenses." If his conduct is characterized by a pattern of repetitive, compulsive behavior and violence, or his victim under 15 years of age, and the offender is an adult aggressor, he is to be submitted to a program of specialized treatment for his mental and physical aberrations.
N.M. Stat. Ann. (1964)	
N.Y. Mental Hygiene Law (McKinney 1951)	
N.C. Gen. Stat. (1963)	
N.D. Cent. Code (1960)	
OHIO Rev. Code (Baldwin 1964) 2947.24(B)	"Psychopathic offender is any person who is adjudged to have a psychopathic personality, who exhibits criminal tendencies and who by reason thereof is a menace to the public. Psychopathic personality is evidenced by such traits or characteristics inconsistent with the age of such person, as emotional immaturity and instability, impulsive, irresponsible, reckless, and unruly acts, excessively self-centered activities, deficient power of self-discipline, lack of normal capacity to learn from experience, marked deficiency of moral sense or control."
OKLA. Stat. (1951)	
ORE. Rev. Stat. (1967) 137.111	Any person convicted of rape, murder or manslaughter or other crimes may in the court's discretion be subjected to a sentence other than that authorized by law if the court finds that such person has mental or emotional disturbance, deficiency or condition predisposing him to the commission of a crime to a degree rendering the person a menace to safety of others. The court may sentence the convicted person to an indeterminate term not exceeding the natural life of such person.

STATE AND CITATION	STATUTORY PROVISIONS
PA. Stat. Ann. (1964) 11, §1166	If the court is of the opinion that a person convicted of indecent assault with intent to commit sodomy, solicitation to commit sodomy or assault with intent to ravish or rape, if at large constitutes a threat of bodily harm to members of the public, or if he is an habitual offender and mentally ill, the court may sentence such person for an indeterminate period of time to a state institution.
R. I. Gen. Laws Ann. (1956)	
S. C. Code Ann. (1962)	
S. D. Compiled Laws Ann. (1967)	
TENN. Code Ann. (1955) 33-1301 (Supp. 1968)	Sex offender means any person who has been convicted of a crime involving the unlawful sexual abuse, molestation, fondling, or carnal knowledge of a child of the age of fourteen years or younger.
TEX. Rev. Civ. Stat. Ann. (1958)	
UTAH Code Ann. (1953) 77-49-1 (Supp. 1967) 77-49-5	Sex offenders. Whenever any person is convicted of, or pleads guilty to, a charge of rape, sodomy, incest, indecent exposure, an attempt to commit any of the aforementioned crimes, assault with attempt to commit rape, assault with attempt to commit sodomy, or indecent assault upon, and taking indecent liberties with, the body of a minor child and if after a mental examination it appears that he suffers from any form of abnormal or subnormal mental illness, or other psychosis, which caused the commission of the sex offense, he shall be committed to the state hospital for life, unless he is paroled or pardoned.
VT. Stat. Ann. (1968) 18, §8501 (Supp. 1969)	"The term 'psychopathic personality' . . . means those persons who by a habitual course of misconduct in sexual matters have evidenced an utter lack of power to control their sexual impulse, and who, as a result, are likely to attack or otherwise inflict injury, loss, pain or other evil on the object of their uncontrolled desire."
VA. Code Ann. (1953)	
WASH. Rev. Code Ann. (1962) 71.06.010	"'Psychopathic personality' means the existence in any person of such hereditary, congenital or acquired condition affecting the emotional or volitional rather than the intellectual field and manifested by anomalies of such character as to render satisfactory social adjustment by such person difficult or impossible. "'Sexual psychopath' means any person who is affected in a form of psychoneurosis or in a form of psychopathic personality, which form predisposes such person to the commission of sexual offenses in a degree constituting him a menace to the health or safety of others. . . . "'Psychopathic delinquent' means any minor who is psychopathic, and who is a habitual delinquent, if his delinquency is such as to constitute him a menace to the health, person, or property of himself or others, and the minor is not a proper subject for commitment to a state correctional school, to a state school for the mentally deficient as a mentally deficient person, or to a state hospital as a mentally ill person."
W. VA. Code Ann. (1966)	
WIS. Stat. Ann. (1957)	
WYO. Stat. Ann. (1957)	

Table 10.2 PSYCHOPATHY AND THE LAW

STATE	APPLIES TO	PROCEEDINGS INITIATED BY — Public Official	PROCEEDINGS INITIATED BY — Defense Attorney or Accused	TIME OF PROCEEDINGS — Preconviction	TIME OF PROCEEDINGS — Presentence	TIME OF PROCEEDINGS — After Sentence	MEDICAL EXAMINATION — Psychiatrist	MEDICAL EXAMINATION — Physician	MEDICAL EXAMINATION — Other	HEARING	JURY	COMMITMENT PERIOD — Indeterminate	COMMITMENT PERIOD — Specified Term	RELEASED WHEN — Cured	RELEASED WHEN — Improved	RELEASE — Petition by Patient	RELEASE — Administrative	RELEASE — Judicial	TYPE OF RELEASE — Absolute	TYPE OF RELEASE — Probation or Parole	DISPOSITION OF ORIGINAL OFFENSE — Returned for Trial or Sentence	DISPOSITION OF ORIGINAL OFFENSE — Defense to Original Charge	APPEAL
Draft Act	"The Scope of the Draft Act," page 1, states: "The Act will also by reason of the definition [mentally ill individual] include persons who are psychopaths. . . ." No specific provisions relating only to psychopaths are included, however.																						
ALA. Code (1958)	criminal sexual psychopaths. 15, §434 (Supp. 1967)	prosecuting solicitor or attorney general. 15, §436 (Supp. 1967)		15, §436 (Supp. 1967)	15, §436 (Supp. 1967)		2 psychiatrists must conclude defendant is a sexual psychopath as a requirement to a hearing. 14, §437 (Supp. 1967)			15, §438		until fully & permanently recovered. 15, §438		"fully recovered." 15, §440				hearing as to "full recovery." 15, §440		"fully recovered & discharged, placed on probation for such reasonable time as circumstances may justify. 15, §441	discretionary with court if probation violated. 15, §441		
ALAS. Stat. (1962)																							
ARIZ. Rev. Stat. Ann. (1956)																							
ARK. Stat. Ann. (1964)																							
CAL. Welf. & Inst'ns Code (West 1966) (Supp. 1968)	mentally disordered sex offender; inapplicable to person under sentence of death. 6300 6301	both judge & prosecuting attorney may initiate. 6302(a)	6302		after conviction, suspend or adjourn proceedings. 6302(a)		at least 2 required, other technical requirements. 6307			6305 to 6315	persons committed to department for placement in state hospital following observation placement in county hospital may demand jury. 6318	fn.1 6316	fn.1 90-day observational placement 6316	not a danger to health & safety of others. 6325	fn.2 will not benefit from further medical treatment & not a danger to health & safety of others.	may petition committing court each 6 months for medical report leading to release. 6327		court may on its own motion every 6 months seek medical report leading to release. 6327		fn.3 criminal court may place person on probation for not less than 5 years; not applicable to those persons not recovered & still a menace to society. 6325	ultimately all mentally disordered sex offenders must face criminal charge; never a defense. 6325 6326 6327		6318
	mentally abnormal sex offenders 6450; proceedings may be instituted although no criminal charge. 6451		only by parent, spouse or child of person himself. 6451		pending criminal charge must be prosecuted to final judgment. 6456		2. 6307 6453	certificate to accompany petition. 6451		6305 to 6315 6452			not to exceed 2 years. 6454				6455						

Table 10.2 PSYCHOPATHY AND THE LAW continued

STATE	APPLIES TO	PROCEEDINGS INITIATED BY		TIME OF PROCEEDINGS			MEDICAL EXAMINATION			HEARING	JURY	COMMITMENT PERIOD		RELEASED WHEN		RELEASE			TYPE OF RELEASE		DISPOSITION OF ORIGINAL OFFENSE		APPEAL
		Public Official	Defense Attorney or Accused	Preconviction	Pre-sentence	After Sentence	Psychiatrist	Physician	Other			Indeterminate	Specified Term	Cured	Improved	Petition by Patient	Administrative	Judicial	Absolute	Probation or Parole	Returned for Trial or Sentence	Defense to Original Charge	
COLO. Rev. Stat. Ann. (1964)	sex offenders. 39-19-1	district court. 39-19-1			postpone sentence a maximum of 45 days for psychiatric examination. 39-19-3		complete written report containing facts, findings & recommendations. 39-19-2 (2), (3)		psychiatric reports shall contain opinion whether person could be adequately supervised on probation 39-19-2 (3)			fn. 4 minimum: 1 day; maximum: natural life. 39-19-1 39-19-6		after sentence by court to a state institution, state board of parole assumes exclusive and complete control of person. Board shall review case within first 6 months and every year thereafter. It has power to parole and to give an absolute release if such is in best interest of justice; consult medical reports. 39-19-6, 39-19-7, 39-19-8			state board of parole has complete power of absolute release as interest of justice and welfare of society may dictate. 39-19-6 39-19-7 39-19-8		39-19-7	parole or reparole. 39-19-7			
CONN. Gen. Stat. Ann. (1960)	convicted of certain sex crimes. 17-244(a)	state's attorney or court on own motion. 17-244(a) 17-244(b)	either 17-244 (b)		17-244 (d) (4)		commit to diagnostic center of security treatment for a period not to exceed 60 days; examine, report and recommend. 17-244(a) 17-244(c) 17-244(d)					court may sentence in accord with conviction, place on probation, require outpatient psychiatric treatment or sentence in accord with conviction to diagnostic center. 17-245	though court may commit to diagnostic center, commitment shall not go beyond maximum period specified in criminal sentence. 17-245	fn. 5,6	advisory and review board has wide powers as to parole, leave of absence, and discharge; see 17-251 for complex procedures 17-254		advisory and review board must examine each case at least once each year; may parole or discharge. 17-250, 17-251		17-251	17-251	17-251		habeas corpus 17-256
DEL. Code Ann. (1953)																							
D.C. Code Ann. (1967)	fn. 7 sexual psychopath 22-3503 proceedings may be instituted though no criminal charge or conviction. 22-3504(a)	22-3504 (b) 22-3504 (c)		before trial. 22-3504 (d)(1)	22-3504 (d)(2)	before completion of probation. 22-3504(d) (3)	two 22-3506 (a)			22-3507	if demanded. 22-3508	22-3508			sufficiently recovered so as not to be dangerous to other persons. 22-3509		22-3509			22-3509	22-3509 22-3510		22-3508

Table 10.2   PSYCHOPATHY AND THE LAW   continued

STATE	APPLIES TO	PROCEEDINGS INITIATED BY — Public Official	PROCEEDINGS INITIATED BY — Defense Attorney or Accused	TIME OF PROCEEDINGS — Preconviction	TIME OF PROCEEDINGS — Pre-sentence	TIME OF PROCEEDINGS — After Sentence	MEDICAL EXAMINATION — Psychiatrist	MEDICAL EXAMINATION — Physician	MEDICAL EXAMINATION — Other	HEARING	JURY	COMMITMENT PERIOD — Indeterminate	COMMITMENT PERIOD — Specified Term	RELEASED WHEN — Cured	RELEASED WHEN — Improved	RELEASE — Petition by Patient	RELEASE — Administrative	RELEASE — Judicial	TYPE OF RELEASE — Absolute	TYPE OF RELEASE — Probation or Parole	DISPOSITION OF ORIGINAL OFFENSE — Returned for Trial or Sentence	DISPOSITION OF ORIGINAL OFFENSE — Defense to Original Charge	APPEAL
FLA. Stat. Ann. (1965)	mentally disturbed sex offenders. 917.12(1) (1944) (Supp. 1969)	both judge on his own motion and attorney. 917.12 (2)(a) (1944) (Supp. 1969)	by affidavit on behalf of defendant. 917.12(2) (a)(1944) (Supp. 1969)		adjourn proceedings or suspend sentence. 917.12 (2)(a) (1944) (Supp. 1969)		not less than 2 nor more than 3; each must file with court a separate written report. 917.12(2) (c)(1944) (Supp. 1969)			917.12(2) (d)(1944) (Supp. 1969)		commit to board of state institutions until reasonable grounds to believe such person has recovered. 917.12(2) (d)(1944) (Supp. 1969)		if recovered so as not to be a menace to others; commit to criminal court. 917.12(3) (1944) (Supp. 1969)				hearing upon petition of director of corrections. 917.12(3) (Supp. 1969)	if recovered to a degree that he will not be a menace to others, discharge from institution; return to criminal court. 917.12(3) (Supp. 1969)		return to criminal court to stand trial if proceedings still pending. 917.12(3) (1944) (Supp. 1969)		
	fn. 8 child molesters. 801.041 (Supp. 1969)	court 801.051 (Supp. 1969)	defendant may also ask court for psychiatric psychological examination of complaining witness. 801.161 (Supp. 1969)		801.051 (Supp. 1969)		2 or 3 psychiatrists. 801.051 (Supp. 1969)					commit to or sentence to newly created state research and treatment center for an indeterminate period. 801.091 (1)(b) (Supp. 1969)	commit to or sentence to prison for not more than 25 years and treatment center for an indeterminate period. 801.091(1) (a) (Supp. 1969)	mental health staff board of review must re-examine case of committed person within 6 months and every 2 years thereafter. 801.13(1) (Supp. 1969)	when patient has received available treatment and center has exhausted curative abilities. 801.111 (Supp. 1969)		to custody of court. 801.111 (Supp. 1969)	801.121 (Supp. 1969)	801.121 (3) (Supp. 1969)	801.121(1) (Supp. 1969)	sentence. 801.121 (2) (Supp. 1969)		
GA. Code Ann. (1960)																							
HAWAII Rev. Stat. Ann. (1968)																							
IDAHO Code Ann. (1947)																							
ILL. Stat. Ann. (Smith-Hurd 1964)	sexually dangerous persons. 38, §105-1.01	attorney general or state's attorney. 38, §105-3		when any person is charged with a criminal offense. 38, §105-3			2 psychiatrists shall personally examine and make written report to court. 38, §104-4			38, §105-5	on demand. 38, §105-5	commit to director of public safety who shall act as guardian and retain custody until "recovered and released." 38, §105-8		released if recovered after hearing; conditionally released if believed to be recovered, but uncertain. 38, §105-9 38, §105-10		committing court shall discharge any person recovered after hearing. 38, §105-9	conditional release by court if director of public safety thinks patient has recovered but cannot tell for certain under hospital con- [cont'd]		discharge if court-after hearing upon application finds person "recovered." 38, §105-9	if conditionally released, person is on probation and may be recommitted if violation. 38, §105-10			as provided by the Civil Practice Act. 38, §105-3.01

Table 10.2 PSYCHOPATHY AND THE LAW *continued*

STATE	APPLIES TO	Proceedings: Public Official	Proceedings: Defense Attorney or Accused	Time: Preconviction	Time: Pre-sentence	Time: After Sentence	Med. Exam: Psychiatrist	Med. Exam: Physician	Med. Exam: Other	HEARING	JURY	Commitment: Indeterminate	Commitment: Specified Term	Released: Cured	Released: Improved	Release: Petition by Patient	Release: Administrative	Release: Judicial	Type: Absolute	Type: Probation or Parole	Disp.: Returned for Trial or Sentence	Disp.: Defense to Original Charge	APPEAL
ILL. Ann. Stat. (Smith-Hurd 1964) (continued)																	ditions. 38, §105-10						
IND. Ann. Stat. (1956)	fn. 9 criminal sexual psychopathic persons. 9-3401	county prosecuting attorney. 9-3402	someone on behalf of person charged. 9-3402	9-3402	or placed on probation. 9-3402			court ordered examination by 2 physicians mandatory if petition by prosecuting attorney; discretionary if by accused. 9-3404(a) (Supp. 1969)		do not hold hearing unless both physicians conclude person is a criminal sexual psychopath. 9-3404(b) to 9-3404(d) (Supp. 1969)		mandatory observation period not to exceed 60 days; if then committed, period is until "fully and permanently recovered." 9-3404(d) (Supp. 1969)		may be released only when "fully recovered;" 2 physicians are to examine once each year and report findings. 9-3408	9-3408	9-3408		if court after petition finds him "fully recovered". 9-3408	if "fully recovered" 9-3408	council for mental health has right to release person on parole. 9-3407		no person adjudged a psychopath shall thereafter be tried or convicted. 9-3409	as in any criminal case. 9-3406
IOWA Code Ann. (1969)	criminal sexual psychopath. 225A.1	fn. 10 225A.2		225A.2			at discretion of court. 225A.4, 225A.7			225A.4 225A.8	if requested by defendant. 225A.9	225A.11			fn. 11 225A.12	if supported by opinion of 3 psychiatrists. 225A.12		225A.12		minimum of 3 years. 225A.12(1)	fn. 12 225A.13		225A.5
KAN. Stat. Ann. (1964)	offense against public morals and decency. 62-1534	62-1534	62-1534		62-1534		at state hospital. 62-1535 62-1536					62-1536		62-1537				62-1537	62-1537	62-1537	62-1537		65-1536
KY. Rev. Stat. Ann. (1969)																							
LA. Rev. Stat. Ann. (1967)																							
ME. Rev. Stat. Ann. (1964)																							
MD. Ann. Code (1967)	defective delinquent. 31B, § 5 31B, § 5	31B, § 6(b)	31B, § 6(b)			31B, § 6(c)	fn. 13 31B, § 7(a) 31B, § 7(b)	31B, § 7(a)	psychologist. 31B, § 7(a)	31B, § 8(a) 31B, § 7	31B, § 8(c)	31B, § 9(b)		31B, § 10(a)	fn. 14 31B, § 10(f)	fn. 15 31B, § 10(a)	31B, § 13(b) 31B, § 10(d)	31B, § 10 31B, § 13(f)	31B, § 10(a) 31B, § 13(f)	31B, § 10(d) 31B, § 13(f)	31B, § 10(f)		31B, § 11

Table 10.2 PSYCHOPATHY AND THE LAW continued

STATE	APPLIES TO	PROCEEDINGS INITIATED BY: Public Official	Defense Attorney or Accused	TIME OF PROCEEDINGS: Preconviction	Pre-sentence	After Sentence	MEDICAL EXAMINATION: Psychiatrist	Physician	Other	HEARING	JURY	COMMITMENT PERIOD: Indeterminate	Specified Term	RELEASED WHEN: Cured	Improved	RELEASE: Petition by Patient	Administrative	Judicial	TYPE OF RELEASE: Absolute	Probation or Parole	DISPOSITION OF ORIGINAL OFFENSE: Returned for Trial or Sentence	Defense to Original Charge	APPEAL
MASS. Ann. Laws (1965)	sexually dangerous person. 123A, § 1	123A, § 4			123A, § 4	fn. 16 / 123A, § 6	123A, § 4			123A, § 5	123A, § 5	123A, § 5			125A, § 9 (Supp. 1967)	123A, § 9 (Supp. 1968)	123A, § 9 (Supp. 1968)	123A, § 9 (Supp. 1968)	123A, § 9 (Supp. 1968)	123A, § 5; and in Supp. 1968, 123A, § 9			
fn. 17 MICH. Comp. Laws. Ann.																							
MINN. Stat. Ann. fn. 18 (1969)	psychopathic personality. 526.09 526.10	526.10						526.10		526.10											526.11		526.10
MISS. Code Ann. (1952)																							
MO. Rev. Stat. (1959)	criminal sexual psychopath 202.700	202.710		202.710				202.720.2	fn. 19 / 202.720.2	202.720	202.720.4	202.730		202.740				202.730	202.740	202.740	202.750		202.720.4
MONT. Rev. Codes Ann. (1961)																							
NEB. Rev. Stat. fn. 20 (1964)	sexual psychopath 29-2901	county attorney 29-2902				fn. 21 / 29-2902(1)		fn. 22 two 29-2902(2)		29-2902(2) 29-2904	unless waived. 29-2904	29-2906		at court's discretion after superintendent's recommendation. 29-2906			at court's discretion after superintendent of institution's recommendation. 29-2906		at court's discretion 29-2906				may appeal directly to Supreme Court. 29-2902
NEV. Rev. Stat. (1967)																							
N.H. Rev. Stat. Ann. fn. 23 (1964)	sex offender. 173-A:2 (Supp. 1969)			173-A:3 (1) (Supp. 1969)						173-A:4 (Supp. 1969)	no right to trial by jury. 173-A:4 (VI) (Supp. 1969)	173-A:5 (Supp. 1969)		recovered or improved to such extent that patient is not dangerous & further treatment is without benefit. 173-A:9(I) (Supp. 1969)		fn. 24 / 173-A:9 (II) (Supp. 1969)	fn. 25 / 173-A:6 (III) / 173-A:9(I) (Supp. 1969)	fn. 26 / 173-A:6 (II) / 173-A:9 (I,III) (Supp. 1969)	173-A:9 (III) (Supp. 1969)	fn. 25 / 173-A:6 (III) (Supp. 1969)	173-A:10 (Supp. 1969)		

Table 10.2 PSYCHOPATHY AND THE LAW *continued*

STATE	APPLIES TO	PROCEEDINGS INITIATED BY		TIME OF PROCEEDINGS			MEDICAL EXAMINATION			HEARING	JURY	COMMITMENT PERIOD		RELEASED WHEN		RELEASE			TYPE OF RELEASE		DISPOSITION OF ORIGINAL OFFENSE		APPEAL
		Public Official	Defense Attorney or Accused	Preconviction	Pre-sentence	After Sentence	Psychiatrist	Physician	Other			Indeterminate	Specified Term	Cured	Improved	Petition by Patient	Administrative	Judicial	Absolute	Probation or Parole	Returned for Trial or Sentence	Defense to Original Charge	
N.J. Stat. Ann. (1953)	sex offender. 2A:164-3 (Supp. 1970)	fn. 27 2A:164-2			2A:164-2				fn. 27 2A:164-2			but not to exceed period specified by law for the criminal offense. 2A:164-6			capable of making an acceptable social adjustment in the community 2A:164-8		2A:164-8		fn. 28 2A:164-6	2A:164-6 (a) 2A:164-8			
N.M. Stat. Ann. (1964)																							
N.Y. Mental Hygiene Law (McKinney 1951)																							
N.C. Gen. Stat. (1963)																							
fn. 29 N.D. Cent. Code (1960)																							
OHIO Rev. Code (Baldwin 1964)	mentally deficient offender; psychopathic offender. 2947.24(A) 2947.24(B)	trial court. 2947.25 (Supp. 1968)			2947.25 (Supp. 1968)		2947.25 (Supp. 1968)		2947.25 (Supp. 1968)	2947.25 (Supp. 1968)		fn. 30 2947.25 (Supp. 1968)			recovered or his condition appears to have improved so that he no longer needs special custody, care, or treatment. 2947.27 (Supp. 1968)	fn. 31 2947.28	2947.27 (Supp. 1968)	2947.28	fn. 32 2947.27 (Supp. 1968)		if confined for less than the period of maximum sentence for the offense of which convicted. 2947.27(A) (Supp. 1968)		2947.25 (Supp. 1968)
OKLA. Stat. (1951)																							
ORE. Rev. Stat. (1967)	persons convicted of certain sex offenses. 137.111	137.111			137.111		137.112			137.114		137.111										commitment is in lieu of any other sentence authorized by law for such crime. 137.111	

Table 10.2 PSYCHOPATHY AND THE LAW *continued*

STATE	APPLIES TO	PROCEEDINGS INITIATED BY — Public Official	PROCEEDINGS INITIATED BY — Defense Attorney or Accused	TIME OF PROCEEDINGS — Preconviction	TIME OF PROCEEDINGS — Pre-sentence	TIME OF PROCEEDINGS — After Sentence	MEDICAL EXAMINATION — Psychiatrist	MEDICAL EXAMINATION — Physician	MEDICAL EXAMINATION — Other	HEARING	JURY	COMMITMENT PERIOD — Indeterminate	COMMITMENT PERIOD — Specified Term	RELEASED WHEN — Cured	RELEASED WHEN — Improved	RELEASE — Petition by Patient	RELEASE — Administrative	RELEASE — Judicial	TYPE OF RELEASE — Absolute	TYPE OF RELEASE — Probation or Parole	DISPOSITION OF ORIGINAL OFFENSE — Returned for Trial or Sentence	DISPOSITION OF ORIGINAL OFFENSE — Defense to Original Charge	APPEAL
PA. Stat. Ann. (1964)	persons convicted of certain sex crimes. 19-1166	court. 19-1166			19-1166		19-1167		facilities of department of public welfare. 19-1167	arraigned and sentenced. 19-1170 (a)		19-1166				fn. 33 19-1172	fn. 34 19-1172			19-1172 19-1173		in lieu of sentence provided by law for certain sex offenders, the court may sentence such person to a state institution for an indeterminate period. 19-1166	
R.I. Gen. Laws Ann. (1956)																							
S.C. Code Ann. (1962)																							
S.D. Compiled Laws Ann. (1967)																							
TENN. Code Ann. (1955) (Supp. 1968)	sex offender 33-1301	33-1304				33-1303	33-1304			33-1305		33-1304		33-1305 (Supp. 1968)				33-1305	33-1305		33-1305		
TEX. Rev. Civ. Stat. Ann. (1958)																							
UTAH Code Ann. (1953)	persons convicted of certain sex crimes. 77-49-1 (Supp. 1967)	by the court. 77-49-1 (Supp. 1967)			77-49-1 (Supp. 1967)		77-49-2						for life unless paroled or pardoned. 77-49-5		fn. 35 77-49-7 (Supp. 1967)		77-49-7 (Supp. 1967)		77-49-7 (Supp. 1967)	77-49-7 (Supp. 1967)		77-49-5	
VT. Stat. Ann. (1968)	mentally defective delinquents, mentally deficient or psychopathic personalities 18, §8501 (Supp. 1969) 18, §8502	18, § §8504 (Supp. 1969)			18, §8504				to be examined at place of commitment. 18, §8504		18, §8505							18, § 8506 (Supp. 1969)		18, §850c (Supp. 1969)		

Table 10.2 PSYCHOPATHY AND THE LAW continued

STATE	APPLIES TO	PROCEEDINGS INITIATED BY		TIME OF PROCEEDINGS			MEDICAL EXAMINATION			HEARING	JURY	COMMITMENT PERIOD		RELEASED WHEN			RELEASE		TYPE OF RELEASE		DISPOSITION OF ORIGINAL OFFENSE		APPEAL
		Public Official	Defense Attorney or Accused	Preconviction	Pre-sentence	After Sentence	Psychiatrist	Physician	Other			Indeterminate	Specified Term	Cured	Improved	Petition by Patient	Administrative	Judicial	Absolute	Probation or Parole	Returned for Trial or Sentence	Defense to Original Charge	
VA. Code Ann. (1967)	sexual abnormality. 53-278.2	53-278.2	53-278.2		defer sentence until report of mental examination 53-278.2		one employed in any state hospital 53-278.3																	
WASH. Rev. Code Ann. (1962)	sexual psychopath. 71.06.010 71.06.020	prosecuting attorney 71.06.020		71.06.020		fn. 36 71.06.020 & in Supp. 1968, 71.06.030		fn. 37 71.06.040		71.06.070	defendant may demand jury. 71.06.070	fn. 38 71.06.130 (Supp. 1968)			until safe to be at large. 71.06.130 (Supp. 1968)			71.06.130 (Supp. 1968)	fn. 39 71.06.130 (Supp. 1968)	conditional release. 71.06.130 (Supp. 1968)	at court's discretion. 71.06.030, 71.06.060, 71.06.130 (Supp. 1968)		
W. VA. Code Ann. (1966)	persons convicted of incest, crimes against nature, rape, and other sex crimes (provided in case of rape the sentence is not death.) 27-6A-1 27-6A-2	the court. 27-6A-1 27-6A-2			27-6A-1 27-6A-2				27-6A-1 27-6A-2				every person who has not been discharged shall be discharged at expiration of maximum term prescribed by law for offense or at expiration of 1 year, whatever is greater, unless commissioner of public institutions has made an order directing that patient remain subject to commissioner's control for a longer period and has applied to the committing court for review of such order. 27-6A-12		control no longer necessary for protection of public or expiration of term for offense. 27-6A-11 27-6A-12		27-6A-11 27-6A-12		27-6A-11 27-6A-12				if court affirms order of commissioner of public institutions, the person whose liberty is involved may appeal to proper appellate court for reversal or modification of order. 27-6A-16
WIS. Stat. Ann. (1957)	persons convicted of certain sex crimes 959.15(1) 959.15(2)				959.15(1)				facilities of state department of public welfare. 959.15(1) 959.15(2)				fn. 40 959.15(11) (12), (13), (14), and (15)		retained as long as necessary for the protection of public 959.15(11)		959.15 (10) 959.15 (11)		fn. 41 959.15 (11)	959.15 (6), 959.15 (10) (Supp. 1968)		959.15(12)	959.15(7) (b) and 959.15(16)
WYO. Stat. Ann. (1957)	persons convicted of certain sex crimes. 7-348(a) (Supp. 1969)	7-348(b) (Supp. 1969)			7-348(b) (Supp. 1969)		7-349 (Supp. 1969)	7-349 (Supp. 1969)				may have specified commitment period but in no case is detention to exceed maximum period of sentence for the crime. 7-356 (Supp. 1969)			capable of acceptable social adjustment in the community 7-357			7-357		7-352 (Supp. 1969) 7-357			

1. After examination and hearing, the person adjudged a mentally dis-ordered sex offender shall be placed temporarily in a county or state hospital for observation and diagnosis for a period not to exceed 90 days. The hospital superintendent shall within 90 days cause the person to be examined and shall furnish a report, diagnosis, and recommendations for the person's future welfare to the court. Three categories of offense may be reported:

   (1) If not a mentally disordered sex offender, return to criminal court to await further action.
   (2) If a mentally disordered sex offender who will not benefit from medical treatment, return to criminal court. If the criminal court so desires, it may send the patient to the superior court for in-determinate commitment to a state hospital.
   (3) If a mentally disordered sex offender who could benefit from medical treatment, the court may commit for an indeterminate period to the state hospital.

   Various technical procedures for hearings, witnesses, etc., are provided but are beyond the scope of this footnote. "No person shall be committed for an indeterminate period as a mentally disordered sex offender unless an [90-day] observation placement has been made and reported, diagnosed and recommended. . ." Cal. W. & I. 6316 (Supp. 1968).

2. A mentally disordered sex offender who has not recovered and is still a menace shall be returned to the criminal court to stand trial or the superior court may recommit him to the hospital for a further indeterminate period. Cal. W. & I. 6325, 6326 (Supp. 1968).

3. When the patient is released, he is to be returned to the court which had jurisdiction over the criminal proceedings. If the offense was one for which probation is available, the court may put him on probation for a minimum of 5 years. Cal. W. & I. 6325 (Supp. 1968).

4. The state board of parole may authorize detention in a county jail, penitentiary, industrial school or any other state institution. Colo. 39-19-6.

5. At least annually the defendant must be reexamined by the diagnostic center and a report of the examination made to the advisory and review board. The board will then determine whether the defendant should receive further treatment or be granted a leave of absence, parole, or discharge. If the defendant's condition has so improved as to warrant his discharge before the expiration of his sentence, he must be placed on parole before he may be discharged absolutely. Conn. 17-251.

6. Within 6 months prior to the expiration of the maximum period of detention, the Advisory and Review Board may recommend that the Commissioner of Welfare initiate civil commitment proceedings. Conn. 17-254.

7. The sexual psychopath law does not apply to persons charged with or convicted of rape or assault with intent to rape. D.C. 22-3504(e).

8. Child Molester Law may become operative upon a conviction for at-tempted rape, sodomy, attempted sodomy, crimes against nature, at-tempted crimes against nature, lewd and lascivious behavior, incest, attempted incest, assault (when a sexual act is committed or at-tempted), when said acts are committed against, to, with, or in the presence of a person 14 years of age or under. Fla. 801.041 (Supp. 1968).

9. Criminal sexual psychopath law does not apply when a defendant is charged with murder, manslaughter, or rape of a female child under 12 years old. Ind. 9-3403.

10. Also any reputable person may inform the county attorney when he has any knowledge that the defendant is a criminal sexual psycho-path. Iowa 225A.2 (Supp. 1968).

11. If a defendant has obtained maximum hospital benefit and his re-lease is not incompatible with public welfare. Iowa 225A.12 (Supp. 1968).

12. The fact that a person is found to be a criminal sexual psychopath does not constitute a defense to any criminal action. Iowa 225A.13.

13. If petition is not filed by the state's attorney or assistant state's attorney or by the court itself, the defendant is entitled to 1 psychiatrist of his own choice at the expense of the state in addition to the regular examination. Md. 31B, §7(b).

14. If Board of Review believes patient has sufficiently improved to warrant unconditional release, it informs whichever court has juris-diction over the person and the court in turn makes such further study of such person as seems necessary to determine the course of action to take. Md. 31B, §13(f).

15. After defendant has been committed for 2 years, he or anyone in his behalf may petition for judicial redetermination of his condition. If found still to be defective delinquent, a new petition may not be submitted for 3 years. Md. 31B, §10(a) and (b).

16. Special proceedings for commitment of prisoners under sentence in jail exist. Mass. 123A, §6.

17. Michigan's sexual psychopath statute (the Goodrich Act) was recently repealed in its entirety and the legal category of criminal sexual psychopath abolished (Public Act 143, effective Aug. 1, 1968). Michigan retains provisions on "sexually delinquent" persons who may be sentenced to prison indeterminately (Mich. Comp. Laws Ann. §§750.10a, 750.335a et seq. (1968).

Notes to Table 10.2 PSYCHOPATHY AND THE LAW *continued*

18. Statute does not specify a charge or conviction of a criminal offense as prerequisite to initiation of proceedings. Minn. 526.10.

19. Or "2 members of the medical staff of any state mental hospital." Mo. 202.720.2.

20. "The term sexual psychopath shall mean any person who, by a course of misconduct in sexual matters, has evidenced an utter lack of power to control his sexual impulses and who, as a result, is likely to attack or otherwise inflict injury, loss, pain, or other evil on the objects of his uncontrolled and uncontrollable desires." Neb. 29-2901.

21. "Whenever facts are presented to the county attorney which satisfy him that good cause exists for judicial inquiry as to whether a person is a sexual psychopath, he shall prepare a petition setting forth such facts." Neb. 29-2902(1).

22. Two years' special training in mental diseases. Neb. 29-2902(2).

23. Any person "suffering from such conditions of emotional instability or impulsiveness of behavior, or lack of customary standards of good judgment, or failure to appreciate the consequences of his acts, or a combination of any such conditions, as to render such person irresponsible with respect to sexual matters and thereby dangerous to himself or other persons." N.H. 173-A:2 (Supp. 1969).

24. Petition must be accompanied by affidavit of psychiatrist that defendant has improved. N.H. 173-A:9 (II) (Supp. 1969).

25. Commission on Mental Health with approval of court may parole patient for 1 year. N.H. 173-A:6(III) (Supp. 1969).

26. Commission on Mental Health is to make annual report on patient's condition to court. N.H. 173-A:6(II) (Supp. 1969).

27. Judge before imposing sentence may order a mental and physical examination of defendant by county clinic of county wherein sentence is to be imposed and which clinic is set up for that purpose, or by one of the state institutions. N.J. 2A:164-2.

28. No "person can be confined or subject to parole supervision for a period of time greater than that provided by law for the crime of which the person was convicted." N.J. 2A:164-6.

29. Warden may cause any person convicted of rape and carnal abuse to be given psychiatric treatment or to be transferred to state hospital for diagnosis and disposition according to such conditions as may be prescribed by warden after consulting with prison psychiatrist or psychologist. N.D. 12-30-12 (Supp. 1969).

30. Court is to impose proper sentence for the crime and at same time as court orders indefinite commitment to Department of Public Welfare. Ohio 2947.25 (Supp. 1968).

31. Patient may apply to court for release any time after expiration of time equivalent to maximum sentence. Court need not hear subsequent application until year after previous hearing. Ohio 2947.28.

32. If defendant has been confined for period less than maximum sentence, he shall be transferred to proper institution, and suspended sentence shall go into effect. For parole or discharge purposes, time spent in confinement shall count as time served. If he has been confined for a period longer than maximum sentence, he is to be placed on trial visit until director feels it is safe to discharge him. Ohio 2947.27 (Supp. 1968).

33. "Nothing in this section shall be construed to prohibit a person sentenced under the provisions of this act from making application for parole in the manner now provided by law." Pa. 19, §§1172, 1057. Pa. 19, §1057, sets out the general procedure for parole of one sentenced for indefinite term.

34. Within 3 months after commitment and at least every 6 months thereafter, Parole Board must examine records of patients and determine whether they may be paroled. Pa. 19, §1172.

35. If it is for best interest of patient and of public, then he shall be paroled or pardoned. Utah 77-49-7 (Supp. 1967).

36. Petition alleging defendant is a sexual psychopath must be filed and served on defendant 10 days before trial of criminal charge. Court may proceed to hear criminal charge. If defendant is convicted or has previously pleaded guilty to charge, sentence is pronounced; court then proceeds to hear sexual psychopathy allegation. Acquittal does not suspend hearing on issue of psychopathy. Wash. 71.06.020, 71.06.030 (Supp. 1968).

37. At preliminary hearing on charge of sexual psychopathy, court may require testimony of 2 physicians who have examined defendant. If court finds there are reasonable grounds to believe defendant is a psychopath, it shall commit him to state hospital for no more than 90 days for observation. Wash. 71.06.040.

38. Sexual psychopath shall be retained by institution superintendent until in superintendent's opinion it is safe for him to be at large, or until he has received maximum benefit of treatment; or if he is not amenable to treatment, he shall be retained if superintendent is unable to render an opinion that it is safe for him to be at large. Thereupon, superintendent shall so inform whatever court committed the sexual psychopath. From reports, investigation and possible hearing, court shall determine whether person before it shall be released unconditionally from custody as a sexual psychopath, released conditionally, returned to custody of institution as sexual psychopath, or returned to department of institutions to serve original sentence imposed on him. Wash. 71.06.091 (Supp. 1968).

39. When defendant has been conditionally released for 5 years, committing court may discharge him if superintendent is satisfied that he should be at large. Wash. 71.06.130 (Supp. 1968).

40. Detention is not to exceed period specified in sentence for the criminal offense unless department obtains order from committing court to continue person in control of department. Wis. 959.15(11) to 959.15(15).

41. Department of public welfare is authorized to parole or discharge patients, but no patient convicted of a felony may be discharged prior to 2 years after commitment. Wis. 959.15(11).

Chapter Eleven

Mental Disability and the Criminal Law

I. INTRODUCTION

The preceding chapter, in describing the treatment afforded the sexual psychopath, explored but one aspect of a much broader social and legal problem. That problem concerns the impact which the mental condition of a person accused of a criminal act should have on the action society takes against him. The present chapter will attempt to survey this problem more extensively.

Although the mental condition of a person who commits a criminal act can influence the action taken in regard to him at many times and in many ways,[1] the discussion in this chapter will be concerned primarily with three major possible effects. First, the mental condition of the defendant may absolve him completely of responsibility for the crime and shield him from the imposition of any criminal punishment. Second, the degree of the crime and/or the severity of the punishment exacted may be reduced if the defendant's mental condition made him only partially responsible for his acts. And third, criminal proceedings against the accused may have to be suspended pending his recovery from a present mental condition.

II. CRIMINAL IRRESPONSIBILITY: RELIEVING ACCUSED OF RESPONSIBILITY

All adult persons, including the mentally disabled, are presumed by the law to be responsible for their criminal acts. However, Anglo-American legal tradition—stemming from developments during the reign of Edward III (1326–77)—has relieved an amorphous group of the mentally disabled of criminal liability on the grounds of "madness" or "insanity."[2] With reference to the complexity of this tradition, it has been observed that a good deal of confusion in this field can be avoided by postulating that the term "insanity" is a legal concept which has no medical counterpart.[3] Thus the concept has been defined as follows:

> In criminal law "insanity," by whatever test it may be ascertained, may be said to be that *degree* or *quantity* of mental disorder which relieves one of the criminal responsibility for his actions.[4]

While this definition clarifies the function of the defense, it says nothing about the purposes of, or the philosophy behind, the defense of insanity, or to whom it applies and why. It is also quite circular. Thus the definition may *not* avoid confusion; in fact, it may well be the very source of misapplication and misunderstanding.[5]

2. Biggs, *The Guilty Mind* 83 (1955).

3. Id. at 117: "[T]he divergence between law and psychiatry is caused in part by the legal fiction represented by the words 'insanity' or 'insane,' which are a kind of lawyer's catchall and have no clinical meaning."

4. Sollars v. State, 73 Nev. 248, 316 P.2d 917, 919 (1957).

5. It may be doubted whether it is acceptable, realistic, or even possible to regard insanity as an exclusively legal concept. Can any concept be "strictly legal"? Can one ignore the relevance of medical and sociological considerations in determining "legal" feasibility or desirability? For example, if one attempted to evaluate the various formulations of the defense of insanity, it would not do to stop at the linguistic (legal?) clarity of the formulation; even this limited inquiry into the desirability of one formula over another must involve our conception of the criminal law in its entirety, a highly philosophical conception demanding that questions from a broad spectrum of disciplines be asked and answered. Why should we broaden the defense of insanity, or restrict its application? Whom do we want to "punish-incarcerate," who should be "treated-hospitalized"? What is the rationale behind this dichotomy of dispositions? What is the practical difference? Why is insanity a separate defense distinguishable from all other instances where the requisite criminal intent may be absent? Is it a separate concept merely because the legal system is unable to make determinations about it without the aid of medical expertise? Or is the defense a means of easing the harshness of our system of punishment? Is "legal" insanity therefore more accurately a humanist concept? How much weight then should be given to medical testimony? Why not have expert testimony—psychological or socio-

1. For instance, under many modern sentencing procedures the type of sentence imposed may be modified by the defendant's mental condition. (See Weihofen, *Mental Disorder as a Criminal Defense* 206–10, 487–89 (1954), for a discussion of existing and proposed sentencing procedures which employ an inventory of the defendant's mental condition in deciding the proper disposition for him.) After sentence has been pronounced and the defendant committed to the prison system, another mental assessment may influence the mode of treatment he receives within the system. The prison administration may send a convict suffering from a mental condition to a psychiatric ward within the prison or to a special hospital for the criminally insane. Or, at the expiration of his sentence he may be subjected to civil hospitalization.

In general, our criminal laws are premised on the view that human beings are normally capable of free and rational choice between alternative modes of behavior, that an individual who chooses to harm another is morally blameworthy or guilty, and that he is liable to punishment if his behavior and the resulting harm have been proscribed by law. Seen from this viewpoint, punishment of the offender serves society in several ways: (1) it implements and publicizes the community's concepts of morality; (2) it protects society from further wrongdoing through the incarceration of the offender; (3) it serves to deter the individual punished and others from doing similar wrongs; (4) it may in some instances be used to rehabilitate the offender and allow his return to society as a more useful citizen.[6]

Two primary reasons have been given for the exclusion of certain mentally disabled individuals from the traditional sanctions of the criminal law. The earlier edition of this Report phrased the arguments as follows:

---

logical—in all criminal trials, regardless of the defense asserted? These are just some of the questions. They and others are dealt with individually or comprehensively in the virtually innumerable articles in legal and medical journals, treatises, books, and pamphlets on the subject of the defense of insanity. The mere volume of these writings testifies to the fundamental nature of the defense in relation to the criminal law as a whole. The questions raised cannot all be discussed with any degree of thoroughness in this Report. But they give a measure of the range of controversy and confusion that surrounds "legal" insanity, and suggest that definitional oversimplification in this area is not likely to aid the analysis.

6. Hall, "Psychiatry and Criminal Responsibility," 65 *Yale L.J.* 761, 765 (1955–56). More often the purposes served by punishment are stated as retribution, individual prevention, rehabilitation of the offender, and general deterrence. It is recognized that these goals are often in conflict with each other. Waelder, "Psychiatry and the Problems of Criminal Responsibility," 101 *U. Pa. L. Rev.* 378, 386–89 (1952–53). Waelder also points out that the complete elimination of the concept of retribution from our legal system may not be desirable, since it would "tend to dissociate the law entirely from moral sentiment." Id. at 387. Hill states that most modern writers in the field believe that if society were to forgo punishment of the criminal, it would be deprived of one of its major outlets for its repressed antisocial aggressiveness. Hill, "The Psychological Realism of Thurman Arnold," 22 *U. Chi. L. Rev.* 377, 388 (1955). Thus it may be said that if the concept of retribution is accepted as a separate goal of punishment which does serve society, it is possible that the punishment of the mentally disabled will not frustrate this aim. However, even if this were so, punishing the mentally disabled would satisfy only one of several objectives while frustrating the others, and on this ground the exclusion of the mentally disabled from the traditional sanctions of the penal law could still be rationalized. See Biggs, *supra* note 2, at 174–76 and Hill, *supra* at 387–89.

First, an established requirement for criminal culpability is *mens rea*—the intent to commit a criminal act. Those who do not possess sufficient capacity to avoid forming a criminal intent are deprived of "free will" or rational choice. Since the very concept of *mens rea* or the "guilty mind" assumes rational choice, persons deprived of this capacity do not come within the concept.[7]

The circularity of this reasoning is evident and reinforces the suggestion that in the area of criminal responsibility we are dealing with a set of historic, cultural, perhaps intuitive responses which are exceptionally difficult to articulate rationally or convincingly.

Second, the punishment of certain of the mentally disabled may not serve society in the same manner as would the punishment of other offenders. For instance, since some of the mentally disabled do not have the capacity to make rational choices or understand either the law or the nature of their actions, it may be doubted whether the threat or imposition of criminal punishment will have any significant deterrent effect on their behavior.[8] In fact, certain mentally disabled persons commit criminal acts precisely because they seek to be punished.[9]

It may be suggested, though, that these propositions apply equally well to offenders who are found clearly "sane" under any of the existing tests of criminal responsibility, traditional or modern. Can the "ordinary" offender be said to have made a rational choice? What was the law's deterrent effect on him? May not his motivation have been in part a desire to seek punishment?

The traditional rationale of the criminal justice system further recognizes that punishment of a mentally ill (and thus nondeterrable) offender does not help to deter other persons in the community from behaving similarly. Presumably, the general public is well aware that such people are different and do not deserve the same treatment; moreover, punishing them would not serve to implement and publicize social concepts of morality. In addition, rehabilitation of the mentally disabled offender cannot generally be accomplished merely through long-term incarceration. It is appropriate to ask, how-

7. Lindman & McIntyre, *The Mentally Disabled and the Law* 331 (1961).

8. Ibid.

9. Ibid., citing Guttmacher & Weihofen, *Psychiatry and the Law* 417 (1952).

ever, whether long-term incarceration is a successful method of rehabilitating any offender; and alternatively, whether long-term institutionalization of the mentally disabled offender in our present facilities for the criminally insane can justifiably be said to conform to rehabilitative ideals.

A. Abolishing Defense of Insanity

Abandonment of the insanity defense is hardly a novel proposal or an isolated one. In 1911, Dr. William White in effect proposed abandonment when he recommended that the jury's duty be confined to determining whether the accused was the true transgressor.[10] More recently, scholars of the stature of Chief Justice Weintraub, Dr. Karl Menninger, former Justice Fortas (as attorney on appeal of the *Durham* case), Lady Barbara Wootton, Professor H. L. A. Hart, Dr. Thomas Szasz, Professor Norval Morris, and various others have similarly suggested that the defense be abolished.[11]

The rationales behind the proposal are many and varied, and represent opposite poles of perception about mental disability and the criminal law.[12] A common and fundamental feature, however, is an expression of doubt about the validity of the prison–hospital (custody–treatment) dichotomy and the process of selective stigmatization. Basic objections are made on abstract as well as on practical grounds. Should the criminal law distinguish among offenders, prescribe imprisonment for some and treatment for others? And can the criminal law rationally make such distinctions? Do existing dispositional institutions of custody and treatment bear any relation to these distinctions, or do they merely reflect a common disregard for all social deviates disguised only by self-serving semantics? Has the defense of insanity any philosophic validity, and is any formulation of it workable? What is the propriety of psychiatric testimony at a criminal trial, and what is its value, sincerity, reliability? And so forth. Generally, it may also be said that those who wish to abolish the defense of insanity believe that in addition to being of dubious premise and practicability the defense misplaces the focus of the criminal process: it overemphasizes the public deterrence and morality aspects of the process, whereas the focus should be more on the offender and how to deal humanely and effectively with him; thus, dispositional determinations should be based (idealistically) on neutral principles to be applied to any offender whether sane or insane, responsible or irresponsible by present standards.

The constitutionality of eliminating the defense of insanity is historically quite dubious.[13] Three states have enacted statutes to this effect at one time in their history, but the laws in all three states were quickly struck down. In 1909 the state of Washington adopted a statute providing that insanity at the time of the crime should no longer be a defense but that the trial court, sitting without a jury, if it found the accused insane at the time of the offense, was to order him committed to a mental institution. A year later, the statute was held to violate the defendant's right to a jury trial.[14] Mississippi, in 1928, enacted a provision to the effect that insanity should not be a defense to murder; on conviction the defendant would be imprisoned for life, the governor being empowered to order him transferred to a hospital for the insane if the defendant's mental condition so warranted. Three years later, the Mississippi Supreme Court held that the statute violated due process.[15] Louisiana, also in 1928, enacted a law providing that in case of a plea of insanity, the defendant was to be tried before a lunacy commission which could commit if the defendant was found insane, or order trial if he was found sane, at which trial the defendant would be precluded from raising the insanity defense. The Louisiana Supreme Court found the statute to be unconsti-

---

10. Guttmacher, *The Role of Psychiatry in Law* 93 (1968).

11. See Justice Weintraub's address to the Annual Judicial Conference of the Second Federal Circuit, 37 F.R.D. 365 (1964); Wootton, *Crime and the Criminal Law,* chaps. 2, 3 (1963); Menninger, *The Crime of Punishment* (1968); Hart, *The Morality of the Criminal Law,* chap. 1 (1965); Szasz, *Law, Liberty and Psychiatry* (1963); Morris, "Psychiatry and the Dangerous Criminal," 41 *S. Cal. L. Rev.* 514 (1968); Guttmacher, *supra* note 10. See especially the appendix to Morris, *supra,* at 544, for a summary of several of the arguments advanced for abolishing the defense of insanity.

12. Contrast, for instance, the arguments of Szasz and Menninger. Szasz sees consideration of the accused's mental condition as a totally inappropriate intrusion into the criminal process, the aim of which is to identify and penalize offenders of the law. He thus advocates that psychiatric expertise be eliminated as irrelevant to this process. Menninger, on the other hand, seems to say that psychiatric considerations are ultimately relevant to the criminal process, his objection to the defense being that psychiatric expertise is presently being constricted and abused by artificial rules and notions inherent in the criminal process which tend to turn considerations of mental condition into a farcical exercise.

13. See Weihofen, *supra* note 1, at 477–80 for a brief discussion of the constitutional aspect.

14. State v. Strasberg, 60 Wash. 106, 110 P. 1020 (1910).

15. Sinclair v. State, 161 Miss. 142, 132 So. 581 (1931).

tutional as violating both due process and the right to a jury trial.[16]

Support for elimination of the defense of insanity has sometimes been based on an analogy to strict liability statutes, some of which have been constitutionally upheld. On the whole, however, courts have·been reluctant to construe statutes as imposing criminal liability without fault. The well-known case of *Morrisette v. United States*[17] held criminal intent essential to the crime of "knowingly converting" government property. It has been argued, though perhaps not very persuasively, that the reasoning of such cases makes it doubtful, on constitutional grounds, that attempts to eliminate insanity as a defense would be judicially sanctioned.

In any case, criminal irresponsibility remains a defense in all Anglo-American jurisdictions. The paradox is that the more glaring shortcoming of our existing dispositional institutions have been interpreted both as signaling the need for, and as militating against, abolition of the defense: the mental institutions to which we now send mentally ill defendants acquitted under the defense are woefully inadequate, but the prisons to which they would be sent instead if convicted, after abolition of the defense, are no better. It would seem that if our penal and treatment facilities underwent drastic reform, much of the controversy concerning "legal" insanity would disappear.

The various formulations of the defense of insanity will now be examined.

B. Tests of Criminal Responsibility

1. CURRENT TESTS

Unlike the civil area, in which a variety of standards have been formulated to determine the need for hospitalization, at present there are basically only four carefully drawn standards of criminal responsibility used in connection with persons suffering from a mental condition. These are the M'Naghten rules, the M'Naghten rules accompanied by the irresistible-impulse test, the New Hampshire or Durham test (the product test), and the test recommended by the American Law Institute's Model

Penal Code. These four formulations will be briefly outlined below. A detailed analysis and criticism will follow in the next section.

a) M'Naghten Rules

In 1843 the following test was announced in the celebrated case of Daniel M'Naghten:[18]

> [T]o establish a defense on the ground of insanity, it must be clearly proved that, at the time of the committing of the act, the party accused was laboring under such a defect of reason, from disease of the mind, as not to know the nature and quality of the act he was doing; or, if he did know it, that he did not know he was doing what was wrong.[19]

Two features of this formulation should be noted. First, the alternative tests, i.e., not knowing the nature and quality of the act, *or* not knowing that the act is wrong, apply only in cases where the defendant has a defect of reason from disease of mind, and either alternative must flow from the diseased mind. And second, if the defendant was otherwise sane but acted under an insane delusion[20] in which the facts, as they appeared to the defendant, would constitute a defense to the crime charged, he is not responsible for the crime.[21]

Despite the inclusion of alternative tests in the original M'Naghten case, the most common form in which the M'Naghten test now appears is "whether the defendant had the capacity to know right from

---

16. State v. Lange, 168 La. 958, 123 So. 639 (1929). Compare People v. Wells, 33 Cal. 2d 330, 202 P.2d 53 (1949), which upheld the California bifurcated procedure in criminal trials, emphasizing that the consideration of insanity as a separate issue "is but a departure in procedure. Each issue must still be tried by a jury of 12 impartial persons. . . . The guaranteed right of a trial by jury is as inviolate and just as much secured to all under the new system as it was under the old." 202 P.2d at 68.

17. 342 U.S. 246 (1951).

18. M'Naghten's Case, 10 Clark & Fin. 200, 8 Eng. Rep. 718 (1843). For a comprehensive study of the M'Naghten rules and a comparison with earlier tests, see Biggs, *supra* note 2, at 79–119.

19. 10 Clark & Fin. at 210.

20. The theory of partial insanity or monomania, i.e., that a person could be sane in all other respects and yet have an insane delusion, has been exploded by the more modern theory of the integrated psyche. See Guttmacher & Weihofen, *supra* note 9, at 417–18.

21. On the specific question of insane delusion, the answer of the judges in the *M'Naghten* case (an answer intended to set the pattern for a supplementary instruction in like cases) was as follows: "[M]aking the same assumption as we did before, namely that he labours under such partial delusion only, and is not in other respects insane, we think he must be considered in the same situation as to responsibility as if the facts with respect to which the delusion exists were real. For example, if under the influence of his delusion he supposes another man to be in the act of attempting to take away his life and kills that man, as he supposes, in self defense, he would be exempt from punishment. If his delusion was that the deceased had inflicted injury to his character and fortune, and he killed him in revenge for such supposed injury, he would be liable for punishment." 10 Clark & Fin. at 211.

wrong in respect to the particular act charged."[22] Most jurisdictions which apply M'Naghten seem to assume that the requirement of "knowing the nature and quality of the act" adds nothing to the right-wrong test.[23] A cogent argument might be made that a person may be able to retain intellectual knowledge of right and wrong and yet not understand the "nature and quality" of his act (i.e., its social significance).[24] From this point of view, omission of the "nature and quality" phrase might narrow the class of mentally disabled who are not criminally responsible. Since this distinction is not made by most courts, however, it is primarily the right-wrong facet of the M'Naghten formulation that will be evaluated in a later section.

The right-wrong M'Naghten formulation has been subjected to much criticism, and its status in both federal and state jurisdictions is less secure than it was a decade ago. Today M'Naghten is the sole test of criminal responsibility in fewer than half of the states. In at least fifteen states, the rule is supplemented and broadened by the irresistible-impulse test.[25] Several other states which reject the irresistible-impulse modification nonetheless recognize "insane delusions" as a defense.[26] Furthermore, perhaps a third of the states, notably California, accept the doctrine of diminished (or partial) responsibility[27]—albeit for limited purposes only. Most significant, twelve states, the District of Columbia, and eight of the federal circuits have specifically rejected M'Naghten and supplementary rules in favor of more "modern" formulations of criminal responsibility: the Durham rule or the American Law Institute's Model Penal Code test. Finally, the courts

in some of the jurisdictions which adhere to M'Naghten by statutory mandate have clearly expressed dissatisfaction with the rule and have refused to discard it only on the grounds that such a decision should be left to the legislature.[28]

Despite the decline of M'Naghten as the only criterion for criminal irresponsibility, the rule and its wording retain a good measure of their prominence. In fact it has been suggested that since the modern rules in effect broaden and add to the right-wrong test,

> it would appear that [M'Naghten remains] a defense in all Anglo-American jurisdictions and that the only controversy is over whether there are some cases in which the right and wrong test is not met, but in which a defense on grounds of insanity should nevertheless be recognized.[29]

b) Irresistible-Impulse Test

The irresistible impulse test is nowhere relied on as the sole criterion of criminal responsibility. It has been entirely rejected in England, Canada, and some 22 of our states, but in at least fifteen states it is accepted in conjunction with the M'Naghten right-wrong test, thus liberalizing the gauge of criminal irresponsibility. In addition, those jurisdictions employing the Model Penal Code formulation may be said to have given recognition to the basic thrust of the irresistible-impulse test.

This test applies to a defendant who may know the nature and quality of his act and may be aware that it is wrong, but who, nevertheless, may be irresistibly driven to commit a criminal act by an overpowering impulse resulting from a mental condition. The rule probably had its genesis in 1834 in Ohio[30] but assumed a progressively more definite form in subsequent decisions in other states.[31]

22. Weihofen, *supra* note 1, at 70.

23. Id. at 73. See also Guttmacher & Weihofen, *supra* note 9, at 403–4.

24. Weihofen, *supra* note 1, at 73.

25. The states which clearly recognize the irresistible impulse test as modifying M'Naghten are: Alabama, Arkansas, Colorado, Connecticut, Delaware, Indiana, Kansas, Michigan, New Mexico, Nevada, South Carolina, Texas, Utah, Virginia, and Wyoming. See 21 *Am. Jur.* 2d "Criminal Law" §§ 31–41 (1965); 22 C.J.S. "Criminal Law" §§ 55–61 (1961); Annot., 45 A.L.R.2d 1447 (1956 and Later Case Service, 1969, 1970).

26. Ibid. Whether recognition of "insane delusions" implies a broadening of the M'Naghten formula is debatable. First of all the delusion theory can be said to be part of the original M'Naghten test. Secondly, the delusion defense is in most jurisdictions infused with a limitation of substantial rigidity—that the accused's action be rationally consistent with the delusion—which is hardly a liberalization of the strict right-wrong formula.

27. See this chapter, § II B 3, Diminished Responsibility: An Alternative Approach?

28. See, e.g., State v. D'Haemers, 276 Minn. 332, 150 N.W.2d 66 (1967); State v. Schantz, 98 Ariz. 200, 403 P.2d 521 (1965); People v. Nash, 52 Cal. 2d 36, 338 P.2d 416 (1959).

29. 21 *Am. Jur.* 2d § 33 (1965). Compare Blocker v. United States, 320 F.2d 800 (D.C. Cir. 1963), holding that if the accused did not know right from wrong, the jury should conclude that his act was the product of mental disease. See also Wright v. United States, 250 F.2d 4 (D.C. Cir. 1957), stating that "[w]hile capacity to distinguish right from wrong is no longer *the* earmark of legal *sanity*, the lack of that capacity is *one* of the earmarks of legal *insanity*." Id. at 12.

30. State v. Thompson, Wright's Ohio Rep. 617 (1834). See also Clark v. State, 12 Ohio Rep. 483 (1843); Blackburn v. State, 23 Ohio 146 (1872); Weihofen, *supra* note 1, at 85–89.

31. Commonwealth v. Rogers, 48 Mass. 500 (1844); Commonwealth v. Mosler, 4 Pa. 264 (1846); State v. Felter, 25 Iowa

There has been some confusion surrounding the use of the term "irresistible impulse." The so-called irresistible impulse should not be confused with "unresisted impulse." Where reason is temporarily blinded by anger, jealousy, or other overriding passion not the result of a mental condition, the irresistible impulse test as stated above does *not* apply.[32]

c) The Product Rule: The New Hampshire and Durham Test

The New Hampshire Supreme Court in 1871 rejected the M'Naghten rules as inadequate, stating that "the verdict should be 'not guilty by reason of insanity' if the killing was the offspring or product of mental disease in the defendant."[33] New Hampshire stood alone in the use of this formulation until 1954 when the United States Court of Appeals for the District of Columbia Circuit in *Durham v. United States* held that "an accused is not criminally responsible if his unlawful act was the product of mental disease or mental defect."[34]

Quite clearly the Durham rule was an attempt to release the law from the century-old manacles of moral abstraction fastened to it by the judges in the case of Daniel M'Naghten. The Durham rule also encompasses those instances of "irresistible impulse" which are not sudden but rather the result of brooding and reflection. The test is supposedly factual and not legal or moralistic. Relevant inquiry is thus intended to be directed toward medical concepts of mental disability rather than conjecture as to the defendant's capacity to make moral judgments.

Since 1954 the Durham rule has been clarified and modified by subsequent decisions of the United States Court of Appeals for the District of Columbia Circuit.[35] In 1959, the Committee on Criminal Responsibility of the Bar Association of the District of Columbia stated the rule as follows:

> The accused is not responsible for a criminal act if such act was the product of a mental disease or mental defect. A mental disease is a diseased mental condition which may get better or get worse; a mental defect is a diseased mental condition which cannot get better and cannot get worse. The criminal act was the product of the mental disease or mental defect if the act would not have occurred except for the disease or defect; and that is so whether the disease or defect was the only cause of the act, or the principal one of several causes, or one of several causes.[36]

The *McDonald* decision in 1962 and the *Washington* decision in 1967,[37] redefining "mental disease or defect" and limiting to some extent the scope and impact of psychiatric testimony, represent a further evolution of the rule to a point where it is now viewed by some as virtually indistinguishable from the Model Penal Code test.[38]

Despite much favorable comment the Durham rule has not been widely accepted, and has been specifically rejected in at least twenty states.[39] Aside from the District of Columbia and New Hampshire where the test originated, only two other jurisdictions have adopted its formulation, both by statute: the Virgin Islands in 1956 and Maine in 1963.[40] Thus, only four jurisdictions follow Durham as the test of criminal responsibility.

36. Bar Association of the District of Columbia, Committee on Criminal Responsibility, "Report," 26 *J.B.A.D.C.* 301, 304 (1959) [hereinafter cited as Committee on Criminal Responsibility Report]; in Wright v. United States, 250 F.2d 4, 12–13 (D.C. Cir. 1957), the court, in striking down the trial judge's instruction which had intimated that the defendant's mental disease must be the principal cause of his act, cited Carter v. United States, 252 F.2d 608, 616–17 (D.C. Cir. 1957) and quoted therefrom: "When we say the defense of insanity required that the act be a 'product' of a disease we do not mean that it must be a direct emission, or a proximate creation, or an immediate issue of the disease in the sense, for example, of Hatfield's delusion that the Almighty had directed him to shoot George III."

37. McDonald v. United States, 312 F.2d 847 (D.C. Cir. 1962); Washington v. United States, 390 F.2d 444 (D.C. Cir. 1967).

38. For the view that *Durham* as modified by *McDonald* is much the same as the ALI formulation, see, e.g., United States v. Smith, 404 F.2d 720 (6th Cir. 1968) and commentary like Allen, Ferster, & Rubin, *Readings in Law and Psychiatry* 423–27 (1968).

39. See 22 C.J.S. "Criminal Law" §§ 55–61 (1961).

40. *Me. Rev. Stat. Ann.* tit. 15 § 102 (1964); *Virgin Is. Code* tit. 14, § 14(4) (1964). See also Virgin Islands v. Smith, 278 F.2d 169 (1960).

---

67 (1868); for citations to cases see Perkins, *Criminal Law* 760 n.16 (1957). See also Annot., 70 A.L.R. 659 (1931) and Annot., 173 A.L.R. 391 (1948). Perkins disagrees with Weihofen on whether the cases prior to *Commonwealth v. Mosler, supra,* actually refer to an irresistible impulse. He contends that they are no more than ambiguous phrasings of the M'Naghten rules. See Perkins, *supra* at 759–60, especially 759 n.1.

32. Perkins, *supra* note 31, at 757–58.

33. State v. Jones, 50 N.H. 369, 398, 9 Am. R. 242, 264 (1871). See also State v. Pike, 49 N.H. 399, 6 Am. R. 533 (1869).

34. Durham v. United States, 214 F.2d 862, 874–75 (D.C. Cir. 1954).

35. See Douglas v. United States, 239 F.2d 52 (D.C. Cir. 1956); Lyles v. United States, 254 F.2d 725 (D.C. Cir. 1958); Carter v. United States, 252 F.2d 608 (D.C. Cir. 1957); Fielding v. United States, 251 F.2d 878 (D.C. Cir. 1957); Wright v. United States, 250 F.2d 4 (D.C. Cir. 1957); and Williams v. United States, 250 F.2d 19 (D.C. Cir. 1957).

Minnesota, in 1956 in *Anderson v. Grasberg,*[41] adopted the Durham rule for some purposes in civil cases, but the court later explicitly declared in the 1960 *Finn* case[42] that the rule did not obtain in criminal trials, stating that the Minnesota statute on criminal responsibility (§ 610.10)[43] calling for application of M'Naghten was "clear and unambiguous [and] not subject to judicial construction or modification." By contrast, the Michigan Supreme Court has deviated to some extent from such judicial passivity: in the *Krugman* case in 1966 it indicated that application of Durham would be considered "if properly presented."[44] The Michigan court's attitude may be explained by the fact that M'Naghten is not a statutory test in that state.

One of the thrusts of the Durham rule has been seen to be that it allows the complete psychiatric picture of the defendant to be presented before the judge and jury. Thus Judge David L. Bazelon, author of the opinion, explained four years after the *Durham* decision:

> The thesis of *Durham* is not complicated and it is not revolutionary. It is simply that juries should be told what is known about the dynamics of human behavior. . . .
>
> The psychiatrist in the courtroom must understand that his function is *not* to make a *legal* determination of whether an accused is suffering from a mental disease or defect. That is for the judge and jury to decide. The psychiatrist's role is to supply the medical data—observed facts or opinions or both—upon which a legal determination can be based.[45]

The assumption underlying this view is that M'Naghten unduly restricted the scope of psychiatric testimony. This assumption has been questioned, however: a number of studies have argued that the M'Naghten rule never had such effect.[46] It may be difficult to ascertain which view of the impact of Durham is the correct one. It is clear, however, that

a rule which permits sensible psychiatric testimony is a goal sought even by some of the jurisdictions which continue to operate under M'Naghten. In the 1960 New Jersey case of *State v. Di Paolo,*[47] for example, the court felt bound to adhere to the M'Naghten rules, yet permitted the defense to present "the complete psychiatric picture *unrestrained by the M'Naghten concept.*" A similar situation obtains in military proceedings.[48] Admissibility of full psychiatric testimony has presumably also been a primary goal in those jurisdictions which have chosen to discard M'Naghten in favor of the Model Penal Code test—a variant of the Durham formulation.

d) The Model Penal Code and Vermont Test

In 1957, Vermont abolished the use of the M'Naghten rules and substituted for them a formulation very similar to that recommended by the American Law Institute's Model Penal Code.[49]

As enacted in Vermont this test provides that:

> (1) A person is not responsible for criminal conduct if at the time of such conduct as a result of mental disease or defect he lacks adequate capacity either to appreciate the criminality of his conduct or to conform his conduct to the requirements of law.
>
> (2) The terms "mental disease or defect" do not include an abnormality manifested only by repeated criminal or otherwise antisocial conduct. *The terms "mental disease or defect" shall include congenital and traumatic mental conditions as well as disease.*[50]

The Vermont test differs from that suggested by the Model Penal Code in only two aspects: It substitutes the word "adequate" for the word "substantial" in the Code's phrase "substantial capacity"; and it adds a sentence which elaborates on the meaning of "mental disease or defect."

The comment to the Model Penal Code[51] accepts the theory of the combined M'Naghten and irresistible-impulse tests that takes "account of the impairment of volitional capacity no less than of impairment of cognition." However, it rejects both of these tests as too narrow. The Durham test was rejected by the drafters of the Code as ambiguous, since it does not set forth a specific concept of causality.

41. 247 Minn. 538, 78 N.W.2d 450 (1956).

42. State v. Finn, 257 Minn. 138, 100 N.W.2d 508 (1960).

43. Later codification: *Minn. Stat. Ann.* § 611.026 (1964).

44. People v. Krugman, 377 Mich. 559, 141 N.W.2d 33 (1966). The Durham test was not properly presented in *Krugman*, the question of causality or "product" having been omitted in the trial court's instructions.

45. Bazelon, "Implications of the Durham Decision," 9 *Mental Hospitals* 3 (No. 2, February 1958).

46. See Goldstein, *The Insanity Defense* 54 (1967). Matthews, *Mental Disability and the Criminal Law: A Field Study* 44 (1970), observes: "We have not found psychiatric testimony excluded or even seriously limited under *M'Naghten*."

47. 34 N.J. 279, 168 A.2d 401 (1960). (Emphasis added.)

48. *Manual for Courts-Martial United States* 200 (1951).

49. *Model Penal Code* § 4.01 (1962).

50. *Vt. Stat. Ann.* tit. 13, § 4801 (1959). (Emphasis added.)

51. *Model Penal Code* § 4.01, Comments, at 156–59.

One of the major criticisms of the M'Naghten–irresistible-impulse formulation is that it requires complete impairment of cognitive capacity and of capacity for self-control (volitional capacity). Psychiatrists generally feel that total impairment of the cognitive and volitional faculties is rarely, if ever, reached.[52] Therefore, the Code does not demand total impairment of capacity but requires only "substantial" impairment.[53] The Vermont requirement of "adequate" rather than "substantial" capacity is probably not of great significance in the setting of an actual trial. In terms of language analysis it is not even clear whether "adequate" capacity demands greater or less impairment than the Code's "substantial" capacity.

The phrase "to appreciate the criminality of his conduct" in the Code and Vermont statute seems to be a substitute for the M'Naghten wording "to know the nature and quality of the act he was doing." Again, this distinction may be too subtle to be appreciated by a lay jury[54] and seems to be aimed primarily at placating the M'Naghten critics. However, the new phrase does suggest that integrated knowledge—both cognitive and effective knowledge[55]—is required and it may thus affect the scope of psychiatric testimony.

The Code "accepts the criticism of the 'irresistible-impulse' formulation as inept insofar as it may be impliedly restricted to sudden, spontaneous acts as distinguished from insane propulsions that are accompanied by brooding or reflection."[56] In order to remedy this defect, the drafters of the Code used the phrase "to conform his conduct to the requirements of law." This language was also adopted by the Vermont legislature.

The second paragraph of the Model Penal Code formulation, according to the Comments, is designed to exclude the so-called psychopathic personality.[57] The reason for this exclusion is that the psychopath is defined only in terms of his recidivist conduct, with no explanation of the cause of his abnormality. As stated by the Comments,

While it may be feasible to formulate a definition of "disease," there is much to be said for excluding a condition that is manifested only by the behavior phenomena that must, by hypothesis, be the result of disease for irresponsibility to be established.[58]

Vermont apparently accepted this rationale but in addition sought to clarify the meaning of "mental disease or defect" by stipulating that these terms shall include "congenital and traumatic mental conditions as well as disease." Whether the Model Penal Code was intended to include these conditions is not made clear by the Comments.

In summary, it may be said that the Code and the Vermont formulations contemplate a further broadening of the M'Naghten–irresistible-impulse combination in an effort to reflect some of the shades in the spectrum between complete mental collapse and complete understanding. At the same time, these formulations attempt to state a reasonably workable standard of criminal irresponsibility. In terms of general acceptance the Model Penal Code test has fared considerably better than the Durham rule. As of this writing, ten states and eight of the eleven federal circuits have explicitly adopted its formulation either verbatim or with minor modifications. Six states in addition to Vermont have incorporated the rule statutorily:[59] Connecticut, Illinois, Maryland, Missouri, Montana, and New York. Three others—Kentucky, Massachusetts, and Wisconsin—have adopted it by judicial decision.[60] Wisconsin's espousal of the test is unique in that ordinarily the jury shall be instructed under the traditional

52. Id. at 158.

53. Id. at § 4.01.

54. Hall, "Mental Disease and Criminal Responsibility—M'Naghten versus Durham and the American Law Institute's Tentative Draft," 33 *Ind. L.J.* 212, 224–25 (1957–58).

55. *Model Penal Code* § 4.01, Comments, at 157; see Zilboorg, "Misconceptions of Legal Insanity," 9 *Am. J. Orthopsychiat.* 540, 552–53 (1939).

56. *Model Penal Code* § 4.01, Comments, at 157.

57. Id. at 160.

58. Ibid. Compare the "medical" definition of *"Psychopathic Personality (Psychopath)*: A person whose behavior is predominantly amoral or antisocial and characterized by impulsive, irresponsible actions satisfying only immediate and narcissistic interests without concern for obvious and implicit social consequences accompanied by minimal outward evidence of anxiety or guilt." American Psychiatric Association, Committee on Public Information, *Psychiatric Glossary* (1964).

59. *Conn. Gen. Stat. Ann.* § 54-82(a) (Supp. 1969); *Ill. Rev. Stat.* ch. 38, § 6-2 (1967); *Md. Ann. Code* art. 59, § 9(a) (1968); *Mo. Ann. Stat.* § 552.030 (Supp. 1969); *Mont. Rev. Codes Ann.* § 95-501 (1968); *N.Y. Penal Law* § 30.05 (McKinney 1967); *Vt. Stat. Ann.* tit. 13, § 4801 (1958). Listing New York as having adopted the Model Penal Code test is questionable, though many studies do so. It may certainly be argued that New York's present formulation represents no significant departure from the traditional *M'Naghten* wording. See the "Practice Commentary" to the statute and People v. Moseley, 20 N.Y.2d 64, 281 N.Y.S.2d 762, 228 N.E.2d 765 (1967).

60. Terry v. Commonwealth, 371 S.W.2d 862 (Ky. 1963); Commonwealth v. McHoul, 352 Mass. 544, 226 N.E.2d 556 (1967); State v. Shoffner, 31 Wis. 2d 412, 143 N.W.2d 458 (1966).

M'Naghten rule, *unless* the defendant elects to be tried under the Model Penal Code test, in which case the burden of proof ("by greater weight of the credible evidence") then shifts to him.[61]

On the federal level, six of the circuit courts of appeals have adopted the Model Penal Code test as is.[62] The Third and Eighth Circuits, in the *Currens* and *Dusky* decisions respectively,[63] have sanctioned the American Law Institute formulation in slightly different fashion. *Currens* deletes the phrase "to appreciate the criminality of his conduct" on the grounds that it is too reminiscent of M'Naghten in its stress on the cognitive aspect. The *Dusky* case, on the other hand, citing Chief Justice Burger (then a judge on the District of Columbia Circuit Court of Appeals) to the effect that the American Law Institute formulation is little more than M'Naghten plus irresistible impulse in modern terminology, states that any test which considers the three essential elements—cognition, volition, and capacity to control behavior—is acceptable, regardless of the label.[64] Since the *Dusky* court regarded the Model Penal Code phraseology as at least favorable, if not absolutely essential, the Eighth Circuit is uniformly listed as having "adopted" the test. The First and Ninth Circuits are said to "have open minds on the question" of the desirability of adopting the Model Penal Code formulation.[65]

The chances for even wider acceptance of the American Law Institute test seem favorable. The Massachusetts Supreme Court in the *McHoul* case[66] supported its own acceptance of the test with a reference to the fact that the Code definition had been proposed for adoption or was under consideration in a number of other jurisdictions. In the meantime, the United States Supreme Court has given "at least tacit recognition" to the development of tests other than M'Naghten, as the Sixth Circuit Court noted in *Smith*,[67] citing Justice Marshall's approval of "fruitful experimentation" and "the developing dialogue between law and psychiatry."[68] The Supreme Court has also refused to grant certiorari in cases where the debate concerned the relative appropriateness of the various tests of criminal responsibility, a policy that the Second Circuit Court in *Freeman*[69] characterized as "no coincidence." The 1897 *Davis* case,[70] sometimes noted as the United States Supreme Court's sanction of M'Naghten, has not been regarded as binding by many courts, and it would seem that the present Supreme Court is not about to take issue with that interpretation.

2. CRITICISM OF CURRENT TESTS

a) General Criticism

The problem of articulating a test of criminal responsibility is essentially that of drafting a verbal formula which will enable the judicial process to discriminate effectively between those cases where a punitive-correctional disposition is thought to benefit society and those in which a medical-custodial disposition is believed to be proper.[71] Although a crystal-clear definition of responsibility may be impossible and perhaps undesirable,[72] an operational definition is not out of reach. Any definition of criminal irresponsibility should be consistent with the framework of our penal laws. In other words, such a test would presently be premised on the rationality of man—i.e., on the concept that man is a being who has free choice—and would retain irrationality as a minimum criterion of insanity.[73] Second, it should harmonize law and modern medical science, thus enabling the psychiatrist to make a maximum contribution unhampered by moral and

61. State v. Shoffner, 31 Wis. 2d 412, 143 N.W.2d 458 (1966).

62. Wion v. United States, 325 F.2d 420 (10th Cir. 1963); United States v. Freeman, 357 F.2d 606 (2d Cir. 1966); United States v. Shapiro, 383 F.2d 680 (7th Cir. 1967); United States v. Chandler, 393 F.2d 920 (4th Cir. 1968); United States v. Smith, 404 F.2d 720 (6th Cir. 1968); Blake v. United States, 407 F.2d 908 (5th Cir. 1969).

63. United States v. Currens, 290 F.2d 751 (3d Cir. 1961); Dusky v. United States, 295 F.2d 743 (8th Cir. 1961).

64. Two Eighth Circuit cases reiterating the *Dusky* outlook are: Feguer v. United States, 302 F.2d 214 (1962); Pope v. United States, 372 F.2d 710 (1967).

65. Blake v. United States, 407 F.2d 908, 914 (1969), citing Amador Beltran v. United States, 302 F.2d 48 (1st Cir. 1962) and Ramer v. United States, 390 F.2d 564 (9th Cir. 1968).

66. Commonwealth v. McHoul, 226 N.E.2d 556 (Mass. 1967).

67. United States v. Smith, 404 F.2d 720 (6th Cir. 1968).

68. Powell v. Texas, 392 U.S. 514 (1968).

69. United States v. Freeman, 357 F.2d 606 (2d Cir. 1966).

70. Davis v. United States, 165 U.S. 373 (1897).

71. *Model Penal Code* § 4.01, Comments, at 156.

72. "Lord Blackburn well expressed the difficulties involved more than 50 years ago when he said: 'I have read every definition (of insanity) which I could meet with and never was satisfied with one of them, and I have endeavored in vain to make one satisfactory to myself. I verily believe it is not in human power to do it.'" Quoted in Bar Association of the District of Columbia, Committee on Criminal Responsibility, "Memorandum of Dissent," 26 *J.A.B.D.C.* 316, 336 (1959).

73. Hall, *supra* note 6, at 781. See Carter v. United States, 252 F.2d 608, 616 (D.C. Cir. 1957): "The problem . . . is not one of philosophy. It is one of translating the accepted philosophy into practical rules of action for everyday use in the courtroom."

legal abstractions and oversimplifications. If possible, the test should be unblemished by hypertechnical concepts, speculation, vagueness, and ambiguity which will sever communications between the medical expert and the jury. Third, the test should be stated in such a manner that it is readily applicable and easily understood by a jury of laymen. Fourth, any test of criminal responsibility should relieve from responsibility all those whose imprisonment in the traditional manner would not satisfy the purposes of the penal law, while at the same time making certain that the accountability of other persons for their actions is in no way undermined.

Before analyzing each of the four specific tests, it might be well to consider two more general questions. First, on a linguistic level, is there really much significant difference in meaning between the various tests of criminal irresponsibility, such that it could be appreciated by, for instance, a jury instructed according to one test or another? Second, a related query, what would be the practical effect of such difference: i.e., would application of one rule lead to conviction but of another to acquittal, assuming the facts of the case were similar? Or do most juries and judges operate on the basis of a rough, intuitive sense of justice which tends to obliterate fine and even not-so-fine distinctions? Are there any data that demonstrate or disprove such possible effect?

In answer to the first question, it has already been pointed out that according to a number of legal thinkers, the American Law Institute Model Penal Code test is little more than the traditional M'Naghten–irresistible-impulse combination in modern form.[74] Similarly, it has been suggested that Durham, particularly as "clarified" by McDonald, is no different from the American Law Institute formulation.[75] One could put forth, therefore, something like the following equation: M'Naghten $+$ Irresistible Impulse $=$ American Law Institute $=$ Durham-McDonald. Much of the controversy over the relative desirability of the respective rules would then seem superfluous. However, such logic may be viewed as too simplistic to be acceptable. One would expect the differences in nuance and emphasis, explicit references to scope and conclusiveness of expert testimony, and varying standards of cognition and volition to have some impact of greater than mere artistic appreciability.

The question of actual outcome of similar cases under the different rules thus becomes the important one. Unfortunately, data on this point are scant and subject to manipulation depending on what a researcher desires to demonstrate. Information regarding the impact of the Durham rule on criminal dispositions in the District of Columbia may be taken as illustrative. Thus the *American Law Reports Annotated* indicate that between 1953 and 1961 the "proportion of acquittals by reason of insanity rose . . . from 0.9 percent to 14 percent,"[76] the implication being that *Durham* (decided in 1954) provides a far more liberal standard. The majority report of the President's Commission on Crime in the District of Columbia, on the other hand, emphasizes that since *McDonald* (1962), "insanity acquittals have stabilized at two to three percent of all defendants."[77] Yet another study[78] cites acquittals by reason of insanity as being between 0.2 percent and 0.6 percent of all criminal dispositions in the three years immediately preceding *Durham,* but for 6.0 percent 1961.[79] This study also points out that most of the increase in acquittals by reason of insanity appears to have come at the expense of what previously would have been not-guilty verdicts.[80] The suggestion has been made that the number of incompetency findings has been similarly affected by the liberalization of the insanity test.[81] In line with its general defensive posture, the President's Commission on Crime in the District of Columbia seeks to emphasize that defendants found not guilty by reason of insanity under Durham are indeed ill and remain in St. Elizabeths Hospital "for substantial periods of time," adding that even many of those *convicted* under Durham rule have been

74. See Dusky v. United States, 295 F.2d 743 (8th Cir. 1961).

75. See United States v. Smith, 404 F.2d 720 (6th Cir. 1968). See also Allen et al., *supra* note 38, at 423–27.

76. Annot., 45 A.L.R.2d 1447 (Later Case Service 1969).

77. President's Commission on Crime in the District of Columbia, *Report* 550 (1966).

78. Simon, *The Jury and the Defense of Insanity* 203, Table 61 (1967).

79. Note how markedly at variance the figures given in the several sources are. Such inconsistency may be explained by the fact that different relative categories are used, resulting therefore in different percentages. For other statistics on the District of Columbia, see, e.g., Matthews, *supra* note 46, at 33, Table 3. Matthews considers at length the interrelationships among the various possible dispositions of criminal cases. Thus facilitation of the insanity defense through Durham is shown to have had a quantitative effect on the utilization of alternative disposition possibilities such as not-guilty verdicts, incompetency findings, and even civil commitment.

80. Simon, *supra* note 78, at 204.

81. See Guttmacher, *supra* note 10, at 48; Matthews, *supra* note 46, at 69 and at 33, Table 3.

shown to suffer from "mental problems"—presumably supportive of the conclusion that "[t]he Durham rule does not appear to offer a readily available opportunity for criminal offenders to escape the consequences of their acts."[82] In sum, the statistics available are inconsistent and the implications to be derived from them vary—a fact which would probably persist even if statistical consistency were achieved.

An attempt to ascertain the practical impact of the various rules by means of mock jury situations was made in a 1967 study[83] growing out of the American Jury Project directed by Harry Kalven, Jr., and Hans Zeisel. Again, however, the results are inconclusive. Juries given no instructions at all returned the highest proportion of verdicts of not guilty by reason of insanity. Juries instructed under M'Naghten produced the least such verdicts, with Durham in between. Though the difference between M'Naghten and Durham was 12 percent, the author concludes that "there was no significant difference." She *does* conclude that "the criterion for criminal responsibility as defined under Durham is closer to the jury's natural sense of equity [because the results coincide more closely with uninstructed jury verdicts] than is the M'Naghten rule." These conclusions appear as open to dispute as those drawn from the actual numerical statistics for the District of Columbia given above.

Since reliable inferences as to actual impact appear impossible, a brief look may profitably be directed at the major theoretical criticisms and evaluations of the various rules.

b) The M'Naghten Rules

Even before the M'Naghten rules were handed down, Isaac Ray, in his classic *Medical Jurisprudence of Insanity,* sharply criticized the use of knowledge of right and wrong as the test of criminal responsibility.[84] Since their promulgation the M'Naghten rules have been subjected to a constant stream of criticism from both the medical and the legal professions.[85] The primary objections of the

medical profession and others to the M'Naghten formulation have been reiterated throughout the past century in substantially the same form. As stated by the Royal Commission on Capital Punishment in 1953,

> Briefly, they have contended that the M'Naghten test is based on an entirely obsolete and misleading conception of the nature of insanity, since insanity does not only, or primarily, affect the cognitive or intellectual faculties, but affects the whole personality of the patient, including both the will and the emotions. An insane person may therefore often know the nature and quality of his act and that it is wrong and forbidden by law, but yet commit it as a result of the mental disease.[86]

Most of the objections to the M'Naghten formulation are based on the view that it "reflects what may be called a *minimalistic policy* regarding the members of this class of irresponsibles."[87] In other words these critics believe that M'Naghten is not adequate for the task of selecting all those mentally disabled persons whose punishment will not aid society and/or who are incapable of making rational choices between alternative modes of behavior.[88]

Proponents of the above view point out that the great majority of patients in mental hospitals, even the "grossly insane" and the psychotic, know what conduct is proscribed by the rules of the hospital and that breach of these rules may result in the forfeiture of some privilege.[89] This observation reflects the immense difficulty psychiatrists have in giving expert testimony under the M'Naghten formulation.[90] This test requires total impairment of cogni-

---

82. President's Commission, *supra* note 77, at 550, 559.

83. Simon, *supra* note 78.

84. Cited in Durham v. United States, 214 F.2d 862, 870 (D.C. Cir. 1954). Dr. Henry Maudsley declared, soon after the rules appeared, that the judges were holding to "an absurd dictum which has long been discredited by medical science." See Guttmacher, "The Psychiatrist as an Expert Witness," 22 *U. Chi. L. Rev.* 325 (1954–55).

85. Guttmacher, *supra* note 84, at 325–26. Testifying before the British Royal Commission on Capital Punishment, Justice

Frankfurter said of the M'Naghten rules: "They are in large measure abandoned in practice and therefore I think the M'Naghten rules are in large measure shams. That is a strong word, but I think the M'Naghten rules are difficult for conscientious people and not difficult enough for people who say, 'We'll just juggle them!'" Royal Commission on Capital Punishment 1949–53, *Report,* CMD. NO. 8932, at 102 (1953). See also Durham v. United States, 214 F.2d 862, 870, 871 n.25 (D.C. Cir. 1954).

86. Royal Commission on Capital Punishment, *supra* note 85, at 80.

87. Waelder, *supra* note 6, at 379; see Royal Commission on Capital Punishment, *supra* note 85, at 88; Group for the Advancement of Psychiatry, "Criminal Responsibility and Psychiatric Expert Testimony" 4 (Rep. No. 26, May 1954) [hereinafter cited at G.A.P. *Rep.*].

88. Guttmacher & Weihofen, *supra* note 9, at 420.

89. Royal Commission on Capital Punishment, *supra* note 85, at 103; see also *Model Penal Code* § 4.01, Comments, at 158.

90. Guttmacher, *supra* note 84; G.A.P. *Rep., supra* note 87, at

tive capacity (to distinguish right from wrong) whereas "clinical experience reveals only a graded scale with marks along the way."[91] Whether a psychiatrist is at all capable of determining the existence or nonexistence of an individual's capacity to make ethical judgments has been seriously questioned.[92] One eminent psychiatric authority[93] has said,

> To force a psychiatrist to talk in terms of the ability to distinguish between right and wrong and of legal responsibility is . . . to force him to violate the Hippocratic Oath, even to violate the oath he takes as a witness to tell the truth and nothing but the truth. . . .

Dr. Bernard Diamond elaborates on this concept of "psychiatric perjury," stating that if the psychiatrist is to be truthful on the witness stand, he must say that

> just about every defendant, no matter how mentally ill, no matter how advanced his psychosis, knows the difference between right and wrong in the literal sense of the phrase—[thus the psychiatrist] becomes an expeditor to the gallows or the gas chamber.[94]

Specifically, one source of difficulty is the dual meaning which may be attached to the word "wrong" used in the test. Does it refer to legal or moral wrong? The significance of this ambiguity was recognized in the latter part of the nineteenth century by Sir James Stephen.[95] His classic illustration was that of A killing B with knowledge of his act and its illegality, but under an insane delusion that the murder of B was directed by God and would result in the salvation of the human race.[96] If the word "wrong" means illegal, A's act is a crime; if it means morally wrong, A would not be criminally responsible for his act.

Oddly enough, though the word has been used throughout the past hundred years by the courts, most of them have not bothered to define it.[97] However, in 1915, Judge Cardozo review the history of the M'Naghten rules and concluded, in his opinion for the court in *People v. Schmidt,*[98] that "wrong" means moral wrong. The courts of Tennessee and Texas as well as the Court of Criminal Appeals in England have taken the opposite position, interpreting "wrong" to mean legally wrong.[99] This view might result in holding some of the most disordered of the mentally ill responsible for their criminal acts.[100]

Of greater significance is the latent ambiguity created by the word "know." Did the defendant "know" the act was wrong? One of the earlier commentators to advocate a broad interpretation of the word "know" was Sir James Stephen, who summarized his views as follows:

> Knowledge and power are the constituent elements of all voluntary action, and if either is seriously impaired the other is disabled. It is as true that a man who cannot control himself does not know the nature of his acts as that a man who does not know the nature of his acts is incapable of self-control.[101]

From this analysis, Stephen concluded that under the M'Naghten formulation, "a man who by reason

---

4, 6. Even assuming the validity of the contention that M'Naghten does not in practice restrict the scope of psychiatric testimony (see sources at note 46 *supra*), this would not necessarily alleviate the courtroom psychiatrist's problems. The psychiatrist may still be faced with questions prompted by the M'Naghten formula which tend to elicit what he would consider unrealistic, unscientific, and irrelevant opinions.

91. *Model Penal Code* § 4.01, Comments, at 158; but see Hall, *supra* note 54, at 218–19.

92. Roche, "Criminal Responsibility and Mental Disease: Medical Aspects," 26 *Tenn. L. Rev.* 222, 228–30 (1959); Roche, "Criminality and Mental Illness—Two Faces of the Same Coin," 22 *U. Chi. L. Rev.* 320, 321 (1954–55); Guttmacher, *supra* note 84; *Model Penal Code* § 4.01, Comments, at 173; G.A.P. *Rep., supra* note 87, at 6.

93. Gregory Zilboorg, quoted in Guttmacher & Weihofen, *supra* note 9, at 406.

94. Diamond, "Criminal Responsibility of the Mentally Ill," 14 *Stan. L. Rev.* 59 (1961).

95. "Sir James Stephen probably had a wider knowledge of forensic psychiatry than any other legal commentator of his time." Weihofen, *supra* note 1, at 63 n.30.

96. 2 Stephen, *A History of the Criminal Law of England* 149 (1883).

97. Guttmacher & Weihofen, *supra* note 9, at 405. Weihofen, *supra* note 1, at 78.

98. 216 N.Y. 324, 110 N.E. 945 (1915).

99. Guttmacher & Weihofen, *supra* note 9, at 405. See Weihofen, *supra* note 1, at 77–80, for a discussion of the cases involving interpretations of the word "wrong."

100. One authority in this field believes that the distinction between the two meanings of the word "wrong" is irrelevant since the vast majority of cases in which criminal irresponsibility is pleaded as a defense involves acts which are universally condemned as morally wicked as well as illegal. Perkins, *supra* note 31, at 729. See also Glueck, *Mental Disorder and the Criminal Law* 184 (1925). The paucity of cases since 1843 defining the word "wrong" adds weight to this argument. At least under our present conceptions of culpability, "moral wrong" would seem to be a preferable interpretation, since the punishment of persons acting illegally but without "guilt" is generally repugnant to our concept of *mens rea*. But then again, what is "morally wrong" in a pluralistic society?

101. Stephen, *supra* note 96, at 171.

of mental disease is prevented from controlling his own conduct is not responsible for what he does."[102] Thus Stephen would interpret the word "know" to include within the M'Naghten formulation what is today termed the "irresistible-impulse" test, which relieves an individual of criminal responsibility, despite the fact that he knew the nature and quality of his act and that it was wrong, if the act was the result of an overpowering impulse stemming from a mental disability.

Stephen saw the personality as an integrated unit, all parts of which are impaired by mental disorder.[103] This view contrasted sharply with the traditional one of the compartmentalized personality as reflected in the M'Naghten rules, which were laid down in an age when the pseudoscience of phrenology was still influencing theories of insanity.[104]

The thrust of the M'Naghten formulation is that "there is a little man in the top of one's head called reason whose function it is to guide another unruly little man called instinct, emotion, or impulse in the way he should go."[105] The M'Naghten rules assume that if an individual "knows" right from wrong, his ratiocinative powers are intact and he is therefore capable of governing his conduct accordingly.

Zilboorg, in a very illuminating article, articulates the ambiguity inherent in the word "know" as follows:

> This fundamental difference between verbal or purely intellectual knowledge and the mysterious other kind of knowledge is familiar to every clinical psychiatrist; it is the difference between knowledge divorced from affect and knowledge so fused with affect that it becomes a human reality.[106]

Knowledge divorced from the rest of the personality is nonintegrated knowledge. It has no social significance or contact with reality and fails to qualify as moral knowledge.[107] If the word "know" were given a broad interpretation so as to encompass affective as well as verbal or intellectual knowledge, much of the criticism directed against the M'Naghten right-

wrong formulation would be silenced.[108] Although it is axiomatic in the field of criminal law that to be a crime an act must be the result of volition,[109] the English and most of the American courts which adhere to a strict M'Naghten test have in essence refused to recognize this postulate in those instances where the lack of volition is caused by mental disability.[110] Thus, the interpretation of the word "know" advocated by Stephen met, at least at first, with a cool reception by the judiciary and most members of the legal profession.[111] However, a growing acceptance of this interpretation has become discernible in the emergence of irresistible impulse and later formulations of legal insantiy.

c) Irresistible-Impulse Test

The irresistible-impulse test emphasizes the volitional aspect of "knowing," and though this doctrine initially encountered widespread rejection, today it is accepted in more than half of the states and most federal circuits—as a supplement of M'Naghten or as (arguable) included in a modern formulation of criminal responsibility such as the American Law Institute rule.

Traditional criticism of the irresistible-impulse concept has centered around the following points: (1) An impulse to do harm by one who can distinguish right from wrong cannot be irresistible but only unresisted. (2) It is difficult to prove the existence of an "irresistible impulse" in a given case. (3) The test is too impractical in its application. (4) Its use would be dangerous to society because it would dilute the deterrent effect of the law. (5) This defense is not needed since postconviction clemency can be granted to persons "irresistibly" driven to commit crimes.[112]

---

102. Id. at 167.

103. See Hall, *supra* note 6, at 775.

104. Biggs, *supra* note 2, at 93; Guttmacher & Weihofen, *supra* note 9, at 418; see also Roche, *supra* note 92 (1959), at 224.

105. Holloway v. United States, 148 F.2d 665, 667 (D.C. Cir. 1945), *cert. denied,* 334 U.S. 852 (1948).

106. Zilboorg, "Misconceptions of Legal Insanity," 9 *Am. J. Orthopsychiat.* 540, 552–53 (1939); see also Wertham, *The Show of Violence* 86 (1949).

107. Ibid. See Hall, *supra* note 54, at 217–18.

108. Hall, *supra* note 6, at 780–81. Hall is a vigorous advocate of giving the word "know" such a broad interpretation; see also Hall & Menninger, "Psychiatry and the Law—A Dual Review," 38 *Iowa L. Rev.* 687, 696 (1952–53).

109. Keedy, "Irresistible Impulse as a Defense in the Criminal Law," 100 *U. Pa. L. Rev.* 956, 968 (1952). "Since our criminal law is based on the assumption of free will, we should not punish men for what they cannot avoid. As an abstract proposition, this is unquestioned. 'All the several pleas and excuses,' said Blackstone, 'which protect the committer of a criminal act from the punishment which is otherwise annexed thereto, may be reduced to this single consideration, the want or defect of will' "; Guttmacher & Weihofen, *supra* note 9, at 408–9.

110. Guttmacher & Weihofen, *supra* note 9, at 409.

111. Royal Commission on Capital Punishment, *supra* note 85, at 80.

112. Guttmacher & Weihofen, *supra* note 9, at 409; Keedy, *supra* note 109, at 987–88.

Whether or not an "irresistible impulse" can exist in a person able to distinguish right from wrong is not a question which can be decided by judicial fiat.[113] The view that certain impulses which result from mental disorders may be "irresistible" has formidable medical support.[114] Opinions contrary to this view are held "by relatively few members of the profession."[115]

Although the problem of proving the existence of such an impulse (assuming it can exist) is difficult, it may be no more difficult than proving capacity to know right from wrong.[116] The contention that refusal to use the test will help to deter crime is said to have no empirical support,[117] and the argument for postconviction clemency has been termed an "evasion of judicial responsibility"[118]—not to mention the fact that such clemency is not likely to be granted.

The irresistible-impulse test has also been criticized by those who agree with its basic rationale of taking the volitional element into account. Their criticism is directed at the misleading interpretation of the term as implicitly "restricted to sudden spontaneous acts as distinguished from insane propulsions that are accompanied by brooding or reflection.[119] A closely related criticism is that irresistible impulse implies total impairment of volitional capacity, yet medical science asserts that impulses which are entirely overwhelming and absolutely impossible to resist are rare occurrences, especially in the commission of serious crimes.[120]

Accordingly, many commentators feel that even though the M'Naghten–irresistible-impulse combination contains no inherent or necessary inadequacies, the close ties of the test with traditional limitations on inquiry demand at least a revolutionary rewording. A primary aspect of such a reformulation would be eliminating the restrictions applied by the traditional rule that limits psychiatric inquiry—if perhaps not testimony—to isolated symptoms of behavior. This goal is sought not merely for the comfort of testifying medical experts; its end is more fundamental. As the Second Circuit Court of Appeals saw it:

> The true vice of M'Naghten is not . . . that psychiatrists will feel constricted in artificially structuring their testimony, but rather that the ultimate deciders —the judge and the jury—will be deprived of information vital to their final judgment.[121]

d) The Product Rule: The New Hampshire and Durham Test

Although the *Durham* decision in 1954 merely adopted the position taken by the New Hampshire court nearly a century before, it brought forth a deluge of commentary.[122] Psychiatrists for the most part applauded the decision, while the legal profession accepted it with some skepticism;[123] some mem-

---

113. Ibid. See also a leading case on irresistible impulse, Parsons v. State, 81 Ala. 577, 586, 2 So. 854, 860 (1887), Sommerville J.,: "It will not do for the courts to dogmatically deny the possible existence of such a disease, or its pathological and psychical effect."

114. Keedy, *supra* note 109, at 988, 989 n.201, lists medical authorities who support his proposition; see also Royal Commission on Capital Punishment, *supra* note 85, at 109.

115. Keedy, *supra* note 109, at 989 n.202; see Hall, *supra* note 6, at 775–78, who argues that the concept of will as separated totally from emotion and reason is untenable if the psyche is viewed as integrated; but see Guttmacher & Weihofen, *supra* note 9, at 410, for an answer to Hall's point; see also Wertham, *supra* note 106, at 13–14: "There is with one exception no symptom in the whole field of psychopathology that would correspond to a really ungovernable or uncontrollable impulse. . . . The medico-legal theory of the irresistible impulse is advocated only by laymen and by psychiatrists who are scientifically not sufficiently oriented. It lends an air of scientific literalness and accuracy to a purely legal definition without any foundation in the facts of life or science."

Waelder, *supra* note 6, at 383, observes: "The concept of an irresistible impulse is well-defined only in a central area where certain impulses are irresistible to all people. We may say, for example, that the need to sleep becomes irresistible after a certain time. . . . But when we enter the territory of impulses that are resisted by some and not by others . . . we are on shaky ground. There are no criteria for this decision."

116. Guttmacher & Weihofen, *supra* note 9, at 409; Keedy, *supra* note 109, at 990–91; Royal Commission on Capital Punishment, *supra* note 85, at 109. But see Perkins, *supra* note 31, at 761.

117. Keedy, *supra* note 109, at 991; Guttmacher & Weihofen, *supra* note 9, at 409.

118. Keedy, *supra* note 109, at 991.

119. *Model Penal Code* § 4.01, Comments, at 157; but see Hall, *supra* note 6, at 777–78, for the view that the test in practice actually does not require "sudden" impulses but only "inability to conform." See also Wechsler, "The Criteria of Criminal Responsibility," 22 *U. Chi. L. Rev.* 367, 370 n.14 (1954–55); *Manual for Courts-Martial United States* 120b (1951), which phrases the military version of irresistible impulse as completely depriving "the accused of his ability . . . to adhere to the right."

120. Guttmacher & Weihofen, *supra* note 9, at 410–11.

121. United States v. Freeman, 357 F.2d 606 (2d Cir. 1966).

122. Perkins, *supra* note 31, at 764; see also at 764 n.47 for bibliography of some of the commentary greeting the *Durham* decision.

123. Comment, "Proposed Revisions of the M'Naghten Rule," 4 *Catholic Law.* 297, 303 (1957–58).

bers of each profession, however, chose to cross the aisle.[124]

Despite the great enthusiasm which the *Durham* opinion generated in many commentators, it has been adopted only in Maine and the Virgin Islands.[125] It has been specifically rejected in nearly thirty jurisdictions (at least twenty states and most of the federal circuits).

One of the chief targets of *Durham* critics is the uncertainty surrounding the key terms "mental disease," "mental defect," and "product."[126] Exculpation from criminal responsibility requires that the criminal act be the "product" of a "mental disease" or "mental defect." The term "mental disease" is actually not defined in the *Durham* opinion, but is merely differentiated from the term "mental defect."[127] Much of the criticism concerning the vagueness and general lack of guidance of the Durham rule has since been obviated by later opinions of the United States Court of Appeals for the District of Columbia Circuit. The *McDonald* case (1962)[128] defines the term "mental disease or defect." The *Wright, Carter,* and *Douglas* decisions (1956–57)[129] have dealt with the causal problem of when the act can be said to be the "product" of the accused's mental disability. Finally, the recent *Washington* case (1967)[130] and to some extent the *McDonald* decision circumscribe the scope and conclusiveness of expert testimony.

Anxiety as to whether "mental disease" will be an exclusively psychiatric determination, or alternatively an exclusively jural decision, is no longer appropriate if it ever was. *McDonald* outlines a balance, stating that what may be a "mental disease" for psychiatric purposes is not necessarily mental disease for jural-legal purposes. At the same time, the decision gives a measure of direction in that the jury is to be told that disease or defect "includes any abnormal condition of the mind that substantially affects mental or emotional processes and substantially impairs behavior controls."[131] Perhaps this is in some sense still less precise than the rigid right-wrong formulation, but it might be profitable to remember in this context that "what we ought to fear above all is not the absence of a definition, but being saddled with a false definition."[132]

Similarly, the "product" concept has been particularized by judicial decisions. The *Wright, Douglas,* and *Carter* cases[133] speak of a "but for" test; thus, if the jury can "reasonably" infer that the accused would not have committed the act were it not for his disease, the product test is satisfied. In addition to these substantive guidelines, the District of Columbia Circuit Court laid down an important procedural rule in the *Washington* case[134] when it held that the term product "has no clinical significance" and that therefore there was "no justification" for a psychiatrist to testify on this "ultimate issue." The *Washington* ruling against psychiatric testimony on the "product" issue probably stems in part from the fears expressed by some commentators that even under a theoretically stringent "but for" causation test, the modern psychiatric view of the integrated personality would rarely permit the answer that absent the accused's illness he would

124. Ibid. Legal comments ran the gamut from "careful and psychologically literate," Kalven, "Insanity and the Criminal Law—A Critique of *Durham v. United States: Introduction*," 22 *U. Chi. L. Rev.* 317, 318 (1954–55), to Judge Hand's "it did not seem to me to give us any guidance that perceptibly would help," letter from Judge Learned Hand to editors of the University of Chicago Law Review, 22 *U. Chi. L. Rev.* 319 (1954–55). Psychiatric commentary ranged from "unadulterated nonsense," Szasz, "Psychiatry, Ethics, and the Criminal Law," 58 *Colum. L. Rev.* 183, 190 (1958), to "both psychiatry and jurisprudence ought to be grateful for the enlightened courage of the three judges who were responsible for the new turn in our criminal jurisprudence," Zilboorg, "A Step toward Enlightened Justice," 22 *U. Chi. L. Rev.* 331, 335 (1954–55).

125. *Me. Rev. Stat. Ann.* tit. 15, § 102 (1964); *Virgin Is. Code* tit. 14, § 14(4) (1964).

126. See Commonwealth v. Chester, 337 Mass. 702, 712, 150 N.E.2d 914, 920 (1958); Wechsler, *supra* note 119, at 368. One psychiatrist goes so far as to say: "I will say there is neither such a thing as 'insanity' nor such a thing as 'mental disease.' These terms do not identify entities having separate existence in themselves." Roche, "A Panel, Criminal Responsibility and Mental Disease: Legal Aspects," 26 *Tenn. L. Rev.* 232, 240 (1959).

127. Committee on Criminal Responsibility, "Report," *supra* note 36, at 306.

128. McDonald v. United States, 312 F.2d 847 (D.C. Cir. 1962); see also Hawkins v. United States, 310 F.2d 849 (D.C. Cir. 1962).

129. Douglas v. United States, 239 F.2d 52 (D.C. Cir. 1956); Wright v. United States, 250 F.2d 4 (D.C. Cir. 1957); Carter v. United States, 252 F.2d 608 (D.C. Cir. 1957).

130. Washington v. United States, 390 F.2d 444 (D.C. Cir. 1967); McDonald v. United States, 312 F.2d 847 (D.C. Cir. 1962).

131. McDonald v. United States, 312 F.2d 847, 851 (D.C. Cir. 1962). Note the similarity to the ALI test this chapter, § II B 1 d.

132. Roche, *The Criminal Mind* 251 (1958), quoting Simon E. Sobeloff.

133. Wright v. United States, 250 F.2d 4 (D.C. Cir. 1957); Douglas v. United States, 23 F.2d 52 (D.C. Cir. 1956); Carter v. United States, 252 F.2d 608 (D.C. Cir. 1957).

134. Washington v. United States, 390 F.2d 444 (D.C. Cir. 1967).

still have committed the act.[135] The rule may well be a reaction against some psychiatric opinion which would equate criminal behavior with mental illness[136]—an approach which, it has been said, "clearly undermines the pillars of our present penal system."[137] Presumably a jury of laymen is more likely to uphold those pillars.

One commentator[138] has suggested that strict application of Durham would require a finding of not guilty in 90 percent of all criminal cases, including in this group most sociopaths. This in turn would greatly overtax already overcrowded hospital facilities. The *Blocker* decisions,[139] holding eventually that the sociopathic personality may indeed fit the Durham definition of mental disease (after a series of interchanges which may be seen to raise some serious doubts about the efficacy of psychiatric-legal dialogue), do support this suggestion. On the other hand, overall experience with the Durham rule decidedly negates this fear. Moreover, assuming the viability of our dual system of "punishment" and "treatment," the question still remains whether within this system it is more desirable to acquit only a small proportion of offenders by using a rule that is generally regarded as unsound than to acquit by reason of insanity a percentage which may potentially overcrowd our hospitals.

e) The Model Penal Code Test

The expansion or reformation of the M'Naghten and irresistible-impulse tests by the Model Penal Code test meets many of the criticisms aimed at the narrow scope of these formulations. Its adoption in ten states and eight of the eleven federal circuits,[140] as well as its use as a model for other proposed tests,[141] tends to substantiate this evaluation.

Nonetheless, the Code test has been criticized as retaining the inadequacies of the M'Naghten–irresistible-impulse formulation and even those of Durham. Some justification for this criticism exists: the possible interchangeability of the three rules has been noted earlier.[142] But this type of criticism seems often to reflect the view that all tests of criminal responsibility are destined to be inadequate, rather than a positive attempt to devise the best formulation within the present framework of the criminal law.

On the specific level, Professor Hall has argued that the Model Penal Code formulation—i.e., incapacity "to conform [one's] conduct to the requirements of law"—allows a defendant to rest his defense entirely on the independent and autonomous alternative of "irresistible impulse," the change being merely one of expression, not one of substance. Hence he believes the Code's test is worth only as much as the "irresistible-impulse" test and is subject to the same criticisms as were previously leveled at that test.[143] On the other hand, Judge Biggs states that the phrase "conform his conduct to the requirements of law" is "substantially the same rule of responsibility as that laid down by the *Durham* case . . . though the reporters . . . in their comments expressly repudiate the doctrine of the *Durham* decision."[144]

Another objection to the Code formulation is that through the use of the words "result of" it introduces the most objectionable aspects of the Durham test.[145] Also, the use of the phrase "appre-

135. *Model Penal Code* § 4.01, Comments, at 159; Wechsler, *supra* note 119, at 371.

136. "Mental illness does not cause one to commit a crime nor does mental illness produce a crime. Behavior and mental illness are inseparable—one and the same thing." Roche, *supra* note 92 (1954–55), at 322; see also De Grazia, "The Distinction of Being Mad," 22 *U. Chi. L. Rev.* 339, 343 (1954–55); Roche, *supra* note 132, at 267–68; cf. United States v. Smith, 5 U.S.C.M.A. 314, 324–26, 17 C.M.R. 314, 324–26 (1954). But see Matthews, *supra* note 46, regarding the nature of psychiatric testimony generally. Matthews' description of courtroom psychiatric opinion as anything but independent professional opinion would tend to alleviate many of the fears expressed above. He notes that often competency and responsibility procedures are in effect vehicles for dispositional decision: in many cases the psychiatrist's contribution is in the nature of a contribution to a "dispositional conference very much like a sentencing hearing." Id. at 132. Matthews' perspective may not be comforting, but it shifts attention to what might be the "real" problems concerning expert psychiatric testimony.

137. Wechsler, *supra* note 119, at 367.

138. Gasch, "Prosecution Problems under the Durham Rule," 5 *Catholic Law.* 5, 33 (1959).

139. Blocker v. United States, 274 F.2d 572 (D.C. Cir. 1959); Blocker v. United States, 320 F.2d 800 (D.C. Cir. 1963).

140. See notes 59 and 60 *supra* for a listing of the jurisdictions adopting the Code test; see notes 62 and 63 *supra* for federal circuit cases.

141. For alternative proposals, see, e.g., Report of the Committee on Criminal Responsibility 301–2 (New York, 1958); The District of Columbia Bar Association Report, as in Weihofen, *The Urge to Punish* 34 (1956); Royal Commission on Capital Punishment, *supra* note 85, at 276.

142. See "equation" in § II A 2 a of this chapter.

143. Hall, *supra* note 54, at 222–24; see also Roche, *supra* note 132, at 180–91.

144. Biggs, *supra* note 2, at 60.

145. Comment, *supra* note 123, at 307; but see Cutler, "Insanity as a Defense in Criminal Law," 5 *Catholic Law.* 44, 55 (1959), where this objection is refuted.

ciate the criminality of his conduct" has been interpreted to reject the concept of "moral wrong" as opposed to "legal wrong."[146] The *Currens* court,[147] deleting this phrase from the test, agreed with this objection, arguing that "appreciation of the criminality of one's conduct" retained too much of the M'Naghten strictness on the element of cognition. Nor has the phrase "substantial capacity" escaped the critics. It has been described as too nebulous for a jury to grasp and as likely as M'Naghten to force the psychiatrist back into the "ultimate extreme of total incapacity,"[148] at which point only the most severe cases could meet the standard set forth.

The second paragraph of the Model Penal Code formulation "is designed to exclude from the concept of 'mental disease or defect' the case of so-called psychopathic personality."[149] Judge Biggs expresses the opinion that since there is doubt as to whether the psychopathic personality constitutes a valid psychiatric classification, no rigid exclusionary rule should be attempted at present.[150] One medical commentator[151] questions the validity of equating "psychopathic personality" with repetitious "criminal or otherwise anti-social conduct," since it is doubtful that any psychiatrist would predicate a finding of psychopathy "only" on a history of "repeated criminal or otherwise anti-social conduct." The exclusion of the psychopathic personality by the Model Penal Code is described by this observer as "tantamount to the usurpation of the functions of the psychiatrists in helping to formulate realistic legislation." It may be recalled here that one major objection to the Durham rule was precisely the opposite: Durham *would* include the class of sociopaths. (A psychiatric usurpation of the lawmakers' function?)

Many of the criticisms of the Model Penal Code (and Durham-McDonald as well) are appropriately summarized by the observation of Dr. Roche:

> To some it may seem that in abandoning some words and replacing them with others the Code points to the promised land. But a real change can scarcely be

effected by the use of words which bear a dictionary synonymity with those erased.[152]

Granting that the "modern" tests of criminal responsibility indeed fail to lead to a sociolegal "promised land," the problem with such observations is that they often become the parlance of those who are unwilling to advocate or even entertain the thought of any "real change" in our conceptions and institutions such as might bring the criminal justice system closer to ideals of consistency and rationality, and tend to justify the principle of inertia, espousing old rules and formulations by default.

Justice Weintraub, who surely does not fall in the above class, observed in *State v. Lucas:*

> No one will dispute that society must be protected from the insane as well as the sane. The area of disagreement is whether a civil or criminal process should be employed when forbidden acts have been committed. If we could think of a conviction simply as a finding that the mortal in question has demonstrated his capacity for anti-social conduct, most of the battle would be decided. What would remain is the employment of such post-conviction techniques as would redeem the offender if he can be redeemed and secure him if he cannot.[153]

This may be a very cogent observation. More questionable, however, is its sequitur that within the framework of our present assumptions "M'Naghten is unassailable," coupled with Justice Weintraub's assertion that "until a basis for personal blameworthiness can be *scientifically established,* [he] would not tinker with the existing law of criminal accountability."[154] If we have to wait for this Godot, we will never tinker with anything.

3. DIMINISHED RESPONSIBILITY: AN ALTERNATIVE APPROACH?

The doctrine of diminished or partial responsibility grew up as a reaction to the all-or-nothing aspect of the insanity defense, particularly as formulated and administered along M'Naghten lines. Rather than having to convict an accused whose state of mind is clearly abnormal or acquit one whose presence in society is likely to be unsafe,[155] the deciders

---

146. Comment, *supra* note 123, at 310.

147. United States v. Currens, 290 F.2d 751 (3d Cir. 1961).

148. Roche, *supra* note 132, at 179; Comment, *supra* note 123, at 307; see also *Model Penal Code* § 4.01, Comments, at 159.

149. *Model Penal Code* § 4.01, Comments, at 160.

150. Biggs, *supra* note 2, at 160.

151. Kozol, "The Psychopath before the Law," 44 *Mass. L.Q.* 106, 116 (No. 2, July 1959); see also Roche, *supra* note 132, at 179–80.

152. Roche, *supra* note 132, at 180.

153. State v. Lucas, 30 N.J. 37, 83, 152 A.2d 50, 75 (1959) (concurring opinion).

154. Ibid. (Emphasis added.)

155. This choice is of course mythical: virtually all those acquitted by reason of insanity are committed to mental institu-

of the accused's fate under the doctrine of partial responsibility can take comfort in being permitted a less rigorous choice. This doctrine also reflects the feeling that

> among those who are sane and legally responsible there are appreciable degrees of mental impairment, and it is unjust to ignore that and impose uniform sentences. Within the rule of law there can and should be a substantial measure of individualization.[156]

The thrust of the doctrine of diminished responsibility is twofold.[157] First, evidence of abnormal mental condition, though not sufficient to constitute legal insanity, may be introduced to negate the requisite state of mind for the crime charged (e.g., premeditation and deliberation for first degree murder). If successful, the accused can be convicted only of a lesser crime, one which does not require proof of such state of mind.[158] Second, evidence of mental abnormality may be presented for the purpose of reducing punishment.[159] Reduced imprisonment, but *not* hospitalization, is the result of each approach.

Historically, the concept of diminished responsibility was first recognized in Anglo-American law by the Scottish decision of *Dingwall* in 1867.[160] In England, the doctrine was sanctioned in 1957 when Parliament passed the Homicide Act providing for partial responsibility in homicide cases:

> [The defendant] shall not be convicted of murder if he was suffering from such abnormality of mind (whether arising from a condition of arrested or retarded development of mind or any inherent causes

or induced by disease or injury) as substantially impaired his mental responsibility for his acts and omissions in doing or being a party to the killing.[161]

The Homicide Act has been viewed as a substitute for the recommendation made in 1953 by the Royal Commission on Capital Punishment that M'Naghten be abandoned—a recommendation the English Parliament chose not to follow. It applies to homicides only, whereas the law of Scotland had general application to all types of offenses.[162] In the United States the doctrine of diminished responsibility has been in existence in one form or another since the 1880s.[163]

The question of when the doctrine of diminished responsibility applies has a variety of answers. In Scotland, where the doctrine is of judicial origin, a later case[164] outlined what has been interpreted as a rather strict standard: "[T]here must be a state of mind which is bordering, though not amounting to insanity." The Homicide Act of England speaks of "such abnormality of mind . . . as substantially impaired [the defendant's] mental responsibility."[165] Judicial decisions have construed this language as meaning "insanity . . . in its broad popular sense" or "a state of mind so different from that of ordinary human beings that the reasonable man would term it abnormal."[166] Jurisdictions in this country have generally been less specific and have emphasized the evidentiary character of the rule. Accordingly, the American Law Institute Model Penal Code, in adopting the defense, has followed this approach:

> Evidence that the defendant suffered from a mental disease or defect shall be admissible whenever it is relevant to prove that the defendant did or did not have a state of mind which is an element of the offense.[167]

The doctrine of diminished responsibility, in its application to reduce the grade or degree of the

---

tions; such commitment is in fact mandatory by statute or automatic by practice (absent such statutory provision) in many states—a finding of present insanity not being required. It is more accurate, therefore, to postulate that the diminished responsibility doctrine seeks to alleviate the rigor of the criminal process in its entirety, including considerations of the appropriateness of stigmatization, deterrence, and publicizing the community's moral concepts.

156. Hall, *General Principles of Criminal Law* 462–63 (2d ed. 1960).

157. Annot., 22 A.L.R.3d 1228 (1968).

158. See, e.g., People v. Gorshen, 51 Cal. 2d 716, 336 P.2d 492 (1959).

159. E.g., People v. Moseley, 281 N.Y.2d 762, 228 N.E.2d 765 (1967). Compare State v. Rodriguez, 25 Conn. Supp. 350, 204 A.2d 37 (1964).

160. H. M. Advocate v. Dingwall, 5 Irvine 466 (1867). See Glueck, *Law and Psychiatry* 23–30 (1962); Guttmacher, *supra* note 10, at 47–50.

161. The Homicide Act § 2 (1957).

162. Guttmacher, *supra* note 10, at 47.

163. See Annot., 22 A.L.R.3d 1228 (1968), citing: United States v. Lee, 4 Machey 489 (D.C. Cir. 1886); State v. Holloway, 156 Mo. 222, 56 S.W. 734 (1900); State v. Kotovsky, 11 Mo. App. 584, *aff'd,* 74 Mo. 247 (1882).

164. H. M. Advocate v. Savage (1923), cited in Glueck, *supra* note 160, at 26; and Guttmacher, *supra* note 10, at 48.

165. The Homicide Act § 2 (1957).

166. Guttmacher, *supra* note 10, at 48.

167. *Model Penal Code* § 4.02(1).

offense (as opposed to its application for purposes of mitigating punishment), it not clearly recognizable as a distinct doctrine.[168] An accused should of course always be able to assert that an element of the crime with which he has been charged was absent at the time he committed the act. For example, premeditation may be an element of the offense charged. Mental abnormality, like other circumstances, may well contradict the supposition that the accused actually had this type of intent. Consequently, the diminished responsibility concept has been designated as at most a rule of evidence,[169] and arguably a superfluous one at that. This difficulty of recognition has cropped up in studies which have attempted to catalog those jurisdictions "adopting" the doctrine. Most jurisdictions have accepted the concept of diminished responsibility in cases involving intoxication—that is, intoxication (even if voluntary) as a defense to a crime involving specific intent[170]—but fewer states have extended the principle beyond such circumstances. The *American Law Reports Annotated* list eighteen states as recognizing diminished responsibility in situations *not* involving intoxication;[171] Guttmacher counts only eleven states.[172] Most of these jurisdictions allow evidence of mental abnormality falling short of insanity to be introduced only in homicide cases or cases where the charge is first degree murder.[173] It is of course debatable whether jurisdictions which limit the defense to homicides can be said to have "adopted" the concept of diminished responsibility, since the degrees of homicide are expressly based on a specific intent which must be proved, and evidence negating such intent could not justifiably be excluded. It is suggested therefore that the classification of states where diminished responsibility is operative turns largely on the admissibility of expert psychiatric testimony,[174] a suggestion which would

also explain why jurisdictions limiting the concept to circumstances involving intoxication—i.e., where psychiatric expertise is less relevant—are usually not classified as having "adopted" diminished responsibility.

Jurisdictions allowing evidence of mental abnormality in nonhomicide cases or for purposes of fixing punishment, or those entitling the defendant to special instructions on diminished responsibility can less hesitatingly be said to operate under a distinct concept of criminal responsibility. That is, the doctrine of diminished responsibility is simply more observable in these settings. For example, a specific intent often appears to be a less integral part of the offense in nonhomicide cases than it is when the degree of murder is the issue; hence permitting evidence of mental abnormality in nonhomicide cases appears less consonant with the traditional sequence of the criminal trial. Similarly, when mental abnormality is introduced and considered in order to mitigate punishment, this too indicates a more perceptibly distinct procedure than when the evidence is used to disprove an element of the offense, though the dispositional result may be indistinguishable. Special instructions on the issue of diminished responsibility speak for themselves in regard to observability.

California, Connecticut, Iowa, Kentucky, New Jersey, New Mexico, and Utah have judicially held that the defendant is entitled to special instructions drawing attention to evidence of mental abnormality short of insanity.[175] California, Colorado, and New York have allowed diminished responsibility in nonhomicide cases.[176] The concept is known to have been used for purposes of fixing punishment in Arizona, Connecticut, Georgia, New Jersey, New York, Oregon, Pennsylvania, Tennessee, and Texas.[177]

---

168. This observation is in an abstract sense also applicable to the defense of criminal irresponsibility.

169. Annot., 22 A.L.R.3d 1228 (1968).

170. See 22 C.J.S. "Criminal Law" § 68 (1961).

171. Annot., 22 A.L.R.3d 1228 (1968): California, Colorado, Connecticut, Indiana, Iowa, Kentucky, Nebraska, Nevada, New Jersey, New Mexico, New York, Ohio, Oregon, Rhode Island, Utah, Virginia, Wisconsin, and Wyoming. At least one jurisdiction, Colorado, has interpreted diminished responsibility to be part of its statute on criminal responsibility; see Gallegos v. People, 159 Colo. 379, 411 P.2d 956 (1966)—a case which concerned intoxication, however.

172. Guttmacher, *supra* note 10, at 49.

173. Ibid.; see also Annot., 22 A.L.R.3d 1228 (1968).

174. This distinctiveness of the defense of diminished respon-

sibility is indicated in a California case which held that in a separate trial on the issue of legal insanity, evidence of the diminished responsibility type is not admissible. People v. Wells, 33 Cal. 2d 330, 202 P.2d 53 (1949). But see note 231 *infra* and text for precisely the opposite conclusion.

175. Annot., 22 A.L.R.3d 1228 (1968).

176. Ibid. California: People v. Wells, 33 Cal. 2d 330, 202 P.2d 53 (1949), assault on prison guard; People v. Gorshen, 51 Cal. 2d 716, 336 P.2d 492 (1959), where the court cited with approval a case involving voting more than once at an election (People v. Harris, 29 Cal. 678 (1866)). Colorado: Schwickrath v. People, 159 Colo. 390, 411 P.2d 961 (1966), felonious escape. New York: People v. Colavecchio, 11 App. Div. 2d 161, 202 N.Y.S.2d 119 (1960), larceny.

177. Annot., 22 A.L.R.3d 1228 (1968).

Neither the volume nor the percentage of cases in which the defense of diminished responsibility is asserted appears to be high in American jurisdictions. Only in California, and perhaps Colorado, has the doctrine been utilized with any frequency or regularity. By contrast, in England during the first six years after passage of the Homicide Act of 1957, pleas of partial responsibility were made in 150 of 223 murder cases, three-quarters of them successfully.[178] An interesting sidelight to the English experience has been a closely proportionate reduction of findings of incompetency to stand trial during that same period.[179]

Opposition to the doctrine of diminished responsibility has come in a variety of forms and from all extremes. Thus, it has been argued on the one hand that the concept does nothing more than make explicit the admissibility of evidence which is already admissible: if, on the basis of relevant facts, the accused desires to show absence of a necessary element of the offense, the law has always permitted him to do so. At the other extreme, it has been said that acceptance of the doctrine "would involve a fundamental change in the common law theory of responsibility."[180]

On a different level, diminished responsibility has been criticized as requiring juries to "answer questions which are . . . by their very nature unanswerable."[181] Specifically, it has been contended that juries would be incapable of distinguishing that degree of mental impairment which does not prevent the sufferer from harboring an intent to kill and yet does prevent him from premeditating or deliberating.[182] This is indeed a telling argument, but

proponents of the doctrine have replied that difficulties of administration do not excuse denial of this defense to an afflicted person. The question may also be asked whether the queries posed by diminished responsibility are in essence any more unanswerable than those posed by the traditional defense of insanity.

Another objection to the defense of diminished responsibility is that through its application those criminals who are most dangerous to society—persons who have exhibited criminality, lack of self-control, and in many cases extreme brutality—would be the first to be released from prison and at a time when they still pose a threat to society.[183] The argument is that though the logic and humanity of the law might favor showing leniency to those affected by an involuntary mental condition as it does to those who offend while intoxicated,[184] the safety of society prohibits such extension. In response, those who defend diminished responsibility have advocated the procedural expedient of retaining custody of such socially dangerous persons in mental hospitals after completion of their prison sentences until it is determined that they are no longer dangerous.[185]

Finally, there have been general questions concerning the wisdom of modifying the all-or-nothing

---

178. Guttmacher, *supra* note 10, at 47.

179. Ibid. An analogous situation has occurred in the District of Columbia under the Durham rule: While acquittals by reason of insanity have increased, the increase has been at the expense of findings of incompetency and not-guilty verdicts. See sources in notes 79–81 *supra*. Such experience seems to suggest that rather than producing radical changes of outlook and result, the replacement of old rules by new ones serves primarily to direct the deciders' sense of rough justice and fairness into new (and perhaps more appropriate) channels.

180. Fisher v. United States, 328 U.S. 463 (1946), applying the law of the District of Columbia.

181. Guttmacher, *supra* note 10, at 48, quoting Barbara Wootton.

182. "The Courts do not ask the jury to undertake the impossible task of discriminating between degrees of insanity so as to find a prisoner incapable of forming a deliberate and premeditated intent to kill, while he has still so much sanity that he is a person of sound memory and discretion, as he must be to be

guilty of murder even in the second degree." Commonwealth v. Hollinger, 190 Pa. 155, 160, 42 A. 548, 549 (1899); State v. Van Vlack, 57 Idaho 316, 65 P.2d 736 (1937); see also Note, "Partial Responsibility: Adequacy of Present Law," 43 *Cornell L.Q.* 283, 284 (1957–58).

183. "It is apparent that one who is a mental defective, who has criminal tendencies, and who has committed what would be unquestionably first degree murder were he normal, is a lasting social menace. . . . Acceptance here of the doctrine of reduced responsibility . . . means that after a period of years any such defendant surviving at the expiration of sentence for second degree murder will be turned loose on society. It may be logical . . . to do so, but not practical. . . ." Commonwealth v. Scott, 14 Pa. D. & C. 191, 198 (1930). See also Note, *supra* note 182, at 286–87.

184. As argued in, e.g., State v. Noel, 102 N.J.L. 659, 694, 133 A. 274, 285 (1926): "The law is not the creation of such barbarous and insensible animal nature as to extend a more lenient legal rule to the case of a drunkard, whose mental faculties are disturbed by his own will and conduct, than to the case of a poor demented creature afflicted by the hand of God."

185. "The judge should have power to order the defendant confined for the period proper as punishment for the offense of which he has been found guilty, if any, and in addition, retained for medical care until safe to be at large. This procedure could probably be adopted in most states without any additional statutory authority. . . ." Weihofen & Overholser, "Mental Disorder Affecting the Degree of Crime," 56 *Yale L.J.* 959, 980–81 (1947).

aspects of the insanity defense by means of a doctrine that takes into account shades or degrees of responsibility producing "compromise verdicts."[186] A case in point is *State v. Rodriguez* (1964),[187] where responsibility (punishment) was reduced partially on the basis of the accused's cultural background. Opponents of the diminished responsibility concept would argue that this "compromise" represents the ultimate in the process of undermining the traditional principles of criminal justice. Others might view *Rodriguez* as a very desirable extension of the principle of diminished responsibility, a salutary example of individualized justice not at all inconsistent with traditional principles and practices of criminal justice, giving official sanction to a process which goes on daily in our courts in a more covert manner.

C. Implementation of Tests of Criminal Responsibility

A plea of insanity[188] is conceptually not unlike any other defense to crime that operates to acquit the accused. But insanity defenses have been singled out for extensive special treatment in the procedural provisions of the criminal law.

1. Raising the Defense

Criminal irresponsibility may, in several jurisdictions, be pleaded initially at trial and in most states under a general plea of "not guilty."[189] However, in recognition of the technical difficulty of proof raised by the plea and the desirability of adequate notice to the state,[190] it has been provided in at least twenty

states that the plea shall be entered at the time of arraignment.[191] A few states require the defendant either to plead at arraignment or to file not later than four days before trial with the court and with the prosecuting attorney a notice of intent to raise the defense. In at least one state, failure to plead insanity results in conclusive presumption of sanity, except that the court may allow a change in plea at any time prior to the commencement of the trial.[192] In Colorado,

> a defendant who does not thus [appropriately] plead not guilty by reason of insanity shall not be permitted to rely on insanity as a defense . . . : provided, that evidence of mental condition may be offered in a proper case as bearing upon the capacity of the accused to form the specific intent essential to constitute a crime.[193]

Failure to plead insanity in Colorado thus leaves the defendant only the defense of diminished responsibility.[194] Another state gives the court power to declare a mistrial if, without prior notice but in good faith, the plea is made during the trial. Following a declaration of mistrial, the court may then order the defendant hospitalized for purposes of examination.[195]

The notice provisions are generally consistent with modern "no surprise" pleading concepts,[196] yet their strict application in criminal cases would be unduly harsh.

> The defendant who has an insanity defense, and who wishes to assert it, should not be barred from doing so because of inadequate procedures or inadequate lawyers. The only way to assure he will not is to discard the fiction that all defendants come equally well equipped to make the decisions, and the choices,

---

186. Note, *supra* note 182, at 284.

187. 25 Conn. Supp. 350, 204 A.2d 37 (1964). The sentence of manslaughter was reduced because the court felt that the defendant's Puerto Rican background precluded him from making the choice that the law imposes on citizens of our culture.

188. Insanity, as used in the phrases "insane person," "insanity as a defense," or "plea of insanity," is the standard legal term designating those mentally disabled whom the law recognizes as criminally irresponsible. Because of the prevalence of this terminology in the statutes and other writings in the field, "insanity" will be used interchangeably with "criminal irresponsibility" in this section to denote a mental condition serious enough to relieve the accused of responsibility for his criminal acts.

189. Weihofen, *supra* note 1, at 357.

190. "In a criminal case the defendant learns from the preliminary examination substantially what will be shown against him, while the prosecuting attorney is often in ignorance until the defendant's evidence is presented at the trial. Occasionally the prosecuting attorney is forced to prepare on rebuttal what proves to be the real case. As a result of grave abuses of the

insanity defense, some jurisdictions more than a generation ago provided by statute that insanity was to be pleaded specially." Orfield, *Criminal Procedure from Arrest to Appeal* 303 (1947). But compare note 198 *infra*.

191. See Table 11.1, Insanity as a Defense to Crime, Time of Pleading columns.

192. *Ohio Rev. Code Ann.* § 2943.03 (Baldwin 1968).

193. *Colo. Rev. Stat. Ann.* § 39-8-1(1) (1963).

194. See this chapter § II B 3 on Diminished Responsibility alluding to the difficulty of classifying language like that of the Colorado provision as embracing the concept of diminished responsibility.

195. *Ark. Stat. Ann.* § 43-1301 (1964).

196. See Orfield, *supra* note 190, at 321; Millar, "The Function of Criminal Pleadings," 12 *J. Crim. L.C. & P.S.* 500 (1922). *Model Penal Code* § 4.03(2) also adopts notice requirements.

called for by procedural rules; and to adopt a liberal view of "good cause" [whereby the defendant can raise the insanity issue despite noncompliance with the notice requirements].[197]

The notice provisions make sense only to the extent that they are conducive to an orderly trial by confirming expectations—usually already quite clear[198]—of the issues to be raised. Enforcement of notice requirements against the defendant[199] should occur only in circumstances where assertion of the defense and failure to give notice are clearly without legitimate reason or justification.

In at least eight states the grand jury may refuse to indict in a case of insanity.[200] This constitutes a departure from the usual rule that no matters in defense are considered at the grand jury hearing. Whether refusal to indict operates as an acquittal or merely postpones further criminal prosecution would seem to depend on whether the refusal is based on a finding of insanity at the time of the alleged act or at the time of the grand jury proceeding. While one state, West Virginia,[201] specifies insanity at the time of the act charged, the other statutes appear to cover both situations. Four states provide that, upon notice of a refusal to indict, the court *may* hospitalize the accused in a mental institution; in the other four hospitalization is mandatory.[202] Only Mississippi provides for the initiation of regular civil hospitalization proceedings,[203] while North Carolina and Utah require a special detailed procedure.[204] In two states the accused may be incarcerated in prison or jail.[205]

Although the defense of criminal irresponsibility is normally raised upon arraignment, when the defendant in a felony case is required to plead to the indictment,[206] in some instances the defendant may fail to raise the defense until after conviction; convictions are rarely upset by this sort of attack, however. In those cases where the accused is allowed to raise a belated defense of insanity, he must be able to show clearly why the defense was not presented in a timely fashion. In a few cases in which the defendant has raised the defense for the first time on a motion for a new trial, the motion has been granted where the defendant was tried without benefit of counsel.[207] But the cases are not uniform on the reasons for granting such a motion.[208] Generally, the defense cannot be raised by writ of habeas corpus,[209] because the attack is not directed against the jurisdiction of the convicting court. In a few jurisdictions, however, it can be raised by writ of *error coram nobis*,[210] designed specifically to correct errors not known by the trial court.[211]

A belated defense of irresponsibility has traditionally been treated in the same unsolicitous fashion as any other belated defense. The fact that the defendant has had an opportunity and elected not to exercise it, and the concomitant elements of public expense and inconvenience, are the obvious reasons for the absence of judicial leniency toward such a defense. Furthermore, belated insanity defenses may be suspect in that they represent, in some instances, a last-ditch stand by the defendant to avert criminal punishment. Such suspicion is not entirely justified, because the result of a successful defense of irresponsibility is usually confinement in a mental hospital, imposing nearly the same restraint as that involved in imprisonment.[212] Furthermore, since

197. Goldstein, *supra* note 46, at 109.

198. "In practice, however, the prosecutor [already] has at his disposal a wide variety of devices by which he can learn what the defense will be." Goldstein, *supra* note 46, at 107–8.

199. See 32 A.L.R.2d 434, 464 (§ 13). E.g., State v. Messer, 194 La. 238, 193 So. 633 (1940).

200. *Ala. Code* tit. 15, § 429 (1959); *Mass. Ann. Laws* ch. 277, § 16 (1967); *Miss. Code Ann.* § 2574 (1956); *N.H. Rev. Stat. Ann.* §§ 607:1, 607:3 (1955); *N.C. Gen. Stat.* § 122-84 (1963); *Utah Code Ann.* § 77-48-2 (Supp. 1967); *Vt. Stat. Ann.* tit. 13, § 4804 (1958); *W. Va. Code Ann.* §§ 62-2-12, 62-3-9 (1966).

201. *W. Va. Code Ann.* § 62-2-12 (1966).

202. Discretionary: Massachusetts, New Hampshire, Vermont, West Virginia. Mandatory: Alabama, Mississippi, North Carolina, Utah. See note 200 *supra*.

203. *Miss. Code Ann.* § 2574 (1956).

204. *N.C. Gen. Stat.* § 122-84 (1963); *Utah Code Ann.* § 77-48-2 (Supp. 1967).

205. *N.H. Rev. Stat. Ann.* § 607.3 (1955); *Vt. Stat. Ann.* tit. 13, § 4804 (1958).

206. Weihofen, *supra* note 1, at 355.

207. E.g., Gardner v. State, 82 Tex. Crim. 38, 198 S.W. 312 (1917).

208. Annot., 1918B L.R.A. 1146.

209. Ford v. Warden, Md. House of Corrections, 218 Md. 646, 145 A.2d 773 (1958); Ferguson v. Hoffman, 180 Kan. 139, 299 P.2d 596 (1956); see also Annot., 29 A.L.R.2d 703 (1953). But see notes 427, 428 and accompanying text concerning the erosion of this traditional limitation on habeas corpus.

210. Putnam v. People, 408 Ill. 582, 97 N.E.2d 841 (1951); Swain v. State, 215 Ind. 259, 18 N.E.2d 921 (1939); cf. Blodgett v. State, 245 S.W.2d 839 (Mo. 1952); People v. Boehm, 309 N.Y. 362, 130 N.E.2d 897 (1955); see also Annot., 29 A.L.R.2d 703 (1953).

211. Weihofen, *supra* note 1, at 387–88.

212. "Aristotle observed long ago that 'punishment is a sort of medicine.' We have considerable cause today to observe that

as a practical matter raising the issue of insanity is tantamount to an admission by the defendant that he committed the alleged act, an unsuccessful defense of insanity significantly increases the likelihood of conviction. In sum, if there is any other defense, it is preferable to insanity, and in fact the insanity defense is seldom raised—belatedly or otherwise—in all except capital cases.

About fifteen states have provisions covering the *form* of insanity pleas. A number of them require a special plea of "not guilty by reason of insanity," or its equivalent, in order to raise the defense. In the other states the form of the plea is more permissive.[213] The special pleas appear to be required in order to give the state time to proceed with a pretrial mental examination of the accused and otherwise prepare proofs on the cumbersome insanity issue.[214] This same rationale is perceptible in the statutes of some seven other states which, though not providing for a special plea, *do* require written notice of intent to raise the insanity defense.[215]

2. TRIAL

The actual trial of cases involving insanity defenses raises a few procedural variations. In forty-four jurisdictions statutes provide that the determination of all issues raised, including responsibility, is to be made by the jury.[216] However, the defendant may often waive the jury if he so chooses. In New Hampshire[217] the prosecutor may accept the defendant's plea of insanity and quash the criminal proceedings. Under this special procedure the defendant cannot complain if his plea is accepted, regardless of the fact that the court has not ruled on it.

In California a special plea is used in order that a separate trial may be conducted for the purpose of determining the question of responsibility raised by the plea.[218] Thus the defendant who pleads only

"not guilty by reason of insanity" is tried on the issue of irresponsibility alone. If he is found responsible, he is presumed conclusively by statute to have admitted commission of the offense and is sentenced forthwith. But if the defendant pleads both "not guilty" and "not guilty by reason of insanity," then a trial is held first on the former plea alone. If he is found guilty, a second trial is held on the plea of insanity. Only if the defendant is found responsible at the later trial is he sentenced forthwith.[219] When an accused is found not guilty but the insanity issue has been raised, he is not released until a proper hearing is held to determine the issue of insanity.[220]

Separate trials on the issue of criminal responsibility have been held constitutional, whether the special trial is held before[221] or after the criminal trial.[222] The procedure does not deprive the defendant of his right to a jury, since he expressly receives a jury determination in both proceedings.[223]

The bifurcated trial concept may well be a concept of the past.[224] Even in California, the only state where it has remained statutorily intact and mandatory, the procedure has been greatly undermined in practice and by adverse commentary.[225] The separate trial provisions in California were devised

---

medicine can be a sort of punishment." De Grazia, *supra* note 136, at 355; see also chap. 5, "Rights of Hospitalized Patients," this volume.

213. Weihofen, *supra* note 1, at 357–58.

214. In State v. Gunter, 208 La. 694, 23 So. 2d 305 (1954), it was held that the defense cannot be raised if the special plea is not made, and the form seems to be as strictly construed as the time for raising the defense.

215. Weihofen, *supra* note 1, at 354.

216. See Table 11.1, Finding By columns.

217. *N.H. Rev. Stat. Ann.* § 607:2 (1955).

218. *Cal. Penal Code* § 1026 (West 1956). In Colorado it is in the discretion of the court to order a bifurcated trial or to try all issues in one trial. *Colo. Rev. Stat. Ann.* § 39-8-3 (1963).

219. This procedure has been held constitutional. People v. Walker, 33 Cal. 2d 250, 201 P.2d 6 (1948). See also Annot., 67 A.L.R. 1451 (1930).

220. See *Cal. Penal Code* § 1026 (West 1956).

221. State v. Toon, 172 La. 631, 135 So. 7 (1931). But see note 224 *infra* to the effect that Louisiana no longer allows separate trials.

222. People v. Walker, 33 Cal. 2d 250, 201 P.2d 6 (1948).

223. See People v. Wells, 33 Cal. 2d 330, 202 P.2d 53 (1949), upholding constitutionality; but see Weihofen, *supra* note 1, at 360, criticizing the constitutionality of this procedure.

224. Texas has recently abandoned the separate trial approach. *Tex. Code Crim. Proc.* art. 46.02 (1966); see "Special Commentary," at p. 561. The Texas provision still allows separate determination of the insanity issue by agreement ("upon written application on behalf of the accused with the consent of the state's attorney and the approval of the trial judge") but only as an exception to the general rule that "no issue of insanity shall be tried in advance of trial on the merits." Louisiana, the only other state which has had a separate trial procedure during recent years, has also abandoned it. See Louisell & Hazard, "Insanity as a Defense: The Bifurcated Trial," 49 *Cal. L. Rev.* 805, 827 (1961), citing State v. Dowdy, 217 La. 773, 47 So. 2d 496 (1950).

225. See Louisell & Hazard, *supra* note 224, at 805; Comment, "The Gradual Decay of the Bifurcated Trial System in California and the Emergence of Partial Insanity: 1966," 3 *Cal. Western L. Rev.* 149 (1967); Guttmacher, *supra* note 10, at 16, citing Bernard Diamond.

in 1925 by a commission which has been labeled "prosecution minded" and which "seems to have regarded the claim of insanity as a sham defense used by the obviously guilty to gull juries into verdicts of acquittal."[226] It has been charged that in separating the trials of guilt and sanity, the proponents of bifurcation relied on two unarticulated suppositions which are highly questionable: that criminal intent can be separated from sanity, and that the criminal act can be established without regard to intent.[227]

The infusion of the concept of diminished responsibility (or partial insanity) into California law[228] has served to emphasize the artificiality of separate trials and has been responsible for what has been termed "the gradual decay"[229] of the bifurcated system. The *Wells, Gorshen, Conley*[230] line of cases on diminished responsibility appears to illustrate that evidence permitted to be presented on the trial of the general issue (evidence of mental abnormality to negate specific intent) is now virtually indistinguishable in scope and effect from that which would be permitted on the insanity issue. Thus it has been concluded that the diminished responsibility decisions have "entirely done away with the bifurcated trial system as anything more than a second chance for the defendant to achieve acquittal."[231]

3. BURDEN OF PROOF

To analyze properly the various positions assumed by the states in assigning the burden of proof, it is valuable to separate the concept of burden of proof into two constituent elements: the initial burden of going forward with the evidence,[232] and the burden of persuasion.[233]

On the issue of criminal responsibility, the states seem to be unanimous in imposing the initial bur-

den of going forward with the evidence on the accused.[234] This burden is discharged when sufficient evidence of *irresponsibility* is introduced, by either side, to create a question for the jury.[235] If this minimum amount of evidence is not forthcoming, the judge will direct a verdict for the prosecution on this issue. In terms of presumptions it could be said that the accused is presumed sane because, as a generalization, most men are sane. But this presumption is overcome when evidence of insanity is offered sufficient to raise doubt whether the underlying generalization can validly be applied to the defendant. Although in agreement on where this burden should be placed, the states do not agree on the quantum of evidence required to discharge the burden. The prevailing requirement is for evidence sufficient to raise reasonable doubt of the defendant's mental responsibility for the criminal act.[236] A few jurisdictions are satisfied with the lesser standard of "some evidence."[237] Earlier cases in the District of Columbia suggested that in that jurisdiction the accused must only introduce a "scintilla" of evidence to fulfill his obligation of producing "some evidence."[238] But the more recent *McDonald* decision[239] appears to revert to the prevailing view; regarding the quantum of proof the court said that "certainly it means *more* than a scintilla, yet, of course, the amount need not be so substantial as to require, if uncontroverted, a directed verdict of acquittal."[240]

Once adequate evidence of irresponsibility has been introduced to bring the issue to the jury, there still remains the problem of which party must bear the responsibility of convincing the jury. This responsibility is sometimes referred to as the burden of persuasion, the risk of nonpersuasion, or less precisely, the burden of proof.[241] In reality, it is a question of which party must *lose* if, by all the evidence presented by both sides, the jury is not per-

---

226. Louisell & Hazard, *supra* note 224, at 807–8.

227. Comment, *supra* note 225, at 150.

228. People v. Wells, 33 Cal. 2d 330, 202 P.2d 53 (1949).

229. Comment, *supra* note 225, at 149.

230. People v. Wells, 33 Cal. 2d 330, 202 P.2d 53 (1949); People v. Gorshen, 51 Cal. 2d 716, 336 P.2d 492 (1959); People v. Conley, 64 Cal. 2d 310, 411 P.2d 911 (1966).

231. Comment, *supra* note 225, at 156.

232. Also referred to as the duty of going forward with the evidence, 9 Wigmore, *Evidence* § 2487 (3d ed. 1940), or the risk of nonproduction of the evidence, Morgan, Maguire, & Weinstein, *Cases and Materials on Evidence* 422 (4th ed. 1957).

233. Also referred to as the risk of nonpersuasion, Wigmore, *supra* note 232, at § 2485.

234. Weihofen, *supra* note 1, at 227.

235. Wigmore, *supra* note 232, at §§ 2487, 2489.

236. C.J.S. "Criminal Law" § 924 (1940); Weihofen, *supra* note 1, at 227.

237. Flowers v. State, 236 Ind. 151, 139 N.E.2d 185 (1956); Torske v. State, 123 Neb. 161, 242 N.W. 408 (1932).

238. Tatum v. United States, 190 F.2d 612 (D.C. Cir. 1951); *In re* Rosenfield, 157 F. Supp. 18 (D.D.C. 1957); Goforth v. United States, 269 F.2d 778 (D.C. Cir. 1959).

239. McDonald v. United States, 312 F.2d 847 (D.C. Cir. 1962).

240. Id. at 849.

241. Wigmore, *supra* note 232, at § 2485.

suaded to the requisite degree of certainty of the responsibility or irresponsibility of the accused. The federal government and approximately half the states places this burden or risk on the prosecution,[242] which must establish responsibility beyond a reasonable doubt. The remainder of the states impose on the defendant the burden of convincing the jury of his *irresponsibility,* but only by the civil standard of a preponderance of the evidence.[243] Oregon, which formerly required the defendant to prove his irresponsibility beyond a reasonable doubt,[244] amended its statute in 1957 to conform with those states requiring proof by a preponderance of the evidence.[245]

Since the Supreme Court has explicitly held that due process does not guarantee any particular allocation of the burden of persuasion on the issue of criminal responsibility,[246] there has been no pressure to resolve the dichotomy which has grown up among the states. Those who urge placing the burden on the prosecution contend that the fundamental proposition of the criminal law calling upon the state to prove the defendant's guilt beyond a reasonable doubt should logically extend to the issue of criminal responsibility.[247] They argue that the basic elements of a crime are first, the act, and second, the intent or *mens rea.* To place the burden of persuasion on the accused is to force him to *disprove* an essential element of his alleged guilt,[248]

and is equivalent to requiring him to *disprove* his commission of the criminal act. This step, it is urged, undermines the presumption of innocence, which is the traditional cornerstone of American criminal jurisprudence. Another very practical consideration in favor of assigning this burden to the state, at least in the case of indigent or poor defendants, is that the state has greater resources at its command with which to obtain the expensive psychiatric evidence inherently involved in litigation over criminal responsibility.

The opposing view, which would impose the burden of persuasion on the accused, seems to have gained more adherents in recent years.[249] Supporters of this position look upon the issue of criminal irresponsibility as an affirmative defense to be established by the defendant, rather than seeing criminal *responsibility* as an element of the criminal charge to be proven by the prosecution. The usual presumption of innocence is considered offset by the presumption of sanity.[250] The chief policy consideration underlying this allocation of the burden appears to be the fear that a "reasonable doubt" about a defendant's responsibility can be too easily created,[251] especially in light of the imprecise, often conflicting nature of psychiatric testimony.[252] This fear has become especially perceptible with the adoption of tests of criminal responsibility less stringent than the M'Naghten rules. Accordingly, the minority report of the President's Commission on

---

242. Annot., 17 A.L.R.3d 146 (1968).

243. Ibid.

244. *Ore. Rev. Stat.* § 136.390 (1955). See Leland v. Oregon, 343 U.S. 790 (1952), *aff'g* 190 Ore. 598, 227 P.2d 785 (1951).

245. *Ore. Rev. Stat.* § 136.390 (1959).

246. "[W]e adopted a rule of procedure for the federal courts which is contrary to that of Oregon. But '[i]ts procedure does not run afoul of the Fourteenth Amendment because another method may seem to our thinking to be fairer or wiser or to give a surer promise of protection to the prisoner at the bar.' . . . We are therefore reluctant to interfere with Oregon's determination of its policy with respect to the burden of proof on the issue of sanity since we cannot say that policy violates generally accepted concepts of basic standards of justice." Leland v. Oregon, 343 U.S. 790, 798–99 (1952). See also Note, "Two Constitutional Problems in Proving Insanity," 48 *Nw. U.L. Rev.* 94 (1953–54).

247. Glueck, *supra* note 100, at 41; Hopps v. State, 31 Ill. 385, 83 Am. Dec. 231 (1863); Leland v. Oregon, 343 U.S. 790 (1952) (Frankfurter, J., dissent); Note, "Burden of Proof of Insanity in Criminal Cases," 15 *Md. L. Rev.* 157, 168 (1955); Note, *supra* note 246, at 97–98.

248. "[I]t is a deprivation of life without due process to send a man to his doom if he cannot prove beyond a reasonable doubt that the physical events of homicide did not constitute murder

because under the State's theory he was incapable of acting culpably." Leland v. Oregon, 343 U.S. 790, 804 (1952) (Frankfurter, J., dissent).

249. Wigmore, *supra* note 232, at § 2501; Underhill, *Treatise on the Law of Criminal Evidence* § 452 (5th ed. 1957); Thomas v. State, 206 Md. 575, 112 A.2d 913 (1955); Note, *supra* note 247, at 167–68. But see Weihofen, *supra* note 1, at 238.

250. "The theory is that sanity is the natural condition of men, and that therefore the law presumes all men to be sane until the contrary is proved; insanity is therefore an affirmative defense, which the defendant must establish," Weihofen, *supra* note 1, at 220.

251. "Merely doubtful evidence of insanity would fill the land with acquitted criminals. . . . The danger to society from acquittals on the ground of a doubtful insanity demands a strict rule. It requires that the minds of the triers should be satisfied of the fact of insanity." Ortwein v. Commonwealth, 76 Pa. 414, 425, 18 Am. R. 420 (1874). See also State v. Barton, 361 Mo. 780, 236 S.W.2d 596 (1951); Holober v. Commonwealth, 191 Va. 826, 62 S.E.2d 816 (1951).

252. A reasonable doubt of a defendant's responsibility may not always be as easily created in the mind of the jury as the adherents of this position fear; see People v. Horton, 308 N.Y. 1, 123 N.E.2d 609 (1954).

Crime in the District of Columbia registered its disenchantment with the Durham rule partly in terms of the view that the burden of proof was misplaced. The minority felt that the liberality of Durham's rule of criminal responsibility had made the prosecution's burden too onerous, and suggested placing the burden of persuasion on the defendant "by a preponderance of the evidence."[253] Similarly, the Wisconsin procedure announced in the *Shoffner* case[254] allows the defendant to elect to be tried under the Model Penal Code test rather than M'Naghten, but if he does so, the burden of persuasion shifts to him and he must prove insanity "by the greater weight of the evidence."

An intermediate approach has been to assign the burden of persuasion to the prosecution, regardless of what test of responsibility is applied, but to reduce the weight of the burden by requiring proof only by a preponderance of the evidence rather than beyond a reasonable doubt.[255] This proposal, however, does not seem to have received much serious consideration.

4. MEDICAL EXAMINATION AND TESTIMONY

Statutes in at least twenty-five states specifically provide that defendants who plead insanity shall be examined by impartial experts.[256] Many of these statutes specify that the accused shall be hospitalized in an appropriate institution for a stated period while such examination is being made.[257] These latter statutes have been generally upheld,[258] though they have been attacked on the ground that the defendant is merely confined for a period of time, often without the notice and hearing attendant upon

the usual order of civil hospitalization. But recent judicial decisions in several jurisdictions have thrown doubt upon the constitutionality of this procedure. One state[259] has held that a similar statute would be unconstitutional if construed to deny the defendant notice and hearing, and the validity of such a procedure is doubtful in another.[260] Even more recently a New York case and one in California have indicated similar doubts by analogy. The 1968 New York decision[261] held that an alleged narcotics addict, before being required to undergo a medical examination, must be given a hearing to determine "whether there are reasonable grounds to order him to undergo [such an] examination." More closely analogous is the 1967 California *Succop* case,[262] which stated that a person suspected of being a mentally ill sex offender could not be temporarily committed to a state institution without a hearing to determine whether there were sufficient grounds to warrant such confinement.

Compulsory mental examinations have also been challenged as violating other basic rights of the defendant. Violation of the right against self-incrimination has been successfully asserted in several cases.[263] The basis for the self-incrimination challenge has been the *Escobedo-Miranda* line of decisions[264] which, though aimed primarily at police interrogations and the dangers of involuntary or untrustworthy confessions, may well be applicable to the compulsory psychiatric examination. Intimating the broad applicability of its decision, the Supreme Court said in *Miranda*:

> [T]oday, then, there can be no doubt that the Fifth Amendment privilege is available outside of criminal court proceedings . . . to protect persons *in all settings* in which their freedom of action is curtailed in any significant way from being compelled to incriminate themselves.[265]

253. President's Commission, *supra* note 77, at 897.

254. State v. Shoffner, 143 N.W.2d 458 (Wis. 1966).

255. Wigmore, *supra* note 232, at § 2501. Wigmore cites several cases suggesting that some states require the prosecution to establish responsibility by a mere preponderance of the evidence. See Cutcliff v. State, 17 Ala. App. 586, 87 So. 706 (1920); Witty v. State, 69 Tex. Crim. 125, 153 S.W. 1146 (1913); People v. Nino 149 N.Y. 317, 43 N.E. 853 (1896). Only one of these, *People v. Nino,* seems actually to support such interpretation. This case was overruled by later New York authority: see People v. Egnor, 175 N.Y. 419, 67 N.E. 906 (1903).

256. See Table 11.1, Medical Certification column.

257. The Model Penal Code provides that when the defendant files notice of intent to plead insanity the court shall appoint one qualified psychiatrist to examine and report on the defendant's mental condition; the court may order the defendant committed for a period not greater than sixty days for purposes of such examination. *Model Penal Code* § 4.05.

258. See cases collected in 32 A.L.R.2d 434 (1953).

259. See In the Matter of Lutker, 274 P.2d 786 (Okla. Crim. 1954).

260. Alabama. See Weihofen, "Procedure for Determining Defendant's Mental Condition under the American Law Institute's Model Penal Code," 29 *Temp. L. Q.* 235, 240 (1956).

261. Narcotic Addiction Control Commission v. James, 293 N.Y.S.2d 531 (1968).

262. People v. Succop, 67 Cal. 2d 785, 433 P.2d 473 (1967).

263. See Comment, "Changing Standards for Compulsory Mental Examinations," 1969 *Wis. L. Rev.* 270, upon which the following discussion is based.

264. Escobedo v. Illinois, 378 U.S. 478 (1964); Miranda v. Arizona, 384 U.S. 436 (1966).

265. Miranda v. Arizona, 384 U.S. 436, 467. (Emphasis added.)

At least three recent cases[266] in the state supreme courts of Colorado, Illinois, and Minnesota have held explicitly that Fifth Amendment rights obtain in the context of compulsory mental examinations. However, all three decisions rested on particular fact situations which preclude a flat statement to the effect that any and all compulsory mental examinations violate the defendant's rights. The Minnesota *Olson* decision[267] held that in view of the absence of statutory authorization in Minnesota, the trial court could not constitutionally compel the accused to undergo an examination without his consent. It further added that the essence of statutory authorization would be to provide procedural protections to the accused, but intimated that even such a statute could not compel the accused to be a witness against himself. This dictum of the Minnesota court was made explicit in the Illinois case of *People v. Wax,*[268] which held that a defendant could properly assert his Fifth Amendment right by standing mute at a psychiatric examination. Along similar lines, the Colorado court in the *French*[269] case had held that a defendant could refuse to cooperate with psychiatrists during the period of observational hospitalization and that the trial court could not constitutionally strike the insanity plea on the basis of the defendant's refusal.

It would appear that these decisions against compulsory examination could be circumvented by statutes which respect the right against self-incrimination (e.g., by allowing the defendant to remain silent), and protect it (e.g., by giving appropriate warnings, and providing counsel at the examination and proper jury instructions at trial). The constitutionality of such statutes or orders for compulsory mental examinations would be bolstered by an already existing line of authority in opposition to the *Olson-Wax-French* decisions.[270] The thrust of

this authority is that *Escobedo* and *Miranda* refer exclusively to custodial-police interrogations and have no applicability to the setting of the psychiatric examination, the purpose of which is not to incriminate but to discover the accused's state of mind; that furthermore a defendant who raises the issue of insanity has no right to limit the inquiry he himself initiated; and that at any rate it would be anomalous for the state to be compelled to provide psychiatric service without being able to verify resulting psychiatric opinion. A lack of realism would seem to pervade these arguments. The accused is seen as equal to the state which prosecutes: discrepancies of choice in terms of legal strategy and availability of expert assistance are overlooked. Furthermore, there is a failure to perceive the range of impact and utilization of the psychiatric inquiry at the time of trial. The virtue of a decision such as *State v. Olson*[271] is its acceptance of these oft-ignored actualities. This perception argues strongly for the application of procedural protections implementing the defendant's Fifth Amendment rights at the stage of the psychiatric examination as a minimum of due process.

In the sense that the compulsory examination statutes are not operative until the defendant enters a plea of insanity, initiative to commence psychiatric inquiry lies with the defendant. This has often been considered a serious defect in the existing provisions on impartial examination.[272] Massachusetts has sought a remedy in the Briggs Law,[273] which provides for routine psychiatric examination of all defendants in cases where the possibility of capital punishment exists, or where the defendant has been previously convicted of a felony or indicted more than once for any other offense. Experts are appointed by the state's Department of Mental Diseases, and examinations are normally conducted promptly after the accused has been arrested, usually at the jail where he is being held. Kentucky has a similar provision, restricted to repeated offender cases.[274] There have been proposals to go even further than the Briggs Law "remedy": to expand

266. French v. District Court, 153 Colo. 10, 384 P.2d 268 (1963); People v. Wax, 75 Ill. App. 2d 163, 220 N.E.2d 600 (1966); State v. Olson, 274 Minn. 225, 143 N.W.2d 69 (1966).

267. State v. Olson, 274 Minn. 225, 143 N.W.2d 69 (1966).

268. 75 Ill. App. 2d 163, 220 N.E.2d 600 (1966). But note the recent statutory change in Illinois as reported in the Chicago Daily Law Bulletin, Sept. 9, 1969, at 3, col. 3: "A defendant in a criminal case who intends to plead insanity . . . must submit to an examination by experts appointed by the court at the state's request. . . . A defendant's experts may not testify in support of such defense if the defendant refuses to submit to the examination." See Ill. Ann. Stat. ch. 38, § 115-6 (Smith-Hurd Supp. 1969).

269. French v. District Court, 153 Colo. 10, 384 P.2d 268 (1963).

270. For authority contrary to *Olson-Wax-French,* see cases

listed in Comment, *supra* note 263, at 273–76. See also discussion in State v. Olson, 274 Minn. 225, 143 N.W.2d 69 (1966), where the court refers to, and disposes of, some of the authority *contra* its decision.

271. 274 Minn. 225, 143 N.W.2d 69 (1966).

272. Weihofen, "Eliminating the Battle of Experts in Criminal Insanity Cases," 48 *Mich. L. Rev.* 961, 971 (1950).

273. *Mass. Ann. Laws* ch. 123, § 100A (1965).

274. *Ky. Rev. Stat.* § 203.340 (1963).

the role of the impartial expert to "all phases (. . . the earliest and latest phases . . .) of the criminal process."[275]

Doubts may be expressed regarding the desirability of such expansion of psychiatric functions. For the trial itself, the appointment of impartial experts claims merit chiefly as a procedure which attempts to eliminate or minimize the confusion resulting from the usual "battle of partisan experts" over the insanity issue.[276] Since any physician can normally qualify as an expert,[277] both sides are invited to "shop" for an expert of the proper opinion to give testimony in evidence on the issue of criminal responsibility. However, even where the witnesses are in fact experts on mental disorders, astute counsel may completely obscure the value of their diverse opinions by clever hypothetical questioning.[278] On the other hand, when court-appointed experts essentially agree, their agreement can be minimized and their disagreement magnified by examination of counsel, while the fact of their appointment and initial unanimity may raise questions concerning their independence and impartiality. Finally, the attempt to make insanity a totally nonadversary issue, especially where insanity is the only defense offered by the defendant, faces constitutional obstacles. Where impartial examiners are appointed, each party may still present his own experts; and the denial of this right has been held unconstitutional.[279]

In sum, the movement toward expanded and more "impartial" psychiatric intervention in the criminal process is in need of clearer practical and constitutional justification. Court appointment does not assure impartiality, and may well deprive judge and jury of validly diverging opinions. Furthermore, whatever benefits are thought to be derived from expanded and nonadversary psychiatric intervention in the criminal process should be weighed against the element of compulsion inherent in this approach and the attendant possibilities of detention and incrimination without due process.

5. NONMEDICAL TESTIMONY

In virtually all states[280] the opinion of a layman about the sanity of the accused is held admissible in evidence.[281] This is the accepted common-law rule.[282] In the few excepted states it appears that lay opinion is, in fact, often admitted as a result of "finespun distinctions between what a layman may testify to and what he may not."[283] Generally, the lay witness must have had an opportunity to form an intelligent opinion on the matter. Although some states adopt a contrary rule, the great majority of states allow lay witnesses to express their opinions about the defendant's capacity to distinguish right from wrong under the M'Naghten test.[284]

6. VERDICT

Statutory specifications concerning the form and content of jury verdicts in criminal cases involving insanity are imposed in order that the court may determine the proper disposition of the defendant after verdict. A verdict of "not guilty" is insufficient where several defenses in addition to irresponsibility have been raised. If the defendant is found irresponsible, special disposition usually must be made.

The vast majority of states require that if the jury acquits the defendant on grounds of insanity, it must so state in the verdict. Some go further and require the jury to state in the verdict whether it acquits on the sole ground of insanity, and in at least eight states, the jury must also state whether

---

275. Sadoff, "Mental Illness and the Criminal Process: The Role of the Psychiatrist," 54 *A.B.A.J.* 566 (1968).

276. For example, the Federal Rules of Criminal Procedure provide that a court may order the parties to show cause why an expert witness should not be appointed and the court may request the parties to submit nominations for such expert. If one is agreed upon, a potential battle of experts is partially or totally eliminated. *Fed. R. Crim. P. 28.*

277. 2 Wharton, *Criminal Evidence* § 508 (12th ed. 1955); cases collected in 54 A.L.R. 862 (1928). The statutes covering appointments of experts rarely specify their qualifications, and in one instance where this was attempted the statute was later amended to require only "disinterested physicians," apparently because there was a scarcity of qualified persons. See *La. Rev. Stat.* § 15:268 (1950); Weihofen, *supra* note 272, at 964. Under these court-appointment statutes, just as with "partisan" experts, any physician may qualify as an expert, regardless of his particular knowledge or ignorance in the field of mental disorders.

278. For a prime example, see People v. Horton, 308 N.Y. 1, 123 N.E.2d 609 (1954).

279. State v. Lange, 168 La. 958, 123 So. 639 (1929).

280. See Weihofen, *supra* note 1, at 301–2.

281. See cases collected in 72 A.L.R. 579 (1931). For a recent case, see People v. Wax, 75 Ill. App. 2d 163, 220 N.E.2d 600 (1966).

282. Wharton, *supra* note 277, § 532 at 371.

283. Weihofen, *supra* note 1, 304–5.

284. Id. at 311. This permission is interesting since this capacity is the primary component of the M'Naghten test for responsibility. Thus courts generally permit lay witnesses to utter opinion on one of the tests the jury must apply to decide the issue, although it is not proper to ask either layman or expert directly whether the defendant was responsible, since that is an ultimate issue for the jury.

the defendant is still insane.[285] This latter requirement has been criticized as logically anomalous
since supposedly the defendant should not have
gone to trial at all if he was insane at the time of
trial. However, the requirement is defensible on the
ground that the jury is here concerned with insanity
for purposes of hospitalization and thus with a
state of mind at least theoretically distinct from that
standard which would warrant postponement of the
trial.

7. DISPOSITION OF DEFENDANT UPON ACQUITTAL

The form of the verdict often influences the nature
of the subsequent procedure. If the jury declares the
defendant not guilty by reason of insanity, but not
presently insane, then the defendant in those states
authorizing such a verdict will be set free. This is
an infrequent practice. If, as is far more common,
the jury states in its verdict simply that the defendant is not guilty by reason of insanity, then the
court in most instances must order the defendant
hospitalized, either for observation or until discharged as sane. In about one-third of the states
hospitalization following such acquittal is automatic
or mandatory. In several others commitment is conditioned on a finding of continued insanity by the
acquitting court or jury. A number of states provide that the court "may" commit after an acquittal
by reason of insanity, emphasizing the discretionary
aspect of this disposition, and four jurisdictions provide a special procedure.[286]

In some instances the statutes providing for discretionary hospitalization also provide for an examination of the defendant by the court in such a
way as it deems necessary for the proper exercise
of its discretion. In at least one state the judge
may impanel a jury to determine the defendant's
present mental condition for purposes of hospitalization.[287] By the terms of most statutes the accused
can be released unless the judge feels that public
safety would be threatened.

At common law the power of the courts to dispose of persons acquitted as insane was normally
limited to commitment to penal institutions, but
today this power is broad enough to include hos-

pitalization in mental institutions.[288] The statutes in
nearly all states specify by name the institution or
institutions to which the criminally insane or those
acquitted for insanity shall be assigned. Some statutory provisions are not specific, however, and provide only for commitment to prison, jail, or the
"custody of the sheriff."[289] This discretionary commitment power has also been exercised by an order
of confinement to the care of a relative or friends,
upon bond.

Any model procedure concerning disposition following acquittal on the grounds of insanity should
discountenance commitment to a penal facility and
should preclude mandatory commitment procedures
which fail to consider the defendant's present mental condition.[290] The proposal of the Special Committee on Mental Illness of the Association of the
Bar of the City of New York[291] might serve as such
a model. The Committee's recommendation regarding persons acquitted of crime by reason of insanity
is as follows:

> Any person acquitted of crime by reason of insanity
> must automatically and immediately be ordered ex-
> amined as to his present mental health and possible
> need for hospitalization. The procedures governing
> observation and examination of mentally ill defend-
> ants should apply. Incarceration or hospitalization for
> such purpose should not exceed 30 days, except that
> the court may extend the period to a maximum of 60
> days.
>
> If, following a hearing upon the results of such
> examination, the acquitted defendant is determined
> to be in need of hospitalization for mental illness, the
> court should commit him to the custody of the Com-

285. Id. at 363–64.

286. See Table 11.1, Dispositions columns.

287. *Idaho Code Ann.* § 19-2320 (1947). For the view that
due process does not demand a trial by jury, see Dowdell,
Petitioner, 169 Mass. 387, 47 N.E. 1033 (1897); but defendant
must have had a hearing and an opportunity to prove facts.

288. See Weihofen, *supra* note 1, at 372.

289. E.g., *N.D. Cent. Code* § 29-22-36 (1959).

290. In many of the states where commitment following acquittal by reason of insanity is automatic, the presumption is
that insanity at the time of the crime continues through the
verdict to support an order of hospitalization. It is usually held
that the defendant who is successful in establishing insanity as a
defense cannot object to the presumption of continuing insanity.
See State v. Toon, 172 La. 631, 135 So. 7 (1931). The logic of
the presumption seems indefensible on both theoretical and
practical grounds.

291. Association of the Bar of the City of New York, Special
Committee on the Study of Commitment Procedures and the
Law Relating to Incompetents, "Mental Illness, Due Process
and the Criminal Defendant," Recommendation No. 18 (1968).
For a comparably sound provision see, e.g., *Ill. Rev. Stat.* ch.
38, § 118-2(a) (1967), stating that the court and jury (unless
waived) must make a finding as to the defendant's present sanity: if found presently insane the defendant will be placed in
custody of the Department of Mental Health.

missioner of Mental Hygiene for care and treatment at an institution within the Department of Mental Hygiene under the procedures regulating other civil patients, including periodic review, notice of applications to retain the patient, jury trial review of orders authorizing retention, assistance of the Mental Health Information Service, and eligibility for transfer and release.

This proposal was scheduled to be introduced as a bill before the New York legislature in 1970.[292]

Recent legal developments in the District of Columbia with regard to mandatory commitment provisions upon acquittal by reason of insanity may be seen to exemplify the trend indicated in the New York proposal. The District of Columbia has an unequivocal mandatory or automatic commitment statute,[293] but judicial decisions have gradually construed it out of existence. The first modification of the provision came by way of the United States Supreme Court case, *Lynch v. Overholser,*[294] which held that mandatory commitment applied only to a defendant who raised the defense of insanity himself, and not to an accused who had the defense thrust upon him. This holding was subsequently amplified in the second *Rouse v. Cameron* decision[295] by the United States Court of Appeals for the District of Columbia Circuit. But the death blow to mandatory commitment was dealt by the 1968 *Bolton* case.[296] In *Bolton,* the District of Columbia Circuit Court of Appeals indicated that mandatory commitment was an ill-conceived reac-

tion to the liberality of the Durham test and added that the presumption of continuing insanity after a finding of insanity at the time of the crime was unwarranted. It rejected dispositional distinctions based on criminal indictment or method of defense as inconsistent with the equal protection principles enunciated in 1966 by the United States Supreme Court in the *Baxstrom* decision.[297] The court stated that for purposes of commitment it made no difference whether the defendant raised the issue of insanity himself or whether it was thrust upon him. In neither case could he be deprived of the type of protection offered by the 1964 Hospitalization of the Mentally Ill Act:[298] henceforth, "persons found not guilty by reason of insanity must be given a judicial hearing substantially similar to those in civil commitment proceedings."[299]

8. DISCHARGE

Orders for hospitalization uniformly provide that a defendant shall not be released until his sanity is restored, and some states further provide that the defendant shall not be released, even if presently sane, if there is any danger of relapse.[300]

In more than half the states either the court which ordered the defendant hospitalized or some other designated court is to decide the issue of restoration in a discharge proceeding.[301] Sixteen states provide for a rehearing of the hospitalization order. This hearing is in some states in lieu of, and in others in addition to, a release procedure.[302] Twelve states and the District of Columbia require notice to the prosecutor prior to either a rehearing of the hospitalization order or a discharge proceeding.[303] In several states the court may act only after hospital authorities or a commission of experts certify that a person is now recovered,[304] and in a number of other states the mental institution itself may discharge a hospitalized person without a court order.[305]

292. The present New York law regarding disposition of one acquitted by reason of insanity is *N.Y. Code Crim. Proc.* § 454 (McKinney Supp. 1969). This provision is essentially similar to *Model Penal Code* § 4.08. No finding of present insanity is required, commitment is indefinite, release is at the option of the Commissioner of Mental Hygiene, and the burden of persuasion at a court hearing on release is on the defendant.

293. *D.C. Code Ann.* § 24-301(d) (1967): "If any person tried upon an indictment or information for an offense . . . is acquitted solely on the ground that he was insane at the time of its commission, the court *shall* order such person to be confined in a hospital for the mentally ill." (Emphasis added.)

294. 369 U.S. 705 (1962).

295. Rouse v. Cameron, 387 F.2d 241 (D.C. Cir. 1967). The first Rouse v. Cameron, 373 F.2d 451 (D.C. Cir. 1966), held that the right to treatment was cognizable in habeas corpus and remanded the case to determine the facts concerning treatment. When the case came before the court the second time, the right of treatment issue was avoided, the court holding that on the basis of Lynch v. Overholser, 369 U.S. 705 (1962), the defendant was committed without due procedural protections since he had not raised the defense himself.

296. Bolton v. Harris, 395 F.2d 642 (D.C. Cir. 1968).

297. Baxstrom v. Herold, 383 U.S. 107 (1966).

298. *D.C. Code Ann.* §§ 21-501 to 21-591 (1967).

299. Bolton v. Harris, 395 F.2d 642, 651 (D.C. Cir. 1968).

300. See Table 11.1, Release from Institution columns.

301. Id. at Release from Institution columns. Only a few states specifically call for a jury trial in these proceedings. See *Colo. Rev. Stat. Ann.* § 39-8-4(4) (1963); *Tex. Code Crim. Proc.* art. 46.02(3)(a) (Supp. 1969); *Wash. Rev. Code* § 10.76.070 (Supp. 1968).

302. See Table 11.1, Rehearing columns.

303. Id. at Notice columns.

304. E.g., *Colo. Rev. Stat. Ann.* § 39-8-4(3) (1963).

305. E.g., *Kan. Stat. Ann.* § 62-1532 (Supp. 1968).

In North Carolina it is provided by statute that a person acquitted of a capital crime because of insanity may be discharged from hospitalization only by a special act of the legislature; if the crime charged was less than a capital crime, discharge may be ordered by the governor.[306] Colorado provides that when the superintendent of the hospital deems the person sufficiently recovered, he shall so inform the court which issued the hospitalization order. Thereafter the court is to notify the prosecutor and have the person transferred to the Colorado Psychopathic Hospital for a period not exceeding one month for observation and examination. Then, if the court is satisfied as to the person's sanity, it may discharge him on such condition as it sees fit.[307]

Habeas corpus proceedings may be brought as a matter of right in all but a very few states[308] for the adjudication of recovery of a person hospitalized after being acquitted as insane. If a statute gives the defendant power to initiate release proceedings himself or through friends, these statutory procedures, as well as any remedy available through appeal or writ of error, must be exhausted before habeas corpus can be sought.[309]

An adjudication on a petition for release, regardless of the form it takes, does not have a continuing force; it operates only as an adjudication of fact as of the time the petition was presented. To prevent unduly repeated requests for release,[310] several states have enacted statutes restricting the frequency of such petitions. The intervals generally range from one to two years.[311]

Today habeas corpus, in at least one jurisdiction,[312] is also available to adjudicate whether treatment is being provided for a committed criminal or civil patient. The rationale for its availability is that the justification for commitment disappears when some minimal form of treatment is not provided.[313]

Periodic judicial review for criminal patients to determine the feasibility of discharge may also be a developing trend. Such right of review is based on the equal protection principles of decisions like *Baxstrom*[314] which state that all mentally disabled patients—whether civil or criminal—should be accorded substantially the same rights. In New York, the criminal patient's right to periodic judicial review has recently been established by judicial decision.[315]

Great variety exists in the criteria for release and discharge of acquitted defendants. No rigid tests for establishing fitness for release have been set up, but the standard questions apparently are: (1) Is this person likely to repeat his offense? and (2) Is it safe to release him into society? However, liberal provisions covering probation, conditional release, and court or administrative supervision of the hospitalized person after discharge have made it possible to release from mental institutions a number of acquitted defendants who might otherwise have remained in confinement for a considerable length of time.[316] In general, it would appear that the focus for reform in this area has been on the *procedural* steps that enable these questions to be raised; i.e., emphasis has been placed on procedures which facilitate a determination of the discharge issue rather than on the criteria applied in such determination.

Procedures for rehospitalization after release or discharge are provided for by statute in a few instances. Thus in Connecticut, where the hospitalization of a person acquitted because of insanity is

306. *N.C. Gen. Stat.* § 122-86 (1963). But the person hospitalized also has a right to bring discharge proceedings by habeas corpus.

307. *Colo. Rev. Stat. Ann.* § 39-8-4(3) (1963).

308. Weihofen, *supra* note 1, at 380.

309. Ibid. But see note 312 *infra* and accompanying text.

310. Goodman, "Use and Abuse of the Writ of Habeas Corpus," 7 F.R.D. 313 (1947).

311. See Table 11.1, Rehearing columns; e.g., one year in California, two years in Indiana.

312. The District of Columbia: see Rouse v. Cameron, 373 F.2d 451 (D.C. Cir. 1966).

313. The District of Columbia procedure may be seen to be the

beginning of a new development in the law: an enforceable "right to treatment" for criminal and civil patients. For further discussion see this chapter, § III, Present Incompetency, and chaps. 5 and 10 relating to civil patients and sexual psychopaths respectively.

314. Baxstrom v. Herold, 383 U.S. 107 (1966).

315. United States *ex rel.* Schuster v. Herold, 410 F.2d 1071 (2d Cir. 1969), declaring unconstitutional the denial of periodic judicial review to criminal patients where New York law provided for such review for civil patients. The *Schuster* court quoted, and by its holding adopted, Recommendations No. 1 and 2 of the New York City Bar Association Special Committee Report, *supra* note 291, which proposed that this right be extended to criminal patients.

316. *D.C. Code Ann.* § 24-301(e) (Supp. 1959); *Kan. Stat. Ann.* § 62-1532 (1949); *Me. Rev. Stat. Ann.* tit. 27, § 120 (1954); *Md. Ann. Code* art. 59, § 8 (1957); *Mich. Comp. Laws* § 767.27 (1948); *Ohio Rev. Code Ann.* § 2945.39 (Baldwin 1958); *Pa. Stat. Ann.* tit. 50, §§ 1321(a), 1301(1) (1954); *Wis. Stat. Ann.* § 51.21(6) (1957); *Wyo. Stat. Ann.* § 25-23 (1957).

always for a definite term, the welfare commissioner must obtain a new hospitalization order after the expiration of the original term.[317] In Washington a person acquitted because of insanity and subsequently released from a mental institution may be hospitalized again on the petition of the prosecutor for a jury hearing on the question of whether the person previously discharged "has suffered a relapse or recurrence of his mental unsoundness."[318]

9. CIVIL STATUS

Connecticut provides that the court hospitalizing a person who has been acquitted by reason of insanity shall appoint "an overseer" for him.[319] The overseer is given the same powers and duties as a conservator appointed by courts of probate. In the other states the statutes covering the hospitalization orders emanating from criminal proceedings say nothing of guardianships or limitations on civil rights.

10. TRANSFER FROM PRISON TO MENTAL INSTITUTION

Though the mental disability which might cause a convicted prisoner to be transferred to a mental institution is conceptually distinct from mental disability which operates to excuse from criminal responsibility, a brief discussion of the transfer process at this point is not entirely out of place. It may be that in many cases the only distinction between mental disability as related to transfer and mental disability as related to responsibility is the time of detection or assertion of the disability. If so, the rationale of the criminal law which makes exceptions for the mentally disabled at trial should be relevant to the mentally disabled in prison. This obtains even if it is shown in a particular case that the disability did indeed not develop until after trial: those aspects of the criminal law and punishment having to do with deterrence and morality have no applicability to a mentally ill prisoner.[320]

From the foregoing discussion it would appear that the problem of mental disability developed or detected in prison is one of the prisoner's trying to assert his disability and obtain transfer to a treatment-oriented institution. As it turns out, however,

the thrust of the problem is usually the reverse: it is the prison authorities who seek to effectuate a transfer, and the prisoner who resists it. Recent New York experience regarding transfer from prison to a mental institution bears this out and will be analyzed briefly as representative of the problems and remedial trends in this area.

The leading case is *People v. Johnston* (1961).[321] The appellant, having been sentenced to hard labor at a state prison, brought habeas corpus to challenge his subsequent transfer to Dannemora State Hospital for the criminally insane. The lower court refused to inquire into the propriety of the transfer on the basis of the then-prevailing rule that "[o]nce a valid commitment [disposition] is made, the place of detention is an administrative matter not subject to court intervention."[322] The Court of Appeals disagreed, stating:

> [W]e do not feel that the courts should sanction, without question, removals in cases of alleged insane prisoners, which can conceivably be uncontrolled and arbitrary.
>
> The issue here is . . . whether the courts below may properly refuse to even inquire into the nature of his condition and the possibility that [the appellant] may be *illegally* confined with deranged persons who are liable to harm and/or adversely affect him. . . . [I]t seems quite obvious that any *further* restraint *in excess* of that permitted by the judgment or constitutional guarantees should be subject to inquiry. . . . [The prisoner] is not to be divested of all rights and unalterably abandoned and forgotten by the remainder of society.[323]

The *Johnston* decision spelled the end of administrative transfers in New York. A year after the

---

317. *Conn. Gen. Stat. Ann.* § 54-39 (Supp. 1969).

318. *Wash. Rev. Code Ann.* § 10.76.080 (1961).

319. *Conn. Gen. Stat. Ann.* § 54-37 (Supp. 1969).

320. See this chapter, § III, Present Incompetency, particularly concerning insanity subsequent to crime with respect to sentencing and execution.

321. 9 N.Y.2d 482, 174 N.E.2d 725 (1961). See also the related decisions of Baxstrom v. Herold, 383 U.S. 107 (1966) and United States v. McNeill, 294 F.2d 117 (2d Cir. 1961). In *Baxstrom,* the United States Supreme Court held that the commitment process in the case of a mentally ill prisoner whose sentence has expired must in all respects be similar to any other civil commitment. In *McNeill,* the Second Circuit Court of Appeals applied the equal protection clause to hold that an ex-convict committed civilly to a mental hospital could not be transferred to an institution for the criminally insane without a hearing, where a hearing was available to all others considered for such transfer.

322. People v. Johnston, 9 N.Y.2d 482, 174 N.E.2d 725 (1961), quoting the lower court [203 N.Y.S.2d 355 (App. Div. 1960)], which relied on People v. Shaw, 4 App. Div. 2d 817, N.Y.S.2d 750 (1957).

323. People v. Johnston, 9 N.Y.2d 482, 483, 174 N.E.2d 725, 726 (1961). (First emphasis added.)

decision the legislature amended § 383 of the Correction Law; whereas previously transfer of a state prisoner to Dannemora State Hospital could be accomplished solely on the certificate of a single doctor without a hearing or judicial review, the amended law provided for notice, examination upon court order by physicians not connected with the state prison, and opportunity for a judicial hearing. The new provisions went into effect in 1964.[324] The Association of the Bar of the City of New York in its 1968 report[325] fully endorsed the provisions, seeking only to expand prisoners' rights further by having the transfer statutes "amended to provide . . . that the assistance of Mental Health Information Service should apply to prisoners hospitalized while serving a sentence." These statutory changes and recommendations were fully implemented in 1969 when the United States Court of Appeals for the Second Circuit, relying heavily on the *Baxstrom* case,[326] held in *Schuster v. Herold* that

> before a prisoner may be transferred to a state institution for insane criminals, he must be afforded substantially the same procedural safeguards as are provided in civil commitment proceedings, including proper examination, a hearing upon notice, period-review of the need for commitment, and trial by jury.[327]

III. PRESENT INCOMPETENCY: SUSPENDING PROCEEDINGS AGAINST ACCUSED

The present mental condition of an accused may be sufficiently disabling to require postponement of criminal proceedings against him pending his recovery. There are several stages at which proceedings may be suspended: trial, sentencing, execution, and in some jurisdictions, appeal. Suspension at the trial stage is the most significant point of postponement; recent United States Supreme Court decisions have indicated that an accused is *constitu-*

tionally entitled to a determination on the issue of competency to stand trial.[328]

A. PRESENT COMPETENCY: TESTS AND RATIONALES

1. TRIAL

It is a basic tenet of the common law[329]—one which is probably included in the constitutional protection of due process[330]—that an accused may not be tried or sentenced while "insane." Two fundamental policy goals are furthered by requiring a certain level of mental competence in the defendant. First, his full assistance, or as much as he volunteers to provide, will be available in developing the "true facts" of the case. The testimony of other witnesses will constantly be checked against the defendant's own version by his counsel and discrepancies brought to the attention of the court. If he chooses, the accused may take the stand and give the court the benefit of his knowledge of what took place. Through the type of assistance which only a competent accused can provide, the probability that a correct determination will result from the trial is greatly increased. A second reason for requiring a competent defendant relates to the fundamental fairness of the trial proceedings. Only if he is mentally competent will the defendant be able to exercise effectively the rights which this society extends to persons charged with committing a crime.[331] Among these are the rights to choose and assist counsel, to act as a witness in one's own behalf, and to confront opposing witnesses. A trial at which the defendant is mentally incapable of exercising these rights is, in essence, one at which these rights do not exist. It is clear that postponement of trial because of the defendant's

324. See *N.Y. Correc. Law* § 383 (McKinney 1968); see also § 408 concerning transfer and commitment to Matteawan State Hospital.

325. Association of the Bar of the City of New York, *supra* note 291, Recommendations Nos. 1 and 2.

326. Baxstrom v. Herold, 383 U.S. 107 (1966).

327. United States *ex rel.* Schuster v. Herold, 410 F.2d 1071, 1073 (2d Cir. 1969); see especially 1083–84, where the court discusses and quotes in full Recommendations Nos. 1 and 2 of the New York City Bar Association Report.

328. Pate v. Robinson, 383 U.S. 375 (1966); Bishop v. United States, 350 U.S. 961 (1956).

329. Blackstone, *Commentaries* 24, 395 (9th ed. 1783); Annot., 3 A.L.R. 94 (1919).

330. "The trial, adjudication, sentence, or execution of a person charged with a criminal offense, while insane, is a violation of due process of law." People v. Burson, 11 Ill. 2d 360, 143 N.E.2d 239 (1957); see Brown v. People, 8 Ill. 2d 540, 134 N.E.2d 760 (1956); United States *ex rel.* Smith v. Baldi, 344 U.S. 561, 571 (1953) (Frankfurter, J., dissent); cf. Massey v. Moore, 348 U.S. 105 (1954); People v. Berling, 115 Cal. App. 2d 255, 251 P.2d 1017 (1953); Pate v. Robinson, 383 U.S. 375 (1966); Bishop v. United States, 350 U.S. 961 (1956).

331. "[M]ere physical presence without mental realization of what was going on would be of no value to the accused—the accused person must be both physically and mentally present." Note, "Ability to Stand Trial—Amnesia," 8 *Kan L. Rev.* 132, 134 (1959); cf. People v. Berling, 115 Cal. App. 2d 255, 251 P.2d 1017 (1953).

present incompetency has much to commend itself in theory. It is submitted, however, that procedural implementation often appears to contradict the theoretical goals. Possible and actual abuses of the incompetency issue will be discussed later.

The common-law test of mental competency for criminal defendants is geared very closely to the theoretical goals mentioned. An accused is eligible for trial if he is

> capable of understanding the nature and object of the proceedings going on against him; if he rightly comprehends his own condition with reference to such proceedings and can conduct his defense in a rational manner, . . . although on some other subject his mind may be deranged or unsound.[332]

The key elements of this definition, which run through most of the relevant appellate cases,[333] are the defendant's ability to comprehend his position and his ability to participate rationally in his defense.

2. SENTENCE

The test for competency to be sentenced is usually framed in much the same terms as that for competency to stand trial.[334] The accused must be able to relate to his counsel any matters relevant to his sentence. The policies which require that an accused have a substantial degree of mental competency at trial apply equally well at the pronouncement of sentence. At this stage, matters are being considered which might serve to aggravate or mitigate his punishment, matters which he must be mentally capable of refuting or urging. It has also been suggested that imposition of a sentence of a person incapable of understanding its meaning has little deterrent value and hardly serves to publicize the morality of the law. However, the validity of this suggestion relates to the accused's inability to comprehend the nature and purpose of the sentence, a state of mind presumably more similar to legal insanity than to competency to assist and participate in the trial and sentencing process.

3. EXECUTION

It is usually held that the death penalty cannot be inflicted upon a convicted defendant who is unable

to meet a mental standard similar to that for trial or sentence.[335] However, unlike the delay of trial or sentence, a stay of execution is considered by many authorities to be a matter of grace and not of right.[336] It is debatable whether the policy opposing execution of an incompetent is so "implicit in the concept of ordered liberty" as to be included within the scope of the due process clause of the Fourteenth Amendment.[337] It has been argued that denying the existence of that right would be consistent with basic fairness because the defendant's assistance is no longer required in bringing the defenses available at this stage;[338] but in effect such interpretation ignores the deterrence and morality aspects of punishment alluded to above.

4. APPEAL

A minority of jurisdictions delay an appeal of a conviction pending recovery of a defendant mentally incapable of aiding in that appeal.[339] These jurisdictions fear that possible grounds for reversal will be irretrievably lost if an appeal proceeds while a defendant is unable to render the assistance neces-

332. State v. Severns, 184 Kan. 213, 336 P.2d 447, 452 (1959). "The test is not whether he is of unsound mind or mentally ill, but whether he is rendered incompetent to make a rational defense thereby." *Ex parte* Hodges, 166 Tex. Crim. App. 433, 314 S.W.2d 581, 584 (1958).

333. See cases collected in 3 A.L.R. 94 (1919).

334. Weihofen, *supra* note 1, at 431.

335. *In re* Lang, 77 N.J.L. 207, 71 A. 47 (1908); see also cases collected in 49 A.L.R. 804 (1927).

336. "The plea at this stage is only an appeal to the humanity of the court to postpone the punishment until a recovery takes place or as a merciful dispensation." Laros v. Commonwealth, 84 Pa. 200 (1877). "A trial of the question of the insanity of a convict, suggested after the verdict and sentence, is at common law in the discretion of the judge, without an absolute right on his part to have the issue tried before a court and jury." *In re* Smith, 25 N.M. 48, 176 P. 819, 823 (1918); *accord,* Nobles v. Georgia, 168 U.S. 398 (1897); see also Weihofen, *supra* note 1, at 464; Annot., 49 A.L.R. 804 (1927).

337. Solesbee v. Balkcom, 339 U.S. 9 (1950); People v. Riley, 37 Cal. 2d 510, 235 P.2d 381 (1951); cf. Louisiana v. Resweber, 329 U.S. 459 (1947); but see Caritativo v. California, 357 U.S. 549 (1958) (Frankfurter, J., Harlan, J., separate opinions). It is clear that due process does not make any procedural demands. *Solesbee v. Balkcom, supra,* approved the governor as arbiter of preexecution sanity under a statute which did not provide for judicial review of his decision. *Caritativo v. California, supra,* upheld a statute placing the initial decision within the absolute discretion of the prison warden.

338. "After the trial is over, after the jury has heard all that the defendant may have to say in his defense, after the punishment has been legally assessed and all permissible appeals finished, no question of fair trial remains. . . . New facts, such as the issuance of a pardon, will be at least as well known to his counsel as to himself, and can be pleaded for him without his help." Guttmacher & Weihofen, *supra* note 9, at 434.

339. See, e.g., United States v. Washington, 6 U.S.C.M.A. 114, 19 C.M.R. 240 (1955); Williams v. State, 135 Tex. Crim. 585, 124 S.W.2d 990 (1938); People v. Skwirsky, 213 N.Y. 151, 107 N.E. 47 (1914).

sary to make the grounds known or effective.[340] On the other hand, it has been suggested with more cogency that because of the negligible role a defendant usually plays in the preparation and presentation of an appeal, the same concern for his mental capacity as pertains to the original trial is not justified.[341] A strong objection to delay of appeal lies in the obstacle it erects to obtaining the reversal of a clearly unjustified conviction.[342]

5. STATUTORY FORMULATIONS OF THE TESTS: CONSEQUENCES OF MISFORMULATIONS

The exact state of mind required for the postponement of criminal proceedings[343] has been variously phrased in state statutes, but few of them lay down an explicit test such as appears in proceedings to establish criminal irresponsibility. Whatever the statutory formulation of the tests of present competency, most jurisdictions have retained the common-law criteria of ability to comprehend the proceedings and ability to assist in the defense as interpretive guidelines for the statutory language.[344] However, statutory terminology turns out to be a source of confusion: the competency provisions of most states speak only in terms of "insanity," or insanity in conjunction with terms denoting other inapposite mental conditions such as idiot, lunatic, unsound mind, imbecile, mentally deranged, and so forth.[345] Field experience has shown that such language serves to obscure the more appropriate common-law criteria: determinations of an accused's competency have often been based on standards applicable to questions of criminal responsibility. In no small measure this confusion is reinforced by the common practice of ordering a single psychiatric examination to determine both competency and re-

sponsibility.[346] Both judicial and psychiatric thought have been shown to be affected. Many courts are said to be less than vigilant in cases involving the competency issue, permitting the relatively unrestricted introduction of less than pertinent expert testimony.[347]

A Michigan field study of 1960[348] is demonstrative. At the time of the study Michigan operated under a competency statute which outlined the common-law criteria for incompetency, but then went on to state, "If such person is found *insane,* [he shall be committed to the state hospital]."[349] The study postulates that the use of the term "insane" in an otherwise sound competency statute may be sufficient to lead court and psychiatrist astray. It quotes as typical a psychiatric recommendation to the court concerning an accused's fitness to stand trial:

> This man does not know right from wrong, he is incompetent, he is not able to help his counsel, he should be committed to an institution because he is insane, and should be released only when he is found to be sane.[350]

The Michigan legislature has since eliminated this source of confusion by reformulating its incompetency statute to employ only the terminology of incompetency.[351]

As indicated earlier, the statutorily created problems are often compounded by the fact that the psychiatrist is asked to determine both competency and responsibility in one examination. Sometimes the purpose of the examination remains entirely unclear to the examiner, a situation not ameliorated by the fact that he is often given no information about the accused's offense and present legal

340. "This is probably because an insane defendant is unable . . . in the event of an appeal, to confer with his counsel in reference to the argument thereof; . . . ." People v. Skwirsky, 213 N.Y. 151, 152, 107 N.E. 47 (1914).

341. Suttles v. Davis, 215 F.2d 760 (10th Cir. 1954); Note, "Appellate Proceedings Stayed during Insanity of Accused," 56 *Colum. L. Rev.* 133, 135 (1956).

342. Note, *supra* note 341, at 135.

343. A very few courts have held that even though a person is now insane he may nonetheless be tried, convicted, sentenced, or executed since he was insane even before the crime and hence does not meet the requirement, "became insane after the crime." See Walker v. State, 46 Neb. 25, 64 N.W. 357 (1895); State v. Brinyea, 5 Ala. 241 (1843).

344. Annot., 3 A.L.R. 94 (1919).

345. See Table 11.2, Insanity Subsequent to Crime, Condition Requirement columns.

346. See Matthews, *supra* note 46, at 85.

347. Guttmacher, *supra* note 10, at 97.

348. Comment, "Criminal Law—Insane Persons—Competency to Stand Trial," 59 *Mich. L. Rev.* 1078 (1961).

349. *Mich. Stat. Ann.* § 28.967 (1954). (Emphasis added.) See also the Colorado competency statute, formerly often cited as a model provision, which contains a similar defect: "The defendant is not to be considered *insane* if he has sufficient intelligence to understand the nature and object of the proceeding against him and to rightly comprehend his own condition with reference to such proceeding, and has sufficient mind to conduct his own defense in a rational and reasonable manner, although on some other subject his mind may be deranged or unsound." *Colo. Rev. Stat. Ann.* § 39-8-6(8)(a) (1963). (Emphasis added.)

350. Comment, *supra* note 348, at 1081–82.

351. *Mich. Stat. Ann.* § 28.966(11) (Supp. 1968); *Mich. Comp. Laws Ann.* § 767.27a (1968).

status.[352] In view of these several potential sources of confusion regarding competency standards, the following recommendation by the Association of the Bar of the City of New York merits serious attention:

> The Mental Hygiene Department and the judiciary should jointly develop, establish, and supply to every examining psychiatrist a uniform form of the report of the results of the examination required to be completed by the examiners and filed with the court. It should contain a reasonably detailed explanation of the legal criteria of capacity to be tried.[353]

One jurisdiction that has made a complete break with common-law standards is Pennsylvania, which stipulates that no person should be tried whose mental illness is severe enough to make it "necessary or advisable for him to be under care."[354] This break with traditional criteria is justified on grounds similar to those adduced in favor of the Durham rule.[355] It seeks to center the court's attention on the defendant's total personality instead of merely the cognitive aspects of his mind.[356] Such a test, it is also urged, will automatically remain abreast of latest psychiatric knowledge as new discoveries in the field modify the meaning of "necessary or advisable."[357]

A cautious approach to this modification of the prevailing test is suggested by two considerations. First, the mental characteristics of a person which make it "necessary or advisable" that he be hospitalized do not strictly parallel those which fundamental fairness dictates must of necessity delay the trial of an accused pending his recovery.[358] Although the common-law test has been criticized as being too narrow in isolating certain factors as determinative of competency, the Pennsylvania test may err even more in the opposite direction, shifting the focus to factors that are not relevant.[359] Second, the Pennsylvania test seems to fail to give due weight to the interest of society and the defendant in a reasonably speedy trial. The difficulties inherent in preparing a case which has long laid dormant because of the defendant's immunity from prosecution accrue to the detriment of both the prosecution and the defense.[360] Furthermore, a defendant could be confined for years without being given the opportunity to clear his record of the pending criminal charge.[361] The too-liberal granting of lengthy delays which this test might encourage is not without its social cost.

Several commentators have extended these qualifications regarding the Pennsylvania test for incompetency to the issue of incompetency in general. They suggest that the statutory obfuscation of the common law is more than a coincidence, and that in many jurisdictions the criteria for unfitness to stand trial have been deliberately expanded to a point where the competency issue has become a legal ploy used to solve difficult cases—"a means of handling situations . . . and problems for which there seems

---

352. See Matthews, *supra* note 46, at 85: "[P]sychiatrists . . . reveal profound confusion not only about the purpose of the examination but also about the content of the legal standard. Some doctors stated that they were unsure whether they were determining competency to stand trial, responsibility, or need for treatment."

353. Association of the Bar of the City of New York, *supra* note 291, Recommendation No. 9a. The proposal, at least implicitly, also deals with the problems of perfunctory examinations ("boiler-plate" reports) and examinations by unqualified experts. On these questions generally, see Matthews, *supra* note 46, chap. 3, for a description of competency examinations. See also Millard v. Cameron, 373 F.2d 468 (D.C. Cir. 1966), where the trial court was reversed in part because of its acceptance of totally inadequate psychiatric reports.

354. Commonwealth v. Cook, 390 Pa. 516, 135 A.2d 751 (1957); Commonwealth v. Bechtel, 384 Pa. 184, 120 A.2d 295 (1956); cf. Commonwealth v. Moon, 383 Pa. 18, 117 A.2d 96 (1955).

355. Ironically, Pennsylvania steadfastly adheres to M'Naghten as the test for criminal responsibility.

356. "The controlling factor is the degree or extent to which the mind has been affected. If the mind is impaired to such a degree as to require care, then the person is incompetent. Thus the cognitive aspect of the common law is enlarged to include conative and affective aspects of mental disease, and the law is brought closer to psychiatric truths." Note, "Criminal Law—Mental Competency at Time of Sentence—New Standard under Pennsylvania Mental Health Act of 1951," 29 *Temp. L.Q.* 389, 391 (1955–56).

357. "With growth of psychiatric knowledge, what is either 'necessary' or 'advisable' may change, but the test itself will remain effective from a medical standpoint." Ibid.

358. See Aponte v. State, 30 N.J. 441, 153 A.2d 665 (1959), for a discussion of the distinction between the criteria for hospitalization and the criteria for competency to stand trial.

359. One jurisdiction, at least, has recognized the accused's right to be tried if he meets the conditions of the common-law test of present sanity, even though, judged by other criteria, he should remain hospitalized. See State v. Swails, 223 La. 751, 66 So. 2d 796 (1953); Note, "Present Insanity—Right to Trial," 28 *Tul. L. Rev.* 137 (1953–54).

360. Williams v. United States, 250 F.2d 19 (D.C. Cir. 1957).

361. "The decision of the lower court in the instant case would have resulted in the imprisonment without criminal conviction of a presently sane person simply because of the likelihood of danger to society involved in his release." Note, *supra* note 359, at 139.

to be no other recourse under the law."[362] Expansion of the concept of incompetency, procedurally facilitated by the admission of loose expert testimony, has been hailed by some as producing greater rationality and humanity in the field of criminal justice.[363] But others have felt that the infusion of psychiatric theory into competency law "has been accomplished with too little consideration of the practical consequences for the defendant."[364] They see incompetency determinations being used as "instruments of preventive detention, with prosecutors and courts less concerned about whether the individual involved understands the nature of the proceedings than in detaining him until he has 'recovered.' "[365]

The suggestion of abuse in competency determinations is a serious one. A finding of incompetency to stand trial often leads to a deprivation of liberty as severe as a prison sentence while "safeguards comparable to those surrounding criminal conviction are lacking."[366] The fact that in most jurisdictions the competency issue may be raised by the court or prosecution as well as by the accused, and may be raised by them over the accused's objection,[367] creates a situation where it "may be used against persons whose offenses are sufficiently minor that they . . . would never think of raising the insanity defense, and who may not be sufficiently dangerous to warrant civil commitment."[368] The accused may be confined for a crime he did not commit, or for which he could not be convicted. The criteria used in determining incompetency,

from which confinement follows, are often unclear or not adhered to. Expert testimony is relatively unchecked and does not appear to be subject to limitations such as those imposed in determinations of criminal responsibility or need for civil commitment. Confinement is usually in institutions for the criminally insane where considerations of security and custody are paramount and rehabilitative possibilities minimal.[369] Time served in such institutions may be "dead time," not credited against a subsequent sentence.[370] Postponement of the trial often results in loss of evidence, which may well be more damaging to the defendant than to the prosecution.

An example of how an incompetency determination can work to the disadvantage of the accused is provided in *United States v. Barnes* (1959).[371] The case involved four defendants accused of a murder committed ten years prior to the indictment. Three of the accused were acquitted on the grounds that they had been denied a speedy trial as guaranteed by the Sixth Amendment. But the fourth, Coons, even though he had the same defense, was found incompetent and committed until fit to stand trial. Clearly competency law was here abused to achieve the desired end of commitment.[372] Since

362. Comment, *supra* note 348, at 1078–1100; see also Guttmacher, *supra* note 10, at 97–103; Note, "Incompetency to Stand Trial," 81 *Harv. L. Rev.* 454 (1967). See also Matthews, *supra* note 46, at 89–100, 179–92, regarding utilization of the competency issue for dispositional purposes.

363. See, e.g., Sadoff, *supra* note 275.

364. Note, *supra* note 362, at 454.

365. Goldstein, "The Mentally Disordered Offender and the Criminal Law," in *The Mentally Abnormal Offender* 188, 190 (de Reuck & Porter eds. 1968).

366. Note, *supra* note 362, at 454.

367. See this chapter, § II C, Implementation of Tests of Criminal Responsibility. It has been noted by one commentator that the competency concept in general, and the possibility of the issue being raised by parties other than the accused or his counsel specifically, made sense in the days when indigent defendants had no constitutional right to appointed counsel, but that the rule is no longer so appropriate, the historical rationale having disappeared. Note, *supra* note 362, at 467.

368. Goldstein, *supra* note 365, at 190. Several studies have pointed out that a large percentage of incompetents in institutions have committed offenses against property only.

369. See the discussion of the Ezra Pound case in Szasz, *supra* note 11, at 199–210. Szasz, among other criticisms of the proceedings, points out that it took the jury exactly three minutes to determine from the psychiatric testimony that the defendant should be confined in an institution on account of his present incompetency. Pound remained in the institution for thirteen years despite the fact that within a year after the incompetency adjudication, the hospital director testified that continued institutionalization would be of no benefit to Pound and was extremely unlikely to restore him to competency.

Isolated cases have questioned the propriety of incompetency commitments where recovery to competence appeared unlikely in view of the accused's condition: see United States v. Klein, 325 F.2d 283 (2d Cir. 1963); Miller v. Overholser, 206 F.2d 415 (D.C. Cir. 1953). Wells v. Attorney General, 201 F.2d 556 (10th Cir. 1953), even interpreted the federal power to commit an accused on grounds of incompetency as limited to cases where it was shown that the accused's recovery was a possibility. The *Wells* court's interpretation of 18 *U.S.C.A.* § 4246, however, was overruled by the United States Supreme Court in Greenwood v. United States, 350 U.S. 366 (1956).

370. Guttmacher, *supra* note 10, at 99. However, some states do credit this time. See e.g., *Ill. Ann. Stat.* ch. 38, § 104-3(c) (Supp. 1969).

371. United States v. Barnes, 175 F. Supp. 60 (S.D. Cal. 1959). The defendants were first indicted and convicted in a military court, which conviction was subsequently vacated. The present case involves a second indictment, this time in a civilian court ten years later.

372. That the controversey over the uses and abuses of the

Coons's defense was unassailable, the finding of incompetency had nothing to do with postponement of trial or protection of the accused's constitutional right to a fair trial. If the state felt that hospitalization was indicated for Coons, it should have used civil commitment procedures.

A rational application of the criteria of incompetency in the *Barnes* case would not have resulted in a finding of incompetency, because the nature of the issues precluded a need for the defendant's assistance and understanding in a trial on the merits. But *Barnes* further suggests that the possibility of abuse may persist even where the standards of incompetency are adequately formulated and reasonably applied. The factual situation in *Barnes* can be interpreted to demonstrate that deference to, and clarification of, traditionally espoused competency standards (the common-law criteria) may not in themselves be sufficient to guarantee fairness to the accused: a more drastic reevaluation of the competency principles is needed.

To meet this need, a number of fairly revolutionary proposals have been put forward. The essence of these proposals has been the attempt to avoid unnecessary hardship to the incompetent that might ensue from complete postponement of his trial. Thus the Model Penal Code advocates that the accused be given the opportunity to contest the issues which are "susceptible of fair determination prior to trial and without the personal participation of the defendant."[373] Various formulations of this principle exist,[374] all to the effect that the suspension of

proceedings against the incompetent be only partial, going only so far as the principle of due process—the basic rationale of the competency law[375]—requires. Generally, a determination of the accused's physical participation in the act with which he is charged is seen as one major issue which may be contested by preliminary motions, despite the accused's incompetency and at no prejudice to him upon subsequent trial. A few states, notably Texas, have sought to remedy existing competency law by providing that determination of competency and trial on the merits may be held at the same proceeding.[376]

The practicability of the above proposals will probably emerge as the central point of debate. Unassailable, however, is the essential principle of only partial suspension of trial in accordance with the guiding rationale of fairness to the accused. This principle is worthy of serious efforts to find its most acceptable formulation.

B. IMPLEMENTATION OF THE REQUIREMENTS OF PRESENT COMPETENCY

Technically speaking, the incompetency of the defendant is not a defense, since a finding of incompetency does not alter the ultimate criminal liability of the accused. Yet, so important is the competency of the defendant to the course of the subsequent criminal proceedings that it has inspired the crea-

---

competency procedure is not merely a debate by theorists over abstractions is shown by the large number of cases disposed of on the issue of competency. Many of our hospitals for the criminally insane have large percentages of patients found incompetent to stand trial. Until recently, approximately 50 percent of the patients at Ionia State Hospital in Michigan and 60 percent of those in Matteawan State Hospital in New York, for example, were "incompetents." The respective populations of these institutions in 1962 were 1,500 and 2,100. The situation in New York has since changed radically: the population of Matteawan has been greatly reduced over the past three years through "Operation Baxstrom" (see note 399 *infra*).

373. *Model Penal Code* § 4.06(3).

374. The Association of the Bar of the City of New York, *supra* note 291, proposes in Recommendation No. 13 that "the suspension [of trial] should not operate to disadvantage the defendant unnecessarily. Only those aspects of the proceedings requiring participation of the defendant should be postponed. Counsel should be permitted to make pre-trial motions otherwise available to the defendant and, in the circumstances, not requiring his assistance. Denial of relief should be without prejudice to renewal after defendant's recovery. There should also be provision to take and preserve essential evidence." This

recommendation, along with others proposed by the Special Committee, was introduced in substantially similar form as a "Study Bill" during the 1968 session of the New York legislature. Presently, efforts to have the recommendation enacted as law are continuing. (Personal letter from Dean Malachy Mahon, director of the Special Committee.)

The Judicial Conference of the District of Columbia Circuit, *Report of the Committee on Problems Connected with Mental Examination of the Accused in Criminal Cases, Before Trial* 57 (1965), recommended a similar approach: "*Recommendation 15.* . . . [L]egal objections that do not require the assistance or participation of the accused may be presented to and passed upon by the court after the adjudication of an accused as incompetent; the court's disposition . . . would be as final as any order of the same kind in any other criminal proceeding except that if, after restoration to competence, the accused demonstrates that the presentation of any such request was prejudiced by his inability to participate, an order adverse to the accused would be reopened by the court." See also the English case of Regina v. Roberts, 2 Q.B. 329 (1954), the Queen's Bench holding that the general issue of the accused's guilt could be tried by the defense counsel prior to the competency determination without sacrifice of the incompetency plea. Professor Foote of the University of Pennsylvania has proposed a plan similar to the *Roberts* holding; see Allen et al., *supra* note 38, at 386.

375. See Pate v. Robinson, 383 U.S. 375 (1966).

376. *Tex. Code Crim. Proc.* art. 46.02(1), (2) (1966).

tion of a set of special procedures comparable in scope to those pertaining to the defense of criminal irresponsibility. The methods of determining competency at the time of trial and at the time of pronouncing sentence are so similar that they will be treated together in the first part of this discussion. A different problem is posed by the mental condition of a prisoner condemned to death. This will be discussed separately.

In general, incompetency as a ground for postponing criminal proceedings may be raised at any stage from arraignment to execution of sentence. The issue is usually raised before the trial and most statutes deal mainly with the capacity to stand trial.

1. RAISING THE QUESTION BEFORE CONVICTION

The term "pleading" is not generally applicable to incompetency since at common law there existed no plea or formality designed to raise the question.[377] Only two states have elevated the application for inquiry into competency to the stature of requiring a "special plea."[378] In most jurisdictions capacity to stand trial may be raised in almost any manner, even orally, as long as the supporting matter is sufficient to raise a reasonable doubt about the accused's mental condition. Similarly, almost anyone can bring the question of the defendant's mental state to the attention of the court, including the prosecution, the defense, the court, or "any person." Moreover, once the issue of incompetency has been raised, the defendant cannot prevent its determination.[379] The shortcomings and possible impropriety of this procedure, now that all criminal defendants are constitutionally entitled to counsel, have already been noted.

In a few states, the application for an inquiry into the accused's competency must be accompanied by the certificate of a reputable physician.[380] Whether showing of incapacity is made by affidavits, medical certificates, or direct testimony, in all cases it must be sufficient to raise a reasonable doubt.

377. 14 *Am. Jur.* "Criminal Law" §§ 44, 51 (1938).

378. *Ga. Code Ann.* § 27-1504 (1953); *Wyo. Stat. Ann.* § 7-240(b) (1957). While the Georgia statute does not expressly require a special plea, the courts have held that it is mandatory. Danforth v. State, 75 Ga. 614, 58 Am. R. 480 (1885).

379. See Seidner v. United States, 260 F.2d 732 (D.C. Cir. 1958).

380. For example, *Colo. Rev. Stat. Ann.* § 39-8-6(4)(a) (1963); *Ohio Rev. Code Ann.* § 2945.37 (Baldwin 1964).

2. HEARING

When the issue of capacity to stand trial is raised, a determination of it must be made. Many states allow the courts the same discretion over the way the determination shall be made as was enjoyed by common-law courts.[381] In forty-two jurisdictions the determination may be made by the judge, but he is frequently authorized to employ experts or impanel juries to assist him in reaching a conclusion. Thus, in three states the court may at its discretion impanel a jury for purposes of deciding the question but in fifteen states a jury is mandatory, at least if requested by one of the parties.[382] Jury determination of the accused's competency has been criticized on the implied grounds that the issue is of preliminary, technical, or jurisdictional character and therefore "clearly an issue for judicial determination."[383] There exists some case law which may be interpreted to support this position.[384] The statutory trend has been in accordance with such cases and commentary.

Use of a panel of experts to determine the question is provided for in nine jurisdictions. In a few states the court may order the defendant hospitalized to permit observation by expert personnel.[385]

Special provisions have been designed to aid in the early detection of present incompetency among criminal defendants. The Massachusetts Briggs Law,[386] for example, requires routine expert examination of all persons charged with certain crimes. Though this law ostensibly aims at determining the accused's "criminal responsibility," the examining commission reports on both present and past mental condition; in practice, therefore, the law pertains to and focuses on the question of competency as well. Thus in the *Devereaux* case, the court stated illustratively:

381. Orfield, *supra* note 190, at 280.

382. See Table 11.2, Finding By columns.

383. Guttmacher, *supra* note 10, at 98.

384. See, e.g., Higgins v. United States, 205 F.2d 650 (9th Cir. 1953), upholding the constitutionality of 18 *U.S.C.* §§ 4244, 4246 despite failure of these provisions to provide for a jury trial. Myers v. Blalock, 214 F. Supp. 853, 855 (W.D. Va. 1963), states that there is "no federal constitutional right . . . to a jury trial" on the issue of insanity or incompetency; "in fact . . . the reverse might be thought," i.e., that a mandatory jury trial on the issue would be unconstitutional. Id. at 856. See also Annot., 142 A.L.R. 961, 997 (1943); 33 A.L.R.2d 1145 (1954); 21 *Am. Jur.* 2d "Criminal Law" § 68 (1965).

385. See Table 11.2, Finding By columns.

386. *Mass. Ann. Laws* ch. 123, § 100A (1965).

The examination is required in order that no person so indicted may be put upon his trial unless his mental condition is thereby determined to be such as to render him responsible to trial and punishment for the crime charged against him. . . .[387]

Although, as previously discussed, time requirements for raising incapacity to stand trial are usually not of critical importance, a belated "plea" may determine the tribunal before which the question is tried. Thus, in a situation where the issue was not raised until after the criminal trial had started, the court at common law could submit the issue of incompetency to the same jury trying the criminal charge.[388] The use of this common-law procedure has been held in a number of states to be an allowable exercise of the judge's discretion. On the other hand, in at least one state it has been held to constitute reversible error.[389]

If an accused who has pleaded guilty later appears to have been incompetent at the time of pleading, he may in most instances have the plea withdrawn, if such a request is made prior to conviction. Once convicted, however, few defendants manage to have the conviction upset by such an attack. The trial judge must normally satisfy himself that the defendant knows the consequences of the plea of guilty before accepting it.[390] The need for such an inquiry has, in at least one jurisdiction, been grounded on the extraordinary presumption that any person who pleads guilty to a crime is prima facie not competent.[391] The inquiry into the competency of an accused who pleads guilty may be regarded as an additional method of raising the issue of the defendant's capacity to stand trial.

3. DISPOSITION OF PERSONS INCAPABLE OF STANDING TRIAL OR BEING SENTENCED

In at least forty-two jurisdictions hospitalization is mandatory for persons adjudged incapable of standing trial or being sentenced.[392] In the remaining jurisdictions hospitalization is entirely discretionary or, in some states, conditioned upon the court's finding that release of the accused would be "dangerous" or a "menace."[393] Often statutes give the court power to hospitalize the accused in an "appropriate" institution, presumably an appropriate mental institution. However, the dispositional power is not restricted to hospitalization, and the statute of at least one state expressly gives the court authority to order the accused to "prison" or to a "hospital."[394]

The statutory phraseology providing for "mandatory" commitment and/or commitment to "appropriate" institutions has recently come under considerable attack. It has been suggested that commitment should not be automatic upon a finding of the accused's incompetency: that after a determination of unfitness to stand trial and the postponement of the trial, the court should consider disposition as a separate question.[395] The theory is that the criteria used to determine incompetency are not determinative of the defendant's need for hospitalization. It is of course a fact that in determining incompetency questions, many courts in effect do seem to apply standards akin to those of civil commitment proceedings while others appear to employ standards which call for either greater or lesser impairment of mental capacity—or no discernible standards at all; but whatever the situation in a particular court or jurisdiction, the proposal that commitment be considered as a separate question remains valid. The disposition of one adjudged unfit to stand trial should depend on explicit standards as to his need for care or treatment and the danger which his release would pose to himself and/or society—and *not* on the finding of incompetency as such.

It would be difficult to view jail as an "appropriate" facility for the commitment of a person found incompetent to stand trial. It is of course possible that an accused who is found incompetent not be

387. Commonwealth v. Devereaux, 257 Mass. 391, 396, 153 N.E. 881, 883 (1926). The merging of the issues of criminal responsibility and incompetency at the examination obtains as a practical matter in many other jurisdictions where there is no statutory provision such as the Briggs Law to authorize it. The potential and actual disadvantages of this practice have already been noted.

388. Orfield, *supra* note 190, at 280.

389. See State v. McIntosh, 136 La. 1000, 68 So. 104 (1915). For a description of the actual operation of a judicial inquiry into the capacity to stand trial, see Matthews, *supra* note 46, chap. 4.

390. Robinson v. Johnston, 50 F. Supp. 774 (N.D. Cal. 1943), aff'd, 144 F.2d 392 (6th Cir. 1944), aff'd, 324 U.S. 282 (1945); State v. Brown, 60 Wyo. 379, 151 P.2d 950 (1944).

391. Sanders v. State, 18 Tex. App. 372 (1885); but see Spero v. State, 109 Tex. Crim. 392, 5 S.W.2d 145 (1928).

392. See Table 11.2, Disposition columns.

393. Ibid.

394. *Vt. Stat. Ann.* tit. 13, § 4805 (1959). On the face of it, the Vermont statute applies to defendants acquitted by reason of insanity. But in the context of the entire Vermont criminal procedure law, the provision can be interpreted to apply to incompetents as well.

395. Note, *supra* note 362, at 462.

in need of treatment and yet be dangerous to the safety of society; in such a case custodial incarceration may be the proper disposition. But it must be recalled that in most states commitment follows automatically upon a finding of incompetency; no determination as to need of treatment or dangerousness is made. Given that fact, an accused who has not been tried and convicted cannot—in consistency with the principles of criminal justice—be placed in an institution designed by the criminal justice system for convicted offenders. Expanding on this assertion, the Special Committee of the Association of the Bar of the City of New York has proposed that an incompetent may not be committed to a mental institution for the criminally insane either.[396] On grounds that such a disposition would offend constitutional guarantees, the Committee recommends that those adjudicated as unfit to stand trial be treated in all respects as *civil* patients. Effectuation of this principle would involve both changes which may be largely semantic in character and provisions of practical import. Henceforth jurisdiction over an incompetent would lie with the Department of Mental Hygiene rather than with the Department of Corrections. Responsibility for an accused would be vested in civil agencies, including hospitals as well as outpatient clinics; placement in a security institution could occur only upon a special showing of dangerousness.[397] In addition, the incompetent patient would be afforded such protections accorded to civil patients as periodic judicial review and legal aid from the Mental Health Information Service.[398] In essence these proposals are an extension of the United States Supreme Court's holding in *Baxstrom* (1966)[399] that a men-

tally ill prisoner, upon expiration of his sentence, is entitled to the same rights, protections, and procedures as those available to any prospective civil patient in that jurisdiction. In the *Baxstrom* case, this meant that the prisoner could not be placed in a security institution by administrative decision alone, but was entitled to a judicial determination on the issue of whether he was dangerously mentally ill; furthermore, his transfer to any other mental institution could not be effected without the availability of de novo review by jury trial, a right available to all others civilly committed in New York. The thrust of the Committee's recommendations is that an individual adjudged unfit to stand trial should be entitled to nothing less.

4. RESTORATION

In many states the certificate of the superintendent of the institution in which the accused has been hospitalized, to the effect that the accused is now recovered, is sufficient to warrant his removal to penal custody for the resumption of criminal proceedings.[400] This statutory procedure, however, is not exclusive; if the superintendent refuses to act, habeas corpus is available to the accused, being expressly permitted in a number of states. Whichever way the issue of recovery comes to court, the question of capacity to stand trial ultimately rests with the court which is trying the criminal charge. At this stage the court may make the same use of experts and juries as in determining the issue for purposes of the initial order of hospitalization. A small number of jurisdictions expressly require the court to conduct a hearing and in Colorado this hearing is to be a formal jury trial.[401]

The unsatisfactory aspect of the restoration question is essentially the same as that which plagues the initial adjudication of incompetency: that is, often the wrong criteria are applied. Statutes in many jurisdictions speak of recovery of "sanity," rather than fitness to stand trial, and courts have been shown to follow such terminology literally.

396. Association of the Bar of the City of New York, *supra* note 291, Recommendations Nos. 9–12. These recommendations reflect the fundamental principle of the Committee's entire report: "a rejection of the notion that the mere fact of a criminal charge or conviction is a proper basis upon which to build unnecessary, unprofitable, and essentially unfair distinctions among the mentally ill." Id. at 1.

397. Id. at 228: "[C]linical experience raises questions concerning the need and wisdom of placing the mentally ill in special security facilities just because of their legal status."

398. These recommendations are presently being considered by the New York legislature. (Personal letter, *supra* note 374.)

399. Baxstrom v. Herold, 383 U.S. 107 (1966), held that *N.Y. Correc. Law* § 384, relating to the retention of mentally ill prisoners after expiration of their terms, was unconstitutional as applied. The equal protection principle of *Baxstrom* has been interpreted to require, and has already resulted in, the transfer of over 900 New York patients—many of whom were incompetent to stand trial—from correctional to civil institutions. The relocation of these patients has appropriately been labeled

"Operation Baxstrom." See Association of the Bar of the City of New York, *supra* note 291, Recommendations Nos. 7–8 and the appended discussion at 228. Recommendations Nos. 9–12, *supra* note 396, represent a further extension of the *Baxstrom* holding.

400. Weihofen, *supra* note 1, at 458.

401. *Colo. Rev. Stat. Ann.* § 39-8-6(5)(b) (1963); *Conn. Gen. Stat. Ann.* § 54-40 (1959); *Ore. Rev. Stat.* § 136.160(2) (1967). The Connecticut and Oregon statutes provide for a recovery hearing which shall be in all respects the same as the hearing of the first instance.

The hospitals that harbor incompetent patients almost inevitably employ criteria of release which have to do with the patient's ability to go back to the community—an inappropriate standard since what is at issue is the accused's competency to stand trial. One field study reports the case of a twenty-five-year-old male who was held as an incompetent patient for four years while hospital personnel worked toward his achieving "insight into his behavior" and, even more inappropriately, "confession of his crime."[402] Since primary responsibility to initiate the restoration procedure rests with the hospital, such misapplication of standards is a serious matter.

The resumption of criminal proceedings upon recovery of the accused is everywhere contemplated, and all but eight states have statutes covering the matter.[403] Some statutes, although quite detailed, in effect merely codify the common-law procedures. Thus, if an accused was hospitalized as incompetent after conviction but before sentencing, he is regularly sentenced forthwith upon recovery. If the accused was hospitalized because he was incapable of pleading or standing trial, he is required to plead or proceed with trial upon recovery. In other words, the entire hospitalization process is essentially a pause in criminal proceedings: when the accused recovers, proceedings will take up where they left off.

Resumption of criminal proceedings, however, is not nearly as smooth a process as the above exposition indicates. The courts in many jurisdictions have shown pronounced reluctance to consider restoration cases, reflecting perhaps the notion that the finding of incompetency represents a "final disposition" of the case.[404] The attitude of some courts may thus serve to lengthen a confinement already made unduly long by hospital criteria of "recovery." Remedial proposals or legislation have been of an indirect variety. The Special Committee of the Association of the Bar of the City of New York recommends that the court be empowered to dismiss the criminal proceedings at its discretion if the incompetent defendant has been hospitalized for a long time. Should the defendant at that time still be in need of care, the court must issue a new order committing him as a civil patient.[405] A number of state statutes employ a slightly different approach, crediting the time served in the hospital by the accused incompetent against his eventual sentence if convicted.[406]

The statutes of three states[407] provide for the parole of certain persons who may safely be released although not sufficiently recovered to stand trial. In all instances notice must first be given to the prosecutor and to the court which issued the hospitalization order, and then parole is granted only with the consent of the court. In two states the accused is paroled to the care of a public agency, which must also be notified. The agency has the responsibility for continued supervision over the person of the accused. Parole provisions have been criticized as inconsistent with the rationale behind the competency provisions. It has been persuasively argued that as a practical matter any accused found eligible for parole is certainly fit to stand trial.[408] On a theoretical level, of course, the argument is less compelling, since the criteria for parole and those for restoration to competency are not congruent.

A final note on recovery concerns the right to treatment of patients who are in mental institutions because of incompetency to stand trial. The development of this right for other types of patients has already been discussed.[409] Its extension to incompetent persons was highlighted by a recent New York case which granted $300,000 damages as part of the remedy for denial of the right to treatment.[410]

---

402. See Comment, *supra* note 348, at 1084. The same point is illustrated in Matthews, *supra* note 46, at 144–47.

403. See Table 11.2, Recovery columns.

404. See Matthews, *supra* note 46, at 147–49. The charge of judicial reluctance to consider restoration cases was often heard from hospitals in the course of field work for the ABF study, Brakel & South, "Diversion from the Criminal Process in the Rural Community," 7 *Am. Crim. L.Q.* 122 (1969).

405. Association of the Bar of the City of New York, *supra* note 291, Recommendation No. 15.

406. E.g., *Ill. Ann. Stat.* ch. 38, § 104-3(c) (Supp. 1969).

407. Kansas, Michigan and Wisconsin. See Table 11.2, Parole Provisions column.

408. Comment, *supra* note 348, at 1087.

409. Regarding persons acquitted by reason of insanity, see § II C 8, Discharge, at text accompanying notes 312 and 313; for civil patients and sexual psychopaths, respectively, see chaps. 5 and 10.

410. Whitree v. State, 56 Misc. 2d 693, 290 N.Y.S.2d 486 (Ct. Cl. 1968). The case is discussed in Comment, "Insane Persons — . . . Inmate of State Institution for the Criminally Insane May Recover Damages for Inordinate Length of Incarceration Due to Lack of Proper Psychiatric Care," 82 *Harv. L. Rev.* 1771 (1969). The plaintiff Whitree was committed to Matteawan State Hospital in 1947 as unfit to stand trial. He had been arrested for a probation violation, his probation status growing out of a suspended sentence for an assault in the third degree to which he pleaded guilty in 1946. The maximum penalty for the original offense was three years. Whitree was discharged from Matteawan on writ of habeas corpus in 1961, fourteen

There is, of course, nothing startling about extending the right of treatment to incompetency cases if this right is appropriate in cases involving civil patients, sexual psychopaths, or those acquitted because of insanity at the time of the offense. By the same token, an award for damages in an incompetency case assumes importance because of its logical applicability to other types of cases which differ only in terms of the legal status of the aggrieved patient. Thus, the facts and reasoning of the New York decision bear close scrutiny to determine the limits of this logic: Were the particular circumstances of this case so extreme as to preclude its applicability as a general precedent? Did the court consider the duty of treatment owed to an incompetent defendant—whose commitment is in theory explicitly premised on speedy recovery so that the ordinary criminal processes may proceed—to be greater than the duty owed to patients of different legal status?

The answer to these questions appears to be negative. Though the court found the hospital's treatment record to be as inadequate as any it had ever examined, the facts are not extraordinary, but on the contrary may well be fairly typical of many institutions with similarly limited physical and personnel resources, and hence typical of the experience of many patients—whatever their legal status. In addition, the criterion by which the court judged the

hospital's performance was conformity to the standards in the community.[411] It may be that the court felt that the hospital had fallen below this standard on the basis of the inadequacy of the record—as opposed to inadequacy of overall performance—though a reading of the case suggests that the court was significantly influenced by the evidence relating to the total treatment picture. At any rate, it is clear that the court's decision was based on general notions as to what constitutes adequate or inadequate care, and not on any special standards resulting from the patient's legal status of incompetency. It is thus not unreasonable to postulate that the *Whitree* case will have broad applicability and concomitantly significant impact. The prospect of large money judgments may encourage institutions to adopt better treatment practices. It may influence prosecutors to urge commitment for incompetency less often. Judges may become more reluctant to commit on this ground. It might encourage legislatures to make more adequate appropriations for mental health facilities generally,[412] whether the institutions be civil or criminal by designation, and whatever the diagnostic or legal status of their patients. At this point in time, however, all this is still speculation.[413]

5. RAISING THE ISSUE OF INCOMPETENCY AFTER CONVICTION

Conviction of an accused person who is incompetent violates due process.[414] In accordance with this fundamental principle, a defendant suffering from a mental condition, who for some reason did not have a hearing on his competency to be proceeded against, may under certain conditions obtain a determination of that issue even after his conviction. The major premise behind the availability of such postconviction remedy is that by definition a mentally incompetent defendant cannot be expected to raise the issue of his incompetency and thus his

---

years after commitment. The court held the state liable for failure to provide proper psychiatric treatment; arbitrarily choosing 1949 as the date that plaintiff would have been restored had proper treatment been provided, it estimated damages over these twelve years (1949–1961) to be $300,000, including compensation for moral and mental degradation, physical injuries, pain and suffering, and loss of earnings. The court's finding that the plaintiff had not received adequate care was based on its examination of the hospital record—"as inadequate a record as we have ever examined." 290 N.Y.S.2d at 495. Evidently the court measured the hospital's performance by criteria similar to those in medical malpractice cases, stating that the "record did not conform to the standards in the community." Ibid. The court further took note of the beatings administered to the plaintiff by guards and fellow inmates. Explaining that the hospital has no positive duty to prevent all such assaults, the court must have considered them as supporting evidence for the conclusion that the level of psychiatric care was anything but proper. These facts also balanced the equities further in favor of the plaintiff. But the most fundamental finding upon which the court rested its decision was the total lack of careful examinations: Whitree had been examined only seven times in six years, the majority of even these few examinations had been perfunctory at most, and no acceptable diagnostic evaluation was ever made of the plaintiff. From this the court concluded that adequate care was lacking: this "was the primary reason for the inordinate length of [plaintiff's] incarceration." Ibid.

411. Ibid. The question might be posed: "What community?" The community of hospital officials? Of general hospitals, psychiatric hospitals, or the medical profession at large? The judicial community? Or even the general public of New York State?

412. These possible results are suggested in Comment, *supra* note 410, at 1776–77. The efficacy of these speculations is of course also in part dependent on how states other than New York have dealt with the sovereign immunity concept. For the New York approach, see the Court of Claims Act: N.Y. Judiciary Law (McKinney 1963).

413. As yet this Whitree case has not been cited on any of its major propositions.

414. Bishop v. United States, 350 U.S. 961 (1956). See also 21 *Am. Jur.* 2d "Criminal Law" § 73 (1965); Annot., 10 A.L.R. 213 (1921); 121 A.L.R. 267 (1939).

case should not be prejudiced by his failure to do so.[415] If it is found at the postconviction hearing that the defendant was incompetent at the time of the prior proceeding, that proceeding will usually be voided and a new one be required to be initiated.

Following conviction, there are two basic methods for raising the issue of prior incompetency. One is appeal, which is a continuation of the former proceeding. The other is collateral attack, which is an independent action brought to void the conviction on the grounds that the prisoner was not competent at the time of the former proceedings.

a) Appeal

Under the prevailing view, if the question of the defendant's competency was not raised during the trial, it may not be considered on an appeal of the conviction.[416] The appellate courts of a few jurisdictions will hold a separate hearing to ascertain the defendant's mental condition if the record and the conduct of the accused create a strong suspicion of incompetency.[417]

If the possibility of present incompetency was suggested in the lower court and a hearing held, the special hearing itself, as a mere interlocutory decision, generally is not subject to review.[418] But as a component of the total trial proceedings, that hearing will come under the scrutiny of the upper court on the issue of substantial compliance with the prescribed procedure.[419] The refusal to hold a requested special hearing on the defendant's competency to stand trial may, in a given case, constitute an abuse of discretion.[420]

b) Collateral Attack Procedures Available to State Prisoners

At common law an accused could bring a writ of *error coram nobis* to challenge the validity of his conviction on the grounds that he was not mentally capable of understanding the proceedings or of making an intelligent defense.[421] This writ was not available, however, if the mental condition was known to the court or suggested at the trial.[422] Some jurisdictions have retained this means of collateral attack, at least in modified form.[423] The right to raise the question by motion for new trial has been recognized in several cases,[424] and motion in arrest of judgment may be proper in some jurisdictions.[425]

Since the common-law writ of habeas corpus has usually been interpreted as limited to questioning the *jurisdiction* of the convicting court, it has ordinarily not been considered a proper means of raising the issue of incompetency.[426] But in the unusual situation of the trial and conviction of an accused while there is outstanding an unreversed order for hospitalization in a mental institution, at least one state has indicated habeas corpus to be the proper remedy.[427] The United States Supreme Court has held habeas corpus available under other special circumstances, such as where the accused was not represented by counsel.[428] Where the accused was represented at trial, relief has been denied if evidence of incompetency was known to his attor-

415. Pate v. Robinson, 383 U.S. 375 (1966); Taylor v. United States, 282 F.2d 16 (8th Cir. 1960).

416. O'Neal v. State, 111 Ark. 42, 163 S.W. 793 (1914); People v. Schmitt, 106 Cal. 48, 39 P. 204 (1895); Weihofen, *supra* note 1, at 470.

417. E.g., Jordan v. State, 124 Tenn. 81, 135 S.W. 327 (1911); see Weihofen, *supra* note 1, at 470.

418. People v. Riley, 37 Cal. 2d 510, 235 P.2d 381 (1951); *Ex parte* Chesser, 93 Fla. 590, 112 So. 87 (1927); People v. Cornelius, 332 Ill. App. 271, 74 N.E.2d 900 (1947). *Contra, D.C. Code Ann.* § 24-301 (1951).

419. People v. Jackson, 105 Cal. App. 2d 811, 234 P.2d 261 (1951); People v. Geary, 298 Ill. 236, 131 N.E. 652 (1921). See *Pate v. Robinson*, where the defendant challenged first by way of appeal: 22 Ill. 2d 162, 174 N.E.2d 820 ,1961), *cert. denied,* 368 U.S. 995 (1962); *subsequently by way of habeas corpus:* 345 F.2d 691 (1965), 383 U.S. 375 (1966).

420. People v. Aparicio, 38 Cal. 2d 565, 241 P.2d 221 (1952); Shipp v. State, 215 Miss. 541, 61 So. 2d 329 (1952); State v. Folk, 56 N.M. 583, 247 P.2d 165 (1952).

421. Adler v. State, 35 Ark. 517, 37 Am. R. 48 (1880); Howie v. State, 121 Miss. 197, 83 So. 158 (1919); cases collected in 10 A.L.R. 213 (1921) and 121 A.L.R. 267 (1939); Orfield, *supra* note 190, at 523. *Contra,* Mitchell v. State, 179 Miss. 814, 176 So. 743 (1937).

422. Kelley v. State, 156 Ark. 188, 246 S.W. 4 (1922); People v. Walton, 10 Cal. App. 2d 413, 51 P.2d 1117 (1935); Turner v. State, 225 Ark. 146, 279 S.W.2d 818 (1955); see cases collected in 10 A.L.R. 213 (1921) and 121 A.L.R. 267 (1939).

423. E.g., Arkansas, Illinois, Indiana, Nebraska, and New York.

424. See 21 *Am. Jur.* 2d "Criminal Law" § 73 (1965).

425. Ibid.

426. See People v. Lawes, 230 N.Y. 553, 130 N.E. 890 (1920); *Ex parte* Potts, 89 Okla. Crim. 89, 205 P.2d 522 (1949); Lewis v. Tinsley, 138 Colo. 117, 330 P.2d 532 (1958); Scott, "Post-Conviction Remedies in Colorado Criminal Cases," 31 *Rocky Mt. L. Rev.* 249, 255–57 (1958–59).

427. Horace v. Gulver, 111 So. 2d 670 (Fla. Sup. Ct. 1959); Perkins v. Mayo, 92 So. 2d 641 (Fla. Sup. Ct. 1957); see also Ashley v. Pescor, 147 F.2d 318 (8th Cir. 1945).

428. Massey v. Moore, 348 U.S. 105 (1959). See also Fay v. Noia, 372 U.S. 391 (1963), for the broad applicability of habeas corpus generally.

neys or could have been discovered by them with ordinary diligence.[429] But the mere fact of representation by counsel at trial does not make the habeas corpus form of collateral attack unavailable to the defendant.[430]

Some states have enacted statutes establishing special postconviction procedures.[431] These statutes are ordinarily written in terms broad enough to allow a review of the defendant's competency to stand trial and be sentenced. Typically, these provisions expressly cover any constitutional right which may have been violated by the proceeding.[432]

The primary objections to the remedial procedures of individual states have been their inadequacy and confusion. To meet these criticisms the Commissioners of Uniform State Laws have drafted a Post-Conviction Procedure Act[433] couched in language similar to the corresponding federal procedures.[434] The federal procedures themselves, however, are not free from ambiguity or exempt from criticism.[435]

c) Collateral Attack Procedures Available to Federal Prisoners

Because of some relatively recent statutory additions to the arsenal of postconviction remedies, a defendant convicted of a federal crime now has two and possibly three other methods of raising the issue of his competency at the time of trial or sentence.

(i) Motion to vacate sentence.[436] This motion must be brought in the sentencing court and may be carried to the Court of Appeals. Under existing

law, in order to qualify for this remedy the convicted defendant must allege that (a) he was incompetent at the time of trial or sentencing; (b) this issue was not adjudicated in the prior proceeding; and (c) a certificate of probable cause has *not* been issued by the Director of the Bureau of Prisons.[437]

(ii) Petition for certification of probable cause from Director of Bureau of Prisons.[438] A Board of Examiners conducts an examination of the petitioner and submits a report to the director. If the director considers that the report indicates probable cause for believing the petitioner was incompetent at the time of trial or sentence, he may submit the certification of probable cause to the court. It must appear not only that the petitioner was probably incompetent but that his incompetency was not suggested at the former proceeding.[439]

(iii) Common-law writ of error coram nobis. In the present state of the law it is not clear whether *coram nobis* has been abolished in the federal courts and superseded by the motion to vacate sentence.[440] In any case, the latter remedy parallels *coram nobis* both in function and procedural requirements.[441]

6. DETERMINING THE COMPETENCY OF PRISONER SENTENCED TO DEATH

Since many authorities view the postponement of the execution of a condemned incompetent as a matter of grace or humanity rather than as a requirement

---

429. E.g., Morris v. State, 356 P.2d 757 (1960).

430. See, e.g., Gregori v. United States, 243 F.2d 48 (5th Cir. 1957).

431. E.g., *Ill. Rev. Stat.* ch. 38 § 122 (1967).

432. Ibid.

433. 9B *U.L.A.* 541 (1957), adopted, for example, by Arkansas in 1957.

434. "If any proposition can be stated dogmatically in this field it is this: the state courts must provide post-conviction corrective process which is at least as broad as the requirements which will be enforced by the federal courts in habeas corpus through the due process clause of the 14th Amendment. A state can call this remedy whatever it wants, but it must provide some corrective process." Conference of Chief Justices, "Report of the Special Committee on Habeas Corpus," Appendix, at 12 (June 1953).

435. Swadron, "Collateral Attack of Federal Convictions on the Ground of Mental Incompetency," 39 *Temp. L.Q.* 117 (1966).

436. 28 *U.S.C.A.* § 2255 (1950). See Floyd v. United States, 365 F.2d 368 (5th Cir. 1966).

437. Bistram v. United States, 171 F. Supp. 258 (D.N.D. 1959); Simmons v. United States, 253 F.2d 909 (8th Cir. 1958); Gregori v. United States, 243 F.2d 48 (5th Cir. 1957); Bishop v. United States, 350 U.S. 961 (1956). *Contra,* Gordon v. United States, 250 F.2d 676 (10th Cir. 1957), holding 18 *U.S.C.A.* § 4245 (1950) the sole remedy available to a prisoner declared insane after conviction whose incompetency was not raised at trial. See Note, "Insanity during Trial—Assertion after Conviction," 43 *Iowa L. Rev.* 142, 146 (1957–58).

438. 18 *U.S.C.A.* § 4245 (1950). See Nunley v. Chandler, 308 F.2d 223 (10th Cir. 1962). But see also Floyd v. United States, 365 F.2d 368 (5th Cir. 1966).

439. Bistram v. United States, 171 F. Supp. 258, 259 (D.N.D. 1959); United States v. Fooks, 132 F. Supp. 533 (D.D.C. 1955).

440. In the United States v. Jones, 147 F. Supp. 265 (D. Md. 1956), a "motion in the nature of Coram Nobis" was sufficient to gain the prisoner a hearing. See also United States v. King, 128 F. Supp. 664 (D. Wyo. 1955). Cf. United States v. Morgan, 346 U.S. 502 (1954). For further discussion suggesting the continued availability of *coram nobis* in the federal courts see Note, *supra* note 437, at 145–46.

441. The motion to vacate sentence (28 *U.S.C.A.* § 2255) is in the nature of, but much broader than, *coram nobis*. It "broadly covers all situations where the sentence is 'open to collateral attack.' As a remedy, it is intended to be as broad as habeas corpus." United States v. Hayman, 342 U.S. 205, 216–17 (1952).

of due process, it is not surprising that the states employ a wide variety of procedures in ascertaining incompetency at this stage. There seem to be virtually no minimal constitutional standards to which the means afforded must conform.[442]

The typical statute places upon the warden or other custodial official primary responsibility for notifying the court, or other authority possessing the power to stay the execution, of any apparent mental incapacity on the part of the prisoner.[443] However, most states allow the appropriate authority to grant relief if knowledge of the prisoner's condition is acquired in some other manner.[444]

Most states have chosen to vest in the trial courts this power to stay execution on grounds of incompetency. Although it is not a constitutional mandate,[445] many jurisdictions provide for a jury hearing of this issue. Others rest the ultimate decision with the judge,[446] usually affording him the assistance of a report from a mental examination of the prisoner. A number of states, however, have withdrawn this power from the courts and delegated it to other governmental authorities. The governor is the official most often given the responsibility,[447] but one state has named the Board of Pardons[448] as the final arbiter of the competency of condemned prisoners.

IV. CONCLUSIONS AND RECOMMENDATIONS

1. *It is desirable to broaden and modernize the M'Naghten test of criminal responsibility as traditionally administered by substituting the Model*

442. Solesbee v. Balkcom, 339 U.S. 9 (1950); Caritativo v. California, 357 U.S. 549 (1958); 61 *W. Va. L. Rev.* 141 (1958–59).

443. Weihofen, *supra* note 1, at 465–66.

444. Grossi v. Long, 136 Wash. 133, 238 P. 983 (1925); Lewis v. State, 155 Miss. 810, 125 So. 419 (1930); *contra,* Howell v. Kincannon, 181 Ark. 58, 24 S.W.2d 953 (1930); Caritativo v. California, 357 U.S. 549 (1958).

445. Nobles v. Georgia, 168 U.S. 398 (1897); cf. Solesbee v. Balkcom, 339 U.S. 9 (1950).

446. E.g., *Conn. Gen. Stat. Ann.* § 54-101 (Supp. 1969); *Neb. Rev. Stat.* § 29-2590 (1964); *N.M. Stat. Ann.* § 41-14-4 (1964). See also *Ariz. Crim. Code* §§ 13-1691 to 13-1694 (1956).

447. *Fla. Stat. Ann.* § 922.07 (1959); *Ga. Code Ann.* § 27-2602 (1953); *Mass. Ann. Laws* ch. 279, § 48 (1968); *N.Y. Code Crim. Proc.* § 495-a (McKinney 1958). Indiana has adopted this policy by judicial decision; see Diamond v. State, 195 Ind. 285, 144 N.E. 250 (1924). See again *Ariz. Crim. Code* §§ 13-1691 to 13-1694 (1956).

448. *N.D. Cent. Code* § 12-50-17 (1960).

Penal Code test or a substantially similar formulation.

Although it is difficult to document the point in terms of practical effects and results, the traditional M'Naghten rule appears to define too narrowly the class of persons who should be hospitalized rather than imprisoned for their criminal acts and tends to place unnecessary and unwarranted restrictions on psychiatric testimony. The Model Penal Code test, though not without imperfection, presently represents the most careful and acceptable formulation of the criteria for criminal irresponsibility. More radical proposals such as abolition of the defense of insanity are not without merit, but as they are premised on a complete reorientation of the criminal law and its dispositional institutions, this Report does not recommend their adoption at this time.

2. *It is not unreasonable to require that notice of intent to raise the issue of criminal irresponsibility be served on the prosecutor and the court at a stated time before trial. However, any statute on this matter should be worded and construed so as to give a defendant who has failed to give notice every opportunity to explain and correct the omission.*

Notice requirements should take into account the facts that many defendants are not as well equipped to make decisions and choices as existing procedural rules seem to presume, and that prosecutors generally have at their disposal a variety of means other than statutory notice by which they can anticipate the defense. Furthermore, the serious hardship which results from strict enforcement of the notice requirement against the defendant must be fully recognized. The courts should adopt a liberal view of "good cause" whereby a defendant can raise the issue of insanity despite noncompliance with the notice statute. If unprepared, the prosecution should be given time to meet the "surprise" defense.

3. *A thorough mental examination by a panel of impartial experts should be available to all persons accused of serious crime and should be mandatory for all defendants raising the issue of criminal irresponsibility, provided that the procedural protections of a criminal proceeding be made applicable to such examination.*

Availability of expensive psychiatric testimony to an accused who otherwise may lack the necessary funds removes the label "rich man's defense" from the insanity plea. An impartial panel may help to avoid the "battle of experts" by offering to the jury a presumably neutral body of psychiatric testimony. Compulsory examination of defendants raising the issue of insanity is justifiable on grounds that in such instances the state is entitled to an expert assessment of the defendant's mental condition. The risk to the defendant inherent in such an examination can to a large extent be obviated by allowing him a voice in the selection of the panel of examiners. Furthermore, the defense should always be permitted to introduce its own independent expert testimony. Application of the procedural protections of a criminal trial represents an additional safeguard: at a minimum it should include the right to presence of counsel at the examination and the right against self-incrimination, i.e., the right not to cooperate with the examiners and the exclusion at trial of involuntary confessions.

4. *Defendants acquitted by reason of insanity at the time of the offense should be examined as to present mental condition, preferably by way of a mandatory but short period of observational hospitalization. Findings of the examination shall be made relevant and analogous to civil standards of hospitalization, such as need of treatment and dangerousness to self and others.*

The defense of criminal irresponsibility becomes a mockery when those acquitted by it are automatically and indeterminately institutionalized. Once the verdict of acquittal is reached, the issue becomes present mental condition, which should be determined by criteria applicable to any other allegedly mentally ill person. Subsequent to and on the basis of the examination or period of observation, the court shall determine whether the acquitted is to go free or be hospitalized. Public fear that the criminally insane will thus be loosed upon society can be assuaged by ensuring that the procedure take public safety into consideration, as well as by emphasizing that the determination of dangerousness or need of treatment is bound to be greatly influenced (rightly or wrongly) by the acquitted person's alleged crime.

5. *Discharge of persons hospitalized after a verdict of acquittal by reason of insanity should be guided by the substantive and procedural rights and standards pertaining to civil discharge, including administrative discharge, habeas corpus, periodic judicial review of the need for continued hospitalization, and the right to treatment.*

Distinctions among the mentally disabled based on the extraneous fact of a prior criminal charge or trial have no more applicability during the discharge process than they do at the stage of hospitalization. Equal protection dictates that avenues to and criteria for release substantially similar to those obtaining for civil patients be available to people institutionalized following acquittal of a criminal charge.

6. *All persons charged with serious crimes shall be informed of the availability of an examination by impartial experts as to present mental condition to determine competency to stand trial. This issue shall be resolved by focusing on the accused's capacity to participate and assist in his defense.*

Fundamental fairness prohibits the trial of a mentally incompetent defendant: neither the purpose of the criminal law nor the defendant is well served by the trial or conviction of the latter while he is unable to understand the nature of the proceedings against him and incapable of assisting in his defense. The detection of potential incompetents is therefore a primary interest which, as balanced against other rights of the accused, is best served by informing the accused of the availability of an impartial examination. Prompt detection and diagnosis of the accused's mental condition also mean earlier treatment, enhancing the chances of recovery.

7. *The issue of competency to stand trial should be permitted to be raised during the trial as well as prior to it by the defendant or by the court.*

In view of the basic, even constitutional, principle that an accused may not be tried while incompetent, it should be permissible to raise the issue of incompetency at any time during the trial prior to the verdict. Furthermore, if during the proceedings the court doubts the defendant's present competency, it should be the court's duty to raise the issue. However, in order to preclude use of the issue as a convenient dispositional alternative and to preserve the defense's choice of strategy, the question of the defendant's competency should not be determined over his counsel's objection, when such objection is *prima facie* not unreasonable.

8. *Following a determination of incompetency to stand trial the court shall hospitalize the accused for observation. If continued hospitalization—as determined by criteria analogous to those for civil commitment—is thereupon indicated, the court shall so order. The accused so hospitalized shall have substantially the same rights as a civil patient.*

Although present incompetency is an indication of some degree of mental imbalance, a finding of incompetency to stand trial is not a determination of need for treatment or of dangerousness. The most desirable means of determining these issues is through observational hospitalization. Thus the initial disposition shall be limited to observational hospitalization. If on the basis of the observational report the court finds the accused in need of treatment or dangerous to self or others, it shall order continued hospitalization. Outpatient care may be sufficient in some cases.

A hospitalized incompetent shall have the rights of a civil patient; differential treatment of mentally disabled persons against whom a criminal charge is pending is neither medically nor legally justifiable. If anything, the incompetent patient is entitled to a higher degree of attention and protection than a civilly committed patient because the hospitalization of one incompetent to stand trial presumes and is defensible only on the prospect of speedy recovery. Moreover, the recovery of an incompetent is measured by his projected ability to participate in the postponed trial, thus by criteria which are significantly different from those involved in determining fitness to reenter life in the community. Thus restoration to competency is much more a legal question, to be determined by the judiciary, rather than to be left exclusively to hospital personnel. Consequently in the case of an incompetent, though frequent medical review is important, a right to judicial review and a right to treatment as enforced by judicial review are paramount.

9. *A finding that the accused has sufficiently recovered to stand trial shall result in an immediate return to the court for continuation of the suspended criminal proceedings.*

Field studies have shown that lengthy delays between restoration to competency and return to trial are common. Judicial or prosecutorial reluctance to pursue old cases of recovered incompetents must not be allowed to result in indefinitely pending charges; the case against the accused should be dismissed if there is no intention to prosecute. If the case is pursued, time spent in a hospital by the incompetent should be credited against an eventual sentence.

10. *The proceedings against an accused who has been found incompetent to stand trial should be suspended only to the point which the reason for suspension dictates. Those aspects of the trial which can be resolved without the understanding and assistance of the defendant, or those issues which will be dispositive of the need for any further proceeding, should be resolved without the defendant's participation.*

The principle of only partial postponement is essential in efforts to prevent the injustices that may result, incidentally or by design, to mentally disabled persons accused of crime who may not have committed or could not possibly be convicted of that crime. Though difficult to administer and to formulate acceptably, the concept of only partial suspension would permit certain issues—such as the question of the accused's physical participation in the act with which he is charged—to be contested by preliminary motions or otherwise, despite the accused's incompetency and at no prejudice to him. In the absence of practical experience with partial postponement, questions regarding its impact on the fair and efficient administration of justice must be limited to speculation and an element of vagueness in formulating the proposal is unavoidable.

11. *Statutes should take cognizance of the civil rights and property interests of persons hospitalized in connection with criminal proceedings.*

When it is anticipated that the period of hospitalization will extend over any significant length of time, the courts should initiate an inquiry into the property interests of the person being hospitalized to ascertain whether measures should be taken to protect those interests while the person is unable to protect them himself. In addition, the hospitalized person should be guaranteed the free exercise of all civil rights not inconsistent with his personal welfare, the public welfare, or the exigencies of hospital administration.

BIBLIOGRAPHY

Allen, Richard C.; Ferster, Elyce Z.; and Rubin, Jesse G. *Readings in Law and Psychiatry.* Baltimore: Johns Hopkins Press, 1968.

American Jurisprudence. San Francisco: Bancroft-Whitney Co. Rochester, N.Y.: Lawyers Co-operative Publishing Co.

"Criminal Law." 14 (1938) §§ 44, 51; 2d ser. 21 (1965) §§ 31–41, 68, 73.

American Law Reports Annotated. San Francisco: Bancroft-Whitney Co.; Rochester, N.Y.: Lawyers Co-operative Publishing Co.

"Competency of Physician or Surgeon as an Expert Witness as Affected by the Fact That He Is Not a Specialist." 54 (1928) 860.

"Competency of Testimony of Nonexperts on Questions of Sanity or Insanity in Criminal Cases." 72 (1931) 579.

"Comment Note—Mental or Emotional Condition as Diminishing Responsibility for Crime." 3d ser. 22 (1968) 1228.

"Constitutional Right to Jury Trial in Proceeding for Adjudication of Incompetency or Insanity or for Restoration." 2d ser. 33 (1954) 1145.

"Constitutionality of Statutes Relating to Determination of Plea of Insanity in Criminal Cases." 67 (1930) 1451.

"Hearing by Trial Judge." 142 (1943) 997.

"Insanity of Accused at Time of Commission of Offense, Not Raised at Trial, as Ground for Habeas Corpus or Coram Nobis after Conviction." 2d ser. 29 (1953) 703.

"Insanity Supervening after Conviction and Sentence of Death." 49 (1927) 804.

"Irresistible Impulse as an Excuse for Crime." 70 (1931) 659, 173 (1948) 391.

"Modern Status of M'Naghten 'Right-and-Wrong' Test of Criminal Responsibility." 2d Ser. 45 (1956) 1447.

"Modern Status of Rules as to Burden and Sufficiency of Proof of Mental Irresponsibility in Criminal Case." 3d ser. 17 (1968) 146.

"Remedy of One Convicted of Crime while Insane." 10 (1921) 213; 121 (1939) 267.

"Test of Present Insanity Which Will Prevent Trial for Crime or Punishment after Conviction." 3 (1919) 94.

"Validity and Construction of Statutes Providing for Psychiatric Examination of Accused to Determine Mental Condition." 2d ser. 32 (1953) 434.

American Psychiatric Association. Committee on Public Information. *Psychiatric Glossary.* 2d ed. New York: Basic Books, Inc., 1964.

Bazelon, David L. "Implications of the Durham Decision." 9 *Mental Hospitals* 3 (February 1958).

Biggs, John, Jr. *The Guilty Mind.* New York: Harcourt, Brace & Co., 1955.

Blackstone, Sir William. *Commentaries on the Laws of England.* 9th ed. by RI. Burn, LL.D., vol. 1. London: W. Strahan, T. Cadell, & D. Prince, 1783.

Brakel, Samuel J., and South, Galen R. "Diversion from the Criminal Process in the Rural Community." 7 *American Criminal Law Quarterly* 122 (Spring 1969). Reprinted as *Research Contribution No. 6.* Chicago: American Bar Foundation, 1969.

Comment, "Changing Standards for Compulsory Mental Examinations." 1969 *Wisconsin Law Review* 270.

———. "Criminal Law—Insane Persons—Competency to Stand Trial." 59 *Michigan Law Review* 1078 (1961).

———. "The Gradual Decay of the Bifurcated Trial System in California and the Emergence of Partial Insanity: 1966." 3 *California Western Law Review* 149 (1967).

———. "Insane Persons— . . . Inmate of State Institution for the Criminally Insane May Recover Damages for Inordinate Length of Incarceration due to Lack of Proper Psychiatric Care." 82 *Harvard Law Review* 1771 (1969).

———. "Proposed Revisions of the M'Naghten Rule." 4 *Catholic Lawyer* 297 (1957–58).

Conference of Chief Justices. Special Committee on Habeas Corpus. *Report.* June 1953.

Corpus Juris Secundum. Brooklyn: American Law Book Co. "Criminal Law." 23 (1940) § 924; 22 (1961) §§ 55–61, 68.

Cutler, Oley, S.J. "Insanity as a Defense in Criminal Law." 5 *Catholic Lawyer* 44 (1959).

Diamond, Bernard L. "Criminal Responsibility of the Mentally Ill." 14 *Stanford Law Review* 59 (1961).

District of Columbia. Bar Association Committee on Criminal Responsibility. "Memorandum of Dissent." 26 *Journal of the Bar Association of the District of Columbia* 316 (1959).

———. "Report." 26 *Journal of the Bar Association of the District of Columbia.* 301 (1959).

Gasch, Oliver. "Prosecution Problems under the Durham Rule." 5 *Catholic Lawyer* 5 (1959).

Glueck, Sheldon. *Law and Psychiatry.* Baltimore: Johns Hopkins Press, 1962.

———. *Mental Disorder and the Criminal Law.* Boston: Little, Brown & Co., 1925.

Goldstein, A. "The Mentally Disordered Offender and the Criminal Law." In *The Mentally Abnormal Offender,* edited by A. V. S. de Reuck and Ruth Porter for the Ciba Foundation. Boston: Little, Brown & Co., 1968.

Goldstein, Abraham S. *The Insanity Defense.* New Haven: Yale University Press, 1967.

Goodman, Louis E. "Use and Abuse of the Writ of Habeas Corpus." 7 *Federal Rules Decisions* 313 (1947).

de Grazia, Edward. "The Distinction of Being Mad." 22 *University of Chicago Law Review* 339 (1954–55).

Great Britain. Royal Commission on Capital Punishment 1949–53. *Report.* Cmd. No. 8932. London: Her Majesty's Stationery Office, 1953.

Group for the Advancement of Psychiatry. *Criminal Responsibility and Psychiatric Expert Testimony.* Report no. 26. New York: Group for the Advancement of Psychiatry, May 1954.

Guttmacher, Manfred S. "The Psychiatrist as an Expert Witness." 22 *University of Chicago Law Review* 325 (1954–55).

———. *The Role of Psychiatry in Law.* Springfield, Ill.: Charles C Thomas, 1968.

Guttmacher, Manfred S., and Weihofen, Henry. *Psychiatry and the Law.* New York: W. W. Norton & Co., 1952.

Hall, Jerome. *General Principles of Criminal Law*. 2d ed. Indianapolis: Bobbs-Merrill Co., 1960.

————. "Mental Disease and Criminal Responsibility—M'Naghten versus Durham and the American Law Institute's Tentative Draft." 33 *Indiana Law Journal* 212 (1957–58).

————. "Psychiatry and Criminal Responsibility." 65 *Yale Law Journal* (1955–56).

Hall, Jerome, and Menninger, Karl. "Psychiatry and the Law—A Dual Review." 38 *Iowa Law Review* 687 (1952–53).

Hand, Judge Learned. Extracts from letters to the editors. 22 *University of Chicago Law Review* 319 (1954–55).

Hart, H. L. A. *The Morality of the Criminal Law*. New York: Oxford University Press, 1965.

Hill, Warren. "The Psychological Realism of Thurman Arnold." 22 *University of Chicago Law Review* 377 (1955).

Judicial Conference of the District of Columbia Circuit. Committee on Problems Connected with Mental Examination of the Accused in Criminal Cases, before Trial. 1965.

Kalven, Harry, Jr., "Insanity and the Criminal Law—A Critique of Durham v. United States: Introduction." 22 *University of Chicago Law Review* 317 (1954–55).

Keedy, E. R. "Irresistible Impulse as a Defense in the Criminal Law." 100 *University of Pennsylvania Law Review* 956 (1952).

Kozol, Harry L. "The Psychopath before the Law." 44 *Massachusetts Law Quarterly* 106 (July 1959).

Lawyers' Reports Annotated. Rochester, N.Y.: Lawyers Co-operative Publishing Co.
"Insanity of Accused at the Time of the Offense, Raised for the First Time on Motion for New Trial." 1918B (1918) 1146.

Lindman, Frank T., and McIntyre, Donald M., Jr. *The Mentally Disabled and the Law*. A Report of the American Bar Foundation on the Rights of the Mentally Ill. Chicago: University of Chicago Press, 1961.

Louisell, David W., and Hazard, Geoffrey C., Jr. "Insanity as a Defense: The Bifurcated Trial." 49 *California Law Review* 805 (1961).

Matthews, Arthur R., Jr. *Mental Disability and the Criminal Law: A Field Study*. Chicago: American Bar Foundation, 1970.

Menninger, Karl. *The Crime of Punishment*. New York: Viking Press, 1968.

Millar, Robert Wyneff. "The Function of Criminal Pleadings." 12 *Journal of Criminal Law, Criminology and Police Science* 500 (1922).

Morgan, Edmund M.; Maguire, John M.; and Weinstein, Jack B. *Cases and Materials on Evidence*. 4th ed. Brooklyn: Foundation Press, 1957.

Morris, Norval. "Psychiatry and the Dangerous Criminal." 41 *Southern California Law Review* 514 (1968).

New York. Association of the Bar of the City of New York. Special Committee on the Study of Commitment Procedures and the Law Relating to Incompetency. *Report*. "Mental Illness, Due Process and the Criminal Defendant." Recommendation no. 18. New York: Fordham University Press, 1968.

————. Committee on Criminal Responsibility. *Report*. 1958.

Note, "Ability to Stand Trial—Amnesia." 8 *Kansas Law Review* 132 (1959).

————. "Appellate Proceedings Stayed during Insanity of Accused." 56 *Columbia Law Review* 133 (1956).

————. "Burden of Proof of Insanity in Criminal Cases." 15 *Maryland Law Review* 157 (1955).

————. "Criminal Law—Mental Competency at Time of Sentence—New Standard under Pennsylvania Mental Health Act." 29 *Temple Law Quarterly* 389 (1955–56).

————. "Due Process in Determination of Sanity of Condemned Prisoner—Remedial Procedures." 61 *West Virginia Law Review* 141 (1958–59).

————. "Incompetency to Stand Trial." 81 *Harvard Law Review* 454 (1967).

————. "Insanity during Trial—Assertion after Conviction." 43 *Iowa Law Review* 142 (1957–58).

————. "Partial Responsibility: Adequacy of Present Law." 43 *Cornell Law Quarterly* 283 (1957–58).

————. "Present Insanity—Right to Trial." 28 *Tulane Law Review* 137 (1953–54).

————. "Two Constitutional Problems in Proving Insanity." 48 *Northwestern University Law Review* 94 (1953–54).

Orfield, Lester Bernhardt. *Criminal Procedure from Arrest to Appeal*. New York: New York University Press, 1947.

Perkins, Rollin M. *Criminal Law*. Brooklyn: Foundation Press, 1957.

President's Commission on Crime in the District of Columbia. *Report*. Washington, D.C.: Government Printing Office, 1966.

Roche, Philip Q. "Criminality and Mental Illness—Two Faces of the Same Coin." 22 *University of Chicago Law Review* 320 (1954–55).

————. *The Criminal Mind*. New York: Farrar, Straus & Cudahy, 1958.

————. "Criminal Responsibility and Mental Disease: Medical Aspects." 26 *Tennessee Law Review* 222 (1959).

———. "A Panel, Criminal Responsibility and Mental Disease: Legal Aspects." 26 *Tennessee Law Review* 232 (1959).

Sadoff, Robert L. "Mental Illness and the Criminal Process: The Role of the Psychiatrist." 54 *American Bar Association Journal* 566 (1968).

Scott, Austin W., Jr. "Post-Conviction Remedies in Colorado Criminal Cases." 31 *Rocky Mountain Law Review* 249 (1958–59).

Simon, Rita James. *The Jury and the Defense of Insanity.* Boston: Little, Brown & Co., 1967.

Stephen, Sir James Fitz James. *A History of the Criminal Law of England.* Vol. 2. London: Macmillan & Co., 1883.

Swadron, Barry B., "Collateral Attack of Federal Convictions on the Ground of Mental Incompetency." 39 *Temple Law Quarterly* 117 (1966).

Szasz, Thomas S. "Psychiatry, Ethics, and the Criminal Law." 58 *Columbia Law Review* 183 (1958).

———. *Law, Liberty and Psychiatry.* New York: Macmillan Co., 1963.

Underhill, Harry C. *Treatise on the Law of Criminal Evidence.* 5th ed rev. by Phillip T. Herrick. Indianapolis: Bobbs-Merrill Co., 1956.

Uniform Laws Annotated. Brooklyn: Edward Thompson Co. "Uniform Post-conviction Procedure Act." Commissioners' Prefatory Note. 9B (1957) 541.

United States. *Manual for Courts-Martial.* 1951.

United States Code Annotated. St. Paul: West Publishing Co.
"Federal Rules of Criminal Procedure." 18 (1950) § 4245.
"Judiciary and Judicial Procedure." 28 (1950) § 2255.

Waelder, Robert. "Psychiatry and the Problem of Criminal Responsibility." 101 *University of Pennsylvania Law Review* 378 (1952–53).

Wechsler, Herbert. "The Criteria of Criminal Responsibility." 22 *University of Chicago Law Review* 367 (1954–55).

Weihofen, Henry. "Eliminating the Battle of Experts in Criminal Insanity Cases." 48 *Michigan Law Review* 961 (1950).

———. *Mental Disorder as a Criminal Defense.* Buffalo, N.Y.: Dennis & Co., 1954.

———. "Procedure for Determining Defendant's Mental Condition under the American Law Institute's Model Penal Code." 29 *Temple Law Quarterly* 235 (1956).

———. *The Urge to Punish.* New York: Farrar, Straus & Cudahy, 1956.

Weihofen, Henry, and Overholser, Winfred. "Mental Disorder Affecting the Degree of Crime." 56 *Yale Law Journal* 959 (1947).

Weintraub, Justice Joseph. Address to the Annual Judicial Conference, Second Judicial Circuit of the United States. 37 *Federal Rules Decisions* 365 (1964).

Wertham, Fredric. *The Show of Violence.* Garden City, N.Y.: Doubleday, Doran Co., 1949.

Wharton, Francis. *Criminal Evidence.* 12th ed. by Ronald A. Anderson. Vol. 2 Rochester, N.Y.: Lawyers Co-operative Publishing Co., 1955.

Wigmore, John Henry. *A Treatise on the Anglo-American System of Evidence in Trials at Common Law.* 3d ed. vol. 9. Boston: Little, Brown & Co., 1940.

Wootton, Barbara. *Crime and the Criminal Law.* London: Stevens and Sons, Ltd., 1963.

Zilboorg, Gregory. "Misconceptions of Legal Insanity." 9 *American Journal of Orthopsychiatry* 540 (1939).

———. "A Step toward Enlightened Justice." 22 *University of Chicago Law Review* 331 (1954–55).

CASES

Adler v. State, 35 Ark. 517, 37 Am. R. 48 (1880).

Amador Beltran v. United States, 302 F.2d 48 (1st Cir. 1962).

Anderson v. Grasberg, 247 Minn. 538, 78 N.W.2d 450 (1956).

Aponte v. State, 30 N.J. 441, 153 A.2d 665 (1959).

Ashley v. Pescor, 147 F.2d 318 (8th Cir. 1945).

Baxstrom v. Herold, 383 U.S. 107 (1966).

Bishop v. United States, 350 U.S. 961 (1956).

Bistram v. United States, 171 F. Supp. 258 (D.N.D. 1959).

Blackburn v. State, 23 Ohio 146 (1872).

Blake v. United States, 407 F.2d 908 (5th Cir. 1969).

Blocker v. United States, 274 F.2d 572 (D.C. Cir. 1959).

Blocker v. United States, 320 F.2d 800 (D.C. Cir. 1963).

Blodgett v. State, 245 S.W.2d 839 (Mo. 1952).

Bolton v. Harris, 395 F.2d 642, (D.C. Cir. 1968).

Brown v. People, 8 Ill. 2d 540, 134 N.E.2d 760 (1956).

Caritativo v. California, 357 U.S. 549 (1958).

Carter v. United States, 252 F.2d 608 (D.C. Cir. 1957).

Clark v. State, 12 Ohio 483 (1843).

Commonwealth v. Bechtel, 384 Pa. 184, 120 A.2d 295 (1956).

Commonwealth v. Chester, 337 Mass. 702, 150 N.E.2d 914 (1958).

Commonwealth v. Cook, 390 Pa. 516, 135 A.2d 751 (1957).

Commonwealth v. Devereaux, 257 Mass. 391, 153 N.E. 881 (1926).

Commonwealth v. Hollinger, 190 Pa. 155, 42 A. 548 (1899).

Commonwealth v. McHoul, 226 N.E.2d 556 (Mass. 1967).

Commonwealth v. Moon, 383 Pa. 18, 117 A.2d 96 (1955).

Commonwealth v. Mosler, 4 Pa. 264 (1846).

Commonwealth v. Rogers, 48 Mass. 500 (1844).

Commonwealth v. Scott, 14 Pa. D & C 191 (1930).

Cutcliff v. State, 17 Ala. App. 586, 87 So. 706 (1920).

Danforth v. State, 75 Ga. 614, 58 Am. R. 480 (1885).

Davis v. United States, 165 U.S. 373 (1897).

Douglas v. United States, 239 F.2d 52 (D.C. Cir. 1956).

Dowdell, Petitioner, 169 Mass. 387, 47 N.E. 1033 (1897).

Durham v. United States, 214 F.2d 862 (D.C. Cir. 1954).

Dusky v. United States, 295 F.2d 743 (8th Cir. 1961).

Escobedo v. Illinois, 378 U.S. 478 (1964).

Ex parte Chesser, 93 Fla. 590, 112 So. 87 (1927).

Ex parte Hodges, 314 S.W.2d 581 (Tex. Crim. App. 1958).

Ex parte Potts, 89 Okla. Crim. 89, 205 P.2d 522 (1949).

Fay v. Noia, 372 U.S. 391 (1963).

Feguer v. United States, 302 F.2d 214 (1962).

Ferguson v. Hoffman, 180 Kan. 139, 299 P.2d 596 (1956).

Fielding v. United States, 251 F.2d 878 (D.C. Cir. 1957).

Fisher v. United States, 328 U.S. 463 (1946).

Flowers v. State, 236 Ind. 151, 139 N.E.2d 185 (1956).

Floyd v. United States, 365 F.2d 368 (5th Cir. 1966).

Ford v. Warden, Md. House of Corrections, 218 Md. 646, 145 A.2d 773 (1958).

French v. District Court, 153 Colo. 10, 384 P.2d 268 (1963).

Gallegos v. People, 159 Colo. 379, 411 P.2d 956 (1966).

Gardner v. State, 82 Tex. Crim. 38, 198 S.W. 312 (1917).

Goforth v. United States, 269 F.2d 778 (D.C. Cir. 1959).

Greenwood v. United States, 350 U.S. 366 (1956).

Gregori v. United States, 243 F.2d 48 (5th Cir. 1957).

Grossi v. Long, 136 Wash. 133, 238 P. 983 (1925).

H. M. Advocate v. Dingwall, 5 Irvine 466 (1867).

H. M. Advocate v. Savage (1923).

Hawkins v. United States, 310 F.2d 849 (D.C. Cir. 1962).

Higgins v. United States, 205 F.2d 650 (9th Cir. 1953).

Holloway v. United States, 148 F.2d 665 (D.C. Cir.), *cert. denied,* 334 U.S. 852 (1948).

Holober v. Commonwealth, 191 Va. 826, 62 S.E.2d 816 (1951).

Hopps v. State, 31 Ill. 385, 83 Am. Dec. 231 (1863).

Horace v. Culver, 111 So. 2d 670 (Fla. Sup. Ct. 1959).

Howell v. Kincannon, 181 Ark. 58, 24 S.W.2d 953 (1930).

Howie v. State, 121 Miss. 197, 83 So. 158 (1919).

In re Lang, 77 N.J.L. 207, 71 A. 47 (1908).

In re Rosenfield, 157 F. Supp. 18 (D.D.C. 1957).

In re Smith, 25 N.M. 48, 176 P. 819 (1918).

In the Matter of Lutker, 274 P.2d 786 (Okla. Crim. 1954).

Jordan v. State, 124 Tenn. 81, 135 S.W. 327 (1911).

Kelley v. State, 156 Ark. 188, 246 S.W. 4 (1922).

Laros v. Commonwealth, 84 Pa. 200 (1877).

Leland v. Oregon, 343 U.S. 790 (1952), *aff'g* 190 Ore. 598, 227 P.2d 785 (1951).

Lewis v. State, 155 Miss. 810, 125 So. 419 (1930).

Lewis v. Tinsley, 138 Colo. 117, 330 P.2d 532 (1958).

Louisiana v. Resweber, 329 U.S. 459 (1947).

Lyles v. United States, 254 F.2d 725 (D.C. Cir. 1958).

Lynch v. Overholser, 369 U.S. 705 (1962).

McDonald v. United States, 312 F.2d 847, (D.C. Cir. 1962).

M'Naghten's Case, 10 Clark & Fin. 200, 8 Eng. Rep. 718 (1843).

Massey v. Moore, 348 U.S. 105 (1954).

Millard v. Cameron, 373 F.2d 468 (D.C. Cir. 1966).

Miller v. Overholser, 206 F.2d 415 (D.C. Cir. 1953).

Miranda v. Arizona, 384 U.S. 436 (1966).

Mitchell v. State, 179 Miss. 814, 176 So. 743 (1937).

Morris v. State, 356 P.2d 757 (1960).

Morrisette v. United States, 342 U.S. 246 (1951).

Myers v. Blalock, 214 F. Supp. 853 (W.D. Va. 1963).

Narcotic Addiction Control Commission v. James 293 N.Y.S.2d 531 (1968).

Nobles v. Georgia, 168 U.S. 398 (1897).

Nunley v. Chandler, 308 F.2d 223 (10th Cir. 1962).

O'Neal v. State, 111 Ark. 42, 163 S.W. 793 (1914).

Ortwein v. Commonwealth, 76 Pa. 414, 18 Am. R. 420 (1874).

Parsons v. State, 81 Ala. 577, 2 So. 854 (1887).

Pate v. Robinson, 22 Ill. 2d 162, 174 N.E.2d 820 (1961), *cert. denied,* 368 U.S. 995 (1962); *subsequently by way of habeas corpus:* 345 F.2d 691 (1965), 383 U.S. 375 (1966).

People v. Aparicio, 38 Cal. 2d 565, 241 P.2d 221 (1952).

People v. Berling, 115 Cal. App. 2d 255, 251 P.2d 1017 (1953).

People v. Boehm, 309 N.Y. 362, 130 N.E.2d 897 (1955).

People v. Burson, 11 Ill. 2d 360, 143 N.E.2d 239 (1957).

People v. Colavecchio, 11 App. Div. 2d 161, 202 N.Y.S.2d 119 (1960).

People v. Conley, 64 Cal. 2d 310, 411 P.2d 911 (1966).

People v. Cornelius, 332 Ill. App. 271, 74 N.E.2d 900 (1947).

People v. Egnor, 175 N.Y. 419, 67 N.E. 906 (1903).

People v. Geary, 298 Ill. 236, 131 N.E. 652 (1921).

People v. Gorshen, 51 Cal. 2d 716, 336 P.2d 492 (1959).

People v. Harris, 29 Cal. 678 (1866).

People v. Horton, 308 N.Y. 1, 123 N.E.2d 609 (1954).

People v. Jackson, 105 Cal. App. 2d 811, 234 P.2d 261 (1951).

People v. Johnston, 9 N.Y.2d 482, 174 N.E.2d 725 (1961).

People v. Krugman, 141 N.W.2d 33 (1966).

People v. Lawes, 230 N.Y. 553, 130 N.E. 890 (1920).

People v. Moseley, 20 N.Y.2d 64, 281 N.Y.S.2d 762, 228 N.E.2d 765 (1967).

People v. Nash, 52 Cal. 2d 36, 338 P.2d 416 (1959).

People v. Nino, 149 N.Y. 317, 43 N.E. 853 (1896).

People v. Riley, 37 Cal. 2d 510, 235 P.2d 381 (1951).

People v. Schmidt, 216 N.Y. 324, 110 N.E. 945 (1915).

People v. Schmitt, 106 Cal. 48, 39 P. 204 (1895).

People v. Shaw, 164 N.Y.S.2d 750 (App. Div. 1957).

People v. Skwirsky, 213 N.Y. 151, 107 N.E. 47 (1914).

People v. Succop, 67 Cal. 2d 785, 433 P.2d 473 (1967).

People v. Walker, 33 Cal. 2d 250, 201 P.2d 6 (1948).

People v. Walton, 10 Cal. App. 2d 413, 51 P.2d 1117 (1935).

People v. Wax, 75 Ill. App. 2d 163, 220 N.E.2d 600 (1966).

People v. Wells, 33 Cal. 2d 330, 202 P.2d 53 (1949).

Perkins v. Mayo, 92 So. 2d 641 (Fla. Sup. Ct. 1957).

Pope v. United States, 372 F.2d 710 (1967).

Powell v. Texas, 392 U.S. 514 (1968).

Putnam v. People, 408 Ill. 582, 97 N.E.2d 841 (1951).

Ramer v. United States 390 F.2d 564 (9th Cir. 1968).

Regina v. Roberts, 2 Q.B. 329 (1954).

Robinson v. Johnston, 50 F. Supp. 774 (N.D. Cal. 1943), *aff'd,* 144 F.2d 392 (6th Cir. 1944), *aff'd,* 324 U.S. 282 (1945).

Rouse v. Cameron, 373 F. 2d 451 (D.C. Cir. 1966).

Rouse v. Cameron, 387 F.2d 241 (D.C. Cir. 1967).

Sanders v. State, 18 Tex. App. 372 (1885).

Schwickrath v. People, 159 Colo. 390, 411 P.2d 961 (1966).

Seidner v. United States, 260 F.2d 732 (D.C. Cir. 1958).

Shipp v. State, 215 Miss. 541, 61 So. 2d 329 (1952).

Simmons v. United States, 253 F.2d 909 (8th Cir. 1958).

Sinclair v. State, 161 Miss. 142, 132 So. 581 (1931).

Solesbee v. Balkcom, 339 U.S. 9 (1950).

Sollars v. State, 73 Nev. 248, 316 P.2d 917 (1957).

Spero v. State, 109 Tex. Crim. 392, 5 S.W.2d 145 (1928).

State v. Barton, 361 Mo. 780, 236 S.W.2d 596 (1951).

State v. Brinyea, 5 Ala. 241 (1843).

State v. Brown, 60 Wyo. 379, 151 P.2d 950 (1944).

State v. D'Haemers, 276 Minn. 332, 150 N.W.2d 66 (1967).

State v. Di Paolo, 34 N.J. 279, 168 A.2d 401 (1960).

State v. Dowdy, 217 La. 773, 47 So. 2d 496 (1950).

State v. Felter, 25 Iowa 67 (1868).

State v. Finn, 257 Minn. 138, 100 N.W.2d 508 (1960).

State v. Folk, 56 N.M. 583, 247 P.2d 165 (1952).

State v. Gunter, 208 La. 694, 23 So. 2d 305 (1954).

State v. Holloway, 156 Mo. 222, 56 S.W. 734 (1900).

State v. Jones, 50 N.H. 369, 9 Am. R. 242 (1871).

State v. Kotovsky, 11 Mo. App. 584, *aff'd,* 74 Mo. 247 (1882).

State v. Lange, 168 La. 958, 123 So. 639 (1929).

State v. Lucas, 30 N.J. 37, 152 A.2d 50 (1959).

State v. McIntosh, 136 La. 1000, 68 So. 104 (1915).

State v. Messer, 194 La. 238, 193 So. 633 (1940).

State v. Noel, 102 N.J.L. 659, 133 A. 274 (1926).

State v. Olson, 274 Minn. 225, 143 N.W.2d 69 (1966).

State v. Pike, 49 N.H. 399, 6 Am. R. 533 (1869).

State v. Rodriguez, 25 Conn. Supp. 350, 204 A.2d 37 (1964).

State v. Schantz, 98 Ariz. 200, 403 P.2d 521 (1965).

State v. Severns, 184 Kan. 213, 336 P.2d 447 (1959).

State v. Shoffner, 31 Wis. 2d 412, 143 N.W.2d 458 (1966).

State v. Strasberg, 60 Wash. 106, 110 P. 1020 (1910).

State v. Swails, 223 La. 751, 66 So. 2d 796 (1953).

State v. Thompson, Wright's Ohio Rep. 617 (1834).

State v. Toon, 172 La. 631, 135 So. 7 (1931).

State v. Van Vlack, 57 Idaho 316, 65 P.2d 736 (1937).

Suttles v. Davis, 215 F.2d 760 (10th Cir. 1954).

Swain v. State, 215 Ind. 259, 18 N.E.2d 921 (1939).

Tatum v. United States, 190 F.2d 612 (D.C. Cir. 1951).

Taylor v. United States, 282 F.2d 16 (8th Cir. 1960).

Terry v. Commonwealth, 371 S.W.2d 862 (Ky. 1963).

Thomas v. State, 206 Md. 575, 112 A.2d 913 (1955).

Torske v. State, 123 Neb. 161, 242 N.W. 408 (1932).

Turner v. State, 225 Ark. 146, 279 S.W.2d 818 (1955).

United States *ex rel.* Schuster v. Herold. 410 F.2d 1071 (2d Cir. 1969).

United States *ex rel.* Smith v. Baldi, 344 U.S. 561 (1953).

United States v. Barnes, 175 F. Supp. 60 (S.D. Cal. 1959).

United States v. Chandler, 393 F.2d 920 (4th Cir. 1968).

United States v. Currens, 290 F.2d 751 (3d Cir. 1961).

United States v. Fooks, 132 F. Supp. 533 (D.D.C. 1955).

United States v. Freeman, 357 F.2d 606 (2d Cir. 1966).

United States v. Hayman, 342 U.S. 205 (1952).

United States v. Jones, 147 F. Supp. 265 (D. Md. 1956).

United States v. King, 128 F. Supp. 664 (D. Wyo. 1955).

United States v. Klein, 325 F.2d 283 (2d Cir. 1963).

United States v. Lee, 4 Machey 489 (D.C. Cir. 1886).

United States v. McNeill, 294 F.2d 117 (2d Cir. 1961).

United States v. Morgan, 346 U.S. 502 (1954).

United States v. Shapiro, 383 F.2d 680 (7th Cir. 1967).

United States v. Smith, 5 U.S.M.C.A. 314, 17 C.M.R. 314 (1954).

United States v. Smith, 404 F.2d 720 (6th Cir. 1968).

United States v. Washington, 6 U.S.M.C.A. 114, 19 C.M.R. 240 (1955).

Virgin Islands v. Smith, 278 F.2d 169 (1960).

Walker v. State, 46 Neb. 25, 64 N.W. 357 (1895).

Washington v. United States, 390 F.2d 444 (D.C. Cir. 1967).

Wells v. Attorney General, 201 F.2d 556 (10th Cir. 1953).

Whitree v. State, 56 Misc. 2d 693, 290 N.Y.S.2d 486 (Ct. Cl. 1968).

Williams v. State, 135 Tex. Crim. 585, 124 S.W.2d 990 (1938).

Williams v. United States, 250 F.2d 19 (D.C. Cir. 1957).

Wion v. United States, 325 F.2d 420 (10th Cir. 1963).

Witty v. State, 69 Tex. Crim. 125, 153 S.W. 1146 (1913).

Wright v. United States, 250 F.2d 4 (D.C. Cir. 1957).

Table 11.1   INSANITY AS A DEFENSE TO CRIME

STATE	TIME OF PLEADING			MEDICAL CERTIFICATION	FINDING BY			DEFINITION OF INSANITY	DISPOSITION			REHEARING		RELEASE FROM INSTITUTION			NOTICE TO		HEARING BEFORE RELEASE	CIVIL RIGHTS	OTHER PROVISIONS
	At Arraignment	At Trial	With Court Permission		Court	Jury	Other		Commitment Mandatory	Discretionary	Other	Right to	Frequency	On Probation	Administrative	Judicial	Prosecutor	Other			
DRAFT ACT	Does not specifically deal with the criminally insane. See "The Scope of the Draft Act," The Mentally Ill, page 111, in Appendix A of this volume																				
ALA. Code (1958)	raise only by special plea. 15, §423			commission of lunacy composed of institution superintendent and 2 medical staff members shall examine and report to court; only applicable to capital cases. 15, §425		special verdict. 15, §424			only if judge, after careful inquiry determining the person's insanity, continues. 15, §429												
ALAS. Stat. (1962)						12.45.090			if court considers his being at large dangerous to the public peace or safety. 12.45.090						when he becomes sane. 12.45.090	by authority of law. 12.45.090					
ARIZ. Rev. Stat. Ann. (1956)		no later than 4 days prior to trial; notice of intention to the prosecutor. R. Crim. P. 192(A)	when two trials are used to decide question of guilt and, second, sanity. 13-162.01 (Supp. 1970) / if "good cause" shown for failure to file and serve notice. R. Crim. P. 192(A)			special verdict R. Crim. P. 288					if jury verdict specifically finds defendant was insane when criminal act committed, court shall direct petition to be filed as a mentally ill person in accordance with 36-502. R. Crim. P. 288										
ARK. Stat. Ann. (1964)	43-1301 43-1304 43-1305	judge may declare mistrial. 43-1301 43-1304		commitment to and observation and examination of person in, state hospital. 43-1301 43-1304 43-1305		special verdict 43-2135															

430

Table 11.1   INSANITY AS A DEFENSE TO CRIME   continued

STATE	At Arraignment	At Trial	With Court Permission	MEDICAL CERTIFICATION	Court	Jury	Other	DEFINITION OF INSANITY	Commitment Mandatory	Discretionary	Other	Right to	Frequency	On Probation	Administrative	Judicial	Prosecutor	Other	HEARING BEFORE RELEASE	CIVIL RIGHTS	OTHER PROVISIONS
CAL. Penal Code (West 1956)		trial without regard to insanity defense first; if found guilty, then trial on issue of insanity. 1026		must be examined by 2 or 3 court-appointed psychiatrists, who may be called to testify by either party. 1027		fn. 1 1026			unless court finds defendant has fully recovered his sanity. 1026			by person committed or superintendent of hospital; only manner of release from hospital. 1026; and in Supp. 1968, 1026a	no application for 90 days after commitment order; if adverse court ruling, no application for 1 year. 1026; and in Supp. 1968, 1026a		on petition of superintendent of hospital. 1026a (Supp. 1968)		for rehearing 1026		1026		
COLO. Rev. Stat. Ann. (1964)	39-8-1 (Supp. 1965)	fn. 2 39-8-1 (Supp. 1965)	prior to trial. 39-8-1 (Supp. 1965)	commitment for observation; physicians and specializing in mental diseases may use polygraph and sodium pentathol as evidence on which to base their opinion. 39-8-2 (Supp. 1965)	if agreed by all parties and court. 39-8-3(1) (Supp. 1965)	upon issue of insanity only. 39-8-1(3)(a) (Supp. 1967) 39-8-3(1) (Supp. 1965) 39-8-4 (Supp. 1965)		fn. 3 39-8-1 (2) (Supp. 1965)	39-8-4(2)(a) (Supp. 1965)							fn. 4 39-8-4(3) to 39-8-4(6) (Supp. 1965)	39-8-4(3) (Supp. 1965)		none if judge agrees after observation & medical reports; if judge disagrees, hearing is held, & issue of person no longer being insane is put to a normal jury. 39-8-4(3) to 39-8-4(6) (Supp. 1965)		
CONN. Gen. Stat. Ann. (1958)									fn. 5 to state hospital or to a person who requests custody and gives a bond; appoint overseer if any property. 54-37 (Supp. 1969)			54-38 (Supp. 1969)				54-38 (Supp. 1969)	to town selectmen and to person, if any, upon whom offense was committed. 54-38 (Supp. 1969)		54-38 (Supp. 1969)		
DEL. Code Ann. (1953)		11, §4701				11, §4701				court may commit on motion of attorney general or court may set at large if satisfied public safety will not be endangered thereby. 11, §4702 (a), 11, §4702 (c) (Supp. 1970)					11, §4702 (c) (Supp. 1970)					

431

Table 11.1 INSANITY AS A DEFENSE TO CRIME continued

STATE	TIME OF PLEADING			MEDICAL CERTIFICATION	FINDING BY			DEFINITION OF INSANITY	DISPOSITION			REHEARING		RELEASE FROM INSTITUTION			NOTICE TO		HEARING BEFORE RELEASE	CIVIL RIGHTS	OTHER PROVISIONS
	At Arraignment	At Trial	With Court Permission		Court	Jury	Other		Commitment Mandatory	Discretionary	Other	Right to	Frequency	On Probation	Administrative	Judicial	Prosecutor	Other			
D.C. Code Ann. (1967)						24-301(c)						habeas corpus 24-301(g)		conditional release is by court on filing of certificate by hospital superintendent. 24-301(e)		in both conditional and unconditional releases, after filing of proper certificate by hospital superintendent. 24-301(e)	24-301(e)		in both conditional and unconditional releases, court may hold hearing; it must hold one if prosecutor objects. 24-301(e)		
FLA. Stat. Ann. (1967)	R. Crim. P. 1.210(b)		R. Crim. P. 1.210(b)	court may cause defendant to be examined. R. Crim. P. 1.210(b)		special verdict. R. Crim. P. 1.460				discharged unless court considers person's going at large manifestly dangerous to peace and safety. R. Crim. P. 1.460											
GA. Code Ann. (1953)	when special plea is made at arraignment, duty of court to first cause issue to be tried by a special jury, and if found insane, commit to state hospital until discharged by law; this procedure differs from procedures depicted on remainder of table. 27-1502	if defendant contends at the trial that he was insane at time he committed act, court must charge jury to so specify in their verdict should they acquit defendant on this ground. 27-1503				special verdict. 27-1503		"A person shall be considered of sound mind who is neither an idiot, a lunatic, nor afflicted with insanity, and who had arrived at the age of 14 years, or before that age if such person knows the distinction between good and evil." 26-301 26-303	committed until release would be proper in a civil commitment. 27-1503 but this may be ineffectual for continued detention. 195 Ga. 368						27-1503; but see 195 Ga. 308						
HAWAII Rev. Stat. Ann. (1968)	711-91, 711-92	711-93		court may require examination by the state psychiatrist and 2 physicians. 711-91	if court deems medical report conclusive of insanity. 711-91	special verdict 711-93				must commit unless defendant presents due proof of regained sanity. 711-94						711-94					
IDAHO Code Ann. (1947)						fn. 6 19-2320			fn. 6 if still insane. 19-2320												

Table 11.1 INSANITY AS A DEFENSE TO CRIME *continued*

STATE	TIME OF PLEADING			MEDICAL CERTIFI-CATION	FINDING BY			DEFINITION OF INSANITY	DISPOSITION			REHEARING		RELEASE FROM INSTITUTION			NOTICE TO		HEARING BEFORE RELEASE	CIVIL RIGHTS	OTHER PRO-VISIONS
	At Arraign-ment	At Trial	With Court Permission		Court	Jury	Other		Commitment Mandatory	Discre-tionary	Other	Right to	Frequency	On Probation	Admini-strative	Judicial	Prose-cutor	Other			
ILL. Ann. Stat. (Smith-Hurd 1964)		affirma-tive de-fense. 38, §6-4			if trial by court. 38, §115-3 (b) (Supp. 1969)	jury must give ver-dict on both: (1) insane or not at time of commit-ting act; (2) whether or not such person has entirely and perman-ently re-covered. 38, §115-4 (j), 38, §118-2 (a) (Supp. 1969)		fn. 7 38, §6-2	if jury finds per-son entirely and per-manently recovered, court shall dis-charge otherwise commitment is manda-tory. 38, §118-2 (a) (Supp. 1969)			habeas corpus 38, §118-2 (c) (Supp. 1969)				as in civil commitment. 38, §118-2 (a) (Supp. 1967) 98½, §8-12 (Supp. 1969)			38, §118-2 (a) (Supp. 1969) 91½, §8-12 (Supp. 1969)		
IND. Ann. Stat. (1956)		estab1ish defense specially in writing. 9-1701		2 or 3 physicians 9-1702	if no jury 9-1703	special findings. 9-1703			court must make spe-cial findings: if still insane, or sane at time of trial but high prob-ability of recurrence, mandatory commitment. 9-1704(a) (Supp. 1969)			9-1705 (Supp. 1969)	must wait 2 years after com-mitment; if adverse ruling, no applica-tion to court for 2 years. 9-1705 (Supp. 1969)			9-1705 (Supp. 1969)					
IOWA Code Ann. (1950)	777.18					special verdict 785.19 (Supp. 1969)				may commit if dis-charge is dangerous to public peace and safety. 785.19 (Supp. 1969)					when de-fendant demon-strates good men-tal health 785.19 (Supp. 1969)						
KAN. Stat. Ann. (1964) (Supp. 1968)		62-1532				62-1532			62-1532					"Any patient committed under the terms of this section may be granted convalescent leave or dis-charged as an involuntary patient. . . ." 62-1532			62-1532	sheriff 62-1532			
KY. Rev. Stat. Ann. (1969)		9.90(1)				9.90(1)			if jury impaneled for this purpose finds de-fendant insane at time ver-dict ren-dered. 9.90(2)							"confined . .. until his mind is restored. 9.90(2)					

433

Table 11.1 INSANITY AS A DEFENSE TO CRIME *continued*

STATE	TIME OF PLEADING			MEDICAL CERTIFICATION	FINDING BY			DEFINITION OF INSANITY	DISPOSITION			REHEARING		RELEASE FROM INSTITUTION			NOTICE TO		HEARING BEFORE RELEASE	CIVIL RIGHTS	OTHER PROVISIONS
	At Arraignment	At Trial	With Court Permission		Court	Jury	Other		Commitment Mandatory	Discretionary	Other	Right to	Frequency	On Probation	Administrative	Judicial	Prosecutor	Other			
fn. 8 LA. Crim. Proc. Code Ann. (West 1967)		650 651		644 to 646 650					654 (capital case)	fn. 9 654 (other felony cases)		655	initial application after 6 months confinement; then not more frequently than yearly. 655	655 658	superintendent may recommend release to committing court. 655	court may order a re-examination by available members of original sanity commission or others. 656	district attorney from which the person was committed. 655		657		
ME. Rev. Stat. Ann. (1964)		fn. 10 15, §101		15, §101	15, §101		fn. 11 15, §103	fn. 12 15, §102	to custody of commissioner of mental health. 15, §101.1 or on release on bail for further psychiatric care. 15, §101.2	15, §101 (Supp. 1969)	fn. 13 15, §103 (Supp. 1969)	rehearing to determine competence to start trial. 15, §101.2 (Supp. 1969)	not less than 60 days following release on bail or commitment. 15, §101.2 (Supp. 1969)	may be supervised by parole board for up to 2 years. 15, §104 (Supp. 1969)	upon record and opinion of commissioner for release the court shall review the report and may hold a hearing, and may order an unconditional or a court's discretion release. 15, §104 (Supp. 1969)		county attorney or attorney general. 15, §104 (Supp. 1969)		15, §104 (Supp. 1969)		
MD. Ann. Code (1968)		time of pleading. 59, §9(b)	"unless the court for good cause shown shall allow a later plea". 59, §9(b)	59, §9(b), §10	59, §9(b)	59, §9(b)		fn. 14 59, §9(a)		may be committed at court's discretion. 59, §11		59, §11 59, §21	after first 3 months of confinement, then yearly. 59, §11 59, §21	fn. 15 59, §12		59, §12	state's attorney 59, §12	clerk of committing county court. 59, §12			
MASS. Ann. Laws (1965)		fn. 16 court may order the examination of any person coming before it to determine his mental condition. 123, §99 court may commit persons under complaint or indictment found by court to be mentally ill or in need of care until a determination of mental condition can be made. 123, §100		123, §99 123, §100 123, §100A		123, §101			for life if acquitted of murder or manslaughter. 123, §101	fn. 17 277, §16 278, §13					persons acquitted of murder or manslaughter: action by governor by & with consent of the council. 123, §101	persons acquitted of a crime other than murder or manslaughter. 278, §13					

Table 11.1 INSANITY AS A DEFENSE TO CRIME *continued*

STATE	TIME OF PLEADING — At Arraignment	At Trial	With Court Permission	MEDICAL CERTIFICATION	FINDING BY — Court	Jury	Other	DEFINITION OF INSANITY	DISPOSITION — Commitment Mandatory	Discretionary	Other	REHEARING — Right to	Frequency	RELEASE FROM INSTITUTION — On Probation	Administrative	Judicial	NOTICE TO — Prosecutor	Other	HEARING BEFORE RELEASE	CIVIL RIGHTS	OTHER PROVISIONS
MICH. Comp. Laws Ann. (1967)				767.27a (4)	767.27 b	767.27b			767.27b					the person shall not be released on convalescent care or final discharge without first being evaluated and recommended for release by the center for forensic psychiatry. 767.27b							
MINN. Stat. Ann. (1947)		631.19 (Supp. 1969)			631.19 (Supp. 1969)	631.01; & in Supp. 1969, 631.19		"[H]e shall not be excused from criminal liability except upon proof that at the time of committing the alleged criminal act he was laboring under such a defect of reason, from one of these causes, as not to know the nature of his act, or that it was wrong." 611.026	631.19 (Supp. 1969)			631.19 (Supp. 1969)		paroled 631.19 (Supp. 1969)	certificate from superintendent to court. 631.19 (Supp. 1969)	court order 631.19 (Supp. 1969)					
MISS. Code Ann. (1956)	fn. 18 if it appears that prisoner was insane when offense was committed, and is still insane, remand to chancery court for proceedings in accordance with 6909-11. 2573	2575				special finding that person was acquitted on grounds of insanity, and whether accused has since been restored to reason or whether he is dangerous to the community. 2575			if jury certifies such person is still insane and dangerous. 2575												
MO. Rev. Stat. (1949) (Supp. 1969)		plea of not guilty by reason of mental disease or defect excluding responsibility. 552.030(2)	later date as the court for good cause or may permit. 552.030(2)	552.030(4)	fn. 19 552.030(6)	552.030(6)		fn. 20 552.030(1)	552.030(2) 552.040(1)			application for release. 552.040(4)	180 days after last denial. 552.040(4)	552.040(4)		552.040(3)	552.040(4)	head of hospital. 552.040(4)	only upon written objection filed. 552.040(4)		

435

Table 11.1 INSANITY AS A DEFENSE TO CRIME continued

STATE	TIME OF PLEADING — At Arraignment	At Trial	With Court Permission	MEDICAL CERTIFICATION	FINDING BY — Court	Jury	Other	DEFINITION OF INSANITY	DISPOSITION — Commitment Mandatory	Discretionary	Other	REHEARING — Right to	Frequency	RELEASE FROM INSTITUTION — On Probation	Administrative	Judicial	NOTICE TO — Prosecutor	Other	HEARING BEFORE RELEASE	CIVIL RIGHTS	OTHER PROVISIONS
MONT. Rev. Codes Ann. (1947) (Supp. 1969)		95-503(b)	such later time as the court for good cause shall permit. 95-503(b)	95-505	95-507			fn. 21 95-50T(a)	95-508(a)			95-508(e)	1 year 95-508(3)	95-508(c)	application by superintendent to court. 95-508(b)	95-508(c)	95-508(b)		95-508(b)		
NEB. Rev. Stat. (1964)		may be raised by general plea of not guilty or specially pleaded. 29-2203				special finding 29-2203			until sane and discharged by due process of law. 29-2203												
NEV. Rev. Stat. (1967)		when an indictment or reformation is called for trial. 175.445 178.400				fn. 22 175.521	"A person is considered to be of sound mind who is neither an idiot or lunatic or affected with insanity, and who has arrived at the age of 14 years, or before that age if such person knows the distinction between right and wrong." 193.210 "knowing the difference between right and wrong". 178.450 178.455(2)(a)	175.521 178.425							175.521						
N.H. Rev. Stat. Ann. (1953)	"Whenever the grand jury shall omit to find an indictment against a person, for reason of insanity or mental derangement, or a person prosecuted for an offense shall be acquitted by the petit jury for the same reason such jury shall certify the same to the court." 607:1	607:2	fn. 23 135:17 (1964) (Supp. 1967)			or plea accepted by state's counsel. 607:2				the court may commit person it considers dangerous to prison or state hospital for life until or unless earlier discharged, released, or transferred by due course of law. 607:1, 607:2 & in Supp. 1967, 607:3											governor and his council or the superior court may discharge any such person from prison, or may transfer any prisoner who is insane to the state hospital, whenever they are satisfied that such discharge or transfer will be conducive to health and comfort of the person and the welfare of the public. 607:4

Table 11.1 INSANITY AS A DEFENSE TO CRIME *continued*

STATE	TIME OF PLEADING: At Arraignment	At Trial	With Court Permission	MEDICAL CERTIFICATION	FINDING BY: Court	Jury	Other	DEFINITION OF INSANITY	DISPOSITION: Commitment Mandatory	Discretionary	Other	REHEARING: Right to	Frequency	RELEASE FROM INSTITUTION: On Probation	Administrative	Judicial	NOTICE TO: Prosecutor	Other	HEARING BEFORE RELEASE	CIVIL RIGHTS	OTHER PROVISIONS
fn. 24 N.J. Stat. Ann. (1953)		2A:163-3	assignment Judge or county court judge may, upon application and certi- ficate in accordance with tit. 30, ch. 4, inquire in- to person's mental con- dition both at present time and time when act commit- ted; court may use testimony of quali- fied psy- chiatrists and in its discretion may also use jury to resolve in- sanity. 2A:163-2		court in its dis- cretion may decide both whether person in- sane now or at time of crimi- nal act or may impanel a special jury for this pur- pose 2A:163-2	if acquit- ted by jury at trial on ground of insanity, jury must find person was insane at time of act, wheth- er he was ac- quitted for such reason and or not such in- sanity con- tinues. 2A:163-3			if jury ac- quits and specially finds that such insan- ity con- tinues. 2A:163-3 if insane now, re- gardless sane or in- sane at time of criminal act; other- wise dis- miss. 2A:163-2							can only be released by order of court by which per- son was committed and only then when restored to reason; does not prevent use of writ of habeas corpus. 2A:163-2					
N.M. Stat. Ann. (1964) (Supp. 1969)	41-13-3			mental ex- amination court pays cost for indigent. 41-13-3.2	in non- jury trials. 41-13-3	fn.25 special verdict required. 41-13-3				fn.26 41-13-3											
N.Y. Code Crim. Proc. (McKinney 1958)		fn. 27 336, 454 (Supp. 1970)	at later times for good cause as the court may permit. 336, 454 (Supp. 1970)			if acquit- ted on ground of insanity, state fact in its ver- dict. 454 (Supp. 1970)		fn. 28 Penal Code 1120 (1967)	454 (Supp. 1970)					condition- al re- lease. 454 (Supp. 1970)		by court order after application by commis- sioner of mental hy- giene and an examina- tion. 454 (Supp. 1970)					
N.C. Gen. Stat. (1964)	all per- sons who commit certain crime while mentally disorder- ed upon arraign- ment shall be com- mitted to proper state hospital by "due course of law". 122-83 (Supp. 1967)	if person who has committed enumerated crimes "or other crimes" has es- caped in- dictment or was ac- quitted at trial, the judge shall de- tain such person & inquire into his mental *cont.*			.-122-84	122-84			if upon inquisi- tion judge shall find that men- tal con- dition or disease renders person dangerous to himself or others, he shall be commit- ted to the proper state hospital. 122-84						No person acquitted of of a capital felony on the ground of mental illness and committed to state hospital shall be discharged unless an act authorizing his discharge be passed by the general assembly. A person acquitted of a crime of a lesser degree shall not be discharged except upon order from the Gover- nor. Nothing, however, shall prevent the use of a writ of habeas corpus, but a discharge on a writ of habeas corpus shall not be granted unless the hos- pital superintendent *cont.*					

Table 11.1 INSANITY AS A DEFENSE TO CRIME *continued*

STATE	TIME OF PLEADING			MEDICAL CERTIFICATION	FINDING BY			DEFINITION OF INSANITY	DISPOSITION			REHEARING		RELEASE FROM INSTITUTION			NOTICE TO		HEARING BEFORE RELEASE	CIVIL RIGHTS	OTHER PROVISIONS
	At Arraignment	At Trial	With Court Permission		Court	Jury	Other		Commitment Mandatory	Discretionary	Other	Right to	Frequency	On Probation	Administrative	Judicial	Prosecutor	Other			
N.C. Gen. Stat. (1964)--*cont.*		condition. An inquisition with witnesses, notices, etc., shall be held. 122-84														finds person sane. 122-84, 122-86					
N.D. Cent. Code (1960)		29-20-03		29-20-03 29-20-04		12-05-03 29-22-36		mental deficients incapable of knowing wrongfulness of act charged against them. 12-02-01.3 (Supp. 1969) "at the time of committing the act charged against them they were incapable of knowing its wrongfulness" 12-02-01.4		12-05-03 29.22-36 can be committed until sane.											
OHIO Rev. Code (Baldwin 1964)	2943.02 2943.03			2945.40		2945.39			2945.39					release final or on condition, or on parole. 2945.39	no release until judge, superintendent of Lima State Hospital, an alienist selected by such judge and superintendent, or a majority of them, upon a hearing find defendant's sanity restored. 2945.39		2945.39		2945.39		
OKLA. Stat. (1958)		22, §1161				22, §1161		"at the time committing of the act charged against them they were incapable of knowing its wrongfulness" 21, §152.4		if jury acquitting defendant deems the discharge of such person dangerous to the public safety. 22, §1161											
ORE. Rev. Stat. (1967)		136.390			136.730	136.730				fn. 29 136.730											
fn. 30 PA. Stat. Ann. (1969)			50, §4408; & 50, 19, §1351 19, §1354 19, §1381 (1964)	50, §4408 (b)	50, §4408 (b)	19, §1351, 19, §1352, 19, §1353 (1964)	commission 50, §4408 (b)			19, §1352, 19, §1353 (1964) 50, §4408					50, §4409						

438

Table 11.1   INSANITY AS A DEFENSE TO CRIME   *continued*

STATE	TIME OF PLEADING – At Arraignment	At Trial	With Court Permission	MEDICAL CERTIFICATION	FINDING BY – Court	Jury	Other	DEFINITION OF INSANITY	DISPOSITION – Commitment Mandatory	Discretionary	Other	REHEARING – Right to	Frequency	RELEASE FROM INSTITUTION – On Probation	Administrative	Judicial	NOTICE TO – Prosecutor	Other	HEARING BEFORE RELEASE	CIVIL RIGHTS	OTHER PROVISIONS
R.I. Gen. Laws Ann. (1956)		26-4-7	fn. 31 26-4-3 26-4-4		fn. 31 26-4-3 26-4-4	26-4-7				fn. 31 26-4-3 26-4-4	fn. 32 26-4-7					fn. 33 26-4-5					
S.C. Code Ann. (1962) (Supp. 1968)			fn. 34 32-969	fn. 35 32-970	fn. 34 32-970					fn. 34 32-969						fn. 35 32-970					
S.D. Compiled Laws Ann. (1967)	to be specially pleaded. 23-37-1		fn. 36 23-37-4	examination by medical experts selected by state. 23-37-2		23-45-12			if dangerous to public peace and safety. 23-38-6					23-38-6							
fn. 37 TENN. Code Ann. (1955)																					
TEX. Rev. Civ. Stat. Ann. (1966)		fn. 38 C. Cr. P. 46.02(1) (Supp. 1969)		C. Cr. P. 46.02(9)		C. Cr. P. 46.02(2)(b)(1) 46.02(2)(b)(3) 46.02(2)(g) (Supp. 1969)			if still insane. C. Cr. P. 46.02(d)(1); 46.02(2)(e) (Supp. 1969)	C. Cr. P. 46.02(2) 46.02(d)(3) (Supp. 1969)						person previously acquitted because insane at time of offense. C. Cr. P. 46.02(3)(a) (Supp. 1969)			46.02(3)(a) (Supp. 1969)		
UTAH Code Ann. (1953)	notice to be given defendant. 77-22-16		there is also a procedure to inquire, at various times, as to present insanity-- on complaint; court may even direct prosecutor to make same. 77-22-16; in Supp. 1968, 77-48-2	trial-in-chief--2 alienists at to examine and testify. 77-24-17; insanity inquiry-- 2 or more physicians to examine and certify. 77-48-4	insanity inquiry 77-48-5 (Supp. 1967)	trial-in-chief 77-24-15			insanity inquiry. 77-48-5 (Supp. 1967)	person acquitted because insane-- court commits if still insane. 77-24-15		person acquitted because insane and committed. 77-24-16	annually as to person acquitted because insane and committed. 77-24-16			77-24-16 77-48-5			person acquitted because insane and committed. 77-24-16		
VT. Stat. Ann. (1959)		notice of insanity plea to be given at least 48 hours before trial. 13, §6561		court may have person detained and observed by hospital superintendent. 13, §4803		13, §4805		fn. 39 13, §4801 (1)		if person is acquitted because insane and is dangerous to community, court may confine. 13, §4805		upon petition to county court which ordered confinement. 13, §4808				13, §4808	13, §4808		13, §4812		

Table 11.1 INSANITY AS A DEFENSE TO CRIME continued

STATE	TIME OF PLEADING			MEDICAL CERTIFICATION	FINDING BY			DEFINITION OF INSANITY	DISPOSITION			REHEARING		RELEASE FROM INSTITUTION			NOTICE TO		HEARING BEFORE RELEASE	CIVIL RIGHTS	OTHER PROVISIONS
	At Arraignment	At Trial	With Court Permission		Court	Jury	Other		Commitment Mandatory	Discretionary	Other	Right to	Frequency	On Probation	Administrative	Judicial	Prosecutor	Other			
VA. Code Ann. (1960)	defendant must plead or the court plead him before the trial may proceed. 19.1-240					19.1-239(1) (Supp. 1968)					if acquittal by reason of insanity the defendant shall be examined and committed if he is insane and dangerous; otherwise he is discharged. 19.1239(1) (Supp. 1966)	19.1-239(5) (Supp. 1968)	every 6 months 19.1-239(5) (Supp. 1968)		19.1-239(2) 19.1-239(3) (Supp. 1968)	19.1-239(2) 19.1-239(3) (Supp. 1968)		attorney for city or court. 19.1-239(2) (Supp. 1968)	if court does not agree with commission's report. 19.1-239(3) (Supp. 1968)		
WASH. Rev. Code Ann. (1961)	10.76.020	if condition at time of crime was not before known to any person authorized to plea. 10.76.020				there is also a separate procedure whereby prosecutor may petition as to person acquitted because of condition and not in custody. 10.76.040		fn. 40 10.76.010	only if found that condition still exists or that person is so liable to relapse or reoccurrence of condition as to be unsafe to be at large. 10.76.040			provided certification by director of institutions of change of mental condition. 10.76.070 (Supp. 1968)				10.70.060, 10.70.070 (Supp. 1968)	notice as to petition for rehearing. 10.76.070 (Supp. 1968)		10.76.070 (Supp. 1968)		
W. VA. Code Ann. (1966)	Judge of court of record involved may, on own motion, inquire into mental condition of person charged with or convicted of a crime, or acquitted thereof because of mental condition; when inferior court not of record involved, proper court of record shall so inquire on application of such inferior court. 63-3-9			if judge makes inquiry, court appoints 2 physicians to examine and report. 63-3-9	63-3-9					judge on inquiry may commit 63-3-9											
WIS. Stat. Ann. (1957)	957.11(1)	at arraignment, unless court, for cause shown, otherwise orders. 957.11(1)						finding of not guilty because insane, if defendant was insane, or if a reasonable doubt of sanity or mental responsibility at time of commission. 957.11(1)	957.11(3)			957.11(4)	after first reexamination, court is to be satisfied that there is reasonable cause to believe condition has improved. 957.11(4)	parole 51.21(6) (Supp. 1968)	parole, unless committing court files objection within time allowed. 51.21(6) (Supp. 1968)	discharge 957.11(4)		parole 51.21(6) (Supp. 1968)	discharge 957.11(4)		
WYO. Stat. Ann. (1957)	7-240	court may allow at time later than arraignment "for good cause shown." 7-240		where any plea of insanity made, court to order commitment for examination and observation for prescribed period. 7-241		insanity at time of commission 7-242(b) 7-242(c)	if plea is not triable because of present insanity, county attorney to file petition under 25-1 to 25-15; 25-17 to 25-48 for determination. 7-241(c)				if insane at time of offense--discharged, prior to discharge, petition to be filed under 25-1 to 25-15; 25-17 and 25-17 to 25-48; and sanity hearing arranged. 7-242(b)					no discharge except upon order of court. 25-75				25-72 25-25	

1. If plea of insanity is joined with other pleas, trial continues as if question of sanity had not been raised. If defendant is found guilty, the question of sanity is promptly tried, either before the same jury or before a new jury at the court's discretion. Cal. Penal Code 1026.

2. "A defendant who does not thus plead not guilty by reason of insanity shall not be permitted to rely on insanity as a defense to any accusation of crime; provided, however, that evidence of mental condition may be offered in a proper case as bearing upon the capacity of the accused to form the specific intent essential to constitute a crime." Colo. 39-8-1 (Supp. 1965).

3. ". . . so diseased in mind at the time of the commission of the act as to be incapable of distinguishing right from wrong with respect to that act, or being able so to distinguish, has suffered an impairment of mind by disease as to destroy the will power and render him incapable of choosing the right and refraining from doing the wrong. . . ." Colo. 39-8-1(2) (Supp. 1965).

4. If in the opinion of the superintendent of the institution the person is no longer insane, he shall so certify to the court. If the judge agrees, he shall discharge the person or place him on probation. If he disagrees, provisions for a hearing with a jury are made. Colo. 39-8-4(3) to (6) (Supp. 1965).

5. When a person committed to a state hospital for any specific term following his acquittal on the ground of insanity or dementia is at the expiration of such term still suffering from the insanity or dementia, the superintendent shall initiate civil proceedings for commitment in accordance with provisions of 17-197. Conn. 54-39 (Supp. 1969).

6. The single provision dealing with the chart is: "if the jury render a verdict of acquittal on the ground of insanity the court may order a jury to be summoned . . . to inquire [whether] the defendant continues to be insane. The court may cause the same witnesses to be summoned who testified on the trial, and other witnesses and direct the prosecuting attorney to conduct the proceedings, and counsel may appear for the defendant. The court may direct the sheriff to take the defendant and retain him in custody until the question of continuing insanity is determined. If the jury find the defendant insane he shall be committed by the sheriff to the state insane asylum. If the jury find the defendant sane, he shall be discharged." Idaho 19-2320. The provisions of Idaho 19-3301 to 19-3307 appear to apply only to Table 11.2, Insanity Subsequent to Crime.

7. A person is not criminally responsible for conduct if at the time of such conduct, as a result of a mental disease or mental defect, he lacks substantial capacity either to appreciate the criminality of his conduct or to conform his conduct to the requirements of the law. The terms "mental disease" and "mental defect" do not include an abnormality manifested only by repeated criminal or otherwise antisocial conduct. Ill. 38, §6-2.

8. The new Louisiana Code of Criminal Procedure formed 2 procedures for the defense of insanity at the time of the crime (a defense on the merits) and present insanity (a bar to present trial). La. Crim. Pro. Code Ann. Art. 641-649, 650-658.

9. When defendant is found not guilty by reason of insanity in any other felony case (apart from capital cases) the court shall hold promptly a contradictory hearing to see if defendant can be discharged or released on probation. The defendant may be discharged or paroled if not dangerous to others, or the court may order him committed to a proper state mental institution. La. Code of Crim. Proc. Art. 654.

10. "When a finding of probable cause has been made or an indictment has been returned against a person or a person has taken an appeal to the superior court . . . a justice may order respondent examined. . . . If it is made to appear to the court by the report that the respondent suffers or suffered from a mental disease or mental defect affecting his criminal responsibility or his competence to stand trial or that further observation is indicated, the court may order the respondent committed . . . to ascertain his mental condition. Me. 15, §101 (Supp. 1969)."

11. When respondent is acquitted by reason of mental disease or mental defect excluding responsibility, the verdict and judgment shall so state. In such case the court shall order such person committed to custody of the commissioner of mental health and corrections to be placed in an appropriate institution. Notice of commitment or transfer shall be given by the commissioner to the committing court. Me. 15, §102.

12. An accused is not criminally responsible if his unlawful act was the product of mental disease or mental defect; the terms "mental disease" or "mental defect" do not include an abnormality manifested only by repeated criminal conduct or excessive use of drugs or alcohol. Me. 15, §102.

13. The commissioner may, in cases deemed appropriate by him, receive for observation persons committed by the judge of the U.S. district court. Me. 15, §105 (Supp. 1969).

14. A defendant is not responsible for criminal conduct and shall be found insane at the time of the commission of the alleged crime if, at the time of such conduct as a result of mental disease or defect, he lacks substantial capacity either to appreciate the criminality of his conduct or to conform his conduct to the requirements of law. As used in this section, the terms "mental disease or defect" do not include an abnormality manifested only by repeated criminal or otherwise antisocial conduct. Md. 59-9(a).

15. The court may make a conditional release of defendant upon satisfactory proof of permanent or temporary recovery. Md. 59, §12.

16. If a person is indicted by the grand jury for a capital offense or if a person, known to have been indicted for any offense more than

once or previously to have been convicted of a felony, is so indicted, an investigation of his mental condition is ordered. Mass. 123, §100A.

17. If the grand jury fails to indict on grounds of insanity, or if a person is acquitted on grounds of insanity for a crime other than murder or manslaughter, the court if it is satisfied that the defendant is still insane and finds that he has been a criminal or is of vicious tendency, may, under such limitations as it deems proper, commit him. Mass. 277, §16; 278, §13.

18. If grand jury shall not find a true bill by reason of insanity of the accused, the grand jury shall certify the fact to the circuit court and state whether such person is dangerous to community. Chancery court may then proceed in accordance with 6909-11. Miss. 2574.

19. When defendant is acquitted on the ground of mental disease or defect excluding responsibility, the verdict and the judgment shall so state. Mo. 552.030(c) (Supp. 1969).

20. A person is not responsible for criminal conduct if at the time of such conduct as a result of mental disease or defect he did not know or appreciate the nature, quality, or wrongfulness of his conduct or was incapable of conforming his conduct to the requirements of law. Mo. 552.030(1) (Supp. 1969).

21. A person is not responsible for criminal conduct if at the time of such conduct as a result of mental disease or defect he was unable either to appreciate the criminality of his conduct or to conform his conduct to the requirements of law. Mont. Code of Crim. Proc. 95-501-(a) (Supp. 1969).

22. Where on a trial a defense of insanity is interposed by the defendant and he is acquitted by reason of that defense, the finding of the jury shall have the same force and effect as if he were regularly adjudged insane as now provided by law and the judge thereupon shall forthwith order that the defendant be confined in the Nevada state hospital until he be regularly discharged therefrom in accordance with law. Nev. 175.-521.

23. When a person is indicted or is in jail awaiting trial and a plea of insanity is made in court or the question of sanity is raised, the court may commit him to the state hospital for observation until further order of court or until hospital declares such person to be sane. N.H. 135:17 (Supp. 1967).

24. New Jersey has 2 distinct procedures, both of which are plotted on the chart. 2A:163-3 relates only to those cases where the jury acquits the defendant upon regular trial on the ground of insanity at the time the offense was committed. The jury must make special findings, and if the jury finds the insanity continues, the person shall be committed. 2A:163-2 applies not only to insanity at any time, whether at the time of the proceeding or at the time of commission of the offense or both, but also to a time other than the normal trial, i.e.,

any person in confinement under commitment, indictment, or under any process. Hence 2A:163-2 conceivably could arise prior to, at the same time as, or subsequent to the normal criminal trial with which 2A:163-3 is concerned. N.J. 2A:163-2, 2A:163-3.

25. The issue shall be determined in nonjury trials by the court and in jury trials by a special verdict of the jury. If the defense is raised in the course of trial in a court other than the district court, the proceeding shall be suspended and the cause transferred to the district court, but this transfer requirement does not apply to preliminary hearings. When the determination is made and the defendant is acquitted on the ground of the insanity, the court shall proceed to make a further determination, without a jury, of the present sanity of the defendant. N.M. 41-13-3 (Supp. 1969).

26. The determination of the defendant's present sanity shall be in accordance with the provisions of law governing proceedings for the involuntary hospitalization of the mentally ill except that in lieu of an application the proceeding shall be initiated upon the court's own motion. N.M. 41-13-3 (Supp. 1969).

27. Written notice to rely on defense of insanity in section 30.5 of the penal law must be filed within 20 days from the date of entry of plea of not guilty, or at such later time as the court for good cause may permit. N.Y. Code Crim. Proc. 336.

28. A person is not criminally responsible for conduct if at the time of such conduct as a result of mental disease or defect he lacks substantial capacity to know or appreciate either: (a) the nature and consequence of such conduct; or (b) that such conduct was wrong. N.Y. Penal Law 1120.

29. If the defendant is found not guilty on the ground of insanity, the court shall, if it deems his being at large dangerous to the public peace and safety, order him to be committed to a hospital or institution until he becomes sane or is otherwise discharged therefrom by authority of law. Ore. 13.730.

30. In title 19, "Criminal Procedures," §§1351, 1354, and 1381 to 1383 also relate to proceedings after acquittal on grounds of insanity. Title 19, §1352, relates to proceedings when the defendant is found insane on arraignment and title 19, §1353, deals with the procedure when a prisoner who is brought up for discharge for want of prosecution appears insane.

31. There is also a procedure whereby, on petition of the director of social welfare or the officer having custody of a person awaiting trial setting forth that such person is insane, the court may make an examination of such person and, if satisfied as to the insanity, order transfer to the criminal insane ward. R.I. 26-4-3, 26-4-4.

32. If the court feels that release of a defendant who was acquitted because of insanity at the time of the offense would endanger the public

peace it shall so certify to the governor, who may commit defendant to the criminal insane ward. R.I. 26-4-7.

33. Upon recovery, the person who was awaiting trial and, on petition, was transferred to the criminally insane ward may be remanded by the presiding judge to the place of original confinement to await trial. R.I. 26-4-5.

34. The judge may order admitted to the state hospital any person charged with the commission of any criminal offense who shall, upon the trial before him, be adjudged mentally ill or in whom there is a question as to the relation of mental illness to the alleged crime, whether this question is raised by the prosecution or defense or appears to the judge from any evidence brought before him or upon his own recognition. S.C. 32-969 (Supp. 1968).

35. At the end of 30 days, the admitted person is to be returned to the court, if found to be mentally competent. If found mentally ill, the hospital superintendent so certifies to the court, and the person is retained at the state hospital. Upon the patient's recovery, the court is notified and advises the hospital superintendent as to further disposition. S.C. 32-970 (Supp. 1968).

36. If during the trial of a case, where the plea of insanity has not been made, and the court deems that a substantial suggestion of the defendant's insanity has been raised as a defense, the defendant will be deemed to have consented to a mistrial and a second trial shall be had. S.D. 23-37-4.

37. When a person is acquitted of a criminal charge on a verdict of not guilty by reason of insanity, the judges having criminal jurisdiction thereof shall have authority, upon petition filed by the district attorney general, or the attorney for defendant, and after hearing, to order defendant hospitalized in a state mental hospital for observation, care, and treatment for a period not exceeding 30 days. The superintendent of the hospital in which an individual is hospitalized shall, not later than 30 days after admission, certify to the court whether or not the conditions which justified hospitalization still exist. If so, the individual shall be detained in the hospital and an order for his hospitalization shall be entered, and if otherwise, he shall be returned to the court for such disposition or further proceeding as is appropriate to the case. Tenn. 33-701 (Supp. 1968).

38. No issue of insanity shall be tried in advance of trial on the merits, except upon written application on behalf of the accused with the consent of the state's attorney and the approval of the trial judge. Tex. C. Cr. P. 46.02(1) (Supp. 1969).

39. The test of insanity when used as a defense in criminal cases is that a person is not responsible for criminal conduct if at the time of such conduct as a result of mental disease or defect he lacks adequate capacity either to appreciate the criminality of his conduct or to conform his conduct to the requirements of law. Vt. 13, §4801(1).

40. Any person who shall have committed a crime while insane, or in a condition of mental irresponsibility and in whom such insanity or mental irresponsibility continues to exist shall be deemed criminally insane. No condition of mind induced by the voluntary act of a person charged with a crime shall be deemed mental irresponsibility. Wash. 10.76.010.

Table 11.2 INSANITY SUBSEQUENT TO CRIME

STATE / DRAFT ACT	CONDITION REQUIREMENT				FINDING BY				DISPOSITION			REHEARING		RECOVERY			PAROLE PROVISIONS
	Insane	Deficient	Incapable of Defense	Other	Court	Jury	Commission	Other	Commitment Mandatory	Other	Continuing Court Supervision	Right to	Frequency	Trial Mandatory	Parole Without Trial	Discharge	Parole by
DRAFT ACT	The Act contains no specific provisions.				See "The Scope of the Draft Act,"				"The Mentally Ill," page 1, in			Appendix A of this volume.		this volume			
ALA. Code (1958)	trial or pre-trial. 15, §425 15, §426 sentence of death. 15, §427 15, §428 15, §429				15, §427 15, §428	trial 15, §426 sentence of death. 15, §427 court may im-panel jury. 15, §428	fn. 1 15, §428		mandatory 15, §426 15, §429 permissive 14, §428					15, §426			
ALAS. Stat. (1962)	12.45.100	12.45.100	12.45.100		may order psychiatric examination. 12.45.100					commitment discretion-ary 12.45.110 (Supp. 1969)		only upon application 12.45.115(a) (Supp. 1969)		hearing by court upon application of custodian. 12.45.115(b) (Supp. 1969)			
ARIZ. Rev. Stat. Ann. (1956)	time of trial or after con-viction but prior to sentencing. 13-1621A (Supp. 1970) 13-1622 under sen-tence of death. 13-1691 to 13-1694		13-1621(A) (Supp. 1970)		13-1621(B)	13-1691A 13-1693			13-1621(H)(2) (Supp. 1970) 13-1693 13-1694B					13-1621(H)(3) to (5) (Supp. 1970) warrant for execution. 13-1694C			
ARK. Stat. Ann. (1964)	43-1301				may declare mistrial. 43-1301 43-1303 43-1304 43-1305 43-1306 43-1307 43-1312			fn. 2 43-1301 to 43-1307	for observa-tion and ex-amination. 43-1301 to 43-1307								
CAL. Penal Code (West 1956)	1367 1368				1368	if demanded 1368 1369 1370 (Supp. 1968)			1370 (Supp. 1968)								
COLO. Rev. Stat. Ann. (1964)	fn. 3 trial, post-conviction, preexecution. 39-8-6(1) 39-8-6(8)		fn. 3 39-8-6(8)		39-8-6(2) 39-8-6(3) 39-8-6(4)	39-8-6(2) 39-8-6(3) 39-8-6(4)			39-8-6(2)(5) (a)					39-8-6(5)(c)			
CONN. Gen. Stat. Ann. (1960) (Supp. 1969)	54-40(a)	mental de-fective. 54-40(a)	54-40(a)		54-40(c)				until time of trial; if hospital su-perintendent does not be-lieve person insane, court shall have second full hearing. 54-40					54-40(c)			

Table 11.2 INSANITY SUBSEQUENT TO CRIME continued

STATE	CONDITION Insane	CONDITION Deficient	REQUIREMENT Incapable of Defense	REQUIREMENT Other	FINDING BY Court	FINDING BY Jury	FINDING BY Commission	FINDING BY Other	DISPOSITION Commitment Mandatory	DISPOSITION Other	DISPOSITION Continuing Court Supervision	REHEARING Right to	REHEARING Frequency	RECOVERY Trial Mandatory	RECOVERY Parole Without Trial	RECOVERY Discharge	PAROLE PROVISIONS Parole By
DEL. Code Ann. (1953)	mentally ill after conviction and before sentence. 11, §4703 after confinement. 11, §4704				11, §4703(c)		fn. 4 11, §4703(a) 11, §4703(c)		11, §4703(c)					serves sentence 11, §4703(c)			
D.C. Code Ann. (1967)	unsound mind 24-301(a)	mentally incompetent 24-301(a)			fn. 5 24-301(a)				24-301(a)			habeas corpus 24-301(g)		fn. 5 24-301(b)			
FLA. Stat. Ann. (1967)	before trial R.Crim. P. 1.210(a) before sentencing R.Crim. P. 1.740(a)				R. Crim. P. 1.210(a) 1.740(b)				R.Crim. P. 1.210(a) 1.740(b)					R. Crim. P. 1.210(a) sentence R. Crim. P. 1.740(b)			
GA. Code Ann. (1953)	27-1504 after capital conviction. 27-2601				when convict under capital offense has been committed to hospital by governor as per 27-2602, 27-2604	special jury 27-1502		only governor has power to act to commit to hospital an insane convict under capital crime. 27-2601 27-2602	trial 27-1502	governor only may commit to hospital an insane convict under capital crime. 27-2602							
HAWAII Rev. Stat. Ann. (1968)	711-91 711-92				if court finds medical report conclusive of insanity. 711-91	711-92			711-91 711-92					711-92			
IDAHO Code Ann. (1947)	trial or for judgment on conviction. 19-3302					19-3302 to 19-3304				fn. 6 19-3304				proper custody until trial or judgment or legally discharged. 19-3306			
ILL. Ann. Stat. (Smith-Hurd 1964)	38, §104-1 (Supp. 1969)	38, §104-1 (Supp. 1969)	38, §104-6 (Supp. 1969)		if jury waived or not requested by defendant. 38, §104-2(a) 38, §104-2(b)	38, §104-2(a) 38, §103-2(b)			38, §104-3(a) (Supp. 1969)			rehearing to be held when "reasonable grounds exist". 39, §104-3(b) (Supp. 1969)		38, §104-3(b) (Supp. 1969)		fn. 7 38, §104-3 (c) (Supp. 1969)	
IND. Ann. Stat. (1956) (Supp. 1969)	9-1706a	9-1706a	9-1706a		fn. 8 9-1706a				9-1706a					9-1706a			
IOWA Code Ann. (1950)	783.1				separate trial, as on charge. 783.2	separate trial, as on charge. 783.2			if discharge will endanger public peace or safety, mandatory commitment until sane. 783.3 (Supp. 1969)					proper custody until trial, judgment, or legally discharged. 783.4 (Supp. 1969)			

445

Table 11.2 INSANITY SUBSEQUENT TO CRIME *continued*

STATE	CONDITION REQUIREMENT				FINDING BY				DISPOSITION			REHEARING		RECOVERY			PAROLE PROVISIONS
	Insane	Deficient	Incapable of Defense	Other	Court	Jury	Commission	Other	Commitment Mandatory	Other	Continuing Court Supervision	Right to	Frequency	Trial Mandatory	Parole Without Trial	Discharge	Parole by
KAN. Stat. Ann. (1964) (Supp. 1968)	62-1531	idiot, imbecile 62-1531	62-1531		62-1531	idiot imbecile 62-1531	62-1531		62-1531					fn. 9 unless paroled by hospital superintendent. 62-1531	fn. 9 62-1531		fn. 9 Institution 62-1531
KY. Rev. Stat. Ann. (1969)	8.06				8.06	8.06 431.240 (1963)			8.06	if execution suspended, commissioner of welfare may commit. 431.240(2) (1963)				8.06			
LA. Crim. Pro. Code Ann. (West 1967)	28:59 La. Rev. Stat (1951)	641	641	defendant's mental incapacity to proceed may be raised at any time by the defense, the district attorney, or the court. 642	the issue shall be determined by the court in a contradictory hearing with the sanity commission report admissible in evidence. 643 645 647 La. Rev. Stat 15:211		court shall appoint a sanity commission. 644 report of the sanity commission shall be filed with the court. 645	defendant or district attorney has the right to an independent mental examination by a physician of his choice. 646	648			district attorney or defense may apply to court to have proceedings resumed on ground that defendant presently has mental capacity to proceed. 649		649			institution 648
ME. Rev. Stat. Ann. (1964)	convict in county jail who becomes mentally ill. 15, §2211A (Supp. 1969) inmates of county jails and persons under indictment who become insane before final conviction. 15, §2215 persons insane when motion for sentence made. 15, §2217				15, §2215				may be committed to department for criminal insane if crime punishable by imprisonment in state prison; otherwise commitment to hospital for mentally ill. 15, §2217	court may commit inmates of county jails and persons under indictment. 15, §2215	15, §2215						
MD. Ann. Code (1968)		fn. 10 59, §7			123, §100 123, §103 123, §104 277, §16		department of Mental Hygiene. 59, §7			court, in its discretion, may direct confinement or set bail. 59, §8	59, §8	59, §8 59, §21	1 year 59, §8 59, §21	59, §8, 11 59, §21		conditional release 59, §12	institution 59, §9
MASS. Ann. Laws (1965)	person under complaint or indictment for any crime. 123, §100 prisoner in correctional institution. 123, §102 123, §103				123, §100 123, §103 277, §16				if certain conditions met. 123, §103 123, §104	court may commit. 123, §103 277, §16					if complaint or indictment dismissed or nol prossed. 123, §105	if complaint or indictment dismissed or nol prossed. 123, §105	institution 123, §88 123, §105

Table 11.2 INSANITY SUBSEQUENT TO CRIME *continued*

STATE	CONDITION REQUIREMENT				FINDING BY				DISPOSITION			REHEARING		RECOVERY			PAROLE PROVISIONS
	Insane	Deficient	Incapable of Defense	Other	Court	Jury	Commission	Other	Commitment Mandatory	Other	Continuing Court Supervision	Right to	Frequency	Trial Mandatory	Parole Without Trial	Discharge	Parole by
MASS. Ann. Laws--*cont'd*	prisoner under sentence in a jail house of correction or prison other than in section 102, 123, §104 where grand jury does not indict. 277, §16																
MICH. Comp. Laws Ann. (1967)			fn. 11 767.27a(1)		767.27a(5)		767.27a(3)		if incompetent, 60-day period. 767.27a(3)					fn. 12 767.27a(6)		fn. 13 767.27a(8)	fn. 13 institution 767.27a(8)
MINN. Stat. Ann. (1947)	611.026	611.026	611.026		631.18 (Supp. 1969)				631.18 (Supp. 1969)					631.18 (Supp. 1969)			
fn. 14 MISS. Code Ann. (1956)	if sheriff satisfied that any convict in his custody under sentence is insane. 2558					2558		sheriff 2558	2558								
MO. Rev. Stat. (1949) (Supp. 1969)			552.020(1)	fn. 15 552.010	522.020(4)				552.020(4)	fn. 16	552.020(4)	552.020(4)		fn. 17 552.020(4)		fn. 18 552.020(4)	
MONT. Rev. Code Ann. (1947) (Supp. 1969)			fn. 19 95-504		95-506				95-506(6)			on request 95-506(b)		fn. 17 95-506(b)		95-506(b)	
NEB. Rev. Stat. (1964)	29-1822				29-1823 (Supp. 1967)				29-1823 (Supp. 1967)					29-1822 29-1823 (Supp. 1967)			
NEV. Rev. Stat. (1967)	178.400 178.405				178.415(3)				if court finds defendant insane. 178.425.1 178.445		178.450	examination by sanity commission. 178.455		178.425.2			
N.H. Rev. Stat. Ann. (1955)	indicted or committed to jail to await grand jury action. 135:17 transfer from prison. 607:4 607:5				135:17 607:4 607:5			governor and council. 607:4	135:17	607:4 607:5				135:17			
N.J. Stat. Ann. (1953)	2A:163-2, 30:4-82 (Supp. 1970)	mentally retarded. 30:4-82 (Supp. 1970)			in discretion of judge. 2A:163-2, 30:4-82 (Supp. 1970)				2A:163-2, 30:4-82 (Supp. 1970)		30:4-82 (Supp. 1970)			2A:163-2, 30:4-82 (Supp. 1970)		30:4-82 (Supp. 1970)	
N.M. Stat. Ann. (1964) (Supp. 1969)			fn. 20 41-13-3.1		41-13-3.1		41-13-3.2		41-13-3.1		fn. 21 41-13-3.1	fn. 22 41-13-3.1		41-13-3.1			institution 41-13-3.1

Table 11.2 INSANITY SUBSEQUENT TO CRIME *continued*

STATE	Insane	Deficient	Incapable of Defense	Other	Court	Jury	Commission	Other	Commitment Mandatory	Other	Continuing Court Supervision	Right to	Frequency	Trial Mandatory	Parole Without Trial	Discharge	Parole by
	CONDITION REQUIREMENT				FINDING BY				DISPOSITION			REHEARING		RECOVERY			PAROLE PROVISIONS
N.Y. Code of Crim. Proc. (McKinney 1958) (Supp. 1970)	658 870	idiocy, imbecility 658 870	658 870		fn. 23 662-b		fn. 23 if counsel does not object. 658, 659, 660, 662		662-b	870 to 876				proper custody until trial or legal discharge. 662-b			
N.C. Gen. Stat. (1963)			122-84	mentally ill 122-83 122-85	122-83 122-84				122-83 122-84 122-85					122-84 122-87			
N.D. Cent. Code (1960) (Supp. 1969)	29-20-01	mentally defective 29-20-01	29-20-01		29-20-01 29-20-02				29-20-02					court shall conduct hearing as original hearing recommit if still insane, continue trial if now sane. 29-20-02			
OHIO Rev. Code (Baldwin 1964)	2945.37				2945.37 2945.38	discretionary 2945.37 2945.38			2945.38					2945.38			
fn. 24 OKLA. Stat. (1958)	22, §1161					22, §1162, 22, §1167 (Supp. 1969)				committed if court deems his discharge dangerous to the public peace or safety. 22, §1167 (Supp. 1969)				sheriff places him in custody until he be brought to trial or judgment. 22, §1169		or be legally discharged. 22, §1169	
ORE. Rev. Stat. (1967)			insane or mentally defective to the extent that he is unable to understand the proceedings against him or to assist in his defense. 136.150		136.150				fn. 25 136.160					136.160			
PA. Stat. Ann. (1969)	lunatic 19, §1352 (1964) 50, §4102 50, §4407(a)	50, §4102 50, §4407(a)		50, §4102 50, §4407(a)	50, §4408(b) (4)	fn. 26 19, §1351 (1964) 19, §1352	50, §4408(b) (2)	50, §4408(b) (1) 50, §4408(b) (3)	19, §1351 (1964) 19, §1352	fn. 27 50, §4408(d)				50, §4410		50, §4410	
R.I. Gen. Laws Ann. (1956)	26-4-3	idiotic 26-4-4			26-4-3				"may order," however. 26-4-4					discretionary by justice of superior court. 26-4-5			
S.C. Code Ann. (1962) (Supp. 1968)	mentally ill 32-969				fn. 28 32-969				"may" 32-969					court shall advise superintendent as to further disposition. 32-970			
S.D. Compiled Laws Ann. (1967)	mentally ill 23-38-1					23-38-2				23-38-6				23-38-9		23-38-9	

448

Table 11.2 INSANITY SUBSEQUENT TO CRIME continued

STATE	CONDITION REQUIREMENT				FINDING BY				DISPOSITION			REHEARING		RECOVERY			PAROLE PROVISIONS
	Insane	Deficient	Incapable of Defense	Other	Court	Jury	Commission	Other	Commitment Mandatory	Other	Continuing Court Supervision	Right to	Frequency	Trial Mandatory	Parole Without Trial	Discharge	Parole by
TENN. Code Ann. (1955) (Supp. 1968)	mentally ill 33-701	fn. 29 33-50T(4)			fn. 30 33-70T					court, on petition, may commit for observation and treatment, not to exceed 30 days; then may order commitment or proceed otherwise. 33-701							
TEX. Code Crim. Proc. (1966)	fn. 31 at trial 46.02(2)(a) (Supp. 1969) felony between conviction and sentence, or while appeal from conviction pending. 46.02(4) death sentence. 46.02(5)					requires competent medical or psychiatric testimony. 42.06(9) 46.02(c) (1), 46.02(f) (1) (Supp. 1969)			order according to Jury's finding of need of hospitalization. 46.02(2)(b) (2)(,)(,) (Supp. 1969)					fn. 7 person insane at time of trial but not acquitted of offense. 46.02(7)			
UTAH Code Ann. (1953)	77-48-2 (Supp. 1967)	77-48-2 (Supp. 1967)			fn. 32 77-48-4 77-48-6				77-48-5 (Supp. 1967)					77-48-5 (Supp. 1967)			
VT. Stat. Ann. (1959)	13, §4803				commit to state hospital to determine truth or falsity of such plea of insanity. 13, §4803					fn. 33 permission 13, §4803 13, §4804							
VA. Code Ann. (1960)	19.1-227 pretrial 19.1-228 other 19.1-229 (Supp. 1968)	feebleminded 19.1-227 pretrial 19.1-228 19.1-229 (Supp. 1968)	competent to plead 19.1-228 (Supp. 1968)		commitment for observation. 19.1-228 (Supp. 1968)		pretrial 19.1-230.1 (Supp. 1968) postconviction but presentence 19.1-234 (Supp. 1968) after sentence 19.1-235 (Supp. 1968)		19.1-231 19.1-234 19.1-235 (Supp. 1968)					fn. 7 19.1-230 (Supp. 1968)			
fn. 34 WASH. Rev. Code Ann. (1961)																	
W. VA. Code Ann. (1966)		mentally defective; charged with or convicted. 62-3-9		mentally ill; charged with or convicted. 62-3-9	appoint 2 physicians to examine and report. 62-3-9					court may commit either person charged with or convicted of crime. 62-3-9				62-3-9			

Table 11.2 INSANITY SUBSEQUENT TO CRIME   continued

STATE	CONDITION REQUIREMENT				FINDING BY				DISPOSITION			REHEARING		RECOVERY			PAROLE PROVISIONS
	Insnae	Deficient	Incapable of Defense	Other	Court	Jury	Commission	Other	Commitment Mandatory	Other	Continuing Court Supervision	Right to	Frequency	Trial Mandatory	Parole Without Trial	Discharge	Parole by
WIS. Stat. Ann. (1957)	957.13(1)	957.13(1)			957.13(2) (Supp. 1968)				957.13(2) (Supp. 1968)			957.13(4)	subsequent rehearings depend upon court having reasonable cause to believe there is improvement in mental condition. 957.13(4)	957.13(2), 957.13(3) (Supp. 1968)	fn. 9 51.2T(6) (Supp. 1968)		institution 51.21(6) (Supp. 1968)
WYO. Stat. Ann. (1957)	7-239 7-240(b)					7-241(c)	7-241(c)		7-241(c)					7-241(c)		fn. 35 25-75	

1. When defendant is charged with a capital offense the judge shall, if notified in writing by the superintendent of Alabama State Hospital, or by 3 reputable specialists that defendant is insane, deliver him to such superintendent for observation. The superintendent and 2 of his medical staff shall constitute a commission on lunacy, examine the defendant, and file a full written report with the court. Ala.' 14, §425.

2. If the circuit judge has grounds to believe that the defendant has become insane, the court shall commit the defendant to the state hospital for examination for a period not to exceed 30 days. Ark. 43-1301 to 43-1307.

3. Even though defendant's mind may be deranged or unsound on some subjects, he is not to be considered insane if he has sufficient mind to assist in his own defense in a rational and reasonable manner. See specific tests set forth in the statute for trial, presentence, and preexecution of sentence. Colo. 39-8-6(8).

4. Whenever in a capital case the prisoner has become mentally ill after conviction and before sentence, the court may, with a view to informing its own mind on the subject, appoint a commission to be composed of experienced and practical men, at least 2 of whom shall be practicing physicians, to inquire into the mental condition of the prisoner. Del. 11, §4703(a) (Supp. 1970).

5. Certification by the superintendent of the hospital that the accused is restored shall be sufficient to authorize the court to enter an order thereon adjudicating him to be competent to stand trial unless the accused or the government objects, in which case the court after hearing without a jury shall determine the issue. D.C. 24-301(b).

6. Court may, if it feels defendant's discharge would be dangerous to the public peace or safety, order that he be committed to the state insane asylum until he is able to stand trial. Idaho 19-3304.

7. If a defendant so committed is thereafter sentenced for the offense charged, he shall be credited with the time of his commitment and that portion of his sentence shall be considered served. Ill. 38, §104-3(c) (Supp. 1969); Tex. 46.01; Va. 19.1-234, 19.1-235 (Supp. 1968).

8. When court has reason to believe defendant is insane it shall immediately fix a time for a hearing and shall appoint 2 experts who shall examine defendant and testify at the hearing as to their findings. Ind. 9-1706a (Supp. 1969).

9. If the medical superintendent of the state security hospital believes that the defendant should be paroled rather than returned to court, he should notify the court. If the court does not object within 60 days, the superintendent with the approval of the department may parole the defendant to a legal guardian or some other person. Kan. 62-1531 (Supp. 1968); Wis. 51.21(6).

10. Such person is unable to understand the nature or the object of the proceedings against him or to assist in his defense. Md. 15, §7.

11. Incompetent person shall not be proceeded against in trial while he is incompetent. A person is incompetent to stand trial within the meaning of this section if he is incapable of understanding the nature and object of the proceedings against him, of comprehending his own condition in reference to the proceedings against him, or of assisting in his defense in a rational or reasonable manner. Mich. 767.27a(1).

12. The Michigan statutes in regard to persons incompetent to stand trial include several procedures. Once the issue of incompetency is raised (767.27a(2)) and a showing of incompetency is made (767.-27a(3)) the court commits defendant to the center for forensic psychiatry for a period not to exceed 60 days. The center's report is then transmitted to the committing court (767.27a(4)) and the defendant is returned to the court's custody, and the competency of the defendant is determined. If found incompetent to stand trial (767.27a(5)), the defendant shall be committed to the department of mental health for treatment in a public institution. If at any time within 18 months of the commitment order defendant has regained competence to stand trial in the opinion of the department, the defendant shall be returned to the court (767.27a(6)) to stand trial. If the department does not believe defendant can recover competence to stand trial within 18 months, a certified opinion will be sent the probate court in the county from which the defendant was originally committed, that court to proceed under 330.21 relating to general commitment, and 767.27a(7), which allows the probate court to decide proper care. If it decides not to commit, the case will be transferred to the circuit court which originally determined incompetency to stand trial, and which will proceed to a hearing de novo that may overrule the probate court, causing defendant to be committed, with discharge governed by sections 330.11 to 330.71 (767.27a(8)).

13. Discharge shall be in accordance with Michigan statutes (330.11 to 330.71). The person shall not be released on convalescent care or final discharge without first being evaluated and recommended for release by the center for forensic psychiatry. Mich. 767.27a(8).

14. The annotations to sections 2573 and 2574 indicate that present insanity prevents trial or punishment. Miss. 2573, 2574.

15. The terms "mental disease or defect" include congenital and traumatic mental conditions as well as disease. They do not include an abnormality manifested only by repeated criminal or otherwise antisocial conduct, whether or not such abnormality may be included under mental illness, mental disease, or defect in some classifications of mental abnormality or disorder. Ther terms do not include an abnormality manifested only by criminal sexual psychopathy as defined in section 202.700 R.S. Mo., nor shall anything in this chapter be construed to repeal or modify the provisions of sections

Notes to Table 11.2   INSANITY SUBSEQUENT TO CRIME   *continued*

202.760 to 202.770 R.S. Mo. Mo. 552.010 (Supp. 1969). No person who as a result of mental disease or defect lacks capacity to understand the proceedings against him or to assist in his own defense shall be tried, convicted, or sentenced for the commission of an offense so long as the incapacity endures. Mo. 552.020(1) (Supp. 1969).

16. There are provisions for commitment of inmates of correctional institutions to state mental hospitals. Mo. 552-050 to 552-080 (Supp. 1969).

17. The court shall commit him to the custody of the director of the division of mental diseases for so long as the unfitness endures or until the charges on proceedings are disposed of according to law. Mo. 552.020(4) (Supp. 1969). If, however, the prosecuting or circuit attorney determines that enough time has elapsed since the commitment of the accused that it would be unjust to resume the criminal proceedings, the court may dismiss the charges. Mo. 552.020(4) (Supp. 1969); Mont. 95-506(b) (Supp. 1969).

18. If the charges against any accused person are dismissed either by the state or by the court and if he is then in custody of the director of the division of mental diseases, he shall not be retained in such custody or in any hospital unless proper proceedings have been instituted and held, as provided in sections 202.780 to 202.875, in which use these sections and no others shall be applicable to his continued retention, hospitalization and discharge. Mo. 552.020(5) (Supp. 1969).

19. No person who as a result of mental disease or defect is unable to understand the proceedings against him or to assist in his own defense shall be tried, convicted, or sentenced for the commission of an offense so long as such incapacity endures. Mont. 95-504 (Supp. 1969).

20. Lacks mental capacity to stand trial. N.M. 41-13-3.1 (Supp. 1969).

21. Defendants committed under section 41-13-3.1 shall be treated as other patients committed involuntarily to the New Mexico state hospital except that they may not be released from custody without an order of the court. N.M. 41-13-3.1 (Supp. 1969).

22. Defendants committed under section 41-13-3.1 shall have the question of their mental capacity to stand trial redetermined by the court whenever the medical authorities of the New Mexico state hospital any medical authority appointed by the court report to the court that, in their opinion, the defendant is mentally competent to stand trial. N.M. 41-13-3.1 (Supp. 1969).

23. The court upon its own motion or upon the motion of either party may cause the defendant to be examined by 2 psychiatrists from the staff of a state hospital. To facilitate the examination the defendant may be committed to an institution for a maximum of 60 days. Elaborate procedural provisions are set forth. N.Y. Code Crim. Proc. 658 to 662, 870 (Supp. 1970).

24. Oklahoma has 2 different methods. The method charted is when there is doubt of the sanity of the defendant when an indictment or information is called for trial or upon conviction. The other method is for when there is doubt as to the sanity of the person held for trial before the actual trial. In the latter case the judge of the district court will have that person committed to the state hospital and suspend all proceedings pending the report of the doctors of the hospital. If the doctors are of the opinion that the defendant is sane, the order suspending the proceedings shall be dissolved and the question of present sanity shall not be again questioned until the calling of the indictment or information for trial. If, in the opinion of the doctors, such individual is presently insane the district court shall order him committed to the state hospital for treatment until such time as he may be declared presently sane. There is a right to a hearing before a jury. Okla. 22, §1171; 22, §1172; 22, §1173; 22, §1174 (Supp. 1969).

25. If the court determines that care other than that available through commitment of a mentally defective defendant would better serve the defendant and the community, the court at any time may suspend the order of commitment upon condition that the defendant comply with the directors of the court and receive such care as the court may determine and that the defendant is able to understand the proceeding and to assist in his defense. Ore. 136.160(3).

26. If the issue is raised at the time of the arraignment, a jury may at that time be impaneled to try the issue. If the issue is raised during the trial, the trial jury shall determine the issue. Pa. 19, §1352 (1964).

27. After consideration of the petition and all evidence presented, the court may order the commitment of such person to a designated facility if satisfied that the person is mentally disabled and that his commitment is necessary. Pa. 50, §4408(d).

28. The court may commit the defendant to the state hospital for a period of 30 days for observation. S.C. 32-969, 32-970 (Supp. 1968).

29. If at any stage of a court proceeding against any person charged with a criminal offense other than murder or rape it appears to the court that there is reason to believe that the person is mentally retarded, the court shall appoint 2 examiners to examine the person and certify their findings to the court. The procedures to be followed are the same as if there is a civil filing for admission to a hospital or a school. Tenn. 33-501(4) (Supp. 1968).

30. The court can order the defendant hospitalized for observation, care, and treatment for a period not to exceed 30 days. The superintendent of the hospital no later than 30 days after admission shall certify to the court whether the conditions which justified hospitalization still exist. If so, defendant shall be detained in the hospital and an order for his hospitalization shall be entered; if otherwise, he

shall be returned for appropriate disposition to the court which ordered his hospitalization. If he is detained in the hospital, the superintendent shall examine him or have him examined as often as practical, but not less often than every 6 months. Tenn. 33-701 (Supp. 1968).

31. Code of Criminal Procedure 46.01 relates to mental illness after conviction and deals with transfer of prisoners to state mental hospital for treatment. It has not been charted here. Tex. Code Crim. Proc. Ann. 46.01.

32. Before proceeding with the examination, court may order the accused committed for observation and treatment for a period not to exceed 30 days. In such event, hospital superintendent or assistant is to be present at examination and, at the close, is to certify to court. Two or more disinterested physicians are to aid court in examination and, at the close, are to certify to court. Utah 77-48-4.

33. If court feels that discharge of the accused would be dangerous to public, it shall order him confined in state prison or hospital or other suitable institution at his own expense if he has sufficient estate for the purpose. It is unclear whether this provision applies to this table. Vt. 13, §4804.

Appendix A

A Draft Act Governing Hospitalization of the Mentally Ill[1]

STATEMENT BY
GEORGE S. STEVENSON, M.D.

Some 300,000 citizens each year are admitted to our mental hospitals, and a large percentage of these are given no alternative. For the most part these sick people are like the unconscious victim of an auto accident—unable to make the decisions necessary for adequate treatment. A few of the more aggressive, like the carriers of an infectious disease, are a source of danger to others. For this reason, society requires that they submit to conditions that will safeguard both themselves and the community.

But no matter how justified we are in depriving a person of a freedom that we consider basic in a democracy, society, in committing a patient, takes on a clear obligation to make that deprivation an act of good faith. To begin with, the procedure of certification or commitment should be even more surely equitable than if the ill person were able to speak for himself. Anything that aggravates his illness unnecessarily is a violation of this principle. This Draft Act will help States to follow this principle, for it is oriented toward service to a sick person.

But the law cannot fully replace common sense. Peremptory or superficial medical examinations are able to negate a wise law. Recent advances in medical education have been designed to help all doctors meet their psychiatric obligations more skillfully and to improve the quality of medical service. The inclusion of psychiatric services in general hospitals should obviate the use of jails in detention of patients pending admission to a mental hospital.

Beyond this society has an obligation to fully justify enforced hospitalization by making that hospitalization as effective as possible. The responsibility to these patients is clear—to provide all that makes for a good hospital: good medical care, good food, good housing without overcrowding, adequate clothing, respect for and protection of the patient both psychologically and physically, preservation of his relation with and place in a family and community, and opportunity for such work and play as his condition will permit. He should be given such help as will tide him over into the stream of normal community life. This includes help in returning him to wholesome occupation.

There are many steps needed to improve our provisions for the care of the mentally ill. Basic to all these improvements, however, is adequate provision in law for all aspects of proper treatment of the mentally ill. One primary consideration in such basic legislation has to do with statutes that can adequately protect the rights of individuals and at the same time make possible suitable and medically sound commitment procedures. The provisions of this Draft Act can be sincerely recommended as a forward step in our handling of the mentally ill and in the maximum utilization of our mental hospital facilities.

GEORGE S. STEVENSON, M.D.
Medical Director
National Association for Mental Health
September 1952

Reprinted from Public Health Service Publication No. 51, United States Government Printing Office, Washington, 1952.

1. Public Health Service Publication No. 51 is entitled *A Draft Act Governing Hospitalization of the Mentally Ill* (revised September 1952) and was prepared in the Federal Security Agency by the National Institute of Mental Health and the Office of General Counsel. It consists of (1) a Statement by George S. Stevenson, Medical Director of the National Association for Mental Health, (2) Foreword, (3) Scope of the Draft Act, (4) text of the Act, and (5) Commentary. The title page and table of contents for the publication have not been reprinted herein.

FOREWORD

The general objectives of the Draft Act were stated in 1869 by Isaac Ray:

> In the first place, the law should put no hindrance in the way to the prompt use of those instrumentalities which are regarded as most effectual in promoting the comfort and restoration of the patient. Secondly, it should spare all unnecessary exposure of private troubles, and all unnecessary conflict with popular prejudices. Thirdly, it should protect individuals from wrongful imprisonment. It would be objection enough to any legal provision, that it failed to secure these objects, in the completest possible manner.

To broaden the access of the mentally ill to hospital facilities, the Act includes provisions for voluntary admission to mental hospitals which eliminate some of the restrictions now present in the laws of some States, and provisions for admission on medical certification.

To avoid the well-known traumatic effects of "exposure of private troubles" and subjection of sick people to popular prejudices about mental illness, the Draft Act, in addition to providing for voluntary admission and admission on medical certification, includes provisions for formal proceedings for indeterminate involuntary hospitalization which eliminate most, if not all, medically objectionable features of many current procedures. Thus, for example, the jury and the compulsory presence of the proposed patient are excluded. Affirmatively, the hearing body, which would be a court advised by a panel of qualified physicians, would be required to hold a hearing in a physical setting which would not be likely to be harmful; in addition, it would be authorized to exclude persons having no legitimate interest.

To protect individuals from wrongful imprisonment, the Draft Act limits compulsory apprehension and detention to dangerous situations and those in which the individual has had an opportunity for a hearing. It contains detailed provisions for notice to the proposed patient and other interested persons and full opportunity for a hearing in the case of indeterminate involuntary hospitalization. This type of hospitalization would be under judicial control from the beginning. In the medical certification cases, initially without such control, the full procedure could be invoked upon request in writing for the patient's release. Such a request would in effect be a request for a hearing which would be required to be accorded or the patient released. Finally, the Act contains provisions seeking to assure continuing review of the propriety of detention as well as provisions for access to the courts to effect discharges.

In the last few years, the problem of mental hospital legislation has received increased attention, notably by the last three Conferences of State Governors. During this time, the Federal Security Agency has received many requests for suggestions from officials and groups interested in revision of State laws.

Work on this Act was started early in 1949 at the request of the National Advisory Mental Health Council. A working committee was formed in the Federal Security Agency, consisting of the writers of this Foreword and the following members: Dr. James V. Lowry and Riley H. Guthrie of the National Institute of Mental Health; Mrs. Israel L. Sonenshein of the Office of the General Counsel; Dr. Winfred Overholser, Superintendent of Saint Elizabeths Hospital; and also Mr. Franklin N. Flaschner, attorney, of Boston, who was appointed as special consultant because of his prior extensive research in this field. Upon Mrs. Sonenshein fell the principal burden of organizing material for the discussions of the committee, and of drafting the text of the Draft Act and commentary.

During the 2 years that have elapsed since the Draft Act was first formulated, it became apparent that certain changes in its terminology and text would better promote the welfare of the individual member of society and the community at large. Accordingly, representatives of the Federal Security Agency, the National Association for Mental Health, Inc., and the National Institute of Mental Health exchanged views on the suggested changes. The members of the original committee who had passed on the Draft Act were also polled for their views on the proposed amendments. After the representatives and committee members concurred in the proposed changes, it was agreed to amend the Draft Act. The following is a brief recapitulation of the revisions.

Under the general heading *Scope of the Draft Act,* the first paragraph has been revised to clarify the basic criteria used in identifying individuals in need of hospitalization for mental illness. Under Section 2, Part II, and Section 5, Part III, a duty to admit an individual in emergency situations is specifically indicated in the text. As rewritten, Section 6(*a*–2) provides latitude to the central administration in developing certification procedures on the basis of its best judgment. In Section 8, the possibility of the individual's injuring himself or others constitutes the grounds for recommendation by a health or police officer to hospitalize the individual. An added recommendation in this section calls for a report to be made by the head of the hospital admitting the individual. Under section 9(*f*) revised language specifically excludes all persons not having a legitimate interest in hospitalization proceedings. A new subsection (*j*) has been added to Section 9. Under Section 14(*a*) emphasis has been placed on the importance of family ties to the restoration of the patient. Under Section 16(*a*) and (*b*) greater emphasis has been placed on the truly convalescent aspects of the patient's status. Section 23(*b*) clarifies the types of information that may be disclosed about a patient's confidential medical record. Section 25 has been amended to emphasize the additional powers of the central administration in maintaining constant vigilance over the interest of patients.

The assistance of all the legal and medical authorities who participated in this revision of the Draft Act is deeply appreciated.

R. H. FELIX, M.D.
Director
National Institute of Mental Health
GLADYS HARRISON
Assistant General Counsel
Federal Security Agency

Appendix A

SCOPE OF THE DRAFT ACT

THE MENTALLY ILL

The Draft Act deals with hospitalization of the mentally ill. "Mentally ill individual" is defined (sec. 1*a*) as "an individual having a psychiatric or other disease which substantially impairs his mental health." The definition embodies the basic criteria for identifying those potentially in need of hospitalization for a mental condition—i. e. the presence of disease and the consequent impairment of mental health. This type of functional definition seems preferable to an enumeration of categories not in themselves pertinent to the purpose of the Act.

The definition has, of course, the effect of excluding those who are mentally defective. This follows the pattern of many existing statutes. Although the legal principles may be similar for any formal procedures, a separate statutory approach for the two groups appears advisable because they frequently present entirely different problems and substantive needs. The Act will also by reason of the definition include persons who are psychopaths, chronic alcoholics, or members of other special groups, but it will do so only to the extent that the individual meets the criteria set forth in the definition.

CENTRAL ADMINISTRATION; ROLE OF LOCAL HEALTH AUTHORITIES

It is beyond the scope of this Act to deal in any comprehensive way with the administration of the State's mental health or mental hospital programs. As will be seen, the Act reflects the view that the soundness of a program for hospitalization of the mentally ill depends in large measure on centralized State administration, integration with other public health programs of the State, and a larger role for local health officers than they now enjoy. However, details of administrative organization, the general powers and duties of the administering authorities at State and local levels, the tenure of personnel, supervisory relationships, and similar items must necessarily be tailored to the varying governmental patterns of the several States and cannot be reduced to uniform statutory provisions. Thus, while the necessity and desirability of a centralized over-all agency within the State is assumed, the Act would be equally consistent with placing responsibility for hospitalization of the mentally ill in the State health department, in a specialized mental health commission or department, or in a mental hospital department. In regard to administration at the community level, the Act suggests throughout that responsibility be lodged in the "local health authority." The authorities designated could be municipal, county, or district health officers, health departments, boards of health, or similar agencies.

ABILITY TO PAY

The matter of payment for care is not dealt with in the Act because it entails a host of considerations inextricably tied up with special factors and policies of a local character varying from State to State. The Act aims only to carry out the double principle that access to mental hospital facilities, whether on a voluntary or involuntary basis, should not be conditioned on ability to pay, and that the question of ability to pay should be separated procedurally from the question of hospitalization.

GUARDIANSHIP AND INCOMPETENCY

A statute having to do with the mentally ill is necessarily one which deals with individuals who as a class are peculiarly in need of the protective forces of society; public provision of hospital care for the mentally ill generally is itself a recognition of this need. Decision as to hospitalization in the individual case, however, is one which as a rule needs to be made in the light of the individual's entire situation, including the availability of alternatives which may be sufficient or preferable, even from the medical point of view, in the particular case. In those cases where a guardian of the person has previously been appointed, the guardian should be helpful and will have a more or less authoritative role, depending upon the law of the State, in arriving at decisions in the interest of the sick individual. Appointment of a guardian by the court may frequently be a desirable first step in meeting problems growing out of the individual's mental condition of which his need for hospitalization may be only one.

The Act, however does not deal with guardianship as such, nor does it make the status of incompetency a prerequisite to, or a consequence of, hospitalization. It recognizes the basic right of every individual to make his own decision as to the acceptance of medical care or hospitalization and would enforce hospitalization in the case of mental illness only when necessary to do so for the protection of the individual or other members of society or when the individual, because of his illness, has lost the ability to make a responsible decision for himself. Because the conditions justifying the appointment of a guardian are in some respects similar to those justifying court orders for involuntary hospitalization, it is desirable that jurisdiction for both types of proceedings should be in the same court, and that this court should be able to call upon competent social as well as medical advisers. Procedurally, however, the determination that hospitalization is justified should be separated from the adjudication of incompetency and the appointment of a guardian. It is a fundamental theory of the Act that an order of hospitalization decides no more than the question of hospitalization.

Availability of Care Outside the Act

The Act does not make provision for placing individuals, with respect to whom hospitalization proceedings have been commenced, in the custody of private individuals or organizations able and willing to provide care and treatment adequate to the individuals' medical needs. Such matters, of course, impinge on guardianship even though a State might not think it necessary to limit such custody to legally appointed guardians. It has been thought preferable to leave this matter to individual treatment in the light of the family law of the several States. It may be suggested, however, that where it is desired to make it possible to place mentally ill individuals in the custody of private persons or organizations as an alternative to involuntary hospitalization, a distinction should be made between individuals likely to cause injury to themselves or others and those who may be ordered to be hospitalized on other grounds. (See sec. 9.)

AN ACT GOVERNING HOSPITALIZATION OF THE MENTALLY ILL

[Be it enacted, etc.]

PART I—DEFINITIONS

SECTION 1. *Definitions.*—As used in this Act, terms shall have the following meanings:

(*a*) *Mentally ill individual.*—An individual having a psychiatric or other disease which substantially impairs his mental health.

(*b*) *Patient.*—An individual under observation, care, or treatment in a hospital pursuant to this Act.

(*c*) *Licensed physician.*—An individual licensed under the laws of this State to practice medicine and a medical officer of the Government of the United States while in this State in the performance of his official duties.

(*d*) *Designated examiner.*—A licensed physician registered by the (*central administration*) as specially qualified, under standards established by it, in the diagnosis of mental or related illness.

(*e*) *Hospital.*—A public or private hospital or institution, or part thereof, equipped to provide in-patient care and treatment for the mentally ill.

(*f*) *Head of hospital.*—The individual in charge of a hospital, or his designee.

(*g*) (*Central administration*).—The (State) (Department of Health) (Mental Health Commission) (Department of Mental Hygiene).

PART II—VOLUNTARY HOSPITALIZATION

SEC. 2 *Authority to receive voluntary patients.*—The head of a private hospital may and, the head of a public hospital, subject (except in case of medical emergency) to the availability of suitable accommodations, shall admit for observation, diagnosis, care, and treatment any individual who is mentally ill or has symptoms of mental illness and who, being 16 years of age or over, applies therefor, and any individual under 16 years of age who is mentally ill or has symptoms of mental illness, if his parent or legal guardian applies therefor in his behalf.

SEC. 3. *Discharge of voluntary patients.*—The head of the hospital shall discharge any voluntary patient who has recovered or whose hospitalization he determines to be no longer advisable. He may also discharge any voluntary patient if to do so would, in the judgment of the head of the hospital, contribute to the most effective use of the hospital in the care and treatment of the mentally ill.

SEC. 4. *Right to release on application.*—(*a*) A voluntary patient who requests his release or whose release is requested, in writing, by his legal guardian, parent, spouse, or adult next of kin shall be released forthwith except that

(1) if the patient was admitted on his own application and the request for release is made by a person other than the patient, release may be conditioned upon the agreement of the patient thereto, and

(2) if the patient, by reason of his age, was admitted on the application of another person, his release prior to becoming 16 years of age may be conditioned upon the consent of his parent or guardian, and

(3) if the head of the hospital, within 48 hours from the receipt of the request, files with the (*probate*) court or a judge thereof, whether in session or in vacation, a certification that in his opinion the release of the patient would be unsafe for the patient or others, release may be postponed on application for as long as the court or a judge thereof determines to be necessary for the commencement of proceedings for judicial hospitalization, but in no event for more than 5 days.

(*b*) Notwithstanding any other provision of this Act, judicial proceedings for hospitalization shall not be commenced with respect to a voluntary patient unless release of the patient has been requested by himself or the individual who applied for his admission.

PART III—INVOLUNTARY HOSPITALIZATION

Subpart A—Admission Provisions

SEC. 5. *Authority to receive involuntary patients.*—The head of a private hospital may and the head of a public hospital, subject (except in case of medical emergency) to the availability of suitable accommodations, shall receive therein for observation, diagnosis, care, and treatment any individual whose admission is applied for under any of the following procedures:

(*a*) Hospitalization on medical certification; standard nonjudicial procedure.

(*b*) Hospitalization on medical certification; emergency procedure.

(*c*) Hospitalization without endorsement or medical certification; emergency procedure.

(*d*) Hospitalization on court order; judicial procedure.

SEC. 6 *Hospitalization on medical certification; standard nonjudicial procedure.*—(*a*) Any individual may be admitted to a hospital upon

(1) written application to the hospital by a friend, relative, spouse, or guardian of the individual, a health or public welfare officer, or the head of any institution which such individual may be, and

(2) certification by two designated examiners that they have examined the individual and that they are of the opinion that

(A) he is mentally ill, and

(B) because of his illness is likely to injure himself or others if allowed to remain at liberty, or

(C) is in need of care or treatment in a mental hospital, and because of his illness, lacks sufficient insight or capacity to make responsible application therefor.

The certification by the designated examiners may be made jointly or separately, and may be based on examination conducted jointly or separately, as the regulations of the (*central administration*) may prescribe. An individual with respect to whom such certification has been issued may not be admitted on the basis thereof at any time after the expiration of 15 days after the date of examination, exclusive of any period of temporary detention authorized under section 11. The head of the hospital admitting the individual shall forthwith make a report thereof to the (*central administration*).

(*b*) Such certification, if it states a belief that the individual is likely to injure himself or others if allowed to remain at liberty, shall, upon endorsement for such purpose by the head of the (*local health authority*) or by a judge of any court of record of the county in which the individual is resident or present, authorize any health or police officer to take the individual into custody and transport him to a hospital designated in the application.

SEC. 7. *Hospitalization on medical certification; emergency procedure.*—(*a*) Any individual may be admitted to a hospital upon

(1) written application to the hospital by any health or police officer or any other person stating his belief that the individual is likely to cause injury to himself or others if not immediately restrained, and the grounds for such belief, and

(2) a certification by at least one licensed physician that he has examined the individual and is of the opinion that the individual is mentally ill and, because of his illness, is likely to injure himself or others if not immediately restrained.

An individual with respect to whom such a certificate has been issued may not be admitted on the basis thereof at any time after the expiration of 3 days after the date of examination. The head of the hospital admitting the individual shall forthwith make a report thereof to the (*central administration*).

(*b*) Such a certificate, upon endorsement for such purpose by the head of the (*local health authority*) or a judge of any court of record of the county in which the individual is present, shall authorize any health or police officer to take the individual into custody and transport him to a hospital as designated in the application.

SEC. 8. *Hospitalization without endorsement or medical certification; emergency procedure.*—Any health or police officer who has reason to believe that

(*a*) an individual is mentally ill and, because of his illness, is likely to injure himself or others if allowed to remain at liberty pending examination and certification by a licensed physician, or

(*b*) an individual who has been certified under section 6 or 7 as likely to injure himself or others and therefore cannot be allowed to remain at liberty pending the endorsement of the certificate as provided in those sections, may take the individual into custody, apply to a hospital for his admission, and transport him thereto. The application for admission shall state the circumstances under which the individual was taken into custody and the reasons for the officer's belief. The head of the hospital admitting the individual shall forthwith make a report thereof to the (*central administration*).

SEC. 9. *Hospitalization upon court order; judicial procedure.*—(*a*) Proceedings for the involuntary hospitalization of an individual may be commenced by the filing of a written application with the (*probate*) court by a friend, relative, spouse, or guardian of the individual, or by a licensed physician, a health or public welfare officer, or the head of any public or private institution in which such individual may be. Any such application shall be accompanied by a certificate of a licensed physician stating that he has examined the individual and is of the opinion that he is mentally ill and should be hospitalized, or a written statement by the applicant that the individual has refused to submit to examination by a licensed physician.

(*b*) Upon receipt of an application the court shall give notice thereof to the proposed patient, to his legal guardian, if any, and to his spouse, parents, and nearest known other relative or friend. If, however, the court has reason to believe that notice would be likely to be injurious to the proposed patient, notice to him may be omitted.

(*c*) As soon as practicable after notice of the commencement of proceedings is given or it is determined that notice should be omitted, the court shall appoint two designated examiners to examine the proposed patient and report to the court their findings as to the mental condition of the proposed patient and his need for custody, care, or treatment in a mental hospital.

(*d*) The examination shall be held at a hospital or other medical facility, at the home of the proposed patient, or at any other suitable place not likely to have a harmful effect on his health. A proposed patient to whom notice of the commencement of proceedings has been omitted shall not be required to submit to an examination against his will, and on the report of the designated examiners of refusal to submit to an examination the court shall give notice to the proposed patient as provided under paragraph (*b*) of this section and order him to submit to such examination.

(*e*) If the report of the designated examiners is to the effect that the proposed patient is not mentally ill, the court may without taking any further action terminate the proceedings and dismiss the application; otherwise, it shall forthwith fix a date for and give notice of a hearing to be held not less than 5 nor more than 15 days from receipt of the report.

(*f*) The proposed patient, the applicant, and all other persons to whom notice is required to be given shall be afforded an opportunity to appear at the hearing, to testify, and to present and cross-examine witnesses, and the court may in its discretion receive the testimony of any other person. The proposed patient shall not be required to be present, and all persons not necessary for the conduct of the proceedings shall be excluded, except as the court may admit persons having a legitimate interest in the proceedings. The hearings shall be conducted in as informal a manner as may be consistent with orderly procedure and in a physical setting not likely to have a harmful effect on the mental health of the proposed patient. The court shall receive all relevant and material evidence which may be offered and shall not be bound by the rules of evidence. An opportunity to be represented by counsel shall be afforded to every proposed patient, and if neither he nor others provide counsel, the court shall appoint counsel.

(*g*) If, upon completion of the hearing and consideration of the record, the court finds that the proposed patient

(1) is mentally ill, and

(2) because of his illness is likely to injure himself or others if allowed to remain at liberty, or

(3) is in need of custody, care or treatment in a mental hospital and, because of his illness, lacks sufficient insight or capacity to make responsible decisions with respect to his hospitalization,

it shall order his hospitalization for an indeterminate period or for a temporary observational period not exceeding 6 months; otherwise, it shall dismiss the proceedings. If the order is for a temporary period the court may at any time prior to the expiration of such period, on the basis of report by the head of the hospital and such further inquiry as it may deem appropriate, order indeterminate hospitalization of the patient or dismissal of the proceedings.

(*h*) The order of hospitalization shall state whether the individual shall be detained for an indeterminate or for a temporary period and if for a temporary period, then for how long. Unless otherwise directed by the court, it shall be the responsibility of the (*local health authority*) to assure the carrying out of the order within such period as the court shall specify.

(*i*) The court is authorized to appoint a special commissioner to assist in the conduct of hospitalization proceedings. In any case in which the court refers an application to the commissioner, the commissioner shall promptly cause the proposed patient to be examined and on the basis thereof shall either recommend dismissal of the application or hold a hearing as provided in this section and make recommendations to the court regarding the hospitalization of the proposed patient.

(*j*) The head of the hospital admitting a patient pursuant to proceedings under this section shall forthwith make a report of such admission to the (*central administration*).

SEC. 10. *Hospitalization by an agency of the United States.*—(*a*) If an individual ordered to be hospitalized pursuant to the previous section is eligible for hospital care or treatment by any agency of the United States, the court, upon receipt of a certificate from such agency showing that facilities are available and that the individual is eligible for care or treatment therein, may order him to be placed in the custody of such agency for hospitalization. When any such individual is admitted pursuant to the order of such court to any hospital or institution operated by any agency of the United States within or without the State, he shall be subject to the rules and regulations of such agency. The chief officer of any hospital or institution operated by such agency and in which the individual is so hospitalized, shall with respect to such individual be vested with the same powers as the heads of hospitals or the (*central administration*) within this State with respect to detention, custody, transfer, conditional release, or discharge of patients. Jurisdiction is retained in the appropriate courts of this State at any time to inquire into the mental condition of an individual so hospitalized, and to determine the necessity for continuance of this hospitalization, and every order of hospitalization issued pursuant to this section is so conditioned.

(*b*) An order of a court of competent jurisdiction of another State, or of the District of Columbia, authorizing hospitalization of an individual by any agency of the United States shall have the same force and effect as to the individual while in this State as in the jurisdiction in which is situated the court entering the order; and the courts of the State or District issuing the order shall be deemed to have retained jurisdiction of the individual so hospitalized for the purpose of inquiring into his mental condition and of determining the necessity for continuance of his hospitalization, as is provided in subsection (*a*) of this section with respect to individuals ordered hospitalized by the courts of this State. Consent is hereby given to the application of the law of the State or District in which is located the court issuing the order for hospitalization with respect to the authority of the chief officer of any hospital or institution operated in this State by any agency of the United States to retain custody, transfer, conditionally release, or discharge the individual hospitalized.

SEC. 11. *Transportation; temporary detention.*—(*a*) Whenever an individual is about to be hospitalized under the provisions of section 6, 7, 8, or 9, the (*local health authority*) shall, upon the request of a person having a proper interest in the individual's hospitalization, arrange for the individual's transportation to the hospital with suitable medical or nursing attendants and by such means as may be suitable for his medical condition. Whenever practicable, the individual to be hospitalized shall be permitted to be accompanied by one or more of his friends or relatives.

(*b*) Pending his removal to a hospital, a patient taken into custody or ordered to be hospitalized pursuant to this Act may be detained in his home, a licensed foster home, or any other suitable facility under such reasonable conditions as the (*local health authority*) may fix, but he shall not, except because of and during an extreme emergency, be detained in a nonmedical facility used for the detention of individuals charged with or convicted of penal offenses. The (*local health authority*) shall take such reasonable measures, including provision of medical care, as may be necessary to assure proper care of an individual temporarily detained pursuant to this section.

Subpart B—Post-Admission Provisions

SEC. 12. *Notice of hospitalization.*—Whenever a patient has been admitted to a hospital pursuant to section 6, 7, or 8 on the application of any person other than the patient's legal guardian, spouse, or next of kin, the head of the hospital shall immediately notify the patient's legal guardian, spouse, or next of kin, if known.

SEC. 13. *Medical examination of newly admitted patients.*—(*a*) Every patient admitted pursuant to the provisions of section 6, 7, 8, or 9 shall be examined by the staff of the hospital as soon as practicable after his admission.

(*b*) The head of the hospital shall arrange for examination by a designated examiner of every patient hospitalized pursuant to the provisions of section 7 or 8. If such an examination is not held within 5 days after the day of admission, or if a designated examiner fails or refuses after such examination to certify that in his opinion the patient is mentally ill and is likely to injure himself or others if allowed to remain at liberty, the patient shall be immediately discharged.

SEC. 14. *Transfer of patients.*—(*a*) The (*central administration*) may transfer, or authorize the transfer of, an involuntary patient from one hospital to another if the (*central administration*) determines that it would be consistent with the medical needs of the patient to do so. Whenever a patient is transferred, written notice thereof shall be given to his legal guardian, parents, and spouse, or, if none be known, his nearest known relative or friend. In all such transfers, due consideration shall be given to the relationship of the patient to his family, legal guardian or friends, so as to maintain relationships and encourage visits beneficial to the patient.

(*b*) Upon receipt of a certificate of an agency of the United States that facilities are available for the care or treatment of any individual heretofore ordered hospitalized pursuant to law or hereafter pursuant to section 9 of this Act in any hospital for care or treatment of the mentally ill and that such individual is eligible for care or treatment in a hospital or institution of such agency, the (*central administration*) may cause his transfer to such agency of the United States for hospitalization. Upon effecting any such transfer, the court ordering hospitalization, the legal guardian, spouse, and parents, or if none be known, his nearest known relative or friend shall be notified thereof immediately by the (*central administration*). No person shall be transferred to an agency of the United States if he be confined pursuant to conviction of any felony or misdemeanor or if he has been acquitted of the charge solely on the ground of mental

illness unless prior to transfer the court originally ordering confinement of such person shall enter an order for such transfer after appropriate motion and hearing. Any person transferred as provided in this section to an agency of the United States shall be deemed to be hospitalized by such agency pursuant to the original order of hospitalization.

SEC. 15. *Discharge.*—The head of a hospital shall as frequently as practicable, but not less often than every 6 months, examine or cause to be examined every patient and whenever he determines that the conditions justifying involuntary hospitalization no longer obtain, discharge the patient and immediately make a report thereof to the (*central administration*).

SEC. 16. *Convalescent status; rehospitalization.*—(*a*) The head of a hospital may release an improved patient on convalescent status when he believes that such release is in the best interests of the patient. Release on convalescent status shall include provisions for continuing responsibility to and by the hospital, including a plan of treatment on an out-patient or nonhospital patient basis. Prior to the end of a year on convalescent status, and not less frequently than annually thereafter, the head of the hospital shall reexamine the facts relating to the hospitalization of the patient on convalescent status and, if he determines that in view of the condition of the patient hospitalization is no longer necessary, he shall discharge the patient and make a report thereof to the (*central administration*).

(*b*) Prior to such discharge, the head of the hospital from which the patient is given convalescent status may at any time readmit the patient. If there is reason to believe that it is to the best interests of the patient to be rehospitalized, the (*central administration*) or the head of the hospital may issue an order for the immediate rehospitalization of the patient. Such an order, if not voluntarily complied with, shall, upon the endorsement by a judge of a court of record of the county in which the patient is resident or present, authorize any health or police officer to take the patient into custody and transport him to the hospital, or if the order is issued by the (*central administration*) to a hospital designated by it.

SEC. 17. *Right to release; application for judicial determination.*—(*a*) Any patient hospitalized under the provisions of section 6, 7, or 8 of this Act who requests to be released or whose release is requested, in writing, by his legal guardian, spouse, or adult next of kin shall be released within 48 hours after receipt of the request except that, upon application to the court or a judge thereof, whether in session or in vacation, supported by a certification by the head of the hospital that in his opinion such release would be unsafe for the patient or

for others, release may be postponed for such period not to exceed 5 days as the court or a judge thereof may determine to be necessary for the commencement of proceedings for a judicial determination pursuant to section 9.

(*b*) The head of the hospital shall provide reasonable means and arrangements for informing involuntary patients of their right to release as provided in this section and for assisting them in making and presenting requests for release.

SEC. 18. *Petition for re-examination of order or hospitalization.*—Any patient hospitalized pursuant to section 9 shall be entitled to a re-examination of the order for his hospitalization on his own petition, or that of his legal guardian, parent, spouse, relative, or friend, to the (*probate*) court of the county in which he resides or is detained. Upon receipt of the petition, the court shall conduct or cause to be conducted by a special commissioner proceedings in accordance with such section 9, except that such proceedings shall not be required to be conducted if the petition is filed sooner than 6 months after the issuance of the order of hospitalization or sooner than 1 year after the filing of a previous petition under this section.

PART IV—PROVISIONS APPLICABLE TO PATIENTS GENERALLY

SEC. 19. *Right to humane care and treatment.*— Every patient shall be entitled to humane care and treatment and, to the extent that facilities, equipment, and personnel are available, to medical care and treatment in accordance with the highest standards accepted in medical practice.

SEC. 20. *Mechanical restraints.*—Mechanical restraints shall not be applied to a patient unless it is determined by the head of the hospital or his designee to be required by the medical needs of the patient. Every use of a mechanical restraint and the reasons therefor shall be made a part of the clinical record of the patient under the signature of the head of the hospital or his designee.

SEC. 21. *Right to communication and visitation; exercise of civil rights.*—(*a*) Subject to the general rules and regulations of the hospital and except to the extent that the head of the hospital determines that it is necessary for the medical welfare of the patient to impose restrictions, every patient shall be entitled

(1) to communicate by sealed mail or otherwise with persons, including official agencies, inside or outside the hospital;

(2) to receive visitors; and

(3) to exercise all civil rights, including the right to dispose of property, execute instruments, make

purchases, enter contractual relationships, and vote, unless he has been adjudicated incompetent and has not been restored to legal capacity.

(*b*) Notwithstanding any limitations authorized under this section on the right of communication, every patient shall be entitled to communicate by sealed mail with the (*central administration*) and with the court, if any, which ordered his hospitalization.

(*c*) Any limitations imposed by the head of the hospital on the exercise of these rights by the patient and the reasons for such limitations shall be made a part of the clinical record of the patient.

SEC. 22. *Writ of habeas corpus.*—Any individual detained pursuant to this Act shall be entitled to the writ of habeas corpus upon proper petition by himself or a friend to any court generally empowered to issue the writ of habeas corpus in the county in which he is detained.

SEC. 23. *Disclosure of information.*—(*a*) All certificates, applications, records, and reports made for the purpose of this Act and directly or indirectly identifying a patient or former patient or an individual whose hospitalization has been sought under this Act shall be kept confidential and shall not be disclosed by any person except insofar

(1) as the individual identified or his legal guardian, if any (or, if he is a minor, his parent or legal guardian), shall consent, or

(2) as disclosure may be necessary to carry out any of the provisions of this Act, or

(3) as a court may direct upon its determination that disclosure is necessary for the conduct of proceedings before it and that failure to make such disclosure would be contrary to the public interest.

(*b*) Nothing in this section shall preclude disclosure, upon proper inquiry, of information as to his current medical condition, to any members of the family of a patient or to his relatives or friends.

(*c*) Any person violating any provision of this section shall be guilty of a misdemeanor and subject to a fine of not more than $500 and imprisonment for not more than 1 year.

SEC. 24. *Detention pending judicial determination.*—Notwithstanding any other provision of this Act, no patient with respect to whom proceedings for judicial hospitalization have been commenced shall be released or discharged during the pendency of such proceedings unless ordered by the court or a judge thereof upon the application of the patient, or his legal guardian, parent, spouse, or next of kin, or upon the report of the head of the hospital that the patient may be discharged with safety.

SEC. 25. *Additional powers of* (*central administration*).—In addition to the specific authority granted by other provisions of this Act, the (*central administration*) shall have authority to prescribe the form of applications, records, reports, and medical certificates provided for under this Act and the information required to be contained therein; to require reports from the head of any hospital relating to the admission, examination, diagnosis, release, or discharge of any patient; to visit each hospital regularly to review the commitment procedures of all new patients admitted between visits; to investigate by personal visit complaints made by any patient or by any person on behalf of a patient; and to adopt such rules and regulations not inconsistent with the provisions of this Act as it may find to be reasonably necessary for proper and efficient hospitalization of the mentally ill.

SEC. 26. *Unwarranted hospitalization or denial of rights, penalties.*—Any person who wilfully causes, or conspires with or assists another to cause, (1) the unwarranted hospitalization of any individual under the provisions of this Act, or (2) the denial to any individual of any of the rights accorded to him under the provisions of this Act, shall be punished by a fine not exceeding $ . . . . . or imprisonment not exceeding . . . . , or both.

COMMENTARY

PART I—DEFINITIONS

SECTION 1. *Definitions.*—(*a*) *Mentally ill individual.*—This definition serves to indicate the general classification of individuals to whom the various provisions of the Act have potential application. A reading of the remainder of the Act will make it plain that a mere determination that an individual is mentally ill, while it makes him eligible for voluntary hospitalization does not conclude the question of his involuntary hospitalization. Hospitalization on other than a voluntary basis will depend on whether his illness is of such a nature or at such a stage as to make him a source of probable danger to himself or others or whether he has lost his capacity to make responsible decisions on the question of his hospitalization.

(*b*) *Patient.*—This term is defined for convenience only.

(*c*) *Licensed physician.*—This definition makes it possible to utilize for purposes of examination and certification the professional experience and capacity of medical officers of the United States who may be available in the State.

(*d*) *Designated examiner.*—Ideally, all medical judgments required by this Act should be made by fully qualified psychiatrists. However, since the availability of psychiatrists varies greatly from State to State and even between parts of the same State, the Act entrusts the making of such judgments to specially qualified physicians known as "designated examiners," who may or may not be psychiatrists, and, in emergencies, to any licensed physician. Except for the obvious requirement of licensure, standards of qualification for carrying out the special functions assigned to "designated examiners" are left for determination by the central authority. The definition includes a guide for that authority; namely, the training or experience of the physician in the diagnosis of mental and related illness. However, within the limits established by this requirement, the central authority would be free, depending upon the actual situation in the State, to require national board certification, successful completion of a certain number of courses in psychiatry, a number of years of experience in dealing with mental illness, or a combination of these or similar factors.

(e) *Hospital.*—The principal purpose of this definition is to include within the purview of the Act the mental or psychopathic wards of general hospitals, public or private, as possible places for the hospitalization of the mentally ill.

(f) *Head of hospital.*—This definition reflects the need for placing at the highest level responsibility for the important functions to be carried out in the hospitals. The performance of those functions, however, involves in major part the exercise of medical judgment. In any State in which mental hospitals are not headed by licensed physicians, the definition should be adjusted to assure that those judgments will be made by the highest medical official of the hospital.

(g) (*Central administration*).—The definition "central administration" obviously provides only the framework for a definition of the body or officer performing in the State the functions assigned throughout this Act to the "central administration." When completed, the definition would read somewhat like this: "*Department.* The (State) Department of Public Health"; or "*Commission.* The (State) Mental Health Commission"; or "*Commissioner.* The Commissioner of Mental Health." Inclusion of such a definition would then simplify references to the central authority throughout the Act.

PART II—VOLUNTARY HOSPITALIZATION

The guiding purpose of this Part is to increase the scope and effectiveness of voluntary hospitalization. A fully operating program of voluntary admissions will reduce materially the harmful experiences often associated with compulsory hospitalization and at the same time encourage the mentally ill and their families to obtain care at an early stage, when the promise of recovery is greatest. Another important consideration is the need, from the standpoint of effective treatment, for the patient's cooperation with his physician. This is most likely to be obtained if the patient is in a hospital environment because he recognizes his need for it and affirmatively seeks it. Making hospitalization so far as possible as readily available to the mentally ill as to the physically ill should reduce the financial and human cost of mental illness which is greatest when the patient's condition has been aggravated by delay in treatment or by the experience of forcible hospitalization, and when, recovery having become impossible, lifelong custody is the only prospect.

SEC. 2. *Authority to receive voluntary patients.*— This section states the basic provisions governing voluntary admission to mental hospitals. Admission to private hospitals is, of course, at the discretion of their heads. Mentally ill individuals are, however, accorded a right to admission to public hospitals if suitable accommodations are available. In view of the latter limitation and the discharge provisions of section 3, below, the necessary freedom of the head of a public hospital to manage its affairs would not seem to be unduly restricted. A duty to admit in emergency situations is, however, specifically indicated in the text. On the other hand, there is the view that a mentally ill individual who needs hospitalization, even if he does not present a medical emergency, should have an unqualified right of admission to a public hospital. If this view is preferred, the limitation on the right of admission to a public hospital—the availability of suitable accommodations—in this section and in section 5 should be deleted.

Potential voluntary patients are divided into two categories: Those who are less than 16 years old and those who have attained that age. If the proposed patient is not yet 16 years old, he will be admissible only upon the application of his parent or legal guardian. If he is 16 years old or older, his admission will depend on his own application. The specified line of division is necessarily arbitrary just as 17, 15, or 18 would be, and should therefore be considered only suggestive. However, the age of 21 which is used in a number of statutes is considered too high. Individuals in their later teens carry responsibilities which are often commensurate with those of older persons—responsibility for infractions of law, for example. Hence it is believed that they should not by reason of their age alone be denied the opportunity to apply for hospital care. It may be noted in this connection that, in cases involving the consent of a minor to the performance of surgery upon him, our courts have generally held the consent to be effective where the minor was over 15 years old and sufficiently mature to realize the dangers and benefits of the operation, although this fact has not been elevated to a rule of law.

The possibility that an adolescent's application may be ill advised is strongly balanced (1) by the fact that the hospital will be unauthorized to accept him or to keep him if his mental condition does not meet the statutory requirements, and (2) by later provisions in the Act which make it possible for his parents to request his release and, if release should be refused unjustifiably, to obtain it by recourse to the courts.

It has already been pointed out that the definition of "mentally ill" formulates the general basis for potential application of the Act. In relation to this Part, an individual who is mentally ill would be eligible for reception as a voluntary patient. However, in furtherance of the principle that it is medically more effective and administratively more economical to bring medical science to bear on the problem of mental health at the earliest possible moment, the Act also makes eligible for admission as voluntary patients those whose mental illness is only in the process of developing. There will be many cases in which symptoms of mental illness are plainly discernible but have not yet reached the point where the individual may be said to be "mentally ill" in the full sense. Opening hospital facilities to such individuals can contribute to the reduction of the State's total hospitalization problem. Many such individuals may recover after a short course of treatment, whereas if they fail to receive it, they will need substantially longer hospitalization later.

SEC. 3. *Discharge of voluntary patients.*—The use of voluntary hospitalization procedures will be increased if the governing statute makes it abundantly clear that this kind of hospitalization is not a one-way street. This is achieved in part by imposing on the head of the hospital a clear duty to discharge a patient immediately upon recovery or when hospital care is no longer advisable. In the case of public hospitals, such a provision entails the additional consideration that it will minimize the possibility that persons no longer ill or needing hospitalization will be allowed to continue their stay at public expense. In recognition of the possible necessity for the head of the hospital to make choices as between types of patients if he is to intelligently administer the hospital for the benefit of all, he is empowered to discharge a voluntary patient if he determines it to be necessary to do so in order to make the most effective use of the hospital for its intended purpose.

SEC. 4. *Right to release on application.*—(a) This subsection, by providing the easiest possible egress, contributes to the assurance that voluntary admission is not an irrevocable act. A voluntary patient's release can be requested by the patient himself, or by his parent, spouse, adult next of kin, or legal guardian. This provision is, however, subject to certain limitations.

(1) While it is obviously desirable to permit persons other than the patient himself to request his release, it should nevertheless be possible for the patient's wishes to prevail in case of a disagreement between him and the parent or spouse, for example, who demands his release. Accordingly, this section makes it possible to make the release depend on the patient's agreement. The head of the hospital can permit the patient to remain if he agrees with the patient's own judgment as to the latter's best medical interests. (The parent or spouse can of course still seek release through judicial proceedings.)

(2) On the other hand, a patient disqualified by reason of age from obtaining admission on his own application should not be able to obtain his release entirely at will while still under 16 years of age. This section, therefore, provides that release in response to such a patient's request may be conditioned by the head of the hospital on the consent of the person in legal control, that is, the patient's parent or guardian. If the disqualifying condition has ceased to exist, that is, the patient has become 16 years of age, this limitation on his right to release will no longer apply.

(3) The right of release is subject, in some cases, to provision for the institution of formal proceedings for involuntary hospitalization. When release is requested, the head of the hospital will have to determine whether the patient may be released without danger to himself or others. The condition of a patient harmless upon admission may have become so aggravated that his release would result in a suicide or a homicide.

The authority to detain is, however, severely circumscribed. If the head of the hospital forms the opinion that the patient is dangerous, whether to himself or others, and cannot safely be released, the head of the hospital is authorized to file with the (*probate*) court, or a judge of that court, a certificate stating his opinion to that effect. ("Probate" as used in this section of the Act and elsewhere is intended only to suggest a court having special responsibilities in the field of family law.) Should such a certificate not be filed within 48 hours from receipt of the request, the patient could not be further held. If the certificate is filed the patient's release can then be postponed by order of the court or a judge thereof for as long as is determined to be necessary for the institution of formal proceedings, not to exceed 5 days. (Under sec. 24, once proceedings are commenced, the patient may be detained pending their conclusion unless his prior release should be judicially ordered.)

This limitation on release may appear inconsistent with the objectives of encouraging voluntary hospitalization by assuring prospective patients and their families that admission to the hospital is subject to revocation. However, if the condition of the person is such that it is unsafe for him to go unrestrained, the necessity of steps to secure his detention and treatment is the same whether he is outside or inside the hospital at the time the condition develops.

(*b*) Under this subsection, it is possible for a patient to retain his voluntary status as long as he (or in the case of a child, his parent or guardian) so desires. Proceedings for his judicial hospitalization cannot be commenced until he or the person who applied for his admission seeks the patient's release. In many cases, individuals contemplating application for voluntary admission will be concerned lest, by doing so, they make themselves subject to proceedings for involuntary hospitalization.

PART III—INVOLUNTARY HOSPITALIZATION

Voluntary admission is generally considered the ideal procedure for hospitalization for mental illness. This view is reenforced by the growing awareness that, apart from treatment techniques, sharp lines between mental illness and physical illness are quite artificial. Yet it must be expected that, no matter how extensive the educational effort along this line, there will continue to be many mentally ill individuals who will not use voluntary procedures. The problem then becomes to determine which of the mentally ill who do not or cannot seek hospitalization for themselves ought to be hospitalized on grounds of public policy and to devise procedures which will at once reduce the danger of harmful effects inherent in many existing procedures and insure against unconstitutional deprivation of the liberty of the individuals involved. In the latter case, a duty to admit in emergency situations is specifically indicated in the text. The provisions of Part III constitute a possible solution of this difficult problem.

Subpart A—Admission Provisions

SEC. 5. *Authority to receive involuntary patients.*— This section simply sets forth the basic authority of the private hospital and the obligation of the public hospital to receive patients on other than a voluntary basis. The four enumerated procedures, which are elaborated in subsequent sections, differ from each other as to the occasions for and consequences of their use. Two are intended for emergency situations, two for cases permitting of deliberate consideration of the individual's condition and medical needs. One procedure involves a full judicial hearing and determination. The others are substantially nonjudicial. All, however, pertain to the situation in which there has been failure or refusal on the part of the individual or, if he is under 16 years of age,

on the part of his parents or guardian to initiate voluntary action looking to hospital care.

Although the possibility of forcible apprehension is involved in each of these procedures, it should be emphasized that "involuntary hospitalization" as used in this Act is not coextensive with compulsory hospitalization. The terms "voluntary" and "involuntary" are used only to mark off the area in which there is affirmative original action by the individual (or, in appropriate cases, his parent or guardian) from the area in which hospitalization is achieved despite the lack of such action. Thus, a sick individual who has been unwilling to apply for voluntary admission may, after a medical certification has been made under section 6 or 7, accept the judgment of others and go along without protest to the hospital with a friend or member of his family. Legal authority, however, for a health or police officer to take the individual into custody and remove him to the hospital is provided, under proper safeguards, when the individual refuses hospitalization and his condition is such as to require his restraint. The term "involuntary hospitalization" should be understood therefore as encompassing both the passive and nonvoluntary entry into a hospital as well as the entry which must be accomplished against the will and despite the resistance of the individual.

SEC. 6. *Hospitalization on medical certification; standard nonjudicial procedure.*—This section sets out the standard nonjudicial procedure for use in situations other than emergencies compelling resort to more summary procedures. The basic elements of this procedure are the written application for admission and the medical certification by two "designated examiners."

(*a*) The application must be in writing and under section 25 may be required to be on a prescribed form. It can be made by a friend, relative, spouse, or guardian of the individual or by a health or public welfare officer, or by the head of any hospital or other institution in which the individual may happen to be. The application need not be made by the person who actually brings the mentally ill individual to the hospital. For example, a husband might make the application and then invoke the assistance of a trained public welfare officer to escort his wife to a hospital. Again, the head of a nonmental hospital could make application with respect to a patient who, while being treated for some physical illness, has become mentally ill and could arrange directly for the patient's transfer to the mental hospital or could call upon a friend or relative of the patient or a health officer to assist.

Certification under this section must be made by two "designated examiners" based upon examination, by each, of the individuals thought to be ill. It is left to the central administration to prescribe whether these certifications or examinations shall be made jointly or separately and on the basis of joint or separate examinations. Some experts favor a single certification that will represent a joint judgment reached after consultation by two trained examiners on the basis of independent examination and consider also that some interval between examinations is desirable. Some experts, on the other hand, consider that there are advantages in a joint judgment by two trained examiners observing the individual under the same conditions. The section as written provides latitude to the central administration in developing procedures on the basis of its best judgment and in the light of developing experience.

To be effective under this section the certificate must show that the examiners have concluded that the individual is mentally ill. In addition, either of two other conditions must exist in their opinion. Either the nature or stage of the individual's illness must be such that he is likely to injure himself or others if allowed to go unrestrained or he must be in need of care or treatment in a mental hospital but, because of his illness, lacks sufficient insight or capacity to make a responsible application in his own behalf. The provisions of this subsection are readily usable for the individual who is not mentally fit to apply for voluntary hospitalization. If hospitalization in the opinion of the examiners might be beneficial, but the individual is capable of making decisions for himself in such matters, authoritative intervention is necessary only in case there is a real threat of injury if he remains at liberty. (See, in this connection, the discussion of sec. 9g.)

A medical certification issued under this section will be effective as authority for the admission to the hospital if the individual certified is presented within 15 days after the date of the examination. Specification of a short period on the life of the certificate is designed to forestall unscrupulous use of stale certificates. Periods of temporary detention are not counted because the risk sought to be guarded against will no longer exist after action has been taken under the certificate. (See sec. 11.)

(*b*) Hospitalization under this procedure cannot be legally compelled unless the examiners certify that in their opinion there is an element of danger present; namely, that the individual is likely to injure himself or others if allowed to remain at liberty. Given the latter circumstance, the certificate may be presented for endorsement by the judge of any court of record of the country in which the individual is resident or present, or by the head of the local health authority. Endorsement has the effect of authorizing any health or police officer to take the individual into custody and transport him to a hospital. The officer is, of course, not authorized

to take any such action if 15 days have gone by since the date of the examination.

Under this procedure the person executing the application and the medical examiners in making their certifications are acting as private individuals rather than as agents of the State or of any court. The endorsement is a means by which the regularity of the certification may be checked by a judge or the local health authority before the compulsory forces of the State may be invoked. The requirement for endorsement is somewhat analogous to that of a magistrate's warrant for arrest upon a showing of "propable cause." As another safeguard, a State may also wish to consider addition of a requirement that the designated examiners be in each case assigned, selected, or approved by a specified State or local authority.

SEC. 7. *Hospitalization on medical certification; emergency procedure.*—(*a*) The procedure set forth in the previous section is based on the premise that the important medical judgment at the root of a hospitalization procedure should be made by persons who have acquired a certain expertness in the diagnosis of mental illness. Hence the requirement for examination and certification by two "designated examiners," whose status implies that they have that expertness. However, critical situations will arise in which it will not be possible to comply with such requirements without real danger to the sick individual, members of his family or others in the community. Hence, the emergency provisions of sections 7 and 8.

The issuance of the certificate under section 7 is conditioned on an examination by a licensed physician and his determination, stated in the certificate, that the individual is mentally ill and, because of his illness, is likely to injure himself or others if not *immediately* restrained.

As in the standard procedure, hospitalization under this section requires also the filing of an application with the hospital. However, there are differences between the application requirements of the two procedures. Because of the emergency nature of the procedure under section 7, the application can be made by any health or police officer or by any other person. The applicant, however, must state his belief that the individual is likely to cause injury to himself or others if not immediately restrained, and must state also the grounds for his belief. The latter would not necessarily be limited to the results of the applicant's own observation but could be based on credible reports by others.

(*b*) Endorsement of the certificate by a judge or by the head of the local health authority is required, as under section 6, to give it the effect of a warrant for apprehension and forcible removal to a hospital.

SEC. 8. *Hospitalization without endorsement or medical certification; emergency procedure.*—Apprehension of an individual, and his admission solely on the application of a police or health officer on a strictly provisional basis (see sec. 13*b*), is authorized purely as a safety measure where circumstances make it impossible to delay action before completion even of the emergency procedure of section 7. The officer acting on his own responsibility in such a case must set forth in his application the circumstances under which the individual was placed in custody and the reason for the officer's belief that it would be unsafe for the individual to be allowed to remain at liberty pending examination by a licensed physician or pending the procurement of the endorsement of a medical certificate by the local health authority or a judge.

This section is intended to supply, for those situations in which an unbalanced person threatens immediate violence, authority for emergency detention in a hospital. This is comparable to the authority, recognized at common law, for the emergency detention in jail of a person arrested without warrant because of an immediately threatened breach of the peace.

As will be seen below (sec. 13*b*), the individual apprehended, like an individual hospitalized under section 7, would have to be certified by a "designated examiner" within 5 days after admission, or be released. He would be released in any event if it is found upon examination by the hospital staff that he is not mentally ill or that his hospitalization is not justified.

SEC. 9. *Hospitalization on court order; judicial procedure.*—Many patients admitted under one of the nonjudicial procedures described above could become voluntary patients and remain as long as hospitalization is needed. Those who do not choose or are unable to exercise this prerogative may, nevertheless, remain in the hospital for an indeterminate period as medically necessary. (This is, of course, subject to the requirements of sec. 13*b* for perfecting admission in certain cases.) Thus, there is opportunity procedurally for hospitalization for an indeterminate period without resort of formal judicial proceedings. The chances for successful treatment will generally be enhanced if such procedural possibilities are utilized.

There will, however, be cases in which enforced hospitalization for an indeterminate period will be necessary. While all sound procedures for hospitalization of the mentally ill seek to assure that medical factors will be given the fullest emphasis, liberty of movement is one of the most elemental of human rights and one of which no person in this country may constitutionally be deprived without due process of law. Final authority and responsibility for compulsory hospitalization is therefore here placed in an arm of the State customarily exercising a judicial function. Under the Act, except in emergency situations, only a judicial decision can compel the hospitalization of an individual against his will. The central role of the physician in the determination and evaluation of data within the field of his special expertness is nevertheless given full recognition.

(*a*) Judicial proceedings are commenced by the filing of a written application with the probate or other designated court.

An application may be filed by a friend, relative, spouse, parent, or guardian of the individual, or by a licensed physician, a health or public welfare officer, or the head of any public or private institution in which the individual might be. Thus, for example, the superintendent of a mental hospital may file an application with respect to one of his voluntary patients. Similarly, the head of a nonmental hospital may institute the proceedings with respect to an individual who, while admitted because of a physical complaint, is discovered to be or becomes mentally ill.

To reduce the possibility of frivolous or malicious applications, each application is required to be accompanied by a certificate of a licensed physician to the effect that he has examined the individual and is of the opinion that he is mentally ill and should be hospitalized. Lest commencement of the proceedings be thwarted by the individual's refusal to submit to medical examination and the consequent inability of a licensed physician to make the certification, the applicant may, in lieu of the certificate, file a written statement that there has been such a refusal.

(*b*) The court receiving the application will notify the individual involved, as well as his legal guardian, if any, his parents, spouse, and his other nearest known relative or friend. If there should be reason, however, to believe that it would be injurious to the individual, the notice that an application has been filed may be omitted as to him.

(*c*) Having given notice of the institution of proceedings, the court is required to appoint two "designated examiners" to examine the proposed patient and make a report of their findings as to his mental condition, and his need for custody and treatment in a mental hospital. It is a matter for the discretion of the court whether the "designated examiners" are appointed on an *ad hoc* or an indefinite basis. From the statutory duty imposed on the court to have the proposed patient examined, authority to issue the necessary process to compel the submission to examination when necessary would seem to be implied; in a particular State, however, express provision therefore may be desirable.

(*d*) The examination itself must be held at a place

not likely to have a harmful effect on the proposed patient's condition. Whenever possible the examination should be held in the individual's home or in a medical facility, but the provisions of this subsection are flexible enough to permit use of other places, if necessary. No individual, however, can be required to submit to a medical examination, except on court order, if the notice to him of the commencement of proceedings has been omitted. It is anticipated, of course, that in most cases in which it is determined by the court that notice of proceedings should not be given, the individual will not refuse to be examined.

(*e*) Upon receipt of the report of the examining physicians, the court is required to fix a date for a hearing within a specified period. The requirement to hold a hearing upon receipt of the medical report is subject to the discretion of the court to terminate the proceedings without further action if the report is to the effect that the individual examined is not mentally ill.

(*f*) While seeking to avoid the medically undesirable results of overformal proceedings, this subsection includes provisions to assure full and fair consideration of all relevant data so that the question of the proposed patient's hospitalization may be considered in the light of his total situation. Not only the proposed patient but also the applicant and those required to be notified of the proceedings are entitled to be present, to testify, and to present and cross-examine witnesses. The court is empowered in addition to receive the testimony of any other person. The court is not bound by the rules of evidence lest important matter be barred on technical grounds. Finally, the proposed patient is entitled to be represented by counsel of his choice and, if counsel should not be retained, the court is under a duty to appoint counsel.

In order to reduce the harmful possibilities inherent in formal proceedings, compulsory presence of the patient at the hearing is expressly excluded. He has a right to participate in the hearing and, if he chooses to exercise it, the court is under a legal obligation to give him the opportunity to do so. There will be instances, however, in which a proposed patient's appearance would, in the view of his physician, aggravate his illness; there is no reason why he should not be permitted to accept such medical advice. The basic constitutional right of an opportunity to appear and be heard is provided for. As a corollary to the provisions on compulsory presence, this subsection authorizes the court to ban from attendance all persons having no legitimate interest in the proceedings.

On the affirmative side, there is imposed on the court the express obligation to conduct the hearing in a physical setting not likely to be injurious to the individual's health, and in as informal a manner as may be consistent with orderly procedure. There is widespread agreement that a hearing held in physical circumstances or in an atmosphere suggestive of criminal proceedings or formal adjudication often retards recovery and sometimes intensifies the condition from which the proposed patient is suffering.

Section 9 makes no provision for a jury "trial." Since mental illness is not a crime, there is no justification for treating as criminals those thought to be suffering with it. It has, moreover, come to be widely recognized that the appearance of the proposed patient before a jury of laymen increases the likelihood of harmful effects. Equally important is the consideration that the jury is a questionable instrument for evaluating the preeminently medical ingredients of a determination in this field. As the proceeding is designed in this section, nothing is involved except the hospitalization of the individual thought to be ill.

(*g*) The next step is the court's action upon completion of the hearing. If, upon consideration of the record, the court should find that the proposed patient is mentally ill and (1) because of his illness is likely to injure himself or others if allowed to remain at liberty, or (2) is in need of hospitalization and, because of his illness, lacks sufficient insight or capacity to make responsible decisions with respect to his hospitalization, it is required to order his hospitalization for an indeterminate period or for a temporary observational period not exceeding 6 months. On the other hand, if it should appear to the court that the individual is not mentally ill, or that, while he is mentally ill, he is neither likely to cause any injury nor is in need of hospitalization nor lacking in capacity to make the requisite decisions, the application must be dismissed and the proposed patient discharged.

If an individual should be ordered hospitalized for a temporary period, a report must be made by the head of the hospital at the expiration of the period. After considering the report and making such further inquiry as might seem appropriate, the court is required to decide whether the individual should be hospitalized for an indeterminate period or discharged.

Special reference should be made to the grounds upon which the involuntary hospitalization of a mentally ill individual may be ordered under this subsection. The grounds established are in the alternative: (1) The likelihood that the individual will injure himself or others if he is not confined, and (2) need of hospitalization and lack of sufficient insight or capacity to make responsible decisions with respect to the question of hospitalization.

Individuals to whom the first ground is applicable are those traditionally called "dangerous," and they clearly should be hospitalized. Other mentally ill individuals are usually referred to as "harmless." The second alternative ground is based on the premise that within the "harmless" class there are some individuals who may also be ordered to be hospitalized; namely, those who need care, custody, or treatment in a mental hospital and lack sufficient capacity to make a decision on the question of their hospitalization which would have a reasonable relation to relevant factors.

Within the wide range of mental illnesses there are cases in which the sick individual, like the individual who is physically sick, retains sufficient capacity to make a responsible decision on the question of his hospitalization, weighing it against other factors in his life and affairs. On the other hand, without being "dangerous," a mentally ill individual may because of the nature or stage of his illness lose his power to make choices or become so confused as no longer to have the capacity to make a decision having any relation to the factors bearing on his hospitalization. It is in the latter situation that the Act permits compulsory hospitalization. The mentally ill individual who is found to have retained this capacity cannot be compelled to enter a hospital unless he is "dangerous."

It should be emphasized that it is not a question of the individual agreeing or disagreeing with medical judgment as to the nature of his illness or the need for hospital care, but rather of whether he is *capable* of making a responsible, not necessarily a wise, decision in the premises.

In short, the State through its courts is here authorized to make for the individual a decision which, by reason of his illness he is incapable of making for himself.

(*h*) Orders of hospitalization are required to state the duration of the hospitalization. Normally, it would be the responsibility of the local health authority to see to it that the order is carried out in accordance with its terms. There is, however, sufficient flexibility to permit designation of persons, officers, or agencies not connected with the local health authority to have this responsibility. It is not intended to require that the person or agency so designated shall take the individual into custody and deliver him to a hospital. Once the order is issued the individual may come or be brought to the hospital without need for any official intervention.

(*i*) Provision for designation of a special commissioner or similarly named officer to assist the court in disposition of cases under this section is made in order to facilitate their prompt handling. Promptness is especially important in cases in which proceedings have been instituted following a request for release of a voluntary patient or one admitted under a nonjudicial procedure. Since the probate or other court designated to conduct the hospitalization proceedings normally has

responsibility for decision on a wide variety of other problems as well, it would be extremely valuable to have available a commissioner who would through experience become expert in this special field and be able to give the court the benefit of that expertness.

The commissioner has no power of decision. Upon referral of an application to him, he is required to conduct the proceedings as provided in subsections (*c*) and (*f*), inclusive, and at their conclusion to make recommendations to the court as to the hospitalization of the proposed patient.

(*j*) Reports of admission are required so that the (central administration) will have a complete record on all patients in State institutions at the earliest possible moment.

SEC. 10. *Hospitalization by an agency of the United States.*—This section follows very closely the provisions of paragraphs (1) and (2) of section 18 of the Uniform Veterans' Guardianship Act which have been adopted by about three-fourths of the States. Section 10 varies from the cited portions of the Uniform Act only insofar as is necessary to make the terminology consistent with that used in the Draft Act generally. Accordingly, for the 35 or more States having provisions patterned after those of the Uniform Act, adoption of section 10 of the Draft Act as part of a revised whole would not materially affect existing procedures for hospitalization of the mentally ill in Federal facilities. The matter of transfer of patients originally hospitalized in non-Federal facilities is covered by section 14 of this Act, which follows very closely the provisions of section 18 (3) of the Uniform Act already referred to.

If a State chooses not to accept the principle of the Draft Act that final authority and responsibility for compulsory hospitalization should be exclusively in the judicial arm, it will of course be necessary, as the case may be, to substitute for or add to the word "court" in section 10 (and at other appropriate points) the designation of other agencies or officials given such authority and responsibility in place of or in addition to a court.

As pointed out by the Uniform Commissioners, provisions of the type set out in section 18 of the Uniform Act "will facilitate the placing of patients in appropriate Federal institutions especially equipped to treat a particular type of mental trouble and save the patient distress and sometimes definite harm incident to a second adjudication experience in the State to which transferred." An example is the case of a psychosis involving narcotic addiction. The Public Health Service operates two institutions devoted to care and treatment of narcotic addicts. If a patient ordered hospitalized under section 9 is eligible for care under the auspices of the Service and accommodations are available, he can be placed in the custody of the Service at the time of adjudication or, as will be seen below, transferred to it after his admission to a State hospital. The Service can then place him in one of its institutions treating narcotic addicts—one is in Kentucky, the other in Texas—irrespective of the State in which he is ordered to be hospitalized.

Sec. 11. *Transportation; temporary detention.*—(*a*) The matter of transportation of mentally ill individuals to hospitals has been a sore point medically. Expert opinion is agreed that transportation of mental patients by police officers and sheriffs, using as they do conveyances and equipment pertinent to criminals, causes the patient to enter the course of his treatment under the worst possible circumstances. Accordingly, this section of the Act seeks to reduce to a minimum the occasion for that type of transportation. In all cases it is possible under the Act for the sick individual's family or friends to arrange for transportation by private means. On the other hand, anyone having a proper interest in or responsibility for the admission of an individual to a mental hospital under any of the procedures enumerated in section 5 of this Act can request the local health authority to make arrangements for transporting the patient to the hospital. The local health authority is required to comply with such requests. Its responsibility includes provision of suitable medical or nursing attendants and arrangement for the use of such means as would be most consistent with the patient's medical condition. While the language used in this section is by design flexible to permit variations based on the judgment of the responsible officials, it is hard to visualize a situation—short of extreme urgency—in which a Black Maria could be said to be such a means. With regard to the attendants, the Act does not indicate their source, leaving it to the local health authority to provide personnel from its own staff or by temporary retainer, or to arrange for personnel from the hospital staff to accompany the patient. The latter practice is now in use in many places and is highly favored by medical men.

In general, the transportation provisions seek to make available at this important prehospitalization stage the skill and training of public officers or employees whose primary interest can be expected to be the health of the patient.

(*b*) The Act talks repeatedly of taking the individual to a hospital as defined in section 1; i.e., to a medical facility able to provide the indicated therapy or custody. Yet it must be anticipated that it will on some occasions be impracticable to place the individual in a hospital immediately. Detention in jails and similar places is among the worst of current practices in this whole field and this section of the Act expressly excludes such places as normal points of temporary detention. Patients may,

however, on occasion have to be kept in a jail as a matter of sheer necessity. The Act attempts to deal with this problem realistically, authorizing detention in a jail or similar facility only in cases of extreme emergency. When the emergency ends, the detention must also end.

In any case of temporary detention the local health authority has supervisory responsibility, which includes the imposition of reasonable conditions. In addition, that authority is under a duty to take such reasonable measures, including provision of medical care, as may be necessary to assure proper care of the individual temporarily detained. This is to be contrasted with confinement in a hospital where such matters are entirely in the hands of the head of the hospital.

Subpart B—Postadmission Provisions

Sec. 12. *Notice of hospitalization.*—The provisions of this section are applicable only to a patient admitted pursuant to section 6, 7, or 8 on the application of a person other than his legal guardian, spouse, or next of kin. It is an important adjunct to admission under those sections because notice prior to hospitalization such as is provided under section 9 is not included in those three sections.

Sec. 13. *Medical examination of newly admitted patients.*—(*a*) This subsection simply requires prompt examination by the hospital staff of every involuntary patient. Every hospital will want to examine every new patient, irrespective of any statutory requirement, if only for the purpose of classification. Specific statutory provision is, nevertheless, desirable as a safeguard against unjustified hospitalization because as to a good portion of the patients admitted to hospitals such an examination would be the first by physicians specially trained in psychiatry. See section 15, which provides for discharge of patients with respect to whom conditions justifying hospitalization no longer obtain. It is recognized that the maintenance of contact with family and friends during hospitalization is frequently conducive to the early improvement of the patient and his subsequent adjustment at home. Where family relationships and visits are beneficial to the patient, this factor should be taken into account in considering the transfer of patients.

(*b*) The purpose of the provision for examination within a short specified period by a "designated examiner" of all patients admitted under emergency procedures (sec. 7 or 8) is to perfect their admission and, from the viewpoint of the protection of the patient against unwarranted hospitalization, to bring it substantially up to the level of the standard nonjudicial procedure. Once such an examination and an effective certification have been made, the patient has the same status as one admitted under the standard procedure established by section 6. The net effect of this subsection is that a patient admitted under one of the emergency procedures is admitted only provisionally and must be discharged at the end of 5 days unless steps have been taken to "complete" his admission. A valuable aspect of this type of provision is that it protects the involuntary patient admitted without certification of two "designated examiners" against any undue delay in complying with the requirements of subsection (a) of this section.

SEC. 14. *Transfer of patients.*—(a) With the increasing specialization of mental hospital facilities and the swelling of hospital populations, the problem of transfer of patients has grown in importance. This section of the Act declares only the basic authority to transfer, who shall have that authority, and a requirement that interested persons be notified. In contrast to the power to discharge which is localized in the head of the hospital, the assignment of the transfer power to the central administration is most likely to assure rational distribution of patients among a State's general and specialized facilities.

(b) See discussion under section 10.

SEC. 15. *Periodic examination; discharge.*—Advances in medicine now make it likely that many mental patients will, after a suitable period in a hospital environment, become so improved as to make their further hospitalization unjustified. This may take years, but it may also sometimes be achieved in months. In many cases the patients or their relatives or friends may become aware of the improvement and take steps to secure release. It is not enough, however, to leave such an important matter to voluntary private action. This section therefore imposes on those who have readiest access to the facts; namely, the hospital staff acting under its head, the duty to take the initiative in assuring that involuntary patients will not remain in the hospital when the statutory conditions justifying hospitalization have ceased to exist. It must, of course, be recognized that adequate execution of the responsibilities imposed by this section, as well as some of those imposed by other sections, will depend largely upon the existence of adequate hospital staffs.

SEC. 16. *Convalescent status; rehospitalization.*—(a) Ancillary to the discharge provisions is the one for release on convalescent status set out in this subsection. Patients frequently advance toward recovery to such a degree that it is advisable to dispense tentatively with hospital care. In such cases the head of the hospital is authorized to release the patient on convalescent status. This status contemplates the continued exercise of responsibility by the hospital and the establishment of a plan of treatment, as for example, that the patient receive

treatment at an outpatient clinic or at a psychiatrist's office and not engage in certain types of work.

The release is tentative because of the uncertainty as to the effect the change of environment may have on the improved patient. In order to avoid the possibility of a patient released under this subsection remaining indefinitely in the position of being outside the hospital and yet somehow within its jurisdiction, provision is made for complete reconsideration of his status prior to the completion of a year on convalescent status. Where a hospital has an outpatient clinic closely connected with it, it is, of course, relatively easy to keep current on the patient's medical condition so that his complete discharge under section 15 can be effected as soon as he recovers his mental health. Where the outpatient care is beyond the hospital's control, this is more difficult to achieve and the main reliance has to be on the requirement for review prior to the end of the first year of convalescent status and not less frequently than annually thereafter.

(b) Rehospitalization of a patient released under the previous subsection may be called for because of a failure to comply with the terms of convalescent status or because of a change in the patient's condition. Prior to discharge, the patient may voluntarily request readmission for hospital care. In the absence of such action, it would serve no useful purpose to require the institution of fresh proceedings in order to reestablish the individual's status as a hospital patient. This subsection therefore provides that the central administration or the head of the hospital may order the rehospitalization of a patient if there is reason to believe that rehospitalization is to the best interests of the patient. Upon issuance of the order and its endorsement by a judge of any court of record of the county in which the patient is resident or present, any health or police officer may take the patient into custody and transport him to the hospital, or if the order is issued by the central administration, to a hospital designated by it.

SEC. 17. *Right to release; application for judicial determination.*—(a) This section relates only to the patient admitted with out the full judicial proceedings established under section 9. It sets forth his right and the right of his legal guardian, spouse, or adult next of kin to request the patient's release at any time. In order to avoid disputes as to whether or not a request had been made, the request is required to be in writing. The patient has to be released within 48 hours unless an application is filed with the probate or other designated court for postponement of release. The application may be filed by the head of the hospital or by someone else, but it must in any case be supported by a certification by the head of the hospital that in his opinion release would be unsafe for the patient or for others. If the application and certification are filed within 48 hours from receipt of the request, the court or one of its judges may authorize the detention of the patient for not more than 5 days for the purpose of allowing time for commencement of judicial proceedings for hospitalization. Should the application and certification not be filed within the specified period, the patient must, of course, be released.

(*b*) This subsection imposes an obligation on the head of the hospital to assure that patients admitted under nonjudicial procedures will be informed of their right to request release and be assisted in making the request. Without such a requirement, the right provided by subsection (*a*) might have no real meaning in many cases.

SEC. 18. *Petition for re-examination of order of hospitalization.*—The provisions of this section apply to the patient judicially hospitalized and serve in regard to him the same basic purpose as the previous section serves in regard to a patient admitted under a nonjudicial procedure. Any judicially hospitalized patient is entitled to have the order for his hospitalization re-examined by the probate court of the county in which he resides or is detained. A petition for re-examination may be filed by the patient himself or by his legal guardian, spouse, relative, or friend. The proceedings conducted upon receipt of such a petition are identical with those provided for original applications for judicial hospitalization. Although the court is free to entertain petitions for re-examination at any time, a provision is included by which the court can protect itself against petitions filed before there has been time for a change in the patient's condition. Thus, the court is not required to set the proceedings in motion during the first 6 months after the original order of hospitalization and, also, if a new petition is filed before a year has elapsed since the last re-examination proceeding. The duty of the hospital to periodically examine every involuntary patient with a view to possible discharge operates independently of the provisions of this section and is not affected by the court's rejection of an untimely petition.

PART IV—PROVISIONS APPLICABLE TO PATIENTS GENERALLY

As the title suggests, the provisions of sections 19–26, inclusive, apply equally to voluntary and involuntary patients. Section 24 apart, these provisions are largely concerned with the rights of patients. Some of the individual rights specified would seem to be necessarily implied from the function of a mental hospital. The creation of a sympathetic public attitude toward the operation of this Act will, however, be facilitated by express provisions guaranteeing such rights.

SEC. 19. *Right to humane care and treatment.*—The right prescribed by this section states a practical ideal

for the care and treatment of mental patients. While demanding adherence to the highest medical standards, it takes account of limitations on facilities, equipment, and personnel which often make adherence to those standards difficult or impossible.

SEC. 20. *Mechanical restraints.*—Although use of mechanical restraints has decreased materially, they are still recognized as medically permissible in some cases. The provisions of this section seek to assure against improvident use of such restraints in preference to more desirable but more difficult measures. This is sought to be accomplished by prohibiting the use of mechanical restraints unless directed by the head of the hospital, or his designee, as medically necessary. The requirement for a record of each resort to such restraints and of the reasons therefor is an additional measure of control.

SEC. 21. *Right to communication and visitation; exercise of civil rights.*—(*a*) The right of communication and visitation is stated as broadly as it is possible to do so consistently with the orderly execution of the functions of the hospital. Thus, for example, while every patient is entitled to receive visitors, he is entitled to receive them only during such visiting hours as the hospital may by rule establish. In addition, his right to receive visitors may be limited if the hospital head determines that receiving visitors may worsen the patient's condition or impede his recovery.

The right to full enjoyment of personal rights as specified in paragraph (3) follows naturally from the fact that, under the theory of the Act, a determination that hospitalization is justified is entirely different and separate from an adjudication of incompetency. Loss of the right to vote, to dispose of property, and similar rights flows only from the latter type of judicial action.

(*b*) This subsection contains a special provision overriding the authority of the hospital head to limit by regulation or other action the right of communication. The judicially hospitalized patient, as well as others, is thus, guaranteed an opportunity to call attention to a claim of unjustified hospitalization without having to resort to judicial proceedings as provided in section 18.

(*c*) The requirement of a record of limitations imposed on the exercise of rights specified in this section and the reasons for such limitations is a measure of control assuring compliance with the requirements of subsection (*a*) and in case of controversy would facilitate determination of the facts.

SEC. 22. *Writ of habeas corpus.*—This section does no more than preserve the right to petition for a writ of habeas corpus, leaving the matter of the scope of the judicial inquiry to be governed by the law and practice of the individual State. If a State wishes to make certain that the hearing on the petition will not be limited to consideration of the propriety of the original hospitalization, thought might well be given to expressly requiring or permitting the court to go into the question of the patient's condition at the time of the hearing.

SEC. 23. *Disclosure of information.*—(*a*) The purpose of this section is to protect patients and those whose hospitalization has been sought under the Act against the morbidly or maliciously curious who may, by taking advantage of the stigma which mental illness still connotes to many minds, cause social or economic injury to the individuals involved and their families. Inclusion of this protection should encourage those in need of hospital care as well as their families to seek to bring the provisions of the Act into play at an earlier stage than might otherwise be the case. At the same time, this section seeks to satisfy the legitimate public interest in the protected information. To that end, the information is permitted to be disclosed insofar as it is necessary to carry out the provisions of the Act—for example, in reports by the head of a hospital to the central administration—or insofar as a court may determine disclosure to be necessary for the conduct of proceedings and required by the public interest.

(*b*) No comment.

(*c*) No comment.

SEC. 24. *Detention pending judicial determination.*—It is made clear under this section that once section 9 proceedings for judicial hospitalization have been commenced with respect to a patient, that is, an individual who is under observation, care, or treatment in a hospital, the court's jurisdiction is complete. This provision applies equally to voluntary and involuntary patients. The effect of this section is to freeze all provision of the Act for release or discharge whenever judicial proceedings have been commenced. The prohibition is not, however, absolute since release can still be obtained upon application to the court handling the case, or to a judge of that court.

The additional provision for release upon receipt of a report from the head of the hospital that release would not be unsafe should be read in relation to the provisions of sections 4 (*a*) (3) and 17 (*a*). Under those sections a voluntary or involuntary (nonjudicial) patient whose release has been requested must be released unless the head of the hospital certifies within 48 hours that the patient cannot safely be released. It is possible that sometime subsequent to such a certification the head of the hospital may be able to report to the court that the patient may now be safely released. The court is upon the receipt of such a report empowered to order release.

SEC. 25. *Additional powers of central administration.*—As has already been indicated, it is beyond the scope of the Act to deal comprehensively with the State's programs in the mental health field. This section therefore does not enumerate the general powers and duties of the central administration and is limited to (1) those authorizations which, while necessary to the administration of the Act, would involve endless repetition if they were specified at each appropriate point, and (2) the authority to issue reasonable rules necessary to carry out the Act effectively. There are a host of details involved in the administration of the Act which can be better handled by administrative rules such as would be authorized by this section than by specific statutory provision.

SEC. 26. *Unwarranted hospitalization or denial of rights; penalties.*—Two types of offenses are covered by this section: Those resulting in unwarranted hospitalization and those resulting in denial of rights accorded by the Act. In either case, the willful character of the conduct in question would be an essential element of the crime at which this section is directed. With respect to both offenses, not only the direct agent but anyone who conspires with or assists him would be criminally liable as well.

Although the acts made punishable by this section might be punishable under the general criminal laws of many States, special provision in this Act has the advantages of leaving no room for doubt if there should be any under the general laws and emphasizing one of the principle objectives of the Act; namely, to protect mentally ill individuals from wrongful confinement and deprivation of rights.

Appendix B

Summary of Admission, Hospitalization, and Discharge Provisions of Guam, Virgin Islands, and the Commonwealth of Puerto Rico

GUAM

The provisions for admission, hospitalization, and discharge of the mentally ill on the island of Guam have been fashioned after the Draft Act. Any individual sixteen years of age or over who is mentally ill or has symptoms of mental illness may be admitted to a hospital on the basis of a voluntary application. The application for a person under sixteen may be made by a parent or legal guardian.[1] Mental illness is defined in the Guam Code as "a psychiatric or other disease which substantially impairs mental health."[2]

A patient admitted to a hospital on a voluntary basis must be released upon request.[3] However, the head of the hospital may, within forty-eight hours after receipt of the request, file with a court an application for the restraint of such an individual until judicial hospitalization proceedings can be commenced.[4] This procedure is followed if the hospital head determines that it would be unsafe to release the patient. An individual's release may not be postponed beyond five days in any event.[5]

There are several admission procedures for the involuntary commitment of the mentally ill. For an emergency situation there are two. In one instance, any individual may make an application for emergency admission provided the application is accompanied by a medical certificate.[6] The application must state that the individual is likely to cause injury to himself or others if not immediately restrained.[7] In the other, application may be made only by the Director of Medical Services or a police officer.[8] It does not require a medical certificate but must state a belief that the individual cannot go unrestrained pending examination by a physician.[9] The provisions governing the right to release of such patients are identical to the release provisions for the voluntary patient.[10]

Only certain people specifically enumerated by statute may make an application for admission by medical certification.[11] Such application must be certified by two designated examiners who have found the subject "mentally ill, and because of his illness . . . likely to injure himself or others if allowed to remain at liberty, or . . . in need of care or treatment in a mental hospital, and because of his illness, [lacking] sufficient insight or capacity to make responsible application therefor."[12] Upon receiving this type of application, the head of a hospital may admit any individual for care and treatment. Again, the release provisions pertaining to an individual admitted to a hospital upon medical certification are the same as the provisions governing the release of voluntary and emergency patients.[13]

Proceedings for the judicial commitment of an individual may also be commenced only by certain people specifically listed by statute.[14] The fact that the person is mentally ill must be verified by a physician.[15] After the proceedings have been initiated, the court orders its own examination, to be conducted by two court-appointed examiners.[16] If the report of the examiners is to the effect

1. *Guam Gov't Code* § 9801 (1961). All subsequent references are to sections within Guam Gov't Code (1961).

2. § 9800(a).

3. § 9803(a).

4. § 9803(a)(3).

5. § 9803(b).

6. § 9806.

7. Ibid.

8. § 9807.

9. Ibid.

10. § 9816.

11. § 9805(a)(1).

12. § 9805(a)(2).

13. § 9816.

14. § 9808(a).

15. Ibid.

16. § 9808(c).

that the person is mentally ill, a hearing is set by the court.[17]

The hearing is conducted in an informal manner so as not to be harmful to the patient. Also, every patient is to be represented by counsel.[18] If the court finds the proposed patient mentally ill and likely to injure himself or others, or in need of custody and care, it can order the patient hospitalized for an indeterminate period or for a temporary observation period not to exceed six months.[19] A patient so hospitalized may petition for reexamination of the hospitalization order within six months of its issuance.[20] Any individual detained in a mental hospital pursuant to any of the proceeding provisions is entitled to a writ of habeas corpus.[21]

A mental patient may be discharged at any time by the head of the hospital if the conditions justifying involuntary hospitalization no longer obtain.[22] An improved patient may also be released on a conditional basis.[23] However, the conditionally discharged patient may be immediately rehospitalized if he fails to comply with the conditions of his release. The Director of Medical Services is empowered to issue such an order.[24]

VIRGIN ISLANDS

In the Virgin Islands, the only people who may be voluntarily admitted to a mental hospital are the so-called private patients,[25] who are defined as being "maintained at the mental hospital at their own expense or at the expense of their relatives or friends."[26] All other patients must be committed to a mental hospital pursuant to a judicial hospitalization proceeding.

Application for judicial admission may be made by anyone and is directed to the judge of the district or municipal court. Such application must allege that the person "is mentally ill and that the welfare of himself or of others requires that he be placed under restraint."[27]

If the judge finds satisfactory justification for the application, he issues a warrant for the apprehension of the individual and fixes a day for a hearing.[28] The judge may also certify the individual to the care and custody of the Commissioner of Health for up to fifteen days pending the outcome of the hearing.[29] At the time the warrant is issued, the judge designates two or more qualified physicians to examine the individual.[30] Their testimony is presented at the hearing.[31] The alleged mentally ill person is entitled to the appointment of legal counsel[32] and a jury trial may be requested.[33]

If the patient is found to be of unsound mind and in need of restraint, he is ordered to an appropriate hospital.[34] There is no special provision for the appeal of such a judgment. A patient thus admitted may be discharged upon recovery or at any time by unanimous decision of the Sanity Board.[35]

Statutory provision is also made for the consideration of cases of mental illness "when occasion arises," by the Sanity Board.[36] It is not made clear exactly when such occasion arises, but such a procedure most probably comes into play in emergency situations. The Sanity Board is authorized to restrain and treat an individual in any place and in any manner it deems necessary, pending commencement of and during judicial proceedings.[37]

PUERTO RICO

Puerto Rico has statutory provisions for the hospitalization of the mentally ill by both voluntary and involuntary means. Little detail is given on the voluntary admission procedure, other than that any person may voluntarily enter any hospital or other facility in order to receive treatment for a mental disorder.[38]

There are two varieties of involuntary admission in Puerto Rican law. One is a judicial commitment proceedings,[39] the other an emergency procedure whereby a

17. § 9808(e).

18. § 9808(f).

19. § 9808(g); compare § 9805(a)(2), n. 12.

20. § 9817.

21. § 9821.

22. § 9814.

23. § 9815(a).

24. § 9815(b).

25. *V. I. Code Ann.* tit. 19, § 1175 (1964). All subsequent references are to sections within *V. I. Code Ann.* tit. 19.

26. § 1174(2).

27. § 1131(a) (Supp. 1970).

28. Ibid.

29. Ibid.

30. § 1135.

31. § 1139.

32. § 1136.

33. § 1134.

34. § 1141(a).

35. § 1201.

36. § 1112. The Sanity Board is a part of the Department of Health; it is composed of three members appointed by the governor and the Commissioner of Health, who is an ex officio member. No professional qualifications are established for membership. *V. I. Code Ann.* tit. 3, § 416 (1964).

37. §1113.

38. *P. R. Laws Ann.* tit. 24, § 141 (1964). All subsequent references are to sections within *P. R. Laws Ann.* tit. 24.

39. § 147a–147k.

patient requiring immediate care and treatment can be admitted without the delays and deferments of a judicial proceeding.[40] Apparently, any person may have an individual hospitalized under the emergency procedure. The sole requirement of this procedure is that within twenty-four hours of such an admission, notice of the admission must be given to the prosecuting attorney of the superior court where the hospital is located.[41]

To safeguard the individual liberty of those people hospitalized without the benefit of a judicial hearing, it is the responsibility of the prosecuting attorney after receiving such notification to conduct an investigation into the causes and reasons for the admission.[42] If the prosecuting attorney has reason to believe the admission was unjustified, he may file with the Superior Court a petition requesting the appearance of the person at whose request the admission was made.[43] Unless such person is satisfactorily able to show cause why the patient should remain in the hospital, the patient may be released by the court.[44]

Provision is also made for any relative or friend of a person committed by the emergency procedure to petition the court for a hearing; this contingency becomes operative, however, only if the prosecuting attorney refuses to take action on the case.[45]

Other than by means of the above emergency procedure, no person may be committed to a hospital for the treatment of a mental disorder without a previous declaration of insanity by a competent court.[46] The criterion for such an admission is that the person be "suffering from mental disorder, and that his own welfare and that of others requires that he be placed under restraint."[47] If a judge, after proper investigation, believes such an allegation to be true he issues a warrant for the apprehension of the individual and his provisional admission to a medical facility.[48] A hearing date is then set.

The hearing is held before a judge with the patient being entitled to counsel.[49] At the hearing, one or more practicing physicians are required to testify.[50] If, after hearing the evidence, the judge concludes that the patient is mentally ill, he orders him hospitalized.[51] The person adjudged to be mentally ill is entitled to appeal if he does so within fifteen days after the rendition of judgment.[52] A patient committed to a mental hospital remains there unless he is discharged either by being certified sane or by a declaration that his mental condition is no longer such as to constitute a danger to the community.[53]

40. § 141 (Statement of motives).

41. § 141.

42. § 142.

43. Ibid.

44. Ibid.

45. § 146.

46. § 141.

47. § 147a.

48. Ibid.

49. § 147c.

50. § 147d.

51. § 147e.

52. § 147g.

53. § 147s (B).

Index

An asterisk after certain page numbers indicates that those pages contain recommendations or conclusions of the Report. No attempt has been made in this index to list the numerous authors and names appearing in the footnotes. For further references the reader should consult the bibliography and list of cases at the end of each chapter.